# THE HOLY BIBLE

## THE MATTHEWS BIBLE OF 1537 VOL. II

### PSALMS – REVELATION

The text of the Matthews Bible is in the public domain in the United States.

This book may be used and reproduced freely,
in whole or in part, for non-commercial purposes.

\*\*\*

For more information, or to be notified of subsequent volumes and
projects, contact the editors/compilers, Robert & Anne Kelly, at
**The.Sola.Scriptura.Prayer.Book@gmail.com**

Volume 1: Genesis to Job, ISBN 9798304724449
Volume 2: Psalms to Revelation, ISBN 9798304724456

# EDITOR'S NOTE TO THE READER
## 2024

While the spellings in this text may appear to us as typos, spelling errors, etc., these spellings, along with their variations and inconsistencies, are original to the manuscript and were acceptable in their historical context. The thorn (þ) character is pronounced "th," so "þat" is the word "that."

Some verses that we have today are not included in the Matthews translation of 1537. Those are idnciated by pointed brackets: <>

This is not a scholarly work. The text we used is text we found online and are making assumptions about its reliability, having spot-checked it in areas against a facsimile of the original. This book does not attempt to be a representation of the entire 1537 Matthews Bible, but only of the text itself. Moreover, we have created it for our own use, but are making it available, royalty-free, to anyone who might want a physical copy from which to read the Biblical text.

Concerning the text, deliberate deviations from the original 1537 Matthews Bible are as follows (there may be others we have overlooked):

- We did not include any external and internal illustrations or the original book separator materials.
- We did not include any prefatory and explanatory materials, charts, tables, etc.
- We did not include any marginal notes or study notes.
- We did not include any extended book and chapter titles, headings, or explanatory text, but used conventional book titles.
- We did not include the any apocryphal texts.
- We did not include any apocryphal additions to Esther or Daniel.

We simply included the 1537 Great Bible translation of the text that you would find, generally speaking, in any 66-book Bible.

We hope you understand and enjoy.

God bless you.

*Thanks be to God for His Holy Word.*

*Even so, come, Lord Jesus.*
*~Revelation 22:20b*

To Mr. and Mrs. RF Clerk, who love the Word.

## ACKNOWLEDGEMENTS

*We are grateful to all who worked to bring us God's Word in the English language and other native languages.*

# Table of Contents

(Bold text indicates books in this volume.)

| | |
|---|---|
| Genesis | 1 |
| Exodus | 47 |
| Leviticus | 85 |
| Numbers | 113 |
| Deuteronomy | 151 |
| Joshua | 183 |
| Judges | 207 |
| Ruth | 231 |
| 1 Samuel | 235 |
| 2 Samuel | 265 |
| 1 Kings | 289 |
| 2 Kings | 319 |
| 1 Chronicles | 347 |
| 2 Chronicles | 373 |
| Ezra | 405 |
| Nehemiah | 415 |
| Esther | 429 |
| Job | 437 |
| **Psalms** | **463** |
| **Proverbs** | **523** |
| **Ecclesiastes** | **545** |
| **Song of Solomon** | **553** |
| **Isaiah** | **557** |
| **Jeremiah** | **603** |
| **Lamentations** | **655** |
| **Ezekiel** | **661** |
| **Daniel** | **707** |
| **Hosea** | **723** |
| **Joel** | **731** |
| **Amos** | **735** |
| **Obadiah** | **741** |
| **Jonah** | **743** |
| **Micah** | **745** |

| | |
|---|---|
| **Nahum** | **751** |
| **Habakkuk** | **753** |
| **Zephaniah** | **757** |
| **Haggai** | **761** |
| **Zechariah** | **763** |
| **Malachi** | **771** |
| **Matthew** | **775** |
| **Mark** | **805** |
| **Luke** | **825** |
| **John** | **857** |
| **Acts** | **881** |
| **Romans** | **913** |
| **1 Corinthians** | **927** |
| **2 Corinthians** | **939** |
| **Galatians** | **947** |
| **Ephesians** | **953** |
| **Philippians** | **959** |
| **Colossians** | **963** |
| **1 Thessalonians** | **967** |
| **2 Thessalonians** | **971** |
| **1 Timothy** | **973** |
| **2 Timothy** | **977** |
| **Titus** | **981** |
| **Philemon** | **983** |
| **Hebrews** | **985** |
| **James** | **995** |
| **1 Peter** | **999** |
| **2 Peter** | **1003** |
| **1 John** | **1007** |
| **2 John** | **1011** |
| **3 John** | **1013** |
| **Jude** | **1015** |
| **Revelation** | **1017** |

# The Old Testament

# Psalms

## PSALM 1

O blessed is the man, þt goeth not in the counsayll of the vngodly: that abydeth not in þe waie of sinners and sitteth not in the seate of þe scorneful.

2 But deliteth in the lawe of the Lord, and exercyseth hym self in hys lawe, bothe daye and nyght.

3 Suche a man is lyke a tree planted by the watersyde, that bringeth forthe hys frute in due season. His leaues shall not fall af, & loke whatsoeuer he doth, it shall prospere.

4 As for the vngodly, it is not so with them but they are lyke the dust, wych the wynde scatered awaye from the grounde.

5 Thefore þe vngodly shall not be able to stande in the iudgement, nether the synners in the congregacyon of the ryghtuous.

6 For the Lorde aloweth the waye of the righteous, but the waye of the vngodly shal peryshe.

## PSALM 2

VVHY do the Heathen grudge? why do the people ymagyne vayne thinges?

2 The kynges of the earth stande vp, and the rulers are come to gether, agaynste the Lorde and agaynste hys anoynted.

3 Let vs breake their hondes a sunder, and cast away their yock from vs.

4 Neuerthelesse he that dwelleth in heauen, shall laughe them to scorne: yea euen the Lorde hym selfe shall haue them in derysyon.

5 Then shal he speake vnto them in hys wrath, and vexe them in hys sore displeasure.

6 Yet haue I sette my kyng vpon my holy hyll of syon.

7 As for me, I wyll preache the law, wherof the Lord hath sayde vnto me: Thou arte my sonne, this day haue I begotten the.

8 Desyre of me, and I shall geue the Heathen for thyne enherytaunce. Yea the vttermost partes of the worlde for thy possessyon.

9 Thou shalt rule them wyth a rodde of yron, and breake them in peces lyke an earthen vessell.

10 Be wyse nowe therfore, O ye Kinges, be warned, ye that are iudges of the earthe.

11 Serue the Lorde wyth feare, and reioyse before hym wyth reuerence.

12 Kysse the sonne, lest the Lorde be angrye and so ye peryshe from the ryght way. For his wrath shalbe kindled shortly: blessed are all they that put their trust in hym.

## PSALM 3

*A Psalme of Dauid when he fledde from the face of Absalom.*

WHY are they so many, O Lord that trouble me? a great multytude are they that ryse agaynst me.

2 Yea many one ther be that say of my soule: there is no helpe for hym in God Selah.

3 But thou, O Lord, arte my defender, my worshippe, and the lifter vp of my head.

4 I call vpon the Lord wyth my voyce, and he heareth me out of hys holy hyll. Selah.

5 I layed me downe and slepte, but I rose vp agayne, for the Lorde sustayned me.

6 I am not afrayed for thousandes of the people, that compasse me rounde aboute.

7 Vp Lorde, and helpe me O my God for thou smitest al mine enemyes vpon þe cheke bones and breakest the teeth of the vngodly.

8 Helpe belongeth vnto the Lorde, therfore let thy blessynge be vpon thy people.

## PSALM 4

*To the Chanter in Neginoth, a Psalme of Dauid.*

HEARE me when I call, O God of my ryghteousnes: thou that comfortest me in my trouble: haue mercy vpon me, herken vnto my praier.

2 O ye sonnes of men, howe longe wyll ye blaspheme myne honour? why haue ye suche pleasure in vanytye, and seke after lyes? Selah.

3 Knowe thys, that the Lorde dealeth maruelously wyth hys saynt: and when I cal vpon the Lorde, he heareth me.

4 Be angrye, but synne not: comen wyth youre owne hertes vpon youre beddes, and remember youre selues. Selah.

5 Offer thy sacrifyce of ryghtuousnes, and put your trust in the Lord.

6 There be many that saye: who wyll do vs any good? Lord lift vp vpon vs the lyghte of thy countenaunce.

7 Thou reioyseste myne herte, thoughe their encrease be great both in corne & wyne.

8 Therfore wyll I laye me downe in peace, and take my rest: for thou Lorde only settest me in a sure dwellynge.

## PSALM 5

*To the Chaunter by Nehiloh, a Psalme of Dauid.*

HEARE my wordes (O Lorde) consyder my callynge.

2 O marke the voice of my petition my Kynge and my God, for vnto the wyl I make my prayer.

3 Heare my voyce by tymes (O Lorde) for early in the mornyng wyll I get me vnto the, yea and that with diligence.

4 For thou art not the God that hath pleasure in wickednesse, ther may no vngodly person dwel with the.

5 Suche as be cruell maye not stande in thy syght, thou art an enemye vnto all wycked doers.

6 Thou destroiest the lyers: the Lord abhorreth the bloude thursty and disceatful.

7 But as for me, I wyl come into thy house euen vpon the multytude of thy mercy: and in thy feare wyll I worshippe towarde thy holy temple.

8 Lede me (O Lord) in thy ryghtuousnesse; because of myne enemyes, & make thy waye playne before me.

9 For there is no faithfulnesse in their mouthes: they dessemble in their hertes: their throt is an open sepulcher: with their tonges thy disceaue.

10 Punysh them (O God) that they may perysh in their owne ymaginacions: cast them out because of the multytude of their vngodlynesse, for they rebell agaynste the.

11 Agayne, let all them that put their truste in the, reioyse: yea let them euer be geuynge of thankes, because thou defendest: them: that they whyche loue thy name, be ioyfull in the.

12 For thou Lord geuest thy blessynge vnto the ryghtuous: and with thy fauorable kindnes thou defendest him, as wyth a shylde.

## PSALM 6

*To the chaunter by Negynoth vpon Sheminith, a Psalme of Dauid.*

OH Lorde rebuke me not in thyne anger: Oh chasten me not in thy heuy dyspleasure.

2 Haue mercye vpon me (O Lorde) for I am weake: O Lorde heale me for all my bones are vexed.

3 My soule also is in great trouble, but lord how longe?

4 Turne the (O Lord) and deliuer my soule Oh saue me for thy mercyes sake.

5 For in death no man remembreth the: Oh who wyll geue the thankes in the hell?

6 I am wery of gronyng euery nyght wash I my bedde, and water my couche wyth my teares.

7 My countenance is chaunged for verye inwarde grefe. I consume awaye I haue so many enemyes.

8 Awaye fro me all ye wicked dors, for the Lorde hath hearde the voyce of my wepyng

9 The Lord hath hearde myne humble petycyon, the Lorde hath receaued my prayer.

10 All myne enemies shalbe confunded and sore vexed: yea they shalbe turned backe and put to shame, and that ryght soone.

## PSALM 7

*Sigaion of Dauid, whych he sang for the wordes of Cus the sonne of Iemini.*

O Lord my god, in the do I trust: saue me from al them that persecute me, and delyuer me.

2 Lest he deuoureth vp my soule lyke a lion and teare it in peces whyle ther is none to helpe,

3 O Lorde my God, if I haue done anye suche thyng, if there be any vnrightuousnes in my handes:

4 If I haue rewarded euyl vnto them that dealt frendly wyth me, or hurt them that wyth out any cause are myne enemies.

5 Then let myne enemye persecute my soule, and take mo: ye let hym treade my life downe in the earth, and laye myne honour in the dust. Selah.

6 Stande vp (O Lorde) in thy wrath, lyft vp thy selfe ouer the furyous indygnacyon of myne enemyes: aryse vp (for me) in the vengeaunce that thou hast promysed.

7 That the congregacion of the people maye come about the, for their sakes therfore lyfte vp thy selfe agayne.

8 The Lord is iudge ouer the people: auenge me then (O Lord) accordynge to my ryghtuousnes and innocency.

9 Oh let the wickednes of the vngodly come to an ende: but maynteyne the iust, thou

# PSALMS

righteous God, that triest the very hertes and the reynes.

10 My helpe commeth of God, which preserueth them that are true of herte.

11 God is a ryghtuous iudge, and God is euer threatnynge,

12 If men wyll not turne, he hath whette his swearde: he hath bent his bowe and made it ready.

13 He hath prepared hym the weapons of death, & ordeined his arrowes to be destroied.

14 Beholde, he trauyleth wyth mischefe, he hath conceaued vnhappinesse, and broughte forth a lye.

15 He hath grauen & digged vp a pyt, but he shall fall hym selfe into the pitte that he hath made.

16 For hys vnhappinesse shall come vpon hys owne head, and hys wyckednes shal fal vpon hys owne pate.

17 As for me, I wyll geue thankes vnto the Lorde for hys ryghtuousnes sake, and wyll prayse the name of the Lorde the most hyest.

## PSALM 8

*To the chaunter vpon Githith, a Psalme of Dauid.*

O Lord our gouernour: how wonderfull is thy name in all the worlde? howe excellente is thy glory aboue the heauens?

2 Out of the mouth of þe very babes and sucklynges thou haste ordeyned prayse, because of thyne enemyes, that thou mightest destroye the enemye & the auenger.

3 For I considre thy heauens, euen þe worke of thy fingers: the moone & the starres which thou hast made.

4 Oh what is man, that thou art so myndfull of hym? either the sonne of man that thou visitest hym?

5 After thou haddest for a season made him lower then the aungels, thou crounedest him with honour and glory.

6 Thou haste set him aboue the workes of thy handes: and thou hast put all thynges in subiection vnder his fete.

7 All shepe and oxen, yea, and the beastes of the felde.

8 The foules of the ayre, the fish of the sea, and whatsoeuer walketh thorow the wayes of the sea.

9 O Lorde our gouernoure, how wonderfull is thy name in all the worlde?

## PSALM 9

*To the chaunter vpon Almuth Laben, a Psalme of Dauid.*

I wyll geue thankes vnto the (O Lord) with my whole hert I will speake of all thy meruelous workes.

2 I will be glad, and reioyse in þe, yea, my songes wil I make of thy name O thou moost hyest.

3 Because thou hast dryuen myne enemyes abacke, they were disconfited, and perished at thy presence.

4 For thou hast maynteyned my right and my cause: thou sittest in the throne that arte the true iudge.

5 Thou rebukest the Heythen, & destroyest the vngodly, thou puttest out their name for euer and euer.

6 The enemyes sweardes are come too an ende, thou haste ouerthrowen their cytyes, their memorial is perished with them.

7 But the Lorde endureth for euer, he hath prepared his seate vnto iudgement.

8 He gouerneth the worlde with righteousnes, and ministreth true iudgement vnto the people.

9 The Lorde is a defence for the poore, a defence in the tyme of trouble.

10 Therfore they that know thy name, putte their trust in the: for thou (Lorde) neuer faylest them that seke the.

11 O prayse the Lorde, whiche dwelleth in Syon, shewe the people of hys doynges.

12 And why? he maketh inquisicion for their bloude, and remembreth theym: he forgetteth not th complaynte of the poore.

13 Haue mercy vpon me (O Lord) considre the trouble that I am in amonge myne enemyes, thou that liftest me vp from the gates of death.

14 That I maye shewe all thy prayses within the portes of the daughter of Sion, and reioyse in thy sauynge health.

15 As for the Heathen, thei are suncken doune in the pytte that they made: in the same nette which they spred out priuely, is their owne feete taken.

16 Thus the Lord is knowen to execute true iudgemente, when the vngodly is trapped in the woorkes of hys owne handes. Selah.

17 The wicked must be turned vnto hell, & all the Heythen that forget God.

18 But the poore shall not all waye be oute of remembraunce, the pacyent abydynge of suche as be in trouble shall not peryshe for euer.

19 Vp Lorde, let no man haue the vpperhand let the Heythen be condemned before the.

20 O Lorde set a scholemaster ouer them, that the Heathen maye knowe theim selfes to be but men. Selah.

## PSALM 10

WHY arte thou gone so far of, O Lord? wylt thou hyde thy selfe in tyme of trouble?

2 While the vngodlye hath þe ouer hand, the pore must suffer persecutyon. O that they were taken in the ymagynacion which they go aboute.

3 For the vngodly maketh bost of his owne hertes desyre, the couetous blesseth him selfe

and blasphemeth the Lorde.

4 The vngodlye is so proude and full of indignacyon, that he careth not mether is God before hys eyes.

5 Hys wayes are al waye filthye, thy iudgementes are farre out of his sight, he defyeth all his enemyes.

6 For he sayth in hys herte: Tushe, I shall neuer be cast downe, ther shal no harme happen vnto me.

7 His mouth is ful of cursyng, fraude & disceate vnder hys tonge is trauayle and sorowe.

8 He sytteth lurckynge in the gardens, that he may pryuely murther the innocente, hys eyes are set vpon the poore.

9 He lyeth waytynge secretlye, as ti were a lyon in hys denne. He lurketh that he maye rauyshe the pore, yea, to rauysh the poore, when he hath gotten him into hys net.

10 Then smyteth he, then oppresseth he and casteth downe the pore with his authoritye.

11 For he sayeth in hys herte: Tushe, God hath forgotten, he hath turned awaye hys face, so that he wyll neuer se it.

12 Aryse Lorde God, lyfte vp thyne hande and forget not the poore.

13 Wherfore should the wycked blaspheme God and saye in his herte: tush, he careth not for it:

14 Thys thou seyst, for thou consyderest the mysery and sorowe. The poore geueth him selfe ouer into thy hande, and committeth hym vnto the, for thou art the helper of the frendlesse.

15 Breake thou the arme of the vngodly and malycyous, search out the wickednes which he hath done, that he maye perysh.

16 The Lord is kynge for euer, the Heithen shal perish out of his land.

17 Lord, thou hearest the desyrous longing of the poore: theyr hert is sure, that thine eare herkeneth therto.

18 Helpe the fatherlesse and poore vnto their ryght, that the vngodlye be no more exalted vpon earh.

## PSALM 11

*To the chaunter, of Dauid.*

IN þe Lord put I my trust: how will ye then saye too my soule: that she shoulde fle as a byrde vpon your hyll?

2 For lo, the vngodly haue bent their bowe, and made ready their arrowes in the quyuer, that they maye pryuely shute at them, which are true of hert.

3 The verye foundacion haue they caste doune, what can the righteous then do with all?

4 But the Lorde is in hys holy temple, the Lordes seate is in heauen: He considereth it with hys eyes, hys eye lyddes beholde the chyldren of men.

5 The Lorde seith bothe the righteous and vngodly, but who so delyteth in wickednes, hym hys soule abhorreth.

6 Vpon the vngodly he shall rayne snares, fyre, brymstone, storme and tempest: thys rewarde shall they haue to drynke.

7 For the Lord is righteous, and he loueth righteousnes: hys countenaunce beholdeth the thinge that is iust.

## PSALM 12

*To the chaunter vpon Sheminith, a Psalme of Dauid.*

HELPE Lord, for there is not one saincte more: very fewe faythfull are there amonge the chyldren of men.

2 Euery man telleth lyes too his neyghbour, they do but flatter with their lyppes and dissemble in their herte.

3 O that the Lorde wolde rote out all disceatfull lyppes, and the tonge that speaketh proude thynges.

4 Which saye: oure tonge shoulde preuayle we are they that oughte too speake, who is Lord ouer vs?

5 Now for the troubles sake of the oppressed, and because of the complainte of the poore I will vp (sayeth the Lord) I wil helpe them, & set them at rest.

6 The wordes of the Lord are pure wordes euen as the siluer, which from earth is tryed and purified .vij. tymes in the fyre.

7 Kepe them therfore (O Lorde) and preserue vs from this generacion for euer.

8 And why? when vanite & ydelnes getteth the ouerhande among the chyldren of men, all are full of the vngodly.

## PSALM 13

*To the chaunter, a Psalme of Dauid.*

HOW longe wilt thou forget me O Lorde? for euer? howe longe wilt thou hyde thy face fro me?

2 Oh how long shal I seke counsayl in my soule? how longe shall I be so vexed in myne hert? howe longe shall myne enemye triumphe ouer me?

3 Considre, & heare me, O Lorde my God: lighten myne eyes, that I sleape not in death.

4 Lest myne enemye saye: I haue preuayled agaynst hym: for if I be cast doune, they that troble me will reioyse at it.

5 But my trust is in thy mercy, & my herte is ioyfull in thy sauynge health.

6 I will singe of the Lorde, that dealeth so louingly with me. (Yea, I wil prayse the name of the Lorde the moost hyest.)

## PSALM 14

*To the chaunter, of Dauid.*

THE folyshe bodyes saye in their hertes: tushe, there is no

God. They are corrupt, & become abhominable in their doynges, there is not one þt doth good.

2 The Lorde loked doune from heauen vpon the chyldren of men, too se if there were any that wolde vnderstande and seke after God.

3 But they are all gone out of the waye, they are altogether become vnprofitable: there is none that doeth good, no not one.

4 How can they haue vnderstandinge, that worke mischiefe, eatynge vp my people, as it were bread, & call not vpon the Lord?

5 Therfore shall they be brought in greate feare, for God standeth by the generacion of the righteous.

6 As for you ye haue made a mocke at the counsail of the poore, because he putteth hys trust in the Lorde.

7 Oh that the sauynge healthe were geuen vnto Israel out of Sion. Oh that the Lord wolde deliuer his people out of captiuitie. Then shoulde Iacob reioyse, & Israell should be right glad.

## PSALM 15

*A Psalme of Dauid.*

LORDE, who shal dwel in thy tabernacle? who shall reste vpon thy holy hyl?

2 Euen he that leadeth an vncorrupt life: that doth the thing which is right, and that speaketh þe trueth from hys hert.

3 He that vseth no disceat in his tongue: he that doth no euell to hys neyghbour, & sclaundreth not hys neyghbours.

4 He that setteth not by the vngodly, but maketh muche of them that feare the Lorde: he that sweareth vnto his neyghbour, & dispoynteth hym not.

5 He that geueth not his money vpon vsury, and taketh no rewarde agaynste the innocent. Who so doth these thinges, shall neuer be remoued.

## PSALM 16

*Michtam of Dauid.*

PRESERUE me (O God) for in the do I trust.

2 I haue saide vnto the Lord: thou art my God, my goodes are nothing vnto the.

3 All my delytes is vpon the saynctes that are in the earth, and vpon suche lyke.

4 But they that runne after another, shall haue greate trouble. Their drinckoffringes of bloude will not I offre, neither make mencion of their name in my mouth.

5 The Lorde him selfe is my good and my porcion, thou mayntaynest myne enherytaunce.

6 The lot is fallen vnto me in a fayre ground, yea, I haue a goodly heritage.

7 I will thanke the Lorde for geuynge me warnynge: my reynes also haue chastened me in the night season.

8 Afore hand sawe I God always before me, for he is on my righte hande, that I should not be moued.

9 Therfore dyd my hert reioyce, & my tunge was glad, my flesh also shal rest in hope.

10 For why? thou shalt not leaue my soule in hell, neither shalt thou suffre thy saincte to se corrupcion.

11 Thou hast shewed me the wayes of lyfe: thou shalte make me full of ioye wyth thy countenaunce. At thy ryght hande there is pleasure and ioye for euermore.

## PSALM 17

*A prayer of Dauid.*

HEARE the right (O Lord) considre my complaynte: herken vnto my prayer, that goeth not oute of a fayned mouth.

2 Let my sentence come forth from thy presence: and loke vpon the thinge that is equall.

3 Thou hast proued & visited myne herte in the night season: thou hast tryed me in the fyre: & hast founde no wickednes in me: for I vtterly purposed that my mouthe shoulde not offende.

4 Because of the woordes of thy lippes, I haue kepte me from the workes of men, in the waye of the murtherer.

5 Oh ordre thou my goinges in thy pathes: that my fote steppes slippe not.

6 For vnto the I crie: heare me O God: encline thine eares to me: & herken vnto my woordes.

7 Shewe thy maruelous louing kindnesse, thou that sauest them whiche put their trust in the, from suche as resist thy right hande.

8 Kepe me as the apple of an eye, defende me vnder the shadow of thy wynges.

9 From the vngodly that trouble me, fro myne enemyes which compasse my soule round about.

10 Which manteyne their owne welthinesse with oppression, and their mouthe speaketh proude thynges.

11 They lye wayting in our waye on euery side, turnyng their eyes doune to the ground.

12 Like as a Lyon that is gredy of his pray, and as it were a Lyons whelpe lurkynge in hys denne.

13 Vp Lord, disapoynte hym and cast him doune: deliuer my soule with thy swerde from the vngodly.

14 From the men of thy hande (O Lord) from the men of the worlde, which haue theyr porcion in this lyfe: whose bellyes thou fyllest with thy treasure. They haue chyldren at

theyr desyre, and leaue the rest of of theyr substaunce for their babes.

15 But as for me, I wil beholde thy presence in righteousnes: and when thy glory appeareth, I shall be satisfied.

# PSALM 18

*To the chaunter of Dauid, seruaunt of the Lorde, whiche sayde vnto the Lorde the woordes of thys songe, on the daye in which the Lorde delyuered hym from the hande of all hys enemyes, and from the hande of Saul, and sayde.*

I wyll loue the (O Lorde) my strength.

2 The Lorde is my succour, my refuge, my sauyoure: my God, my helper in whome I trust: my buckler, the horne of my health, and my proteccion.

3 I will prayse the Lorde, and call vppon hym, so shall I be safe fro myne enemyes.

4 The sorowes of deathe compassed me, and the brokes of vngodlynes made me afrayed.

5 The paynes of hell came aboute me, the snares of death toke holde vpon me.

6 Yet in my trouble I called vpon the Lord, and complayned vnto my God. So he hearde my voyce out of hys holye temple, and my complaynte came before hym ye euen into hys eares.

7 Then the earth trembled and quaked, the verye foundacyones of the hylles shoke and were remoued, because he was wroth.

8 There wente a smoke oute of hys nostrels and a consuming fyre out of his mouth so that coales were kyndled at it.

9 He bowed the heauens & came downe, and it was darke vnder his fete.

10 He rode vpon the Cherubyns & dyd fle: he came flyenge wyth the wynges of the wynde.

11 He made darcknesse his pauylion rounde aboute hym, wyth darcke water and thycke cloudes to couer him.

12 At the brightnes of his presence the cloudes remoued, wyth hayle stones and coales of fyre.

13 The Lord also thondred out of the heauen and the heygth gaue his thonder wyth haile stones and coales of fyre.

14 He sente oute hys arrowes and scattered them, he cast sore lyghtenynges, and destroied them.

15 The sprynges of waters were sene, and the foundacyons of the rounde worlde were discouered at thy chidynge (O Lorde) at the blastynge and breth of thy displeasures.

16 He sente doune from the heygth to fetch me, and toke me out of greate waters.

17 He delyuered me fro my stronge enemies & fro my foes whych were to myghtye for me

18 They preuented me in the time of my trouble, but the Lorde was my defence.

19 He broughte me forthe also into lybertye: and delyuered me, because, he had a fauoure vnto me.

20 The Lorde shall rewarde me after my righteous dealynge, and accordynge to the clennesse of my handes shall he recompense me.

21 For I haue kepte the wayes of the Lord: and haue not behaued my selfe wickedly agaynst my God.

22 I haue an eye vnto all hys lawes, and caste not oute hys commaundementes fro me.

23 Vncorrupte wyll I be before him, and will eschue myne owne wyckednes.

24 Therfore shall the Lorde rewarde me after my ryghtuous dealynge, and accordinge vnto the clennesse of my handes in his eye sighte.

25 With the holye thou shalte be holye, and wyth the innocente thou shalte be innocente.

26 With the cleane thou shalt be cleane, and with the frowarde thou shalte be frowarde.

27 For thou shalte saue the poore oppressed, and brynge doune the hye lokes of the proude.

28 Thou lyghtest my candell, O Lorde my God: thou maketh my darcknesse to be light

29 For in the I can dyscomforte an hoste of men: yea in my God I can leape ouer the walle.

30 The waye of God is a perfecte waye: the wordes of the Lorde are tryed in the fire: he is a shylde of defence, for all them that truste in hym.

31 For who is God, but the Lord? Or who hath any strength, but our God?

32 It is God that gyrded me with strength, and made my way vncorrupt.

33 He hathe made my fete lyke hertes fete, and set me vpon hye.

34 He teacheth myne handes to fyght, & maketh myne armes to breake euen a bowe of stele.

35 Thou haste geuen me the defence of thy healthe, thy ryghte hande vpholdeth me, and thy louynge correctyon maketh me greate.

36 Thou hast made roume ynough vnder me for to go, that my fote steppes shuld not slyde.

37 I wyll folowe vpon myne enemyes, and take them: I wyll not turne tyll they be dyscomforted.

38 I wyll smyte them, they shall not be able to stand, but fal vnder my fete.

39 Thou hast gyrded me with strength vnto the battel, thou hast throwen them al downe vnder me that rose vp agaynst me.

40 Thou hast made myne enemyes to turne heir backes

vpon me, thou haste destroyed them: that hated me.

41 They cryed, but there was none to helpe them: yea euen vnto the Lorde, but he heard them not.

42 I wyll beate them as smalle as the duste claye in the wynde, I wyll cast them out as the clay in the stretes.

43 Thou shalt delyuer me from the striuynges of þe people, thou shalt make me þe head of the Heathen. A people whom I haue not knowne shal serue me.

44 As soone as they heare of me, they shall obey me, but the straung chyldren dyssemble with me.

45 The straunge chyldren are waxen olde, and go haltynge out of their pathes.

46 The Lorde lyueth: and blessed be, my helper, praysed be the God of my health.

47 Euen the God which seyth that I be auenged, and subdueth the people vnto me.

48 It is he that delyuereth me from my cruell enemyes: thou shalt lyfte me vp from them that ryse against me, thou shalt rid me from the wycked man.

49 For this cause I wyll geue thankes vnto the (O lorde) among the gentiles, and synge prayses vnto thy name.

50 Greate prosperitye geueth he vnto hys Kynge: and sheweth louynge kyndnesse vnto Dauyd hys anoynted yea & vnto his sede for euermore.

## PSALM 19

*To the chaunter, a Psalm of Dauid.*

THE very heauens declare the glory of God, and the very firmament sheweth his handy worcke.

2 One daye telleth another, and one nyght certifyeth another.

3 There is neyther speach ner language, but their voices are hard among them.

4 Their sounde is gone oute into all landes, and their wordes into the endes of the worlde.

5 In them hathe he sette a tabernacle for the Sunne, whych commeth forthe as a brydegrome out of his chamber, and reioyseth as a giaunt to runne his course.

6 It goeth forth from the one ende of the heauen, and runneth aboute vnto the same ende agayne, and there maye no man hyde hym selfe from the heate therof.

7 The lawe of the Lorde is a perfecte lawe it quickeneth the soule. The testimonye of the Lorde is true, and geueth wisdome euen vnto babes.

8 The statutes of the Lord are ryght, and reioyse the hert: the commaundement of the lord is pure, and geueth lyght vnto the eyes.

9 The feare of the Lorde is cleane, and endureth for euer: the iudgementes of the Lord are true and ryghtuous altogether.

10 More pleasaunt are they then golde, yea then much fyne golde: sweter then hony and the hony combe.

11 These thy seruaunt kepeth, & for kepynge of them there is great reward.

12 Who can tell, how oft he offendeth? Oh clense thou me fro my secrete fautes.

13 Kepe the seruaunt also from presumptuous synnes, lest they get the dominion ouer me: so shall I be vndefyled and innocent from the greate offence.

14 Yea the words of my mouth and the meditacion of my herte shalbe acceptable vnto the, O Lorde, my helper and my redemer.

## PSALM 20

*To the chanter, a Psalme of Dauid.*

THE Lorde heare the in the tyme of trouble, þt name of the God of Iacob defend the.

2 Send the helpe from the Santuary, and strength the oute of Sion.

3 Remember all thy offerynges, and accept thy brent sacrifice, Selah.

4 Graunte the thy hertes desyre, and fulfill all thy mynde.

5 We wyll reioyse in thy health, & triumphe in the name of the Lorde our God: the Lord perfourme all thy peticion.

6 Now knowe I, that the Lord helpeth hys anoynted, and will heare hym from his holy heauen: myghtye is the helpe of hys ryghte hande.

7 Some put their trust in charettes, & some in horses: but we will remember the name of the Lorde oure God.

8 They are broughte doune and fallen, but we are rysen and stande vp right.

9 Saue, Lorde, and helpe vs, O kyng, when we call vpon the.

## PSALM 21

*To the chaunter, a Psalme of Dauid.*

LORDE, how ioyfull is the kyng in thy strength? O how exceadyng glad is he of thy sauynge health?

2 Thou haste geuen him hys hertes desyre, and hast not put him from the request of hys lippes. Selah.

3 For thou hast preuented him with liberal blessinges, and set a croune of golde vpon hys head.

4 He asked lyfe of the, and thou gauest him a longe lyfe, euen for euer and euer.

5 His honour is great in thy sauing health, glory and great worship shalt thou laye vpon hym.

6 For thou shalt geue hym euerlastinge felicitie, and make hym glad with the ioye of thy

countenaunce.

7 And why? because the kynge putteth hys trust in the Lord, and in the mercy of þe most hyest he shall not miscary.

8 Let all thyne enemyes fele thy hande: let thy right hande fynde out all theym that hate the.

9 Thou shalt make them like a fyry ouen in tyme of thy wrath: the Lorde shall destroye them in hys displeasure, and the fyre shal consume them.

10 Their frute shalte thou rote oute of the earth, and their sede from amonge the chyldren of men.

11 For they intended mischief agaynst the, & ymagined suche deuyces, as they were not able to perfourme.

12 Therfore shalte thou put them to flighte, & with thy strynges thou shalte make ready thyne arrowes agaynst the faces of them.

13 Be thou exalted, Lorde in thyne owne strength, so wyll we synge and prayse thy power.

## PSALM 22

*To the chaunter vppon Aieleth of the dawnyng, a Psalme of Dauid.*

MY God, my God: why haste thou forsaken me? the wordes of my complaynte are farre fro my health.

2 O my God, I crye in the daye tyme, but thou hearest not: and in the night season also I take no rest.

3 Yet dwellest thou in the sanctuarye, O thou worshyppe of Israel.

4 Oure fathers hoped in the, they trusted in the, and thou dyddest deliuer them.

5 They called vpon the, & were helped: they put their trust in the, & were not confounded.

6 But as for me, I am a worme & no man: a very scorne of men and the outcaste of the people.

7 Al they that se me, laugh me to scorne: thei shute out their lippes, & shake their heades.

8 He trusted in God, let hym delyuer hym: let him helpe hym, if he will haue hym.

9 But thou art he that toke me out of my mothers wombe: thou waste my hope, when I hanged yet vpon my mothers brestes.

10 I haue bene left vnto the euer sence I was borne, thou art my God, euen fro my mothers wombe.

11 O go not fro me then, for trouble is harde at hande, and here is none to helpe me.

12 Great bulles are come about me, fatte oxen close me in on euery syde.

13 They gape vpon me with their mouthes, as it were a rampynge and roarynge Lyon.

14 I am poured out lyke water, all my boones are out of ioynt: my herte in the middest of my body is euen lyke meltyng waxe.

15 My strength is dryed vp lyke a potsherde, my tunge cleueth to my goomes, & thou haste brought me into the dust of death.

16 For dogges are come about me, the counsail of þe wicked hath layed seage against me. They pearsed my handes and my fete,

17 I might haue tolde all my bones: as for them, they stode staryng and lokyng vpon me.

18 They haue parted my garmentes among them, and cast lottes vpon my vesture.

19 But be not thou farre fro me, O Lorde: thou art my succoure, haste the to helpe me.

20 Delyuer my soule from the swearde, my dearlyng from the power of the dogge.

21 Saue me from the Lyons mouth, & heare me from amonge the hornes of the Vnicornes.

22 So wyll I declare thy name vnto my brethren, in the middest of the congregacion wyl I prayse the.

23 O praise the Lord ye that feare him: Magnify hym all ye sede of Iacob, and let al the sede of Israel feare hym.

24 For he hath not despised nor abhorred the miserable estate of the poore: he hath not hid hys face fro me, but when I called vnto him he herde me.

25 I wyll prayse the in the great congregacion, and perfourme my vowes in the sighte of all them that feare the.

26 The poore shall eate & be satisfied: they þt seke after the Lord shal prayse hym: our hert shall lyue for euer.

27 All the endes of the worlde shall remembre them selfes, and be turned vnto the Lorde: & all the generacions of the Heithen shal worshippe before hym.

28 For the kyngdom is the Lordes, & he shal be the gouernour of the Heythen.

29 All such as be fat vpon earth, shall eate also and worshippe. All they that lye in the dust, and lyue so hardly, shall fall doune before hym.

30 The sede shall serue hym, and preache of the Lord for euer.

31 They shall come, and declare hys ryghteousnes: vnto a people that shallbe borne, whome the Lorde hath made.

## PSALM 23

*A Psalme of Dauid.*

THE Lord is my shepherde, I can want nothynge.

2 He fedeth me in a grene pasture, and ledeth me to a freshe water.

3 He quickeneth my soule, and bryngeth me forth in the waye of righteousnes for his names sake.

4 Though I should walke now in þe valley of þe shadow of death, yet I feare not euel for thou arte with me: thy staffe & thy shepehoke comforte me.

5 Thou preparest a table before me agaynste myne enemyes: thou anoyntest my head with oyle, and fyllest my cuppe ful.

6 Oh let thy louing kyndnes and mercy folowe me all the dayes of my life, that I may dwell in the house of the Lorde for euer.

## PSALM 24

*A Psalme of Dauid.*

THE earth is the Lordes, & all þt therin is: the compase of the world, & al that dwell therein.

2 For he hath founded it vpon the seas, and buylded it vpon the floudes.

3 Who shall go vp into the hyll of þe Lord? Or who shal remayne in his holy place?

4 Euen he that hath innocent handes and a cleane hert: which lifteth not vp his minde vnto vanite, and sweareth not to disceaue.

5 He shal receaue the blessing from the Lord, and mercy from God his sauiour.

6 This is the generation of them that seke hym, of them that seke thy face, O Iacob. Selah.

7 Open your gates (O ye princes) lette the euerlastynge dores be opened, that the kyng of glory may come in.

8 Who is this kyng of glory? It is þe Lorde strong and myghtie, euen the Lorde myghty in batell.

9 Open youre gates (O ye princes) let the euerlastynge dores be opened, that the kyng of glory may come in.

10 Who is this king of glory? It is the Lord of Hoostes, he is the kynge of glorye. Selah.

## PSALM 25

*Of Dauid.*

VNTO the (O Lorde) I lyft vp my soule.

2 My God, I trust in the: Oh lette me not be confounded, leste myne enemyes tryumphe ouer me.

3 For all they that hope in the shall not be ashamed: but suche as be scornefull despysers without a cause they shall be put to confucyon.

4 Shewe me thy wayes, O Lord, & teach me thy pathes.

5 Lede me in thy trueth and learne me, for thou art the God of my healthe, and in the is my hope al the day long.

6 Call to remembrance, O Lorde, thy tender mercyes and thy louynge kyndenesses, which haue bene euer of olde.

7 Oh remembre not the synnes and offences of my youth, but accordynge vnto thy mercye thynke vpon we, O Lord, for thy goodnesse.

8 O how frendly & rightuous is the Lord, therfore will he teach synners in the way.

9 He ledeth the symple a right, & suche as be meke them lerneth he his wayes.

10 All the wayes of the Lord are verye mercy and faythfulnes, vnto suche as kepe hys testament and couenaunte.

11 For thy names sake, O Lorde, be mercyfull vnto my synne, for it is greate.

12 Whatsoeuer he be that feareth the Lorde he shall shewe hym the waye that he hathe chosen.

13 Hys soule shall dwell at ease, and his sede shal possesse the lande.

14 The secrete of the Lorde is amonge them that feare him, and he sheweth them hys couenaunt.

15 Myne eyes are euer lokynge vnto the Lorde, for he shall plucke my fete oute of the net.

16 Turne the vnto me and haue mercy vpon me, for I am desolate and in misery.

17 The sorowes of my herte, are greate, O brynge me out of my troubles.

18 Loke vpon myne aduersyty and misery, & forgeue me all my synnes.

19 Consyder how myne enemyes are many, and beare a malicious hate against me.

20 O kepe my soule, and delyuer me: let me not be confounded, for I haue put my trust in the.

21 Let inocencye and ryghtuous dealynge walie vpon me, for my hope is in the.

22 Delyuer Israell, O God oute of all hys trouble.

## PSALM 26

*Of Dauid.*

BE thou my iudge, O Lord, for I walke innocently: my trust is in the Lorde therfore shal I not fal.

2 Examen me. O Lorde, and proue me: trye out my raines and my hert

3 For my louynge kindnesse is before mine eyes, and I walke in thy truth.

4 I syt not amonge vayne personnes, & haue no feloshippe with the disceatfull.

5 I hate the congregacyon of the wycked, and I wyll not syt amonge the vngodlye.

6 I wash my handes with innocencye, O Lorde, and so go I to thyne alter.

7 That I may shewe the voice of thy praise and tell of all thy wonderous workes,

8 Lorde, I loue the habitacion of thy house, and the place where thy honoure dwelleth.

9 O destroy not my soule wyth the sinners nor my lyfe with the bloudthursty.

10 In whose handes is wyckednesse, and their right hande is full of gyftes.

11 But as for me I wyll walcke innocentely: O deliuer me, and be mercyfull vnto me.

12 My fote standeth right: I wyll prayse the (O Lorde) in the

congregations.

## PSALM 27

*Of Dauid.*

THE Lorde is my lyghte and my health: whome then shoulde I feare? the Lorde is the strength of my life, for whom then shuld I be afraied?

2 Therfore when the wycked, euen myne enemies and my foes, came vpon me, to eate vp my flesh, stombled and fell.

3 Thoughe an hooste of men were layed agaynst me, yet shall not my hert be afrayed: and though there rose vp warre agaynst me, yet wyll I put my trust in him.

4 One thynge haue I desyred of the Lorde, which I wyll requyre: namelye, that I maye dwel in the house of the Lorde all the dayes of my lyfe, to beholde the fayre beutye of the Lorde, and to viset his temple.

5 For in the tyme of trouble he hath hydde me in his tabernacle, yea in the secrete place of his dwellynge hath he kept and set me vp vpon a rocke of stone.

6 And now hath he lift vp my head aboue myne enemyes, that compassed me rounde aboute. Therfore wyll I offer in hys dwellynge. the oblacyon of thankesgeuynge: I wil singe and speake prayses vnto the Lorde.

7 Herken vnto my voyce, O Lorde, when I crye vnto the: haue mercye vpon me and heare me,

8 My hert speketh vnto the, my face seketh the, yea Lorde, thy face wyll I seke.

9 O hyde not thou thy face fro me, caste not in thy seruaunt of displeasure. Thou art my succour, leaue me not, nether forsake me, O God my sauioure.

10 For my father and my mother haue forsaken me, but the Lord hath taken me vp.

11 Shewe me thy waye O Lord and lede me in the right path, because of myne ennemyes

12 Delyuer me not into the wyles of myne aduersaryes, for there are false wytnesses risen vp against me, and they ymagyne myschyefe.

13 Neuerthelesse I beleue verelye to se the goodnesse of the Lorde in the lande of the lyuynge.

14 O tary thou the Lordes leisure, be strong let thyne hert be of good comfort, and wayte thou still for the Lorde.

## PSALM 28

*Of Dauid.*

VNTO the wil I crye, O my strong defence: thinke no scorne of me, leste if thou make the as thoughe thou herdeste not, I be come lyke them, that go downe in to the pyt.

2 Heare the voyce of my humble peticyon, when I cry vnto the, and hold vp my handes toward thy holy temple.

3 O plucke me not awaye amonge the vngodly and wickeddoers, which speake frendly to their neyghboure, but ymagin mischefe in their hertes.

4 Rewarde them accordynge to their dedes and wyckednesse of their owne inuencyons. Recompence them after the worckes of their handes, paye them that they haue deserued.

5 For they regarde not the worckes of the Lorde, nor the operacyon of his hands: therfore shall he breake them down, and not bild them vp.

6 Praysed be the Lorde, for he hath herd the voyce of myne humble petycyon.

7 The Lord is my strength and my shylde: my hert hoped in hym, and I am helped: therfore my hert daunseth for ioy, and I wil sing praises vnto hym.

8 The Lord is the strength of his people, he is the defender and Sauioure of his anoynted.

9 O helpe thy people, geue thy blessyng vnto thyne enheritaunce: fede them, and set them vp for euer.

## PSALM 29

*A Psalme of Dauid.*

ASCRIBE vnto the Lorde, O ye mightie, ascribe vnto the Lord worship and strength.

2 Geue the Lord the honour of his name bow your selues to the holy magesty of the Lord,

3 It is the Lorde that commaunded the waters: It is the gloryus God that maketh the thonder: it is the Lorde that ruleth the sea.

4 The voyce of the Lorde is mighty in operacyon, the voice of the Lorde is a glorius voyce.

5 The voyce of the Lorde breaketh the Cedre trees: yea the Lorde breaketh the Ceders of Libanus.

6 He maketh them to skyppe lyke a calfe: Libanus and Sirion lyke a younge vnicorne

7 The voyce of the Lorde deuydeth the flames of fyre:

8 the voice of the Lorde shaketh the wylderuesse, yea the Lorde shaketh the wildernesse of Cades.

9 The voyce of the Lorde moueth the hyndes and discouereth the thicke bushes: in hys temple shall euerye man speake of hys honoure.

10 The Lord stilleth the water floud, and the Lord remaineth a king for euer.

11 The Lorde shall geue power vnto hys people, the Lord shall geue his people the blessyng of peace.

## PSALM 30

*A Psalme and songe of the dedicatiou of the house of Dauid.*

I wyll magnifye the, O Lord, for thou hast set me vp, and not suffred my foes to triumphe ouer me.

2 O Lord my God, I cried vnto the, and thou hast healed me.

3 Thou Lord hast brought my soule out of hell: thou hast kepte my lyfe, where as they go downe to the pyt.

4 Singe prayses vnto the Lord (O ye saintes of hys) geue thankes vnto hym for a remembraunce of hys holynesse.

5 For his wrath endureth but the twincling of an eie, and his pleasure is in lyfe: heuinesse may well endure for a nyght, but ioye commeth in the morning.

6 As for me, when I was in prosperytye, I sayd: Tush I shal neuer fall more.

7 And why? thou Lord of thy goodnesse hadest made my hyll so stronge. But as soone as thou turnedest thy face fro me, I was brought in feare.

8 Then cryed I vnto the, O Lorde, yea vnto the Lord made I my praier.

9 What profyt is ther in my bloude, if I go downe to corruption? May the dust geue thankes vnto the? Or shal it declare thy faythfulnesse?

10 Heare, O Lorde, and haue mercye vpon me: Lord be thou my helper.

11 And so thou hast turned my heuynesse into ioye: thou haste put of my sacke cloth, & gyrded me with gladnesse.

12 That mine honoure myght synge praises vnto the without ceasyng: O Lord my God, I wil geue thankes vnto the for euer.

## PSALM 31

*To the chaunter a Psalme of Dauyd.*

In þe O lord, is my trust: let me neuer be put to confusyon, but delyuer me in thy rightuousnesse.

2 Bow downe thyne eare to me, make haste to delyuer me: be thou my strong rocke and a house of defence, that thou mayest saue me.

3 For thou arte my stronge holde and my castel: O be thou my gide and lede me for thy names sake.

4 Drawe me out of the nette that they haue layed pryuelye for me, for thou arte my strength

5 In to thy handes I commende my spirite: thou hast delyuered me O Lorde thou God of truth.

6 I hate them that holde of vanites, and my trust is in the Lord.

7 I wil be glad and reioyse in thy mercy for thou hast consydered my trouble, thou haste knowne my soule in aduersity.

8 Thou hast not delyuered me ouer into the handes of the enemye, but hast set my fete in a large rowme.

9 Haue mercy vpon me, O Lorde, for I am in trouble, myne eye consumed for verye heuynesse, yea my soule and my body.

10 My lyfe is waxen olde with heuines, and my yeares with moornyng. My strength fayleth me because of mine aduersitie, and my bones are corrupt.

11 I am become a verye reprofe amonge all myne enemyes, my neyghbours and they of myne owne aquayntaunce are afraied of me they that se me in the streate, conueye them selues fro me.

12 I am cleane forgotten and oute of mynde as a dead man: I am become lyke a broken vessell.

13 For I haue harde the blasphemy of the multytude: euerye man abhorreth me: they haue gathered a councell together agaynste me, and are purposed to take awaye my lyfe.

14 But my hope is in the Lord, and I say thou art my God.

15 My tyme is in thy hande: deliuer me from the hand of mine enemies, and from them þt persecute me.

16 Shewe thy seruaunte the lyghte of thy countenaunce, helpe me for thy mercyes sake.

17 Let me not be confounded, O Lorde, for I calle vpon the: lette the vngodlye rather be put to confusyon, and broughte vnto the hell.

18 Let the lieng lippes be put to silence which cruely, disdainefully, and despitefully speake against the rightuous.

19 O howe greate and manyfolde is thy good, whyche thou haste hyd for them that feare the? O what things bringest thou to passe for them, that put their truste in the, euen before the sonnes of men?

20 Thou hydest them priuely by thyne owne presence from the proude men, thou kepeste them secretly in thy tabernacle, from þe strife of tonges.

21 Thankes be to the Lorde, for he hath shewed me maruelous greate kyndenesse in a strong cytye.

22 For when the suddaine feare cam vpon me I said: I am cast out of thy sighte. Neuerthelesse, thou herdest myne humble prayer, when I cried vnto the.

23 O loue the Lorde (all ye hys sayncts) for the Lorde preserueth the faythfull, and plenteusly rewardeth he the proud doer.

24 Be strong therfore and take a good herte vnto you, all ye þt put your trust in the Lord.

## PSALM 32

*An instruccyon of Dauid.*

Blessed are they, whose vnryghtuousnes is forgeuen, and whose sinnes are couered.

2 Blessed is the man, vnto whom the Lord imputeth no synne, in whose, spirite ther is no gyle.

3 For while I helde my tonge my bones consumed awaye thorowe my daylye complaynynges.

4 And because thy hand was so heuy vpon me both daye and nyght, my moysture was lyke the drouth in Sommer. Selah.

5 Therfore I confessed my sinne vnto the & hyd not myne vnryghtuousnes. I sayde: I wyll knowledge myne offence and accuse my selfe vnto the Lord, & so þu forgauest me þe wickednesse of my synne Selah.

6 For thys shall euerye sayncte make hys prayer vnto the in due season, therfore shall not, the great water fludes, come nie hym.

7 Thou art my defence in the trouble that is come aboute me, O compasse thou me about also with the ioy of deliuerance. Selah

8 I wyl enforme the, and shew the the waie wherin thou shalt go I wyll fasten myne eyes vpon the.

9 Be not ye now like horses & mules, which haue no vnderstandyng. Whose mouthes thou must hold with bit and bridle, if they wil not obey the.

10 Great plages shal the vngodly haue, but who so putteth hys trust in the Lorde, mercy shall compasse him on euery syde.

11 Be glad, O ye ryghtuous, and reioyse in the Lord, be ioyful al ye þt are true of herte.

## PSALM 33

Reioyse in the Lord, O ye righteous, for it becommeth well þe iust to be thankefull.

2 Prayse the Lord with harpe: singe psalmes vnto him wyth the lute and instrument of ten strynges.

3 Singe hym a new songe, yea, sing lustely vnto hym, and with a good corage.

4 For the woorde of the Lorde is true, & all hys workes are faythful.

5 He loueth mercy and iudgement, the earth is full of the goodnesse of the Lorde.

6 By the worde of the Lorde were the heauens made, and all the hoostes of theym by the breth of hys mouth.

7 He gathereth the waters together as it were in a bottell, and layeth vp the depe in secret.

8 Let all the earth feare the Lorde, and lette all them that dwell in the worlde, stande in awe of hym.

9 For loke what he sayeth, it is done: and loke what he commaundeth, it standeth fast.

10 The Lorde bryngeth the counsayl of the Heythen to naught, and turneth the deuyces of the people.

11 But the counsayll of the Lorde endureth, and the thoughtes of his herte from generacion to generacion.

12 Blessed are the people that holde þe Lorde for their God, & blessed are the folke whome he hath chosen to be hys heretage.

13 The Lorde loketh doune from heauen, & beholdeth all the chyldren of men:

14 from hys stronge seate he considreth all them that dwell in the worlde.

15 He onely hath fashyoned all the hertes of them, and knoweth all their workes.

16 A kynge is not helped by hys owne great hoost, neyther is a giaunte saued thorow the myght of hys owne strength.

17 A horse is but a vayne thing to saue a man, it is not the power of hys strengthe that can delyuer hym.

18 Beholde, the eye of the Lorde loketh vnto them that feare hym, & put their trust in hys mercy.

19 That he maye delyuer their soules frome death, & to fede them in the deare tyme.

20 Let oure soule paciently abyde the Lord, for he is oure helpe and shylde.

21 So shall oure hert reioyse in him, because we haue hoped in hys holy name.

22 Let thy mercifull kyndnesse, O Lorde, be vpon vs, lyke as we put our trust in the.

## PSALM 34

*Of Dauid, when he fayned hym self too be madde before Abimelech: whyche droue hym awaye, and he departed.*

I wyll alwaye geue thanckes vnto the LORD, hys prayse shall euer be in my mouth.

2 My soule shall make her boast in the Lord: the humble shall heare therof, & be glad.

3 O prayse the Lord wyth me, and let vs magnyfye hys name together.

4 I sought the Lorde, and he herde me, yea he delyuered me out of all my feare.

5 They that haue an eye vnto hym, shalbe lightened, & ther faces shal not be ashamed.

6 This poore man cryed vnto the Lorde, & he hearde hym, yea, and delyuered hym oute of all hys troubles.

7 The Aungel of the Lorde pytcheth hys tente rounde aboute hym that feare hym, & delyuereth them.

8 O taste and se how frendly the Lorde is, blessed is the man that trusteth in hym.

9 O feare the Lord, ye that be hys sayntes: for they that feare hym, lacke nothyng.

10 The ryche shall wante and suffre hunger, but they which seke the Lord, shal want no maner of thyng, that is good.

11 Come hyther, O ye chyldren, herken vnto me, I wil teache you the feare of the Lorde.

12 Who so lysteth to lyue, and wolde fayne se good dayes.

13 Let hym refrayne his tonge from euell, & hys lyppes that

they speake no gyle.

14 Let hym eschue euell, and do good: Lette hym seke peace and ensue it.

15 For the eyes of the Lorde are ouer the righteous, and his eares are open vnto theyr prayers.

16 But the face of the Lorde beholdeth them that do euell, to destroye the remembraunce of them out of the earth.

17 When the righteous crye, the Lorde heareth them, & delyuereth them out of all theyr troubles.

18 The Lorde is nye vnto them that are contryte in hert, and will helpe suche as be of an humble sprete.

19 Great are the troubles of the righteous, but the Lorde delyuereth them out of all.

20 He kepeth all their bones, so that not one of them is broken.

21 But misfortune shall slaye the vngodly, & they that hate the righteous shalbe gylty.

22 The Lorde deliuereth the soules of hys seruauntes, and all they that put their truste in hym, shall not offende.

## PSALM 35

*Of Dauid.*

STRYUE thou with them, O lord, that stryue with me, fight thou against them that fight against me.

2 Laye hande vpon the shylde and speare, and stande vp to helpe me.

3 Drawe out thy swearde, and stoppe the waye agaynst them that persecute me, saye vnto my soule: I am thy helpe.

4 Let them be confounded & put to shame, that seke after my soule: let theym be turned back and brought to confusion, that ymagin mischiefe for me.

5 Let them be as the dust before the winde, and the aungel of the Lord scateryng them.

6 Let their waye be darcke and slippery, & the aungell of the Lorde to persecute them.

7 For they haue priuely layed their nette to destroye me without a cause, yea, & made a pytte for my soule, which I neuer deserued.

8 Let a soden destruccion come vpon hym vnwares, & the nette that he had layed pryuely, catche hym selfe, that he maye fall into hys owne mischief.

9 But let my soule be ioyfull in the Lorde, and reioyse in hys helpe.

10 All my bones shall saye: Lorde who is lyke vnto the? which deliuerest the poore from those that are to strong for him, yea, the poore and the nedy from hys robbers.

11 False witnesses are rysen vp, and laye to my charge thinges that I know not.

12 They rewarde me euell for good, too the great discomforte of my soule.

13 Neuerthelesse, when they were sycke, I put on a sacke cloth: I humbled my soule with fastyng, and my prayer turned into myne owne bosome.

14 I behaued my selfe as though it had bene my frende or my brother, I went heuely, as one that mourneth for hys mother.

15 But in myne aduersitie they reioyse, & gather them together. Yea, the very lame come together agaynste me vnwares, makynge mowes at me, and ceasse not.

16 With the gredy and scorneful hypocrites they gnasshed vpon me with their teeth.

17 Lorde, whan wilt thou loke vpon thys? O restore my soule from the wycked rumoure of them, my dearlynge from the lyons?

18 So will I geue the thanckes in the great congregacion, and prayse the among muche people.

19 O let them not triumphe ouer me, that are myne enemyes for naught: O let them not winke with their eyes, that hate me without a cause.

20 And why? their comening is not for peace but they ymagyn false wordes agaynste the outcastes of the lande.

21 They gape vpon me with their mouthes, saying: there, there: we se it with our eyes.

22 This thou seist, O lorde: holde not thy tonge then, go not farre fro me, O lorde.

23 Awake lorde, and stande vp: auenge thou my cause, my God, and my lorde,

24 Iudge me, O lorde my God, accordynge to thy righteousnesse, that they triumphe not ouer me.

25 O let them not saye in their hertes: there there, so wolde we haue it: O let them not saye: we haue ouercome hym.

26 Let them be put to confusion & shame, that reioyse at my trouble: let them be clothed wt rebuke and dishonoure, that boost them selfes agaynst me.

27 Let them also be glad and reioyse, that fauoure my righteous dealynge: yea, let them saye alwaye: blessed be the lord, whiche hath pleasure in the prosperitie of hys seruaunt.

28 And as for my tonge, it shalbe talkyng of thy righteousnes and of thy prayse, all þe day longe.

## PSALM 36

*To the chaunter, of Dauid the seruaunt of the Lorde.*

MY hert sheweth me the wickednesse of the vngodly, that there is no feare of God before hys eyes.

2 For he dissembleth before his face, so longe tyll hys abhominable sinne be founde out.

3 The woordes of hys mouth are vnrighteousnes and disceate,

he will not be learned to do good.

4 He ymagineth mischief vpon his bedde he wil come in no good waye, nor refuse the thyng that is euel.

5 Thy mercy, O Lorde, reacheth vnto the heauen, and thy faythfulnesse vnto the cloudes.

6 Thy righteousnesse standeth lyke þe strong mountaynes, and thy iudgemente lyke the great depe. Thou Lord preseruest both men and beastes.

7 How precious is thy mercy, O God, that the chyldren of men maye put their trust vnder the shadowe of thy wynges?

8 They shalbe satisfied with the plenteousnesse of thy house, and thou shalte geue them drynke of the ryuer of thy pleasures.

9 For by the is the wel of lyfe, and in thy lyght, shall we se lyght.

10 O sprede forth thy louing kyndnesse vnto them that knowe the, and thy ryghteousnesse vnto them that are true of hert.

11 O let not the fote of pride ouertake me, O let not the hande of the vngodly caste me doune.

12 As for wycked doers, they fall, they are cast doune, and are not able to stande.

## PSALM 37

*A Psalme of Dauid.*

FRET not thy selfe at the vngodly be not thou enuious agaynst the euel doers.

2 For they shall soone be cutte doune lyke the grasse, & be wythered euen as the grene herbe.

3 Put thou thy trust in the Lorde, and be doyng good: so shalt thou dwel in the lande, & verely it shall fede the.

4 Delyte thou in the Lorde, & he shall geue the thy hertes desire.

5 Committe thy waye vnto the Lorde, sette thy hope in hym, and he shall brynge it too passe.

6 He shal make thy righteousnesse as cleare as the light, & thy iust dealynge as the noone daye.

7 Holde the styl in the Lord, and abyde paciently vpon hym: but greue not thy selfe at one that hath prosperytie, and lyueth in abhominacion.

8 Leaue of from wrath, let go displeasure, let not thy gelousy moue the also to do euell.

9 For wycked doers shalbe roted oute, but they that paciently abyde the Lord, shall enheret the lande.

10 Suffre yet a litle whyle, and the vngodly shalbe cleane gone: thou shalt loke after hys place, and he shalbe awaye.

11 But the meke spreted shall possesse þe earth, and haue pleasure in muche rest.

12 The vngodly layeth wayte for the iust, & gnassheth vpon him with his tethe.

13 But the Lord laugheth him to scorne, for he seyth that his daye is commyng.

14 The vngodly drawe oute the swerde & bende their bowe, to caste doune the simple and poore, and to slaye suche as go the right waye.

15 Neuertheles, their swerde shal go thorow their owne hert, and theyr bowe shalbe broken.

16 A small thinge that the righteous hath, is better then great ryches of the vngodly.

17 For the armes of the vngodly shalbe broken, but the Lorde vpholdeth the ryghteous.

18 The Lord knoweth the dayes of þe Godly and their inheritaunce endureth for euer.

19 They shall not be confounded in the perlous tyme, and in the daies of derth thei shal haue ynough.

20 As for the vngodly, they shall perysh: and when the enemyes of the Lorde are in theyr floures, they shall consume, yea, euen as the smoke shall they consume awaye.

21 The vngodly boroweth and payeth not agayne, but the righteous is mercyfull and lyberall.

22 Such as be blessed of hym, shall possesse þe lande: and they whome he curseth, shalbe roted out.

23 The Lorde ordreth a good mans goynge, and hath pleasure in hys waye.

24 Though he fall, he shall not be hurte, for the Lorde vpholdeth him with his hande.

25 I haue bene yonge, and now am olde: yet sawe I neuer the righteous forsaken, nor hys sede to seke their bread.

26 The righteous is euer mercifull, and lendeth gently, therfore shal his sede be blessed.

27 Fle from euell, and do the thynge that is good, so shalt thou dwell for euer.

28 For the Lorde loueth the thynge that is ryght, he forsaketh not hys sainctes, but thei shalbe preserued for euermore: as for the sede of the vngodly, it shalbe roted out.

29 Yea, the righteous shal possesse the land, and dwell therein for euer.

30 The mouth of the righteous is exercised in wysdome, and hys tonge talketh of iudgement.

31 The lawe of his God is in his hert, therfore shall not his fotesteppes slyde.

32 The vngodly seyth the righteous, & goeth aboute to slaye hym.

33 But the Lorde will not leaue him in hys handes, nor condempne him when he is iudged.

34 Hope thou in the Lord, & kepe his waye, & he shal so promote the, that thou shalt haue the lande by enheritaunce, and

se, when the vngodly shall perishe.

35 I my selfe haue sene the vngodly in great power, & florishinge lyke a grene baye tree:

36 but when I went by, lo, he was gone: I sought hym, but he coulde no where be founde.

37 Kepe innocency, and take hede vnto the thynge that is ryghte, for that shall brynge a man peace at the last.

38 As for the transgressours, they shall peryshe together, and the vngodly shall be roted out at the laste.

39 The helpe of the righteous commeth of the Lorde, he is their strength in the tyme of trouble.

40 The Lorde shall stande by them, and saue them: he shall delyuer them from the vngodly and helpe them, because they put their truste in hym.

## PSALM 38

*To the chaunter, to brynge too remembraunce.*

PVTTE me not too rebuke (Oh Lorde) in thyne anger: Oh chasten me not in thy heuy displeasure.

2 For thyne arrowes stycke fast in me, and thy hande presseth me sore.

3 There is no whole parte in my body, because of thy displeasure: there is no reste in my bones, by reason of my synnes.

4 For my wyckednesses are gone ouer my head, and are like a sore burthen, to heuy for me to beare.

5 My woundes styncke and are corrupte, thorow my folyshnesse.

6 I am broughte into so greate trouble and mysery, that I go mournynge all the daye longe.

7 For my loynes are cleane dryed vp, and there is no whole parte in my body.

8 I am feble & sore smytten, I roare for the very disquietnes of my hert.

9 Lorde, thou knowest all my desyre, & my gronynge is not hyd from the.

10 My hert panteth, my strengthe hath fayled me, and the lighte of myne eyes is gone fro me.

11 My louers and frendes stande lokynge vpon my trouble, and my kynsmen are gone afarre of.

12 They that sought after my lyfe, and to do me euell, spake of lyes & ymagined disceate all the daye longe.

13 As for me, I was lyke a deaf man & herde not: and as one that were domme, not openynge hys mouth.

14 I am become as a man that heareth not: and that can make no resistaunce wyth hys mouth.

15 For in the, O Lorde, is my truste, thou shalt heare me, O Lorde my God.

16 My desyre is, that myne enemyes triumphe not ouer me: for if my foote slyppe, they reioyse greatly agaynst me.

17 I am ready to suffre trouble, and my heuinesse is euer in my sight.

18 For I confesse my wyckednesse, and my synne greueth me.

19 But myne enemyes lyue, & are mightye: and they that hate me without a cause, are many in numbre.

20 They þt rewarde me euel for good, speake euell of me, because I folowe the thyng that good is.

21 Forsake me not (O Lord my God) O go not farre fro me.

22 Haste the to helpe me, O Lorde my succoure.

## PSALM 39

*To the chanter for Iduthun, a Psalme of Dauid.*

I sayde: I wyll kepe my wayes that I offende not in my tonge And so I shutte my mouthe whyle the vngodly layed wait for me.

2 I helde my tonge, I was domme, I kept sylence, yea euen from good wordes, but it was payne and grefe to me.

3 My hert was hote within me, and whyle I was thus musyng, the fyre kindled: so that I spake wyth my tong.

4 Lorde, let me knowe myne ende, and the numbre of my dayes: that I may be certified what I want.

5 Behold, thou hast made my dayes a span longe, and my lyfe as it were nothynge before the. O how vayne are all men liuing? Selah

6 Yea euery man walketh as it were a shadow, and disquieth him selfe in vayne: he heapeth vp ryches, and can not tell to whome he gathereth them.

7 And now Lorde wherin shall I comforte me? my hope is in the.

8 Delyuer me from all myne offences, and make me not a scorne vnto the folish.

9 I kepe sylence, and open not my mouthe, for thou hast done it.

10 Turne thy plages awaye fro me, for I am consumed thorow the feare of thy hande.

11 When thou punishest man for sinne. thou chastenest him: so þt his beutye consumeth awaye, lyke as it were a moth. O how vayne are al men? Selah.

12 Heare my prayer O Lorde, and consyder my callynge: shewe not thy selfe as though thou sawest not my teares. For I am a straunger and pilgrymme wyth the, as all my forefathers were.

13 Oh spare me a lytle that I may refreshe my selfe, before I goo hence, and be no more sene.

## PSALM 40

*To the chaunter, a Psalme of*

*Dauid.*

I waited pacyently for þe Lord, which enclined hym selfe vnto me: and herd my callynge.

2 He brought me out of the horryble pitte, out of the myre and claye: he set my fete vpon the rocke, & ordred my goinges.

3 He hath put a newe songe in my mouthe, euen a thanckes geuynge vnto oure God. Many men seing this shal feare the Lord, and put their trust in hym.

4 Blessed is the man that setteth his hope in the Lorde, and turneth not vnto the proud, & to such as go aboute with lyes.

5 O Lorde my God, greate are thy wonderous worckes whiche thou haste done: and in thy thoughtes toward vs there maye none be likened vnto the. I wold declare them, and speake of them: but they are so manye, that they can not be tolde.

6 Sacryfyce and offerynge thou wouldeste not haue but a bodye haste thou ordeyned me: burnt offerynges and sacrifyce for synne thou hast not alowed.

7 Then sayde I: Lo, I come. In the begynnynge of the boke is it written of me,

8 that I shoulde fulfyl thy wyl O my God, and that am I content to do: yea thy lawe is wythin my hert.

9 I will preach of thy ryghtuousnesse in the great congregacyon: Lo. I wyl not refraine my lippes, O Lorde, and that thou knowest.

10 I do not hyde thy ryghtuousnes in my hert, my talkinge is of thy trueth and sauing health: I kepe not thy louyng mercy & faythfulnesse backe from the greate congregacyon.

11 Turne not thou thy mercy fro me O Lord but let thy louynge kyndnesse and trueth alwaye preseue me.

12 For innumerable troubles are come about me: my synnes haue taken suche holde vpon me that I am not able to loke vp: yea they are mo in number then the heares of my head and my hert hath fayled me.

13 O Lorde, let it be thy pleasure to delyuer me make hast (Lord) to help me.

14 Let them be ashamed and confunded, that seke after my soule, to destroye it: let them fall backwarde and be put to confusion, that wish me euell.

15 Let them soone be broughte to shame, that crye ouer me, there there.

16 But let all those that seke the, be ioyfull and glad in the: & let al such as delyte in thye sauyng health, say alway: þe Lord be praised.

17 As for me, I am poore and in miserye, but the Lord careth for me. Thou art my helper and redemer, make no long tariyng, O my God.

## PSALM 41

*To the chaunter, a Psalme of Dauid.*

BLESSED is he, that consydereth the poore: the Lord shal deliuer him in þe tyme of trouble.

2 The Lord shal preserue him & kepe him aliue: he shall make him to prospere vpon earth, and shall not delyuer him into the wyl of his enemeyes.

3 The Lord shal refresh him, when he lyeth sicke vpon his bed, yea thou makest hys bed in al his sicknesse.

4 I sayd: Lord be mercifull vnto me, heale my soule, for I haue synned agaynst the.

5 Myne enemyes speake euel vpon me: when shal he die, and his name perishe.

6 Though he came in to se, yet meaned he falsede in his hert, heapyng myscheyfe vpon hym selfe.

7 All they that hate me, runne together agaynst me, and ymagyn euell against me.

8 They haue geuen a wycked sentence vpon me: when he lyeth, he shall ryse vp no more.

9 Yea euen myne owne famylyer frende, whom I trusted, whiche dyd eate my breade hath lyfte vp his hele agaynste me.

10 But be thou mercyful vnto me (O Lord) rayse thou me vp, and I shall reward them

11 By this I know thou fauourest me, that. my enemy shal not triumphe ouer me.

12 Thou hast vpholden me because of my innocency, and set me before thy face for euer.

13 O blessed be the Lorde God of Israel, from hence forth and for euermore. Amen. Amen.

## PSALM 42

*To the chaunter, a monicion of the sonnes of Corah.*

LIKE as the hert desyreth the water brokes, so longeth my soule after the, O God.

2 My soule is a thurste for God, yea euen for the lyuynge God: when shall I come, and behold the face of God?

3 My teares are my meate daye and nighte whyle it is daylye sayed vnto me: where is now thy God?

4 Now when I thincke ther vpon, I poure out my hert by my self: for I would faine go hence wyth the multytude and passe ouer wt them vnto the house of God, in the voyce of prayse and thankes geuynge, amonge suche as kepe holy daye.

5 Why art thou so full of heuynes, (O my soule) and why arte thou so vnquyet wythin me? O put thy trust in God, for I wyl yet geue him thankes, for the helpe of his countenance

6 My God, my soule is vexed wythin me: therfore I remembre the lande of Iordaine, and the little hyl of Hermonim.

7 One depe calleth another

wyth the voyce of thy whistles, al thy waues and water floudes are gone ouer me.

8 The Lorde hath promysed hys louynge kyndnesse daylye, therfore will I prayse him in the night season, and make my prayer vnto the God of my lyfe.

9 I wyll say vnto God my stony rock: why host thou forgotten me? why go I thus heuely, whyle the enemye oppresseth me?

10 Whyle my bones are broken, whyle mine enemyes cast me in the teeth, daylye saiynge vnto me: where is now thy God?

11 Why art thou so heuy (O my soule) & why art thou so disquieted within me? O put thy trust in God, for I wyll yet thanke hym for the helpe of hys countenaunce, and because he is my God.

## PSALM 43

Geue sentence vpon me (O God) and defende my cause agaynst the vnholy people: Oh delyuer me from the dysceatefull, and wycked man.

2 For thou (O God) art my strength: why hast thou shut me from the? Why go I then so heuely, whyle the enemye oppresseth me?

3 Oh sende out thy light any thy truth, that they maye leade me and brynge me vnto thy holy hyll, and to thy dwellyng.

4 That I maye go into the aulter of God, euen vnto the God whyche is my ioye & pleasure, and vpon the harpe to geue thankes vnto the, O God, my God.

5 Why art thou so heuy (O my soule) and why art thou so disquyeted wythin me? O put thy trust in God, for I wyll yet geue hym thanckes for the helpe of hys countenaunce, and because he is my God.

## PSALM 44

*To the chaunter an instruccyon of the sonnes of Corah.*

WE haue herde with our eares (O God) our fathers haue told vs, what thou hast don in their tyme of olde

2 Howe thou hast dryuen out the Heythen wyth thy hand, and planted them in: how thou hast destroyed the nacions and cast them out.

3 For they gat not the lande in possessyon thorowe their owne swearde, neyther was it their owne arme that helped them. But thy ryght hande, thyne arme and the lyght of thy countenaunce, because thou haddest a fauoure vnto them.

4 Thou arte the Kynge and my God, thou sendest helpe vnto Iacob.

5 Thorow the, wyll we ouerthrow our enemyes: and in thy name wyll we treade them vnder, that ryse vp agaynst vs.

6 For I wyll not trust in my bowe, it is not my sweard that shall helpe me.

7 But it is thou that sauest vs from our enemyes: and puttest them to confusyon that hate vs.

8 We wyll alway make our boast of God, and prayse thy name for euer. Selah.

9 But now thou forsakest vs, and puttest vs to confusyon, and goest not forth wyth oure Hostes.

10 Thou makest vs to turne oure backes vpon oure enemyes, so that they which hate vs spoyle our goodes.

11 Thou lettest vs be eaten vp lyke shepe, & scaterest vs among the Heathen.

12 Thou sellest thy people for naught, and takest no money for them.

13 Thou makeste vs to be rebuked of oure neyghboures, to be laughed to scorne & had in derision, of them that are rounde about vs

14 Thou hast made vs, a very by word among the Heathen, and that the people shake their heades at vs.

15 My confusion is dayly before me, and the shame of my face couereth me.

16 For the voyce of the sclaunderer and blasphemer, for the enemye and auenger.

17 All this is come vpon vs, and yet haue we not forgotten the ner behaued oure selues vnfaythfully in thy couenaunt.

18 Oure herte is not turned backe, neyther our steps gone out of thy way.

19 For thou hast smitten vs in the place of dragones, and couered vs with the shadow of death.

20 If we had forgotten the name of our God and holden vp oure handes to any straunge God.

21 Should not God fynde it out? for he knoweth the very secretes of the herte.

22 But for thy sake we are kylled all the daye longe, and are counted as shepe apoynted to be slayne.

23 Vp Lorde, why slepest thou? wake, and cast vs not of for euer.

24 Wherfore hydest thy face? wylte thou cleane forget oure mysery and oppression

25 For oure soule is brought low euen vnto the dust, and our bely cleueth vnto the ground

26 Arise O Lord, helpe vs and delyuer vs for thy mercy sake.

## PSALM 45

*To the chaunter, vpon Sosanim, an instruccion of the chyldren of Corah, a songe of loue.*

MI herte is endytinge of a godd matter, I speake of that, which I haue made of the kynge: My tonge is the penne of a ready wryter.

2 Thou arte the fayrest amonge the chyldren of men,

full of grace are thy lyppes, therfore God blesseth the for euer.

3 Gyrde the with thy swerde vpon thy thyghe (O thou mightye) with worshippe and renowne.

4 Good lucke haue thou with thyne honor, ryde on with the trueth, mekenesse & righteousnes: and thy righthand shall teach the wonderfull thynges.

5 Thy arrowes are sharpe, þe people shal be subdued vnto the, euen in the myddest amonge the kynges enemyes.

6 Thy seate (O God) endureth for euer: the scepter of thy kyngdome is a right scepter.

7 Thou hast loued righteousnesse, & hated iniquitie: wherfore God (which is thy God) hath anoynted the with the oyle of gladnes aboue thy felowes.

8 All thy garmentes are lyke myrre, Aloes & Cassia, when thou commest out of thine yuerye palaces in thy beutifull glory.

9 Kynges daughters go in thy goodly aray and vpon thy right hande standeth the quene in a vesture of the most fyne golde.

10 Herken (O daughter) considre, & enclyne thyne eare: forget thyne owne people, & thy fathers house.

11 So shall the kynge haue pleasure in thy beuty, for he is thy Lorde, & thou shalte worshyp hym.

12 The daughters of Tire shalbe there with gyftes, the ryche amonge the people shall make their supplication before the.

13 The kynges daughter is all glorious within, her clothyng is of wrought golde.

14 She shalbe brought vnto the kyng in rayment of nedle worke, & maidens after her: such as be next her shalbe brought vnto the.

15 Wyth ioye and gladnesse shall they be brought, & go into the kynges palace.

16 In steade of thy fathers thou hast gotten chyldren, whome thou shalt make princes in all landes.

17 I wyll remembre thy name from one generacion to another: therfore shall the people geue thankes vnto the, worlde withoute ende.

## PSALM 46

*To the chaunter, a songe of the children of Corah vpon almuth.*

IN oure troubles & aduersitye, we haue founde, that God is oure refuge, oure strength and helpe.

2 Therfore wyl we not feare though the earth fell, and though the hylles were caryed into the myddest of the sea.

3 Though the waters of the sea raged and were neuer so troublous, and thoughe the mountaynes shoke at the tempest of the same. Selah.

4 For there is a floude, which with hys ryuers reioyseth the cytye of God, the holy dwellyng of the moost hyest.

5 God is in the middest of her, therfore shal she not be remoued: for God helpeth her, & that right early.

6 The Heythen are madde, the kingdomes make muche a do: but when he sheweth hys voyce, the earth melteth awaye.

7 The Lord of hoostes is with vs, the God of Iacob is oure defence. Selah.

8 O come hither, and beholde the woorkes of the LORD, what destruccions he hathe brought vpon the earth.

9 He hath made warres to cease in all the worlde: he hathe broken the bowe, he hathe knapped the speare in sonder, and brente the charettes in the fyre.

10 Be styll then and confesse that I am God I will be exalted amonge the Heythen, and I will be exalted vpon earth.

11 The Lord of hostes is with vs, the God of Iacob is our defence. Selah.

## PSALM 47

*To the chaunter, a Psalme of the chyldren of Corah.*

O clappe youre handes together (all ye people) O synge vnto God with the voyce of thankesgeuynge.

2 For the Lord the most hyest is to be feared, and he is the great kyng vpon all the earth.

3 He shal subdue the people vnder vs, and the Heythen vnder oure fete.

4 He choseth vs for an heretage, the beutye of Iacob whome he loued. Selah.

5 God is gone vp with a mery noyse, & the Lord with the sownde of the trompet.

6 O singe prayses, singe prayses vnto God O singe prayses, singe prayses vnto oure kynge.

7 For God is kyng of all the earth, O sing prayses vnto hym with vnderstandynge.

8 God is kyng ouer the Heythen, God sitteth in hys holy seate.

9 The pryncess of the people are gathered together vnto the God of Abraham: for God is farre hyer exalted, then the mighty lordes of the earth.

## PSALM 48

*A songe of a Psalme of the chyldren of Corah.*

GREATE is the Lorde & hyely too be praysed, in the cytye of oure God, euen vpon hys holy hyl.

2 The hyll of Syon is lyke a fayre plante, whereof all the lande reioyseth: vpon the north side lyeth the cytye of the great kyng.

3 God is well knowen in her palaces, that he is the defence of the same.

4 For lo, kynges are gathered, and gone by together.

5 They marueled, to se suche thynges: they were astonied, and sodenly cast doune.

6 Feare came there vpon them, and sorow as vpon a woman in her trauayle.

7 Thou shalt breake the shyppes of the sea, thorow the East wynde.

8 Lyke as we haue herde, so se we in the cytye of the Lord of hoostes, in the citie of oure God. God vpholdeth the same for euer. Selah.

9 We wayte for thy louynge kyndnesse (O God) in the middest of thy temple.

10 O God, according vnto thy name, so is thy praise vnto the worldes ende: thy right hande is full of righteousnes.

11 Oh let the mount Sion reioyse, and the daughters of Iuda be glad because of iudgementes.

12 Walke about Sion, go rounde about her and tell her towres.

13 Marke well her walles, sette vp her houses. that it may be tolde them that come after.

14 For this God is our God for euer & euer, and he shall alwaye be oure guyde.

# PSALM 49

*To the chaunter, a Psalme of the chyldren of Corah.*

O heare thys, all ye people: pondre it wel, all ye that dwel vpon the earth.

2 Hye & lowe, & rych & poore, one wyth another.

3 My mouth shall speake of wysdome, and my hert shall muse of vnderstandynge.

4 I will enclyne myne eare to the parable, and shewe my darke speach vpon the harpe.

5 Wherfore should I feare the euel dayes, when the wickednesse of my heles compaseth me rounde aboute?

6 They that put their trust in their good, & boast theym selfes in the multitude of theyr ryches.

7 No man may deliuer his brother, nor make agrement vnto hym for God.

8 For it costeth more to redeme their soules so that he must let that alone for euer.

9 Yea, though he liue longe, and se not the graue.

10 For it shalbe sene, that such wyse men shal dye and perysh together, as wel as the ignoraunt and folysh, and leue their goodes for other.

11 Loke what is in their houses, it contynueth still: their dwellyng places endure from one generacion to another, and are called after their owne names vpon the earth.

12 Neuerthelesse man abydeth not in suche honour, but is compared vnto the brute beastes, and becommeth lyke vnto them.

13 This waye of theirs is very folyshnesse, and yet their posteritie prayse it wyth theyr mouth. Selah.

14 They lye in the hell like shepe, death shall gnawe vpon theim, and the righteous shall haue dominacion of theim in the mornynge by tymes: their strength shall consume, and hell shalbe their dwellynge.

15 But God shall deliuer my soule from the power of hell, when he receyueth me. Selah.

16 O be not thou afraied, when one is made ryche, & the glory of hys house increased.

17 For he shall cary nothynge away wyth hym when he dyeth, neither shall his pompe folowe hym.

18 Whyle he lyueth, he is counted an happy man: and so long as he is in prosperitie, men speake good of hym.

19 But when he foloweth his fathers generacion, he shall neuer se light any more.

20 When a man is in honour and hath no vnderstandinge, he is compared vnto the brute beastes, and becommeth lyke vnto them.

# PSALM 50

*A Psalme of Asaph.*

THE Lord euen the mighty God hath spoken, & called the world from the risyng vp of the sunne vnto the goynge doune of the same.

2 Out of Sion apeareth the glorious beuty of God.

3 Oure God shal come, and not kepe silence there goeth before him a consuming fyre, and a mighty tempest round about him.

4 He shall call the heauens from aboue, and the earth, that he may iudge his people.

5 Gather my saynctes together vnto me, those that set more by the couenant then by any offering.

6 And the heauens shal declare his rightuousnes, for God is iudge him selfe. Selah

7 Heare, O my people: let me speake, let me testify among you, O Israell: I am God, euen thy God.

8 I reproue the not because of thy sacryfice thy burnteofferynges are allwaye before me.

9 I wil take no bullockes out of thy house, nor gotes out of thy foldes.

10 For all the beastes of the felde are myne, and thousandes of cattell vppon the hylles.

11 I know al the foules vpon the mountaynes, and the wylde beastes of the felde are in my sight.

12 If I be hongry, I wyll not tell the: for the whole worlde is myne, & all that therein is.

13 Thynkest thou, that I will

eate the fleshe of oxen, or drynke the bloude of goates?

14 Offre vnto God prayse and thankesgeuynge, and paye thy vowes vnto the most hyest.

15 And call vpon me in the tyme of trouble, so wyll I heare the, that thou shalte thanke me.

16 But vnto the vngodly sayeth God? Why doest thou preach my lawes, and takest my couenaunt in thy mouth?

17 Where as thou hatest to be refourmed, and castest my woordes behynde the?

18 If thou seist a thefe, thou runnest wyth him, and art partaker with the aduouterers.

19 Thou lettest thy mouthe speake wickednesse, and thy tonge paynteth disceate.

20 Thou sittest & speakest agaynste thy brother, yea, & sclaundrest thyne owne mothers sonne.

21 This thou doest, whyle I holde my tonge and thynkest me to be euen suche one as thy self: but I wyll reproue the, and set my selfe agaynst the.

22 O considre this, ye that forget God: lest I plucke you awaye, and there be none too delyuer you.

23 Who so offreth me thankes and prayse, he honoureth me: & this is the way, wherby I wyll shewe hym the sauynge healthe of God.

## PSALM 51

*To the chaunter, a Psalme of Dauid, when the prophet Nathan came vnto hym, after he was gone into Bethsabe.*

HAUE mercy vpon me (O God) after thy goodnes, & according vnto thy great mercyes, do awaye myne offences.

2 Wash me well fro my wickednesse, and clense me fro my synne.

3 For I knowledge my fautes, & my synne is euer before me.

4 Agaynst the only, agaynst the haue I sinned, & done euel in thy sight: that thou mightest be iustified in thy saynges, and shouldest ouercome when thou art iudged.

5 Beholde, I was borne in wickednesse, & in synne hath my mother conceyued me.

6 But lo, thou hast a pleasure in the trueth, and hast shewed me secrete wisdome.

7 O purge me with Isope, and I shall be cleane: wash thou me, and I shalbe whyter then snowe.

8 Oh let me heare of ioye & gladnesse, that the bones which thou hast broken, maye reioyse.

9 Turne thy face from my synnes, & put oute all my misdedes.

10 Make me a cleane hert, O God, & renue a right sprete within me.

11 Cast me not awaye from thy presence, & take not thy holy sprete from me.

12 O geue me the comforte of thy helpe agayne, and stablish me with thy sprete.

13 Then shall I teache thy wayes vnto the wicked, þt sinners may be conuerted vnto the.

14 Deliuer me from bloude giltinesse, O God, thou that art the God of my health, that my tonge may prayse thy righteousnesse.

15 Open my lyppes, O LORD, that my mouth maye shewe thy prayse.

16 For if thou haddest pleasure in sacrifice, I wolde geue it the: but thou delytest not in burntofferinges.

17 The sacryfice of God is a troubled spirit a broken and a contrite hert, O God, shalte thou not despyse.

18 O be fauourable gracyous vnto Syon, that the walles of Ierusalem maye be buylded,

19 For when shalt thou be pleased wyth the sacrifice of ryghtuousnes, with the burntofferinges and oblations: then shal they laye bullockes vpon thine alter.

## PSALM 52

*To the chaunter, an exortacyon of Dauid when Doeg the Edomite came to Saul, and shewed hym, sayinge: Dauid is come to the house of Ahimelech.*

WHY boastest thou thy self, thou Tyrraunt, that thou canste do myschiefe? Wher as the goodnesse of God endureth yet dayly.

2 Thy tonge ymagyneth wyckednesse, and with lyes it cutteth like a sharpe rasoure.

3 Thou loueste vngratiousnesse more then good, to talke of lyes more then ryghtuousnesse. Selah.

4 Thou louest to speake al wordes that may do hurte. O thou false tonge.

5 Therfore shall God cleane destroye the, smyte the in peces, pluke the out of thy dwellynge, and rote the out of the lande of the lyuynge. Selah.

6 The rightuous shal se this, and feare, and laugh him to scorne,

7 Lo, this is the man, that toke not God for his strength but trusted vnto the multitud of his riches, & was myghty in his wickednes.

8 As for me, I am lyke a grene olyue tree in the house of God: my truste is in the tender mercy of God for euer and euer.

9 I wyll alwaye geue thankes vnto the, for that thou hast done: & wil hope in thy name, for thy sayntes lyke it wel.

## PSALM 53

*To the chaunter vpon Mahalath, an instruccyon of Dauid.*

THE folysh bodyes saye in their hertes: Tush, there is no

God. Corrupte are they & become abhomynable in their wyckednesse: there is not one, that doth good.

2 God loked downe from heauen vpon the chyldren of men, to se if there were any that would vnderstand, or seke after God.

3 But they are all gone out of the waye they are al become vnprofitable: ther is none that doth good, no not one.

4 How can they haue vnderstandynge, that are the worckers of wyckednes, eatynge vp my people as it were breade, and call not vpon God?

5 They are afrayed, where no feare is: for God breaketh the bones of them that beseige the: thou puttest them to confusion, for God despiseth them.

6 Oh that the sauynge healthe were geuen vnto Israel out of Sion: Oh that the Lorde woulde delyuer his people out of captiuity. Then shoulde Iacob reioyse, and Israell should be ryght glad.

## PSALM 54

*To the chaunter in Neginoth, an instruccyon of Dauyd, when the Zephytes came and sayed vnto Saul: Dauid is hydde amongest vs.*

HELPE me (O God) for thy names sake, and deliuer me in thy strength.

2 Heare my prayer (O God) considre þe wordes of my mouth.

3 For straungers are rysen vp agaynst me, and the mighty (which haue not God before their eyes) seke after my soule. Selah.

4 But lo, God is my helper: it is he that vpholdeth my soule.

5 He shall reward euel vnto myne enemies and in thy trueth shalt thou destroy them.

6 A fre will offerynge will I geue the, and prayse thy name O Lorde, because it is so comfortable.

7 For thou hast deliuered me out of all my trouble, so that myne eye seith his desire vpon myne enemyes.

## PSALM 55

*To the chaunter in Neginoth, an instruccion of Dauid.*

HEARE my prayer, O God, and hyde not thy self fro my petycion.

2 Take hede vnto me & heare me, how piteously I mourne and complayne.

3 The enemye cryeth so, and the vngodly commeth on so fast: for they are mynded too do me some mischief, so maliciously are they set agaynst me.

4 My hert is heuy within me, and the feare of death is fallen vpon me.

5 Fearfulnesse and tremblynge are come vpon me, and an horrible drede hathe ouerwhelmed me.

6 And I sayde: O that I had wynges lyke a doue, that I might fle somwhere, and be at rest.

7 Lo, then wolde I get me awaye farre of, and remayne in the wildernesse. Selah.

8 I wolde make haste to escape, from the stormy wynde and tempest.

9 Destroye their tonges (O Lorde) and deuyde them, for I se vnrighteousnes & stryfe in the cytye.

10 Thys goeth daye and nyght aboute the walles, mischief and vyce are in the middest of it.

11 Wickednesse is therin, disceate and gyle go not out of her stretes.

12 If it were myne enemye that reuyled me, I could beare it: or if one that ought me euel wyll dyd threaten me, I wolde hyde my self from hym.

13 But it is thou my companyon, my gyde & myne owne familier frende.

14 We had swete and secrete communicacion together in the house of God.

15 Let death come hastely vppon them, and let them goo doune quyck into hell, for wickednes is amonge theym in their dwellynges.

16 As for me, I will call vnto God, and the Lord shall helpe me.

17 In the euenynge, mornyng and at noone daye will I mourne and complayne: and he shall heare my voyce.

18 It is he that deliuereth my soule in peace, from them that laye wayte for me: for they are many agaynst me.

19 Yea, euen God that endureth for euer, shall heare me, and bring them doune. Selah. For they will not turne: and why? they feare not God.

20 Yea, they laye handes vpon such as be at peace with hym, & so they breake hys couenaunt.

21 Their mouthes are softer then butter, & yet haue they battayll in theyr mynde: theyr wordes are smoother then oyle, and yet be they very swerdes.

22 O cast thy burthen, or care, vpon the Lord he shall norysh the, and not leaue the ryghteous in vnquyetnesse.

23 But as for them, thou (O God) shalt cast doune into the pytte of destruccion. The bloudthrustye & disceatfull shall not lyue out half their dayes. Neuerthelesse my trust is in the.

## PSALM 56

*To the chaunter, vpon the domme stock doue: whiche flyeth ferre of, Michtam of Dauid, when the Phylystynes toke hym in Geth.*

BE mercifull vnto me (O God) for men will treade me doune: they are dayly fightynge and troublynge me.

2 Myne enemyes treade me dayly vnder their fete, for they

be many that proudly fighte agaynste me.

3 Neuerthelesse, when I am afrayed, I put my trust in the.

4 I will comforte my selfe in Gods worde, yea, I will hope in God, & not feare: What can flesh then do vnto me?

5 They vexe my dayly in my wordes: all þt they ymagyne, is to do me euell.

6 They holde alltogether, & kepe them selues close they marcke my steppes, how they may catch my soule.

7 But in vayne, for it shall escape them: and why? thou (O God) in thy dyspleasure shalt cast doune suche people.

8 Thou tellest my flytynges, thou puttest my teares in thy bottel, and numbrest them.

9 When soeuer I call vpon the, myne enemyes are put to flight: whereby I knowe that thou art my God.

10 In Goddes worde wyll I reioyse, in the Lordes worde wyll I comforte me.

11 Yea, in God do I trust, and am not afraied what can man than do vnto me?

12 Vnto the (O god) wil I paye my vowes, vnto the wyll I geue thankes and prayse.

13 For thou haste delyuered my soule from death, and my fete frome fallynge, þt I may walke before God in the lyght of the lyuyng.

## PSALM 57

*To the Chaunter destroy not Michtam of Dauid, when he fledde from Saull into the caue.*

BE mercyfull vnto me, O God, be mercyfull vnto me, for my soule trusteth in the: and vnder the shadow of thy winges shal be my refuge, vntyll wyckednes be ouer past.

2 I call vnto God the moste hyest, euen the God that shal helpe me vp agayne.

3 He shal send from heauen, and saue me from the reproue of him that would swalowe my vp. Selah. This shall God sende, for his mercye and faythfulnes sake.

4 I lye wyth my soule among the cruel lions euen among the chyldren of men, whose teeth are speares and arrowes, and their tonge a sherpe sweard.

5 Set vp thy selfe, O God, aboue the heauens, and thy glory aboue al the earthe.

6 They haue layed a net for my fete, and pressed doune my soule: they haue dygged a pytte before me, and are fallen into it them selues. Selah.

7 My hert is redy, O God, my herte is ready to synge and geue prayse.

8 Awake, O my glorye, awake lute and harpe, I my selfe wil awake ryght early.

9 I wil geue thanckes vnto the, O Lorde, amonge the people, I wyll synge prayses vnto the among the Heithen.

10 For the greatnes of thy mercye reacheth vnto the heauens, and thy faythfulnes vnto the cloudes.

11 Set vp thy selfe, O God, aboue the heauens, and thi glory aboue al the earth.

## PSALM 58

*To the chaunter Destroye not Michtam of Dauid.*

IF youre myndes be vpon righteousnes in deede, then iudge the thyng that is ryght, O ye sonnes of men,

2 But ye ymagyn mischefe in youre hertes and youre handes deale with wickednes.

3 The vngodly are froward, euen from their mothers wombe: as soone as they be borne, they go a stray and speake lyes.

4 They are as furyous as the serpent, euen lyke the deaf Ader that stoppeth her eares.

5 That she shoulde not heare the voyce of the charmer, charme he neuer so wisely.

6 Breake their teeth (O god) in their mouthes, smite the chaft bones of the lions whelpes in sonder, O Lord.

7 That they maye fall awaye, lyke water that runneth a pace: and that when they shote their arrowes, they maye be broken.

8 Let them consume away lyke a snaile, and lyke the vntymely frute of a woman, and let them not se the sunne.

9 Or euer your thorns be sharpe, the wrath shall take them awaye quicke, like a stormy wynde.

10 The ryghteous shal reioyse when he seith the vengeaunce, and shall washe hys fete in the bloud of the vngodly.

11 So that men shall saye, verelye there is a rewarde for the righteous: doutles, there is a God that iudgeth the earth.

## PSALM 59

*To the chaunter destroye not Michtam of Dauid, when Saull sende to watche the house, to thintent to kyll hym.*

DELYUER me fro myne enemyes (O my God) and defende me from them that rise vp against me.

2 O delyuer me from þe wycked doers, and saue me from the bloudthursty men.

3 For lo, they lye waytinge for my soule: the mighty men are gathered together agaynste me, withoute any offence or faulte of me, O Lorde.

4 They runne, & prepare them selfes, without my faute: Arise, come thou helpe me, and beholde.

5 Stande vp O Lord God of hostes, thou God of Israel to viset all Heythen: be not mercifull vnto theym that offende of malicious wyckednesse. Selah.

6 Let them go to and fro, and

runne aboute the cytye, houlynge lyke dogges.

7 Beholde, they speake (agaynste me) wyth their mouth, swerdes are vnder their lippes for who reproueth them?

8 But thou (O Lorde) shalte haue theim in derision, thou shalte laugh all Heythen too scorne.

9 My strength do I ascrybe vnto the, for thou (O God) art my defender.

10 God sheweth me his goodnes plenteously, God letteth me se my desyre vppon myne enemyes.

11 Slaye them not, leste my people forget it: but scatre them abroade with thy power, & put them doune, O Lord my defence.

12 For the synne of their mouth, for the wordes of their lyppes, & because of their pryde, let them be taken: and why? their preachyng is of cursing and lyes.

13 Consume them in thy wrath, consume them that they maye perishe, and knowe that it is God, whyche ruleth in Iacob and in all the worlde. Selah.

14 Set them go to and fro, and runne aboute the cytye, houlyng lyke dogges.

15 Let them runne here and there for meate, and grudge when they haue not ynough.

16 As for me, I will synge of thy power, and prayse thy mercy by tymes in the mornyng: for thou art my defence & refuge in the tyme of my trouble.

17 Vnto the (O my strengthe) wyll I singe, for thou (O God) art my defence, & my mercifull God.

## PSALM 60

*To the chaunter, vpon the rose of wytnesse Michtam of Dauid, for too teache when he fought agaynst Syria of Mesopotania, & Syria of Zoba: and when Ioab turned backe, and slue .xij. thousand Edomytes. in the valley of Salt.*

O God, thou that hast cast vs out and scatered vs abroade, thou that hast bene so sore displeased at vs, comforte vs agayne.

2 Thou that hast remoued the lande & deuided it, heale the sores therof, for it shaketh.

3 Thou hast shewed thy people heuy thinges, thou hast geuen vs a drynke of wyne, that we slombre with all.

4 Yet hast thou geuen a token for suche as feare the, that they maye caste it vp in the trueth. Selah.

5 That thy beloued myghte be delyuered, healpe them wyt thy ryghthande, and heare me.

6 God hath spoken in his Sanctuary (which thing reioyseth me) I wyll deuyde Sichem, and meate aut the valley of Suchoth.

7 Galaad is myne, Manasses is myne, Ephraim is the strength of myne head, Iuda is my Captayne.

8 Moab is my washpotte, ouer Edom will I stretche oute my shoue, Phylystea shalbe glad of me.

9 Who will leade me into the strong cytie? Who will bryng me into Edom?

10 Shalt not thou do it O God, thou that hast cast out: thou God, that wenteste not out with our hostes?

11 O be thou our helpe in trouble, for vayne is the helpe of man.

12 Thorow God we shal do great actes, for it is he that shall treade downe oure enemies.

## PSALM 61

*To þe chaunter vpon Neginoth, of Dauid*

HEARE my crying (O god) geue hede vnto my prayer.

2 From the endes of þe earth will I call vnto the, when my herte is in trouble:

3 Oh sette me vp vpon an hye rocke. For thou art my hope, a strong tower for me agaynst the enemye.

4 I wyll dwell in thy tabernacle for euer, that I maye be safe vnder the couerynge of thy wynges. Selah.

5 For thou, O Lord, hast harde my desyres, thou hast geuen an heretage vnto those that feare thy name.

6 Thou shalte graunte the Kynge a longe lyfe, that his yeares may endure thorow out all generacyons.

7 That he maye dwel before God for euer: Oh let thy louynge mercy and faythfulnes preserue hym.

8 So wyl I al away syng prayses vnto thy name, þt I may dayly perfourme my vowes.

## PSALM 62

*To the chaunter, for by Iduthun a Psalme of Dauyd.*

MY soule wayteth onely vpon God, for of hym commeth my helpe.

2 He only is my strength, my saluation, my defence, so that I shal not greatly fall.

3 How longe wyll ye ymagyn myschiefe agaynste euerye man? ye shalbe slayne all the sorte of you: yea as a tottrynge wall shall ye be, and lyke a broken hedge.

4 Their deuyce is only how to put hym out, their delite is in lyes: they geue good wordes wyth their mouth, but curse wyth the herte. Selah.

5 Neuerthelesse, my soule abideth only vpon God, for he is my God.

6 He only is my strength my saluacion, and my defence: so that I shall not fal.

7 In God is my helth, my glory, my might, and in God is my trust.

8 O put your trust in him alway (ye people) poure oute

youre hertes before hym, for God is our hope. Selah.

9 As for men, they are but vayne, men are dysceatfull: vpon the weyghtes they are all together lyghter than vanitye it selfe.

10 O trust not in wronge and robbery, geue not youre selues vnto vanitye: if ryches encrease, set not your herte vpon them.

11 God spake once a worde, twyse haue I hearde the same: that power belongeth vnto God

12 That thou Lorde arte mercyfull, and that thou rewardeste euerye man accordynge to his worckes.

## PSALM 63

*A Psalme of Dauid, when he was in the wildernes of Iuda.*

O God, thou art my God: earlye wyll I seke the. My soule thrusteth for the, my flesh longeth after the in a baren and drye lande wher no water is.

2 Thus do I loke for the in thy Sanctuary, that I myght beholde thy power and glorye,

3 For thy louynge kyndnesse is bettrr then lyfe, my lyppes shall prayse the.

4 As longe as I lyue wyll I magnyfye the and lyft vp my handes in thy name.

5 My soule is satisfied euen as it were with mary and fatnesse, when my mouth prayseth the with ioyful lyps.

6 In my bedde wyll I remember the, and when I wake my talkynge shalbe of the.

7 For thou hast bene my helper, and vnder the shadow of thy wynges wyl I reioyse.

8 My soule hangeth vpon the, thy ryghte hande vpholdeth me.

9 They seke after my soule, but in vayne, for they shall go vnder the earth.

10 They shall fall into the swerd, and be a porcyon for foxes.

11 But the Kynge shall reioyse in God: all they that sweare by him, shalbe commended for the mouth of lyers shalbe stopped.

## PSALM 64

*To the chaunter a Psalme of Dauid.*

HEARE my voice, O God, in my complaynte, preserue my lyfe from feare of the enemye.

2 Hide me from the gathering together of the frowarde, from the heape of wycked doers.

3 Which whet their tonges lyke a sweard, and shote wyth their veneymous words like as with arowes.

4 That they maye preuely hurt the innocent sodenly to hyt him wythout any feare.

5 They haue deuysed myschefe, and communed amonge them selues, how they may laye snares: tush (saye they) who shall se them?

6 They ymagyn wyckednes, and kepe it secrete amonge them selues, euerye man in the depe of his herte.

7 But God shal sodenly shote wyth an arow that they shalbe wounded.

8 Yea their owne tonges shall make them fall, in somuch that who so seyth them, shall laugh them to scorne.

9 And all men that se it shal saye: thys hath God done, for they shall perceyue that it is hys worcke.

10 The righteous shal reioyse in the Lorde, and put his trust in him: and all they that are true of hert, shalbe glad therof.

## PSALM 65

*To the chaunter, a Psalme and song of Dauid.*

THOU, O God art, praised in Syon, and vnto the is the vow perfourmed.

2 Thou hearest the praier, therfore commeth all fleshe vnto the.

3 Oure misededes preuaile agayust vs, Oh be thou mercyfull vnto our synnes.

4 Blessed is the man whom thou chosest and receauest vnto the, that he may dwell in thy courtes: he shalbe satisfied wyth the pleasures of thy house, euen of thy holy temple.

5 Heare vs, according vnto thy wonderfull rightuousnesse, O God oure saluation: thou that art the hope of all the endes of the earth, and of the broade sea.

6 Which in his strength setteth fast the mountaynes, and is gyrded aboute wyth power.

7 Which stilleth the ragynge of the sea, the roarynge of his waues, and the woodnes of the people.

8 They that dwell in the vttermoste partes are afrayed at thy tokens, thou makest both the mornyng and euenyng starres to prayse the.

9 Thou visitest the earth, thou waterest it. and makest it very plenteous. The riuer of god is ful of waters, thou preparest man hys corne, and thus thou prouydeste for the earth.

10 Thou waters, her forowes, thou breakest the harde clottes thereof, thou makest it softe with the droppes of rayne, and blessest the increase of it.

11 Thou crownest the yeare wyth thy good and thy fotsteppes droppe fatnesse.

12 The dwellinges of the wildernes are fat also, that they droppe wyth all: and the lytle hylles are pleasaunt on euerye syde.

13 The foldes are full of shepe, the valleyes stande so thicke with corne that they laughe and synge.

## PSALM 66

*To the chaunter, a Psalme of*

*Dauyd.*

O be ioyfull in God, all ye landes,

2 synge prayses vnto the honoure of his name, make hys prayse to be gloryous.

3 Saye vnto God: O howe wonderful are thy worckes? thorowe the greatenesse of thy power shall thine enemyes be confounded.

4 O that all the worlde woulde worshippe the, synge of the, and prayse thy name. Selah

5 O come hyther and beholde the worckes of God, which is so wonderful in his doinges amonge the chyldren of men.

6 He turned the sea into drye lande, so that they wente thorow the water on fote: therefore wyll we reioyse in him.

7 He ruleth wyth hys power for euer, hys eyes beholde the people: the rennagates shall not be able to exalte them selues. Selah.

8 O magnyfye oure God, ye people, make the voyce of his prayse to be hearde.

9 Whych holdeth oure soule in life, and suffreth not our fete to slyppe.

10 For thou, O God, hast proued vs, thou hast tryed vs lyke as syluer is tryed.

11 Thou hast broughht vs into captyuyty, & layed trouble vpon oure loynes.

12 Thou haste suffred men to ryde ouer oure heades, we went thorow fyre and water, but thou hast broughte vs out, and refreshed vs.

13 Therfore wyll I go into thy house wyth brentoffrynges, to paye the my vowes,

14 which I promysed with my lippes, and spake wyth my mouth, when I was in trouble.

15 I wyll offer vnto the fat brentsacrifyces wyth the smoke of rammes, I wyl offer bullockes and goates. Selah.

16 O come hither, and herken, all ye that feare God, I wyll tell you, what he hath done for my soule.

17 I called vnto hym wyth my mouthe, and gaue hym prayses wyth my toung.

18 If I enclyne vnto wyckednesse wyth my herte, the Lorde wyll not heare me.

19 Therfore God hath herde me, and consydred the voyce of my prayer.

20 Praysed be God, which hath not cast out my prayer, ner turned his mercy fro me.

## PSALM 67

*To the chaunter, in Neginoth, a Psalm and songe.*

GOD be mercyfull vnto vs, blesse vs, and shewe the lyght of hys countenaunce vpon vs. Selah

2 That we maye knowe thy waye vpon earth, thy sauynge helth among al Heathen.

3 Let the people prayse the, O God, yea let all people prayse the.

4 O let the people reioyse and be glad, that thou iudgest the folke ryghtuouslye, and gouernest the nacions vpon earth.

5 Let the people prayse the, O God, let al people prayse the.

6 God, euen oure owne God, geue vs hys blessynge, that the earth maye brynge forth her encrease.

7 God blesse vs, and let all the endes of the world feare hym.

## PSALM 68

*To the chaunter, a Psalm and song. of Dauid.*

LET God aryse, so shall hys enemyes be scattered, and they that hate hym, shall flee before hym.

2 Lyke as the smoke vanysheth, so shalt thou dryue them away: and lyke as waxe melteth at the fyre so shal the vngodly perysh at the presence of God.

3 But the ryghtuous shalbe glad and reioyce before God, they shalbe mery and ioyfull.

4 Oh synge vnto God, synge prayses vnto his name: magnify hym that rydeth aboute the heauens (whose name is þe Lord) & reioyce before hym.

5 He is a father of the fatherlesse, he is a defender of widdowes: euen God in his holy habytacyon.

6 He is the God that maketh men to be of one mynde in a house, and bryngeth the presoners out of captyuity in due season, but let the rennagates contynue in scarcenesse.

7 O God, when thou wenteste forth before the people, when thou wentest thorowe the wyldernesse. Selah.

8 The earth shoke, and the heauens dropped at the presence of God in Sinai, at the presence of God, whyche is the God of Israell.

9 Thou O God sendest a gracyous raine vpon thyne enherytaunce, and refreshest it when it is dry.

10 That thy beastes may dwel therin, which thou of thy goodnesse haste prepared for the poore.

11 The Lorde shall geue the worde, wyth great hostes of Euangelystes.

12 Kynges wyth their armyes shall fle, and they of the housholde shall deuyde the spoile

13 If so be that ye lye amonge the pales, the doues fethers shalbe couered with syluer, & her wynges of the colour of golde.

14 When the Almyghty setteth Kynges vpon þe earth, it shalbe cleare euen in þe darknes

15 The hyll of Basan is Gods hyl, the hil of Basan is a plenteous hyl.

16 Why hoppe ye so, ye greate hylles? It pleaseth God to dwell vpon thys hyll yea the Lorde wyll abide in it for euer.

17 The charettes of God are many .M. tymes thousande, the Lorde is among them in the holy Sinai.

18 Thou art gone vp an hye, thou hast ledde captiuitie captiue, and receyued gyftes for men: Yea, euen for thyne enemyes, that they might dwell with the Lord God.

19 Praysed be the Lord dayly, euen the God whiche helpeth vs, & poureth hys benefites vpon vs. Selah.

20 The God that is our sauiour, euen God the Lord by whome we escape death.

21 The God that smyteth the enemies vpon the heades and vpon the heary scalpes: such as go on styll in their wickednes.

22 The Lorde hath sayde: some wil I bryng agayne from Basan, some wyll I brynge agayne from the depe of the sea.

23 That thy fote may be dipped in the bloud of thyne enemyes, and that thy dogges may licke it vp.

24 It is well sene, O God, how thou goest, howe thou my God and kynge goest in the Sanctuary.

25 The singers go before, and then the mynstrels amonge the maydens with the tymbrels.

26 O geue thankes vnto God the Lorde in the congregacion, for the welles of Israel.

27 There lytle Beniamin, the princes of Iuda, the princes of Zabulon, & the princes of Nephthaly beare rule amonge them.

28 Thy God hath commytted strength vnto the, stablyshe the thynge, O God, that thou hast wrought in vs.

29 For thy temples sake at Hierusalem shall kynges brynge presentes vnto the.

30 Reproue the beastes amonge the reedes, the heape of bulles with the calues: those þt dryue for money. Oh scatre þe people that delite in battaile.

31 The princes shall come out of Egipt, the Morians land shall stretch out her handes vnto God.

32 Synge vnto God, O ye kyngedomes of the earth: O syng prayses vnto the Lorde. Selah.

33 Which sitteth in the heauens ouer all from the beginnynge: Lo, he shall sende oute hys voyce, yea, and that a mighty voyce.

34 Ascrybe ye the power vnto God, his glory is in Israel, and his might in the cloudes.

35 God is wonderfull in his Sanctuary, he is the God of Israel, he will geue strength and power vnto hys people. Blessed be God.

## PSALM 69

*To the chaunter vpon Sosanim of Dauid.*

HELPE me, O god, for the waters are come in, euen vnto my soule.

2 I stycke fast in þe depe myre where no ground is: I am come into depe waters, and the floudes wyll drowne me.

3 I am weery of crying, my throte is drye, my sight fayleth me, for waytinge so longe, vpon my God.

4 They that hate me without a cause, are mo then the heeres of my head: they that are myne enemyes & wolde destroye me giltlesse are mighty: I am fayne to paye the thinges that I neuer toke.

5 God thou knowest my simplenesse, and my faultes are not hyd from the.

6 Let not them that trust in the, O Lord God of hoostes, be ashamed for my cause: let not those that seke the, be confounded thorowe me, O God of Israel.

7 And why? for thy sake do I suffre reprofe, shame couereth my face.

8 I am become a straunger vnto my brethren, and an aleaunt vnto my mothers chyldren.

9 For the zele of thyne house hath euen eaten me, and the rebukes of them that rebuked the, is fallen vpon me.

10 I wepte and chastened my selfe with fastyng, and that was turned to my reprofe.

11 I put on a sacke cloth, and therefore they iested vpon me.

12 They that sate in the gate, spake agaynste me, & the dronkardes made songes vpon me.

13 But Lorde I made my prayer vnto the in an acceptable tyme. Heare me, O God, with thy great mercy and sure helpe.

14 Take me out of the myre, that I sinke not Oh let me be deliuered from them that hate me, and out of the depe waters.

15 Lest the water floud drowne me, that the depe swalowe me not vp, and that the pytte shut not her mouth vpon me.

16 Heare me, O Lord, for thy louyng kyndnesse is comfortable: turne the vnto me according vnto thy great mercy.

17 Hyde not thy face from thy seruaunt, for I am in trouble: O haste the to helpe me.

18 Drawe nye vnto my soule, & saue it: Oh deliuer me because of myne enemyes.

19 Thou knowest my reprofe, my shame & my dishonoure: myne aduersaries are all in thy sight.

20 The rebuke breaketh my herte, and maketh me heuy: I loke for some to haue pytye vpon me, but ther is no man: and for some to comforte me, but I fynde none.

21 They gaue me gall to eate, & when I was thurstye, they gaue me vinegar to dryncke.

22 Let their table be made a snare to take them selues with

# PSALMS

all, an occasyon to fall and a reward vnto them.

23 Let their eyes be blinded, that they se not: and euer bow downe their backes.

24 Power out thyne indignacyon vpon them, and let thy wrathfull dyspleasure take holde of them.

25 Let theyr habytacyon be voyd, and no man to dwel in ther tentes.

26 For they persecute hym whom thou hast smytten, and besyde thy woundes they haue geuen him mo.

27 Let them fall from one wyckednesse to another, and not come into thy ryghtuousnesse.

28 Let them be wyped out of the boke of the lyuynge, and not be wrytten amonge the ryghtuous.

29 As for me, I am poore and in heuines, let thy helpe defend me O God.

30 That I may praise the name of God, with a songe and magnyfye it wyth thanckesgeuynge.

31 Thys shall please the Lord better then a bullocke, that hath hornes and hoofes.

32 O consyder this and be glad (ye that be in aduersytye) seke after God, and youre soule shall lyue.

33 For the Lorde heareth the poore, and despyseth not hys priesoners.

34 Let heauen and earth praise him, the sea & all that moueth ther in.

35 For God wyll saue Syon, and buyld the cityes of Iuda, that men may dwel ther, and haue them in possession.

36 The sede of his seruauntes shall inherette it, and they that loue hys name shall dwell therein.

## PSALM 70

*The chaunter, of Dauid to bryng to remembraunce.*

HAST the, O God, to deliuer me, and to helpe me, O Lord.

2 Let them be shamed and confounded that seke after my soule let them be turned backward and put to confusyon, that wysh my euyl.

3 Let them sone be broughte to shame, that crye ouer me, there there.

4 But let all those that seke the, be ioyfull & gladde in the: and let al suche as delyte in thy sauynge health, saye alwaye: the Lorde be praysed.

5 As for me, I am poore and in misery, hast the God for to helpe me. Thou art my helpe, my redemer and my God: Oh make no long tarying.

## PSALM 71

IN the, O Lord, is my trust, let me neuer be put to confusyon,

2 but rydde me, and delyuer me thorow thy ryghtuousnesse: enclyne thyne eare vnto me, and helpe me.

3 Be thou my strong hold (wher vnto I may all waye fle) thou that hast promised to helpe me: for thou art my house of defence and my castell.

4 Deliuer me, O my God, out of the hand of the vngodly, oute of the hande of the vnryghtuous and cruell man.

5 For thou, O Lord God, art the thing that I long for, þu art my hope euen fro my youth.

6 I haue leaned vpon the euer sence I was borne, thou art he that toke me out of my mothers wombe therfore is my prayse all waye of the.

7 I am become a wonder vnto the multytude, but my sure trust is in the.

8 Oh let my mouth be filled with thy praise and honour all the day long.

9 Cast me not away in myne old age forsake me not when my strength fayleth me.

10 For myne enemyes speake agaynst me & they that laye wayte for my soule, take their councell together,

11 sayinge: God hath forsaken hym, persecute hym, take hym, for there is none to helpe hym.

12 Go not farre fro me, O God: my God, haste the to helpe me.

13 Let them be confounded and perysh, that are agaynste my soule: let theym be couered with shame and dishonoure, that seke too do me euell.

14 As for me, I wil paciently abyde alwaye, and will euer encrease thy prayse.

15 My mouth shall speake of thy righteousnesse and sauyng health all the day longe, for I knowe no ende therof.

16 Let me go in (O Lorde God) and I wyll make mencion of thy power and righteousnesse onely.

17 Thou, O God, haste learned me fro my youth vp vntyll now, therfore wyll I tell of thy wonderous workes.

18 Forsake me not, O GOD, in myne olde age, when I am gray headed: vntyll I haue shewed thyne arme vnto chylders chyldren, and thy power to all them that are yet for to come.

19 Thy righteousnes, O God, is very hye, thou that doest great thinges: O God, who is lyke vnto the?

20 O what great troubles and aduersityes hast thou shewed me? and yet dyddest thou turne and refreshe me: yea, & broughtest me from the depe of the earth agayn.

21 Thou hast brought me to great honoure, and comforted me on euery syde.

22 Therfore wil I prayse the and thy faythfulnesse, O God, playing vpon þe lute, vnto the will I singe vpon the harpe, O thou holy one of Israell.

23 My lippes wolde fayne singe prayses vnto the: and so wolde my soule, whom thou hast deliuered.

24 My tongue talketh of thy righteousnesse all the daye longe, for they are confounded and brought vnto shame, that soughte to do me euell.

## PSALM 72

*Of Salomon.*

GEUE the king thy iudgement, O God, and thy righteousnesse vnto the kynges sonne.

2 That he maye gouerne thy people accordynge vnto ryght and defende thy poore.

3 That the mountaynes maye brynge peace, and the litle hylles righteousnesse vnto the people.

4 He shall kepe the symple folke by theyr ryght, defende the chyldren of the poore, and punish the wronge doer.

5 Thou shalt be feared as longe as þe sunne and moone endureth, from one generacyon to another.

6 He shall come doune lyke the rayne into a fleise of wolle, & like the droppes that water the earth.

7 In hys tyme shall righteousnesse florysh, yea, and aboundaunce of peace, so longe as the moone endureth.

8 Hys dominion shalbe from the one sea to the other, & from the floud vnto the worldes ende.

9 They that dwell in the wyldernes shall knele before him, & his enemyes shal licke the dust.

10 The kynges of the sea & of the Iles shall bringe presentes, the kynges of Araby and Saba shall offre gyftes.

11 All kynges shall worshyppe hym, and all Heathen shall do hym seruyce.

12 For he shall delyuer the poore when he cryeth, and the neady that hath no helpe.

13 He shalbe fauorable to þe simple & poore, he shall preserue the soules of suche as be in aduersitie.

14 He shall delyuer their soules from extorcyon and wrong, and deere shall their bloud be in hys sight.

15 He shall lyue, and vnto hym shalbe geuen of the golde of Arabia: Prayer shalbe made euer vnto hym, and daylye shall he be praysed.

16 There shalbe an heape of corne in þe earth hye vpon the hilles, his frute shal shake like Libanus, and shalbe grene in the cytye, lyke grasse vpon the earth.

17 Hys name shal endure for euer, his name shall remayne vnder the sunne amonge the posterites, which shalbe blessed thorow him and all the Heathen shall prayse hym.

18 Blessed be the Lorde God, euen the God of Israell, whiche onely doeth wonderous thinges.

19 And blessed be the name of his maiesty for euer, and al landes be fulfilled with his glory. Amen, Amen.

20 Here ende the prayers of Dauid the sonne of Iesse.

## PSALM 73

*A Psalme of Asaph.*

O how louyng is God vnto Israel, to suche as are of a cleane hert?

2 Neuerthelesse my fete were almost gone, my treadynges had well nye slypte.

3 And why? I was greued at the wicked, to se the vngodly in suche prosperitie.

4 For they are in no parell of deathe, but stande fast lyke a palace.

5 They come in no misfortune lyke other folke, neither are they plaged like other men.

6 And this is þe cause that they be so puft vp in pryde, and ouerwhelmed with crueltie & vnrighteousnesse.

7 Their eyes swell for fatnesse, they do euen what they lyst.

8 Corrupte are they, and speake blasphemyes maliciouslye, proude and presumpteous are their wordes.

9 They stretche forth their mouthe vnto the heauen, and their tongue goeth thorow the worlde.

10 Therfore fall the people vnto them, and thereout sucke they no small auauntage.

11 Tush (saye they) howe shoulde God perceiue it? is there knowlege in the most hyest?

12 Lo, these are the vngodly, these prospere in the worlde, these haue ryches in possession.

13 Shoulde I then clense my herte in vayne (thougt I) and washe my handes in innocency?

14 Wherefore shoulde I be then punyshed dayly, & be chastened euery mornynge?

15 Yea, I had almoost also sayd euen as they: but lo, then shoulde I haue condemned the generacion of thy chyldren.

16 Then thought I, to vnderstande this, but it was to harde for me.

17 Vntyll I wente into the Sanctuary of God, and considred the ende of these men.

18 Namely, how thou hast set them in a slippery place, that thou mayst cast them doune headlinges and destroye them.

19 O how sodenly do they consume, perysh, and come to a fearful ende?

20 Yea, euen like as a dreame when one awaketh, so makest thou their ymage too vanysh out of the cytye.

21 Thus my hert was greued, and it wente euen thorow my reynes.

22 So folysh was I and ignoraunte, and as it were a beast before the.

23 Neuerthelesse I am al waye by the, thou holdest me by my right hande.

24 Thou leadest me with thy counsayll, and afterwarde receyuest me vnto glory.

25 O what is there prepared for me in heauen? there is nothinge vpon earthe, that I desyre in comparyson of the.

26 My fleash & my hert fayleth, but God is the strength of my herte, and my porcion for euer.

27 For lo, they that forsake the shall perysh: thou destroyest all them that committe fornicacion agaynst the.

28 But it is good for me, to holde me fast by God, to put my trust in the Lorde God, and to speake of all thy workes.

## PSALM 74

*An instruccion of Asaph.*

O God, wherfore doest thou cast vs so cleane away? why is thy wrath so hoote agaynste the shepe of thy pasture?

2 O thynke vpon thy congregacion, whome thou hast purchased from the beginnyng: the stafe of thyne enheritaunce, whome thou hast redemed, euen this hyll of Sion wherein thou dwellest.

3 Treade vpon them with thy fete, and cast them doune to the grounde, for the enemye hath DESTROYED altogether in the Sanctuary.

4 Thyne aduersaries roare in thy houses, & set vp their banners for tokens.

5 Men may se the axes glyster aboue, lyke as those that hewe in the wood.

6 They cut doune all the syelyng worke of the Sanctuary with bylles and axes.

7 They haue set fyre vpon the Sanctuary, they haue defyled the dwellyng place of thy name, euen vnto the grounde.

8 Yea, they say in their hertes: let vs spoyle them altogether, thus haue they brent vp all the houses of God in the lande.

9 We se oure tokens no more, there is not one Prophet more, no not one that vnderstandeth any more.

10 O God, how long shall the aduersary do this dishonoure? how longe shall the enemy blaspheme thy name? for euer?

11 Why withdrawest thou thine hand? why pluckest thou not thy right hande out of thy bosome, to consume thyne enemyes?

12 But God is my Kynge of olde, the helpe that is done vpon earth, he doth it hym selfe.

13 Thou deuidest the sea thorow thy power thou breakest the heades of the dragons in the waters.

14 Thou smitest the heades of Leuiathan in peces, and geuest him to be meate for people in the wyldernes.

15 Thou diggest vp welles and brokes, thou dryest vp myghty waters.

16 The daye is thyne, and the nyght is thine thou hast prepared the lightes and the sunne.

17 Thou hast set all the borders of the earth, thou hast made both sommer and winter.

18 Remember this, O Lord, how the enemy rebuketh, and howe the folyshe people blaspheme thy name.

19 O delyuer not the soule of thy turtle doue vnto the beastes, and forget not the congregacyon of the poore for euer.

20 Loke vpon the couenaunte, for the darcke houses of the earth are full of wyckednesse.

21 O let not the symple go awaye ashamed: for the poore and nedy geue prayses vnto thy name.

22 Aryse, O God, and mayntaine thine own cause, remember howe the folyshe man blasphemeth the daylye.

23 Forget not the voyce of thyne enemyes, for the presumptyon of them that hate the, increaseth euer more and more

## PSALM 75

*To the chaunter destroye not, a Psalme and song of Asaph.*

VNTO the, O God, wil we geue thankes, yea vnto the wyll we geue thanckes, and seynge thy name is so ny, we wil tel of thy wonderous worckes.

2 When I maye get a conuenyent tyme, I shall iudge accordyng vnto ryght.

3 The earh is weake and al that is therein, but I beare vp her pyllers.

4 I sayde vnto the madde people, deale not so madly, and to þe vngodly set not vp your hornes.

5 Set not vp your hornes on hie, and speake not wyth a styfe necke.

6 For promocyon commeth neyther from the East ner from the weste, ner yet from the wyldernesse

7 And why? God is the Iudge: he putteth downe one, and setteth vp another.

8 For in the hand of þe Lord ther is a cup full of strong wyne, and he poureth oute of the same: As for the dregges therof, al the vngodly of the earth shall dryncke them, and sucke them oute.

9 But I wyll talke of the God of Iacob, & prayse him for euer.

10 Al the hornes of the vngodly wil I breake and the hornes of the ryghtuous shall be exalted.

## PSALM 76

*To the chaunter, in Neginoth, a Psalm and songe of Asaph.*

IN Iuda is God knowne, hys name is great in Israel.

2 At Salem is hys tabernacle, and his dwellinge in Sion.

3 Ther breaketh he the arowes of the bow, the shylde, the swearde, and the whole battaylle, Selah.

4 Thou art of more honour and might then the hylles of robbers.

5 The proude shalbe robbed and slepe their slepe, and the myghtye shalbe able to do nothyng with their handes.

6 When thou rebukest them, O God of Iacob, both the charrettes and horsemen shall fal on slepe.

7 Thou art fearful, for who maye abyde in thi sight, when thou art angry?

8 When thou lettest thy iudgment be heard from heauen, the earth trembleth and is stil.

9 Yea when God aryseth to geue iudgment and to helpe all them that be in aduersyty vpon earth. Selah.

10 When thou punyshest one man, he muste knowledge that thou arte readye to punyshe other mo.

11 Loke what ye promise vnto the Lord your God, se that, ye kepe it, all ye that be rounde about him: brynge presentes vnto hym that ought to be feared.

12 Which taketh awaye the breth of Pryncers, and is wonderfull amonge the Kynges of the earth.

## PSALM 77

*To the chaunter, for Iduthun. a Psalme of Asaph.*

I cryed vnto God wyth my voyce, yea vnto God cryed I wyth my voyce, and he hearde me.

2 In the tyme of my trouble I soughte the Lorde, I helde vp myne handes vnto him in the night season, for my soule refused all other comforte.

3 When I was in heuinesse, I thought vpon God: when my hert was vexed, then dyd I speake Selah.

4 Thou heldest myne eyes wakyng, I was so feble, that I coulde not speake.

5 Then remembred I the tymes of old, and the yeares that were past.

6 I called to remembraunce my song in the night, I communed wyth myne owne herte, and sought out my spirite.

7 Wyll the Lorde cast out for euer? Wyl he be no more intreated?

8 Is hys mercye cleane gone? Is hys promyse come vtterlye to an ende for euermore?

9 Hath the Lord forgotten to be gracyous? Or, hath he shut vp hys louynge kyndnes in dyspleasure? Selah.

10 At the last, I came to thys poynte, that I thought: O why art thou so folysh? the right hande of the moost hyest can chaunge all.

11 Therefore wyll I remembre the worckes of the Lorde, and call to mynde thy wonders of olde tyme.

12 I wyll speake of all thy worckes, and my talkynge shalbe of thy doynges.

13 Thy waye, O God, is holye: who is so great and myghty as God?

14 Thou arte the God that doeth wonders, þu hast declared thy power amonge the people

15 Thou wyth thyne arme hast delyuered thy people, euen the sonnes of Iacob and Ioseph. Selah.

16 The waters saw the, O God, the waters sawe the, & were afrayed, the deapthes were moued.

17 The thicke cloudes poured out water, the cloudes thondered, and thyne arowes went abroade.

18 The thonder was hearde rounde aboute, the lyghtenynges shone vpon the grounde, the earth was moued and shoke wyth al.

19 Thy waye was in the sea, and thy pathes in the greate waters, yet coulde noman know thy fotesteppes.

20 Thou leddeste thy people lyke a flocke of shepe, by the hande of Moyses and Aaron.

## PSALM 78

*An instruccyon of Asaph.*

Heare my lawe, O my people, enclyne your eares vnto the wordes of my mouth.

2 I wyll open my mouth in parables, and speake of thynges of olde.

3 Whych we haue herde and knowne, and such as our fathers haue told vs.

4 That we shoulde not hyde them from the chyldren of the generations to come: but to shewe the honoure of the Lorde, hys myghte and wonderfull worckes that he hath done.

5 He made a couenaunte wyth Iacob, and gaue Israel a lawe, whiche he commaunded oure forefathers to teache their chyldren.

6 That their posterytye myghte knowe it, and the chyldren whych were yet vnborne. To thintent that when they came vp they myghte shewe their chyldren the same.

7 That they also myghte put their truste in God, & not to forget what he had done, but to kepe his commaundementes,

8 And not to be as their forefathers, a froward and ouerthwarte generatyon, a generation that set not their herte a ryghte, and whose spirite was not true towarde God.

9 Lyke as the chyldren of Ephraim, which beyng harnessed and carieng bowes, turned them selues backe in tyme of battayl.

10 They kept not þe couenant of god, and wold not walke in his

law.

11 They forgate what he had done, and the wonderfull workes that he had shewed for them.

12 Maruelous thynges dyd he in the sighte of our fathers in the lande of Egipt, euen in the felde of Zoan.

13 He deuided the sea & let them go thorowe it, & made the waters to stande like a wall.

14 In the daye tyme he ledde them with a cloude, and all the night thorow with a light of fyre.

15 He cloaue the harde rockes in the wildernesse, & gaue them drynke therof, as it hadde bene out of the great deapth.

16 He brought waters out of the stony rock, so that they gusshed out lyke the ryuers.

17 Yet for all this they synned agaynste hym, and prouoked the moost hyest in the wyldernes.

18 They tempted God in their hertes, and requyred meate for their lust.

19 For they spoke agaynst God, & sayde: yea yea, God shall prepare a table in the wildernesse, shall he?

20 Lo, he smote the stony rocke, that the watery streames gusshed out, and the streames flowed with all: but how can he geue bread and prouyde flesh for hys people?

21 When þe Lord hearde this, he was wroth so the fyre was kyndled in Iacob, and heauy displeasure agaynst Israel.

22 Because they beleued not in God, & putte not their trust in hys helpe.

23 So he commaunded the cloudes aboue, & opened the dores of heauen.

24 He rayned doune Manna vpon them for to eate, and gaue them bread from heauen.

25 Then eate they aungels fode, for he sentte them meate ynough.

26 He caused the East wynd to blowe vnder the heauen, & thorow hys power he brought in the South wynde.

27 He made flesh to raine vpon them as thicke as dust, and fethered foules like as the sande of the sea.

28 He let it fall amonge their tentes rounde about theyr habitacions.

29 So they eate, and were fylled, for he gaue them their owne desyre.

30 They were not disapoynted of their lust. But whyle þe meate was yet in their mouthes:

31 the heuy wrath of God came vpon them, slewe the welthiest of them, & smote doune the chosen men of Israel.

32 But for all this they sinned yet more, and beleued not hys wonderous workes.

33 Therfore their dayes were consumed in vanyte, and sodenly their yeares were gone.

34 When he slewe them, they sought hym, & turned them early vnto God.

35 They thoughte then that God was theyr succour, and that the hye God was their redemer.

36 Neuerthelesse they dyd but flatter him in their mouthes, and dissembled with hym in their tonges.

37 For their herte was not whole with him, neither continued they in his couenaunt.

38 But he was so mercifull, that he forgaue their misdedes, and destroyed them not. Yea, many a tyme turned he hys wrathe awaye, and wolde not suffre hys whole dyspleasure to aryse.

39 For he considered that they wer but flesh: euen a wynde that passeth awaye, and commeth not agayne.

40 O how ofte haue they greued hym in the wyldernesse? How many a tyme haue they prouoked hym in the deserte?

41 They turned backe, and tempted God, & moued the holy one in Israel.

42 They thought not of hys hand, in the day when he delyuered them from the hande of the enemye.

43 Howe he had wroughte hys myracles in Egypte, and hys wonders in the lande of Zoan.

44 How he turned their waters into bloude, so that they myghte not dryncke of the ryuers.

45 How he sent lyce among them, to eate them vp, and frogges to destroye them.

46 How he gaue their frutes vnto the catyrpyller, & their labour vnto the greshopper.

47 How he bete doune theyr vyneyardes wt hayle stones, and their molbery trees wyth the frost.

48 How he smote theyr cattel with haylestones, & their flockes with hote thonder boltes.

49 How he sent vppon them the furiousnesse of his wrath, anger & displeasure: with trouble and falling in of euell aungels.

50 When he made a waye to hys fearful indignacion, and spared not their soules from death, yea, & gaue their cattell ouer to the pestilence.

51 When he smote al the first born in Egipt, the mooste principall and mightyest in the dwellynges of Ham.

52 But as for his owne people, he lead them forth lyke shepe, and caried them in the wyldernesse lyke a flocke.

53 He brought them out safely, þt they shoulde not feare, and ouerwhelmed their enemyes with the sea.

54 He caryed them vnto the borders of his Sanctuary: euen into thys hyl, which he purchased with hys ryghthande.

55 He dyd cast out the Heathen before them, caused their lande to be deuyded among them for an heritage, and made the trybes of Israel to dwell in their tentes.

56 For all this they tempted & displeased the most hye God, and kept not hys couenaunt.

57 But turned their backes, and fell awaye lyke their forefathers, startynge asyde like a broken boowe.

58 And so they greued hym with theyr hye places, & prouoked him with their ymages.

59 When God hearde thys, he was wroth, and toke sore dyspleasure at Israell.

60 So that he forsoke the Tabernacle in Silo, euen his habitacyon wherin he dwelte amonge men.

61 He delyuered their power into captuitye and their glory into the enemies hande.

62 He gaue his people ouer into the swearde for he was wroth wyth hys herytage.

63 The fyre consumed their yonge men, and their maydens were not geuen to mariage.

64 Their Prestes were slaine with the swerd and there were no wyddowes to make lamentacyon.

65 So the Lorde, awaked as one oute of slepe, and lyke a gyaunte refreshed wyth wyne.

66 He smote hys enemyes in the hynder partes, and put them to perpetuall shame.

67 He refused the tabernacle of Ioseph, and chose not the trybe of Ephraim.

68 Neuertheles, he chose the trybe of Iuda, euen the hyll of Syon which he loued.

69 And there he buylded hys temple on hye, and layd the foundation of it like the ground that it myght perpetually endure.

70 He chose Dauid also hys seruaunte, and toke hym away from the shepe foldes.

71 As he was folowynge the yewes greate with yonge, he toke him, that he myghte fede Iacob hys people, & Israel hys enherytance.

72 So he fedde them wyth a fayethfull and true herte, and ruled them wyth diligence of of his power.

## PSALM 79

*A Psalme of Asaph.*

O God, the Heathen are fallen into thyne heritage: the holy temple haue they defiled, and made Ierusalem an heape of stones.

2 The deade bodye of thy seruauntes haue they geuen vnto the foules of þe ayre to be deuoured, and the flesh of thy saintes vnto the beastes of the lande.

3 Their bloude haue they shed lyke water on euery syde of Ierusalem, and ther was no man to bury them.

4 We are become an open shame vnto oure enemyes, a verye scorne and derysyon vnto them that are rounde aboute vs.

5 Lorde, howe longe wylt thou be angrye? shall thy ielousy burne lyke fyre for euer?

6 Poure oute thyne indignacyon vpon the Heathen that knowe the not, and vpon the Kyngdomes that call not vpon thy name.

7 For they haue deuoured Iacob, and laied wast his dwellynge place.

8 O remembre not oure olde synnes, but haue mercye vpon vs, and that soone, for we are come to greate mysery.

9 Helpe, vs, O God oure sauyoure, for the glory of thy name: O deliuer vs, and forgeue vs oure synnes for thy names sake.

10 Wherfore shall the Heathen say: wher is now their God? O lette the vengeaunce of thy seruauntes bloude that is shed, be openly shewed vpon the Heathen in our syght.

11 O Let the sorowfull sighehyng of the presoners come before the, and accordinge vnto the power of thyne arme, preserue those that are appoynted to dye.

12 And for the blasphemye wherewyth oure neyghboures haue blasphemed the, rewarde them, O Lorde, seenu folde into theyr bosome.

13 So we that be the people and shepe of thy pasture, shall geue the thanckes for euer, and wyll all waye be shewynge forth thy prayse more and more.

## PSALM 80

*To the chaunter, vpon Sosanim, a Psalme of Asaph.*

HEARE O thou shepeherde of Israel, thou that leadest Iacob lyke a flocke of shepe: shew thy self, thou that sittest vppon the Cherubyns.

2 Before Ephraim, Beniamin, and Manasses: stirre vp thy power, & come help vs.

3 Turne vs agayn, O God, shew the light of thy countenaunce, and we shalbe whole.

4 O Lord God of hostes, howe longe wilt thou be angry ouer the praier of thy people?

5 Thou hast fed them with the bread of teares, yea, thou hast geuen them plenteousnes of teares to drynke.

6 Thou haste made vs a verye stryfe vnto oure neyghbours, and oure enemyes laugh vs to scorne.

7 Turne vs agayne, thou God of hoostes, shewe the light of thy countenaunce, & we shalbe whole.

8 Thou hast broughte a vyneyarde oute of Egypte, thou diddest cast out the Heathen, & planted it.

9 Thou madest rowme for it, and caused it to take rote, so that it fylled the lande.

10 The hylles were couered with þe shadow of it, and so were the stronge Cedre trees wt the bowes therof.

11 She stretched out her braunches vnto the sea, and her

bowes vnto the water.

12 Why haste thou then broken doune her hedge, that all they whiche go by, plucke of her grapes?

13 Then wylde bore out of the wood hath roted it vp, and the beastes of the felde haue deuoured it.

14 Turne the agayne, thou God of hoostes, loke doune from heauen, beholde and vyset this vyneyarde.

15 Maynteyne it, that thy rightehande hath planted, and the sonne whom thou madest so muche of for thy self.

16 For why? it is brent with fyre, and lyeth waste: O let them peryshe at the rebuke of thy wrath.

17 Let thy hande be vpon the man of thy right hande, and vpon the man whome thou madest so much of for thyne owne selfe.

18 And so will not we go back from the: Oh let vs lyue, & we shall call vpon thy name.

19 Turne vs agayne, O Lorde God of hoostes, shewe the light of thy countenaunce, & we shalbe whole.

## PSALM 81

*To the chaunter vpon Githith, of Asaph.*

SINGE merely vnto God which is our strengthe, make a chearfull noyse vnto the god of Iacob.

2 Take the Psalme, brynge hyther the tabret, the mery harpe & lute.

3 Blowe vp the trompettes in the new mone, vpon our solempne feast daye.

4 For this is the vse in Israel, and a lawe of the God of Iacob.

5 This he ordeined in Ioseph for a testimony, when he came out of Epipt, & had heard a straunge language.

6 When he eased hys shoulder from the burthen, and when hys handes were deliuered from the pottes.

7 When thou callest vpon me in trouble, I helped the, and hearde the, what tyme as the storme fell vpon the, I proued the also at þe water of stryfe. Selah.

8 Heare, O my people, for I assure the O Israel, if thou wilt herken vnto me:

9 There shal no straunge God be in the, neither shalt thou worshippe any other God.

10 I am the Lord thy God, which broughte the out of the lande of Egipt, open thy mouth wyde, and I shall fyll it.

11 But my people wolde not heare my voice and Israel wolde not obey me.

12 So I gaue them vp vnto their owne hertes luste, and let them folowe theyr owne ymaginacions.

13 O that my people wolde obeye me, for if Israel wolde walke in my wayes:

14 I should soone put doune their enemyes, and turne myne hande againste their aduersaries.

15 The haters of the Lord should mysse Israel, but their tyme shoulde endure for euer.

16 He should feade them with the finest wheat floure, and satisfye them with hony out of þe stony rocke.

## PSALM 82

*A Psalme of Asaph.*

GOD standeth in the congregacion of the Goddes, and is a iudge amonge the iudges.

2 How long will ye geue wrong iudgement, and accept the personnes of the vngodly? Selah.

3 Defende the poore and fatherlesse, se that suche as be in nede & necessitie haue right.

4 Deliuer the outcaste & poore, & saue hym from the hande of the vngodly.

5 Neuerthelesse, they will not be learned & vnderstande, but walke on styll in darkenesse: therfore must all the foundacions of the lande be moued.

6 I haue sayde: ye are Goddes, ye all are the chyldren of the moost hyest.

7 But ye shall dye lyke men, and fall lyke one of the tyrauntes.

8 Aryse, O God, & iudge thou the earth, for all the Heathen are thyne by enheritaunce.

## PSALM 83

*A songe and Psalme of Asaph.*

HOLDE not thy tongue, O God, kepe not styll silence, refrayne not thy self O God.

2 For lo, thyne enemies make a murmurynge, and they that hate the, lyft vp their heade.

3 They ymagyn craftely agaynst thy people, and take counsayll agaynste thy secrete ones.

4 Come (saye they) let vs rote them out from amonge the people, that the name of Israell maye be put out of remembraunce.

5 For they haue caste their heades together with one consent, & are confederate agaynst the.

6 The tabernacles of the Edomites and Ismaelytes, the Moabytes and Hagarenes.

7 Gebal, Ammom, and Amalech: the Philistines with them that dwell at Tyre.

8 Assur also is ioyned vnto them, and helpe the chyldren of Loth. Selah.

9 But do thou to them as vnto the Madianites, vnto Sisera, and vnto Iabin by the broke of Kyson.

10 Whych peryshed at Endor, & became as the donge of the earth.

11 Make their prynces lyke Oreb & Zeb. Yea, make all their prynces lyke as Zebea & Salmana.

12 Whiche saye: we will haue

the houses of God in possession.

13 O my God, make them lyke vnto a whele, and as the stubble before the wynde.

14 Lyke as a fyre that burneth vp the wood, and as the flame that consumeth the mountaynes.

15 Persecute them euen so with thy tempest, and make them afrayed with thy storme.

16 Make their faces ashamed, O Lord that they maye seke thy name.

17 Let them be confounded and vexed euer more and more: let them be put to shame and perishe.

18 That they may know that thou art alone that thy name is the Lorde, & that thou onely art the moost hyest ouer all the earth.

## PSALM 84

*Vpon Githith, a Psalm of the sonnes of Corah.*

O howe amiable are thy dwellinges, thou Lord of hoostes?

2 My soule hath a desyre & longing for the court of the Lord, my hert and my fleshe reioyse in the lyuyng God.

3 For the sparow hath founde her an house and the swalow a nest, where she maye laye her yonge: euen thy aulters O Lorde of hostes, my kynge and my God.

4 O how blessed are they that dwell in thy house, they are all way praysing the. Selah.

5 Blessed are the men whose strengthe is in the, in whose herte are thy wayes.

6 Which goinge thorow the vale of misery vse it for a well, and the poles are filled with water.

7 They go from strength to strength, and so the God of Goddes appeareth vnto them in Sion.

8 O Lord God of hostes, heare my prayer: herken O God of Iacob.

9 Beholde O God our defence, loke vpon the face of thyne anoynted.

10 For one daye in thy courte is better then a thousande. I had rather be a dore keper in the house of my God, then to dwell in the tentes of the vngodly.

11 For the Lord God is a light and defence, the Lorde wyll geue grace and worshyppe, and no good thynge shall he wytholde from them that lyue a godly lyfe.

12 O Lorde God of Hostes, blessed is the man that putteth his truste in the.

## PSALM 85

*To the chaunter, a Psalme of the sonnes of Corah.*

LORDE, thou barest a loue vnto thy land thou dydest brynge agayne the captyuyte of Iacob.

2 Thou dydest forgeue the offence of thy people, and couerdest al their synnes. Sela.

3 Thou takest away al thy displeasure, and turnedest thy selfe from thy wrathfull indignacyon.

4 Turne vs then. O God oure Sauyoure, and let thyne anger ceasse from vs.

5 Wylt thou be dyspleased at vs for euer? wylt thou stretch out thy wrath from one generacyon to another?

6 Wylt thou not turne agayne and quycken vs, that thy people maye reioyse in the?

7 <>

8 I wyll herken what the Lorde God wyll saye for he shall speake peace vnto hys people and to hys saynctes, that they turne not them selues vnto folyshnes.

9 For hys saluacyon is nye them that feare hym so, that glory shall dwell in oure lande.

10 Mercy and trueth are met together, ryghtuousnesse and peace kysseth eche other.

11 Trueth shall ryse oute of the earthe, and ryghtuousnesse shal loke downe from heauen

12 And why? the Lorde shall shewe louynge kyndnesse, and oure lande shal geue her encrease.

13 Rightuousnes shall go before hym, and prepare the waye for his commynge.

## PSALM 86

*A prayer of Dauyd.*

BOw downe thine eare, O Lord and heare me, for I am comfortles and poore.

2 O kepe my soule, for I am holy my God, helpe thy seruante that putteth his trust in the.

3 Be merciful vnto me, O Lord, for I cal dayly vpon the.

4 Comfort the soule of thy seruaunt, for vnto the, O Lord, do I lyft vp my soule.

5 For thou Lorde arte good and gracyous, and of greate mercye vnto all them that call vpon the.

6 Geue eare Lord vnto my praier, and ponder my humble desyre.

7 In the tyme of my trouble I cal vpon the, for thou hearest me.

8 Amonge the Goddes ther is none like vnto the, O Lorde, there is not one that can do as thou doest.

9 All nacyons whom thou hast made, shall come and worship before the, O Lorde, and shal gloryfy thy name.

10 For thou art great, thou dost wonderous thinges, thou art God alone.

11 Leade me in thy way, O Lord, that I may walke in thy trueth: O let my herte delyte in fearyng thy name.

12 I thanke the. O Lorde my God, and will prayse thy name for euer.

13 For great is thy mercy towarde me, thou hast delyuered my soule from the nether most

hell.

14 O God the proude are rysen agaynst me, and the congregacyon of the myghtye seketh after my soule, and sette not the before theyr eyes.

15 But thou, O Lord God, art ful of compassion, and mercy, long suffring, great in goodnes and truth.

16 O turne the then vnto me, haue mercy vpon me: geue thy strength vnto thy seruante, and helpe the sonne of thyne handmayde.

17 Shew some token vpon me for good, that they which hate me, maye se it, and be ashamed: because thou Lord hast helped me, and comforted me.

## PSALM 87

*A Psalme and songe of the sonnes of Corah*

HER foundatyons are vpon the holye hylles:

2 the Lorde loueth the gates of Syon more then all the dwellynges, of Iacob.

3 Very excellent thynges are spoken of the thou cyty of God. Selah.

4 I wyll thynke vpon Rahab and Babilon so that they shall know me. Yea the Philistines also, and they of Tire wyth the Morians. Lo ther was he borne.

5 And of Sion it shalbe reported, that he was borne in her, euen the most hyest whych hath buylded her.

6 The Lorde shall cause it to be preached & wrytten amonge the people, that he was borne ther. Selah.

7 Therfore the dwellynge of all syngers & daunsers is in the.

## PSALM 88

*A Psalme and songe, of the sonnes of Corah, to the chaunter vpon Mahelath, for affliccyon, an instruccyon of Heman the Ezrathyte.*

O Lord God my sauiour, I cry day and nyghte before the:

2 Oh let my praier enter into thy presence, incline thyne eare vnto my callynge.

3 For my soule is full of trouble, and my lyfe draweth nye vnto hell.

4 I am counted as one of them that go downe vnto the pitte, I am euen as a man that hath no strength.

5 Fre among the dead, like vnto them that lye in the graue, whyche be out of remembraunce, and are cutte away from thy hand.

6 Thou hast layed me, in the lowest pytte, in the darcknesse and in the depe.

7 Thyne indignacion lieth harde vpon me, and thou vexest me wyth all thy floudes Selah.

8 Thou hast put awaye myn acquaintance farre fro me, and made me to be abhorred of them: I am so faste in pryson, that I can not get forth.

9 My syght fayleth for very trouble: Lord I call dayly vpon the, and stretch oute myne handes vnto the.

10 Doest thou shewe wonders amonge the deade? Can the Phisicions raise them vp againe that they maye prayse the?

11 Maye thy louynge kyndnes be shewed in the graue or thy faythfulnesse in destruccyon:

12 May thy wonderous workes be knowne in the darcke, or thy ryghtuousnes in the land wher al thinges are forgotten?

13 Vnto the I crye, O Lorde, and early commeth my prayer before the.

14 Lorde, why putteste thou awaye my soule? Wherfore hydest thou thy face fro me?

15 My strength is gone for very sorow & myserye, wyh fearfulnesse do I beare thy burthens.

16 Thy wrathfull dyspleasure goeth ouer me the feare of the, oppresseth me.

17 They come rounde about me dayly lyke water, and compasse me together on euerye side.

18 My louers, and frendes hast thou put awaye fro me, and turned awaye myne acquayntaunce.

## PSALM 89

*An instruccyon yf Ethan the Ezrahyte.*

MY songe shalbe alway of the louynge kyndnesse of the Lorde, wyth my mouth wyl I euer be shewynge thy faythfulnes from one generacyon to another.

2 For I haue sayed, mercy shalbe set vp for euer, thy faythfulnesse shalt thou stablysh in the heauens.

3 I haue made a couenaunt wyth my chosen, I haue sworne vnto Dauid my seruant.

4 Thy sede wyll I stablyshe for euer, and set vp thy trone from one generacyon to another Selah.

5 O Lorde the verye heauens shall prayse thy wonderous, worckes, yea and thy faythfulnes in the congregation of the sayinctes.

6 For who is he amonge the cloudes, that may be compared vnto the Lord. Yea, what is he among the Gods þt is like vnto þe lord?

7 God is greatly to be feared in the councel of the saintes and to be had in reuerence of al them that are aboute hym.

8 O Lorde God of Hostes who is lyke vnto the in power? thy trueth is round about þe

9 Thou rulest the pryde of the sea, thou stillest the waues therof, when they aryse.

10 Thou breakest the proude, like one that is wounded, thou scatrest thine enemies abroad with thy mightye arme.

11 The heauens are thine, the

earth is thine: thou hast layed the foundation of the rounde world, and al that therin is.

12 Thou hast made the north and the south, Tabor and Hermon shal reioyse in thy name

13 Thou hast a myghty arme, stronge is thy hande, and hye is thy righthande.

14 Righteousnes and equite is the habitacion of thy seate, mercy and truethe go before thy face.

15 Blessed is the people, O Lorde, that can reioyse in the, & walketh in the lyghte of thy countenauce.

16 Their delyte is in thy name all the daye longe, and thorowe thy righteousnesse they shalbe exalted.

17 For thou art the glory of their strength, & thorow thy fauoure shalt thou lyfte vp oure hornes.

18 The Lorde is our defence, and the holy one of Israel is our kyng.

19 Thou spakest sometyme in visions vnto thy saynctes, and saydest: I haue layed helpe vpon one that is mighty, I haue exalted one chosen out of the people.

20 I haue founde Dauid my seruaunt, with my holy oyle haue I anoynted hym.

21 My hande shal holde him fast, and myne arme shall strengthen hym.

22 The enemye shall not ouercome hym, & the sonne of wyckednesse shall not hurte hym.

23 I shall smyte doune hys foes before hys face, and plage them that hate hym.

24 My trueth also & my mercy shalbe wyth hym, and in my name shall hys horne be exalted.

25 I will set hys hande in the sea, & his right hande in the floudes.

26 He shall call me, thou art my father, my God, and the strength of my saluacion.

27 And I will make hym my fyrste borne, hyer then the kynges of the earth.

28 My mercy wyll I kepe for hym for euermore, and my couenaunte shall stande faste with hym.

29 Hys sede wyll I make to endure for euer, yea, and his trone as the dayes of heauen.

30 But if hys chyldren forsake my law, and walke not in my iudgementes.

31 If they breake myne ordynaunces, & kepe not my commaundementes.

32 I will vyset their offences wyth the rodde, and their synnes wit scourges.

33 Neuerthelesse, my louinge kyndnesse wil I not vtterly take from hym, nor suffre my trueth to fayle.

34 My couenaunt wyl I not breake, nor disanulle the thynge that is gone out of my lippes.

35 I haue sworne once by my holinesse, that I will not fayle Dauid.

36 Hys sede shall endure for euer, and hys seate also lyke as the sunne before me.

37 He shall stande faste for euermore as the moone, and as the faythfull wytnesse in heauen. Selah.

38 But now thou forsakest & abhorrest thine anoynted, and art displeased at hym.

39 Thou hast turned backe the couenaunte of thy seruaunt, and caste hys croune to the grounde.

40 Thou hast ouerthrowen all his hedges, & broken doune his stronge holdes.

41 All they that go by, spoyle hym, he is become a rebuke vnto hys neyghbours.

42 Thou settest vp the righthande of his enemyes, and makest all hys aduersaries to reioyse.

43 Thou hast taken awaye the strengthe of his swerde, and geuest him not victory in the battayle.

44 Thou hast put out his glory, and cast his trone doune to the grounde.

45 The dayes of his youth hast thou shortened, & couered him with dishonoure. Selah.

46 Lord, how longe wilt thou hyde thy self? For euer? shall thy wrathe burne lyke fyre?

47 O remembre how shorte my time is, hast thou made all men for nought?

48 What man is he that lyueth, and shall not se death? Maye a man deliuer his owne soule from the hande of hell? Selah.

49 Lorde, where are thy olde louing kyndnesses, whyche thou sworest vnto Dauid in thy trueth?

50 Remembre Lord the rebuke that the multitude of the people do vnto thy seruauntes, and how I haue borne it in my bosome.

51 Wherwith thyne enemyes blaspheme þe, and sclaunder the footesteppes of thyne anoynted.

52 Thankes be too the Lorde for euermore: Amen: Amen.

## PSALM 90

*A prayer of Moyses the man of God.*

LORDE thou art oure refuge from one generacion to another.

2 Before the mountaines were broughte forthe, or euer the earthe and the worlde were made, thou art God from euerlastynge and worlde without ende.

3 Thou turnest man to destruccyon, Agayne, thou sayest: come agayne ye chyldren of men

4 For a thousande yeares in thy sighte are but as yesterdaye that is past, and lyke as it were a nyght watch.

5 As sone as thou scatrest them, they are euen as a slepe, & fade awaye sodenly like the

grasse.

6 In the mornyng it is grene and groweth vp, but in the euenynge it is cut doune and wythered.

7 For we consume awaye in thy displeasure, and are afrayed at thy wrathful indignacion.

8 Thou settest our misdedes before the, and our secrete sinnes in the light of thy countenaunce.

9 For when thou art angrye, all oure dayes are gone, we brynge our yeares to an ende, as it were a tale that is tolde.

10 The dayes of oure age are .iij. score yeares and ten: and though men be so strong that they come to foure score yeares, yet is their strength then but laboure, & sorowe: so soone passeth it awaye, and we are gone.

11 But who regardeth þe power of thy wrath thy fearfull and terrible displeasure?

12 O teach vs to numbre our daies, that we maye apply our hertes vnto wisdome.

13 Turne the agayn (O Lorde) at the last, & be gracious vnto thy seruauntes.

14 O satisfie vs with thy mercy, & that sone, so shall we reioyse and be glad all the dayes of our lyfe.

15 Comforte vs agayne, now after the tyme that thou hast plaged vs, and for the yeares wherin we haue suffred aduersitie.

16 Shewe thy seruauntes thy worke, & their chyldren thy glory.

17 And the glorious maiesty of the Lord our God be vpon vs: O prospere thou þe worke of our handes vpon vs, O prospere thou our handy worke.

## PSALM 91

WHO so dwelleth vnder the defence of the most hyest, & abydeth vnder the shadowe of the almightye.

2 He shal say vnto the Lorde: O my hope, and my strong holde, my God, in whome I will trust.

3 For he shall delyuer the from the snare of the hunter, and from the noysome pestylence.

4 He shall couer the vnder hys wynges, that thou mayest be safe vnder his fethers: his faythfulnesse & trueth shalbe thy shylde and buckler.

5 So that thou shalt not nede to be afrayed for any bugges by night, nor for the arrowe that flyeth by daye.

6 For the pestilence that crepeth in þe darkenesse, nor for the sikenesse that destroyeth in the noone daye.

7 A thousande shall fall beside the, and ten thousande at thy righthande, but it shall not come nye the.

8 Yea, with thyne eyes shalt thou beholde, and se the rewarde of the vngodly.

9 For thou Lorde art my hope, thou hast set thyne house of defence very hye.

10 There shall no euell happen vnto the, neither shall any plage come nye thy dwelling.

11 For he shall gyue his aungels charge ouer the, to kepe the in all thy wayes.

12 They shall beare the in their handes, that thou hurt not thy fote agaynst a stone.

13 Thou shalt go vpon the Lyon and Adder the yonge lyon and the Dragon shalte thou treade vnder thy fete.

14 Because he hath set his loue vppon me, I shall deliuer hym: I shal defende him, for he hath knowen my name.

15 When he calleth vpon me, I shall heare hym: yea, I am with hym in hys trouble, wherout I will deliuer him, and bring hym to honoure.

16 With longe lyfe will I satisfye him, and shewe hym my saluacion.

## PSALM 92

*A Psalme of the songe for the Sabboth daye.*

IT is a good thynge too geue thankes vnto the Lord, and to synge prayses vnto thy name, O moost hyest.

2 To tell of thy louyng kyndnesse early in the mornyng. and of thy trueth in the night season.

3 Vpon an instrument of ten strynges, vpon the lute and with a songe vpon the harpe.

4 For thou lord hast made me glad thorow thy workes, and I will reioyse ouer the operacion of thy handes.

5 O Lorde, how glorious are thy workes, thy thoughtes are very depe.

6 An vnwyse man will not knowe thys, and a foole will not vnderstande it.

7 That the vngodly are grene as the grasse and that all the workes of wickednes do florish to be destroyed for euer.

8 But thou Lorde O mooste hyest, abydest worlde without ende.

9 For lo, thyne enemyes, O Lord, lo, thyne enemyes shall perishe, and all the workers of wickednes shalbe scatred abroade.

10 But my horne shalbe exalted like þe horne of an Vnicorne, & shalbe anoynted wyth fresh oyle.

11 Myne eye also shall se hys luste of myne enemyes, and myne eare shall heare his desire of the wicked that ryse vp agaynst me.

12 The righteous shall florish lyke a palme tree, and growe like a Cedre of Libanus.

13 Suche as be planted in the house of the Lorde, be frutefull,

14 plenteous and grene.

15 That they maye shew, how true þe Lorde my strength is, and that there is no vnrighteousnesse in hym.

## PSALM 93

THE Lorde is kyng, and hath put on glorious apparell, the Lorde hath put on his apparell, & gyrded him selfe with strengthe: he hath made the rounde world so sure, that it can not be moued.

2 From that tyme forth hath thy seate bene prepared, thou art from euerlastyng.

3 The floudes aryse (O Lorde) the floudes lyft vp their noyse, the floudes lyfte vp theyr waues.

4 The waues of the sea are mightye, & rage horribly: but yet the Lorde that dwelled on hye, is mightier.

5 Thy testimonies, O LORD, are very sure, holynesse becommeth thyne house for euer.

## PSALM 94

O Lorde God, to whome vengeaunce belongeth: thou God to whome vengeaunce belongeth shewe thy self.

2 Aryse thou iudge of þe world & rewarde the proude after their deseruyng.

3 Lorde how longe shall the vngodly, how longe shall the vngodly triumphe?

4 How longe shall all wicked doers speake so disdaynfully, and make such proude boastynge?

5 They smyte doune thy people, O Lorde, and trouble thine heritage.

6 They murthur the wydowe & the straunger, and put the fatherlesse to death.

7 And yet they saye: Tushe, the Lorde seyth not, the God of Iacob regardeth it not.

8 Take hede, ye vnwyse among the people: O ye fooles, when will ye vnderstande?

9 He that planted the eare, shal he not heare? he that made the eye, shal not he se?

10 He that nurtureth the Heathen, and teacheth a man knowlege, shall not he punish?

11 The Lord knoweth the thoughtes of men, that they are but vayne.

12 Blessed is the man, whome thou learnest (O LORDE) and teacheste hym in thy lawe.

13 That thou mayest geue hym pacience in tyme of aduersitie, vntil the pytte be dygged vp for the vngodly.

14 For the Lorde will not fayle his people, neither will he forsake his inheritaunce.

15 And why? iudgement shalbe turned agayn vnto righteousnesse, and all suche as be true of hert shall folow it.

16 Who ryseth vp with me agaynst the wicked? who taketh my parte agaynste the euell doers?

17 If the Lord had not helped me, my soule had almost bene put to silence.

18 When I sayde: my fote hath slypped, thy mercy (O Lord) helde me vp.

19 In the multitude of the sorowes that I had in my herte, thy comfortes haue refreshed my soule.

20 Wilt thou haue any thing to do with the stoole of wickednesse, which ymagineth mischief in the lawe?

21 They gather them together agaynste the soule of the righteous, and condemne the innocent bloude.

22 But the Lord is my refuge, my God is þe strength of my confidence.

23 He shall recompence them their wickednesse, & destroye them in their owne malyce: yea, the Lorde our God shall destroy them.

## PSALM 95

O come let vs prayse þe Lord, let vs hertely reioyse in þe strength of our saluacion.

2 Let vs come before his presence with thankesgeuynge, & shewe oure selfe gladde in hym with Psalmes.

3 For the Lord is a great God, and a great kyng aboue all Goddes.

4 In his hand are al the corners of the earth, and the strength of the hylles is his also.

5 The sea is his, for he made it, & his handes prepared the drye lande.

6 O come, let vs worshippe & bowe doune our selfes: Let vs knele before the Lord our maker.

7 For he is oure God: & we are the people of his pasture, and the shepe of his handes. To daye if ye wil heare his voyce,

8 harden not youre hertes, as when ye prouoked in tyme of temptacion in the wildernes.

9 Where your fathers tempted me, proued me, and sawe my workes.

10 .xl. yeares long was I greued with the generacion, & sayd: they euer erre in their hertes, they verely haue not knowen my wayes.

11 Therfore I sayd vnto them in my wrath, that they should not enter into my rest.

## PSALM 96

O synge vnto the Lorde a newe songe, singe vnto the Lorde all the whole earth.

2 Synge vnto the Lord, and prayse his name, be tellyng of his saluacion from daye to daye.

3 Declare his honour among the Heathen, and his wonders among all people.

4 For the Lord is great, and can not worthely be praysed: he is more to be feared then all goddes.

5 As for all the goddes of the Heathen, they be but Idols, but it is the Lorde that made the heauens.

6 Thankesgeuynge and worshippe are before hym,

power & honoure are in hys Sanctuary.

7 Ascribe vnto the Lord (O ye kynredes of the Heathen) ascribe vnto the Lord worship and strength.

8 Ascribe vnto the Lord the honoure of his name, brynge presentes, and come into hys courte.

9 O worship the lorde in the beuty of holynesse, lette the whole earthe stande in awe of hym.

10 Tell it out amonge the Heathen, that the Lorde is kynge: and that it is he, which hath made the rounde worlde so faste, that it can not be moued, and howe that he shall iudge the people righteously.

11 Let the heauens reioyse, and let the earth be glad: let the sea make a noyse, yea, and all that therin is.

12 Let the felde be ioyfull and all that is in it, lette all the trees of the woode leape for ioye.

13 Before the lorde, for he commeth: for he commeth to iudge the earth: yea, with ryghteousnesse shall he iudge the worlde, and the people with his trueth.

## PSALM 97

THE Lord is king, the earth may be glad therof: yea, the multitude of the Iles may be glad therof.

2 Cloudes & darkenesse are round about him, righteousnesse & iudgement are þe habitacion of hys seate.

3 There goeth a fyre before hym, to burne vp hys enemyes on euery syde.

4 Hys lightenynges geue shyne vnto the worlde, the earth seyth it, and is afrayed.

5 The hilles melt like waxe at the presence of the lord of the whole earth.

6 The very heauens declare his righteousnes, and all the people se his glory.

7 Confounded be all thei that worship ymages, and delyte in their Idols: worship him all ye Goddes.

8 Sion heareth of it & reioyseth: yea, & all þe daughters of Iuda are glad because of thy iudgementes, O lorde.

9 For thou lorde art the most hyest ouer all the earth, thou arte exalted farre aboue all goddes.

10 O ye that loue the lorde, se that ye hate þt thyng whiche is euell: the lorde preserueth þe soules of his saynctes, he shall deliuer them from the hande of the vngodly.

11 There is sprong vp a lighte for the ryghteous, and a ioyfull gladnesse for suche as be true herted.

12 Reioyse therfore in the lorde, ye ryghteous: and geue thankes for a remembraunce of hys holinesse.

## PSALM 98

*A Psalme.*

O synge vnto the Lorde a new song, for he hath done maruelous thynges. With hys owne rygt hande and with his holy arme hathe he gotten the victory.

2 The lord hath declared his sauyng health & hys righteousnes hathe he openly shewed in the sight of the Heathen.

3 He hath remembred his mercy and trueth towarde the house of Israel: so that all þe endes of the worlde, se the sauing health of our God.

4 Shewe youre selfes ioyfull vnto the Lorde all ye landes, synge, reioyse, and geue thanckes.

5 Prayse the Lordes, vpon the harpe, synge to the harpe wyth a psalme of thanckesgeuynge

6 With trompettes also and shawmes: O shewe youre selues ioyfull before the Lorde the kynge.

7 Let the sea make a noyse and all that therin is, yea the whole worlde, and al that dwel therein.

8 Let the floudes clappe their handes, and let al the hylles be ioyful together.

9 Before the Lorde, for he is come to iudge the earth. Yea wyth ryghtuousnes shall he iudg the worlde, and the people wyth equyte.

## PSALM 99

THE Lorde is kynge, be the people neuer so vnpaciente: he sytteth vpon the Cherubyns, be the earth neuer so vnquiete.

2 The Lord is greate in Sion, & hye aboue all people.

3 O let men geue thanckes vnto thy greate and wonderfull name, for it is holye.

4 The kinges power loueth iudgment, thou preparest equite, thou executest iudgment and ryghtuousnes in, Iacob.

5 O magnyfy the Lorde oure God, fal down before his fote stole, for he is holye.

6 Moyses ond Aaron amonge hys pryestes and Samuell amonge such as call vpon hys name: these called vpon the Lorde, and he hearde them.

7 He spake vnto them out of the cloudy piller for he kepte hys testymonyes, and the lawe that gaue them.

8 Thou heardest them, O Lorde oure God thou forgauest them O God, and punyshedst their owne inueucions.

9 O magnyfye the Lorde oure God, and worshyppe hym vpon hys holy hyll, for the Lorde oure God is holy.

## PSALM 100

*A Psalme of praise.*

O be ioiful in God (al ye landes)

2 serue the Lorde with gladnes, come before his presence wyth ioye.

3 Be ye sure, that the Lord he is God: It is he that hath made vs, and not we our selues: we are but his people, and the shepe of his pastoure.

4 O go youre waye into hys gates then with thanckesgeuynge, and into his courtes with prayse, be thanckefull vnto hym, and speake good of his name.

5 For the Lorde is gracyous, hys mercie is euerlastynge, and hys trueth endureth from generatyon to generacyon.

## PSALM 101

*A Psalme of Dauid.*

MY songe shalbe of mercye and iudgment yea vnto the, O Lord wyll I synge.

2 O let me haue vnderstandynge in the way of Godlynesse vntyll the tyme that thou come vnto me: and so shall I walcke in my house wyth an innocent herte.

3 I wyl take no wycked thynge in hande, I hate the synne of vnfaythfulnesse, it shal not cleaue vnto me.

4 A frowarde harte shall departe fro me I wyll not knowe a wicked personne.

5 Who so preuely sclaundereth hys neyghboure. hym wyl I destroye: Who so hath a prowd loke and an hye stomacke, I may not awaye with him.

6 Myne eyes shal loke for such as be faythfull in the lande, that they maye dwell wyth me: and who so leadeth a godly liue, shall be my seruaunt.

7 There shall no disceatfull personne dwell in my house he that telleth lyes shall not tary in my syght.

8 I shalll soone destroye all the vngodlie of the lande, that all wycked doers maye be roted out of the cytie of the Lord.

## PSALM 102

*A prayer of the afflycte, when he was in woo, and powered oute hys complaynte before the Lord.*

HEARE my prayer, O Lord, & and lette my crienge come vnto the.

2 Hyde not thy face fro me in the tyme of my trouble encline thyne eares vnto me when I call, O heare me, and that ryghte sone.

3 For my dayes are consumed awaye lyke smoke, and my bones are brent vp as it were a fyre brande.

4 My herte smytten doune and wythered lyke grasse, so that I forgette too eate my bread.

5 For the voyce of my gronynge, my bone wil scarse cleue to my flesh.

6 I am be come lyke a Pellicane in þe wildernes, and lyke an owle in a broken wal.

7 I wake, and am euen as it were a sparow sittinge alone vpon the house toppe.

8 Myne enemyes reuyle me all the daye longe, they laugh me to scorne, & are sworne together agaynst me.

9 I eate ashes with my bread, and myngle my drynke with wepynge.

10 And that because of thyne indignacion & wrath, for thou hast taken me vp, and caste me awaye.

11 My dayes are gone lyke a shadowe, and I am wythered lyke grasse.

12 But thou O Lord, endurest for euer, and thy remembraunce thorow out all generacyons.

13 Aryse therfore & haue mercy vpon Sion, for it is time to haue mercy vpon her, yea, þe tyme is come.

14 And why? thy seruauntes haue a loue too her stones, and it pitieth them to se her in the dust.

15 The Heathen shal feare thy name, O Lord, and all the kynges of the earth thy maiesty.

16 For the Lorde shall buylde vp Sion, and shall apeare in hys glory.

17 He turneth him vnto the prayer of the poore destitute, & despiseth not their desyre.

18 This shalbe wrytten for those that come after, that the people whiche shalbe borne, maye prayse the Lorde.

19 For he loketh doune from hys Sanctuary, out of the heauen doth the Lorde beholde the earth.

20 That he maye heare the mournynges of such as be in captiuitie, and deliuer the chyldren of death.

21 That they maye preache the name of the Lorde in Sion, and his worshippe at Hierusalem.

22 When the people are gathered together, & the kyngdomes also to serue the Lord.

23 He hath brought doune my strength in my iourney, and shortened my dayes.

24 Yet will I saye: O my God, take me not away in the myddest of myne age: as for thy yeares, they endure thorowe out all generacions.

25 Thou Lorde in the beginnyng hast layed the foundacion of the earth, and the heauens are the workes of thy handes.

26 They shal perish, but thou shalt endure: they all shall wexe olde as doth a garment, & as a vesture shalt thou chaunge them, & they shalbe chaunged.

27 But thou art the same, & thy yeares shall not fayle.

28 The chyldren of thy seruauntes shall continue, and their sede shall prospere in thy sighte.

## PSALM 103

*Of Dauid.*

PRAYSE the Lorde O my soule: & all that is within me prayse hys holy name.

2 Prayse the Lord O my soule & forget not all his benefites.

3 Whych forgeueth all thy synnes, & healeth all thyne infirmities.

4 Which saueth thy lyfe from destruccion, and crouneth the with mercy, and louynge kyndnesse.

5 Whiche satisfeth thy desyre wyth good thynges, makyng the yonge and lusty as an Aegle.

6 The Lorde executeth righteousnesse and iudgement, for all theim that suffre wronge.

7 He shewed his wayes vnto Moses, & his workes vnto the chyldren of Israel.

8 The Lord is ful of compassion and mercy, long sufferyng, & of great goodnesse.

9 He will not alwaye be chydynge, neither will he kepe his anger for euer.

10 He hath not dealt with vs after oure sinnes, nor rewarded vs according to our wickednesse.

11 For loke how hye the heauen is in comparison of the earth, so greate is his mercy also towarde them that feare hym.

12 Loke how wyde the East is from þe West, so farre hath he set oure sinnes from vs.

13 Yea, like as a father pitieth his owne children, euen so is the Lord mercifull vnto them that feare hym.

14 For he knoweth whereof we be made, he remembreth that we are but dust.

15 That a man in hys time is but as grasse, and florisheth as a floure of the felde.

16 For as sone, as the wynde goeth ouer it, it is gone, and the place thereof knoweth it no more.

17 But the mercyfull goodnesse of the Lorde endureth for euer and euer, vpon them that feare him, and his righteousnesse vpon their chyldren.

18 Suche as kepe hys couenaunte, & thynke vpon hys commaundementes to do them.

19 The Lorde hath prepared his seate in heauen, and his kingedome ruleth ouer all.

20 O prayse the Lorde ye aungels of his, ye that be myghty in strength fulfyllynge hys commaundement that men may here the voice of hys wordes.

21 O prayse the Lorde all ye his Hostes, yea seruauntes of his, that do hys pleasure.

22 O speake good of the Lorde al ye workes of his, in euery place of his dominion: praise thou the Lorde, O my soule.

## PSALM 104

PRAYSE the Lorde O my soule: O Lord my God, thou art become excedinge glorious, thou arte clothed with maiesty and honoure.

2 Thou deckest thy self with light, as it were with a garment, thou spredest out the heauen lyke a curtayne.

3 Thou voltest it aboue with waters, thou makest the cloudes thy charet, & goest vpon the wynges of the wynde.

4 Thou makest thyne aungels sprites, and thy ministers flammes of fyre.

5 Thou hast layed the earth vpon her foundacion, that it neuer moueth at any tyme.

6 Thou couerest it with the depe lyke as wt a garmente, so that the waters stande aboue the hylles.

7 But at thy rebuke they fle, at the voyce of thy thonder they are afrayed.

8 (Then are the hylles sene alofte, and the valleis beneth in their place which thou hast appoynted for them.)

9 Thou hast set them their boundes, which they maye not passe, that they turne not agayne to couer the earth.

10 Thou causest the welles to sprynge vp amonge the valleys, and the waters to runne amonge the hylles.

11 That all beastes of the felde maye haue drynke, & that the wilde asses maye quenche their thyrste.

12 Aboue vpon the hylles haue the foules of the ayre their habitacion, and singe amonge the braunches.

13 Thou waterest the hilles from aboue, the earth is filled wt the frutes of thy workes.

14 Thou bringest forth grasse for the cattell, and grene herbes for the seruice of men. Thou bringest fode out of the earth:

15 wyne to make glad the herte of man, oyle to make hym a chearfull countenaunce and bread to strength mans herte.

16 The trees of the Lord are ful of sappe, euen the trees of Libamis whiche he hathe planted.

17 There make the byrdes their nestes, & the fyrre hylles are a dwellyng for the storke.

18 The hilles are a refuge for the wilde goates, & so are the stony rockes for the conyes.

19 Thou hast appoynted the moone for certayne seasons, the sunne knoweth hys going doune.

20 Thou makest darkenesse, that it maye be night, wherin all the beastes of the forest do moue.

21 Yea, and the yonge lyons which roare after their praye, and seke their meate at God.

22 But when the sunne aryseth, they get them awaye together, and lye them doune in their dennes.

23 Then goeth man forth to hys worke, and to tyll hys lande vntyll the euenynge.

24 O Lord, how manifolde are thy workes, right wisely hast thou made them al: yea, the earth

is full of thy ryches.

25  So is this great & wyde sea also, wherein are thynges creping innumerable, both smal and great beastes.

26  There go the shippes ouer, and there is þe Leuiathan, whom thou hast made, to take hys pastyme therein.

27  They wayte all vpon the, that thou mayest geue them meate in due season.

28  When thou geuest it them, they gather it: when thou openest thyne hande, they are filled with good.

29  But when thou hydest thy face, they are sorowfull: if thou takest awaye their breth, they dye, & are turned agayne to their dust.

30  Agayne, when thou lettest thy brethe goo forth, they are made, and so thou renuest the face of the earth.

31  The glorious maiesty of the Lorde endureth for euer, & the Lorde reioyseth in hys workes.

32  The earth trembleth at the loke of hym, he doethe but touche the hylles and they smoke.

33  I wyll synge vnto the Lorde as longe as I lyue, I will prayse my God whyle I haue my beyng.

34  O that my wordes might please hym, for my ioye is in the Lorde.

35  As for synners, they shalbe consumed out of the earth, and the vngodlye shall come to an ende: but prayse thou the Lorde, O my soule. Prayse the euerlastynge.

## PSALM 105

O geue thankes vnto the Lord, and cal vpon his name: tel the people what thynges he hath done.

2  O let your songes be of him prayse hym, and let your talking be of al hys wonderous workes.

3  Gyue hys holye name a good report lette their hertes reioyse that seke the Lord.

4  Seke the Lord, and his strength, seke his face euermore.

5  Remember the maruelous worckes that he hath done, his wonders and the iudgementes of his mouth.

6  O ye sede of Abraham hys seruaunte, ye chyldren of Iacob hys chosen.

7  He is the Lorde oure God, whose punishmentes are thorow oute all the worlde.

8  He is alwaye myndeful of his couenaunt and promyse that he made to a thousand generations.

9  Yea the couenant that he made with Abraham, and the oth that, he sware vnto Isaac,

10  And appoynted the same vnto Iacob for a lawe, and to Israell for an euerlastynge testamente.

11  Sayenge: vnto the wyl I geue the land of Canaan, the lot of your heritage.

12  When there was yet but a fewe of them, and the straungers therin.

13  What tyme as they wente from one nacyon to another, from one kyngedome to another.

14  He suffered no man to hurt them, but reproued euen kynges for their sakes.

15  Touch not myne anoynted, do my prophetes no harme.

16  Moreouer he called for a dearth vpon the lande, and destroyed all the prouysyon of breade.

17  But he had sente a man before them, euen Ioseph whiche was solde to be a bonde seruaunte.

18  They hurte hys fete in the stockes the yron pearsed hys hert.

19  Vntill the tyme that his worde, and tyll the word of þe Lorde had tryed hym.

20  Then sent the kyng & caused him to be deliuered, the prince of þe people bad let him go

21  He made him Lorde of hys house, and ruler of all hys substaunce.

22  That he might enfourme his princes after hys wyl, & teach his Senatoures wisedom.

23  Israell also came into Egipte, and Iacob was a straunger in the lande of Ham.

24  But he increased hys people exceadyngly and made them stronger then their enemyes.

25  Whose hert turned so that they hated his people: and dealt vntruly wt hys seruauntes.

26  Then sente he Moses his seruaunte, and Aaron, whome he had chosen.

27  These dyd his tokens amonge them, and wonders in the lande of Ham.

28  He sente darcknesse and it was darcke, for they were not obedyent vnto hys worde.

29  He turned their waters into bloude, and slew theyr fysh.

30  Their land brought forth frogges, yea euen in their kynges chambers.

31  He spake the worde, and their came all maner of flyes and lyce in al their quarters

32  He gaue them hayle stones for rayne, and flammes of fyre in their land.

33  He smot their vineyeardes & figge trees, & destroyed the trees that were in their coastes.

34  He spake the worde, and ther were greshoppers and catyrpyllers innumerable.

35  These eate vp all the grasse in their land, and deuoured their frutes of the grounde.

36  He smote al the fyrst borne in the lande, euen the chefe of al their substaunce.

37  He broughte them forth wyth syluer and gold, ther was not one feble person amonge theyr trybes.

38 Egypte was glad of their departinge, for they were afrayed of them.

39 He spred out a cloude to be a coverynge, and fyres to geue lyght in the nyght season.

40 At their desyre, ther came quailes, and he fylled them wyth the breade of heauen.

41 He opened the rocke of stone, and the waters flowed out: so that ryuers ranne in the wyldernesse.

42 For why? he remembred his holy promes whyche he had made vnto Abraham his seruaunte.

43 Thus he broughte forth hys people wyth ioy, and his chosen with gladnesse.

44 And gaue them the landes of Heathen, where they toke þe laboures of þe people in possessyon.

45 That they myghte kepe hys statutes, and obserue his lawes. Prayse the euerlastynge.

## PSALM 106

PRAYSE the euerlastynge. O geue thankes vnto the Lorde, for he is gracyous, and hys mercy endureth for euer.

2 Who can expresse the noble actes of the Lord, or shewe forth al hys prayse?

3 Blessed are they that allwaye kepe iudgement, and do ryghtuousnes.

4 Remember vs, O Lorde, accordynge to the fauour that thou bearest vnto thy people O vyset vs wyth thy sauynge health.

5 That we myght se the pleasure of thy chosen, that we myght reioyse in the gladnesse of thy people, and geue thanckes with thine enherytaunce.

6 We haue synned wyth oure fathers, we haue done amysse, we haue dealt wyckedlye.

7 Oure fathers regarded not thy wonders in Egypte, they kepte not thy great goodnes in remembraunce: but were dysobedyent at the sea, euen at the reed sea.

8 Neuertheles, he helped them for hys names sake, that he myghte make hys power to be knowne.

9 He rebuked the read sea, and it was dryed vp: so he led them thorowe the depe as in a wyldernes.

10 Thus he saued them from the hand of the hater, and delyuered them from the hande of the enemye.

11 As for those that troubled them the waters ouerwhelmed them, ther was not one of them left.

12 Then beleued they in his worde, and sang prayse vnto hym.

13 But within a whyle they forgat his workes, and wold not abyde his councel.

14 A lust came vpon them in the wildernesse, so that they tempted God in the deserte.

15 Yet he gaue them their desire, and sent them ynough at their wylles.

16 They angred Moyses in þe tentes, & Aaron the saynct of the Lord.

17 So the earth opened & swalowed vp Dathan, & couered the congregatyon of Abyram.

18 The fyre was kyndled in their companie, the flamme brent vp the vngodly.

19 They made a calfe in Horeb, and worshipped the molten ymage.

20 Thus they turned their glorye into the similitude of a calfe, that eateth hay.

21 They forgat God their Sauiour, whyche had done so greate thynges in Egypte.

22 Wonderous workes in the land of Ham and fearful thynges in the read sea.

23 So he sayde he wuld haue destroyed them had not Moses hys chosen stand before him in that gappe: to turne awaye his wrathfull indignatyon, lest he should destroy them.

24 Yea, they thought scorne of that pleasaunt lande, and gaue no credence vnto hys worde

25 But murmured in their tentes, and herkened not vnto the voyce of the Lord.

26 Then lyft he vp his hand against them to ouerthrowe them in the wildernes.

27 To cast out their sede among the nacions. and to scatter them in the landes.

28 They ioyned them selues vnto Baal Peor and eate the offeringes of the dead.

29 Thus they prouoked him vnto anger with their owne inuencyons, and the plage was great among them.

30 Then stode vp Phynehes and executed iustice, and so the plage ceased.

31 And that was counted vnto him for ryghtuousnesse, amonge all posterityes for euermore.

32 They angeryd hym also at the waters of strife, so that Moyses was punished for ther sakes.

33 Because they prouoked his spirite, and he told them plainly with his lippes.

34 Nether destroied they the Heathen, as the Lorde commaunded them.

35 But were mingled among the Heathen, and lerned their workes.

36 In so much that they worshipped their images, which turned to their owne decay.

37 Yea they offred their sons and their daughters vnto deuels.

38 And shed the innocent bloud of their sonnes and of their daughters, whom they offered vnto the ymages of Canaan, so that the land was defiled with bloud.

39 Thus were they stayned with their owne workes, and went a whoring with their owne inuencyons.

40 Therfore was the wrath of the Lord kindled agaynst hys people, in so much that he abhorred his owne enheritaunce.

41 And gaue them ouer into the hand of the Heathen, and they that hated them, were lordes ouer them.

42 Their enemyes oppressed them, and had them in subieccion.

43 Many a tyme did he delyuer them but they prouoked him wyth theyr owne inuencyons and were broughte downe for theyr wyckednesse.

44 Neuertheles when he saw their aduersitie he herd their complaynt.

45 He thought vpon hys couenaunt, and pytyed them, accordyng vnto the multytude of hys mercyes.

46 Yea he made all those that had led them awaye captyue, to pitiye them.

47 Delyuer vs, O Lorde oure God, and gather vs from amonge the Heathen: that we maye geue thanckes to thy holye name, and make our boast of thy prayse.

48 Blessed be the Lorde God of Israel from euerlastyng and world without ende, and let all people saye: Amen, Amen. Prayse the euerlastynge.

## PSALM 107

O geue thankes vnto the Lord, for he is gracious, & his mercy endureth for euer.

2 Let them geue thankes whome the Lord hath redemed, & deliuered from the hande of the enemye.

3 And gathered them out of the landes, from the East, from the West, from the North and from the South.

4 They went astraye in the wildernesse in an vntroden waye, and founde no cytye too dwell in.

5 Hungry & thirsty, and their soule faynted in them.

6 So they cryed vnto the Lorde in theyr trouble, and he deliuered them from theyr distresse.

7 He ledde them forth by the ryghte waye, that they myghte go to the cytye where they dwelt.

8 O that men wolde praise the goodnesse of the Lorde, and the wonders that he doth for the chyldren of men.

9 For he satisfied the empty soule, & fylled the hungry soule with good.

10 Such as sat in darkenesse and in the shadow of death, beyng fast bounde in mysery and yron.

11 Because they were not obedient to the commaundementes of God, but lightely regarded the counsayll of the moost hyghest.

12 Their hert was vexed with labour, they fel doune, and there was none to helpe them.

13 So they cryed vnto the LORD in their trouble, and he deliuered them oute of theyr dystresse.

14 He brought them out of darkenesse & oute of the shadow of death, & brake their bondes in sonder.

15 O that men wolde prayse the goodnesse of the Lord, and the wonders that he doth for the chyldren of men.

16 For he hath broken the gates of brasse, and smytten the barres of yron in sonder.

17 Folysh men were plaged for their offence and because of their wickednesse.

18 Their soule abhorred all maner of meate, they were euen harde at deaths dore.

19 So they cryed vnto the Lorde in their trouble, and he deliuered them oute of theyr distresse.

20 He sent hys worde and healed them, and saued them from destruccion.

21 O that men woulde prayse the goodnesse of the Lorde, and the wonders that he doth for the chyldren of men.

22 That they wolde offre vnto him the sacrifice of thankesgeuyng, & tell out hys workes with gladnes.

23 They that go doune to the sea in shippes, and occupy their businesse in great waters.

24 These men se the workes of the Lorde, & his wonders in the deape.

25 For at his worde, the stormy winde aryseth, and lifteth vp the waues therof.

26 They are caryed vp to the heauen, & doun agayne too the deape, their soule melteth awaye in the trouble.

27 They rele to and fro, they stacker lyke a dronken man, and are at their wittes ende.

28 So they crye vnto the Lorde in their trouble, and he delyuereth them oute of their distresse.

29 He maketh the storme to ceasse, so that the waues are styll.

30 Then are they glad because they be at rest & so he bringeth them vnto the hauen, where they wolde be.

31 O that men wolde prayse the goodnes of the Lorde, and the wondres that he doth for the chyldren of men.

32 That they wolde exalte him in the congregacion of the people, & loane hym in the seate of the elders.

33 Which turneth the floudes into drye land, and drieth vp the water sprynges.

34 A frutefull lande maketh he baren, for the wickednesse of them that dwell therin.

35 Agayn, he maketh the wildernes a standinge water, and water springes of a drye grounde.

36 There he setteth the hongrye, that they maye buylde them a cytye to dwell in.

37 That they may sow their grounde, plante vyneyardes, to

yelde them frutes of increase.

38 He blesseth them, so that they multiplye excedingly, and suffreth not their cattel to decrease.

39 When they are minished & brought lowe thorowe oppression, thorowe any plage or trouble.

40 Though he suffre them to be euell intreated thorow tyrauntes, or lette them wandre out of the waye in the wildernesse.

41 Yet helpeth he the poore out of misery (at the last) and maket hym an housholde lyke a flocke of shepe.

42 The righteous will considre this & reioyse, the mouth of all wyckednesse shalbe stopped.

43 Who so is wyse, & pondreth these thynges well, shal vnderstande the louyng kyndnesses of the Lorde.

## PSALM 108

*A songe of Psalme of Dauid.*

OGod, my herte is ready to synge, and to geue prayse. Awake, O my glorye,

2 awake lute and harpe, I my selfe wyll awake ryght early.

3 I wyll geue thanckes vnto the, O Lord, amonge the people. I wil syng prayses vnto the among the Heathen.

4 For the greatenesse of thy mercy is higher then the heauens, and thy faithfulnesse reacheth vnto the cloudes.

5 Set vp thy selfe, O God, aboue the heauens, and thy glory aboue al the eartth.

6 That thy beloued may be delyuered: helpe them with thy right hand and heare me

7 God hath spoken in his Sanctuary, whych thyng reioyseth me. I wyll deuyde Sichem, and meate out the valley of Suchoth.

8 Galaad is myne, Manasses is myne, Ephraym is the strength of my head, Iuda is my captaine.

9 Moab is my washpotte, ouer Edom will I stretch oute my shue, Phylystea shall be glad of me.

10 Who wyll lead me into the stronge cyty? Who wyll brynge me into Edom?

11 Shalt not thou do it (O God) which hast cast vs: out thou God, that wentest not forth with our Hostes?

12 O be thou our helpe in trouble, for vayne is the helpe of man.

13 Thorow God we shal do great actes, for it is he that shal treade downe our enemyes.

## PSALM 109

*To the chaunter, a Psalme of Dauyd.*

HOLDE not thy tong: O God of my praise.

2 For the mouth of the vngodlye yea and þe mouth of the disceatfull is opened vpon me, and speake agaynste me wyth false tonges.

3 They compase me aboute with wordes of hatred, and fight against me without a cause

4 For the loue that I had vnto them, they take now my contrary parte, but I geue my selfe vnto prayer.

5 Thus they reward me euel for good, and hatred for my god wyll.

6 Set an vngodly man to be ruler ouer him and let Satan stande at his ryghte hande.

7 When sentence is geuen vpon him, let him be condempned, and let his prayer be turned into synne.

8 Let his daies be few, and his bishopricke let another take.

9 Let hys chyldren be fatherlesse, and hys wyfe a wydowe.

10 Let his children be vagabaundes, and bege their breade: lette them seke it, as they that be destroyed.

11 Let the extorcioner consume al that he hath and let straungers spoyle his laboure.

12 Let ther be no man to pytye, ner to haue compassyon vpon his fatherles chyldren.

13 Let hys ende be destruccyon, & in the next generacion let his name be cleane put oute.

14 Let the wickednesse of his fathers be had in remembraunce in the syght of the Lorde & and let not the synne of hys mother be done awaye.

15 Let them alway be before the Lorde, but as for the memoryall of them selues, let it perysh from out of the earth.

16 And that because hys mynde was not to do good. but persecuted the poore helplesse, and hym that was vexed at the harte, to slay hym.

17 Hys delyte was in cursynge, and therfore shall it happen vnto hym: he loued not blessynge and that shall be far from hym.

18 He clothed hym selfe wyth cursynge lyke as wyth a rayment: yea it wente into hys bowels lyke water, and lyke oile into his bones

19 Let it be vnto hym as the cloke that he hath vpon hym, and as the gyrdle that he is gyrded with al.

20 Let it thus happen from the Lorde vnto myne enemyes, and to those that speake euel agaynst my soule.

21 But deale thou wyth me, O Lorde God, accordynge vnto thy name, for swete is thy mercy. O deliuer me,

22 for I am helplesse, and pore and my herte is wounded within me.

23 I go hence lyke the shadowe that departeth, & am driuen away as the greshoppers.

24 My knees are weake thorow fastynge my flesh is dryed vp for want of fatnesse.

25 I am become a rebuke vnto

them, they loke vpon me and shake their heades.

26 Helpe me, O Lorde my God, oh saue me for thy mercies sake.

27 That they maye knowe, how that thys is thy hand, and that thou hast done it.

28 Though they curse, yet blesse thou: and let them be confounded, that ryse vp agaynst me, but let thy seruaunt reioyse.

29 Let myne aduersaryes be clothed wyth their owne shame, as with a cloke.

30 As for me, I wyl geue thanckes vnto the Lord wyth my mouth, and praise hym among the multitude.

31 For he standeth at the ryght hand of the pore, to saue hym from suche as condempne hys soule.

## PSALM 110

*A Psalme of Dauyd.*

THE Lorde sayde vnto my Lord: Syt thou on my ryght hande, vntyll I make thyne enemies thy fotestole.

2 The Lord shal sende the rod of thy power out of Sion; be thou ruler euen in the myddest amonge thyne enemyes.

3 In the daye of thy power shal thy people offer the frewyll offerynges wyth an holye worshyppe, the dewe of thy byrthe is of the wombe of the mornynge.

4 The Lorde sware, and wyll not repente: Thou arte a priest for euer after the order of Melchisedec.

5 The Lorde vpon thy ryghte hande, shall smyte euen kinges in the daye of hys wrath.

6 He shall be iudge amonge the Heathen, he shall fyl them wyth deade bodyes, and smite in sunder the heades ouer diuerse countres.

7 He shall dryncke of the broke in the waye, therfore shall he lyft vp his head.

## PSALM 111

PRAYSE the euerlastynge. I wyll geue thanckes vnto the Lorde wyth my whole herte: secretly amonge the faythful and in the congregacyon:

2 The worckes of the Lorde are greate, sought oute of all them, that haue pleasure therin.

3 Hys worcke is worthy to be praysed and had in honoure, and his rightuousnes endureth for euer.

4 The mercyfull and gracyous Lord hath so done his maruelous workes, þt they ought to be had in remembraunce.

5 He geueth meat vnto them, that feare him he is euer myndfull of hys couenaunte.

6 He sheweth hys people the power of hys worckes, that he may geue them the herytage of the Heathen.

7 The worckes of his hands are veryte and iudgment, all hys commaundementes are true.

8 They stand fast for euer and euer, and are done in truth and equyte.

9 He sent redempcyon vnto hys people, he hath commaunded his couenaunte for euer, holy and reuerente is his name

10 The feare of the Lorde is the beginning of wysdome, a good vnderstandyng haue al they that do therafter: the prayse of it endureth for euer.

## PSALM 112

PRAYSE the euerlastynge. Blessed is the man that feareth the Lord, and hath great delite in hys commaundementes.

2 Hys sede shal be mighty vpon earth the generacyon of the faythfull shalbe blessed.

3 Ryches and, plenteousnesse shalbe in hys house, and hys ryghtuousnesse endureth for euer.

4 Vnto the godly there aryseth vp lyghte in the darcknesse: he is mercyfull, louynge and ryghtuous.

5 Well is he that is mercyfull, and lendeth gladly, and pondereth his wordes wyth discrecyon,

6 For he shall neuer be moued, the ryghtuous shall be had in an euerlastynge remembraunce.

7 He wyll not be afrayed for anye euyll tydynges, his herte standeth fast, and beleueth in the Lord.

8 Hys hert is stablished, he wyl not shrynke, vntyl he se hys desyre vpon hys enemyes.

9 He hath sparsed abrode, and geuen to the poore, hys ryghtuousnes remayneth for euer his horne shalbe exealted with honoure

10 The vngodly shall se it, and it shall greue them: he shall gnash with his teeth, and consume awaye. and the desyre of the vngodlye shall perysh.

## PSALM 113

PRAYSE the euerlastynge. Prayse the Lord (O ye seruauntes) O prayse the name of þe Lorde.

2 Blessed be the name of þe lord, from this time forth euermore

3 The Lords name is worthy to be praysed from the risynge vp of the Sun vnto the going downe of the same.

4 The Lorde is hye aboue all Heathen, and his glory aboue the heauens.

5 Who is lyke vnto the Lorde oure God, that hath his dwellynge so hye,

6 whyche humbleth him selfe, to beholde that is in heauen and earth.

7 Which taketh vp the simple out of the dust and lyfteth the poore out of the myre.

8 That he may sette him amonge the prynces, euen

amonge the prynces of hys people.

9 Whyche maketh the baren woman to kepe house, and to be a ioyfull mothere of chyldren. Prayse the euerlastyng.

## PSALM 114

WHEN Israel came out of Egypt and the house of Iacob from among that straunge people.

2 Iuda was his Sanctuary, Israell his domynyon.

3 The sea saw þt & fled, Iordan turned backe.

4 The mountaynes skipped like rammes, and the lytle hylles like yong shepe.

5 What ayled the, O thou sea, that thou fleddest so thou Iordan, þt thou turnedest backe?

6 Ye mountaynes that ye skypped lyke rammes: and ye litle hilles, like yong shepe?

7 The earth trembled at the presence of the Lorde, at the presence of the God of Iacob.

8 Whyche turned the harde rocke into a staudynge water, and the flynte stone into a spryngyng well.

## PSALM 115

NOT vnto vs, O Lorde not vnto vs. but vnto thy name geue þe praise for thy louing mercye & faythfulnesse.

2 Wherfore shal the Heathen say wher is now their God?

3 As for oure God, he is in heauen, he doeth whatsoeuer it pleaseth him.

4 Their ymages are but syluer and gold, euen the worke of mens handes.

5 They haue mouthes, and speake not: eies haue they, but they se not.

6 Thei haue eares, and heare not: noses haue they, but they smell not.

7 They haue handes, and handle not, fete haue they, but they cannot goo, neyther can they speake thorow their throte.

8 They that made them, are lyke vnto them and so are all suche as put theyr truste in them.

9 But let Israell trust in the Lorde, for he is their succoure and defence.

10 Let the house of Aaron put their truste in the Lorde for he is their succoure and defence

11 They that feare the Lorde, lette them put their trust in the Lord, for he is their succour and defence.

12 The Lorde is myndfull of vs, and blesseth vs: he blesseth the house of Israel, he blesseth the house of Aaron.

13 Yea he blesseth al them that feare the Lord both smale and great.

14 The Lorde encrease you more and more: you, and your children.

15 For ye are the blessed of the Lord, whych made heauen and earth.

16 Al the whole heauens are the Lordes, but þe earth hath he geuen vnto þe chyldren of men.

17 The dead prayse not the (O Lorde) nether all they that go downe into sylence.

18 But we wil prayse the Lord, from this time forth for euermore. Prayse the euerlastynge.

## PSALM 116

I am wel pleased, that the Lord hath hearde the voyce of my prayer.

2 That he hath enclyned his eare vnto me, therfore wil I cal vpon him as long as I lyue.

3 The snares of death compased me round aboute, the paynes of hell gat hold vpon me I founde trouble and heauynesse.

4 Then called I vpon the name of the Lord O Lorde: delyuer my soule.

5 Gracious is the Lord, and rightuous, yea oure God is mercyfull.

6 The Lorde preserueth the symple, I was brought downe, and he helped me.

7 Turne agayne then vnto thy rest, O my soule, for the Lord hath geuen the thy desire.

8 And why thou haste delyuered my soule from death, myne eyes from teares, and my fete from fawlyng.

9 I wyll walcke before the Lorde, in the land of the lyuyng.

10 I beleued, and therfore haue I spoken, but I was sore troubled.

11 I sayde in my hast: Al men are liers.

12 What rewarde shall I geue vnto the Lorde, for all the benyfytes that he hath done vnto me?

13 I wyl receyue the, cuppe of saluacion, and call vpon the name of the Lord.

14 I wyll paye my vowes in the presence of al his people,

15 right deare in the syghte of the Lorde is the death of his saynctes.

16 O Lorde, I am thy seruaunt, I am thy seruant, and the son of thy handmaide, thou hast broken my bondes in sonder.

17 I wyl offre to the sacrifyce of thanckesgegeuynge, and wyll call vpon the name of the Lord.

18 I wyll paye my vowes vnto the Lord in the syght of al his people,

19 in the courtes of þe Lordes house, euen in the middest of the, O Ierusalem. Prayse the euerlasting.

## PSALM 117

O prayse the Lorde all ye Gentyles, laude him al ye people.

2 For his mercyfull kyndnes is euer more and more toward vs, and the truth of the Lorde eudureth for euer. Prayse the euerlasting.

# PSALM 118

O geue thankes vnto the Lord, for he is gracyous, & hys mercy endureth for euer.

2 Let Israel now confesse, that his mercy eudureth for euer.

3 Let the house of Aaron now confesse, that his mercy endureth for euer.

4 Yea let them now that feare the Lorde confesse, that his mercy endureth for euer.

5 I called vpon the lord in trouble, and the lord heard me at large.

6 The lord is my helper, I wyll not feare what man doeth vnto me.

7 The lord is my helper, and I shall se my desyre vpon myne enemyes.

8 It is better to trust in the lord, then to put any cofydence in man.

9 It is better to trust in the lord then to put any confydence in pryncces.

10 All Heathen compassed me round about but in the name of the lorde wyll I destroye them.

11 They kepe me in on euery side, but in the name of the lord, I wyll destroy them.

12 They came aboute me lyke bees, and wer as hote as the fyre in the thornes, but in the name of the Lorde I wyll destroye them.

13 They thrust at me, that I myght fall, but the lorde was my helpe.

14 The lorde is my strength, and my songe and is become my saluation.

15 The voice of ioy and meyth is in þe dwellynges of the rightuous, for the ryght hand of the Lord hath gotten the victory.

16 The ryght hande of the Lord hath þe preemynence, the ryght hande of the Lorde hath gotten the victory.

17 I wyll not dye, but lyue, and declare the workes of the lord.

18 The Lorde hath chastened and correcte me, but he hath not geuen me ouer vnto deathe.

19 Open me the gates of ryghtuousnes, that I maye go in there thorowe, and geue thanckes vnto the Lord.

20 This is the dore of the Lorde, the rightuous shall enter in thorow it.

21 I thancke, the that thou hast herd me, and are become my saluatyon.

22 The same stone whych the builders refused, is become the heade stone in the corner

23 Thys was the Lordes doynge, and it is maruelous in our eyes.

24 This is the, daye whych the Lorde hath made, let vs reioyse and be glad in it.

25 Helpe now O lord O, lord sende vs now prosperity.

26 Blessed be he that commeth in the name of the Lorde, we wysh you good lucke, ye that be of the house of the Lord.

27 God is the lord, and hath shewed vs light O garnysh the solempne feaste wyth grene braunches, euen vnto the hornes of the aulter.

28 Thou art my God, and I wil thancke the: thou art my God, and I wyll prayse the.

29 O geue thanckes vnto the lorde, for he is gracyous, and his mercy endureth for euer.

# PSALM 119

Blessed are those that be vndefyled in the way: which walcke in the law of the Lord.

2 Blessed are they that kepe hys testimonies, and seke him with their whole herte.

3 Which walcke in hys wayes, and do no wickednes.

4 Thou haste geuen strayte charge to kepe thy commaundementes.

5 O that my wayes were stablished to kepe thy statutes.

6 So shoulde I not be confounded while I haue respecte vnto all thy commaundementes

7 I wyll thancke the wyth an vnfayned herte, because I am learned in the iudgmentes of thy ryghtuousnesse.

8 I wyll kepe thy statutes, O forsake me not vtterly.

Where withall shall a yonge man clense his waye? Euen by rulynge hym selfe after thy worde.

10 Wyth my whole herte do I seke the, O let me not go wronge out of thy commaundementes.

11 Thy wordes haue I hyd wythin my hert that I should not synne against the.

12 Praysed be thou O Lorde, O teache me thy statutes.

13 With my lippes wil I be tellyng out all the iudgmentes of thy mouth.

14 I haue as greate delyte in the way of thy the testimonies, as in al maner of ryches.

15 I wyl exercise my selfe in thy commaundementes, and haue respect vnto thy fotepathes

16 My delite shalbe in thy statutes, I wyll not forget thy wordes.

O do well vnto thy seruant, that I maye lyue and kepe thy wordes.

18 Open thou myne eyes, and so shall I spy out wonderous thynges in thy lawe.

19 I am a straunger vpon earth, O hide not thy commaundementes fro me.

20 My soule breaketh out, for the very feruent desire that I haue alwaie vnto the iudgementes.

21 Thou rebukest the proud, cursed are they that departe from thy commaundementes.

22 O turne fro me shame and rebuke, for I kepe thy testimonies.

23 Princes also syt and speake against me but thy seruaunt is occupied in thy statutes.

24 In thy testomonyes is my delite, they are my councelers.

MY soule cleaueth to the dust, O quicken thou me accordyng to thy word.

26 I knowledged my waies, and thou herdest me, O teach me then thy statutes.

27 Make me to vnderstand the waye of thy commaundementes, and so shall I talcke of thy wonderous workes.

28 My soule melteth awaye for verye heuynesse, O set me vp accordyng vnto thy word

29 Take fro me þe waye of lyeng, and graunte me thy lawe.

30 I haue chosen the way of truth, thy iudgementes haue I layed before me.

31 I stycke vnto thy testimonies, O Lorde confound me not.

32 I wyll runne the waye of thy commaundementes, when thou haste comforted my herte.

TEACH me O lord the way of thy statutes and I shall kepe it vnto the ende.

34 O geue me vnderstandyng, & I shall kepe thy lawe, yea I shal kepe it wyth my whole herte.

35 Leade me in the pathe of thy commaundmentes, for that is my desyre,

36 Enclyne myne herte vnto thy testymonies, and not to couetousnes.

37 O turne awaye myne eyes, leste they behold vanite, and quycken me in thy way.

38 O stablish thy word in thy seruaunt, that I may feare the.

39 Take awaie the rebuke that I am afraied of, for thy iudgmentes are amyable.

40 Beholde, my delyte is in thy commaundementes, O quicken me in thy ryghtuousnesse.

LET thy louynge mercy come vnto me, O Lorde, and thy sauynge health accordynge vnto thy worde.

42 That I may geue answere vnto my blasphemers, for my trust is thy word.

43 O take not the worde of treuth vtterly out of my my mouthe, for my hope is in thy iudgementes.

44 So shall I alwaye kepe thy lawe, yea for euer and euer.

45 And I wyll walcke at lybertye, for I seke thy commaundementes.

46 I wyll speake of thy testimonyes euen before kynges, and wyll not be ashamed.

47 My delyte shalbe in thy commaundementes whych I loue.

48 My handes also wyll I lyft vp vnto thy commaundementes which I loue, and my talkinge shalbe of thy statutes.

O thyncke vpon thy seruaunt as concernynge thy worde, wherin thou haste caused me to put my trust.

50 For it is my comfort in my trouble, yea thy word quyckeneth me.

51 The proude haue me greatly in derysyon yet shryncke not I from thy law.

52 I remember thyne euerlasting iudgementes O Lorde, and am comforted.

53 I am horrible afraied for the vngodly, that forsake thy law.

54 Thy statutes are my songes in the house of my pylgremage.

55 I thyncke vpon thy name, O Lorde, in the nyghte esason, and kepe thy lawe.

56 It is mine owne, for I kepe thy commaundementes.

THou art my porcion, O lord, I am purposed to kepe thy law.

58 I make myne humble petycyon in thy presence wyth my whole herte, O be mercyfull vnto me accordynge vnto thy word.

59 I cal myne owne wayes to remembrance, and turne my fete into thy testimonies.

60 I make haste, and prolonge not the time, to kepe thy commaundementes.

61 The congregacyons of the vngodly haue robbed me, but I forget not thy law.

62 At midnight stand I vp, to geue thanckes vnto the, for the iudgmentes of thy ryghtuousnesse.

63 I am a companyon of all them that feare the, and kepe thy commaundementes.

64 The earth, O Lord, is ful of thy mercy. O teach me thy statutes.

O Lord, thou hast dealt frendly wyth thy seruaunt, according vnto thy word.

66 O learne me thy kyndnesse, nourtoure and knowlege, for I beleue thy commaundementes.

67 Before I was troubled, I wente wronge but now I kepe thy word.

68 Thou art good & frendly, O teach me the statutes.

69 The proud ymagyn lyes vpon me, but I kepe thy commaundementes with my whole herte.

70 Their herte is as fat as brawne, but my delyte is in thy law.

71 It is good for me that I haue bene in trouble, that I may learne thy statutes.

72 The law of thy mouth is dearer vnto me, then thousandes of golde and siluer.

THY hands haue made me and fashyoned me, O geue me vnderstandyng, that I may learne thy commaundementes.

74 They that feare the, wyll be glad when they se me, because I put my truste in thy worde.

75 I knowe, O Lorde, that thy iudgmentes are right, and that thou of very faithfulnes hast caused me to be troubled.

76 O let thy mercyful kyndnesse be my comforte, accordynge to the promes that thou hast made vnto thy

seruaunt.

77 O let thy louyng mercies come vnto me, that I may lyue, for thy law is my delite.

78 Let the proud be confounded, which handle me so falslye.

79 But let such as feare the, and knowe the testimonies, be turned vnto me.

80 O let myne herte be vndefyled in thy statutes that I be not ashamed.

MY soule longeth for thy sauynge health, for my trust is in thy word,

82 Myne eyes long sore for thy word, saing: O when wylt thou comforte me?

83 For I am become like a botel in þe smoke, yet do not I forget thy statutes.

84 How many are the dayes of thy seruaunt? When wilt thou be auenged of myne aduersaryes?

85 The proude haue dygged pyttes for me, which are not after thy lawe.

86 All thy commaundementes are true, they persecute me falsely, O be thou my helpe.

87 They haue almooste made an ende of me vpon earth, but I forsake not thy commaundementes.

88 O quycken me after thy louynge kyndenes, and so shall I kepe the testimonyes of thy mouth.

O Lorde, thy worde endureth for euer in heauen.

90 Thy trueth also remayneth from one generacion to another: thou hast layed the foundacion of the earth, and it abydeth.

91 They contynue this daye accordinge too thyne ordinaunce, for all thinges serue the.

92 If my delyte were not in thy lawe, I should perysh in my trouble.

93 I will neuer forget thy commaundementes, for with them thou quickenest me.

94 I am thyne, Oh helpe me, for I seke thy commaundementes.

95 The vngodly laye wayte for me too destroye me, but I considre thy testimonyes.

96 I se that all thynges come to an ende, but thy commaundement is exeeadyng broade.

O what loue haue I vnto thy law? all the daye longe is my talkyng of it.

98 Thou thorow thy commaundement hast made me wyser then myne enemyes, for it is euer by me.

99 I haue more vnderstandyng then all my teachers, for thy testimonies are my studye.

100 Yea, I am wyser then the aged, for I kepe thy commaundementes.

101 I refrayne my fete from euery euell waye, that I maye kepe thy woordes.

102 I shrynke not from thy iudgementes, for thou teachest me.

103 O howe swete are thy woordes vnto my throte? Yea, more then hony vnto my mouth.

104 Thorow thy commaundementes I gette vnderstandynge, therefore I hate all false wayes.

THY woorde is a lanterne vnto my fete and a light vnto my pathes.

106 I haue sworne and am stedfastly purposed, to kepe the iudgementes of thy righteousnesse.

107 I am troubled aboue measure, quycken me, O Lord, according vnto thy worde.

108 Let the frewill offeringes of my mouthe please the, O Lorde, and teache me thy iudgementes.

109 My soule is alwaye in my hande, yet do not I forget thy lawe.

110 The vngodly haue layed a snare for me, but yet swarue not I from thy commaundmentes.

111 Thy testimonyes haue I claymed as myne heritage for euer: and why? thei are the very ioye of my herte.

112 I applye myne herte to fulfil thy statutes alwaye, euen vnto the ende.

I hate the vngodly, but thy law do I loue.

114 Thou art my defence & shylde, my truste is in thy woorde.

115 Away fro me ye wycked, I will kepe the commaundementes of my God.

116 O stablish me according vnto thy worde, that I maye lyue, & let me not be disapoynted of my hope.

117 Holde thou me vp, and I shall be safe: yea I shall euer be talkyng of thy statutes.

118 Thou treadest doune all them that departe from thy statutes, for they ymagin but disceate.

119 Thou puttest awaye all the vngodly of the earth lyke drosse, therfore I loue thy testymonies,

120 My flesh trembleth for feare of the, and I am afrayed of thy iudgementes.

I deale wt the thinge þt is lawfull & ryght, O geue me not ouer vnto mine oppressours.

122 Be thou suertye for thy seruaunte too do hym good, that the proude do me no wronge.

123 Myne eyes are waysted awaye with lokyng for thy health, and for the worde of thy righteousnesse.

124 O deale with thy seruaunt according vnto thy louing mercy, & teach me thy statutes.

125 I am thy seruaunt, O graunte me vnderstanding, that I may know thy testimonies.

126 It is tyme for the (O Lord) to lay to thine hande, for they haue destroyed thy lawe.

127 For I loue thy commaundementes aboue golde and precious stone.

128 Therfore holde I streyght all thy commaundementes, and all false wayes I vtterly abhorre.

THY testimonyes are wonderfull, therefore doth my soule kepe them.

130 When thy woorde goeth forthe, it geueth light & vnderstandyng, euen vnto babes.

131 I open my mouth and draw in my breath, for I desyre thy commaundementes.

132 O loke thou vpon me, & be mercifull, as thou vsest to do vnto those þt loue thy name.

133 Ordre my goinges after thy woorde that no wickednesse raygne in me.

134 O delyuer me from the wrongeous dealinges of men, and so shall I kepe thy commaundementes.

135 Shewe the light of thy countenaunce vnto thy seruaunt, and learne me thy statutes.

136 Myne eyes gusshe out with water, because men kepe not thy lawe.

RYGHTEOUS art thou, O Lorde, and true is thy judgement.

138 Thy testimonyes that thou hast commaunded are exceadyng, righteous and true.

139 My zeale hath euen consumed me, because myne enemyes haue forgotten thy wordes.

140 Thy worde is tryed to the vttermost, and thy seruaunt loueth it.

141 I am small and of no reputacion, yet do not I forget thy commaundementes.

142 Thy righteousnesse is an euerlastyng righteousnes, and thy lawe is true.

143 Trouble and heuynesse haue taken holde vpon me, yet is my delite in thy commaundementes.

144 The righteousnes of thy testimonyes is euerlastyng, O graunt me vnderstandinge, and I shall lyue.

I call with my whole herte, heare me, O Lorde, I will kepe thy statutes.

146 Yea, euen vpon the do I call, helpe me, & I shall kepe thy testimonies.

147 Early in the mornyng do I crye vnto the, for in thy worde is my trust.

148 Myne eyes preuente the night watches, that I might be occupyed in thy wordes.

149 Heare my voyce, O Lorde, accordynge vnto thy louyng kyndnesse, quycken me accordyng as thou art wont.

150 They drawe nye that of malyce persecute me, and are farre from thy lawe.

151 Be thou nye at hande also, O Lorde, for thy promyses are faythfull.

152 As concernynge thy testimonies, I haue knowen euer sens the beginnuing, that thou hast grounded them for euer.

O considre myne aduersite, & deliuer me, for I do not forget thy lawe.

154 Manteyn thou my cause and defende me, quycken me according vnto thy worde.

155 Health is farre from the vngodly, for thei regarde not thy statutes.

156 Great is thy mercy, O Lorde, quicken me as thou art wont.

157 Many there are that trouble me, & persecute me, yet do not I swarue from thy testimonies.

158 It greueth me, when I se, that the transgressours kepe not thy law.

159 Considre, O Lorde, how I loue thy commaundementes, O quycken me with thy louyng kyndnesse.

160 Thy worde is true from euerlastyng, all the iudgementes of thy righteousnesse endure for euer more.

THE princes persecute me withoute cause, but my herte standeth in awe of thy woordes.

162 I am as gladde of thy worde, as one that fyndeth great spoyles.

163 As for lyes, I hate and abhorre them, but thy law do I loue.

164 Seuen times a daye do I prayse the, because of thy righteous iudgementes.

165 Great is the peace that they haue whych loue thy law, and they are not offended at it.

166 Lord, I loke for thy sauynge healthe, and do after thy commaundementes.

167 My soule kepeth thy testimonies, and loueth them exceadingly.

168 I kepe thy commaundementes and testimonies, for all my wayes are before the.

LET my complaynte come before the, O Lorde, geue me vnderstanding, accordynge vnto thy worde.

170 Oh let my supplicacion come before the, deliuer me according to thy promes.

171 My lyppes shall speake of thy prayse, seyng thou hast taught me thy statutes.

172 Yea, my tonge shall synge of thy worde, for all thy commaundementes are right.

173 Let thine hande helpe me, for I haue chosen thy commaundementes.

174 I longe for thy sauyng health, O Lorde, and in thy law is my delyte.

175 Oh let my soule lyue and prayse the, that thy iudgementes maye helpe me.

176 I go astraye, lyke a shepe that is lost: Oh seke thy seruaunt, for I do not forget thy commaundementes.

## PSALM 120

*The song of the steares*

WHEN I am in trouble, I cal vpon the Lorde, and he answereth me.

2 Delyuer my soule, O Lord

from liyng lippes, and from a disceatful tonge.

3 What rewarde shalbe geuen or done vnto the, thou false tonge.

4 Euen myghty and sharpe arowes, wyth hote burnynge coales.

5 Who is me that my banyshmente endureth so longe: I dwel in the tabernacles of the sorowfull.

6 My soule hath long dwelt amonge them that be enemies vnto peace,

7 I laboured for peace, but when I spake therof, they made them to battayle.

## PSALM 121

*The song of the steares.*

I lyft vp myne eyes vnto the hylles, from whence commeth my helpe.

2 My helpe commeth euen from the Lord which hath made heauen and earth.

3 He wyll not suffer thy fote to be moued, and he that kepeth the slepeth not.

4 Beholde, he that kepeth Israell, doth nether slomber nor slepe.

5 The Lorde him selfe is thy keper, þe Lorde is thy defence vpon thy ryght hande.

6 So that the sunne shall not burne the by daye, nether the mone by nyght.

7 The Lorde preserueth the from all euyll, yea it is the Lorde that kepeth thy soule.

8 The Lorde preserueth thy goyng out and thy commynge in, from thys tyme forth for euer more.

## PSALM 122

*The songe of the steares.*

I was glad, when they sayed vnto me: we wyll go into the house of the Lorde.

2 Oure fete shall stande in thy gates O Ierusalem.

3 Ierusalem is buylded as a cytye, that is at vnyte in it selfe.

4 For ther the tribes go vp, euen the tribes of the Lorde: to testyfye vnto Israel, to geue thanckes vnto the name of the Lorde.

5 For there is the seate of iudgmente, euen the seate of the house of Dauyd.

6 O praye for the peace of Ierusalem, they shall prospere that loue the.

7 Peace be wyth thy walles, and plenteousnes within thy palaces.

8 For my brethren and companions sakes, I wyll wysh the prosperite.

9 Yea because of the house of the Lord oure God, I wyll seke to do the good.

## PSALM 123

*The songe of the steares.*

VNTO the lyft I vp mine eies, thou that dwelleste in the heauens.

2 Beholde euen, as the eyes of seruauntes loke vnto the handes of their maysters: and as the eyes of a maiden vnto the handes of her mastresse, euen so oure eyes wayte vpon the Lorde our God vntylll he haue mercy vpon vs.

3 Haue mercy vpon vs, O Lord, haue mercy vpon vs, for we are vtterly despysed.

4 Our soule is filled with the scornefull reprofe of the welthy, and wyth the despitefulnes of the proude.

## PSALM 124

*The songe of the steares.*

IF þe Lord had not bene of oure side (now may Israel say)

2 If þe Lord had not bene of oure syde when men rose vp against vs.

3 They had swalowed vs vp quicke when thei were so wrathfully displeased at vs.

4 Yea the waters had drowned vs, þe streame had gone ouer oure soule.

5 The depe waters of the proud had gon euen vnto our soule.

6 But praysed be the Lord, which hath not geuen vs ouer for a praie vnto their teeth.

7 Oure soule is escaped, euen as a byrde out of the snare of the fouler: the snare is broken and we are delyuered.

8 Oure helpe standeth in the name of the Lord, which hath made heauen and earth.

## PSALM 125

*The song of the steares.*

THEY that put their truste in the Lord, are euen as the mounte Syon, which may not be remoued, but standeth fast for euer.

2 The hylles stande about Ierusalem, euen so standeth the Lorde rounde about hys people, from this tyme forthe for euermore.

3 That the rodd of the vngodly come not into the lot of the righteous, lest the righteous put their hande vnto wickednesse.

4 Do wel, O Lord, vnto those that be good and true of herte.

5 As for suche as turne backe vnto their owne wickednesse, the Lorde shall leade them forth with the euell doers: but peace be vpon Israell.

## PSALM 126

*The songe of the steares.*

WHEN the Lorde turneth agayn the captiuitie of Syon, then shall we be lyke vnto them that dreame.

2 Then shal our mouth be filled wyth laughter, and oure tonge with ioye. Then shall it be sayd among the Heathen: the Lord hath done greate thynges

for them.

3 Yea, the Lorde hath done greate thynges for vs all ready, wherof we reioyse.

4 Turne oure captiuitie, O Lorde, as the ryuers in the south.

5 They that sowe in teares, shall reape in ioye.

6 He that now goeth in hys waye wepyng and beareth forthe good sede, shall come agayne with ioye, & bryng hys sheaues wyth hym.

## PSALM 127

*The song of the steares.*

EXCEPT the Lord buylde þe house, their laboure is but loste that buylde it. Except the Lord kepe the cytye, the watchman waketh but in vayne.

2 It is but lost labour that ye ryse vp early and take no rest, but eate the breade of carefulnesse: for loke to whom it pleaseth him, he geueth it in slepe.

3 Lo, chyldren & the frute of the wombe are an heritage & gift, that commeth of the Lorde.

4 Lyke as the arrowes in the hande of the gyaunt, euen so are the yonge chyldren.

5 Happy is the man, that hathe his quyuerful of them: they shal not be ashamed, when they speake with their enemyes in the gate.

## PSALM 128

*The song of the steares.*

BLESSED are all they that feare þe Lord, & walke in his wayes.

2 For thou shalte eate the laboures of thyne owne handes: O well is the, happy art thou.

3 Thy wyfe shalbe as the frutefull vyne vpon the walles of thy house. Thy chyldren lyke the Olyue braunches rounde about thy table.

4 Lo, thus shal the man be blessed, that feareth the lorde.

5 The lord shall so blesse the out of Syon, that thou shalt se Hierusalem in prosperytie all thy lyfe longe.

6 Yea, that thou shalt se thy chylders chyldren, and peace vpon Israel.

## PSALM 129

*The song of the steares.*

MANY tyme haue they foughte agaynst me fro my youth vp (may Israel now saye.)

2 Yea, many a tyme haue they fought gaainst me fro my youth vp, but thei haue not ouercome me.

3 The plowers plowed vpon my backe, & made longe forowes.

4 But the righteous lorde hath hewen the yocke of the vngodly in peces.

5 Let them be confounded & turned backewarde, as many as haue euell will at Syon.

6 Let them be euen as the haye vppon the house toppes, whyche wythereth afore it be pluckte vp.

7 Wherof the mower fylleth not his hande, neither he that byndeth vp the sheaues, hys bosome.

8 So þt they which go by, saye not so much as: þe Lord prospere you, we wish you good lucke in the name of the Lord.

## PSALM 130

*The song of the steares.*

OVT of the depe cal I vnto þe O Lord,

2 Lord heare my voice Oh let thyne eares consider wel the voice of my complaint

3 If thou Lorde wylte be extreme to marke what is done amysse. Oh Lord who may abide it?

4 But ther is mercy wyth the, that thou maiest be feared.

5 I loke for the Lord, my soule doth wayte for hym, and in his word is my trust.

6 My soule doth paciently abide the Lorde from the one morning to the other.

7 Let Israel trust in the Lord, for wyth the Lorde there is mercy and plenteouse redempcyon.

8 And he shal redeme Israel from al his synnes.

## PSALM 131

*The songe of the steares.*

LORDE, I am not hye mynded, I haue no proude lokes. I do not exercise my selfe in greate matters, whych are hye for me.

2 But I refrayne my soule and kepe it lowlye as a childe that is weaned from his mother: yea my soule is euen as a weaned child

3 Let Israel trust in þe Lord, from this time forth for euermore.

## PSALM 132

*The song of the steares.*

LORDE, remember Dauyd and all his trouble.

2 How he swore vnto the Lorde, and vowed a vowe vnto the allmyghty one of Iacob:

3 I wyll not come within the tabernacle of my house, nor clyme vp in my bedde.

4 I wyll not suffer myne eyes to slepe, nor myne eye lyddes to slomber.

5 Vntill I fynde out a place for the Lorde, an habitacion for the mightye one of Iacob.

6 Lo we herde of the same at Ephrata, and found it in the woode.

7 We wyll go into hys tabernacle, and fall downe before his fote stole.

8 Aryse, O Lord, into thy restynge place, thou and the arcke of thy strength.

9 Let thy Preastes be clothed wyth rightuousnesse, and let thy saynctes reioyse.

10 For thy seruaunte Dauyds

sake turne not awaye the presence of thyne anoynted.

11 The Lord hath made a faythful ooth vnto Dauyd, and he shall not shrynke from it Of the frute of thy body shal I set vpon thy seate.

12 If thy chyldren wyll kepe my couenaunt, and my testimony that I shal lerne them: their chyldren also shal syt vpon thy seate for euermore.

13 For the Lord hath chosen Syon, to be an habitacyon for him selfe hath he chosen her.

14 This shalbe my rest, here wyll I dwel for I haue a delyte therin.

15 I wyll blesse her vytalles wyth increase, and wyll satysfye her poore with bread.

16 I wyl decke her Preastes with health and her saynctes shall reioyse and be glad.

17 Ther shall I make the horne of Dauid to floryshe, I haue ordeyned a lanterne for myne anoynted.

18 As for hys enemyes, I shall clothe them wyth shame, but vpon hym selfe shall hys crowne florysh.

## PSALM 133

*The song of the steares of Dauyd.*

BEHOLD, how good and ioyfull a thinge it is, brethren to dwel together in vnitie.

2 It is like the preacious oyntment vpon the heade, that ranne downe vnto the beard: euen vnto Aarons bearde, and wente downe to the skyrtes of his clothyng.

3 Like the dewe of Hermon, which fell vpon the hil of Sion. For there the Lorde promysed hys blesyng, and lyfe for euermoe.

## PSALM 134

*The song of the steares*

BEHOLD, O praise the Lord, al ye seruantes of the Lorde, ye þt by night stande in the house of the Lord.

2 O lyfte vp youre handes in the Sanctuary, and prayse the Lorde.

3 The lorde that made heauen and earthe blesse the out of Sion.

## PSALM 135

PRAYSE the euerlastynge. O praise the name of the Lord prayse it O ye seruauntes of the Lorde.

2 Ye that stande in the house of the Lorde, in the courtes of the house of our God.

3 O prayse þe lord for þe lord is gracious: O sing prayses vnto hys name, for it is louely.

4 For why the Lorde hath chosen Iacob vnto hym selfe, and Israel for his owne possession.

5 For I know that the Lorde is greate, and that our Lorde is aboue all goddes.

6 Whatsoeuer the Lord pleaseth that doth he in heauen and in earth, in the sea, and in all deape places.

7 He bryngeth forth the cloudes from the endes of the worlde, he turneth the lyghtenynges vnto rayne, bryngynge the wyndes out of their treasuryes.

8 Which smote the fyrst borne of Egypte both of man and of beast.

9 He hath sent tokens and wonders into the middest of the, O thou lande of Egypt, vpon Pharao and al his seruauntes.

10 Whych smote dyuerse nacyons, and slew myghty Kynges.

11 Sehon Kynge of the Amorytes, Og the Kynge of Basan, and all the Kyngdomes of Canaan.

12 And gaue their land for an heritage, for an heritage vnto Israel his people.

13 Thy name. O Lorde, endureth for euer, so doeth thy memoryall, O Lorde, from one generacyon to another.

14 For the Lorde wil auenge his people, and be gracyous vnto hys seruauntes.

15 As for the ymages of the Heathen, they are but siluer and golde, the worcke of mens handes.

16 They haue mouthes, and speake not: eyes haue they, but they se not.

17 They haue eares, and yet they heare not, neyther is ther any breath in their mouthes.

18 They that make them, are lyke vnto them, and so are all they that put their trust in them.

19 Prayse the Lord ye house of Israel, praise the Lorde ye house of Aaron.

20 Prayse the Lorde, ye house of Leui, ye þt feare the Lorde, prayse the Lorde.

21 Praysed be the Lord out of Sion, whych dwelleth at Ierusalem. Praise the euerlastynge.

## PSALM 136

O geue thankes vnto the Lord, for he is gracious, and his mercy endureth for euer.

2 O geue thankes vnto the God of all goddes, for his mercy endureth for euer.

3 O thancke the Lord of all Lordes, for his mercy endureth for euer.

4 Whych only doth greate wonders, for his mercy endureth for euer.

5 Which by hys wisdome made the heauens for his mercy endureth for euer.

6 Which layed out the earth aboue the waters, for his mercy endureth for euer.

7 Whych hath made great lyghtes, for hys mercy endureth for euer.

8 The sunne to rule the daye, for hys mercy endureth for euer.

9 The mone and the starres

to gouerne the nyght, for his mercy endureth for euer.

10 Whych smote Egypt wyth their fyrste borne, for his mercy endureth for euer.

11 And brought out Israell from among them, for his mercy endureth for euer.

12 With a myghtye hand and stretcheth out arme, for his mercy endureth for euer.

13 Whych deuyded the reed sea into partes, for his mercy endureth for euer.

14 And made Israell to go thorow the myddest of it, for his mercy endureth for euer.

15 But as for Pharao, and his host, he ouerthrewe them in the read sea, for his mercy endureth for euer.

16 Which led hys people thorow the wyldernesse, for his mercy endureth for euer.

17 Whiche smote greate Kynges, for hys mercy endureth for euer.

18 Yea, and slue myghtye Kynges, for hys mercy endureth for euer.

19 Sehon Kyng of the Amorytes, for hys mercy endureth for euer.

20 And Og the Kyng of Basan, for his mercy endureth for euer.

21 And gaue awaye their lande for an herytage, for his mercy endureth for euer.

22 Euen for an heritage vnto Israel hys seruaunt, for his mercy endureth for euer.

23 Which remembreth vs, when we are in trouble, for hys mercy endureth for euer.

24 <>

25 Which geueth fode vnto al flesh, for his mercy endureth for euer.

26 O geue thankes vnto the God of heauen, for his mercy endureth for euer.

## PSALM 137

BY the waters of Babylon we sat downe and weapte, when we remembred Syon.

2 As for our harpes, we hanged them vpon the trees, that are therin.

3 Then they that led vs awaye captyue, requyred of vs a songe and melody in our heauynes: synge vs one of the songes of Syon.

4 How shall we synge the Lordes songe in a straunge land?

5 If I forget the, O Ierusalem, let my right hande be forgotten.

6 If I do not remember the, lette my tonge cleue to the rofe of my mouth: yea, if I preferre not Ierusalem in my myrth.

7 Remember the children of Edom, O Lorde in the daye of Ierusalem, howe they sayde: doune wyth it, doune wyth it: euen to the grounde.

8 O daughter of Babilon, thou shalt come to mysery thyselfe: yea, happye shall he be, that rewardeth the as thou hast serued vs.

9 Blessed shall he be, that taketh thy chyldren, and throweth them agaynst the stones.

## PSALM 138

*Of Dauid.*

I wyll geue thankes vnto the. O Lord, wyth my whole herte, euen before the Gods, wil I singe prayses vnto the.

2 I wyll worshyp toward thy holy temple and prayse thy name, because of thy louyng kyndenesse and trueth, for thou hast magnyfyed thy worde, accordyng vnto thy greate name.

3 When I call vpon the, thou hearest me, & endewest my soule wyth muche strength.

4 All the Kynges of the earthe shall prayse the, O Lord, when they heare the wordes of thy mouth.

5 Yea, they shall singe in the wayes of the Lorde, that great is the glory of the Lord.

6 For though the Lorde be hye, yet hath he respecte vnto the lowly: as for the proude, he beholdeth theim a farre of.

7 Though I walke in the middest of trouble, yet shalte thou refreshe me: thou shalte stretche forth thyne hande vpon the furiousnes of myne enemyes, and thy righte hande shall saue me.

8 The Lord shall make good for me, yea, thy mercy, O LORDE, endureth for euer despyse not then the worcke of thyne awne handes.

## PSALM 139

*To the chaunter, a Psalme of Dauid.*

O Lorde, thou searchest me out, and knowest me.

2 Thou knowest my doune sittyng and myne vprysinge, thou vnderstandest my thoughtes a farre of.

3 Thou art about my path & about my bed and spyest out all my wayes.

4 For lo, there is not a worde in my tonge, but thou, O Lorde knowest it altogether.

5 Thou hast fashioned me behynde and before, and layed thyne hande vpon me.

6 Such knowlege is to wonderfull and excellent for me, I can not atteyne vnto it.

7 Whither shal I go then from thy sprete? or, whyther shall I go then frome thy presence?

8 If I clyme vp into heauen, thou art there if I go doune to hel, thou art there also.

9 If I take the wynges of the mornynge, & remayne in the vttermost parte of the sea:

10 Euen there also shall thy hande leade me, and thy right hand shall holde me.

11 If I saye: peraduenture the darkenesse shall couer me, then shall my nyghte be turned to daye.

12 Yea, the darkenesse is no darkenesse with the, but the nyght is as cleare as the day, the darkenesse and light are both a lyke.

13 For my reynes are thyne, thou hast couered me in my mothers wombe.

14 I will geue thankes vnto the, for I am wonderously made: maruelous are thy workes, & that my soule knoweth right well.

15 My bones are not hyd from the, though I be made secretly, and fashyoned beneth in the earth.

16 Thyne eyes se myne vnperfectnesse, they stande all written in thy boke: my dayes were fashyoned, when as yet there was not one of them.

17 How deare are thy counsails vnto me O God? O how greate is the summe of them?

18 If I tell them, they are mo in numbre then the sande: when I wake vp, I am presente with the.

19 Wylt thou not slaye the wycked (Oh God) that the bloudthyrsty myghte departe fro me?

20 For they speake vnright of the, thyne enemyes exalte them selfes presumpteously.

21 I hate them, O Lorde, that hate the: and I maye not awaye wyth those that ryse vp agaynst the.

22 Yea I hate them right sore, therefore are they myne enemyes.

23 Trye me, O God, and seke the grounde of myne herte: proue me, and examen my thoughtes.

24 Loke well if there be any way of wickednesse in me, and leade me in the way euerlastynge.

## PSALM 140

*To the chaunter, a Psalme of Dauid.*

DELIUER me, O Lorde, from the euel men, Oh preserue me from the wycked men.

2 Which ymagin mischief in their hertes, and stere vp strife all the daye longe.

3 They sharpen their tonges lyke a serpent: adders poyson is vnder their lippes. Selah.

4 Kepe me, O Lorde, from the hande of the vngodly: preserue me from the wycked men, which are purposed to ouerthrowe my goynges.

5 The proude haue layed a snare for me, & spred a net abroade wyth coardes, yea, and set trappes in my waye. Selah.

6 But my sayinge is vnto the Lorde: thou art my God, heare the voyce of my prayer O Lord.

7 O Lord God, thou strength of my health thou hast couered my head in the day of battayle.

8 Let not the vngodly haue hys desyre, O Lord, let him not haue hys purpose, lest they be to proude. Selah.

9 Let the mischief of their owne lippes fall vpon the head of theym, that compase me about.

10 Let hote burnyng coales fall vpon them let them be cast into the fyre, & into the pytte, that they neuer ryse vp agayne.

11 A man full of woordes shall not prosper vpon the earth: a malicious & wicked person shalbe hunted awaye, and destroyed.

12 Sure I am, that the Lorde wyll auenge the poore, & maynteyne the cause of the helpelesse.

13 The righteous also shall geue thanckes vnto thy name, and the iust shall continue in thy sight.

## PSALM 141

*A Psalme of Dauid.*

LORDE, I call vpon the: hast the vnto me, & consider my voyce, when I crye vnto the.

2 Let my prayer be setforth in thy sight as the incense, and let the lifting vp of my handes be an euenynge sacrifice.

3 Set a watch, O lorde, before my mouth, yea, a watch at the dore of my lippes.

4 O let not myne herte be enclyned to any euell thyng, to be mynded as the vngodly or wicked men, lest I eate of suche thynges as please them.

5 Let the righteous rather smite me frindly, & reproue me: so will I take it, as though he had poured oyle vpon my head: it shall not hurt my head, yea, I will praye yet for theyr wickednesse.

6 Their iudges stomble at the stone, yet heare they my wordes, that they be ioyfull.

7 Oure bones lye scatered before the pyt, lyke as when one graueth and dyggeth vp the grounde.

8 But myne eyes loke vnto the, O Lorde God: in the is my trust, Oh caste not out my soule.

9 Kepe me from the snare whiche they haue layed for me, and from the trappes of the wicked doers.

10 Let the vngodly fall into their owne nettes together, vntyll I be gone by them.

## PSALM 142

*The instruccion of Dauid, a prayer when he was in the caue.*

I crye vnto the Lorde with my voyce, yea, euen vnto the Lord do I make my supplicacion.

2 I poure out my complaynte before hym, and shewe hym of my trouble.

3 When my sprete is in heuynesse, for thou knowest my path: in þe way wherin I walke haue they preuely layed a snare for me.

4 I loke vpon my right hande, & se, there is no man that will know me. I haue no place to fle vnto, no man careth for my

# PSALMS

soule.

5 Therfore do I crye vnto the, O Lorde, & say: thou art my hope and my porcion in the londe of the liuing.

6 Considre my complaynt, for I am brought very lowe. O deliuer me fro my persecuters, for thei are to stronge for me.

7 Bryng my soule out of pryson, that I may geue thankes vnto thy name: which thyng if thou wilt graunt me, then shall the righteous resorte vnto my company.

## PSALM 143

*A Psalme of Dauid.*

HEARE my prayer, O Lord, considre my desire: aunswere me for thy trueth and righteousnesse sake.

2 And entre not into iudgement with thy seruaunt, for in thy sighte shall no man lyuyng be iustefied.

3 For the enemye persecuteth my soule, he smyteth my lyfe doune too the grounde, he layeth me in the darkenesse, as the dead men of the worlde.

4 Therefore is my sprete vexed within me, and my herte within me is desolate.

5 Yet do I remembre the times past, I muse vpon all thy workes, yea, I exercise my selfe in the workes of thy handes.

6 I stretche forthe myne handes vnto the, my soule cryeth vnto the oute of the thyrstye lande. Selah.

7 Heare me, O Lorde, & that soone, for my sprete waxeth faynte: hyde not thy face fro me, lest I be lyke vnto theym that go doune into the graue.

8 O let me heare thy louyng kyndnesse by tymes in the morning, for in þe is my trust: shew thou me the waye that I should walke in, for I lift vp my soule vnto the.

9 Deliuer me, O Lord, fro myne enemies, for I resorte vnto the.

10 Teache me to do the thynge that pleaseth the, for thou arte my God: lette thy louinge sprete leade me forth vnto the lande of righteousnes.

11 Quicken me, O Lord, for thy names sake and for thy righteousnesse sake brynge my soule out of trouble.

12 And of thy goodnesse scater myne enemyes abroade, & destroye all them that vexe my soule, for I am thy seruaunt.

## PSALM 144

*Of Dauid.*

BLESSED be the Lorde my refuge which teacheth my handes to warre, and my fyngers too fyght.

2 My hope and my castell, my defence and my deliuerer, my shylde in whome I trust, which gouerneth the people that is vnder me.

3 Lorde what is man, that thou hast suche respect vnto hym? Or the sonne of man, that thou so regardest hym?

4 Man is like a thing of naught, hys tyme passeth awaye like a shadow.

5 Bowe thy heauens, O Lorde, & come doune, touche the mountaynes, that thei may smoke with all.

6 Sende forthe the lightenynge and scater them, shute out thyne arrowes, and consume them.

7 Sende doune thyne hande from aboue, deliuer me, & take me out of the great waters, from the hande of straunge chyldren.

8 Whose mouth talketh of vanitie, & theyr right hande is a right hande of falsede,

9 That I maye singe a new songe vnto the O God, and singe prayses vnto the vpon a tenstrynged lute.

10 Thou that geuest victory vnto kynges, & hast deliuered Dauid thy seruaunt from the parell of the swerde.

11 Saue me, and deliuer me from the hande of straunge chyldren, whose mouth talketh of vanitie, and their ryght hande is a ryghte hande of falsede.

12 That oure sonnes maye growe vp as the yong plantes, & that our daughters may be as the polyshed corners of the temple.

13 That oure garners may be full and plenteous with all maner of stoare: þt oure shepe maye brynge forth thousandes and hundreth thousandes in our vyllages.

14 That our oxen may be strong to laboure, that there be no mischaunce, no decaye, & no complaynyng in our stretes.

15 Happy are the people that be in suche a case: yea, blessed are the people, whiche haue the Lord for their God.

## PSALM 145

*A prayse of Dauid.*

I wyll magnifie the, O God my kyng, I wil prayse thy name for euer & euer.

2 Euery daye wil I geue thankes vnto the, & praise thy name for euer and euer.

3 Great is the Lord, & maruelous worthy to be praysed, there is no ende of his greatenesse.

4 One generacion shall prayse thy workes vnto another, and declare thy power.

5 As for me I will be talkynge of thy worshyp, thy glory, thy prayse, and wonderous workes.

6 So that men shal speake of the myght of thy maruelous actes, and tell of thy greatenes.

7 The memorial of thyne aboundant kyndnes shalbe shewed, & men shall synge of thy rightuousnesse.

8 The Lord is gracious and merciful, longe sufferyng, and of great goodnesse.

9 The Lorde is louynge vnto euery man, & hys mercy is ouer all hys workes.

10 All thy workes prayse the (O Lorde) and thy saynctes geue thankes vnto the.

11 They shew the glory of the kyngdome, & talke of thy power.

12 That thy power, thy glory & mightinesse of thy kyngedome myghte be knowen vnto men.

13 Thy kyngdome is an euerlastyng kyngedome, and thy dominion endureth thorowe out all ages.

14 The Lord vpholdeth all such as shoulde fall, and lifteth vp all those that be doune.

15 The eyes of all wayte vpon the, and thou geuest them their meate in due season.

16 Thou openest thyne hande, and fyllest all thinges liuing with plenteousnesse.

17 The Lord is righteous in all his wayes, and holy in all hys workes.

18 The Lord is nye vnto them that call vpon him, yea, al such as call vpon hym faithfully.

19 He fulfilleth the desire of them that feare him, he heareth their crie, and helpeth them.

20 The Lord preserueth all theym that loue hym, but scatreth abroade all the vngodly.

21 My mouth shall speake the prayse of the Lord, and let all flesh geue thankes vnto his holy name for euer and euer. Prayse the euerlastynge.

## PSALM 146

PRAYSE the euerlastyng. Prayse the Lorde, O my soule:

2 whyle I lyue will I prayse the Lorde: yea, as longe as I haue any beyng, I will sing prayses vnto my God.

3 O put not your trust in pryces, nor in any chylde of man, for there is no helpe in them.

4 For when the breath of man goeth forth, he shall turne agayne to his earth, and so all hys thoughtes perysh.

5 Blessed is he that hath the God of Iacob for his helpe, and whose hope is in the Lord hys God.

6 Which made heauen and earth, the sea, & all that therin is, which kepeth hys promise for euer.

7 Which helpeth them to righte that suffre wrong, which fedeth the hongry. The Lord louseth men out of pryson,

8 the Lord geueth sight to the blynde. The Lorde helpeth them vp that are fallen, the Lord loueth the righteous.

9 The Lorde careth for the straungers, he defendeth the fatherlesse and wydow: as for the way of the vngodly, he turneth it vpside doune.

10 The Lord thy God, O Syon, is kyng for euermore, & thorow out all generacions. Prayse the euerlastynge.

## PSALM 147

PRAYSE the euerlastyng. O prayse þe Lord, for it is a good thyng to sing prayses vnto our God: yea, a ioyful & pleasaunt thing is it to be thankeful.

2 The Lorde shall buylde vp Hierusalem, & gather together the outcastes of Israel.

3 He healeth the contryte in herte, and byndeth vp their woundes.

4 He telleth the numbre of the starres, and calleth them all by their names.

5 Great is our Lord, & great is his power: yea, hys wysdome is infinitie.

6 The Lord setteth vp the meke, and bryngeth the vngodly doune to the grounde.

7 O singe vnto the Lorde with thankesgeuyng, sing prayses vpon the harpe vnto our God.

8 Which couereth the heauen wyth cloudes, prepareth rayn for the earth, & maketh the grasse to growe vpon the mountaynes.

9 Which geueth fodre vnto the cattell, and fedeth the yong rauens that call vpon hym.

10 He hath no pleasure in the strengthe of an horse, neither deliteth he in any mans legges.

11 But the Lordes delyte is in them that feare hym, and put their trust in his mercy.

12 Prayse the Lord O Ierusalem, prayse thy God O Sion.

13 For he maketh fast þe barres of the gates, and blesseth the chyldren within the.

14 He maketh peace in thy borders, & filleth the with the floure of wheate.

15 He sendeth forth hys commaundemente vpon earth, his worde runneth swyftly.

16 He geueth snow lyke wolle, & scatereth þe hore frost lyke ashes.

17 He casteth forth hys yse lyke morsels, who is able to abyde hys frost?

18 He sendeth out hys woorde and mealteth them, he bloweth with hys wynd, & the waters flowe.

19 He sheweth hys woorde vnto Iacob, hys statutes and ordinaunces vnto Israel.

20 He hath not dealte so with all the Heathen, neither haue they knowlege of hys lawes. Prayse the euerlastyng.

## PSALM 148

PRAYSE the euerlastyng. O prayse the Lorde of heauen, prayse hym in the heygth.

2 Prayse hym all ye aungels of hys, prayse hym all hys hoost.

3 Prayse hym Sunne and Moone, prayse hym all ye starres and light.

4 Prayse hym all ye

heauens, and ye waters that be vnder the heauens.

5 Let them prayse the name of the Lorde, for he commaunded, and they were made.

6 He hath made them fast for euer and euer, he hath geuen them a lawe whiche shall not be broken.

7 Prayse the Lord vpon earth, ye whalfysshes, and al depes.

8 Fyre and hayle, snow and vapors, wynde and storme, fulfillynge his worde.

9 Mountaynes and al hilles, fruteful trees and all Cedres.

10 Beastes and cattel, wormes and fethered foules.

11 Kynges of the earth and all people, Pryncones and iudges of the worlde.

12 Yonge men and maydens, olde men and chyldren:

13 let them prayse the name of þe Lord, for his name only is excellent, and his prayse aboue heauen and earth.

14 He exalteth the horne of his people, all hys saynctes shall prayse hym, the chyldren of Israell, euen the people that serueth him. Prayse the euerlastyng.

## PSALM 149

Prayse the euerlastynge. O synge vnto the Lorde a newe songe, let the congregacion of saynctes prayse hym.

2 Let Israell reioyse in hym that made hym, & let the chyldren of Sion be ioyfull in their kyng.

3 Let them prayse his name in the daunce, let them singe prayses vnto hym with tabrettes and harpes.

4 For the Lorde hath pleasure in hys people, and helpeth the meke harted.

5 Let the saynctes be ioyfull with glory, let them reioyse in their beddes.

6 Let the prayses of God be in their mouth and sharpe swerdes in their handes.

7 To be auenged of the Heathen, and to rebuke the people.

8 To bynde their Kynges in cheynes, and their nobles with lynckes of yron.

9 That they may be auenged of them, as it is written, such honour haue all his saynctes. Prayse the euerlastynge.

## PSALM 150

Prayse the euerlastyng. O prayse the Lord in his Sanctuary, prayse hym in the fyrmament of hys power.

2 Prayse hym in his noble actes, prayse him in hys excellent greatnesse.

3 Prayse hym in the sounde of the trompet, prayse hym vpon the lute and harpe.

4 Prayse hym in the cymbales and daunse prayse hym vpon the strynges and pype.

5 Prayse hym vpon the weltuned cymbals prayse him vpon the loude cymbales.

6 Let euery thing that hath breth, prayse þe Lorde. Prayse the euerlastynge.

# Proverbs

## CHAPTER 1

THE Prouerbes of Salomon the sonne of Dauid king of Israell:

2 too lerne wisdome instruccion, vnderstanding prudence,

3 righteousnesse, iudgement & equite.

4 That the very babes might haue wit, and that yongmen might haue knowlege & vnderstanding.

5 By hearing, the wyse man shall come by more wysedome: & by experience

6 he shalbe more apte to vnderstande a parable, & the interpretacion therof, þe wordes of the wise, & the darke speaches of the same.

7 The feare of the Lord is the begynnynge of wysdome. But fooles despise wysdome & destruccion.

8 My sonne, heare thy fathers doctryne, & forsake not the lawe of thy mother:

9 for that shall bryng grace vnto thy head, & shall be a cheyne about thy necke.

10 My sonne, consent not vnto sinners,

11 if they entise þe, & say: come with vs, let vs leye wayte for bloud, and lurke preuely for þe innocent without a cause:

12 let vs swalow them vp like þe hel, let vs deuour them quicke & whole, as those þt go doune into the pyt.

13 So shal we finde al maner of costely riches, & fil our houses wt spoiles.

14 Cast in thy lot among vs, we shall haue all one purse.

15 My sonne, walke not thou with them, refrayn thy fote from their ways.

16 For their fete runne to euel, & are hasty to shed bloud.

17 But in vayn is þe net laied forth before þe byrdes eyes.

18 Yea, they themselfes laye wayte one for anothers bloud, & one of them wolde sley another.

19 These are þe ways of all suche as be couetous, þt one wolde rauish anothers life.

20 Wisdome crieth without, & putteth forth her voyce in the stretes.

21 She calleth before þe congregacion in the open gates, & sheweth her wordes thorow the citie, saying:

22 O ye chyldren, how longe will ye loue chyldyshnesse? how long wil the, scorners delite in scorning & the vnwise be enemies vnto knowlege?

23 O turne you vnto my correccion: lo. I wil expres my mynde vnto you, & make you vnderstande my wordes.

24 Seing then that I haue called & ye refused it: I haue stretched out my hand, & no man regarded it,

25 but all my counsayls haue ye despysed, & set my corrections at naught.

26 Therfore shall I also laugh in your destruccion, & mocke you, when the thyng that ye feare cometh vpon you:

27 euen when þe thing that ye be afrayed of, falleth in sodenly lyke a storme, & your miseri like a tempest: yea, when trouble & heuinesse commeth vpon you.

28 Then shal they call vpon me, but I will not heare: they shal seke me early, but thei shal not find me:

29 And þt because thei hated knowlege, & receyued not the feare of þe Lord,

30 but abhorred my counsail, & despised my correction.

31 Therfore shal they eate the frutes of their owne way, & be filled with their oune counsayls:

32 for the turning away of the vnwyse shal sley them, & the prosperitie of foles shalbe their owne destruccion.

33 But who so harkeneth vnto me shal dwel safely, and haue ynough without any feare of euell.

## CHAPTER 2

MY sonne, if thou wilt receyue my wordes, & kepe my commaundementes by the,

2 þt thyne eare may herken

vnto wisdome, applie thyne hert then to vnderstanding.

3 For if thou cryest after wysdome, & callest for knowledge:

4 if thou sekest after her as after money, & dyggest for her as for treasure:

5 then shalt thou vnderstande þe feare of the Lord, & fynde the knowlege of God.

6 For it is the Lord that geueth wysdome, out of hys mouth commeth knowlege & vnderstandyng.

7 He preserueth the welfare of the righteous, & defendeth them that walke innocently:

8 he kepeth them in the right path, & preserueth the waye of his saynctes.

9 Then shalt thou vnderstande righteousnesse, iudgement and equite, yea, & euery good path.

10 If wisdome entre into thyne hert, and thy soule delyte in knowlege:

11 then shall counsayl preserue the, & vnderstanding shall kepe the.

12 That thou mayest be delyuered from the euell waye, & from the man that speaketh frowarde thinges

13 From suche as leaue the hye strete, & walke in the wayes of darkenesse:

14 whiche reioyse in doinge euel, and delite in wicked thinges:

15 whose wayes are croked, and their pathes sclaunderous.

16 That thou mayest be deliuered also from the straunge woman, & frome her that is not thyne owne: whiche geueth swete woordes,

17 forsaketh the housbande of her youth, & forgetteth the couenaunt of her God.

18 For her house is enclined vnto death, & her pathes vnto hel.

19 Al thei that go in vnto her, come not agayn, neither take they holde of the way of lyfe.

20 That thou mayest walke in the good way, & kepe the pathes of þe righteous.

21 For the iust shal dwell in the lande, & the innocentes shall remayne in it:

22 but the vngodly shalbe roted oute of the lande, and the wicked doers shalbe taken out of it.

## CHAPTER 3

O my sonne, forget not my law but se that thyne hert kepe my commaundementes.

2 For they shall prolong the dayes & yeares of thy life, & bring þe peace.

3 Let mercy & faythfulnes neuer go from the: bynde them about thy necke, & write them in the tables of thyne hert.

4 So shalt thou fynde fauour & good vnderstanding in the sight of God & men.

5 Put thy trust in the Lord wyth all thyne hert, and leane not vnto thyne own vnderstandinge.

6 In all thy wayes haue respecte vnto hym, & he shal ordre thy goinges.

7 Be not wyse in thyne own conceyte, but feare the Lord, & departe from euell:

8 so shall thy nauell be whole, & thy bones strong.

9 Honour the Lord with thy substaunce, & with the firstlinges of all thyne encrease:

10 so shall thy barnes be filled with plenteousnesse, and thy presses shall flowe ouer with swete wyne.

11 My sonne, despise not the chastening of the Lorde, neyther faynte when thou arte rebuked of hym.

12 For whome the Lord loueth hym he chasteneth: & yet deliteth in him euen as a father in his owne sonne.

13 Well is hym that findeth wysdome, and opteyneth vnderstandinge,

14 for the gettinge of it is better then any marchaundise of syluer, and the profet of it is better then golde.

15 Wysdome is more worth then precyous stones, and all thinges that thou canste desyre, are not to be compared vnto her.

16 Vpon her righte hande is longe lyfe, and vppon her lefte hande is ryches and honour.

17 Her wayes are pleasaunte wayes, and al her pathes are peaceable.

18 She is a tree of lyfe to them that laye holde vpon her, and blessed are they that kepe her fast.

19 With wysdome hath the Lorde layed the foundacion of the earth, & thorow vnderstanding hath he stablished the heauens.

20 Thorow hys wysdome the deapthes breake vp, and the cloudes droppe downe of the dewe.

21 My sonne, let not these thinges depart from thyne eyes, but kepe my lawe and my councel:

22 so shal it be life vnto thy soule, and grace vnto thy mouth.

23 Then shalt thou walke safely in thy waye, and thy fote shal not stomble.

24 If thou slepest, thou shalt not be afraied, but shalt take thy rest and slepe swetelye.

25 Thou nedest not to be afrayed of any sodaine feare nether for the vyolent rushynge in of the vngodly, when it commeth.

26 For the Lorde shal be besiege the, and kepe thy fote that thou be not taken.

27 Refuse not to do good vnto hym that shoulde haue it, so longe as thyne hande is able to do it.

28 Say not vnto thy neyghbour go thy waye and come agayne, to morowe wyll I geue the:

29 where as thou hast nowe to

geue him. Intend no hurt vnto thy neighbour seing he hopeth to dwel in rest by the.

30 Striue not lightely with any man, wher as he hath done the harme.

31 Folowe not a wycked man, and chose none of hys wayes:

32 for the Lorde abhorreth the froward, but hys secrete is amonge the rightuous.

33 The curse of the Lord is in the house of the vngodly, but he blessed the dwellynges of the rightuous.

34 As for the scornefull, he shall laugh them to scorne, but he shal geue grace vnto the lowly.

35 The wise shall haue honour in possession, but shame is the promocion that foles shall haue.

# CHAPTER 4

Heare, O ye children, the fatherly exhortation, and take good hede, that ye maye learne wysdome.

2 Yea I shall geue you a good rewarde, if ye wyll not for sake my lawe.

3 For when I my selfe was my fathers deare sonne, and tenderlye beloued of my mother,

4 he taughte me also, saiyng: Let thyne herte receaue my wordes, kepe my commaundementes, and thou shalt lyue.

5 Get the wysdome, get the vnderstanding forget not the wordes of my mouth, & shrinke not from them.

6 Forsake her not, she shall preserue the: loue her, and she shal kepe the.

7 The chyefe poynte of wisdom is, that thou be willing to optayne wysdome, and before all thy goodes to gett the vnderstandynge.

8 Make muche of her and she shall promote the: Yea if thou embrace her, she shall brynge the vnto honoure.

9 She shall make the a gracyous head, and garnyshe the wyth a crowne of glorye.

10 Heare my sone, and receyue my wordes, that the yeares of thy lyfe maye be many.

11 I wyll shewe the, the waye of wysdome, and leade the in the ryght pathes,

12 So that if thou goost therin, ther shall not straytenesse hynder the and when thou runnest thou shalte not fall,

13 Take fast holde of doctryne, let her not go: kepe her, for she is thy lyfe.

14 Come not in the path of the vngodly, and walke not in the waye of the wycked.

15 Eschue it, and go not therein: departe a syde, and passe ouer by it.

16 For they can not slepe, except they haue first done some myschefe: neither take they anye rest, except they haue fyrst done some harme

17 For they eate the breade of wickednesse, and dryncke the wyne of robberye.

18 The path of the ryghtuous shyneth as the lyghte, and is euer brighter and brighter vnto the perfecte daye.

19 But the waye of the vngodly is as the darcknes, wherin men fal, or thei be aware.

20 My sonne, marcke my words, and encline thyne eare vnto my saiynges.

21 Let them not depart from thine eyes, kepe them euen in the myddest of thyne herte.

22 For they are lyfe vnto all those that fynde them, and health vnto all their bodyes.

23 Kepe thyne herte wyth all dilygence, for there vpon hangeth lyfe.

24 Put awaye from the a frowarde mouth, and let the lippes of sclander be farre from the.

25 Let thyne eyes beholde the thinge that is righte, and let thine eye liddes loke straight before the.

26 Pondre the path of thy fete, so shal al thy waies be sure.

27 Turne not a side, neither to the righte hande ner to the lefte, but withholde thy fote from euel.

# CHAPTER 5

O my sonne, geue hede vnto my wysdome, and bow thyne eare vnto my prudence:

2 that thou mayest regarde good councel, and that thy lyppes may kepe nourtoure.

3 For the lyppes of an harlot are a droppynge combe, and her throte is softer then oyle.

4 But at the laste she is as bytter as worme wode, and as sharpe as a two edged sweard.

5 Her fete go downe vnto death, and her steps pearse thorow vnto hel.

6 She regardeth not the path of life, so vnstedfast are her waies, that thou canst not know them.

7 Heare me therefore (O my sonne) and departe not from þe wordes of my mouth.

8 Kepe thy way far from her, and come not nye the dores of her house.

9 That thou geue not thyne honoure vnto another, and thy yeares to the cruell.

10 That other men be not filled wt thy goods & þt thy labours come not in a strang house.

11 Yea þt thou mourne not at þe last (when thou hast spent thy body & goods)

12 and then say: Alas why hated I nourtoure? why dyd my herte despys correction.

13 Wherfore was not I obedyente vnto þe voyce of my teachers, & herkened not vnto them that infourmed me?

14 I am come almoste into all mysfortune, in the middest of the multytude and congregacion.

15 Drinke of the water of

thine owne wel, and of the riuers that runne out of thine owne springes.

16 Let thy welles flowe out abroad, that ther may be ryuers of water in the stretes:

17 but let them be only thyne owne, and not strangers wyth the.

18 Let thy well be blessed, and be glad wyth the wyfe of thy youth.

19 Louyng is the hind, & frendly is þe Roo: let her brestes alway satisfye the, and holde the euer content wyth her loue.

20 My sonne, why wilt thou haue pleasure in an harlotte, and embrace the bosome of another woman?

21 For euery mannes waies are open in the sight of the Lorde, and he pondreth all their goynges.

22 The wyckednesses of the vngodly shal catch him selfe, and with the snares of of his owne synnes shall he be trapped.

23 Because he wold not be refourmed he shall dye: and for his greate folyshnesse he shalbe destroyed.

## CHAPTER 6

My son, if thou be suerty for thy neyghboure, thou hast fastened thyne hand wyth another man:

2 yet thou art bound with thyne owne wordes, & taken wt thine owne speache.

3 Therfore, my sonne, do thys discharge thy selfe, for thou art come into thy neyghboures daunger. Go thy way then sone and intreate thy neighbour:

4 let not thine eies slepe ner thyne eye lyddes slomber.

5 Saue thy selfe as a doo from the hande, and as a byrde from the handes of the fouler.

6 Go to the Emmet (thou slogard) consyder her wayes, and lerne to be wise.

7 She hath no guide, no teacher, no leader:

8 yet in the Sommer she prouideth her meate, and gathereth her foode together in the haruest,

9 How longe wilt thou slepe? thou slogysh man? When wylte thou aryse out of thy slepe?

10 Yea slepe on stil a litle, slomber a lytle, folde thyne handes together yet a lytle, that thou mayest slepe:

11 so shall pouerte come vnto the as one that trauaileth by the way, and necessitie lyke a weaponed man.

12 A dissembling person, a wycked man goeth with a frowarde mouth,

13 he wyncketh wyth hys eyes, he tokeneth wyth hys fete, he poynteth wyth his fingers,

14 he is euer ymagining mischefe and frowardnesse in his hert, & causeth dsscord.

15 Therfore shal his destruccyon come hastely vpon him, sodenly shal he be al to broken, and not be healed.

16 There be sixe thinges which the Lorde hateth, and the seuenth he vtterly abhorreth:

17 A proude loke, a dyssemblynge tonge, handes that shede innocent bloud,

18 an hert that goeth about with wicked ymaginacions, fet that be swift in rening to do mischefe,

19 a false witnes that bringeth vp lies, and such one as soweth dyscord amonge brethren,

20 My son kepe thy fathers commaundementes, and forsake not the law of thy mother.

21 Put them vp together in thine herte, and bind them about the neck.

22 That they may leade the where thou goest, preserue the when thou art a sleape, and that when thou awakest, thou maiest talke of them

23 For the commaundement is a lanterne, and the lawe a lyghtie, a chastening, and nurtour is the waye of lyfe:

24 that they maye kepe the from the euell woman, and from the flattering tong of the harlot:

25 that þu lust not after he beuty in thine herte, & lest þu be taken wt her fayre lokes.

26 An harlot will make a man to begge his breade, but a maried woman wyl hunte for þe precyous lyfe.

27 May a man take fyre in his bosome and his clothes not be brent?

28 Or can one go vpon hoate coales, & hys fete not be hurte?

29 Euen so, whosoeuer goeth into hys neyghbours wyfe, and toucheth her can not be vngilty.

30 Men do not vtterly despise a thefe that stealeth to satisfye hys soule, when he is hongry:

31 but if he may be gotten, he restoreth agayne seuen tymes as muche, or els he maketh recompense with al the good of his house

32 But who so comitteth aduoutry wyth a womanne, he is a fole, and bringeth hys lyfe to destruccyon.

33 He getteth him selfe also shame & dishonour, such as shal neuer be put out.

34 For the gelousy and wrath of the man wil not be intreated,

35 no though thou woldest offer him greate giftes to make amendes, he wyll not receiue them.

## CHAPTER 7

My sonne, kepe my wordes, and lay vp my commaundementes by the.

2 Kepe my commaundementes and my lawe, euen as the apple of thyne eie, and thou shalt liue.

3 Bind them vpon thy fingers, and wryte them in the table of thyne herte.

4 Saye vnto wysdome: thou art my sister, and cal

vnderstandyng thy kynswoman:

5 that she may kepe þe from the starnge woman, and from the harlot which geueth swete wordes,

6 For out of þe window of my house I loked thorow the trealesse,

7 & beheld the simple people: and among other yong folkes I spyed one yonge fole

8 going ouer the stretes, by the corner in the way toward the harlots house

9 in the twylight of þe euening, when it beganne now to be nyght and darke.

10 And beholde, ther met him a woman in an harlots apparel,

11 a dysceatful, wanton & vnstedfast woman: whose fet could not abide in þe house,

12 now is she without, now in þe stretes, lurketh in euery corner,

13 she caught the yonge man, kyssed hym, & was not ashamed, sayinge:

14 I had a vowe to paye, & thys daye I perfourme it.

15 Therfore came I forth to mete the, that I mighte seke thy face, and so I haue founde the.

16 I haue deckte my bed with coueryngs & clothes of Egypte.

17 My bed haue I made to smell of myrre, Aloes, and Cynamon.

18 Come let vs lye together, and take our pleasure tyll it be daye lyghte.

19 For the good man is not at home, he is gone farre of.

20 He hath taken the bagge of money with hym: who can tell when he commeth home?

21 Thus with many swete woordes she ouercome hym, and with her flatteryng lippes she wanne hym.

22 Immediatly he folowed her, as it were an oxe led to the slaughter (& lyke as it were to the stockes, where foles are punyshed)

23 so longe tyll she had wounded hys lyuer with her dart: like as if a byrde hasted to the snare not knowyng that the parell of his lyfe lieth therupon.

24 Heare me now therfore (O my sonne) and marke the wordes of my mouth.

25 Let not thyne herte wandre in her wayes, & be not thou disceyued in her pathes.

26 For many one hath she wounded and cast doune yea, many a stronge man hath she slayne.

27 Her house is the waye vnto hell, where men go doune into the chambers of death.

# CHAPTER 8

Doth not wysdome crye? doeth not vnderstanding put forth her voyce?

2 Standeth she not in the hye places in the stretes & ways

3 doth she not crie before þe whole citie, and in the gates where men go out & in?

4 It is you, O ye men (saieth she) whom I cal? Vnto you (O ye chyldren of men) lyft I vp my voyce.

5 Take hede vnto knowlege O ye ignoraunt, be wyse in hert O ye foles.

6 Geue eare, for I will speake of great matters, and open my lyppes to tell thinges that be right.

7 For my throte shalbe talking of the trueth, & my lyppes abhorre vngodlinesse.

8 All þe wordes of my mouth are righteous, there is no frowardenesse nor falsede therin.

9 They are all playne to suche as will vnderstande, and ryght to them that fynde knowlege.

10 Receiue my doctrine therfore, & not siluer: & my knowledge, more then fyne golde.

11 For wysdome is more worth then precious stones, yea, all the thinges that thou canst desire, are not to be compared vnto it.

12 I wysdome haue my dwelling wt knowledge, & prudent counsaill is myne owne.

13 With me is the feare of the Lorde, and the eschuyng of euell. As for pryde, dysdayne, & euell waye, & a mouth that speaketh wicked thinges, I vtterly abhorre them.

14 I can geue counsayl, & be a gyde: I haue vnderstanding I haue strength.

15 Thorow me, kinges reygn: thorow me, prynces make iust lawes.

16 Thorow me, lordes beare rule, and all iudges of the earth execute iudgement.

17 I am louyngevnto those that loue me, & they that seke me early, shall fynde me.

18 Riches and honoure are with me, yea, excellent goodes & righteousnes.

19 My frute is better then golde & precious stone, & myne encrease more worth then fyne siluer.

20 I walke in the waye of righteousnes, and in the strete of iudgement.

21 That I may sende prosperitie to those that loue me, & to encrease their treasure.

22 The Lord hym self had me in possession in the begynning of hys wayes, or euer he beganne hys workes afore tyme.

23 I haue bene ordeyned from euerlasting, & from the beginning or euer the earthe was made.

24 When I was borne, there were nether depthes nor springs of water.

25 Before the foundacions of the mountaynes were layed, yea, before al hylles was I borne.

26 The earth & all that is vpon the earth was not yet made, no not the grounde it selfe.

27 For when he made the heauens, I was present: when he

sette vp the depthes in ordre:

28 when he hanged the cloudes aboue: when he fastened the sprynges of the depe:

29 When he shut the sea within certayn boundes, that the waters should not go ouer their markes. When he layed the foundacions of the earth

30 I was with hym, ordering all thinges, delytynge dayly, and reioysinge all waye before hym.

31 As for the rounde compase of his worlde, I make it ioyfull: for my delyte is to be among the chyldren of men.

32 Therfore herken vnto me, O ye chyldren, for blessed are they þt kepe my wayes.

33 O geue eare vnto nurtour, be wyse, and refuse it not.

34 Blessed is the man that heareth me, watchynge dayly at my gates, & geuynge attendaunce at the postes of my dores.

35 For who so findeth me, findeth life and shall obtayne fauour of the Lorde.

36 But who so offendeth agaynste me, hurteth hys owne soule. All they that hate me, are the louers of death.

## CHAPTER 9

WYSDOME hath buylded her selfe an house, & hewen out seuen pyllers:

2 she hath kylled her vitayles, poured out her wyne, & prepared her table.

3 She hath sent forth her maydens to crye vpon the hyest place of þe citie:

4 Who so is ignoraunt, let hym come hither. And to the vnwise she sayd:

5 O come on your way, eat my bred, & drinke my wyne, which I haue poured out for you.

6 Forsake ignoraunce, & ye shall lyue: & se þt ye go in the way of vnderstandinge.

7 Who so reproueth a scornefull personne, getteth hym self dishonour: & he that rebuketh þe vngodly stayneth him self.

8 Reproue not a scorner, lest he owe þe euel wil: but rebuke a wise man, & he wil loue the.

9 Geue a discrete man but an occasion, & he wilbe the wiser, teache a righteous man, and he will increase.

10 The feare of the Lorde is the beginning of wisdome, and the knowledge of holy thinges is vnderstandynge.

11 For thorow me thy dayes shalbe prolonged, and the yeares of thy lyfe shalbe manye.

12 If thou be wyse thy wysdome shall do thy selfe good: but if thou thynckeste scorne therof, it shalbe thyne owne harme.

13 A folysh restles woman, ful of words, and such one as hath no knowledge,

14 sitteth in the dores of her house vpon a stoole aboue in the cytye,

15 to cal such as go by, & walke streght in their waies,

16 Who so is ignorant (sayeth she) let him come hyther, and to the vnwyse she sayeth:

17 stollen waters are swete, and the bread that is preuely eaten, hath a good tast.

18 But they consyder not that death is there, and that her gestes go doune to hell.

## CHAPTER 10

THE Parables of Salomon. A wyse sonne maketh a glad father, but an vndiscrete sonne is the heuinesse of hys mother.

2 Treasures that are wyckedlye gotten, profit nothing, but righteousnesse deliuereth from death,

3 The lorde wyll not let the soule of the ryghtuous suffer honger, but he putteth the vngodly from his desire.

4 An ydle hand maketh pore, but a quicke laboryng hand maketh ryche.

5 Who so gathereth in Sommer, is wyse: but he that is slougysh in haruest, bryngeth him selfe to confusyon.

6 Louynge and fauourable is the face of the rightuous, but the forehead of the vngodly is past shame and presumptuous.

7 The memoryall of the iust shall haue a good reporte but the name of the vngodly shal styncke.

8 A wyse man wyll receyue warnyng, but a fole wyll soner be smytten in the face.

9 He that leadeth an innocente lyfe, walketh surelye: but who so goeth a wrong way, shalbe knowne,

10 He that wyncketh wyth hys eye, wyl do some harme: but he that hath a folysh mouth shalbe beaten.

11 The mouth of a ryghtuos man is a wele of lyfe, but the mouth of the vngodly is past shame, and presumptuous.

12 Euyll wyll stereth vp strife, but loue couereth the multytude of synnes.

13 In the lyppes of hym that hath vnderstandynge a man shall fynde wysdome, but the rod belongeth to the backe of the folysh.

14 Wyse men laie vp knowledge, but the mouth of the folysh is nye destruction.

15 The rich mans goodes are his strong hold, but pouerte oppresseth the poore.

16 The ryghtwyse laboureth to do good, but the vngodly vseth his encrease vnto sinne.

17 To take hede vnto the chastenyng of nurtoure, is the way of lyfe: but he that refuseth to be refourmed, goeth wrong.

18 Dissembling lippes kepe hatred secretly, and he that speaketh any sclander, is a foole.

19 Where much babling is, ther must nedes be offence: he that refraineth his lippes is wisest of all.

20 An innocent tong is a noble treasure, but the hert of the vngodly is nothynge worthe.

21 The lyppes of the rightuous fed a whole multitude, but foles shal die in their owne folye.

22 The blessing of the Lord maketh rich men, as for carefull trauayle, it doth nothynge therto.

23 A fole doth wyckedly and maketh but a sport of it: neuerthelesse it is wysdome for a man to beware of suche.

24 The thinge that the vngodly are afrayed of, shall come vpon them, but the rightuous shall haue their desyre.

25 The vngodly is lyke a tempest that passeth ouer, and is no more sene but the rightuous remayneth sure for euer

26 As vyneger is to the tethe, and as smoke is vnto the eyes, euen so sa slougysh person to them that send him forth.

27 The feare of the Lorde maketh a long lyfe but the yeares of the vngodly shalbe shortened.

28 The paciente abydynge of the rightuous shalbe turned to gladness, but þe hope of þe vngodli shal perish.

29 The waye of the Lorde geueth a corage vnto the godly, but it is a fear for wicked doers

30 The righteuous shall neuer be ouerthrowen but the vngodly shal remaine in the land.

31 The mouth of the iust wilbe talkyng of wisdome, but the tonge of the frowarde shall perysh.

32 The lyppes of the ryghtuous are occupied in acceptable thinges, but the mouth of the vngodly take them to the worst.

# CHAPTER 11

A false balance is an abhomynation vnto the Lord, but a true weight pleaseth him.

2 Wher pryde is, ther is shame also and confusion: but where as is lowlynes, there is wysdome.

3 The innocente dealyng of the iust shal leade them, but the vnfaithfulnesse of the despisers shalbe their owne destruccion

4 Riches helpe not in the day of vengeaunce, but rightuousnes deliuereth from death.

5 The rightuousnes of the innocent ordereth his way, but the vngodly shall fall in his owne wyckednesse.

6 The rightuousnes of the iuste shall delyuer them, but the despisers shalbe taken in their owne vngodlynesse.

7 When an vngodlie man dieth, his hope is gone, the confydence of ryches shal perish

8 The righteous shalbe delyuered out of trouble, and the vngodly shal come in his steade.

9 Thorow the mouth of the dyssembler is hys neyghboure destroyed, but thorowe knowledge shall the iust be deliuered.

10 When it goeth well with the righteous, the cytye is mery: and when the vngodly perish, there is gladnesse.

11 When the iust are in wealth, the citie prospereth: but when the vngodly haue the rule, it decayeth.

12 A foole bringeth vp a sclaunder of his neyghbour, but a wyse man wil kepe it secrete.

13 A dissembling person will discouer preuy thinges, but he that is of a faythful hert, wil kepe counsayl.

14 Where no good counsail is there the people decaye: but where as many are that can geue counsayll, there is wealth.

15 He that is suerty for a straunger, hurteth him self: but he that medleth not with suertiship, is sure.

16 A gracious woman manteyneth honesty, as for the mighty, they manteyne ryches.

17 He that hath a gentle liberall stomack is merciful: but who so hurteth hys neyghbour, is a tyraunt.

18 The labour of the vngodly prospereth not, but he þt soweth righteousnes, shal receyue a sure rewarde.

19 Like as righteousnes bringeth lyfe: euen so to cleue vnto euel, bringeth death.

20 The Lord abhorreth a fayned hert, but he hath pleasur in them that are vndefiled.

21 It shal not helpe the wicked, though they laye all their handes together, but the sede of þe righteous shalbe preserued.

22 A fayre woman without discrete maners, is like a ringe of golde in a swynes snoute.

23 The iust labour for peace and tranquyllite, but the vngodly for disquietnesse.

24 Some man geueth out hys goodes, & is the rycher, but the nygard (hauyng ynough) will departe from nothynge, and yet is euer in pouerty.

25 He that is liberal in geuyng, shal haue plentye: and he that watereth, shalbe watered also him self.

26 Who so hoordeth vp hys corne, shalbe cursed amonge the people: but blessing shall light vppon hys head that selleth it.

27 He þt laboureth for honesty findeth hys desire: but who so seketh after mischiefe, shall happen vnto hym.

28 He that trusteth in hys ryches shall haue a fall, but the righteous shall florish as the grene leaf.

29 Who so maketh disquyetnes is his owne house, he shall haue wynde for hys heritage, and the foole shalbe seruant to the wyse.

30 The frute of the righteous is as the tree of lyfe, a wyse man also wynneth mens soules.

31 If the righteous be recompensed vppon earth, how much more then the vngodly and the sinner?

## CHAPTER 12

WHO so loueth wysdome, wil be content to be refourmed: but he that hateth to be reproued, is a foole.

2 A good man is acceptable vnto the Lord, but the wicked will he condempne.

3 A man can not endure in vngodlinesse, but the rote of þe righteous shall not be moued.

4 A stedfast woman is a croune vnto her husband: but she that behaueth her selfe vnhonestly is a corrupcion in hys bones.

5 The thoughtes of the righteous are righte, but the ymaginacion of the vngodly are disceatfull.

6 The talkyng of the vngodlye is howe they maye laye wayte for bloud, but the mouthe of the righteous wyll deliuer them.

7 Or euer thou canst turne the about, the vngodly shalbe ouerthrowen: but the house of the righteous shall stande.

8 A man shalbe commended for hys wysdome, but a fole shalbe despised.

9 A simple man which laboureth & worketh, is better then one that is gorgyous and wanteth bread.

10 A righteous man regardeth the lyfe of his cattell, but the vngodly haue cruel hertes.

11 He that tilleth his lande, shal haue plenteousnesse of bread: but he that foloweth ydelnes, is a very foole.

12 The desyre of the vngodly hunteth after mischief, but the rote of the righteous bryngeth forth frute.

13 The wicked falleth into the snare thorow the malyce of his own mouth, but the iust shal escape out of parel.

14 Euery man shall enioye good accordyng to the innocency of his mouth, & after the workes of his handes shal he be rewarded.

15 Loke what a foole taketh in hande, he thynketh it wel done: but he that is wyse, wil be counsayled.

16 A foole vttereth his wrath in all the hast, but a discrete man forgeueth wrong.

17 A iust man wil tel the trueth, & shewe the thynge that is right: but a false witnesse disceyueth.

18 A sclaunderous personne pricketh like a swerd, but a wise mans tonge is wholsome.

19 A true mouth is euer constant, but a dissemblyng tonge is soone chaunged.

20 They that ymagyn euell in their mynde, will disceyue: but the counsaylers of peace shall haue ioy folowing them.

21 There shall no misfortune happen vnto þe iust but the vngodly shalbe filled with misery.

22 The Lord abhorreth disceatful lyppes, but they that laboure for trueth please hym.

23 He that hath vnderstanding, can hyde his wisdome: but an vndiscrete hert telleth oute hys folishnesse.

24 A diligent hande shal beare rule, but the ydle shalbe vnder tribute.

25 Heauinesse discorageth the hert of man, but a good worde maketh it glad again.

26 The righteous is liberall vnto hys neyghbour, but the waye of þe vngodly will disceyue them selfs.

27 A disceatfull man shall fynde no vauntage, but he that is content with that he hath, is more worthe then golde.

28 In the waye of righteousnesse there is lyfe, as for any other waye it is the pathe vnto death.

## CHAPTER 13

A wyse sonne wyll receaue hys fathers warnynge, but he that is scornefull, wyl not heare when he is reproued.

2 A good man shall enioye the fruite of hys mouth, but he that hath a froward mind shalbe spoyled.

3 He that kepeth his mouth, kepeth his lyfe: but who so speaketh vnaduised findeth harme.

4 The slogarde woulde fayne haue, and can not get his dsyre: but the soule of the diligente shall haue plenty.

5 A ryghtuous man abhorreth lyes, but the vngodlye shameth both other and hym selfe.

6 Ryghtuousnesse kepeth the innocente in the waye, but vngodlynesse shal ouerthrow the sinner.

7 Some men are rych, thoughe they haue nothynge: againe some men are pore hauing greate ryches.

8 With goodes euery man deliuereth his lyfe, and the poore wyll not be reproued.

9 The lyght of the rightuous maketh ioyfull, but the candle of the vngodly shalbe put out.

10 Among the proud ther is euer strife, but amonge those that do all thynges wyth aduysemente, ther is wysdome.

11 Hastely gotten goodes are sone spent, but they that be gathered together with the hand, shall increase

12 Longe taryenge for a thing that is differred, greueth the hert: but when þe desyre commeth, it is a tre of lyfe.

13 Who so despiseth þe word destroyeth hym selfe: but he that feareth the commaundemente shal haue peace.

14 The law is a wel of life vnto the wise, that it may kepe him from the snares of death,

15 Good vnderstanding geueth fauour, but hard is the way of the despisers.

16 A wyse man doth al thinges with dyscrecyon, but a

foole wyl declare his folly.

17 An vngodly messanger bryngeth myschyefe, but a faythfull embassytour is wholsome.

18 He that thynketh scorne to be refourmed, commeth to pouertie & shame: but who so receaueth correction, shal come to honour

19 When a desyre, is brought to passe, it delyteth the soule: but fooles abhorre him that eschueth euell.

20 He that goeth in the company of wyse men, shalbe wyse: but who so is a companyon of foles, shalbe hurte.

21 Mischefe foloweth vpon synners, but the ryghtuous shal haue a god reward.

22 Which their chylders chyldren shal haue in possession, for the riches of the synner is layed vp for the iuste.

23 Ther is plentuousnesse of fode in the feldes of the pore, and shalbe increased out of measure.

24 He that spareth the rod, hateth hys son: but who so loueth hym, holdeth hym euer in nurtoure.

25 The ryghtuous eateth, and is satisfied, but the belly of þe vngodly hath neuer ynough.

# CHAPTER 14

A wise woman vpholdeth her house but a folish wife plucketh it doun

2 Who so feareth the Lorde, walketh in the ryght path: and regardeth not hym that abhorreth the wayes of the Lord.

3 In the mouth of the folyshe is the boastynge of lordshyppe, but the lyppes of the wyse wylbe ware of such.

4 Where no oxen are, ther þe cribbe is empty: but where the oxen labour ther is much frute.

5 A faithful witnesse will not dyssemble, but a false recorde wyll make a lye.

6 A scorneful body seketh wisdom, and findeth it not: but knowlege is easy to come by, vnto him that wyl vnderstand

7 Se that thou meddle not with a foole, and do as though thou haddest no knowledge.

8 The wysdome of hym that hath vnderstanding is, to take hede vnto hys way but the folyshnes of the vnwyse disceaueth.

9 Foles make but a sporte of synne, but ther is fauourable loue amonge the rightuous.

10 The hert of him that hath vnderstandyng wyll neyther dyspaire for any sorow, ner be to presumptuous for any sodaine ioy.

11 The houses of the vngodly shalbe ouerthrowne, but þe tabernacles of the rightuous shal florish.

12 Ther is a waye whiche some men thinke to be ryght, but the ende thereof leadeth vnto death.

13 The herte is sorowfull euen in a laughter, and the ende of mirth is heuinesse.

14 An vnfaythful personne shalbe filled wyth hys owne wayes, but a good man wyl beware of suche.

15 An ignoraunt boddy beleueth all thynges, but who so hath vnderstandyng, loketh well to his goinges.

16 A wyse man feareth, and departeth from euel, but a foole goeth on presumptuously.

17 An vnpacient man dealeth folyshly, but he that is well aduysed doth other wayes.

18 The ignoraunte haue folyshnes in possession, but the wyse are crowned with knowledge.

19 The euel shal bow hem selues before the good, and the vngodly shall wayte at the dores of the ryghtuous.

20 The poore is hated euen of his owne neyghbours, but the rich hath many frends.

21 Who so despyseth his neyghbour, doth amysse: but blessed is he that hath pytye of the poore.

22 They that ymagyn wyckednes, shall be disapoynted: but they that muse vpon good thinges, vnto suche shall happen mercy and faythfulnesse.

23 Diligent laboure bringeth ryches, but wher many vayne wordes are, trulye ther is scarcenesse.

24 Ryches are an ornamente vnto the wyse, but the ignoraunce of fooles is very folyshnesse,

25 A faythfull wytnesse delyuereth soules, but a lyar disceaueth them,

26 The feare of the Lord in a strong hold for vnto his he wyl be a sure defence,

27 The feare of the lorde is a well of lyfe, to auoide the snares of death.

28 The increase and prosperite of the commens is the Kynges honoure, but the decaye of the people is the confusion of the Prince.

29 Pacyence is a token of wisdom, but wrath & hasty displasure is a token of folyshnesse.

30 A merye hert is the life of the bodye, but rancoure consumeth awaye the bones.

31 He that doeth a poore man wrong, blasphemeth hys maker: but who so hathe pytye of the poore, doeth honoure vnto God,

32 The vngodlye is afrayed of euery parel, but the ryghtuous hath a good hope euen in death.

33 Wysdome resteth in the herte of him that hath vnderstandynge, and he wyll teach theym that are vnlearned.

34 Ryghtuousnes setteth vp the people, vut wickednes bringeth folke to destruccyon.

35 A dyscrete seruaunt is a pleasure vnto the Kynge, but one

þt is not honest prouoketh hym vnto wrath.

## CHAPTER 15

A soft answere putteth downe displeasure. but frowarde words prouoke vnto anger.

2 A wise tonge commendeth knowledg, a folysh mouth blabbeth oute no thynge but folyshnesse.

3 The eyes of the Lord loke on euery place, both vpon the good and badde.

4 A wholsome tonge is a tree of lyfe but he that abuseth it, hath a broken mynde.

5 A foole despyseth hys fathers correccyon, but he that taketh hede whan he is reproued shalhaue þe more vnderstandyng.

6 In the house of the ryghteous are greate rytches, but in the increase of the vngodlye ther is mysorder.

7 A wyse mouth poureth out knowledge, but the herte of the folysh doth not so.

8 The Lorde aborreth the sacryfyce of the vngodlye, but the prayer of the rightuous is acceptable vnto hym.

9 The waye of the vngodlye is an abhomynacyon vnto the Lorde, but who so foloweth rightuousnesse, hym he loueth.

10 He that forsaketh the ryghte strete, shalbe sore punyshed: and who so hateth correccyon, falleth into death.

11 The hell wyth her payne is knowne vnto the Lorde, howe muche more then, the hertes of men?

12 A scorneful body loueth not one that rebuketh hym, nether wyll he come amonge the wyse.

13 A mery hert maketh a chearful countinance but an vnquiet mynd maketh it heuy.

14 A wise hert wil seke after knowledge, but the mouth of foles medleth with folishnesse.

15 All the dayes of the pore are myserable, but a quyet herte is as a continnual feaste.

16 Better is a litle with the feare of the Lord then great tresure, for they are not without sorowe.

17 Better is a messe of potage with loue, then a far oxe wyth euel wyll.

18 An angry man stereth vp strife, but he that is pacient stilleth discord.

19 The way of þe slouthful is ful of thornes, but þe strete of the rightuous is wel cleansed.

20 A wyse son maketh a glad father, but an vndiscrete body shameth hys mother.

21 A foole reioiseth in folyshe thynges but awyse man loketh wel to hys own goinges.

22 Vnaduised thoughts shal come to naught but wher as men are þt can geue councel, ther is stedfastnes.

23 O howe ioyfull a thing is it, a man to geue a conuenyente answere? O how pleasaunt is a word spoken in due season.

24 The waye of lyfe leadeth vnto heauen, that a man shoulde beware of hell beneth.

25 The Lord wyl breake downe the house of the proud, but he shal make fast the borders of the widdowe,

26 The Lorde abhorreth the ymaginacons of þe wycked, but pure wordes are pleasaunt vnto him.

27 The couetous man roteth vp his owne house, but who so hateth rewardes shall liue.

28 A ryghtuous man museth in hys mynde howe to do good, but the mynde of the vngodly ymagineth, howe he may do harme,

29 The Lorde is farre from the vngodly, but he heareth the praier of the rightuous.

30 Lyke as the clearenesse of the eyes reioiseth the herte so doth a good name fede the bones.

31 The eare that herkeneth vnto wholsome warnnynge, and enclyneth therto, shal dwell amonge the wyse.

32 He that refuseth to be refourmed, despyseth his owne soule: but he that submytteth hym selfe to correccyon, is wyse.

33 The feare of the Lord is þe righte scyence of wysdome, and lowlines goeth before honure.

## CHAPTER 16

A man may wel purpose a thinge in his herte, but the answere of the tong commeth of the Lord,

2 A man thynketh al his waies to be cleane, but it is þe Lord that fashyoneth the mindes

3 Commit thy workes the Lord, and loke what thou deuisest, it shal prospere.

4 The Lorde doth al thynges for hys owne sake, yea when he kepeth the vngodly for the day of wrath.

5 The Lorde abhorreth all presumptuous & proude hertes, ther may neyther strength ner powere scape.

6 With louyng mercye and fayethfulnesse synnes be forgeuen, and who so feareth the Lorde, he eschueth euell.

7 When a mans ways please the Lord, he maketh his very enemies to be hys frendes.

8 Better is it to haue a lyttle thinge with rightuousnes, then greate rentes wrngeously gotten.

9 A man deuyseth awaye in his herte, but it is the Lorde that ordreth hys goynges.

10 When the prophecye is in the lyppes of the kynge, hys mouth shal not go wronge in iudgment.

11 A true measure and a true balaunce are the Lordes, he maketh all weightes.

12 It is a great abhominatyon when kynges are wycked, for a kinges seat should be holden vp

wyth ryghtuousnesse

13 Ryghtuous lyppes are pleasaunte vnto kynges, and they loue hym that speaketh the trueth.

14 The kynges dyspleasure is a messaunger of deathe, but a wyse man wyll pacyfye hym.

15 The chearefull conntenaunce of the kynge is lyfe, and hys louynge fauoure is as the euenynge dewe.

16 To haue wysdome in possesstion is better then gold, & to get vnderstanding is more worth then siluer.

17 The path of þe rightuous eschueth euel, & who so loketh wel to his waies, kepeth hys owne soule.

18 Presumptuousnes goth before destruction, & after aproud stomake ther foloweth a fall.

19 Better is it to be of humble mynde with the lowly, then to deuyde the spoyles wyth the proud.

20 He that handleth a matter wisely, opteineth good: and blessed is he, that putteth his trust in the Lord

21 Who so hath a wyse vnderstanding, is called to councel but that canne speake faire getteth more riches.

22 Vnderstanding is a wel of lyfe vnto him that hath it, as for the chastenyng of foles, it is but folishnesse.

23 The hert of the wyse enfourm his moueth, and amendeth the doctryne in his lyps.

24 Fayre wordes are an hony combe, a refreshynge of the mynde, and helth of the bones.

25 Ther is away þt men thinke to be right but the ende thereof leadeth vnto death.

26 A troublous soule dysquyeteth her selfe, for her owne mouth hath brought her therto.

27 An vngodly personne styreth vp euell, and in hys lipps he is as an whote burnyng fyre.

28 A frowarde bodye causeth stryfe, and he that is a blabbe of his tonge, maketh deuisyon amonge princes.

29 A wycked man begyleth hys neyghbour, and leadeth hym the waye that is not good.

30 He that wyncketh wyth his eyes, ymagineth mischife: and he that byteth his lyppes wyll do some harme.

31 Age is a crowne of worshippe, if it be founde in the waye of ryghtuousnes.

32 A pacyente man is better then one stronge: and he that can rule him selfe, is more worth then he that winneth a city.

33 The lotts are caste into the lappe, but there fal standeth in the Lorde.

# CHAPTER 17

BETTER is a dry morsell with quietnes, then a full house and many fat catell with stryfe.

2 A discrete seruaunt shall haue more rule then the sonnes that haue no wysdom, and shal haue like heritage with the brethren.

3 Lyke as syluer is tryed in the fyre and golde in the fornace, euen so doeth the Lorde proue the hertes.

4 A wycked bodye holdeth muche of false lippes, and a dissemblyng personne geueth eare to a dysceatefull tonge.

5 Who so laugheth the pore to scorne blasphemeth hys maker: & he that is glad of another mans hurt, shall not be vnpunished.

6 Chylders chyldren are a worshyppe vnto the elders, & the fathers are the honoure of þe children.

7 An eloquent speach becommeth not a fole, a dissemblyng mouth also besemeth not a prince.

8 Liberalite is a precyous stone vnto hym þt hath it, for whersoeuer he becometh, he prospereth.

9 Who so couereth another mans offence seketh loue: but he þt discloseth þe faut setteth frends at variance.

10 One reprofe only doth more good to him þt hath vnderstandinge then an .C. stripes vnto a fole.

11 A sedicious personne seketh myschefe, but a cruell messaunger shall be sent against hym.

12 It were better to come against a shee Bere robbed of her whelpes, then agaynst a fole in his foolyshnes.

13 Who so rewardeth euell for good, the plage shall not departe frome hys house.

14 He that soweth discord & strife, is lyke one that dyggeth vp a water broke: but an open enemy is like the water that breaketh out & renneth abroad.

15 The Lord hateth as wel hym þt iustifyeth the vngodly, as him that condemneth the innocent,

16 What helpeth it to geue a foole mony in his hand, wher as he hath no mind to bye wysdome?

17 He is a frende that alway loueth, and in aduersite a man shal know who is hys brother.

18 Whoso promyseth by the hande, and is suertye: or another, he is a foole.

19 He that loueth stryfe, delyteth in synne: & who so setteth his dore to hye, seketh after a fall.

20 Who so hath a frowarde herte obtayneth no good: & he that hath an ouerthwarte tonge, shall fall into myschyefe.

21 An vnwyse body bringeth him selfe into sorow, and the father of a foole can haue no ioye.

22 A merye hert maketh a lusty age, but a sorowful mind dryeth vp the bones.

23 The vngodlye taketh

gyftes out of the bosome, to wrest the waies of iudgment.

24 Wysdome shineth in the face of hym that hath vnderstanding, but the eies of fooles wander thorow out all landes.

25 An vndiscrete sonne is a grefe vnto his father, & an heuynesse vnto hys mother that bare him

26 To punish the innocent, and to smite the princes that geue true iudgmente, are both euell.

27 He is wyse and discrete, that tempereth his wordes: and he is a man of vnderstandinge, that maketh much of his spirite.

28 Yea a verye foole (when he holdeth his tonge) is counted wyse, and to haue vnderstandinge, when he shutteth his lyppes.

## CHAPTER 18

WHO so hath pleasure to sow dyscorde, pyketh a quarel in euery thyng.

2 A foole hath no delite in understanding, but only in those thynges wherin his herte reioyseth.

3 Wher vngodlynes is, there is also disdayne: and so there foloweth shame and dishonoure.

4 The wordes of mans mouth are lyke depe waters, and the well of wysdome is lyke a full streame.

5 It is not good to a regarde the personne of the vngodly, or to put backe the ryghteous in iudgmente.

6 A fooles lippes are euer brawling, and his mouth prouoketh vnto battayll.

7 A fooles mouth is hys owne destruccion and his lippes are the snare for his owne soule.

8 The words of a sclanderer are very woundes, and go thorow vnto the inmost parts of þe body.

9 Who so is slouthful & slacke in his laboure, is the brother of him that is a waster.

10 The name of þe Lord is a strong castel, the righteous flieth vnto it, and shalbe saued.

11 But þe rich mans goods are his strong hold, yea he taketh them for an hie wall rounde aboute hym.

12 After pryde commeth destruccion, and honour after lowlines.

13 He þt geueth sentence in a matter before he heare it, is a foole, & worthy to be confounded.

14 A good stomacke driueth awaye a mans disease, but when the sptrite is vexed, who may abide it?

15 A wyse herte laboureth for knowledge, and a prudent eare seketh vnderstanding

16 Liberalitye bryngeth a man to honoure and worship, and setteth him among great men.

17 The rightuous accuseth hym selfe firste of al, if his neyghbour come, he shal fynd him.

18 The lot pacifieth the variaunce, and parteth þe mighty a sunder.

19 The vnitie of brethren is stronger then a castel, and they that hold together are like the barre of a palayce.

20 A mans belly shalbe satisfied wyth the fruyte of hys owne mouthe, and wyth the increase of hys lyppes shall he be fylled.

21 Death & lyfe stand in the power of the tong, he that loueth it shal enioy the frute thereof.

22 Who so fyndeth a wyfe fyndeth a good thynge, and receyueth an wholsome benefyte of þe Lord.

23 The poore maketh supplicacyon & prayeth mekelye, but the ryche geueth a rough aunswere.

24 A frende that delyteth in loue, doeth a man more frenshyppe, and stycketh faster vnto hym then a brother.

## CHAPTER 19

BETTER is the poore that lyueth godly then the blasphemer that is but a foole.

2 Where no discrecion is, ther the soule is not well: and who so is swyft on fote, stombleth hastly,

3 Folyshuesse maketh a man to go out of his waye, and then is his hert vnpacient agaynst the Lorde.

4 Ryches make many frendes, but the poore is forsaken of his own frendes.

5 A false witnesse shall not remayne vnpunished, & he that speaketh lyes shal not escape.

6 The multitude hangeth vpon great men, and euery man fauoureth him that geueth rewardes.

7 As for the poore, he is hated amonge all hys brethren: yea, hys owne frendes forsake hym, & he that geueth credence vnto wordes getteth nothyng.

8 He that is wyse, loueth his owne soule: & who so hath vnderstandynge, shall prospere.

9 A false witnesse shall not remayne vnpunished, & he þt speaketh lyes shal perish.

10 Delicate ease becommeth not a foole much more vnsemely is it, a bonde man too haue the rule of princes.

11 A wyse man putteth of displeasure, & it is his honour to let some fautes passe.

12 The kynges disfauour is lyke the roaryng of a Lyon, but hys frendship is lyke the dewe vpon the grasse.

13 An vndiscrete sonne is the heuynes of hys father, & a braulyng wyfe is lyke the top of an house, where thorow it is euer droppyng.

14 House & ryches maye a man haue by the heritage of hys elders, but a discrete woman is

the gifte of the Lord.

15 Slouthfulnes bringeth slepe, & an ydel soule shall suffer hunger.

16 Who so kepeth the commaundement, kepeth hys owne soule: but he that regardeth not hys way, shal dye.

17 He that hath pittie vppon the poore, lendeth vnto the Lord: & loke what he layeth oute, it shalbe payed hym agayn.

18 Chasten thy sonne whyle there is hope, but let not thy soule be moued to sleye hym.

19 For great wrath bryngeth harme, therfore let hym go, & so mayest thou teache hym more nurtoure.

20 O geue eare vnto good counsayll, & be content to be refourmed, that thou mayest be wyse here after.

21 There are many deuises in a mans hert, neuertheles the counsayll of the Lorde shall stande.

22 It is a mans worship to do good & better it is to be a poore man, then dissembler.

23 The feare of the Lord preserueth the life yea, it geueth plenteousnes, without the visitacion of any plage.

24 A slouthful body shuteth hys hande into hys bosome, so that he cannot put it to his mouth.

25 If thou smitest a scorneful personne, the ignoraunt shall take better hede: & if thou reprouest one that hath vnderstanding, he will be þe wyser.

26 He that hurteth hys father or shuteth out his mother, is a shamefull & an vnworthy sonne.

27 My sonne, heare nomore the doctrine that leadeth the awaye from the wordes of vnderstandyng.

28 A false witnes laugheth iudgement to scorn & the mouth of the vngodly eateth vp wickednes.

29 Punishmentes are ordeyned for the scornefull, and strypes for fooles backes.

# CHAPTER 20

WINE is a volupteous thynge, & dronckennes causeth sedicion: who so deliteth therin, shal neuer be wyse.

2 The kyng oughte to be feared as the roarynge of a Lyon, who so prouoketh hym vnto anger, offendeth agaynst hys owne soule.

3 It is a mans honour to kepe him selfe from stryfe, but they that haue pleasure in braulinge, are fooles euery one.

4 A slouthfull body will not go to plowe for colde, therefore shall he go a beggynge in Sommer, and haue nothynge.

5 Wyse counsayll in the herte of man is lyke a water in the depe of the earth, but he þt hathe vnderstanding, bringeth it forth.

6 Many there be that are called good doers, but whereshal one fynde a true faythful man?

7 Who so leadeth a godly and an innocent lyfe, happy shal his chyldren be whome he leaueth behynde hym.

8 A kynge that sitteth in iudgement, and loketh well aboute hym, dryueth awaye all euell.

9 Who can saye: my herte is cleane, I am innocent from sinne?

10 To vse two maner of weyghtes, or twoo maner of measures, both these are abhominable vnto the Lorde.

11 A chylde is knowen by hys conuersacion, whether hys workes be pure & right.

12 As for the hearing of the eare & the sight of the eye, the Lord hath made them both.

13 Delyte not thou in slepe, lest thou come vnto pouerte: but open thyne eyes, and thou shalt haue bread ynough.

14 It is naught, It is naught (say men) when they haue it, but when it is gone, they geue it a good woorde.

15 A mouth of vnderstanding is more worth then gold, many precious stones, & costly iewels.

16 Take his garment that is suerty for a straunger, & take a pledge of him for the vnknowen mans sake.

17 Euery man liketh the bread that is gotten with disceate, but at the laste hys mouth shalbe filled with grauell.

18 Thorow counsayl the thynges that men deuise go forward: and with discrecion ought warres to be taken in hande.

19 Medle not with hym that bewrayeth secretes, and is a sclaunderer, and disceaueth with hys lippes.

20 Whoso curseth hys father and mother, hys lyght shalbe put outin the myddest of darcknesse.

21 The herytage that commeth to hastely at the fyrste, shall not be praised at the ende.

22 Saye not thou: I wyll recompence euel, but put thy truste in the Lorde, and he shall defende the.

23 The Lorde, abhorreth two maner of weyghtes, and a false balaunce is an euell thinge.

24 The Lorde ordreth euery mans goinges, for what is he that vnderstandeth his owne wayes?

25 It is a snare for a man to to blaspheme that which is holy, and then to go aboute wyth vowes.

26 A wyse kynge destroyeth the vngodly, & bringeth the whele ouer them.

27 The lanterne of þe Lord is the breath of man, and goeth thorow al the inward partes of the body.

28 Mercy and faithfulnes preserue the kynge, and wyth louyng kyndnes his seate is holden vp.

29 The strength of yong men is their worship, and a gray head,

is an honour vnto the aged.

30 Woundes dryue away euel, and so do strips the inward partes of the body.

## CHAPTER 21

THE kinges hert is in the hand of the Lord, lyke as are the ryuers of water: he maye turne it whether so euer he wyll.

2 Euery man thynketh hys owne waye to be ryght, but the Lord iudgeth the herts.

3 To do ryghtuousnes & iudgment is more acceptable to the Lorde then sacrifyce.

4 A presumptuous loke, a proude stomacke, and the lanterne of the vngodly is synne.

5 The deuyces of one þt is diligente, brynge plentuousnes: but he that is vnaduised, commeth vnto pouerte.

6 Who so hoordeth vp ryches wyth the disceatfulnes of his tonge, he is a foole, and lyke vnto them þt seke their own death.

7 þe robberies of the vngodlye shalbe their owne destruccyon, for they wolde not do the thinge that was right.

8 The waies of the froward are straunge, but the worckes of him that is cleane, are ryght

9 It is better to dwell in a corner vnder the house toppe, then wyth a braulynge woman in a wyde house.

10 The soule of the vngodlye wysheth euell, and hath no pytye vpon hys neyghboure.

11 When the scornefull is punyshed, the ignoraunt take the better hede: and when a wyse man is warned, he wyll receaue the more vnderstandynge.

12 The ryghtuous enfourmeth the house of the vngodlye, but the vngodlye goo on styll after their owne wyckednesse.

13 Who so stoppeth hys eare at the cryenge of the pore he shal cry him selfe and not be herd

14 A preuy rewarde pacyfyeth displeasure & a gift in the bosome stilleth furiousnes.

15 The iust delyteth in doinge the thing that is ryghte, but the worckers of wyckednesse abhorre the same.

16 The man that wandereth out of the way of wysdome, shall remayne in the congregacion of the dead.

17 He that hath pleasure in banckettes, shalbe a poore man: Who so deliteth in wyne and delicates, shall not be ryche.

18 The vngodlye shalbe geuen for the ryghtuous, and the wicked for þe iust.

19 It is better to dwell in a wyldernesse, then wyth a chidynge and an angrye woman.

20 In a wyse mans house there is a greate treasure and a plenteousnesse, but a foolish body spendeth vp all.

21 Who so foloweth ryghtuousnes and mercy, fyndeth both life, ryghtuousnes and honoure.

22 A wyse man wynneth the citye of the mighty, and as for strength that they trust in, he bryngeth it downe.

23 Who so kepeth his mouth and his tong, the same kepeth hys soule from troubles.

24 He that is proud & presumptuous, is called a scorneful man, whyche in wrath darre worke malycyouslye.

25 The voluptuousnesse of the slouthfull is hys owne death, for hys handes wyll not laboure.

26 He coueteth and desyreth all the day longe, but the ryghtuous is alwaye geuynge, and kepeth nothynge backe.

27 The sacrifyce of the vngodly is abhominacion, for they offer the thyng that is gotten with wickednes.

28 A false witnesse shall perish, but he that wilbe content to heare, shall alway haue power to speake him selfe.

29 An vngodly man goeth forth rashlye, but the iuste refourmeth his owne waie.

30 There is no wysdome ther is no vnderstandyng, there is no councell agaynste the Lorde.

31 The horse is prepared against the day of battail, but the Lord geueth the victory.

## CHAPTER 22

A good name is more worthe then greate ryches. and louyng fauoure is better then siluer and golde.

2 Whether ryches or pouerty do mete vs, it commeth al of God.

3 A wise man seith the plage and hideth him self, but the folysh go on styl and are punished.

4 The ende of lowlines and þe feare of God, is riches, honour, prosperity and health.

5 Speres and snares are in the way of the froward, bot he that wyll kepe his soule, let hym fle from such.

6 If thou teachest a child in his youth what waye he shuld go, he shal not leaue it when he is old

7 The rich ruleth þe pore, & þe borower is seruant to the lender.

8 He þt soweth wickednes shal repe sorow, & þe rod of his plage shal destroy him

9 A louing eie shalbe blessed, for he geueth of his bread vnto þe pore.

10 Cast out þe scorneful man, & so shal strife go out wt him, yea variance & sclander shal cease.

11 Who so deliteth to be of a cleane herte and of gracious lyppes, the king shall be his frend.

12 The eies of the Lord preserue knowledge, but as for þe words of þe despyteful, he bringeth them to naught.

13 The slouthful body sayeth: ther is a lyon wythoute, I myghte be slayne in the strete.

14 The mouth of an harlot is a

depe pyt, wherein he falleth þt the Lorde is angrye wyth all.

15 Foolishnes sticketh in þe herte of the lad, but the rod of correccion dryueth it awaye.

16 Who so doth a pore man wrong to increase his owne riches, geueth (commenly) vnto the rych, & at the last commeth to pouerte him selfe.

17 My sonne, bow down thine eare, and herken vnto the wordes of wysdome, applye thy mynde vnto my doctryne:

18 for it is a plesaunt thyng if thou kepe it in thyne hert, and practise it in thy mouth:

19 that thou mayest alwaye put thy truste in the Lorde.

20 Haue not I warned the very oft with counsel & lerning?

21 that I might shew the truth andt that thou with the verity myghtest answere them that lay any thynge agaynst the?

22 Se that thou robbe not the pore because he is weake, & oppresse not the simple in iudgment:

23 for the Lorde him selfe wyll defende their cause, and do vyolence vnto them that haue vsed vyolence.

24 Make no frendship with an angry wilful man, and kepe no company wt the furious:

25 lest thou learne hys wayes, and receaue hurte vnto thy soule.

26 Be not thou one of them that bind their hand vpon promyse, and are suerttye: for dett:

27 for if thou hast nothing to paye, he shall take awaye thy bed from vnder the.

28 Thou shalte not remoue the lande marke, which thy fore elders haue sette.

29 Seyst thou nat, that they whyche be diligent in ther busines stand before kinges and not among the simple people?

# CHAPTER 23

WHEN thou syttest at the table to eate with a lorde, order thy selfe manerly with the thinges that are set before þe.

2 Measure thine appetite: and if thou wilt rule thyne owne selfe,

3 be not ouer gredye of his meate, for meate begyleth and disceaueth

4 Take not ouer greate trauayle and labour to be ryche, beware of suche a purpose.

5 Why wylt thou set thyne eie vpon the thing, which sodenly vanysheth awaye? For ryches make them selues wynges, & take their flight lyke an Aegle into the ayre.

6 Eat not þu wt the enuious, & desire not his meat,

7 for he hath a meruelus hert. He saith vnto the: eate & drinke as wher, as his hert is not wt þe.

8 Yea, þe morsels þt thou hast eaten shalt þu perbrake, & lese those swete wordes.

9 Tel nothyng into the eares of a fole, for he wyll despise the wysdome of thy wordes.

10 Remoue not the olde lande marke, and come not within the feld of the fatherles

11 For he that delyuereth them is myghty, euen he shall defend their cause agaynste the.

12 Applie thine herte vnto learning, and thine eare to þe words of knowledge.

13 With holde not correction from the childe, for if thou beatest him with the rodde, he shall not dye thereof.

14 Thou smitest him with the rod. but thou deliuerest his soule from hel.

15 My son, if thy herte receaue wysdome, my herte also shal reioyce

16 yea my reines shalbe very gladde, if thy lyppes speake the thynge that is ryght.

17 Let not thine herte be gelous to folowe synners, but kepe the styl in the feare of the Lord al the daye long:

18 for the ende is not yet come & thy pacient abydyng shal not be in vaine.

19 My sone, geue eare and be wise, so shal thine herte prospere in the way.

20 Kepe no company with wine bybbers & ryotous eaters of flesh

21 for such as be dronkards & riotous shal come to pouerte, & he þt is geuen to much slepe shall go wt a ragged cote.

22 Geue eare vnto thy father þt begat þe, & despise not thy mother when she is olde.

23 Labour for to get þe truth: sell not away wisdome, nurtour and vnderstanding

24 (for a rightuous father is maruelous glad of a wyse son, and deliteth in him)

25 so shal thy father be glad, & thy mother þt bare the shal reioyse.

26 My sonne, geue thyne hert, & let thyne eies haue pleasure in my wayes.

27 For an whore is a depe graue, and an harlot is a narow pyt.

28 She lurketh lyke a thefe, and those þt be not aware she bryngeth vnto her.

29 Wher is wo? wher is sorow? where is strife? where is brauling? wher are wounds without cause? wher be reed eies?

30 Euen among those that be euer at the wyne, and seke out where the best is.

31 Loke not thou vpon the wyne, how redde it is, & what a coloure it geueth in the glasse

32 It goeth downe softly, but at the laste it byteth lyke a serpent, & styngeth, as an Adder.

33 So shall thyne eyes loke vnto straunge wemen, and thyne herte shal muse vpon froward thyngs.

34 Yea thou shalt be as thoughe thou sleptest in the middest of þt sea, or vpon þe toppe of the mast.

35 They wounded me (shalte thou say) but it hath not hurte me, they smote me, but I felt it not. When I am well wakened, I will go to the dryncke agayne.

## CHAPTER 24

Be not thou gelous ouer wycked men, and desyre not thou to be among them.

2 For their herte imagineth to do hurte, and their lippes talke of mischiefe.

3 Thorow wysdome an house shalbe builded, & wt vnderstandyng shalbe set vp.

4 Thorow discrecion shal the chambers he fylled wyth al costly & plesant ryches.

5 A wise man is strong, yea a man of vnderstanding is better then he þt is myghti of strength

6 For wt discrecion must warres be taken in hand, & wher as are many þu can geue councell, there is the victorye.

7 Wisdome is an hye thyng, yea euen to the foole for he dar not open his mouth in the gate.

8 He that Imagyneth myschefe, maye welbe called an vngracious personne.

9 The thoughte of the folysh is synne, & the scorneful is an abhominacion vnto men.

10 If þu be ouersene & negligent in tyme of nede, then is thy strength but smale

11 Delyuer them þt go into death, and are led away to be slayne, & be not negligent therin.

12 If thou wylt saye: I knewe not of it. Thinkest thou þt he which made the herts, doth not consider it? & þt he which regardeth thy soule, seyth it not? Shall not he recompence euerye man accordynge to his workes?

13 My sonne, thou eatest hony & the swete hony combe. because it is good & swete in thy mouthe.

14 Euen so shall the knowledge of wysedome be vnto thy soule, as soone as thou hast gotten it. And there is good hope, yea thy hope shall not be in vanyte.

15 Laye no preuy waite wyckedly vpon the house of the rightuous, and disquiete not his resting place.

16 For a iust man falleth seuen tymes, and riseth vp againe, but the vngodly fal into wickednes.

17 Reioyce not thou at the fall of thyne enemye, and let not thyne herte be glad when he stombleth.

18 Lest the Lord (when he seyth it) be angrie, & turne hys wrath from him vnto the.

19 Let not thy wrath and gelosy moue the, to folowe the wycked and vngodlye.

20 And why? the wycked hath nothyng to hope for, and the candle of the vngodly shal be put oute.

21 My sonne, feare thou the Lord and the kyng, and kepe no company with the sclaunderous:

22 for their destruccion shal come sodenly, and who knoweth the far of them both?

23 These are also the sayenges of the wyse. it is not good, to haue respect ofe any person in iudgment.

24 He that saieth to the vngodly: thou art rightuous, him shal the people curse yea the comenty shal abhorre hym.

25 But they that rebuke the vngodly shalbe commended and a ryche blessynge shall come vpon them.

26 He maketh him selfe to be well loued, that geueth a good answere.

27 Fyrste make vp thy worke that is wythout, & loke wel vnto that which þu hast in the felde, & then buyld thyne house.

28 Be no false witnesse against thy neighbour hurte hym not with thy lyppes.

29 Saye not I wil handle him, euen as he hath delte wt me and wil reward euery man according to his dedes.

30 I went by the felde of þe slouthful, and by the vineiarde of the feld of the slouthful and by the vyneyeardes of þe folish man.

31 And lo, it was all couered wyth nettels, and stode ful of thistles. and the stone wall was broken doune.

32 Thys I saw, and consydered it well I loked vpon it, and toke it for a warnyng.

33 Yea slepe on styl a lytle, slomber a lytle, fold thyne handes together yet a lytle,

34 so shal pouertye come vnto the as one that trauayleth by the way, and necessite like a weapened man.

## CHAPTER 25

These also are the sayinges of Salomon, which the men of Ezekiah Kynge of Iuda gathered together.

2 It is þe honour of God to kepe a thing secret, but the kings honour is to serch out a thing

3 The heauen is hye, the earth is depe, þe kings hert is vnsearcheable.

4 Take the drosse from the syluer, and ther shalbe a cleane vessel therof.

5 Take awaye vngodlynes from the king, & his seat shalbe stablished wt ryghtuousnes

6 Put not forth thy self in the presence of þe king, & prayse not into the place of great men.

7 Better is it that it be sayde vnto the: come vp hyther, then thou to be set doun in the presence of the prince whom thou seist with thine eyes.

8 Be not hastye to go to the law, lest happely thou order thy selfe so at the laste, that thy neighbour put the to shame.

9 Handle thy mater wt thy neyghbour him self, and dyscouer not an other mans secrete:

10 lest when men heare therof, it turne to thy dishonoure, and lest thine euell name do not ceasse.

11 A worde speken in due season, is lyke apples of golde in a syluer dish.

12 The correction of the wise is to an obedient eare, a golden cheine & a Iewel of gold.

13 Lyke as the wynter coole in the haruest, so is a faithfull messenger to him þt sent him, & refresheth his masters mynd.

14 Whoso maketh great boasts & geueth nothing, is like cloudes & wind without rain.

15 With pacience may a prince be pacified, & wt a soft tong may rigoriousnes be broken.

16 If thou findest hony, eate so much as is sufficient forth lest thou be ouerful, & perbrake it out agayne.

17 Wythdraw thy fote from thy neighbours house, lest he be wery of the, and so abhor the.

18 Who so beareth false wytnesse agaynst hys neyghboure, he is a verye speare, a sweardе, and a sharpe arowe.

19 The hope of the vngodlye in tyme of neade, is lyke a rotten toth and a slippery fote.

20 Who so singeth a song to a wycked her hert, clotheth him wt rags in the cold & poureth vynegar vpon chalke.

21 If thyne enemy honger, fead him: if he thyrst, geue hym drinke:

22 for so shalt þu heape coles of fyre vpon his head, and the Lord shal reward the.

23 The North wind driueth away the raine, euen so doth an earnest sober countenances backbyters tong.

24 It is better to sit in a corner vnder þe rose, then wt a brauling woman in a wide house

25 A good reporte out of a farre contre, is like could water to a thirsty soule.

26 A ryghtuous man falling down before þe vngodlye, is like a troubled wel & a spring þt is destroyed.

27 Like as it is not good to eate to much hony, euen so he þt wil search out hyghe things, it shalbe to heuy for him.

28 He þt can not rule him self, is like a city which is broken doune, & hath no walles.

# CHAPTER 26

Like as snow is not mete in sommer, nor raine in haruest: euen so is worship vnsemelye for a foole

2 Like as the bryd and the swalowe take their flyght and fle here and ther, so the curse that is geuen in vayne, shall not lighte vpon a man.

3 Vnto the horse belongeth a whyppe, to the Asse a brydle, and a rodde to the fooles backe.

4 Geue not the foole an answere after hys folyshnesse, lest thou become lyke vnto hym:

5 but make the fole an answer to his folishnes, lest he be wise in his own conceat.

6 He is lame of his fete yea dronken is he in vanite, þt committeth any thing to a fole.

7 Like as it is an vnsemely thing to haue legs & yet to halt euen so is a parable in þe foles mouthe.

8 He that setteth a foole in hye dignity, that is euen as if a man did cast a precious stone vpon the gallous.

9 A parable in a fooles mouth is lyke a thorne that prycketh a dronken man in the hand.

10 A man of experience dyscerneth all thynges well, but whoso hyreth a foole, hyreth such one as will take no hede.

11 Lyke as the dogge turueth agayne to hys vomyte, euen so a foole beginneth hys folishnesse agayne a fresh.

12 If thou seiest a man that is wyse in his owne conceate, there is more hope in a fole then in him.

13 The slouthful sayeth: there is a leopard in the way, and a lion in the myddest of the stretes.

14 Lyke as the dore turneth aboute vpon the thresholde, euen so doth the slouthfull welter hym self in his bedde.

15 The slouthful bodye thrusteth his hand into his bosome, and it greueth him to put it agayne to his mouth.

16 The slogard thynketh hym selfe wyser then? .vij. men þt sit & teach.

17 Who so goeth by & medleth wyth other mens stryfe, he is lyke one that taketh a dog by the eares.

18 Lyke os one shutteth deadly arowes and dartes out of a preuy place, euen so doth a dissembler wyth his neighboure.

19 And then saith he: I dyd it but in sporte.

20 Where no wodde is, there the fyre goeth oute: and where the backcbyter is taken awaye, there the stryfe ceaseth.

21 Coales kyndle heate, and wode the fire: euen so doth a braulynge felowe stere vp varyaunce.

22 A slaunderers wordes are lyke flaterye, but they pearse the inwarde partes of the bodye.

23 Venimous lippes and a wicked herte, are lyke a potsherde couered with syluer drosse.

24 An enemy dissembleth with hys lyps, and in the meane season he ymagineth mischefe:

25 but when he speaketh fayre, beleue hym not, for ther are seuen abhomynacons in hys herte.

26 Who so kepeth euel wil, secretly to do hurte, his malice shalbe shewed before the whole congregacion.

27 Who diggeth vp a pyt, shal fal therin: and he that weltreth a stone shal stomble vpon it him selfe.

28 A dissembling tong hateth one that rebuketh hym, and a flattering mouth worketh mischefe.

## CHAPTER 27

MAKE not thy boaste of to morow, for thou knowest not what maye happen to day.

2 Let another man praise the, & not thine own mouth yea other folkes lips, & not thine.

3 The stone is heuy, and the sand weyghty: but a foles wrath is heuier then then they both

4 Wrath is a cruel thing, and furyousnesse is a verye tempeste: yea who is able to abyde enuye?

5 An open rebuke is beter then a secrete loue.

6 Faythfull are the woundes of a louer, but the kysses of an enemy are disceatful

7 He that is ful, abhorreth an hony combe: but vnto him that is hongry, euery sower thing is swete.

8 He that oft times flytteth, is like a bird þt forsaketh her nest.

9 The hert is glad of a swet ointment and sauoure, but a stomake that can geue good councel, reioiseth a mans neyghboure.

10 Thine owne frend, and thy fathers frend se thou forsake not, but go not into thy brothers house in tyme of thy trouble. Better is a frend at hand, then a brother far of.

11 My son, be wyse, and thou shalt make me a glad herte: so that I shall make answere vnto my rebukers.

12 A wyse man seynge the plage wyll hyde hym selfe, as for fooles they go on styll, and suffer harme.

13 Take hys garmente that is suertye for a straunger, & take a pledge of him for the vnknowne mans sake.

14 He that is to hasty to prayse his neyghbour aboue measure, shalbe taken as one þt geueth hym and euel report.

15 A braulling woman and the rose of the house dropping in a rainy day may wel be compared together.

16 He that refrayneth her, refrayneth the wynde, and holdeth oyle fast in hys hande.

17 Lyke as one yron whetteth another, so doth one man conforte another.

18 Who so kepeth his fyggetre, shall enioye the fruytes therof he that wayteth vpon hys master, shal come to honoure.

19 Lyke as in one water there appeare diuerse faces, euen so diuerse men haue dyuerse hertes.

20 Lyke as hell and destruccyon are neuer full, euen so the eyes of men canne neuer be satysfyed.

21 Siluer is tryed in the mold, and golde in the fornace and so is a man, when he is openlye praysed to his face.

22 Though thou shouldest bray a foole wyth a pestell in morter like otemel, yet wyll not his folyshnesse go from hym.

23 Se that thou know the number of thy catell thy selfe, and loke wel to thy flockes.

24 For riches abyde not alway, & the crowne endureth not for euer.

25 The hey groweth, the grasse commeth vp, & herbes are gathered in the mountaynes.

26 The lambes shall clothe the, and for the gotes

27 thou shalt haue goates mylcke ynough to fede the, to vpholde thy housholde, and to susteyne thy maydens.

## CHAPTER 28

THE vngodly flyeth no man chasyng him, but the rightuous standeth styf as lyon.

2 Because of synne the lande doth oft chang her prynce: but thorowe men of vnderstandynge and wysdome a realme endureth long.

3 One pore man oppressinge another by uiolence is lyke a continuall rayne that destroieth the fruyte.

4 They that forsake the lawe, prayse the vngodly: but such as kepe the law abhorre them.

5 Wycked men discerue not the thynge that is ryght, but they that seke after the Lord, discusse al thynges.

6 A poore man leadyng a godly lyfe, is better then the rych þt goeth in froward wayes.

7 Who so kepeth the lawe, is a childe of vnderstandynge: but he that fedeth ryotous men shameth hys father.

8 Who so increaseth hys ryches by vauntage and wynnynge, let hym gather them to helpe the poore wyth al.

9 He that turneth away his eare from hearing the lawe, his prayer shalbe abhorred.

10 Who so leadeth the ryghtuous into an euel waye, shal fal into his owne pit, but, the iust shall haue the good in possession.

11 The rych man thyncketh him selfe to be wyse, but the poore that hath vnderstandynge can perceaue him well ynough.

12 When ryghtuous men are in prosperite, then doth honoure floryshe: but when the vngodly come vp, the state of men chaungeth.

13 He that hydeth hys synnes, shall not prosper: but who so knowledgeth them and forsaketh them shal haue mercy.

14 Well is hym þt standeth alwaye in awe: as for hym that hardeneth his hert, he shall fal into myschyefe.

15 Lyke as a rorarynge lyon and an hongry beare, euen so is an vngodly prynce ouer the pore people.

16 Wher the prynce is wythout vnderstandyng, ther is greate oppression and wronge: but if he be such one as hateth

couetousnesse he shall longe raygne.

17 He that by vyolence sheddeth anye mannes bloude, shall be a rennagate vnto his graue, and no man shall be able to succoure hym.

18 Who so leadetth a godly and an inocent life, shalbe, safe: but he that goeth frowarde wayes, shall once haue a fall.

19 He that tylleth his lande, shall haue plenteousnesse of bread: but he that foloweth ydilnesse, shall haue pouerte ynough.

20 A faithfull man is greatlye to be commended, but he that maketh to much haste for to be rych, shall not be vngyltye.

21 To haue respecte of persons in iudgment is not good: And why? he wil do wrong, yea euen for a pece of bread.

22 He that wyll be ritch all to soone, hath an euell eye, and considereth not, that pouertye shall come vpon him.

23 He that rebuketh a man, shal fynde more fauoure at the laste, then he that flattereth him.

24 Who so robbeth hys father and mother, and sayeth it is no synne: the same is like vnto a murtherer.

25 He that is of a proud stomacke, stereth vp strife but he that putteth hys truste in the Lorde, shalbe wel fedde.

26 He that trusteth in his own hert, is a foole: but he þt dealeth wysely, shal be safe.

27 He that geueth vnto the poore, shall not wante: but he that turneth awaye hys eyes from suche as be in necessytye, shal suffer greate pouertye hym selfe.

28 When the vngodlye are come vp, men are fayne to hyde them selues: but when they perysh, the ryghtuous increase.

## CHAPTER 29

HE that is styfnecked and wyll not be refourmed, shal sodenly be destroied without any helpe

2 Wher the rightuous haue the ouer hand the people are in prosperitye: but wher the vngodly beareth rule, ther the people mourne.

3 Who so loueth wysdome, maketh his father a glad man: but he þt kepeth harlottes, spendeth away þt he hath.

4 With true iudgment the kyng setteth vp the land, but if he be a man that taketh giftes, he turneth it vpsyde downe.

5 Whoso flattereth hys neyghboure, layeth a nette for hys fete.

6 The synne of the wycked is his owne snare, but the ryghtuons shall be glad and reioyse.

7 The righteous consydereth the cause of þe poore, but the vngodly regardeth no vnderstandynge.

8 Wycked people brynge a cytye in decay, but wyse men sette it vp agayne.

9 If a wyse man go to lawe wyth a foole (whether he deale wyth hym frendly or roughly) he getteth no rest.

10 The bloude thyrstye hate the ryghtuous, but the iust seke his soule.

11 A foole poureth out his spirit altogether, but a wyse man kepeth it in till afterwarde.

12 If a prynce delyte iu lyes, all his seruauntes are vngodly.

13 The pore and the lender mete together, the Lord lyghteneth both their eies

14 The seate of the Kynge that faythfully iudgeth the poore, shall contynue sure for euermore.

15 The rod and correction myuister wysdome, but if a chylde be not loked vnto, he bringeth his mother to shame.

16 When the vngodly come vp, wyckednesse increaseth: but the righteous shall se their fal.

17 Nurtour thy sonne with correction, and he shall comforte the, yea he shall do the good at thyne herte.

18 Wher no Prophete is ther the people perysh: but wel is hym that kepeth the law.

19 A seruaunte wyll not be the better for wordes for thoughe he vnderstande, yet wyll he not regarde them,

20 Yf thou seist a man that is hastye to speake vnaduysed, thou, mayest trust a foole more then hym.

21 He that delicately bringeth vp his seruaunt from a chyld, shall make hym hys master at length.

22 An angrye man stereth vp stryfe, and he that beareth euell wyll in hys mynde, doeth muche euill.

23 After pryde commeth a fal, but a lowly spirit bringeth great worshippe.

24 Who so kepeth companye wyth a thyefe, hateth hys owne soule: he heareth blasphemyes, and telleth it not fourth.

25 He that feareth men, shall haue a fall: but whoso putteth his trust in the Lorde shall come to honoure.

26 Manye there be that seke the Princes fauoure, but euery mans iudgement commeth from the Lorde.

27 The ryghtuous abhorreth the vngodlye: but as for those that be in the ryght way, the wicked hate them.

## CHAPTER 30

THE wordes of Agur the sunne. of Iakeh. The prophecye of a true faithful man, whom God hath helped, whom God had comforted and norished.

2 For though I am þe least of al, & haue no mans vnderstanding

3 (for I neuer learned wysdom) yet haue I vnderstanding, & am wel

infourmed in godly thinges.

4 Who hath climed vp into heauen? Who hath come down from thence? Who hath holden the wynd fast in his hand? Who hath comprehended the waters in a garment? Who hath set al the endes of the worlde? What is his name, or his sonnes name? Canst thou tel?

5 All the wordes of God are pure & cleane, for he is a shyeld vnto al them, þt put theyr trust in him.

6 Put thou nothing therfore vnto hys wordes, lest he reproue the, and thou be founde a lyar.

7 Two thynges I requyre of the, that thou wilt not denye me before I dye,

8 Remoue fro me vanite and lyes: geue me neither pouerte nor ryches, onely graunte me a necessary lyuyng.

9 Lest if I be to full, I denye the, & say: what felow is the Lord? And lest I beynge constrayned thorow pouerte, fall vnto stealyng, and forsweare the name of my God.

10 Accuse not a seruaunt vnto hys master, lest he speake euell of the also, and thou be hurt.

11 He that bringeth vp an euell reporte vpon þe generacion of hys father and mother, is not worthy to be commended.

12 The generacion that thynke them selfes cleane, shall not be clensed from their filthynesse.

13 There are people that haue a proude loke, and cast vp their eye lyddes.

14 This peoples teth are swerdes, and with their chafte bones they consume and deuour the simple of the earth, and the poore from among men.

15 This generacion (whiche is lyke an horslech) hath two daughters: the one is called, fetch hither, and the other bring hyther.

16 There be thre thinges that are neuer satisfied, and the forth sayeth neuer hoo. The hell, a womans wombe, and the earthe hath neuer water ynough. As for fyre, it sayeth neuer, hoo.

17 Who so laugheth hys father to scorne, and setteth his mothers commaundement at naughte: the rauens pycke out hys eyes in the valley, and deuoured be he of the yonge Aegles.

18 There be thre thinges to hye for me, and as for the forth, it passeth my knowledge.

19 The way of an Aegle in the ayre, the way of a serpent ouer a stone, the waye of a shyp in the sea, and the waye of a man with a yonge woman.

20 Such is the way also of a wife that breaketh wedlocke, which wipeth her mouth like as when she hath eaten, & sayeth. As for me, I haue done no harme.

21 Thorow thre thinges the earth is disquieted, & the fourthe may it not beare:

22 Thorow a seruaunt that beareth rule, thorow a foole that hath greate ryches,

23 thorow an ydle houswyfe, & thorow an handmayden that is heyre to her mastres.

24 There be foure thinges in the earth, þt which are very litle: but in wysedome they exceade the wyse.

25 The Emmettes are but a weake people, yet gather they their meate together in the haruest.

26 The Conyes are but a feble folke, yet make they their couches amonge the rockes.

27 The greshoppers haue not a gyde, yet go thei forth together by heapes.

28 The spyder laboureth with her handes, & that in the kynges palace.

29 There be thre thinges that go stifly, but the going of the fourth is the godlyest of all.

30 A Lyon, which is kinge of beastes, & geueth place to no man:

31 A cock ready to fight: A ramme and a kyng that goeth forth with his people.

32 If thou be so folish to magnifie thy selfe, or medlest with any such thing, then laye thine hande vpon thy mouth.

33 Who so cherneth mylke, maketh butter: he that rubbeth hys nose, maketh it blede: and he that causeth wrath, bringeth forth stryfe.

# CHAPTER 31

THE wordes of kyng Lamuell, and the Prophecye that his mother taughte hym.

2 My sonne, thou sonne of my body: O my deare beloued sonne,

3 geue not ouer thy substaunce & mynde vnto women, whiche are the destruction euen of kinges.

4 O Lamuel, geue kynges no wyne, geue kynges & princes no strong drincke:

5 lest they beyng dronken forget the law, & regarde not the cause of the poore, and of al such as be in aduersite.

6 Geue strong drinke vnto suche as are condempned to death, & wyne vnto those that mourne:

7 that they may drinke it, & forget their misery and aduersitie.

8 Be thou an aduocate, and stande in iudgement thy selfe, to speake for all such as be domme & socourles.

9 With thy mouth defende the thyng that is lawful and right, and the cause of þe poore and helpelesse.

10 Aleph. Who so fyndeth an honest faythfull woman, she is much more worth then pearles.

11 Beth. The hert of her husband may safely trust in her, so þt he shal haue no nede of spoyles.

12 Gimel. She will do him good & not euell all the dayes of

her lyfe.

13 Daleth. She occupyeth woll and flax, and laboureth gladly with her handes.

14 He. She is lyke a merchauntes shyppe, that bringeth her vitayles from a farre.

15 Vau. She is vp in the night season, to prouyde meate for her housholde, and foode for her maydens.

16 Zain. She considreth lande, & byeth it, & wyth þe frute of her handes she planteth a vyneyarde.

17 Heth. She gyrdeth her loynes with strength, and courageth her armes.

18 Teth. And if she perceyue that her houswyfrye doth good, her candle goeth not out by night.

19 Iod. She layeth her fingers to the spyndle, & her hande taketh holde of the rocke.

20 Caph. She openeth her hande to the poore, yea, she stretched forthe her handes too suche as haue nede.

21 Lamed. She feareth not that the colde of wynter shall hurte her house, for all her housholde folkes are double clothed.

22 Mem. She maketh her selfe fayre ornamentes, her clothyng is whyte silke and purple.

23 Nun. Her husband is much set by in the gates, when he sitteth among the rulers of the lande.

24 Samech. She maketh cloth of silke & selleth it, and deliuereth a gyrdle vnto the marchaunt.

25 Ain. Strength and honour is her clothynge, & in the latter daye she shall reioyse.

26 Phe. She openeth her mouth with wysdome, and in her tonge is the lawe of grace.

27 Zade. She loketh well to the wayes of her housholde, & eateth not her bread with ydelnes.

28 Koph. Her chyldren arise, and call her blessed: & her husbande maketh much of her.

29 Res. Many daughters there be that gather riches together, but thou goest aboue them all.

30 Sin. As for fauour, it is disceatfull, & beuty is a vayne thing: but a woman that feareth the Lord, she is worthy to be praysed.

31 Thau. Geue her of the frute of her handes, & let her owne workes prayse her in the gates.

# Ecclesiastes

## CHAPTER 1

THESE arethe wordes of the Preacher, þe sonne of Dauid, king of Ierusalem

2 All is but vanitie (sayeth þe preacher) all is but playne vanite.

3 For what els hath a man, of all the laboure that he taketh vnder the Sunne?

4 One generacion passeth away, another commeth, but the earth abideth styll.

5 The Sunne aryseth, the sunne goeth doune, and returneth to his place, that he may there ryse vp agayn.

6 The wynde goeth towarde the South, & fetcheth hys compasse about vnto the North, & so turneth into him self agayn.

7 All floudes runne into the sea, & yet the sea is not filled: for loke vnto what place the waters runne, thence they come agayn.

8 All thinges are so harde, þt no man can expresse them. The eye is not satisfied with sight, the eare is not filled with hearing.

9 The thing that hath bene cometh to passe agayn: & the thing that hath bene done, is done agayn, there is no new thyng vnder the Sunne.

10 Is there any thyng wherof it may be sayd: lo, this is new? For it was longe a goo in the tymes that haue bene before vs.

11 The thing that is past, is out of remembraunce: Euen so the thynges that are for to come, shal no more be thought vpon among theim that come after.

12 I myself the Preacher, beynge kynge of Israel & Hierusalem,

13 applied my mynde to seke out & search for the knowlege of all thinges that are done vnder heauen. Such trauayle and labour hath God geuen vnto the chyldren of men, too exercyse them selfes therein.

14 Thus I haue considred all the thynges þt come to passe vnder the Sunne, & so, they are all but vanitie & vexacion of mynde.

15 The croked can not be mayde strayght, & the fautes can not be numbred.

16 I commoned wyth myne owne hert, saying: lo, I am come to a greate estate, & haue gotten more wisdome, then all they that haue bene before me in Ierusalem. Yea, my hert had great experience of wysedome & knowlege,

17 for there vnto I applyed my mynde: that I might knowe what were wisdome & vnderstanding, what were errour & folishnes. And I perceyued that this also was but a vexacion of minde:

18 for where much wysdome is, there is also great trauayle and disquietnes: and the more knowledge a man hath, the more is his care.

## CHAPTER 2

THEN sayde I thus in my herte: Now go to, I will take myne ease and haue good dayes. But lo, that was vanitie also:

2 in so much that I sayd vnto laughter: thou art mad, and to myrthe: what doest thou?

3 So I thought in my hert, to withdrawe my flesh from wyne, to apply my mynde vnto wysdome, & to comprehende folishnes vntill þe time that (among all þe thinges which are vnder the sunne) I might se what were best for men to do, so long as they lyue vnder heauen.

4 I made Gorgious fayre workes. I buylded me houses, & planted vineyardes.

5 I made me ortchardes & gardens of pleasure, & planted trees in them of al maner frutes.

6 I made poles of water, to water þe grene & frutefull trees withall.

7 I bought seruauntes and maidens and had a greate housholde, As for catell and shepe, I had more substance of them then all they that were before me in Ierusalem,

8 I gathered syluer and gold together, euen a treasure of kynges and landes. I prouyded

me syngers and wemen which coulde playe of instrumentes, to make men myrth and pastime. I gat me drinckyng cuppes also and glasses.

9 Shortly, I was greater and in more worshippe, then all my predecessours in Ierusalem. For wysdome remained with me

10 and loke what soeuer myne eyes desyred, I let them haue it: and wherein soeuer my herte delited or had any pleasure, I wyth helde it not from it. Thus my herte reioysed in all that I dyd, and this I toke for the porcion of all my trauayle.

11 But when I consydered all the workes that my handes had wrought, and all the laboures that I had taken therein, lo, all was but but vanytye and vexacion of mind, & nothyng of any value vnder the Sunne.

12 Then turned I me to consyder wysdome, erroure and folyshnesse (for what is he amonge men, that myght be compared to me the kyng in suche workes?)

13 and I saw that wysdome excelleth folishnesse, as farre as lyght doth darcknesse.

14 For a wyse man beareth his eyes about in his head, but the foole goth in the darcknesse. I perceaued also that they both had one end.

15 Then thought I in my mynde: If it happen vnto the foole as it doeth vnto me, what nedeth, me then to laboure anye more for wysdome? So I confessed wythin my herte, that thys also was but vanitye.

16 For the wyse are euer as lytle in remembraunce as the folish, and al the daies for to come shalbe forgotten, yea the wyse man dyeth as well as the fole.

17 Thus began I to be werye of my lyfe, in so muche that I coulde awaie wyth nothynge that is done vnder the Sunne, for all was but vanytye and vexacion of mynde:

18 Yea I was weerye of al my laboure, which I had taken vnder the Sunne, because I shoulde be fayne to leaue them vnto another man, that commeth after me

19 for who knoweth, whether he shalbe a wyse man or afole? And yet shall he be lorde of al my laboures, which I wyth suche wysdome haue taken vnder the Sunne. Is not this a vayne thynge.

20 So I turned me to refraine my mynd from all such trauayle, as I toke vnder the Sunne

21 for somuch as a man shuld weery hym selfe with wisdome, wt vnderstanding & oportunyte & yet be faine to leaue his laboures vnto another, that neuer swet. for them. This is also a vayne thinge and a greate miserie.

22 For what getteth a man of all the laboure and trauaile of his mind, þt he taketh vnder þe Sunne,

23 but heauinesse, sorow and disquietnes al þe daeis of his life? In so much that his herte can not rest in þe night. Is not this also a vaine thing?

24 Is it not better then, for a man to eat & drinke, and his soule to be mery in his labour? Yea I sawe that thys also was a gyfte of God:

25 For who may eat, drinke, or bring any thing to passe wythout hym? And why?

26 he geueth vnto man, what it pleaseth him: whether it be wysdome, vnderstandyng, or gladnesse. But vnto the sinner he geueth werines and sorow þt he may gather and heape togather the thing that afterward shalbe geuen vnto him whom it pleaseth God. This is now a vayne thynge yea a very disquietnes and vexacion of mind.

# CHAPTER 3

Every thynge hath a tyme, yea all that is vnder the heauen, hath his conuenient season.

2 Their is a tyme to be borne, & a tyme to dye. Ther is tyme to plant, and a time to plucke vp the thing, that is planted.

3 A tyme to slay, and a tyme to make whole. A time to breake down, & a time to bild vp.

4 A time to wepe, and a time to laugh: A time to mourne, and a tyme to daunce:

5 A time to cast away stones, and a tyme to gather stones together: A tyme to enbrace, and a tyme to refrayne from enbrasyng.

6 A time to win, and a tyme to lose: A time to spare, and a tyme to spend:

7 A time to cut in peces, and a time to sowe together: A time to kepe silence, and a time to speake:

8 A tyme to loue, and a tyme to hate: A tyme of war, and time of peace:

9 What hath a man els (þt doth any thinge) but werines & labour?

10 For as touchyng the trauayle and carefulnes which God hath geuen vnto men, I se þt he hath geuen it them, to be exercised in it.

11 Al this hath he ordeyned maruelous goodly: to euery thing his due tyme He hath planted ignorance also in the hertes of men, þt thei shuld not find out þe ground of his workes, whiche he doth from þe beginning to the end.

12 So I perceiued, þt in these thinges their is nothinge better for a man, then to be mery and to do wel so long as he liueth.

13 For al þt a man eateth & drinketh, yea whatsoeuer a man enioyeth of al his labour, the same is a gyfte of God.

14 I considered also that whatsoeuer God doth, it continueth for euer, & þt no thing can be put vnto it nor taken

# ECCLESIASTES

from it: & þt god doth it to the intent, that men shuld feare him.

15 The thing þt hath bene, is now: & þt thing that is for to come, hath bene afore time, for God restoreth agayne the thynge that was paste.

16 Moreouer, I saw vnder the sunne vngodlyenesse in the steade of iudgemente, and iniquitye in steade of ryghtuousnesse.

17 Then thought I in my mind: God shal separat the rightuous from þe vngodly, & then shalbe þt time and iudgment of al councels and worckes.

18 I comened with mine own hert also concerning the children of men how God hath chosen them & yet letteth them apeare: as though they were beastes:

19 for it hapeneth vnto men as it doth vnto beastes, & as the one dieth, so dyeth the other: yea, thei haue both one maner of byrth so that (in this) a man hathe no preemynence aboue a beast, but al are subdued vnto vanitie.

20 They go all vnto one place, for as they be all of dust, so shal they all turne vnto dust agayne.

21 Who knoweth the sprete of man that goeth vpwarde, & the breath of the beast that goeth doune into the earth?

22 Wherefore I perceyue, that there is nothing better for a man, then to be ioyfull in his labour, for that is hys porcion. But who will bring him to se the thing that shall come after hym?

## CHAPTER 4

So I turned me, & considred al the violent wrong that is done vnder the sunne: & beholde, the teares of such as were oppressed, & there was no man to comforte them or that wolde deliuer & defende them from the violence of their oppressours.

2 Wherfor I iudged those that are dead, to be more happy then such as be alyue:

3 yea, hym that is yet vnborne to be better at ease then they both, because he seith not the miserable workes that are done vnder the sunne.

4 Agayn, I sawe that all trauayle and diligence of labour was hated of euery man. This is also a vayn thinge, and a vexacion of mynde.

5 The foole foldeth his handes together, and eateth vp hys owne flesh.

6 One hand full (sayeth he) is better with rest, then bothe the handes full with labour and trauayle.

7 Moreouer, I turned me, & beholde yet another vanitie vnder the Sunne.

8 There is one man, no mo but him self alone, hauing neither childe nor brother: yet is there no ende of his carefull trauayle, hys eyes can not be satysfied with ryches, (yet doth he not remembre him selfe, & saye:) For whome do I take such trauayle? For whose pleasure do I thus consume away my lyfe? This is also a vayne & miserable thynge.

9 Therfore two are better then one, for they may well enioy the profyt of their labour.

10 If one of them fall, hys companion helpeth hym vp agayn: But wo is hym that is alone, for if he fall, he hathe not another to helpe hym vp.

11 Agayn, when two slepe together, they are warme: but how can a body be warme alone?

12 One maye be ouercome, but two may make resistaunce: A three folde cable is not lightly broken.

13 A poore chylde beynge wyse, is better then an olde kynge, that doteth, & can not beware in tyme to come.

14 Some one commeth out of pryson, & is made a kyng: and another which is born in the kyngdome, commeth vnto pouerte.

15 And I perceyued, that al men lyuyng vnder þe Sunne, go with the seconde chylde, that commeth vp in the steade of the other.

16 As for the people that haue bene before hym, and that come after him, they are innumerable: yet is not their ioy the greater thorow hym. This is also a vayne thyng and a vexacion of mynde.

## CHAPTER 5

When thou commest into the house of God, kepe thy fote & draw nye, that thou mayest heare: that is better then the offeringes of fooles, for they knowe not what euell they do.

2 Be not hasty with thy mouth, & let not thyne herte speake any thyng rashly before God. For God is in heauen, & thou vpon earth, therfore let thy wordes be few.

3 For where muche carefulnesse is, there are many dreames: and where many wordes are, there men may heare fooles.

4 If thou make a vowe vnto God, be not slacke to perfourme it. As for folish vowes, he hath no pleasure in them.

5 If thou promise any thynge, paye it: for better it is that thou make no vowe then that thou shouldest promyse, and not paye.

6 Vse not thy mouth to cause thy flesh for to synne, that thou say not before the aungell: my foolishnesse is in the faute. For then God will be angry at thy voyce, & destroye all the workes of thyne handes.

7 And why? where as are many dreames and many wordes, there are also diuerse vanities: but loke that thou feare God.

8 If thou seyst the poore to be oppressed and wrongeously dealt withall, so that equite & the

right of the law is wrasted in the lande: maruell not thou at such iudgement, for one great man kepeth touch with another, and the mightye helpe them selfes together.

9 The whole lande also with the feldes and all that is therin, is in subiection & bondage vnto the kyng.

10 He þt loueth money, will neuer be satisfied wyth money: and who so deliteth in ryches, shall haue no profit therof. Is not this also a vayn thyng?

11 Where as much ryches is, there are many also that spende them away. And what pleasure more hath he that possesseth them, sauyng that he may loke vpon them with hys eyes?

12 A labouryng man slepeth swetely, whether it be litle or much that he eateth: but the aboundaunce of the ryche wil not suffre him to slepe.

13 Yet is there a sore plague, whiche I haue sene vnder the sunne (namely) ryches kept to the hurt of him that hath them in possession.

14 For oft tymes they perishe with his greate misery & trouble: and if he haue a chylde, it getteth nothynge.

15 Lyke as he came naked out of his mothers wombe, so goeth he thyther agayn, and carieth nothing away with hym of all his labour.

16 This is a miserable plage, that he shal go away euen as he came. What helpeth it hym then, that he hath labored in the wynde?

17 All the dayes of his life also muste he eate in the darke, with greate carefulnesse, syckenesse and sorowe.

18 Therefore me thincke it a better and a fayrer thinge a manne to eate and drynck, and to be refreshied of all hys laboure, that he taketh vnder the Sunne all the dayes of hys lyfe which God geueth hym, for this is hys porcyon.

19 For vnto whom soeuer God geueth ritches, goodes and power, he geueth it him to enioy it, to take it for hys porcyon, and to be refreshed of his laboure: thys is nowe the gyfte of God.

20 For he thyncketh not muche how longe he shall lyue, for so much as God fylleth his herte with gladnesse.

## CHAPTER 6

Here is yet a plage vnder the Sunne, and it is a general thing among men:

2 when God geueth a man rytches, goodes and honoure, so that he wanteth nothynge of all that hys herte can desyre: and yet God geueth hym not leaue to enioye the same, but another man spendeth them. Thys is a vayne thynge and a myserable plage.

3 If a man begette an hundred chyldren, and lyue manye yeares, so that his dayes are many in number, and yet cannot enioy his good neyther be buried: as for him I saye, that an vntymely byrth is better then he.

4 For he commeth to naughte, and goeth hys waye into darckenes, and his name is forgotten.

5 More ouer, he seith not the Sunne, and knoweth of no rest neyther here ner there:

6 Yea thoughe he lyued two thousande yeares, yet hath he no good lyfe. Come not all to one place?

7 All the laboure that a man taketh, is for him selfe, and yet hys desyre is neuer fylled after hys mynde.

8 For what hath the wyse moore then the foole. What helpeth it the poore, that he knoweth to walcke before the lyuynge?

9 The syght of the eyes is better, then that the soule shoulde so departe awaye. How be it thys is also a vayne thynge and a dysquyetnesse of mynde.

10 What is more excellente then man? yet can he not in the lawe get the vyctorye of him that is myghtyer then he:

11 A vaine thing is it to cast out many wordes, but what hath a man els?

12 For who knowth what is good for man lyuynge, in the dayes of hys vayne life, whych is but a shadowe? Or, who wyll tell a man, what shall happen after him vnder the Sunne.

## CHAPTER 7

A good name is more worth then a precious oyntemente, and the day of death is better then the daye of byrthe.

2 It is better to go into an house of mourning, then into a bancketynge house. For there is the ende of all men, and he that is lyuyng, taketh it to hert.

3 It is better to be sory then to laugh, for when the countenaunce is heauye, the herte is ioyfull.

4 The herte of the wyse is in the mournyng house, but the hert of the folish is in the house of myrthe.

5 It is better to geue eare to the chastenyng of a wyse man, then to heare the song of fooles.

6 For the laughing of fooles is lyke the crackinge of thornes vnder a pot, And that is but a vayne thing.

7 Who so doeth wronge, maketh a wyse man to goo out of hys wytte, and destroyeth a gentle herte.

8 The ende of a thyng is better then the begynnynge. The pacient of spirite is better then the hye mynded.

9 Be not hastelye angrye in thy mynde, for wrath resteth in the bosome of a foole.

10 Saye not thou: What is the cause that the dayes of the olde tyme were better, then they that

be now? for that were no wyse question.

11 Wysdome is better then ritches, yea much more worth then the eye syght.

12 For wysdome defendeth as well as money, and the excellent knowledge and wysdome geueth life vnto him that hath it in possession.

13 Consyder the worke of God, how that no man can make þe thyng strayght whych he maketh croked.

14 Vse well the tyme of prosperyty, and remembre the time of misfortune: for God maketh the one by þe other. so that a man can fynd nothyng els.

15 These .ij. things also haue I considered in the tyme of vanytye: that þe iust man perisheth for hys ryghtuousnes sake, and the vngodly lyued in hys wickednesse.

16 Therefore be thou nether to rightuous ner ouer wyse, that thou perysh not:

17 be nether to vnrightuous also ner to folyshe, lest thou dye before thy tyme.

18 It is good for the to take hold of thys, and not to let that go out of thy hand. For he þt fereth God shal escape them al.

19 Wisdom geueth more corage vnto the wise then ten myghty men of the cyty:

20 for there is not one iuste vpon earth, that doth good, and synneth not.

21 Take not hede vnto euery word that is spoken, leste thou heare thy seruaunt curse the:

22 for thyne owne herte knoweth, that thou thy selfe also hast ofte tymes spoken euell by other men.

23 All these thynges haue I proued because of wysdome: for I thought to be wise, but she went farther fro me

24 then she was before, yea and so depe that I might not reach vnto her

25 I aplied my minde also vnto knowledg, and to seke out science wysdome and vnderstandynge: to know the foolishnesse of the vngodly, and the erroure of dotynge fooles.

26 And I founde, that a woman is bytterrer then death: for she is a very angle, her herte is a net, and her handes are cheynes. Who so pleaseth God shall escape from her, but the synner wil be taken wt her.

27 Beholde (sayeth the preacher) this haue I dilygently searched oute and proued, that I myght come by knowledge: whych as yet I seke, and fynde it not.

28 Amonge a thousande men I haue founde one, but not one woman amonge all.

29 Lo thys onely haue I founde, that God made man iust and right, but they seke dyuerse soteltyes,

## CHAPTER 8

Wher as no man hath wysdome and vnderstandynge, to geue answere thereunto. (8:1) Wysdome maketh a mans face to shyne, but malyce putteth it oute of fauoure.

2 Kepe the kynges commaundemente (I warne the) and the othe that thou haste made vnto god.

3 Be not hasty to go out of hys syght, and se thou contynue in no euell thynge: for whatsoeuer it pleaseth him, that doth he,

4 Lyke as when a kynge geueth a charge, hys commaundemente is myghtye: Euen so who maye saye vnto hym what doest thou?

5 Who so kepeth the commaundement, shal fele no harme: but a wise mans herte discerneth tyme and maner:

6 For euerye thinge wil haue oportunite and iudgement, and thys is the thynge that maketh men ful of carefulnes and sorowe.

7 And why a man knoweth not what is for to come, for who wyll tell him?

8 Nether is there any man that hath power ouer the spirite, to kepe styll the spirite, ner to haue any power in the tyme of death: it is not he also that can make an ende of the battail, nether maye vngodlynes delyuer him that medleth with al.

9 All these thynges haue I consydered, and applyed my mynde vnto euerye worcke that is vnder the Sonne: howe one man hath lordshyppe vpon another to hys owne harme.

10 For I haue oft sene the vngodly broughte to their graues, and fallen downe from the hye & glorious place: in so muche that they were forgotten in the cytye, where they were had in so hye and greate reputacyon. This is also a vayne thynge.

11 Because now that euell worckes are not hastely punyshed the herte of man geueth hym selfe ouer vnto wyckednesse.

12 But thoughe an euell persone offende an hundred tymes, and haue a longe life: yet am I sure, that it shall go well wyth them that feare God, because they haue hym before their eyes.

13 Againe, as for the vngodly, it shal not be well wyth hym, neyther shall he prolonge his dayes: but euen as a shaddowe, so shal he be that feareth not God.

14 Yet is there a vanitye vpon earth: There be iust men, vnto whome it happeneth, as thoughte they had the workes of the vngodly: Agayne, there be vngodly, wyth whom it goeth as though they had the worckes of the ryghtuousnes, Thys me thynke also a vayne thyng.

15 Therfore I commaunde

gladnesse, because a man hath no better thynge vnder the Sonne, then to eate and dryncke, and to be mery: for that shal he haue of his laboure al þe dayes of hys lyfe, whych God geueth hym vnder the Sonne.

16 When I applied my mind to learne wysdome, and to knowe the trauail that is in the worlde (and that of such a fashion, that I suffred not myne eyes to slepe nether daye ner nyghte)

17 I vnderstode of all the workes of god, that it is not impossyble for a man, to attaine vnto the workes that are done vnder the Sunne: and thoughe he bestowe his laboure to seke them oute, yet can he not reach vnto them: yea though a wise man would vndertake to knowe them, yet myght he not fynde them.

## CHAPTER 9

For all these thynges purposed I in my mynd to seke out. The ryghtuous and wyse yea and their workes also are in the hande of God: and their is no man knoweth eyther the loue or hate of the thyng þt he hath before him.

2 It happeneth vnto one as vnto another: It goeth wt the ryghtuous as wt the vngodli wt the good & cleane as wt the vncleane: wt him that offereth as wt him that offereth not: lyke as it goeth wyth þe vertuous, so goeth it also wyth the sinner: As it happeneth vnto the periured, so happeneth it also vnto him þt is afraied to be forsworne.

3 Amonge all thynges that come to passe vnder the Sunne, this is a mysery, that it happeneth vnto all alyke. This is the cause also that the hertes of men are ful of wyckednes, and mad folishnes is in their hertes as longe as they liue, vntyl they dye.

4 And why? As longe as a man lyueth, he is careles: for a quicke dogg (saye they) is better then a dead lyon:

5 for they that be lyuyng, knowe that they shall dye: but they that be dead, knowe nothinge, neyther deserne they any more. For their memoriall is forgotten,

6 so that they be nether loued, hated ner enuied nether haue they animore parte in the world, in al that is done vnder the Sonne.

7 Go thou thy waye then, eate thy bread wyth ioy, and dryncke thy wyne wyth gladnesse, for thy worckes please God.

8 Let thy garments be alway white, and let thy head want none oyntment.

9 Vse thy selfe to lyue ioyfully with thy wyfe whom thou leuest, all the dayes of thy life, which is but vaine, that God hath geuen the vnder the Sunne, all the dayes of thy vanite: for that is thy porcion in this lyfe, of all thy laboure and trauayle that thou takeste vnder the Sunne.

10 Whatsoeuer thou takest in hande to do, that do wyth all thy power: for among the dead, wher as thou goest vnto, ther is nether worcke, councel, knowledge ner wysdome.

11 So I turned me vnto other thynges vnder the Sonne, and I sawe, that in runnyng, it helpeth not to be swift: in battayll, it helpeth not to be stronge, to fedynge, it helpeth not to be wyse: to ryches, it helpeth not to be suttell: to be had in fauoure, it helpeth not to be cunnynge: but that all lyeth in tyme and fortune.

12 For a man knoweth not his tyme, but like as the fishes are taken wyth the angle and as the byrdes are catched with the snare Euen so are men taken in the perilous time, when it commeth sodenly vpon them.

13 This wysdome haue I sene also vnder þe Sunne, and me thought it a great thynge.

14 There was a litle citie, and a fewe men within it: so there came a great kyng and beseged it, and made great bulwarkes agaynste it

15 And in the cytye there was founde a poore man (but he was wyse) which with hys wisdome deliuered the cytye: yet was there no body, that had any respect vnto such a symple man.

16 Then sayde I: wysdome is better then strengthe. Neuertheles, a simple mans wysedome is despised, & his wordes are not herde.

17 A wyse mans counsayl that is folowed in silence, is farre aboue the cryeng of a captayne among fooles.

18 For wysdome is better then harnesse: but one vnthryft alone destroyeth much good.

## CHAPTER 10

Dead flyes that corruppe swete oyntment and make it to stinke are somthyng more worth then the wysdome and honour of a foole.

2 A wyse mans hert is vpon the right hande, but a fooles hert is vpon the left.

3 A dotyng foole thynketh, that euery man doth as folishly as hym selfe.

4 If a principall sprete be geuen the to beare rule, be not negligente then in thine office: for so shall great wickednesse be put doun, as it were wt a medecine.

5 Another plage is there, which I haue sene vnder the sunne: namely, the ignoraunce that is commenly among princes:

6 in that a foole sitteth in great dignitie, and the ryche are set doune beneth:

7 I se seruauntes ryde vpon horses, & princes going vpon theyr fete as it were seruauntes.

8 But he that dyggeth vp a pyt, shal fal therin hym self: & who so breaketh doune the hedge, a serpente shall byte hym.

9 Who so remoueth stones,

# ECCLESIASTES

shall haue trauayl withal: & he that heweth wood shalbe hurt therwith.

10 When an yron is blont, and the poynt not sharpened, it muste be whet agayn, and that with might: Euen so doth wysdome folowe diligence.

11 A babler of his tonge is no better then a serpent that styngeth without hyssyng.

12 The wordes of out a wyse mans mouth are gracious, but þe lippes of a fole wil destroy hym self.

13 The begynnyng of his talkynge is foolishnes, and the last worde of his mouth is great madnesse.

14 A foole is so full of woordes, that a man can not tell what ende he will make: who will then warne hym to make a conclusion?

15 The labour of the folish is greuous vnto them, whyle they know not how to go into the cytye.

16 Wo be vnto the (O thou realme & lande) whose kyng is but a chylde, & whose princes are early at their bankettes.

17 But well is the (O thou realme and lande) whose kynge is is come of nobles, and whose pryncks eate in due seasou, for strength and not for luste.

18 Thorow slothfulnesse the balkes fal doune, and thorowe ydle handes it raineth in at the house.

19 Meate maketh men to laugh, and wine maketh them mery: but vnto money are all thynges obedyente.

20 Wyshe the kynge no euell in thy thoughte, and speake no hurte of the ryche in thy preuy chambre: for a byrde of the ayre shall betraye thy voyce, and wyth her fethers shall she bewraye thy wordes.

## CHAPTER 11

SENDE thy vyttuayls ouer the waters, and so shalt thou finde them after many yeares.

2 Geue it awaye amonge seuen or eyghte, for thou knoweste not what mysery shall come vpon earth.

3 When the cloudes are full, they poure oute rayne vpon the earthe. And when the tree falleth (whether it be towarde the South or North) in what place soeuer it fall, there it lyeth.

4 He that regardeth the wynde, shall not sowe: and he that hath respecte vnto the cloudes, shall not reape.

5 Nowe lyke as thou knowest not the waye of the wynde, nor how the bones are fylled in a mothers wombe: Euen so thou knoweste not the worckes of God, whych is the worckemaster of all.

6 Cease not thou therefore with thy handes to sowe thy sede, whether it be in the mornynge or in the euenynge: for thou knoweste not whether this or that shall prospere, and if they both take, it is the better.

7 The lyghte is swete, and a pleasaunte thinge is it for the eyes to loke vpon the Sunne.

8 If a man lyue manye yeares, and be gladde in them all, let hym remember the dayes of darckenesse, whiche shalbe many: and when thei come, al thynges shalbe but vanytye.

9 Be glad then (O thou yong man) in thy youth, and let thine herte be mery in thy yonge daies: folowe the wayes of thine owne herte, and the luste of thyne eyes: but be thou sure, that God shall brynge the into iudgement for all these thinges.

10 Pvt awaye displeasure oute of thine hert, & remoue euel from thy body: for childhode & youth is but vanitie.

## CHAPTER 12

REMEMBRE thy maker in thy youth, or euer the dayes of aduersitie come, and or the yeares drawe nye, when thou shalt saye: I haue no pleasure in them

2 before the sunne, the lyght, the moone and starres be darkened, and or the cloudes turne agayn after þe rayne:

3 when the kepers of the house shall tremble, & when the strong men shall bowe them selfes: when the myllers stande styll, because they be so fewe, & when the sight of þe wyndowes shal waxe dymme:

4 when the dores in the stretes shalbe shut, & when the voyce of the myller shalbe layed doune: when men shall ryse vp at the voyce of the byrde, and when all the daughters of musicke shalbe brought lowe:

5 when men shall feare in hye places, and be afrayed in the stretes: when the Almonde tree shalbe despised, the greshopper borne out, & when great pouerte shall breake in: when man goeth to his longe home, and the mourners go about the stretes.

6 Or euer the siluer lace be taken awaye, and or the golden bande be broken: Or the pot be broken at the wel, and the whele vpon the cysterne:

7 Or dust be turned agayn vnto earth from whence it came, and or the sprete returne vnto God, whyche gaue it.

8 All is but vanitie (sayeth the Preacher) all is but playne vanite.

9 The same Preacher was not wyse alone, but taught the people knowlege also: he gaue good hede, sought out the ground & set forth many parables.

10 His diligence was to fynde out acceptable wordes, right scripture, and the wordes of trueth.

11 For the wordes of the wise are like prickes and nayles that go thorow, wherewith men are kepte together: for they are geuen of one shepeherde onely.

12 Therfore be ware (my sonne) þt aboue these thou make the uot many and innumerable bokes, nor take diuerse doctrynes in hande, to weery thy body withall.

13 Let vs heare the conclusion of all thinges Feare God, and kepe his commaundementes, For that toucheth al men:

14 For God shal iudge all workes and secrete thynges, whether they be good or euell.

# Song of Solomon

## CHAPTER 1

O that thy mouthe woulde geue me a kysse, for thy brestes are more pleasaunt then wyne,

3 & that because of the good & pleasaunt sauoure. Thy name is a swete smelling oyntment, therfore do the maydens laue the:

4 yea, that same moueth me also to runne after the. The King hath brought me into his preuy chambre. We wil be glad and reioyce in the, we thynke more of thy brestes then of wyne: well is them that loue the.

5 I am black (O ye daughters of Hierusalem) like as the tentes of the Cedarenes, and as the hanginges of Salomon:

6 but yet am I fayre & welfauoured withal. Maruell not at me that I am so blacke: & why? þe sunne hath shyned vpon me. For when my mothers chyldren had euel will at me, they made me the keper of þe vyneyarde. Thus was I fayne to kepe a vyneyarde, which was not myne owne.

7 Tell me (O thou whom my soule loueth) where thou fedest, where thou restest at the noone daye: lest I go wrong, and come vnto the flockes of thy companyons.

8 If thou knowe not thy selfe (O thou fayrest among women) then go thy waye forthe after the fotesteppes of the shepe, as though thou woldest fede thy goates beside þe shepeherdes tentes.

9 There will I tary for the (my loue) with myne host and mith my charettes which shalbe no fewer then Pharaos.

10 Then shall thy chekes & thy neck be made fayre, & hanged with spanges & goodly iewels:

11 a neck bande of golde will we make the with siluer butons.

12 When the king sitteth at the table, he shal smell my Nardus:

13 for a bondel of Myrre (O my beloued) lyeth betwixte my breastes.

14 A cluster of grapes of Cypers, or of þe vyneyardes of Engaddi art thou vnto me, O my beloued.

15 O how fayre art thou (my loue) how fayre art thou? thou hast doues eyes.

16 O how fayre art thou (my beloued) how wel fauored art thou? Our bed is decketh wt floures,

17 the sylinges of our house are of Cedre tree, and our balkes of Cypresse.

## CHAPTER 2

I am the floure of the felde, and Lylye of the valleys:

2 as the Rose amonge the thornes, so is my loue among the daughters.

3 Lyke as the apple tree among the trees of the wood, so is my beloued among the sones. My delyte is to sit vnder hys shadowe, for hys frute is swete vnto my throte.

4 He bringeth me into hys wyne seller, and loueth me specially well.

5 Refreshe me wyth grapes, comforte me with apples, for I am sycke of loue.

6 His left hand lyeth vnder my head, and hys right hande embraceth me.

7 I charge you (O ye daughters of Ierusalem) by the Roes & hyndes of the felde, that ye wake not vp my loue nor touche her, tyll she be content her selfe.

8 Me thynke I heare the voyce of my beloued: lo, there commeth he hoppyng vpon the mountaynes, & leapyng ouer the litle hylles.

9 My beloued is lyke a Roo or a yong hart. Beholde, he standeth behynde oure wall, he loketh in at the wyndow, and pepeth thorow the grate.

10 My beloued aunswered & sayde vnto me. O stande vp my loue, my doue, my beutifull, & come:

11 for lo, the wynter is now

paste, & the rayne is away & gone.

12 The floures are come vp in the felde, the twystynge tyme is come, the voyce of the turtle doue is hearde in our lande.

13 The fygge tree bringeth forthe her figges, the vynes beare blossoms, & haue a good smell. O stande vp my loue, my beutifull, & come

14 (O my doue) oute of the caues of the rockes, out of the holes of the wal: O let me se thy countenaunce & heare thy voyce, for swete is thy voyce and fayre is thy face.

15 Get vs the foxes, yea, the litle foxes that hurt þe vynes, for our vines beare blossoms.

16 My loue is myne, and I am hys, whych fedeth among the Lilies,

17 vntill the day breake, and till the shadowes be gone. Come agayn preuely (O my beloued) lyke as a Roo or a yong hart vnto the mountaynes.

# CHAPTER 3

BY night in my bedde I soughte hym, whome my soule loueth: yea, diligently soughte I hym, but I founde him not.

2 I will get vp (thought I) & go aboute the citie, vpon the market & in all the stretes will I seke him whome my soule loueth: but when I sought hym, I founde him not.

3 The watchemen that go aboute the citie, founde me. Sawe ye not him whom my soule loueth?

4 So when I was a litle past them, I founde hym whom my soule loueth. I haue gotten holde vpon him, & will not let hym go, vntil I bryng hym into my mothers house, and into her chambre that bare me.

5 I charge you, O ye daughters of Ierusalem, by the Roes & Hyndes of the felde, that ye wake not vp my loue nor touche her, tyll she be content her selfe.

6 Who is thys þt commeth out of the wildernesse lyke pylers of smoke as it were a smell of Myrre, franckencence and al maner spyces of the Apotecary?

7 Behold, aboute Salomons bedstede ther stande .lx. valeaunt men of the myghty in Israel.

8 Thei holde swerdes euery one & are experte in warre. Euery man hath his swerde vpon his thygh, because of feare in the nighte.

9 Kynge Salomon hath made him selfe a bedstead of the wood of Libanus,

10 the pilers are of syluer, the coueryng of golde, the seate of purple, the ground pleasauntly paued for þe daughters of Ierusalem.

11 Go forth (O ye daughters of Sion) and beholde Kynge Salomon in the crowne wherwyth his mother crowned him in the day of his mariage, and in the daye of the gladnesse of hys herte.

# CHAPTER 4

O how fayre arte thou, my loue, how fayre art thou? thou haste doues eyes, beside that whych lyeth hyd wythin.

2 They hearye lockes are lyke a flocke of shepe that be clipped, which go first vp from the washing place: where euery one beareth two twynes, and not one vnfruteful among them.

3 Thy lyppes are lyke a rose coloured rybonde, thy wordes are louely: thy chekes are like a pece of a pomgranate, besides that whych lyeth hyd wythin.

4 Thy necke is lyke the tower of Dauyd buylded wyth bulworkes, where vpon there hange a thousaunde shyldes, yea all the weapens of the gyauntes.

5 Thy two brestes are lyke two twins of yong roes, which fede among the lilies.

6 O that I myght go to the mountayne of Myrre, and to the hyll of franckincense: tyll the day breake, and tyl the shadowes be past awaye.

7 Thou arte all fayre, O my loue, and no spot is therin the.

8 Come to me from Lybanus, O my house, come to me from Libanus come soone the next way from the top of Amana, from the top of Sanir and Hermon, from the lyons dennes & from the mountaynes of þe leopardes.

9 Thou hast wounded my hert. O my syster, my spouse, thou hast wounded my hert, with one of thyne eyes, & wyth one cheyne of thy neck.

10 O howe fayre and louely are thy brestes, my syster, my spouse? Thy brestes are more pleasaunte then wyne, and the smell of thyne oyntmentes passeth al spices.

11 Thy lyps, O my spouse, drop as the hony combe, yea milcke and hony is vnder thy tonge, and the smel of thy garmentes is lyke the smell of frankyncense.

12 Thou arte a well kepte garden, O my syster, my spouse, thou art a well kepte waterspringe, a sealed well.

13 The frutes that sprute in the, are like a very Paradyse of pomegranates with swete frutes:

14 as Cypresse, Nardus, Saffron, Calmus, and all the trees of Libanus: Myrre, Aloes, and all the best spyces.

15 Thou art a well of gardens, a well of lyuyng waters, whyche reune doune from Libanus.

16 Vp thou Northwynde, come thou southwynde, & blowe vppon my garden, that the smell therof may be caryed on eueryside: yea that my beloued may come into my garden, and eate of the frutes and apples that grow therein.

# SONG OF SOLOMON

## CHAPTER 5

COME into my garden O my sister, my spouse: I haue gathered my Myrre with my spyce. I wil eate my hony and my hony combe, I will drinke my wyne and my mylke. Eate, O ye frendes, drynke & be mery, O ye beloued.

2 As I was a slepe, & my hert wakynge, I hearde the voyce of my beloued, when he knocked. Open to me (sayde he) O my sister, my loue, my doue, my derlynge: for my heade is full of dewe, and the lockes of my heere are full of the night droppes.

3 I haue put of my cote, how can I do it on agayn? I haue washed my fete, how shall I fyle them agayn?

4 But when my loue put in his hand at the hole, my hert was moued toward hym:

5 so þt I stode vp to open vnto my beloued. My handes dropped with Myrre, & the Myrre ranne doune my fingers vpon the locke.

6 Neuerthelesse when I had opened vnto my beloued, he was departed and gone his waye. Now lyke as afore tyme when he spake, my hert coude not longer refrayne: Euen so now I soughte hym, but I coulde not fynde hym: I cryed vpon him, neuerthelesse he gaue me no aunswere.

7 So the watchmen that wente aboute the cytye, founde me, smote me, & wounded me: Yea, they that kept the walles, toke awaye my garment fro me.

8 I charge you therfore, O ye daughters of Ierusalem, if ye fynde my beloued, that ye tell hym how that I am sycke for loue.

9 Who is thy loue aboue other louers, O thou fayrest among women? Or what can thy loue do, more then other louers, þt thou chargest vs so straytely?

10 As for my loue, he is whyte and read coloured, a singular personne amonge mauy thousandes:

11 his head is the most fine golde, the lockes of hys heer are bushed, broune as the euenyng:

12 Hys eyes are as the eyes of doues by the water brokes, washen with mylke and remaynyng in a plenteous place:

13 Hys chekes are lyke a garden bed, where in the Apotecaries plante all maner of swete thinges: His lyppes droppe as the floures of þe most principal Myrre,

14 hys handes are full of golde rynges & precious stones. His body is as the pure yuery, decte ouer with Saphires:

15 His legges are as the pylers of Marbel set vpon sokettes of golde: His face is as Libanus, and as the bewty of the Cedre trees:

16 Hys throte is swete, yea, he is altogether louely. Such one is my loue, O ye daughters of Ierusalem, such one is my loue.

## CHAPTER 6

WHITHER is thy loue gone then (O thou fayrest amonge women) whither is thy loue departed, that we may seke hym with the?

2 My loue is gone doune into hys garden, vnto the swete smelling beddes, that he maye refreshe him self in the garden, and gather floures.

3 My loue is myne and I am hys, which fedeth among the Lylyes.

4 Thou art pleasaunt (O my loue) euen as louelynesse it self, thou art fayre as Ierusalem, glorious as an army of men, with their banners.

5 (Turne awaye thyne eyes fro me, for thei make me to proude.) Thy heery lockes are lyke a flocke of goates vpon þe mount of Galaad.

6 Thy teth are like a flocke of shepe that be clypped, which go out of the wasshyng place: where euery one beareth twoo twynes, and not one vnfruteful among them.

7 Thy chekes are lyke a pece of pomegranate besydes that which lyeth hyd within.

8 There are thre score Quenes, foure score concubines, & yong women without numbre.

9 But one is my doue, my derling. She is the onely beloued of her mother, and deare vnto her þt bare her. When the daughters sawe her, they sayde, she was blessed: Yea the Quenes and concubynes praysed her.

10 What is she this, that pepeth out as the mornynge? fayre as the moone, excellent as the sunne, glorious as an army of men with their baners.

11 I went doune into the nutte garden, to se what grew by þe brokes, to loke if þe vineyarde florished, & if þe pomegranates were shot forth.

12 Then the charettes of the prynce of my people made me sodenly afrayde.

13 Turne agayn, turne agayn, O thou Sulamite, turne agayne, turne agayne, that we may loke vpon the. (7:1) What pleasure haue ye more in the Sulamite, than when she daunseth among the men of warre?

## CHAPTER 7

O how pleasaunt are thy treadinges with thy shoes, thou princes daughter? Thy thinges are like a fayre iewel, which is wrought by a connyng worke master:

2 Thy nauell is like a round goblet, which is neuer without drynke: Thy wombe is like an heap of wheat, set about with Lylies:

3 Thy two brestes are lyke two twynnes of yong roes:

4 Thy necke is as it were a

tower of yuery: thyne eyes are lyke the water poles in Hesebon, beside the porte of Bathrabbim: thy nose is like the tower of Libanus, which loketh toward Damascus:

5 That head that standeth vpon the is lyke Carmel: the heare of thy head is like the kynges purple folden vp in plates.

6 O how fayre & louely art thou, my dearlyng, in pleasures?

7 Thy stature is like a date tree, and thy brestes like the grapes. I sayde:

8 I will clymme vp into the date tree, and take holde of hys braunches. Thy brestes also shalbe as the vyne grapes, the smell of thy nostrels lyke the smell of apples,

9 and thy throte like the beste wine. This shalbe pure and cleare for my loue, his lippes & teth shal haue their pleasure.

10 There wyll I turne me vnto my loue, and he shall turne hym vnto me.

11 O come on my loue, let vs go forth into the felde, and take oure lodgynge in the vyllages.

12 In the mornyng wyll we ryse by tymes, and go se the vyneyarde: if it be sprong forth, if the grapes be growne, & if the pomegranates be shut out. There wil I geue the my brestes:

13 there shall the Mandragoras geue their smell besyde oure dores: there, O my loue, haue I kepte vnto the all maner of frutes, both newe and olde.

# CHAPTER 8

O that I myght fynde the without, and kisse the, whom I loue as my brother whiche sucked my mothers brestes: and that thou woldest not be offended,

2 if I toke the, and broughte the into my mothers house: that thou mightest teache me, & that I might geue the drinke of spiced wyne and of the swete sappe of my pomgranates.

3 Hys left hand lyeth vnder my head and hys right hande embraceth me.

4 I charge you, O ye daughters of Ierusalem. that ye walke not vp my loue, nor touch her, tyll she be content her self.

5 What is she this, that commeth vp from the wyldernes, and leaneth vpon her loue? I am the same that waked the vp among the apple trees, where thy mother bare the, where thy mother brought the into þe world.

6 O set me as a seale vpon thyne herte, and as a seale vpon thine arme: for loue is mightye as the death, and gelousy as the hell. Her cooles are of fyre, and a very flamme of the Lord:

7 so that many waters are not able too quenche loue, neither may þe streames droun it. Yea, if a man wolde geue al the good of his house for loue, he should counte it nothinge.

8 When our loue is tolde our yong syster, whose brestes are not yet growen, what shal we do vnto her?

9 If she be a wall, we shall buylde a siluer bulwerke there vppon: if she be a tower, we shall fasten her with borders of Cedre tree.

10 If I be a wall, & my brestes like towres, then am I as one that hath founde fauoure in hys sight.

11 Salomon had a vyneyarde at Baal Hamon, thys vyneyarde delyuered he vnto the kepers: that euery one for the frute thereof should geue hym a thousand peces of siluer.

12 But my vyneyard, O Salomon, geueth the a thousand, and two hundreth to the kepers of the frute.

13 Thou that dwellest in the gardens, O let me heare thy voyce, that my companyons may herken to the same.

14 O get the awaye, my loue, as a roo or a yong hert vnto the swete smellynge mountaynes

# Isaiah

## CHAPTER 1

THE prophecye of Esai the sonne of Amos, whiche he shewed vpon Iuda & Ierusalem: In the tyme of Oziah, Ioatham, Ahaz, and Iehezekiah Kynges of Iuda.

2 Heare O heauen, herken O earth, for the Lord speaketh: I haue norysshed & brought vp chyldren, and they are fallen awaye from me.

3 An oxe knoweth hys Lorde, & an Asse his masters stall: but Israel knoweth nothynge, my people hath no vnderstanding.

4 Alas for thys synfull people, whiche are ouerladen with blasphemyes, a frowarde generacyon, wicked chyldren. They haue forsaken the Lorde, they haue prouoked the holy one of Israell vnto anger, and are gone backwarde.

5 Wherfore shulde ye be plaged any more? For ye are euer fallyng away. The whole head is sick, & the herte is very heauy.

6 From the sole of the fote vnto the head, there is no whol parte in all youre bodye: but all are woundes, botches, sores, and stripes, whiche can nether be helped, bound vp, molifyed, nor eased with any oyntment.

7 Youre lande lyeth waste, youre cyties are brent vp, youre enemyes deuoure your lande, and ye muste be fayne to stand, and loke vpon it: and it is desolate, as it were wyth enemyes in a battell.

8 Moreouer the doughter of Syon is lefte alone lyke a cotage in a vyneyard like a watche house in tyme of warre, lyke a beseged cytye.

9 And excepte the Lord of hostes had lefte vs a fewe alyue: we shulde haue ben as Sodoma, and lyke vnto Gomorra.

10 Heare the worde of the Lorde ye tyrauntes of Sodoma, and herken vnto the lawe of oure God, thou people of Gomorra.

11 Why offre ye so manye sacrifyces vnto me? I am discontent for the brentofferinges of wethers and with the fatnesse of fedbeastes. I haue no pleasure in the bloude of bullockes, lambes & gootes.

12 When ye appeare before me, who requyreth you to treade wythin my porches?

13 Offre me no mo oblacions, for it is but loste laboure. I abhorre youre incense. I maye not awaye with youre new moones, youre Sabbathes and solempne dayes. Youre fastinges are also in vayne.

14 I hate youre newe holye dayes and fastynges, euen from my very hert. They make me weerye, I can not abyde them.

15 Though ye holde oute your handes, yet turne I myne eyes from you. And though ye make manye prayers, yet heare I nothynge at all, for youre handes are full of bloude.

16 Washe you, make you cleane, put awaye youre euill thoughtes out of my sighte, cease from doynge of euyll and vyolence.

17 Lerne to do right, applye youre selues to equite, delyuer the oppressed, helpe the fatherlesse to hys ryght, let the wyddowes complaynte come before you.

18 Nowe go to (sayth the Lorde) we will talke together. Is it not so? Thoughe youre synnes be as reade as scarlet, shal they not be whyther then snowe? And though they were lyke purple, shall they not be lyke white wolle?

19 Is it not so? If ye be louynge and obedyent, ye shall enioye the best thynge that groweth in the lande.

20 But yf ye be obstynate and rebellyous, ye shalbe deuoured wt the swerde: for thus the Lorde hath promysed wyth hys owne mouthe.

21 Howe happeneth it then that þe ryghtuous cytye (whiche was full of equyte) is be come vnfaythful as an whore? ryghteousnes dwelt in it, but now murthur.

22 Thy syluer is turned to

drosse, and thy wyne mixte wyth water.

23 Thy prynces are traytours and companyons of theues. They loue gyftes altogether, & folowe rewardes. As for the fatherles, they helpe hym not to hys ryght, nether wyll they let the wydowes causes come before them.

24 Therfore speaketh the Lorde God of hostes þe myghtye one of Israel: Ah I muste ease me of myne enemyes, and avenge me vpon them.

25 And therfore shall I laye my hande vpon the and burne oute thy drosse from the fyneste and pureste, and put oute all the leade,

26 and set thy iudges agayne as they were some tyme, and thy Senatours as they were from the begynninge. Then shalte thou be called þe ryghtuous cytie, the faithful citye.

27 But Syon shalbe redemed with equite, and her captyuyte with ryghteousnesse.

28 For the transgressours and vngodlye, and suche as are become vnfaythfull vnto the Lorde, muste altogether be vtterlye destroyed.

29 And except ye be ashamed of the oke trees wherein ye haue so delyted, and of the gardens that ye haue chosen:

30 ye shalbe as an oke whose leaues are fallen awaye, and as a garden that hath no moystnesse.

31 And as for the glorye of these thynges, it shalbe turned to drye straw, and he that made them to a sparke. And they shall both burne together, so that no man shalbe able to quenche them.

## CHAPTER 2

MOREOUER this is þe word that was opened vnto Esay the sonne of Amoz, vpon Iuda & Ierusalem.

2 It will be also in processe of tyme: That þe hyl where the house of the Lorde is buylded, shal be the chefe amonge hylles, and exalted aboue al lytle hylles. And all the Heathen shall preache vnto hym, & the multytude of people shall go vnto hym,

3 speakynge thus one to another: vp let vs go to the hyll of the Lorde, & to þe house of the God of Iacob: that he maye shewe vs hys waye, and that we maye walcke in hys pathes. For the lawe shall come out of Syon and the worde of God from Ierusalem,

4 and shall geue sentence amonge the Heathen, and shall reforme the multytude of people. So that they shal breake theyr swerdes & speares to make sythes, sycles and sawes thereof. From that tyme forth shall not one people lyfte vp weapen agaynste another, neyther shall they learne to fight from thence forth.

5 It is to the þt I crye (O house of Iacob) vp, let vs walck in the lyghte of the Lorde,

6 But thou art scatered abroade with thy people (O house of Iacob) for ye go farre beyonde youre fathers, whether it be in Sorcerers (whome ye haue as the Phylystynes had) or in calkers of mens byrthes, whereof ye haue to manye.

7 As soone as youre lande was full of syluer and golde, and no ende of youre treasure: so soone as youre lande was full of stronge horses and no ende of youre charettes:

8 Immediatlye was it full of Idols also, euen workes of youre owne handes, which ye youre selues haue fashyoned, & your syngers haue made.

9 There kneleth þe man there falleth the man doune before them, so that thou canste not brynge hym a waye from thence.

10 And therfore get the soone into some rock, & hyde the in the grounde from the sighte of the fearful iudge, & from the glorye of his mageste:

11 Which casteth doune the hygh lokes of presumptuous personnes, & bryngeth lowe the pryde of man, & he only shall be exalted in the daye.

12 For the daye of the Lorde of Hostes shall go ouer all pryde & presumpcyon, vpon all them that exalte them selues, & shall brynge them all doune:

13 vpon all high & stoute Cedre trees of Lybanus, and vpon all the okes of Basan,

14 vpon all hygh hylles, and vpon al stoute mountaynes,

15 vpon all costlye towres, and vpon al strong walles,

16 vpon all shyppes of the sea, and vpon euerye thynge that is gloryous and pleasaunte to loke vpon.

17 And it shall bryng doune the pryde of man, & laye mans presumptuousnesse ful lowe, and the Lorde shall onelye haue the vyctorye in that daye.

18 But the ydoles shall vtterly be roted oute.

19 Men shall crepe into holes of stone, and into caues of the earthe, from the syghte of the fearfull iudge, and from the glorye of hys magesty: what tyme as he shall make hym vp to shake the earthe.

20 Then then, shall man caste awaye hys Goddes of syluer and golde (whiche he neuerthelesse had made to honoure them) vnto Moles and Backes:

21 that he maye the better crepe into the caues & rockes, and into the cliffes of harde stones, from the syghte of the fearfull iudge & from the glorye of hys Magestye.

22 Every man can eschue a persone moued in anger, for what doeth he wyselye?

## CHAPTER 3

EUEN so shall the Lorde of Hostes take awaye from

Ierusalem & Iuda, all possessyons and power, al meate and drincke,

2 the captayne & the soudyar, the iudge & the Prophete the wyse and the aged man,

3 the worshipful of fyftye yeare olde, and the honorable: the Senatours, and men of vnderstandyng: the maisters of craftes and oratours.

4 And I shal geue you chyldren to be youre prynces (sayeth the Lord) & babes shall haue the rule of you.

5 One shall euer be doynge vyolence & wronge to another. The boye shall presume agaynste the elder, and the vyle persone agaynst the honorable.

6 Ye one shal take a frend of his owne kynred by the bosome and saye: thou haste clothynge, thou shalt be oure heade, for thou mayest kepe vs from thys fall and parell.

7 Then shall he sweare and saye: I can not helpe you. Moreouer, there is neyther meate nor clothynge in my house, make me no ruler of the people.

8 For Ierusalem and Iuda muste decaye, because that bothe theyr wordes and councels are agaynste the Lorde, they prouoke the presence of his magesty vnto anger.

9 The chaungynge of their countenaunce bewrayeth them, yea they declare theyr owne synnes them selues, as the Sodomites, and hyde them not. Wo be vnto theyr soules, for they shalbe heuely rewarded.

10 Then shall they saye. O happye are the godly, for they maye enioye the frutes of theyr studyes.

11 But wo be to the vngodlye & vnryghtuous for they shall be rewarded after theyr worckes.

12 O my people rybaudes oppresse the, and wemen haue rule of the. O my people, thy leaders deceyue the, and treade oute the waye of thy foteseppes.

13 The Lorde is her to comen of the matter, and standeth to geue iudgement wyth the people.

14 The Lorde shall come forth to reason wyth the Senatours and pryncks of hys people, and shal saye thus vnto them: It is ye that haue burnt vp my vyneyarde, the robberye of the poore is in your house.

15 Wherfore do ye oppresse my people, and marre the faces of the innocentes? thus shall the God of Hostes reuyle them.

16 Moreouer thus sayth the Lorde: Seynge the doughters of Sion are become so proude, and come in with stretched oute neckes, and with vayne wanton eyes: seynge they come in tryppynge so nycely with their fete:

17 Therfore shall the Lorde shaue the heades of the doughters of Syon, and make theyr bewtye bare in that daye.

18 In that daye shall the Lord take awaye the gorgyousnes of theyr apparel & spanges, chaynes, parlaftes,

19 and colares, bracelettes & hooues,

20 the goodly floured wide & broderd rayment, brusshes & headebandes,

21 rynges and garlandes,

22 holye daye clothes & vales, kerchues & pynnes,

23 glasses & smockes, bonettes and taches.

24 And in steade of good smell there shalbe styncke amonge them. And for theyr gyrdles there shalbe louse bandes. And for well set hearre there shalbe baldnesse. In steade of a stomacker, a sackclothe, and for theyr bewtye wytherydnesse & sunneburninge.

25 Their housbandes and theyr myghtye men shall perysh with the swerde in batell.

26 At that time shal their gates mourne & complayne, and they shall sitte as desolate folck vpon the earth.

# CHAPTER 4

THEN shall seuen wyues take holde of one man, and saye: we wil laye all oure meate and clothing together in comen, only that we may be called thy wyues, & that this shameful reprofe may be taken from vs.

2 After that tyme shall the braunche of the Lorde be bewtyfull & myghtye, & the frute of the earth shall be fayre & pleasaunte for those Israelites that shall bringe thereof.

3 Then shall the remnaunt in Syon and the remnaunte at Ierusalem be called holye: namelye all suche as are wrytten amonge the lyuynge at Ierusalem:

4 what time as the Lorde shall washe awaye the desolacion of the doughters of Syon, & pourge þe bloude out from Ierusalem wt the wynde of his smoke & fyre.

5 Moreouer vpon al the dwellynges of þe hyl of Syon, and vpon their whole congregacyon, shal the Lord prouyde a cloude & smoke by daye, and the shynynge of a flammynge fyre by nyght: for all their glorye shalbe preserued.

6 And Ierusalem shall be a tabernacle for a shadowe because of hete in the daye tyme, a place and refuge where a man may kepe him for wether and rayne.

# CHAPTER 5

NOWE wel then, I wyl syng my beloued frende a songe of hys vyneyarde. My beloued frende hath a vyneyard in a very frutefull plenteous grounde.

2 This he hedged, this he walled rounde about, & planted with goodly grapes. In the myddest of it buylded he a toure, & made a wyne presse therein. And afterwarde when he loked that it shulde bringe him grapes,

it broughte forthe thornes.

3 I shewe you nowe my cause (O ye Cytesens of Ierusalem & whole Iuda:) Iudge I praye you betwixte me, & my vyneyarde.

4 What more coulde haue bene done for it, that I haue not done? Wherfore then hath it geuen thornes, where I loked to haue had grapes of it?

5 Well, I shall tell you how I wyl do with my vineyarde: I will take the hedge from it, that it maye perishe, & breake doune the wall, that it maye be troden vnder fote.

6 I wyl laye it waste, that it shall neyther be twisted nor cut, but beare thornes and breares. I wil also forbydde the cloudes, that they shall not raine vpon it.

7 As for the vyneyarde of the Lorde of Hostes it is the house of Israel, & whole Iuda hys fayre plantynge. Of these he loked for equyte, but se there is wronge: for rightuousnesse, lo, It is but miserye.

8 Wo be vnto you that ioyne one house to another, & bring one land so nyghe vnto another, tyll ye can get no more grounde. Wyll ye dwel vpon the earth alone?

9 The Lorde of Hostes roundeth me thus in myne eare: shall not many greater and more gorgyous houses be so waste, that no man shall dwell in them?

10 And ten akers of vynes shal geue but a Quarte, & .xxx. bushels of sede shall geue but thre.

11 Wo be vnto them that ryse vp earlye to vse them selues in dronkennes, & yet at nyght are more superfluous wyth wyne.

12 In those companies are harpes and lutes, tabrettes & pipes and wyne. But they regarde not the worck of the Lorde, and consydre not the operacyon of hys handes.

13 Therfore commeth my folcke also in captyuite, because they haue no vnderstandynge. Theyr glory shalbe mixte with hunger and theyr pryde shalbe marred for thyrste.

14 Therfore gapeth hell, and openeth her mouth maruelous wyde: that pryde, boastyng & wysdome, with suche as reioyse therein, may descende into it.

15 Thus shall man haue a fall, he shalbe brought lowe, & the hygh lokes of the proude layde doune.

16 But the Lorde of hostes, that holye God shalbe exalted and vntouched, when he shall declare hys equyte and ryghtuosnesse after thys maner:

17 Then shall the lambes eate theyr appoynted foder, & shall fede plenteouslye in the mountaynes.

18 Wo be vnto vayne persones, that drawe wyckednes vnto them, as it were with a coorde: & synne, as it were wt a carte rope.

19 Whiche vse to speake on thys maner: let hym make haste nowe, & go forthe with his worcke, that we maye se it. Let þe councell of the holye one of Israel come, and draw nye, that we maye knowe it.

20 Wo be vnto them that cal euyll good, and good euyll: which make darckenesse lyghte, & lyghte darckenesse, that make sower swete and swete sower.

21 Wo be vnto them that are wyse in theyr owne syght, and thyncke them selues to haue vnderstandynge.

22 Wo be vnto them, that are connynge men to suppe oute wyne, and experte to set vp dronckennesse.

23 These geue sentence wyth the vngodlye for rewardes, but condempne the iust cause of the ryghtuous.

24 Therfore lyke as fyre lycketh vp the straw & as the flamme consumeth the stubble: Euen so (when theyr rote is full) theyr blossome shall vanyshe awaye lyke duste or smoke: for they despyse the lawe of the Lorde of Hostes, and blaspheme the worde of the holye maker of Israel.

25 Therfore is the wrath of the Lorde kyndeled also agaynst his people, and he shaketh hys hande at them: yea he shall smyte so, that the hylles shall tremble. And theyr karcases shall lye in the open stretes, lyke myre. After all thys, the wrathe of God shall not ceasse, but he shall stretche hys hande wyder.

26 And he shall geue a token vnto a straunge people and call vnto them in a farre countrey: and beholde, they shall come hastelye wyth spede.

27 There is not one faynte nor feble amonge them, no not a slogyshe nor sleperye personne. There shall not one of them put of the gyrdle from hys loynes, nor louse their lachet of his shue.

28 Theyr arowes are sharpe, and theyr bowes bent. Their horse hoofes are lyke flynt, & theyr cartwheles lyke a stormy wynde.

29 Theyr crye is as it were of a lyon, and the roarynge of them lyke lyons whelpes. They shal roare and hantch vp the praye, and no man shal recouer it, or get it from them.

30 In that day they shalbe so fearce vpon them, as the sea. And yf we loke vnto the lande, beholde, it shalbe all darckenesse and sorowe. If we loke to heauen: beholde, it shalbe darcke wyth careful desperacyon.

# CHAPTER 6

IN the same yeare þe kynge Oziah dyed, I sawe the Lorde sytting vpon an high & gloryous seate, and hys trayne fylled the palace.

2 From aboue flakred the Seraphins, whereof euery one had six wynges. With twayne

# ISAIAH

eche couered his face, with twayne his fete, & with twayne dyd he flye.

3 They cryed also eche one to other on this maner: holy holy holy, is the Lord of hostes. The whole world is ful of his glory.

4 Yea the gestes and dorecheckes moued at their crieng, & the house was ful of smoke.

5 Then I sayde: O wo is me. For I was astonished: þt I (which am a man of vncleane lippes and dwell amonge people that hath vncleane lyppes also) shulde se the kynge and þe Lorde of hostes wyth myne eyes.

6 Then flue one of the Seraphins vnto me, hauynge a hote cole in hys hande, whiche he had taken from the aulter wyth the tounges,

7 and touched my mouthe, and sayde: lo, thys hath touched my mouth, and thyne vnryghtuousnes is taken awaye, and thy synne forgeuen.

8 After thys I heard the voyce of the Lord takyng aduysement on thys maner: Whome shall I sende, & who wylbe oure messenger? Then I sayde: here am I, sende me.

9 And so he sayde: go, and tell thys people: ye shall heare in dede, but ye shall not vnderstande, ye shall playnelye se, & not perceyue.

10 Harden þe hart of thys people, stoppe theyr eares, and shutte theyr eyes, that they se not with theyr eyes, heare not wyth theyr eares, and vnderstande not wyth theyr hertes, and conuerte and be healed.

11 Then spake I: Lorde, howe longe? he aunswered: vntyll the cytyes be vtterlye without inhabytours, and the houses wythoute men, tyll the lande be also desolate, & lye vnbuylded.

12 For the Lorde shall take the men farre awaye, so that the lande shall lye waste.

13 Neuertheles, the tenthe part shall remayne there in, for it shall conuerte and be frutefull. And lykewyse as the Terebyntes and Oketrees brynge forthe theyr frutes, so shall the holye sede haue frute.

## CHAPTER 7

IT happened in the time of Ahaz the sonne of Ioatham, whiche was the sonne of Oziah kyng of Iuda: that Razin the kyng of Syria, and Phakeh the sonne of Romeliah, kynge of Israel wente vp towarde Ierusalem to besege it, but wanne it not.

2 Nowe when the house of Dauid (that is Ahaz) hearde worde thereof, that Syria and Ephraim were confederate together: hys herte quaked (yea and the hertes also of hys people) lyke as a tree in the felde, that is moued wyth the wynde.

3 Then sayde God vnto Esay: go mete Ahaz (thou and thy sonne Sear Iasub) at the heade of the ouer pole, in the fote pathe by the fullers grounde,

4 and saye vnto hym: Take hede to thy selfe and be styll, but feare not, neyther be fayntharted, for these two tales: that is: for these two smokynge fyre brandes, the wrathe and furyousnes of Razin the Syryan and Romelyes sonne:

5 because that the kynge of Siria Ephraim & Romelyes sonne haue wickedlye conspyred agaynst the,

6 sayinge: We wyll go doune into Iuda, vexe them, and bryng them vnder vs, and set a kynge there, euen the sonne of Tabeel.

7 For thus sayth the Lorde GOD therto, It shall not so go forthe, nether come so to passe:

8 for the head cytye of the Syryans is Damascus, but the head of Damascus is Razin. And after fyue and threscore yeare, shall Ephraim be no more a people.

9 And the chefe cytye of Ephraim is Samaria, but the heade of Samaria is Romelies sonne. And yf ye beleue not, there shall no promyse be kepte wyth you.

10 Moreouer, God spake vnto Ahaz, saying:

11 requyre a token of the Lorde thy God, whether it be towarde the depthe benethe or towarde the heyght aboue.

12 Then sayde Ahaz: I wyll requyre none, neyther will I tempte the Lorde.

13 The Lord aunswered: Then heare to, ye of the house of Dauid: Is it not ynough for you, that ye be greuous vnto men, but ye muste greue my God also?

14 And therfore the Lorde shall geue you a token of hym selfe: Beholde, a vyrgyn shall conceyue and beare a sonne, and shall call hys name Emmanuel.

15 Butter and honye shall he eate, that he maye knowe the euyll, and chose the good.

16 But or euer the chylde come to knowledge, to eschue the euyll and chose the good: The lande (that thou arte so afrayde for) shalbe desolate of both her kynges.

17 The Lorde also shall sende a tyme vpon the, vpon thy people, and vpon thy fathers house (suche as neuer came sence the tyme that Ephraim departed from Iuda) thorowe the kynge of the Assyryans.

18 For at the same tyme shall the Lorde whistle for the flies that are aboute the water of Egypte, and for the bees in the Assyryans lande.

19 These shall come, and shall lyght all in the valeys, in the vawtes of stone, vpon all greue thynges, and in all corners.

20 At the same tyme shall the Lorde shaue the hearre of the heade and the fete and the beerd cleane of, with the rasoure þt he shall paye them wyth all

beyonde the water: namelye wyth the kynge of the Assyryans.

21 At the same tyme shall a man lyue wyth a cowe, and two shepe.

22 Then because of the aboundaunce of mylcke, he shall make butter and eate it. So that euerye one whiche remayneth in the lande, shall eate butter and honye.

23 At the same tyme all vyneyardes (thoughe there be a thousande vynes in one, and were solde for a thousande syluerlynges) shalbe turned to brears and thornes.

24 Lyke as they shall come into the lande wyth arowes and bowes, so shall al the land be come brears and thornes.

25 And as for all hylles that nowe are hewen doune, thou shalt not come vpon them, for feare of brears and thornes. But the catell shall be dryuen thyther, and the shepe shall fede there.

# CHAPTER 8

MOREOUER the Lorde sayde vnto me: Take the a great leaf, and wryte in it, as men do wyth a penne, that he spede hym to robbe and haste him to spoyle.

2 And immediatly I called vnto me faythfull wytnesses, Vriah the priest, and Zachariah þe sonne of Barachiah.

3 After that went I vnto the Prophetisse, that nowe had conceiued and borne a sonne. Then sayde the Lorde to me: geue him this name: Maherschalal haschbas (that is, a spedie robber: an hastie spoyler.)

4 For why, or euer the child shall haue knowledge to saye: Abi and Im (that is father, and mother): shall the ryches of Damascus, and the substaunce of Samaria be taken awaye, thorowe the kynge of the Assirians.

5 The Lorde spake also vnto me, sayinge:

6 for so muche as the people refuseth the styll runnynge water of Silo, and put their delyte in Razin and Romelies sonne:

7 Beholde, the Lorde shall brynge mightye and greate floudes of water vpon them: namely the kinge of the Assirians with all his power. Whyche shall poure oute his furiousnesse vpon euery man, and runne ouer all their banckes.

8 And shall breake in vpon Iuda, increasyng in power, tyll he get him by the throte. He shal fyl also the wydenesse of thy lande with hys broade wynges, O Emanuell.

9 Go together ye people, and gather you, herken to all ye of farre countreyes. Mustre you, & gather you: mustre you and gather you,

10 take your councel together, yet must youre councell come to nought: go in hand with all, yet shall it not prosper. Excepte Emanuel: (that is God) be with vs.

11 For the Lord chastised me, & toke me by the hande, and warned me, sayinge vnto me, that I shoulde not walcke in the waye of thys people. He sayde moreouer:

12 rounde with none of them, whosoeuer saye: younder people are bounde together. Neuertheles feare them not, neyther be afraide of them,

13 but sanctifye the Lorde of hostes, let him be youre feare and drede.

14 For he is the sanctifyeng, and stone to stomble at the rocke to fall vpon, a snare and net to both the houses, to Israell, and the inhabitours of Ierusalem.

15 And many shall stomble, fall, & be broken vpon him: yea they shalbe snared and taken.

16 Now laye the witnesses together (said the Lorde) and seale the lawe with my disciples.

17 Thus I wayte vpon the Lorde that hath turned his face from the house of Iacob, and I loke vnto him.

18 But lo, as for me, and the children whiche the Lorde hath geuen me: we are a token and a wondre in Israel, for the Lorde of hostes sake, whiche dwelleth vpon the hill of Syon.

19 And therfore yf they saye vnto you: aske councel at the sothesayers, wytches, charmers and coniurers, then make them thys answere: Is there a people any where, that asketh not councel at his God, whether it be concerning the deade, or the lyuynge?

20 Yf any man want lyght, let hym loke vpon the lawe and the testimony, whether they speake not after thys meaninge.

21 Yf he do not thys, he stombleth & suffereth hunger. And yf he suffre hunger, he is out of pacience, and blasphemeth hys kynge and his God. Then loketh he vpwarde, and dounewarde to the earthe,

22 and beholde, there is trouble & darcknesse, vexacyon is rounde aboute him, and the cloude of erroure. And oute of suche aduersitie, shall he not escape.

# CHAPTER 9

EVEN lyke as in time past it hath bene well sene, that the lande of Zabulon and the land of Nephtali (where thorow the sea way goeth ouer Iordane into the land of Galilee) was at the fyrst in lytle trouble, but afterwarde sore vexed.

2 Neuertheles the people that haue dwelt in darcknesse, shall se a greate lyght. As for them that dwell in the lande of the shadowe of death, vpon them shall the lyght shyne.

3 Shalt thou multyplye the people, and not increase the ioye

also? They shall reioyse before the euen as men make mery in haruest and as men that haue gotten the vyctorye, when they deale the spoyle.

4 For thou shalte breake the yocke of the peoples burthen, the staffe of his shoulder, and the road of hys oppressoure, as in the daye of Madian.

5 Moreouer all temerariours and sedicious power (yea where there is but a cote fylled with bloude) shalbe burnt, and fede the fyre.

6 For vnto vs a chylde shalbe borne, and vnto vs a sonne shalbe geuen. Vpon his shoulder shall the kyngedome lye, and he shalbe called with hys owne name. The wonderous geuer of councel, the myghty God, the euerlastinge father, the prynce of peace,

7 he shall make no ende to encrease the kyngedome and peace, and shall sytte vpon the seate of Dauid, and in his kyngedome, to set vp the same, to stablyshe it wyth equyte and ryghteousnesse, from thence forth for euermore. This shall the gelousy of the Lorde of hostes brynge to paste.

8 The Lord sent a word into Iacob, the same is come into Israell.

9 And the people also of Ephraim, and they that dwell in Samaria, can saye wyth pryde and hye stomackes, on this maner:

10 The tyle worcke is fallen doune but we wyll buylde it wyth harder stones. The Molbery tymbre is broken, but we shal set it vp agayne with Cedre.

11 Neuertheles, the Lorde shall prepare Razin the enemy against them, and so ordre their aduersaryes,

12 that the Sirians shall laye holde vpon them before, & the Philistines behinde, and so deuoure Israell wyth open mouth. After all thys, the wrath of the Lord shall not ceasse, but yet his hande shall be stretched oute styll.

13 For the people turneth not vnto hym, that chastyseth them, nether do they seke the Lorde of Hostes.

14 Therfore the Lorde shal rote oute of Israel bothe head & tayle, braunch and twigge in one daye.

15 By the heade, is vnderstande the Senatoure and honorable man, and by the tayle, the Prophet that preacheth lyes.

16 For al they whiche enfourme the people that they be in a righte case, suche be disceyuers. Suche as men thyncke also to be perfecte amonge these, are but cast awaye.

17 Therfore shall the Lorde haue no pleasure in their yonge men, neyther fauoure their fatherlesse and wyddowes. For they are all together ypocrytes and wicked, and all their mouthes speake foly. After all this shall not the Lordes wrathe ceasse, but yet his hande shalbe stretched oute still.

18 For the vngodlye burne as a fyre in the bryers and thornes. And as it were oute of a fyre in a wood or a read bushe, so ascendeth the smoke of their pryde.

19 For this cause shall the wrath of the Lorde of Hostes fal vpon the lande, and the people shalbe consumed, as it were with fyre, no man shall spare his brother.

20 Yf a man do turne him to the ryght hande, he shall famishe, or to the lefte hande to eate, he shall not haue ynough. Euery man shall eate the fleshe of his owne arme.

21 Manasses shall eat Ephraim and Ephraim Manasses, and they both shall eate Iuda. After al this shall not the Lordes wrath cease, but yet shall his hande be stretched oute styll.

# CHAPTER 10

Wo be vnto you that make vnryghteous lawes, and deuyse thinges, whiche be to harde for to kepe:

2 where thorow the pore are oppressed on euery syde, & the innocentes of my people are therwyth robbed of iudgement: that wyddowes maye be youre praye, and that ye maye robbe the fatherlesse.

3 What wyll ye do in tyme of the visitacion and destruccyon, that shall come from farre? Tho whome wyll ye runne for helpe? or to whome will ye geue your honour that ye maye kepe it?

4 that ye come not among the presonners, or lye amonge the deade? After all this shall not the wrath of the Lord cease, but yet shall hys hande be stretched out styll.

5 Wo be also vnto Assur, whiche is a staffe of my wrathe, in whose hande is the roade of my punishement.

6 For I shall send him among those ypocrytish people, amonge the people that haue deserued my disfauour shall I send him: that he maye vtterly robbe them, spoyle them, and tread them doune lyke the myre in the strete.

7 How be it, his meaninge is not so, neither thinccketh his hert of this fasshion. But he ymagineth only, how he may ouerthrowe and destroye muche people,

8 for he sayth: are not my princes al kinges?

9 Is not Calno as easye to winne, as Charchamis? Is it harder to conquere Antiochia then Arphad? Or is it lyghter to ouercome Damascus then Samaria?

10 As wo say: I were able to

winne the kingedome of the Idolatres and their Goddes, but not Ierusalem and Samaria.

11 Shall I not do vnto Ierusalem and their ymages, as I dyd vnto Samaria and their ymages?

12 Wherfore the Lorde sayeth: As sone as I haue perfourmed my whole worcke vpon the hyll of Sion and Ierusalem, then wyll I also vpset the noble and stoute kynge of Assiria, wyth his wisedom and pryde.

13 For he standeth thus in hys owne conceyte. Thys do I thorow the power of myne owne hand, and thorowe my wysedome: For I am wyse I am he that remoue the landes of the people I robbe the princes, and (lyke one of the worthies) I dryue them from their hye seates.

14 My hande hathe founde out the hostes of the people, as it were arnest. And lyke as egges, that were layde here and there, are gathered togegether. So do I gather all countreyes. And there is no man, that darre be so bolde, as to touche a fether, that darre open his mouth, or ones whisper.

15 But doth the axe boost it selfe, agaynste hym, þt he heweth therwyth, or doth the sawe make any krackynge, agaynst hym that ruleth it? That were euen lyke, as yf the roade dyd exalte it selfe, against him that beareth it: or as though the staffe shoulde magnyfye it selfe, as who saie: it were no wode.

16 Therfore shall the Lorde of Hostes sende him pouerte in his ryches, and burne vp hys power, as it were wyth a fyre.

17 But the lyght of Israell shalbe that fyre, and his Sanctuarye shalbe the flamme, and it shal kyndle, and burne vp his thornes and breers in one daye,

18 ye all the glory of his woodes and feldes shalbe consumed with body and soule. As for hym selfe, he shalbe as one chased away.

19 The trees also of his felde shalbe of suche a nombre, that a chylde may tell them.

20 After that daye shall the remnaunt of Israel, & suche as are escaped out of the house of Iacob, seke no more comfort at him that smote them, but shall comforte them selues wyth faythfulnesse and truthe in the Lorde, the holy one of Israell.

21 The remnaunt, yea and the posteryte of Iacob, shall conuerte vnto God the myghty one.

22 For thoughe thy people (O Israel) be as the sande of the sea, yet shall but the remnaunt of them onely conuerte vnto hym. Perfecte is the iudgement of hym that floweth in ryghteousnesse,

23 and therfore the Lorde of Hostes shall perfectlye fulfyll the thynge, that he had determyned in the myddest of the whole world.

24 Therfore thus sayth the Lorde God of Hostes: Thou my people thrt dwellest in Sion, be not afrayed for the king of þe Assirians: He shall wagge his staffe at the, yea and beate the with the road, as the Egypcians did some tyme.

25 But soone after, shal my wrathe and mine indignacion be fulfilled agaynst their blasphemies.

26 Moreouer the Lorde of Hostes shall prepare a scourge for him, lyke as was the punyshement of Madian vpon the mount of Oreb. And he shall lyft vp his road ouer the sea, as he dyd somtyme ouer the Egipcians.

27 Then shall his burthen be taken from thy shoulders, and his yock from thy neck, yea þe same yocke shall be corrupt for very fatnesse.

28 He shall come to Aiath, & go thorow towarde Migron. But at Machmas shall he muster his hoste,

29 and go ouer the foorde. Gabaah shalbe their restinge place, Rhamah shalbe afrayed, Gabaah Saul shall fle awaye.

30 The voyce of the noyse of thy horses (O doughter Gallim) shalbe hearde vnto Lais and to Anathoth, which also shalbe in trouble.

31 Madmena shall tremble for feare, but the cytesyns of Gabin are manlye,

32 yet shall he remayne at Nob that daye. After that, shall he lyft vp his hande agaynst the mount of Sion, and against the hyll of Ierusalem.

33 But se the lorde God of hostes shall take awaye the proude from thence with feare. He shall hew doune the proude, and fel the hye minded.

34 The thornes of the wood shalbe roted out with yron, and Libanus shall haue a myghtye fall.

# CHAPTER 11

AFTER this there shall come a road forth of the kynrede of Iesse, & a blossome oute of his rote.

2 The spyryt of the Lorde shall lyghte vpon it, the spyryte of wisedome and vnderstandynge: the spirit of councell, & strength: the spirite of knowledge, and of the feare of God:

3 and shall make him feruent in the feare of God. For he shall not geue sentence, after the thinge that shall be brought before his eyes, neyther reproue a matter at the fyrst hearing

4 but wyth ryghteousnesse shall he iudge the poore, and with holynes shal he refourme the symple of the worlde. He shall smyte the worlde wyth the staffe of hys mouthe, & with the breathe of his mouth shall he slay the wicked.

5 Ryghteousnesse shalbe þe gyrdle of his loynes, truthe & faythfulnesse, the gyrdynge vp of hys raynes.

6 Then shall the wolfe dwell wyth the lambe, and the leoparde shall lye doune by the gote. Bullockes, lions and catel shal kepe company together, so that a lytle childe shall dryue them forthe.

7 The cowe and the Beare shall fede together, & their younge ones shall lye together. The Lyon shall eate strawe like the oxe, or the cowe.

8 The chylde whyle he sucketh, shal haue a desyre to the serpentes nest, and when he is weaned, he shall put his hand into the Cochatryce denne.

9 No man shall do euyl to another, no man shall destroye another, in all the hyll of my Sanctuarye. For the earth shalbe full of the knowledge of the Lorde, euen as thoughe the water of the sea floweth ouer the earth.

10 Then shal the Gentyles enquere after the rote of Iesse (whiche shalbe set vp for a token vnto the Gentyles) for hys dwellinge shalbe glorious.

11 At the same tyme shal the Lord take in hande agayne, to conquere the remnaunt of hys people (whiche are left alyue.) From the Assirians, Egypcians, Arabians, Morians, Elamites, Ealdeyes, Antiochiaus, and Ilandes of the sea.

12 And he shal set vp a token amonge the Gentyles, and gather together the dispersed of Israel, yea and the out castes of Iuda from the foure corners of the world.

13 The hatred of Ephraim and the emnyte of Iuda shalbe cleane roted oute. Ephraim shall beare no euyll wyll to Iuda, and Iuda shall not hate Ephraim:

14 but they bothe together shall flee vpon the shoulders of the Philistines towarde the West, and spoyle them together that dwell towarde the Easte. The Idumytes and the Moabites shall let their handes, fal & the Ammonites shalbe obedient vnto them.

15 The Lorde also shall cleaue the tunges of the Egypcyans sea, and with a mighty wind shal he lift vp his hande ouer Nilus, & shall smyte hys seuen streames and make men go ouer drye shod.

16 And thus shall he make a waye for his people, that remayneth from the Assirians, lyke as it happened to the Israelytes, what tyme they departed oute of the lande of Egypt.

## CHAPTER 12

So that then thou shalt saye: O Lord I thanke the, for thou wast displeased at me, but thou haste refrained thy wrath, & hast mercy vpon me.

2 Beholde, God is my health, in whom I trust, & am not afraid. For the Lorde God is my strength and my praise, he also shalbe my refuge.

3 Therefore wt ioye shal ye drawe water out of the welles of the Sauioure,

4 & then shall ye saye: Let vs geue thankes vnto the Lorde, and call vpon his name, & declare his councels amonge the people, and kepe them in remembraunce for his name is excellente.

5 O synge prayses vnto the Lorde, for he doth great thinges, as it is knowne in al the worlde.

6 Crye oute, and be glad, thou that dwellest in Sion, for greate is thy prince, the holy one of Israell.

## CHAPTER 13

Thys is the heauy burthen of Babilon, whiche Esai the sonne of Amos dyd se.

2 Make some tokens to the hye hilles, call vnto them, hold vp youre hande, that the Princes maye go in at the dore.

3 For I will send for my debites & my gyauntes (sayth the Lorde) and in my wrath I wil call for suche, as triumphe in my glory.

4 With that, me thought I heard in the mountaynes a noyse, like as is hath bene of a great people: & a russhynge, as though the kyngedomes of al nacions had come together. (And the Lorde of Hostes was the captayne of the whole armye)

5 As they had not come only out of farre countreyes, but also from the endes of the heauens: Euen the Lorde him selfe with the ministres of his wrath, to destroye the whole lande.

6 Mourne therfore, for the daye of the Lorde is at hande, & commeth as a destroyer from the Almyghtye.

7 Then shall all handes be letten doune, and all mens hertes shall melt awaie,

8 they shall stande in feare, carefulnesse and sorowe shal come vpon them, and they shal haue payne, as a woman that trauaileth with childe. One shal euer be abasshed of another, and their faces shall burne lyke the flamme.

9 For lo, the daye of the Lorde shall come, terrible, full of indignacion and wrathe, to make the lande waste, and to rote oute the synne therof.

10 For the sterres and planetes of heauen shal not geue their lyght, the sunne shalbe quenched in the risinge, and the mone shall not shyne with his light.

11 And I will punysh the wickednesse of the worlde, and the synnes of the vngodly, sayeth the Lorde. The hye stomackes of the proude wyl I take awaye, and will laye doune the boastynge of tyrauntes.

12 I wyll make a man dearer

then fyne goulde, and a man to be more worthe, then a goulden wedge of Ophir.

13 Moreouer, I wil so shake the heauen, that the earth shall remoue oute of her place. Thus shall it go with Babilon in the wrath of the Lorde of Hostes in the daye of his fearfull indignacyon.

14 And Babilon shalbe as an hunted or chased do, and as a flocke wythout a sheperde. Euery man shal turne to his own people, and flee eche one into his owne land.

15 Whoso is founde alone, shalbe shot thorow. And whoso gather together, shalbe destroied with the swerd.

16 Their chyldren shalbe slaine before their eyes, their houses spoyled, and their wyues rauyshed.

17 For lo, I shall brynge vp the Medes agaynst them, whiche shall not regarde siluer, nor be desyrous of gould.

18 Then shall young mens bowes be knapped a sunder. The Medes shall haue no pytye vpon wemen with chylde, and their faces shal not spare the chyldren.

19 And Babylon (that glory of kingedomes and bewtye of the Caldees honoure) shalbe destroied, euen as God destroyed Sodome and Gomorra.

20 It shall neuer be more inhabyted, neyther shal there be any more dwellynge there from generacion to generacyon. The Arabians shall make no more tentes there, neyther shall the shepardes make their foldes ther any more:

21 but wild beastes shal lye there, & the houses shalbe full of greate Oules. Estriches shall dwel there, and Apes shall daunse there:

22 the lytle Oules shal crye in the palaces, one after another, and Dragons shalbe in the plesaunt parlours. And as for Babilons tyme it is at hande, & her dayes maye not be longe absent.

# CHAPTER 14

Bvt the Lorde wylbe mercyfull vnto Iacob, and wil take vp Israel agayne, and set them in their owne lande. Straungers shall cleaue vnto them, and get them to the house of Iacob.

2 They shall take the people, and cary them home with them. And the house of Israell shall haue them in possession for seruauntes and maydens in the lande of the Lorde. They shall take those presonners, whose captyues they had bene afore, and rule those that had oppressed them.

3 When the lord now shall bringe the to rest, from the trauail, feare, and harde boundage that thou wast laden wyth all,

4 then shalte thou vse thys mockage vpon the Kynge of Babylon, and saye: Howe happeneth it, that the oppressoure leaueth of? Is the goulden trybute come to an ende?

5 Douteles the Lorde hathe broken the staffe of the vngodlye, and the scepter of the lordly.

6 Whyche when he is wrothe, smyteth the people with durable strokes, and in his wonders he persecuteth them, and tameth them continually.

7 And therfore the whole worlde is now at reste and quyetnesse, and men sing for ioye.

8 Yea, euen the Fyrre trees and Cedres of Libanus reioyse at thy fall, sayinge: Nowe that thou arte laide doune, there come no mo vp to destroye vs.

9 Hell also trembleth at thy commynge, all myghtye men, and Prynces of the earth, steppe forth before the. All Kynges of the earth stande vp from their seates,

10 that they may all (one after another) synge & speake vnto the. Art thou wounded also as we? art thou become lyke vnto vs?

11 Thy pompe and thy pryde is gone doune to hell. Mothes shalbe layde vnder the, and wormes shalbe thy coueringe.

12 How art thou fallen from heauen (O Lucifer) thou faire mornyng childe? hast thou gotten a fal euen to the ground, thou that (not withstanding) diddest subdue the people.

13 And yet thou thoughtest in thyne herte: I wyll climme vp into heauen, and make my seate aboue the starres of God, I wyl syt vpon the glorious mounte toward the North,

14 I wyll climme vp aboue the cloudes, and wylbe like the hyghest of all.

15 Yet darre I saye, that thou shalt be brought doune to þe depe of hel.

16 They that se the, shal narowly loke vpon the, and thinke in them selues, sayenge: Is thys the man, that brought all landes in feare, and made the kyngedomes afrayde.

17 Is this he þt made the worlde in a maner waste, and layde the cytyes to the grounde, whyche let not his prisoners go home?

18 How happeneth it, that the kynges of all people lye, euery one at home in his owne palace, with worshyppe,

19 and thou art cast oute of thy graue, like a wild braunch: like as dead mens raiment that are shot thorow wyth the swerde: as they that go doune to the stones of the depe, as a deade coarse that is troden vnder fete:

20 and art not buryed with them? Euen because that thou hast wasted thy lande, and destroyed thy people. For the generacion of the wycked shalbe

wythoute honoure foreuer.

21 There shall a way be sought to destroye their chyldren, for their fathers wyckednes: they shall not come vp agayne to possesse the lande, and fyll the worlde ful of castels and townes.

22 I will stande vp against them (sayeth the Lorde of Hostes) and rote out the name & generacyon of Babylon (sayeth the Lorde)

23 and wyll geue it to the Oiters, and wyl make water podles of it. And I wyll swepe them oute with the besome of destruccyon, sayeth the Lorde of Hostes.

24 The Lorde of Hostes hathe sworne an othe, sayinge: It shal come to passe as I haue determyned: and shalbe fulfylled as I haue deuysed.

25 The Assyryans shalbe destroyed in my lande, and vpon my mountaynes wyll I treade them vnder fote. Where thorow hys yock shall come from you, & hys burthen shalbe taken from youre shoulders.

26 This deuyce hath God taken thorowe the whole worlde, and thus is hys hand stretched out ouer al people.

27 For yf the Lorde of Hostes determen a thynge, who wyl dysanulle it? And yf he stretch forth hys hande, who wil holde it in agayne?

28 The same yeare that kynge Ahaz dyed, God threatened by Esay on thys maner:

29 Reioyse not (thou whole Palestina) as thoughe the road of him that beateth the were broken: for out of the serpentes rote, there shall waxe a kockatrice, & the frute shalbe a fyrie worme.

30 But the poore shall fede of the best thynges, and the simple shal dwel in safety. Thy rotes wil I destroye with hunger, and it shall slay thy remnaunt.

31 Mourne ye portes, wepe ye cities, and feare thou (O whole Palestina) for there shall come from the North a smoke, whose power noman may abyde.

32 Who shall then maynteyne the messages of the Gentyles? But the Lorde stablisheth Sion, and the poore of my people shall put their truste in hym.

# CHAPTER 15

THIS is the heauy burthen vpon Moab: Ar of Moab was destroyed (as me thought) in the night season: the walles of Moab perished in the night, and vanished awaye.

2 They wente to Baith and Dibon in the hie places, for to wepe: Moab dyd mourne from Nebo to Medba. All their heades were colled, and all their beardes shauen.

3 In their stretes were they girded aboute with sacke clothe. In al the toppes of their houses and stretes was there nothinge but mourninge and wepinge.

4 Hesebon and Eleale cryed, that their voyce was hearde vnto Iahaz. The worthyes also of Moab bleared and cryed for very sorowe of their mindes.

5 Wo is my herte for Moabs sake. They fled vnto the cyty of Zoar, whiche is lyke a faire frutefull bullocke, they went vp to Luhith, weping. The waye toward Horonaim was ful of lamentacion for the hurte.

6 The waters of Nimrim were dried vp, the grasse was withred, the herbes destroied, and what necessary grene thing there was beside.

7 In lyke maner the thing that was left them of their substaunce, they caryed it by water to Arabye.

8 The crye wente ouer the whole lande of Moab: from Eglaim vnto Beer was there nothinge but mournyng.

9 The waters of Dimon were full of bloude, for the enemye hath sent thyther a bonde of men, which as a lyon laye awayte for the remnaunt of the lande, and for them that were escaped.

# CHAPTER 16

THEN sent the Lordes of the lande a man of warre, from the rocke that lyeth toward the deserte vnto the hyl of þe doughter Sion.

2 (For as for the doughters of Moab, they were as it had bene a trembling byrd, that is put oute of her nest, by the fery of Arnon) whiche messaunger sayde:

3 gather you councell, come together couer vs wyth your shadowe in the middaye, as the nyght doeth: hyd the chased, and be wray not them that are fled,

4 let the persecuted Moabites dwel among you, be you open refuge against the destroyer: for the aduersarye oppresseth vs, the robber vndoeth vs, & the tiraunt driueth vs oute of oure lande.

5 But the trone of youre Kyngedome is full of grace, therfore he that sitteth vpon it with faythfulnesse and trueth in the house of Dauid, knowe the thing, and do his diligence to helpe shortly, according to equite and ryghteousnes.

6 As for Moabs pride (shal they answere) it is well knowne. And all thoughe they be excellent, proude, arrogante and hye minded: yet is their strength nothing lyke.

7 And therfore Moab complayneth vnto Moab, where thorowe they come all to mourne: and now that they be smytten, they take their deuyce beneth by the bryckwall, & make theyr complaynte.

8 The suburbes also of Hesebon were made waste, & the Princes of the Gentyles hewed doune the vyneyardes of Sibma, whyche were planted

# ISAIAH

with noble grapes, and spred vnto Iazer, and wente vnto the ende of the deserte, whose braunches stretched their selues forth beyonde the sea.

9 Therfore I mourned for Iazer, & for the vineyardes of Sibma with great sorowe. I poured my teares vpon Hesebon and Eleale, for al their songes were layde doune, in their haruest and gatherynge of their grapes.

10 Myrth and there was gone out of the felde and vyneyardes, in so muche that noman was glad nor songe. There went no treader into the wynepresse, their merye chere was layde doune.

11 Wherfore my belye rombled (as it had bene a lute) for Moabs sake and mine inward membres, for the brickwalles sake.

12 For it happened thus also: when Moab sawe that she was turned vpsyde doune: she went vpon on hye into her Sanctuarie, to make her prayer there, but she might not be helped.

13 This is the deuyce, whyche the Lorde toke in hande at that tyme agaynste Moab.

14 But now the Lorde sayeth thus: In the yeare shall the power of Moab wyth their pompe (whiche is greate) be minished, lyke as the burthen of an hyred seruaunt. And as for the remnaunt of them, they shalbe lesse then a fewe, and not rekened muche worth.

## CHAPTER 17

THIS is the heauy burthen vpon Damascus: Behold Damascus shalbe no more a citie, but an heape of broken stones.

2 The cyties of Aroer shalbe waste: the catell shal lye there, and no man shal fray them awaye.

3 Ephraim shal no more be strong, and Damascus shal no more be a kingedom. And as for the glory of the remnaunt of the Sirians it shalbe as the glory of the children of Israel sayeth the Lorde of Hostes.

4 At that tyme also shal the glory of Iacob be very poore, and his fatnes leane.

5 It shal happen to them, as when one sheareth in haruest, which cutteth his handfull with the sickle, and when one gathereth þe sheaues together in the valley, of Raphaim

6 there remaineth yet some eares ouer: Or as when one shaketh an olyue tre, whiche fyndeth but two or thre olyue beries aboue in the toppe, & foure or fyue in the braunches. Thus the Lorde God of Israel hath spoken.

7 Then shall man conuerte agayne vnto his maker, and turne his eyes to the holy one of Israel.

8 And shall not turne to the aulters that are the worcke of his owne handes, neyther shal he loke vpon groues & ymages, which his fingers haue wrought.

9 At the same tyme shall their stronge cities be desolate, lyke as were ones the forsaken plowes & corne, which they forsoke, for feare of the children of Israel.

10 So shalt thou (O Damascus) be desolate because thou hast forgotten God thy Sauyoure, & hast not called to remembraunce the rocke of thy strength. Wherfore thou hast also set a fayr plat, & grafted a straung branch.

11 In the day when thou diddest plant it, it was greate, and gaue sone the frute of thy sede. But in the daye of haruest, thou shalt reape and heape of sorowes and myseries.

12 Wo be to the multitude of muche people, that rush in lyke the sea, and to the heape of folke, that runne ouer al lyke greate waters.

13 For thoughe so manye people increase as the flowynge waters, and though they be armed yet they fle farre of, and vanyshe awaye lyke the dust with the winde vpon an hill, and as the whirle winde thorow a storme.

14 Thoughe they be fearfull at night, yet in the morninge it is gone with them. This is their porcyon, that do vs harme, and heritage of them, that robbe vs.

## CHAPTER 18

WO be to the land of flieng shippes, whyche is of thys side the floude of Ethiopia:

2 whych sendeth her message ouer the sea in shyppes of redes vpon the water: and sayeth: go sone & do youre message vnto a straunge and harde folke, to a fearful people, and to a people that is forther then this: to a desperate and pylled folke, whose lande is deuyded from vs with riuers of water.

3 Yea, al ye that syt in the compasse of the worlde, and dwell vpon the earthe, when the token shalbe geuen vpon the mountaynes, then loke vp: & when the horne bloweth, then herken to,

4 for thus hath the Lorde sayde vnto me. I layde me doune, and pondred the matter in my house, at the noone day when it was hote. And there fell a mistynge shower, lyke a dewe, as it happened in Haruest.

5 But the frutes were not yet type cut of, and the grapes were but younge and grene. Then one smote of the grapes wyth an hoke, yea he hewed doune also the bowes and the braunches and dyd cast them awaye.

6 And thus they were layde waste, for the foules of the mountaynes, and for the beastes of the earthe together. So that the foules sat there vpon, and the beastes of the earth wyntered

there.

7 Then shall there be a present brought vnto the Lord of Hostes, euen that harde folke, that fearful folke, and that forther is then thys: that desperate and pylled folke (whose lande is deuided from vs with floudes of water) vnto the place of the name of the Lorde of Hostes: euen vnto the hyll of Syon.

## CHAPTER 19

THIS is the heauy burthen vpon Egipt: Beholde, the Lord wyll ryde vpon a swyft cloude, & come into Egipt. And the Goddes of Egypte shall tremble at hys comminge, and the herte of Egypt shal quake within her.

2 For thus sayeth the Lord: I wil stere vp the Egypcyans one agaynste another among them selues, so that one shalbe euer against his brother & neyghbour, yea one city against another, & one kingdome against another.

3 And Egypt shalbe choked in her selfe. When they aske councel at their goddes, at their prophetes, at their sothsayers & witches, then will I brynge their councell to naught.

4 I wil delyuer Egipt also into þe handes of greuous rulers, and a cruel king shal haue þe rule of them.

5 The water of the sea shalbe drawen out, Nilus shal sinck away, & be droncken vp.

6 The riuers also shalbe drawen out, þe welles shal decreace and drye away. Rede & rush shal faile,

7 the grasse by the water syde or vpon the riuers banck, yea & whatsoeuer is sowen by the waters, shalbe withered, destroyed, & brought to naught.

8 The fishers shal mourne al suche as cast angles in the water, shal complayne, & they that sprede their nettes in the water, shalbe faynt harted.

9 Such as laboure vpon flax & sylck, shal come to pouerte, and they also that weeue fyne worckes.

10 All the poundes of Egypte, all the pollycye of their Moates and dyches shall come to naught.

11 Yea the vndiscrete Princes of Zoan, the councel of the wise Senatoures of Pharao, shall turne to folyshenesse. Those that darre boast & saye of Pharaos behalfe: I am come of wyse people,

12 I am come of the olde regall Progeny. But where are now thy wyse men? Let them tel the & shewe the, what the Lorde of hostes hath taken in hande agaynst Egipt.

13 Fooles are these Prynces of Zoan, & proude are the Princes of Noph: yea they disceyue Egypte with the nobilitye of their stock.

14 For the Lorde hath made Egypte droncken with the spirit of erroure, and they shal vse it in al matters, euen lyke as a droncken man goeth spewynge aboute.

15 For Egypte shall lacke good councell, so that they shall not knowe what to do, neyther beginning nor ende, neyther vpon the lande nor water.

16 Then shal the Egipcyans be lyke vnto wemen, afrayde & astonied, at the liftynge vp of the head, which the Lorde of Hostes shal lyft vp ouer them.

17 The land of Iuda also shall make the Egipcians afrayde, who so doeth but speake vpon it, shal put them in feare. And that because of the councel, whiche the Lorde of Hostes hath deuysed agaynst them.

18 Then shall the fyue cyties of Egypte speake wyth the Cananytes tonge, and swere by the Lorde of Hostes, & Heliopolis shalbe one of them.

19 At the same tyme shall the Lorde of Hostes haue an aulter in the middest of the lande of Egypt, with thys tytle therby: Vnto the Lord.

20 This shalbe a token or testimony vnto the Lorde of hostes in the lande of Egypt, when they shall crye vnto him, because of those that oppresse them, that he shal sende them a Captayne and a Sauioure to delyuer them.

21 Moreouer, Egypte shalbe boughte vnto the Lorde, and the Egipcians also shal know the Lorde at the same tyme: they shall do him reuerence with peaceofferinges, & with meatofferinges: they shal promyse him offeringes, yea and paye him also.

22 Thus the Lorde shall smyte Egipt, and heale it agayn: and so shal they turne to the Lorde, & he also shall haue mercy vpon them, and saue them.

23 Then shall there be a commen waye out of Egipt, into Assiria. The Assirians shal come into Egipt, and the Egipcians into Assiria. The Egipcians also and the Assirians shall bothe haue one Goddes seruyce.

24 Then shal Israel with honour be the thirde to Egipt and Assur,

25 and the Lorde of hostes shall blesse them, saying: Blessed is my people of the Egipcians, Assur is the worcke of my handes, but Israel is mine enheritaunce.

## CHAPTER 20

IN the same yeare that Tharthan came to Asdod, where Sargon the kynge of the Assirians sent him, what tyme as he also beseged Asdod, and wanne it the same season.

2 Then spake the Lorde vnto Esai the sonne of Amos, sayinge: go and louse of that sacke clothe from thy loynes: and put of thy shoes from thy fete. And so he did, going naked

and barefote.

3 Then sayde the Lorde: where as my seruaunt Esai goeth naked and barefote, it is a token and signifyenge of the thinge, that after thre yeare shall come vpon Egipt and Ethiopia.

4 For euen thus shall the kinge of the Assirians dryue bothe younge & olde, as presonners naked and barefote, oute of Egipte and Ethiopia. And shall discouer the shame of Egipt.

5 They shalbe also at their wittes ende, and ashamed one of another: the Egipcians of the Morians, and the Morians of the Egipcians, at the syght of their glorye.

6 Moreouer they that dwell in the Iles shall se euen the same daye: behold, this is our hope to whom we fled to seke helpe, that we might be delyuered from the kynge of the Assirians. How wil we escape?

## CHAPTER 21

THYS is the heauy burthen of the waste sea: A greuous vysion was shewed vnto me, lyke as when a storme of winde & rayn russheth in from the wildernesse that terrible land.

2 Who so may disceyue (said the voyce) let him disceyue. Who so may destroye, let him dystroye. Vp Elam, besege it O Madai, for I wyl styl al their groninges.

3 With this the raynes of my backe were full of payne: Panges came vpon me, as vpon a woman in her trauayle. When I hearde it, I was abasshed, and when I loked vp, I was afrayde.

4 Myne herte panted, I trembled for feare. The darcknesse made me fearfull in in my mynde.

5 Yea sone make ready the table (sayde this voyce) kepe the watch, eate & dryncke. Vp ye Captaynes, take you to youre shild,

6 for thus the Lorde hath charged me: go thy waye, and set a watche man, þt he may tel what he seith.

7 And when he had wayted dylygentlye, he sawe two horsemen: the one rydynge vpon an Asse, the other vpon a Camel.

8 And the lyon cryed: Lorde, I haue stande waytynge all the whole daye, and haue kepte my watch all the night.

9 Wyth that came there one rydinge vpon a charet, whyche answered, and sayde: Babilon is fallen, she is turned vp syde doune and al the ymages of her Godes are smytten to the grounde.

10 This (O my felowe thresshers and fanners) haue I hearde of the Lorde of Hostes the God of Israel, to shewe it vnto you.

11 The heauy burthen of Duma. One of Seir cryed vnto me: Watche man what hast thou espyed by nyght, whatcheman what hast thou espyed by nyght.

12 The watchman answered: The daye breaketh on, and the nyght is commyng: Yf youre request be earnest, then aske and come agayne.

13 The heauy burthen of Arabia. At euen ye shall abyde in the wood, in the way toward Dedanim.

14 Mete the thursty wt water (O ye cytesins of Hema) mete those wt bread þt are fled.

15 For they shal runne away from the weapen, from the drawen swearde, from the bent bowe, and from the greate battel.

16 For thus hath the Lorde spoken vnto me: ouer a yeare shall all the power of Cedar be gone, lyke as when the offyce of an hyred seruaunt goeth oute.

17 And the remnaunte of the good Arthers of Cedar, shalbe very fewe: For the Lorde God of Israel hath spoken it.

## CHAPTER 22

THE heauy burthen vpon the valley of vysyons. What haste thou there to do, that thou clymmest vp into the house toppe,

2 O thou cytye of miracles, sedycyous and wylfull seynge, thy slayne men are neyther kylled wyth swearde, nor deade in battell.

3 For all thy captaynes gat them to their horses from their ordinaunce, yea they are all together ridden aweye, & fled farre of.

4 When I perceyued that, I sayde: aweye from me, that I may wepe bitterly. Take no laboure for to comforte me, as thouchinge the destruccion of my people.

5 For this is the daye of the lord of hostes, wherin he will plage, treade doune, & wede out the valleye of visions, and breake doune the walles with suche a cracke, that it shal geue a sounde in the mountaynes.

6 I sawe the Elamites take the quyuers to carte and to horse, and that the walles were bare from harnesse.

7 Thy goodly valleys were ful of charettes, the horse men made them sone to besege the gates.

8 Then was the couerynge of Iuda put from thence, and then was sene the sege of the tymbre house.

9 There shall ye se the ryftes in the walles of the cyty of Dauid, whereof there shalbe many. Ye shall gather together the waters of the lower pole,

10 and tell the houses of Ierusalem, and breake of some of them to kepe the walles.

11 And ye shal make a pyt betwyxte the two walles of the water of the old pole, and nothing regard him, that toke it in hande, & made it.

12 And at the same tyme shall

the Lorde of Hostes call men to wepinge, mourninge, to baldnesse & puttynge on of sacke clothe.

13 But they to fulfil their lust and wilfulnes, slaughter oxen: they kyll shepe, they eate costly meate, and drincke wyne, let vs eate and drincke, to morow we shall dye.

14 Neuerthelesse when the Lorde of Hostes hearde of it, he sayde: yea, yf this wyckednes of yours shalbe remytted, ye must dye for it. This hathe the Lorde of Hostes spoken.

15 Thus sayeth the Lorde God of Hostes: Go into the treasury vnto Sobna the gouernoure, & saye vnto him:

16 What hast thou here to do, & from whence comest thou? that thou hast made the a graue here? For he had caused a costly tombe of stone to be made for him selfe, & a place to lye into be hewen out of a rocke.

17 Beholde, the Lorde shal cast the out by violence, he wyl deck the of another fashyon, & put vpon the a straunge cloth.

18 He shall carye the into a farre countre, lyke a ball with hys handes. There shalt thou dye, there shal the pompe of thy charettes haue an ende: thou villeyne of the house of the Lorde:

19 I wyl shut the oute of thyne offyce, and put þe from thine estate.

20 After this wil I cal my seruaunt Eliakim, the sonne of Helkiah,

21 & aray with him thy cote & gyrde him with the gyrdle, & I wil geue thy power into his hande. He shalbe a father of þe cytesins of Ierusalem and of the kinred of Iuda:

22 I will also laye the keye of Dauids house vpon his shoulders, & yf he open, noman shall shut: and yf he do shut, noman shal open.

23 I wyl fasten him to a nayle in the place of þe moost hye faithfulnesse, and he shalbe vpon the glorious trone of his fathers house.

24 They shall hange vpon him all the glorie of his fathers house, of the children and childers children, al apparel small and great, al instrumentes of measure & musike.

25 This shal come to passe (sayeth the Lorde of Hostes) when the nayle that is fastened to þe place of the highest faythfulnesse, shalbe pluckt of. And when the weyght that hangeth vpon it, shall fal, be broken, and hewen in peces. For the Lorde hym selfe hath sayde it.

# CHAPTER 23

AN heauy burthen vpon Tyrus. Mourne ye shippes of Tarsis, for she is throwen doune to the grounde, and conquered of them that are come from Cethim.

2 The in dwellers of the Ilandes, the marchauntes of Sidon, & they that occupied the sea (of whom thou wast full sometyme) are at a poynt.

3 For by sea were there frutes brought vnto the, & all maner of corne by water. Thou wast the romen market of all people.

4 Sidon is sorye for it, yea and all the power of the sea complaineth, and sayeth: O that I had neuer trauayled with child, that I had neuer borne any that I had neither norished boye, nor brought vp doughter.

5 As sone as Egipte perceyueth it, she wilbe as sory as Tirus it selfe.

6 Go ouer the sea, mourne ye that dwel in the Iles.

7 Is not that the glorious cytye, whiche hath bene of longe antiquitie? whose natiues dwelling farre of, commende her so greatly?

8 Who hath deuysed suche thinges vpon Tirus the croune of al cities, whose marchauntes and captaines were the highest & principal of the world?

9 Euen the Lord of Hostes hath deuysed it, that he may put doune al pompe, & minish al the glory of the worlde.

10 Go thorowe thy land (O thou doughter of the sea) as men go ouer the water, and there is not a gyrdle more.

11 Thus the Lord hath remoueth the kyngedomes, & hathe taken inhande agaynste that mighty Canaan to rote it out: hath stretched oute his hande ouer the sea,

12 and saide: From henceforth shalt thou make no more myrthe, O thou doughter of Sidon: for thou shalt be put doune of the Cethens. Stand vp therfore and go where the enemy will cary the, where thou shalt also haue no reste.

13 Beholde (for thine ensample) The Chaldees were suche a people, that no man was like them, Assur builded them: he set vp his castels and palaces, & broke them doune agayn.

14 And therfore mourne (ye shippes of the sea) for youre power shalbe throwne doune.

15 After that, shall the .lxx. yeares of Tyrus (euen as longe as their kinges lyfe was) be forgotten. And after .lxx. yeares, it shall happen to Tirus as with an harlot that playeth vpon a lute.

16 Take the lute (saye men to her) and go aboute the citie, thou art yet an vnknowne whence, make pastyme wyth dyuerse balettes, wherby thou mayest come into acquayntaunce.

17 Thus shall it happen after .lxx. yeares. The Lorde shall vyset the cytye of Tyrus, and it shall come agayne to her marchaundyse, and shal occupye with all the kingedomes that be in the worlde.

18 But al her occupyinge and winninge shalbe halowed vnto the Lorde. For then shal they laye vp nothinge behind them, nor vpon heapes: but the marchaundyse of Tyrus shall belong vnto þe cytesins of the Lorde, to the feadynge and susteninge of the hungrye, and to the clothinge of the aged.

## CHAPTER 24

BEHOLDE, the Lorde shal waste & plage the worlde, he shal make the face of the earthe desolate, & scatre abroade the inhabitoures therof.

2 Then shal the pryeste be as the people, the mayster as the seruaunt, þe dame lyke the mayde, the seller lyke the byer he that lendeth vpon vsurye, lyke vnto him þt boroweth vpon vsury, the creditoure, as the detter.

3 Yea miserably shall the worlde be wasted & clean destroied. For the Lorde hath so determed in him selfe.

4 The earth shalbe heauy & decay. The face of the earth shal perishe & fal awaye, the proude people of the worlde shal come to naught.

5 For the earth is corrupt of her indwellers. For why? they haue offended the law chaunged the ordynaunces, & made the euerlasting testament of none effecte.

6 And therfore shall the course deuoure þe earth: for they that dwel theron haue sinned, wherfore they shal be brent also, and those that remaine shalbe very few.

7 The swete wyne shal mourne, the grapes shalbe weake, and al that haue bene mery in harte, shall sighe.

8 The myrth of tabrettes shalbe layde doune, the chere of the ioyfull shall cease & the pleasure of lutes shal haue an ende

9 there shal no more wyne be droncke wyth myrth, the beere shalbe bytter to them that dryncke it,

10 the wicked cytyes shalbe broken donne, al houses shalbe shut, þt no man maye come in.

11 In the stretes shall there be lyft vp a crye because of wine, al mens chere shall vanyshe awaye & al ioye of the earth shal passe.

12 Desolacion shal remayne in the cytyes, and the gates shalbe smytten wyth wastnesse.

13 For it shall happen vnto al landes & to all people, lyke as when a man smyteth donne the olyues, that are left vpon the tree: or seketh after grapes, when the wyne gatherynge is oute.

14 And those same (that remayne) shall lyft vp their voyce, and be glad, & shal magnifye the glorye of the Lord, euen from the sea,

15 & praise the name of the Lorde God of Israel, in the valeys, and Ilandes.

16 We heare sunges sung to the prayse of the righteous, from al þe endes of the worlde. Therefore I must speake: O myne vnfrutefulnesse, O my pouerte. Wo is me, all is full of synners, whiche offende of purpose and malice.

17 And therfore (O thou that dwellest vpon the earth) there is at hand for the, feare, pyt and snare.

18 Who so escapeth the terrible crye, shal fal into the pyt. And yf he come out of the pit, he shalbe taken with the snare. For the wyndowes aboue shalbe opened, and the foundacion of the earth shall moue.

19 The earthe shall geue a greate cracke, it shall haue a sore ruyne, & taken an horrible fall.

20 The earth shal stacker lyke a drocken man, & be taken awaye like a tente. Her mysdedes shal lie so heauy vpon her, that she must fal, and neuer ryse vp agayne.

21 At the same tyme shall the Lorde mustre together the hye hooste aboue, and the kynges of the worlde vpon the earth.

22 These shalbe coupled together as prysoners be, and shalbe shut in one ward and punished innumerable daies.

23 The Mone and the Sunne shalbe ashamed, when the Lorde of Bostes shall rule them at Ierusalem vpon the mount Sion, before and wyth his excellent councel.

## CHAPTER 25

O Lorde, thou arte my God, I wil praise the, & magnifie thy name. For thou bryngest maruelous thinges to passe, accordinge to thyne olde councels, truly & stedfastly.

2 Thou makest of townes, heapes of stone, and of head cities, broken walles: The palaces of the wicked destroyest thou out of þe citie that they shal neuer be buylded again.

3 Therfore the very rude people must magnifie the, & the cities of the cruel Heathen muste feare the.

4 For thou art the poore mans helpe, a strength for the neadful in his necessyte. Thou art a defence against euyll wether, a shadow agaynst the hete. But vnto the presumptuous, thou art lyke a stronge whyrle wynde, that casteth doune

5 the boastynge of the vngodly: thou kepest men from heate, wt the shadow of the cloudes, thou cuttest of the braunches of tyrauntes.

6 Moreouer the Lorde of Hostes shall ones prepare a feaste, for all people vpon the hyll: A plenteous, costly, pleasaunt feaste, of fat & wel fede beastes, of swete & most pure thinges.

7 Vpon the hil shal he take away the side vale that hangeth before the face of al people and

the couerynge wherwith al Gentiles are couered.

8 As for death, he shal vtterly consume it. The Lord God shall wype awaye teares from all faces, & take away the confusion of his people thorow the whole worlde. For the lord hym selfe hath sayde it.

9 At the same tyme shall it be sayde: lo, thys is oure God in whom we put oure trust, and he hath healed vs. This is the Lorde that we haue wayted for. Let vs reioyse and delyte in hys health.

10 For the hand of the Lorde ceaseth vpon thys hyll. But Moab shalbe thresshen doune vnder him, lyke sa the straw is troden vnder fete in a donge hill.

11 For he shal stretche out his handes vpon him, lyke as a swimmer doth to swimme. And with the power of his handes shal he rast doune his hye pompe.

12 As for his strong holdes and hye walles: he shal bowe them, that cast them doune, & fel them to the grounde into dust.

## CHAPTER 26

THEN shal thys songe be sung in the lande of Iuda. We haue a stronge cyty, the walles and the ordynaunce shal kepe vs.

2 Open the gates, that the good people maye go in, whiche laboureth for the truthe.

3 And thou, whiche art the doar & hast the matter in hand, shalt prouyde for peace, euen the peace that men hope for in the.

4 Hope styl in the lord for in the Lorde God is euerlastyng strength.

5 For why, it is he, that bringeth low the hye mynded citesins, & casteth doune the proude cytyes. He casteth them to the grounde, yea euen into myre that they may be troden

6 vnder the fete of the symple, and wyth the steppes of the poore.

7 Thou (Lorde) consydrest the path of the ryghteous, whether it be ryghte, whether the waye of the ryghteous be ryght.

8 Therfore (Lorde) we haue a respecte vnto the waye of thy iudgementes, thy name & thy remembraunce reioyse thy soule.

9 My soule lusteth after the all the nyght longe, and my mynde hasteth frely to the. For as soone as thy iudgemente is knowne to the worlde, then the inhabytours of the earth learne rightuousnesse.

10 But the vngodly (though he haue receyued grace) yet lerneth he not ryghtuousnesse, but in the place where he is punished, he offendeth, & feareth not the glorye of the Lorde.

11 Lorde, they wyll not se thyne hye hande, but they shall se it, and be confounded: when thou shalte deuoure them with the wrathe of the people, & wyth the fyre of thyue enemyes.

12 But vnto vs, O Lorde, prouyde for peace: for thou worckest in vs all oure worckes.

13 O Lord oure God thoughe soith Lordes haue domynacyon vpon vs as knowe not the: yet graunt that we maye hope onelye in the, and kepe thy name in remembraunce.

14 The malycyous Tyrauntes when they dye, are nether in lyfe nor in the resurreccyon, for thou vysytest them and rootest them oute, and destroyest all the memory all of them.

15 Agayne, thou increaceste the people, O Lorde, thou increaceste the people, thou shalte be praysed and magnyfyed in all the endes of the worlde.

16 The people that seke vnto the in trouble, that same aduersite which they complayne of is vnto them a chastening before the.

17 Lyke as a wyfe wyth chylde (when her trauyle commeth vpon her) is ashamed, cryeth and suffreth the payne: Euen so are we O Lorde, in thy sight.

18 We are with chyld, we trauyle, & beare, & with the spryte we bring forth healthe, where thorowe the earth is vndestroyed, and the inhabytours of the worlde perysh not.

19 But as for thy dead men and oures, that be departed, they are in lyfe and resurreccion. They lye in the earthe, they wake, & haue ioy: for thy dewe is a dew of lyfe and light. But the place of the malycyous Tyrauntes is fallen awaye.

20 So go now my people into thy chambre, & shut the dore to the, and suffre now the twincklynge of an eye, tyll the wrathe be ouerpaste.

21 For beholde, the Lorde wyl go out of his habitacyon, and vpset the wyckednesse of them that dwell vpon earthe. He wyl dyscouer the bloud that she hath deuoured, she shal neuer hyde them, that she hath murthered.

## CHAPTER 27

THEN the Lorde with his heauye, great, & longe swerd shall vyset Leuyathan that inuyncible serpent: euen Leuiathan that croked serpent & shall slaye the whalfysh in þe sea.

2 At the same tyme shal men synge of the vyneyarde of Muscatel.

3 I the Lorde kepe it, and water in it due ceason. I watche daye and nyght, that no man breake into it. I beare no euil wil in my mynd.

4 Who wyll compell me, that I greatly forgettynge all faythfulnesse, shulde burne it vp at ones with thornes & bushes?

5 Or who wyll enforce me to kepe or make peace.

6 It wyll come to thys

poynte, that Iacob shalbe roted agayne, & Israel shallbe grene, and beare floures, and they shall fyll the whole worlde with theyr frute.

7 Smyteth he not hys smyter, as euyl as he is smyten him selfe: Destroyeth he not the murtherers, as he is murthered?

8 Euery man recompenseth with the measure that he receyueth: He museth vpon hys sore wynde, as vpon the dayes of extreame heate.

9 And therfor shall þe iniquite of Iacob be thus reconcyled. And so shall he take away all the frute of hys sinnes. As for aulter stones, he shall make them all as stones beaten to poulder: the groues & Idols shall not stande.

10 The stronge cytyes shalbe desolate, & the fayre cytyes shalbe lefte lyke a wyldernes. The cattell shall fede and lye there, & the shepe shall eate it vp.

11 Theyr haruest shalbe brente, theyr wyues which were theyr bewtye when they came forth: shalbe defyled. For it is a people wythout vnderstandynge, & therfore he that created them, shall not fauoure them, and he that made them shal not be mercyful to them.

12 In that time shal the Lorde shute from the swyfte water of Euphrates, vnto the ryuer of Egypte. And there shal the chyldren be chosen oute one by one.

13 Then shall the greate trompette be blowen, so that those whiche haue bene destroyed in the Assyryans lande, and those that be scatred abroad in Egypte: shall come and worshyppe þe Lord at Ierusalem, vpon the holy mount.

## CHAPTER 28

Wo be to the croune of pryde, to the droncken Ephraemytes, & to the faydynge floure, to the glorye of hys pompe, that is vpon the toppe of the plenteous valleye: whiche men be ouerladen with wine.

2 Beholde, the strength and power of the Lord shall breake into the lande on euerye syde, like a tempest of hayle, that beareth doune strong holdes, and lyke an horryble, myghty & ouerflowynge water.

3 And the proude croune of þe droncken Ephraemytes, shalbe troden vnder fote.

4 And as for the faydynge floure, the glory of hys pompe, whiche is vpon the toppe of þe plenteous valleye: it shall happen vnto hym, as to an vntymelye frute before the harueste come. Which as soone as it is sene, is by and by deuoured, or euer it come well in a mans hande.

5 And then shall the Lorde of Hostes be a ioyfull croune, and a gloryous garlande vnto the remnaunt of hys people.

6 Vnto the lowly, he shalbe a sprete of iudgement, and vnto them that dryue away the enemyes from the gates he shalbe a spryte of strength.

7 But they go wronge by the reason of wyne, they fall and stacker because of stronge drincke. Yea euen the Priestes and Prophetes them selues go amysse, they are droncken with wyne, & weake braynd thorowe stronge drincke. They erre in seynge, and in iudgemente they fayle.

8 For all tables are so full of vomyte and fylthynes, that no place is cleane.

9 What is he amonge them, that can teache, instructe or enfourme the chyldren, whiche are wened from sucke or taken from the brestes: of anye other fashyon then:

10 Commaunde that maye be commaunded, byd that maye be bydden, forbidde that maye be forbidden, kepe backe that maye be kepte backe, here a lytle, there a lytle.

11 And therfore the Lorde also shall speake wyth lispynge lippes and with a straunge language vnto this people to whome he spake afore of thys maner.

12 This shall bringe reste, yf one refreshe the weerye, ye this shall bringe reste. But they had no will to heare.

13 And therfore the Lorde shall aunswere theyr stubbournes (Commaunde that maye be commaunded, byd that may be bidden, forbid that may be forbidden, kepe backe that maye be kept backe, here a lytle, there a lytle) That they maye go forth fall back warde, be brosed, snared and taken.

14 Wherfore heare the worde of the Lorde, ye mockers that rule the Lordes people, whiche is at Ierusalem.

15 For ye comforte youre selues thus: Tushe, death & we are at a poynte, and as for hell, we haue made a condicyon with it, that thoughe there breake out anye sore plage it shall not come vpon vs. For wyth disceyte wyll we escape, and with nymblenes wil we defende oure selues.

16 Therfore sayth the Lorde God: Beholde, I wyll laye a stone in Syon a great stone, a costly corner stone for a sure foundacyon: that who so putteth hys truste in hym, shall not be confounded.

17 Ryghtuousnes will I set vp agayne in the balaunce, and iudgement in the weyghtes. The tempeste of haile shall take awaye your refuge, that ye haue to disceyue wythall, & the ouerflowynge waters shall breake doune youre stronge holdes of dyssimulacion:

18 Thus the appoyntmente that ye haue made with deathe, shalbe done away and the condition that ye made with hell,

shal not stande. When the great destruccyon goeth thorowe, it shal all to treade you. It shal take you quyte away before it.

19 For it shal go forth earlye in the mornynge, and contynue onelye that daye & that nighte. And the very feare only shall teache you, when ye heare it.

20 For the bedde shall be so narrowe that a man can not lye vpon it: And the coueryng to small, that a man maye not wynde hym selfe therein.

21 For the Lorde shall steppe forthe as he dyd vpon the mounte Perazim, and shall take on as he dyd vpon the dale of Gabaon: that he maye bryng forthe his deuyce his straunge deuyce: and fulfyll hys worcke, hys wonderful worcke.

22 And therfore make no mockes at it, that youre captiuite increase not: for I haue hearde the Lorde of Hostes saye, that there shall come a soden destruccyon & plage vpon the whole earthe.

23 Take hede, and heare my voyce, pondre and marcke my wordes well.

24 Goeth not the housbande man euer in due season earnestlye to hys lande: he moweth and ploweth hys grounde to sowe.

25 And when he hath made it playne, he soweth it wyth fetches or comyn. He soweth the wheate & Barlye in theyr place, Mylyum and Rye also in theyr place.

26 And that he maye do it ryght, hys God teacheth hym and sheweth hym.

27 For he treadeth not the fytches oute wyth a wayne, neyther bringeth he the carte here & there ouer the comyn, but he tresseth the fitches out with a flayle, and the comyn with a rod.

28 As for the wheate he gryndeth it to make breade thereof In as muche as he can not brynge it to passe with treadynge oute. For nether the brosyng that the carte wheles make, nor hys beastes can grynde it.

29 This and suche lyke thynges come of the Lorde of Hostes whiche is maruelous in councell, and greate in ryghtuousnesse.

# CHAPTER 29

Wo be vnto the O Ariel, thou citye that Dauid wanne. Take yet some years, & let some feastes yet passe ouer:

2 then shall Ariel be beseged, so that she shall be heuy and sorowfull, & shall be vnto me euen as a lyon.

3 For I will laye sege to the rounde aboute, & kepe the in with towers, and graue vp dykes against the.

4 And thou shalte be brought lowe, and speake oute of the earth and thy wordes shall go humbly oute of the grounde.

5 Thy voyce shall come oute of the earthe, lyke the voyce of a witch, and thy talkynge shall grone oute of the myre. For the multytude of thyne enemyes shalbe lyke mealduste. And the nombre of Tyrauntes shalbe as the duste that the wynde taketh awaye sodenlye.

6 Thou shalte be vysyted of the Lorde of hostes with thondre, earthequake, & wyth a greate crack, with the whyrle wynde, tempeste, & with the flamme of a consumynge fyre.

7 But nowe the multytude of all the people, that wente oute agaynste Ariel: the whole hoste, the stronge holdes and sege, is lyke a breame whiche appeareth in the nyghte.

8 It is lyke as when an hungrye man dreameth that he is eatynge, and when he awaketh, he hath nothynge: lyke as when a thyrstye man dreameth that he is drinckynge, and when he awaketh, he is faynte, and hys soule vnpacyent. So is the multitude of all people that mustre them selues agaynste the hyll of Syon.

9 But ye shalbe at youre wyttes ende, ye shall be abashed, ye shall stackre, and rele to & fro. Ye shalbe droncken, but not of wyne. Ye shall fall, but not thorowe dronckennes.

10 For the Lorde shall geue you an harde slepynge spryte, and holde doune youre eyes: namelye youre Prophetes and heades which shuld se, them shall he couer.

11 And all vysyons shalbe vnto you, as the wordes that stande in a sealed lettre, when one offereth it to a man that is learned, and sayeth: reade vs thys lettre. Then he aunswereth: I cannot read it, for it is shut.

12 But yf it be geuen to one that is not learned, or sayd vnto him: reade this lettre: Then saith he: I can not reade.

13 Therfor thus sayth the Lord: For so much as thys people draweth nye me with theyr mouthe, and prayseth me hyghlye wyth theyr lyppes (where as theyr herte neuerthelesse is farre from me, & the feare which they owe vnto me, that turne they to mens lawes and doctrynes)

14 therfore will I also shewe vnto thys people a maruelous, terryble, and great thing (Namelye thys:) I wyll destroye the wysdom of theyr wyse, & the vnderstandynge of theyr learned men shall peryshe.

15 Wo be vnto them that seke to depe, to hyde theyr ymagynacion before the Lorde, which reherse theyr councels in the darcknes, & saye: who seyth vs, or who knoweth vs?

16 Whiche ymagynacyon of yours is euen as when the potters clay taketh aduysemente, as thoughe the worcke myghte saye to the worckemaister: make me not, or as when an earthen vessell sayeth of the potter: he

vnderstandeth not.

17 Se ye not that it is harde by, that Lybanus shalbe turned into Charmell, and that Charmell shalbe taken as a woode?

18 Then shall deaf men vnderstande the wordes of the boke, and the eyes of the blynd shall se wythoute anye cloude or darckenes.

19 The oppressed shall holde a merye feaste in þe Lorde, and the poore people shall reioyse in the holye one of Israell.

20 Then shall the furyous people ceasse, and the mockers shalbe put awaye, and all they that do wronge shalbe plucked oute,

21 suche as laboure to drawe men vnto synne: & that dysceyue hym, whiche reproueth them in the gate, and such as turne good personnes to vanite.

22 And therfore the Lord (euen the defender of Abraham) sayeth thus vnto the house of Iacob: Now shall not Iacob be ashamed, nor hys face confounded,

23 when he seyth amonge hys children (whome my handes haue made) suche as halowe my name amonge them: that they maye sanctyfye the holye one of Iacob, and feare the God of Israell:

24 and that they which afore tyme were of an erroneous sprite haue nowe vnderstandynge, and that such as before coulde not speake, are nowe learned in my lawe.

## CHAPTER 30

Wo be to those shrynkynge children (sayeth the Lorde) whiche seke councell, but not at me: whiche take a webbe in hande but not after my wil: that they may heape one synne vpon another.

2 They go doune into Egypte (and aske me no councell) to seke helpe at the power of Pharao, and comforte in the shadowe of the Egypcians.

3 But Pharaos helpe shalbe youre confusyon, & the comfort in the Egypcyans shadowe shalbe your owne shame.

4 Youre rulers haue bene at Zoan, and youre messaungers came vnto Hanes.

5 But ye shall al be ashamed of the people that maye not helpe you, whiche shall not brynge you strength or comforte, but shame and confusyon.

6 Youre beastes haue borne burthens vpon theyr backes towarde the Southe, thorow the way that is full of parell and trouble, because of the lyon & lyones, of the Cockatryce & shutynge dragon. Yea the Mules bare youre substaunce, & the Camels brought your treasure vpon their croked backes, vnto a people that can not helpe you.

7 For the Egipcians helpe shalbe but vayne and lost. Therfore I tolde you also, that your pryde shulde haue an end.

8 Wherfore go hence, and wryte them thys in theyr tables, & note it in a boke: that it may remayne by theyr posteryte, & be styll kept.

9 For it is an obstynate people, vnfaythful children children that will not heare the lawe of þe Lord.

10 They darre saye to the Prophetes: Intromytte youre selues with nothynge, and vnto the Sothsayers: tell vs of nothynge for to come, but speake frendlye wordes vnto vs, & preache vs false thinges.

11 Treade oute of the waye, go out of the path, turne the holye one of Israel from vs.

12 Therfore thus sayeth the holye one of Israel: In as muche as ye haue caste of youre bewtye, and comforted youre selues with power and nymblenesse, and put youre confidence therin:

13 therfore shal ye haue this myschefe agayne for youre destruccyon and fall, lyke as an hye wall, that falleth because of some ryft (or blast) whose breakynge cometh sodenly.

14 And youre destruccyon shalbe lyke as an earthen pot, whiche breaketh no man touching it, yea and breaketh so sore, that a man shall not fynde a sheuer of it to fetche fyre in, or to take water wyth all oute of the pyt.

15 For the Lorde God, euen the holy one of Israell hath promysed thus: Wyth styll syttynge and rest shall ye be healed, in quyetnesse & hope shall youre strength lye.

16 Notwithstandynge ye regarde it not, but ye wyll saye: No, for thus are we constrayned to fle vpon horses. And therfore shall ye fle, we muste ryde vpon swift beastes, and therfore youre persecutours shal yet be swyfter.

17 A thousand of you shall fle for one, or at the moste for fyue, whiche do but only geue you euyll wordes? vntyll ye be desolate, as a shyp mast vpon an hye mountayne, and as a beaken vpon on hyll.

18 Yet standeth the Lorde waytynge, that he maye haue mercye vpon you, and lyfteth hym selfe vp, þt he maye receyue you to grace. For the Lorde God is ryghtuous. Happy are all they that wayte for him.

19 For thus (O thou people of Syon and ye citisens of Ierusalem) shall ye neuer be in heauynes, for doutlesse he wyll haue mercy vpon the. As sone as he heareth the voyce of thy crye, he wyl helpe the.

20 The Lorde geueth you the bread of aduersite, and the water of trouble. But thyne instructer flyeth not farre from the, yf thyne eyes loke vnto thyne instructer,

21 and thyne eares harken to his worde, that cryeth after the,

and sayeth: thys is the waye, go thys, and turne neyther to the right hande nor to the lefte.

22 Moreouer yf ye destroye the syluer worckes of youre Idoles, and caste awaye the golden coppes that ye deckte them wythall (as fylthynes) & saye get you hence:

23 Then wyll he geue rayne to the sede that ye shall sowe in the earthe, and geue you bread of the encrease of the earthe, so that all shalbe plentuous and aboundaunt. Thy cattel also shall he fede in þe brode medowes,

24 yea thyne oxen & Mules that tyll the grounde, shall eate good fodder, which is purged with the fanne.

25 Goodly ryuers shall flowe out of all hys mountaynes and hylles. In the daye of the greate slaughter when the towers shall fall,

26 the mone shall shyne as the sunne, and the sunne shyne shalbe seuen folde, and haue as much shyne, as in seuen dayes besyde. In that daye shall the Lorde bynde vp the brosed sores of hys people, and heale theyr woundes.

27 Beholde the glory of the Lord shal come from farre, hys face shal burne, that no man shalbe able to abyde it, hys lyppes shall wagge for verye indignacyon, and hys tonge shalbe as a consumynge fyre.

28 His breath like a vehement floude of water, whiche goeth vp to the throte. That he may take away the people, whiche haue turned them selues vnto vanite, and the brydle of erroure, that lyeth in other folkes chawes.

29 But ye shall synge, as the vse is in þe night of the holy solempnyte. Ye shall reioyse from youre herte, as they that come with the pype, when they go vp to the mounte of the Lorde, vnto the rocke of Israel.

30 The Lorde also shall set vp the power of his voyce, and declare his terryble arme, wyth hys angry countenaunce yea and the flamme of the consumynge fyre, with earthquake, tempest of wynde, and haile stones.

31 Then shall the Assyryans feare also, because of the voyce of the Lorde, which shall smyte him with the rodde.

32 And the same rodde which the Lorde wil sende vpon hym, shall moue the whole foundacyon with trompet, with noyse of warre and battell to destroye.

33 For he hath prepared the fyre of payne from the begynnynge, yea euen for Kynges also. This hath he made depe & wyde, þe noryshing thereof is fyre & woode innumerable, whiche the breathe of the Lorde kyndleth, as it were a matche of brymstone.

## CHAPTER 31

Wo be vnto them that go doune into Egypte for help, and trust in horses, & comforte themselues in charettes, because they be many, & in horse men because they be lusty & strong. But they regarde not the holy one of Israel, and they aske no question at the Lorde.

2 Where as he neuertheles plageth the wicked, and yet goeth not from hys word when he steppeth forthe, and taketh the victory agaynste the housholde of the frowarde, & agaynste the helpe of euyll doars.

3 Nowe the Egypcyans are men, and not God, and theyr horses fleshe and not sprete. And as soone as the Lorde stretched oute his hande, then shall the helper fall, and he that shuld haue ben helped, and shall all together be destroyed.

4 For thus hath the Lorde spoken vnto me: Lyke as the lyon or lyons whelpe roareth vpon the praye that he hath gotten, and is not afrayed, thoughe the multitude of shepardes crye oute vpon hym, nether abashed for all the heape of them: So shal the Lord of Hostes come doune from the mounte of Sion, and defend his hil.

5 Lyke as the brydes flotre about theyr nestes, so shall the Lord of Hostes, kepe, saue, defend & delyuer Ierusalem.

6 Therfore, O ye children of Israel, turne agayne, lyke as ye haue exceaded in youre goynge backe.

7 For in that daye euerye man shall caste oute hys Idols of syluer and gold, which ye haue made with your synfull handes.

8 Assur also shalbe slayne with the swerde, not with a mans swerde. A swerd shall deuoure hym, but not a mans swerde. And he shall fle from the slaughter, and hys seruauntes shalbe taken prysoners.

9 He shall go for feare to hys stronge holdes, and hys Prynces shal fle from hys badge. Thys hath the Lorde spoken, whose lyght burneth in Syon, and hys fyre in Ierusalem.

## CHAPTER 32

Beholde, the kynge shal gouerne after the rule of ryghtuousnes, & the princes shal rule according to the balaunce of equyte.

2 He shalbe vnto men as a defence for the wynde, & as a refuge for the tempeste, like as a riuer of water in a thurstye place, and the shadowe of a great rocke in a drye land.

3 The eyes of the seynge shall not be dymme, & the eares of them that heare, shall take dylygente hede.

4 The herte of the vnwyse, shall attayne to knowledge, & the vnparfyte tung shal speake playnely and distinctely.

5 Then shal þe nygard be no

more called gentle, nor the churle liberal.

6 But the churle wyll be churlyshly mynded, & his hert wil worcke euil & playe the Ipocrite, & ymagyn abhominacyons against God, to make the hungry leane, & to withhold drincke from the thurstie.

7 These are the perlous weapons of the couetous, these be hys shamefull councels: that he maye begyle the poore with disceatfull workes, yea euen there as he shuld geue sentence with the poore.

8 But the lyberall person ymagyneth honest thynges, and commeth vp with honestye.

9 Vp (ye ryche and ydell cytyes) harken vnto my voyce. Ye carelesse cytyes, marke my wordes.

10 After yeares & dayes shal ye be broughte in feare, O ye carelesse cytyes. For Harueste shalbe oute, and the grape gatherynge shall not come.

11 O ye ryche ydell cytyes ye that feare no parell, ye shalbe abashed and remoued, when ye se the barennesse, the nakednesse and preparynge to warre.

12 Ye shall knocke vpon youre brestes, because of the pleasaunte felde, and because of the frutefull vyneyarde.

13 My peoples felde shall brynge thornes & thystels for in euerye house is voluptuousnes, and in the cytyes, wylfulnes.

14 The palaces also shalbe broken, and the greatly occupied cities desolate. The towers and bulworkes shalbe become deunes for euermore, the pleasure of Mules shalbe turned to pasture for shepe:

15 vnto the tyme that the spryte be poured vpon vs from aboue. Then shall the wyldernesse be a fruteful felde and the plenteous felde shalbe rekened for a wodde.

16 Then shall equyte dwell in the deserte, and righteousnesse in a fruteful land.

17 And the rewarde of ryghtuousnesse shalbe peace, and her frute reste and quyetnesse for euer.

18 And my people shall dwell in the ynnes of peace, in my tabernacle and pleasure where there is ynough in them all.

19 And when þe hayle falleth, it shal fal in the wodde and in the cytie.

20 O how happy shall ye be, when ye shall safely sowe youre sede besyde all waters and dryue thyther the fete of youre oxen and asses.

# CHAPTER 33

THERFORE wo be vnto the (O robber) shalte not thou be robbed also? and vnto the that layeste wayte, as who say: there shuld no waite be layde for the: Wo vnto the whiche doest hurte, euen so shalte thou be hurte also. And as thou layest wayte, so shall waite be layde for the also.

2 Lorde be mercyful vnto vs, we wayte for the. Thyne arme is at a poynte to vyset vs, but be thou oure health in the tyme of trouble

3 Graunt that the people maye fle at the anger of thy voyce, & that at thyne vpstandynge the Gentyles maye be scatred abroade,

4 and that theyr spoyle maye be gathered, as the gresshoppers are comonly gathered together into the pyt.

5 Stande vp Lorde, thou that dwellest on hye: Let Syon be fylled wyth equyte & rightuousnesse.

6 Let trueth and faythfulnesse be in her tyme: power, health, wisdome, knowledge and the feare of God are her treasure.

7 Beholde, theyr aungels crye wythout, þe messaungers of peace wepe bytterly.

8 The stretes are waste, there walketh no man therein, the appoyntment is broken, the cyties are despysed, they are not regarded,

9 the desolate earthe is in heuynes. Lybanus taketh it but for a sporte, that it is hewen doune: Saron is lyke a wyldernes: Basan and Charmel are turned vpsyde doune.

10 And therfore sayeth the Lorde. I wyll vp, now wyll I get vp, nowe wil I aryse.

11 Ye shall conceyue stubble, & bear straw, & youre sprete shall be the fyre, that it maye consume you:

12 and the people shalbe burnt like lyme, and as thornes burne that are hewen of, and caste in the fyre.

13 Now herken to, ye that are farre of, howe I do with them, & consydre my glorye, ye that be at hande.

14 The synners at Syon are afrayd a sodane fearfulnesse is come vpon the ypocrytes. What is he among vs (saye they) that will dwell by that consumynge fyre whyche of vs maye abyde that euerlastinge heate?

15 He that ledeth a godly lyfe (saye I) and speaketh the trueth: He that abhorreth to do vyolence and dysceyte: he that kepeth his hande that he touche no rewarde: which stoppeth hys eares that he heare no councel agaynste the innocent: which holdeth doune hys eyes, that he se none euyll.

16 He it is, that shall dwell on hye whose sauegarde shalbe in the true rocke, to him shal be geuen the right true meate and drincke.

17 His eyes shall se the kynge in hys glory: and in the wyde worlde,

18 and hys herte shal delyte in the feare of God. What shall then become of the scrybe? of the Senatoure what of hym that teacheth chyldren?

19 There shalt thou not se a people of a straunge tounge to haue so diffused a language, that it may not be vnderstande: neyther so straunge a speache but it shall be perceyued.

20 There shal Sion be sene, the head cytye of oure solempne feastes. There shal thyne eyes se Ierusalem that gloryous habytacyon: the tabernacle that neuer shal remoue, whose nayles shall neuer be taken oute worlde wythout ende, whose coardes euerychone shall neuer corrupte:

21 for the gloryous Magestye of the Lorde shall there be present amonge vs. In that place, where fayre broade ryuers & streames are, shall neyther Galeyrowe, nor great shyppe tayle.

22 For the Lorde shalbe oure captayne, the Lorde shalbe oure lawe geuer. The Lorde shalbe oure kynge, and he hym selfe shalbe oure sauyoure.

23 There are the coardes so layde abroad, that they cannot be better: The maste set vp of suche a fashyon, that no banner nor sayle hangeth theron: but there is dealed great spoyle, ye lame men runne after the praye.

24 There lyeth no man that sayeth: I am syck, but all euyll is taken awaye from the people, that dwell there.

## CHAPTER 34

COME ye Heithen & heare, take hede ye people. Herken thou earth & all that is therin: thou rounde compasse & all that groweth there vpon

2 for the Lord is angrye with all people, & hys displeasure is kindled agaynst all the multytude of them, to curse them, & to sleye them.

3 So that their slayne shalbe cast out, and their bodyes styncke: that euen the verye hilles shalbe wet with the bloude of them.

4 All þe starres of heauen shalbe consumed, & the heauen shall folde together lyke a roll, & all the starres therof shal fall, lyke as the leaues fall from the vynes & fygetrees.

5 For my swearde (saieth he) shalbe bathed in heauen, and shall immediatly come downe vpon Idumea, and vpon the people which I haue cursed for my vengeance.

6 And þe Lordes swearde shalbe full of bloude, and be rustye wyth the fatnesse & bloude of lambes & gootes, wyth the fatnesse of the kydneys of wethers. For the Lorde shall kyl a greate offringe in Bosra, and in the lande of Idumea.

7 There shall the Vnycornes fall with the Bulles (that is with the gyauntes) and theyr lande shalbe washed wyth bloude, and their grounde corrupte wyth fatnesse.

8 Vnto the also (O Syon) shall come the daye of the vengeaunce of God, & the yeare when thyne owne iudgmentes shalbe recompensed.

9 Thy floudes shalbe turned to pytch, and thyne earthe to brymstone, and ther wyth shall the lande be kyndled,

10 so that it shall not be quenched daye ner nyght: But smoke euermore, and so forth to lye waste. And no man shall go thorowe thy lande for euer:

11 But Pellicanes, Storkes, great Dules, and Rauens shall haue it in possessyon, and dwell therin. For God shall sprede out the lyne of desolacyon vpon it, and weye it with the stones of emptynes.

12 When kinges are called vpon there shalbe none, and all prynces shalbe awaye.

13 Thornes shall growe in their palaces, nettels and thistles in theyr stronge holdes, that the dragons maye haue their pleasure therin, and that they maye be a courte for Estriches.

14 There shall straunge visures and monstruous beastes mete one another, and the wilde kepe companye together. There shall the lamya lye, and haue her lodginge.

15 There shall the hedghoge buylde, digge, be there at home, and brynge forth hys younge ones. There shall the kytes come together, ech one to his lyke.

16 Seke thorow the scrypture of the Lorde & rede it. There shall none of these thynges be left out, there shall not one (ner soche lyke) fayle. For what his mouth commaundeth, that same doth hys sprete gather together (or fulfylleth.)

17 Vpon whom soeuer the lot falleth, or to whom he dealeth it with the lyue: those shall possesse the enheritaunce from generacyon to generacyon, and dwell therin.

## CHAPTER 35

BVT the deserte & wyldernes shall reioyse, the waste ground shalbe glad, and florysh as the lylly.

2 She shall floryshe pleasauntlye, & be ioyfull, & euer be geuyng of thanckes more and more. For the glory of Libanus, the bewty of Charmel and Saron shalbe geuen her. These shall knowe the honour of the Lorde, and the magestie of oure God.

3 And therfore strengthen the weake handes, and comforte the feble knees.

4 Saye vnto them that are of a fearfull herte: Be of good there, & feare not. Beholde youre God cometh, to take vengeaunce, and to rewarde, God commeth his owne selfe, & wyll delyuer you.

5 Then shall the eyes of the blynde be lyghtened, & the eares of the deafe opened.

6 Then shall the lame man leape as an herte, and the domme mans tunge shal geue thanckes.

In the wyldernesse also there shall welles spryge, and floudes of water in the deserte.

7 The drye grounde shall turne to ryuers, and the thurstye to springes of water. Where as drrgons dwelt afore, there shall growe swete floures and grene russhes.

8 There shalbe fote pathes and comen stretes, this shalbe called the holy waye. No vncleane person shall go thorow it, for the Lorde hym selfe shall go with them that waye, and the ignoraunt shall not erre,

9 There shalbe no lyon, and no rauyshynge beast shall come therin, nor be there, but men shall go there fre and safe.

10 And the redemed of þe Lorde shall conuerte, and come to Syon with thankesgeuynge. Euerlastinge ioye shall they haue, pleasure and gladnesse shall be amonge them. And as for all sorowe and heuynes, it shall vanysh awaye.

## CHAPTER 36

IN .xiiij. yeare of Kyng Hezekiah, came Sennaherib kyng of the Assyrians downe, to laye sege vnto all the stronge cyties of Iuda.

2 And the Kynge of the Assyrians sent Rabsakeh from Lachis towarde Ierusalem, agaynst Kynge Hesekiah, wyth a greuous Hoste, which set hym by the condite of þe ouerpole, in the waye that goeth thorowe the fullers lande.

3 And so there came forth vnto hym Eliakim Helkiahs sonne the Presydent, Sobna þe Scribe, & Ioah Asaphs sonne the Secretary.

4 And Rabsakeh sayde vnto them: Tell Hezekiah, that the greate kyng of Assyria sayeth thus vnto hym: What presumpcton is this, that thou trustest vnto?

5 Thou thinckest (peraduenture) that thou hast councell and power ynough to mayntene this warre: or els wherto trustest thou, that thou castest thy selfe of frome?

6 lo, thou puttest thy truste in a broken staffe of rede (I meane Egypte) whyche he that leaneth vpon, it goeth in to hys hande & shutteth hym thorowe. Euen so is Pharao the Kyng of Egypt, vnto all them that trust in him.

7 But yf thou woldest saye to me: we trust in the Lorde oure God: A goodlye God in dede: whose Hye places and aulters Hezekiah toke downe, & commaunded Iuda & Ierusalem, to worshyppe onely before the aulter.

8 Abyde the, thou haste made a condycyon with my lorde the kyng of the Assyrians, that he shuld geue the two thousand horses: art thou able to set men ther vp?

9 Seyng now that thou canst not resiste the power of the smallest prynce, that my Lorde hath, how darrest thou truste in the charettes and horse men of Egipt:

10 Moreouer, thinckest thou that I am come downe hether, to destroye thys lande without þe Lordes wil? The Lord sayde vnto me, go downe in to the lande, that thou mayest destroye it.

11 Then sayde Eliakim, Sobua & Ioah vnto Rabsakeh: Speake to vs thy seruauntes (we praye the) in the Sirians language, for we vnderstande it well: And speake not to vs in the Iewes tonge, leste the folcke heare, whych lyeth vpon the wall.

12 Then answered Rabsakeh: Thyncke ye, that the kynge sent me to speake this only vnto you? Hath he not sent me to them also, that lye vpon the wall? that they be not compelled to eate their owne donge, and drincke theyr owne stale wyth you?

13 And Rabsakeh stode styf, and cryed with a loude voyce in the Iewes tunge: and sayd: Now take hede, how the greate kynge of the Assirians geueth you warning.

14 Thus sayeth the kynge: Let not Hezekiah disceyue you, for he shal not be able to delyuer you.

15 Moreouer let not Hezekiah conforte you in the Lorde, when he sayeth: The Lorde without doute shall defende vs, and shall not geue ouer this citie into the handes of The kynge of the Assyrians, beleue hym not.

16 But thus sayth þe king of Assyria: opteyne my fauoure, enclyne to me: so maye euery man enioye his vineyardes and fygetrees, and drincke the water of hys cisterne:

17 vnto the tyme that I come my selfe, and bringe you into a lande that is like youre owne: wher in is wheate and wyne, whyche is both sowen wyth sede, and planted wyth vyneyardes.

18 Let not Hezekiah dysceyue you, when he sayeth vnto you: the Lorde shall delyuer vs? Myght the Goddes of the Gentiles kepe euery mans lande, from the power of the Kinge of the Assyrians?

19 Where is the God of Hemath and Arphad? Where is the God of Sepharnaim? And who was able to defende Samaria out of my hande?

20 Or which of all þe Goddes of the landes, hath delyuered their countre out of my power, so þt the Lorde shuld delyuer Ierusalem fro my hande?

21 Vnto this Hezekiahs messaungers helde their tunges, & answered not one worde: for the Kyng had charged them, that they shulde geue hym none answere.

22 So came Eliakim Helkiahs sonne the President, Sobna the Scrybe, and Ioah Asaphs sonne

the Secretarye vnto Hezekiah with rente clothes, and tolde him the wordes of Rabsakeh.

## CHAPTER 37

WHEN Hezekiah hearde that, he rente his clothes, and put on a sack cloth, & went into the temple of the Lorde.

2 But he sent Eliakim the Presydent, Sobna the Scrybe, wyth the eldest preastes clothed in sacke, vnto the Prophet Esay the sonne of Amoz,

3 & they sayde vnto hym: Thus sayeth Hezekiah: This is þe daye of trouble, of plage and of wrath: lyke as when a chylde cometh to the byrth, but the woman hath no power to brynge it forth.

4 The Lorde thy God (no doute) hath well consydered the wordes of Rabsakeh, whom hys lorde the Kynge of the Assyrians hath sent, to defye & blaspheme the lyuynge God: with soch wordes as the Lord thy God hath heard right well. And therfore lyfte vp thy prayer for the remnaunt, that yet are left.

5 So the seruauntes of Kyng Hezekiah came to Esay.

6 And Esay gaue them this answere. Saye thus vnto youre lorde: thus sayeth the Lord: Be not afrayed of the wordes that thou hast hearde, wherwith the Kyng of the Assyrians seruauntes haue blasphemed me.

7 Beholde, I wyll cause a wynde go ouer hym, as sone as he heareth it, he shall go agayne into hys countre, there wyll I destroye hym with the swerde.

8 Now when Rabsakeh returned, he founde the kynge of Assyria layenge sege the Lobnah, for he had vnderstande, that he was departed from Lachis.

9 For there came a rumoure, that Tharhakah kynge of Ethiopia was come forth to warre agaynst hym. And when the Kynge of Assyria hearde that, he sent other messaungers to Kynge Hezekiah with this commaundement:

10 Saye thus to Hezekiah Kyng of Iuda: Let not thy God disceyue the, in whom thou hopest, & sayeste: Ierusalem shall not be geuen in to the handes of the Kyng of Assyria.

11 For thou knowest well how the Kynges of Assyria haue handled all the landes that they haue subuerted, and hopest thou to escape?

12 Where the people of the Gentyles (whom my progenytours conquered) delyuered at any tyme thorow their goddes? As namely, Gozan, Haran, Rezeph, and the chyldren of Eden, which dwell at Thalassar.

13 Where is the Kynge of Hemah, & the Kynge of Arphad, & the Kyng of the cytye Sepharuaim, Ena and Aua?

14 Nowe when Hezekiah had receyued the lettre of the messaungers, and read it, he went vp into the house of the Lorde and opened the letter before the Lord.

15 And Hezekiah prayed before þe Lorde on this maner:

16 O Lorde of Hostes, thou God of Israel, which dwellest vpon Cherubyn. Thou art the God, that only is God of all þe Kyngdomes of the world, for thou only hast created heauen & earth.

17 Enclyne thyne eare Lord & consydre, open thyne eyes, O Lorde, & se, & pondre all þe wordes of Sennaherib, whiche hath sent hys embage to blaspheme the lyuynge God.

18 It is true, O Lorde, that the Kynges of Assyria haue conquered all Kyngdomes and landes,

19 and cast their goddes in the fyre. Not wythstandynge those were no goddes but the worckes of mens handes, of wod or stone, therfore haue they destroyed them.

20 Delyuer vs then, O Lorde oure God, from the handes of Sennaherib, that all Kyngdomes of the earth maye knowe, that thou only art the Lorde.

21 Then Esay the sonne of Amoz sent vnto Hezekiah, sayinge: Thus sayth the Lorde God of Israel: Where as thou haste made thy prayer vnto me, as touchyng Sennaherib,

22 thys is the answere, that the Lorde hath geuen concernynge hym: Despised art thou, & mocked, O daughter of Syon, he hath shaken his head at the, O doughter of Ierusalem.

23 But thou Sennaherib, whom hast thou defyed & blasphemed? And agaynst whom hast thou lyfted vp thy voyce, & exalted thy proude lokes? euen agaynst the holy one of Israel.

24 Thou with thy seruauntes hast blasphemed the Lord, and thus holdest thou of thy selfe: I couer the hye mountaynes, and sydes of Libanus with my horsmen. And there wyll I cut downe the hye Cedre trees & the fayreste Fyrre trees. I will vp into the heyght of it, & into the chefest of his tymbre woddes.

25 If there be no water, I wyl graue & drynke. And as for waters of defence, I shall drye them vp wyth the fete of myne Hoste.

26 Yee (sayest thou) hast thou not hearde, what haue taken in hande, and brought to passe of olde tyme? That same wyll I do now also: waste, destroye, & bringe stronge cities vnto hearpes of stones.

27 For theyr inhabitours shal be lyke lame men, brought in feare and confounded. They shalbe lyke the grasse and grene herbes in the felde, lyke the haye vpon house toppes, that withereth a fore it be growne vp.

28 I knowe thy wayes, thy

goinge forth and thy commyne home, yee & thy madnesse agaynst me.

29 Therfore thy furiousnesse agaynst me, & thy pryde is come before me. I will put a ringe in thy nose, and a bridle byt in the chawes of the, & turne the aboute, euen the same waye thou comest.

30 I will geue the also thys token (O Hezekiah) this yeare shalt thou eate that is kept in stoare, & the next yeare soch as groweth of him selfe, and in the thyrde yeare ye shall sowe & reape, yee ye shall plante vyneardes, and enioye the fruytes therof.

31 And soch of the house of Iuda as are escaped, shall come together, and the remnaunt shall take rote beneth, and bringe forth fruyte aboue.

32 For the escaped shall go out of Ierusalem, and the remaunte from the mount Syon. And this shall the gelousy of the Lorde of hostes bringe to passe.

33 Therfore thus sayeth the Lorde, concernynge the kynge of the Assyrians: He shall not come in to the cytye, and shall shote no arowe in to it, there shall no shilde hurte it, nether shall they graue aboute it.

34 The same waye that he came, shall he retourne, & not come at thys cytie, sayeth the Lorde.

35 And I wyll kepe and saue the cytie (sayeth he) for myne owne, and for my seruaunte Dauyds sake.

36 Thus the angel went forth, and slewe of the Assyrians hoste, an .clxxxv. thousande. And when men arose, vp earlye (at Ierusalem:) Beholde, all laye full of deed bodyes.

37 So Sennaherib the kynge of the Assyrians brake vp, and dwelt at Niniue.

38 Afterwarde it chaunsed, as he prayed in the temple of Nesrah hys god, that Adramalech and Sarazer hys owne sonnes slewe hym with þe sweard, and fled in to the lande of Ararat. And Asarhadon hys sonne reygned after hym.

# CHAPTER 38

Not longe afore thys, was Hezekiah sick vnto the deeth: and the Prophet Esay the sonne of Amoz came vnto hym, & sayde: Thus commaundeth the Lord: Set thine house in ordre: for thou must dye, and shalt not escape.

2 Then Hezekiah turned hys face towarde the wall, and prayed vnto the Lorde,

3 and sayde: Remembre (O Lorde) that I haue walcked before the in treuth and a stedfast herte, and haue done the thyng that is pleasaunt to the. And Hezekiah wepte sore.

4 Then sayde God vnto Esay:

5 Go and speake vnto Hezekiah: the Lorde God of Dauid thy father sendeth the thys worde: I haue herde thy prayer, and consydred thy teares: beholde I wyll put fyftene yeares mo vnto thy lyfe,

6 and delyuer the and the cytie also, from the hande of the kynge of Assiria, for I wyll defende the citie.

7 And take the this token of the Lord, that he wyll do it, as he hath spoken:

8 Beholde, I will returne the shadowe of Ahaz dial, that now is layed out wyth the Sunne & brynge it ten degrees backe warde. So the Sunne turned ten degree backward, the which he was descended a fore.

9 A thanckesgeuynge, whiche Hezekiah Kynge of Iuda wrote, when he had bene sycke, and was recouered.

10 I thought I shulde haue gone to the gates of hell in my best age, and haue wanted the resydue of my yeares.

11 I spake with in my selfe: I shall neuer viset the Lorde God in this lyfe: I shall neuer se man amonge the dwellers of the worlde.

12 Myne age is folden vp together, and taken awaye fro me, lyke a shepherdes cotage: my lyfe is hewen of, lyke as a weeuer cutteth of his webb. Whyle I was yet takynge my rest, he hewed me of, & made an ende of me in one day.

13 I thought I wolde haue lyued vnto the morow, but he brosed my bones lyke a lyon, and made an ende of me in one daye.

14 Then chatred I lyke a swalowe, and lyke a crane, and mourned as a doue. I lyfte vp myne eyes into the heyght: O Lorde (sayde I) vyolence is done vnto me, be thou suertye for me.

15 What shall I speake or saye, that he may this do? That I may lyue out all my yeares, yee in the bytternesse of my lyfe?

16 Verely (Lorde) men must lyue in bytternesse, & all my life muste I passe ouer therin: For thou raysest me vp, and wakest me. But lo, I wyllbe well content with this bytternes.

17 Neuertheles my conuersacyon hath so pleased the, that thou woldest not make an ende of my lyfe: so þt thou hast cast all my synnes behynde thy back.

18 For hell prayseth not the, death doth not magnyfye the. They þt go downe into þe graue, prayse not thy treuth:

19 but the lyuyng, yee the liuinge acknowledge the, lyke as I do thys daye. The father telleth hys chyldren of thy faythfulnesse.

20 Delyuer vs (O Lorde) and we wyll singe prayses in thy house, all þe dayes of oure life.

21 And Esay sayde: take a playster of fygges, and laye it vpon the sore, so shall it be whole.

22 Then sayd Hezekiah: O what a great thinge is this, that I shall go vp into the house of the Lorde.

## CHAPTER 39

AT the same tyme Merodach Baladam, Baladams sonne Kynge of Babylon, sent lettres and presentes to Hezekiah. For he vnderstode how that he had bene sick, and was recouered agayne.

2 And Hezekiah was glad therof, and shewed them the commodytes of hys treasure, of syluer, of golde, of spyces and rootes, of precyous oyles, all that was in hys cubbordes & treasure houses. There was not one thing in Hezekiahs house, & so thorow out all hys kyngdome, but he let them se it.

3 Then came Esay the Prophete of Kynge Ezekiah, and sayde vnto hym. What haue þe men sayde, & from whence came they vnto the? Hezekiah answered: they came out of a farre countre vnto me, out of Babylon.

4 Esay sayd: what haue they loked vpon in thyne house? Hezekiah answered: All þt is in myne house haue they sene: and there is nothinge in my treasure, but I shewed it them.

5 Then sayde Esay vnto Hezekiah: Vnderstande the worde of the Lord of Hostes:

6 Beholde the tyme wyll come, that euery thynge which is in thyne house, and al that thy progenytoures haue layde vp in stoare vnto this daye, shalbe caried to Babylon, & nothinge left behynde. Thys· sayeth the Lorde.

7 Yee & parte of thy sonnes, that shall come of the, & whom thou shalt get, shalbe caried hence, & become gelded chamberlaynes in the Kynge of Babylons courte:

8 Then sayde Hezekiah to Esay: Now God prosper hys owne councell, which thou hast told me. He sayde more ouer: So that there be peace and faythfulnesse in my tyme.

## CHAPTER 40

BE of good chere my people, be of good chere (sayeth youre God)

2 conforte Ierusalem, and tell her: that her trauayle is at an ende that her offence is pardoned, that she hath receyued of the Lordes hande sufficient correccyon for all her synnes.

3 A voyce cryeth: Prepare the waye for the Lorde in the wyldernesse, make streyght the path for oure God in the deserte.

4 Let all valleyes be exalted, & euery mountayne & hyll be leyed lowe. What so is croked, let it be made streyght, & lett the rough places be made playne feldes.

5 For the glory of the Lorde shall apeare, & all flesh shall se it, for why, the mouth of the Lorde hath spoken it.

6 The same voyce spake: Now crye. And I sayde: what shall I crye? Then spake yt: that all flesh is grasse, and that all the bewtye therof, is as the floure of the felde.

7 When the grasse is withered, the floure falleth awaye. Euen so is the people as grasse, when the breath of the Lorde bloweth vpon them.

8 Neuerthelesse whether the grasse wyther, or the floure fade awaye: Yet the worde of oure God endureth for euer. Moreouer the voyce cried thus:

9 Go vp vnto the hyll (O Sion) thou tha bryngest good tydynges, lyft vp thy voyce with power, O thou preacher Ierusalem. Lyft it vp without feare, & saye vnto the cities of Iuda: Beholde youre God,

10 beholde the Lorde, euen the Allmyghtie shall come with power, and beare rule with hys arme. Beholde, he bryngeth his treasure with hym, & hys worckes go before hym.

11 He shall fede his flock lyke an herdman. He shall gather the lambes together with his arme, and carie them in hys bosome, and shall kyndlye intreate those that beare yonge.

12 Who hath holden the waters in hys fyst? Who hath measured heauen with his spanne, and hath comprehended all the earth of the worlde in thre fyngers? Who hath weyed the mountaynes and hylles?

13 Who hath refourmed the mynde of the Lord? Or who is of hys councell to teach him?

14 At whom hath he asked councell, to make hym vnderstand, and to lerne hym the waye of iudgment: to teach him science: and to enstructe hym in the waye of vnderstandynge.

15 Beholde, all people are in comparyson of hym, as a droppe to a boket full, and are counted as the leste thing that the balaunce weyeth. Beholde, the Iles are in comparyson of hym, as the shadowe of the sonne beame.

16 Libanus is not suffycyent to mynystre fyre for his offringe, and all the beastes therof are not ynough to one sacryfyce.

17 All people in comparyson of hym are rekened as nothing, yee vayne vanyte and emptynesse.

18 To whom then will ye liken God? or what simylitude wyll ye set vp vnto hym?

19 Shall the caruer make hym carued ymage? and shall the goldsmyth couer hym with golde, or cast hym in to a fourme of syluer plates?

20 Moreouer shall the ymage maker (that the poore man whyche is dysposed, maye haue some thynge to set vp also) seke out & chose a tree, that is not rotten, and came therout an

ymage, that moueth not?

21 Knowe ye not this? Hearde ye neuer of it? Hath it not bene preached vnto you sence the begynnyng? Haue ye not bene enfourmed of this, sence the foundacyon of the earth was layde:

22 That he sytteth vpon the circle of the worlde, and that al the inhabytours of the worlde are in comparison of him, but as greshoppers: That he spredeth out the heauens as a coueryng, that he stretcheth them out, as a tent to dwell in:

23 That he bryngeth Pryncs to nothyng, and the iudges of the earth to dust:

24 so that they be not planted nor sowen agayne, nether theyr stocke roted agayne in þe earth? For as sone as he bloweth vpon them, they wither & fade awaye, lyke the strawe in a whyrle wynde.

25 To whom now will ye lyken me, & whom shall I be lyke, sayeth the holy one?

26 Lyft vp youre eyes on hye, and consydre. Who hath made those thynges, whyche come out by so greate heapes? And he can call them all by their names. For there is nothynge hyd vnto the greatnesse of his power, strength, and myght.

27 How maye then Iacob thyncke, or how maye Israel saye: My wayes are hyd from the Lorde, and my God knoweth not of my iudgementes.

28 Knowest thou not, or hast thou not hearde, that the euerlastynge God the Lorde whiche made all the corners of the earth, is nether weery nor faynt, & that his wysdome can not be comprehended,

29 but that he geueth strength vnto the weery, and power vnto the faynte?

30 Chyldren are weery and faynt, and the strongest men fall:

31 But vnto them that haue the Lorde before their eyes, shal strength be encreased, Aegles wynges shall growe vpon them: When they runne they shall not fal: and when they go, they shal not be weery.

# CHAPTER 41

Be styll (ye Ilandes) and herken vnto me. Be stronge ye people, Come hether, and shewe youre cause, we wyll go to the lawe together.

2 Who rayseth vp the iuste from the rysynge of the Sunne, and calleth him to go forth? Who casteth downe the people, and subdueth þe kynges before him: that he maye thorowe them all to the grounde wyth hys swearde, and scatre them lyke stuble with hys bowe?

3 He foloweth vpon them, & goeth safely hym selfe, and cometh in no fote path with his fete.

4 Who hath made, created, and called the generacions from the begynnyng? Euen I the Lorde, whiche am the fyrst, and with the last.

5 Beholde ye Iles? that ye maye feare, and ye endes of the earth, that ye maye be abasshed, draw nye, and come hether.

6 Euery man hath exorted hys neyghboure, and brother, and bydden him be stronge.

7 The Smyth conforted the moulder, and the Ironsmyth the hammerman, sayenge: It shalbe good, that we fasten this cast worcke: and then they fastened it with nayles, that it shulde not be moued.

8 And thou Israell my seruaunte: Iacob my electe sede of Abraham my beloued,

9 whom I led from the endes of þe earth by the hande: For I called the from farre, and sayde vnto the: Thou shalt be my seruaunt: I haue chosen the, and will not cast the awaye:

10 be not afrayd, for I will be with the. Loke not behynde the, for I will be thy God, to strength the, helpe the, and to kepe the with this right hand of myne.

11 Behold, all they that resyst þe, shall come to confusyon and shame: & thine aduersaries shalbe destroyed and brought to naught.

12 So that who so seketh after them, shall not fynde them. Thy destroyers shall perysh and so shall they that vndertake to make batell agaynst the:

13 For I thy Lorde and God, will strengthen thy ryght hande. Euen I þt saye vnto the: Feare not. I will helpe the.

14 Be not a frayde thou lytle worme Iacob, & thou despysed Israell for I will helpe the, sayeth the Lorde, and the holy one of Israel thyne auenger.

15 Beholde, I will make þe a treadyng cart & a new flayle, that thou mayest thresshe and grynd the mountaynes, and brynge the hylles to poulder.

16 Thou shalt fanne them, & the wynde shall carye them awaye, and the whyrlwynde shall scater them. But thou shalt reioyse in the Lorde, and shalt delyte in praysinge the holy one of Israel.

17 When the thyrstye & poore seke water and fynde none, and when their tonge is drye of thyrst: I geue it them sayth the Lorde. I the God of Israel forsake them not.

18 I bringe forth floudes in the hylle, and welles in the playne feldes. I turne the wildernes to riuers, & the drye lande to condythes of water.

19 I plante in the waste grounde trees of Cedre, Boxe, Myrre & Olyues. And in the drye I set Fyre trees, Elmes, and Hawthornes together.

20 All thys do I, that they altogether may se & marcke, perceyue with their hertes & consydre, that the hande of the Lorde maketh these thinges, and that the holye one of Israel

bringeth them to passe.

21 Stande at your cause (sayeth the Lorde) & brynge forth your stroungest grounde, counceleth the Kynge of Iacob.

22 Let the goddes come forth them selues, & shewe vs the thynges that are past, what they be: let them declare them vnto vs, that we maye take them to herte, and knowe them herafter.

23 Ether, let them shewe vs thynges for to come, and tell vs what shalbe done her after: so shal we knowe, that they be goddes. Shewe somthing, ether good or bad: so wyll we both knowledge the same, and tell it out.

24 Beholde, ye goddes are of naugth, & your makynge is of naught but abhomynacyon hath chosen you.

25 Neuertheles, I haue waked vp one from the North, and he shall come. And another from the East, which shall call vpon my name, & shall come to the Princes, as the Potter to his claye, and as the Potter treadeth downe the myre.

26 Who tolde that afore? So wyll we confesse and saye, that he is rightuous: But there is none that sheweth or declareth any thynge, there is none also that heareth youre wordes.

27 Beholde, I wyll fyrst graunte them of Sion and Ierusalem to be Euangelistes.

28 But when I consydre: there is not one amonge them that prophecyeth, nether (when I aske hym) that auswereth one worde.

29 Lo, wicked are they and vayne, with the thynges also that they take in hande: yee wynde are they, and emptynesse, with theyr ymages together.

## CHAPTER 42

Beholde now therfore, thys is my seruaunte whom I wyll kepe to my selfe: myne electe, In whom my soule shalbe pacified. I wyll geue hym my sprete, that he may shewe forth iudgement & equyte amonge the Gentyles.

2 He shall not be an outcryer, ner an hye mynded person. Hys voyce shall not be hearde in the stretes.

3 A brossed rede shall he not breake, and the smokyng flax shall he not quench, but faythfully and truly shall he geue iudgement.

4 He shall nether be ouersene ner hastye, that he maye restore ryghtuousnes vnto the earth: and the gentyles also shall kepe his lawes.

5 For thus sayeth God the Lord vnto hym (euen he that the made heauens, and spred them abrode & seth forth the earth with her increase, whych geueth breath vnto the people that is in it, & to them that dwell therin)

6 I the Lorde haue called the in rightuousnesse, & led the by the hande. Therfore wyll I also defende the, and geue the for a couenaunt of the people, and to be þe lyght of þe Gentyles.

7 That thou mayest open the eyes of the blynde, let out the prisoners, & them that syt in darknesse, out of the dongeon house.

8 I my selfe, whose name is the Lorde, whych geue my power to none other nether myne honoure to the Goddes:

9 shewe yow these newe tydynges, and tell you them or they come, for olde thynges also are come to passe.

10 Synge therfore vnto the Lorde, a newe songe of thanckes geuynge, blowe out hys prayse vnto the ende of the world. They that be vpon the sea, and all that is therin, prayse hym, the Iles and they that dwell in them.

11 Let the wyldernes with her cities lyft vp her voyce, the townes also that be in Cedar. Let them be glad that syt vpon rockes of stone, & let them crie downe from the hye mountaynes:

12 ascribinge almightynes vnto the Lorde, and magnifying hym amonge the Gentyles.

13 The Lord shal come forth as a gyaunte, and take a stomacke to hym lyke as a freshe man of warre. He shall roare and crye, and ouercome hys enemyes.

14 I haue longe holden my peace (sayeth the Lorde) shulde I therfore be styll, and kepe sylence for euer? I wyll crye lyke a trauelynge woman, and ones wyl I destroye, & deuoure.

15 I wyll make waste both mountayne & hyll, & drye vp euery grene thynge that groweth theron. I wyll drye vp the floudes of water, and drincke vp the ryuers.

16 I will brynge the blynde into a strete, that they knowe not: & lede them into a fote path, that they are ignoraunt in. I shall make darckenesse light before them, and the thinge that is croked to be streyght. These thinges wyll I do, & not forget them.

17 And therfore let them conuerte, and be ashamed earnestlye, that hope in Idoles, and saye to fashyoned ymages: ye are oure godes.

18 Heare, O ye deaf men, and sharpen youre sightes to se (O ye blynde.)

19 But who is blinder, then my seruaunt? Or so deaf, as my messaungers, whom I sent vnto them? For who is so blinde as my people, & they þt haue the rule of them?

20 They are lyke, as yf thou vnderstodest moch, & keptest nothyng: or yf one herde well, but were not obedient.

21 The Lord be mercyfull vnto them for his rightuousnesse sake, that his worde myght be magnyfyed & praysed.

22 But it is a myscheuous and wycked people. Their younge

men belonge all to the snare, & shalbe shut into preson houses. They shalbe caryed awaye captyue, and no man shall lowse them. They shalbe troden vnder fote, & no man shall laboure to bringe them agayne.

23 But who is he amonge you, that pondreth this in hys mynde, that consydreth it, & taketh it for a warnynge in tyme to come?

24 Who suffred Iacob to be trodden vnder fote, and Israel to be spoyled? Dyd not the Lorde? Now haue we synned agaynst hym, & haue had no delyte to walcke in his wayes nether bene obedyent vnto his lawe.

25 Therfore hath he poured vpon vs hys wrathfull dyspleasure, & stronge batell, whiche maketh vs haue to do on euery syde, yet wyll we not vnderstande: He burneth vs vp, yet syncketh it not in to oure hertes.

## CHAPTER 43

BUT now, the Lorde that made the O Iacob, & he that fashyoned the O Israel, sayeth thus: Feare not, for I wyll defende the. I haue called the by name thou art myne owne.

2 When thou wentest in the water, I was by the, that the stronge floudes shuld not pluck the awaye. When thou walkest in the fyre, it shall not burne the, and the flame shall not kindle vpon the.

3 For I am the Lorde thy God, the holy one of Israel, thy Sauyour. I gaue Egypte for thy delyueraunce, the Moryans, and the Sabees for the:

4 because thou wast deare in my sight, and because I set by the, and loued the. I pylled all men for the, & delyuered vp al people for thy sake,

5 that thou shuldest not feare, for I was wyth the. I wyll brynge thy sede from the East, and gather the together from the West.

6 I wyll saye to the North, let go. And to þe South, kepe not backe: but bringe me my sonnes from farre, and my daughters from the endes of the worlde:

7 Namelye, all those that be called after my name: For them haue I created, fasshyoned, and made for myne honoure.

8 Brynge forth that people, whether they haue eyes or be blynde, deafe or haue eares.

9 All nacyons shall come in one, and be gathered in one people. But whiche amonge yonder goddes shall declare suche thynges, & tell vs what is to come? Let them bringe theyr wytnesses, so shall they be fre: for then men shall heare it, & saye, it is trueth.

10 But I bring you wytnesses (sayth the Lorde) euen those that are my seruauntes, whom I haue chosen: to the intent that ye myght be certyfyed and geue me faythfull credence: yee & to consydre, that I am he, before whom there was neuer any God, and that there shalbe none after me.

11 I am only the Lorde, and wythout me is there no Sauyour.

12 I geue warnynge, I make whole, I teach you that there shulde be no straunge God amonge you. And thys recorde must ye beare me your selues (sayth the Lorde) that I am God.

13 And euen he am I from the begynnynge, & there is none that can take any thynge out of my hande. And what I do, can no man chaunge.

14 Thus sayeth the Lorde the holy one of Israel youre redemer: For youre sake I wyll sende to Babylon, & brynge all the strongest of them from thence: Namely, the Chaldees that boost them of their shyppes:

15 Euen I the Lorde youre holy one whiche haue made Israel, and am youre Kynge.

16 Moreouer, thus sayeth the Lorde, euen he that maketh a waye in the sea, and a footpath in the myghtye waters:

17 which bryngeth forth the charettes and horses, the hoste & the power, that they maye fall a slepe & neuer ryse, and be extincte, lyke as towe is quenched.

18 Ye remembre not thynges of olde, and regarde nothing that is past

19 Therfore beholde, I shall make a new thynge, & shortly shall it appeare: ye shall well knowe it, I told it you afore, but I wil tel it you agayne. I wyll make stretes in the deserte, & ryuers of water in þe wyldernes

20 The wylde beastes shall worshyppe me: the dragon, and the Estryche. For I shall geue water in the wyldernesse, and streames in the deserte: that I may geue dryncke to my people, whom I chose.

21 This people haue I made for my self, & they shall shewe forth my prayse.

22 For thou (Iacob) woldest not call vpon me, but thou haddest an vnlust towarde me, O Israel.

23 Thou gauest me not thy younge beastes for burntoffrynges, nether dydest honoure me with thy sacryfices. Thou boughtest me no deare spice wyth thy money, nether pouredest the fatt of thy sacrifices vpon me. Howbeit I haue not bene chargeable vnto the in offringes, nether greuous in incense.

24 But thou hast laden me wyth thy synnes, and weeried me wyth thyne vngodlynes.

25 Where as I yet am euen he onlye, that for myne owne selfes sake do awaye thyne offences, & forget thy synnes: so that I wyll neuer thyncke vpon them.

26 Put me now in remembraunce (for we wyll reason together) & shew what

thou hast for the, to make the quyte.

27 Thy fyrst father offended sore, & thy rulers haue synned agaynst me.

28 Therfore I ether suspended, or slue the chefest Prynces: I dyd curse Iacob, and gaue Israel into reprofe.

## CHAPTER 44

So heare now, O Iacob my seruaunt, and Israel whom I haue chosen.

2 For thus sayth the Lord that made the: fashyoned the, and helped the, euen from thy mothers wombe: Be not afrayed, O Iacob my seruaunt, thou rightuous, whom I haue chosen.

3 For I shall pouer water vpon the drye grounde and ryuers vpon the thurstye. I shall poure my sprete vpon thy sede, and myne encerase vpon thy stocke.

4 They shall growe together, lyke as the grasse, and as the Willies by the waters syde.

5 One wyll saye: I am the Lordes. Another will call vnder the name of Iacob. The thyrde shall descrybe wyth hys hande vnto the Lorde, and geue hym selfe vnder the name of Israel.

6 Moreouer, thus hath the Lorde spoken: euen the Kynge of Israel, and his auenger, the Lorde of Hostes: I am þe fyrst & the last, and with out me is there no God.

7 For what is he, that euer was lyke me, which am from euerlastinge? Let hym shewe hys name, and do where thorow he may be likened vnto me. Let him tell you forth planely thinges, that are past & for to come:

8 yee and that without any feare or stoppe. For haue not I euer tolde you hytherto, and warned you? Ye can beare me recorde youre selues. Is there any God excepte me? or any maker, that I shuld not knowe hym.

9 Wherfore all caruers of Idoles are but vayne, & their labour lost. They must beare recorde them selues, that (seyng they came nether se ner vnderstande) they shalbe confounded.

10 Who shulde now make a God, or fashion an Idole, that is profytable for nothynge?

11 Beholde, all the felowshyppe of them must be brought to confusyon. Let all the worckmaisters of them come and stande together from amonge men: they must be abashed and confounded one with another.

12 The smith taketh yron, and tempereth it with hoate coales, and fashyoneth it with hammers, and maketh it with all the strength of his armes: yee sometyme he is faynt for very hunger, & so thurstye, that he hath no more power.

13 The carpenter, (or ymage caruer) taketh meat of the tymbre: & spredeth forth hys lyne: he maketh it with some coloure: he playneth it, he ruleth it, & squareth it, & maketh it after the ymage of a man, and accordynge to the bewtye of a man: that it maye stande in the temple.

14 Moreouer, he goeth oute to hewe downe Cedre trees: He bryngeth home Elmes and Okes, and other tymbre of the wod. Or els the Fyrre trees which he planted hym self, & soch as the rayne hath swelled,

15 whyche wod serueth for men to burne. Of this he taketh and warmeth him selfe with all: he maketh a fyre of it to bake bred. And afterwarde maketh a God there of, to honoure it: & an Idole to knele before it.

16 One pece he burneth in the fyre, with another he rosteth flesh, þt he maye eate roste hys bely full: wyth the thyrde he warmeth hym self, & sayeth: Aha, I am well warmed, I haue bene at the fyre.

17 And of the resydue he maketh hym a God, and an Idole for hym selfe. He kneleth before it, he worshyppeth it, he prayeth vnto it, and sayeth: deliuer me, for thou art my God.

18 Yet men nether considre ner vnderstande, because their eyes are stopped, that they can not se: and their hertes, that they cannot perceyue.

19 They pondre not in their myndes, for they haue nether knowledge ner vnderstandyng, to thyncke thus: I haue brent one pece in the fyre: I haue baked bred with the coles there of, I haue rosted flesh with all, & eaten it: shall I now of the resydue make an abhomynacyon, & fall downe before a rotten pece of wodd?

20 The kepyng of dust, and folishnesse of herte hath turned them asyde: so that none of them can haue a fre conscience to thyncke maye not I erre?

21 Consydre this (O Iacob & Israel) for thou art my seruaunt. I haue made the, that thou mightest serue me. O Israel, forget me not.

22 As for thyne offences, I dryue them awaye lyke the cloudes, and thy synnes as the mist. Turne the agayne vnto me, and I wyl delyuer the.

23 Be glad ye heauens, whom the Lorde hath made, let al that is here beneth vpon þe earth, be ioyfull. Reioyse ye mountaynes & woddes, with all the trees that are in you: for the Lord shall redeme Iacob, & shewe his glory vpon Israel.

24 For thus sayth the Lorde thy redemer euen he that fashioned the from thy mothers wombe: I am the Lorde, whiche do all thinges my selfe alone. I onlye haue spred oute the heauens and I only haue layde the foundacyon of the earth.

25 I destroye the tokens of witches, and make the Soth sayers go wronge. As for the wyse, I turne them backwarde, and make their connynge folyshnesse.

26 But I set vp the purpose of my seruauntes, and fulfill the councell of my messaungers. I saye to Ierusalem: turne agayne: And to the cyties of Iuda, be ye buylded agayne: and I repayre their decayed places.

27 I saye to the ground: be drie. And I drye vp thy water floudes.

28 I saye to Cyrus: thou art myne herd man: so that he shall fulfill all thinges after my will. I saye to Ierusalem: be thou buylded, & to the temple: be thou fast grounded.

# CHAPTER 45

THUS sayeth the Lorde vnto Cyrus his anoynted, whom he ledeth by the righthande: that the people maye fal downe before hym: I will lowse the gyrdle of kynges: that they shall open the gates before thy face, & not to shut their dores.

2 I wil go before the, & make the croked streyght I shall breake þe brasen dores, & burst þe yron barres.

3 I shall geue the the hyd treasure & the thinge which is secretly kepte: þt thou maiest knowe that I the God of Israel haue called the by thy name:

4 & that for Iacob my seruauntes sake and for Israel my chosen. For I called the by thy name, & ordened the or euer thou knewest me:

5 Euen I the Lorde, before whom there is none other: for without me, tere is no God. I haue prepared the or euer thou knewest me

6 that it myght be knowne from the rysyng of the sunne to the goynge downe of the same, that all is nothing without me. For I am the Lord, & there is els none.

7 It is I that created the lyght and darcknes, I make peace & trouble yee euen I the Lorde do all these thinges.

8 The heauens aboue shall droppe downe, & the cloudes shall rayne ryghtuousnes. The earth shall open it self, & brynge forth health, & therby shall ryghtuousnes florishe. Euen I the Lorde shall brynge it to passe.

9 Wo be vnto hym that chydeth wyth hys maker, the potsherde with þe potter: Sayeth the claye to the potter: What makest thou? or thy worcke serueth for nothynge?

10 Wo be vnto hym, þt sayeth to his father: Why begettest thou? And to hys mother: why bearest thou?

11 Thus sayeth the Lorde, euen the holy one & maker of Israel: Aske me of thynges for to come, concernynge my sonnes: and put me in remembraunce, as touchyng the worckes of my handes:

12 I haue made the earth, & created man vpon it. Wyth myne handes haue I spred forth heauen, and geuen a commaundment for all the Host therof.

13 I shall wake hym vp with ryghtuousnesse, & ordre all hys wayes. He shall buylde my cytye, and lett out my prisoners: and that nether for gyft nor rewardes, sayeth the Lorde of Hostes.

14 The Lorde hath sayde moreouer: The occupiers of Egypte, the marchauntes of the Morians and Sabees, shall come vnto the with trybute, they shalbe thyne, they shall folowe the, & go with cheynes vpon their fete. They shall fall downe before the, and make supplicacyon vnto þe. For God (without whom there is none other God) shall be with the.

15 O how profunde art thou O God, thou God & Sauioure of Israel?

16 Confounded be ye, and put to dishonour: go hence together with shame, all ye þt be worckmaysters of erroure: (that is worshippers of Idols)

17 But Israell shalbe saued in the Lorde, which is the euerlastinge saluacion: They shall not come to shame ner confusyon, worlde without ende.

18 For thus sayeth the Lorde: euen he þt created heauen, God that made the earth, that fashioned it, & sett it forth: I haue not made it for naught, but I made it to be enhabited Euen I the Lorde, wythout whom there is none other.

19 I haue not spoken secretely, nether in darcke places of the earth. It is not for naught, that I sayde vnto the sede of Iacob: seke me. I am þe Lord, which when I speake, declareth the thing that is ryghtuous & true.

20 Let them be gathered and come together, lett them drawe nye hyther, that are escaped of the people: Haue they eny vnderstandynge, that set vp the stockes of their Idols, & praie vnto a God, that cannot helpe them?

21 Lett men drawe nye, let them come hyther, & aske councell one at another, and shewe forth: What is he, that tolde this before? or who spake of it, euer sence the begynnynge? Haue not I the Lorde done it: wythout whom there is none other God? the true God and Sauioure, and there is els none but I?

22 And therfore turne you vnto me (all ye endes of þe earth) so shall ye be saued, for I am God, and there is els none.

23 I sweare by my selfe, out of my mouth commeth the worde of ryghtuousnesse, and that maye no man turne: but all knees shall bowe vnto me, and

# ISAIAH

all tunges shall sweare by me,

24 sayinge: Verelye in the Lorde is my ryghtuousnes and strength. To hym shall men come: but all they that thyncke scorne of hym, shalbe confounded.

25 And the whole sede of Israel shalbe iustyfyed, and praysed in the Lorde.

## CHAPTER 46

Neuertheles Bell shall fall, and Nabo shalbe broken: whose ymages are a burthen for the beastes and cattell, to ouerlade them, and to make them weery.

2 They shall syncke downe, and fall together: for they maye not ease them of their burthen, therfore muste they go in to captyuyte.

3 Herken vnto me, O house of Iacob, & all ye that remayne yet of the housholde of Israel: whom I haue borne from youre mothers wombe, & brought you vp from your birth, tyll ye weere growen:

4 I whych shall beare you vnto youre laste age: I haue made you, I wyll also noryshe you, beare you and saue you.

5 Whom wyll ye make me lyke, in fashion or ymage, that I maye be lyke him?

6 Ye fooles (no doute) wyll take out syluer & golde oute of youre purses, and weye it, and hyre a gold smith to make a God of it, þt men maye knele downe & worshippe it.

7 Yet muste he be taken on mens shoulders & borne, & set in hys place that he maye stande and not moue. Alas that men shulde crye vnto hym, which geueth no answere: and delyuereth not the man that calleth vpon hym, from hys trouble.

8 Consydre this well, & be ashamed Go in to youre owne selues (O ye runnagates.)

9 Remembre the thynges which are past, sence the begynnyng of þe worlde: that I am God, & that there is els no God, yee & that there is nothynge lyke vnto me.

10 In the beginning of a thynge, I shewe the ende therof: & I tell before, thynges that are not yet come to passe. With one worde is my deuyce accomplyshed, & fulfylleth all my pleasure.

11 I call a byrde out of the East, & all that I take in hande, out of farre countrees, as soone as I commaunde, I brynge it hether: as soone as I thyncke to deuyse a thynge, I do it.

12 Heare me, O ye þt are of an hye stomack, but farre from ryghtuousnesse.

13 I shall brynge forth my ryghtuousnesse. It is not farre, and my health shall not traye longe awaye. I wyll laye health in Sion, and geue Israel my glorye.

## CHAPTER 47

But as for the (O daughter thou virgin Babylon) Thou shalt syt in the dust thou shalt sit vpon the grounde, & not in a trone (O thou mayden of Chaldea.) Thou shalt no more be called tender and pleasaunt.

2 Thou shalt bringe forth the querne and grind meele, put downe thy stomacher make bare thy knees & shalt wade thorow þe water ryuers.

3 Thy shame shalbe discouered, & thy preuyties shalbe sene. For I wyll auenge me of the, and no man shall lett me:

4 sayeth oure redemer, which is called the Lorde of Hostes the holy one of Israel.

5 Syt styll, holde thy tunge, & get the in to some darcke corner, O daughter Chaldea, for thou shalt nomore be called lady of kyngdomes.

6 I was so wroth with my people, þt I punished myne enheritaunce, & gaue them into thy power. Neuertheles, thou shewedeste them no mercy, but euen the very aged men of them, didest thou oppresse ryght sore wyth thy yock,

7 & thou thoughtest thus. I shalbe lady for euer. And desyde all that, thou hast not regarded these thinges, nether cast, what shuld come after.

8 Heare now therfore, thou wylful, þt syttest so carelesse, & speakest thus in thine herte: I am alone, & without me is there none I shall neuer be wydowe, ner desolate agayne.

9 And yet both these thinges shall come to the vpon one daye in þe twyncklyng of an eye: Namely wyddowhead, & desolacyon. They shall mightely fall vpon the, for the multitude of thy witches, & for the greate heape of thy coniurers.

10 For thou hast comforted thy selfe in thy dysceitfulnes, and hast sayde: No man seyth me. Thyne owne wysdome & connyng hath disceueyd the. In that thou hast sayde: I am alone, and without me there is none.

11 Therfore shall trouble come vpon the, & thou shalt not knowe, from whence it shall aryse. Myschefe shal fall vpon the, which thou shalt not be able to put of. A sodane myserye shall come vpon the, or euer thou be a warre.

12 Now go to thy coniurers, and to the multitude of thy witches (whom thou haste bene acquainted withall from thy youthe) yf they maye helpe the, or strengthen the.

13 Thou haste hytherto had manye councels of them, so let the heauengasers & the beholders of starres come on now and delyuer the: yea & let them shewe, when these new thynges shal come vpon the.

14 Beholde, they shalbe lyke

strawe, whiche yf it be kindled with fyre, no man may rydde it for the vehemence of the flame: And yet it geueth no synners to warme a man by, nor cleare fyre to sit by.

15 Euen so shall they be vnto the whome thou haste vsed and occupied from thy youthe. Euery one shall shewe the hys erroneous waye, yet shall none of them defende the.

## CHAPTER 48

Heare this, O thou house of Iacob: ye that are called by the name of Israel, and are come oute of one stocke with Iuda, whiche sweare by the name of the Lorde, & beare wytnesse by the God of Israell (but not with trueth & righte)

2 whiche are called fre men of the holye citie, as they that loke for comforte in the God of Israel, whose name is the Lorde of hostes.

3 The thinges that I shewed you euer sence the begynnynge: Haue I not broughte them to passe, immedyatly as they came out of my mouthe, & declared them? And they are come.

4 Howebeit I knewe that thou arte obstynate, & that thy neck hath an yron veyne, & that thy browe is of brasse.

5 Neuertheles I haue euer sence the beginning shewed the of thinges for to come, and declared them vnto the, or euer they came to passe: that thou shouldest not saye: myne Idoll hathe done it, my carued or caste ymage hath shewed it.

6 Heare and consyder all these thynges whether it was ye that prophecyed them: But as for me, I tolde the before at the beginning, new and secrete thinges that thou knewest not of.

7 And some done nowe not of olde tyme, whereof thou neuer heardest, before they were brought to passe, þt thou canst not saye: I knewe of them.

8 Moreouer there be some whereof thou haste neyther hearde nor knowne, neyther haue they ben opened vnto thyne eares afore tyme. For I knew that thou woldest maliciously offende, therfor haue I called the a transgressoure, euen from thy mothers wombe.

9 Neuertheles for my names sake, I haue withdrawen my wrath, and for myne honours sake I haue ouersene the, so that I haue not roted the oute.

10 Beholde I haue pourged the, & not for moneye. I haue chosen the in the fyre of pouerte,

11 And that onely for myne owne sake, for I geue myne honoure to none other, þt thou shuldest not despyse me.

12 Herken vnto me O Iacob, and Israel whom I haue called I am euen he that is, I am the fyrst & the last.

13 My hande is the foundacyon of the earthe, & my ryghte hande spanneth ouer the heauens. As sone as I called them they were there.

14 Gather you al together, and herken: Whiche of yonder goddes hath declared this, that the Lorde wyll do by the kyng of Babylon (whom he loueth & fauoureth) & by the Caldees hys arme?

15 I my self alone haue tolde you this before. Yea I shall call him and brynge him forth & geue him a prosperous iourneye.

16 Come nye and heare this, haue I spoken anye thynge darcklye sence the begynnynge? when a thing begynneth, I am there. Wherfore the Lorde God with his spryte hathe sent me,

17 And thus sayeth the Lord God thyne auenger, the holye one of Israell: I am the Lorde thy God, whiche teache the profitable thynges, & leade the the waye, þt thou shuldest go.

18 Yf thou wilt now regarde my commaundement, thy welthynes shalbe as the water streame, and thy ryghteousnes as the waues flowynge in the sea.

19 Thy sede shalbe lyke as the sande in the sea, and the frute of thy body, lyke the grauel stones therof. Thy name shal not be roted oute, nor destroyed before me.

20 Ye shall go awaye from Babylon, and escape the Calders with a merye voyce. This shalbe spoken of, declared abroad, and go forth vnto the ende of the worlde, so that it shalbe sayde: The Lorde hathe defended hys seruaunte Iacob,

21 that they suffred no thurste, when they trauayled in the wyldernesse. He claue the rockes a sonder, and the water gusshed out.

22 As for the vngodlye, they haue no peace, sayeth the Lorde.

## CHAPTER 49

Ye Iles, herken vnto me, & take hede ye people from farre. The Lorde hath called me from my byrth, and made mencion of my name from my mothers womb:

2 he hath made my mouth like a sharp swerd vnder the shadowe of hys hande hath he defended me, & hyd me in hys quyuer, as a good arowe,

3 and sayde vnto me: Thou arte my seruaunt Israel, I wylbe honoured in the.

4 Then aunswered I: I shall lese my laboure, I shall spende my strength in vayne. Neuertheles, I wyll commytte my cause and my worcke vnto the Lorde my God.

5 And now sayth þe Lord euen he that fashioned me from my mothers wombe to be his seruaunte, that I may bring Iacob agayne vnto him: howbe it, Israel wil not be gathered vnto hym agayne. In whose syght I am greate; whiche also is my Lorde my God and my strength.

# ISAIAH

6 Let it be but a smal thynge, that thou arte my seruaunte, to set vp the kynredes of Iacob, & to restore the destruccyon of Israel: yf I make the not also the light of the Gentiles. that thou mayest be my helthe vnto the ende of the worlde.

7 Moreouer thus sayth the Lorde the auenger and holye one of Israel, because of the abhorrynge and despysynge amonge the Gentyles, concernynge the seruaunte of all them that beare rule: Kynges and prynces shall se, and aryse and worshyppe, because of the Lord that he is faythfull: and because of the holye one of Israell, which hath chosen the.

8 And thus sayth the Lorde: In the tyme apointed wyll I be present with the. And in the houre of healthe wyll I helpe the, and delyuer the. I wyll make the a pledge for the people, so that thou shalte helpe vp the earthe agayne, and chalenge agayne the scatred herytages:

9 That thou mayest saye to the presonners: go forth, & to them that are in darknesse: come into the lyght, that they may fede in the hye wayes, and get theyr lyuynge in all places.

10 There shall neyther hunger nor thurste, heate nor sunne hurte them. For he that fauoureth them, shall leade them, and geue them drincke of the sprynge welles.

11 I wyll make wayes vpon all my mountaynes, & my fote pathes shalbe exalted.

12 And beholde, they shall come from farre: lo, some from the north and weste, some from the south.

13 Reioyse ye heauens, and synge prayses thou earthe: Talke of ioye ye hylles, for God wyll comforte hys people, and haue mercye vpon hys, that be in trouble.

14 Then shal Syon saye: God hath forsaken me, and the Lorde hath forgotten me.

15 Doth a wyfe forget the chylde of her wombe, & the sonne whom she hath borne? And though she do forget, yet wyll not I forget the.

16 Beholde, I haue written the vp vpon my handes, thy walles are euer in my syght.

17 They that haue broken the doune, shall make haste to build the vp agayne: and they that made the waste, shall dwell in the.

18 Lyft vp thyne eyes, & loke aboute the: all these shall gather them together, and come to the. As truly as I lyue (saith the Lorde) thou shalte put them all vpon the, as an apparell, and gyrde them to the, as a bryde doth her Iewels.

19 As for thy lande that lyeth desolate, wasted & destroyed: it shalbe to narowe for them, that shall dwell in it. And they that wolde deuoure the, shalbe farre awaye.

20 Then the childe whom the baren shal bringe forth vnto the, shall saye in thyne eare: thys place is to narowe, syt nye together, that I maye haue roume.

21 Then shalt thou thincke by thy self: Who hath begotten me these: seing I am baren & alone, a captyue & an oute cast? And who hath noryshed them vp for me? I am desolate and alone, but from whence come these?

22 And therfore thus sayth the Lorde God. Beholde, I wyll stretch out myne hand to the Gentyles, and set vp my token to the people, They shal bryng the thy sonnes in theyr lappes, and carye thy doughters vnto the vpon theyr shoulders.

23 For kynges shalbe thy noursynge fathers, and Quenes shalbe thy noursynge mothers. They shall fall before the wt theyr faces flat vpon the earth, and lycke vp the duste of thy fete: that thou mayest knowe, how that I am the Lord. And wo so putteth his trust in me, shal not be confounded.

24 Who spoyleth the gyaunte of hys praye? or who taketh the presoner from the mightye?

25 And therefore thus sayeth the Lorde: The prysoners shalbe taken from the gyaunte, & the spoyle delyuered from the vyoleute: for I wil maintayne thy cause agaynste thyne aduersaryes, and saue thy sonnes.

26 And wyl fede thyne enemyes with their owne fleshe, and make them dryncke of theyr owne bloude, as of swete wyne. And all fleshe shall knowe (O Iacob) that I am the Lorde thy Sauyoure & stronge auenger.

# CHAPTER 50

THUS sayeth the Lorde: Where is the byll of your mothers deuorcement, that I sente vnto her or who is the vsurer, to whome I solde you? Beholde, for youre owne offences are ye solde: & because of youre transgression, is youre mother forsaken.

2 For why wolde no man receyue me, when I came and when I called, no man gaue me aunswere. Was my hande clene smyten of, that it might not helpe? or had I not power to delyuer? lo, at a worde I drincke vp the sea, and of water floudes I make drye lande: so that for want of water, the fysh corruppe and dye of thurst.

3 As for heauen, I clothe it wyth darcknesse, & put a sack vpon it.

4 The Lorde God hath geuen me a wel learned tunge, so that I can comforte them whiche are troubled, yea & that in due ceason. He waked myne eare vp by tymes in the mornynge (as the scolemasters do) that I myght herken.

5 The Lord God hath opened

myne eare, therfore can I not saye naye, nor withdrawe my selfe,

6 but I offre my backe vnto the smyters, & my chekes to the uyppers. I turne not my face from shame & spyttynge,

7 for the Lorde God helpeth me, therfore shall I not be confounded. I haue hardened my face like a flynt stone, for I am sure, that I shall not come to confusyon.

8 Myne aduocate speaketh for me, who wyl then go with me to law? Let vs stand one agaynste another: yf there be any þt wyll reason with me, let him come here forth to me.

9 Beholde the Lord God standeth by me, what is he that can condempne me? lo, they shalbe all lyke as an olde clothe, whiche the mothes shall eate vp.

10 Therfore who so feareth the Lorde among you let hym heare the voyce of hys seruaunt, Who so walketh in darcknesse, and no lyghte shyneth vpon hym, let hym hope in the Lord, and holde hym by his God.

11 But take hede ye haue all kyndled a fyre, and gyrded youre selues with the flamme: Ye walcke in the glysteryng of youre owne fyre, and in the flamme that ye haue kyndled. This cometh vnto you from my hande, namely that ye shall slepe in sorowe.

# CHAPTER 51

Herken vnto me, ye that hold of ryghtuousnes, ye that seke the Lord. Take hede vnto the stone whereout ye are hewen, and to the graue whereoute ye are digged.

2 Consydre Abraham youre father, & Sara that bare you: how that I called him alone prospered hym well, & encreased him:

3 how the Lorde comforted Syon, and repayred all her decaye: makynge her deserte as a Paradyse, & her wyldernesse as the garden of the Lorde. Myrth and ioye was there, thanckesgeuynge and the voyce of prayse.

4 Haue respecte vnto me then, O my people, and laye thyne eare to me: for a lawe and an ordynaunce shall go forth from me, to lyghten the Gentyles.

5 It is harde by, that my health & my ryghteousnesse shall go forthe, and the people shalbe ordered wyth myne arme. The Ilandes (that is the Gentyles) shall hope in me, & put theyr truste in myne arme.

6 Lyfte vp youre eyes towarde heauen, & loke vpon the earthe beneth. For the heauens shall vanyshe awaye lyke smoke, & the earthe shall teare lyke a clothe, & they that dwell therein, shall perysh in lyke maner. But my healthe endureth for euer, & my ryghtuousnes shall not cease.

7 Therfore herken vnto me, ye that haue pleasure in rightuousnes, thou people that bearest my lawe in thyne herte. Feare not the curse of men, be not afrayde of theyr blasphemies & reuylynges:

8 for wormes and mothes shal eate them vp lyke cloth and wol. But my ryghtuousnesse shall endure for euer, & my sauinge health from generacion to generacyon,

9 Wake vp, wake vp, and be strong: O thou arme of the Lorde: wake vp, lyke as in tymes paste, euer and sence the worlde beganne.

10 Arte not thou he, that haste wounded that proude lucyfer, & hewen the dragon in peces? Arte not thou euen he, whiche haste dryed vp the depe of the sea, whiche haste made playne the sea grounde, that the delyuered myght go thorow?

11 That the redemed of the Lord, which turned agayne, myghte come wyth ioye vnto Syon, there to endure for euer? That myrthe and gladnesse might be with them, that sorow & wo myght fle from them?

12 Yea I, I am euen he, that in all thynges geueth you consolacion. What arte thou then, that fearest a mortal man, the chylde of man, whiche goeth awaye as doeth the floure?

13 And forgettest the Lord that made the, that spred oute the heauens, & layde the foundacyon of the earthe. But thou arte euer afrayde for the syght of thyne oppressour whiche is ready to do harme: Where is the wrath of the oppressoure?

14 It commeth on fast it maketh haste to apeare: It shall not perysh, that it shulde not be able to destroye, neyther shall it fayle for faute of noryshyng.

15 I am the Lorde thy God, that make the sea to be styl, & to rage: whose name is the Lorde of Hostes.

16 I shall put my worde also in thy mouth, & defende the with the turninge of my hande: that thou mayest plante the heauens, and laye the foundacyns of the earth, and saye vnto Sion: thou arte my people.

17 Awake, awake, and stande vp, O Ierusalem, thou that from the hande of the Lorde, hast droncken oute the cuppe of hys wrath, thou that hast supped of, and sucked oute the slombrynge cuppe to the bottome.

18 For amonge all the sonnes whome thou haste begotten, there is not one that maye holde the vp: and not one to leade the by the hande, of al the sonnes that thou hast noryshed.

19 Both these thynges are happened vnto the, but who is sorye for it: Yea, destruccyon, wastynge, hunger, & swerde: but who hath conforted the?

20 Thy sonnes lye comfortles at the heade of euery strete lyke

a taken venyson, and are full of the terryble wrath of the Lorde, & punyshmente of thy God.

21 And therfore thou myserable & droncken (howbe it not with wyne) Heare this:

22 Thus sayth thy Lorde, thy Lorde & God, the defender of his people: Beholde, I wyll take the slombrynge cuppe oute of thy hande, euen þe cuppe with the dregges of my wrathe: that from hence forthe thou shalt neuer drincke it more,

23 & wyll put it in theyr hande that trouble the: whiche haue spoken to thy soule: stoupe doune, that we maye go ouer the: make thy body eauen with the grounde, and as the strete to go vpon.

## CHAPTER 52

Vp Syon vp, take thy strengthe vnto the: put on thyne honeste rayment O Ierusalem, thou citie of the holye one. For from thys tyme forthe, there shall no vncyrcumcysed nor vncleane person come in the.

2 Shake the from the dust, aryse and stand vp, O Ierusalem. Plucke oute thy necke from the bonde. O thou captyue doughter Syon.

3 For thus sayth the Lord: ye are solde for naughte, therfor shal ye be redemed also without anye moneye.

4 For thus hath the Lorde sayde: My people wente doune afore tyme into Egypte, there to be straungers. Afterwarde dyd the kynge of the Assyryans oppresse them, for naughte.

5 And nowe what profyt is it to me (sayeth the Lorde) that my people is frely caryed awaye, & brought into heuynes by theyr rulers, and my name euer styll blasphemed? saith the Lorde.

6 But that my people maye knowe my name, I my selfe will speache in that daye. Beholde, here am I.

7 O howe bewtyfull are the fete of the Embassytoure, that bryngeth the message from the mountaine, and proclameth peace, that bringeth the good tydynges, and preacheth health, and sayeth vnto Syon. Thy God is the kynge.

8 Thy watchemen shall lyft vp theyr voyce with loude voyce shall they preache of him: for they shall se him presente, when the Lorde shall come agayne to Syon.

9 Be glad, O thou desolate Ierusalem, and reioyce together, for the Lorde wyll comforte hys people, he wyll delyuer Ierusalem.

10 The Lorde wyl make bare hys holye arme, and shewe it forthe in the sight of al the Gentyls, & all the endes of the earthe shall se the sauing healthe of oure God.

11 Awaye, awaye, get you oute from thence, and touche no vnclean thing. Go oute from amonge suche. And be cleane, ye that beare the vessell of the Lorde.

12 But ye shall not go oute with sedicion, nor make hast as they that fle awaye: for the Lord shall go before you, and the God of Israel shal kepe the watche.

13 Beholde, my seruaunt shall deale wysely, therfore shall he be magnyfyed, exalted and greatly honoured.

14 Lyke as the multitude shal wondre vpon hym, because his face shalbe so deformed & not as a mans face, & hys bewtye lyke no man:

15 Euen so shall the multitude of þe Gentyles loke vnto hym, & the kinges shall shut theyr mouthes before hym. For they that haue not bene tolde of hym, shall se hym, and they that hearde nothynge of hym, shall beholde hym.

## CHAPTER 53

Bvt who geueth credence vnto oure preachynge? Or to whome is the arme of the Lorde knowne?

2 He shall growe before the Lorde lyke as a braunche, and as a rote in a drye grounde, he shall haue neither bewtye nor fauoure. When we loke vpon him there shalbe no fayrenesse: we shall haue no lust vnto him

3 He shalbe the most simple, and despysed of all, which yet hath good experience of sorowes & infyrmyties. We shall reken him so symple and so vyle, that we shall hyde our faces from hym.

4 Howbeit (of a trueth) he only taketh awaye oure infyrmyte, and beareth our payne: Yet we shal iudge him, as though he were plaged & caste doune of God:

5 where as he (notwithstanding) shal be wounded for oure offences, & smytten for oure wickednes. For the payne of oure punyshmente shalbe sayde vpon hym, and with hys strypes shall we be healed.

6 As for vs, we go all astraye (lyke shepe) euery one turneth hys owne waye. But thorow hym, the Lorde pardoneth all oure synnes.

7 He shall be payned & troubled, and shal not open his mouth. He shalbe led as a shepe to be slayne, yet shall he be as styll as a lambe before the shearer, and not open hys mouthe.

8 He shall be had awaye, hys cause not hearde, & wythout any iudgement: Whose generacion yet no man maye nombre, when he shalbe cut of from the grounde of the lyuyng: Which punishment shall go vpon him, for the transgression of my people.

9 His graue shalbe geuen hym with the condempned, & hys crucyfyenge with the theues. Where as he dyd neuer vyolente nor vurygght, neyther had there

bene any disceytfulnesse in hys month.

10 Yet hath it pleased the Lorde to smyte him with infirmite, that when he had made hys soule an offerynge for synne, he myght se longe lasting sede. And this deuyce of the Lord shall prospere in hys hande.

11 Wyth trauayle and laboure of hys soule, shall he obtayne great ryches. My ryghtuous seruaunte shall wyth hys wysdome iustifye & delyuer the multitude, for he shal beare away theyr synnes,

12 Therfore wyll I geue him the multytude for hys parte, and he shall deuyde the stronge spoyle because he shall geue ouer hys soule to death, & shalbe rekened amonge the transgressours, which neuertheles shall take away the sinnes of the multytude, and make intercessyon for the mysdoers.

## CHAPTER 54

THERFORE be glad nowe, thou baren that bearest not. Reioyce, singe, and be mery, thou that arte not with chyld. For the desolate hath mo children, then the maried wife sayeth the Lorde.

2 Make thy tente wyder, and sprede out the hanginges of thyne habytacion: spare not, laye forth thy coardes, and make faste thy stakes,

3 for thou shalt breake oute on the ryght syde and on the left, & thy sede shall haue the Gentyles in possessyon, & dwell in þe desolate cities.

4 Feare not, for thou shalte not be confounded: Be not ashamed, for thou shalt not come to confusyon. Yea thou shalt forget the shame of thy youth, and shalt not remember the dyshonoure of thy wedowheade.

5 For he that made the, shalbe thy Lorde & husband (whose name is the Lorde of hostes) & thyne auenger shalbe euen the holy one of Israel, þe Lorde of the whole worlde.

6 For the Lord shal call the, beynge as a desolate sorowful woman and as a younge wyfe that hath broken her wedlocke: sayeth thy God.

7 A lytle whyle haue I forsaken the, but with greate mercyfulnes shall I take the vp vnto me.

8 When I was angry, I hyde my face from the for a lytle season, but thorowe euerlasting goodnes shall I pardon the, sayeth the Lorde thyne auenger.

9 And this must be vnto me as the water of Noe: for as lyke I haue sworne that I wyll not brynge the water of Noe any more vpon the worlde: so haue I sworne that I wil neuer be angrye with the, nor reproue the:

10 The mountaynes shal remoue and the hylles shal fal doune: but my louing kindnesse shall not moue, & the bonde of my peace shal not fal doune from the, saith þe lord thy mercifull louer.

11 Beholde thou pore, vexed and despysed: I will make thy walles of precious stones, & thy foundacyon of Saphires,

12 thy wyndowes of Christal, thy gates of fyne cleare stone, and thy borders of pleasaunt stones.

13 Thy children shall all be taught of god & I wyll geue them plenteousnes of peace.

14 In rightuousnes shalt thou be grounded, and be farre from oppressyon: for the whiche thou nedeste not be afrayed, nether for hynderaunce for it shall not come nye the.

15 Beholde, the aleaunt that was farre from the, shal dwel with the: & he that was sometyme a straunger vnto the. shalbe ioyned with the:

16 Beholde, I make the smyth that bloweth the coales in the fyre, & he maketh a weapen after hys handy worck. I make also the waster to destroye:

17 but al the weapens that are made agaynste the, shal not prospere. And as for all tunges, that shall resiste the in iudgement, thou shalte ouercome them, and condempne them. This is the herytage of the Lordes seruauntes, and the ryghtuousnes that they shal haue of me, sayeth the Lorde.

## CHAPTER 55

COME to the waters all ye, þt be thurstye, & ye that haue no money. Come, bye, þt ye maye haue to eate. Come bye wine & mylcke, without any money or money worth.

2 Wherfore do ye laye oute youre moneye, for the thing that fedeth not, and spende youre laboure aboute the thynge that satisfyed you not. But herken rather vnto me, & ye shall eate of the beste, & youre soule shall haue her pleasure in plentuousnes.

3 Encline youre eares, & come vnto me, take hede, & your soule shall lyue. For I wyll make an euerlastynge couenaunt wyth you, euen the sure mercyes of Dauid.

4 Beholde, I shall geue him for a wytnesse amonge the folke, for a Prynce and Captaine vnto the people.

5 Lo, thou shalte call an vnknowne people: & a people that had no knowledge of the, shall runne vnto the: because of the Lorde thy God, the holye one of Israell, which glorifieth the.

6 Seke the Lorde, whyle he maye be founde, & call vpon hym whyle he is nye.

7 Let the vngodly man forsake his wayes & the vnrighteous his ymaginacions, & turne agayne vnto the Lorde: so shall he be mercyfull vnto

him: & to oure God, for he is redy to forgeue.

8 For thus saith the Lorde: my thoughtes are not youre thoughtes, & youre wayes are not my wayes,

9 but as farre as the heauens are hyer then the earth, so farre do my wayes exceade yours, and my thoughtes yours.

10 And lyke as the rayne & snowe commeth doune from heauen, & returneth not thyther agayne, but watereth the earthe, maketh it frutefull and grene, that it maye geue corne and breade vnto the sower:

11 So the worde also that commeth oute of my mouthe shall not turne agayne voyde vnto me, but shall accomplysh my wil & prospere in the thinge, whereto I sende it.

12 And so shall ye go forth with ioye, & be led with peace. The mountaynes & hilles shal sing with you for ioye, and all the trees of the feld shall clappe theyr handes.

13 For thornes, there shall growe. Fyrre trees, & the Myrre tre in the steade of breres. And thys shall be done to the prayse of the Lorde, and for an euerlasting token, that shall not be taken awaye.

## CHAPTER 56

THUS sayth the Lord Kepe equite, and do ryght, for my sauing health shal come shortly, & my righteousnes shalbe opened.

2 Blessed is the man that doth this & the mans chylde which kepeth the same. He that taketh hede, that he vnhalow not þe Sabboth (that is) he that kepeth him self that he do no euyll.

3 Then shall not the straunger, which cleaueth to the Lorde, saye: Alas the Lorde hath shut me cleane oute from his people. Nether shall the gelded man say: lo, I am a drye tre.

4 For thus sayth the Lorde, fyrste vnto the gelded that kepeth my Sabboth: Namelye: þt holdeth greately of the thynge that pleaseth me, and kepeth my couenaunte:

5 Vnto them wyll I geue in my housholde and within my walles, a better herytage and name then yf they had bene called sonnes and doughters I wyll geue them an euerlastynge name, that shall not peryshe.

6 Agayne, he sayeth vnto the straungers that are dysposed to stycke to the Lorde, to serue hym, and to loue hys name: That they shalbe no bonde men. And all they whiche kepe them selues, that they vnhalowe not the Sabboth, namely that they fulfil my couenaunt.

7 Then wyll I brynge to my holye mountayne, and make them ioyfull in my house of prayer. Their burnt offeringes & sacryfyces shalbe accepted vpon mine aulter, for my house shalbe an house of prayer for all people.

8 Thus sayeth the Lorde God whiche gathered together the scatred of Israel: I wil bring yet another congregacion to him.

9 Al the beastes of the felde, and al the beastes of þe wood shal come to deuoure hym.

10 For hys watch men are al blind, they haue altogether no vnderstandyng, they are al domme dogges, not beyng able to barcke, they are slepery: slogish are they, & lye snortynge:

11 they are shamelesse dogges, that be neuer satisfyed. The sheperdes also in lyke maner haue no vnderstanding but euery man turneth his owne way, euery one after his owne couetousnes with all hys power.

12 Come (saye they) I wil fetche wyne, so shall we fyll oure selues, that we maye be droncken. And to morowe, lyke as to daye, yea and much more.

## CHAPTER 57

BVT in the meane season the righteous perysheth, and no man regardeth it in his herte. Good godly people are taken awaye, and noman consydreth it. Namely: that the righteous is conuayed awaye thorowe the wicked,

2 that he him selfe myght be in reste, lye quietly vpon his bed, & lyue after his owne pleasure.

3 Come hyther therfore ye charmers children, ye sonnes of the aduoutrer & the whore:

4 Wherin take ye your pleasure? Vpon whom gape ye with your mouth and bleare out your tonge? Are ye not children of aduoutry, and a sede of dissimulacion?

5 Ye take youre pleasure vnder the okes, and vnder all grene trees, the childe beyng slayne in the valleys, and dennes of stone.

6 Thy part shalbe with the stony rockes by þe ryuer. Yea euen these shalbe thy part. For there thou hast poured meat and drinckeofferinges vnto them. Shoulde I ouerse that?

7 Thou hast made thy bed vpon hye mountaynes, thou wentest vp thither, and there hast thou slayne sacryfyces.

8 Behinde the dores and postes, hast thou set vp thy remembraunce. When thou haddest discouered thy selfe to another then me, when thou wentest doune & made thy bed wyder (that is) when thou diddest carue the certayne of yonder Idols, & louedest their couches, where thou sawest them.

9 Thou wentest streyght to kinges with oyle & diuerse oyntmentes (that is) thou hast sente thy messaungers farre of, and yet arte thou fallen into the pyt therby.

10 Thou hast had trouble for þe multitude of thine owne

waies, yet saydest thou neuer: I will leaue of. Thou thynkest to haue lyfe (or health) of thy selfe, & therfore thou beleuest not that thou art syck.

11 For when wilt thou be abashed or fear seinge: thou hast broken thy promise, and remembrest not me, neyther hast me in thyne herte? Thinkest thou, that I also will holde my peace (as a fore tyme) that thou fearest me not?

12 Yea verely I wil declare thy goodnes and thy workes, but they shal not profyt that

13 when thou criest, let thy chosen heape deliuer the. But þe winde shall take them al away, & cary them into the ayre. Neuertheles, they that put there trust in me, shal inheret the lande, and haue my holy hill in possession.

14 And therfore thus he sayeth: Make ready, make ready, & clense the strete, take vp what ye can oute of the waye that ledeth to my people.

15 For thus sayeth the hye and excellent, euen he that dwelleth in euerlastingnesse, whose name is the holy one. I dwell hye aboue & in the sanctuary, and with him also, that is of a contrite & humble spirite: that I maye heale a troubled mind, & a contrite hert.

16 For I chide not euer, & am not wroth without ende. But þe blastinge goeth from me, though I make the breath.

17 I am wroth with him for his couetousnes and lust, I smyte him, I hyd me, and am angry, when he turneth him selfe, & foloweth the by the waye of his owne herte.

18 But yf I may se his right way againe, I make hym whole, I lede him and restore him vnto them, whome he maketh ioyfull, and that were sorye for him.

19 I make the frutes of thankesgeuynge. I geue peace vnto them that are farre of, and to them that are nye. saye I the Lord, that make hym whole.

20 But the wycked are lyke the raryng sea, that can not reste, whose water fometh with the myre and grauel.

21 Euen so the wycked haue no peace, saieth my God.

# CHAPTER 58

AND therfore crye now, as loude as thou canst. Leaue not of, lyft vp thy voyce like a trompet, and shewe my people their offences, and the house of Iacob their synnes.

2 For they seke me daylye and wyll knowe my waies, euen as it were a people that did right & had not forsaken the statutes of their God. They argue with me concerninge right iudgement, and wil pleate at the lawe with their God.

3 Wherfore fast we (saye they) and thou seist it not? we put oure lyues to straytnesse, & thou regardest it not?

4 Beholde, when ye fast, your lust remayneth still: for ye do no lesse vyolence to youre detters: lo, ye falle to stryfe and debate, and to smite hym wyth youre fyst that speaketh vnto you. Ye fast not (as som tyme) that your voyce might be hearde aboue.

5 Thyncke ye this fast pleaseth me, that a man shoulde chasten him self for a daye, and to writhe his head aboute lyke an hoke in an hearry cloth, and to lye vpon the earth? Shoulde that be called fasting, or a daye that pleaseth the Lord.

6 But this fastyng pleaseth not me, til the tyme be thou louse him out of bondage, that is in thy daunger: that thou breake the ooth of wicked barginnes, that thou let the oppressed go fre and take from them all maner of burthens.

7 It pleaseth not me, tyll thou deale thy breade to the hungry, and brynge the poore fatherlesse home into thy house, when thou seyste the naked that thou couer him, and hyde not thy face from thyne owne fleshe.

8 Then shall thy lighte breake forthe as the morninge, and thy healthe florysshe ryghte shortlie: thy righteousnesse shall go before the, and the glorye of the Lorde shall embrace the.

9 Then yf thou callest, the Lorde shall answere the: yf thou cryest, he shall saye: here I am. Yea, yf thou layest awaie thy burthens, and holdest thy fingers, and ceasest from blasphemous talkinge,

10 yf thou hast compassyon vpon the hongrye, and refresshest the troubled soule: Then shall thy light sprynge oute in the darcknesse, and thy darckenesse shalbe as the noone day.

11 The Lord shal euer be thy gyde, and satisfye the desire of thyne herte, and fyl thy bones with marye. Thou shalt be like a freshwatred garden, and lyke the founteyne of water, that neuer leaueth running.

12 Then the places that haue euer bene waste, shalbe buylded of the: there shalt thou lay a foundacion for many kinredes: thou shalt be called the maker vp of hedges, and the buylder againe of the waye of the Sabboth.

13 Yea yf thou turne thy fete from the Sabboth, so that thou do not the thynge whyche pleaseth thy selfe in my holy daye: then shalte thou be called vnto the pleasaunt, holy, & gloryous Sabboth of the Lorde, where thou shalt be in honoure: so that thou do not after thyne owne ymaginacion, neyther seke thine owne wyll, nor speake thyne owne wordes.

14 Then shalt thou haue thy pleasure in the lord whyche shal carye the hye aboue the earthe, & fede the wt the heretage of

Iacob thy father for the lordes owne mouthe hath so promised.

# CHAPTER 59

Beholde, the Lordes hand is not so shortened, that it can not helpe, neyther is his care so stopped, that it maye not heare.

2 But youre misdedes haue separated you from youre God, and youre synnes hyde his face from you, that he heareth you not.

3 For your handes are defiled with bloud and youre fyngers with vnryghteousnesse. Youre lippes speake lesinges, and your tong setteth oute wickednes.

4 Noman regardeth righteousnes, and noman iudged truely. Euery man hopeth in vayne thinges, and ymagyneth disceyte, conceyueth werynesse, and bringeth forth euyl.

5 They brede cockatrice egges, and weue the spyders webbe Who so eateth of their egges, dyeth. But yf one treade vpon them, there commeth vp a serpent.

6 Their webbe maketh no clothe and they maye not couer them with their laboures. Their dedes are the dedes of wickednes, and the worck of robbery is in their handes:

7 Their fete runne to euyll, & they make haste to shed innocent bloude. Their councels are wycked councel, harme and destruccion are in their wayes.

8 But the way of peace they know not. In their goinge is no equite, their wayes are so crocked, that whosoeuer goeth therin, knoweth nothinge of peace.

9 And this is the cause that equyte is so far from vs, and that ryghteousnes commeth not nye vs. We loke for light, lo, it is darcknesse: for the morninge shine, se we walke in the darcke.

10 We grope like the blinde vpon the wal, we grope euen as one þt hath none eyes. We stomble at the none daye, as thoughe it were toward night, in the fallynge places, lyke men that are halfe deade.

11 We roare all lyke Beeres, and mourne still like doues. We loke for equyte, but there is none: for health, but it is farre from vs.

12 For oure offences are many before the, and oure sinnes testifie against vs. Yea we must confesse þt we offende, and knowledge that we do amysse:

13 Namely transgresse and dissemble agaynst the Lorde, and fall awaye from oure God: vsinge presumptuous and trayterous ymaginacions, and castynge false matters in oure hertes.

14 And therfore is equyte gone a syde, & ryghteousnes standeth farre of: truthe is fallen doune in the strete, and the thinge that is playne and open, maye not be shewed.

15 Yea, the truth is layde in preson, and he that refraineth him selfe from euyl, must be spoyled. When the Lorde sawe this, it dyspleased him sore, that there was no where any equite.

16 He sawe also, that there was noman, whiche had pitie thereof, or was greued at it. And he helde him by hys owne power, and cleued to his owne ryghteousnes.

17 He put ryghteousnes vpon him for a brest plate, and set the helmet of health vpon his heade. He put on wrath steade of clothinge, and toke gelousye aboute hym for a cloke

18 (lyke as when a man goeth forth wrothfully to recompence his enemies, and to be auenged of his aduersaryes.) Namely that he might recompence and rewarde the Ilandes,

19 where thorowe the name of the Lorde might be feared, from the rysynge of the Sunne: and his magesty, vnto the goinge doune of the same. For he shall come as a vyolente waterstreame, whyche the winde of the Lorde hath moued.

20 But vnto Sion there shall come a redemer, and vnto them is Iacob that turne from wyckednesse, sayeth the Lorde.

21 I wyll make this couenaunt with them (sayeth the Lorde): My spirite that is come vpon the, and the wordes whyche I haue put in thy mouthe, shall neuer go out of thy mouthe, nor oute of the mouth of thy childers chyldren, from this tyme forth for euermore.

# CHAPTER 60

And therfore get the vp by tymes, for thy lyght cometh, and the glory of the Lorde shall ryse vp vpon the.

2 For lo, whyle the darcknesse and cloude couered the earth and the people, the Lorde shal shew the lyght, and hys glorye shalbe sene in the.

3 The Gentyles shal come to thy light, & kynges to the brightnes that springeth forth vpon the.

4 Lyft vp thyne eyes, & loke round aboute the: All these gather them selues, and come to the. Sonnes shal come vnto the from farre, and doughters shal gather them selues to the on euery syde.

5 When thou seyst this, thou shalt maruel exceadingly, and thine hert shal be opened: when the power of the sea shalbe conuerted vnto the (that is) when the strength of the Gentiles shall come vnto the.

6 The multitude of Camels shall couer the, the dromedaries of Madian and Epha. Al they of Saba shal come, bringinge golde and incense, and shewinge the prayse of the Lorde.

7 All the catel of Cedar shalbe gathered vnto the, the

rammes of Nabaioth shall serue the, to be offred vpon myne aulter, whiche I haue chosen, and in the house of my glory, whiche I haue garnyshed.

8 But what are these that fle here like the cloudes, and as the doues flyenge to their wyndowes?

9 The Iles also shall gather them vnto me, and specially the shippes of the sea: that they maye bringe the sonnes from farre, and their syluer and their goulde with them, vnto the name of the Lorde thy God, vnto the holye one of Israel, that hath glorifyed the.

10 Straungers shall buylde vp thy walles, and their kinges shall do thy seruice. For when I am angrie, I smyte the: & when it pleaseth me, I pardon the.

11 The gates shall stande open still both daye and night, and neuer be shut: that the hoste of the Gentiles may come, and that their kinges may be brought vnto the.

12 For euery poeple & kingedom that serueth not the, shal perysh, and be destroyed with the swerd.

13 The glorye of Libanus shall come vnto the. The Fyrre trees, Boxes and Cedres together, to garnish the place of my Sanctuarye, for I will glorifie the place of my fete.

14 Moreouer those shall come knelinge vnto the, that haue vexed the: and al they that despised the, shal fall doune at thy fote. Thou shalt be called the citie of the Lorde, the holye Sion of Israel.

15 Because thou hast bene forsaken and hated, so that noman went thorowe the: I wyl make the glorious for euer and euer, and ioyfull thorowe oute all posterities.

16 Thou shalt sucke the mylcke of the Gentiles, and kinges brestes shal fede the. And thou shalt knowe that I the Lorde am thy Sauyoure and defender, the mightie one of Iacob.

17 For brasse, will I geue the golde, and for yron siluer: for wood brasse, & for stones yron. I will make peace thy ruler, and ryghteousnes thyne officer.

18 Violence and robbery shall neuer be heard of in thy land, neither harme and destruccyon within thy borders. The walles shalbe calleth healthe, and thy gate the prayse of God.

19 The Sunne shall neuer be thy day lyght, and the light of the Mone shal neuer shyne vnto the, but the Lorde hym selfe shalbe thyne euerlasting lyght, and thy God shalbe thy glory.

20 Thy Sunne shall neuer go doune, & thy Mone shal not be taken awaye, for the Lorde him selfe shalbe thy euerlastynge light, & thy sorowfull dayes shalbe rewarded the.

21 Thy people shalbe all godly, and possesse the land for euer: the floure of my plantinge, þe worcke of my handes, whereof I wyll reioyce.

22 The youngest and leest shall growe into a thousande, and the symplest into a strong people. I the Lorde shall shortly bringe this thinge to passe in hys tyme.

## CHAPTER 61

THE spirite of the Lorde God is with me, for the Lorde hath annointed me, & sent me, to preache good tydinges vnto the poore, that I myght binde vp the wounded hertes, that I myght preach delyueraunce to the captyue, and open the preson to them that are bounde:

2 that I myght declare the acceptable yeare of the Lorde, and the daye of the vengeaunce of oure God: that I myghte comforte al them that are in heauynesse,

3 that I might geue vnto them that mourne in Sion bewtye in the steade of ashes, ioyful oyntment for syghing, pleasaunt rayment for an heauy mynde: That they might be called excellente in ryghteousnesse, a plantinge of the Lord for hym to reioyce in.

4 They shal builde the longe roughe wyldernes, and set vp the olde deserte, They shal repayre the waste places, & such as haue bene voyde thorow out many generacions.

5 Straungers shall stande and fede your catel, and the Aleauntes shalbe your ploumen and repers.

6 But ye shalbe named the priestes of the lord, & men shall call you the seruauntes of oure God. Ye shall enioye the goodes of the Gentiles and triumphe in their substaunce.

7 For your greate reprofe & shame, shall they haue ioy þt ye may haue parte with them. For they shall haue double possession in their lande, & euerlastinge ioy shalbe with them.

8 For I the Lorde, whiche loue right and hate robberye (though it were offred me) shal make their worckes of faithfulnes, and make an euerlastinge couenaunt with them.

9 Their sede also and their generacion shalbe knowne amonge the Gentiles, and amonge the people. All they that se them, shal knowe that they are the hye blessed sede of the Lord.

10 And therfore I am ioyful in the Lorde, and my soule reioyseth in my God. For he shall put vpon me the garment of health, & couer me with the mantle of righteousnes. He shal decke me lyke a brydegrom, and as a bryde þt hath her apparell vpon her.

11 For lyke as the ground bringeth forth frute, & as the garden shuteth forth sede. So

shall the Lorde God cause ryghteousnesses, and the feare of God to floryshe forthe before all the Heathen.

## CHAPTER 62

For Syons sake therfore wyll I not holde my tonge, and for Ierusalems sake I wil not ceasses vntil their righteousnesses breake forth as the shininge lyghte, & their health as a burninge lampe.

2 Then shal the Gentiles se thy ryghteousnesses and all kinges thy glorye. Thou shalt be named wyth a newe name, whyche the mouthe of the Lorde shal shewe.

3 Thou shalt be a croune in the hande of the Lorde, and a glorious garlande in the hande of thy God.

4 From this tyme forthe thou shalt neuer be called þe forsaken, & thy land shal no more be called the wildernesse. But thou shalt be called Hephribah, & thy lande Beula: for the Lorde loueth the, and thy land shalbe inhabyted.

5 And lyke as a younge man taketh a doughter to mariage, so shall God mary him selfe vnto thy sonnes. And as a brydegrome is glad of his bride, so shall God reioyse ouer the.

6 I wyll set watchmen vpon thy walles (O Ierusalem) whiche shall neyther ceasse daye nor night to preache the Lorde. And ye also shal not kepe him close,

7 nor leaue to speake of him, vntill Ierusalem be set vp, & made the prayse of the worlde.

8 The Lorde hath sworne by his right hande, and by his strong arme, þt from thence forthe he will not geue thy corne to be meate for thine enemies, nor thy wyne (wherin thou hast laboured) to be dryncke for þe straungers.

9 But they þt haue gathered in þe corne shall eate it, and geue thanckes to the Lorde: and they that haue borne in the wyne, shal drincke it in in the court of my sanctuary.

10 Stande backe, and depart a sunder, ye that stand vnder the gate: make roume ye people, repayre the strete, and take awaye the stones, & set out a token for the people.

11 Beholde, the Lorde proclameth in the endes of the worlde: tell the doughter Syon: se, thy saluacyon commeth, beholde he bryngeth his treasure wyth hym, and hys worckes go before hym.

12 For they whome the Lorde delyuereth, shalbe called the holy people: and as for the, thou shalt be named the greatly occupied, and not the forsaken.

## CHAPTER 63

What is he thys, that cometh from Edom, with stayned read clothes of Bolra: (whyche is so costly cloth) and cometh in so nimbly wyth all his strength: I am he that teachech ryghteousnes, and am of power to helpe.

2 Wherfore then is thy clothinge reade, and thy rayment lyke his that treadeth in the wyne presse?

3 I haue troden the presse my self alone, and of al people, there was not one with me. Thus haue I troden doune myne enemyes in my wrath, and set my fete vpon them in my indignacyon. And their bloude sprange vpon my clothes, and so haue I stayned al my raiment.

4 For the day of vengeaunce that I haue taken in hande, and the yeare of my delyueraunce is come.

5 I loked aboute me, and there was noman to shewe me any helpe, I fell doune, & no man helde me vp. Then I held me by myne owne arme, and my feruentnesse susteyned me:

6 and thus haue I troden doune the people in my wrath, and bathed them in my displeasure: In so muche that I haue shed their bloude vpon the earth.

7 I wyl declare the goodnesse of the Lorde, yea and the prayse of the Lorde for all that he hath geuen vs, for the great good that he hath done for Israel: whyche he hath geuen them of hys owne fauoure, and accordynge to the multytude of hys louynge kyndnesses.

8 For he sayde: These no doute wylbe my people and no shrynkynge chyldren, and so he was their sauyoure.

9 In their troubles he forsoke them not, but the aungel that went forthe from his presence delyuered them. Of very loue & kindnesse that he had vnto them, redemed he them. He hath borne them, and caryed them vp euer, sence the worlde beganne.

10 But after they prouoked hym to wrath, and vexed hys holy mynd, he was their enemye, and fought against them him selfe.

11 Yet remembred he þe olde tyme of Moses and hys people: How he brought them from the water of the sea, as a sheperde doth wyth his shepe: how he had geuen his holy spyryte amonge them:

12 howe he had led Moses by the ryght hande with hys glorious arme: how he had deuided the water before them (wherby he gat him selfe an euerlasting name)

13 how he led them in þe depe as an horse is led in the playne, that they shoulde not stomble.

14 The spirite of the Lorde led them, as a tame beast goeth in the felde. Thus (O God) hast thou led thy people, to make thy selfe a glorious name wyth all.

15 Loke doune then from heauen, and beholde the

dwellinge place of thy sanctuary and thy glory: how is it, that they gelousy, thy strength the multitude of thy mercyes, & thy louynge kindnesse, will not be entreated of vs.

16 Yet art thou oure father: For Abraham knoweth vs not, neither is Israel acquainted with vs. But thou Lorde art oure father and redemer and thy name is euerlastinge.

17 O Lord wherfore hast thou led vs out of thy waye? wherfore hast thou hardened our hertes, that we feare the not? Be at one with vs agayne, for thy seruauntes sake that are of the generacion of thine heretage.

18 Thy people hath had but litle of thy Sanctuarye in possession, for oure enemies haue taken it in.

19 And we are become euen as we were from the beginninge: but thou art not their Lorde, for they haue not called vpon thy name.

## CHAPTER 64

O that thou wouldest cleaue the heauen in sonder, & come doune that þe mountaynes might melt awaye at thy presence,

2 lyke as at an hote fyre: and that the malicious might boyle, as the water doth vpon þe fyre: Wherby thy name might be knowne amonge thyne enemies, and that the Gentiles might tremble before the.

3 That þu mightest come doune, with thy wonderous straung workes, then shoulde the hilles melt at thy presence.

4 For sence the beginninge of the worlde there was none (except thou O God) that hearde or perceyueth, neyther had anye eye sene, what thou dost for them, that put their trust in the.

5 Thou helpest him that doeth ryght with cherefulnesse, and them that thyncke vpon thy wayes. But lo, thou art angry, for we offend and haue euer be in sinne, there is not one whole.

6 We are al as vncleane thinge, and all oure ryghteousnesses are as the clothes defyled with the floures of a woman: we fall euerychone as the leafe, for oure synnes carye vs awaie like the winde.

7 There is no man þt calleth vpon thy name, þt standeth vp to take hold by the. Therfore hydest thou thy face from vs, and consumest vs, because of oure synnes.

8 But now O Lorde, thou father of oures: we are al the claye, and thou art our potter & we are al the worke of thy handes.

9 Be not to sore displeased (O Lorde) and kepe not our offences to longe in thy remembraunce, but considre that we are all thy people.

10 The cytyes of thy Sanctuary lye waste, Sion is a wildernesse, and Ierusalem a deserte.

11 Oure holy house whiche is oure bewty, where oure fathers praysed the, is brent vp: yea all oure commodities & pleasures are wasted awaye.

12 Wylt thou not be intreated (Lorde) for all this? Wylt thou holde thy peace, and scourge vs so sore?

## CHAPTER 65

THEY shal seke my, that hytherto haue not asked for me: they shall fynde me, that hitherto haue not sought me. Then shal I say immediatly to the people that neuer called vpon my name: I am here, I am here.

2 For thus longe haue I euer holden out my handes to an vnfaithfull people, that go not the ryght waye, but after their owne ymaginacyons:

3 To a people that is euer defyinge me to my face. They make their oblacyons in gardens, and their smoke vpon aulters of brycke,

4 they lurcke amonge the graues, and lye in the dennes all nyght. They eat swyne fleshe, and vncleane broth is in their vessels.

5 Yf thou comest nye them, they saye, touch me not, for I am holyer then thou. All these men when I am angry, shalbe turned to smoke and fyre, that shall burne for euer.

6 Beholde it is written before my face and shal not be forgotten, but recompenced. I shall rewarde it them in their bosome.

7 I meane youre misdedes, and the misdedes of youre fathers together (sayeth the Lorde) whyche haue made their smokes vpon the mountaynes, and blasphemed me vpon the hylles: therefore wyll I measure their olde dedes into their bosome agayne.

8 Moreouer thus sayeth the Lord: lyke as when one would gather holy grapes, men say vnto him: breake it not of for it is holy: euen so wyll I do also for my seruauntes sake, that I wyll not destroye them all.

9 But I wyl take a sede oute of Iacob, and out of Iuda one, to take possession of my hyl. My chosen shal possesse these thinges, and my seruauntes shal dwell there.

10 Saron shalbe a shepefolde, and the valleye of Achor shall geue the stallinge for the catel of my people, that feare me.

11 But as for you, ye are they, that haue forsaken the Lorde, and forgotten my holy hil. Ye haue set vs an aulter vnto fortune, and geuen ryche drincke offerynges vnto treasure.

12 Therfore will I nombre you with the swerde, that ye shalbe destroyed altogether. For when I called, noman gaue me answere: when I spake, ye

herkened not vnto me, but dyd wyckednes before myne eyes, & chose the thing that pleased me not.

13 Therfore thus saieth the Lorde God: Beholde, my seruauntes shall eate, but ye shall haue honger. Beholde, my seruauntes shall dryncke, but ye shall suffre thurste. Beholde my seruauntes shalbe mery, but ye shalbe confounded.

14 Beholde, my seruauntes shall reioyce for very quyetnesse of herte: But ye shal crye for sorowe of herte, and complayne for vexacyon of mynde.

15 Youre name shal not be sworne by amonge my chosen, for God the Lorde shall slay you, and cal his seruauntes by another name.

16 Who so reioyseth vpon earthe shall reioyse in the true God. And who so sweareth vpon earth, shal sweare in the true God. For the olde emnyte shalbe forgotten and taken awaye out of my syght.

17 For lo, I shall make a newe heauen, and a newe earthe. And as for the olde, they shall neuer be thought vpon, nor kept in minde:

18 but men shalbe glad and euermore reioise, for the thinges, that I shall do. For why: Behold, I shal make a ioyfull Ierusalem,

19 yea and my selfe wyl reioyse with Ierusalem, and be glad with my people: And the voyce of wepynge and waylinge shall not be heard in her from thenceforth.

20 There shal neuer be chylde, nor olde man, that haue not their full dayes. But when the childe cometh to an hundreth yeare olde it shall dye. And yf he that is an hundreth yeare of age do wronge, he shalbe cursed.

21 They shalt buylde houses, and dwell in them: they shall plante vyneyardes, and eate the frute of them.

22 They shall not buylde, and another possesse: they shall not plante, and another eate. But the lyfe of my people shalbe lyke a tree, and so shall the worcke of their handes.

23 My chosen shall lyue longe, they shal not laboure in vayne, nor beget with trouble, for they that are the hye blessed sede of the Lord, and their frutes with them.

24 And it shalbe, that or euer they call, I shall answere them. While they are yet but thinckinge howe to speake. I shal heare them.

25 The wolfe and the lambe shall fede together, and the lyon shall eate haye like the bullocke. But earthe shalbe the serpentes meate. There shal noman hurte nor slaye another, in al my holy hyll, sayeth the Lorde.

# CHAPTER 66

THUS sayeth the Lorde: Heauen is my seat, and the earth is my fote stole Where shal nowe the house stande, that ye wyll buylde vnto me. And where shalbe the place, that I dwell in?

2 As for these thynges, my hande had made them all, and they are all created, sayeth the Lorde. Whyche of them shall I then regarde? Euen hym, that is of a lowly troubled spyryte, and standeth in awe of my wordes.

3 For who so slaieth an oxe for me, doth me so great dishonour as he that killeth a man. He that kylleth a shepe for me, choketh a dogge. He that bryngeth me meateofferinges, offereth swynes bloude. Who so maketh me a memory all of incense, prayseth the thinge that is vnryght. Yet take they suche wayes in hand, and their soule delyteth in these abhomynacyons.

4 Therfore wyll I also haue pleasure in laughing him to scorne, & the thing þt they feare wyll I brynge vpon them. For when I called, no man gaue answere: when I spake, they woulde not heare. But dyd wickednesse before myne eyes, and chose the thynges that displease me.

5 Heare the worde of God all ye, that feare the thynge whyche he speaketh. Your brethren that hate you, and cast you out for my names sake, saye: Let the Lorde magnyfye him selfe, that we may see youre gladnesse: and yet they shalbe confounded.

6 For as thouchinge the cytie and the temple, I heare the voyce of the Lorde, that wyll rewarde, and recompence his enemies,

7 lyke as when a wyfe bryngeth forth a man chylde, or euer she suffre the payne of the byrth, and anguysh of the trauayle.

8 Who euer hearde or sawe suche thinges? doth the grounde beare in one daye? or are the people borne all at ones, as Sion beareth her sonnes?

9 For thus sayeth the Lorde: Am I he that maketh other to beare, and beare not my selfe? Am not I he that beareth, and maketh baren? sayeth thy God

10 Reioyse with Ierusalem, and be glad with her, all ye that loue her. Be ioyful with her, all ye that mourneth for her.

11 For ye shall sucke comforte oute of her brestes, and be satysfyed. Ye shall taste, and haue delite in the plenteousnesse of her power.

12 For thus sayeth the Lorde: Beholde, I wyll let peace into her, lyke a water floude, and the myght of the Heathen lyke a flowinge streame. Then shall ye sucke, ye shalbe borne vpon her sides and be ioyfull vpon her knees.

13 For lyke as a chylde is comforteth of hys mother, so shall I comforte you, and ye shalbe comforted in Ierusalem.

14 And when ye se thys, youre herte shall reioyse, and

youre bones shall floryshe lyke an herbe. Thus shall the hande of the Lorde be knowne amonge his seruauntes, and his indignacyon amonge his enemyes.

15 For behold the Lorde shall come with fyre, and hys charet shalbe lyke a whirle winde, that he maye recompence his vengeaunce in his wrath and hys indignacyon wt the flamme of fyre.

16 For the Lorde shall iudge all fleshe with the fyre, and with his swearde, & there shalbe a greate nombre slayne of the Lorde.

17 Suche as haue made them selues holy and cleane in the gardens, and those that haue eaten swyne fleshe, myce, and other abhomynacyons, shalbe taken awaye together, sayeth the Lorde.

18 For I wyl come to gather all people and tonges wt their workes and ymaginacyons: these shall come, and se my glory.

19 Vnto them shall I geue a token, and geue a certayne of them (that be delyuered) amonge the Gentyles: into Celycia, Africa and Lidia (where men can handle bowes) into Italye also and Greke lande. The Iles farre of, that haue not hearde speake of me, and haue not sene my glorye, shall preache my prayse amonge the Gentyles,

20 and shall bringe all oure brethren for an offerynge vnto the Lorde, oute of all people vpon horses, charettes and horse litters, vpon Males and cartes to Ierusalem my holy hill (sayeth the Lorde) like as the children of Israel brynge the offerynge in cleane vessels, to the house of the Lorde.

21 And I shall take oute certayne of them for to be Pryestes and Leuytes, sayeth the Lorde.

22 For lyke as the newe heauen and the newe earthe whyche I will make, shalbe fast stablyshed by me, (sayeth the Lorde.) So shall youre seade and youre name contynue

23 and there shalbe a newe Mone for the other, and a newe Sabboth for the other, and all fleshe shall come to worshyppe, before me (sayeth the Lord.)

24 And they shall go forth and loke vpon the carions of them, that haue transgressed against me. For their wormes shall not dye, neyther shall their fyre be quenched, and al fleshe shall abhorre them.

# Jeremiah

## CHAPTER 1

THESE are the Sermons of Ieremy the sonne of Helkiah the prieste, one of them that dwelt at Anathoth in the land of Beniamin:

2 when the Lorde had fyrste spoken wyth him in the tyme of Iosiah the sonne of Amon kinge of Iuda, in the .xiij. yeare of his kingdome,

3 and so during vnto the tyme of Iehoakim the sonne of Iosiah kynge of Iuda, and vntill .xi. yeares of Zedekiah the sonne of Iosiah kinge of Iuda were ended: when Ierusalem was taken, euen in the fyfth Moneth.

4 The worde of the Lord spake thus vnto me:

5 Before I fashyoned the in thy mothers wombe, I did know the. And or euer thou wast borne, I sanctifyed the, and ordeyned the, to be a Prophete vnto the people.

6 Then sayde I: Oh Lorde God, I am vnmete, for I am yet but younge.

7 And the Lorde answered me thus: Saye not so, I am to younge. For thou shalt go to al that I shall sende the vnto, and whatsoeuer I commaund the, that shalt thou speake.

8 Be not afrayed of their faces, for I wilbe with the, to delyuer the, sayeth the Lorde.

9 And with that, the Lorde stretched oute his hande, and touched my mouthe, and sayde moreouer vnto me. Beholde I put my wordes in thy mouth,

10 & this daye do I set þe ouer the people & kingedomes, that thou mayest rote oute, breake of, destroye, & make waste: and that thou mayest buylde vp and plante.

11 After thys, the Lorde spake vnto me sayinge: Ieremy, what seyst thou? And I sayde: I se a wakinge roade.

12 Then sayde the Lord: thou hast sene ryght, for I will watch diligentlye vpon my worde, to perfourme it.

13 It happened afterwarde, that the Lorde spake to me againe, and sayde: What seyst thou? And I sayd: I do se a seethinge pot, lokinge from oute of the North hytherward.

14 Then saide the Lorde vnto me: Oute of the Northe shall come a plage vpon all the dwellers of the lande.

15 For lo, I wil cal all the officers of the kingdomes of the north (saieth the Lorde.) And they shall come, and euery one shall set the seate in the gates of Ierusalem, and in al their walles round aboute and thorowe al the cytyes of Iuda.

16 And thorowe them shall I declare my iudgement, vpon all the wyckednesse of those men that haue forsaken me: that haue offered vnto straunge Goddes, and worshipped the workes of their owne handes.

17 And therfore gyrde vp thy loines, arise, and tell them al, that I geue the in commaundement. Feare them not, I will not haue the to be afrayed of them.

18 For beholde, this daye do I make the a strong fensed towne, an yron pyler, and a wall of stele agaynst the whole lande, against the kinges and myghtye men of Iuda, agaynste the priestes and people of the lande.

19 They shall fyght against the, but they shall not be able to ouercome the: for I am with the, to delyuer the, sayeth the Lord.

## CHAPTER 2

MOREOUER, the worde of the Lord commaunded me thus:

2 Go thy waye, crye in the eares of Ierusalem, and saye: Thus sayeth the Lorde: I remembre r þe kindnesse of thy youth, and because of thy stedfast loue: in that thou folowdest me thorowe the wildernesse, in an vntilled lande.

3 Thou Israel wast halowed vnto the Lorde, and so was his fyrst frutes. Al they that

deuoured Israel, offended: mysfortune fell vpon them, sayeth the Lorde.

4 Heare therfore the worde of the Lorde, O thou house of Iacob, and al the generacion of the house of Israell.

5 Thus sayeth the Lorde vnto you. What vnfaythfulnesse founde youre fathers in me, that they wente so farre awaye from me, fallinge to lightnesse, and beynge so vaine?

6 They thought not in their hertes: Where haue we left the Lorde, that broughte vs oute of the lande of Egipte, that led vs thorowe the wildernesse, thorow a desert and roughe lande, thorow a drye and deadly land yea a lande that no man had gone thorowe, and wherin noman had dwelt.

7 And when I had brought you into a plasaunt welbuilded lande, that ye might enioye the frutes and all the commodities of the same: ye went forth, and defyled my lande, and brought myne heretage to abhomynacion.

8 The pryestes them selues sayde not once: where is the Lorde? They that haue the lawe in their handes, knowe me not. The sheperdes offende against me. The Prophetes do seruice vnto Baal, and folowe suche thinges as shall brynge them no profyt.

9 Wherfore I am constrayned (sayeth the Lorde) to make my complaynte vpon you, and vpon youre chyldren.

10 Go into the Iles of Cethim, and loke well: sende vnto Cedar, take diligent hede, and se, whether suche thinges be done there,

11 whether the Gentiles them selues deale so fastly and vntruly with their goddes (whiche yet are no Goddes in dede.) But my people hath geuen ouer their hye honoure, for a thinge that maye not helpe them.

12 Be astonished (O ye heauens) be afrayde and abashed at such thinge, sayeth the Lorde.

13 For my people hath done two euyls. They haue forsaken me the well of the water of life and dygged them pyttes, yea vyle & broken pittes, that holde no water.

14 Is Israell a bond seruaunt, or one of the housholde? Why is he then so spoiled?

15 Why do they roare, and crye then vpon him, as a lyon? They haue made his lande waste, his cities are so brent vp, that there is noman dwellynge in them.

16 Yea the chyldren of Noph and Taphnes haue defyled thy neck.

17 Commeth not this vnto the, because thou hast forsaken the Lorde thy God, euer sence he led the by the waye.

18 And what hast thou nowe to do in the strete of Egipte? to drincke foule water? Ether, what makest thou in the way to Assiria? To drincke water of þe floud?

19 Thyne owne wickednesse shall reproue the, and thy turnynge awaye shal condemne the: that thou maiest know and vnderstand, how euyl and hurtful a thinge it is, that thou hast forsaken thy Lorde thy God, and not feared him, sayeth the Lorde God of Hostes.

20 I haue euer broken thy yocke of olde, and burste thy bondes: yet sayest thou: I wil nomore serue, but (lyke an harlot) thou runnest aboute vpon all hye hilles, and amonge all grene trees,

21 where as I planted the out of noble grapes & good rotes. How art thou turned then into a bitter, vnfrutefull, and straunge grape?

22 Yea, & that so sore: that thoughe thou wasshe the with Nitrus, and make thy self to fauoure with that swete smelling herbe of Borith: yet in my sight thou art stayned with thy wyckednesse, sayeth the Lorde thy God.

23 Saye not now: I am not vncleane, and I haue not folowed the Goddes. Loke vpon thyne owne wayes in the woddes, valleyes and dennes, so shalt thou knowe, what thou hast done. Thou art lyke a swyft Dromedary, that goeth easely in his waye:

24 and thy wantonnes is like a wilde Asse, that vseth the wildernesse, and that snoffeth and bloweth at his wyll. Who can tame the? All they that seke the, shal not fayle, but finde the in thine owne vnclennes.

25 Thou kepest thy fote from nakednes, and thy throte from thyrste, and thynkest thus in thy selfe: tushe, I will take no sorow, I will loue the straunge Goddes, and hang vpon them.

26 Lyke as a thefe that is taken with the dede commeth to shame, euen so is the house of Israell come to confusyon, the comen people their kynges and rulers, their priestes & prophetes.

27 For they saye to a stocke: thou art my father, and to a stone: thou hast be gotten me, yea they haue turned their backe vpon me, & not their face. But in the tyme of their trouble, when they saye: stande vp, and helpe vs,

28 I shal answere them: Where are now thy Goddes, that thou hast made the? byd them stande vp, & helpe the in the time of nede? For loke how many cityes thou hast (O Iuda) so many Goddes hast thou also.

29 Wherfore then will ye go to lawe wyth me, seynge ye are all synners agaynste me, sayeth the Lorde?

30 It is but lost laboure, that I smyte youre children, for they receyue not my correccyon. Youre owne swearde destroyeth

youre Prophetes, lyke a deuourynge lyon.

31 Yf ye be the people of the Lorde, then herken vnto this worde: Am I then become a wyldernesse vnto the people of Israel? or a lande that hath no light? Wherfore sayeth my people then: we are fallen of, and we wyl come no more vnto the?

32 Doth a mayden forget her rayment, or a bryde her stomacher? And doth my people forget me so long?

33 Why boastest thou thy wayes so hylye (to obtayne fauoure there thorowe) when thou hast yet stayned them with blasphemyes?

34 Vpon thy wynges is founde the bloude of poore and innocent people, and that not in corners and holes onlye, but openly in all these places.

35 Yet darrest thou saye: I am giltlesse: Tush, his wrath can not come vpon me. Beholde, I will reason with the because thou darrest say: I haue not offended.

36 O how euill wil it before the, to abyde it, when it shalbe knowne, how oft thou hast gone bacwarde? For thou shalt be confounded, as well of Egipte, as of the Assirians:

37 yea thou shalt go thy waye from them, and smyte thine handes together vpon thy heade. Because the Lorde shall brynge that confydence and hope of thyne to naught, and thou shalt not prospere with all.

# CHAPTER 3

COMENLY, when a man putteth awaye his wife, and she goeth from him, and marieth with another, then the question is: should he resorte vnto her any more after that? Is not this felde then defiled and vnclean? But as for the thou hast played the harlot with many louers, yet turne againe to me, sayeth the Lorde.

2 Lyft vp thine eyes on euery side, and loke, yf thou be not defyled. Thou hast wayted for them in stretes, and as a murtherer in the wildernesse. Thorowe thy whordome and shameful blasphemies, is the lande defyled.

3 This is the cause, that the rayne and eueninge dew hath ceased. Thou hast gotten the an whores foreheade, and canst not be ashamed.

4 Els wouldest thou saye vnto me: O my father, thou art he that hast brought me vp, and led me from my youth.

5 Wilt thou then put me awaye, and cast me of for euer? Or wilt thou withdrawe thy selfe cleane from me? Neuertheles, thou speakest suche wordes, but thou art euer doynge worse and worse.

6 The Lord sayd also vnto me: in the time of Iosiah the kinge, hast thou sene what that shrinkinge Israel hath done? howe she hathe runne vp vpon all the hilles, and amonge all thicke trees, and there playeth the harlot?

7 hast thou sene also (when she had done all thys) how I sayde vnto her: that she sholde turne agayne vnto me, and yet she is not returned? Iuda that vnfaythfull syster of hers also saw this:

8 Namely, that after I had well sene the aduoutrye of the shrynkynge harlot Israel. I put her awaye, and gaue her a byl of deuorcement. For al this, her vnfaithfull syster Iuda was not ashamed, but went backe and plaied the whore also.

9 Yea and the noise of her whordome that defyled the whole lande. For she hath commytted her aduoutrye with stones and stocke.

10 Neuerthelesse, her vnfaythfull syster Iuda is not turned vnto me again with ther whole herte, but faynedly, sayeth the Lorde.

11 And the Lorde sayde vnto me. The bacslyder Israel is more ryghteous, then the vnfaythfull Iuda:

12 and therfore go preache these wordes towarde the North, and saye: Thou shrenkinge Israel, turne agayne (sayeth the Lord) and I wyll not turne my face from you, for I am mercyfull, sayeth the Lorde, and I will not alwaye beare displeasure agaynste the:

13 but on this condicion, that thou knowe thy greate blasphemy: Namely, that thou haste vnfaithful forsaken the Lorde thy God, and hast made thy selfe partaker of straung goddes vnder all grene trees, but hast had no wil to heare my voyce, sayeth the Lorde.

14 O ye shrinkinge children, turne agayne, sayeth the Lorde: and I wilbe maried wyth you. For I will take one oute of the citie, and two oute of one generacyon from amonge you, and bring you out of Sion:

15 and wil geue you herdmen, after mine owne mynd, which shal fede you with learninge and wysedome.

16 Moreouer, when ye be increased and multyplied in the land, then (sayeth the Lorde) there shall no more boost be made of the arcke of the Lordes Testament: No man shal thincke vpon it, neyther shall any man make mencion of it: for from thence forth it shall neyther be visited, nor honoured with gyftes.

17 Then shal Ierusalem be called the Lordes seate, and all Heathen shalbe gathered vnto it, for the name of the Lordes sake, whyche shalbe set vp at Ierusalem. And from that tyme forth, they shal folow no more the ymaginacion of their owne frowarde herte.

18 Then those that be of the house of Iuda, shal go vnto the

house of Israel, and they shal come together out of the North, into the same land, that I haue geuen youre fathers.

19 I haue shewed also, howe I toke the vp beynge but a chylde, & gaue the a pleasaunt lande for thyne heretage, yea & a goodly Hoste of the heathen: & how I commaunded the, that þu shouldest cal me father only, & not to shrynck from me.

20 But lyke as a woman fayleth her louer, so are ye vnfaithfull vnto me (O ye house of Israel) sayeth the Lorde.

21 And therfore the voyce of the chyldren of Israel was heard in euery side, wepinge & waylinge: for they haue defyled their waye, and forgotten God their Lorde.

22 O ye shrinkynge chyldren, turne agayne, (sayinge: lo, we are thyne, for thou arte the Lorde oure God:) And so shall I heale your bacturnynges.

23 The hylles fal, and al the hye pryde of the mountaynes, but the healthe of Israel standeth onely vpon God oure Lorde.

24 Confusion hath deuoured oure fathers laboure from our youth vp: yea their shepe and bullockes, their sonnes and doughters.

25 So do we also slepe in oure confusyon, and shame couereth vs: for we and oure fathers from oure youth vp vnto thys daye haue sinned agaynste the Lorde oure God, and haue not obeyed the voyce of the Lord oure God.

# CHAPTER 4

O Israel, yf thou wylt turne the, then turne vnto me, sayeth the Lorde. And yf thou wilt put awaye thine abhominacyons out of my sight, thou shalt not be moued.

2 And shalt sweare: The Lorde liueth: in truthe, in equyte and ryghteousnesse: and al people shalbe fortunable and ioyful in him.

3 For thus sayeth the Lorde, to al Iuda and Ierusalem: plowe your lande, and sowe not amonge the thornes.

4 Be circumcised in the Lorde, and cut away the foreskinne of youre hertes, all ye of Iuda and all the indwellers of Ierusalem: that my indignacion breake not oute like fyre & kindle so that no man may quenche it, because of the wickednes of youre ymaginacions.

5 Preache in Iuda and Ierusalem, crye out and speake: blow the trompettes in the land, crie that euery man may heare, and saye: Gather you together, and we will go into strong cyties.

6 Set vp the token in Syon, spede you, and make no taryenge: for I will bringe a greate plage, and a greate destruccyon from the north.

7 For the spoyler of the Gentyles is broken vp from his place, as a lyon oute of his denne, that he may make the land waste, and destroie the cities, so that noman maye dwell therin.

8 Wherfore girde youre selues about with sacke clothe mourne and wepe for the fearfull wrath of the Lorde shall not be withdrawen from you.

9 At the same tyme (saieth the Lorde) the hert of the kinge and of the Princes shalbe gone, the pryestes shalbe astonished, and the prophetes shalbe sore afraied.

10 Then sayde I: O Lord God, hast thou disceyued then thys people and Ierusalem, saienge: ye shall haue peace, & now the swerde goeth thorowe their lyues?

11 Then shall it be sayde to the people & to Ierusalem: There commeth a warm wind from the North thorow the waye of my people, but nether to fanne, nor to clense.

12 After that shall there come vnto me a strong winde, and then will I also geue sentence vpon them.

13 For lo, he commeth doune lyke as a cloude, and his charettes are lyke a stormye winde: hys horsemen are swyfter then the Aegle. Wo vnto vs, for we are destroyed.

14 O Ierusalem wash thine herte from wyckednesse, that thou mayest be helped. Howe longe shal thy noysome thoughtes remayne with the.

15 For a voice from Dan and from the hil of Ephraim speaketh out, and telleth of a destruccion.

16 Beholde, the Heathen geue Ierusalem warninge, and preache vnto her, that her destroyers are comming from farre countrees. They tell the cities of Iuda the same also,

17 they shal geue him warninge in euery place, lyke as the watchmen in the felde. For they haue prouoked me to wrath, sayeth the Lorde.

18 Thy wayes and thy thoughtes, haue brought the vnto this, thys is thyne owne wickednesse and disobedience, that hath possessed thine herte:

19 Ah my belye, ah my belye, (shalt thou crye) how is my hert so sore? my herte painteth within me, I can not be styl, for I haue hearde the cryeng of the trompettes and peales of warre.

20 They crye murthur vpon murthur, the whole lande shall perishe. Immediatly my tentes were destroied, and my hanginges, in the twinckelinge of an eye.

21 Howe longe shall I se the tokens of warre, and heare the noyse of the trompettes.

22 Neuertheles this shal come vpon them, because my people is become folysh, and hath vtterly no vnderstandynge. They are the children of folishnes, and without any dyscrecion. To do

euill, they haue wyt ynoughe: but to do wel, they haue no wisdome.

23 I haue loked vpon the earth, and se it is waste, and voyde. I loked toward heauen, and it had no shyne.

24 I behelde the mountaynes, and they trembled, and al the hilles were in a feare.

25 I loked aboute me, and there was no bodye, and all the birdes of the ayre were awaye.

26 I marked wel, and the plowed felde was become wast: yea all their cytyes were broken doune, at the presence of the Lorde, and indignacyon of his wrath.

27 For thus hath the Lorde sayde: The whole lande shalbe desolate, yet will I not then haue done.

28 And therfore let the earth mourne and let the heauen be sory aboue: for the thing that I haue purposed and taken vpon me to do, shall not repente me, and I wil not go from it.

29 The whole lande shall fle, for the noyse of the horsmen and bowmen, they shal runne into dennes into woddes, and climme vp the stony rockes. All the cyties shalbe voyde, and noman dwellinge therin.

30 What wilt thou now do, for thou beynge destroyed? For though thou clotest thy selfe wyth scarlet, and deckest the wyth goulde: thoughe thou payntest thy face with colours yet shalt thou trymme thy selfe in vayne. For those that hytherto haue bene thy great fauourers, shall abhorre the, and go aboute to slaye the.

31 For (me thincke) I heare a noyse like as it were of a woman trauaylyng, or one laboringe of her fyrste chylde. Euen the voyce of the doughter of Syon, that casteth oute her armes, and souneth, sayenge: Ah wo is me, how sore vexed and faynte is my herte for them that are slayne?

# CHAPTER 5

LOKE thorow Ierusalem, beholde and se: Seke thorow the her stretes also wythin, yf ye can fynde one man, that doth equall and right, or that laboureth to be faythfull: and I shall spare hym (sayeth the Lorde.)

2 For though they can saye: the Lorde liueth, yet do they sweare to disceyue:

3 Where as thou (O Lorde) lokest only vpon faythe and truthe. Thou hast scourged them, but they toke no repentaunce: thou hast correcte them for amendement, but they refused thy correccion. They made their faces harder then a stone, and woulde not amende.

4 Therfore I thought in my selfe: peraduenture they are so symple and folish, that they vnderstande nothinge of the Lordes waye, and iudgementes of our God.

5 Therfore wil I go vnto their heades and rulers, and talke with them: yf they knowe the waie of the lord and the iudgementes of oure God. But these (in like maner) haue broken the yocke, and burste the bandes in sonder.

6 Wherfore a lyon out of the wood shall hurte them, and a wolfe in the euenyng shall destroy them. The cat of the mountayne shal lye lurking by their cities, to teare in peces al them, that come thereoute. For theyr offences are manye, and theyr departynge awaye is greate.

7 Shulde I then for al thys haue mercy vpon the? Thy chyldren haue forsaken me, & sworne by them that are no Goddes. And albe it they were bounde to me in maryage, yet they fell to aduoutrye, and haunted harlottes houses.

8 In the desyre of vnclenly luste they are become lyke the stoned horse, euery man neyeth at hys neyghbours wyfe:

9 Shulde I not correcte thys, sayeth the Lorde. Shulde I not be auenged of euerye people that is lyke vnto this?

10 Clymme vp vpon theyr walles, beate them doune, but destroye them not vtterlye cut of theyr braunches, because they are not þe Lordes.

11 For vnfaythfully hath the house of Israell and Iuda forsaken me, (sayth the Lorde).

12 They haue denyed þe Lord, & sayde: it is not he. Tush, there shall no mysfortune come vpon vs, we shall se nether swerd nor hunger.

13 As for the warnynge of the Prophetes, they take it but for wynde, yea there is none of these, which wyll tell them, þt suche thynges shall happen vnto them.

14 Wherfore thus sayth the Lord thy God of Hostes: because ye speake suche wordes, beholde: The wordes that are in thy mouth wyl I turne to fyre, & make the people to be wood, that it maye consume them.

15 Lo, I wyll bryng a people vpon you from farre, O house of Israel (sayeth the Lorde) a myghtye people, and olde people, a people whose speache thou knowest not, neyther vnderstandest what they saye.

16 Theyr arowes are sodane death, yea they them selues be very gyauntes.

17 Thys people shall eate vp thy frute & thy meate, yea they shall deuoure thy sonnes and thy doughters, thy shepe and thy bullockes. They shall eate vp thy grapes & fygges. As for thy stronge and well fensed cytyes, wherein thou dyddest trust, they shal destroy them with the swerde.

18 Neuerthelesse I wyll not then haue done with you, saith the Lorde.

19 But yf they saye: wherfore

doeth the Lord our God all this vnto vs? Then answere them: because, that lyke as ye haue forsaken me, & serued straunge goddes in your owne lande, euen so shall ye serue other Goddes also in a straunge lande.

20 Preach this vnto the house of Iacob, and crye it oute in Iuda, and saye thus:

21 Heare thys (thou folyshe and vndiscrete people) ye haue eyes, but ye se not: eares haue ye, but ye heare not.

22 Feare ye not me, sayeth the Lorde? Are ye not ashamed, to loke me in the face? which bynde the sea wyth the sande, so that it can not passe hys boundes: For thoughe it rage, yet can it do nothynge, and thoughe the waues thereof do swell, yet maye they not go ouer.

23 But thys people hath a false and an obstinate herte, they are departed & gone awaye fro me.

24 They thincke not in theyr hertes: O let vs feare the Lorde oure God, that geueth vs rayne early and late, when nede is, which kepeth euer styll the harueste for vs yearlye.

25 Neuertheles youre mysdedes haue turned these from you, and your synnes haue robbed you hereof.

26 For amonge my people are founde wicked personnes, that pryuelye laye snares & wayte for men, to take them & destroye them.

27 And lyke as a net is ful of byrdes, so are their houses full of that which they haue gotten wt falshed and disceyte. Hereof commeth theyr greate substaunce and ryches,

28 hereof are they fat and welthy, and are runne awaye fro me wyth shameful blasphemyes. They mynistre not the lawe, they make no ende of the fatherlesses cause, they iudge not the poore according to equite.

29 Shulde I not punyshe these thynges, saith the Lorde? shulde I not be auenged of al suche people, as these be?

30 Horryble and greuous thinges are done in the lande.

31 The Prophetes teache falsely, and the priestes folowe them, and my people hath pleasure therein. What wyll come thereof at the laste.

# CHAPTER 6

COME out of Ierusalem, ye strong children of Ben Iamin: blowe vp the trompettes ye Tecuytes, set vp a token vnto Bethcarem, for a plage and a greate myserye pepeth oute from the Northe.

2 I wyll licken the doughter Syon to a fayr and tendre woman, and to her shall come the shepeherdes with theyr flockes.

3 Theyr tentes shall they pytch rounde aboute her, and euery one shall fede them that are vnder his hand.

4 Make battell agaynst her (shall they say) Aryse, let vs go vp, whyle it is yet daye. Alas, the daye goeth awaye, & the nyghte shadowes fal doune:

5 Aryse, let vs go vp by nyght, and destroye her stronge holdes,

6 for thus hath the Lorde of hostes commaunded. Hewe doune her trees, and set vp bulworkes agaynste Ierusalem. Thys is the cytye that must be punyshed, for in her is all malyciousnes.

7 Lyke as a conduyte abounde th in water, euen so thys cytye aboundeth in wyckednes. Robberye and vnrightuousnesse is heard in her, sorow and woundes are euer there in my sight.

8 Amende the (O Ierusalem) leste I withdrawe my herte from the, and make the desolate: & thy lande also, that no man dwell in it.

9 For thus sayeth the Lorde of hoostes: The resydue of Israell shalbe gathered, as the remnaunt of grapes. And therfore turne thyne hande agayne into the basket, like the grape gatherer.

10 But vnto whome shall I speake, whome shall I warne that he maye take hede? Theyr eares are so vncircumcyced, þt they maye not heare. Beholde, they take the worde of God but for a scorne, & haue no luste therto.

11 And therfore I am so ful of thyne indignacyon (O Lorde) that I maye suffre no longer. Shede oute thy wrath vpon the children that are withoute, and vpon all younge men. Yea the man must be taken presoner with the wife, and the aged with the crepel.

12 Theyr houses with their landes and wyues shall be turned vnto straungers, when I stretche oute myne hande vpon the inhabitours of this land, sayeth the Lord.

13 For from the leaste vnto the moost, they hang all vpon couetousnes: & from the Prophet vnto the prieste, they go all aboute wyth falshed and lyes.

14 And besyde that, they heale the hurte of my people with swete wordes, sayinge: peace peace, when there is no peace at all.

15 Therfore they must be ashamed, for they haue committed abhomynacyon. But howe shulde they be ashamed, when they knowe nothinge, neither of shame nor good nurtoure? And therfore they shall fall amonge the slayne, and in the houre when I shall vyset them, they shall be brought doune, sayeth the Lorde.

16 Thus sayth the Lorde: go into the streates considre and make inquisicion for the old way and yf it be the good and right waye, then go therein, that ye

# JEREMIAH

maye fynde rest for your soules. But they saye: we wyll not walcke therin

17 and I wil set watchemen ouer you, & therfore take hede vnto the voyce of the trompet. But they saye: we wyll not take hede.

18 Heare therfore ye Gentyles, and thou congregacion shalt knowe, what I haue deuised for them.

19 Heare thou earth also: beholde, I wyll cause a plage come vpon this people, euen the frute of theyr owne ymagynacions. For they haue not bene obedyente vnto my wordes and to my lawe, but abhorred them.

20 Wherfore brynge ye me incense from Saba, & swete smellinge Calamus from farre countrees? Youre burntofferynges displease me, & I reioyse not in youre sacrifices.

21 And therfore thus sayth the Lorde: beholde I will make this people fall, & there shall fall from amonge them the father with the chyldren, one neyghboure shall peryshe with another.

22 Moreouer thus sayeth the Lorde: Behold, there shall come a people from the North, and a greate people shall aryse from the endes of the earthe,

23 with bowes & with dartes shall they be weapened: It is a roughe & fearce people, an vnmercyfull people: theyr voyce roareth lyke the sea, they ryde vpon horses wel appoynted to þe battel agaynst the, O doughter Sion.

24 Then shall thys crye be heard: Our armes are feble, heuynes & sorowe is come vpon vs, as vpon a woman trauaylynge with chylde.

25 No man go forth into the felde, no man come vpon the hye strete: for the swerde and feare of the enemye shalbe on euerye syde.

26 Wherfore, gyrde a sack clothe aboute the (O doughter of my people) sprinkle thy selfe wyth ashes, mourne and wepe bytterlye, as vpon thy onely beloued sonne: For the destroyer shall sodenly fall vpon vs.

27 The haue I set for a prouer of my harde people, to seke oute, and to trye theyr wayes.

28 For they are al vnfaythfull and fallen awaye, they hange vpon fylthy lucre, they are cleane brasse & yron for they hurte and destroye euerye man.

29 The bellous are brent in the fyre, the lead is consumed, the melter melteth in vayne, for the euyll is not taken awaye from them.

30 Therfore shal they be called naughtye syluer, because the Lorde hath caste them oute.

# CHAPTER 7

THESE are the wordes that GOD spake vnto Ieremie:

2 Stande vnder the gates of the Lordes house & crye oute these wordes there, wt a loude voyce, and saye: Heare þe worde of the Lorde all ye of Iuda, that go in at thys dore, to honoure the Lord.

3 Thus saith the Lorde of Hostes the God of Israel. Amend youre wayes and youre councels, and I wyll let you dwell in thys place.

4 Truste not in false lyenge wordes, sayenge: here is the temple of the Lorde, here is the temple of the Lorde, here is the temple of the Lorde.

5 For yf ye wyll amende youre wayes & councels, yf ye wyll iudge righte betwixte a man and hys neyghboure:

6 yf ye wyl not oppresse the straunger, the fatherles & the wyddowe: yf ye wyll not shede innocent bloud in this place: yf ye wyll not cleue to straunge goddes to youre owne destruccyon:

7 then wil I let you dwell in thys place, yea in the land þt I gaue afore tyme vnto youre fathers for euer.

8 But take hede, yea trust in councels, that begyle you & do you no good.

9 For when ye haue stolen, murthered, committed aduoutrye, and periury: When ye haue offred vnto Baal, folowyng straunge & vnknowne Goddes.

10 Then come ye, and stande before me in thys house, whiche hath my name geuen vnto it and say: Tush, we are absolued quite, though we haue done all these abhominacions.

11 What? thincke you thys house þt beareth my name, is a denne of theues? And these thinges are not done priuelye, but before myne eyes sayeth the Lorde.

12 Go to my place in Silah, wherevnto I gaue my name afore tyme, & loke wel what I did to the same place for the wyckednes of my people of Israell.

13 And now, thoughe ye haue done all these dedes (sayth the Lorde) & I my selfe rose vp euer by tymes to warne you & to comen wyth you yet wolde ye not heare me: I called, ye wolde not aunswere.

14 And therfore euen as I haue done vnto Siloh, so wil I do to thys house, þt my name is geuen vnto (and that ye put your trust in) ye vnto the place that I haue geuen to you & youre fathers.

15 And I shal thrust you of my syght, as I haue cast out all youre brethren the whole sede of Ephraim.

16 Therfore thou shalt not praye for this people, thou shalt nether geue thankes, nor byd prayer for them: thou shalt make no intercessyon to me for them for in no wyse wil I heare the.

17 Seyst thou not what they do in the cyties of Iuda, and

wythoute Ierusalem?

18 The chyldren gather stickes the fathers kyndle þe fyre, the mothers kneade the doughe, to bake cakes for the quene of heauen, They poure out drincke offerynges vnto straunge goddes, to prouoke me vnto wrath:

19 Howe be it they hurte not me (sayth the Lord) but rather confounde, and shame themselues.

20 And therfore thus saith the Lorde God: beholde, my wrath and my indignacyon shalbe poured out vpon this place, vpon men & catel vpon the trees in the felde & all frute of the lande, and it shall burne so, that no man maye quenche it.

21 Thus sayth the Lorde of Hostes, the God of Israel. Ye heape vp youre burntofferinges with youre sacrifyces, & eate the fleshe.

22 But when I broughte youre fathers out of Egipt I spake no worde vnto them of burntofferynges & sacrifyces:

23 but this I commaunded them, sayinge: herken & obeye my voyce, & I shalbe youre God, and ye shall be my people: so that ye walcke in all the wayes, whiche I haue commaunded you, that ye maye prospere.

24 But they were not obedyent, they inclined not theyr eares there vnto, but wente after theyr owne ymagynacyons and after the mocyons of theyr owne wycked herte, & so turned them selues awaye, and conuerted not vnto me.

25 And thys haue they done, from the tyme that youre fathers came oute of Egypte, vnto thys daye. Neuertheles, I sente vnto them my seruauntes all the Prophetes. I rose vp earlye & sente them worde,

26 yet wolde they not herken, nor offre me theyr eares, but were obstynate and worse then theyr fathers.

27 And thou shalt now speake all these wordes vnto them, but they shall not heare the: thou shalte crye vpon them but they shall not aunswere the.

28 Therfore shalte thou saye vnto them: This is the people that neyther heareth the voyce of the Lord theyr God, nor receyueth hys correccyon. Faithfulues & trueth is cleane roted oute of theyr mouth.

29 Wherfore cut of thyne hearre, and cast it awaye, take vp a complaynte in the whole lande for the Lorde shal caste awaye, and scatre the people, that he is displeased withall.

30 For the chyldren of Iuda haue done euyll in my sight sayeth the Lord. They haue set vp theyr abhominacyons, in the house that hath my name, & haue defyled it.

31 They haue also buylded an aulter at Topheth, which is in the valley of the chyldren of Hennom: that they might burne theyr sonnes and doughters, whiche I neuer commaunded them, neyther came it euer in my thought.

32 And therfore beholde, þe dayes shall come (sayeth the Lorde) that it shall no more be called Topheth, or the valleye of the chyldren of Hennom, but the valleye of the slayne, for in Topheth, they shall be buryed because they shall els haue no roume.

33 Yea the dead bodyes of this people shall be eaten vp of the foules of the ayre & wylde beastes of þe earth, and no man shall fraye them awaye.

34 And as for the voyce of myrth and gladnesse of the cytyes of Iuda, and Ierusalem the voyce of the brydegrome & of the bryde: I wil make them ceasse, for the lande shall be desolate.

## CHAPTER 8

At the same tyme sayeth þe Lord þe bones of the kinges of Iuda, the bones of hys prynces, þe bones of þe priestes & prophetes, yea & the bones of the citesens of Ierusalem, shalbe broughte oute of theyr graues

2 & layed against þe sunne, the Mone and all the heauenlye hoste, whom they loued, whome they serued whome they rayne after, whome they soughte & worshypped. They shall nether be gathered together nor buryed, but shall lye vpon the earthe, to theyr shame and despysynge.

3 And all they that remayne of thys wycked generacyon, shall desyre rather to dye then to lyue: wheresoeuer they remayne, & where as I scatre them, sayth the Lorde of hoostes.

4 This shalte thou saye vnto them also: Thus sayeth the Lorde: Do men fall so, that they aryse not vp agayne? And turne they so farre awaye, that they neuer conuerte?

5 Wherfore then is this people and Ierusalem gone to farre backe, that they turne not agayne. They are euer the longer the more obstynate, & wyl not be conuerted.

6 For I haue loked, & consydered: but there is no man that speaketh a good worde: there is no man that taketh repentaunce for hys synne, that wyll so muche as saye: wherfore haue I done thys? But euerye man (as sone as he is turned backe) runneth forth styl, lyke a wylde horse in a battayle.

7 The Storke knoweth hys appoynted tyme, the Turtledoue, þe Swalowe & the Crane consydre the tyme of theyr trauayle: but my people wyll not know the tyme of the punyshmente of the Lorde.

8 Howe darre ye saye then: we are wyse, we haue the lawe of the Lorde amonge vs. Beholde, the disceytfull penne of the scrybes, setteth forth lyes:

9 therfore shall the wyse be confounded, they shalbe afrayed

and taken: for lo, they haue caste oute the worde of the Lorde: what wysdom can then be among them?

10 Wherfore I will geue their wyues vnto aleauntes, and their feldes to destroyers. For from the loweste vnto the hyeste, they folowe all fylthy lucre: & from the Prophete vnto the prieste, they deale al with lyes.

11 Neuertheles, they heale the hurte of my people with swete wordes, saying: peace, peace wher there is no peace at all.

12 Fye for shame, how abhominable thinges do they? and yet they be not ashamed, yea thei knowe of no shame. Wherfore in the tyme of theyr vysytacion they shall fall among the dead bodyes, sayeth the Lorde.

13 Moreouer I wyll gather them in (sayth the Lorde) so that there shall not be one grape vpon the vyne, neyther one fygge vpon the fygge tree, and the leaues shalbe plucte of. Then wyll I cause them to departe, & saye:

14 why prolong we the tyme? Let vs gather our selues together, & go into the stronge cytye, there shall we be in reste: For the Lorde oure God hath put vs to sylence, and geuen vs water myxte with gal, to drincke: because we haue synned agaynst hym.

15 We loked for peace, and we fare not the better, we wayted for the tyme of health, and lo, here is nothynge but trouble.

16 Then shall the noyse of his horses be hearde from Dan, the whole lande shall be afrayed at the neyenge of his stronge horses: for they shal go in, & deuoute the lande, with al that is in it: the cities, and those that dwel therin.

17 Moreouer, I will sende Cockatryces and serpentes amonge you (which wyl not be charmed) & they shall byte you, sayeth the Lorde.

18 Sorowe is come vpon me, and heuynes vexeth my herte,

19 for lo, the voyce of the crieng of my people is hearde from a farre countre: Is not the Lorde in Syon? Is not the kynge in her? Wherfore then haue they greued me (shall the Lorde saye) with theyr ymages and folyshe straunge fashyons?

20 The harueste is gone, the Sommer hath an ende, and we are not helped.

21 I am sore vexed, because of þe hurte of my people: I am heuye and abashed,

22 for there is no more Tryacle at Galaad, & there is no Physycyen, that can heale the hurte of my people.

# CHAPTER 9

O who wil geue my heade water ynough, and a wel of teares for myne eyes: that I may wepe night and day, for the slaughter of my people?

2 Wold God that I had a cotage some where farre from folcke that I myghte leaue my people, & go from them for they be all aduoutrers and a shrynkynge sorte.

3 They bende theyr tunges lyke bowes, to shute oute lyes. As for the trueth, they may nothynge awaye with all in the worlde. For they go from one wyckednes to another, & hold nothinge of me, sayeth the Lorde.

4 Yea one must kepe him selfe from another no man maye safely truste his owne brother: for one brother vndermyneth another, & one neyghboure begyleth another.

5 Yea one dyssembleth with another, & they deale wyth no trueth. They haue practysed theyr tunges to lye, and taken greate paynes to do myschefe.

6 They haue set theyr stole in the myddest of dysceyte, and for very dyssemblynge falshede they wyll not knowe me, sayeth the Lorde.

7 Therfore thus sayeth the Lorde of Hostes: beholde, I wyll melte them, and trye them, for what shulde I els do to my people?

8 Their tunges are lyke sharpe arowes, to speake disceyte. Wyth theyr mouthe they speake peaceably to theyr neyghboure, but preuely they laye wayte for hym.

9 Shulde I not punyshe them for these thynges, sayeth the Lorde? Or shulde I not be auenged of any suche people as thys?

10 Vpon the mountaynes wyl I take vp a lamentacyon and sorowfull crye, and a mournynge vpon the fayre playnes of the wyldernes: Namely, howe they are so brente vp, that no man goeth there anye more. Yea a man shall not heare one beaste crye there. Byrdes and catell are al gone from thence.

11 I wyll make Ierusalem also an heape of stones, and a denne of venymous wormes. And I wyll make the cytyes of Iuda so wast, that no man shall dwell therein.

12 What man is so wyse, as to vnderstande thys? Or to whome hath the Lorde spoken by mouth, that he may shewe this, and saye: O thou lande, why peryshest thou so? Wherfor art thou so brent vp, & lyke a wyldernesse, that no man goeth thorowe?

13 Yea the Lorde hymselfe tolde the same vnto them, that forsoke hys lawe, and kepte not the thynge that he gaue them in commaundement, neither lyued thereafter:

14 but folowed the wyckednes of theyr owne hertes, and serued straunge Goddes, as theyr fathers taught them.

15 Therfore, thus sayeth the Lorde of Hostes the God of

Israell: Beholde, I wyll fede this people with wormewood, and geue them gal to drincke.

16 I wyll scatre them also among the Heathen, whome neyther they nor theyr fathers haue knowne: & I will sende a sweard amonge them, to persecute them, vntyl I bring them to naughte.

17 Moreouer, thus sayeth the Lorde of Hostes: loke that ye call for mournynge wyues, and send for wyse wemen: that they come shortly,

18 & synge a mournyng song of you: that the teares maye fall oute of oure eyes, and that oure eye lyddes maye gusshe oute of water.

19 For there is a lamentable noyse heard of Sion: O how are we so sore destroyed? O howe are we so piteously confounded? We muste forsake oure owne naturall countreye, & we are shote out of oure owne lodgynges.

20 Yet heare the worde of the Lorde (O ye wemen) and let your eares regard the wordes of hys mouth: that ye may learne your doughters to mourne, and that euerye one maye teache her neighbouresse, to make lamentacyon.

21 Namely thus Death is climminge vp in at oure windowes he is come into oure houses, to destroye the chylde before the dore, and the younge man in the strete.

22 But tell thou planelye, thus sayeth the Lorde: The dead bodyes of men shall lye vpon the grounde, as the dong vpon the felde, and as the heye after the mower, and there shalbe no man to take them vp.

23 Moreouer, thus sayeth the Lorde: Let not the wyse man reioyse in his wisdome, nor the stronge man in hys strength, neyther the ryche man in hys ryches:

24 But who so wyl reioyse, let hym reioyse in this, that he vnderstandeth and knoweth me: for I am the Lorde, which do mercy, equite, and ryghtuousnes vpon the earth. Therefore haue I pleasure in suche thynges, sayeth the Lorde.

25 Beholde, the tyme commeth (sayth the Lorde) that I will vyset all them, whose foreskinne is vncyrcumcysed.

26 The Egypcians, the Iewes, the Edomytes, the Ammonytes, the Moabites, and the shauen Madyanites, that dwell in the wildernes. For all the Gentyles are vncyrcumcysed in the fleshe, but all the house of Israell are vncyrcumcysed in the herte.

# CHAPTER 10

HEARE the worde of the Lorde, þt he speaketh vnto the, O thou house of Israell:

2 Thus sayth the Lorde: Ye shall not learne after the maner of the Heathen, & ye shall not be afrayed for the tokens of heauen: for the Heathen are afrayed of suche:

3 yea all the customes and lawes of the Gentiles are nothinge, but vanite. They hewe doune a tree in the wood with the handes of þe worcke man, and fashyon it with the axe:

4 they couer it ouer with gold or siluer, they fasten it with nayles and hammers, that it moue not.

5 It standeth as styfe as the palmetree, it can not neyther speake nor go, but must be borne. Be not ye afrayed of suche, for they can do neyther good nor euill.

6 But there is none lyke vnto þe, O Lorde, & great is the name of thy power.

7 Who wolde not feare the? Or what Kinge of the Gentyles wolde not obeye the. For amonge all the wyse men of the Gentyles, & in all their kyngdomes, there is none that maye be lickened vnto the.

8 They are all together vnlearned and vnwyse. All theyr conninge is but vanyte:

9 namelye, woode, syluer, whiche is brought oute of Tharsis, and beaten to plates: and golde from Ophir, a worcke þt is made with the hande of the craftesmen and the caster, clothed with yelowe sylcke & scarlet: euen so is the worcke of theyr wyse men altogether.

10 But the Lorde is a true God, a lyuynge God, and an euerlastinge kyng. Yf he be wroth, the earthe shaketh: all the Gentiles maye not abyde his indygnacyon.

11 As for theyr Goddes, it maye well be sayde of them: they are Goddes, that made neyther heauen nor earthe: therfore shall they peryshe from the earthe, & from al thynges vnder heauen

12 But (as for oure God) he made the earth with his power, and with hys wysdom hath he fynished the whole compasse of the worlde, wyth hys discrecion hath he spred oute the heauens.

13 At his voyce the waters gather together in þe ayre, he draweth vp the cloudes from the vttermoste partes of the earth: he turneth lyghtenyng to rayne, & bryngeth forth the windes oute of theyr treasures:

14 Hys wysdom maketh all men fooles. And confounded be all casters of ymages, for that they cast, is but a vayne thynge, and hath no lyfe.

15 The vayne craftesmen with theyr worckes, that they in theyr vanite haue made, shall peryshe one with another in the tyme of vysitacyon.

16 Neuertheles, Iacobs porcyon is not suche: but it is he, that hath made all thynges, and Israel is the rode of hys enherytaunce: The Lorde of Hostes is his name.

17 Put away thyne

vnclennesse oute of the lande, thou that arte in the stronge cyties.

18 For thus sayth the Lorde: Beholde, I wyl nowe thruste oute the inhabitours of this land a greate waye of, and trouble them of suche a fashyon, that they shall no more be founde.

19 Alas how am I hurte? Alas, howe paynefull are my scourges vnto me? For I consydre this sorowe by my selfe, & I must suffre it.

20 My tabernacle is destroyed, and al my coardes are broken. My children are gone fro me, & can no where be found. Nowe haue I none to sprede oute my tente, or to set vp my hanginges.

21 For the herdmen haue done folyshly, that they haue not soughte the Lorde. Therfor haue they dealt vnwysely wyth theyr cattell, and all are scatred abroade.

22 Beholde, þe noyse is harde at hande, and greate sedycyon out of the north: to make the cytyes of Iuda a wyldernesse, and a dwellynge place for Dragons.

23 Now I knowe (O Lorde) that it is not in mans power to ordre hys owne wayes, or to rule hys owne steppes and goinges.

24 Therfor chasten thou vs, O Lorde, but wyth fauoure and not in thy wrath, brynge vs not vtterlye to naught.

25 Poure oute thyne indygnacion rather vpon the Gentyles, that knowe the not, and vpon the people that call not on thy name: And that because they haue consumed, deuoured and destroyed Iacob, and haue roted out hys glorye.

## CHAPTER 11

THIS is another Sermon, which the Lorde commaunded Ieremy for to preache, saying:

2 Hear the wordes of the couenaunt, & speake vnto all Iuda, and to all them that dwell at Ierusalem.

3 And saye thou vnto them: Thus sayth the Lorde God of Israell. Cursed be euerye one that is not obedient vnto the wordes of this couenaunt:

4 whiche I commaunded vnto youre fathers, what tyme as I brought them oute of Egypte, from the yron fornace, sayinge: Be obedient vnto my voyce, & do accordynge to all that I commaund you: so shall ye be my people, & I wilbe youre God,

5 and will kepe my promyse, that I haue sworne vnto youre fathers: Namelye, that I wolde geue them a lande which floweth with mylcke and hony, as ye se, it is come to passe vnto this daye. Then aunswered I, and sayd: Amen. It is euen so Lorde, as thou sayest.

6 Then the Lorde sayde vnto me agayne: preache this in the cytyes of Iuda & round about Ierusalem, & saye: Heare the wordes of this conuenaunt, that ye maye kepe them.

7 For I haue diligently exorted youre fathers, euer sence the tyme that I broughte them oute of þe land of Egipte, vnto this daye. I gaue them warnyng by tymes, sayenge: herken vnto my voyce:

8 Neuertheles, they wolde not obeye me nor enclyne theyr eares vnto me, but folowed the wicked ymaginacions of theyr owne hertes. And therfore haue I accused them as transgressours of all the wordes of this couenaunt, that I gaue them to kepe, whiche they (not with vnderstandynge) haue not kepte.

9 And the Lorde sayde vnto me: It is founde oute, that whole Israell and all these citesens of Ierusalem are gone backe.

10 They haue turned them selues to the blasphemyes of theyr forefathers, whiche had no luste to heare my worde. Euen lykewyse haue these also folowed straunge Goddes, and worshypped them. The house of Israell and Iuda haue broken my couenaunt, whiche I made wyth their fathers.

11 Therfore thus sayth the Lorde: Beholde, I wyll sende a plage amonge you, whiche ye shall not be able to escape: and though ye crye vnto me, I wyll not heare you.

12 Then shal the tounes of Iuda and the cytezyns of Ierusalem go, and call vpon theyr Goddes, vnto whom they made theyr oblacyons: but they are not able to helpe them in tyme of theyr trouble.

13 For as manye cytyes as thou haste, O Iuda, so many Goddes haste thou also: And loke how many stretes there be in the (O Ierusalem) so manye shamefull aulters haue ye set vp, to offre vpon them vnto Baal.

14 But praye not thou for thys people, byd neyther prayse nor prayer for them, for thoughe they crye vnto me in theyr trouble, yet wyl I not heare them.

15 O thou beloued, why doest thou so shamefull greate blasphemyes in my house, euen as though that holy flesh myght absolue the, specially when thou haste made thy boaste of thy wickednes.

16 The Lorde called the a grene olyue tree, a fayre one, a fruteful one, a goodly one, but nowe that there is a contrarye reporte of the abroade, he wyl burne the vp, & destroye thy braunches.

17 For the Lorde of hostes that planted the, hath deuysed a plage for the, (O thou house of Israell and Iuda) for the euyll that ye haue done to prouoke hym to wrath, in that ye dyd seruyce vnto Baal.

18 This (O Lord) haue I learned of the, and vnderstand it, for thou hast shewed me theyr ymaginacions.

19 But I (as a meke lambe) was caried awaye to be slayne: not knowing, that they had deuised soche a councell agaynst me sayenge: We wyll destroye hys meate wyth woed, & dryue hym out of the lande of the lyuing: þt his name shall neuer be thought vpon.

20 Therfore I wyll beseche the now (O Lord of hostes) thou righteous iudge, thou that tryest the reynes and the hertes: lett me se the aunged of them, for vnto the haue I committed my cause.

21 The Lord therfore spake thus of þe citezyns of Anothoth, that sought to slaye me, sayenge: Preache not vnto vs in the name of the Lord, or els thou shalt dye of oure handes.

22 Thus (I saye) spake the Lorde of hostes: Beholde, I will viset you. Youre yonge men shall peryshe wyth the swearde, your sonnes & your daughters shall vtterlye dye of honger,

23 so that none shall remayne. For vpon þe cytezyns of Anathoth wil I bring a plage, the yeare of their visitacion.

## CHAPTER 12

O Lorde, thou art more rightuous then that I shulde dyspute with the: Neuertheles, lett me talke wyth the in thynges resonable. How happeneth it, that the waye of the vngodlye is so prosperous: and that it goeth so well with them, which (without eny shame) offende and lyue in wyckednesse?

2 Thou plantest them, they take rote, they growe, and brynge forth fruite: They booste moch of the, yet doest thou not punish them.

3 But thou Lorde (to whom I am well knowne) thou that hast sene, and proued my herte, take them awaye, lyke as a flocke is caryed to the slaughter house, & apoynte them for the daye of slaughter.

4 Howlonge shall the lande mourne, and al the herbes of the felde perysh, for the wyckednes of them that dwell therin? The catell and the byrdes are gone, yet saye they: tush, God wyll not destroye vs vtterly.

5 Seing thou art weery in runninge with þe fote men, how wilt thou then runne with horses? In a peaceable sure lande thou mayest be safe, but how wilt thou do in the furyous pryde of Iordane?

6 For thy brethren and thy kynred haue all together despised the, & cried out vpon the in thine absence. Beleue them not, though they speake fayre wordes to the

7 As for me (saye I) I haue forsaken myne owne dwellyng place, & left myne heretage. My life also that I loue so well, haue I geuen in to the handes of myne enemyes.

8 Myne heretage is become vnto me, as a Lyon, in the wod. It cried out vpon me, therfore haue I forsaken it.

9 Myne heretage is vnto me, as a speckled byrde, a byrde of dyuerse coloures is vpon it. Go hence, and gathere all the beastes of the felde together, that they maye eate it vp.

10 Dyuerse herdmen haue broken downe my vyneyarde, and troden vpon my porcyon. Of my pleasaunt porcion, they haue made a wyldernes & deserte.

11 They haue layed it waste: and now that it is waste, it sygheth vnto me. Yee the whole lande lyeth waste, and no man regardeth it.

12 The destroyers come ouer the heeth euery waye, for the swearde of þe Lorde shall consume from the one ende of the lande to the other, & no flesh shall haue reste.

13 They shall sowe wheate, and reepe thornes. They shall take heretage in possession, but it shall do them no good. And ye shalbe confounded of youre owne wynnynges, because of the greate wrath of the Lorde.

14 Thus sayeth the Lorde vpon all myne euell negbours, that laye hande on myne heretage, whiche I haue geuen my people of Israel: Beholde, I will plucke them (namely Israel) out of their lande, & put out the house of Iuda from amonge them.

15 And when I haue roted them out, I wylbe at one wyth them agayne, and wyll haue mercye vpon them: & brynge them agayne, euery man to hys owne heritage, and in to his land.

16 And yf they (namely that trouble my people) wyll lerne the wayes of them, to sweare by my name: The Lorde lyueth (lyke as they lerned my people to sweare by Baal) then shall they be rekened amonge my people.

17 But yf they will no obeye then wyll I rote out the same folke & destroy them, sayeth the Lorde.

## CHAPTER 13

MOREOUER, thus sayde the Lorde vnto me: go thy waye, and gett the a lynen breche, and gyrde it aboute thy loynes, and let it not be wet.

2 Then I got me a breche, accordynge to the commaundement of the Lorde, and put it about my loynes.

3 After this, þe Lord spake vnto me agayn:

4 Take the breche that thou hast prepared and put aboute the, and gett the vp, and go vnto Euphrates, and hyde it in a hole of the rock.

5 So went I, and hydde it, as the Lorde commaunded me.

6 And it happened longe after this, that the Lorde spake vnto me: Vp, and get the to Euphrates, and fet the breche from thence, which I commaunded the to hyde there.

7 Then went I to Euphrates, & dygged vp, & toke the breche from the place where I had hyd it: & beholde, the breche was corrupt, so that it was profytable for nothinge.

8 Then sayde the Lorde vnto me:

9 Thus sayeth the Lord: Euen so wyll I corrupte the pryde of Iuda, & the hye mynde of Ierusalem.

10 This people is a wycked people, they wyll not heare my worde, they folowe the wicked ymagynacyons of their owne herte, & hange vpon straunge Goddes, them haue they serued & worshypped: & therfore they shalbe as this breche, that serueth for nothynge.

11 For as straytelye as a breche lyeth vpon a mans loynes, so strately dyd I bynde þe whol house of Israell, and the whole house of Iuda vnto me, sayeth the Lorde: that they myght be my people: þt they myght haue a gloryous name: þt they myght be in honoure: but they wolde not obeye me.

12 Therfore laye thys rydle before them, and saye: Thus sayeth the Lorde God of Israel: Euery pot shalbe fylled with wyne. And they shall saye: thinckest thou we knowe not, that euery pot shalbe fylled with wyne?

13 Then shalt thou saye vnto them: Thus sayeth the Lorde: Beholde: I shall fyll all the inhabytours of this lande with dronckennes, the Kynges that syt vpon Dauids stole, the Prestes and Prophetes, with all that dwell at Ierusalem.

14 And I wyll shute them one agaynst another, yee the fathers agaynst the sonnes, sayeth the Lorde. I wyll not pardon them, I will not spare them, ner haue pytye vpon them: but destroye them.

15 Be obedient, geue are, take no dysdayne at it, for it is the Lorde hym selfe that speaketh.

16 Honoure the Lorde youre God herein, or he take hys lyght from you, and or euer youre fete stomble in darcknesse at the hylle lest when ye loke for the lyght, he turne it into the shadowe and darcknesse of death.

17 But yf ye wyll not heare me, that geue you secrete warnyng, I will mourne fro my whole hert for youre stubburnesse. Pyteouslye wyll I wepe, and the teares shall gusshe out of myne eyes. For the Lordes flocke shall be caryed awaye captyue.

18 Tell the kynge and the rulers: Humble youre selues, sett you downe lowe, for the crowne of youre glory shall fall from your head.

19 The cities towarde þe south shalbe shut vp, and no man shall open them. All Iuda shalbe caried away captyue, so that none shall remayne.

20 Lyft vp youre eyes, and beholde them, that come from the North: Lyke a fat flocke shall they fall vpon the.

21 To whom wylt thou make thy mone, when they come vpon the? for thou hast taught them thy selfe, and made them maysters ouer the. Shall not sorowe come vpon the, as on a woman trauaylinge with childe:

22 And yf thou woldest saye then in thyne herte: Wherfore come these thinges vpon me? Euen for the multitude of thy blasphemyes, shall thy hinder partes and thy fete be discouered.

23 For lyke as the man of Iude maye chaunge hys skyne, and the cat of the mountayne her spottes: so maye ye that be exercysed in euell, do good.

24 Therfore will I scatre you, lyke as the stobble that is taken awaye with the south wynde.

25 This shall be youre porcyon, and the porcyon of youre measure, wher with ye shal be rewarded of me, sayeth the Lorde: because ye haue forgotten me, and put youre trust in disceytfull thinges.

26 Therfore shall I turne thy clothes ouer thy head, and discouer thy thyghes, that thy preuities maye be sene,

27 thy aduoutrye, thy deedly malice, thy beastlinesse and thy shamefull whordome. For vpon the feldes and hylles I haue sene thy abhominacions. Wo be vnto the (O Ierusalem) when wylt thou euer be clensed eny more?

# CHAPTER 14

THE worde of the Lorde shewed vnto Ieremye, concernynge the derth of the fruites.

2 Iuda shal mourne, men shall not go moch more thorow hys gates: the lande shalbe no more had in reputacyon, and the crie of Ierusalem shall breake out.

3 The Lordes shall sende their seruauntes to fetch water, and when they come to the welles, they shall fynde no water, but shall carye their vessels home emptye. They shall be ashamed and confounded, & shall couer their heades.

4 For the grounde shalbe dried vp, because there commeth no rayne vpon it. The plowmen also shalbe a shamed, & shall couer their heades.

5 The Hynde shall forsake the yonge fawne, that he bringeth forth in the felde because there shalbe no grasse.

6 The wylde Asses shall stande in the Mosse, and drawe in their wynde lyke þe Dragons, their eyes shall fayle for want of grasse.

7 Doutles oure owne wickednesse rewarde vs: But Lorde do thou according to thy name, though oure transgressyons and synnes be

many.

8 For thou art the comforte & helpe of Israel in þe tyme of trouble. Why wilt thou be as a straunger in the Lande, and as one that goeth ouer the felde, and commeth in onely to remayne for a night?

9 Why wilt thou make thy self a cowarde, and as it were a gyaunte that yet maye not helpe? For thou art ours (O Lorde) and we beare thy name, therfore forsake vs not.

10 Then spake the Lorde, concernynge this people that haue pleasure to go so nymblye with their fete, and leaue not of, and therfore displease the Lorde: in so much, that he wyll now bringe agayne to remembraunce al their mysdedes, and punysh all their synnes.

11 Yee euen thus sayde the Lorde vnto me: Thou shalt not praye to do this people good.

12 For though they fast, I wyll not heare theyr prayers. And though they offre burntoffringes & sacrifices, yet wyll not I accepte them. For I will destroye them with þe swearde, honger and pestilence.

13 Then answerede I: O Lorde God, the prophetes saye vnto them: Tush, ye shal se no swearde, and no honger shall come vpon you, but the Lorde shall geue you continuall rest in this place.

14 And the Lorde sayde vnto me: The prophetes preach lyes vnto them in my name. I haue not spoken wyth them, nether gaue I them eny charge, nether dyd I sende them: yet they preach vnto you false visions, charming vanite, & disceytfulnesse of their owne herte.

15 Therfore thus saieth the Lorde: As for those prophetes that preache in my name (whom I neuertheles haue not sent) and that saye: Tush, there shall nether batell ner honger be in this lande: Wyth swearde and with honger shall those prophetes perysh,

16 and the people to whom they haue preached shalbe cast out of Ierusalem, dye of honger, and be slayne wyth the swearde (and there shallbe no man to burye them) buth they and their wyues, their sonnes and their daughters. For thus wyll I poure their wyckednes vpon them.

17 This shalt thou saye also vnto them: Myne eyes shall wepe without ceassynge daye and night. For my people shalbe destroyed wyth great harme, and shall perysh wyth a great plage.

18 For yf I go in to the felde, lo, it lyeth all full of slayne men. If I come in to the cytye, lo, they be all fameshed of honger. Yee their prophetes also and prestes shall be led in to an vnknowne lande.

19 Haste thou then vtterlye forsaken Iuda? (sayde I) Doest thou so abhorre Syon? Or hast thou so plaged vs, that we can be healed nomore? We loked for peace, and there commeth no good: for the tyme of health, and lo, here is nothynge but trouble:

20 We knowlege (O Lorde) all oure mysdedes, & the synnes of oure fathers, that we haue offended þe.

21 Be not dyspleased (O Lorde) for thy names sake, forgett not thy louynge kyndnes: Remembre the trone of thyne honoure, breake not the couenaunt, that thou hast made with vs.

22 Are there eny amonge the goddes of the Gentiles that sende rayne or geue the showers of heauen? Doest not thou it O Lorde oure God, in whom we trust? Yee Lorde, thou doest all these thinges.

## CHAPTER 15

THEN spake the Lorde vnto me, & sayde: Though Moses and Samuel stode before me, yet haue I no herte to thys people. Dryue them awaye, that they maye go out of my syght.

2 And yf they saye vnto the: Whyther shall we go? Then tell them: The Lorde geueth you thys answere: Some vnto death, some to the swearde, some to honger, some in to captyuyte.

3 For I will bryng foure plages vpon them sayeth the Lorde. The swearde shall strangle them, the dogges shal deuoure them, the foules of the ayre, and beastes of the earth shall eate them vp, and destroye them.

4 I wyll scatter them aboute also in all kyngdomes and landes to be plaged, because of Manasseh the sonne of Hezekiah kynge of Iuda, for the thinges that he dyd in Ierusalem.

5 Who shall then haue pyte vpon the O Ierusalem? Who shall be sory for the? Or who shall make intercession, to opteyne peace for the?

6 seynge thou goest fro me, & turnest backwarde, sayeth the Lorde? Therfore I will stretch out myne hand agaynst the, to destroy the, and I wyll not be intreated.

7 I will scatre the abrode with fanne no euery side of the lande: I wyll waste my people and destroye them, for they haue had no luste to turne from their owne wayes.

8 I wyll make their wyddowes mo in nombre, then the sandes of the sea. Vpon the mothers of their chyldren, I shall brynge a destroyer in the noone daye. Sodenlye & vnawarres, shall I sende a feare vpon their cyties.

9 She that hath borne .vij. chyldren, shall haue none, here herte shal be full of sorowe. The Sunne shall fayle her in the cleare daye, when she shalbe confounded and faynte for very heuynesse. As for those þt

remayne, I wyll delyuer them vnto the swearde of their enemyes, sayth the Lorde.

10 O mother, alas that euer thou dydest beate me, an enemye and hated of the whose lande: Though I neuer lente ner receyued vpon vsury, yet all men speake euell vpon me.

11 And the Lorde answered me: Lede not I þe then vnto good? Come not I to the, when thou art in trouble: & helpe the, when thyne enemye oppresseth the?

12 Doth one yron hurte another, or one metall that commeth from the North, another?

13 As for youre ryches and treasure, I wyll geue them out in to a praye, not for eny money, but because of all your synnes, that ye haue done in all youre coastes.

14 And I wyll brynge you with youre enemyes in to a lande, that ye knowe not: for the fyre that is kyndled in my indignacyon, shall burne you vp.

15 O Lorde (sayde I then) thou knowest all thinges, therfore remembre me, & vyset me, delyuer me fro my persecuters: Recyeue not my cause in thy longe wrath, yet thou knowest, þt for thy sake I suffre rebuke.

16 When I had found thy wordes, I ate them vp gredely: they haue made my herte ioyfull & glad. For I call vpon thy name, O Lorde God of Hostes.

17 I dwell not amonge the scorners, nether is my delyte therin: but I dwell only in the feare of thy hand, for thou hast fylled me with bytternes.

18 Shall my heuynes endure for euer? Are my plages then so greate, that they maye neuer be healed? Wilt thou be as a water, that falleth, and can not continue?

19 Vpon these wordes, thus sayde the Lorde vnto me: If thou wylt turne agayne, I shall set the in my seruyce: and yf thou wylt take out the thynge that is precious from the vile, thou shalt be euen as myne owne mouth. They shall conuerte vnto the, but turne not thou vnto them:

20 & so shall I make the a stronge wall of stele agaynst this people. They shall fyght agaynst the, but they shall not preuayle. For I my selfe will be with the, to helpe the, and delyuer the, sayeth the Lorde.

21 And I wyll rydd the out of the handes of the wycked, and delyuer the out of the hande of Tirauntes.

## CHAPTER 16

Moreouer, thus sayde the Lorde vnto me:

2 Thou shalt take þe no wyfe, ner beget chyldren in this place.

3 For of the chyldren þt are borne in thys place, of their mother þt haue borne them, and of their fathers that haue begotten them in thys lande, thus sayeth the Lorde:

4 They shal dye an horrible deeth, no man shall mourne for them, ner burye them, but they shall lye as donge vpon the earth. They shall perishe thorow the swearde and honger, and their bodyes shall be meate for the foules of the ayre, & beastes of the earth.

5 Agayne, thus sayeth the Lorde: Go not vnto them, that come together, for to mourne and wepe: for I haue taken my peace from this people (saieth the Lorde) yee my fauoure & my mercy.

6 And in this lande shall they dye, olde and yonge, and shall not be buryed: no man shall bewepe them, no man shall clyppe or shaue hym selfe for them.

7 There shal not one viset another, to mourne with them for their deed, or to comforte them. One shall not offre another the cuppe of consolacyon, to forget their heuynes for father & mother.

8 Thou shalt not go in to their feaste house, to syt downe, moche lesse to eate or drincke with them.

9 For thus sayeth the Lorde of Hostes the God of Israell: Beholde, I shall take awaye out of this place, the voyce of myrth and gladnesse, the voyce of the brydegrome and of the bryde: yee & that in youre dayes, that ye maye se it.

10 Now when thou shewest thys people all these wordes, and they saye vnto the: Wherfore hath the Lorde deuysed all thys greate plage for vs? Or what is the offence & synne, þt we haue done agaynst the Lord oure God?

11 Then make thou them this answere: Because youre fathers haue forsaken me (sayth þe Lord) and haue cleued vnto straunge goddes, whom they haue honoured and worshypped: but me haue they forsaken, & haue not kepte my lawe.

12 And ye with youre shamefull blasphemyes, haue exceaded the wyckednes of youre fathers. For euery one of you foloweth the frowarde and euell ymagynacyon of his owne herte, and is not obedient vnto me.

13 Therfore wyll I cast you oute of this lande, in to a lande that ye and youre fathers knowe not: and there shall ye serue straunge goddes daye and nyght, there wyll I shewe you no fauoure.

14 Behold therfore (sayeth the Lorde) the dayes are come, that it shall nomore be sayed: The Lorde lyueth, whyche brought the chyldren of Israell out of the lande of Egypte:

15 but, it shall be sayde, þe Lord lyueth, that brought the

chyldren of Israell from the North, and from all landes where I had scatred them. For I wyll brynge them agayne in to the lande, that I gaue vnto their fathers.

16 Beholde (sayeth the Lorde) I wyll sende out many fyshers to take them, & after þt wyll I sende out manye hunters to hunte them out, from all mountaynes and hylles & out of þe caues of stones.

17 For myne eyes beholde all their wayes, and they can not be hyd fro my face, nether can their wycked dedes be kepte close out of my syght.

18 But firste wyll I sufficientlye rewarde their shamefull blasphemies and synnes, wherwyth they haue defyled my lande: Namely, wyth their stinckyng Idols and obhominacions, wherwith they haue fylled myne heretage.

19 O Lorde, my strength, my power, and refuge in tyme of trouble. The Gentyles shall come vnto þe from the endes of the worlde, and saye: Verely our fathers haue cleued vnto lyes, their Idols are but vayne & vnprofitable.

20 How can a man make those his goddes, which are not able to be goddes.

21 And therfore I wyll ones teach them, sayeth the Lorde, I wyll shewe them my hande & my power, that they maye knowe, that my name is the Lorde.

## CHAPTER 17

Y OURE synne (O ye of the trybe of Iuda) is written in the table of youre hertes, and grauen so vpon the edges of your aulters wyth a penne of yron and wyth an adamant clawe:

2 that youre chyldren also maye thincke vpon youre aulters, woddes, thicke trees, hie hylles, mountaynes & feldes.

3 Wherfore, I will make all youre substaunce & treasure be spoyled, for the great synne that ye haue done vpon your hye places thorow out all the coastes of youre lande.

4 Ye shall be cast out also from the heretage, that I gaue you. And I wyll subdue you vnder the heuy bondage of youre enemyes, in a lande that ye knowe not. For ye haue mynystred fyre to my indignacyon, whyche shall burne euermore.

5 Thus sayeth the Lorde: Cursed be the man that putteth his trust in man, & that taketh flesh for hys arme: and he, whose herte departeth from the Lorde.

6 He shall be lyke the heeth, that groweth in the wildernes. As for the good thing that is for to come, he shal not se it: but dwell in a drye place of the wildernes, in a salt and vnoccupied lande.

7 O blessed is the man, that putteth hys trust in the Lorde, and whose hope is the Lorde hym selfe.

8 For he shalbe as a tre, that is planted by the water syde: which spredeth out þe rote vnto moystness, whom the heate can not harme, when it commeth, but his leaues are grene. And though there growe but lytle frute because of drouth, yet is he not carefull, but he neuer leaueth of to brynge forth fruite.

9 Amonge all thynges lyuinge, man hath the moste disceytfull and vnsercheable herte. Who shall then knowe it?

10 Euen I the Lorde search out the grounde of the herte, & trye the reynes, and rewarde euery man accordinge to hys wayes, and acordynge to the fruyte of his councels.

11 The dysceytfull maketh a nest, but bryngeth forth no yonge. He commeth by ryches, but not ryghtuously. In þe middest of his life must he leaue them behinde hym, and at the last be founde a very foole.

12 But thou (O Lord) whose trone is moste gloryous, excellent and of most antyquite, whych duellest in the place of oure holye reste:

13 Thou art the comforte of Israell. All they that forsake the, shal be confounded: all they that departe from the, shalbe wrytten in earth, for they haue forsaken the Lorde the very condyte of the waters of lyfe.

14 Heale me, O Lord, and I shall be whole: saue thou me, and I shalbe saued, for thou art my prayse.

15 Beholde, these men saye vnto me: Where is the worde of þe Lord: Lett it come.

16 Where as I neuertheles ledynge the flocke in thy wayes, haue compelled none by violence. For I neuer desyred eny mans deeth, this knowest thou well. My wordes also were right before the.

17 Be not now terryble vnto me, O Lorde, for thou art he in whom I hope, when I am in parell.

18 Let my persecuters be confounded, but not me: let them be afrayed, and not me. Thou shalt bringe vpon them the tyme of their plage, and shalt destroye them right sore.

19 Agayne, thus hath the Lorde sayde vnto me: Go and stande vnder the gate, where thorow the people and the kynges of Iuda go out and in, yee vnder all the gates of Ierusalem,

20 and saye vnto them: Heare þe worde of the Lorde, ye kynges of Iuda, and al thou people of Iuda, and all ye cytesyns of Ierusalem, that go thorowe thys gate:

21 Thus the Lorde commaundeth: Take hede for youre lyues, that ye carye no burthen vpon you in the Sabboth, to brynge it thorowe the gates of Ierusalem:

22 ye shall beare no burthen also out of youre houses in the Sabboth. Ye shall do no laboure therin, but halowe the Sabboth, as I commaunded youre fathers.

23 How be it they obeyed me not, nether herkened they vnto me: but were obstynate & stubburne, & nether obeyed me, nor receyued my correccyon.

24 Neuertheles, yf ye will heare me (sayet þe Lord) & beare no burthen in to þe cytie thorow this gate vpon the Sabboth: If ye wyll halowe the Sabboth, so that ye do no worcke therin:

25 then shall there go thorowe the gates of this cytie, kynges and prynces, that shall syt vpon the stole of Dauid: They shall be caried vpon charettes, and ryde vpon horses, both they and their prynces. Yee whole Iuda and all the cytesyns of Ierusalem shall goo here thorowe, and this cytye shall euer be the more and more inhabyted.

26 There shall come men also from the cyties of Iuda, from aboute Ierusalem, & from the lande of BenIamin, from the playne feldes, from the mountaynes and from the wyldernesse: whiche shall brynge burntofferynges, sacrifyces, oblacions, and incense, and offre vp thanckesgeuyng in the house of the Lord.

27 But yf ye wyll not be obedyent vnto me, to halow the Sabboth, so þt ye will beare youre burthens thorow the gates of Ierusalem vpon the Sabboth: Then shall I set fyre vpon the gates of Ierusalem, and it shall burne vp the houses of Ierusalem, and no man shall be able to quench it.

## CHAPTER 18

THIS is another communicacion, that God had with Ieremye, sayinge:

2 Aryse, and go downe into the Potters house, and there shall I tell the more of my mynde.

3 Now when I came to the Potters house, I founde hym makynge his worcke vpon a whele.

4 The vessell þt the Potter made of claye, brake amonge hys handes: So he beganne a new, and made another vessell, accordynge to hys mynde.

5 Then sayde the Lorde thus vnto me:

6 Maye not I do with you, as this Potter doth, O ye house of Israel, sayeth the Lord? Beholde, ye house of Israell: ye are in my hande, euen as the claye in the Potters hande.

7 When I take in hande to rote out, to destroye, or to waste awaye eny people or kingdome:

8 yf that people (agaynst whom I haue this deuysed) conuerte from their wickednes: Immediatly, I repente of the plage, that I deuysed to brynge vpon them.

9 Agayne. When I take in hande, to buylde, or to plante a people or a kyngdome:

10 yf the same people do euell before me, and heare not my voyce: Immediatly, I repente of the good, that I deuyse to do for them.

11 Speake now therfore vnto whole Iuda, and to them that dwell at Ierusalem: Thus sayeth the Lorde: Beholde, I am deuysynge a plage for you, and am takynge a thynge in hande agaynst you. Therfore let euery man turne from hys euell waye, take vpon you the thinge that is good, and do ryght.

12 But they saye: No more of this, we wyll folowe oure owne ymagynacyons, and do euery man accordyng to the wylfulnesse of his owne mynde.

13 Therfore thus sayeth þe Lord: Aske amonge the Heathen, yf eny man hath hearde soch horryble thynges, as the daughter of Syon hath done.

14 Shall not the snowe (that melteth vpon the stony rockes of Libanus) moysten the feldes? Or maye the sprynges of waters be so grauen awaye, that they runne no more, geue moystnesse, ner make fruitefull?

15 But my people hath so forgotten me, that they haue made sacryfyce vnto vayne Goddes. And whyle they folowed their owne wayes they are come out of the hye strete, & gone in to a fote waye not vsed to betroden.

16 Where thorowe they haue brought their lande in to an euerlastyng wyldernesse and scorne: So that whosoeuer trauayleth therby: shalbe abashed, and wagge their heades.

17 With an East wynde will I scatre them, before their enemyes. And when their destruccion commeth, I wyll turne my backe vpon them, but not my face.

18 Then sayde they: come, let vs ymagyn smothynge agaynst this Ieremy. Yee thys dyd euen the prestes, to whom the lawe was commytted: the Senatours, that were the wysest, and the prophetes, whiche wanted not the worde of God. Come (sayde they) lett vs cut out hys tunge, & let vs not regarde his wordes.

19 Consydre me, O Lorde, and heare the voyce of myne enemies.

20 Do they not recompence euell for good, when they dygg a pyt for my soule? Remembre, how that I stode before the, to speake for them, and to turne awaye thy wrath from them.

21 Therfore let their chyldren dye of hunger and lett them be oppressed with the swearde. Let their wyues be robbed of their chyldren, and become widdowes: let their housbandes be slayne, lett their yonge men

be kylled with the swearde in the felde.

22 Let the noyse be herde out of their houses, when the murtherer commeth sodenly vpon them: For they haue digged a pyt to take me, and layed snares for my fete.

23 Yet Lorde, thou knowest all their councell, that they haue deuysed, to slaye me. And therfore forgeue them not their wyckednes, and let not their synne be put out of thy syght: but lett them be iudged before the as the gyltye: Thys shalt thou do vnto them in the tyme of thy indygnacyon.

## CHAPTER 19

MOREOUER, thus sayde the Lorde vnto Ieremy: Go thy waye, and bye the an erthen pytcher, & bringe forthe the Senatours, & chefe preastes

2 in to the valley of the chyldren of Hennon, which lieth before the porte that is made of bryck, & shewe them there the wordes, that I shall tell the,

3 & saye thus vnto them: Heare the worde of the Lorde, ye kynges of Iuda, and ye cytesyns of Ierusalem: Thus sayeth the Lord of Hostes the God of Israel: Beholde, I will bring soche a plage vpon this place, that the eares of all that heare it, shall glowe.

4 And that because they haue forsaken me, and vnhalowed this place, and haue offred in it vnto straunge goddes: whome nether they, their fathers, ner þe kynges of Iuda haue knowne. They haue fylled this place also with the bloude of innocentes,

5 for they haue sett vp an aulter vnto Baall, to burne their children for a burntofferynge vnto Baall, which I nether commaunded, ner charged them, nether thought ones there vpon.

6 Beholde therfore, the time commeth (saieth the Lorde) that this place shall nomore be called. Topheth, ner the valley of the children of Hennom, but the valley of slaughter.

7 For in thys place wyll I slaye the Senatours of Iuda and Ierusalem, and kyll them downe with the swearde in þe syght of their enemyes and of them that seke their lyues. And theyr deed carcases wyll I geue to be meate for the foules of the ayre, and beastes of the felde.

8 And I wyll make this cytie so desolate, and despysed, that who so goeth ther by, shall be abashed and ieast vpon her, because of al her plages.

9 I wyll fede them also with the fleshe of their sonnes and their daughters. Yee euery one shall eate vp another in the besegynge & straytnesse, wherwith their enemyes (þt seke their lyues) shall kepe them in.

10 And the pytcher shalt thou breake in the syght of the men, that shalbe wyth the, and saye vnto them:

11 Thus sayeth the Lorde of Hostes: Euen so wyll I destroye thys people and cytie: as a Potter breaketh a vessell, that can not be made whole agayne. In Topheth shall they be buried, for they shall haue none other place.

12 Thus wyll I do vnto this place, also sayeth the Lorde, and to them that dwell therin: yee I wyl do to thys citie as vnto Topheth.

13 (For the houses of Ierusalem & the houses of the kynges of Iuda are defyled, lyke as Topheth) because of all þe houses, in whose parlers they dyd sacryfyce vnto all the hooste of heauen and poured out drincke offringes vnto straunge goddes.

14 And so Ieremye came from Topheth, where the Lorde had sent hym to prophecye, and stode in the courte of the house of the Lorde, and spake to all the people:

15 Thus sayeth the Lord of Hostes the God of Israell: Beholde, I will brynge vpon this cytie and vpon euery towne aboute it, all the plages that I haue deuysed agaynst them: for they haue bene obstinate, & wolde not obeye my warnynges.

## CHAPTER 20

WHEN Phashur the preaste, the sonne of Emer, chefe in the house of the Lorde, herde Ieremy preache so stedfastly:

2 he smote Ieremye, & put hym in the stockes, that are by the hye gate of BenIamim, in the house of the Lorde.

3 The nexte daye folowynge Phashur brought Ieremye out of the stockes agayne. Then sayde Ieremy vnto hym: The Lorde shall call the nomore Phashur (that is excellent and increasynge) but Magor (that is fearfull and afrayed) euery where.

4 For thus sayeth the Lorde: beholde, I wyll make the afrayed, the thy selfe, and all that fauoure the: which shall peryshe wyth the swearde of their enemyes, euen before thy face. And I wyll geue whole Iuda vnder the power of the kynge of Babylon, which shall carie some vnto Babylon presoners, & slaye some with the swearde.

5 Moreouer, all the substaunce of this lande, all their precyous and gorgeous worckes, all costlynesse, & all the treasure of the Kynges of Iuda: wyll I geue in to þe handes of their enemyes, which shall spoyle them, and carie them vnto Babylon.

6 But as for þe (O Phashur) thou shalt be caried vnto Babylon with all thine housholde, & to Babylon shalt thou come, where thou shalt dye, and be buryed: thou & all thy fauourers, to whom thou hast

preached lyes

7 O Lorde, thou makest me weake, but thou refreshest me, & makest me stronge agayne. All the daye longe am þe despysed, & laughed to scorne of euery man:

8 because I haue now preached longe agaynst malycious Tyranny, & shewed them of destruccion. For the which cause they cast the worde of the Lorde in my teeth, and take me euer to the worst.

9 Wherfore, I thought from hence forth, not to speake of hym, ner to preach eny more in hys name. But the worde of the Lorde was a very burnynge fyre in my herte and in my bones, which when I wolde haue stopped I might not.

10 For why, I herde so many derisyons and blasphemies, yee euen of myne owne companions, and of soch as were conuersaunte with me: whiche wente aboute, to make me afrayed, sayinge, vpon hym, let vs go vpon him to feare hym and make hym holde his tonge: þt we maye ouer come hym, and be auenged of hym.

11 But the Lorde stode by me, lyke a myghtie giaunte: therfore my persecuters fell, and coulde do nothing. They shall be sore confounded, for they haue done vnwysely, they shall haue an euerlastynge shame.

12 And now, O Lorde of Hostes, thou ryghtuous sercher (which knowest the reynes and the very hertes:) let me se them punished, for vnto the I commytte my cause.

13 Synge vnto the Lorde, and prayse hym, for he hath deliuered the soule of the oppressed, from the hande of the violent.

14 Cursed be the daye, wher in I was borne: vnhappye be the daye, wherin my mother brought me forth.

15 Cursed be the man, that brought my father þe tydinges, to make hym glad, saying: thou hast gotten a sonne.

16 Lett it happen vnto that man, as to the cyties whiche the Lorde turned vp syde downe (when he had hearde longe the wicked rumoure of them)

17 because he slewe me not, as sone as I came out of my mothers wombe, & because my mother was not my graue her selfe, that the byrth mighte not haue come out, but remayned styl in her.

18 Wherfore came I forth of my mother wombe? To haue experience of all laboure & sorow? & to leade my lyfe wyth shame?

# CHAPTER 21

THESE are þe wordes that þe Lord spake vnto Ieremye what time as Kynge Zedekiah sent vnto hym Pashur the sonne of Melchiah, and Sophoniah the sonne of Maasiah preaste, saying:

2 Aske councell at the Lorde (we praye the) of oure behalfe, for Nabuchodonosor the Kynge of Babylon besegeth vs, yf the Lorde (peraduenture) wyll deale wyth vs, accordynge to his maruelous power, and take hym from vs.

3 Then spake Ieremy. Geue Zedekiah this answere.

4 Thus sayeth the Lorde God of Israell, beholde, I wyll turne backe the weapens, that ye haue in youre handes, wherwith ye fyght agaynst the kynge of Babylon and the Caldees, whyche besege you rounde aboute the walles, and I wyl brynge them together in to the myddest of this cytie

5 and I my selfe wyll fight agaynst you, with an outstretched hande, and with a mightye arme, in great displeasure and terrible wrath

6 and wyll smyte them, that dwell in this cytye: yee both men and catell shall dye of the pestilence.

7 And after this (sayeth the Lorde) I shall delyuer Zedekiah the kynge of Iuda, & hys seruauntes, his people (& soch as are escaped in the cytie, from the pestilence, swearde, and honger) in to the power of Nabuchodonosor kynge of Babylon: yee in to the handes of their enemyes, in to the handes of those that folowe vpon their lyues, whiche shall smyte them with the swearde: they shall not pytie them, they shall not spare them, they shall haue no mercye vpon them.

8 And vnto this people thou shalt saye: Thus sayeth the Lord: beholde, I laye before you the waye of lyfe and death.

9 Who so abydeth in this cytie, shall perish: ether wt þe swearde, with honger, or with pestilence. But who so goeth out to holde on the Chaldees parte, þt besege it, he shall saue hys lyfe, and, shall wynne hys soule for a praye.

10 For I haue sett my face agaynst this cytie (sayeth the Lord) to plage it, and to do it no good. It muste be geuen in to the hande of the kynge of Babylon, and be brent with fyre.

11 And vnto the house of the kynge of Iuda, saye thus: Heare the worde of the Lorde

12 (O thou house of Dauid) for thus saieth þe Lord: Ministre ryghtuousnes, and that soone, delyuer the oppressed from vyolent power: or euer my terryble wrath breake oute lyke a fyre, and burne so, that no man maye quench it, because of the wyckednes of youre ymagynacions.

13 Beholde (sayeth the Lorde) I will come vpon you, that dwell in the valleyes, rockes & feldes, & saye: Tush: who will make vs afrayed? or who will come into oure houses?

14 For I wyll vyset you (sayeth the Lorde) because of the wickednes of youre inuencions and wyll kyndle soch a fyre in youre wod, as shall consume all, that is aboute you.

# CHAPTER 22

THUS sayde the Lorde also: Goo downe in to þe house of the kyng of Iuda, and speake there these wordes,

2 & saye: Heare the worde of the Lorde, thou kyng of Iuda that syttest in the kyngly seate of Dauid: thou and thy seruauntes and thy people, that go in and out at this gate.

3 Thus the Lorde commaundeth: kepe equyte and ryghtuousnesse, delyuer the oppressed from the power of the violent: do not greue ner opppresse the straunger, the fatherlesse ner the wyddowe, and shede no innocent bloude in this place.

4 And yf ye kepe these thinges faythfully, then shall there come in at the dore of thys house kynges, to syt vpon Dauids seate: they shall be caryed in Charettes and ryde vpon horses, both they & their seruauntes, & their people:

5 But yf ye wyll not be obedient vnto these commaundementes, I sweare by myne owne selfe (sayeth the Lorde) this house shall be waste.

6 For thus hath the Lord spoken vpon the kynges house of Iuda: Thou art the head as Galaad is in Libanus. What wylt thou saye of it, yf I make the not so waste (& thy cyties also) that no man shall dwell therin?

7 I will prepare a destroyer with his weapons for þe, to hew downe thy specyall Cedre trees and to cast them in the fyre.

8 And all the people that go by this cytie, shall speake one to another: Wherfore hath the Lorde done thus vnto thys noble cytye?

9 Then shall it be answered: because they haue broken the couenaunt of the Lorde their God, & haue worshipped & serued straunge goddes.

10 Mourne not ouer the deed, & be not wo for them, but be sory for hym that departeth awaye: for he commeth not agayne, and seeth his natyue countre no more.

11 For thus sayeth the Lorde, as touchynge Selum the sonne of Iosiah kynge of Iuda, whiche raygned after his father, and is caryed oute of this place: He shall neuer come hether agayne,

12 for he shall dye in the place, whervnto he is led captiue, and shall se this lande nomore.

13 Wo worth him, that buyldeth hys house with vnrightuousnes, and hys parlers with the good that he hath gotten by violence: which neuer recompenseth hys neyghbours laboure, ner payeth hym his hyre.

14 He thyncketh in hym selfe: I wyll buylde me a wyde house, and gorgeous parlers: He causet windowes to be hewen therin, and the sylynges and geastes maketh he of Cedre, & paynteth them with Zenober.

15 Thinckest thou to raigne, now that thou prouokest me to wrath wyth the Cedre trees? Dyd not thy father eate and drincke, and prospere well, as longe as he dealt wt equite and ryghtuousnesse?

16 Yee when he helped the oppressed and poore to their ryght then prospered he well. From whence came this, but onlye because he had me before hys eyes, sayth the Lorde.

17 Neuertheles, as for thyne eyes & thine herte, they loke vpon couetousnesse, to shede innocent bloude, to do wronge and violence.

18 And therfore, thus sayeth the Lorde agaynst Iehoakim, the sonne of Iosiah kynge of Iuda: They shall not mourne for hym (as they vse to do) alas brother, alas syster: Nether shall they saye vnto hym: Alas syre, alas for that noble prynce.

19 But as an Asse shall he be buried, corrupte and be cast without the gates of Ierusalem.

20 Clymme vp the hyll of Libanus (O thou daughter Sion) lyft vp thy voyce vpon Basan, crye from all partes: for all thy louers are destroyed.

21 I gaue the warnynge, whyle thou wast yet in prosperyte. But thou saydest: I wyll not heare. And thys maner haste thou vsed from thy youth, that thou woldest neuer heare my voyce.

22 All thy herdmen shalbe dryuen wyth the wynde, and thy derlynges shalbe caryed awaye in to captyuite: Then shalt thou be brought to shame & confusyon, because of all thy wickednes:

23 þt thou dwellest vpon Libanus, & makest thy neste in the Cedre trees. O how greate shall thy mourning be, when thy sorowes come vpon the, as a woman trauelynge with chylde?

24 As truelye as I lyue (sayeth the Lorde) Though Conaniah þe sonne of Iehoakim kynge of Iuda were the sygnet of my ryght hande, yet wyll I plucke hym of:

25 And I wyl geue the in to the power of them that seke to slaye the, and in to the power of the in that thou fearest: in to the power of Nabuchodonosor the Kynge of Babylon, and in to the power of the Caldees.

26 Moreouer, I wyll sende the, and thy mother that bare the, into a straunge lande, where ye were not borne, and there shall ye dye.

27 But as for the lande that ye will desyre to returne vnto ye shall neuer come at it agayne.

# JEREMIAH

28 This man Conaniah shall be lyke an ymage robbed and torne in peces, which pleaseth no man, for all hys apparell. Wherfore both he & hys sede shal be sent awaye, and cast out in to a lande, that they knowe not.

29 O thou earth, earth, earth: heare þe worde of the Lorde:

30 Wryte this man amonge the outlawes, for no prosperite shall this man haue all hys lyfe longe. Nether shall eny of his sede be so happie, as to syt vpon the seate of Dauid, and to beare rule in Iuda.

## CHAPTER 23

Wo be vnto the shepherdes, that destroye, and scatre my flocke, sayeth the Lorde.

2 Wherfore, thys is the commaundement of the Lorde God of Israel, vnto the shepherdes that fede my people: Ye scatre and thrust out my flocke, & loke not vpon them. Therfore now wyll I vyset the wickednes of youre ymaginacyons, sayeth the Lorde:

3 And will gather together the remnaunt of my flocke, from all landes that I had dryuen them vnto, & will bringe them agayne to their pastures, that they maye growe and increase.

4 I wyll sett shepherdes also ouer them whiche shall fede them. They shall no more feare and drede, for there shall none of them be loste, sayeth the Lorde.

5 Beholde, the tyme commeth, sayeth the Lorde, that I will rayse vp the ryghtuous braunche of Dauid, which shall beare rule, and discusse matters wyth wysdome, & shall sett vp equyte & rightuousnes agayne in the earth.

6 In hys tyme shall Iuda be saued and Israell shall dwell without feare. And thys is the name that they shall call hym: euen the Lorde oure ryghtuous maker.

7 And therfore beholde, the tyme commeth, sayeth the Lorde, that it shall no more be sayde: the Lorde lyueth, which brought the chyldren of Israell out of the lande of Egypte:

8 But the Lorde lyueth, which brought forth, and led the sede of the house of Israell, out of the North lande, and from all countrees where I had scatred them, & they shall dwell in their owne lande agayne.

9 My herte breaketh in my bodye because of the false prophetes, all my bones shake: I am become lyke a droncken man (that by the reason of wyne can take no reste) for verye feare of the Lorde, and of hys holy wordes:

10 Because þe lande is full of adulterers, where thorow it is destroyed and mourneth, and the pleasaunt pastures of the deserte are dryed vp. Yee the waye that men take, is wycked, and their gouernaunce is nothinge lyke the holy worde of the Lorde.

11 For the prophetes & the prestes them selues are poluted ypocrytes, and their wyckednes haue I founde in my house, sayeth the Lorde.

12 Wherfore, their waye shall be slypperye in the darcknesse, where in they maye stacker and fall. For I wyll bringe a plage vpon them, euen the yeare of their visytacyon, sayeth the Lorde.

13 I haue sene foly amonge the Prophetes of Samaria that they preached for Ball, & disceyued my people of Israel.

14 I haue sene also amonge the Prophetes of Ierusalem foule aduouterye, and presumptuous lyes. They take the moste shamefull men by the hande, flatryng them, so that they can not returne from their wickednes. All these wyth their cytesyns are vnto me, as Sodom, and as the inhabitours of Gomorre.

15 Therfore thus sayeth the Lorde of Hostes concernynge the prophetes: Beholde, I wyll fede them with wormwod, and make them dryncke the water of gall. For from the prophetes of Ierusalem is the syckenes and ypocrisye come in to all the lande.

16 And therfore the Lorde of Hostes geueth you this warnynge: Heare not the wordes of the prophetes, that preach vnto you, and disceyue you: for they speake the meanynge of their owne herte, and not out of the mouth of the Lorde.

17 They saye vnto them, that despyse me: The Lorde hath spoken it: Tush, ye shall prospere ryght well. And vnto all them, that walcke after the luste of their owne herte, they saye: Tushe, there shall no misfortune happen you.

18 For who hath sytten in the councell of the Lord, that he hath hearde and vnderstande, what he is aboute to do? Who hath marcked hys deuyce, and herde it?

19 Beholde, the stormy wether of the Lorde (that is his indignacyon) shall go forth, and shall fal downe vpon the head of the vngodlye.

20 And þe wrath of the Lorde shall not turne agayne, vntyll he perfourme and fulfull þe thoughte of his herte. And in the latter dayes ye shall knowe his meanynge.

21 I haue not sent these Prophetes (sayeth the Lorde) and yet they ranne. I haue not spoken to them, and yet they preached.

22 But yf they had contynued in my councell and herde my wordes: they had turned my people from their euell wayes and wycked ymagynacyons.

23 Am I then God that seyth but the thynge, whiche is nye at hande, and not that is farre of? Sayeth the Lorde.

24 Maye eny man hyde hym self so, that I shal not se him? sayeth the Lorde. Do not I fulfyll heauen and earth? sayeth the Lorde.

25 I haue herde well ynough, what the prophetes saye, that preache lyes in my name, sayinge: I haue dreamed, I haue dreamed.

26 How longe wyll this continue in the prophetes hertes, to tell lyes, and to preach þe craftye sotylete of their owne herte?

27 Whose purpose is (wyth the dreames that euery one tell) to make my people forgete my name, as their forefathers dyd, when Baal came vp.

28 The prophet that hath a dreame, let hym tell it: and he that vnderstandeth my worde, lett hym shewe it faythfully. For what hath chaffe and wheate to do together? sayeth the Lorde.

29 Is not my worde lyke a fyre, sayeth the Lorde, and lyke an hammer, that breaketh the harde stone?

30 Therfore thus sayeth the Lorde: beholde, I wyll vpon the prophetes, that steale my worde priuely from euery man.

31 Beholde, here am I (sayeth the Lorde) agaynst the prophetes, that take vpon their tunges to speake: The Lorde hath sayde it.

32 Beholde, here am I (sayeth the Lorde) agaynst those prophetes, that darre prophecye lyes, and dysceyue my people with their vanities, and myracles, whom I neuer sent, ner commaunded them. They shall do thys people greate harme, sayeth the Lorde.

33 If this people, ether eny prophet or preste aske the, and saye: what is the burthen of the Lorde? Thou shalt saye vnto them: What burthen? Therfore wyll I cast you fro me (sayeth the Lord) because ye youre selues are a burthen.

34 And the prophet, preste or people that vseth this terme (the burthen of the Lord) hym wyll I viset, and hys house also.

35 But thus shall ye saye, euery one to another: What answere hath the Lorde geuen? or, what is the Lordes commaundement?

36 And as for the burthen of the Lorde, ye shall speake nomore of it: for euerye mans owne worde is his burthen, because ye haue altered the wordes of the lyuynge God the Lorde of Hostes oure God.

37 Thus shall euerye man saye to the Prophetes: what answere hath the Lorde geuen the? Or, what sayeth the Lord?

38 And not ones to name the burthen of the Lorde. Therfore thus sayeth the Lord: For so moch as ye haue vsed thys terme (the burthen of the Lorde) where as I not withstandinge sent vnto you and forbade you to speake of the Lordes burthen.

39 Beholde therfore, I wyll repute you as a burthen, & will cast you out of my presence: yee and the cytie also, that I gaue you and youre fathers:

40 & will brynge you to an euerlastynge confusyon, and in to soch a shame, as shall neuer be forgotten.

## CHAPTER 24

THE Lorde shewed me a vysion: Beholde, there stode two maundes of fygges before the temple of the Lord, after that Nabuchodonosor kynge of Babylon had led awaye captyue Iechoniah the sonne of Iehoakim kynge of Iuda, the mightie men also of Iuda, with the worckmaysters, and connynge men of Ierusalem, vnto Babylon.

2 In the one maunde were verye good fygges, euen lyke as those that be fyrst rype. In the other maunde were verye naughtye fygges, which might not be eaten, they were so euell.

3 Then sayde the Lorde vnto me, what seyste thou Ieremy? I sayde: fyges, wherof some be verye good, and some so euell, that no man maye eate them.

4 Then came the worde of the Lorde vnto me, after this maner:

5 Thus sayeth the Lorde the God of Israell: lyke as thou knowest the good fyges, so shall I knowe the men led awaye, whom I haue sent out of thys place in to the lande of the Caldees, for their profyte:

6 and I wyll set myne eyes vpon them for the best, for I will brynge them agayne in to this lande: I wyll buylde them vp, and not breake them downe: I will plante them, and not rote them out.

7 And I wyll geue them an herte, to knowe, how that I am the Lorde. They shalbe my people, and I wyll be their God, for they shall returne vnto me wt their whole herte.

8 And lyke as thou knowest the naughtye fyges, whyche maye not be eaten, they are so euell: Euen so wyll I (sayeth the Lorde) lett Zedekiah the Kynge of Iuda (ye and all hys princes, and the resydue of Ierusalem that remayne ouer in this lande, and them also that dwell in Egypte) to be vexed & plaged in all kyngdomes & landes.

9 And wyll make them to be a reprofe, a comen by worde, a laughinge stocke and shame, in all the places, where I shall scatre them.

10 I wyll sende the swearde, honger & pestilence amonge them, vntyll I haue cleane consumed them out of the lande, that I gaue vnto them and their fathers.

## CHAPTER 25

A sermon that was geuen vnto Ieremy, vpon all the people

of Iuda: In the fourth yeare of Iehoakim the sonne of Iosiah Kynge of Iuda, that was, in the fyrste yeare of Nabuchodonosor kynge of Babilon,

2 Which sermon, Ieremy the prophet made vnto all the people of Iuda, and to all the inhabitours of Ierusalem, on thys maner.

3 From the .xiij. yeare of Iosiah the sonne of Amon kynge of Iuda, vnto this present daye (that is euen .xxiij. yeare) the worde of the Lorde hath bene commytted vnto me. And so I haue spoken to you, I haue rysen vp early I haue geuen you warnyng in season, but ye wolde not heare me.

4 Though the Lorde hath sent his seruauntes, all the prophetes vnto you in season: Yet wolde ye not obeye, ye wolde not enclyne youre eares to heare.

5 He sayde: turne agayne euery man from hys euell waye, & from your wicked ymaginacions, and so shall ye dwell for euer in the lande, that the Lorde promesed you & youre forefathers:

6 And go not after straunge goddes serue them not, worshipe them not, and angre me not wyth the worckes of youre handes: then wyll not I punish you.

7 Neuertheles, ye wolde not heare me (sayeth þe Lorde) but haue defyed me with the worckes of youre handes, to youre owne greate harme.

8 Wherfore thus sayeth þe Lorde of Hostes: Because, ye haue not herkened vnto my worde,

9 lo, I wyll sende out, call for all the people, that dwell in the North, sayeth the Lorde, and will prepayre Nabuchodonosor the kynge of Babylon my seruaunt, and will bringe them vpon this lande, & vpon all that dwell therin, and vpon all the people that are aboute them, & will vtterly rote them oute. I wyll make of them a wyldernesse, a mockage and a continuall deserte.

10 Moreouer, I will take from them the voyce of gladnesse and solace, the voyce of the brydegrom & þe bryde, the voyce of þe anoynted, wyth the cresshettes:

11 and this whole lande shall become a wyldernes, & they shall serue þe sayde people & the kynge of Babylon, thre score yeares and ten.

12 When the .lxx. yeares eare expyred, I wyll vyset also the wickednesse of the kynge of Babylon & hys people sayeth the Lorde: ye and the land of the Caldees, and wyll make it a perpetuall wyldernes,

13 and will fulfyl al my wordes vpon that land, which I haue deuysed agaynst it: ye all that is wrytten in this boke, whyche Ieremy hath prophecyed of al people:

14 so that they also shal be subdued vnto diuerse nacyons and greate kinges, for I wil recompense them, accordyng to theyr dedes and worckes of their owne handes.

15 For thus hath the Lord God of Israel spoken vnto me: Take this wyne cuppe of indignacion fro my hande, that thou mayeste cause al the people, to whom I sende the, for to drincke of it:

16 that when they haue drouncken therof, they may be mad, and out of their wyttes, when the swearde commeth, that I wyll sende amonge them.

17 Then toke I the cuppe from the Lordes hande, and made all the people dryncke therof, vnto whom the Lorde had sent me.

18 But fyrst the cytie of Ierusalem, and all the cytyes of Iuda, theyr kinges and princes to make them desolate, waste, despised & cursed according as it is come to passe this day.

19 Ye & Pharao the kinge of Egipt, his seruauntes, his prynces & hys people altogether one with another

20 & al kinges of the land of Hus, al kinges of the Philistines lande, Ascalon, Azah, Accaron & the remnaunt of Asdod,

21 the Edomites, the Moabites & the Ammonites:

22 al the kinges of Tirus & Sidon: the kynges of the Iles, that are beyonde the se:

23 Dedan, Thema, Buz and the shauen Ismaelites:

24 all the kynges of Araby, and (generally) all the kynges that dwell in the deserte:

25 all the kynges of Zamri, al the kinges of Elam, all the kynges of the Meedes,

26 all kynges towarde the North, whether they be farre or nye, euery one with his neyghboures: Ye and all the kyngdomes that are vpon the whole earth. The kynge of Sezach, sayde he, shal drincke with them also.

27 And saye thou vnto them: This is the commaundement of the Lorde of hostes the God of Israel: Drincke and be droncken, spewe & fall, that ye neuer ryse: and that thorow the swearde, whyche I wyll sende amonge you.

28 But yf they wyl not receyue the cuppe of thy hande, and drincke it, then tell them: Thus doeth the Lord of Hostes threaten you: drinck it ye shal, and that shortly.

29 For lo, I begynne to plage the cyty, that my name is geuen vnto: thynke ye then, that I will leaue you vnpunyshed? Ye shal not go quyte. For why, I call for a swearde vpon al the inhabitours of the earth, sayeth the Lord of Hostes.

30 Therfore tell them all these wordes, and saye vnto them: The Lorde shall crye from aboue, and let hys voyce be hearde from his holy habitacion. Wyth a greate

noyse shall he crye from his courte regall. He shall geue a greate voyce (like the grape gatherers) and the sounde thereof shalbe hearde vnto þe endes of the worlde.

31 For the Lorde had a iudgement to geue vpon all people, and wyll holde hys courte of iustice with all fleshe and punyshe the vngodly, sayeth the Lorde.

32 For thus sayeth the Lorde of hostes: Beholde, a miserable plage shall go from one people to another, and a greate stormye water shall aryse from all the endes of the earth.

33 And the same daye shall the Lorde hym selfe slaye them, from one ende of the earth to another. There shall no mone be made for any of them, none gathered vp, none buried: but shal lye as donge vpon the grounde.

34 Mourne (O ye shepeherdes) & crie: sprinkle youre selues wyth ashes, O ye rammes of þe flocke: for the tyme of youre slaughter is fulfilled, and ye shall fall lyke vessels conningly made for pleasure.

35 The shepherdes shall haue no waye to fle, and the rammes of the flocke shall not escape.

36 Then shall the shepeherdes crye horryblye, & the rammes of the flocke shall mourne: for the Lorde shall consume theyr pasture,

37 & theyr best feldes shall lye dead because of the horryble wrath of the Lorde.

38 They shall forsake theyr foldes lyke as a lyon: For theyr landes shalbe waste, because of the wrathe of the destroyer, and because of hys feareful indygnacyon.

## CHAPTER 26

IN the begynninge of the raigne of Iehoakim the sonne of Iosiah kinge of Iuda, came thys worde from the Lorde, saying:

2 Thus sayeth the Lorde: Stand in the courte of the Lordes house, and speake vnto all them whiche (oute of the cyties of Iuda) come to do worshyppe in þe Lordes house, all the wordes that I commaunde the to saye. Loke that thou kepe not one worde backe,

3 yf (peraduenture) they wyll herken, and turne euery man from hys wycked waye: that I maye also repente of the plage, whiche I haue determed to brynge vpon them, because of theyr wycked inuencyons.

4 And after thys maner shalte thou speake vnto them: Thus saith the Lorde: yf ye wyll not obeye me, to walcke in my lawes, whiche I haue geuen you,

5 and to heare the wordes of my seruauntes the Prophetes, whome I sente vnto you, rysynge vp tymelye, and styl sendyng: If ye wyll not folowe them (I saye)

6 then wyll I do to this house, as I dyd vnto Siloh, and wil make this cytie to be abhorred of all the people of the earth.

7 And the priestes the Prophetes and all the people hearde Ieremye preache these wordes, in the house of þe Lorde.

8 Nowe when he had spoken oute all þe wordes, that the Lorde commaunded hym to preach vnto all the people, then the Priestes, þe Prophetes, and all the people toke holde vpon him, and sayde: thou shalte dye.

9 How darrest thou be so bolde, as to saye in the name of the Lord it shall happen to thys house as it dyd vnto Siloh? and this citie shalbe so waste, that no man shall dwell therein?

10 And when all the people were gathered aboute Ieremye in the house of the Lorde, the prynces of Iuda hearde of this rumoure and they came sone oute of the Kynges palace, into the house of the Lorde, and sat them doune before the new dore of the Lorde.

11 Then spake the priestes and the Prophetes vnto þe rulers, & to all the people, these wordes: This man is worthy to dye, for he hath preached agaynste this citie, as ye youre selues haue hearde with youre eares.

12 Then sayde Ieremye vnto the rulers and to all the people: The Lorde hath sente me to preache agaynste this house and agaynst this cytie all the wordes that ye haue hearde.

13 Therfore amende youre wayes, and your aduysementes, and be obedyente vnto the voyce of the Lorde youre God: so shall the Lorde repent of the plage, that he had deuysed against you.

14 Nowe as for me: I am in youre handes, do wyth me, as ye thincke expedyent & good.

15 But thys shal ye know: yf ye put me to death ye shall make youre selues, thys cytye and al the inhabytours thereof, gyltye of innocente bloude. For thys is of a trueth: that the Lorde hath sente me vnto you, to speake al these wordes in youre eares.

16 Then sayde the rulers and the people vnto the priestes and Prophetes: This man maye not be condemned to death, for he hath preached vnto vs in the name of the Lorde oure God.

17 The Elders also of the lande stode vp, and sayde thus vnto all the people:

18 Micheah the Morasthite, which was a Prophet vnder Ezekiah kynge of Iuda, spake to all þe people of Iuda: Thus sayeth the Lorde of Hostes: Syon shalbe plowed lyke a felde, Ierusalem shalbe an heape of stones, and the hyll of the Lordes house shalbe turned to an hye wood.

19 Dyd Ezekiah the kyng of Iuda, & the people of Iuda put

him to death for this? No, verely but rather feared the Lord, & made their prayer vnto hym. For the whiche cause also the Lorde repented of the plage, þt he had deuysed agaynst them. Shulde we then do suche a shamefull dede agaynst oure soules:

20 There was a Prophete also, that preached styflye in þe name of the Lorde, called Vriah the sonne of Semeiah of Cariathiarim: this man preached also agaynst thys cytye and against this lande, accordynge to all as Ieremye sayth.

21 Nowe when Iehoakim the kyng wyth al the estate and pryncen had hearde his wordes, the kynge went about to slaye hym. When Vriah perceyued that, he was afrayed, & fled, and departed into Egypte.

22 Then Iehoakim the kinge sente seruauntes into the lande of Egypte. Namely, Elnathan the sonne of Achabor, and certayne men with him into Egipte,

23 whiche fetched Vriah oute of Egypte, and brought hym vnto kyng Iehoakim that slewe hym with the sweard, and caste hys dead bodye into the comon peoples graue.

24 But Ahikam the sonne of Saphan helped Ieremye, that he came not into the handes of the people to be slayne.

# CHAPTER 27

IN the beginninge of the raigne of Iehoakim the sonne of Iosiah kynge of Iuda, came this word vnto Ieremye from the Lorde, which spake thus vnto me:

2 Make the bondes & chaynes, & put them aboute thy necke,

3 & sende them to the kynge of Edom, the Kynge of Moab, the kynge of Ammon, the Kynge of Tyrus, and to the Kynge of Sydon: and that by the messaungers, whiche shall come to Ierusalem vnto Zedekiah the kynge of Iuda,

4 and byd them saye vnto theyr maisters Thus sayth the Lorde of Hostes the God of Israell, speake thus vnto youre maysters:

5 I am he that made the earthe, the men, & the catell that are vpon the grounde, with my great power and outstretched arme, & haue geuen it vnto whome it pleased me.

6 And nowe wyl I delyuer all these landes into the power of Nabuchodonosor the Kynge of Babylon, my seruuant. The beastes also of the felde shall I geue hym to do hym seruyce.

7 And all people shall serue hym, and hys sonne, and hys chyldes chyldren, vntyll the tyme of the same lande become also: yea many people & greate Kynges shall serue hym.

8 Moreouer, that people and kyngedome whiche wyll not serue Nabuchodonosor, and that wyll not put theyr neckes vnder þe yock of the kynge of Babylon: the same people wil I vpset with the swearde, wyth honger, with pestylence, vntyll I haue consumed them in hys handes, sayeth the Lorde.

9 And therfore folowe not youre Prophetes, sothsayers, expounders of dreames, charmers and wytches whiche saye vnto you: ye shall not serue the Kynge of Babylon.

10 For they preache you lyes: to brynge you farre from your lande, and that I myghte caste you oute, and destroye you.

11 But the people that put theyr neckes vnder the yocke of the Kynge of Babylon, and serue hym, those I wyll let remayne styll in theyr owne lande (sayeth the Lorde) and they shall occupye it, and dwell therein.

12 All these thynges tolde I Zedekiah the Kynge of Iuda, and sayde: Put youre neckes vnder the yocke of the Kynge of Babylon, & serue hym & hys people, that ye maye lyue.

13 Why wylte thou and thy people perysh with the swearde, wyth honger, wyth pestylence: lyke as the Lorde hath deuysed for all people, that wyll not serue the kynge of Babylon?

14 Therfore geue no eare vnto those Prophetes that tell you: Ye shall not serue the kynge of Babylon, for they preache you lyes,

15 neyther haue I sente them, sayeth the Lorde: howebeit they are bolde, falsely to prophecye in my name, that I myghte the sooner dryue you oute, and that ye myghte peryshe wyth youre preachers.

16 I spake to the Pryestes also, and to all the people: Thus sayth the Lorde: Heare not the wordes of those Prophetes, that preache vnto you, and saye: Beholde, the vessels of the Lordes house shall shortly be brought hyther agayne from Babylon: For they prophecye lyes vnto you.

17 Heare them not, but serue the Kynge of Babylon, that ye maye lyue. Wherfore will ye make this citie to be destroyed?

18 But yf they be true Prophetes in very dede, and yf the worde of the Lorde be commytted vnto them, then let them praye þe Lord of Hoostes, that the remnaunte of the ornamentes (whiche are in the house of the Lorde, and remayne yet in the house of the King of Iuda and at Ierusalem) be not caryed to Babylon also.

19 For thus hath the Lorde of hostes spoken concerning the pylers, the lauer, the seate and the resydue of the ornamentes that yet remaine in this citie,

20 which Nabuchodonosor the King of Babylon toke not, when he caryed awaye Iechoniah the sonne of Iehoakim Kynge of Iuda, wyth all the power of Iuda and Ierusalem,

# JEREMIAH

from Ierusalem vnto Babylon, captyue.

21 Yea thus hath the Lorde of hoostes the God of Israell spoken, as touchynge the resydue of the ornamentes of the Lordes house of the kynge of Iudaes house, and of Ierusalem:

22 They shalbe caryed vnto Babylon, & there they shall remayne, vntyll I vpset them sayeth the Lorde. Then wyll I brynge them hyther agayne.

## CHAPTER 28

AND thys was done in the same yeare: euen in the begynnynge of the raygne of Zedekiah kynge of Iuda. (28:1) Bvt in the fourthe yeare of the raygne of Zedekiah kyng of Iuda, in the fyfth moneth, It happened, þt Hananiah þe sonne of Assur þe Prophet of Gabaon, spake to me in þe house of the Lord, in the presence of the priestes & of al the people, & sayd.

2 Thus sayeth the Lorde of Hostes the God of Israel: I haue broken the yocke of the kynge of Babilon,

3 and after two yeare wyll I bryng againe into thys place, all the ornamentes of the Lordes house, that Nabuchodonosor kynge of Babylon caryed away from thys place vnto Babylon.

4 Yea, I wyll brynge agayne Iechoniah the sonne of Iehoakim the kynge of Iuda hym selfe, with all the prysonners of Iuda (þt are caryed vnto Babylon) euen into this place sayeth the Lorde, for I wyll breake the yoeke of the kynge of Babylon.

5 Then the Prophet Ieremye gaue aunswere vnto þe Prophete Hananiah, before the prestes and before all the people that were presente in the house of the Lorde.

6 And the Prophet Ieremye sayd: Amen: the Lord do that, & graunt the thynge, whiche thou hast prophecyed: that he maye brynge agayne all the ornamentes of the Lordes house, and restore all the presonners from Babylon into the place.

7 Neuertheles, herken thou also, what I wyll saye, that thou and all the people maye heare:

8 The Prophetes that were before vs in tymes paste, whiche prophecyed of warre, or trouble, or pestilence,

9 eyther of peace, vpon many nacyons and greate kyngedomes, were proued by this (yf God had sende them in very dede) when þe thynge came to passe, whiche that Prophete tolde before.

10 And Hananiah the Prophete toke þe chaine from the Prophet Ieremies neck, and brake it

11 and with that sayde Hananiah, that all the people myghte heare: Thus hath the Lorde spoken: Euen so wyll I breake the yocke of Nabuchodonosor kynge of Babylon, from the necke of all nacyons, yea & that within thys two yeare. And so the Prophete Ieremye went hys waye.

12 Now after that Hananiah the prophet had taken the chayne from the Prophete Ieremyes necke, and broken it: The worde of the Lord came vnto the Prophete Ieremy saiynge:

13 Go, and tell Hananiah these wordes: Thus sayeth the Lorde: Thou haste broken the chayne of wode, but in steade of woode thou shalte make chaynes of yron.

14 For thus sayth the Lorde of hostes the God of Israel: I will put a yocke of yron vpon the necke of all thys people, þt they maye serue Nabuchodonosor the kynge of Babylon, yea & so shal they do. And I wyll geue him the beastes in the felde.

15 Then sayde the Prophete Ieremye vnto the prophet Hananiah: Heare me (I praye the) Hananiah: The Lorde hath not sent the, but thou bringest this people into a false belefe.

16 And therfore thus sayth the Lorde: beholde, I wyll sende the out of the land, & within a year thou shalte dye because thou haste falsely spoken agaynste the Lord.

17 So Hananiah the Prophete dyed the same yeare in the seuenth moneth.

## CHAPTER 29

THIS is the copye of the lettre, þt Ieremye the Prophete sent from Ierusalem vnto the presoners: the Senatours, priestes, prophetes, and al the people, whome Nabuchodozor had led vnto Babylon:

2 after þe tyme that kynge Iechoniah, and his Quene, hys chamberlaynes the princes of Iuda & Ierusalem the worckemaysters of Ierusalem were departed thyther.

3 Whiche lettre Elasah the sonne of Saphan and Gamariah the sonne of Helkiah dyd beare, whome Zedekiah the kynge of Iuda sente vnto Babylon to Nabuchodonosor the kynge of Babylon: these were the wordes of Ieremyes lettre.

4 Thus hathe the Lorde of hostes the God of Israell spoken vnto all the presonners, that were led from Ierusalem vnto Babilon:

5 buyld you houses to dwell therein: plante you gardens, that ye maye enioye the frutes thereof:

6 take you wyues, to beare you sonnes & doughters: prouyde wyues for youre sonnes, and husbandes for youre doughters, þt they maye get sonnes and doughters, and that ye maye multyplye there. Laboure not to be fewe,

7 but seke after peace & prosperite of the citie, where in ye be presoners, and praye vnto

God for it: For in the peace thereof, shall youre peace be.

8 For thus sayth the Lorde of hostes the God of Israell: Let not those prophetes and sothsayers that be amonge you dysceyue you: and beleue not youre owne dreames.

9 For why, they preach you lyes in my name, and I haue not sente them, sayeth the Lorde.

10 But thus sayeth the Lorde: When ye haue fulfylled .lxx. yeares at Babylon, I wil bring you home, & of myne owne goodnes I wyll carye you hyther agayne vnto this place.

11 For I knowe what I haue deuysed for you sayeth the Lorde. My thoughtes are to geue you peace, and not trouble (whiche I geue you all redye) & þt ye might haue hope agayn.

12 Ye shal crye vnto me, ye shall go & call vpon me, & I shall heare you.

13 Ye shall seke me & fynde me, Yea, yf so be that ye seke me with your whole herte,

14 I wyl be founde of you (sayeth þe Lord) & wil delyuer you out of preson, & gather you together agayne oute of all places, wherein I haue scatred you, sayeth the Lord: & wil bring you agayne to the same place, from whence I caused you to be caryed awaye captyue.

15 But where as ye say, that God hath raysed you vp Prophetes at Babylon:

16 Thus hath the Lorde spoken (concernyng the kyng that sytteth in the stole of Dauid, and all the people that dwell in thys cytye, youre brethren that are not gone with you into captyuyte)

17 Thus (I saye) speaketh the Lorde of hoostes: Beholde I wyll sende a swearde, honger and pestilence vpon them, and wyll make them like vntymelye fyges, that maye not be eaten for bytternes.

18 And I wyll persecute them wyth the swearde, with honger and death. I wyll delyuer them vp to be vexed of all Kyngedomes, to be cursed, abhorred, laughed to scorne, and put to confusyon of all the people, amonge whome I haue scatred them:

19 and that because they haue not bene obedyent vnto my commaundementes (sayeth the Lorde) whiche I sente vnto them by my seruauntes the prophetes. I stode vp earlye, and sent vnto them, but they wolde not heare, sayeth the Lorde.

20 Heare therfore the worde of the Lorde, all ye presonners, whome I sent from Ierusalem vnto Babylon:

21 Thus hath the Lorde of hoostes the God of Israell spoken, of Ahab the sonne of Colaiah, and of Zedekiah the sonne of Maasiah, whiche prophecye lyes vnto you in my name: Beholde I wyll delyuer them into the hande of Nabuchodonozor the kynge of Babylon, that he maye slaye them before youre eyes.

22 And all the presonners of Iuda that are in Babylon, shall take vpon them thys terme of cursynge, and saye: Now God do vnto the, as he dyd vnto Zedekiah & Ahab, whome the kynge of Babylon rosted in the fyre,

23 because they synned shamefullye in Israell. For they haue not onely defyled their neighbours wyues, but also preached lieng wordes in my name, whiche I haue not commaunded them. Thys I testifye, and assure, sayeth the Lorde.

24 But as for Semeiah the Nehelamyte thou shalte speake vnto him:

25 Thus sayeth the Lorde of hoostes the God of Israell: Because thou haste sealed letters vnder thy name, vnto all the people that is at Ierusalem, and to Sophoniah the sonne of Maasiah the priest, yea and sente them to al the priestes: wherein thou wrytest thus vnto hym:

26 The Lorde hath ordened the to be prieste in steade of Iehoiada the prieste, that thou shuldest be the chefe in the house of the Lorde aboue all Prophetes and preachers, and that thou myghteste put them in preson, or in the stockes,

27 How happeneth it then, that thou haste not reproued Ieremye of Anathoth, whiche neuer leaueth of hys prophecyenge,

28 And besyde all thys, he hath sente vs worde vnto Babylon, and tolde vs planelye, that oure captyuyte shall longe endure: that we shuld buylde vs houses to dwel there in, and to plante vs gardens, that we mighte enioye the frutes thereof.

29 Whiche lettre Sophoniah the prieste dyd rede, and let Ieremye the Prophet heare it.

30 Then came the worde of the Lorde vnto Ieremye, sayenge:

31 Sende worde to all them that be in captiuite, on thys maner: Thus hath the Lorde spoken concernynge Semeiah the Nehelamite: Because that Semeiah hath prophecyed vnto you wythoute my commyssyon, & broughte you into a false hope,

32 therfor thus the Lorde doeth certyfye you: Beholde, I wyll vpset Semeiah the Nehelamite, and hys sede: so that none of hys shall remayne amonge thys people, and none of them shall se the good, that I wyl do for thys people, saith the Lorde, For he hath preached falsely of the Lorde.

# CHAPTER 30

THESE are the wordes, that the Lorde shewed vnto Ieremye, sayenge:

2 Thus saith the Lorde God of Israell: Wryte vp dylygentlye al the wordes, that I haue spoken vnto the, in a boke.

3 For lo, þe time commeth (sayth the Lorde) that I wyl brynge agayne the presonners of my people of Israel and Iuda, sayeth the Lord: For I wyl restore them vnto the lande, that I gaue to theyr fathers, and they shall haue it in possessyon.

4 Agayne, these wordes spake the Lorde, concernynge Israell and Iuda:

5 Thus sayeth the Lord: We heare a terryble crye, fear & disquietnesse.

6 For what els doth thys sygnyfye, that I se? Namely, that al strong men smyte, euerye man hys hande vpon hys loynes, as a woman in the payne of her trauayle. Who euer sawe a man trauayle wyth chylde? Enquere thereafter, and se. Yea al theyr faces are maruelous pale:

7 Alas for this daye, whiche is so dredefull, that none maye be lykened vnto it: and alas for the tyme of Iacobs trouble, from the whiche he shall yet be delyuered.

8 For in that daye, sayeth the Lorde, I wyll take his yocke from of thy rocke, & breake thy bondes. They shall no more serue straunge Goddes vnder hym,

9 but they shall do seruyce vnto God their Lorde, and to Dauid theyr Kynge, whome I wyll rayse vp vnto them.

10 And as for the, O my seruaunt Iacob, feare not (sayth the Lord) and be not afrayed, O Israell. For lo, I wyll helpe the also from farre, and thy sede from the lande of theyre captiuite. And Iacob shall turne agayne, he shalbe in rest, and haue a prosperous lyfe, and no man shal make hym afrayed.

11 For I am wyth the, to helpe the, sayeth the Lorde. And thoughe I shall destroye all the people, amonge whome I haue scatred the, yet wyll I not destroy the but correcte the, and that with dyscrecion. For I knowe, that thou arte in no wyse wythoute faute.

12 Therfore thus sayeth the Lorde: I am sory for thy hurte and woundes.

13 There is no man to medle with thy cause, or to bynde vp thy woundes: there maye no man helpe the.

14 All thy louers haue forgotten the, and care nothynge for the. For I haue geuen the a cruell stroke, and chastened the roughly: and that for the multitude of thy mysdedes, for thy synnes haue had the ouer hande.

15 Why makest thou moue for thy harme? I my selfe haue pyte of thy sorowe, but for the multytude of thy mysdedes and synnes, I haue done this vnto the.

16 And therfore all they that deuoure the, shalbe deuoured, and all thyne enemyes shall be led into captiuite. All they that make the wast, shalbe wasted them selues: and al those that robbe the, wyl I make also to be robbed.

17 For I wyll geue the thy healthe agayne, and make thy woundes whole, sayeth the Lorde, because they reuyled the, as one caste awaye, and despysed, O Syon.

18 For thus sayth the Lorde: Beholde, I will set vp Iacobs tentes agayne, and defende his dwellynge place. The cytye shalbe buylded in her olde estate, and the houses shall haue theyr ryghte foundacyon.

19 And oute of them shall go thankesgeuynge, and the voyce of ioye. I wyll multyplye them, and they shall not mynishe: I shall endue them wyth honoure, and no man shall subdue them.

20 Theyr chyldren shalbe as a fore tyme, and theyr congregacyon shall contynue in my syghte. And all those that vexe them, wyll I vyset.

21 A captayne also shall come of them, and a prince shall sprynge oute from the myddest of them: hym wyll I chalenge to my self, and he shall come vnto me. For what is he, that geueth ouer hys herte to come vnto me, sayth the Lorde.

22 Ye shalbe my people also, and I wylbe youre GOD.

23 Beholde, on the other syde shall the wrathe of the Lorde breake oute as a stormye water, as a myghtye whyrle wynde: and shall fall vpon the heades of the vngodly.

24 The terryble dyspleasure of the Lorde shall not leaue of, vntyll he haue done, and perfourmed the intente of hys herte, whiche in the latter dayes ye shal vnderstande.

# CHAPTER 31

AT the same tyme (sayeth the Lorde) shall I be the God of all the generacions of Israel, and they shalbe my people.

2 Thus saieth the Lorde: The people of Israel which escaped in the wyldernes from the sweard, founde grace to come into their rest.

3 Euen so shall the Lorde nowe also apeare vnto me from farre, & saye: I loue the with an euerlastyng loue, therfore do I sprede my mercye before the.

4 I will repayre the agayne (O thou doughter of Israel) that thou mayest be faste and sure. Thou shalt take thy tabrettes againe, and go forth with them, that lede the daunce.

5 Thou shalte plante vynes agayne vpon the hylles of Samaria, and the grape gatherers shall plante, and synge.

6 And when it is tyme, the watche men vpon the mounte of Ephraim shall crye: Aryse, let vs go vp vnto Syon to oure Lorde God,

# JEREMIAH

7 for thus sayeth the Lorde: Reioyce wyth gladnes because of Iacob, crye vnto the heade of the Gentyles: speake oute, synge, and saye: The Lorde shall delyuer hys people, the remnaunte of Israell, and make them whole

8 Beholde, I wyll brynge them agayne from oute of the north lande, and gather them from the endes of the worlde, wyth the blynde and lame that are amonge them, wyth the wemen that be greate wyth chylde, and suche as be also delyuered: and the companye of them that come agayne, shall be greate.

9 They departed from hence in heuynes, but wyth ioye wyll I brynge them hyther agayne. I wyl lede them by the ryuers of water in a straighte waye, where they shall not stomble: For I wyll be Israels father, and Ephraim shalbe my fyrstborne.

10 Heare the worde of the Lorde, O ye Gentyles, preache in the Iles that lye farre of, & saye: he that hath scatred Israell, shall gather hym together agayne, and shall kepe hym as a shepeherde doth hys flocke.

11 For the Lorde shall redeme Iacob, and ryde hym from the hand of the vyolente.

12 And they shal come, & reioyce vpon the hyll of Syon, and shall haue plenteousnes of goodes, whiche the Lorde shall geue them: Namely, wheate, wyne, oyle yonge shepe & calues. And theyr concyence shalbe as well watred garden, for they shal no more be hongrye.

13 Then shall the mayde reioyce in the daunce yea both yonge and olde folkes. For I wyll turne theyr sorowe into gladnesse, and wyll comforte them, and make them ioyfull, euen from theyr hertes.

14 I wyll poure plenteousnes vpon the hertes of the Priestes, and my people shalbe satisfyed with good thinges, saith the Lorde.

15 Thus sayth the Lorde: The voyce of heuynes, wepinge and lamentacyon came vp into heauen: euen of Rachell mournynge for her chyldren, and wolde not be comforted, because they were awaye.

16 But now sayeth the Lorde: leaue of from wepynge and crienge, withholde thyne eyes from feares, for thy laboure shalbe rewarded sayeth the Lorde. And they shall come againe oute of the lande of theyr enemyes:

17 Yea euen thy posterite shall haue consolacion in thys, (saieth the Lorde) that thy children shall come agayne into theyr owne lande.

18 Moreouer I hearde Ephraim, that was led awaye captyue, complayne on thys maner: O Lorde, thou haste correcte me, and thy chastening haue I receyued, as an vntamed calfe. Conuerte thou me, and I shalbe conuerted, for thou arte my Lorde God:

19 Yea as sone as thou turnest me, I shall refourme my self: and when I vnderstande, I shall smyte vpon my thyghe. For verelye I haue committed shamefull thinges: O let my youth beare this reprofe and confusyon.

20 Vpon this complainte, I thoughte thus by my selfe: is not Ephraim my deare sonne? Is he not the chylde, with whom I haue had all myrthe and pastyme? For sence the tyme that I fyrst commened with him, I haue him euer in remembraunce: therfore my verye herte dryueth me vnto hym, gladly and louynglye will I haue mercy vpon him, sayth þe Lorde.

21 Get the watchemen, prouyde teachers for the set thyne herte vpon the right waye, that thou shuldest walcke, and turne agayne (O thou doughter of Israell) turne agayne to these cytyes of thyne.

22 Howe longe wilte thou go astraye, O thou shrinkinge doughter? For the Lorde wil worke a new thynge vpon earthe: A woman shall compasse a man.

23 For thus sayeth the Lorde of hostes the God of Israell: It wil come therto, that when I haue brought Iuda oute of captyuyte, these wordes shalbe hearde in the lande and in his cities: The Lorde, whiche is the fayre brydegrome of ryghtuousnesse, make the frutefull O thou holy hyll:

24 And there shall dwell Iuda, and all her cities, the shepeherdes and husband men.

25 For I shall fede the hongry soule, & refreshe al faint hertes.

26 When I heard this I came agayne to my selfe, and mused, like as I had bene waked oute of a swete slepe.

27 Beholde (sayeth the Lorde) the dayes come, that I will sowe the house of Israell and the house of Iuda, with men & with catell.

28 Yea it shall come therto, that lyke as I haue gone about in tymes paste to rote them out, to scatre them, to breake them doune, to destroye them and chasten them: Euen so wyll I also go dylygentlye aboute, to buylde them vp agayne and to plante them, sayeth the Lorde.

29 Then shall it no more be sayde: the fathers haue eaten a sower grape, and the chyldrens teeth are set on edge:

30 for euerye one shall dye for his owne misdede, so that who so eateth a sower grape, hys teeth shalbe set on edge.

31 Beholde, the dayes come (sayeth the Lord) that I wil make a newe couenaunt with the house of Israell & with the house of Iuda:

32 not after the couenaunte that I made wyth theyr fathers,

when I toke them by the hande, and led them oute of the lande of Egypte: whiche couenaunte they brake, wherfore I punyshed them sore, sayeth the Lorde:

33 But thys shall be the couenaunte that I wyll make with the house of Israel after those dayes, sayeth the Lorde: I wyll plante my lawe in the inwarde partes of them, & wryte it in theyr hertes, and wilbe theyr God, and they shalbe my people.

34 And from thence forth shall no man teache his neyghboure or his brother, and say know the Lorde: But they shall all knowe me, from the loweste vnto the hyeste, sayeth the Lorde. For I wyll forgeue theyr mysdedes, and wil neuer remembre theyr sinnes any more.

35 Thus sayth the Lorde which gaue the sunne to be a lyght for the daye, and the mone and starres to shyne in the night: whiche moueth the sea, so that the floudes thereof waxe fearce: hys name is the Lorde of hostes.

36 Lyke as thys ordynaunce shal neuer be taken out of my sight sayeth the Lorde: So shall the sede of Israell neuer ceasse, but all waye be a people before me.

37 Moreouer, thus sayeth the Lorde: lyke as the heauen aboue can not be measured, and as the foundacyons of the earth beneth may not be soughte oute: So will I also not caste oute the whole sede of Israell, for that they haue committed. sayeth the Lorde.

38 Beholde the dayes come sayeth the Lorde, that the cytie of þe Lord shalbe enlarged from the toure of Hananeel, vnto the gate of the corner wall.

39 From thence shall the ryghte measure be taken before her vnto the hyll toppe of Gareb, and shall come aboute Gaath,

40 and the whole, valleye of the dead karcases, and of the ashes, and all Ceremoth vnto the broke of Cedron: and from thence vnto the corner of the horsgate toward the Easte, where as the Sanctuarye of the Lorde also shall be set. And when it is nowe buylded, and set vp of this fashyon it shall neuer be broken, nor caste doune any more.

# CHAPTER 32

THESE wordes spake the Lord vnto Ieremye, in the tenthe yeare of Zedekiah kynge of Iuda, whyche was the .xviij. yeare of Nabuchodonozor,

2 what tyme as the kinge of Babylons hoste laied seage vnto Ierusalem. But Ieremy the Prophete laye bounde in the courte of the preson, whiche was in the kinge of Iudaes house:

3 where Zedekiah the king of Iuda caused hym to be layed, because he had prophecyed of this maner: Thus sayeth the Lorde: Beholde, I wil delyuer this cytye into the handes of the Kyng of Babilon, which shall take it.

4 As for Zedekiah the Kynge of Iuda, he shall not be able to escape the Chaldees, but surely he shal come into the handes of the kynge of Babylon: whiche shal speake with him mouth to mouth, and one of them shal loke another in the face.

5 And Zedekiah shalbe caryed vnto Babylon, and there shall he be, vnto the tyme that I vyset him, sayeth the Lorde. But yf thou takest in hand to fight against the Caldees, thou shalt not prospere.

6 And Ieremy sayde. Thus hath the Lorde spoken vnto me:

7 Beholde, Hananeel þe sonne of Selum, thyne Vncles sonne shall come vnto the, and require the to redeme the lande, that lyeth in Anathoth vnto thy selfe: for by reason of kinred it is thy parte to redeme it, and to bye it oute.

8 And so Hananeel myne vncles sonne came to me in the courte of the preson (according to the worde of the Lorde) and sayde vnto me: Bye my lande (I pray the) that lyeth in Anathoth in the countreye of Beniamin: for by heretage thou hast right to lowse it oute for thy selfe, therfore redeme it. Then I perceyued, that this was the commaundement of þe lord,

9 and so I lowsed the lande from Hananeell of Anathoth, myne Vncles sonne, and weyed him there the moneye: euen seuen sycles, and ten syluer pens.

10 I caused him also to make me a writtinge and to seale it, and called recorde therby, and weyed him there the money vpon the waightes.

11 So I toke the euydence with the copye (when it was orderly sealed and read ouer)

12 and I gaue the euydence vnto Baruch the sonne of Neriah, the sonne of Maasiah in the sight of Hananeel my cosen, and in the presence of the witnesses, that be named in the euidence, and before all the Iewes that were therby in the courte of the preson.

13 I charged Baruch also before them, saying:

14 The Lorde of Hostes the God of Israel commaundeth the, to take his sealed euydence wt the copie, & to lay it in an earthen vessel, that it may longe continue.

15 For the Lorde of Hostes the God of Israell hath determed, that houses, feldes and vyneyardes shalbe possessed agayne in thys lande.

16 Now when I had delyuered the euydence vnto Baruch the sonne of Neriah, I besought the Lorde, sayinge:

17 O Lorde God, it is thou that hast made heauen and earthe wyth thy greate power, and hye arme, and there is nothinge to harde for the.

18 Thou shewest mercy vpon thousandes, thou recompencest the wickednes of the fathers, into the bosume of the children, that come after them.

19 Thou art the greate and myghtie God, whose name is the Lorde of Hostes, greate in counsel, and infinite in thought. Thine eyes loke vpon all the wayes of mens chyldren, to rewarde euery one after his waye, and according to the frutes of his inuencyons.

20 Thou hast done greate tokens and wonders in the lande of Egipt (as we se this daye) vpon the people of Israel, and vpon those men: to make thy name greate, as it is come to passe this daye.

21 Thou hast brought thy people Israell out of the land of Egipt, with tokens, wt wondres, with a mightye hande, with a stretched out arme, and with greate terriblenes:

22 & hast geuen them this lande, lyke as thou hast promysed vnto their fathers: Namely, that thou wouldest geue them a land, that floweth with mylcke and honye.

23 Now when they came therin, and possessed it, they folowed not thy voyce, and walcked not in thy law: but all that thou commaundedest them to do, that haue they not done, & therfore come al these plages vpon them.

24 Behold, there are bullworckes made now against the citie, to take it: and it shabe wonne of the Caldees that besege it, with swerde, wt honger and death, and loke what thou haste spoken, that same shall come vpon them. For lo, all thinges are present vnto the:

25 Yet sayest thou vnto me (O Lord God) and commaundest me, that I shal louse a pece of land vnto my selfe, and take witnesses therto: and yet in the meane season the citie is delyuered into the power of the Caldees.

26 Then came the worde of the Lorde vnto me sayinge.

27 Beholde, I am the Lorde God of all fleshe, is there any thinge then to harde for me?

28 Therfore thus sayde the Lorde: beholde, I shall delyuer this cytie into the power of the Caldees, and into the power of Nabuchodonozor the kynge of Babilon, they shal take it in.

29 For the Caldees shal come, and wynne this citie, and set fyre vpon it. And burne it, wt the gorgeous houses, in whose parlers they haue made sacrifice vnto Baal, and poured drinckeofferynges vnto straunge goddes, to prouoke me vnto wrath.

30 For seynge the chyldren of Israel, and the chyldren of Iuda haue wrought wickednes before me euer from their youth vp, what haue they els done, but prouoked me wyth the worckes of their owne handes? sayeth the Lorde.

31 Or what hath this cytie bene els, but a prouokinge of my wrath, euer sence the day that I buylded it, vnto this houre? Wherin I cast it out of my sight,

32 because of the great blasphemies of the chyldren of Israell, and Iuda, whiche they haue done to prouoke me: yea, they, their kynges, their princes, their priestes their prophetes, whole Iuda, and al the cytesins of Ierusalem.

33 When I stode vp earlye, and taught them and instructe them, they turned their backes to me, and not their faces.

34 They woulde not heare, to be refourmed and correcte. They haue set their Goddes into the house, that is halowed vnto my name, to defyle it.

35 They haue buylded hyr places for Baal in the valleye of the children of Heunom, to vow their sonnes and doughters vnto Moloch: whiche I neuer commaunded them, neyther came it euer in my thought, to make Iuda sinne with suche abnominacion.

36 Moreouer thus hath the Lorde God of Israel spoken, concerninge this cytie, whiche (as ye youre selues confesse) shalbe deliuered into the hande of the kinge of Babylon, when it is wonne with the swearde, wyth hunger, and with pestilence.

37 Beholde, I wyll gather them together from all landes, wherin I haue scatred them in my wrath, in my fearfull, and greate displeasure: and wyll brynge them agayne vnto this place, where they shal dwell safely.

38 And they shalbe my people, and I wilbe their God.

39 And I wyll geue them one herte and one waye, that they maye feare me all the dayes of their lyfe, that they and their children after them maye prospere.

40 And I wyll set vp an euerlastinge couenaunt with them, Namely, that I will neuer cease to do them good, and that I will put my feate in ther hertes so that they shall not runne awaye from me.

41 Yea I wyll haue a lust and pleasure to do them good, and faythfully to plante them in this lande, with my whole herte, and with al my soule.

42 For thus sayeth the Lorde: lyke as I haue brought all thys great plage vpon this people: so wyll I also brynge vpon them all the good, that I haue promised them.

43 And men shall haue their possessions in thys lande, whereof ye saye now, that it shall neyther be inhabited of people nor of catell, but be delyuered into the handes of the Caldees:

44 Yea lande shalbe bought for money, & euidences made

thervpon and sealed before witnesses in the countre of Beniamin, and round about Ierusalem, in the cyties of Iuda, in the cities that are vpon the mountaynes, and in them that lye beneth, yea and in the cytyes that are in the deserte. For I will bringe their presonners hyther agayne, sayeth the Lorde.

## CHAPTER 33

MOREOUER the worde of the Lord came vnto Ieremye on this maner, when he was yet bound in the courte of the preson.

2 Thus sayeth the Lorde, whiche fulfilleth the thynge that he speaketh, the Lorde whyche perfourmeth the thinge that he taketh in hand: euen he, whose name is the lord:

3 thou hast cryed vnto me, and I haue hearde the: I haue shewed greate and hye thinges, whiche were vnknowen vnto you.

4 Thus (I saye) spake the Lorde God of Israel, concerninge the houses of this citie, and the houses of the kinges of Iuda: that they shalbe broken thorow the ordynaunce & weapens,

5 when the Caldees come to besege them & they shalbe filled wt þe dead karcases of men, whom I will slaye in my wrath and displeasure: when I turne my face from this cytye, because of all her wickednes.

6 Beholde (saieth the Lorde) I will heale their woundes, and make them whole: I wyll open them the treasure of peace and trueth.

7 And I will returne the captyuyte of Iuda and Israell, and I will set them vp agayne, as they were afore

8 From all misdedes (wherein they haue offended against me) I will clense them. And al their blasphemes whiche they haue done agaynst me, when they regarded me not, I will forgeue them.

9 And this shall get me a name, a prayse and honoure, amonge all people of the earthe, whiche shall heare al the good, that I will shewe vnto them: yea they shalbe afrayed and astounded at all the good deedes and benefytes, that I will do for them.

10 Moreouer thus sayeth the Lorde: In this place, wherof ye saye that it shalbe a wyldernesse, wherein neyther people nor catell shall dwel: in lyke maner in the cities of Iuda and wythoute Ierusalem (whyche also shalbe voyde, that neyther people nor catell shal dwel there)

11 Shall the voice of gladnesse be hearde agayne, the voyce of the Brydegrome and of the bryde, the voyce of them that shall synge: Prayse the Lorde of Hostes, for he is louinge and his mercy endureth for euer, and the voyce of them that shall offer vp gyftes in the house of the Lorde. For I will restore the captiuite of this lande, as it was afore, saieth the Lord.

12 Thus sayeth the Lorde of Hostes: It shall come yet therto, that in this lande, whiche is voyde from men and catel, and in al the cities of the land, there shalbe set vp sheperdes cotages:

13 in the cytyes vpon the mountaynes, and in the cyties that lay vpon the plaine, and in the deserte. In the lande of Ben Iamin, in the feldes of Ierusalem, and in the cities of Iuda, shall the shepe be nombred agayn, vnder the hand of him, that telleth them, sayeth the Lorde.

14 Beholde, the tyme commeth, sayth the Lorde that I wil perfourme that good thing, which I haue promysed vnto the house of Israell & to the house of Iuda.

15 In those dayes and at the same tyme, I wil bringe forthe vnto Dauid, the braunche of righteousnes, and he shal do equite and ryghteousnesse in the lande.

16 In those dayes shal Iuda be helped, and Ierusalem shall dwel safe, and he that shal cal her, is euen God our ryghteous maker.

17 For thus the Lorde promyseth: Dauid shal neuer want one, to syt vpon the stole of the house of Israell:

18 neyther shal the priestes and Leuites want one to offre alwaye before me burntofferinges, to kyndle the meatofferynges, and to prepare the sacryfyces.

19 And the worde of the Lorde came vnto Ieremy after this maner.

20 Thus sayeth the lord: May the couenaunt whiche I haue made wt daye and night be broken, that there shoulde not be day and night in due season?

21 Then maye my couenaunt also be broken, whyche I made with Dauid my seruaunte, and so he not to haue a sonne to reygne in hys Trone. So shall also the Priestes and Leuites neuer fayle, but serue me.

22 For lyke as the starres of heauen may not be nombred, neither the sand of the sea measured: so will I multyplie the seade of Dauid my seruaunt, and of the Leuites my mynisters.

23 Moreouer the worde of the Lorde came to Ieremy saying:

24 Considrest thou not what this people speaketh? Two kinredes (saye they) had the Lorde chosen, and those same two hath he cast awaie: for so farre is my people come, that they haue no hope to come together any more, and to be one people again.

25 Therfore thus saieth the Lorde: Yf I haue made no couenaunt with day and night, and geuen no statute vnto heauen and earth:

26 then will I also cast awaye

the sede of Dauid my seruaunt: so that I will take no prynce oute of his sede, to rule the posterite of Abraham, Isaac and Iacob. But yet I will turne again their captiuite, and be mercyfull vnto them.

## CHAPTER 34

THESE are the wordes whiche the Lord spake vnto Ieremy, what tyme as Nabuchodonozor the kinge of Babylon, and all hys Hostes, (out of all the kyngedomes that were vnder hys power) and all his people, fought agaynste Ierusalem, and all the cytyes thereof.

2 Thus saieth the Lord God of Israel: Go, & speake to Zedekiah the kinge of Iuda, and tell him: The Lorde sendeth the this worde: Beholde, I wyll delyuer this cytie into the hande of the kinge of Babylon, he shal burne it,

3 and thou shalt not escape his handes, but shalt be led awaye presoner, and delyuered into hys power. Thou shalt loke the kinge of Babylon in the face, and he shal speake wt þe mouth to mouth, & then shalt thou go to Babylon.

4 Yet heare the worde of the Lorde, O Zedekiah thou Kynge of Iuda. Thus sayeth the Lorde vnto the: Thou shalt not be slayne with the swerde,

5 but shalt dye in peace. Lyke as thy forefathers the kinges thy progenitours, were brente, so shalt thou be brent also, & in the mourninge they shall saye: Oh Lorde. For thus haue I determined sayeth the Lorde.

6 Then spake Ieremy the Prophet all these wordes vnto Zedekiah king of Iuda in Ierusalem:

7 what tyme as the kinge of Babylons hoste beseged Ierusalem, and the remnaunt of the cytyes: Namely, Lachis, and Azecah, whiche yet remayned of the stronge defensed cities of Iuda.

8 These are the wordes that the Lord spake vnto Ieremy the Prophete, when Zedekiah was agreed with al the people at Ierusalem, that there shoulde be proclamed a lyberte,

9 so that euery man shoulde let his seruaunt and handmayde go fre, Hebrue and Hebruesse, & no Iewe to holde his brother as a bond man.

10 Now as they had consented, euen so they were obedient, and let them go fre.

11 But afterward they repented, & toke agayne the seruauntes and handemaydens, whome they had let go fre, and so made them bonde agayne.

12 For the whiche cause the worde of the Lord came vnto Ieremy from the Lorde him selfe, saying.

13 Thus sayeth the Lorde God of Israell: I made a couenaunt with youre fathers when I brought them oute of Egypte, (that they shoulde no more be bondmen) sayinge:

14 When seuen yeares are oute, euery man shall let his bought seruaunte an Hebrue go fre, yf he haue serued him syxe yeares. But your fathers obeyed me not, and herkened not vnto me.

15 As for you, ye were now turned, & dyd ryght before me, in that ye proclamed, euery man to let his neyghboure go fre, & in that ye made a couenaunt before me, in the temple that beareth my name.

16 But yet ye haue turned your selues agayne, and blasphemed my name. In this, that euery man hath required hys seruaunte and handmayden againe whom ye had let go quite and fre, and compelled them to serue you agayne, and to be youre bondmen.

17 And therfore thus sayeth the lord: ye haue not obeyed me, euery man to proclame fredom vnto his brother and neighbour: wherfore I wil call you vnto a fredome, sayeth the Lorde, euen vnto the swerde, to the pestilence, & to honger, & will make you to be plaged in all the kingedomes of the earthe.

18 Yea those men that haue broken my couenaunt, and not kepte the wordes of the appoyntment, which they made before me: when they hewed the calfe in two, and when there wente thorowe the two halfes therof.

19 The Princes of Iuda, the Princes of Ierusalem, the gelded men, the priestes and all the people of the lande, whiche wente thorowe the two sides of the calfe.

20 Those men will I geue into the power of their enemies, & into the handes of them that folowe vpon their lyues. And their dead bodies shalbe meate for the foules of the ayre, and beastes of the felde.

21 As for Zedekiah the Kynge of Iuda and his Princes, I wil delyuer them into the power of their enemies, and of them that desyre to slaye them, and into the hande of the kynge of Babylons hoste whyche now is departed from you.

22 But thorowe my commaundement (sayeth the Lord) they shall come again before this cytye, they shall fyght agaynste it, winne it, and burne it. Moreouer I wyll laye the cities of Iuda so wast, þt no man shal dwell therin.

## CHAPTER 35

THE wordes, whiche the Lorde spake vnto Ieremy, in þe raigne of Iehoakim the sonne of Iosiah Kynge of Iuda, are these:

2 Go vnto the house of the Rechabites, and cal them out, and brynge them to the house of

the Lorde into some commodyous place, and geue them wyne to drycke.

3 Then toke I Iazaniah the sonne of Ieremye, the sonne of Habaziniah, and his brethren and all his sonnes, and the whole houshold of the Rechabytes,

4 and brought them to the house of the Lorde, into the closet of the chyldren of Hanan the sonne of Iegedaliah the man of God: which was by the closet of the Princes, that is aboue the closet of Maasiah the sonne of Selum, whiche is the chefe of the treasurye.

5 And before the sonnes of the kynred of the Rechabites, I set pottes full of wyne, and cuppes, and sayde vnto them: Dryncke wyne.

6 But they sayde: we dryncke no wyne, for Ionadab the sonne of Rechab oure father commaunded vs sayinge: yea and youre sonnes shall neuer dryncke wyne, buylde no houses, sowe no sede, plante no vynes,

7 yea ye shall haue no vyneyardes: but for all youre tyme ye shall dwel in tentes, that ye maye liue longe in the lande wherin ye be straungers.

8 Thus haue we obeyed the commaundement of Ionadab the sonne of Rechab oure father, in al that he hath charged vs, & so we dryncke no wine all oure lyue longe: we nor our wiues, oure sonnes and oure doughters.

9 Neyther buyld we any house to dwell therin we haue also amonge vs neither vyneyardes nor corne lande to sowe:

10 but we dwell in tentes, we obeye, and do accordynge vnto all, that Ionahab oure father commaunded vs.

11 But now that Nabuchodonozor the Kyng of Babilon came vp into the lande, we sayde: come, let vs go to Ierusalem, that we maye escape the Hoste of the Caldees and the Assirians, and so we dwell nowe at Ierusalem.

12 Then came the word of the lord vnto Ieremy sayenge:

13 Thus sayeth the Lorde of Hostes the God of Israel: Go and tell whole Iuda & al the enhabitours of Ierusalem: Wil ye not be refourmed, to obey my wordes? saieth the Lord.

14 The wordes which Ionadab the sonne of Rechab commaunded his sonnes, that they shoulde dryncke no wine, are fast and surely kepte: for vnto this day they drincke no wine, but obeye their fathers commaundemente. But as for me, I haue stand vp early, I haue spoken vnto you, and geuen you earnest warnynge, and yet haue ye not bene obedient vnto me.

15 Yea, I haue sent my seruauntes, al the prophetes vnto you, I rose vp early, and sent you worde, sayinge: O turne you, euery man from his wicked waye: amende your lyues, and go not after straunge Goddes, to worshyppe them, that ye may contynue in the land which I haue geuen vnto you & your fathers but ye would neither heare me, nor folow me.

16 The children of Ionadab Rachabs sonne haue stedfastly kepte their fathers commaundement, that he gaue them, but this people is not obedient vnto me.

17 And therfore thus saieth the Lorde of Hostes the God of Israell: Beholde I will brynge vpon Iuda and vpon euery one that dwelleth in Ierusalem, al þe trouble that I haue deuysed agaynst them. For I haue spoken vnto them, but they woulde not folowe. I haue called vnto them, neuertheles they woulde geue me no answere.

18 Ieremye also spake vnto the housholde of the Rechabites: Thus sayeth the Lorde of Hostes the god of Israel: For so muche as ye haue obeyed the commaundement of Ionadab youre father, & kepte all his preceptes, and done accordynge vnto all that he hath bidden you:

19 Therefore thus sayeth the Lorde of Hostes, the God of Israell: Ionadab the sonne of Rechab shall not fayle, but haue one of his stocke, to stand alway before me.

# CHAPTER 36

IN the fourth year of Iehoakim the sonne of Iosiah King of Iuda, came the worde of the Lorde vnto Ieremye sayinge:

2 Take a boke, & wryte therin all the wordes, that I haue spoken vnto the, to Israel, to Iuda, and to all the people, from the tyme that I beganne for to speake vnto the (in the raygne of Iosiah) vnto thys daye.

3 That when the house of Iuda heareth of the plage whych I haue deuised for them, they may peraduenture turne, euery man from his wicked waye, that I maye forgeue their offences and synnes.

4 Then dyd Ieremy call Baruch the sonne of Neriah, and Baruch wrote in the boke at the mouth of Ieremye, al the wordes of the Lorde, whiche he had spoken vnto him.

5 And Ieremye commaunded Baruch, sayinge: I am in preson, so that I maye not come into the house of the Lorde:

6 therfore go you thyther, and reade the boke, that thou hast written at my mouth: Namely, the wordes of the Lorde, and reade them in the Lordes house vpon the fastynge day: that the people, whole Iuda, and al they that come out of the cyties, maye heare.

7 Peraduenture they will praye mekely before the face of the Lord, and turne euery one from his wicked waie. For great

is the wrath and displeasure, that the Lorde hath taken agaynst this people.

8 So Baruch the sonne of Neriah dyd, accordynge vnto all that Ieremy the Prophete commaunded him, readynge the wordes of the Lorde oute of the boke in the Lordes house.

9 And this was done in the fyfth yeare of Iehoakim, the sonne of Iosiah Kynge of Iuda, in the .ix. moneth when it was commaunded that all the people of Ierusalem shoulde fast before the Lorde, and they also that were come from the cytyes of Iuda vnto Ierusalem.

10 Then read Baruch the wordes of Ieremye oute of the boke within the house of the lorde, out of the treasury of Gamariah the sonne of Saphan the Scrybe, whiche is besyde the hyer lofte of the new dore of the lordes house: that al the people myght heare.

11 Nowe when Micheah the sonne of Gamariah the sonne of Saphan had hearde all the wordes of the Lorde out of the boke,

12 he wente doune to the Kinges palace into the Scrybes chambre, for there al the Prynces were set: Elisama the Scrybe, Dalaiah the sonne of Semei, Eluathan the sonne of Acabor, Gamariah þe sonne of Saphan, Zedekiah the sonne of Hananiah, wyth all the Princes.

13 And Micheah tolde them all the wordes, that he hearde Baruch reade out of the boke before the people.

14 Then all the Prynces sent Iehudi the sonne of Nathaniah, the sonne of Selamiah, the sonne of Chusi, vnto Baruch, sayinge: Take in thyne hande the boke, wherout thou haste read before all the people, and come. So Baruch the sonne of Neriah toke the boke in his hande, & came vnto them.

15 And they sayde vnto him: Syt doune, and read the boke that we may heare also. So Baruch reade, that they might heare.

16 Now when they had heard all the wordes, they were abashed one vpon another, and sayde vnto Baruch: we wyl certifie the kynge of all these wordes.

17 And they examyned Baruch, saying: tell vs, howe diddest thou wrytte all these wordes out of hys mouth.

18 Then Baruch answered them: He spake all these wordes vnto me wt hys mouth and I alone was with him, and wrote them in the boke.

19 Then sayde the Princes vnto Baruch: Go thy waye, and hyd the with Ieremye, so that no man knowe where ye be.

20 And they went in to the Kinge to the courte. But they kepte the boke in the chambre of Elisama the scribe and tolde the Kynge all the wordes that he myghte heare.

21 So the Kynge sent Iehudi to fetch hym the boke, whiche he brought out of Elisama the Scribes chambre. And Iehudi read it, that the King & al the Princes, whiche were about hym, might heare.

22 Now the king sat in the winter house, for it was in the ninth Moneth, and there was a good fyre before him.

23 And when Iehudi had read thre or foure leaues thereof, he cut the boke in peces with a penne knyfe, and cast it into the fyre vpon the herth, vntill the boke was al brente in the fyre vpon the herth.

24 Yet no man was abashed thereof, or rente his clothes: neyther the kinge him selfe, nor his seruauntes, though they hearde all these wordes.

25 Neuerthelesse Elnathan, Dalaiah, and Gamariah besought the Kynge, that he woulde not burne the boke: notwithstanding the kinge woulde not heare them,

26 but commaunded Ierahmeel the sonne of Amalech, Saraiah the sonne of Ezriel and Selamiah the sonne of Abdiel, to laye handes vpon Baruch the Scrybe, and vpon Ieremy the Prophete: but the lord kepte them out of the sight.

27 After now that the Kyng hath brent the boke and the sermons whiche Baruch wrote at the mouthe of Ieremye: The worde of the Lord came vnto Ieremye, sayinge:

28 Take another boke, and wryte in it al the forsayde sermons, that were wrytten in the fyrste boke, whiche Iehoakim the kinge of Iuda hath brente.

29 And tell Iehoakim the kinge of Iuda: thus sayeth the Lorde: thou hast brente the boke, and thoughtest within thy selfe: Why haste thou written therin, that the kynge of Babilon shall come, and make this land waste, so that he shall make bothe people and catell to be oute of it.

30 Therfore thus the Lord sayeth of Iehoakim the king of Iuda. There shal none of hys generacyon syt vpon the throne of Dauid. His dead corse shalbe cast oute, that the heate of the daye, and the frost of the nyghte may come vpon him.

31 And I wil vyset the wickednes of him, of his sede, and of his seruauntes. Moreouer all the euyll that I haue promysed them (thoughe they hearde me not) wil I bringe vpon them, vpon the inhabytoures of Ierusalem, and vpon al Iuda.

32 Then toke Ieremye another boke, and gaue it Baruch the Scrybe, the sonne of Neriah, which wrote therin out of the mouth of Ieremy: all the sermons that were in the fyrst boke, whiche Iehoakim the kynge of Iuda dyd burne. And there were added vnto them many mo sermons, then before.

## CHAPTER 37

Zedekiah the sonne of Iosiah, whiche was made kyng thorow Nabuchodonozor kinge of Babylon, reygned in the lande of Iuda in the head of Cononiah the sonne of Iehoakim.

2 But neyther he, nor hys seruauntes, nor the people in the lande woulde obeye the wordes of the Lord, which he spake by the Prophet Ieremye.

3 Neuerthelesse Zedekiah the Kynge sent Iehucal the sonne of Selemiah and Sophoniah the sonne of Maasiah the pryeste to the Prophet Ieremy, sayinge: O praye thou vnto the lord oure God for vs.

4 Now Ieremy walked fre among the people at that tyme, and was not put in preson as yet.

5 Pharaos Hoste also was come out of Egypte, which when the Caldees that beseged Ierusalem perceyued, they departed from thence.

6 Then came the worde of the Lorde vnto Ieremy the Prophet, sayinge.

7 Thus sayeth the Lorde God of Israel, thys answere shall ye geue to the kinge of Iuda, that sent you vnto me for councell: Beholde, Pharaos host whyche is come forthe to helpe you, shall returne to Egypte into hys owne lande:

8 but the Caldees shall come agayne, and fyght agaynst this cytye, wynne it, and set fyre vpon it.

9 For thus sayeth the Lord dysceyue not your owne myndes, thinckinge on thys maner: tush, the Caldees go now their waye from vs: No, they shall not go their waye.

10 For though ye had slayne the whole hoste of the Caldees, that besege you, and euery one of the slayne laye in his tente, yet should they stande vp, and set fyre vpon this cytie.

11 Nowe when the Hoste of the Caldees was broken vp from Ierusalem, for feare of the Egypcians armye,

12 Ieremy went out of Ierusalem, towarde the lande of BenIamin to do certayne busines there amonge the people.

13 And when he came vnder BenIamins porte, there was a porter, called Ieriah, the sonne of Selemiah the sonne of Hananiah, whiche fell vpon him, and toke hym sayinge: thy mynde is to runne to the Caldees.

14 Then sayde Ieremy: It is not so, I go not to þe Caldees. Neuertheles Ieriah woulde not beleue him, but brought Ieremy bounde before the Prynces.

15 Wherfore the Prynces were angrye wyth Ieremye, causinge hym to beaten, and to be layed in preson in the house of Ionathas the scribe. For he was þe ruler of the prison.

16 Thus was Ieremy put into the dongeon and preson, and so laye there a longe tyme.

17 Then Zedekiah the kinge sent for him, and called him, and asked hym quyetly in hys owne house, sayinge: thynkest thou this busynes (that now is in hande) commeth of the Lorde? Ieremye answered: yea that it doth: and thou (said he) shalt be delyuered in to the kinge of Babylons power.

18 Moreouer, Ieremy sayde vnto kynge Zedekiah. What haue I offended agaynst the, agaynste thy seruauntes, or agaynst this people, þt ye haue caused me to be put in preson?

19 Where are youre prophetes whych haue prophecied vnto you, and sayd, that the kinge of Babilon should not come against you & this lande?

20 And therfore heare now, O my Lord the Kinge: let my prayer be accepte before the and sende me no more into the house of Ionathas the Scrybe, that I dye not there.

21 Then Zedekiah the kinge commaunded to put Ieremye in the fore entrye of the preson, and dayly to be geuen him a cake of breade, & els no dighte meate, vntil al the breade in the cytie was eaten vp. Thus Ieremy remaineth in the fore entre of the preson.

## CHAPTER 38

Saphatiah the sonne of Mathau, Godoliah the sonne of Phashur, Iucal the sonne of Selemiah, & Phashur the sonne of Melchiah perceyued the wordes, that Ieremy had spoken vnto all þe people, namely on this maner:

2 Thus sayeth the Lorde: Who so remayneth in this citie, shall perishe, eyther with the sweard, with honger or with the pestilence. But who so falleth vnto the Caldees shal escape, winninge his soule for a praye, and shall lyue.

3 For thus sayeth the Lord: this cytie (no doute) must be deliuered into the power of the kinge of Babilon, and he also shal winne it.

4 Then sayd the princes vnto the king: Syr, we besech you, let this man to be put to death: For thus he discoraged the handes of the soudyars that be in this cytie, & the handes of al the people, when he speaketh such wordes vnto them. This man verely laboureth not for peace of the people, but mischefe.

5 Zedekiah the kinge answered & sayde: lo he is in youre handes, for the king may denye you nothing.

6 Then toke they Ieremie, and cast him into the dongeon of Melchiah the sonne of Hamelech, that dwelt in the fore entre of the preson. And they let doune Ieremye wyth coardes into a dongeon, where there was no water, but myre.

7 So Ieremy stack fast in the

# JEREMIAH

myre. Now when Abedmelech the Morian beinge a chamberlayne in the kinges courte, vnderstode, that they had cast Ieremy into the dongeon:

8 he went out of the kinges house, & spake to the king (which then sat vnder the porte of Beniamin) these wordes:

9 My Lorde the king where as these men medle with Ieremye the prophet, they do him wrong. Namely, in that they haue put him in preson, there to dye of honger, for there is nomore bread in the city.

10 Then the kynge commaundeth Abedmelech the Morian and sayde: Take from hence .xxx. men whom thou wilt, & drawe vp Ieremy þe prophet oute of the dongeon, before he dye.

11 So Abedmelech toke the men with him, & went to the house of Amalech, and there vnder an almery he gat olde ragges & worne cloutes, and let them doune by a coarde, into the dongeon to Ieremy.

12 And Abedmelech the Morian sayde vnto the prophet Ieremy: O put these ragges and cloutes vnder thine arme holes, betwyxte them and the coardes, & Ieremy dyd so.

13 So they drew vp Ieremy wyth coardes and toke him out of the dongeon, & he remayned in the fore entry of the preson.

14 Then Zedekiah the king sent & caused Ieremy the Prophete be called vnto him, into the thirde entrye, that was by the house of the Lorde. And the kinge sayde vnto Ieremy: I wyll aske the some what, but hyde nothinge from me.

15 Then Ieremye answerde Zedekiah: Yf I be playne vnto the thou wilt cause me suffre death: yf I geue the councel, thou wylt not folow me.

16 So the king swore an oth secretly vnto Ieremye, sayinge: As truely as the Lorde lyueth, that made vs these soules, I wil not slay the, nor geue the into the handes of them that seke after thy lyfe.

17 Then sayde Ieremye vnto Zedekiah: Thus sayeth the Lord of Hostes the God of Israel: Yf case be, that thou wylt go forth vnto the kynge of Babilons Princes, thou shalt saue thy lyfe, and thys cyty shall not be brent, yea both thou and thy housholde shal escape wyth youre lyues.

18 But yf thou wylt not go forth to the kynge of Babylons prync. then shall this cytye be delyuered into the handes of the Caldees whiche shal set fyre vpon it, & thou shalt not be able to escape them.

19 And Zedekiah sayde vnto Ieremy: I am afrayde for the Iewes, that are fled vnto the Caldees, lest I come in their handes, & so they to haue me in derysyon.

20 But Ieremye answerde: No, they shall not betraye the. O herken vnto the voyce of the Lord (I beseche the) whyche I speake vnto þe, so shalt thou be wel, and saue thy lyfe.

21 But yf thou wylt not go forth, the Lord hath told me this planely.

22 Beholde al the wemen that are left in the kynge of Iudaes house, shall go out to the kyng of Babylons princes. For they thincke, that thou art disceyued: and that men in whome thou diddest put thy truste, haue gotten the vnder, & set thy fete fast in the mire, and gone their waye from the.

23 Therefore al thy wyues with their children shall fle vnto the Caldees, and thou shalte not escape their handes, but shalt be the kinge of Babylons presoner, and this cytie shalbe brente.

24 Then sayd Zedekiah vnto Ieremy: loke that no body knowe of these wordes, & thou shalt not dye.

25 But yf the princes perceyue, that I haue talked with the, & come vnto the, saying: O speake, what saide the kinge to the? hyde it not from vs, and we wil not put the to death. Tel vs (we pray the) what saide the kinge to the?

26 Se thou geue them this answere: I haue humbly besought the kinge, that he will let me lye no more in Iehonathans house, that I dye not there?

27 Then came all the princes vnto Ieremy, and asked him. And he tolde them, after the maner as the kinge bad him. Then they helde their peace, for they perceiued nothinge.

28 So Ieremye abode still in the fore entrie of the preson, vntil the daye that Ierusalem was wonne.

## CHAPTER 39

Now when the citie of Ierusalem was taken (for in the .ix. year of Zedekiah kinge of Iuda in the tenth Moneth, came Nabuchodonozor the Kinge of Babilon, and all his Hoste, and beseged Ierusalem.

2 And in the .xi. year of Zedekiah, in the fourth Moneth, the .ix. day of the Moneth, he brake into the citie).

3 Then al the Princes of the king of Babilon came in, and sat them doune vnder the porte: Neregel, Sarezer, Samegarnabo, Sarsachim, Rabsaris, Neregel, Sarezer, Rabmah, with all the other princes of the king of Babilon.

4 And when Zedekiah the king of Iuda wt his soudiars saw them, they fled, and departed out of the citie by night thorow the kinges garden, & thorow the porte that is betwene the two walles, and so they went towarde the wildernesse.

5 But the Caldees Hoste folowed faste after them, and toke Zedekiah in the felde of

Iericho, and brought him presoner to Nabuchodonozor the kinge of Babilon vnto Reblath, that lyeth in the lande of Hemath, where he gaue iudgement vpon him.

6 So the king of Babilon caused the children of Zedekiah and all the nobles of Iuda be slayne, before hys face at Reblath.

7 And made Zedekiahs eyes to be put out, and bounde him with chaynes and sent him to Babilon.

8 Moreouer, the Caldees brent vp the kinges palace, with the other houses of the people, and brake doune the walles of Ierusalem.

9 As for the remnaunt of the people that were in the citie, and suche as were come to helpe them (whatsoeuer was left of the comen sort) Nabuzaradan the chefe captayne caried them to Babilon.

10 But Nabuzaradan the chefe captayne, let the rascal people (and those that had nothinge) dwel still in the lande of Iuda, and gaue them vineyardes and corne feldes at the same tyme

11 Nabuchodonosor also the king of Babilon gaue Nabuzaradan the chefe captayne a charge, concernyng Ieremy, saying:

12 take & cherysh him, and make muche of him: se thou do him no harme, but intreate him after his owne desyre.

13 So Nabuzaradan the chefe captayne, Nabusasban the chefe chamberlayne, Nergalsarezer the treasurer, and all the kinge of Babilons Lordes, sent for Ieremy,

14 and caused him be set out of the fore entrye of the preson, and committed him vnto Godoliah the sonne of Ahikam the sonne of Saphan: that he should carie him home, & so he dwelt among the people.

15 Nowe whyle Ieremy laye yet bounde in the fore entrie of the preson, the worde of the Lord came vnto him, sayinge:

16 Go and tell Abedmelech the Morian: Thus sayeth the Lorde of Hostes the, God of Israel: Beholde the cruell and sharpe plage that I haue deuysed for this citie, will I brynge vpon them, that thou shalt se it:

17 but I will delyuer the, (sayeth the Lorde) and thou shalt not come in the handes of those men, whom thou fearest.

18 For doutles I wyl saue the, so that thou shalte not peryshe with the swerde, but thy lyfe shalbe saued, and that because thou haste put thy trust in me, sayeth the Lorde.

## CHAPTER 40

THIS is þe maner how the lord intreated Ieremy, when Nabuzaradan the chefe captaine had let him go fre from Ramah, whither he had led him bounde amonge all the presonners, that were caried from Ierusalem & Iuda vnto Babilon.

2 The chefe captayn called for Ieremy, & said vnto him: The Lorde thy God spake myghtely before of the misery vpon this place.

3 Now the Lorde hath sent it, & perfourmed it as he had promised: For ye haue sinned agaynst the Lorde, & haue not bene obedient vnto hys voyce, therefore commeth this plage vpon you.

4 Beholde, I louse the boundes from thy handes this daye: yf thou wilt now go with me vnto Babilon, vp then: for I wyll se to the, and prouyde for the. But yf thou wilt not go wyth me to Babilon, then remayne here. Beholde all the lande is at thy wil, loke where thou thinkest conuenient and good for the to abyde, there dwell.

5 Yf thou canst not be contente to dwell alone, then remayne with Godoliah the sonne of Ahicam, the sonne of Saphan: whom the king of Babilon hath made gouernoure ouer the cities of Iuda, & dwell with him among the people, or remayne wheresoeuer it pleaseth the. So the chefe captayne gaue him his expenses with a rewarde, and let him go.

6 Then went Ieremy vnto Godoliah the sonne of Ahicam to Mazphah, & dwelt there with him among the people that were left in the lande.

7 Now when the Captaynes of the hoste of Iuda (which with their felowes were scatred abroad on euery side in the lande) vnderstode that the king of Babilon had made Godoliah the sonne of Ahicam gouernoure in the land, & that man, wyfe & childe, yea & the pore men in the lande (that were not led captyue to Babilon) should be vnder his iurisdiccion.

8 They came to Godoliah vnto Mazphah: Namely, Ismael the sonne of Nathaniah, Iohanan, & Ionathah the sonnes of Kareah, Sareah the sonne of Thanhometh, the sonnes of Ophai the Netophatite, Iesaniah the sonne of Maachati with their companions.

9 And Godoliah the sonne of Ahicam, the sonne of Saphan, swore vnto them, and their felowes on thys maner: Be not afraied to serue the Caldees, dwell in the lande, and do the kinge of Babilon seruice, so shall ye prospere.

10 Beholde, I dwell at Mazphah to be an officer in the Caldees behalfe, & to satisfye such as come to vs. Therfore gather you wine, corne and oyle, & kepe them in youre ware houses, & dwell in youre cities that ye haue in kepynge.

11 Yea, al the Iewes also that dwelt in Moab vnder the Ammonites, in Idumea, and in

# JEREMIAH

all the countreyes, when they hearde, that the Kynge of Babilon had made Godoliah the sonne of Ahicam the sonne of Saphan, gouernoure vpon them that were left in Iuda.

12 All the Iewes (I say) returned out of al places where they fled vnto: and came into the lande of Iuda to Godoliah vnto Mazphah, and gathered wine & other frutes, and that very much.

13 Moreouer Iohanan the sonne of Careah and al the captaynes of the Hoste, that were scatred on euery side in the lande, came to Godoliah in Mazphah, & sayde vnto him:

14 knowest thou not that Baalis kynge of the Ammonites hath sent Ismael the sonne of Nathaniah, to slaye the? But Godoliah the sonne of Ahicam beleued them not.

15 Then sayd Iohanan the sonne of Careah vnto Godoliah in Mazphah these wordes secretely: Let me go, I pray the, and I wil slaye Ismael the sonne of Nathaniah, so that no bodye shall knowe the. Wherfore he will kyll the, that all the Iewes whiche resorte vnto the, myght be scatred, and the remnaunte in Iuda peryshe?

16 Then sayde Godoliah the sonne of Ahicam to Iohanan the sonne of Careah: Thou shalt not do it, for they are but lyes, that men saye of Ismael.

## CHAPTER 41

**B**VT in the seuenth Moneth it happened, that Ismael the sonne of Nathaniah the sonne of Elisama (one of the kinges bloude) came wyth them that were greatest about the king and ten men that were sworne with him: vnto Godoliah the sonne of Ahicam to Mazphah, & ate there together.

2 And Ismael the sonne of Nathaniah with those ten men that were sworne to him, starte vp, and smote Godoliah the sonne of Ahiram the sonne of Saphan with the swerde, and slewe hym, whome the kinge of Babylon had made gouernoure of the lande.

3 Ismael also slewe al the Iewes, that were wtth Godoliah at Mazphah, & all the Caldees that he founde there waytynge vpon him.

4 The next daye after that he had slaine Godoliah (the matter was yet vnknowne)

5 there came certayne men from Sichem, from Siloh and Samaria, to the nombre of .lxxx. whiche had shauen their beardes, rent their clothes, and were al heauy, bringyng meatofferynges, and incense in their handes, to offre it in the house of the Lord.

6 And Ismael the sonne of Nathaniah went forth of Mazphah wepynge, to mete them. Nowe when he met them, he sayde: Go youre waye to Godoliah the sonne of Ahicam.

7 And when they came in the middest of the city, Ismael þe sonne of Nathaniah (with them that were sworne vnto him) slewe them, euen at the myddest of the pyt.

8 Amonge these .lxxx. men there were ten, that sayde vnto Ismael: Oh slay vs not, for we haue yet a great treasure in the feld, of wheat barleye, oyle, and honye. So he spared them, and slewe them not with their brethren.

9 Now þe pit, wherin Ismael dyd cast the dead bodies of the men (whome he slewe because of Godoliah) had Kynge Asa caused to be made, for feare of Baasa the Kynge of Israell, and the same pyt did Ismaell fyll wyth slayne men.

10 As for the remnaunte of the people the kynges doughters and all the people that were yet let at Mazphah, vpon whom Nabuzaradan the chefe Captayne had made Godoliah the sonne of Ahicam gouernoure. Ismaell the sonne of Nathaniah caryed them awaye presoners toward the Ammonites.

11 But when Iohanan the sonne of Careah and all they whyche had bene captaynes ouer the kynges Hoste wyth him, hearde of all the wickednes that Ismael þe sonne of Nathaniah had done,

12 they toke their companions, and wente oute for to fyght wyth Ismael the sonne of Nathaniah, and founde hym by the waters of Rabim in Gabaon.

13 Now when all the people, whowe Ismael led captyue, sawe Iohanan the sonne of Careah, and al the other captaynes of the Hoste, they were glad.

14 So all the people of that Ismael had caryed away from Mazphah, were broughte agayne. And when they returned, they came to Iohanan the sonne of Careah.

15 But Ismaell the sonne of Nathaniah fled from Iohanan with eyght of hys sworne companyons, and went to the Ammonites.

16 Then Iohanan the sonne of Careah & al the captaynes of the Host that were wt hym, toke the remnaunt of the people whome Ismael the sonne of Nathaniah had led awaye (When he had slayne Godoliah the sonne of Ahicam) whome they also had rescued from him: fighting men, wemen and children, and gelded men, whom they brought agayn from Gabaon:

17 & wente from thence, & sat them doune at Geruth Camain, whyche lieth beside Bethlehem, that they might go into Egipte, for feare of the Caldees,

18 of whome they were afrayed, because that Ismael the sonne of Nathaniah had slaine Godoliah Ahikams sonne, whom

the king of Babilon had made gouernoure in the lande.

## CHAPTER 42

So al the rulers, and Iohanan þe sonne of Kareah, Iezaniah the sonne of Osaiah came wyth all the people from the least vnto the most,

2 and sayde vnto Ieremye the Prophet: O heare our peticion, that thou mayest pray for vs vnto the Lord thy God, and for the remnaunt, whereof there be very few left of manye, as thou seyst vs,

3 that the Lorde thy God may shew vs a way to go in & tell vs, what we shoulde do.

4 Then Ieremy the prophete said vnto them: I haue heard you. Behold, I wil pray vnto God your lorde, as ye haue required me: & loke what answere þe lord geueth you, I shal certifye you thereof, & kepe nothing back from you.

5 And they sayd vnto Ieremy: The lord of trueth & faythfulnes be our recorde, that we will do all, that the Lorde thy God commaundeth vs,

6 whether it be good or euill. We will herken vnto the voyce of oure Lorde God to whom we sende the, that we may prospere, when we haue folowed the voice of the Lorde oure God.

7 And after ten dayes came the worde of the Lorde vnto Ieremy.

8 Then called he Iehonan the sonne of Kareah, & al the captaynes of the people that were wyth hym: yea, and all the people from the least to the moost,

9 and sayde vnto them: Thus sayeth the Lord God of Israel, vnto whom ye sent me, to lay forth your prayers before him.

10 Yf ye will dwell in this lande, I shall buylde you vp, and not breake you doune: I shall plante you, and not rote you out: for I am pacified, as concernynge the trouble that I haue done to you.

11 Feare not the kinge of Babilon, of whome ye stand in awe. O be not afrayed of hym, sayeth the Lorde: For I wilbe with you, to helpe you, and deliuer you from his hande.

12 I wil pardon you, I will haue mercy vpon you, and bryng you agayne into youre owne lande.

13 Neuertheles, yf ye purpose not to dwell in this lande, nor to folowe the voyce of the Lorde youre God,

14 but will saye thus, we wil not dwell here, but go into Egypte: where we shall neyther se warre, heare the noyse of batel, nor suffre honger, there wil we dwel.

15 Wherfore heare now the worde of the Lord O ye remnaunt of Iuda. Thus sayeth the Lorde of Hostes the God of Israel: Yf ye be wholy purposed to go into Egipte, and to be there as straungers,

16 the swerde that ye feare, shall ouertake you in Egipte: and the honger wherof ye be here afrayed shall hange vpon you into Egipte, and there ye shall dye.

17 For al they, that of set purpose vndertake to go into Egipte, there to ease them selues of their mysery, shal peryshe with the swerde, wyth honger and pestilence, not one of them shall remayne, there shall none escape the plage, þt I will brynge vpon them.

18 For thus sayeth the Lorde of Hostes the God of Israel: lyke as my wrath and indignacion is come vpon the enhabytoures of Ierusalem, so shall my displeasure go forth vpon you also, yf ye go into Egipte: For there ye shalbe reuyled, abhorred, brought to shame and confusyon: and as for this place, ye shall neuer she it more.

19 The Lorde forbiddeth you (O ye remnaunt of Iuda) that ye shal not go into Egipte. And forget not that I haue warned you earnestly this day,

20 els shall ye begyle youre selues. For ye sent me vnto the Lorde oure God, and sayde: O praye thou the lord oure God for vs: and loke what answere the lorde oure God geueth the, that brynge vs againe & we shall do therafter.

21 Now haue I shewed and declared vnto you the voyce of the Lorde youre God, for the whiche cause he hath sent me to you.

22 Yf ye wyll not folowe it, be sure, that ye shall peryshe with the swearde, wyth honger & pestilence, euen in the same place, where youre lust was to go, and dwell.

## CHAPTER 43

Now when Ieremye had ended all the wordes of the Lord God vnto the people (for their sakes to whome God had sent hym)

2 Azariah the sonne of Osaiah, & Iohanan the sonne of Kareah with al þe proud personnes, sayde vnto Ieremy: Thou lyest, the Lord our God hath not sent the to speake vnto vs, that we shoulde not go into Egypt, and dwel there.

3 But Baruch the sonne of Neriah prouoketh the agaynst vs, that he might brynge vs into the captiuite of the Caldees: that they myght slay vs, and carye vs away presoners vnto Babylon.

4 So Iohanan the sonne of Kareah, & al the captaynes of the Hoste, and al the people folowed not the commaundement of the Lord. Namely, to dwell in the lande of Iuda:

5 But Iohanan the sonne of Kareah, and all the captaynes of the Hoste, caryed awaye al the remnaunte in Iuda, that were

come together agayne from the Heathen (amonge whome they had bene scatred) to dwell in the land of Iuda.

6 Men, wemen, chyldren, the kynges doughters, all those that Nabuzaradan the chefe captayne had left with Godoliah the sonne of Ahikam. They caryed awaye also the prophet Ieremy, Baruch the sonne of Neriah,

7 & so came into Egipte: for they were not obeyent vnto the commaundement of God. Thus came they to Thaphnis.

8 And in Thaphnis the word of the Lorde happened vnto Ieremy, sayinge:

9 Take great stones in thyne hande, and hide them in the bryckwall, vnder the dore of Pharaos house in Thaphnis that all the men of Iuda maye se,

10 and saye vnto them. Thus sayeth the Lord of Hostes the God of Israell: Beholde I wil sende and cal for Nabuchodonozor the kinge of Babilon my seruaunt, and wyll set hys seate vpon these stones that I haue hyd, and he shall sprede hys tente ouer them.

11 And when he commeth, he shall smyte the lande of Egipte with slaughter, with presonment, and with the swerde.

12 He shal set fyre vpon the tempels of the Egipcians Goddes, and burne them vp, & take them selues presoners. Moreouer he shall araye him selfe with the lande of Egipte, lyke as a sheperde putteth on his cote, and shal departe his waye from thence in peace.

13 The pylers also of the temple of the sunne that is in Egipte: shall he breake in peaces, and burne the tempels of the Egypcians Goddes.

# CHAPTER 44

THIS is the worde that was shewed to Ieremy concerninge all the Iewes, whyche dwelt in Egipte, at Magdall, at Thaphnis, at Memphis & in the lande of Patures.

2 Thus saieth the Lorde of Hostes the God of Israel: ye haue sene al the mysery that I haue brought vpon Ierusalem, and vpon al the cities of Iuda, so that this day they are desolate, & no man dwellinge therin:

3 and that because of the great blasphemyes, which they committed, to prouoke me vnto anger. In that they wente backe to do sacrifyce, and worshippe vnto straunge Goddes: whome neyther they, nor ye, nor youre fathers haue knowne.

4 How be it, I sent vnto them my seruauntes al the prophetes: I rose vp earlye, I sent vnto them, and gaue them warninge: O do no such abhominable thinges, & thinges that I hate.

5 But they woulde not folow nor herken, to turne from their wyckednes, and to do no more sacrifice vnto straung Goddes.

6 Wherfore myne indignacion and wrathe was kyndled, and it brente vp the cytyes of Iuda, the feldes with the stretes of Ierusalem, so that they were made waste and desolate as it is come to passe thys day.

7 Now therfore thus sayeth the Lorde of Hostes the God of Israel. How happeneth it, that ye do so great euyl vnto your owne soules, thus to destroy the men and wemen, children and babes of Iuda? so that none of you is left,

8 because ye prouoke me vnto wrath wyth the worckes of your owne handes: when ye offre vnto straung Goddes in the lande of Egipte, where as ye be gone to dwel. That ye myght vtterly peryshe, and that ye myght be reuyled and shamefully intreated of all nacyons.

9 Or haue ye nowe forgotten the wyckednes of your forfathers, the wickednes of the kinges of Iuda & their wyues, þe wickednes that ye your selues and youre wyues haue done in the lande of Iuda, in the cytye and in the lande of Ierusalem?

10 Yet are ye not sory this daye, ye feare not neyther walke ye in my lawe, and in my commaundementes, that I haue geuen vnto you and youre forefathers.

11 Therfore thus sayeth the Lorde of Hostes the God of Israel: I am stedfastlye aduysed and determed, to punysh you, and to rote out al Iuda.

12 As for the remnaunt of Iuda that purposly wente into Egipte, there to ease them of their mysery I wyll take them, and they shall al be destroyed. In the lande of Egipte shall they peryshe beynge consumed with the swerde, and with honger. For from the least vnto the mooste, they shall peryshe with the swerd and with honger. Moreouer they shal be reuyled, abhorred, shamed, and confounded.

13 For I will vpset them that dwel in Egypte, as I haue visited Ierusalem: with the swerde, wyth honger and wyth pestilence:

14 So that none of the remnaunt of Iuda, which are gone to dwell in Egypte, shalbe left to come agayn into the lande of Iuda al though they thincke to come thither againe & to dwel there. For none shall come agayne, but suche as are fled awaye.

15 Then all the men whiche knewe that their wyues haue offered vnto straunge Goddes, and a greate sorte of wyues, that stode there, yea and al the people that dwelt there in Egipte in the cytye of Patures, answerde Ieremy, & sayd:

16 As for the wordes that

thou hast spoken vnto vs in the name of the Lorde, we will in no wyse heare them:

17 but whatsoeuer goeth oute of oure owne mouth, that wyl we do. We wyl do sacryfice, and offre oblacions vnto the Quene of Heauen: lyke as we & our forefathers, our kinges and oure heades haue done in the cities of Iuda, & in the stretes, & feldes of Ierusalem. For then had we plenteousnesse of vytayles, then were we in prosperytie, and no mysfortune came vpon vs.

18 But sence we left, to offre, and to do sacrifice vnto the Quene of Heauen, we haue had scarcenes of all thynges, and peryshe wyth the swerde and honger.

19 Last of all, when we wemen dyd sacryfyce and offred vnto the Quene of heauen, dyd we make her cakes and poure vnto her drynckedofferynges, to do her seruice wythoute oure husbandes wylles.

20 Then sayde Ieremy vnto all the people, to the men, to the wemen and to all the folcke which had geuen hym that answere:

21 Did not the Lorde remember the sacryfyces, that ye youre forefathers, youre kynges and rulers (wyth all the people) haue offred in the cities of Iuda, in the stretes and land of Ierusalem? and hath he not consydred this in his mynde?

22 In so muche, that the Lorde myght no longer suffre the wickednes of youre inuencyons, and the abhominable thinges whiche he dyd? Is not youre lande desolate and voyde, yea & abhorred, so that no man dwelleth therin any more, as it is come to passe this day?

23 Dyd not al this happen vnto you, because ye made suche sacryfyce, and sinned agaynste the Lorde? Ye haue not folowed his voyce, to walcke in his lawe, in hys ordynaunces and statutes. Yea, this is the cause, that all mysfortune happened vnto you, as it is come to passe this daye.

24 Moreouer, Ieremye spake vnto all the people, and to al the wemen: Heare the worde of the Lorde all Iuda, ye that be in the lande of Egipte:

25 Thus sayeth the Lorde of Hostes the God of Israel: Ye & your wyues haue spoken with your own mouth, the thing that ye haue fulfylled in dede. Yea thus haue ye saide: We wyl not fayle but do the thynge that pleaseth vs: we will do sacrifice and poure not drinckofferynges to the Quene of heauen. Purposlye haue ye set vp your owne good meaninges, & hastely haue ye fulfilled youre owne intente.

26 And therefore: heare the worde of the Lorde al Iuda, ye that dwel in the lande of Egipte. Beholde, I haue sworne by my greate name, sayeth the Lorde, that my name shall not be rehearsed thorow any mans mouth of Iuda, in al the lande of Egipte: to saye: The lord God lyueth,

27 for I wil watch, to plage them, and not for their wealth. And al the men of Iuda that be in the lande of Egipte, shal perysh with the swerde and with honger, vntil they be vtterly destroyed.

28 Neuertheles, those that fled away for the swerde, shal come agayne into the land of Iuda, but there shalbe verye fewe of them. And all the remnaunte of Iuda, that are gone into Egypte, there to dwel, shal knowe whose wordes shalbe founde true: theirs or myne.

29 Take this for a token, that I wyll vyset you in this place, sayeth the Lorde, and that ye maye knowe, howe that I (wythoute doute) will perfourme my purpose vpon you, to punishe you.

30 Beholde, sayeth the Lorde, I wyll delyuer Pharao Hophrea kynge of Egipte into the handes of his enemies, that seke after his life: euen as I gaue Zedekiah the kinge of Iuda into the handes of Nabuchodonozor king of Babylon, whiche sought after his lyfe.

## CHAPTER 45

THESE are þe wordes that Ieremy the prophete spake vnto Baruch the sonne of Neriah, after that he had written these Sermons into a boke at the mouthe of Ieremy, In the fourth yeare of Iehoakim the sonne of Iosiah kinge of Iuda.

2 Thus sayeth the Lorde God of Israell vnto the, O Baruch:

3 In so muche as thou thoughtest thus (when thou wast wryttyng.) Wo is me, the Lorde hath geuen me payne for my trauaile: I haue weried my selfe with sighinghe, and shal I finde no rest?

4 Therfore tell him, O Ieremye, that the Lorde sayeth thus: Beholde, the thing that I haue buylded wyll I breake doune agayne, and rote oute the thinge that I haue planted, yea thys whole lande.

5 And sekest thou yet promocyon? Loke not for it, and desire it not. For I wyll bryng a miserable plage vpon all fleshe sayeth the Lord. But thy lyfe will I geue the for a pray wheresoeuer thou goest.

## CHAPTER 46

HERE folowe the wordes of the Lorde to the prophete Ieremy, whiche he spake vnto the Gentyles.

2 These wordes folowing preached he to the Egipcians concerning the Hoste of Pharao Necho king of Egypte, when he was in Charcamis besyde the

water of Euphrates: what tyme as Nabuchodonozor the kinge of Babilon slew him, in the fourth year of Iehoakim the sonne of Iosiah, kynge of Iuda.

3 Ye make ready buckler and shylde, ye go forth to fyght.

4 Ye harnesse youre horsses, and set your selues vpon them. Ye set your salettes fast on, ye bryng forth speares, ye scoure your swerdes, and put on youre brest plates.

5 But alas, howe happeneth it, that I se you so afrayed? why shryncke ye backe? wherfore are youre worthyes slayne? Yea they runne so fast away, that none of them loketh behind hym. Fearfulnesse is fall vpon euerychone of them sayeth the Lord.

6 The lyghtest of fote shall not fle awaye, and the worthies shall not escape. Towarde the North by the water of Euphrates, they shal stomble and fal.

7 But what is he this, that swelleth vp, as it were a floud, roaring & raging like the streames of water?

8 It is Egypte that ryseth vp lyke the floude, & casteth oute the waters wyth so greate noyse. For they saye: We wil go vp, & wyll couer the earth: we will destroy the cities, wyth them that dwel therin.

9 Get you to horse backe, rol forth the Charrettes, come forth ye worthies: ye Morians, ye Libeans with your bucklers ye Lideans with youre bowes:

10 So shall this daye be vnto the Lorde God of Hostes, a day of vengeaunce, that he maye avenge him of his enemies. The swearde shall deuoure, it shalbe satisfyed and bathed in their bloud For the Lorde God of Hostes shall haue a slayne offeringe towarde the North, by the water of Euphrates.

11 Go vp (O Galaad) and bringe tryacle vnto the doughter of Egipte. But in vayne shalt thou go to surgery, for thy wounde shall not be stopped.

12 The Heathen shall heare of thy shame, and the lande shalbe full of thy confusyon: for one stronge man shal stomble vpon another, howe then shoulde they not fall both together?

13 These are the wordes that the Lorde spake to the Prophet Ieremy, concerninge the host of Nabuchodonozor the Kinge of Babilon, which was sent to destroy the land of Egipt:

14 Preache out thorowe the lande of Egipt, and cause it be proclamed at Magdol, Memphys and Taphnis, and saie: Stande still, make the redye, for the swearde shall consume the rounde aboute.

15 How happeneth it that thy mightie worthies are fallen? why stode they not fast? Euen because the Lord thrust them doune.

16 The slaughter was greate, for one fell euer styll vpon another. One cryed vpon another: Vp let vs go againe to oure owne people, and to oure owne naturall countreye, from the swerd of oure enemye.

17 Crye euen there: O Pharao kynge of Egipte, the tyme wyl bringe sedicion.

18 As truely as I liue (sayeth the kynge, whose name is the Lorde of Hostes) it shal come as the mount of Thabor, and as Libanus yf it stond in the sea.

19 O thou doughter of Egipte make ready thy geer to flyt. For Memphis shalbe voyde and desolate, so that no man shal dwel therin.

20 The lande of Egipt is lyke a goodly fayre calfe, but one shal come out of the north to prick her forwarde.

21 Her wagied soudiars that be with her, are like fat calues. They also shal fle away together, and not abide: for the daye of their slaughter and the tyme of their vysytacyon shall come vpon them.

22 The crye of their enemies shall make a noise, as the blast of a trompet. For they shal entre in with their Hoste, and come with axes as it were hewers doune of wood.

23 And they shal cut doune their wood, sayeth the Lord, wythoute any discrecion. For they shall be mo in nombre then the greshoppers, so that no man shalbe able to tel them.

24 The doughter of Egipte shalbe confounded, when she shalbe delyuered into the handes of the people of the North.

25 Moreouer thus sayeth the Lorde of Hostes the God of Israel: Beholde I will vyset that restlesse people of Alexandria, Pharao, and Egipte, yea bothe their Goddes & their kinges, euen Pharao, and all them that put their trust in him.

26 Yea I will delyuer them into the handes of those, that seke after their lyues. Namely, into the power of Nabuchodonozor the kynge of Babylon, and into the power of his seruauntes. And after all these thinges it shalbe inhabited as afore tyme, sayeth the Lorde.

27 But be not thou afrayed (O my seruaunte Iacob) feare not thou, O Israell. For lo, I wyl helpe the from farre, and thy sede from the lande of thy captyuyte. Iacob also shall come agayn, & be in reste: he shal be rych, and no man shall do hym harme.

28 Feare thou not (O Iacob my seruaunte) sayeth the Lord, for I am with the: and wyll destroye all nacions amonge whome I haue scatred the. Neuertheles, I wyll not consume the, but chasten the, and correcte the: yea and that wyth discrecyon: neyther wyll I spare the as one þt were fautelesse.

# CHAPTER 47

THESE are the wordes, that the Lorde spake vnto Ieremye

the Prophete agaynste the Phylystines, before þe Pharao smote the cytye of Azah.

2 Thus sayeth the Lorde: Beholde, there shall waters aryse oute of the Northe: & shall growe to a greate floude, runnynge ouer and coueryng þe land, the cytyes, and them that dwell therein. And the men shall crye, and al they þt dwel in the lande, shall mourne

3 at the noyse & stampynge of theyr stronge barbed horses, at the shakynge of theyr charettes and at the romblynge of the wheles. The fathers shall not loke to theyr chyldren, so feable and wery shall theyr handes be:

4 at the same tyme, when he shall be there, to destroye the whole lande of the Philistines. He shall make waste both Cirus, Sidon and all other that are sworne vnto them. For the Lorde wyll destroye all Palestina and the other Iles, that be deuyded from the countre.

5 Baldnesse is come vpon Azah, Ascalon wyth her other valleys shall kepe her peace. Howe longe wylte thou slaye,

6 O thou sweard of the Lord? Turne agayne into thy sheeth, reste, and leaue of.

7 But howe can it ceasse, when the Lorde hym selfe hath geuen hym a charge agaynste Ascalon, and raysed it vp agaynste the cytyes of the seacoast?

# CHAPTER 48

THUS sayeth the Lorde of hostes the God of Israel agaynste Moab: wo be to the cytie of Nabo, for it shal be layed waste, broughte to confusyon & taken. Yea thy stronge cytye of Kariathiarim shalbe brought to shame, and afrayd:

2 Moab shall no more be had in honoure: Wycked councell shalbe taken vpon Hesebon. Come (shall they saye) let vs rote them oute, þt they maye be no more amonge the nombre of the Gentyles, yea that they maye no more be thought vpon: Thus the swearde shall persecute the:

3 A voyce shall crye from Horonaim: Wyth greate wastynge and destruccyon,

4 is Moab made desolate. And this crye shalbe hearde in all her cytyes.

5 At the goynge vp vnto Luithe there shall aryse a lamentacyon: & doune towarde Horonaim, there shall be hearde a cruell & a deadly crye:

6 Get you away, saue youre lyues, and be lyke vnto the heath in the wyldernes.

7 For because thou haste trusted in thy stronge holdes and treasure, thou shalte be taken Chamos wyth hys priestes and prynces shall go awaye into captiuite.

8 The destroyer shall come vpon all cytyes, none shall escape. The valeys shalbe destroyed, and the feldes shall be layed waste: lyke as the Lorde hath determed.

9 Make a token vnto Moab, that she get her awaye spedelye: for her cytyes shalbe made so desolate, that no man shall dwell there in.

10 Cursed be he that doth the worcke of the Lorde negligentlye, and cursed be he that kepeth backe hys swearde from sheddynge of bloude.

11 Moab hath euer bene ryche and carelesse from her youth vp, she hath sytten and taken her ease wyth her treasure. She was neuer yet put oute of one vessell into another (that is) she neuer wente awaye into captiuite, therfore her taste remayneth, and her sauoure is not yet chaunged.

12 But lo, the tyme cometh, sayeth the Lorde that I shall sende her trussers to trusse her vp, to prepare & season her vessels: yea her tanckerdes rattell, and shake to and fro.

13 And Moab shalbe ashamed of Chamos, lyke as Israel was ashamed of Bethell, wherein she put her truste.

14 Wherfore do ye thincke thus: we are mightye, and stronge men of warre?

15 Moab shall be destroyed, and her cities brente vp: her chosen yong men shall be slayne, sayeth the king, whose name is the Lorde of Hostes.

16 The destruccyon of Moab commeth on a pace, and her fall is at hande.

17 All her neyghbours shall mourne for her, and all they that knowe her name, shall saye: O howe happeneth it, that the stronge staf & the goodlye rode is thus broken?

18 And thou doughter Dibon, come doune from thy glorye, and sit in pouerte. For he that destroyeth Moab, shall come vp to the also, & breake doune thy stronge holdes.

19 And thou that dwelleste in Aroer, get the to the strete, and loke aboute the: aske them that are fled and escaped, and saye: what thinge is happened?

20 O, Moab is confounded and ouercome. Mourne, and crye, tel it oute at Arnon, that Moab is destroyed.

21 And myserye shall come vpon the playne lande: Namely, vpon Holon & Iahazah: vpon Mephaath

22 and Dibon vpon Nabo & the house of Deblathaim,

23 vpon Cariathiarim and Bethgamul, vpon Bethmaon

24 & Carioth, vpon Bozrah and all the cytyes in þe lande of Moab, whether they lye farre or neare.

25 The horne of Moab shall be smitten doune and her arme broken, sayeth the Lorde.

26 Make her droncken, for she magnified her self aboue the

# JEREMIAH

Lord, that men maye clappe theyr handes at her vomyte, and that she also maye be laughed to scorne.

27 O Israel, shalt thou not laugh him to scorne, when he is taken amonge theues? Yea because of thy wordes that thou hast spoken agaynste him, thou shalt be dryuen awaye.

28 Ye Moabites, shall leaue the cytyes, & dwell in rockes of stone, and become like doues, that make theyr nestes in holes.

29 As for Moabs pryde, we haue hearde of it, she is verye hye mynded. I know her stoutnesse, her boastynge, her arrogancye and the pryde of her stomack, sayeth the Lorde.

30 For her furyousnes maye neyther vpholde her wt strength nor dede.

31 Therfore shall there mournynge be made for Moab, and euery man shal crye for Moabs sake: a lamentacion shalbe made to the men that stand vpon the wal.

32 So wil I mourne for the also, O Iazer, and for the, O thou vyneyarde of Sabamah. Thy wyne braunches shall come ouer the sea, & the braunches of Iazer but vnto þe sea: the destroyer shal breake into thy haruest and grape gatheringe:

33 Myrth and cheare shalbe taken awaye from the tymbre feld, and from the whole lande of Moab. There shalbe no swete wyne in the presse, the treader shall haue no stomacke to crye, yea there shalbe none to crye vnto him:

34 which afore time were hearde from Hesebon to Eleale & Iahaz, whiche lyfted vp theyr voyce from Zoar vnto Horonaim, that bullocke of thre yeare olde. The waters also of Memrim shal be dryed vp.

35 Moreouer, I wyll make Moab ceasse (sayeth the Lorde) from the offerynges & censynge that the hath made vnto her Goddes in hye places.

36 Wherfore my hert mourneth for Moab, lyke a croude playenge an heauy song: and for the mens sake of the brycht wall my herte mourneth also, euen as a pype that pypeth a dolefull songe: for they shalbe verye fewe, and destroyed.

37 All heades shalbe shauen, and all beardes clypped of: all handes bounde, and all loynes gyrded aboute with sackclothe.

38 Vpon all the house toppes and stretes of Moab, there shal be mournynge: For I wyll breake Moab lyke an vnprofytable vessell sayeth the Lord.

39 O howe fearfull is she? O howe mourneth she? O howe doeth Moab hange doune her head, and is ashamed? Thus shall Moab be a laughynge stocke, and had in derisyon of all them, that be rounde aboute her.

40 For thus sayeth the Lorde: Beholde, the enemye shall come flyenge as an Aegle, and sprede his winges vpon Moab.

41 They shall clymme ouer the walles, and winne the strong holdes. Then the mighty mens hertes in Moab shalbe lyke the herte of a woman trauaylinge wyth chylde.

42 And Moab shall be made so desolate, that she shall no more be a people, because she hath set vp her selfe agaynste the Lorde.

43 Feare, pyt, and snare shall come vpon the (O Moab) sayeth the Lorde.

44 Who so escapeth the feare, shall fall in the pytte, and whoso getteth oute of the pyt, shalbe taken in the snare. For I wyll bringe a yeare of vysytacyon vpon Moab, sayeth the Lorde.

45 They that are able to flye, shal stande vnder the shadow of Hesebon. For there shall go a fyre oute of Hesebon, and a flamme from Sion, and shal burne vp that proude people of Moab, bothe before and behynde.

46 Wo be vnto the (O Moab) for thou people of Chamos shalte perysh: Yea thy sonnes and doughters shall be led awaye captyue.

47 Yet at the laste wyll I brynge Moab oute of captiuite agayne, sayth the Lord. Thus farre of the plage of Moab.

## CHAPTER 49

As concernynge the Ammonites thus the Lorde sayeth: Hath Israell no chyldren, or is he withoute an heyre? Why hath your kynge then taken Gad in? wherfore both hys people dwel in hys cities?

2 Beholde therfore, the tyme commeth (sayeth the Lorde) that I wyll brynge a noyse of warre into Rabah of the Ammonites. Lahell shalbe desolate, and her cytyes brente vp: and the Israelytes shall be Lordes ouer those that had them in possession afore, sayeth the Lord.

3 Hesebon shall mourne, for it shall be roted out of the grounde, sayeth the Lorde. The cytyes of Rabah shall crye oute, and gyrde them selues wyth sacke clothe: they shall mourne, and runne aboute the walles: for theyr kynge shal be led awaye presonner: yea hys priestes and princes wyth hym.

4 Wherfore trustest thou in the water streames that flowe to and fro, O thou fearre doughter: and thinckest thou arte so safe (by reason of thy treasure) that no man shal come to the?

5 Beholde, I wyll bring a feare vpon the, sayeth the Lord God of Hostes, from al those that be aboute the: so that ye shall be scatered euerye man from another, and no man shall gather them together agayne that be fled.

6 But after that, I wyll brynge the Ammonytes also oute

of captyuite agayne.

7 Vpon the Edomytes hath the Lorde of hostes spoken on thys maner: Is there no more wysdome in Theman? Is there no more good councell amonge hys people? Is theyr wysdome then turned clene to naughte?

8 Get you hence, turne youre backes, crepe doune into the depe, O ye cytesens of Dedan. For I wyll brynge destruccyon vpon Esau yea and the daye of hys visitacion.

9 If þe grape gatherers came vpon the, shuld they not leaue some grapes? If the nyghte robbers came vpon the, shulde they not take so muche as they thoughte were ynough?

10 But I wyll make Esau bare, and discouer hys secretes, so that he shall not be able to hyde them. Hys sede shalbe wasted awaye, yea hys brethren and his neyghbours, and he him selfe shall not be lefte behynde.

11 Thou shalte leaue thy fatherlesse chyldren behynde the, and I wyll kepe them and thy wydowes shall take theyr comforte in me.

12 For thus hath the Lorde spoken: Beholde, they that men thought were vnmete to drinke of the cuppe, haue dronken with the firste: and thynkest thou then to be fre? No, no: thou shalt neyther be quyte nor fre but thou muste drincke also:

13 For why, I haue sworne by my selfe (sayeth the Lord) that Bozrah shal become a wyldernes, an open shame a laughynge stocke and cursynge: and her cytyes shalbe a continuall deserte.

14 For I am perfectly infourmed of þe Lord, that he hath sente a message all readye vnto þe Heathen. Gather you together, and go forthe agaynste them: make you readye to the battayle:

15 for lo, I wyll make the but smal among the Heathen, and lytle regarded among men.

16 Thy hye stomack & the pryde of thy herte haue disceyued the, because thou wylte dwell in the holes of stony rockes, and haue the hye mountaines in possessyon. Neuertheles though thy neste were as hye as the Aegles, yet will I caste the doune, sayeth the Lorde.

17 Moreouer Idumea shall be a wyldernesse: who so goeth by it, shalbe abashed, & wodre at all her myserable plages.

18 Lyke as Sodome Gomor, and the cytyes that laye there about, were turned vp syde doune (sayeth the Lorde) so shall no bodye dwell in Idumea, & no man shall haue hys habytacyon there.

19 Beholde, lyke as the Lyon commeth vp from the pleasaunt medowes of Iordane vnto the grene pastures of Etham, so wyll I dryue hym, and make hym runne agaynste her. But who is þe yongeman that I wyll ordeyne thereto? Who is lyke vnto me? What is he that wyll stryue wyth me? What shepherde may stande in my handes?

20 Therfore heare the councell of the Lorde, þt he hathe taken vpon Idumea: and hys purpose that he hath deuised vpon the cytesyns of Theman: The least of the flocke shall teare them in peces, and loke what faire thing they haue, they shall make it waste, & them selues also.

21 At the noyse of their fall the earthe shall quake, the crie of their voyce shalbe hearde vnto the red sea.

22 Beholde, the enemye shall come & fle vp hyther, lyke as it were an Aegle, and sprede his winges vpon Bozrah. Then shall the hertes of the worthyes in Edom be as the herte of a woman trauailinge of childe.

23 Vpon Damascus, Hemath and Arphad shall come confusion, for they shall heare euill tydinges: they shall be tossed to and fro lyke the sea that can not stande styll.

24 Damascus shalbe sore afrayed, and shall fle, tremblynge shall come vpon her. Sorowe and payne shall ouertake her as a woman trauaylynge of chylde.

25 But howe shulde so worshipful and gloryous a citie be forsaken?

26 Heare therfore: her yonge men shall fall in the stretes, & all her men of warre shall be taken awaye in that tyme, sayeth the Lorde of Hostes:

27 I wyll kyndle a fyre in the walles of Damascus, whiche shall consume the palace of Benhadad.

28 As for Cedar and the kyngdom of Hazor, whome Nabuchodonosor the kynge of Babylon smote doune, the Lorde hath spoken thus vpon them: Aryse, and get you vp vnto Cedar, and destroye the people towarde the easte.

29 Theyr tentes and theyr flockes shal they take awaye, yea theyr hanginges and theyr vessel. Theyr Camels also shall they carye awaye with them. They shall come aboute them on euerye syde with a fearfull crye.

30 Fle, get you sone awaye, crepe into caues, that ye maye dwell there: O ye inhabytours of Hazor, sayeth the Lorde: for Nabuchodonosor the kynge of Babylon hath holden a councell concerning you, and concluded his deuyce agaynst you.

31 Aryse, and get you vp agaynste yonder ryche and carelesse people (sayeth the Lorde) whiche haue neyther gates nor dore barres, and that dwell not together.

32 Theyr camels shalbe stolen, and the droues of theyr catell dryuen awaye. Moreouer, these that be shauen wil I scatre towarde all the wyndes, and

bryng them to destruccyon: yea and that thorowe theyr owne famylyers, sayeth the Lorde.

33 Hazor also shall be a dwellynge for Dragons, and an euerlastynge wyldernesse: so that no bodye shall dwell there, and no man shal haue there hys habytacion.

34 These are the wordes, that the Lord spake to the Prophet Ieremye concernynge Elam, in the beginninge of the raygne of Zedekiah kynge of Iuda.

35 Thus sayeth the Lorde of hostes: Beholde, I wyll breake the bowe of Elam, and take awaye theyr strength:

36 and vpon Elam I wyll brynge the foure wyndes from the foure quarters of heauen, and wyll scatre them agaynste the same foure wyndes. And there shalbe no people, but some of Elam shall fle vnto them.

37 For I wyll cause Elam to be afrayed of theyr enemyes, and of them that seke theyr lyues, and wyll brynge vpon them the indignacyon of my wrathe, sayeth the Lorde. And I wyll persecute them with the swearde so longe tyll I haue broughte them to naughte.

38 I wyll set my stole in Elam, I wyl destroye bothe the kyng and the princes from thence, sayeth the Lorde.

39 But in processe of the, I wil bringe Elam oute of captyuyte agayne, sayeth the Lorde.

## CHAPTER 50

THE wordes that the Lord spake vnto the Prophet Ieremy, concerninge Babylon, & the lande of the Caldees:

2 preache amonge the Gentiles, let youre voyce be hearde, make a token: crye oute, kepe no sylence but saye: Babylon shall be wonne, Bel shalbe confounded, & Merodach shalbe ouercome. Yea their Goddes shalbe brought to shame, and theyr ymages shall stande in feare.

3 For oute of the northe there shall come a people against her, whiche shal make her lande so wast, that no body shall dwell therin: neyther man nor beast, for they shall flye and departe from thence.

4 In those dayes & at that time sayeth the Lorde, the children of Israell shall come, they and the children of Iuda, wepyng & makinge haste, and shall seke the Lord their God.

5 They shall aske the waye to Sion, thyther shall they turne theyr faces, & come and hange vpon the, in a couenaunte that neuer shall be broken.

6 My people hath bene a lost flocke, my shepherdes haue disceyued them, and haue made them go astraye vpon the hylles. They haue gone from the mountayne to the litle hyl, and forgotten their folde.

7 All they that came vpon them, haue deuoured them: & theyr enemyes sayde: We haue made no faute agaynst them for they haue displeased the Lorde, yea euen the Lorde whiche is the bewtie of theyr ryghtuousnes, & that defended theyr fathers.

8 Yet shall ye fle from Babilon, & depart out of the lande of the Caldees, and ye shall be as the rammes that go before the flocke.

9 For lo, I wyll wake vp an hoost of people from the northren lande, and brynge them vpon Babylon: these shall laye sege to it, and winne it: Theyr arowes shall not mysse, like as a connyng archer shuteth not wronge.

10 And the Caldees shalbe spoyled, and all they that spoyle them, shalbe satisfyed, sayeth the Lorde:

11 because ye were so chearfull and glad, to treade doune myne heritage, and fulfylled youre pleasures, as the calues in the grasse: and triumphed ouer them lyke the bulles, when ye had gotten the victory.

12 Youre mothers shalbe sore confounded, and they that bare you, shall come to shame. She shall be the leaste set by amonge the nacions, voyde, waste, and dryed vp.

13 No man shall be able to dwell there, for the feare of the Lorde, but she shall be whole desolate. All they that go by Babylon, shall stande styll, & be abashed, and shall wondre at all her plages.

14 Go forth in your araye againste Babylon rounde aboute, all ye that can handle bowes: shute at her, spare no arowes, for she hath synned agaynst the Lorde.

15 Crye oute: vpon her, vpon her, agaynste her round about: she shall yelde her selfe, her foundacyons shal fall, and her walles shall come doune, for it shalbe the vengeaunce of the Lorde. Yea vengeaunce shalbe taken of her, and as she hath done, so shall she be dealte with al.

16 They shal rote out the sower from Babylon, & hym that handleth the syckle in haruest. For feare of the sweard of the enemye, euery man shal get hym to his owne people, and euery man shall flye to hys owne lande.

17 Israel is a scatred flocke, the Lyons haue dispersed them. Fyrste the kynge of the Assyryans deuoured them, last of all thys Nabuchodonosor Kyng of Babylon hath brosed all theyr bones.

18 Therfore thus saith the Lorde of hostes the God of Israell: Beholde, I wyll vyset the Kynge of Babylon and hys kyngdome, as I haue vysited the kynge of the Assyryans:

19 and wil bringe Israel

agayne to hys pleasaunte pasture, that he maye fede vpon Charmel and Basan, and be satisfyed vpon the mounte of Ephraim & Galaad.

20 In those dayes & at the same tyme (sayeth the Lorde) yf the offence of Israel be soughte for, there shal none be found: Yf men enquere for the sinne of Iuda, there shalbe none: for I wyll be mercyfull vnto them whome I suffre to remayne ouer.

21 Go doune (O thou auenger) into the enemyes lande, and vyset them that dwel therin: doune with them, and smyte them vpon the backes, sayeth the Lorde: do accordyng to all, that I haue commaunded the.

22 There is gone aboute the lande a crye of a slaughter & great murther, namelye on thys maner:

23 How happeneth it, that the hammer of the whole world is thus broken and brosed in sonder? Howe chaunceth it, that Babylon is become a wyldernes amonge the Heathen on this maner?

24 I my selfe haue layed wayte for the, and thou arte taken: vnawarres arte thou trapped and snared: for why, thou haste prouoked þe Lorde vnto anger:

25 The Lorde hath opened his house of ordynaunce, and broughte forthe the weapens of his wrath. For the thing that is done in the lande of the Caldees, it is the Lorde of hostes worcke.

26 These thinges shal come vpon her at the last, they shal breake into her preuye chambres, they shall leaue her as bare as stones, that be layed together vpon heapes. They shal so destroye her, that nothynge shall be lefte.

27 They shall slaye all their mightye soudyars, and put them to death. Wo be vnto them, for þe daye & tyme of their visitacion is at hande.

28 Me thinke I heare allreadye a crye, of them that be fled & escaped oute of the lande of Babylon, which shewe in Syon the vengeaunce of the Lorde oure God the vengeaunce of his temple, yea a voyce of them, that crye against Babylon:

29 Call vp all the archers agaynste Babylon, pytche youre tentes rounde aboute her, that none escape. Recompence her, as she hath deserued: and accordinge as she hath done, so deale wyth her agayne: for she hath set vp her selfe agaynste the Lorde, agaynste the holy one of Israel.

30 Therfore shall her yonge men fal doune in the stretes, and all her men of warre shalbe roted oute in that daye, saith the Lorde.

31 Behold, I speake vnto the (O thou proude) sayeth the Lorde God of hostes: for thy daye shall come, euen the tyme of thy vysitacion.

32 And the proude shall stomble & fall, & no man shall helpe hym vp. I wyl burne vp his cities wyth fyre, and it shal consume al that is rounde aboute hym.

33 Thus sayth the Lorde of hostes: The chyldren of Israell & Iuda suffre violence together. Al they that haue them in captyuyte, kepe them faste, and wyll not let them go:

34 but theyr auenger & redemer is myghtye, whose name is the Lorde of hostes: he shal maintayne theyr cause, he shall make the lande shake, and iudge them that dwell therein, one wyth another.

35 The swearde shall come vpon the Caldees, sayeth the Lorde, vpon them that dwell in Babylon, vpon their princes, & vpon theyr wise men:

36 The swearde vpon theyr soth sayers, as for those (they shal become fooles.) The swearde vpon they: worthies, so þt they shall stande in feare:

37 The swearde vpon theyr horsmen and charettes, and vpon al the comon people that dwell vnder them: so that they shall all become lyke wemen: The swearde vpon their treasure, so that it shall be stolen awaye.

38 The swearde vpon theyr waters, so þt they shalbe dryed vp. For the lande worshippeth ymages, & delyteth in straunge wondrefull thynges.

39 Therfore shall wylde beastes, Apes, and Estriches dwell therin: for there shall neuer man dwell there, neyther shal any man haue his habitacion there for euermore.

40 Lyke as God destroyed Sodome and Gomorre, with the cities that laye there aboute, sayeth the Lord: So shall no man dwell there also, nether shall any man haue there hys habitacyon.

41 Beholde, there shall come a people from the North, with a greate bounde of men and many Kynges shall stande vp from the endes of the earth:

42 They beare bowes & buclers, cruel are they and vnmercyfull. Their voyce roareth lyke the ragyng sea, they ryde vpon horses, & come weapened to fyght agaynst the O Babylon.

43 As sone as the kyng of Babylon heareth tell of them, hys handes shall waxe feable: Sorowe and heuynes shal come vpon him, as a woman trauelynge wyth chylde.

44 Beholde, lyke as the Lyon commeth vp from the pleasaunt medowes of Iordane vnto the grene pastures of Ethan, so wyll I dryue them forth, & make them runne agaynst her. But whom shall I chose out, & ordene to such a thyng? For who is lyke me, or who wyl stryue wt me? or what shepherde maye stande against me?

45 Therfore heare the councel that the Lord hath geuen vpon

Babylon, and the deuyce that he hath taken vpon the lande of the Caldees. The leaste amonge the people shall teare them in peces, & loke what pleasaunte thinge they haue: they shall laye it waste.

46 The noyse at the wynning of Babylon shall moue the earthe, & the crye shalbe hearde amonge the Gentyles.

## CHAPTER 51

THUS hath the Lorde sayd: behold I wyll rayse vp a perlous wind agaynst Babylon & her citezens that beare euyll wyll agaynste me.

2 I wyl sende also into Babylon fanners to fanne her oute, & to destroy lande: for in the daye of her trouble they shalbe aboute her on euery syde:

3 Moreouer, the Lorde hath sayde vnto the bowe men, and to them that clymme ouer the walles in brest plates: He shall not spare her yong men, kil doune all her hoste.

4 Thus the slayne shall fall doune in the lande of the Caldees, & the wounded in the stretes.

5 As for Israel and Iuda, they shal not be forsaken of theyr God, of the Lorde of Hostes, of the holy one of Israel: no, thoughe they haue fylled all theyr lande full of synne.

6 Flye awaye from Babylon, euery man saue hys lyfe. Let no man holde hys tonge to her wyckednes, for the tyme of the Lordes vengeaunce is come, yea he shall rewarde her agayne.

7 Babylon hath bene in the Lordes hande a golden cuppe, that maketh all landes droncken. Of her wyne haue all people droncken, therfore are they oute of theyr wyttes.

8 But sodenly is Babylon fallen, & destroyed. Mourne for her, bryng plasters for her woundes, yf she may peraduenture be healed agayne.

9 We wolde haue made Babylon whole (saye they) but she is not recouered. Therfore wyll we let her alone, & go euery man into hys owne countre. For her iudgemente is come into heauen, and is gone vp to the cloudes.

10 And therfore come on, we wyll shewe Syon the worke of the Lorde oure God.

11 Make sharpe the arowes, and fyll the quyuers: for the Lorde shall rayse vp the sprete of the kynge of the Meedes, which hath already a desyre to destroye Babylon. This shalbe the vengeaunce of the Lordes, and the vengeaunce of hys temple.

12 Set vp tokens vpon the walles of Babylon, make youre watche stronge, set youre watche men in araye, yea holde preuye watches, & yet for all that shall the Lorde go forth with the deuyce, whiche he hath taken vpon them that dwell in Babylon.

13 O thou that dwellest by the greate waters O thou that hast so greate treasure & ryches, thyne ende is come: and the rekenynge of thy winninges.

14 The Lord of hostes hath sworne by him selfe, that he wyll ouer whelme the wt men lyke greshoppers in nombre, which with a corage shall crye Alatum Alarum agaynst the.

15 Yea euen the Lorde of hostes, þt wyth his power made the earthe, with hys wysedome prepared the rounde worlde, and with his discrecyon spred oute the heauens.

16 As soone as he letteth hys voyce be hearde, the waters in the ayre waxe fearce: He draweth vp the cloudes from the endes of the earthe. He turneth the lyghtenynges to rayne, he bryngeth the wyndes oute of theyr secrete places.

17 By the reason of wysdome, all men are become fooles. Confounded be all the casters of ymages for the thynge that they make is but disceyte, and hath no breath.

18 Vayne is it and worthye to be laughed at: and in the tyme of vysitacion it shall peryshe.

19 Neuertheles, the porcyon of Iacob is none soch: but he that made al thinges, whose name is the Lorde of hostes, he is the rode of hys enherytaunce.

20 Thou breakest my weapens of warre, and yet thorowe the I haue scatered the nacyons & kyngdomes:

21 Thorow the haue I scatred horse and horse man: yea the charettes, and suche as sat vpon them:

22 Thorowe the I haue scatred man and woman, olde & yong, bacheler and mayden.

23 Thorowe the I haue scatred the shepherde and hys flocke, the husbandeman and hys cattell, the pryncyes and the rulers.

24 Therfore wyl I rewarde the citie of Babylon and all her cytesens the Caldees with all the euyll whiche they haue done vnto Syon: yea that ye youre selues shall se it, sayeth the Lorde.

25 Beholde, I come vpon the (thou noysome hyll) sayeth the Lorde, thou that destroyest all landes. I wyll stretche out my hande ouer the, and caste the doune from the stony rockes: and wyll make the a brente hyll,

26 so that neyther corner stones, nor pynnacles, nor foundacyon stones shalbe taken anye more oute of the, but waste and desolate shalt thou lye for euer more, sayeth the Lorde.

27 Set vp a token in the lande: blow the trompettes amonge the Heythen, prouoke the nacyons agaynst her, call the kyngedomes of Ararat, Memni, and Ascanes agaynste her: nombre oute Taphsar agaynst her, bryng as greate a sorte of

horses against her, as yf they were greshoppers.

28 Prepare agaynste them the people of the Meedes wyth theyr kynges prynces, and al theyr chefe rulers, yea and the whole lande that is vnder them.

29 The lande also shall shake & be afrayed, when the deuyce of the Lorde shal come forth agaynste Babylon: to make the lande of Babylon so waste, that no man shall dwell anye more therein.

30 The worthyes of Babylon shal leaue the battell, & kepe them selues in stronge holdes, theyr strength hath fayled them, they shalbe lyke wemen. Theyr dwellynge places shal be brente vp, theyr barres shalbe broken.

31 One purseuaunte shal mete another, yea one poste shall come by another, to bring the king of Babylon tydynges: that his citie is taken in on euerye syde,

32 the foordes occupyed, the fennes brente vp, and the soudyares sore afrayed.

33 For thus sayeth the Lorde of hostes the God of Israell: the doughter of Babylon hath bene in her tyme lyke as a threshynge floure, but shortly shal her haruest come.

34 Nabuchodonosor the kynge of Babylon hath deuoured & destroyed me, he hath made me an emptye vessell. He swalowed me vp lyke a dragon, and filled his bely with my delycates: he hath cast me oute,

35 he hath taken my substaunce awaye and the thynge that was lefte me, hath he caryed vnto Babylon, sayeth the doughter that dwelleth in Syon: yea and my bloude also vnto the Caldees, sayeth Ierusalem.

36 Therfore thus sayth the Lorde: Beholde, I wyll defende thy cause, and auenge the: I wil dryncke vp her sea, and drye vp her water springes.

37 Babilon shalt become an heape of stones a dwellinge place for dragons, a fearfulnes and wondrynge, because no man dwelleth there.

38 They shall roare together lyke lyons, and as the yonge lyons when they be angrie, so shall they bende them selues.

39 In their heate I shall sett drinke before them, & they shalbe droncken for ioye: Then shall they slepe an euerlastinge slepe, and neuer wake, sayeth the Lorde

40 I shall carie them downe to be slayne like shepe, like wethers and gootes.

41 O, how was Sesach wonne? O, how was the glorye of the whole lande taken? how happeneth it, that Babilon is so wondred at amonge the Heathen?

42 The see is risen ouer Babilon, and hath couered her with his greate waues.

43 Her cytyes are layed waste, the lande lyeth vnbuylded and voyde: it is a lande where no man dwelleth, and where no man traueleth thorow.

44 Moreouer, I wyll vyset Bell at Babylon: and the thynge that he hath swalowed vp, that same shall I plucke out of hys mouth. The Gentyles also shall runne nomore vnto hym, yee and the walles of Babylon shall fall.

45 O my people, come out of Babylon, that euery man maye saue his lyfe, from the fearfull wrath of the Lorde.

46 Be not faynte herted, and feare not at euery rumoure that shalbe herde in the lande: for euery yeare bringeth new tydinges, yee straunge wyckednes and lordshyppe.

47 And lo, the tyme commeth that I wyll vyset the ymages of Babylon, and the whole lande shalde confounded, yee and her slayne shall lye in the myddest of her.

48 Heauen and earth with all that is therin, shall reioyce ouer Babylon, when the destroyers shall come vpon her from the North, sayeth the Lorde.

49 Like as Babylon hath beaten downe and slayne many out of Israell, so shall there fall many, and be slayne in all her kyngdome.

50 Ye that haue escaped the sweard, haste you, stande not styll, remembre the Lorde afarre of: and thincke vpon Ierusalem,

51 for we were ashamed to heare þe blasphemyes: oure faces were couered with shame, because þe straung aleauntes came into the Sanctuarye of the Lorde.

52 Wherfore beholde (sayeth the Lorde) the tyme commeth, that I will vyset the ymages of Babylon, and thorow the whole lande they shall mourne and fall.

53 Though Babylon clymmed vp into heauen, & kepte her power an hye: yet shal I sende her destroyers, sayeth the Lorde.

54 A pyteous crye shall be hearde from Babylon, and a greate misery from the lande of the Caldees:

55 when the Lorde destroyeth them, and when he dryueth out the hye stomacke & proude boastyng, wherwith they haue bene as furyous as þe waues of greate water floudes, and made greate crakes with their wordes.

56 For the destroyers shall come vpon her (euen vpon Babylon) whyche shall take her worthyes, & breake their bowes: for God is dysposed to auenge hym selfe vpon them, and suffycyentlye to recompence them.

57 Yee (sayeth the Lorde) I will make their Princes their wyse men, their chefe rulers & all their worthyes, droncken: so that they shall slepe an euerlastynge slepe, and neuer wake: Thus sayeth the Kynge, whose name is the Lorde of hostes.

58 Moreouer, thus sayeth the

# JEREMIAH

Lorde of Hostes: The thycke wall of Babylon shalbe broken, & her proude gates shalbe brent vp. And the thynge that the Gentyles and the people haue wrought with greate trauayle and laboure, shal come to naught and be consumed in the fyre.

59 Thys is the charge that Ieremy gaue vnto Saraiah the sonne of Neriah, the sonne of Maasiah, when he went towarde Babylon with Zedekiah the kynge of Iuda, in the .iiij. yeare of his raigne. Now this Saraiah was a peaceable Prince.

60 Ieremye wrote in a boke all the mysery that shulde come vpon Babylon, yee and all these sermons that be wrytten agaynst Babylon,

61 and gaue Saraiah thys charge: When thou commest vnto Babylon se that thou reade all these wordes,

62 and saye: O Lorde, thou art determed to rote out thys place, so that nether people ner catell shall dwell there eny more but to lie waste for euer

63 and when thou hast redde out the boke, bynde a stone to it, and cast it in the myddest of Euphrates,

64 and saye: Euen thus shall Babylon syncke, & be thrust downe with the burthen of trouble, that I will bringe vpon her: so that she shall neuer come vp agayne. Thus farre are the preachinges of Ieremy.

## CHAPTER 52

ZEDEKIAH was .xxi. yeare olde, when he was made kynge, & he raigned .xi. yeare in Ierusalem. His mothers name was Hamistal, Ieremies daughter of Lobnah.

2 He liued wickedly before the Lorde euen as Iehoakim dyd.

3 Wherfore the Lorde was angrie at Ierusalem and Iuda, so longe tyll he had cast them out of his presence. And Zedekiah fell from the kynge of Babylon.

4 But in the .ix. yeare of his raygne, In the tenth Moneth, the tenth daye of the Moneth it happened, that Nabuchodonozor the Kynge of Babylon wyth all hys Hoste came before Ierusalem, and beseged it, and made them bulworckes rounde aboute it.

5 And this beseging of the cytye endured vnto þe .xi. yeare of kyng Zedekiah.

6 And in the fourth Moneth, the .ix. daye of the Moneth, there was so greate honger in the cytye, that there were no more vytayles for the people of the lande.

7 So all þe soudyers brake awaye, & fled out of the cytie by myght thorow the waye of þe porte betwene the two walles by the kynges garden. Now the Caldees had compassed the cytie rounde aboute, yet wente these men their waye to warde the wyldernesse.

8 And so the Caldees folowed vpon them, & toke Zedekiah the kynge in the felde of Ierycho, when his hoost was runne from him.

9 So they caryed the kynge awaye presoner to Reblath, vnto the kynge of Babylon in the lande of Hemath, where he gaue iudgement vpon hym.

10 The kynge of Babylon also caused Zedekiahs sonnes to be slayne before his face, yee & put all the princes of Iuda to death at Reblath.

11 Moreouer he put out the eyes of Zedekiah, caused hym to be bounde with chynes, to be caried vnto Babylon: and lett hym lye in preson, tyll he dyed.

12 Now the tenth daye of the fyfth Moneth in the .ix. yeare of Nabuchodonosor kynge of Babylon, Nabusaradan the chefe captayne & the kynge of Babylons seruantes came vnto Ierusalem,

13 & brent vp the house of the Lorde. He brent vp also the kynges palaces, all the houses & all the gorgeous buildinges in Ierusalem.

14 And the whole Hoost of the Caldees that were with the chefe Captayne, brake downe all the walles of Ierusalem rounde aboute.

15 As for the poore people and soch folcke as yet was left in the cytie, which also were fallen to the Kynge of Babylon, yee and what people as yet remayned: Nabuzaradan the chefe Captayne caryed them awaye presoners.

16 But the poore people of the countre, dyd Nabuzaradan the chefe Captayne leaue in the lande, to occupye the vyneyardes & feldes.

17 The Caldees also brake þe brasen pylers that were in the house of the Lorde, yee the seate & the brasen lauer that was in the house of the Lorde and caryed all the metall of them vnto Babylon.

18 They toke awaye also the Cauldrons, shouels, fleshe hokes, sprynklers, spones, and all the brasen vessell that was occupyed in the seruyce:

19 with the basens, colepannes, sprynklers, pottes, candelstyckes, spones and cuppes: wherof some were of golde, and some of syluer.

20 The chefe Captaynes toke also the two pylers, þe lauer the .xij. brasen bullockes that stode vnder the seate, which Kyng Salomon made in the house of the Lord: & all the vessel conteyned so moch metall, that it myght not be weyed.

21 For euery piler was .xviij. cubytes hye, & the rope that wente aboute it, was .xij. cubytes, and foure fyngers thycke & rounde:

22 Now vpon the rope were brasen knoppes, & euerye knoppe was fyue cubytes hye: & vpon the knoppes weere whopes,

& pomgranates rounde about of cleane brasse.

23 After thys maner were both the pylers fashyoned wyth the pomgranates, wherof there were an hundreth & .xcvi. which hanged vpon the whoopes rounde aboute.

24 The chefe Captayne also toke Sariah the hye preste, & Sophoniah that was chefe next hym, & the thre kepers of the treasury.

25 He toke out the cytie a chamberlayne whyche was a captayne of the souldyers, and seuen men that were the kynges seruauntes, whiche were founde in the cytie: and Sepher a captayne that vsed to muster the men of warre: with .lx. men of the countre that were taken in the cytie.

26 These Nabuzaradan the chefe captayne toke, and caried them to the kyng of Babylon vnto Reblath:

27 and the Kynge of Babylon caused them to be put to death at Reblath in the lande of Hemath. And thus Iuda was ledde awaye captyue, out of hys owne lande.

28 Thys is the summe of the people, whom Nabuchodonosor ledde awaye captyue. In the seuenth yeare of hys reygne, he caried awaye of the Iewes, thre thousand and thre and twenty.

29 In the .xviij. yeare. Nabuchodonosor caryed awaye from Ierusalem eight hundreth and .xxxij. personnes.

30 In the .xxiij. yeare of Nabuchodonosor Nabuzaradan the chefe Captayne, toke awaye seuen hundreth .xlv. Iewes presoners. The whole summe of all the presoners, is foure thousand and syxe hundreth.

31 In the .xxxvij. yeare after that Iehoacin the kynge of Iuda was caryed awaye in the .xxv. daye of the .xij. Moneth, Euilmerodach Kynge of Babylon (the same yeare that he reigned) gaue Iehoacin the kyng of Iuda his pardon, and let him out of preson,

32 and spake louyngly to hym. And set his trone aboue the trones of the other Kynges that were wyth hym in Babylon.

33 He chaunged also the clothes of his preson, yee and he ate with him al hys lyfe longe.

34 And he had a contynuall lyuynge geuen hym of the Kynge of Babylon, euery daye a certayne thynge alowed hym all the dayes of hys lyfe, vntyll he dyed.

# Lamentations

## CHAPTER 1

IT happened, after Israell was brought in to captyuytie & Ierusalem destroyed, that Ieremy the Prophete sate wepynge, & sorowfully bewayled Ierusalem: and syghynge & howlynge wyth an heuy and wofull herte, sayde:

1 Aleph. Alas, how sytteth the citie so desolate, that some tyme was full of people? How is she become lyke a wedowe, whiche was the ladye of all nacyons? How is she brought vnder trybute, that ruled all landes.

2 Beth. She wepeth sore in the nyght, so that the teares runne downe her chekes: for amonge all her louers, there is none that geueth her eny comforte: ye her nexte frendes abhorre her, and are become her enemyes.

3 Gymel. Iuda is taken presoner, because she was defiled: and for seruynge so manye straunge goddes, she dwelleth now amonge the Heythen. She fyndeth no rest, all they that persecuted her, toke her, & so she dwelleth amonge her enemyes.

4 Daleth. The streates of Sion mourne, because no man commeth more to the solempne feastes. All her gates are desolate, her prestes make lamentacyon, her maydens are carefulll, and she her selfe is in greate heuynesse.

5 He. Her enemyes are fallen vpon her head, & haue put her to shame: because þe Lord hath chastened her for her greate wickednes: her children are ledde awaye captiue before their enemye.

6 Vau. All the bewtie of the daughter of Syon is awaye, her princes are become like wethers þt fynd no pastur. They are driuen away befor their enemye, so þt they haue no more power.

7 Zain. Now doth Ierusalem remembre the tyme of her misery & dysobedience, yee the ioye and pleasure þt she hath had in tymes past: seynge her people is brought downe thorow the power of their enemie, & there is no man for to helpe her: her enemies stande lokinge at her & laugh her Sabbath dayes to scorne.

8 Heth. Ierusalem synned euer more & more, therfore is she come in decaye. All they that had her in honour, despyse her: for they haue sene her fylthynesse. Yee she sygheth, and is a shamed of her selfe.

9 Teth. Her skyrtes are defyled, she remembred not what wolde folowe: therfore is her fall so greate, and there is no man to comforte her. O Lord, consydre my trouble, for myne enemye hath the vpperhande.

10 Iod. The enemye hath put his hande to all the precious thynges that she had, yee euen before her eyes came the Heathen in & out of þe Sanctuarye: whom thou (neuertheles) hast forbydden to come within thy congregacyon.

11 Caph. All her people seke their bred wyth heuynes, & loke what precyous thynge euery man hath, that geueth he for meate, to saue his lyfe. Consydre, O Lorde, and se, how vyle I am become.

12 Lamed. O ye all that go fore by, beholde and se, yf there be eny sorow like vnto myne, wherwith the Lord hath troubled me, in the daye of his fearefull wrath.

13 Mem. From aboute hath he sent downe a fyre into my bones and chastened me: he hath layed a net for my fete, and throwen me wyde open: he hath made me desolate, so that I must euer be mournynge.

14 Nun. The yocke of my transgressyon is come at the last, with his hande hath he taken it vp, & put it aboute my neck. My strength is gone: the Lorde hath delyuered me in to those handes, wherout I can not quyte my selfe.

15 Samech. The Lorde hath destroyed all the mightie men, that were in me. He hath proclamed a feast, to slaughter

all my best men. The Lord hath troden downe the daughter of Iuda, like as it were in wyne presse.

16 Ain. Therfore do I wepe, & myne eyes gusshe oute of water: for the comforter that shulde quycken me, is farre fro me. My chyldren are dryuen awaye, for why? the enemie hath gotten the ouer hande.

17 Phe. Sion casteth out her handes, and there is no man to conforte her. The Lord hath layed the enemyes rounde aboute Iacob, and Ierusalem is as it were a menstruous woman, in the myddest of them.

18 Zade. The Lorde is ryghtuous, for I haue prouoked his contenaunce vnto anger. O take hede all ye people, and consydre my heuynes: My maydens and my younge men are led awaye into captyuytye.

19 Koph. I called for my louers (but they begyled me) for my Prestes and councelers, but they peryshed: euen whyle they sought for meate, to saue their lyues.

20 Res. Consydre (O Lorde) how I am troubled, my wombe is dysquyeted, my herte turneth about in me, and I am full of heuynes. The swearde hurteth me without, and within I am lyke vnto death.

21 Sin. They heare my mournynge, but there is none that wyll comforte me. All myne enemyes haue hearde of my trouble, & are glad therof, because thou hast done it. But thou shalt brynge forth the tyme, when they also shalbe lyke vnto me.

22 Thau. From the shall come all their aduersytye: thou shalt plucke them awaye euen as thou hast plucked me, because of all my wyckednes. For my sorowe is very greate, and my herte is heuy.

# CHAPTER 2

ALEPH. Alas, how hath the Lorde darkened the daughter of Syon so sore in hys wrath? As for the honour of Israel, he hath casten it downe from heauen: How happeneth it, that he remembred not hys owne fote stole when he was angrye?

2 Beth. The Lorde hath cast downe all the glorye of Iacob without any fauoure: all the stronge places of the daughter Iuda hath he broken in his wrath, and thorowen them downe to the grounde: her kyngdome & her Princes hath he suspended.

3 Gymel. In the wrath of his indygnacyon he hath broken all the horne of Israel: he hath withdrawen his ryght hande from the enemye: yee a flame of fyre is kyndled in Iacob, and hath consumed vp all rounde aboute.

4 Daleth. Ie hath bent hys bowe lyke an enemye, he hath fastened his ryght hande as an aduersarye: and euerye thynge that was pleasaunt to se, he hath smyten it downe. He hath poured out hys wrath lyke a fyre, into the tabernacle of the daughter of Syon.

5 He. The Lorde is become lyke as it were an enemye, he hath cast downe Israell & all hys places: yee all his stronge holdes hath he destroyed, & fylled the daughter of Iuda wyth moch sorow and heuynesse.

6 Vau. Her tabernacle (which was lyke a garden of pleasure) hath he destroyed: her hye solempne feastes hath he put downe. The Lorde hath brought it so to passe, that the hye solempne feastes & Sabbathes in Sion, are cleane forgotten. In his heuy displeasure hath he made the kynge and prestes to be despysed.

7 Zain. The Lorde hath forsaken hys owne aulter, and is wroth with his owne Sanctuary, and hath geuen the walles of their towres in to the handes of the enemye. Their enemyes made a noyse in the house of þe Lorde, as it had bene in a solempne feast daye.

8 Heth. The Lorde thought to breake downe the walles of the daughter Sion, he spred out his lyne, & drewe not in his hande, tyll he had destroyed them. Therfore mourne the turrettes and the broken walles together.

9 Teth. Her portes are casten downe to the grounde, her barres are broken and smytten in sonder: her kynge & pryncres are caried awaye to the Gentyles. They haue nether lawe ner Prophetes, ner yet eny visyon from the Lorde.

10 Iod. The Senatours of the daughter Syon syt vpon the grounde in sylence: they haue strowed asshes vpon their heades, and gyrded them selues with sack cloth. The maydens of Ierusalem hange downe their heades to the grounde.

11 Caph. Myne eyes begynne to fayle me thorowe wepyng, my body is disquieted, my leuer is poured vpon the earth, for the greate hurte of my people, seynge the chyldren and babes dyd swowne in the stretes of the cytie.

12 Lamed. Euen when they spake to their mothers: where is meate and dryncke? for whyle they so sayde, they fell downe in the stretes of the cytye, lyke as they had bene wounded, and some dyed in their mothers bosome.

13 Mem. What shall I saye of the, O thou daughter Ierusalem, to whom shall I lycken the? To whom shall I compare the, O thou daughter Sion, to conforte the with all? Thy hurte is lyke a many see, who maye heale the?

14 Nun. Thy prophetes haue loked out vayne and folish thinges for the, they haue not shewed the of thy wickednesse, to kepe the from captyuite: but haue ouerladen the, and thorowe falshed scatred the abrode.

15 Samech. All they that go by the, clappe their handes at the: hissynge and waggynge their heades vpon the daughter Ierusalem, and saye: is this the cytie that man call so fayre, wherin the whole lande reioyseth?

16 Ain. All thyne enemyes gape vpon the, whisperynge and bytynge their teth, sayinge: let vs deuoure, for the tyme that we loked for, is come: we haue founde and sene it.

17 Phe The Lord hath fullfylled the thynge, that he was purposed to do: and perfourmed that he had dewysed longe a go: he hath destroyed and not spared. He hath caused thyne aduersary to triumphe ouer the, & set vp the horne of thyne enemye.

18 Zade. Let thyne hert crye vnto the Lorde, O thou cytie of the daughter Sion: let thy teares runne downe lyke a ryuer daye & night: rest not, & let not þe aple of thine eye leaue of.

19 Koph. Stande vp and make thy prayer in þe first watch of the nyght, poure oute thyne herte lyke water before the Lord: lyft vp thyne handes, for the lyues of thy yonge chyldren, that dye of honger in the stretes.

20 Res. Behold, O Lord, and consydre, why hast thou gathered me vp so cleane? Shall the wemen then eate their owne fruyte, euen chyldren of a spanne longe? Shall the prestes and prophetes be slayne thus in the Sanctuarye of the Lorde?

21 Sin. Yonge & olde lye behynde the stretes vpon the grounde, my maydens & yonge men are slayne wyth the swearde: whom thou in the daye of thy wrathfull indignacyon haste put to death: yee euen thou hast put them to death, and not spared them.

22 Thau. My neyghbours þt are rounde aboute me, hast thou called, as it were to a feast daye: so that in the daye of the Lordes wrath none escaped, nether was eny left behinde. Those that I had brought vp and noryshed, hath myne enemy destroyed.

# CHAPTER 3

A LEPH. I am the man, that (thorowe the rodd of hys wrath) haue experyence of mysery.

2 He droue me forth, and led me: yee into darcknesse, but not in to lyght.

3 Agaynst me onely he turneth hys hande, and layeth it euer vpon me.

4 Beth. My flesh & my skynne hath he made olde, and my bones hath he brused.

5 He hath buylded rounde aboute me, & closed me in wyth gall and trauayle.

6 He hath set me in darcknesse, as they that be deed for euer.

7 Gymel. He hath so hedged me in, that I can not get out, and hath layed heuy lynckes vpon me.

8 Though I crye and call piteously, yet heareth he not my prayer.

9 He hath stopped vp my wayes wyth foure squared stones, and made my pathes croked.

10 Daleth. He layeth wayte for me lyke a Bere, & as a lyon in a hole.

11 He hath marred my wayes, and broken me in peces, he hath layed me waste altogether

12 He hath bent his bowe, and made me as it were a marck to shutte at.

13 He. The arowes of his quyuer hath he shot, euen into my reynes.

14 I am laughed to scorne of al my people, they make songes vpon me all þe daye longe.

15 He hath fylled me with bytternesse, and geuen me wormwod to dryncke.

16 Vau. He hath smytten my teth in peces, & rolled me in the dust.

17 He hath put my soule out of rest, I forget all good thynges.

18 I thought in my selfe: I am vndone, there is no hope for me in the Lorde.

19 Zain. O remembre yet my mysery & my trouble the wormwod and the gall.

20 Yee thou shalt remembre them, for my soule melteth awaye in me.

21 Whyle I consydre these thynges in my hert, I get a hope agayne.

22 Heth. Namely, þt the mercyes of the Lord are not cleane gone, and that hys louynge kyndnesse ceasseth not.

23 His faythfulnes is greate, and renueth it selfe as the mournynge.

24 The Lorde is my porcyon, sayeth my soule therfore wyll I hope in hym.

25 Teth. O how good is þe Lord vnto them, þt put their truste in him, & to þe soule þt seketh after him?

26 O how good is it with stylnesse to wate & tarye, for the health of the Lorde?

27 O how good is it for a man, to take the yock vpon hym from hys youth vp.

28 Iod. He sytteth alone, he holdeth hym still, and dwelleth quyetly by him selfe?

29 He layeth his face vpon the earth, yf (percase) there happen to be eny hope.

30 He offreth hys cheke to the smyter, he wyl be content with reproues.

31 Caph. For the Lorde wyll not forsake for euer.

32 But though he do cast of, yet accordynge to þe multitude of hys mercyes, he receyueth to grace agayne.

33 For he doeth not plage, & cast out the chyldren of men from his herte.

34 Lamed. To treade all the

presoners of the earth vnder hys fete.

35 To moue the iudgement of man before the most hyghest.

36 To condemne a man in hys cause: The Lorde hath no pleasure in soche thynges.

37 Mem. What is he then that sayeth: there shuld somethynge be done without the Lordes commaundement:

38 Out of the mouth of the mooste Hyghest goeth not euell and good?

39 Wherfore then murmureth the lyuynge man? let hym murmure at hys owne synne.

40 Nun. Let vs loke well vpon oure owne wayes, and remembre oure selues, and turne agayne to the Lorde.

41 Let vs lyft vp oure hertes with oure handes vnto the Lorde that is in heauen.

42 We haue bene dyssemblers, and haue offended, wylt thou therfore not be intreated?

43 Samech. Thou hast couered vs in thy wrath, & persecuted vs, thou hast slayne vs wythout any fauoure.

44 Thou hast hyd thy selfe in a cloude, that oure prayer shulde not go thorow.

45 Thou hast made vs outcastes, and to be despysed amonge the Heathen.

46 Ain. All oure enemyes gape vpon vs.

47 Feare and snare is come vpon vs, yee despyte and destruccyon.

48 Whole riuers of water gushe out of myne eyes, for the greate hurte of my people.

49 Phe Myne eyes runne, and can not ceasse, for there is no rest.

50 O Lorde, when wylt thou loke downe from heauen and consydre?

51 Myne eye breaketh my herte, because of all the daughters of my cyte.

52 Zade. Myne enemyes hunted me out sharpely, lyke a byrde, yee and that without a cause

53 They haue put downe my life into a pitte and layed a stone vpon me.

54 They poured water vpon my head, then thought I: now am I vndone.

55 Koph. I called vpon thy name, O Lorde, out of the depe pytte.

56 Thou hast herde my voyce, and hast not turned awaye thine eares fro my syghinge & cryenge.

57 Thou hast enclyned thy self vnto me, when I called vpon the, and haste sayde: feare not.

58 Res. Thou (O Lorde) hast mayntened the cause of my soule, and hast redemed my lyfe.

59 O Lorde, thou hast sene my blasphemers take thou my cause vpon the.

60 Thou hast well consydred how they go about to do me harme, and that all their councels are agaynst me.

61 Sin. Thou hast herde their despytefull wordes (O Lorde) yee and all their ymaginacyons agaynst me.

62 The lippes of myne enemyes, and their deuyces that they take agaynst me, all the daye longe.

63 Thou seyst also their syttinge downe and their rysinge vp, they make their songes of nothinge but of me.

64 Thau. Rewarde them (O Lorde) accordynge to the workes of their handes.

65 Geue them the thynge, that their owne herte is afraied of: euen thy curse.

66 Persecute them (O Lorde) with thyne indygnacyon, and rote them out from vnder the heauen.

# CHAPTER 4

ALEPH. O how is the golde become so dymme? How is the goodly coloure of it so sore chaunged? and the stones of the Sanctuarye thus scatred in the corner of euery strete?

2 Beth. The chyldren of Syon that were alwaye in honoure, & clothed with the most precious golde: how are they now becomme lyke the erthen vessels whych be made wyth the potters hande,

3 Gymel. The Lamyes geue their yonge ones suck with bare brestes: but the daughter of my people is cruell, and dwelleth in the wyldernesse: lyke the Eltriches.

4 Daleth. The tonges of the suckyng chyldren, cleue to the rofe of their mouthes for very thyrste. The yonge chyldren aske bred, but there is noman, that geueth it them.

5 He. They that were wonte to fayre delicatly, peryshe in the streates: they that a fore were brought vp in purple, make now moche of donge.

6 Dau. The synne of the daughter of my people is be come greater then the wyckednesse of Sodome, that sodenly was destroyed, & not taken with handes.

7 Zain. Herabsteyners (or Nazarees) were whyter then the snowe or mylke: their coloure was fresh read as the Corall, their beutie lyke the Saphyre.

8 Heth. But now their faces are very black: In so moche, that thou shuldest not knowe them in the streates. Their skynne cleueth to their bones, It is wythered, & become lyke a drye stock.

9 Teth. They that be slayne with the swearde, are happier then soch as dye of honger, and perishe awaye famyshyng for the fruites of the felde.

10 Iod. The wemen (which of nature are pitieful) haue sodden their owne children with their handes that they might be their meate, in the miserable

destruccion of the daughter of my people.

11 Caph. The Lorde hath perfourmed hys heuy wrath: he hath poured out the furiousnes of hys dyspleasure. He hath kyndled a fyre in Sion, which hath consumed the foundacions therof.

12 Lamed. Nether the kinges of the earth, ner all the inhabitours of þe worlde, wolde haue beleued that þe enemie & aduersarye shulde haue come in at the gates of the cytie of Hierusalem.

13 Mem. Whiche neuertheles is come to passe for the synnes of her prophetes, and for the wyckednes of her Prestes that haue shed innocentes bloude with in her.

14 Nun. So that these blynde men wente stomblynge in the streates, & stayned them selues with bloude, whiche els wolde touche no bloudy cloth.

15 Samech. But they cryed vnto euerye man: flee the staynyng, awaye, get you hence touch it not. Yee (sayde they) ye muste be brent, ye muste dwell amonge the Gentiles, and byde no longer here.

16 Ain. The countenaunce of the Lorde hath banished them, and shall neuer loke more vpon them: For they them selues nether regarded the prestes, not pytied their elders.

17 Phe. Wherfore yet oure eyes fayle vs, whyle we loke for vayne helpe: seynge we be euer waytyng vpon a people, þt can do vs no good.

18 Zade. They laye so sharpe waite for vs, that we can not go safe vpon þe streates: for our ende is come, oure dayes are fulfylled, oure ende is here.

19 Koph. Oure persecuters are swyfter then the Aegles of þe ayre, they folowed vpon vs ouer the mountaynes, and layed wayte for vs in the wildernesse.

20 Res. The verye breth of oure mouth: euen the anoynted Lorde him self shalbe taken in oure synnes, of whom we saye: Vnder his shadowe we shalbe preserued amonge the Heythen.

21 Sin. And thou (O daughter Edom) that dwellest in the lande of Huz, be glad and reioyce: for the cuppe shall come vnto the also, which whan thou soppest of thou shalt be droncken.

22 Thau. Thy sinne is well punished (O thou daughter Sion) he shall not suffre the to be caryed awaye eny more. But thy wyckednesse (O daughter Edom) shall he vyset, and for thy synnes sake, he shall lede the in to captiuite.

# CHAPTER 5

Call to remembraunce (O Lorde) what we haue suffred, consydre and se oure confusyon.

2 Oure enherytaunce is turned to the straungers, and oure houses to the aleauntes.

3 We are become carefull and fatherlesse, and oure mothers are as the wydowes.

4 We are fayne to drinke oure owne water for money, and oure owne wod muste we bye wyth moneye.

5 Oure nec are vnder persecucyon, we are weery, and haue no rest.

6 A fore tyme we yelded oure selues to the Egypcians, and now to the Assiryans, onely that we myght haue bred ynough.

7 Oure fathers (whiche now are gone) haue synned, & we must beare their wyckednesse.

8 Seruauntes haue the rule of vs, & no man delyuereth vs out of their handes.

9 We must gett oure lyuynge with the parell of oure lyues because of the drouth of the wyldernesse.

10 Oure skynne is as it had bene brent in an ouen, for very sore honger.

11 The wyues are raueshed in Syon, and the maydens in the cytyes of Iuda.

12 The prynces are hanged vp wyth the hande of the enemyes, they haue not spared the olde sage men,

13 they haue taken yonge mens lyues from them, and the boyes are hanged vp vpon trees.

14 The elders syt no more vnder the gates, and the yonge men vse no more playeng of Musyke.

15 The ioye of oure herte is gone, oure merye quere is turned into mournynge.

16 The garlande of oure head is fallen: alas, that euer we synned so sore.

17 Therfore oure herte is full of heuynesse, and oure eyes dymme:

18 because of the hyll of Syon that is destroyed. In so moch, that the foxes runne vpon it.

19 But thou, O Lord, that remaynest for euermore, and thy seate world wythout ende:

20 wherfore wilt thou styll forgett vs, and forsake vs so longe?

21 O Lord, turne thou vs vnto the, and so shall we be turned. Renne our dayes as in olde tymes,

22 for thou hast banyshed vs now long ynough, & hast bene sore dyspleased at vs

# Ezekiel

## CHAPTER 1

IT chaunsed in the .xxx. yeare the fifth daye of the .iiij. Moneth, that I was amonge the presoners by the ryuer of Cobar: where the heauens opened, and I sawe a vysyon of God.

2 Now the fyfth daye of the moneth made out the fyfth yeare of Kyng Ioacins captiuytye.

3 At the same tyme came the worde of the Lord vnto Ezechiel the sonne of Buzi the Preste, in the lande of the Caldees by the water of Cubar, where the hande of the Lorde came vpon hym.

4 And I loked, and beholde a stormy wynde came out of the North with a greate cloude full of fyre, which with hys glystre lyghtned all rounde aboute. And in the myddest of the fyre it was all cleare,

5 and as it were the lycknesse of foure beastes, which were fashyoned lyke a man: sauyng,

6 that euery one had foure faces and foure wynges.

7 Their legges were streyght, but their fete were lyke bullackes fete, and they glystered, as it had bene fayre scoured metall.

8 Vnder their wynges vpon all the foure corners they had mens handes. Their faces and their wynges were towarde the foure corners:

9 yet were the wynges so, that one euer touched another. When they wente, they turned them not aboute: but echone went streyght forwarde.

10 Vpon the ryght syde of these foure, their faces were lyke the face of a man, and the face of a Lyon: But vpon the left syde, they had the face of an oxe, and the face of an Aegle.

11 Their faces also and their wynges were spred out aboue: so that two winges of one touched euer two wynges of of another, and wyth the other they couered their body.

12 Euery one when it wente, it wente streyght forwarde. Where as the sprete ledd them, thether they went, and turned not aboute in their goynge.

13 The fashyon and countenaunce of the beastes was lyke hoate coales of fyre, euen as though burnynge cressettes had bene amonge the beastes: and the fyre gaue a glystre, and out of the fyre there wente lyghtenynge.

14 When the beastes wente forwarde and backwarde, one wolde haue thought it had lyghtened.

15 Now when I had well considered the beastes, I sawe a worcke of wheles vpon the earth with foure faces also lyke the beastes.

16 The fashyon and worcke of the wheles was lyke the sea. The foure wheles were ioyned and made (to loke vpon) as it had bene one whele in another.

17 When one wente forwarde, they wente all foure, and turned them not about in their goinge.

18 They were large, greate and horryble to loke vpon. Their bodyes were full of eyes round about them all foure. When the beastes wente the wheles wente also with them:

19 And when the beastes lyft them selues vp from the earth, the wheles were lyft vp also.

20 Whether soeuer the sprete wente, thether wente they also, and the wheles were lyft vp, and folowed them: for the sprete of lyfe was in the wheles.

21 When the beastes went forth, stode styll, or lyft them selues vp from the earth: then the wheles also wente, stode styll, and were lyft vp, for the breth of lyfe was in the wheles.

22 Aboue ouer the heades of the beastes there was a fyrmament, whyche was fashyoned as it had bene of the most pure Chrystal, and that was spred out aboue vpon their heades:

23 vnder the same fyrmament were their wynges layed abrode, one toward another, and two winges couered the body of euery beast.

24 And when they wente forth, I hearde the noyse of their wynges, lyke the noyse of greate waters, as it had bene the voyce of the greate God, and a russhynge together as it were of an hoost of men. And when they stode styll, they let downe their wynges.

25 Now when they stode styll, and had letten downe their wynges, it thondred in the fyrmament that was aboue their heades.

26 Aboue the firmament that was ouer their heades, there was the fashyon of a seate, as it had bene made of Saphir. Vpon the seate there sat one lyke a man.

27 I behelde hym, & he was lyke a cleare lyght, as it had bene all of fyre with in from hys loynes vpwarde. And beneth when I loked vpon him vnder the loynes, me thought he was lyke a shynyng fyre, that geueth lyght on euery syde. Yee the shyne & glystre that lyghtened rounde aboute,

28 was lyke a raynbowe, which in a raynye daye appeareth in the cloudes. Euen so was the symylitude, wherin the glory of the Lorde appeared. When I sawe it, I fel vpon my face, and herkened vnto the voyce of him that spake.

## CHAPTER 2

And then sayde he vnto me: Stande vp vpon thy fete (O thou sonne of man) and I wyll talke with the.

2 And as he was commonynge with me, the sprete came in to me, and sett me vp vpon my fete: so that I marcked the thinge, that he sayde vnto me.

3 And he sayde: Beholde, thou sonne of man: I wyll sende the to the chyldren of Israell, to those runnagates and obstynate people: for they haue taken parte agaynst me and are runne awaye fro me: both they and their forefathers vnto this daye.

4 Yee I will sende the vnto a people that haue rough disages and styf stomackes: vnto whom thou shalt saye on this maner: This the Lorde God hym selfe hath spoken,

5 that whether they be obedyent or no (for it is a frowarde housholde) they maye knowe yet that there hath bene a Prophet amonge them.

6 Therfore (thou sonne of man) feare them not, nether be afrayed of their wordes: for they shall rebell agaynst the, and despyse the. Yee thou shalt dwell amonge scorpions: but feare not their wordes, be not abashed at their lokes, for it is a frowarde housholde.

7 Se that thou speake my wordes vnto them, whether they be obedyent or not, for they are obstynate.

8 Therfore, thou sonne of men, obey thou all thynges, that I saye vnto the, and be not thou styfnecked, lyke as they are a styfnecked housholde. Open thy mouth and eate that I geue the.

9 So as I was lokynge vp, beholde, there was sent vnto me an hande, wherin was a closed boke:

10 & the hande opened it before me, & it was wrytten within & wythout, full of carefull mournynges: alas, and wo.

## CHAPTER 3

After this sayde he vnto me: Thou sonne of man, eate that, whatsoeuer it be: yee eate that closed boke & go thy waye, and speak vnto the chyldren of Israel.

2 So I opened my mouth, and he gaue me the boke for to eate,

3 and sayde vnto me: Thou sonne of man, thy bely shall eate, and thy bowels shalbe fylled with the boke, that I geue the. Then dyd I eate the boke, and it was in my mouth sweter then hony.

4 And he sayde vnto me: thou sonne of man, get the soone vnto the house of Israel, and shewe them the wordes, that I commaunde the:

5 for I sende the not to the people that hath a straunge, vnknowne, or harde speache, but vnto the house of Israel:

6 Not to many nacyons, which haue dyuerse speaches & harde languages, whose wordes thou vnderstandest not: Neuerthelesse: yf I sent the to those people, they wolde folowe the:

7 But the house of Israel wyll not folowe the, for they wyll not folowe me: yee all the house of Israell haue styf foreheades and harde hertes.

8 Beholde therfore, I wyll make thy face preuayle agaynst their faces, and harden thy foreheade agaynst their foreheades:

9 so that thy foreheade shalbe harder then an Adamaunte or flynt stone: that thou mayeste feare them the lesse, and be lesse afrayed of them, for they are a frowarde housholde.

10 He sayde moreouer vnto me: thou sonne of man, take dylygent hede wyth thyne eares, to the wordes that I speake vnto the, fasten them in thyne herte:

11 and go to the presoners of thy people, speake vnto them, and saye on this maner: Thus the Lorde God hath spoken: whether ye heare, or heare not.

12 Wyth that the sprete toke me vp. And I hearde the noyse of a greate russhynge and remouynge of the most blessed glory of the Lorde out of his place.

13 I hearde also the noyse of the wynges of the beastes, that russhed one agaynst another, yee

and the ratlynge of the wheles, that were by them, whyche russhynge and noyse was very greate.

14 Now when the sprete toke me vp, and caried me awaye, I wente with an heuy and a sorowfull mynde, but the hande of the Lorde comforted me ryght soone.

15 And so in the begynnynge of the moneth Abib, I came to the presoners, that dwelt by the water of Cobar, and remayned in that place, where they were: And so contynued I amonge them seuen dayes, beinge verye sory.

16 And when the seuen dayes were expired, the Lord sayde vnto me:

17 Thou sonne of man I haue made the a watchman vnto the house of Israell: therfore take good hede to the wordes, and geue them warnyng at my commaundement.

18 If I sayde vnto the, concernynge the vngodly man: that (wythout doute) he muste dye, and thou geuest hym not warnynge, ner speakest vnto hym, that he maye turne from hys euell waye, and so to lyue: Then shalll the same vngodly man dye in hys owne vnryghtuousnes: but hys bloude wyll I requyre of thyne hande.

19 Neuertheles, yf thou geue warnynge vnto the wycked, and he yet forsake not his vngodlynesse: then shall he dye in his owne wyckednesse, but thou hast discharged thy soule.

20 Now yf a ryghtuous man go from his rightuousnesse, and do the thynge that is euell: I will laye a stomblynge blocke before hym, & he shall dye, because thou hast not geuen him warning: yee dye shall he in hys owne synne so that the vertue, which he dyd before, shall not be thought vpon: but hys bloude wyll I requyre of thyne hande.

21 Neuerthelesse, yf thou exhortest the ryghtuous, that he synne not, & so the ryghtuous do not synne: then shall he lyue, because he hath receyued thy warnynge, and thou hast dyscharged thy soule.

22 And there came the hand of the Lorde vpon me, and he sayde vnto me: Stande vp, and go into the felde, that I may there talke wyth the.

23 So when I had rysen vp, and gone forth in to the felde: Beholde, the glory of the Lord stode there, lyke as I saw it afore, by the water of Cobar. Then fell I downe vpon my face,

24 and the sprete came in to me, whych set me vp vpon my fete, & sayde thus vnto me: Go thy waye, and sparre thy self in thyne house.

25 Beholde, (O thou sonne of man) there shall chaynes be brought for the, to bynde the withall, so that thou shalt not escape out of them.

26 And I wyll make thy tunge cleue so to the rofe of thy mouth, that thou shalt be domme, and not be as a chyder wyth them: for it is an obstynate housholde.

27 But when I speake vnto the, then open thy mouth, and saye: Thus sayeth the Lorde God: who so heareth, lett hym heare: who so wyll not, let hym leaue: for it is an obstynate housholde.

# CHAPTER 4

THOU sonne of man: take a tylle stone, & laye it before the, and descrybe vpon it the cytie of Ierusalem,

2 how it is beseged, how bulworckes & stronge dyches are grauen on euery syde of it: descrybe also tentes, and an hooste of men rounde aboute it.

3 Moreouer, take an yron panne, and set it betwixte the and the cyte, insteade of an yron wall. Then set thy face towarde it, besege it, and laye ordynaunce agaynst it, to wynne it. This shalbe a token vnto the house of Israel.

4 But thou shalt slepe vpon thy left syde, and laye the sinne of the house of Israell vpon the. Certayne dayes appoynted, thou shalt slepe vpon that syde, and beare their synnes.

5 Neuerthelesse, I wyll appoynte the a tyme (to put of their sinnes) and the nombre of the dayes: Thre hundreth and .xc. dayes muste thou beare the wyckednesse of the house of Israell.

6 When thou hast fulfylled these dayes lye downe agayne, and slepe vpon thy right syde .xl. dayes, and beare the synnes of the house of Iuda. A daye for a yeare, a daye (I saye) for a yeare, wyll I euer laye vpon the.

7 Therfore set now thy face agaynst that beseged Ierusalem, and dyscouer thyne arme, that thou mayest prophecye agaynst it.

8 Beholde, I wyll laye chaynes vpon the, that thou shalt not turne the frome one side to another, tyll thou haste ended the dayes of thy sege.

9 Wherfore, take vnto the wheate, barlye beanes, growell sede, Millium and fitches: and put these together in a vessell, and make the loaues of bred therof, accordynge to the nombre of the dayes that thou must lye vpon thy side: that thou mayeste haue bred to eate, for thre hundreth and .xc. dayes.

10 And the meate that thou eatest, shall haue a certayne wayght appoynted: namely twentye sicles euery daye. This apoynted meate shalt thou eate daylye, from the begynnynge to the ende.

11 Thou shalt dryncke also a certayne measure of water: Namely, the syxte parte of an Hin shalt thou dryncke daylye from the begynnynge vnto the ende.

12 Barlye cakes shalt thou

eate, yet shalt thou fyrste stracke them ouer with mans donge, that they maye se it.

13 And with that sayde the Lorde: Euen thus shall the chyldren of Israel eate their defiled bred in the myddest of the Gentyles, amonge whom I wyll scatre them.

14 Then sayde I: Oh Lorde God. Beholde, my soule was yet neuer stayned: for fro my youth vp vnto this houre. I did neuer eate of a deed carcase, or of that whiche was slayne of wylde beastes, nether cam there euer eny vncleane flesh in my mouth.

15 Wher vnto he answered me, and sayde Well than, I wyll graunte the to take cowes donge, for the donge of a man, and to strake the bred ouer with all, before them.

16 And he sayde vnto me: Beholde thou sonne of man, I wyll mynishe all the prouisyon of bred in Ierusalem, so that they shall wepe theyr bred, and eate it with scarcenesse. But as for water, they shall haue a verye lytle measure therof, to dryncke.

17 And when they haue nomore bred ner water, one shall be destroyed wyth another, and famyshe awaye for their wyckednesse.

## CHAPTER 5

O thou sonne of man, take the then a sharpe knyfe, namely, a rasoure. Take that, & shaue the hearre of thy head and beerd: Then take the scoales and the waight, and deuyde the hearre a sunder.

2 And burne the thirde parte therof in the fyre in the myddest of the cytie, & cut the other thirde parte in peces with a knyfe. As for the thirde parte that remayneth, cast it in the wynde, & then shewe the bare knyfe.

3 Yet afterwarde take a lytle of the same, and bynde it in thy cote lappe.

4 Then take a curtesy of it, and cast it in the myddest of the fyre: & burne it in the fyre. Out of the same fyre shall there goo a flame, vpon the whole house of Israell.

5 Morouer, thus sayde the Lorde God: This same is Ierusalem. I sett her in the myddest of the Heathen & nacions: that are rounde aboute her,

6 but she hath despysed my iudgmentes more then the Gentiles them selues, and broken my commaundementes more then the nacyons, that lye round aboute her: For they haue cast out myne ordinaunces, & not walcked in my lawes.

7 Therfore, thus sayeth the Lord God: For so moch as ye with youre wickednesse farre exceade the Heathen, that dwell rounde aboute you: (For ye haue not walcked in my lawes, nether haue ye kepte myne ordinaunces)

8 Therfore thus sayeth the Lorde God. I wyll also come vpon the, for in the myddest of the wyll I syt in iudgment, in the syght of the Heathen,

9 and wyll handle the of soch a fashion, as I neuer dyd before, and as I neuer will do from that tyme forth, and that because of all thyne abhominacyons.

10 For in the fathers shall be fayne to eate their owne sonnes, and the sonnes their owne fathers. Soch a courte will I kepe in the, & the whole remnaunt will I scatre in to all the wyndes.

11 Wherfore as trulye as I lyue (sayeth the Lord God) seyng thou hast defiled my Sanctuary, with all maner of abhominacyons and with al thy shameful offences: For this cause will I also destroye the. Myne eye shall not ouer se the, nether will I spare the.

12 One thirde parte within the, shall dye of the pestilence and of honger: Another thirde parte shall be slayne downe rounde aboute the, with the swearde: The other thirde parte that remayneth, will I scatre abroade towarde all the wyndes, and drawe out the swearde after them.

13 Thus I wyll perfourme my indignacion & set my wrath agaynst them, and ease my selfe. So that when I haue fulfylled myne anger agaynst them, they shall knowe that I am the Lorde, whiche with a feruent glousye haue spoken it.

14 Moreouer I wyll make the waste and abhorred, befor all the Heathen that dwell aboute the, & in the syght of all them, that go by the:

15 so that when I punishe the in my wrath, in myne anger, & with the plage of my whote displeasure: thou shalt be a very abhominacion, shame, a gasynge & wondrynge stocke, amonge the Heathen that lye aboute the. Euen I the Lorde haue spoken it, and it shall come to passe,

16 when I shute amonge them the perlous dartes of honger, which shalbe but death: Yee therfore shall I shute them, because I wyll destroye you I will encrease hunger, & mynishe all the prouisyon of bred amonge you.

17 Plages and mysery wyll I sende you, yee and wylde beastes also to destroye you Pestilence & bloudshedynge shall come vpon you, and the swearde will I bringe ouer you. Euen I the Lorde, haue sayde it.

## CHAPTER 6

AND the worde of the Lord came vnto me, sayinge:

2 Thou sonne of man, turne thy face to the mountaynes of Israel, that thou mayest prophecie vnto them,

3 & saye Heare the worde of

the Lorde God, O ye mountaynes of Israell: Thus hath the Lorde God spoken to the mountaynes, hilles, valleyes and dales. Beholde, I wyll brynge a swearde ouer you, & destroye youre hye places:

4 I wyll cast downe youre aulters, & breake downe youre temples. Youre slayne men wyll I laye before youre goddes,

5 and the deed carcases of the chyldren of Israell wyll I caste before their ymages, youre bones will I destroye rounde aboute youre aulters,

6 and dwellynge places. The cyties shalbe desolate, the hyllchapels layed waste: youre aulters destroyed, and broken: youre goddes caste downe and taken awaye, youre tempels layde eauen wyth the grounde, youre owne worckes cleane rote oute.

7 Youre slayne men shall lye amonge you, that ye maye learne to knowe, how that I am the Lorde.

8 Those that amonge you haue escaped the swearde, will I leaue amonge the Gentyles, for I wyll scatre you amonge the nacyons.

9 And they that escape from you, shall thyncke vpon me amonge the Heathen, where they shalbe in captiuyte. As for that whorysh & vnfaythfull herte of theirs, wherwyth they runne awaye fro me, I wyll break it: yee and put oute those eyes of theirs, that commytte fornicacyon with their Idols. Then shall they be ashamed, and displeased wyth their selues, for the wyckednesses & abhomynacions, which they haue done:

10 and shall learne to knowe, how that it is not in vayne, that I the Lorde spake, to brynge soch mysery vpon them.

11 The Lorde sayde moreouer vnto me: Smyte thyne handes together, and stampe wyth thay fete, & saye: Wo worth all the abhominacions and wickednesses of the house of Israel, for because of them, they shall perishe wyth the swearde, with honger & wyth pestilence.

12 Who so is farre of, shall dye of the pestilence: he that is nye at hande, shall perish with the swearde: and the other that are beseged, shall dye of honger. Thus wyll I satisfye my wrothfull displeasure vpon them.

13 And so shall ye learne to knowe, that I am the Lorde, when youre slayne men lye amonge youre goddes, and aboute youre aulters: vpon all hye hylles & toppes of mountaynes, amonge all grene trees, amonge all thycke okes: euen in the places, where they dyd sacrifyce to all their Idols.

14 I wyll stretch myne hande oute vpon them, and wyll make the lande waste: So that it shall lye desolate and voyde, from the wyldernesse of Deblathah forth, thorow all their habitacyons: to learne them for to knowe, that I am the Lorde

## CHAPTER 7

THE worde of the Lorde came vnto me on this maner:

2 The I call, O thou sonne of man. Thus sayeth the Lorde God vnto the lande of Israell: The ende commeth, yee verely the ende commeth vpon all the foure corners of the earth.

3 But now shall the ende come vpon the: for I wyll sende my wrath vpon the, and wyll punishe the accordynge to thy wayes, and rewarde the after all thy abhominacyons.

4 Myne eye shall not ouerse the, nether will I spare the, but rewarde the accordynge to thy wayes, and declare thy abhomynacyons. Then shall ye knowe, that I am the Lorde.

5 Thus sayeth the Lord God: Beholde, one mysery & plage shall come after anothr:

6 the ende is here. The ende (I saye) that wayteth for the, is come all readye,

7 the houre is come agaynst the, that dwellest in the lande. The tyme is at hande, the daye of sedicyon is hard by, and no glad tydynges vpon the mountaynes.

8 Therfore, I will shortly poure out my sore displeasure ouer the, and fulfyll my wrath vpon the. I will iudge the after thy wayes, and recompence the all thy abhominacyons.

9 Myne eye shall not ouerse the, nether will I spare the: but rewarde the after thy wayes, and shewe thy abhomynacions, to learne you for to knowe, how that I am the Lorde that smyteth.

10 Beholde, the daye is here the daye is come, the houre is runne oute, the rodde florisheth, wylfulnesse waxeth grene,

11 malicious violence is growne vp, and the vngodly waxen to a stafe. Yet shall there no complaynte be made for them, ner for the trouble that shall come of these thynges.

12 The tyme commeth, the daye draweth nye: Who so byeth, lett hym not reioyce: he that selleth, let hym not be sory: for why. Trouble shall come in the myddeste of all reste:

13 so that the seller shall not come agayne to the byer, for nether of them both shall lyue. For the vysion shall come so greatly ouer all, that it shall not be hyndered: No man also with his wickednesse shall be able to saue hys owne lyfe.

14 The trompettes shall ye blowe and make you all ready, but no man shall goo to the battel, for I am wroth with all the whole multitude.

15 The swearde shalbe wythout, pestilence and honger wythin: so that who so is in the felde, shalbe slayne with the swearde: and he that is in the

cytie, shall perishe wyth honger and pestilence.

16 And soche as escape and fle from amonge them, shall be vpon the hylles, lyke as the doues in the felde: euery one shalbe afrayed, because of his owne wickednesse.

17 All handes shalbe let downe, and all knees shalbe weake as the water:

18 they shall gyrde them selues with sacke clothe, feare shall fall vpon them. Their faces shalbe confounded, and their heades balde:

19 their syluer shall lye in the stretes, and their golde shalbe despysed: Yee their siluer and golde maye not deliuer them, in the daye of the fearfull wrath of the Lorde. They shall not satysfye their hongry soules, nether fyll their emptye belyes therwith: For it is become their owne decaye thorowe their wickednes:

20 because they made therof not only costly Ieweles for their pompe and pryde, but also abhomynable ymages and Idoles. For this cause wyll I make them to be abhorred.

21 Moreouer, I will geue it into the handes of the straungers to be spoyled: and to the wycked, for to be robbed, and they shall destroye it.

22 My face wyll I turne from them, my treasury shalbe defiled: for the theues shall go in to it, and suspende it.

23 I wyll make clene ryddaunse, for the land is whole defiled with vnrighteous iudgement of innocent bloud & the citie is full of abhomynacyons.

24 Wherfore, I wyll brynge the most cruell tyrauntes from amonge the Heathen, to take theyr houses in possession. I wil make the pompe of the proude to ceasse, and they shall take in theyr sanctuary.

25 When thys trouble commeth they shall seke peace, but they shal haue none.

26 One myschefe & sorowe shall folowe another, and one rumoure shall come after another: Then shall they seke visions in vayne at theyr Prophetes. The lawe shalbe gone from the Priestes, and wysdom from the elders.

27 The king shal mourne, the Princes shalbe clothed with heuinesse, and the handes of the people in the lande shall tremble for feare. I wyll do vnto them after theyr owne wayes, and according to theyr owne iudgementes wyll I iudge them, to learne them for to knowe, that I am the Lorde.

# CHAPTER 8

It happened, that in the syxte yeare the fyfth daye of the syxte moneth I sat in my house, & the Lordes of the councell of Iuda with me: and the hande of the lord God fell euen there vpon me.

2 And as I loked vp, I saw, as it were a lykenesse of fyre from hys loynes douneward, and from hys loines vpwarde it shyned maruelous cleare.

3 This similytude stretched oute an hande, and toke me by the hearry lockes of my head, and the spryte lyfte me vp betwyxte heauen & earthe: and God brought me in a vision to Ierusalem, into the entrye of the inner porte that lyeth towarde the Northe: there stode an ymage, with whome he that hath all thynges in hys power, was very wroth.

4 And beholde, the glorye of the God of Israel was in the same place: euen as I had sene it afore in the felde.

5 And he sayde vnto me: Thou sonne of man, O lyfte vp thyne eyes, and loke towarde the northe. Then lyfte I vp myne eyes towarde the northe, and beholde: besyde the porte Northwarde, there was an aulter made vnto the ymage of prouocacyon in the verye entrynge in.

6 And he sayd further more vnto me: Thou sonne of man, seist thou what these do? Seyst thou the great abhomynacyons that the house of Israel commytte in this place? which oughte not to be done in my sanctuarye? But turne the aboute, and thou shalte se yet greater abhomynacyons.

7 And with that broughte he me to the courtegate, & when I loked, beholde, there was an hole in the wal.

8 Then sayd he vnto me: Thou sonne of man, dygge thorowe the wall. And when I dygged thorow the wal, behold, ther was a dore.

9 And he sayde vnto me: Go thy waye in, & loke what wycked abhomynacions they do there.

10 So I wente in, & sawe: and beholde, there were all maner ymages of wormes & beastes, all Idoles and abhominacions of the house of Israel paynted euery one round aboute the wall.

11 There stode also before the ymages .lxx. lordes of the councell of the house of Israel, and in the myddeste of them stode Iaazamah the sonne of Saphan: and euerye one of them had a censoure in hys hande, and out of the incense, there wente a smoke, as it had bene a cloude.

12 Then sayde he vnto me: Thou sonne of man, haste thou sene what the Senatoures of the house of Israel do secretly euerye one in hys chambre: For they saye: Tush, the Lorde seyth vs not, the Lord regardeth not the worlde.

13 And he sayde vnto me: Turne the yet agayne, and thou shalte se the greate abhomynacyons that they do.

14 And with that he broughte

me to the dore of the port of the Lordes house, towarde the north. And beholde there sate women mournynge for Thamus.

15 Then sayde he vnto me: haste thou sene this thou sonne of man. Turne the about & thou shalte se yet greater abhomynacyons.

16 And so he broughte me into the inward court of the Lordes house: and beholde at the porte of the Lordes house, betwyxte the fore entrye and the aulter, there were fyue and twentye men, that turned theyr backes vpon the temple of the Lorde, and theyr faces towarde the east & these worshipped the sonne.

17 And he sayde vnto me: hast thou sene this, thou sonne of man? Thyncketh the house of Israel, that it is but a tryflle, to do these abhomynacyons here? Shulde they fyll the lande full of wyckednesse, & vndertake to prouoke me vnto anger? Yea and purposelye to caste vp their noses vpon me:

18 Therfore wyll I also do some thynge in my wrothfull displeasure, so that myne eye shall not ouerse them, nether wyll I spare them. Yea and though they crye in myne eares with loude voyce, yet wyll I not heare them.

## CHAPTER 9

He cryed also with a loude voice in myne eares, sayinge: Come here ye rulers of the citie, euery man with hys weapened hand to the slaughter.

2 Then came there sixe men oute of the strete of the vpper porte toward the north, and euery man a weapen in hys hand to the slaughter. There was one amongest them, that had on hym a lynen rayment, & a wryters ynckhorne by hys syde. These wente in, & stode besyde the brasen aulter:

3 for the glorye of the Lorde was gone awaye from the Cherub, & was come doune to the thresholde of the house, and he called the man that had the lynen raymente vpon hym, & the wryters ynckhorne by hys syde,

4 and the Lorde sayde vnto hym: Go thy waye thorow the cytie of Ierusalem, and set thys marcke Than vpon the foreheades of them, that mourne & are sory for all the abhomynacyons, that be done therin.

5 And to the other, he sayde that I myght heare: Go ye after hym thorow the cytye, slaye, ouerse none, spare none:

6 kyl and destroye bothe olde men and yonge, maydens, chyldren, and wyues. But as for those, that haue thys marcke Than vpon them: se that ye touche them not, & begynne at my sanctuarye. Then they began at the elders, whiche were in the temple,

7 for he had sayde vnto them: When ye haue defyled the temple, and fylled the courte wyth the slayne, then go your waye forth. So they went oute, & slewe doune the slaughter,

8 and I yet escaped: I fell doune vpon my face, and cryed sayinge: O Lorde, wylte thou then destroy al the resydue of Israel, in thy sore displeasure, that thou hast poured vpon Ierusalem?

9 Then sayde he vnto me: The wickednesse of the house of Israel and Iuda is very greate: so that the lande is full of bloude, and the citie full of vnfaythfulnesse: For they saye: Tushe, the Lord regardeth not the earth, he seyth vs not.

10 Therfore wyl I vpon them, myne eye shall not ouerse them, neyther wil I spare them, but wil recompense theyr wyckednesse vpon theyr heades.

11 And beholde, the man that had the lynen rayment vpon hym, and the wryters ynckhorne by hys syde: tolde all the matter how it happened, and sayde: Lorde, as thou haste commaunded me, so haue I done.

## CHAPTER 10

And as I loked, beholde in the fyrmament that was aboue the Cherubyns ther apeared the similitude of a stole of Saphir vpon them

2 Then sayd he that sat therin, to him that had the lynen raiment vpon him: Crepe in betwene the wheles that are vnder the Cherubins, and take thyne hande full of hoate coles oute from betwene the Cherubyns, & cast them ouer the citie. And he crept in, that I myght se.

3 Now the Cherubyns stode vpon the right syde of the house, when the man wente in, and the cloude fylled the ynnermer court,

4 But the glory of the Lorde remoued from the Cherubyns, and came vpon the thresholde of the house: so that the temple was full of cloudes, and the courte was full of the shyne of the Lordes glory.

5 Yea and the sounde of the Cherubyns winges was heard into the fore court lyke as it had bene the voyce of the almyghty God, when he speaketh.

6 Now when he had bydden the man that was clothed in lynen, to go and take the hote coales from the myddest of the wheles, whiche were vnder the Cherubyns: he went & stode besyde the wheles.

7 Then the one Cherub reached forth hys hand from vnder the Cherubyns, vnto the fyre that was betwene the Cherubyns, and toke thereof, & gaue it vnto hym that had on the lynen raymente in hys hande: whiche toke it, and went oute.

8 And vnder the wynges of the Cherubyns, there apeared the lykenesse of a mans hande:

9 I sawe also foure wheles besyde the Cherubyns, so that by euerye Cherub there stode a whele. And the wheles were (to loke vpon) after the fashyon of the precyous stone of Tharsis:

10 yet (vnto the syght) were they fashyoned and lyke, as yf one whele had ben in another.

11 When they wente forthe, they wente all foure together, not turnynge aboute in theyr goynge, But where the fyrste wente, thyther wente they after also, so that they turned not aboute in theyr goynge.

12 Theyr whole bodyes theyr backes, theyr handes and wynges, yea and the wheles also, were all full of eyes rounde aboute them all foure.

13 And I hearde hym call the wheles, Galgal (that is) a rounde boule.

14 Euery one of them had foure faces: so that the one face was the face of a Cherub, the seconde of a man, the thyrde of a lyon, the fourthe of an Aegle,

15 and they were lyfted vp aboue. This is the beaste, that I sawe at the water of Cobar,

16 Nowe when the Cherubins wente, the wheles wente wyth them, & when the Cherubyns shoke theyr wynges to lyfte them selues vpwarde, the wheles remayned not behynde, but were with them also.

17 Shortly, when they stode, these stode also: And when they were lyfte vp, the wheles were lyfte vp also with them, for the sprete of lyfe was in the wheles.

18 Then the glory of the Lorde was lyfte vp from the tresholde of the temple, and remayned vpon the Cherubyns.

19 And the Cherubins flackred wyth theyr wynges, & lyft them selues vp from the earth: so that I sawe when they wente, and the wheles with them. And they stode at the east syde of the porte that is in the house of the Lorde. So the glorye of the Lorde was vpon them.

20 Thys is the beast that I saw vnder the god of Israel, by the water of Cobar. And I perceyued, that it was the Cherubyns.

21 Euerye one had foure faces, and euery one foure wynges, and vnder theyr wynges, as it were mens handes.

22 Now the fygure of theyr faces was, euen as I had sene them, by the water of Cobar, & so was the countenaunce of them: Euery one in hys goynge wente strayght forwarde.

# CHAPTER 11

Moreouer, the sprete of the Lorde lyft me vp, & broughte me vnto the Easte porte of the Lordes house. And beholde, there were .xxv. men vnder the dore among whome I sawe Iaazaniah the sonne of Azur, and Pheltiah the sonne of Bananiah, the rulers of the people.

2 Then sayde the Lorde vnto me: Thou sonne of man: these men ymagyn myschefe, and a wycked councel take they in this citie,

3 sayinge: tushe, there is no destruccyon at hande, let vs buylde houses: thys Ierusalem is the cauldron, & we be the fleshe.

4 Therfore shalte thou prophecye vnto them, yea prophecye shalte thou vnto them, O sonne of man.

5 And wyth that fell the spryte of the Lorde vpon me, and sayd vnto me: Speake, thus saith the Lord: On thys maner haue ye spoken (O ye house of Israell) and I knowe the ymagygacyons of youre hertes.

6 Many one haue ye murthered in thys cyte, and fylled the stretes full of the slayne.

7 Therfore, thus sayth the Lord God: The slayne men that ye haue layed on the grounde in thys cytye, are the fleshe, and thys cytie is the cauldron: But I wyll brynge you oute of it:

8 ye haue drawen out the sweard euen so wyll I also brynge a swearde ouer you, sayeth the Lorde God.

9 I wyll dryue you oute of this citie, and delyuer you into youre enemyes hande, and wyll condemne you.

10 Ye shall be slayne in all the coastes of Israell, I wyll be auenged of you: to learne you for to knowe, that I am the Lorde.

11 This cytie shall not be youre cauldron, neyther shall ye be the fleshe therein: but in the coastes of Israell wil I punyshe you,

12 that ye maye knowe, that I am the Lorde: in whose commaundementes ye haue not walcked, nor kepte his lawes: but haue done after the customes of the Heathen, that lye rounde aboute you.

13 Now when I preached, Pheltiah the sonne of Bananiah dyed. Then fell I doune vpon my face, and cried with a loud voyce: O Lord God, wylte thou then vtterlye destroy all the remnaunte in Israell?

14 And so the word of the Lorde came to me on thys maner:

15 thou sonne of man: thy brethren: thy kynsfolke, and the whole house of Iuda, whiche dwell at Ierusalem, saye: They be gone farre from the Lord, but the lande is geuen vs in possessyon.

16 Therfore tell them, thus sayth the Lorde God: I wyll sende you farre of amonge the Gentyles, and scatre you amonge the nacyons, & I wyll halowe you but a lytle, in the landes where ye shal come.

17 Tel them also, thus saith the Lorde God: I wyll gather you

agayne oute of the nacyons, and bryng you from the countrees where ye be scatred, and wyl geue you the lande of Israel agayne:

18 and thyther shall ye come. And as for all impedymentes and all youre abhomynacyons: I wyll take them awaye.

19 And I wil geue you one herte, and I wyll plante a newe sprete wythin youre bowels. That stony herte wyll I take oute of youre body, & geue you a fleshy herte:

20 that ye maye walke in my commaundementes, and kepe myne ordynaunces, & do them: that ye maye be my people, and I youre God.

21 But loke, whose hertes are dysposed to folowe theyr abhomynacyons & wicked lyuynges: those mens dedes wyll I brynge vpon their owne heades, sayeth the Lorde God.

22 After thys did the Cherubins lyft vp theyr wynges, and the wheles wente wyth them, and the glorye of the Lorde was vpon them.

23 So the glorye of the Lorde wente vp from the myddeste of the cytye, and stode vpon the mounte of the cytye towarde the east.

24 But the wynde toke me vp, & in a vision (which came by the spryte of God) it brought me vp agayne into Caldea among the presoners. Then the vision that I had sene, vanyshed awaye fro me.

25 So I spake vnto the presoners, all the wordes of the Lorde, whiche he had shewed me.

## CHAPTER 12

THE worde of the Lorde came vnto me, sayinge:

2 Thou sonne of man, thou dwellest in the myddest of a frowarde housholde: whiche haue eyes to se, and yet se not: eares haue they to hear, & yet heare thei not, for they are an obstinate housholde.

3 Therfore (O thou sonne of man) make thy gere ready to flyt, and go forth by fayre daye lyghte, that they may se. Yea euen in theyr syght shalt thou go from thy place to another place: yf peraduenture they wyll consydre, that they be an vnobedyente housholde.

4 Thy gere that thou hast made redy to flyt withal, shalt thou bear oute by fayre daye lyghte, that they maye se: and thou thy selfe shalte go forth also at euen in theyr sighte, as a man doeth when he flytteth.

5 Dygge thorowe the wall, that they may se, & beare thorowe it the same thing, that thou tokest vp

6 in theyr sight. As for thy selfe, thou shalte go forth in the darcke. Hyde thy face that thou se not the earthe, for I haue made the a shewtoken vnto the house of Israel.

7 Nowe as the Lorde commaunded me, so I dyd: the gere that I had made ready, brought I oute by daye. At euen I brake doune an hole thorowe the wall with my hande: & when it was darcke, I toke the gere vpon my shoulders, and bare them oute in theyr syghte.

8 And in the mornynge, came the worde of the Lorde vnto me, sayinge:

9 Thou sonne of man, yf Israell that frowarde houshold aske the, and saye: what doest thou there?

10 Then tel them: Thus saith the Lorde God: Thys punyshmente toucheth the chefe rulers at Ierusalem, & all the house of Israell, that dwel amonge them:

11 Tell them: I am youre shewtoken: lyke as I haue done, so shall it happen vnto you: Flyt shall ye also, and go into captyuyte.

12 The chefest that is amonge you, shall lade hys shoulders in the darcke, and get him awaye. He shall breake doune the wal, to cary stuf there thorowe: He shall couer hys face, that he se not the grounde, with his eyes.

13 My lyne wyll I sprede oute vpon hym, & catche him in my net, & carye hym to Babylon, in the lande of the Caldees: whiche he shall not se, and yet shall he dye there.

14 As for al his helpers, & all hys hostes, that be aboute hym, I wyll scatre them towarde all the wyndes, and drawe out a sweard after them.

15 So when I haue scatred them amonge the Heathen, and strowed them in the landes, they shall knowe, that I am the Lorde.

16 But I wyll leaue a lytle nombre of them from the swearde, hunger and pestilence: to tell all theyr abhomynacyons amonge the Heathen, where they come, that they maye knowe, howe that I am the Lorde.

17 Moreouer, the worde of the Lorde came vnto me, sayinge:

18 Thou sonne of man: wyth a fearfull tremblynge shalte thou eate thy breade, with carefulnesse & sorowe shalte thou drincke thy water.

19 And vnto the people of the lande, speake thou on thys maner: Thus sayeth the Lorde God, to them that dwell in Ierusalem, & to the lande of Israel: Ye shall eate youre breade with sorowe, and drincke youre water with heuynesse: Yea the lande with the fulnesse therof shalbe layde waste, for the wickednesse of them that dwell therin.

20 And the cyties that nowe be well occupyed, shall be voyde, and the lande desolate: that ye maye knowe, how that I am the Lorde.

21 Yet came the worde of the Lorde vnto me agayne, sayinge:

22 Thou sonne of man, what maner of byworde is that, whiche ye vse in the lande of Israel, sayinge: Thus, seynge that the dayes are so slacke in commynge, all the visyons are of none effecte:

23 Tell them therfore: thus sayth the Lorde God: I wil make that by worde to ceasse, so that it shal no more be commonlye vsed in Israel. But saye this vnto them: The dayes are at hande, that euery thinge whiche hath bene prophecyed, shalbe fulfylled.

24 There shal no visyon be in vayne, neyther anye prophecye fayle amonge the chyldren of Israel:

25 For it is I the Lorde, that speake it: and whatsoeuer I the Lorde speake, it shall be perfourmed, & not be slacke in commynge. Yea euen in youre dayes (O ye frowarde housholde) wyll I deuyce some thynge, and brynge it to passe, sayeth the Lord God.

26 And the worde of the Lorde came vnto me, saying:

27 Beholde, thou sonne of man: The house of Israel saye in this maner: Tushe, as for the vysion that he hath sene, it wil be many a day or it come to passe: Is it farre of it, the thyng that he prophecyeth.

28 Therfore say vnto them: Thus sayth the Lorde GOD: All my wordes shall no more be slacke: Loke what I speake, that same shall come to passe, sayeth the Lorde.

## CHAPTER 13

THE worde of the Lord came vnto me, saying:

2 Thou sonne of man. Speake prophecye agaynst those Prophetes, that preache in Israel: & say thou vnto them that prophecye oute of theyr owne hertes: Heare the worde of the Lorde,

3 thus sayeth the Lorde God: Wo be vnto those folysh prophetes, that folowe their owne spryte, and speake where they se nothyng

4 O Israell, thy prophetes are lyke the foxes vpon the drye felde:

5 For they stande not in the gappes, nether make they an hedge for the house of Israel, that men myght abyde the parell in the daye of the Lord.

6 Vayne thinges they se, & tel lyes, to maintayne their preachynges with al. The Lorde (saye they) hath spoken it, when in very dede the Lorde hath not sent them.

7 Vayne vysions haue ye sene, and spoken false Prophecyes, when ye saye: the Lorde hathe spoken it where as I neuer sayde it.

8 Therfore, thus sayth the Lorde God: Because youre wordes be vayne, & ye seke oute lyes: Beholde, I wyll vpon you, saith the Lord

9 Myne handes shall come vpon the Prophetes that loke out vayne thinges, & preache lies: thei shal not be in the councell of my people, nor writen in the boke of the house of Israel, neyther shall they come in the lande of Israel, that ye maye knowe, how that I am the Lorde God.

10 And that for this cause, they haue disceyued my people, and tolde them of peace, where no peace was. One setteth vp a wal, and they daube it with louse claye.

11 Therfore tell them which dawbe it wyth vntempered morter, that it shal fal. For there shal come a great shower of rayne, greate stones shall fall vpon it, and a sore storme of wynde shal breake it,

12 so shall the wal come doune. Shal it not then be sayde vnto you: where is now the morter, that ye daubed it with all?

13 Therfore thus sayth the Lorde God: I wyll breake oute in my wrothfull displeasure with a stormye wynd, so that in myne anger there shall come a myghtye shower of rayne, & hayle stones in my wrath, to destroye withall.

14 As for the wall, that ye haue dawbed wyth vntempered morter, I wyll breake it doune, make it eauen wyth the grounde, so that the foundacyon therof shall remoue, & it shall fal, yea and ye youre selues shall perysh in the middest therof: to learne you for to knowe, that I am the Lord.

15 Thus wil I perfourme my wrath vpon thys wall, and vpon them that haue dawbed it with vntempered morter, and then wyll I saye vnto you: The wall is gone, and the dawbers are awaye.

16 These are the Prophetes of Israel, whiche prophecye vnto the cytye of Ierusalem, and loke oute vysyons of peace for them, where as no peace is, sayeth the Lorde God.

17 Wherfore (O thou sonne of man) set thy face agaynste the doughters of thy people, whiche prophecye oute of theyr owne hertes: & speake thou prophecye against them,

18 and saye: Thus sayeth the Lorde God: Wo be vnto you, that sowe pylowes vnder all arme holes, and bolsters vnder the heades both of yong and olde, to catche soules wyth all. For when ye haue gotten the soules of my people in your captiuite, ye promise them lyf

19 and dishonoure me to my people, for an handfull of barleye, and for a pece of breade: when ye kyll the soules of them, that dye not, & promes lyfe to them, that lyue not: Thus ye dyssemble with my people, that beleueth youre lyes.

20 Wherfore thus saith the

Lorde God: Beholde, I wyll also vpon the pyllowes, wherwith ye catche the soules in flyenge: then wyl I take from youre armes, and let the soules go, that ye catche in flyenge.

21 Youre bolsters also will I teare in peces, & delyuer my people out of youre hande: so that they shal come no more in youre handes to be spoyled, and ye shall knowe, that I am the Lorde.

22 Seynge that with youre lyes ye discomforte the herte of the ryghteous, whome I haue not discomforted: Agayne. For so muche as ye corage the hande of the wycked, so that he maye not turne from hys wicked waye, and lyue:

23 therfore shall ye spye oute no more vanite, nor prophecye youre owne gessinges: for I wyl delyuer my people oute of youre hande, that ye maye knowe, howe that I am the Lorde.

# CHAPTER 14

THERE resorted vnto me certayne of the elders of Israel, and satte doune by me.

2 Then came the worde of the Lorde vnto me, sayeng:

3 Thou sonne of man, these men beare theyr Idols in their hertes, and go purposly vpon the stomblynge block of their owne wyckednesse: how darre they then aske councell at me?

4 Therfore speake vnto them, & saye: Thus sayth the Lorde God. Euerye man of the house of Israell that beareth hys Idols in his herte, purposynge to stomble in hys owne wickednesse, and commeth to a Prophete, to enquere any thynge at me by hym: vnto that man will I the Lorde my self geue aunswere, accordynge to the multytude of hys Idoles,

5 that the house of Israell maye be snared in theyr owne hertes, because they be cleane gone from me, for theyr Idoles sakes.

6 Wherfore, tell the house of Israell: thus sayeth the Lorde God: Be conuerted, forsake youre Idols, and turne youre faces from all youre abhomynacyons.

7 For euery man (whether he be of the house of Israell or a straunger, that sogeourneth in Israell) whiche departeth fro me, & caryeth Idols in hys herte, purposynge to go still stombling in his owne wickednesse, & commeth to a Prophete, for to aske councell at me thorowe him: vnto that man wyll I the Lorde geue aunswere, by myne owne selfe.

8 I wyll set my face agaynste that man, & will make him to be an example for other, yea & a comon by worde, and wyll rote hym oute of my people, that he maye knowe how that I am the Lorde.

9 And yf that Prophete be deceyued, when he telleth hym a worde: then I the Lorde my selfe haue dysceyued that Prophete, & wyl stretche forth myne hande vpon hym, to rote hym out of my people of Israel,

10 and they bothe shalbe punished for theyr wyckednesse. According to the sinne of hym that asketh, shall the synne of the Prophet be,

11 that the house of Israel be led nomore fro me thorow erroure, & be no more defyled in theyr wyckednesse: but that they maye be my people, & I their God, sayeth the Lorde God,

12 And the worde of the Lorde came vnto me, sayinge:

13 Thou sonne of man, when the lande synneth againste me, & goeth forthe in wyckednesse: I will stretche oute myne hand vpon it, & destroye all the prouysyon of theyr bread, and sende derth vpon them, to destroy man & beast in the lande.

14 And thoughe Noe, Daniel & Iob these thre men were amonge them, yet shal they in their rightuousnesse delyuer but theyr owne soules, sayeth the Lorde God.

15 If I brynge noysome beastes into the lande, to waste it vp, and it be so desolate, that no man maye go therein for beastes:

16 yf these thre men also were in the lande, as truelye as I lyue (sayth the Lorde God) they shall saue neither sonnes nor doughters, but be only delyuered them selues: and as for the lande, it shall be waste.

17 Or yf I bring a swearde into the lande, & charge it to go thorow the land, so that I slay doune man and beast in it,

18 and yf these thre men were therein: As truly as I lyue (sayeth the Lorde God) they shal delyuer neyther sonnes nor doughters, but onelye be saued them selues.

19 If I sende a pestilence into the lande, & poure oute my sore indignacion vpon it in bloude, so that I rote oute of it bothe man & beast,

20 & yf Noe, Daniel and Iob were therin: as truly as I lyue (sayeth the Lorde GOD) they shall delyuer neyther sonnes nor doughters, but saue their owne soules in theyr ryghtuousnes.

21 Moreouer thus sayth the Lord god: Though I sende my foure troublous plages vpon Ierusalem: the swearde, honger, perlous, beastes and pestilence, to destroye man and beaste oute of it:

22 yet shall there be a remnaunte saued therin, whiche shall bryng forth theyr sonnes and doughters. Beholde, they shall come forthe vnto you, & ye shall se theyr waye, and what they take in hande, and ye shall be comforted, as touchynge all the plages that I haue broughte vpon Ierusalem.

23 They shal comforte you, when ye se theyr waye and

worckes: and ye shal knowe, howe that it is not wythoute a cause, that I haue done so agaynste Ierusalem, as I dyd, sayeth the Lorde God.

## CHAPTER 15

THE worde of the Lorde came vnto me, sayinge:

2 Thou sonne of man: What commeth of the vyne amonge al other trees? & of the vyne stock amonge al other timbre of the groaue?

3 Do men take wode of it, to make any worcke withall? Or maye there a nayle be made of it, to hange any thyng vpon:

4 Beholde, it is caste in the fyre to be brente, the fyre consumeth both the endes of it, the myddest is brente to asshes. Is it mete then for any worcke? No.

5 Seyng then that it was mete for no worke being whole: muche lesse maye there any thing be made of it, when the fyre hath consumed & brente it.

6 And therfore thus sayth the Lorde God: Like as I cast the vyne into the fyre for to be brent, as other trees of the wode. Euen so wyll I do with them that dwell in Ierusalem,

7 & set my face against them: they shall go out from the fyre, & yet the fyre shall consume them. Then shall ye knowe, that I am the Lorde, when I set my face agaynst them,

8 and make the lande waste, because they haue so sore offended, sayeth the Lorde God.

## CHAPTER 16

AGAYNE, the worde of the Lorde spake vnto me, sayinge:

2 Thou sonne of man, shewe the citie of Ierusalem theyr abhominacions

3 & saye: Thus sayth the Lorde God vnto Ierusalem: Thy progeny & kinred came oute of the lande of Canaan, thy father was an Amoryte, thy mother a Cethyte.

4 In the daye of thy byrthe, when thou waste borne, the strynge of thy nauel was not cut of: thou wast not bathed in water to make the cleane: Thou wast neyther robbed with salt, nor swedled in cloutes:

5 No man regarded the so muche, as to do any of these thinges for the or to shewe the suche fauoure, but thou waste vtterlye cast oute vpon the felde, yea despised wast thou in the daye of thy byrthe.

6 Then came I by the, and sawe the troden doune in thyne owne bloude, and sayde vnto the: thou shalte be pourged from thyne owne bloude, from thyne owne bloude (I say) shalt thou be clensed.

7 So I planted the, as the blossome of thy felde: thou arte growen vp, and waxen greate: thou haste gotten a maruelous pleasaunt beutie, thy brestes are come vp, thy heare is goodly growen, where as thou wast naked and bare afore.

8 Now when I wente by the, & loked vpon the: beholde, thy tyme was come, yea euen the tyme to vowe the. Then spred I my clothes ouer the, to couer thy dishonesty: yea I made an othe vnto the, and maryed my selfe wyth the (sayeth the Lorde God) and so thou becameste myne owne.

9 Then washed I the wyth water, and pourged thy bloude from the. I anoynted the wyth oyle,

10 I gaue the chaunge of raymentes, I made the shues of Tarus lether: I gyrthed the about with whyte sylcke, I clothed the with kerchues,

11 I decked the wyth costly apparell, I put ryngs vpon thy fyngers: a chayne aboute thy necke,

12 spanges vpon thy fore head, eare rynges vpon thyne eares, and set a beutyfull croune vpon thyne heade.

13 Thus waste thou deckte with syluer & golde, and thy rayment was of fyne whyte sylke, of nedle worke & of dyuerse colours. Thou dyddest eate nothynge but symnels, hony and oyle: maruelous goodly wast thou & beutiful, yea euen a very Quene wast thou:

14 In so muche, that thy beutye was spoken of amonge the Heythen, for thou waste excellent in my beuty, which I put vpon the, sayeth the Lorde God.

15 But thou haste put confidence in thyne owne beutye, & played the harlot, when thou haddest gotten the a name. Thou haste commytted whordome, wyth all that wente by the, & hast fulfilled theyr desyres:

16 yea thou hast taken thy garmentes of dyuerse colours, & deckte thyne aulters therwith, where vpon thou myghtest fulfyll thyne whoredome, of suche a fashyon, as neuer was done, nor shalbe.

17 The goodly ornamentes & Iewels whiche I gaue the of myne owne golde and syluer, hast thou taken, and made the mens ymages thereof, and commytted whordome with al.

18 Thy garmentes of dyuerse coloures haste thou taken, and deckte them ther wyth: myne oyle and incense hast thou set before them.

19 My meate whiche I gaue the, as symnels, oyle & honye (to fede the withall) that haste thou set before them, for a swete sauoure. And thys came also to passe, saieth the Lord God.

20 Thou haste taken thyne owne sonnes & doughters, whom thou hast begotten vnto me, and these haste thou offered vp vnto them, to be theyr meate.

Is this but a smal whordome of thine (thinckest thou)

21 that thou slayest my children and geuest them ouer, to be brent vnto them?

22 And yet in all thy abhominacyons & whordome, thou hast not remembred the dayes of thy youth, howe naked and bare thou wast at that tyme, and troden doune in thyne owne bloude.

23 After all these thy wickednesses (wo wo vnto the, sayeth the Lord)

24 thou hast buylded thy stewes and brodel houses in euery place: yea at the heade of euery stret

25 hast thou builded the an aulter. Thou hast made thy beuty to be abhorred, thou hast laied out thy legges to euery one that came by, and multiplyed thine whoredom.

26 Thou hast committed fornicacyon with the Egipcians thy neyghbours whiche had muche flesh, and thus haste thou vsed thyne whoredome, to anger me.

27 Beholde, I will stretch out mine hande ouer the, and will minishe the stoare of fode, & deliuer the ouer into the willes of the Philistines thine enemies, whiche are ashamed of thy abhominable waye.

28 Thou hast plaied the whore also with the Assirians, whyche might not satisfye the: Yea thou haste played the harlot, and not had ynough.

29 Thus hast thou stil committed thy fornicacyon from the lande of Canaan vnto the Caldees, and yet thy lust not satisfyed.

30 How shoulde I circumcyse thine herte (sayeth the Lorde God) seynge thou doest all these thinges, thou precyous whore:

31 buyldinge thy stewes at the head of euerye strete, and thy brodell houses in all places? Thou hast not ben as another whore that maketh boost of her winninge,

32 but as a wyfe that breaketh wedlock, and taketh other in steade of her husbande.

33 Gyftes are geuen to al other whores, but thou geuest rewardes vnto all thy louers: and offrest them gyftes, to come vnto the out of all places, and to committe fornicacyon wt the.

34 It is come to passe wyth the in thy whordomes contrarye to the vse of other women, yea there had no such fornicacion bene committed after the, seyng that thou proferest gyftes vnto other, and no rewarde is geuen the: thys is a contrarie thing.

35 Therfore heare the worde of the Lorde O thou harlot:

36 thus sayeth the Lorde God: For so much as thou hast spent thy moneye, and discouered thy shame, thorow thy whordome wyth all thy louers, and wyth all the Idols of thy abhominacions in the bloude of thy children, whom thou hast geuen them:

37 Beholde therfore, I wyll gather together all thy louers, vnto whome thou hast made thy selfe comen: yea and all them whom thou fauourest, and euery one that thou hatest: and wil discouer thy shame before them, that they al maye se thy fylthines.

38 Moreouer, I will iudge the as a breaker of wedlocke and a murtherer, & recompence the thyne owne bloud in wrath and gelousy.

39 I will geue the ouer into their power, that shal breake doune thy stewes, and destroye thy brodel houses, they shall stryppe the oute of thy clothes, al thy fayre and beutyfull Iewels shall they take from the, and so let the syt naked and bare:

40 yea they shal bryng the comen people vpon the, whiche shall stone the, and slaye the doune with their sweardes.

41 They shall burne vp thy houses, & punish the in the syght of manye wemen. Thus wyll I make thy whordome to ceasse, so that thou shalt geue out no mo rewardes.

42 Shoulde I make my wrath to be styl, take my gelousy from the, be content, and no more to be displeased?

43 seynge thou remembrest not the dayes of thy youth, but haste prouoked me to wrath in all these thinges? Behold therfore, I wyll brynge thyne owne wayes vpon thyne heade, sayeth the Lorde God: howe be it, I neuer dyd vnto the, accordynge to thy wyckednesse and all thy abhominacions.

44 Beholde, al they that vse comen prouerbes, shall vse this prouerbe also against the: suche a mother, suche a doughter.

45 Thou art euen thy mothers owne doughter, that hast cast of her housbande & their children. Yea, thou art the syster of thy systers, whiche forsoke their husbandes and their children. Youre mother is a Cethite, and youre father an Amorite.

46 Thyne eldest syster is Samaria, she and her doughters that dwel vpon thy left hande. But thy youngest syster that dwelleth on thy ryght hand, is Sodoma & her doughters.

47 Yet hast thou not walked after their wayes, nor done after their abhomynacyons: but in all thy wayes thou hast bene more corrupte then they.

48 As truly as I lyue, sayeth the lorde God: Sodoma thy sister with her doughters hath not done so euyl, as thou and thy doughters.

49 Beholde, the sinnes of thy sister Sodoma were these: Pryde, fulnesse of meate, aboundaunce and Idelnesse: these thynges had she and her doughters. Besydes that, they reached not their hande to the pore and nedy,

50 but were proude, and dyd abhomynable thinges before me:

therfore I toke them awaye, when I had sene it.

51 Neyther had Samaria done halfe of thy synnes, yea thou haste exceded them in wyckednesse. In so muche that in comparyson of all the abhomynacions whyche thou haste done, thou haste made thy systers good wemen.

52 n/a

53 As for their captyuite, namely the captyuite of Sodoma and her doughters: the captiuyte of Samaria and her doughters. I wyll brynge them agayne, so wyl I also brynge agayne thy captiuite amonge them:

54 that thou mayest take thyne owne confusion vpon the, and be ashamed of all that thou hast done, & to comforte them.

55 Thus thy sisters (namelye) Sodoma and her doughters: Samaria and her doughters with thy selfe and thy doughters, shalbe brought agayne to youre olde estate.

56 When thou wast in thy pryde,

57 and before the wyckednes came to lyght, thou wouldest not heare speake of thy sister Sodoma, vntill the tyme that the Sirians with all their townes, and the Philistines with all that lye rounde aboute them, brought the to shame & confusyon:

58 that thou myghtest beare thyne owne fylthines and abhomynacyon, sayeth the Lorde.

59 For thus sayeth the Lorde God: I shoulde (by ryght) deale with the, as thou hast done. Thou hast despysed the ooth, and broken the couenaunte.

60 Neuerthelesse, I wyll remembre the couenaunte, that I made wyth the in thy youth, in so much that it shalbe an euerlastinge couenaunt:

61 so that thou also remembre thy wayes, & be ashamed of them: then shalte thou receyue of me thy elder and younger sisters, whome I will make thy doughters, and that besyde thy couenaunt.

62 And so will I renue my couenaunt with the, that thou mayest know that I am the Lorde:

63 that thou mayest thyncke vpon it, be ashamed, and excuse thine owne confusyon no more: when I haue forgeuen the, all that thou hast done, sayeth the Lorde God.

# CHAPTER 17

THE worde of the Lorde came vnto me, sayinge:

2 Thou sonne of man: put forthe a darcke speakinge, and a parable, vnto the house of Israel,

3 and saye: Thus sayeth the Lorde God. There came a great Aegle with greate wynges, yea with myghty long winges, and full of fethers of dyuerse coloures, vpon the mount of Libanus, and toke a braunche from a Cedre tree,

4 and brake of the toppe of his twigge, and caryed it into the lande of Canaan, and set it in a cytye of marchauntes.

5 He toke also a braunche of the land & planted it in a fruteful ground, he brought it vnto greate waters, and set it as a wyllye tree therby.

6 Then dyd it growe, and was a greate vynestocke, but low by the grounde: thus there came of it a vyne, and it broughte forth blossomes, and spred oute braunches.

7 But there was another Aegle, a great one, whych had great wynges and many fethers: and behold the rotes of this vyne had an hunger after hym, and spred oute his braunches towarde hym, to water hys frutes.

8 Neuertheles it was planted vpon a good grounde besyde greate waters: so that (by reason) it shoulde haue brought out braunches & frute & haue bene a goodly vyne.

9 Speake thou therfore, thus sayeth the lord God: Shall thys vyne prospere? shal not his rotes be pluckte oute, his frute be broken of, his grene braunches withere & fade awaye? yea without eyther strong arme or many people, shall it be plucked vp by the rotes.

10 Beholde it was planted: shall it prospere therfore? Shal it not be dryed vp and wythered, yea euen in the shutynge out of his blossomes, as sone as the east wynde bloweth?

11 Moreouer, the worde of the Lorde came vnto me sayinge:

12 Speake to that frowarde housholde: knowe ye not, what these thinges do signyfye? Tell them: Beholde the king of Babylon came to Ierusalem, and toke the kynge and hys Princes, and ledde them to Babylon.

13 He toke of the kinges sede, and made a couenaunt wyth him, and toke an ooth of him. The Prynces of the lande toke he wyth hym also,

14 that the land myght be holden in subieccyon, and not to rebelle, but kepe the couenaunt, and fulfyll it.

15 But he fell from him, & sent hys Embassitoures into Egipte, that he myght haue horses and much people. Should that prospere? Shoulde he be kept safe, that doeth suche thynges? Or shoulde he escape that breaketh his couenaunt?

16 As truely as I lyue sayeth the Lorde God: He shal dye at Babylon, in the place where the kyng dwelleth, that made him King: whose othe he hath despysed, and whose couenaunte he hath broken.

17 Neyther shall Pharao wyth his greate hoste and multitude of people, maynteyne him in the warre: when they cast vp dyches, and set vp bulworches to destroye much people.

18 For seyng he hath despysed the othe, and broken the couenaunt (where as he yet gaue his hande thervpon) and done all these thynges, he shall not escape.

19 Therfore thus sayeth the Lorde God: As truely as I lyue. I wil bring myne othe that he hath despised, & my couenaunt that he hath broken, vpon his owne heade.

20 I will cast my net aboute hym, and catche him in my yarne. To Babylon wil I carye him, there wyll I punyshe him, because of the greate offence that he made me.

21 As for those that fle from him out of the hoste, they shalbe slayne with the swerd. The residue shalbe scatred toward all the wyndes, and ye shal knowe, that I the Lorde haue spoken it.

22 Thus sayeth the Lord God: I wyll also take a braunche from an hye Cedre tree, & will set it, and take the vttermost twygge, that yet is but tendre, and plante it vpon an hye hill:

23 Namely, vpon the hye hill of Syon wil I plante it: that it may brynge forth twigges, and geue frute, and be a greate Cedre tree: so that all maner of foules maye byde in it, and make their nestes vnder the shadowe of hys braunches.

24 And all the trees of the felde shall knowe that I the Lord haue brought doune the hye tree, and set the low tre vp: that I haue dryed vp the grene tree, and made the drye tree to florysh. Euen I the Lorde that spake it, haue also brought it to passe.

# CHAPTER 18

THE worde of the Lord came vnto me, on this maner:

2 what meane by thys comen prouerbe that ye vse in the land of Israel sayinge: The fathers haue eaten soure grapes, and the childrens teth are set on edge?

3 As truly as I lyue, sayeth the Lord God, ye shall vse thys byworde nomore in Israel.

4 Beholde, all soules are myne. Lyke as the father is mine, so is the sonne myne also. The soul that synneth shal dye.

5 Yf a man be godly and do the thinge that is equall and ryght

6 he eateth not vpon the hilles: he lyfteth not his eyes vp to the Idols of Israel: he defyleth not his neyghboures wyfe, he medleth with no menstruous woman:

7 he greueth no body, he geueth his detter his pledge agayn he taketh none other mans good by vyolence: he parteth his mete with the hongrye: he cloteth the naked:

8 he lendeth nothinge vpon vsury: he taketh nothinge ouer: he wythdraweth his hand from doynge wronge: he handleth faythfully betwixte man & man:

9 he walked in my commaundementes, and kepeth my lawes, and perfourmeth them faithfully: This is a ryghteous man, he shal surely liue sayeth the Lord God.

10 Yf he now get a sonne, that is a murtherer a sheder of bloude: yf he do one of these thinges

11 (though he do not all) he eateth vpon the hilles: he defyled his neyghboures wife:

12 he greueth the poore & nedy: he robbeth and spoiled: he geueth not the detter his pledge againe he lyfteth vp his eyes vnto Idols, & medleth with abhominable thinges:

13 he lendeth vpon vsury, & taketh moreouer. Shall thys man lyue? He shall not lyue. Seynge he hath done all these abhomynacions, he shall dye, hys bloude shalbe vpon him.

14 Now yf this man get a sonne also, that seyth al his fathers synnes, whiche he hath done: and feareth, neyther doth such lyke.

15 Namely he eateth not vpon the mountaynes: he lyfteth not his eyes vp to the Idols of Israel: he defyleth not his neighboures wife:

16 he vexeth no man: he kepeth no mans pledge: he neyther spoyleth, nor robbeth anye man: he dealeth his meate with the hongrye: he clotheth the naked:

17 he oppresseth not the poore: he receyueth no vsury, nor any thinge ouer: he kepeth my lawes, and walcketh in my commaundementes: This man shall not dye in his fathers sinne, but shall lyue withoute fayle.

18 As for his father: because he oppressed and spoiled his brothers, and dyd wyckedly amonge his people: lo, he is dead in his owne sinne.

19 And yet saye ye: Wherfore then should not this sonne beare his fathers sinne? Therfore: because the sonne hath done equitie and ryght, hath kepte al my commaundementes, and done them: therfore shal he leue in dede.

20 The same soule that synneth, shall dye. The sonne shal not beare the fathers offence, neyther shall the father beare the sonnes offence. The ryghteousnes of the righteous shalbe vpon him, and the wickednes of the wycked shalbe vpon him selfe also.

21 But yf the vngodlye will turne away from all his synnes that he hath done, and kepe al my commaundementes, and do the thinge that is equall and ryght, doutles he shall lyue, and not dye.

22 As for all his synnes that he did before, they shall not be thought vpon: but in his ryghteousnes, that he hath done, he shall lyue.

23 For haue I any pleasure in the death of a synner, sayeth the

Lorde God, but rather that he conuerte and lyue.

24 Agayne, yf the righteous turne awaye from his righteousnes, and do iniquytie, according to all the abhomynacyons, that the wycked man doth: shal he lyue? Al the ryghteousnes that he hath done, shal not be thought vpon: but in the faute that he hath offended withall and in the synne that he hath done, he shall dye.

25 And yet ye say: Tush, the waye of the lord is not indifferent. Heare therfor the house of Israel: Is not my way ryght? Or, are not youre wayes rather wicked?

26 When a ryghteous man turneth away from his ryghteousnesse, and medleth with vngodlynes: he must dye therin: yea for the vnryghteousnes that he hath done, must he dye.

27 Agayne, when the wycked man turneth awaye from his wickednesse, that he hath done, & doth the thinge whiche is equall and ryght, he shall saue hys soule alyue.

28 For in so muche as he remembreth hym selfe, & turneth him from all the vngodlynes, that he had vsed, he shall lyue, and not dye.

29 And yet sayeth the house of Israell: Tush the waye of the Lorde is not equall. Are my wayes vnryght, O ye house of Israel: Are not youre wayes rather vnequal?

30 As for me I will iudge euery man, accordynge to hys wayes, O ye house of Israel, sayeth the Lord God. Wherfore be conuerted, and turne you cleane from all youre wickednesse, so shall there no sinne do you harme.

31 Caste awaye from you all your vngodlinesse, that ye haue done: make you new hertes and a new spirit. Wherfore will ye dye, O ye house of Israel?

32 seyng, I haue no pleasure in the death of him that dyeth, sayeth the Lorde God. Turne you then, and ye shall lyue.

# CHAPTER 19

BVt mourne thou for the princes of Israel,

2 & saye: Wherfore laye thy mother that lionesse amonge the lions, & noryshed her yonge ones amonge the lyons whelpes?

3 One of her whelpes she brought vp, and it became a lyon it learned to spoyle, and to deuoure folcke.

4 The Heathen hearde of him, and toke hym in their nettes, and brought him in chaynes vnto the lande of Egipte.

5 Now when the damme sawe, that all her hope and comfort was awaye, she toke another of her whelpes, and made a lyon of him

6 which went amonge the lyons, and became a fearce lion, learned to spoyle and to deuoure folcke:

7 he destroyed their palaces, and made their cities waste. In so muche that the whole lande and euery thinge therin, were vtterlye desolate, thorow the very voyce of his roarynge.

8 Then came the Heathen together on euery side oute of all countreyes againste him, layed their nettes for him, and toke him in their pitte.

9 So they bounde him with chaynes, and brought him to the kinge of Babilon: which put him in preson, that his voyce shoulde nomore be hearde vpon the mountaynes of Israel.

10 As for thy mother, she is like a vyne in thy bloude, planted by the water syde: her frutes and braunches are growen out of many waters,

11 her stalkes were so stronge, that men myght haue made staues thereof for officers: she grow so hye in her stalckes. So when men sawe that she exceaded the heyght and multytude of her braunches,

12 she was roted out in displeasure, and cast doune to the grounde. The East wynde dryed vp her frute, her stronge stalkes were broken of wythered and brent in the fyre.

13 But now she is planted in the wildernesse, in a drye and thurstye grounde.

14 And there is a fyre gone out of her stalckes, which hath brent vp her braunches and her frute: so that she hath no mo stronge stalckes, to be staues for offycers. This is a pyteous and miserable thynge.

# CHAPTER 20

IN the .xvij. yeare the .x. day of the .v. Moneth, it happened, that certayne of the elders of Israel came vnto me, for to aske councell at the Lord, and sat them doune by me.

2 Then came the worde of the Lorde vnto me on this maner.

3 Thou sonne of man: speake vnto the elders of Israel, and say vnto them: Thus sayeth the Lorde God: Are ye come hytherto to aske any thinge at me? As truely as I lyue (sayeth the Lorde)

4 I wyll geue you no answere. Wilt thou not reproue them (thou sonne of man) wilt thou not reproue them? Shew them the abhomynacions of their forefathers,

5 and tell them: Thus sayeth the Lorde God: In the day when I chose Israel, and lyft vp myne hand vpon the sede of the house of Iacob, and shewed my selfe vnto them in the lande of Egypte: Yea, when I lyfte vp myne hande ouer them, and sayd: I am the Lorde youre God,

6 euen in the daye that I lift vp mine hande ouer them, to

bring them out of the lande of Egipte, into a lande that I haue prouided for them, which floweth with milcke and hony, and it is a pleasaunte lande amonge al other:

7 Then sayde I vnto them: Cast awaye euerye man the abhomynacyons that he hath before him, and defyle not youre selues with the Idoles of Egipte, for I am the Lorde youre God.

8 But they rebelled agaynst me, and would not folowe me, to cast awaye euery man the abhominacions of his eyes, & to forsake the Idoles of Egipte. Then I made to poure my indignacion ouer them, and to satisfye my wrath vpon them, yea euen in the myddest of the lande of Egipte.

9 But I woulde not do it, for my names sake, that it shoulde not be vnhalowed before the Heathen, amonge whom they dwelt, and among whom I shewed my selfe vnto them, that it woulde brynge them out of the lande of Egipte.

10 Now when I had caried them out of the lande of Egipte, and brought them into the wildernesse:

11 I gaue them my commaundementes, and shewed them my lawes, whiche who so kepeth, shall lyue in them.

12 I gaue them also my holy dayes, to be a token betwixte me and them, and therby know, that I am the Lorde, whiche haloweth them.

13 And yet the house of Israel rebelled agaynste me in the wildernesse, they woulde not walcke in my commaundementes, they haue cast awaye my lawes (whiche whoso kepeth, shoulde lyue in them) and my Sabboth dayes haue thy greatly vnhalowed. Then I made me to poure oute my indignacion vpon them, and to consume them in the wyldernesse.

14 Yet I would not do it, for my names sake: lest it shoulde be dishonoured before the Heathen, from the which I had caried them away.

15 But I swore vnto them in the wildernesse, that I woulde not byrnge them into the lande, whiche I gaue them, a land that floweth with milck and honye, and is a pleasure of all landes,

16 and that because they refused my lawes, and walcked not in my commaundementes, but and vnhalowed my Sabbathes, for their herte was gone after their Idoles.

17 Neuerthelesse myne eye spared them so that I woulde not vtterly slaye them, and consume them in the wyldernes.

18 Moreouer I sayde vnto their sonnes in the wildernesse: walcke not in the statutes of your forfathers kepe not their ordinaunces, and defyle not youre selues with their Idoles,

19 for I am the Lorde youre God. But walcke in my statutes, kepe my lawes and do them,

20 halowe my Sabbothes: for they are a token betwyxte me and you, that ye may know, howe that I am the Lorde.

21 Notwythstandinge, their sonnes rebelled against me also: they walcked not in my statutes, they kepte not my lawes to fulfyll them (whiche he that doeth shall lyue in them) neyther halowed they my Sabboth dayes. Then I made me againe to poure out my indignacion ouer them, and to satisfye my wrath vpon them in the wildernesse.

22 Neuerthelesse I wythdrewe my hande for my names sake, least it shoulde be vnhalowed amonge the Heathen, before whome I had brought them forth.

23 I lift vp myne hand ouer them also in the wildernesse, that I would scatre them amonge the Heathen, & strowe them amonge the nacions:

24 because they had not kepte my lawes, but cast asyde my commaundementes, vnhalowed my Sabbothes, and lyft vp their eyes to their fathers Idoles.

25 Wherfore I gaue them also commaundementes not good, and lawes thorow the whyche they shoulde not lyue,

26 & I vnhalowed them in their owne gyftes (when I appointed for my selfe all their fyrstborne) to make them desolate: that they might knowe, howe that I am the Lorde.

27 Therfore (O thou sonne of man) tell the house of Israell, thus sayeth the Lorde God: Besyde all this, youre forefathers haue yet blasphemed me more, and greatly offended agaynst me.

28 For after I had brought them in to the lande, that I promysed to geue them, when they sawe euery hye hyll and the thicke trees: they made their offerynges, and prouoked me with their oblacyons, makinge swete sauoures there, and poured oute their drynckeofferynges.

29 Then I asked them: what haue ye to do withall, that ye go thyther? And therefore it is called the hye place vnto thys daye.

30 Wherfore, speake vnto the house of Israel: Thus sayeth the Lorde God: yea are euen as vnclene as youre forefathers, and committe whordome also with their abhominacions.

31 In al youre Idoles, where vnto ye bring your oblacions, and to whose honoure ye burne your children: ye defyle youre selues, euen vnto this day: howe darre ye then come and aske any question at me? O ye housholde of Israel? As truly as I liue (saieth the Lord God) ye get no answere of me:

32 & as for the thinge, that ye go aboute, it shall not come to passe, where as ye saye: we wil be as the heathen, & do as other

people in the lande, wood and stone wyl we worshippe.

33 As truly as I liue, sayeth the Lorde God, I my selfe wyll rule you with a myghty hand with a stretched out arme, and with indignacyon poured out ouer you:

34 and wyll brynge you out of the nacyons and landes, wherin ye are scatred: and gather you together wyth a myghtye hande, with a stretched oute arme and with indignacyon poured out vpon you:

35 and wyll brynge you into the wildernesse of the people, and there I will reason with you face to face.

36 Like as I punished youre forefathers in the wildernesse, so will I punyshe you also, sayeth the Lorde God.

37 I will bring you vnder my iurisdiccion, & vnder the bonde of the coueuaunt.

38 The forsakers also and the transgressours will I take from among you, & bringe them out of the lande of youre habitacion: as for the lande of Israel, they shall not come in it: that they may knowe, howe that I am the Lorde.

39 Go now then (sayeth the Lorde God) ye house of Israel, cast awaye, and destroye euery man his Idoles: then shall ye heare me, & no more blaspheme my holie name with your offeringes and Idoles.

40 But vpon my holye hil, euen vpon the hye hil of Israel shal al the house of Israel and all that is in this lande, worshippe me: and in the same place wyll I fauoure them, and there wil I require youre heaueofferinges, and the fyrstlynges of your oblacions, with all youre holie thinges.

41 I will accepte your swete sauoure, when I bringe you from the nacions, and gather you together oute of the landes, wherin ye be scatred: that I maye be halowed in you before the Heathen,

42 and that ye maye knowe, that I am the Lorde, whiche haue broughte you into the lande of Israel: yea into the same lande, that I swore to geue vnto youre forefathers.

43 There shall ye call to remembraunce your own wayes and all your ymaginacions, wherin he haue bene defiled, and ye shalbe displeased wyth your own selues, for al your wickednes that ye haue done.

44 And ye shall know that I am the Lorde: when I entreate you after my name, not after youre wycked wayes, nor accordynge to youre corrupte workes: O ye house of Israel, sayeth the lord.

45 Moreouer the worde of the Lorde came vnto me saying:

46 Thou sonne of man, set thy face towarde the south, & speake to the south wind,

47 and say to the the wood toward the south: Heare the worde of the Lorde: thus sayeth the Lorde God: Beholde, I wil kindle a fire in the, that shal consume the grene trees with the drye. No man shal be able to quenche hys flamme, but al that loketh from the south to the north, shalbe brent therin:

48 & al flesh shal se, that I the Lord haue kindled it, so that no man maye quenche it.

49 Then saide I: O Lord they will saye of me: Tush, they are but fables, that he telleth.

## CHAPTER 21

THE worde of the Lorde came to me, sayinge:

2 Thou sonne of man set thy face toward Ierusalem, speake against the Sanctuary, & prophecie againste the lande of Israel, saye to the lande of Israel:

3 Thus sayeth the Lorde God: Beholde, I wil vpon the, & wil drawe my swerde out of the sheath, and rote out of the both the righteous & the wycked.

4 Seinge then that I will rote oute of the both the righteous and wicked, therfore shall my swerde go oute of his sheath againste all flesh from the North to the south:

5 that al flesh may know that I the Lord haue drawen my swerde out of the sheath, and it shall not be put in agayne.

6 Mourne therfore (O thou sonne of man) that thy loines crack withal, ye mourne bitterly for them.

7 And yf they saye, wherfore mournest thou? Then tel them: for the tydinges that commeth, at the whiche al hertes shal melt, all handes shalbe letten doune, all stomackes shall faynte, and all knees shal waxe feble. Beholde, it commeth and shalbe fulfilled, sayeth the Lorde God.

8 Agayne the worde of the Lorde came vnto me sayinge:

9 Thou sonne of man, prophecye and speake: Thus sayeth the Lorde God: speake, the sweorde is sharpened and well scoured.

10 Sharpened is it for the slaughter, & scoured that it may be bright. O, the destroyinge staf of my sonne, shall bringe doune all wod.

11 He hath put his sword to the dighting the good holde may be taken of it. This swerd is sharpened & dight, that it may be geuen into the hande of the manslayer.

12 Crie (O thou sonne of man) and howle, for this swerde shall smyte my people, & all the rulers in Israel, which with my people shall be slayne doune to the grounde thorow this swerde.

13 Smyte thou vpon the thyghe, for wherfore shoulde not the plage & staf of iudgement come?

14 Prophecy thou sonne of man, & smite thine handes

together: make the swerd two edged, yea make it thre edged, that manslayers swerde, that swerde of the greate slaughter, whiche shall smyte them, euen in their preuichambres,

15 to make them abashed & faynt at the hertes, and in all gates to make some of them fall. O how bright and sharpe it is, how well dight & mete for the slaughter.

16 Get the to some place alone, ether vpon the ryght hand or on the left, whether soeuer thy face turneth.

17 I wyll smyte my handes together also, & satisfye my wrothful indignacion. Euen I the Lorde haue sayde it.

18 The worde of the Lorde came yet vnto me agayne sayenge:

19 Thou sonne of man, make the two stretes, that the swerde of the kynge of Babylon maye come. Bothe these stretes shall go oute of one lande. He shall set him vp a place, at the heade of the strete shall he chose hym oute of a corner.

20 Make the a strete, that the swerde maye come towarde Kabath of the Ammonites, and to the stronge cytye of Ierusalem.

21 For the kinge of Babylon shall stande in the turning of the waye, at the head of the two stretes, to aske councell at the sothsayers, castynge the lottes with hys arowes to aske councell at the Idols, and to loke in the lyuer.

22 But the sothsayenge shall poynte to the ryght syde vpon Ierusalem, that he maye set men of warre, to smyte it wyth a greate noyse, to crye out Alarum, to set batelrammes agaynst the gates, to graue vp dyches, and to make bulworckes.

23 Neuertheles, as for the sothsayenge, they shal holde it but for vanitie, euen as thoughe a yest were tolde them: yea & they them selues remembre their wyckednesse, so that by ryght they must be taken and wonne.

24 Therfore sayeth the Lord God: For so muche as ye youre selues shew your offence, & haue opened your wickednesse, so that in all your worckes men may se youre synnes: yea in so muche (I say) that ye youre selues haue made mencyon thereof ye shalbe taken by vyolence.

25 O thou shamefull wycked gyde of Israel whose daye is come: euen the tyme that wyckednesse shall haue an ende.

26 Thus sayeth the Lorde God: take away the myre, and put of the croune, and so is it awaye: the humble is exalted, and the proude brought low.

27 Punish punyshe, yea punish them will I, and destroy them: and that shall not be fulfilled vntyll he come, to whome the iudgement belongeth, & to whome I haue geuen it.

28 And thou (O sonne of man) prophecye and speake: Thus sayeth the Lorde God to the children of Ammon, and to their blasphemye, speake thou: The swerde, the swerde is drawen forth al readye to the slaughter, and scoured that it glistreth

29 (because thou hast loked the out vanities, and prophecied lies) that it may come vpon thy necke, like as vpon the other vngodly, which be slayne: whose day came, when their wickednesse was full.

30 Though it were put vp agayn into the sheath, yet wyl I punysh the, in the land where thou wast noryshed and borne,

31 and pour my indignacion vpon the and will blowe vpon the in the fyre of my wrath, and delyuer the vnto cruell people, whych are learned to destroye.

32 Thou shalt fede the fyre and thy bloud shall be shed in the lande, that thou mayest be put out of remembraunce. Euen I the Lord haue spoken it.

## CHAPTER 22

MOREOUER, the worde of the lord came vnto me, & sayd:

2 thou sonne of man, wilt thou not reproue his bluodthursty cityе? Shewe hem their abhomynacions,

3 and tell them: Thus sayeth the Lorde God: O thou cyty, that sheddest bloude in the middest of the, that thy tyme may come also: & makest the Idoles to defyle the withall.

4 Thou haste made thy selfe gyltye, in the bloud that thou hast shed: & defyled the in the Idoles, whiche thou hast made. Thou hast caused thy dayes to drawe nye, & made the tyme of thy yeares to come. Therfore wyll I make the to be confounded among the Heathen, & to be despysed in all the landes,

5 whether they be nye or farre from the: they shal laugh the to scorne, thou that hast gotten the so foule a name, & art full of myschefe.

6 Beholde, the rulers of Israel haue brought euery man his power, to shed bloud in the.

7 In the haue they dispysed father & mother, in the haue they oppressed the straunger, in the haue they vexed the widdowe and the fatherlesse.

8 Thou haste despysed my Sanctuarye, and vnhalowed my Sabboth.

9 Murtherers are there in the, that shede bloude, & eate vpon the hylles, and in the they vse vnhappynesse.

10 In the haue they discouered their fathers shame, in the haue they vexed wemen in their sicknesse.

11 Euery man hath dealte shamefully wyth hys neyghboures wyfe, and

abhomynably defiled his doughter in law. In the hath euery man forced his owne syster, euen his fathers doughter:

12 yea gyftes haue bene receyued in the, to shede bloude. Thou haste taken vsury and encreace, thou haste oppressed thy neyghbours by extorcion, and forgotten me, sayeth the Lorde God.

13 Beholde, I haue smitten my handes vpon thy couetousnesse, that thou hast vsed, and vpon the bloude whyche hath bene shed in the.

14 Is thy herte able to endure it, or may thy handes defende them selues in the tyme that I shall brynge vpon the? Euen I the Lorde that speake it, will brynge it also to passe.

15 I will scatre the amonge the Heathen, and strow the aboute in the landes, & wil cause thy filthinesse to ceasse oute of the:

16 yea and I will haue the possession in the sight of the Heathen, that thou mayest know, that I am the Lorde.

17 And the worde of the Lorde came vnto me sayinge:

18 Thou sonne of man, the house of Israel is turned to drosse. Al they that shoulde be brasse, tynne, yron and leade, are in the fire become drosse.

19 Therfore, thus sayeth the lord God: For so muche as ye all are turned into drosse, beholde, I wyl bringe you together vnto Ierusalem,

20 lyke as syluer, brasse, yron, tynne and leade are put together in the fornace, and the fyre blowen there vnder to melt them. Euen so wil I gather you, put you in together, and melt you in my wrath and indignacyon.

21 I will bringe you together, and kindle the fyre of my cruel displeasure vnder you, that ye may be melted therin.

22 Lyke as the syluer is melted in the fyre, so shal ye also be melted therin, that ye may know, how that I the Lord haue poured my wrath vpon you.

23 And the worde of the Lorde came vnto me sayinge:

24 Thou sonne of man, tell her: thou art an vncleane lande, whiche is not rayned vpon in the daye of the cruell wrath:

25 thy Prophetes that are in the, are sworne together to deuoure soules, lyke as a roarynge Lyon, that lyueth by his praye. They receyue ryches and good, and make many widdowes in the.

26 Thy priestes breake my lawe, and defyle my Sanctuarye. They put no dyfference betwene the holy and vnholy, nether discerne betwene the cleane and vncleane: they turne their eyes from my Sabbothes, & I am vnhalowed among them.

27 Thy rulers in the ate like rauishing wolues, to shed bloude, and to destroye soules, for their owne couetous lucre.

28 As for thy Prophetes, they dawbe wyth vntempered claye, they se vanytyes, and prophecye lyes vnto them, sayinge: the Lorde God sayeth so, where as the Lorde hathe not spoken.

29 The people in the lande vseth wicked extorcyon and robbery. They vexe the poore and nedye and oppresse the straunger agaynste ryghte.

30 And I soughte in the lande for a man, that woulde make vp the hedge, and set him selfe in the gappe before me in the landes behalfe, that I shoulde not vtterlye destroy it: but I coulde fynde none.

31 Therfore will I pour out my cruel displeasure vpon them, and burne them in the fyre in my wrath: their owne wayes will I recompence vpon their heades sayeth the Lorde God.

# CHAPTER 23

THE worde of the Lorde came vnto me, sayinge:

2 Thou sonne of man, there were two wemen, that had one mother:

3 these (when they were younge) beganne to playe the harlottes in Egipte. There were their brestes brosed, and the pappes of their mayden head destroyed.

4 The eldest of them was called Oholah and her youngest syster Oholibah. These two were myne, & bare sonnes and doughters. Their names were, Samaria, and that was Oholah: and Ierusalem, that was Oholibah.

5 As for Oholah she beganne to go a whorynge, when I had taken her to me. She was set on fyre vpon her louers the Assirians,

6 whiche had to do with her: euen the princes & lordes, that were deckte in costly araye: fayre younge men, lusty riders of horses.

7 Thus thorowe her whordome she cleued vnto all the younge men of Assiria. Yea she was made vpon them, and defyled her self with al their Idols.

8 Neyther ceassed she from the fornicacyon, that she vsed wyth the Egyptians, for in her youth they laye wt her, they brosed the brestes of her maydenheade, and poored their whordome vpon her.

9 Wherfore I deliuered her into the handes of her louers euen the Assirians, whom she so loued.

10 These discouered her shame, toke her sonnes and doughters, and slue her with the swerde. An euyll name gat she of all people, and they punyshed her.

11 Her sister Oholibah sawe this, & destroyed her selfe with inordinate loue, more then she, & exceaded her syster in whordome:

12 she loued the Assirians

(which also lay wt her) namelye the princes & greate lordes, that were clothed with all maner of gorgyous apparell, all lustye horsemen and faire younge personnes.

13 Then I sawe, that they bothe were defiled a like.

14 But she increased still in whordome: for when she sawe men paynted vpon the wall, the ymages of the Caldees set forthe wyth freshe colours,

15 with fayre gyrdles aboute them and goodly bonnettes vpon their heades, lokinge all like Princes (after the maner of the Babilonians and Caldees in their owne lande where they be borne)

16 immediatly, as sone as she sawe them, she brent in loue vpon them, & sent messaungers for them into the lande of the Caldees.

17 Now when the Babilonians came to her they laye with her, and defiled her with their whordome, and so was she polluted wyth them. And when her lust was abated from them:

18 her whordome and shame was dyscouered & sene: then my herte forsoke her, lyke as my herte was gone from her syster also.

19 Neuerthelesse she vsed her whordome euer the longer the more, and remembred the dayes of her youth, wherin she hath played the harlot in the lande of Egipte:

20 she brent in lust vpon them, whose flesh was like the fleshe of Asses & their sede like the sede of horses.

21 Thus thou hast renued the filthinesse of thy youth, when thy louers brosed thy pappes, & marred thy brestes in Egipte.

22 Therfore (O Oholibah) thus sayeth the lord God. I will raise vp thy louers (with whom thou hast satisfied thy lust) AGAINST the, and gather them together rounde aboute the:

23 namely, the Babilonians, & all the Caldees: Perod, Schoa and Coa, with al the Assirians: al younge and fayre louers: pryncies and lordes knightes and gentlemen, whiche be all good horsmen:

24 These shal come vpon the with horses, charrettes, and a great multitude of people: whiche shalbe harnessed about the on euery side, with brestplates, sheldes and helmettes. I will punishe the before them, yea they them selues shal punish the, accordinge to their owne iudgement.

25 I will put my gelousy vpon the, so that they shall deale cruelly with the. They shall cut of thine nose and thyne eares, and the remnaunte shall fall thorow the swerde. They shall carie awaye thy sonnes and doughters, and the residue shalbe brent in the fyre.

26 They shall stripe the oute of thy clothes, and cary the costly Iewels away with them.

27 Thus wil I make an ende of thy filthinesse and whordome, whiche thou haste broughte oute of the lande of Egipte: so that thou shalt turne thyne eyes no more after them, and cast thy minde no more vpon Egipte.

28 For thus sayeth the Lorde: behold, I wil deliuer the into the handes of them, whom thou hatest: yea euen into the handes of them, wt whom thou hast fulfilled thy lust,

29 whiche shall deale cruellye with the: Al thy laboure shall they take with them, and leaue the naked & bare, & thus the shame of thy filthy whordome shal come to light.

30 All these thynges shall happen vnto the, because of thy whordome, whyche thou hast vsed amonge the Gentiles wyth whose Idoles thou hast defiled thy selfe.

31 Thou hast walcked in the waye of thy syster, therefore will I geue the her cuppe in thy hande.

32 Thus sayeth the Lorde God: Thou shalte dryncke vp thy sisters cuppe, how depe and farre soeuer it be to the botome. Thou shalte be laughed to scorne, and had as greatlye in derysyon, as is possible.

33 Thou shalte be full of dronckennes and sorowe, for the cuppe of thy sister Samaria is a cuppe of destruccyon and wastynge:

34 the same shalt thou dryncke, & suppe it oute euen to the dregges, yea thou shalt eate vp the broken peces of it, and so feare thine owne brestes: For euen I haue spoken it, sayeth the Lorde God.

35 Therfore thus sayeth the Lorde God: For so muche as thou hast forgotten me, & cast me aside, so beare now thyne owne fylthynesse & whordome.

36 The Lord sayde moreouer vnto me: Thou sonne of man wilt thou not reproue Oholah and Oholibah? Shewe them their abhominacyons:

37 namelye, that they haue broken their wedlocke, and stayned their handes with bloud: yea euen with their ydoles haue they committed aduoutry, & offered them their owne children (to be deuoured) whom they had borne vnto me.

38 Yea, and this haue they done vnto me: also, they haue defiled my Sanctuary in that same daye, & haue vnhalowed my Sabboth.

39 For when they haue slayne their children for their Idoles, they came the same daye into my Sanctuary to defile it. Lo, thys haue they done in my house.

40 Beside all thys, thou hast sent thy messaungers for men oute of farre countreyes: and when they came, thou hast bated, trimmed and set forth thy selfe of the best fashion:

41 thou sattest vpon a goodlye bed, & a table spred before the: whervpon thou hast set mine incense and myne oyle.

42 Then was there greate cheare with her, & the men that were sent from farre countreyes ouer the desert, vnto these they gaue bracelettes vpon their handes, and set glorious crounes vpon their heades:

43 then thought I: no doute, these will vse their harlotry also wyth yonder old whore.

44 And they wente into her, as vnto a comen harlot: Euen so wente they also to Oholah & Oholibah those fylthy wemen.

45 O ye all that loue vertu & ryghteousnes, iudge them, punish them, as aduoutrers and murtherers ought to be iudged & punished. For they are breakers of wedlocke, and the bloude is in their handes.

46 Wherfore thus sayeth the Lorde God: bringe a great multitude of people vpon them, & make them be scatred and spoyled:

47 these shall stone them, & gore them with their swerdes. They shall slaye their sonnes and doughters and burne vp their houses with fyre.

48 Thus will I destroye all such filthynes out of the land: that al wemen may learne, not to do after your vnclennesse.

49 And so they shal lay your filthinesse vpon your owne selues, & ye shalbe punished for the sinnes, that ye haue committed with your Idols, & ye shall know that I am the Lorde.

## CHAPTER 24

IN the .ix. year, in the .x. Moneth the .x. day of the Moneth, came the worde of the Lorde vnto me sayinge:

2 O thou sonne of man wryte vp the name of this daye, yea euen the houre of this present day: when the kinge of Babilon set hym selfe agaynste Ierusalem.

3 Shewe that obstinate housholde a parable and speake vnto them: Thus saieth the Lord God: Get the a pot, se it on, & poure water into it:

4 put al the peces together in it, all the good peces: the loyne and the shoulder, and fyll it with the best bones.

5 Take one of the best shepe, and an heape of bones with all: let it boyle well, and let the bones set well therin.

6 With that sayde the Lorde God on thys maner: Wo be vnto the bloudye citie of the pot, whervpon the rustinesse hangeth, and is not yet scoured awaye. Take out the peces that are in it, one after another: there neade not lottes be cast therfore,

7 for the bloude is yet in it. Vpon a playne drye stone hath she poured it, and not vpon the grounde, that it might be couered with dust:

8 & therfore haue I letten her poure her bloude vpon a playne drye stony rocke, because it should not be hid and that I might bringe my wrothful indignacion and vengeaunce vpon her.

9 Wherfore thus sayeth the Lorde God: O wo be vnto that bloud thursty cyty, for whom I wyll prepare a heape of wood:

10 beare thou the bones together, kindle you the fire, seeth the fleshe, let all be well soden, that the bones maye be suckte oute.

11 Moreouer, set the pot empty vpon the coales, that it may be warme & the metall hote: that the fylth & rustinesse maye be consumed.

12 But it wyl not go of, there is so muche of it: the rustinesse must be brent out.

13 Thy filthinesse is abhominable, for I woulde haue clensed the, but thou wouldest not be clensed. Thou canste not be pourged from thyne vnclennesse, tyll I haue poured my wrothfull indignacyon vpon the.

14 Euen I the Lorde haue so deuysed: Yea, it is come therto already, that I wil do it. I wyll not go backe, I will not spare, I will not be intreated: but accordynge to thy wayes & ymaginacions, thou shalt be punyshed, sayeth the lord God.

15 And the worde of the Lorde came vnto me sayinge:

16 Thou sonne of man, beholde I wil take awaye the pleasure of thyne eyes with a plage: yet shalt thou neyther mourne, nor wepe, nor water thy chekes therfore:

17 thou mayest mourne by thy self alone, but vse no deadly lamentacyon. Hold on thy bonet, and put on thy shues vpon thy fete, couer not thy face, and eate no mourners breade.

18 So I spake vnto the people by tymes in the morninge and at euen my wyfe dyed: then vpon the next morowe, I did as I was commaunded.

19 And the people sayde vnto me: wilt thou not tell vs, what that signifyeth, whyche thou doest?

20 I answered them, the word of the lord came vnto me sayinge:

21 Tell the house of Israell, thus sayeth the Lorde God: beholde, I wyl suspende my sanctuarye: euen the glorye of your power, the pleasure of youre eyes, & the thyng that ye loue, youre sonnes & doughters whome ye haue left, shall fal thorow the swerde.

22 Lyke as I haue done, so shall ye do also: Ye shall not hide youre faces, ye shall eate no mourners bread:

23 your bonnettes shall ye haue vpon youre heades, and shues vpon your fete. Ye shall neyther mourne nor wepe, but in youre sinnes ye shalbe sorowful,

and one repente with another.

24 Thus Ezechiel is your shewtoken. For loke as he hath done, so when this commeth ye shall do also: that ye maye learne to knowe that I am the Lorde God.

25 But beholde, O thou sonne of man: In the daye, when I take from them their power, their ioye and honoure, the lust of their eyes, the burthen of their bodies: namelye, their sonnes and doughters.

26 Then shall there one escape, and come vnto the, for to shew the.

27 In that daye shall thy mouth be opened to him, whiche is escaped, that thou mayest speake, & be no more domme: Yea and thou shalt be their shewtoken, that they may knowe, howe that I am the Lorde.

## CHAPTER 25

THE worde of the Lorde came vnto me, saying:

2 Thou sonne of man, set thy face againste the Ammonites, prophecy vpon them,

3 & say vnto the Ammonites: hear the worde of the Lorde God. Thus sayeth the Lorde God: For so muche as thou speakest ouer my Sanctuarye. A ha, I trow it be now suspended: and ouer the lande of Israel, I trowe it be nowe desolate: ye and ouer the house of Iuda, I trow they be now led away presoners:

4 Beholde, I will deliuer the to the people of the east, that they maye haue the in possession, these shal set their castels and houses in the. They shall eate thy frute, & drincke vp thy milcke.

5 As for Rabath. I will make of it a stall for camels, and of Ammon a shepefolde: & ye shal knowe, that I am the Lord.

6 For thus sayeth the lord God: In so much as thou hast clapped with thine handes, and stamped with thy fete, yea reioysed in thyne herte ouer the lande of Israell with despyte:

7 beholde, I will stretche out myne hand ouer the also, and delyuer the, to be spoyled of the Heathen, and rote the out from amonge the people, and cause the to be destroyed out of al landes: yea, I will make the be layed waste, that thou mayest know, that I am the Lorde.

8 Thus sayeth the Lorde God: For so much as Moab and Seir do say: As for the house of Iuda, it is but lyke as all other Gentyles be.

9 Therfore beholde, I will make the cytyes of Moab weapenlesse, and take awaye their strength: thir cyties and chefe coastes of their lande, whiche are the pleasures of the countrey. As namelye: Bethiesimoth, Baalmeon and Cariathaim:

10 these will I open vnto them of the East, that they maye fall vpon the Ammonites: and wil geue it them in possession, so that the Ammonites shall no more be had in remembraunce amonge the Heathen.

11 Euen thus will I punishe Moab also, that they may knowe, how that I am the Lorde.

12 Moreouer, thus sayeth the Lorde God: Because that Edom hath auenged and eased him selfe vpon the house of Iuda,

13 therefore thus sayeth the Lorde: I wyll reache oute myne hande vpon Edom, and take awaye man and beast oute of it. From Theman vnto Dedan will I make it desolate, they shalbe slayne wt the swearde.

14 Thorowe my people of Israell will I auenge me agayne vpon Edom: they shall handle him, according to my wrath & indignacion, so that they shall know my vengeaunce, sayeth the Lorde God.

15 Thus sayeth the Lorde God: For so much as the Philistines haue done this, namely taken vengeaunce with despitefully stomackes and of an olde euyl will set them selues to destroye.

16 Therfore thus saith the Lorde God: Beholde: I will stretch oute mine hande ouer the Philistines, and destroye the destroyer, and cause all the remnaunt of the sea coaste to perishe.

17 A greate vengeaunce will I take vpon them, & punish them cruelly: that they maye knowe, how that I am the Lorde, which haue auenged me of them.

## CHAPTER 26

IT happened, that in the .xi. yeare the firste daye of the Moneth, the worde of the Lord came vnto me, sayinge:

2 Thou sonne of man, because that Tyre hathe spoken vpon Ierusalem: A ha, now I trow the portes of the people be broken, & she turned vnto me, for I haue destroied my bely ful:

3 yea therfore saieth the lord God. Beholde O Tire I wil vpon the, I wil bring a great multitude of people agaynst the, lyke as when the sea ariseth with his waues:

4 These shal breake the walles of Tire, and cast doune her toures. I wil scrape the ground from her, & make her a bare stone:

5 yea as the drynge place, where the fyshers hange vp their nettes by the sea syde. Euen I haue spoken it, sayeth the Lorde God. The gentyles shal spoile her:

6 her doughters vpon the felde shall peryshe with the swerde, that they may knowe, how that I am the Lorde.

7 For thus sayeth the Lord God: Beholde, I will bringe hither Nabuchodonozor (which

is the Kynge of Babylon, and a kinge of kinges) from the North vpon Tire, with horses charettes, horsmen, and with a greate multytude of people.

8 Thy doughters that are in the lande, shall he slaye with the swearde: but agaynst the, he shal make bulworckes & graue vp diches aboute the, & lyft vp his shylde againste the.

9 His slynges and batelrammes shall he prepare for thy walles, and with his weapons breake doune thy towres.

10 The dust of his horses shall couer the: they shalbe so many: thy walles shall shake at the noyse of the horse men, charettes and wheles: when he cometh to thy portes, as men do into an open cyty.

11 With the hostes of his horse fete, shall he treade doune all thy stretes. He shall sleye thy people with the swerde, & breake doune the pylers of thy strengthe.

12 They shal wast awaye thy riches, and spoile thy marchaundyse. Thy walles shall they breake doune, and destroy thy houses of pleasure. Thy stones, thy timbre and foundacions shal they cast in the water.

13 Thus will I bring the melody of thy songes, and the voyce of thy minstrelsy to an ende, so that they shall no more be hearde.

14 I will make a bare stone of the, yea a dryinge places for nettes, & shalt neuer be builded agayne: For euen I the lord haue spoken it, sayeth the Lorde God:

15 thus hath the Lord God spoken concerning Tire. The Iles shalbe moued at the noyse of thy fall, & at the crye of the slayne, that shall be murthered in the.

16 Al kinges of the sea shall come doun from their seates regal, they shal laye awaye their roabes, & put of their costly clothinge. Yea with tremblinge shal they be clothed, they shall syt vpon the ground: they shalbe afrayed at thy soden fall, and be abashed at the.

17 They shall mourne for the, and saye vnto the: O thou noble city, that hast bene so greatly occupyed of olde, thou that haste bene the strongest vpon the sea with thine inhabitours of whom al men stode in feare: How art thou nowe so vtterlye destroyed?

18 Nowe at the tyme of thy fal the inhabytoures of the Iles, yea and the Iles them selues, shall stande in feare at thyne ende.

19 For thus sayeth the Lord God: when I make the a desolate cytye (as other cities be, that no man dwell in) and when I brynge the depe vpon the, that greate waters maye couer the:

20 Then wyl I cast the doune vnto them, that descende into the pytte: vnto a people that hath bene longe deade, and set the in a lande that is beneth, lyke the olde wildernesse, with them whiche go doune to their graues, so that no man shall dwell more in the. And I wyll make the to be no more in honoure in the lande of the lyuynge.

21 I wil make an ende of the, and thou shalt be gone. Thoughe thou be sought for, yet shalte thou not be founde for euermore, sayeth the Lorde God.

## CHAPTER 27

THE word of the Lorde came vnto me, sayinge:

2 O thou sonne of man, make a lamentable complaynte vpon Tyre,

3 and say vpon Tyre, whyche is a porte of the sea, that occupyeth with muche people and many Iles: thus speaketh the Lord God: O Tire thou hast sayde: what, I am a noble cytye:

4 thy borders are in the middest of the sea, & thy buylders haue made the maruelous goodly.

5 All thy tables haue they made of Cypre trees of the mount Sanir. From Libanus haue they taken Cedre trees, to make the mastes:

6 and the Okes of Basan to make the rowers. Thy boordes haue they made of yuery, & of costly wood out of the Ile of Cethim.

7 Thy sayle was of white small nedle worcke oute of the land of Egipte, to hang vpon thy mast & thy hanginges of yalowe sylcke purple, out of the Iles of Elisah.

8 They of Sydon and Arnah were thy mariners, and the wisest in Tyre were thy shipmaysters.

9 The eldest and wisest at Gebal were they, that mended and stopped thy shippes. All shippes of the sea with their shipmen occupied their marchaundyes in the.

10 The Perses, Lydians and Lybians were in thine host, & helped the to fight: these hanged vp their shildes & helmettes wt the, these set forth thy bewty.

11 They of Arnad were with thine host round about thy walles, and were thy watchmen vpon thy towres, these hanged vp their shildes rounde aboute thy walles, & made the maruelous goodlye.

12 Tharsis occupied wt the in all maner of wares, in siluer, yron, tinne & lead, and made thy market great.

13 Iauan, Tubal, & Mesech were thy marchauntes which brought the men, & ornamentes of metal for thy occupying.

14 They of the house of Thogarma brought vnto the at the tyme of thy marte, horse, horsmen and mules.

15 They of Dedan were thy marchauntes: & many other Iles that occupied with the, brought the whethers, elephant bones and Paycockes for a present.

16 The Sirians occupied wt the, because of thy diuerse worckes, & increased thy marchaundies, with Smaragdes, with scarlet, with nedle worcke, wt white lynen cloth, with silcke and with Christall.

17 Iuda and the lande of Israel occupied with the, and brought vnto thy markettes, wheate balme, hony, oyle and triacle.

18 Damascus also vsed marchaundyes with the, in the beste wine and whyte woll, because the occupying was so greate, & thy wares so manye.

19 Dan, Iauan, and Meusall haue broughte vnto thy markettes, yron redy made, with Casia and Calamus, according to thyne occupyinge.

20 Dedan occupied with the, in fayre tapestrye worcke & quishins.

21 Arabia & al the prynces of Cedar haue occupied with the, in shepe, wethers and goates.

22 The marchauntes of Seba and Rema haue occupied also with the, in al costlye spices, in all precious stones and goulde, which they broughte vnto thy markettes.

23 Haran, Chene and Eden, the marchauntes of Saba, Assiria and Chelmad, were al doers with the,

24 and occupyed with the: In costly raiment, of yalow silcke and nedle worcke (very precious, and therfore packte & bounde together with roapes) Yea and in Cedre wood, of the tyme of thy markettes.

25 The shippes of Tharsis were the chefe of thy occupyinge. Thus thou art ful, and in great worshippe euen in the middest of the sea.

26 Thy mariners were euen bringinge vnto the oute of manye waters. But the East wynde shall ouerbeare the into the myddest of the sea,

27 so that thy wares, thy marchaundies, thy riches, thy mariners, thy shipmaisters, thy helpers, thy occupiers (that brought the thinges necessarye) the men of warre that are in the: yea and all thy commens shall peryshe in the myddest of the sea, in the daye of thy fall.

28 The suburbes shall shake at the loude crye of thy shipmen.

29 All whirry men, and all maryners vpon the sea, shal leape oute of their boates, and let them selues vpon the land.

30 They shal lyft vp their voice because of the, and make a lamentable crye. They shall cast dust vpon their heades, & lye doune in the ashes.

31 They shall shaue them selues, and put sacke clothe vpon them for thy sake. They shal mourne for the with hertfull sorowe,

32 and heauy lamentacion, yea their children also shal wepe for the. Alas, what cytye hath so bene destroyed in the sea, as Tyre is?

33 When thy wares & marchaundies came from the seas, thou gauest al people ynoughe. The kinges of the earth hast thou made ryche, thorowe the multytude of thy wares and occupyinge.

34 But thou art nowe caste doune into the depe of the sea, al thy resorte of people is perished with the.

35 All they that dwell in the Iles are abashed at the, and all their kinges are afrayed, yea their faces haue chaunced colour.

36 The marchauntes of the nacions wondre at the, In that thou arte so cleane broughte to naught, and commeth no more vp.

## CHAPTER 28

THE word of the lord came vnto me saying:

2 Thou sonne of man, tell the Prince of Tyre. Thus saieth the lord god because thou haste a proude hert & hast said: I am a god: I haue my seate in the middest of the sea like a God, where as thou art but a man and not God, & yet standest in thine own conceyt, that thou art God.

3 Behold, thou thinckest thy self wyser then Daniel, that there is no secretes hyd from the.

4 With thy wysedome and thy vnderstanding, thou hast gotten the great welthinesse, and gathered treasure of syluer and goulde.

5 With thy great wysedome and occupying, hast thou increased thy power, and because of thy great ryches, thy hert is proude.

6 Therfore thus sayeth the Lord God: For so muche as thou hast lyft vp thyne herte, as though thou were God:

7 behold, I wil bring enemies vpon the, euen the tyrauntes of the Heathen: these shall drawe out their swerdes vpon thy bewtye and wysedome, and shall defyle thy glory.

8 They shall cast the doune to the pytte, so that thou shalt dye in the middest of the sea,

9 as they that be slayne. Let se, yf thou wylt saye then (before them that slaye the) I am God: where as thou arte but a man and not God, in the handes of them that slay the.

10 Dye shalte thou, euen as the vncircumcysed in the handes of the enemyes: for I my selfe haue spoken it, sayeth the Lord God.

11 Moreouer, the worde of the Lorde came vnto me, sayinge:

12 Thou sonne of man, make a lamentable complaynte ouer the kynge of Tyre, and tell hym: Thus sayth the Lorde God: Thou arte a seale of a lykenesse, full of wysdome & excellente beutye.

13 Thou hast ben in the pleasaunte garden of God: thou art dect with all maner of

precyous stones: wyth Ruby, Topas, Christal, Iacincte, Onic, Iaspys, Saphyr, Smaragde, Carbuncle, and golde. Thy bewty and the holes that be in the, were set forthe in the daye of thy creacyon.

14 Thou arte a fayre Cherub, stretched wyde oute for to couer. I haue set the vpon the holye mounte of God, there hast thou bene, and walked among the fayre glysterynge stones.

15 From the tyme of thy creacyon thou haste bene ryghte excellent, tyll wyckednesse was founde in the.

16 Because of thy greate marchaundyse, thy hert is full of wickednesse, and thou haste offended. Therfore wyll I caste the from the mounte of God (O thou couerynge Cherub) and destroye the among the glisteryng stones.

17 Thy herte was proud in thy fayre beuty, & thorow thy beuty thou haste destroyed thy wysdom. I wil cast the doune to the ground, & that in the sight of kinges.

18 Thou haste defyled thy sanctuarye, wyth the great wyckednesse of thy vnryghteous occupyenge. I wyl brynge a fyre from the myddest of the, to consume the: and wyll make the to ashes, in the syghte of al them that loke vpon the.

19 All they that haue bene acquaynted with the amonge the Heathen shalbe abashed at the, seynge thou arte so cleane brought to naught, and commest no more vp.

20 And the worde of the Lorde came vnto me sayenge:

21 Thou sonne of man, set thy face agaynst Sydon. Prophecy vpon it,

22 and speake Thus sayth the Lorde God: Beholde o Sidon, I wyll vpon the, and get me honoure in the: that it maye be knowne, howe that I am the Lorde, when I punyshe her, and get me honoure in her.

23 For I wyll sende pestilence and bloudsheddyng into her streates, so that those which be slayne with the swearde, shall lye rounde aboute in the myddest of her: and they shall knowe, that I am the Lord.

24 She shal no more be a prickinge thorne, and an hurtynge breer vnto the house of Israel, nor vnto them that lye rounde aboute her, and hate her, and they shall knowe, that I am the Lorde.

25 Thus sayth the Lord God: when I gather the housholde of Israel together agayne from the nacyons amonge whom they be scatered: then shall I be sanctifyed in them, in the sight of the Gentyles, & they shal dwell in the lande that I gaue to my seruaunte Iacob.

26 They shall dwell safely therin, buylde houses, and plante vyneyardes: yea safely shal they dwel therin, when I haue punyshed all those, that despyse them rounde aboute: and then shall they knowe, that I am the Lorde theyr God.

# CHAPTER 29

IN the .x. yeare vpon the .xij. day of the .x. moneth, the word of the Lorde came vnto me, sayinge:

2 O thou sonne of man, set nowe thy face agaynste Pharao the kynge of Egypte, Prophecye agaynst him & against the whole lande of Egypte:

3 Speake, & tel him: thus sayth the Lorde God: Beholde O Pharao thou kynge of Egypte, I wyll vpon the, thou greate dragon, that lyest in the waters: thou that sayest: the water is myne. I haue made it my selfe.

4 I wyl put an hoke in thy chawes, & hange al the fysh in thy waters vpon thy scales, after that I wyl draw the out of thy waters, yea and all the fyshe of thy waters that hange vpon thy scales.

5 I wyll caste the oute vpon the drye lande: wyth the fysh of thy waters, so that thou shalte lye vpon the felde. Thou shalte not be gathered nor taken vp: but shalte be meate for the beastes of the feld, and for the foules of the ayre,

6 that al thei whiche dwell in Egypte, maye knowe, that I am the Lorde: because thou haste bene a staffe of rede to the house of Israel.

7 When they toke hold of the with theyr hand thou brakest & pryekest them on euerye syde, & yf they leaned vpon the, thou brakest & hurtest the reynes of theyr backes.

8 Therfore thus sayeth the Lorde God: beholde, I wyll brynge a swearde vpon the, & rote oute of the bothe man and beaste.

9 Yea the lande of Egypte shalbe desolate and waste, & they shal knowe, that I am the Lord. Because he sayde: the water is myne, I my selfe haue made it.

10 Beholde, therfore, I wyll vpon the & vpon thy waters: I wyll make the lande of Egypte waste and desolate, from the towre of Syenes vnto the borders of the Moryans land,

11 so that in .xl. yeares there shall no fote of man walcke there, neyther fote of cattell go there, neyther shall it be inhabyted.

12 I wyll make the lande of Egypte to be desolate, amonge other waste countreyes, and her cytyes to lye voyde .xl. yeares, among other voyde cytyes: And I wyll scatre the Egypcyans amonge the Heathen and nacyons.

13 Agayne, thus saith the Lorde God: When the .xl. yeares are expyred, I wyll gather the Egypcyans together agayne, oute of the nacyons, among whome they were scatred,

14 and wyll brynge the presoners of Egypte agayne into the lande of Pathures theyr owne natyue countre, that they maye be there a lowlye small kyngdome:

15 yea they shalbe the smallest amonge other kyngedomes, leste they exalte them selues aboue the Heathen, for I wyll so monyshe them

16 that they shal no more rule the Heathen. They shall no more be an hope vnto the house of Israel, neyther prouoke them anye more wyckednesse, to cause them turne backe, & to folowe them: and they shall knowe that I am the Lorde God.

17 In the .xxvij. yeare, the fyrste daye of the fyrste moneth, came the worde of the Lorde vnto me, sayinge:

18 Thou sonne of man, Nabuchodonosor the kynge of Babylon hath made hys hoste, wyth greate trauayle and laboure to come before Tyre: that euerye head may be balde, and euerye shoulder bare. Yet hath Tyre geuen neyther hym nor hys hoost anye rewarde, for the greate trauayle that he hath taken there.

19 Therfore thus sayeth the Lord god: beholde, I wyl geue the lande of Egypt vnto Nabuchodonosor the kynge of Babylon, that he maye take awaye all her substaunce, robbe her robberyes, and spoyle her spoyles, to pay hys hoste theyr wagyes wythall.

20 I wil geue hym the lande of Egypte for hys labour, that he toke for me before Tyre.

21 At the same tyme wyll I cause the horne of the house of Israell to growe forthe, & open thy mouth agayne amonge them: that they maye knowe, howe that I am the Lorde.

# CHAPTER 30

THE worde of the Lord came moreouer vnto me, sayinge:

2 thou sonne of man, prophecye & speake: thus sayth the Lorde God: Mourne wo worth this daye,

3 for the daye is here, the daye of the Lorde is come: the darck daye of the Heathen, the houre is at hande,

4 the swearde commeth vpon Egypte. When the wounded men fall doune in Egypte, when her people are taken awaye, and when her foundacyons are destroyed,

5 the Moryans lande shall be afrayed, yea the Moryans lande, Lybya and Lydia, al theyr comen people, & Chub and al that be confederate vnto them, shal fal with them thorowe the swearde.

6 Thus sayeth the Lorde: The maynteyners of the land of Egypt shall fall, the pryde of her power shall come doune: euen vnto the tower of Syenes shall they be slayne doune wyth the swearde, sayeth the Lorde God:

7 amonge other desolate countreys they shalbe made desolate, & amonge other waste cytyes they shalbe wasted.

8 And they shal know, that I am the Lorde, when I kyndle a fyre in Egypte, and when all her helpers are destroyed.

9 At that tyme, shall theyr messaungers go forth fro me in shippes, to make the carelesse Morians afrayed, and sorowe shall come vpon them in the daye of Egypte for doubtles it shall come.

10 Thus sayth the Lorde God: I wyll make an ende of the people of Egypte thorowe the hande of Nabuchodonosor kynge of Babylon.

11 He and hys people with hym, yea and the cruell Tyrauntes of the heathen shalbe broughte to destroye the lande. They shal drawe oute theyr sweardes vpon Egypte, and fyl the land full of slayne men.

12 I wyll drye vp theyr floudes of water, and sel the lande into the handes of wycked people. The lande and al that is therin, wyl I destroye thorowe the enemyes. Euen I the Lorde haue sayde it.

13 And thus sayth the Lorde God: I wyll destroye the Idols, and bryng the ymages of Noph to an ende. There shal no more be a Prince of Egypte, and a fearfulnes wyl I sende into the Egypcyans lande.

14 As for Pathures, I wyl make it desolate, & kindle a fire in Zoan. Alexandria wyll I punysh

15 and poure my wrothful indignacion vpon Sin, whiche is the strengthe of Egypt. All the substaunce of Alexandria will I destroye,

16 and kyndle a fyre in Egypte. Sin shalbe in greate heauynesse, Alexandria shalbe roted oute, and Noph shall haue daylye sorowe.

17 The beste men of Helyopolis & Bubasto shalbe slayne wyth the swearde, & caryed awaye captyue.

18 At Taphnis the daye shalbe darcke, when I breake there the scepter of the lande of Egypte, and when the pompe of her power shall haue an ende. A cloud shal couer her, & her doughters shalbe led awaye into captyuyte.

19 Thus wyll I punysh Egipte that they may know, how that I am the Lord.

20 It happened in the .xi. yeare, vpon the seuenth daye of the fyrste Moneth, that the Lordes worde came vnto me, sayinge:

21 Beholde, thou sonne of man, I wyl breake the arme of Pharao kynge of Egypte: & lo it shall not be bound vp to be healed, neyther shall any playstre be layed vpon it, for to ease it, or to make it so stronge, as to holde a sweard.

22 Therfore, thus sayth the Lorde God: Beholde, I wyl vpon

Pharao the kynge of Egypte, and bruse hys strong arme (yet is it but a broken one) & wyl smyte the swearde oute of hys hande.

23 As for the Egypcyans, I wyl scatre them amonge the Heathen, & strowe them in the landes aboute.

24 Agayne I wil strength the arme of the kynge of Babilon, & geue him my swerd in hys hande, but I wyl breake Pharaos arme so that he shall holde it before hym pyteously lyke a wounded man.

25 Yea I wyll stablyshe the kyng of Babylons arme, & the armes of Pharao shal fal doune, that it maye be knowne, that I am the Lord, which geue the kynge of Babylon my swearde in his hand, that he may draw it out vpon the land of Egypte:

26 & that when I scatre the Egypcyans amonge the Gentyles, and strowe them in the landes aboute, they maye knowe, that I am the Lorde.

## CHAPTER 31

Moreouer, it happened in the .xi. yeare the fyrst daye of the third Moneth that the worde of the Lorde came vnto me sayinge:

2 Thou sonne of man speake vnto Pharao the kynge of Egypte and to all hys people: Whome arte thou lyke in thy greatenesse?

3 Beholde, Assur was lyke a Cedre tree vpon the mount of Lybanus wyth fayre braunches, so thicke, that he gaue shadowes & shote oute very hye. Hys toppe reached vnto the cloudes.

4 The waters made hym great, & the depe set hym vp an hye. Rounde aboute the rotes of hym ranne there floudes of water, he sente oute hys lytle ryuers vnto al the trees of the felde.

5 Therfore was he hyer then all the trees of the felde, and thorowe the multytude of waters that he sente from hym, he obtayned manye longe braunches.

6 All foules of the ayre made theyr nestes in hys braunches, vnder his bowes gendred all these beastes of the felde and vnder hys shadowe dwelte all people.

7 Fayre and beutyful was he in hys greatnesse and in the length of hys braunches, for hys rote stode besyde great waters,

8 no Cedre tree myght hyde hym. In the pleasaunte garden of God, there was no fyrre tre lyke his braunches, the plaine trees were not lyke the bowes of hym. All the trees in the garden of God myght not be compared vnto hym in hys beuty

9 so fayre and goodly had I made him wyth the multytude of hys braunches: In so muche that al the trees in the pleasaunte garden of God, had enuye at hym.

10 Therfore, thus saith the Lorde God: for so muche as he hath lyfte vp him self so hye, & stretched his toppe into the cloudes, & seynge hys herte is proude in hys hyghnesse:

11 I wyl delyuer hym into the handes of the myghtyest amonge the Heathen, which shall rote hym oute. Accordyng to hys wickednes will I cast him awaye,

12 the enemyes shall destroye hym, and the myghty men of the Heathen shall so scatre hym, that his braunches shall lye vpon all mountaynes & in al valeys: hys bowes shalbe broken doune to the ground thorowoute the lande. Then all the people of the lande shal go from hys shadowe, and forsake hym.

13 When he is fallen, all the foules of the ayre shal syt vpon hym, & all wyld beastes of the felde shall go aboute among his braunches:

14 so that from henceforth, no tre in the water shall attayne to hys hyghnesse, nor reache hys toppe vnto the cloudes, neyther shall any tre of the water stand so hye, as he hath done. For vnto death shall they all be delyuered vnder the earthe, and go doune to the graue, like other men.

15 Moreouer, thus sayeth the Lord God: In the daye when he goeth doune to the graue, I wyl cause a lamentacyon to be made, I wyll couer the depe vpon him, I wyll staunche his floudes, and the great waters shalbe restraigned. I shall cause Lybanus to be sorowful for hys sake, and all the trees of the felde shall be smytten.

16 I wyll make the Heathen shake at the sounde of hys fall, when I caste hym doune to hell, with them that descende into the pytte. All the trees of Eden, with all the chosen and best trees of Lybanus, yea and all they that are planted vpon the waters, shall mourne with him also in the lower habytacyons:

17 for they shall go doune to hell wyth hym, vnto them that be slayne with the swearde, whiche dwelte afore vnder the shadowe of hys arme amonge the Heathen.

18 To whome shalte thou be lykened, that arte so gloryous and greate, amonge the trees of Eden? Yet arte thou cast doune vnder the earthe (amonge the trees of Eden) where thou muste lye amonge vncyrcumcysed, with them that be slayne with the swearde. Euen thus is it with Pharao and al hys people, sayeth the Lorde God.

## CHAPTER 32

In the .xij. yeare, the fyrste day of the .xij. Moneth, the word of the Lorde came vnto me, sayinge:

2 Thou sonne of man, take vp a lamentacyon vpon Pharao the kynge of Egypte, and saye vnto hym: Thou arte reputed as a

# EZEKIEL

Lyon of the Heathen, & as a whalfyshe in the sea. Thou castest thy waters about the, thou troublest the waters with thy fete, and stampest in theyr floudes.

3 Thus sayth the Lorde God: I wyll sprede my nette ouer the, namelye, a greate multytude of people: these shall dryue the into my yarne,

4 for I wyll caste the vpon the lande, and let the lye vpon the felde, that all the foules of the ayre maye syt vpon the: I wyll geue al the beastes of the felde ynoughe of the.

5 Thy flesh wyll I caste vpon the hylles, and fyl the valleyes wt thy hyghnesse.

6 I wyl water the land with the aboundaunce of thy bloude euen to the mountaynes, and the valleys shall be full of the.

7 When thou arte put oute, I wyll couer the heauen, and make hys starres dymme. I wyll sprede a cloude ouer the sunne, and the moone shall not geue her lyghte.

8 All the lyghtes of heauen wyll I put oute ouer the, and brynge darckenesse vpon thy lande, sayeth the Lorde God.

9 I will trouble the hertes of many people, when I brynge thy destruccyon amonge the Heathen & countrees, whom thou knowest not.

10 Yea I wyl make many people with their kynges so afrayed thorowe the, that theyr hearre shal stand vp, when I shake my sweard at theyr faces Sodenly shall they be astonnyed, euerye man in hym selfe, at the day of thy fall.

11 For thus sayeth the Lorde God: the kynge of Babylons swearde shall come vpon the,

12 with the sweardes of the worthyes wyll I smyte doune thy people. Al they that be mightye amonge the Gentyles, shall waste the proude pompe of Egypte, and brynge doune all her people.

13 All the cattell also of Egypte wyll I destroye, that they shall come no more vpon the waters: so that neyther mans fote, nor beastes clawe, shall stere them anye more.

14 Then wyll I make theyr waters cleare, and cause theyr floudes to runne lyke oyle, sayeth the Lorde God:

15 when I make the lande of Egypte desolate, and when the countre wyth al that is therin, shalbe layde waste: and when I smyte all them whiche dwell in it, that they maye knowe, that I am the Lorde.

16 Thys is the mournyng, that the doughters of the Heathen shall make: Yea a sorowe and lamentacyon shal they take vp, vpon Egypte and al her people, sayeth the Lorde God.

17 In the .xij. yeare, the .xv. daye of the Moneth, came the worde of the Lorde vnto me, sayinge:

18 Thou sonne of man. Take vp a lamentacyon vpon the people of Egypte, and caste them doune, yea and the myghtye people of the Heathen also, euen with them that dwell beneth: and with them that go doune into the graue,

19 Downe (how fayre soeuer thou be) and laye the wyth the vncyrcumcysed.

20 Amonge those that be slayne wyth the swearde shall they lye. The swearde is geuen already, he shall be drawen forthe, and all hys people.

21 The myghtye worthyes and hys helpers, that be gone doune, and lye wyth the vncyrcumcysed, and with them that be slayne wyth the swearde, shall speake to hym oute of the hell.

22 Assur is there also with his companye, and theyr graues round about, which were slaine and fell all with the swearde,

23 whose graues lye besyde hym in the lowe pytte. Hys comens are buryed rounde aboute hys graue, all together wounded, and slayne wyth the sweard whiche men afore tyme broughte feare into the lande of the lyuynge.

24 There is Elam also wyth all hys people, and their graues round aboute: which al being wounded and slayne wyth the swearde, are gone doune vncircumcysed vnder the earthe, whiche neuertheles sometyme broughte feare into the lande of the lyuynge: for the whiche they beare theyr shame, wyth the other that be gone doune to the graue.

25 Theyr buryall is geuen them, and al theyr people, amonge them that be slayne. Theyr graues are rounde aboute all them, which be vncyrcumcysed, & with them that be slayne thorowe the sweard: for seyng that in tymes past they made the lande of the lyuynge afrayed, they must now bear theyr owne shame, wt them that go doune to the pytte, and lye among them that be slayne.

26 There is Mesech also and Tubal, & theyr people, and theyr graues rounde about. These al are among the vncircumcysed, & them that be slayne with the swearde, because afore tyme they made the lande of the lyuynge afrayed.

27 Shulde not they then lye also amonge the worthyes, and vncyrcumcysed Gyauntes? which with theyr weapens are gone doune to hell: whose sweardes are layed vnder theyr heades, whose wickednesse is vpon theyr bones: because that as worthyes, they haue broughte feare into the lande of the lyuynge?

28 Yea amonge the vncyrcumcysed shalte thou be destroyed, and slepe wyth them, that perysshed thorowe the swearde.

29 There is the lande of Edom

with her kinges & princes also, whiche with theyr strengthe are layed by them that were slayne with the swearde, yea amonge the vncyrcumcysed, and them whiche are gone doune into the pytte.

30 Moreouer, there be all the prynces of the north wyth all the Sydonyans, whiche are gone doune to the slayne. With theyr feare & strength they are come to confusyon, and lye there vncyrcumcysed, amonge those that be slayne with the swearde: and beare theyr owne shame, with them that be gone doune to the pytte.

31 Nowe when Pharao seyth thys, he shalbe comforted ouer all hys people, that is slayne wyth the swearde both Pharao and all hys host, sayeth the lord God.

32 For I haue geuen my feare in the lande of the lyuynge. But Pharao and all hys people shall lye amonge the vncyrcumcysed, and amonge them that be slayne with the sweard sayeth the Lorde God.

# CHAPTER 33

AGAYNE, the worde of the Lorde came vnto me, sayinge:

2 Thou sonne of man, Speake to the children of thy people, & tell them: When I sende a swearde vpon a lande, yf the people of the lande take a man of their countre, & set him to be their watchman,

3 the same man (whan he seyth the sweard come vpon the lande) shal blowe the trompet, and warne the people.

4 If a man now heare the noyse of the trompet, and wil not be warned, and the swearde come and take him awaye: his bloude shall be vpon hys owne head:

5 for he hearde the sound of the trompet, and wolde not take hede: therfore hys bloude be vpon hym. But yf he wyll receyue warninge, he shall saue hys lyfe.

6 Agayne, yf the watch man se the swearde come and shewe it not wyth the trompet, so that the people is not warned: yf the sweard come then and take any man from amonge them, the same shall be taken awaye in hys owne sinne but hys bloude wyll I requyre of the watchemans hande.

7 And now (O thou sonne of man) I haue made the a watcheman vnto the house of Israell: that where as thou hearest anye thynge oute of my mouthe, thou mayest warne them on my behalfe.

8 If I say vnto the wicked thou wycked, thou shalte surelye dye: & thou geuest hym not warnynge, that he maye bewarre of hys vngodly waye: then shall the wicked dye in hys owne synne, but hys bloude wyll I requyre of thy hand.

9 Neuertheles yf thou warne the wycked of hys waye, to turne from it, where as he yet will not be turned from it, then shall he dye because of hys synne, but thou haste delyuered thy soule.

10 Therfor (O thou sonne of man) speake vnto the house of Israel. Ye saye thus: Oure offences and synnes lye vpon vs, and we be corrupte in them: how shuld we then be restored vnto lyfe?

11 Tell them: As trulye as I lyue, sayeth the Lorde God, I haue no pleasure in the death of the wicked, but moch rather that the wicked turne from his waye and lyue. Turne you, turne you from your vngodlye wayes, O ye of the house of Israell. Oh, wherfore wyll ye dye?

12 Thou sonne of man, tell the chyldren of thy people: The ryghtuousnes of the righteous shall not saue hym, when soeuer he turneth awaye vnfaithfully: Agayne, the wickednesse of the wicked shal not hurt him, when soeuer he conuerteth from hys vngodlynesse. And the ryghtuousnesse of the ryghtuous shall not saue hys lyfe, when soeuer he synneth.

13 If I saye vnto the ryghtuous, that he shall surelye lyue, and so he trust to his owne ryghtuousnesse, and do synne: then shall hys ryghtuousnesse be no more thought vpon, but in the wyckednesse that he hath done he shall dye.

14 Agayne, yf I saye vnto the wycked: thou shalt surely dye: and so he turne from hys synnes, and do the thinge that is lawfull and ryght:

15 In so moch that the same wicked man geueth the pledge agayne, restoreth that he had taken awaye by robbery, walcketh in the commaundementes of lyfe, & doth no wronge: Then shall he surely lyue, and not dye.

16 Yee the synnes that he hath done shall neuer be thought vpon: For in so moch as he doth now the thinge that is lawfull and ryght, he shall lyue.

17 And yet the children of thy people saye: Tushe, the waye of the Lorde is not ryght, where as their owne waye is rather vnright.

18 When the rightuous turneth from his rightuousnesse, & doeth the thinge that is wycked, he shal dye therfore.

19 But yf the wycked turne from hys wyckednesse, doing the thinge that is lawfull & ryght, he shall lyue therfore.

20 Yet ye saye: the waye of the Lorde is not equall. O ye house of Israel, I wyll iudge euery one of you after his wayes.

21 In the .xij. yeare, the .v. daye of the .x. moneth of oure captyuyte, it happened, that one which was fled out of Ierusalem, came vnto me, and sayde: the cytye is destroyed.

22 Now the hande of the Lorde had bene vpon me the euenyng afore this man (which was escaped) came vnto me, & had opened my mouth, vntyll the mornynge that he came to me: yee he opened my mouth, so that I was nomore domme.

23 Then came the worde of the Lorde vnto me, and sayde:

24 Thou sonne of man, these that dwell in the wasted land of Israel, sayde: Abraham was but one man, & he had the lande in possessyon: now are we manye, & the lande is geuen vs to possesse also.

25 And therfore tell them: Thus sayeth the Lorde: In the bloude haue ye eaten, youre eyes haue ye lyft vp to Idoles, & haue shed bloude: shal ye then haue the lande in possessyon?

26 Ye leane vpon youre sweardes, ye worcke abomynacyon, euery one defyleth hys neghbours wyfe: & shall ye then possesse the lande?

27 Saye thou these wordes vnto them: Thus sayeth the Lorde God: As truelye as I lyue all ye that dwell in thys wyldernesse, shalbe slayne with the sweard: what so euer is vpon the feld, will I geue vnto the beastes to be deuoured: those that be in stronge holdes & dennes shall dye of the pestylence.

28 For I wyll make the lande so desolate and waste, and the pompe of her strength shall come to an ende. The mountaynes in Israell shalbe so waste, that no man shall trauayle therby.

29 Then shall they learne to knowe, that I am the Lorde, when I make the lande waste and desolate, because of all theyr abomynacyons, that they haue wrought.

30 And thou sonne of man, the chyldren of thy people that talcke of the, by th walles and in the dores of theyr houses, sayinge one to another: Come, let vs hear what worde is gone forthe from the Lorde:

31 These come vnto the, after the maner of a great people: yea my people syt doune before the, and heare thy wordes, but they do not there after: for in theyr mouthes they shewe them selues, as though they were feruent, but their herte goeth after theyr owne couetous lucre.

32 And as a balet that hath a swete tune, and is pleasaunt to synge, so shalte thou be vnto them: thy wordes shall they heare, but they wil not do thereafter.

33 When thys commeth to passe (for lo, it commeth in dede) then shall they know, that there hath ben a Prophet among them.

# CHAPTER 34

AND the worde of the Lorde came vnto me, saying:

2 Thou sonne of man, prophecy against the shepeherdes of Israel, prophecye and speake vnto them: Thus sayeth the Lorde God: Wo be vnto the shepeherdes of Israel, that fede them selues. Shulde not the shepeherdes fede the flockes?

3 Ye haue eaten vp the fatte, ye haue clothed you wyth the wol: the best fedde haue ye slayne, but the flocke haue ye not noryshed.

4 The weake haue ye not holden vp, the sicke haue ye not healed: the broken haue ye not bounde together, the oute castes haue ye not brought agayne: the lost haue ye not soughte, but churlishly and cruellye haue ye ruled them.

5 Thus are they scatred here and there wythoute a shepherde: yea al the beastes of the felde deuoure them, and they go astraye.

6 My shepe go wandrynge vpon all mountaynes, and vpon euerye hye hyl. Yea they be scatred abroade in al feldes, and there is no man, that careth for them, or seketh after them.

7 Therfore O ye shepeherdes, heare the worde of the Lorde.

8 Thus sayth the Lorde God: As trulye as I lyue, for so much as my shepe are robbed, & deuoured of all the wylde beastes of the felde, hauynge no shepherde: and seinge that my shepeherdes take no regarde of my shepe, but fede them selues onely, and not my shepe:

9 Therfore heare the worde of the Lorde O ye shepherdes:

10 Thus sayth the Lord God: Beholde, I my self wyll vpon the shepherdes and requyre my shepe from theyr handes, and make them ceasse from fedynge of my shepe: yea the shepherdes shall fede them selues no more: For I wyll delyuer my shepe oute of theyr mouthes, so that they shall not deuoure them after this.

11 For thus sayth the Lord god: Beholde, I will loke to my shepe my selfe, & seke them.

12 Lyke as a shepherde amonge the flocke seketh after the shepe that are scatered abroade, euen so wyll I seke after my shepe, & gather them together oute of all places, wher they haue bene scatred in the cloudy & darcke daye.

13 I wyll brynge them oute from all people, and gather them together oute of all landes. I wyll brynge them into theyr owne land, and fede them vpon the mountaynes of Israel, by the ryuers, and in all the places of the countre.

14 I wil fede them in ryght good pastures, and vpon the hye mountaynes of Israell shal there foldes be. There shall they lye in a good folde, and in a fat pasture shall they fede, euen vpon the mountaynes of Israel.

15 I wil fede my shepe my

selfe, and brynge them to theyr rest sayeth the Lorde GOD.

16 Suche as be loste, wyll I seke: suche as go astraye, wyll I bryng agayn: suche as be wounded, wil I bynde vp: suche as be weake, wyll I make stronge: suche as be fat and well lyking, those wil I preserue, and fede them with the thynge that is laufull.

17 And as for you (O my shepe) sayeth the Lorde God: I wyl put a difference amonge the shepe, amonge the wethers & the goates.

18 Was it not ynough for you to eat vp the good pasture, but ye must treade downe the residue of your pasture with your fete also? Was it not ynough for you to drink cleare water, but ye must trouble the resydue also with your fete?

19 Thus my shepe muste be fayne to eate the thynge, that ye haue troden doune with your fete, & to drincke it, that ye with youre fete haue befyled.

20 Therfore, thus saieth the Lorde God vnto them: Beholde, I wyll seuer the fatte shepe from the leane:

21 for so muche as ye haue shot the weake shepe vpon the sydes & shoulders, and runne vpon them with youre hornes, so longe tyll ye haue vtterlye scatred them abroad

22 I will helpe my shepe, so that they shall no more be spoyled: yea, I wyll discerne one shepe from another.

23 I wyll rayse vp vnto them one onelye shepeherde: euen my seruaunt Dauid, he shall fede them, and he shall be theyr shepherde.

24 I the Lorde wyll be theyr God, and my seruaunte Dauid shall be their prince: Euen I the Lorde haue spoken it.

25 Moreouer, I wyll make a couenaunte of yeare with them, and driue al euyl beastes out of the lande: so that they maye dwell safelye in the wyldernes, and slepe in the wooddes.

26 Good fortune and prosperyte wil I geue them, and vnto all that be rounde aboute my hyll. A prosperous shower and rayne wil I sende them in due season,

27 that the trees in the wood maye brynge forthe theyr frutes, & the grounde her increase. They shalbe safe in theyr lande, & shall knowe, that I am the Lorde, whiche haue broken theyr yocke, and delyuered them oute of the handes of those, that helde them in subieccyon.

28 They shal no more be spoyled of the Heathen, nor deuoured with the beastes of the lande: but safely shall they dwell, and no man shall fraye them.

29 I wyll set vp an excellente plante for them, so that they shal suffre no more hunger in the lande, neither beare the reprofe of the Heathen any more.

30 Thus shal they vnderstand that I the Lorde theyr God am with them, & that they (euen the house of Israel) are my people, sayeth the Lorde God.

31 Ye men are my flocke, ye are the shepe of my pasture: and I am youre God, sayeth the Lorde God.

## CHAPTER 35

Moreouer, the worde of the lorde came vnto me, sayinge:

2 Thou sonne of man, turne thy face towarde the mounte Seir, prophecye vpon it,

3 & say vnto it: Thus sayeth the Lord God Beholde (O thou mount Seir) I wil vpon the, I wyl reache out myne hande ouer the, yea waste and desolate will I make the.

4 Thy cytyes wyll I breake doune: and thou shalte lye voyde, that thou mayest knowe, how that I am the Lord.

5 For so much as thou bearesté an olde enemyte agaynst the chyldren of Israel, and with a cruell hande haste made them afrayed, what tyme as they were troubled and punyshed for theyr synne:

6 Therfore as truelye as I lyue, sayeth the Lord GOD, I wyl prepare the vnto bloud, yea bloude shall folowe vpon the: seyng thou layest wayte for bloude, therfore shal bloude persecute the.

7 Thus wyll I make the mounte Seir desolate and waste, and brynge to passe, that there shal no man goo thyther, ner com from thence.

8 Hys mountaynes wyll I fyll wyth hys slayne men: thy hylles, dales and valleys shall lye full of them, that are slayne with the swearde.

9 I wyll make the a perpetuall wyldernesse, so that no man shall dwell in thy cytyes: that ye maye knowe, how that I am the Lorde.

10 And because thou hast sayd: what, both these nacyons and both these landes must be myne, & I wyll haue them in possession, where as the Lorde was there. Therfore, thus sayeth the Lorde God:

11 As trulye as I lyue, I wyll handle the accordynge to thy wrath and gelousy, lyke as thou hast dealt cruellye with them: that I maye be knowen amonge them, how I haue punished the.

12 Yee and that thou also mayest be sure, that I the Lord haue hearde all thy despytefull wordes, whiche thou hast spoken agaynst the mountaynes of Israel, sayinge: Lo, they are made waste, & geuen vs to deuoure.

13 Thus wyth youre mouthes ye haue mayde youre boost agaynst me, yee & multyplyed youre proude wordes agaynst me, which I haue hearde altogether.

14 Wher vnto thus sayeth the Lorde God: when the whole worlde is in wealth, then wyll I make the waste.

15 And like as thou (O mount Seyr) wast glad, because the heretage of the house of Israel was destroyed: euen so wyll I do vnto the also that thou & whole Edom shall be destroyed, and knowe, that I am the Lorde.

## CHAPTER 36

THOU sonne of man, prophecie vpon the mountaynes of Israel, & speake: Heare the worde of the Lorde, O ye mountaynes of Israell:

2 Thus sayeth the Lorde God: Because youre enemye hath sayde vpon you: A ha, the hye euerlastynge places are now become ours:

3 prophecye therfore, and speake: thus sayeth the Lorde God: Seynge ye be wasted & troden downe on euery syde, and become a possessyon vnto the resydue of the Gentyles, whych haue brought you in to mens mouthes & vnto an euell name amonge the people:

4 Therfore heare the worde of the Lorde God, O ye mountaynes of Israell: Thus sayeth the Lorde God vnto the mountaynes and hilles, valleys and dales, to the voyde wildernesses & desolat cytyes, whiche are spoyled, & had in derisyon on euery syde, amonge the resydue of the Heathen:

5 Yee euen thus sayeth the Lord God: In the fyre of my gelousy haue I take a deuyce, agaynst the resydue of the Gentiles, and agaynst all Edom which haue taken in my lande vnto them selues for a possession, which also reioysed from their whole herte with a dyspiteful stomacke to waste it, and to spoyle it.

6 Prophecy therfore vpon the lande of Israell, speake vnto the mountaynes and hilles to valleys and dales, thus sayeth the Lorde God: Beholde, this haue I deuysed in my gelousy and terrible wrath: For so moch as ye haue suffred reprofe of the Heathen,

7 therfore thus sayeth the Lorde God: I haue sworne, that the Gentyles which lye aboute you, shal beare youre confusyon them selues.

8 And as for you (O mountaynes of Israell) ye shall shute out your braunches, and brynge forth youre fruyte to my people of Israell, for it is hard by, that it wyll come.

9 Beholde, I come vnto you, and vnto you wyl I turne me, that ye maye be tylled and sowen.

10 I will sende you moch people, which shal be all of the house of Israel: the cyties shalbe inhabyted, & the decayed places shalbe repayred agayne.

11 I wyll prouyde you wt moch people and catell, whiche shall increase & brynge fruite. I wil restore you also to your old estat & shewe you more kindnes then euer ye had before: wherby ye shal knowe, that I am the Lorde.

12 Yee people wyll I sende vnto you (O my folcke of Israell) whych shall haue the in possessyon, & thou shalt be their inheritaunce so that thou shalt nomore be wythout them.

13 Agayne, thus sayeth the Lorde God: For so moch as they saye vnto you: thou art an eater vp of men, & a waster of thy people:

14 therfore thou shalt eate no mo men, nether destroye thy people eny more, sayeth the Lorde God.

15 And I wyll not suffre the, for to heare thyne owne confusyon amonge the Gentiles from henceforth. Thou shalt not beare the reprofe of the nacions, ner cast out thyne owne people enymore, sayeth the Lorde God.

16 Moreouer, the worde of the Lorde came vnto me, sayeng:

17 O thou sonne of man, when the house of Israell dwelt vpon their owne grounde they defyled them selues with their owne wayes and ymagynacyons: so that in my syght theyr waye was lyke the vnclennesse of a menstrous woman.

18 Wherfore I poured my wrathfull dyspleasure vpon them, because of the bloude that they had shed in the lande, and because of their Idoles, wherwith they had defyled them selues.

19 I scatred them also amonge the Heathen, so that they where strowed aboute in the landes. According to their wayes and after their owne inuencyons, so dyd I punysh them.

20 Now when they were gone vnto the Heathen, & come in amonge them they dyshonoured my holye name: so that it was sayde of them: Are these the people of God, & must go out of their owne lande?

21 Then spared I my holy name, which the house of Israell had dishonoured amonge the Gentyles, to whom they came.

22 Therfore tell the house of Israell: Thus sayeth the Lord God: I do not this for youre sakes (O house of Israell) but for my holye names sake, whyche ye dyshonoured amonge the Heathen, when ye came to them.

23 Therfore, I wyll halowe my greate name agayne, which amonge the Gentiles is euell spoken of: for ye yourselues haue dishonoured it amonge them. And the Gentiles shal knowe that I am the Lord, when I am honoured in you before their eyes, sayeth the Lorde God.

24 As for you, I wyll take you from amonge the Heathen, and gather you together out of all countrees, and brynge you agayne into your owne lande.

25 Then wyll I poure cleare water vpon you, & ye shalbe clene: yee from all your vnclennesse and from all your Idols shal I clense you.

26 A new herte also will I geue you, and a new sprete wyll I put into you: As for that stony herte, I wyll take it out of youre body, & geue you a fleshly herte.

27 I will geue my sprete amonge you, and cause you to walcke in my commaundementes, to kepe my lawes, and to fulfyll them.

28 And so ye shall dwell in the lande, that I gaue to youre forefathers, and ye shalbe my people, & I wilbe youre God.

29 I wyll helpe you out of all youre vnclennesse. I wyll call for the corne, & will increase it, & wyll let you haue no honger.

30 I wyll multiplye the fruites of the trees & the increase of the felde for you, so that ye shall beare no more reprofe of honger amonge the Heathen.

31 Then shall ye remembre your, owne wicked wayes, & youre ymagynacyons, whiche were not good: so that ye shall take displeasure at youre owne selues, by reason of youre synnes & abhominacyons.

32 But I wyll not do this for youre sakes (sayeth the Lorde God) be ye sure of it. Therfore, O ye house of Israell, be ashamed of your synnes.

33 Moreouer, thus sayeth the Lord God: what tyme as I shall clense you from all youre offences, then wyll I make the cytyes to be occupyed agayne, and wyll repayre the places that be decayed.

34 The desolate lande shall be buylded agayne, whiche afore tyme laye waste in the sight of all them that wente by.

35 Then shall it be sayde: this waste lande is become lyke a garden of pleasure, & the voyde, desolate and broken downe cytyes, are now strong, and fensed agayne.

36 Then the resydue of the Heathen that lye rounde aboute you, shall knowe that I am the Lorde, whyche repayre that was broken downe, and plante agayne, that was made waste. Euen I the Lorde haue spoken it, and wyll do it in dede.

37 Thus sayeth the Lorde God: I wyll yet ones be found agayne of the house of Israel & do this for them: I shall increase them as a flocke of men.

38 Lyke as the holy flocke and the flocke of Ierusalem are in the hye solempne feastes: so shall also the wylde wasted cyties be fylled with flockes of men: and they shall knowe that I am the Lorde.

# CHAPTER 37

THE hande of the Lord came vpon me, & caryed me out in the sprete of the Lorde, & let me downe in a playne felde that laye full of bones,

2 and he led me rounde aboute by them: & beholde, the bones that laye vpon the felde, were very many, and maruelous drye also.

3 Then sayde he vnto me: Thou sonne of man: thinkest thou these bones maye lyue agayne? I answered: O Lorde God, thou knowest.

4 And he sayde vnto me: prophecye thou vpon these bones, & speake vnto them: Ye drye bones, heare the worde of the Lorde.

5 Thus sayeth the Lorde God vnto these bones: Beholde, I wyll put breth into you, that ye maye lyue:

6 I wyll geue yow synowes, and make flesh grow vpon you, & couer you ouer with skinne: & so geue you breth, that ye may lyue, and knowe, that I am the Lorde.

7 So I prophecyed, as he had commaunded me. And as I was prophecyinge there came a noyse and a greate mocyon, so that the bones ranne euery one to another.

8 Now when I had loked, beholde, they had synowes, and flesh grewe vpon them: and aboue they were couered with skynne, but there was no breth in them.

9 Then sayde he vnto me: Thou sonne of man, prophecye thou towarde the wynde: prophecy, & speake to the wynd: Thus sayeth the Lord God: Come (O thou ayre) from the foure wyndes, and blowe vpon these slayne, that they maye be restored to lyfe.

10 So I prophecied, as he had commaunded me: then came the breth into them, & they receyued lyfe, & stode vp vpon their fete, a maruelous greate sorte.

11 Moreouer, he sayde vnto me: Thou sonne of man, these bones are the whole house of Israell. Beholde, they saye: Oure bones are dryed vp, oure hope is gone, we are clene cut of.

12 Therfore prophecye thou, & speake vnto them: thus sayeth the Lord God: Beholde, I wyll open youre graues (O my people) & take you out of youre sepulcres, & bringe you in to the lande of Israel agayne.

13 So shall ye know that I am the Lorde, when I open your graues, & bringe you out of them.

14 My sprete also wyll I put in you, & ye shall lyue: I wyll set you agayne in youre owne lande, and ye shal knowe, that I am the Lord, which haue sayd it, and fulfylled it in dede.

15 The worde of the Lorde came vnto me, sayinge:

16 thou sonne of man, take a stycke and wryte vpon it: Vnto Iuda & to the chyldren of Israel his companyons. Then take another sticke, & write vpon it: Vnto Ioseph the stock of Ephraim, & to all the housholde

of Israell his companyons.

17 And then, take both these together in thyne hande, so shall there be one stycke therof.

18 Now yf the chyldren of thy people saye vnto the: wylt thou not shewe vs, what thou meanest by these?

19 Then geue them this answere: thus sayeth the Lorde God: beholde, I wyll take the stock of Ioseph, which is in the hande of Ephraim & of the tribes of Israell his felowes, & will put them to the stock of Iuda, & make them one stocke, & they shall be one in my hande.

20 And the two styckes where vpon thou wrytest, shalt thou haue in thyne hande, that they may se,

21 and shalt saye vnto them. Thus sayeth the Lorde God: beholde, I wyll take awaye the chyldren of Israel from amonge the Heathen vnto whom they be gone, & wyll gather them together on euery syde, & bringe them agayne into their owne lande:

22 yee I wyll make one people of them in the lande, vpon the mountaynes of Israell, and they all shall haue but one kynge. They shall no mor be two peoples from henceforth, nether be deuyded in to two kyngdomes:

23 they shall also defile them selues nomore with their abhomynacyons, Idoles, & all their wicked doinges. I will helpe them out of all their dwellinge places, wherin they haue synned: and will so clense them: that they shalbe my people, & I their God.

24 Dauid my seruaunt shalbe their kinge, & they all shal haue one shepherde onely. They shall walke in my lawes, & my commaundementes shall they both kepe and fulfil.

25 They shal dwel in the lande, that I gaue vnto Iacob my seruaunt, where as youre fathers also haue dwelt. Yea, euen in the same lande shall they, their chyldren, & their childers chyldren dwell for euermore: and my seruaunt Dauid shalbe their euerlastinge prince.

26 Moreouer, I will make a bonde of peace wyth theym, whiche shalbe vnto them an euerlastinge couenaunt. I will satle them also, and multiply them, my Sanctuary wyll I set amonge them for euermore.

27 My dwellynge shalbe wyth them, yea, I will be their God, and they shal be my people.

28 Thus the Heathen also shall knowe, that I the Lorde am the holy maker of Israel: when my Sanctuary shalbe among them for euermore.

# CHAPTER 38

AND the worde of the Lorde came vnto me, sayinge:

2 Thou sonne of man, turne thy face towarde Gog in the lande of Magog, whyche is the chiefe prince at Mesech and Tubal: prophecy agaynst hym,

3 & saye: Thus sayeth the Lord God: O Gog thou chief prince Mesech & Tuball: beholde, I will vpon the,

4 and wil turne the about, and put a bytte in thy chawes: I will bringe the forth & all thine hoost, both horse and horsemen whiche be all weapened of the beste fashion: a great people, that handle altogether speares, shyldes, and swerdes:

5 the Perses, Moryans and with them the Lybians, whiche all beare shyldes & helmettes:

6 Gomer and al his hoostes: the house of Thogorma out of the north quarters, and all his hoostes, yea, & muche people with the.

7 Therfore prepare the, set thy selfe in araye with all thy people, that are come vnto the by heapes, and be thou their defence.

8 After many dayes thou shalt be visited, and in the latter yeares thou shalt come into the lande, that hath bene destroyed wyth the swearde, & now is replenyshed agayne wyth dyuerse people vpon the mountaynes of Israell, which haue longe lyen waste. Yee they be brought out of the nacyons, and dwell all safe.

9 Thou shalt come vp like a stormy wether, to couer the lande, and as it were a darcke cloude: thou wyth all thyne hostes, & a greate multytude of people wyth the.

10 Moreouer, thus sayeth the Lorde God: At the same tyme shall manye thynges come in to thy mynde, so that thou shalt ymagyn myschefe,

11 & saye: I will vp to yonder playne lande, seing they syt at ease, and dwell so safely (for they dwell all wythout any walles, they haue nether barres nor dores)

12 to spoyle them, to robbe them, to laye hande vpon their so well inhabyted wyldernesses: agaynst that people, that is gathered together from amonge the Heathen, whyche haue gotten catell and good, and dwell in the myddest of the lande.

13 Then shall Saba, and Dedan, and the marchauntes of Tharsis wyth all their worthies, saye vnto the: Art thou come to robbe? Hast thou gathered thy people together, because thou wylt spoyle? to take syluer and golde: to carye awaye catell and good: and to haue a greate praye?

14 Therfore, O thou sonne of man, thou shalt prophecye, and saye vnto Gog: Thus sayeth the Lord God: In that daye thou shalt knowe, that my people of Israell dwelleth safe:

15 & shalth come from thy place out of the north partes: thou & moch people with the, whych ryde vpon horses, wherof there is a greate multytude & an

innumerable sorte.

16 Yee thou shalt come vpon my people of Israell, as a cloude to couer the lande. This shall come to passe in the latter dayes: I will bringe the vp into my lande, that the Heathen maye knowe me, when I get me honoure vpon the. O Gog before their eyes.

17 Thus sayeth the Lord God: Thou art he, of whom I haue spoken afore tyme, by my seruauntes the prophetes of Israell, whyche prophecyed in those dayes and yeares, that I shulde brynge the vpon them.

18 At the same tyme, when Gog commeth vp in to the lande of Israell (sayeth the Lorde God) shall my indygnacyon go forth in my wrath.

19 For in my gelousy and hote dyspleasure I haue deuysed, that there shalbe a greate trouble in the land of Israel at that tyme.

20 The very fishes in the sea, the foules of the ayre, the beastes of the felde, and al the men that are vpon the earth, shall tremble for feare of me. The hilles also shalbe turned vp syde downe, the stayres of stone shall fall, & all walles shall syncke to the grounde.

21 I wyll call for a swearde vpon them in all my mountaynes, sayeth the Lorde God: so that euerye mans sweard shall be vpon another.

22 Wyth pestylence and bloude will I punysh hym: stormy rayne & hayle stones, fyre & brimstone, wyl I cause to rayne vpon him & all his heape yee & vpon al that greate people that is with hym.

23 Thus wyll I be magnifyed, honoured, and knowne amonge the Heathen: that they maye be sure, how that I am the Lorde.

## CHAPTER 39

Therfore O thou sonne of man, prophecye agaynste Gog, and speake: Thus sayeth the Lorde God: Behold, O Gog: thou chefe prince at Mesech and Tubal, I wyll vpon the,

2 and turne the aboute, & carie the forth, and leade the from the north partes, and bringe the vp to the mountaynes of Israell.

3 As for thy bowe, I wyll smyte it out of thy left hande, and cast thyne arowes out of thy ryght hande.

4 Thou wyth all thyne heape, and all the people that is wyth the, muste, fall vpon the mountaynes of Israell. Then wyll I geue the vnto the foules & wylde beastes of the felde, to be deuoured:

5 there must thou lye vpon the felde: for euen I the Lorde haue spoken it, sayeth the Lorde God.

6 In to Magog, and amonge those that syt so carelesse in the Iles: will I sende a fyre, & they shall know, that I am the Lorde.

7 I wyll make also the name of my holynesse to be knowne amonge my people of Israell: and I wyll not let my holy name be euell spoken of enymore: but the very Heathen also shal knowe, that I am the Lorde, the holye one of Israell

8 Beholde, it commeth, and shalbe fulfylled in dede, sayeth the Lord God. This is the daye wherof I haue spoken:

9 They that dwell in the cyties of Israel, shall go forth & set fyre vpon the weapens, & burne them: shyldes & speres bowes and arowes, bylles & clubbes: seuen yeares

10 shall they be burnynge therof, so that they shall els bringe no styckes from the felde, nether haue nede to hew downe eny out of the wodde: For they shal haue weapens ynow to burne. They shall robbe those that robbed them, & spoyle those that spoyled them sayeth the Lorde God.

11 At the same tyme wyll I geue vnto Gog, a place to be buried in, in Israel: euen the valley where thorow men go from the east to the see warde. Those that trauayle therby, shall abhorre it. There shall Gog and all hys people be buried: and it shalbe called the valleye of the people of Gog.

12 Seuen monethes longe shall the house of Israell be burienge of them that they maye clense the lande.

13 Yee al the people of the lande shall burye them. O it shall be a glorious daye, when I gett me that honoure, sayeth the Lorde God.

14 They shall ordene men also to be deed buriers, euer going thorow the lande, & appoynte them certayne places to bury those in, which remayne vpon the felde, that the lande maye be clensed. From ende to ende shall they seke, and that .vij. monethes longe.

15 Now those that go thorow the land, where they se a mans bone, they shall set vp a token by it, till the deed buriers haue buried it also, in the valleys of the people of Gog.

16 And the name of the cytye shalbe called. Hamonah: Thus shalt they make the land clene.

17 And thou sonne of man: thus sayth the Lorde God: Speake vnto all the foules and euery byrde, yee and to all the wylde beastes of the felde: heape you together and come, gather you rounde aboute vpon my slaughter, that I haue slayne for you: euen a greate slaughter vpon the mountaynes of Israell: eate flesh, and drincke bloude.

18 Ye shall eate the flesh of the worthies, and drynke the bloude of the prynces of the lande: of the wethers, of the lambes of the goates, and of the oxen that be al slayne at Basan.

19 Eate the fat youre belyfull, & dryncke bloud, tyll ye be

dronken of the slaughter, whyche I haue slayne vnto you.

20 Fyll you at my table, with horses and stronge horsmen: with captaynes and all men of warre, sayeth the Lorde God.

21 I wyll bringe my glorye also amonge the Gentyles, that all the Heathen maye se my iudgement, that I haue kepte, and my hande which I haue layed vpon them:

22 that the house of Israell maye knowe, how that I am the Lorde theyr God, from that daye forth.

23 And the Heathen shall knowe, that where as the house of Israell were led in to captyuite: it was for their wickednes sake, because they offended me. For the whych cause I hyd my face from them, and delyuered them in to the handes of their enemyes, that they myght all be slayne with the sweard.

24 Accordinge to their vnclennesse and vnfaithfull dealinges, so haue I entreated them, and hyd my face from them.

25 Therfore thus sayeth the Lorde God: Now wyll I brynge agayne the captiues of Iacob and haue mercy vpon the whole house of Israell, and be gelous for my holy names sake.

26 All their confusion and offence that they haue done agaynst me, shall be taken awaye: and so safely shall they dwell in their lande, that no man shall make them afrayed.

27 And when I haue brought them agayne from amonge the people, when I haue gathered them together out of their enemyes landes, & am praysed in them before many Heathen:

28 then shall they knowe, that I am the Lorde their God, which suffred them to be led in to cautyuite amonge the Heathen, but now haue brought them agayne in to their owne lande, and not left one of them yonder.

29 After that, wyll I hyde my face nomore from them, but will poure out my sprete vpon the house of Israell, sayeth the Lorde God.

# CHAPTER 40

IN the .xxv. yeare of oure captyuytye, in the beginninge of the yeare, the .x. daye of the moneth: that is the .xiiij. yeare, after that the cyte was smyten downe: the same daye came the hande of the Lorde vpon me, and caried me forth:

2 euen into the lande of Israell brought he me in the vysyons of God: and set me downe vpon a maruelous hye mountayne, where vpon there was a buyldynge (as it had bene of a cyte) towarde the north.

3 Thither he caried me, and beholde, there was a man, whose symylytude was lyke a brasse, which had a thred of flax in his hande, & a metterodde also. He stode in the dore,

4 and sayde vnto me: marcke well with thyne eyes, herken to with thyne eares, & fasten it in thine hert, whatsoeuer I shall shewe the, for to the intent that they myght be shewed the, therfore art thou brought hither. And what soeuer thou seyste, thou shalt certyfye the house of Israel therof.

5 Behalde, there was a wall on the outsyde rounde aboute the house: the meterodde that he had in hys hand, was six cubytes long & a spanne. So he measured the bredth of the buylding, which was a meterodde, & the heygth also a meterodde.

6 Then came he vnto the east dore, and wente vp the stares, and measured the postes of the dore: wherof euery one was a meterodde thicke. Euerye chambre was a meterodde longe & brode:

7 betwene the chambers were fyue cubytes. The poste of the dore within the porche, was one meterodde.

8 He measured also the porche of the ynnermer dore whych conteyned a meterodde.

9 Then measured he the entrye of the dore, that conteyned eght cubytes, and his pylers two cubytes: & this entrye stode inwarde.

10 The chambers of the dore east warde, were thre on euerye syde: a lyke brode and longe. The pylers also that stode of both the sydes, were of one measure.

11 After this, he measured the wydenesse of the dore, which was .x. cubytes, & the heyght of the dore .xiij. cubytes.

12 The edge before the chambres was one cubyte brode vpon both the sydes, and the chambres six cubytes wyde of either syde.

13 He measured the dore from the rygge of one chambre to another, whose wydnesse was .xxv. cubytes, & one dore stode agaynst another.

14 He made pylers also .lx. cubytes hye, rounde aboute the courte dore.

15 Before the inward parte vnto the fore entre of the ynnermer dore, were .L. cubytes.

16 The chambers & their pylers within, rounde about vnto the dore, had sayde wyndowes: So had the fore entries also, whose wyndowes wente rounde about within. And vpon the pylers there stode date trees.

17 Then brought he me in to the fore courte, where as were chambres & paued worckes, made in the fore courte rounde aboute .xxx. chambres vpon one paued worcke.

18 Now the paued worcke was a longe beside the dores, & that was the lower paued worcke.

19 After this, he measured the bredth from the lower dore, vnto the ynnermer courte of the

outsyde, which had an .C. cubytes vpon the east & the north parte.

20 And the dore in the vttermost courte towarde the north, measured he after the length and bredth:

21 his thre chambres also on ether side, wyth his pylers & fore entries: which had euen the measure of the first dore. His heygth was fyfty cubytes, the bredth .xxv. cubytes:

22 his wyndowes & porches wyth hys date tres, had euen lyke measure as the dore towarde the east: there were .vij. steppes to go vp vpon, and their porche before them.

23 Now the dore of the ynnermer court stode streight ouer agaynst the dore, that was toward the north east. From one dore to another, he measured .C. cubytes.

24 After that, he brought me to the southsyde, where there stode a dore towarde the south: whose pilers and porches he measured, these had the fyrste measure,

25 & wyth their porches they had wyndowes rounde aboute, lyke the fyrst wyndowes. The heygth was .l. cubites, the bredth .xxv.

26 with steppes to go vp vpon: his porche stode before hym, with his pylers & date tres on either side.

27 And the dore of the ynnermer courte stode towarde the south, & he measured from one dore to another an .C. cubytes.

28 So he brought me in to the ynnermer courte, thorow the dore of the south syde: whych he measured, & it had the measure afore sayd.

29 In lyke maner, his chambres, pylers, & fore entries, had euen the fore sayde measure also. And he had with hys porches rounde aboute wyndowes of .L. cubytes heyght, and .xxv. cubytes brode.

30 The porches rounde aboute were .xxv. cubytes longe, & .v. cubytes brode:

31 and his porche reached vnto the vttermoste court: vpon his pylers there were date trees, and .viij. steppes to go vp vpon.

32 He brought me also in to the ynmost courte vpon the east syde, and measured the dore, accordyng to the measure afore sayd.

33 His chambers, pylers, and porches had euen the same measure, as the fyrst had: & with his porches he had wyndowes rounde aboute. The heigth was .l. cubytes, the bredth .xxv. cubytes:

34 Hys porches reached vnto the vttermoste courte: his pilers also had date trees on eyther syde, & .viij. steppes to go vp vpon.

35 And he brought me to the north dore, and measured it, which also had the fore sayde measure.

36 His chambres, pylers and porches had wyndowes rounde aboute: whose heygth was .L. cubytes, & the bredth .xxv.

37 His pylers stode towarde the vttermost courte, & vpon them both were date trees, and .viij. steppes to go vp vpon.

38 There stode a chambre also, whose intraunce was at the dore pylers, and there the burntofferynges were wasihed.

39 In the dore porche, there stode on ether syde two tables for the slaughtynge: to sleye the brentofferynges, synne offerynges and trespaceoffrynges ther vpon.

40 And on the out syde as men go forth to the north dore, there stode two tables.

41 Foure tables stode on ether syde of the dore, that is .viij. tables, whervpon they slaughted.

42 Foure tables were of hewen stone for the burntofferynges, of a cubyte & a half longe and brode, and one cubyte hye: wher vpon were layed the vessels and ornamentes, whyche were vsed to the burnt and slayne offerynges, when they were slaughted.

43 And within there were hokes foure fyngers brode, fastened rounde aboute, to hange flesh vpon, & vpon the tables was layed the offryng flesh.

44 On the outsyde of the ynnermerdore were the syugers chambers in the inwarde courte besyde the North dore ouer agaynst the South. There stode one also, besyde the east dore northwarde.

45 And he sayde vnto me: This chambre on the South syde belongeth to the prestes, that kepe the habytacyon:

46 and thys towarde the North, is the Prestes that wayte vpon the aulter: which be the sonnes of Sadoch, that do seruyce before the Lorde in steade of the chyldren of Leui.

47 So he measured the fore courte, whych had in length an .C. cubytes, and as moch in bredth by the foure corners. Now the aulter stode before the house:

48 And he brought me to the fore entre of the house, and measured the walles by the entre dore: which were fyue cubytes longe on ether syde. The thicknesse also of the dore on ether syde, was thre cubytes.

49 The length of the porche was .xx. cubytes, the bredth .xi. cubytes, and vpon steppes went men vp to it: by the walles also were pylers, on ether syde one.

# CHAPTER 41

AFTER this he brought me to the temple, and measured the postes: whyche were of both the sydes .vi. cubytes thicke, accordynge to the wydenesse of the tabernacle.

2 The bredth of the dore was

# EZEKIEL

.x. cubytes and the walles of the dore on either syde fyue cubytes. He measured the length therof, which conteyned .xl. cubytes, and the bredth .xx.

3 Then wente he in, and measured the dore postes, whyche were two cubytes thicke: but the dore it selfe was syxe cubytes, and the bredth of the dore was .xij. cubytes.

4 He measure the length and bredth therof, whych were euery one .xx. cubytes, before the temple. And he sayde vnto me: thys is the holyest of all.

5 He measured also the wall of the house which was syxe cubytes. The chambres that stode rounde aboute the house, were euery one foure cubytes wyde,

6 & one stode harde vpon another, whereof there were .xxxiij. And there stode postes beneth by the walles rounde aboute the house, to beare them vp: but in the wall of the house they were not fastened:

7 The syde chambres were the hyer the wyder, and had steppes thorow them rounde aboute the house. Thus was it wyder aboue, that from the lowest men might go to the hyest & mydd chambers.

8 I sawe also that the house was very hye rounde aboute. The foundacyon of the syde chambres was a meterodde (that is syxe cubytes) brode.

9 The thicknesse of the syde wall without, conteyned fyue cubytes, and so dyd the outwall of the chambres in the house.

10 Betwene the chambers, was the wydenes .xx. cubytes rounde aboute the house.

11 The chambre dores stode ouer agaynst the outwal, the one dore was towarde the north, the other towarde the South: and the thycknesse of the outwal was .v. cubytes rounde aboute.

12 Now the buyldynge that was separated towarde the west, was .lxx. cubytes wyde: the wall of the buyldynge was .v. cubytes thicke rounde aboute, and the length foure score cubytes & ten.

13 So he measured the house which was an .C. cubytes longe, & the separated buyldynge with the wall were an .C. cubytes longe also.

14 The wydnesse before the house and of it that was separated towarde the East, was an .C. cubytes.

15 And he measured the length of the buyldynge before and behynde wyth the chambers vpon both the sydes: and it conteyned an .C. cubites. The yunermer temple, the porch of the fore courte,

16 the side postes, these thre had syde wyndowes, and pylers rounde aboute ouer agaynst the postes, from the grounde vp to the wyndowes: The wyndowes them selues were syled ouer with bordes:

17 and thus was it aboue the dore, vnto the ynmost house & without also: Yee the whole wall on euery syde both within & without was syled ouer with greate bordes.

18 There were Cherubins and date trees made also, so that one date tree stode euer bewixte two Cherubins: One Cherub had two faces,

19 the face of a man lokyng a syde towarde the date tre, and a lyons face on the other syde. Thus was it made rounde aboute in al the house:

20 Yee the Cherubins & date trees were made from the grounde vp aboue the dore, & so stode they also vpon the wall of the temple.

21 The by postes of the temple were foure squared, and the fashion of the Sanctuarye was euen as it appared vnto me a fore in the vision.

22 The table was of wodde, thre cubites hye and two cubytes longe: hys corners, the length and the walles were of wodde. And he sayde vnto me: This is the table, that shal stande before the Lorde.

23 The temple and the holyest of all had ether of them two dores

24 & euery dore had two lytle wyckettes whyche were folden in one vpon another, on euery syde two.

25 And vpon the dores of the temple there were made Cherubins and date trees, lyke as vpon the walles: and a greate thicke balke of wodde was before on the out syde of the porche.

26 Vpon both the sydes of the walles of the porche, there were made depe windowes and date trees, hauyng beames and balkes, lyke as the house had.

## CHAPTER 42

THEN caryed he me out in to the fore court towarde the north, & brought me in to the chambre that stode ouer agaynst the backebuyldynge north warde,

2 which had the length of an .C. cubytes whose dore turned toward the north. The wydenesse conteyned .C. cubites:

3 ouer agaynst the .xx. cubites of the ynnermer courte, and agaynst the paued worke that was in the fore court. Besyde all these thre, therestode pylers, one ouer agaynst another:

4 And before thys chambre there was a walkynge place of .x. cubites wyde, and within was a waye of one cubite wyde, & their dores towarde the north.

5 Thus the hyest chambres were allwaye narower then the loweste and myddell moste of the buylding:

6 for they bare chambre vpon chambre, and stode thre together one vpon another not hauynge pilers lyke the fore courte: therfore were they

smaller then those beneth and in the myddeste, to reken from the grounde vpwarde.

7 The wall with out that stode by the chambres towarde the vtter moste courte vpon the fore syde of the chambres, was .C. cubytes longe:

8 for the length of the vttemost chambres in the fore courte was .C. cubytes also: but the length therof before the temple was an .C. cubytes.

9 These chambres had vnder them an intraunce of the east syde, wherby a man myght go in to them out of the fore courte,

10 thorow the thicke wall of the fore courte towarde the east, right ouer agaynst the separated buyldinge.

11 Before the same buyldynge vpon thys syde there were chambers also whych had awaye vnto them, lyke as the chambers on the north syde of the same length and wydenesse. Their intraunce, fashyon and dores were also of the same maner.

12 Yee euen lyke as the other chamber dores were, so were those also of the south syd. And before the waye toward the fingers steppes on the east side, there stode a dore to go in at.

13 Then sayde he vnto me: The chambers towarde the north and the south whych stande before the backe buyldynge: those be holye habitatyons, wheryn the prestes that do seruyce before the Lorde, muste eate the most holy offeringes: and there must they laye the most holye offerynges: meatofferinges, synne offringes & trespace offerynges, for it is an holy place.

14 When the prestes come therin, they shall not go out in to the fore courte: but (seyenge they be holye) they shall leaue the clothes of their ministracyon, and put on other garmentes, when they haue eny thynge to do with the people.

15 Now when he had measured al the ynnermer house, he brought me forth thorowe the east porte, & measured the same rounde aboute.

16 He measured the east syde with the meterodde, whych rounde aboute conteyned .v.C. meteroddes.

17 And the north syne measured he, whiche conteyned rounde aboute euen so much.

18 The other two sydes also towarde the south

19 and the west (which he measured) conteyned ether of them .v.C. meteroddes.

20 So he measured all the foure sydes where there wente a wall rounde aboute .v.C. meteroddes long and as brode also whych separated the holye from the vnholy.

# CHAPTER 43

So he brought me to the dore, the turneth towarde the east.

2 Beholde, then came the glorye of the God of Israell from out of the east, whose voyce was lyke a greate noyse of waters, and the earth was lyghtened wyth hys glory.

3 His syght to loke vpon was lyke the fyrst, that I sawe, when I wente in, what tyme as the cytye shulde haue bene destroyed: and lyke the vysyon that I sawe by the water of Cobar. Then fell I vpon my face,

4 but the glory of the Lord came in to the house thorow the East dore.

5 So a wyude toke me vp, and brought me into the ynnermer courte: and beholde, the house was full of the glory of the Lorde.

6 I herde one speakyng vnto me out of the house, and there stode one by me,

7 that sayde vnto me: O thou sonne of man, this rowme is my seate, and the place of my fotesteppes: where as I wyll dwell amonge the chyldren of Israell for euermore: so that the house of Israell shall nomore defyle my holye name: nether they, ner their kynges, thorowe their whordome, thorowe their hye places, and thorowe the deed bodyes of their Kynges:

8 whych haue buylded their thresholdes in maner harde vpon my thresholdes, & their postes almoste at my postes: so that there is but a bare wall betwyxte me and them. Thus haue they defyled my holye name wyth their abhominacyons, that they haue commytted. Wherfore I haue destroyed them in my wrath:

9 But now they shall put awaye their whordome and the deed bodyes of their kynges out of my syght, that I maye dwell amonge them for euermore.

10 Therfore (O thou sonne of man) shewe thou the housholde of Israell a temple, that they maye be a shamed of their wickednesse, and measure them selues an example therat.

11 And when they be ashamed of all their worckes, then shewe them the fourme and fashyon of the temple: the commynge in, the goynge oute, all the maner and descripcion therof, yee all the vses and ordynaunces of it that they maye kepe & fulfill all the fashions and customes therof.

12 This is the descripcyon of the house: Aboue vpon the mount rounde aboute all the corners, it shalbe the holyest of all. Beholde, that is the descrypcyon and fashyon of the house.

13 Thys is the measure of the aulter (after the true cubyte: whych is a spanne longer then another cubyte) hys botome in the myddeste was a cubyte longe and wyde, and the ledge that wente rounde aboute it, was a spanne brode. Thys is the heygth

of the aulter:

14 From the grounde to the lower steppes the length is two cubites, and the bredth one cubyte: and from the lower steppes to the higher are foure cubytes, and the bredth but one cubyte.

15 The aulter was foure cubytes hye, & from the aulter vpwarde stode foure hornes,

16 and it was .xij. cubytes longe and .xij. cubytes brode, vpon the foure corners:

17 the coueryinge of the aulter was .xiiij. cubytes longe & brode vpon the foure corners, and the ledge that wente rounde aboute, had half a cubite: and the botome therof rounde aboute one cubyte: hys steppes stode towarde the Easte.

18 And he sayd vnto me: Thou sonne of man, thus saieth the Lorde God: these are the ordynaunces & lawes of the aulter, in the daye when it is made to offre burntoffrynges & to sprenckle bloude ther vpon.

19 To the prestes, to the Leuites that be of the sede of Sadoch, & treade before me to do me seruyce, sayeth the Lorde God: Vnto these geue thou a yonge bullock, for a synofferynge:

20 & take the bloude of hym and sprenckle hys foure hornes withall and the foure corners of the aulter couerynge, with the ledge that goeth rounde aboute: here with shalt thou clense it, & reconcyle it.

21 Thou shalt take the bullock also of the synoffringe, and burne hym in a seuerall place wythout the Sanctuary.

22 The nexte daye, take a gootbuck wythout blemish for a synofferynge, to reconcyle the aulter withall: lyke as it was reconcyled with the bullocke.

23 Now when thou haste made it cleane, then offre a yonge bullocke without blemyshe, and a ramme out of the flocke wythout blemish also:

24 Offre them before the Lorde, and let the prest caste salt thervpon, and geue, them so vnto the Lorde for a burntofferyng.

25 Seuen dayes shalt thou bring, euery daye a gootbuck. A yonge bullocke & a ramme of the flocke (both wythout blemysh) shall they offre.

26 Seuen dayes shall they reconcyle and clense the aulter, and offre vpon it.

27 When these dayes are expired, then vpon the .viij. daye and so forth, the prestes shall offre their burntoffringes & he althoffrynges vpon the aulter: so wyll I be mercyfull vnto you, sayeth the Lorde God.

# CHAPTER 44

AFTER thys, he brought me agayne to the outwarde dore of the Sanctuary on the East syde and that was shut.

2 Then sayde the Lorde vnto me: This dore shall be styll shut, and not opened for enye man to go thorow it, but only for the Lorde God of Israell, yee he shall go thorowe it, els shal it be shut styll.

3 The prynce hym selfe shall come thorow it, that he maye eate bread before the Lorde. At the porche shall he come in, and there shall he go out agayne.

4 Then brought he me to the dore, vpon the North syde of the house. And as I loked aboute me, beholde, the glory of the Lord fylled the house: and I fell downe vpon my face.

5 So the Lord spake vnto me: O thou sonne of man fasten this to thyne herte, beholde, and take dylygent hede to all that I wyll saye vnto the, concernyng all the ordynaunces of the Lord & all his lawes: pondre wel with thyne herte the commynge in of the house and the goinge forth of the Sanctuarye:

6 and tell that obstynate housholde of Israell: Thus sayeth the Lorde God: O house of Israell, ye haue now done ynough withall youre abhomynacyons,

7 seynge that ye haue brought in to my Sanctuary straungers, hauynge vncircumcysed hertes and fleshe, where thorow my Sanctuary is defyled, when ye offre me bred, fat, and bloude. Thus with all youre abhomynacyons ye haue broken my couenaunt,

8 and not kepte the holy ordinaunces of my Sanctuarye: but set kepers of my Sanctuary, euen after your owne mynde.

9 Therfore thus sayeth the Lord God: Of all the straungers that dwell amonge the chyldren of Israell, no straunger (whose herte & fleshe is not cyrcumcysed) shall come within my Sanctuarye:

10 No ner the Leuites that be gone backe frome, and haue dysceyued the people of Israell wyth all erroures, goinge after their ydoles: therfore shall they beare their owne wyckednes.

11 Shulde they be set & ordened to mynystre vnder the dores of the house of my Sanctuarye? And to do seruyce in the house: to slaye burntoffringes and sacrifyces for the people: to stande before them, and to serue them:

12 seynge the seruyce that they do them, is before their Idoles, and cause the house of Israell to stomble thorowe the wyckednes? For the whych cause I haue pluckte out myne hande ouer them (sayeth the Lorde) so that now they must beare their owne iniquyte,

13 and not to come nye me, to serue me with their presthode, in my Sanctuarye, and moost holyest of all: that they maye beare their owne shame & abhomynacyons, which they haue done.

14 Shulde I vse them to be porters of the house, and to all the seruyce that is done therin?

15 But the Prestes the Leuytes the sonnes of Sadoch, that kepte the holye ordynaunces of my Sanctuarye, when the chyldren of Israell were gone fro me: shall come to me, to do me seruyce, to stande before me, & to offre me the fat & the bloude, sayeth the Lorde God.

16 They shall go in to my Sanctuarye, and treade before my table, to do me seruice, and to wayte vpon myne ordynaunces.

17 Now when they go in at the dores of the ynnermer court: they shal put on lynen clothes, so that no wollyne come vpon them: whyle they do seruyce vnder the dores of the ynnermer courte, and within.

18 They shall haue fayre lynen bonettes vpon their heades, and lynen breches vpon their loynes, whyche in their laboure they shall not put about them:

19 And when they go forth to the people in to the outward courte, they shall put of the clothes, wherin they haue mynystred, and laye them in the habytacyon of the Sanctuary, and put on other apparel, lest they vnhalowe the people wyth their clothes.

20 They shall not shaue their heades, ner noryshe the bushe of their heare, but rounde their heades onlye.

21 All the Prestes that go into the ynmost court, shall dryncke no wyne.

22 They shall mary no wydow, nether one that is put from her husband: but a mayde of the sede of the house of Israel, or a wyddowe: that hath had a prest before.

23 They shall shewe my people the dyfference betwene the holye and vnholye, betwyxte the clene and vnclene.

24 If any discorde arise, they shall dyscerne it, and geue sentence after my iudgementes. My solempne feastes, my lawes and ordynaunces shall they kepe, and halowe my Sabbathes.

25 They shall come at no deed persone, to defyle them selues (excepte it be father or mother, sonne or daughter, brother or syster that hath hadyet no husbande) in soch they maye be defyled.

26 And when he is clensed, there shall be rekened vnto hym .vij. dayes:

27 and yf he go in to the Sanctuary agayne to do seruyce, he shall bringe a synoffrynge sayeth the Lorde God.

28 They shall haue an heretage, yee I my selfe wilbe their heretage: els shall ye geue them no possessyon in Israel, for I am their possessyon.

29 The meatoffrynge, synoffrynge & trespaceoffrynge shall they eate, and euery dedycate thing in Israel, shalbe theirs.

30 The firstlynges of all the first fruytes, & all fre wil offrynges shall be the prestes. Ye shal geue vnto the preste also the firstlynges of youre dowe, that God maye prospere the resydue.

31 But no deed caryon shall that perst eate, ner soch as is deuoured of wylde beastes, foules or catell.

# CHAPTER 45

WHEN ye deuyde the lande by the lot, ye shal put a syde one parte for the Lorde, to be holy from other landes: namely .xxv.M. meteroddes longe, and .x.M. brode. This shalbe holye, as wyde as it is rounde aboute.

2 Of thys parte there shall belonge vnto the Sanctuary .v.C. meteroddes in all the foure corners, and .l. cubytes wyde rounde aboute to the suburbes.

3 And from this measure, namelye of .xxv.M. meteroddes longe, and .x.M. brode, thou shalt measure, wherin the Sanctuary and the holyest of all maye stande.

4 The resydue of that holye grounde shall be the prestes, whiche do seruyce in the Sanctuarye of the Lorde, and goo in before the Lorde to serue hym, that they maye haue rowme to dwell in.

5 As for the Sanctuarye, it shall stande for it selfe: and to the Leuites that serue in the house, there shalbe geuen .xx. habytacyons, of the .xxv.M. length and .x.M. bredth:

6 ye shall geue also vnto the cytie a possessyon of .v.M. meteroddes brode, and .xxv.M. longe, besyde the parte of the Sanctuary: that shall be fore the whole house of Israell.

7 Vpon both the sydes of the Sanctuarys parte, and by the cytye, there shalbe geuen vnto the prynce, whatsoeuer lieth ouer agaynst the cytyes, as farre as reacheth westwarde and eastwarde: whiche shalbe as longe as one parte, from the west vnto the east.

8 This shalbe hys owne lande in Israell, that my prync255 be no more chargeable vnto my people. And soch as remayneth yet ouer in the lande, shalbe geuen to the house of Israell accordynge to their trybes.

9 Thus sayeth the Lord God: O ye prynces, ye haue now oppressed and destroyed ynough: now leaue of, handle now accordyng to the thing, that is equall and lauful: and thrust out my people nomore, sayeth the Lorde God.

10 Ye shall haue a true weyght, a true Ephah, and a true Bath.

11 The Ephah and the Bath shalbe a like. One Bath shall conteyne the tenth parte of an

Homer, and so shall one Ephah do: their measure shall be after the Homer.

12 One Sycle maketh .xx. Geras. So .xx. Sicles, and .xxv. & .xv. Sycles make a pounde.

13 This is the heaue offrynge, that ye shall geue to be heaued: namelye, that .xvi. parte of an Ephah, out of an Homer of wheate: and the .xvi. parte of an Ephah, out of an Homer of barly.

14 The oyle shall be measured with the Bath: euen the tent parte of one Bath out of a Cor. Ten Bathes make one Homer: for one Homer sylleth ten Bathes.

15 And one lambe from two hundreth shepe out of the pasture of Israel, for a meatoffringe, burntofferynge and healthoffryng, to reconcyle them, sayeth the Lorde God.

16 All the people of the lande shall geue thys heaue offerynge wyth a fre wyll.

17 Agayne, it shall be the prynces parte to offre burntofferynges, meatofferynges and dryckofferynges vnto the Lorde, in the holy dayes, new Moones, Sabbathes, and in all the hye feastes of the house of Israell. The synoffrynge, meatoffrynge, brentofferynge and healthoffrynge shall he geue, to reconcyle the house of Israell.

18 Thus sayeth the Lord God: The first daye of the first moneth thou shalt take a yonge bullocke wythout blemyshe, and clense the Sanctuarye.

19 So the preste shall take of the bloude of the synoffrynge, and sprenckle it vpon the postes of the house, and vpon the foure corners of the aulter, with the dore postes of the ynnermer courte.

20 And thus shalt thou do also the seuenth daye of the moneth (for soche as haue synned of ygnoraunce, or beynge disceyued) to reconcyle the house withall.

21 Vpon the .xiiij. daye of the fyrste moneth ye shall kepe Easter. Seuen dayes shall the feast contynue wherin there shall no sower ner leuened bred be eaten.

22 Vpon the same daye shall the prynce geue for hym selfe and all the people of the lande, a bullocke for a synoffrynge.

23 And in the feast of the seuen dayes he shall offre euery daye a bullocke and a ram, that are without blemish for a burntoffrynge vnto the Lorde: and an he gaote daylye for a synofferynge.

24 For the meatoffrynges, he shall geue euer an Ephah to a bullocke, an Ephah to a ram, and an Hin of oyle to an Ephah.

25 Vpon the .xv. daye of the seuenth moneth, he shall kepe the seuen dayes holy one after another, euen as the other seuen dayes: with the synoffrynge, burntoffryng, meatoffrynge, and with the oyle.

# CHAPTER 46

THUS sayeth the Lorde God: the dore of the ynnermer courte towarde the East, shall be shut the .vi. worcke dayes: but in the Sabboth & in daye of the newe Moone, it shalbe opened.

2 Then shall that prynce come vnder the dore porche, and stande styll wythout by the dore cheke. So the prestes shall offre vp hys burnt and healthofferynges. And he shall worshyppe at the dore poste and go hys waye forth agayne: but the dore shall nomore be shut tyll the euenynge.

3 On the same maner shall the people of the lande also do their worshipe before the Lord, wythout thys dore vpon the Sabbathes and new Moones.

4 This is now the burntofferynge, that the prynce shall brynge vnto the Lorde vpon the Sabboth: syxe lambes without blemyshe, and a ram without blemyshe,

5 and an Ephah for a meatoffrynge, wyth the ram. As for the lambes, he maye geue as many meatoffrynges to them, as he will, and an Hin of oyle to an Ephah.

6 In the daye of the new moneth, it shall be a yong bullocke without blemysh, syxe lambes & a ram also wythout blemysh.

7 With the bullocke he shall geue an Ephah, and wyth the ram an Ephah also for a meatofferynge: but to the lambes, what he maye come by: And euer an Hin of oyle to an Ephah.

8 When the prynce commeth, he shal go vnder the dore porche, and euen there departe forth agayne.

9 But when the people of the lande come before the Lorde in the hye solempne feaste, as many as come in by the North dore to do worshyppe, shall goo oute agayne at the South dore. And they that come in at the South dore, shall go forth agayne at the North dore. There shall none go oute at the dore where he came in, but shal goo forth ryght ouer on the other syde,

10 & the prince shall go in and out amonge them.

11 Vpon the solempne and hye feaste dayes, this shalbe the meatofferinge: An Epha to a bullock and an Epha to a ram, & to the lambes: as many as he wyll, but euer an Hin of oyle to an Epha.

12 Now when the prynce bryngeth a burntofferynge or an healthofferynge wyth a fre wyll vnto the Lorde, the east dore shalbe opened vnto him, that he maye do with hys burnt and healthofferynges, as he doth vpon the Sabboth, and when he goeth forth, the dore shall be shutt after hym agayne.

13 He shall daylie brynge vnto the Lorde a lambe of a yeare olde without blemyshe for a burntoffringe: this shall he do euerye mornynge.

14 And for a meatofferynge he shall geue the syxte parte of an Epha, and the thyrde parte of an Hin of oyle (to myngle wyth the cakes) euery mournynge. Yee thys shalbe a daylye meatofferinge vnto the Lorde, for an euerlastynge ordynaunce:

15 and thus shall the lambe, the meatofferynge and oyle be geuen euerye mornynge, for a daylie burntofferinge.

16 Moreouer, thus sayeth the Lorde God: If the prynce geue a gyfte vnto eny of hys sonnes, then shall it be hys sonnes heretage perpetuall, that he maye possesse it.

17 But If he wyll geue one of hys seruauntes some of his heretage, it shall be his to the fre yeare, and them to returne agayne vnto the prynce: for hys heretage shalbe hys sonnes ouelye.

18 The prince also shall take none of the peoples enherytaunce, ner put them from their possessyon: but to his owne sonnes shall he geue hys possessyon, that my people be not scatred abrode, but that euerye man maye haue hys owne.

19 And he brought me thorow the intraunce at the syde of the dore to the habytacyon of the Sanctuary, that be longeth to the prestes and stode towarde the north, & beholde, there was a place vpon the West syde,

20 then sayde he vnto me: This is the place, where the prestes shall dight the trespace & synoffrynges and bake the meatofferinges: that they nede not beare them in to the outwarde courte, & so to vnhalowe the people.

21 So he brought me in to the vttemost courte, rounde aboute all the foure corners. Beholde, in euery corner of the fore courte, there was yet a lytle courte.

22 Yee in all the foure corners of the courte, there was made a lytle courte of .xl. cubytes long, and .xxx. cubytes brode: these foure lytle courtes were of one lyke measure,

23 and there went a rygge wall rounde aboute them all foure, vnder the whych there were harthes made rounde aboute.

24 Then sayd he vnto me: This is the kechin, where the mynisters of the house shall dyght the slayne offerynges of the people.

# CHAPTER 47

AFTER this he brought me agayne before the dore of the house: and beholde, there gushed out waters from vnder the postes of the house eastwarde (for the house stode towarde the east) that ranne downe vpon the ryght syde of the house, which lyeth to the aulter south ward.

2 Then caried he me out to the north dore, and brought me forth there rounde aboute by the vttemost dore that turneth eastward. Beholde, there came forth the water vpon the right side.

3 Now whan the man that had the meterodde in his hande wente vnto the east dore, he measured a .M. cubites, and then he brought me thorowe the water, euen to the ancles:

4 so he measured yet a thousand, and brought me thorow the water agayne vnto the knees: yet measured he a thousande, and brought me thorowe the water vnto the loynes.

5 After this he measured a thousande agayne, then was it soch a ryuer that I myght not wade thorow it: The water was so depe, that it was nedefull to haue swimmed, for it myght not be waded ouer.

6 And he sayde vnto me: hast thou sene this, O thou sonne of man? and with that, he brought me to the ryuer banck agayne.

7 Now when I came there, there stode many trees vpon ether syde of the ryuer bancke.

8 Then sayde he vnto me: This water that floweth oute towarde the East, and runneth downe in to the playne felde, commeth in to the sea: and from the sea it runneth out, & maketh the waters whole,

9 Yee all that lyue and moue, where vnto this ryuer commeth, shall recouer. And where thys water commeth, there shalbe moch fyshe. For all that commeth, this water, shalbe lusty and whole.

10 By thys ryuer shall the fysshers stande from Engaddy vnto En Eglaim, and there sprede out their nettes: for there shalbe greate heapes of fish, lyke as in the mayne sea.

11 As for hys claye & pyttes, they shall not be whole, for why, it shalbe occupyde for salt.

12 By this ryuer vpon both the sydes of the shore, there shall growe al maner of fruiteful trees, whose leaues shall not fall of, nether shall their fruyte peryshe: but euer be rype at their monethes, for their water ronneth out of their Sanctuary. His fruite is good to eate and hys leaf profitable for medycyne.

13 Thus sayeth the Lorde God: Let this be the border wherin ye shall deuyde the lande vnto the .xij. tribes of Israell, wyth the lyne.

14 Parte it indyfferently vnto one as vnto another: of the which land I swore vnto youre fathers: that it shulde fall to youre enheritaunce.

15 Thys is the broder of the lande vpon the northside, from

the mayne sea, as men go to Zadada:

16 namelye Hemath, Berotha, Sabarim: from the borders of Damascus and Hemath vnto Hazar Tichon, & that lyeth vpon the coastes of Haueran.

17 Thus the borders from the sea forte, shalbe Hazar Euan, the border of Damascus the North, and the borders of Hemath: that is the North parte.

18 The east syde shall ye measure from Haueran and Damascus, from Galead and the lande of Israell by Iordane and so forth, from the sea coast, that lyeth eastwarde: and this is the east parte.

19 The southsyde is, from Thamar forth to the waters of stryfe vnto Cades, the ryuer, to the mayne sea: and that is the south parte.

20 The west warte: namely the greate sea from the borders therof, tyll a man come vnto Hemath: this is the west parte.

21 Thys lande shall ye parte amonge you, according to the tribes of Israell,

22 & deuide it to be an heretage for you, & for the straungers that dwell amonge you, & begette chyldren. For ye shall take them amonge the chyldren of Israell, lyke as though they were of youre owne housholde and countre, and they shall haue heretage with you amonge the chyldren of Israell.

23 Loke in what tribe the straunger dwelleth, in the same tribe shall ye geue hym hys heretage, sayeth the Lorde God.

# CHAPTER 48

THESE are the names of the trybes that lye vpon the northsyde, by the waye of Hetlon, tyll thou commest vnto Hemath & Hazar Enam, the borders of Damascus towarde the north beside Hemath: Dan shall haue hys porcion from the east quarter vnto the west.

2 Vpon the borders of Dan from the east syde vnto the west, shall Asser haue hys porcyon.

3 Vpon the borders of Asser from the east parte vnto the west shall Nephthali haue hys porcyon.

4 Vpon the borders of Nephthali from the east quarter vnto the west, shall Manasses haue his porcion.

5 Vpon the borders of Manasses from the east syde vnto the west, shall Ephraim haue his porcyon.

6 Vpon the borders of Ephraim from the east parte vnto the west, shall Ruben haue his porcyon.

7 Vpon the borders of Ruben from the east quarter vnto the west shall Iuda haue hys porcyon:

8 Vpon the borders of Iuda from the east parte vnto the west, ye shall set a syde one porcion of .xxv.M. meteroddes longe and brode (like as another porcyon from the east syde vnto the west) wherin the Sanctuary shall stande.

9 As for the porcyon, that ye shall separate out for the Lorde: it shalbe .xxv.M. longe, & .x.M. brode.

10 Which separated holy porcyon shall belonge vnto these: namelye to the prestes, towarde the north .xxv.M. and towarde the west .x.M. brode, towarde the east .x.M. brode also, & toward the south .xxv.M. longe wherin the Sanctuarye of the Lorde shall stande.

11 Yee this same place shalbe the prestes that are of the children of Sadoch, and haue kepte my holy ordynaunce: which wente not astraye in the erroure of the chyldren of Israel lyke as the Leuites are gone astraye:

12 and this separated pece that they haue of the lande shalbe the most holy, harde vpon the borders of the Leuites.

13 And nexte vnto the prestes, shall the Leuites haue .xxv.M. longe. and .x.M. brode. This shalbe on euery syde .xxv.M. longe, and .x.M. brode.

14 Of this porcyon they shall sell nothinge, ner make any permutacyon therof, lest the chefe of the lande fall vnto other, for it is halowed vnto the Lorde.

15 The other .v.M. after the bredth that lyeth by the .xxv.M. shalbe comen: it shall belonge to the cyte and to the suburbes for habytacyons, & the cyte shall stande in the myddest therof.

16 Let this be the measure: towarde the north parte .v.C. and .iiij.M. towarde the sout parte .v.C. and .iiij.M. towarde the east parte .v.C. & .iiij.M. towarde the west part .v.C. and .iiij.M.

17 The suburbes harde vpon the cytye, shall haue towarde the north .L. and .ij.C. towarde the south .L. and .ij.C. towarde the east .L. & two .C. towarde the west also .L. and two .C.

18 As for the resydue of the length, that lyeth harde vpon the separated holy grounde: namely .x. thousande towarde the east, & .x.M. towarde the west, nexte vnto the holye porcion: it and the increase therof shall serue for their meate, that laboure in the cytye.

19 They that laboure for the welth of the cytye, shall manteyne this also, out of what tribe soeuer they be in Israel.

20 All that is separated of the .xxv.M. longe and .xxv.M. brode on the foure partes, that shall ye put a syde for the separated porcyon of the Sanctuarye, & for the possessyon of the cyty.

21 The resydue vpon both the sydes of the Sanctuary and possessyon of the cytye, shall belonge to the prince, before the place of the .xxv.M. vnto the east ende, & before the place of the .xxv.M. westwarde, vnto the

borders of the cytye: this shalbe the princes porcion. Thys shalbe the holy place, and the house of the Sanctuarye shall stande in the myddest.

22 Moreouer from the Leuites and the cytyes possession, that lye in the myddest of the princes parte: loke what remayneth betwixte the border of Iuda & the border of BenIamin, it shalbe the Princes.

23 Now of the other trybes. From the east parte vnto the west, shall Beniamin haue hys porcion.

24 Vpon the borders of BenIamin from the east syde vnto the west, shall Symeon haue his porcion.

25 Vpon the borders of Symeon from the east parte vnto the west, shall Izakar haue hys porcyon.

26 Vpon the borders of Izakar from the east syde vnto the west, shall Sabulon haue his porcion.

27 Vpon the borders of Sabulon from the east parte vnto the west, shall Gad haue hys porcion.

28 Vpon the borders of Gad southwarde, the coastes shall reach from Thamar forth vnto the waters of stryfe to Cades, and to the floude, euen vnto the many sea.

29 This is the lande with his porcions, which ye shall dystribute vnto the trybes of Israel, sayeth the Lorde God.

30 Thus wyde shall the cyte reach: vpon the north parte .v.C. & .iiij.M. measures.

31 The portes of the cyte, shall haue the names of the tribes of Israel. Thre portes of the northside: one Ruben, another Iuda, the thyrde Leui.

32 Vpon the east side .v.C. & .iiij.M. measures, with thre portes: the one Ioseph, another BenIamin, the thyrde Dan.

33 Vpon the south syde .v.C. and .iiij.M. measures, wyth the thre portes: the one Symeon, another Izakar the thyrde Sabulon.

34 And vpon the west side .v.C. and .iiij.M. measures, with thre portes also, that one Gad, another Asser, the thyrde Nephthali.

35 Thus shall it haue .xviij.M. measures rounde about And from that tyme forth, the name of the cyte shalbe: the Lorde is there.

# Daniel

## CHAPTER 1

IN the thyrde yeare of the raygne of Iehoakim kinge of Iuda, came Nabuchodonosor kyng of Babylon vnto Ierusalem, & beseged it

2 and the Lord deliuered Iehoakim the kinge of Iuda into his hande, with certayne ornamentes of the house of God, whiche he caryed awaye vnto the lande of Sennar, to the house of his God, and there he broughte them into hys Goddes treasurye.

3 And the kyng spake vnto Asphanaz the chefe chamberlayne, that he shulde brynge hym certayne of the chyldren of Israel, that were come of the kynges sede & of pryncꝭ,

4 yonge spryngaldes wythout anye blemyshe, but fayre & welfauoured, instructe in all wisdome, connyng and vnderstanding: whiche were able to stande in the kynges palace, to reade and to learne for to speake Caldeish.

5 Vnto these the king appoynted a certayne porcyon of hys owne meate, and of the wyne, which he drancke hym selfe, so to noryshe them thre yeare: that afterwarde they myght stande before the kynge.

6 Amonge these nowe were certayne of the chyldren of Iuda: namely Daniel, Ananias, Misael & Azarias.

7 Vnto these the chefe chamberlayne gaue other names, & called Daniel, Balthazar: Ananias, Sidrach, Misael, Misach, and Asarias, Abednago.

8 But Daniel was at a poynte wyth hym self, that he wolde not be defyled thorowe the kynges meate, nor the wyne whiche he droncke. And this he desyred of the chefe Chamberlaine, leste he shulde defyle hym selfe.

9 So God gaue Daniel fauoure and grace before the chefe chamberlayne,

10 that he said vnto hym: I am afraied of my Lorde the kynge, whiche hath appoynted you youre meate & drinck: lest he spye your faces to be worse lykyng then the other springaldes of youre age, and so ye shall make me lose my head vnto the kynge.

11 Then Daniel aunswered Melassar, whom the chefe chamberlayne had set ouer Daniell, Ananias, Misael and Asarias, & sayde:

12 O proue but ten dayes with thy seruauntes, and let vs haue potage to eate, & water to drincke:

13 then loke vpon oure faces, & theyrs that eate of the kynges meate. And as thou seyst, so deale wyth thy seruauntes.

14 So he consented to them in thys matter, and proued them .x. dayes.

15 And after the ten dayes, theyr faces were better lykyng & fatter, then al þe younge spryngaldes whiche ate of the kynges meate.

16 Thus Melassar toke awaye theyr meate, and wyne, and gaue them potage therefore.

17 God gaue nowe these foure spryngaldes connyng and learnyng in all scrypture and wysdome: but vnto Daniell specyally, he gaue vnderstandynge of all vysyons and dreames.

18 Nowe when the tyme was expyred, that the kynge hath appoynted to bryng in these yonge spryngaldes vnto hym: the chefe chamberlain broughte them before Nabuchodonosor,

19 and the kynge communed with them. But among them all were founde none suche as Daniel, Ananias, Misael, and Asarias. Therfor stode they before the kynge,

20 whiche in all wysdome and matters of vnderstandynge, that he enquered of them, founde them ten tymes better then all the sothsayers and charmers, þt were in all hys realme.

21 And Daniel abode styl, vnto the fyrste yeare of kynge Cyrus.

## CHAPTER 2

IN the seconde yeare of þe raigne of Nabuchodonosor,

had Nabuchodonosor a dreame, wherethorow his sprete was vexed, & hys slepe brake from him.

2 Then the kyng commaunded to cal together all þe sothsayers, charmers, witches & Caldees, for to shew the king his dreame. So they came & stode before þe king.

3 And the king sayd vnto them: I haue dreamed a dreame, and my sprete was so troubled therewith, that I haue clene forgotten, what I dreamed.

4 Vpon thys the Caldees aunswered the kynge in the Syrians speach: O king, God saue thy lyfe for euer. Shew thy seruauntes the dreame, and we shal shewe the, what it meaneth.

5 The kynge gaue the Caldees theyr aunswere, & said: It is gone fro me: Yf ye wyl not make me vnderstande the dreame wyth the interpretacyon thereof, ye shall dye, & youre houses shalbe prysed.

6 But yf ye tell me the dreame & the meanynge therof, ye shall haue of me gyftes, rewardes & greate honoure: onely, shew me the dreame and the sygnifycacyon of it.

7 They aunswered agayne, and sayde: the kynge must shewe his seruauntes the dreame, & so shall we declare what it meaneth.

8 Then þe kinge auswered, sayinge: I perceyue of a trueth, that ye do but prolonge the tyme: for so muche as ye se, that the thing is gone fro me.

9 Therfore ye wil not tell me þe dreame, ye shall all haue one iudgement. But ye fayne & dyssemble with vayne wordes, which ye speake before me, to put of the tyme. Therfore tel me the dreame, & so shal I know yf ye can shewe me, what it meaneth.

10 Vpon this, the Caldees gaue answere before þe king, and sayde: there is no man vpon earthe, that can tell the thynge, whiche the kyng speaketh of, yea there is neyther kyng, prynce nor lord, that euer asked suche thynges at a sothsayer, charmer or Caldeer:

11 for it is a very hard matter, that the kynge requyreth. Neither is there any, that can certyfye the kynge therof, except the Goddes: whose dwellyng is not among the creatures.

12 For the whiche cause the kyng was wroth with greate indignacyon, and commaunded to destroye all the wyse men at Babylon:

13 and the proclamacyon wente forthe, that the wyse men shuld be slayne, They sought also to slay Daniel with hys companions.

14 Then Daniel enquered Arioh the kynges stewarde, of the iudgement and sentence, that was gone forth already to kyll soche as were wyse at Babilon.

15 He aunswered and sayde vnto Arioh brynge then the Kynges debyte: Why hath the kyng proclamed so cruell a sentence? So Arioh tolde Daniel the matter.

16 Vpon this, wente Daniel vp, and desyred the kynge, that he might haue leysoure, to shewe the kynge the interpretacyon:

17 and then came he home agayne, & shewed the thynge vnto Ananias, Misael & Asarias hys companyons:

18 that they shulde beseche the God of heauen for grace in thys secrete, that Daniel and hys felowes wyth other soch as were wyse in Babylon, peryshed not.

19 Then was the mysterye shewed vnto Daniel in a vysyon by nyght And Daniel praysed þe god of heauen.

20 Daniel also cryed loude, and sayd: O that the name of God myghte be praysed for euer and euer, for wysdome and strengthe are hys owne:

21 he chaunged the tymes & ages: he putteth doune kynges, he setteth vp kinges he geueth wysdome vnto the wyse, & vnderstandynge to those that vnderstande,

22 he openeth the depe secretes, he knoweth the thynge that lyeth in darckenesse, for the lyghte dwelleth wyth hym.

23 I thanke the, and prayse the (O thou God of my fathers) that thou haste lente me wysdom and strength, & hast shewed me the thyng, that we desyred of the, for thou haste opened the kynges matter vnto me.

24 Vpon this went Daniel in vnto Arioh, whome the kynge had ordeyned to destroye þe wyse at Babylon: he went vnto hym, & sayde: destroye not suche as are wyse in Babylon, but brynge me in vnto the kynge, and I shall shewe the kynge the interpretacyon.

25 Then Arioch broughte Daniel in to the kyng in all the haste, and sayde vnto hym: I haue founde a man amonge the presoners of Iuda, that shall shewe the kyng the interpretacyon.

26 Then aunswered the kynge, and sayde vnto Daniel, whose name was Balthasar: Arte thou he, that canste shewe me the dreame, whiche I haue sene, & the interpretacyon therof?

27 Daniel aunswered the kynge to hys face, and sayd: As for this secrete, for the whiche the kynge maketh inquisicion: it is neyther the wyse, the sorcerer, the charmer nor the deuyll coniurer, that can certyfye the kynge of it:

28 Onely God in heauen can open secretes, and he it is, that sheweth the kynge Nabuchodonosor, what is for to come in the latter dayes. Thy dreame, & that whiche thou hast sene in thyne heade vpon thy bed, is thys:

29 O kyng thou dyddest caste

ns thy mynde, what shulde come hereafter: So he that is the opener of misteryes, telleth the, what is for to come.

30 As for me, thys secrete is not shewed me, for anye wysdome that I haue, more then anye other lyuynge: but onelye that I myghte shewe the kynge the interpretacyon, and that he myghte know the thoughtes of his owne herte.

31 Thou kynge sawest, & behold, there stode before the a greate Image, whose fygure was marueylous greate, and hys vysage grymme.

32 The Image head was of fyne golde, hys breste & armes of siluer, his body and loynes were of copper,

33 his legges were of yron, his fete were parte of yron, and parte of earthe.

34 Tis thou sawest, tyll the tyme that (wyth oute any handes) there was hewen of a stone whiche smote the Image vpon the fete, that were both of yron and earth, and brake them to poulder:

35 then was the yron, the earthe, the copper, the syluer and gold broken altogether in peces: and be came lyke the chaffe of corne, that the wynde bloweth away from the somer floores, that they can no more be founde. But the stone that smote the Image, became a greate mountayne, whiche fulfilleth þe whole earthe:

36 Thys is the dreame. And nowe wyll we shewe before the kynge, what it meaneth.

37 O kynge, thou arte a kynge of kynges: For the God of heauen hath geuen þe a kyngdome, ryches, strengthe and maiestye:

38 & hathe delyuered the all thynges, that are amonge the children of men: the beastes of the feld, and the foules vnder the heauen, and geuen the dominyon ouer them al. Thou arte that golden head.

39 After þe there shall aryse another kyngdome, whiche shall be lesse then thyne. The thyrde kyngedome shalbe lyke copper, & haue dominacyon in all landes.

40 The fourthe kyngdome shalbe as stronge as yron. For lyke as yron broseth and breaketh all thynges: Yea euen as yron beateth euery thynge doune, so shall it beate doune and destroye.

41 Where as thou sawest the fete and toes, parte of earthe, and parte of yron: that is a deuyded kyngedome, whiche neuertheles shall haue some of the yron grounde myxte with it, for so muche as thou haste sene the yron mixte with the claye.

42 The toes of the fete that were parte of yron and parte of claye, sygnifyeth, that it shalbe a kyngdome partely stronge and partly weake.

43 And where as thou sawest yron myxte wyth claye: they shall myngle them selues wyth the sede of symple people, & yet not contynue one wyth another, lyke as yron wyll not be souldered with a potsherde.

44 In the dayes of these kinges shall the God of heauen set vp an euerlastynge kyngdome whiche shall not peryshe, and hys kyngdome shall not be geuen ouer to another people: yea the same shal breake and destroy al these kingdomes, but it shall endure foreuer.

45 And where as thou saweste, that withoute any handes there was cut oute of the mounte a stone, whiche brake the yron, the copper, the earthe, the syluer and golde in peces: by that hath the greate God shewed the kynge, what wyll come after thys. This is a true dreame, and the interpretacyon of it is sure.

46 Then the kynge Nabuchodonosor fell doune vpon hys face, and bowed hym self vnto Daniel, and commaunded that they shuld offre meate offerynges and swete odours vnto hym.

47 The kynge aunswered Daniel, and sayde: yea of a trueth your God is a GOD aboue all Goddes, a Lorde aboue all kynges and an opener of secretes: seynge thou canste dyscouer thys mysterye.

48 So the kynge made Daniel a greate man, and gaue hym many & greate gyftes. He made hym ruler of all the countrees of Babylon, and Lorde of all the nobles, that were at Babylon.

49 Now Daniel intreated the kynge so: Sidrach, Misach and Abednago, so that he made them rulers ouer all the offyces in the lande of Babylon: But Danyel hymselfe remayned styll in the courte by the kynge.

# CHAPTER 3

Nabuchodonosor the kynge caused a golden Image to be made whiche was .lx. cubytes hye, & sixe cubytes thycke. This he made to be set vp in þe feld of Dura in the lande of Babylon,

2 and sent out to gather together the dukes, lordes and nobles, þe iudges and offycers, the debytes, & shreues, with all the rulers of the lande, þt they mighte come to the dedicacyon of the Image whiche Nabuchodonosor the kynge had set vp.

3 So þe dukes, lordes and nobles, the iudges and offycers, debytes and shreues with all the rulers of the land gathered them together, and came vnto the dedycatynge of the Image, that Nabuchodonosor the kynge had set vp. Now when they stode before the Image, whiche Nabuchodonosor set vp,

4 the bedel cryed out with al his might: O ye people, kynredes and tunges, to you be it sayde:

5 that when ye heare the noyse of the trompettes, whiche shalbe blowen, wyth the harpes, shawmes, Psalteryes, Symphonyes and all maner of Musick: ye fall doune and worshyp ye the golden Image, that Nabuchodonosor the kynge hath set vp.

6 Who so then falleth not downe & boweth hym selfe, shall euen the same houre be caste into an hote burnynge ouen.

7 Therfor when all the folcke hearde the noyse of the trompettes that were blowen, with the harpes, shawmes, Psalteryes, Simphonyes and all kynde of Melody: then all the people, kynredes and nacyons fell doune, and bowed them selues vnto the golden Image, that Nabuchodonosor the kynge had set vp.

8 Now were there certayne men of the Caldees, that wente euen then, and accused the Iewes,

9 and sayde vnto the kynge Nabuchodonosor: O kyng, God saue thy lyfe for euer.

10 Thou beynge kynge, haste geuen a commaundement, that all men when they heare noyse of the trompettes, harpes, shawmes, psalteryes, symphonyes and all the other melodyes: shall fall downe, and bowe them selues towarde the golden Image:

11 who so then fel not doune, and worshypped not, that he shulde be caste into an hote burnynge ouen.

12 Now are there certayne Iewes, whome thou haste set ouer the offyces of the lande of Babylon, namely, Sydrach, Mysach & Abednago. These men (O kynge) regarde not thy commaundement, yea they wyll not serue thy Goddes, nor bowe them selues to the golden Image, þt thou haste set vp.

13 Then Nabuchodonosor in a cruell wrathe, and displeasur, commaunded that Sidrach, Misach and Abednago shulde be broughte vnto hym. So these men were broughte before the kynge.

14 Then Nabuchodonosor spake vnto them, and sayde: what? O Sidrach Misach and Abednago, wyll not ye serue my Goddes, nor bowe youre selues to the golden Image, that I haue set vp?

15 well, be readye here after, when ye heare the noyse of the trompettes blowe wyth the harpes, shawmes, psalteryes, symphonyes and all the other melodyes: that ye fall doune, and worshyppe the Image whiche I haue made. But yf ye worshyppe it not, ye shall be caste immedyatly into an hote burnynge ouen. Let se, what God is there, that maye delyuer you oute of my handes?

16 Sidrach, Misach and Abednago aunswered the kynge, and sayde: O Nabuchodonosor, we oughte not to consente vnto the in this matter, for why:

17 oure GOD whome we serue, is able to kepe vs from the hote burnynge ouen (O kynge) and can right well delyuer vs oute of thy handes.

18 And thoughe he wyll not, yet shalte thou knowe (O kynge) that we wil not serue thy Goddes, nor do reuerence to the Image, whiche thou haste set vp.

19 Then was Nabuchodonosor full of indignacyon, so that the countenaunce of hys face chaunged vpon Sidrach, Misach, and Abednago. Therfor he charged and commaunded, that the ouen shuld be made seuen tymes hoter, then it was wonte to be,

20 and spake vnto the strongeste worthyes that were in hys hoste, for to bynde Sidrach, Misach and Abednago, & to cast them into the hote burnynge ouen.

21 So these men were bounde in theyr cotes hosen, shues with theyr other garmentes, and caste into the hote burnynge ouen:

22 for the kynges commaundemente was so strate, and the ouen was exceadynge hote. As for the men þt put in Sydrach, Mysach & Abednago, the flamme of the fyre destroyed them.

23 And these thre men Sidrach, Misah & Abednago fell doune in the hote burnynge ouen, beinge fast bound.

24 Then Nabuchodonosor the kyng marueyled, & stode vp in al haste: he spake vnto hys councell, and sayde: dyd not ye caste these thre men bounde into the fyre? They aunswered, and sayde vnto the kynge: Yea O kynge.

25 He aunswered and sayde: lo, for all that, yet do I se foure men goynge lowse in the myddeste of the fyre, and nothynge corrupte: and the fourthe is lyke an angell to loke vpon.

26 Vpon thys wente Nabuchodonosor vnto the mouth of the hote burnynge ouen: he spake also, and sayde: O Sydrach, Mysach & Abednago, ye seruauntes of the hye God: go forthe, & come hyther. And so Sydrach, Mysach, and Abednago wente oute of the fyre.

27 Then the dukes lordes and nobles, and the kynges councell came together to se these men, vpon whom the fyre had no maner of power in theyr bodyes: In so much that the very hearre of theyr head was not burnte, & theyr clothes vnchaunged: Yea there was no smel of fyre felt vpon them.

28 Then spake Nabuchodonosor, and sayde: Blessed be the God of Sidrach, Misach and Abednago, whiche hath sente his aungel, &

defended hys seruauntes, that put their trust in him: that haue altered the kynges commaundement: and yeoparde theyr bodyes thervpon, rather then they wolde serue or worshyp any other God, excepte theyr owne God onelye.

29 Therfore I wyll, and commaund, that al people, kynredes and tunges, whiche speake any blasphemye agaynst the God of Sidrach, Misach and Abednago, shall dye, and theyr houses shalbe prysed: Because there is no God þt maye saue, as thys.

30 So the kynge promoted Sidrach, Misach, and Abednago, in the land of Babylon.

# CHAPTER 4

NABUCHODONOSOR Kynge vnto all people, kynreddes and tunges þt dwell vpon the whole earthe: peace be multiplyed among you,

2 I thoughte it good to shew the tokens and meruelous worckes, that the hye God hath wrought vpon me.

3 O how greate are hys tokens, and howe myghtie are hys wonders? His kyngedome is an euerlastynge kyngedome, and hys power lasteth for euer & euer.

4 I Nabuchodonosor beynge at rest in minehouse, and floryshynge in my palace,

5 sawe a dreame, which made me afraied: & the thoughtes that I had vpon my bed, wyth the vysyons of myne heade, troubled me.

6 Then sente I oute a commyssyon, that all they which were of wysdome at Babylon, shulde be broughte before me, to tell me the interpretacyon of the dreame.

7 So there came the sothsayers, charmers, Caldees and coniurers of Deuyls, to whome I tolde the dreame, but what it be tokened, they coulde not shewe me:

8 tyll at the laste, there came one Daniel (otherwyse called Balthazar, accordynge to the name of my God) whiche hath the sprete of the holy Goddes in hym: to whom I tolde the dreame, saying:

9 O Balthasar, thou prince of southsayers: For so muche as I knowe, that thou haste the spryte of the holy Goddes, and no secrete is hyd from the: tell me therfore, what the vysyon of my dreame (that I haue sene) maye sygnifye.

10 I sawe a vysyon in my heade vpon my bed: and beholde, there stode a tre vpon the grounde,

11 whiche was verye hye, greate and myghtye: the heygth reached vnto the heauen, and the bredth extended to all the endes of the earthe,

12 hys leaues were fayre, he had verye muche frute, so that euerye man had ynough to eate therein. The beastes of the feld had shadowes vnder it, and the foules of the ayre dwelte in the bowes therof. Shortly, all creatures fed of it.

13 I sawe in my heade a vysyon vpon my bed: & beholde, a watcher came doune from heauen,

14 & cryed myghtely, sayinge. Hew doune þe tre, breake of hys braunches, shake of hys leaues, and scatre hys frute abroade: that all the beastes maye get them awaye from vnder hym, and the foules from his braunches.

15 Neuertheles leaue the grounde of hys rote styll in the earthe, and bynde hym vpon the playne feld, with cheynes of yron and stele. With þe dewe of heauen shall he be wet, and he shall haue hys parte in the herbes of the grounde wyth other wylde beastes.

16 That mans herte of his shal be taken from him, and a beastes herte shall be geuen hym, tyll seuen yeares be come and gone vpon hym.

17 This erande of the watcher is a commaundement grounded and sought oute in the councell of him, that is most holye, to learne men for to vnderstande, that the hyest hath power, ouer the kyngedomes of men, and geueth them, to whome it lyketh hym, & bryngeth the very oute castes of men ouer them.

18 Thys is the dreame, that I kynge Nabuchodonosor haue sene. Therfore O Balthasar, tell thou me, what it sygnyfyeth: for so muche as the wyse men of my kyngdome are not able to shewe me, what it meaneth. But thou canst do it, for the spryte of the holy Goddes is in the.

19 Then Daniel (whose name was Balthasar) helde hys peace by the space of an houre, and hys thoughtes troubled hym. So the kynge spake, and sayd: O Balthasar, let neyther the dreame nor the interpretacyon therof feare the. Balthazar aunswered, saying: O my Lorde, this dreame happen to thyne enemyes, & the interpretacyon to thyne aduersaryes.

20 As for the tre, that thou sawest, whiche was so great & mighty, whose height reached vnto the heauen, and hys bredth into all the worlde,

21 whose leues were fayre, and the frute muche, vnder the whiche the beastes of þe feld had theyr habitacion, and vpon whose braunches the foules of the ayre dyd syt.

22 Euen thou (O kynge) arte the tre, great & stronge. Thy greatnesse increaseth, and reacheth vnto the heauen, so doth thy power to þe endes of the earthe.

23 But where as the kynge sawe a watcher euen an holye aungel, þt came downe from heauen, and sayde: hewe doune

the tre, and destroye it: yet leaue the grounde of the rote in the earthe, and brynge hym vpon the playne felde with cheynes of yron & stele: He shall be wet with the dewe of heauen, and hys parte shalbe with the beastes of the felde, tyll seuen yeares be come and gone vpon him:

24 This (O Kynge) is the interpretacyon, yea it is the very deuyce of him, that is hyest of all, and it toucheth my Lorde the kynge.

25 Thou shalte be caste oute from men, & thy dwellyng shalbe with the beastes of the feld: with grasse shalte thou be fed lyke an oxe. Thou must be wet with the dewe of the heauen, yea seuen yeares shall come, and go vpon the, tyll thou know, that the hyest hath power vpon the kingedomes of men, & geueth them to whome he lyst.

26 Moreouer, where as it was sayde, that the rote of the tree shulde be lefte styll in the grounde: it betokeneth, that thy kyngedome shall remayne whole vnto the, after thou hast learned to know, that the power commeth from heauen.

27 Wherfore, O Kyng, be content with my councel, that thou mayeste lowse thy synnes wyth ryghtuousnesse, and thyne offences with mercye to poore people: for suche thynges shall prolonge thy peace.

28 All these thynges touche the kynge Nabuchodonosor.

29 So after .xij. monethes, the kynge walked vp & doune in the palace of the kyngedome of Babylon,

30 and sayde: Thys is the greate cytye of Babilon, which I my selfe (wyth my power & strengthe) haue made a kynges courte, for þe honour of my magestye.

31 Whyle these wordes were yet in the kynges mouthe, there fell a voyce from heauen, saying: O king Nabuchodonosor, to þe be it spoken: Thy kingdom shall departe from the,

32 thou shalte be cast oute of mens companye: thy dwelling shalbe with the beastes of þe felde, so that thou shalte eate grasse lyke as an oxe, tyll seuen yeares be come & gone ouer the: euen vntill thou knoweste, þt the hyest hath power vpon the kyngdoms of men, and that he may geue them, vnto whom it pleaseth hym.

33 The very same houre was this matter fulfylled vpon Nabuchodonosor: so that he was cast oute of mens companye, & ate grasse like an oxe. His body was wet with the dewe of heauen, tyll hys hearres were as greate as Aegles fethers, & hys nales like byrdes clawes.

34 When this tyme was passed, I Nabuchodonosor lyfte vp myne eyes vnto heauen, and myne vnderstandynge was restored vnto me agayne. Then gaue I thanckes vnto the hyghest. I magnifyed and praysed hym that lyueth for euermore, whose power endureth alwaye, and his kingdome from one generacion to another:

35 in comparison of whom al they þt dwel vpon the earth, are to be reputed as nothinge. He handleth accordinge to hys wyl, among the powers of heauen & amonge the inhabytours of the earthe: and there is none þt maye resyste hys hande, or say: what doest thou?

36 At the same tyme was myne vnderstandyng geuen me agayne, and I was restored to the honoure of my kingedome, to my dignite, & to myne owne shappe agayne. My greate estates and princes soughte vnto me, and I was set in my kyngdome agayn, so that I had yet greater worshyppe.

37 Then dyd I Nabuchodonosor loue, magnifye and prayse the kynge of heauen: for all hys worckes are true, and hys wayes righte. As for those that go on proudely, he is able to brynge them doune.

# CHAPTER 5

KYNGE Balthazar made a greate bancket to his thousand Lordes: with all these thousand he made great chere,

2 & when he was droncken with wyne, he commaunded to brynge hym the golden and syluer vessels, whiche his father Nabuchodonosor had taken oute of the temple at Ierusalem, that the king and hys lordes with hys quene and concubynes might drincke thereoute.

3 So they broughte the golden vessell, that was taken oute of the temple of the Lordes house at Ierusalem. Then the kynge and hys lordes with his quene & concubynes droncke oute of them.

4 They droncke wyne, and praysed theyr Idoles of golde, syluer, copper, yron woodde and stone.

5 In the very same houre there apeared fyngers, as it had bene of a mannes hande wrytynge, ryght ouer agaynst the candelstycke vpon the playne wall in the kynges palace, & the kynge sawe the palme of the hande that wrote.

6 Then chaunged the kynge hys countenaunce, and hys thoughtes troubled hym, so that the ioyntes of hys bodye shoke, and hys knees smote one against the other.

7 Wherfore the kynge cryed myghtelye, that they shulde brynge hym the charmers, Caldees and coniurers of deuyls. The kynge spake also to the wyse men of Babylon, and sayde: Who so can rede thys wrytynge, and shew me the playne meanyng therof, shalbe clothed wyth purple, haue a

cheyne of golde aboute hys necke, and rule the thyrde parte of my kyngedome.

8 Vpon this, came al the kynges wyse men: but they coulde neyther reade the wrytynge, nor shewe the kinge what it signifyed.

9 Then was the kynge sore afrayed in so muche, that his colour chaunged, and his lordes were sore vexed.

10 So by reason of thys matter, that had happened to the kyng and his lordes, þe quene wente vp her selfe into the banckethouse, and spake vnto the kynge, sayinge: O kyng, God saue thy lyfe for euer: Let not the thoughtes trouble the, and let not thy countenaunce be chaunged.

11 For why? there is a man in thy kingdome, that hath the spryte of the holy Goddes within him, as it was sene in thy fathers dayes. He hath vnderstandynge and wysdome like the Goddes. Yea the kynge Nabuchodonosor thy father made thys man chefe of the sothsayers, charmers, Caldees, and deuilconiurers,

12 because that suche an aboundaunt spryte knowledge & wysdome (to expound dreames, to open secretes, and to declare harde dowtes) was founde in hym: yea euen in Daniel whom the kynge named Balthazar. Let thys same Daniel be sente for, and he shall tell, what it meaneth.

13 Then was Daniel broughte before the kynge. So the kynge spake vnto Daniel, and sayde: Arte thou that Daniel, one of the presoners of Iuda, whome my father the kynge broughte oute of Iewry?

14 I haue heard speake of the, that thou haste the spryte of the holye Goddes, experience and vnderstandyng, and that there hath bene greate wysdome founde in the.

15 Now haue there ben brought me, wyse & conning charmers, to reade thys wrytyng, and to shewe me the meanynge thereof: But they coulde not tell me, what this matter sygnyfyed.

16 Then heard I saye, that thou canste expounde darcke thynges, and declare harde doutes. Well then, yf thou canst reade thys wrytynge, and shewe me the meanynge therof: thou shalte be clothed with purple, haue a cheyne of golde aboute thy necke, and rule þe thyrde parte of my kyngdome.

17 Daniel aunswered, and sayde before the kynge. As for thy rewardes, kepe them to thy selfe, or geue thy ryche gyftes to another: yet not the lesse, I wyll rede the wrytynge vnto þe kynge, and shewe hym the interpretacion therof.

18 O kynge, God the hyest gaue vnto Nabuchodonosor thy father, the dignite of a kynge with worshippe and honoure,

19 so that al people, kynredes and tunge stode in awe & feare of him, by reason of the hye estate, that he had lente him. For why, he slewe whom he wold: he smote, whom it pleased hym. Agayne, whom he wolde, he set vp: and whome he lyst, he put doune.

20 But because hys herte was so proude, and hys stomacke set so fast vnto wilfulnesse: he was deposed from hys kingly trone, & his magesty was taken from hym.

21 He was shote oute from amonge men, his herte was lyke a beastes herte, and hys dwellynge was wyth the wylde asses: he was fayne to eate grasse lyke an oxe, and hys body was wet with the dewe of the heauen: tyll he knewe, that þe hyest had power vpon the kingdomes of men, and setteth ouer them, whome he lyst.

22 And thou hys sonne (O Balthazar) for al this, hast not submytted thyne herte, thoughe thou knewest all these thynges,

23 but hast magnyfyed thy selfe aboue the Lorde of heauen, so that the vessels of hys house were broughte before the, that thou, and thy Lordes, with thy quene and concubynes, myght drincke wyne thereoute: And hast praysed the Idoles of syluer and golde, copper and yron, of wode and stone: As for the God in whose hande consysteth thy breth and all thy wayes: thou haste not loaued hym.

24 Therfore is the palme of thys hande sente hyther from hym, to token vp thys writinge.

25 And thys is the scrypture, that is wryten vp: Mane, Thetel, Phares.

26 Nowe the interpretacyon of the thynge is thys: Mane, God hath nombred the kyngdome, and brought it to an ende:

27 Thetel, thou arte weyed in the balaunce and arte founde to lyghte:

28 Phares, thy kyngdome is delte in partes, and geuen to the Medes and Perses.

29 Then commaunded Balthazar, to clothe Daniel wyth purple, to hange a cheyne of golde aboute hys necke, and to make a proclamacyon concernyng him: that he shulde be the ruler of the thyrde parte of hys kyngedome.

30 The very same nyghte was Balthazar the kynge of the Caldees slayne,

31 and Darius out of Medea toke in the kyngedome, beyng .lxij. yeare of age.

# CHAPTER 6

It pleased Darius to set ouer hys kingedome an .C. and .xx. Lordes, whiche shulde be in all hys kyngdome aboute.

2 Aboue these he set thre princes (of whom Daniel was one) that the Lordes myghte geue accomptes vnto them, and the Kyng to be vndiseased.

3 But Daniel exceaded al

these Princes and Lordes, for the sprete of God was plenteous in him: so that the Kynge was mynded to set hym ouer the whole realme.

4 Wherfore the Prynces and Lordes soughte, to pycke oute in Danyel some quarell agaynst the kyngdom: yet coulde they fynde none occasyon nor faute vpon hym. For why? he was so faythful, that there was no blame nor dyshonestye founde in hym.

5 Then sayde these men: we wil get no quarell agaynste thys Daniel, excepte it be in the lawe of hys God.

6 Vpon this, wente the princes and Lordes together vnto the kynge, and sayde thus vnto him: king Darius God saue thy lyfe for euer.

7 All the greate estates of the realme: as the princes, Dukes, Senatours, and iudges, are determed to put oute a commaundement of the kinge, and to make a sure statute: namely, that who so desireth any peticyon, ether of any god, or man (within this .xxx. dayes) excepte it be onlye of the, O kinge: the same person may be cast into the lions denne.

8 Wherfore, O kynge, confirme thou this statute, and make a wryttynge, that the thynge which the Medes and Perses haue ordeyned be not altered nor broken.

9 So Darius made the writtinge, and confirmed it.

10 Now when Daniel vnderstode that the writtinge was made, he wente into hys house: and the windowes of hys hall toward Ierusalem stode open. There kneled he doune vpon his knees, thre tymes a daye: there he made his peticion, and praysed his God, like as hys maner was to do afore tyme.

11 Then these men made searche, and founde Daniel makinge his petycyon and prayinge vnto his God.

12 So they came to the kynge, & spake before him concerninge his commaundement sayinge: O kinge, hast thou not subscribed the statute, that within .xxx. daies who so requireth hys petycyon of any God or man but onely of thy selfe, O kinge: he shalbe cast into the denne of the lyons? The kinge answered, and sayd: ye, it is true. It must be as a lawe of the Medes and Perses, that maye not be broken.

13 Then answered they, and sayde vnto the kynge: Daniel one of the presoners of Iuda, O kynge, regardeth neyther the, nor thy statute, that thou hast made, but maketh his peticion thre tymes a day.

14 When the king heard these wordes, he was sore greued, and would haue excused Daniel, to deliuer him, and put of the matter, vnto the Sunne wente doune to the intent that he myght saue hym.

15 These men perceyuinge the kinges mind sayde vnto him: knowe thys (O Kinge) that the lawe of the Medes and Perses is, that þe commaundement & statute, whiche the kinge maketh, may not be altered.

16 Then the kynge had them bringe Daniel, and they caste hym into the Lyons denne. The kynge also spake vnto Daniel, & sayde: thy God, whom thou alwaye seruest, euen he shall defende the.

17 And there was broughte a stone, & layed vpon the hole of the denne: this the kinge sealed with his owne ringe, & wyth the signet of his pryncis: that the kinges commaundemente concerninge Daniel, shoulde not be broken.

18 So the kinge wente into his palace, & kepte him sober al night, so that there was no table spred before him, neyther coulde he take any slepe.

19 But by tymes in the morninge at the breake of the day, the kinge arose, and wente in all haste vnto the denne of the Lyons.

20 Now as he came nye vnto the denne, he cried with a pyteous voyce vnto Daniell: yea the Kinge spake, and sayde vnto Daniel: O Daniel, thou seruaunt of the lyuynge God, is not thy God (whom thou alwaye seruest) able to deliuer the from the Lyons?

21 Daniel sayde vnto the Kinge: O King, God saue thy lyfe for euer.

22 My God hath sent his aungell whiche hath shut the lyons mouthes, so that they might not hurte me. For why? myne vngiltinesse is founde oute before him. And as for the, O Kinge, I neuer offended the.

23 Then was the kinge exceadinge glad, and commaunded to take Daniel out of the denne. So Daniel was broughte oute of the denne, and no maner of hurte was found vpon him. For he put his trust in his God.

24 And as for those men which had accused Daniel, the king commaunded to bringe them, and to cast them in the lyons denne: them, their children and their wiues. So the Lyons had the maystry of them, and brake all their bones a sonder, or euer they came at the grounde.

25 After thys, wrote the Kinge Darius vnto all people kinreddes, and tunges, that dwelt in al landes: peace be multiplyed wt you.

26 My commaundement is, in al my dominion & kingedome, that men feare and stande in awe of Daniels God. For he is the liuinge God, whiche abydeth euer: his kingedome shall not fayle, and hys power is euerlasting.

27 It is he that delyuereth and saueth: he doeth wonders & maruelous worckes, in heauen and in earth: he hath preserued

Daniel from the power of the Lyons.

28 This Daniell prospered in the raigne of Darius and Cirus of Persia.

# CHAPTER 7

IN the firste yeare of Balthazar kinge of Babylon, saw Daniel a dreame, and a visyon was in his head vpon his bed. Whiche dreame he wrote, and the summe of the matter is this:

2 Daniel spake, and sayd: I sawe in my vision by nyght, and beholde: the foure wyndes of the heauen stroue vpon the sea,

3 and foure great beastes came vp from the sea one vnlyke another.

4 The fyrste was a lion, and yet had he Aegles winges. I sawe, that hys wynges were plucte from him, and he taken awaye from the earth: that he stode vpon hys fete as a man, and that there was geuen him a mans herte.

5 Beholde, the seconde beaste was lyke a beer & stode vpon the one syde. Amonge his teeth in his mouth he had .iij. greate longe teeth, & it was sayde vnto him: Aryse: eate vp, much fleshe.

6 Then I loked, and beholde, there was another lyke vnto a leoparde: thys had wynges as a foule, euen four vpon the backe. This beaste had foure heades, and there was power geuen him.

7 After this I sawe in a vision by night, and beholde, the fourthe beast was grymme and horrible, and maruelous strong. It had great yron teeth, it deuoured and destroyed, and stamped the resydue vnder hys fete. It was farre vnlyke the other beastes, þt were before it: for it had ten hornes, whereof I toke good hede.

8 And beholde, there came vp amonge them another lyke horne, before whom there were thre of the fyrste hornes pluckte awaye. Beholde, thys horne had eyes lyke a man, and a mouth speakynge presumptuous thynges.

9 I loked tyl the seates were prepared, and tyll the olde aged sat hym doune. His clothynge was as whyte as snowe, and the hearres of hys heade, lyke the pure woll. His trone was lyke the fyrye flamme, and his wheles as the burnynge fyre.

10 There drewe forthe a fyrye streame, and wente out from him. A thousande tymes a thousande serued him .x.M. tymes ten thousande stode before him. The iudgement was set, and the bokes opened.

11 Then toke I hede therunto, because of the voyce of the proude wordes, whyche the horne spake. I behelde, tyll the beaste was slayne, and his bodye destroyed, and geuen ouer to be brent in the fire.

12 As for the power of the other beastes also it was taken awaye, but their lyues were prolonged for a tyme and season.

13 I sawe in a vision by nyght, and beholde, there came one in the cloudes of heauen lyke the sonne of a man, whyche went vnto the olde aged, before whome they broughte hym.

14 Then gaue he hym power and dignitie regal, that al people trybes and tunges shoulde serue him. Hys power is an euerlastynge power, whych shal neuer be put doune, and his kingdome endureth vncorrupte.

15 My herte was vexed, and I Daniel had a troubled spirite within me, and the visions of my heade made me afrayed:

16 til I gat me vnto one of them that stode by, to knowe the trueth, concernynge all these thynges. So he tolde me, and made me vnderstand the interpretacion of these thinges.

17 These foure greate beastes, are foure kynges, whiche shal arise out of the earth.

18 These shall take in the kingedome of the sayntes of the most hyest, and possesse it still more and more for a longe season.

19 After this I requyred diligently to knowe the trueth, concerning the fourth beast, whiche was so farre vnlyke the other beastes, and so horrible: whose teeth were of yron, and his nayles of brasse: which deuoured and destroyed, and stamped the residue vnder his fete.

20 I desired also to knowe the trueth, as touching the ten hornes that he had vpon hys heade, and thys other, whiche came vp afterwarde, before whose face there fell doune thre: whyche horne had eyes, and a mouthe that spake presumptuous thynges, and loked with a grymmer vysage, then his felowes.

21 I behelde, and the same horne made battaile againste the saintes, yea and gat the victorie of them,

22 vntill the tyme that the olde aged came, that the iudgemente was geuen to the chefest sayntes: and till the tyme that the saintes hath the kingedome in possession.

23 He gaue me this answere: That fourthe beast shalbe the fourth kingedome vpon earth: it shalbe more then all other kingedomes, it shall deuoure, treade doune, and destroye all other landes.

24 The ten hornes are ten kinges, that shall aryse out of the kingedom, after whom there shall stande vp another, whiche shalbe greater then the fyrste.

25 He shall subdue thre Kynges, and shal speake wordes against the hyest of all: he shall destroy the saintes of the most hyest, and thincke, that he may chaunge tymes and lawes. They

shalbe geuen vnder his power, vntill a time, two tymes, and half a tyme.

26 But the iudgemente shalbe kepte, so that his power shalbe taken from him, for he shall be destroyed, and perishe at the laste.

27 As for the kingedome, power and all might that is vnder the heauen, it shalbe geuen to the holy people of the most hyest, whose kingedome is euerlastinge, yea all powers shall serue & obeye him.

28 Thus farre extende the wordes. Neuertheles I Daniel was so vexed in my thoughtes, that my countenaunce chaunced, but the wordes I kepte styl in my herte.

# CHAPTER 8

IN the thirde year of the raigne of kinge Balthazar, there apeared a vision vnto me Daniel, after that I had sene the fyrste.

2 I saw in vision (& when I saw it, I was at Susis in the chefe citie, whyche lyeth in the lande of Elam) and in the vision, me thought I was by the ryuer of Vlai.

3 Then I loked vp, and sawe, and beholde there stode before in the riuer, a ramme, whiche had hornes: and these hornes were hye, but one was hyer then another, & the hyest came vp last.

4 I sawe that this ramme pushed with his hornes againste the west, agaynste the north, and againste the south: so that no beastes might stande before him, nor defende them from his power: but he did as him lysted, & waxed greatly.

5 I toke hede vnto this, & then came there an hegoate from the west ouer the whole earthe, and touched not the grounde. This goate had a maruelous goodly horne betwixte his eyes,

6 and came vnto the ramme that had the two hornes (whome I had sene afore by the ryuer syde) and ranne fearcelye vpon him with his might.

7 I sawe him drawe nye vnto the ramme, beynge very fearce vpon him, yea he gaue him suche a stroke, that he brake his two hornes: Neyther had the ramme so much strength as to stande before him: but he cast him doune, trodde him vnder his fete: and no man was able to delyuer the ramme out of his power.

8 The goate waxed exceadinge greate, & when he was at the strongest, his great horne was broken also. Then grewe there other foure suche lyke in the steade, toward the .iiij. windes of the heauen.

9 Yea oute of one of the least of these hornes, there came vp yet another horne, whiche waxed maruelous greate: towarde the southe, towarde the east, and towarde the fayre pleasaunt lande.

10 It grew vp to the host of heauen, wherof it did cast some doune to the grounde, & of the starres also, & trode them vnder fete.

11 Yea it grewe vp vnto the prince of the host from whom the dayly offeringe was taken, & the place of his Sanctuary casten doune:

12 & a certayne ceason was geuen vnto it, against the daylye offeringe (because of wickednesse) that it might cast doune þe verite to the ground and so to prospere in all thynges, that it went aboute.

13 Vpon this I heard one of the sayntes speakinge, whiche saynte sayde vnto one that asked this questyon: How longe shall this vysion of the daylye sacrifice and of the wasting abhominacion endure: that the Sanctuarye and the power shall so be troden vnder fote?

14 And he answered him: Vnto the eueninge & the mornynge, euen two thousand and thre hundreth dayes: then shall the Sanctuarye be clensed againe.

15 Now when I Daniel had sene this vision, and sought for the vnderstandinge of it: beholde, there stode before me a thynge like vnto a man,

16 and I hearde a mans voyce in the ryuer of Vlai, which cryed and sayd: O Gabriel, make this man vnderstande the vysion.

17 So he came, and stode by me. But I was afrayed at his commynge, and fell doune vpon my face. Then he sayde vnto me: O thou sonne of man, marcke well, for in the last tyme shall this vision be fulfylled.

18 Nowe as he was speakynge vnto me, I waxed faynte, so that I suncke doune to the ground. But he toke hold vpon me, and set me vp agayne,

19 sayinge: Beholde, I wyl shewe the, what shall happen in the last wrath, for in the tyme appoynted it shalbe fulfylled.

20 The ramme whyche thou sawest with the two hornes, is the kiuge of the Medes and Perses:

21 but the goate is the king of the Greke lande: the greate horne that stode betwyxte his eyes, that is the pryncypall kynge.

22 But where as it brake, and foure other rose vp in the steade: it sygnifyeth, that out of thys people shall stande vp four kyngdomes, but not so mighty as it.

23 After these kyngedomes (whyle vngodlynes is a growynge) there shall aryse a kynge of an vnshamefast face, whiche shalbe wyse in darcke speakinges.

24 He shalbe myghty and stronge, but not in his owne strength. He shall destroye aboue measure, and all that he goeth aboute shall prospere: he shall slaye the stronge and holye people.

25 And thorowe his craftynes, falshed shall prosper in his hande, hys herte shalbe proude, and many one shall be put to deathe in his welthinesse. He shall stand vp against the Prince of Princes, but he shalbe destroyed wythoute hande.

26 And this vysyon that is shewed vnto the, is as sure as the euenynge & the morninge. Therfore wryte thou vp this sighte, for it wilbe longe, or it come to passe.

27 Vpon this was I Daniel very fainte, so that I lay sicke certayne dayes: but when I rose vp, I wente aboute the kinges busynes, and marueled at the vision, neuertheles no man knewe of it.

# CHAPTER 9

IN the fyrst yeare of Darius þe sonne of Ahasuerus, whyche was the sede of the Medes, & was made king ouer the realm of the Caldees:

2 yea euen in the fyrst yeare of his raygne, I Daniel desyred to knowe the yearly nombre oute of the bokes, whereof the Lorde spake vnto Ieremye the Prophete: that Ierusalem shoulde lye waste .lxx. yeares:

3 and I turned me vnto god the Lorde, for to praye and make myne intercession, with fastinge, sackcloth & ashes,

4 I prayed before the Lorde my God, and knowledged, sayinge: O Lorde, thou greate and fearfull God, thou that kepest couenaunt and mercye wyth them, whiche loue the, and do thy commaundementes.

5 We haue synned, we haue offended, we haue ben disobedient and gone back: yea we haue departed from all thy preceptes and iudgementes.

6 We woulde neuer folowe thy seruauntes the Prophetes, that spake in thy name to our kinges and princes, to oure forefathers, and to all the people of the lande.

7 O Lorde, ryghteousnesse belongeth vnto the, vnto vs pertayneth nothynge but open shame, as it is come to passe this day vnto euery man of Iuda and to them that dwell at Ierusalem: Yea, vnto all Israell, whether they be farre or nye thorow out all landes: wherin thou haste strowed them, because of the offences that they had done agaynst the.

8 Yea O Lorde, vnto vs, to our kinges and princes, to oure forefathers: euen to vs all, that haue offended the, belongeth open shame.

9 But vnto the, O Lorde oure God, pertayneth mercye and forgeuenesse. As for vs, we are gone backe from him,

10 and haue not obeyed the voyce of the Lorde oure God, to walke in his lawes, which he layed before vs by his seruauntes the prophetes:

11 yea all Israel haue transgressed, & gone back from thy law, so þt they haue not herckened vnto thy voyce. Wherfore the cursse & othe, that is written in the lawe of Moses the seruaunte of God (agaynst whom we haue offended) is poured vpon vs.

12 And he hath perfourmed his wordes, whiche he spake against vs, and against oure iudges that iudged vs: to brynge vpon vs suche a greate plage, as neuer was vnder heauen, lyke as it is now come to passe in Ierusalem.

13 Yea all this plage, as it is wrytten in the lawe of Moses, is come vpon vs. Yet made we not our prayer before the Lord our God, that we might turne agayne from our wickednesse, and to be learned in thy verite.

14 Therefore hathe the Lorde made haste, to brynge this plage vpon vs, for the Lorde our God is ryghteous, in all his worckes which he doeth: for why, we woulde not herken vnto his voyce.

15 And now, O Lorde oure God, thou that with a myghty hande haste brought thy people oute of Egipte, to get thy selfe a name, whiche remayneth this day: we haue synned

16 O Lorde, and done wyckedly agaynste all thy ryghteousnes: yet let thy wrothfull displeasure be turned awaye (I besech the) from thy cytye Ierusalem thy holy hill. And why? for oure synnes sake, and for the wickednesse of oure forefathers is Ierusalem and thy people abhorred, of all them that are aboute vs.

17 Now therefore, O oure God, heare the prayer of thy seruaunte, and his intercession. O let not thy face shyne ouer thy Sanctuary that lyeth waste.

18 O my God, enclyne thine eare, and herken (at the leaste for thine owne sake) open thyne eyes: beholde, how we be desolated, yea and the cytye also, whiche is called after thy name: for we do not cast oure prayers before the in oure owne righteousnesse, no: but onely in thy greate mercyes.

19 O Lorde, heare. O forgeue Lorde. O Lorde consydre, tarye not ouer longe: but for thyne owne sake do it. O my God: for the citie and thy people is called after thy name.

20 As I was yet speakinge at my prayers, knoweledginge myne owne sinnes, and the synnes of my people, makinge so mine intercession before the Lorde my God, for the holye hils sake of my God:

21 yea, whyle I was yet speakinge in my prayer, beholde the man Gabrel (whome I had sene afore in the vision) came flying to me, and touched me about the offeringe time in the eueninge.

22 He infourmed me, and

spake vnto me: O Daniel sayde he, I am now come to make the vnderstande it:

23 For as sone as thou begannest to make thy prayer, it was so diuised, and therfore am I come to shewe the. And why? For thou arte a man greatly beloued. Wherfore, pondre the matter well, that thou mayest learne, to vnderstande the vision.

24 .Lxx. weakes are determed ouer thy people, and ouer the holy citie: that the wickednesse maye be consumed, that the sinne maye haue an ende, that the offence may be reconcyled, and to bringe in euerlastinge righteousnesse, to fulfill the visions and the Prophetes, and to annoynte the most holy one.

25 Vnderstande this then, and marcke it well, that from the tyme it shalbe concluded, to go and repayre Ierusalem againe, vnto Christ (or the annointed) prince: there shalbe seuen weakes. Then shal the stretes and walles be buylded again .lxij. weakes, but wyth harde troublous time.

26 After these .lxii. weakes shall Christ be slaine and they shall haue no pleasure in hym. Then shall there come a people with the Prince, and destroye the cytie and the Sanctuarye: & his ende shall come as the water floude. But the desolacion shall continue till the ende of the battell.

27 He shall make a stronge bonde with many, for the space of a weke: and when the weke is halfe gone, he shall put doune the slayne and meateofferinge. And in the temple there shalbe an abhominable desolacion, till it haue destroyed all. And it is concluded, that thys wasting shall continue vnto the ende.

# CHAPTER 10

IN the thirde yeare of king Cirus of Persia, there was shewed vnto Daniel (otherwyse called Balthazar) a matter, yea a true matter, but it is yet a longe tyme vnto it. He vnderstode the matter well, and perceyued what the vision was.

2 At the same time I Daniel mourned for the space of thre weakes,

3 so that I had no lust to eate bread: as for fleshe and wine there came none within my mouth: No, I dyd not ones annoynte my selfe, till the whole thre weakes were oute.

4 Upon the .xxiiii. daye of the first Moneth, I was by the great floude, called Tigris:

5 I lift vp mine eyes, and loked: and beholde, a man clothed in linen, whose loynes were girded vp with fyne goulde of Araby:

6 his body was like the Chrisolite stone, his face (to loke vpon) was like lighteninge, his eyes as the flamme of fyre, his armes and fete were lyke fayre glysterynge metall, but the voyce of his wordes was like the voyce of a multitude.

7 I Daniel alone sawe this vision, the men that were with me, sawe it not: but a greate fearfulnesse fell vpon them, so that they fled away & hid them selues.

8 I was left there my selfe alone, and sawe this greate vision, so longe till there remayned no more strengthe within me: yea I lost my coloure cleane, I waited awaye, and my strength was gone.

9 Yet hearde I the voyce of his wordes: and as sone as I hearde it, fayntnesse came vpon me, and I fell doune flat to the grounde vpon my face.

10 And beholde, an hande touched me, whyche set me vpon my knees, and vpon the palmes of my handes,

11 sayinge vnto me: O Daniel, thou well beloued man: take good hede of the wordes, that I shal say vnto the, and stande ryght, for vnto the am I now sent. And when he had sayde these wordes, I stode vp tremblinge.

12 Then he sayd vnto me: feare not Daniel: for why sence the fyrst day that thou set thyne herte to vnderstande, and diddest chasten thy selfe before thy God: thy wordes haue bene hearde. And I had come vnto the, when thou begannest to speake

13 bad nor the prynce ouer the kingedom of the Perses withstand me .xxi. dayes. But lo, Michael one of the chefe Princes, came to helpe me, hym haue I left by the kyng of Persia,

14 & am come to shewe the, what shall happen vnto thy people in the latter dayes. For it wilbe longe yet or the vision be fulfilled.

15 Nowe when he had spoken these wordes vnto me, I cast doune my head to the ground and helde my tunge.

16 Beholde, there touched my lippes one very lyke vnto a man. Then opened I my mouthe, & sayde vnto him, that stode before me: O my Lorde, my pointes are lowsed in the vision, and there is no more strength within me:

17 Howe may my Lordes seruaunt then talke with my Lorde? seynge there is no strength in me: so that I can not take my breth?

18 Vpon this there touched me agayne, one muche lyke a man, and comforted me,

19 saying: O thou man so well beloued feare not: be content, take a good herte vnto þe, & be strong. So when he had spoken vnto me, I recouered and sayd: Speake on my Lorde, for thou haste refreshed me.

20 Then sayde he: knowest thou wherfore I am came vnto the? now wyl I go again to fyght with the prince of the Perses. As sone as I go forth, lo, the prince of Grekelande shall come.

21 Neuertheles I will shew the the thinge, that is fast noted in the scripture of truethe. And as for all yonder matters, there is none that helpeth me in them, but Michael youre prynce.

## CHAPTER 11

And in the first yeare of Darius of Medea, I stode by him, to comforte him, & to strength him,

2 and nowe wil I shew the the trueth. Beholde, there shall stande vp yet thre kynges in Persia, but the fourth shal be farre rycher then they all. And when he is in the chefest power of his ryches, he shall prouoke euery man against þe realme of Grekelande.

3 Then shall there aryse yet a myghty kinge, that shall rule with greate dominion, and do what him lyst.

4 And as sone as his kingedome cometh vp, it shalbe destroyed, and deuyded toward the foure windes of the heauen. They that come after hym, shall not haue suche power and domynyon as he: but hys kyngedome shalbe scatred, yea euen amonge other then those.

5 And the kyng of the south shal be myghtyer, then his other princes. Agaynste him there shall one make hymselfe stronge, and shal rule his dominyon wt greate power.

6 But after certayne yeares they shalbe ioyned together, and the kinges doughter of the south shall come to the kynge of the Northe, for to make frendshyp, but she shall not obtayne the power of that arme, neyther shall she be able to endure thorow his myght: but she, and such as brought her (yea and he that begat her, & comforted her for hys tyme) shalbe delyuered vp.

7 Oute of the braunches of her rote, there shall one stande vp in his steade: whiche with power of armes shal go thorow the kinges lande of the North, & handle hym according to his strength. As for their Idols & princes, with their costly Iewels of goulde & syluer,

8 he shal carye them awaye captiues into Egipte, & he shall preuayle agaynste the kyng of the north certayne yeares.

9 And when he is come into the kinges realm of the south he shalbe fayne to turne agayne into hys owne lande.

10 Wherfore hys sonnes shalbe displeased, and shall gather together a myghtye greate hoste of people: and one of them shall come, and go thorowe lyke a waterflowed: then shall he returne, and go forth with defyinge and boastinge vnto his owne lande.

11 Then the kynge of the south shalbe angry and shall come forthe to fyght agaynste the kinge of the north: yea he shal brynge a great multitude of people together, & a great heape shalbe geuen into hys hande:

12 these shall he cary awaye with greate pryde, for so muche as he hath cast doune so many thousandes, neuertheles he shall not preuayle.

13 For the king of the north shal gather (of the new) a greater heape of people then afore, & come forth (after a certayne tyme & yeares) wyth a mighty hoste and exceadinge greate good.

14 At the same tyme there shall manye stande vp agaynst the kynge of the south, so that the wycked children of thy people also shall exalte them selues (to fulfyll the vysyon) & then fall.

15 So the kynge of the North shall come to laye sege, & to take the stronge fensed cytyes: And the power of them of the south shal not be able to abyde him, and the best men of the people shal not be so stronge, as to resist him.

16 Shortely, when he commeth, he shall handle him as he list, & no man shalbe so hardy as to stande agaynst hym. He shall stand in þe pleasaunt countreye, whiche thorow him shalbe destroyed.

17 He shal set his face wt al his power to obtayne his kyngedome, and to be lyke it. Yea that shall he do, and geue hym vnto the doughters amonge wemen, to destroye hym. But he shall fayle, neyther shall he obtayne his purpose.

18 After this shall he set hys face vnto the Iles, & take many of them. A prynce shal stoppe him, to do hym a shame, besyde the confusyon that els shall come vnto hym.

19 Thus shall he tourne agayne to hys owne lande, stomble, & fall, and be no more founde:

20 so he that came vpon him & did him violence, shal stande in his place, & haue a pleasaunte kingedom: and after few dayes he shalbe destroyed, and that neyther in wrath, nor in battell.

21 In his steade there shal aryse a vyle person, not holden worthy of a kinges dygnitie: this shal come in craftely, & obtayne the kingedome with fayre wordes:

22 he shall fyghte agaynste the armes of the myghtye (and destroye them) yea and agaynste the prynce of the couenaunte.

23 So after that he hath taken truce with him, he shal handle disceytfully, that he maye get vp, and ouercome him with a small flocke:

24 & so with craftynesse to get him to the fattest place of the lande, and to deale otherwyse, then ether his fathers or graundfathers dyd. For he shall destroy the thinge, that they had robbed and spoiled, yea & al their substaunce: ymageninge thoughtes agaynst the stronge

holdes, and that for a tyme.

25 His power, and herte shalbe sterred vp with a great armye agaynst the kinge of the south: where thorow the king of the south shalbe moued then vnto battell with a great and mighty host also. Neuertheles he shal not be able to stand, for they shal conspire against hym.

26 Yea, they that eat of hys meate, shal hurte him: so that his hoste shall fall, and many be slayne donne.

27 These two kinges shalbe mynded to do myschefe, and talke of disceyte at one table, but they shall not prosper: for why, the ende shal not come yet, vnto the tyme appoynted.

28 Then shal he go home agayne into his owne lande with great good, & set his herte against the holy couenaunt, he shalbe busye againste it, and then returne home.

29 At the time appointed, he shall come agayne, and go toward the south. So shall it happen otherwyse then at the first, yet ones agayn.

30 And why? the shippes of Lithim shall come vpon him, that he may be smytten and turne again: that he may take indignacyon agaynste the couenaunte of holynesse, to medle agaynste it. Yea he shall turne him, and drawe suche vnto hym, as leaue the holy couenaunte.

31 He shall set myghty men to vnhalowe the Sanctuary of strength, to put doune the daylye offerynge, and to set vp the abhomynable desolacyon.

32 And suche as breake the couenaunt shal he flattre wyth fayre wordes. But the people that wyll know their God, shal haue the ouerhand, and prosper.

33 Those also that haue vnderstandyng among the people shall enfourme the multitude: and for a long season, they shalbe persecuted with swerde, with fyre, with captyuyte and with the takinge aweye of their goodes.

34 Nowe when they fall they shalbe set vp with a litle helpe: but many shall clene vnto them fayendly.

35 Yea, some of those whyth haue vnderstandinge shalbe persecuted also: that they maye be tryed, purifyed and clensed, tyll the tyme be oute: for there is yet another tyme appointed.

36 The kinge shal do what him lyst, he shal exalte and magnifye him selfe agaynste all, that is God. Yea he shall speake maruelous thinges against the God of al goddes, wherin he shall prospere, so longe till the wrathe be fulfilled, for the conclusyon is deuysed alredy.

37 He shal not regarde the God of hys fathers, but his lust shalbe vpon wemen: Yea, he shal not care for any God, for he shall magnifye him selfe aboue al.

38 In his place shall he worshippe the mighty Idols: and the god whome his fathers knewe not, shall he honoure with goulde and syluer, with precious stones and pleasaunt Iewels.

39 This shal he do, sekyng helpe and succour at the myghtye Idols and straunge goddes. Suche as wil receyue him, and take him for God, he shall geue them greate worshippe, & power: yea and make them lordes of the multitude, and geue them the lande with rewardes.

40 In the latter tyme shall the kinge of the south stryue with him: & the king of the north in like maner shall come agaynste him wyth charettes, horsemen and wyth a greate nauy of shippes. He shall come into the landes, destroye and go thorowe,

41 he shall entre also into the fayre pleasaunt lande. Manye cytyes and countreyes shall decaye, excepte Edom, Moab & the best of the children of Ammon, whyche shall escape from hys hande.

42 He shal stretch forth his handes vpon the countreyes & the lande of Egipte shall not escape him.

43 For thorowe his goynge in, he shal haue dominion ouer the treasures of siluer and gold & ouer al the precyous Iewels of Egypt, Lybia and Ethiopia.

44 Neuerthelesse the tidinges oute of the easte and north shal trouble hym, for the whiche cause he shall go forthe to destroye & curse a greate multitude.

45 The tentes of his palace shall be pytch betwyxte the two seas, vpon the hill of the noble Sanctuarye, for he shall come to the ende of it, & then shal no man helpe him.

# CHAPTER 12

THE tyme wil come also, that the greate Prince Michael, which standeth on thy people syde, shal aryse vp, for there shall come a tyme of trouble, such as neuer was, sens there beganne to be any people, vnto þt same time. Then shal thy people be deliuered, yea, al those that be found written in the boke.

2 Many of them that slepe in þe dust of the earth, shal awake: some to euerlastinge lyfe, some to perpetual shame and reprofe.

3 The wyse (suche as haue taught other) shall glyster, as the shynninge of heauen: and those that haue instructe the multitude vnto godlynesse, shall be as the starres, worlde without ende.

4 And thou O Daniel, shut vp these wordes, & seale the boke til the last time. Manye shal go aboute here & there, & then shal knowledge encrease.

5 So I Daniel loked, & beholde there stode other two, one vpon thys shore of the water, the other vpon yonder syde.

6 And one of them sayde vnto him, whiche was clothed in lynen, and stode aboue vpon the waters of the floud: How longe shall it be to the ende of the wonderous worckes?

7 Then hearde I the man with the lynen clothes, whiche stode aboue vpon the waters of the floude: when he helde vp his right and lefte hande vnto heauen, and sware, by hym whyche liueth for euer: that it shall tary for a tyme, two tymes and halfe a tyme: & when the power of the holy people is cleane scatred abroade, then shal al these thinges be fulfilled.

8 I hearde it well, but I vnderstode it not. Then sayde I: O my Lord, what shall happen after that?

9 He answered: Go thy waye Daniel, for these wordes shalbe closed vp, & sealed, till the last tyme:

10 & many shalbe purifyed, clensed and tryed. But the vngodly shal lyue wickedly, and those wicked (as many of them as they be) shall haue no vnderstanding. As for suche as haue vnderstandynge, they shall regarde it.

11 And from the time forth that the dayly offeringe shalbe put doune & the abhominable desolacyon set vp, there shalbe a thousande two hundreth & .xc. dayes.

12 O well is him, that wayteth, & commeth to the thousande .iij.C. & .xxxv. dayes.

13 Go thou thy way now, till it be ended: take thy rest, and byde in thy lot, till the dayes haue an ende.

# Hosea

## CHAPTER 1

This is the worde of of the Lord, that came vnto Oseas the sonne of Beery, in the dayes of Oseas, Ioathan, Ahaz and Iezekiah kinges of Iuda: and in the tyme of Ieroboam the sonne of Ioas kynge of Israel.

2 First when the Lorde spake vnto Oseas, he sayde vnto him: Go thy waye, take an harlot to thy wyfe, and get chyldren by her: for the lande hath committed greate whordome agaynst the Lorde.

3 So he wente, and toke Gomer the doughter of Deblaim: whiche conceyued, and brought forth a sonne.

4 And the Lorde sayde vnto him: call his name Iesraell, for I wyll shortly auenge the bloude of Iesrael, vpon the house of Iehu, and wyll brynge the kingedome of the house of Israel to an ende.

5 Then wyl I breake the bowe of Israel, in the valley of Iesrael.

6 She conceyued yet again, and bare a doughter. And he sayde vnto him: Call her name Loruhamah (that is, not obtayninge mercy) for I wyl haue no pyte vpon the house of Israell, but forget them, and put them cleane oute of remembraunce.

7 Neuerthelesse I wyll haue mercy vpon the house of Iuda, and will saue them, euen thorow the Lord their God. But I wyll not delyuer them thorowe anye bowe, sweardoe, battel, horses, or horsemen.

8 Now when she had weaned Loruhamah, she conceyued agayne, and bare a sonne.

9 Then sayd he: cal his name Lo amy. For why? ye are not my people, therfore wyll I not be youres.

10 And thoughe the nombre of the chyldren of Israel be as the sand of the sea, which can neyther be measured nor tolde: yet in the place where it is sayde vnto them, ye be not my people, euen there shal it be thus reported of them: they be the chyldren of the lyuynge God.

11 Then shal the chyldren of Iuda & the children of Israel be gathered together again, & chose them selues one heade, and then depart oute of the lande: for great shalbe the daye of Israel.

## CHAPTER 2

Tell youre brethren, that they are my people: and your sisteren that they haue obtayned mercye.

2 As for youre mother, ye shal chyde with her, & reproue her, for she is not my wyfe, neyther am I her husbande, vnlesse she put awaye her whordom out of my syght, and her aduoutry from her brestes.

3 Yf no I shal strype her naked and sette her, euen as she came into the worlde: yea, I shall lay her waste, and make her like a wildernesse, and slay her for thirst.

4 I shal haue no pyte also vpon her children, for they be the children of fornicacyon.

5 Their mother hath broken their wedlocke, and she that bare them, is come to confusyon. For she sayd: I will go after my louers, that geue me my water and bread, my woll and flax, my oyle and my drincke.

6 But I wyll hedge her awaye wyth thornes, and stoppe it that she shall not fynde her fotesteppes:

7 and thoughe she runne after her louers, yet shall she not get them: she shall seke them, but not fynde them. Then shall she saye: wel I wyll go turne agayne to my firste housbande, for at that tyme was I better at ease, then nowe.

8 But this woulde she not knowe, where as I yet gaue her corne, wyne, oyle, syluer & gold, whiche she hath hangeth vpon Baal.

9 Wherfore now will I go take my corne & wine againe in their season, and set agayne my woll and my flax, whyche I gaue her, to couer her shame.

10 And nowe will I discouer her folyshenesse, euen in the syghte of her louers, and no man shal deliuer her oute of my handes.

11 Moreouer, I wil take awaye all her myrthe, her holye dayes, her newmones, her Sabbothes, and all her solempne feastes?

12 I wil destroy her vyneyardes and figge trees, though she sayeth: lo, here are my rewardes that my louers haue geuen me. I wyll make it a woode, and the wilde beastes shall eate it vp.

13 I will punysh her also for the dayes of Baal, wherin she censed him, deckinge hym with her earynges and cheynes: when she folowed her louers, and forgat me, sayeth the Lorde.

14 Wherfore beholde, I will cal her agayne: bring her into a wildernes, and speake frendly vnto her:

15 there wil I geue her her vineiardes agayne: yea and the valleye of Achor also to shewe her hope and comforte. Then shall she singe there as in the time of her youthe, & lyke as in the day when she came oute of the lande of Egipte.

16 Then (sayeth the Lorde) she shall saye vnto me: O my husbande, and shal call me no more Baal,

17 for I will take awaye those names of Baal from her mouthe, yea, she shal neuer remembre their names anye more.

18 Then will I make a couenaunte with them, with the wilde beastes, with the foules of the ayre, and with euery thing that crepeth vpon the earth. As for bowe, swerde and battel, I will destroye suche out of the lande, & will make them to slepe safely.

19 Thus will I marye the vnto myne owne selfe for euermore: yea, euen to my selfe wil I marye the, in righteousnesse, in equyte, in louinge kindnesse and mercye.

20 In fayth also will I mary the vnto my selfe, and thou shalt know the Lorde.

21 At the same tyme will I shewe my selfe frendlye and gracious vnto the heauens, sayeth the Lorde, & the heauens shal helpe the earth,

22 and the earth shall helpe the corne, wyne and oyle, and they shall helpe Iesrael.

23 I will sowe them vpon earth, for a sede to mine owne selfe, & will haue mercye vpon her, that was without mercy. And to them, which were not my people, I wil say: thou arte my people: and he shal say: thou art my God.

## CHAPTER 3

THEN sayde the Lorde to me: Go yet thy waye, & vowe an aduouterous woman, whom thy neyghboure loueth, as the Lord doeth the children of Israell: how be it they haue respecte to straunge Goddes, and loue the wine kannes.

2 So I gat her for .xv. syluerlinges, & for an Homer & an halt of barley,

3 & sayde vnto her: Thou shalt bide wt me a long season: but se that thou playest not the harlot, and loke thou medle not with none other man, & then wyll I kepe my selfe for the.

4 Thus the children of Israell shall syt a great whyle without king and Prince, withoute offeringe and aulter, without prest and reuelacion.

5 But afterwarde shall the children of Israell conuerte, and seke the Lorde their God: and Dauid their kinge: & in the latter dayes, they shall worshyppe the Lorde, and hys louynge kindnesse.

## CHAPTER 4

HEARE the word of þe lorde o ye children of Israel. For the lord must punish them, that dwel in þe land. And why? There is no faithfulnes, there is no mercy there is no knoweledge of God in the lande:

2 but swearing, lyinge, manslaughter, theft, & aduoutry haue gotten the ouerhande, & one bloudgilthinesse foloweth another.

3 Therfore shall the land be in a miserable case, & al they þt dwel therin, shall mourne: the beastes in the felde, the foules in the ayr, & þe fishes in the sea shal dye.

4 Yet is there none, þe wyl chasten nor reproue another. The priestes which shoulde refourme other men, are become like the people.

5 Therfore stomblest thou in the day tyme & the prophet wt the in the night. I wil bringe thy mother to silence, & why?

6 my people perish, because they haue no knowledge. Seing then þt thou hast refused vnderstanding, therfore wil I refuse the also: so that thou shalt no more be my preste. And for so muche as thou hast forgotten the lawe of thy God, I wil also forget thy children.

7 The more they increased in þe multitude, the more they sinned against me, therfore will I chaunge their honoure into shame.

8 They eat vp the synnes of my people, and corage them in their wyckednesse.

9 Thus the prest is become lyke the people. Wherefore I wil punysh them for their wicked wayes & rewarde them accordinge to their owne ymagynacions.

10 They shall eate and not haue ynoughe: They haue vsed whordome, therfore shall they not prospere, and why? they haue forsaken the Lorde, and not regarded hym.

11 Whordome, wine and drockennesse take the herte

away.

12 My people aske councell at their stockes, their staffes must tell them. For an whoryshe minde hath disceyued them, so that they committe fornycacyon agaynst their God.

13 They make sacrifices vpon the hye mountaynes, and burne their incense vpon the hylles, yea, amonge the okes, groues & bushes, for there are good shadowes Therfore your doughters are become harlottes, and youre spouses haue broken their wedlocke,

14 I wyll not punishe youre doughters for beynge defyled, & youre brydes that became whores: seinge the fathers them selues haue medled wt harlottes & offered wt vnthriftes: but the people þt will not vnderstand, must be punished.

15 Though thou Israel art disposed to play the harlot, yet shouldest not thou haue offended, O Iuda: thou shouldest not haue runne to Galgala, nor haue gone vp to Bethauen, nor haue sworne, the Lord lyueth.

16 For Israel is gone backe like a wanton cow The Lord therfore shall make her fede, as the lambe that goeth astray.

17 And where as Ephraim is become partaker of Idols, wel, let him go.

18 Their dronckennes hath put them backe, and brought them to whordome. Their rulers loue rewardes, bring (say they) to their owne shame.

19 A wind shal take hold of their fethers & they shalbe confounded in their offeringes.

# CHAPTER 5

O ye priestes: hear this, take hede o thou houshold of Israel: geue eare, O thou kyngly house: for thys punyshemente will come vpon you, that are become a snare vnto Myzphah, and a spred net to the mount of Thabor.

2 They kyl sacryfyces by heapes to begyle the people therwith: therfore wyll I punyshe them al.

3 I know Ephraim well ynough, and Israel is not hyd from me: for Ephraim is become an harlot: and Israel is defiled.

4 They are not minded to turne vnto their God, for they haue an whoryshe herte, so that they can not know the Lorde.

5 But the pryde of Israell will be rewarded him in his fate, yea bothe Israel & Ephraim shal fal for their wyckednesse, and Iuda with them also.

6 They shall come with their shepe & bullockes to seke the Lorde, but they shall not fynde him, for he is gone from them.

7 As for the Lorde, they haue refused him, & broughte vp bastarde children: a moneth: therfore shall deuoure them wt their porcyons.

8 Blowe wt the shawmes at Gabea, & with the trompet in Ramah, crye out at Bethaueu vpon the yonsyde of BenIamin.

9 In the tyme of the plage shall Ephraim be layd wast, therfore did I faythfully warne the trybes of Israell.

10 Yet are the princes of Iuda become lyke them, þt remoue the landemarckes, therfore will I poure oute my wrath vpon them lyke water.

11 Ephraim is oppressed, and can haue no right of the lawe: for why? they folowe the doctrynes of men.

12 Therfore wyl I be vnto Ephraim as a moth and to the house of Iuda as a caterpyller.

13 When Ephraim saw his syckenesse, and Iuda hys dysease: Ephraim wente vnto Assur, and sent vnto kinge Iareb: yet coulde not he helpe you, nor ease you of youre payne.

14 I am vnto Ephraim as a lyon, and as a lyons whelpe to the house of Iuda. Euen I, I wyll spoyle them, and go my way. I will take them with me, & no man shall rescue them.

15 I wyll go, and returne to my place, tyll they waxe faynt and seke my.

# CHAPTER 6

IN their aduersite they shal seke me, and said: come, let vs turne againe to the lord: for he hathe smyten vs, & he shall heale vs:

2 He hath wounde vs, & he shall bind vs vp agayne after two dayes shall he quicken vs, in the thirde day he shal rayse vs vp, so that we shal lyue in his sight.

3 Then shall we haue vnderstanding, and endeuoure oure selues to knowe the Lorde. He shall go forth as the springe of the daye, & come vnto vs as the eueninge and morninge rayne vpon the earth.

4 O Ephraim, what shal I do vnto the? O Iuda, how shall I entreate the? seynge youre loue is like a morning cloude, and lyke a dew that goeth early awaye.

5 Therfore haue I cut doune the Prophetes, and let them be slayne for my wordes sake: so that thy punyshment shall come to lyghte.

6 For I haue pleasure in louinge kindnesse, and not in offerynge: yea, in þe knoweledge of God, more then in burnt sacryfyce.

7 But euen like as Adam did, so haue they broken my couenaunt, & set me at naught.

8 Galaad is a city of wycked doers, of malycious people and bloudshedders.

9 The multytude of the priestes is lyke an heape of theues murtherers and bloudthursty: for they haue wroughte abhomynacyon.

10 Horryble thinges haue I sene in the house of Israel, there playeth Ephraim the Harlot, and

Israel is defyled:

11 but Iuda shall haue an haruest for hym selfe, when I returne the captyuyte of my people.

## CHAPTER 7

When I vndertake to make Israel whole, then the vngracyousnes of Ephraim and the wickednes of Samaria commeth to lyght: then go they aboute with lyes. At home, they be theues: & withoute they fall to robbinge.

2 They consydre not in their hertes that I remembre all their wickednes. They go aboute with their owne inuencions, but I se them wel ynough.

3 They make the kinge & the princes, to haue pleasure in their wickednes and lyes.

4 All these burne in aduoutrye, as it were an ouen that the baker heateth, when he hath lefte kneadynge, till the dowe be leuended.

5 Euen so goeth it thys day with oure kinges & princes, for they beginne to be wodde droncken thorowe wine, they vse familarite with suche as disceyue him.

6 They with the ymaginacyon of their herte are lyke an ouen, their slepe is all the nyghte lyke the slepe of a baker, in the morninge is he as hote as the flamme of fyre,

7 they are altogether as hote as an ouen. They haue deuoured their owne iudges, all their kinges are fallen: yet is there none of them that calleth vpon me.

8 Therfore must Ephraim be mirte amonge the heathen. Ephraim is become lyke a cake, that no man turneth:

9 straungers haue deuoured his strength, yet he regardeth it not: he waxeth ful of gray hearres: yet will he not know it,

10 and the pryd of Israell is caste doune before their fare, yet wil they not turne to the Lord their God, nor seke him for all this.

11 Ephraim is lyke a doue, that is begyled, and hathe no herte. Nowe call they vpon the Egipcians, nowe go they to the Assyryans,

12 but whyle they be goynge here and there, I shall sprede my net ouer them, and draw them doune as the foules of the ayre: & accordinge as they haue bene warned, so will I punyshe them.

13 Wo be vnto them, for they haue forsaken me. They must be destroyed, for they haue set me at naught. I am he þt haue redemed them, and yet they dissemble with me.

14 They call not vpon me with their hertes, but lye houlinge vpon their beddes. Where as they come together; it is but for meate and drincke, and me wil they not obeye.

15 I haue taught them, and defended their arme, yet do they ymagin mischefe agaynst me.

16 They turne them selues, but not a right, and are becomen as a broken bowe. Their pryntes shal be slaine with the swerde, for the malyce of their tunges, such blasphemies haue they learned in the lande of Egipte.

## CHAPTER 8

Set the horne to thy mouthe, & blowe: get the swyftly (as an Aegle) vnto the house of the Lorde: for they haue broken my couenaunt, & transgressed my law.

2 Israel can say vnto me thou art my God, we know the,

3 but he hathe refused the thinge that is good, therfore shall the enemy folow vpon him.

4 They haue ordeyned kinges, but not thorowe me: they haue made princes, and I must not know of it. Of their siluer and golde haue they made them Images, to bringe them selues to destruccion.

5 Thy calf, O Samaria, shall be taken away. for my wrothfull indignacion is gone forthe agaynst the. How longe will it be, or they can be clensed?

6 For the calfe came from Israel, the worcke man made it, therfore can it be no God but euen to a spyders webbe shall the calfe of Samaria be turned.

7 They haue sown wind therfore shall they reape a storme. Their sede shal beare no corne, there shal no meel be made of their increase: thoughe they reape, yet shall straungers deuoure it vp.

8 Israel shal perysche, the Gentyles shall intreate him as a foule vessel.

9 Sence they wente vp to the Assirians, they are become lyke a wylde asse in the deserte. Ephraim geueth rewardes to get louers,

10 therfore are they scatred amonge the Heathen, there will I gather them vp. They shall sone be wery of the burthen of kinges & pryncen.

11 Ephraim hath made many aulters to do wickednes, therfore shall the aulters turne to his sinne.

12 Thoughe I shew them my lawe, neuer so muche, they count it but straunge doctrine.

13 Whereas they do sacryfice, offeringe the fleshe and eatinge it: the Lorde wyll haue no pleasure therin: but wyll remembre their wickednes, and punyshe their sinnes. Israel turneth agayne into Egipte,

14 they haue forgotten him that made them, they buylde churches, and Iuda maketh manye stronge cities: therfore will I sende a fyre into their cities, and it shall consume their places.

## CHAPTER 9

Do not thou tryumphe, O Israel, make no boastinge

# HOSEA

more then the Heathen, for thou hast committed aduoutrye againste thy God: straung rewardes hast thou loued more then al þe corneflores.

2 Therfore shal they no more enioy the corneflores & winepresses, & their swete wine shall fayle them.

3 They will not dwell in the Lordes lande, but Ephraim turneth agayne into Egypte, and eateth vncleane thinges amonge the Assirians.

4 They poure oute no wyne for a drinckofferinge vnto the Lord, neyther geue they him their flain offeringes: but they be vnto them as mourners meates, wherin all they that eate them, are defyled. For the breade that they haue suche luste vnto, shall not come into the house of the Lorde.

5 What wyl ye do then in the solempne daies, and in the feaste of the Lorde?

6 Lo, they shall get them awaye for the destruccyon: Egipte shal receyue them, & Noph shall bury them. The netles shal ouergrowe their pleasaunt goodes, and burres shalbe in their tabernacles.

7 Be ye sure (O Israel) the tyme of visitacyon is come, the dayes of recompensynge are at hande. As for the Prophete, ye holde hym for a foole: and him that is ryche in the spyrite for a mad man: so great is youre wickednes and malice.

8 Ephraim hath made him selfe a watchman of my God, a prophet þt is become a snare to do hurte in euery strete and abhomynacyon in the house of his God.

9 They be gone to farre, & haue destroyed themselues, like as they dyd afore tyme at Gabaa. Therfore their wyckednes shalbe remembred, and their synnes punyshed.

10 I founde Israel lyke the grapes in the wildernes, & saw their fathers as the fyrst figges in the top of the fygge tre. But they are gone to Baal Peor, & runne away from me to that shamefull Idoll, and are become as abhominable as their louers.

11 Ephraim flyeth lyke a byrde, so shall their glory also. In so muche, that they shall neyther beget, conceyue nor beare children.

12 And though they bring vp any yet wyll I make them chyldelesse among men. Yea, wo shall come to them, when I departe from them.

13 Ephraim (as me thyncke) is planted in welthynesse, lyke as Tirus, but nowe must she bring her owne children forth to the manslayer.

14 O Lorde thou shalt geue them: what shalte thou geue them? geue them an vnfrutefull wombe and drye brestes.

15 All their wyckednesse is done at Galgal, there do I abhorre them. For the vngracyousnes of their owne inuencyons. I will driue them oute of my house. I will loue them no more, for all their princes are vnfaythfull.

16 Ephraim is hewen doune, their rote is dryed vp, so that they shal brynge no more frute: yea and thoughe they brynge forth any, yet will I slaye euen the best beloued frute of their body.

17 My god shal cast them awaye, for they haue not bene obedient vnto hym, therefore shal they go astray amonge the Heathen.

## CHAPTER 10

ISRAEL was a goodly vyne, but he hath brought forth vnprofytable frute: yea, the more frute he had, þe mo aulters he made: the more good I dyd to their lande, the more frendshyppe shewed they to their Images.

2 Their herte is deuyded, therfore wyll they be destroyed. The Lorde shall breake doune their Images, he shall destroye their aulters.

3 Then shall they saye: we haue no kinge, for why? we haue not feared the Lorde. And what shall then the kinge do to vs?

4 They comen together, and sweare vayn othes: they be confederate together, therefore groweth their punyshement, as the wedes in the forowes of the lande.

5 They þt dwell in Samaria haue worshipped the calfe of Bethauen: therfore shall the people mourne ouer them: yea, and the priestes also, that in their welthynesse reioysed wyth them: and why? it shall passe awaye from them.

6 It shalbe brougthe to the Assyryans, for a present vnto kinge Iareb. Ephraim shal receyue full punishement: Israel shalbe confounded for his owne ymaginacyons.

7 Samaria with his kynge shall vanyshe awaye as the scomme in the water.

8 The hye places of Auen where Israel do synne, shalbe caste doune: thystles and thornes shall growe vpon their aulters. Then shall they saye to the mountaynes: couer vs, and to the hylles, fall vpon vs.

9 O Israel, thou hast synned as Gabaa did afore tyme, where they remayneth, shoulde not the battel then come vpon the wicked children, as wel as vpon the Gabaonites?

10 I wyl chasten them, euen after myne owne desyre, the people shalbe gathered together ouer them, when I punishe them for their greate wyckednesse.

11 Ephraim was vnto me, as a cowe that is vsed to go to plowe, therfore I loued him, & fel vpon his fayre neck, I droue Ephraim, Iuda plowed, and Iacob played the husbande man,

12 that they myght sowe vnto righteousnes, and reape the frutes of weldoynge that they might plowe vp their fresh lande, & seke the Lorde, tyll he came, and learned them ryghteousnes.

13 But nowe they haue plowed them wyckednesse, therfore shall they reape synne, & eat the frute of lyes. Seynge thou puttest thy confydence in thyne owne wayes, and leanest to the multitude of thy worthyes:

14 there shall growe a sedicion amonge thy people. All thy stronge cities shalbe layd waste, euen as Salmana was destroyed with his familiers, thorow him that was auenged of Arbell, in the day of batell, where the mother perysshed wt her children.

15 Euen so shall it go with you (O Bethel) because of youre malicious wickednes. Lyke as the morninge goeth awaye, so shall the kinge of Israel passe.

## CHAPTER 11

WHEN Israel was younge, I loued him: & called him my sonne out of the lande of Egipte.

2 But the more they were called the more they went backe, offeringe vnto Idols, and ceasinge Images.

3 I learned Ephraim to go, & bare them in mine armes, but they regarded not me, that would haue helped them.

4 I led them with coardes of frendshyppe, and bandes of loue. I was euen he, that layed the yocke vpon their neckes. I gaue them my foder my self,

5 that they should not go againe into Egipt. And nowe is Assur their kinge: For they woulde not turne vnto me.

6 Therfore shall the swerde beginne in their cities, the stoare that they haue laied vp, shalbe destroyed and eaten: and that because of their own ymaginacyons.

7 My people had no lust to turne vnto me, their prophetes laye the yocke vpon them, but they ease them not of their burthen.

8 What greate thinges haue I geuen the, O Ephraim? how faythfully haue I defended the, O Israel? haue I dealt wt the as with Adama? or haue I entreated the lyke Seboim? No, my herte is otherwyse minded. Yea, my mercye is to feruent:

9 therfore haue I not turned me to destroye Ephraim in my wrothfull displeasure. For I am God and no man, I am euen that holy one in the middest of the, thoughe I came not within the cyty.

10 The Lorde roareth lyke a Lyon, that they maye folowe him: yea as a lyon roareth he, that they may be afrayed like the children of the sea:

11 that they may be scatred away from Egipt, as men scarre byrdes: & frayed away (as doues vse to be) from the Assirians lande: & that because I woulde haue them to tary at home, sayeth the Lorde.

12 But Ephraim goeth about me with lyes, & the house of Israel dissembleth. Onelye Iuda beholdeth him with God, and with the true holy thinges.

## CHAPTER 12

EPHRAIM kepeth the ayre, and folowed after the east winde: he is euer increasinge lyes & destruccyon. They be confederate with the Assirians, their oyle is caried into Egypte.

2 The Lorde hath a courte to holde with Iuda, and wil punishe Iacob. After their owne wayes and accordinge to their owne inuencyons shall he recompence them.

3 He toke his brother by the hele, when he was yet in his mothers wombe: & in his strengthe he wrestled with God.

4 He stroue with the Aungel, and gat the victorye, so that he praid and desyred hym. He founde him at Bethel, & there he talked with vs.

5 Yet the Lorde God of Hostes, euen the Lorde hym selfe remembred him.

6 Then turne to thy God, kepe mercye and equyte, and hope still in thy God.

7 But the marchaunte hath a false weyght in his hande, he hath a pleasure to occupye extorsion.

8 Ephraim thinketh thus: Tush, I am ryche, I haue good ynoughe. In all my worckes shall not one fawte be founde, that I haue offended.

9 Yet am I the Lorde thy God, euen as when I brought the oute of the lande of Egipte, and fet the in thy tentes, & as in þe hye feaste dayes.

10 I haue spoken thorow the prophetes, and shewed diuerse visions, and declared my self by the ministracyon of the prophetes.

11 But at Galaad is the abhominacyon, they are fallen to vanitye. At Galgal they haue slayne oxen: and as many heapes of stones as they had in their lande forowes, so manye aulters haue they made.

12 Iacob fled into the lande of Siria, and Israel serued for a wyfe, and for a wyfe he kepte shepe.

13 By a prophete the Lorde brought them oute of Egipt, and by a prophet he preserued them.

14 But Ephraim hathe prouoked hym to displeasure thorow his obhominacious, therfore shall his bloude be poured vpon him self and the Lord his God shall rewarde him his blasphemies.

## CHAPTER 13

THE abhominacion of Ephraim is come also into

# HOSEA

Israel: he is gone backe to Baal, therfore must he dye.

2 And now they synne more and more: of their syluer, they make them molten Images, lyke the Idoles of the Heathen, and yet al is nothinge but the worcke of the craftesmre. Notwithstandinge they preach of the same: who so wil kisse the calues, offreth to men.

3 Therfore they shalbe as the morning cloud, & as the dew that early passeth away, & lyke as dust that the wynde taketh awaye from the floure, and as smoke that goeth oute of the chymney.

4 I am the Lorde thy God, whiche broughte the out of the land of Egypte: that thou shouldest know no God, but me onely, & that thou shouldest haue no Sauiour but onlye me.

5 I toke diligent hede of the in the wildernesse þt drye land.

6 But when they were wel fedde & had ynough, they waxed proude, and forgat me.

7 Therfore wyll I be vnto them as a lyon, & as a leoparde in the waye to the Assirians.

8 I wil come vpon them as a she beer, that is robbed of her whelpes, & I will breake that stubburne herte of theirs. There wyll I deuoure them as a lyon: yea the wilde beastes shall teare them.

9 O Israel, thou doest but destroye thy selfe, in me onely is thy helpe.

10 Where are thy kinges now, that shoulde helpe the in all thy cyties? Yea, and thy iudges, of whom thou saydest: geue me a kynge and prynces?

11 well I gaue the a king in my wrath, & in my dyspleasure will I take him from the agayne.

12 The wyckednesse of Ephraim is bounde together and hys sinne lyed hid.

13 Therfore shall sorowes come vpon him, as vpon a woman that trauayleth. An vndyscrete sonne is he: for he consydreth not, that he shoulde not haue bene able to haue endured in the tyme of hys byrth,

14 had not I defended hym from the graue, and delyuered hym from deathe. O death, I wyl be thy death: O hel, I wil be thy stynge.

15 Yet can I se no comforte, for when he is nowe the goodlyest among þe brethren, the East wynde (euen the wynd of the Lorde) shall come doune from the wyldernesse, and drye vp hys condytes, and drincke vp hys welles: he shall spoyle the treasure of all pleasaunte vessels.

16 As for Samaria, they shalbe made waste, and why? they are disobedient vnto their god. They shal perysh with the sweard, their children shalbe slayne, and theyr wemen greate with chylde shalbe rypt vp.

## CHAPTER 14

O Israel, turne the nowe, vnto the Lorde thy God, for thou hast taken a greate fall thorow thy wickednes.

2 Take these wordes with you, when ye turne to the Lorde, & saye vnto him: O forgeue vs all our sinnes, receyue vs gracyouslye, and then wyl we offre the bullockes of oure lyppes vnto the.

3 Assur shalbe no more oure helper, nether wyl we ryde vpon horses any more. As for the worckes of our handes, we wil no more cal vpon them: For it is thou that arte oure God, thou shewest euer mercye vnto the fatherlesse.

4 O (yf they wolde do thys) I shulde heale theyr sores: yea wyth al my herte wolde I loue them: so that my wrath shuld cleane be turned awaye from them.

5 Yea, I wolde be vnto Israel as the dewe, and he shulde growe as the lylye, and hys rote shulde breake oute as Lybanus.

6 His braunches shulde sprede oute abroade, and be as fayre as the olyue tre, and smell sa Lybanus.

7 They that dwell vnder hys shadowe, shulde come agayne, and grow vp as the corne, and floryshe as the vyne: he shulde haue as good a name, as the wyne of Lybanus.

8 O Ephraim what haue I to do wt Idols anye more? I wyll graciously heare him, and lede hym forthe. I will be vnto the as a grene Fyrre tre, vpon me shalt thou find thy trute.

9 Who so is wyse, shall vnderstande thys: & he that is ryght instructe, wyll regarde it. For the wayes of the Lorde are ryghteous, suche as be Godlye wil walcke in them: As for the wicked, they wyll stomble therin.

# Joel

## CHAPTER 1

THYS is the worde of þe lorde that came vnto Ioel þe sonne of Phatuel:

2 Heare O ye elders, pondre this well, al ye that dwell in the lande, yf euer there happened suche a thynge in youre dayes, or in the dayes of youre fathers.

3 Tell youre chyldren of it, and let them shew it vnto theyr chyldren, & so they to certifye their posteryte there of.

4 Loke what the caterpyller hath lefte, that hath the greshopper eaten vp: what the greshopper lefte, that hath the locuste eaten vp: & what the locuste hath lefte, that hath the blastyng consumed.

5 Wake vp ye dronkardes, & wepe: mourne all ye wynesuppers, because of youre swete wyne, for it shall be taken away from your mouth.

6 Yea, a myghtye and an innumerable people shal come vp into my lande: these haue teeth lyke the teethe of Lyons, and chaftbones lyke the lyonesses.

7 They shal make my vyneyarde waste, they shall pyll of the barckes of my fygge trees, strype them bare, cast them away, & make the braunches whyt.

8 Make thy mone as a virgyne doth þe gyrdes her selfe with sacke, because of her brydegrome,

9 For the meat and drinckofferyng shal be taken awaye from the house of the Lorde: and the priestes the Lordes mynysters shall mourne.

10 The felde shalbe wasted, the lande shalbe in a myserable case: for the corne shalbe destroyed, the swete wyne shall come to confusyon, and the oyle vtterlye desolate.

11 The husband men and the wyne gardeners shall loke pyteously & make lamentacyon, for the wheat wyne, and barley & because the haruest vpon the felde is so cleane destroyed.

12 The grape gatherers shall make greate mone, when the vyneyard & figgetrees be so vtterly wasted. Yea all the pomgarnettes, palmetrees, appeltrees & the other trees of the felde shall wyther awaye. Thus the mery cheare of the chyldren of men, shall come to confusyon.

13 Gyrde you, & make youre mone, O ye prestes: mourne ye mynysters of the aulter: go youre way in, and slepe in sackcloth, O ye offycers of my God: for the meate and drinckofferynge shall be taken awaye from the house of youre God.

14 Proclame a fastynge, call the congregacyon, gather the elders & all the inhabiters of the lande together into the house of the Lord your God, & crye vnto the Lorde:

15 alas, alas, for thys daye. And why? the daye of the Lorde is at hand, and commeth as a destroyer from the almighty.

16 Shall not þe meates be taken awaye before oure eyes, the myrthe also & ioye from the house of oure God?

17 The sede shall peryshe in the grounde, the garners shal lye waste, þe floures shalbe broken doune for the corne shalbe destroyed.

18 O what a fyghynge make the cattell? the bullockes are very euyll lykynge, because they haue no pasture: and the shepe are famyshed awaye.

19 O Lord, to the will I crye: for the fyre hath consumed the goodly pastures of the wildernesse, and the flamme hath brente vp all the trees of the felde.

20 Yea, the wylde beastes crye also vnto the: for the water ryuers are dryed vp and the fyre hath consumed the pastures of the wyldernes.

## CHAPTER 2

BLOWE oute the trompet in Sion, & crye vpon my holy

hyl, that al suche as dwell in the land, may tremble at it, for the daye of the Lorde commeth, and is harde at hande:

2 a darcke daye, a gloomynge daye, a cloudye daye, yea & a stormy daye, lyke as the mornynge spredeth oute vpon the hylles: Namely, a great and myghtye people; suche as haue not bene sence the begynnynge, neither shal be after them for euer more.

3 Before hym shall be a consumynge fyre, and behynde him a burnyng flamme. The land shal be as a garden of pleasure before him, but behynde hym shall it be a very waste wyldernes, and there is no man, that shall escape hym.

4 They are to loke vpon lyke barded horses, and runne lyke horse men.

5 They skyppe vp vpon the hylles, as it were the sounde of charettes, as þe flamme of fyre that consumeth the strawe, and as a myghtye people ready to the battell.

6 The folcke shalbe afrayed of hym, all faces shalbe as blacke as a pot.

7 These shal runne lyke gyauntes, and leape ouer the walles lyke men of warre. Euerye man in hys goynge shall kepe hys araye, and not go oute of hys Path.

8 There shall not one dryue another, but eche shall kepe hys owne waye. They shall breake in at the wyndowes, and not be hurte.

9 They shall come into the cytye, and runne vpon the walles: They shal clymme vp vpon þe houses, & slyppe in at the wyndowes lyke a thefe.

10 The earth shall quake before him, yea, the heauens shalbe moued: The sunne & moue shall be darckened, and the starres shal wythdraw theyr shyne,

11 The Lorde shall shewe his voyce before hys hoste, for hys hoste is greate, strong and myghtye to fulfyll hys commaundement. This is that greate and merueylous fearefull daye of the Lorde: And who is able to abyde it.

12 Now therfore sayeth the Lorde: Turne you vnto me wyth all youre hertes, wyth fastynge, wepynge and mournynge,

13 rente your hertes & not youre clothes. Turne you vnto the Lorde youre God, for he is gracyons and mercyfull, longe sufferyng and of great compassyon, & ready to pardone wickednes.

14 Then (no doute) he also shall turne, & forgeue: and after hys chasteninge, he shall let youre increase remayne, for meat & dryncke offerynges vnto the Lorde youre God?

15 Blowe oute with the trompet in Syon, proclame a fastynge, cal the congregacyon,

16 and gather the people together: warne the congregacyon, gather the elders, brynge the chyldren & suckelynges together. Let the brydgrome go forth of his chambre, & the bryde oute of her closet.

17 Let the prestes serue the Lorde betwixte the porche & the aulter, weping and saying: be fauourable (O Lorde) be fauourable vnto thy people: let not thyne herytage be broughte to suche confusyon, leste the Heathen be Lordes therof. Wherfore shulde they saye amonge the Heathen: where is nowe theyr God?

18 Then shall the Lorde be gelous ouer hys lande, & spare his people:

19 yea, the Lorde shall aunswere, and say vnto his people: Behold, I will sende you corne, wyne & oyle, so that ye shall haue plentye of them: & I wyll no more geue you ouer to be a reprofe amonge the heathen.

20 Agayne, as for hym of the Norh, I shal dryue hym farre from you: & shute him out into a drye and waste lande, hys face towarde the east sea, and hys hynder partes towarde the vtmost sea. The styncke of hym shall go vp, and his fylthy corrupcyon shall fal vpon himselfe, because he hath dealte so proudelye.

21 Feare not (O lande) but be glad, and reioyse, for the Lorde wyll do greate thynges.

22 Be not ye afrayed nether (O ye beastes of the felde) for the pastures shalbe greue, and the trees shall beare theyr frute: the fyggetrees & vyneyardes shall geue theyr encrease.

23 Be glad then (O ye chyldren of Syon) & reioyse in the Lorde youre God, for he hathe geuen you a teacher of ryghtuousnes: and he it is þt shall sende you doune shuwers of rayne, early and late in the fyrste moueth,

24 so that the garners shalbe full of corne, and the presses plenteous in wyne and oyle.

25 And as for the yeares þt the greshopper, locuste, blastynge, & caterpyller (my greate hoste, whiche I sente amonge you) haue eaten vp, I shal restore them to you agayne,

26 so that ye shall haue ynoughe to eate, and be satisfyed, and prayse the name of the Lorde youre God, that so meruelouslye hath dealte wyth you. And my people shal neuer be confounded anye more.

27 Ye shall well knowe, that I am in the myddeste of Israel, and that I am youre God: yea, & that there is none other, & my people shal no more be broughte to confusyon.

28 After this, wil I poure out my sprete vpon all fleshe: and your sonnes & your doughters shall prophecye: youre olde men shall dreame dreames, & youre yong men shal se visyons

29 yea in those dayes I wyll poure out my sprite vpon seruauntes and maydens.

30 I wyll shewe wonders in heauen aboue, and tokens in the earth beneth: bloude and fyre, and the vapour of smoke.

31 The sunne shalbe turned into darcknes, & the mone into bloude: before the greate & notable daye of the Lorde come.

32 And þe time shal come, that whosoeuer calleth on the name of the Lorde, shalbe saued. For vpon þe mount Syon & at Ierusalem, there shalbe a saluacion, lyke as the Lorde hath promysed, yea & among the other remnaunte, whome the Lorde shall call.

## CHAPTER 3

FOR take hede: in those dayes & at the same tyme, when I turne agayne the captyuyte of Iuda & Ierusalem:

2 I shal gather al people together, & brynge them in þe valleye of Iosaphat: and there wyl I reason with them: because of my people & herytage of Israel, whom they haue scatred aboute in the nacyons, and parted my lande,

3 yea they haue cast lottes for my people the yonge men haue they set in the bordell house, and solde the Damsels for wine, þt they myghte haue to drincke.

4 Thou Tyrus & Sidon and all ye borders of the Philistines: what haue ye to do with me? Wil ye defye me? wel yf ye wil nedes defye me, I shal recompence you, euen vpon youre head, & þt right shortly:

5 for ye haue taken awaye my syluer and gold, my fayre & goodly Iewels, & brought them into youre goddes houses.

6 The children also of Iuda and Ierusalem haue ye solde vnto the Grekes, that ye myght brynge them farre from the borders of theyr owne countrees.

7 Beholde therfore, I wyll rayse them oute of the place, where ye haue solde them, & wyl rewarde you euen vpon youre heade.

8 Youre sonnes & your doughters wyll I sell thorowe the handes of the chyldren of Iuda, & so they shal geue them forth to sel, vnto them of Saba, a people of a farre countre, for the Lorde hym selfe hath sayde it.

9 Crye out these thinges among the Gentiles, proclame warre, wake vp the gyauntes, let them drawe nye, let them come vp all the lustye warryours of them.

10 Make you sweardes of youre plowshares, and speares of youre sycles & sythes. Let the weake man saye: I am stronge.

11 Mustre you, and come, all ye heathen round about: gather you together, there shall the Lorde laye all thy gyauntes to the grounde.

12 Let the people aryse, & get them to the valleye of Iosaphat, for there wyll I sit, & iudge all Heathen rounde about.

13 Laye to youre sythes, for the haruest is rype: come, get you doune: the winepresse is ful, yea the wynepresses runne ouer, for theyr wickednesse is waxen greate.

14 In the valleye appoynted, there shalbe many, many people: for the daye of the Lorde is nye in the valleye appoynted.

15 The sunne and mone shalbe darkened, & the starres shal withdrawe theyr light.

16 The Lorde shal roare oute of Syon, and crye oute of Ierusalem, that the heauens & the earthe shall quake wythal. But the Lorde shalbe a defence vnto his owne people, & a refuge for the chyldren of Israel.

17 Thus shall ye knowe, that I the Lorde youre God dwell vpon my holy mounte of Syon. Then shall Ierusalem be holy, and there shall no straungers go thorowe her any more.

18 Then shall the mountaines droppe swete wyne, and the hylles shall flowe with mylcke. All the ryuers of Iuda shall haue water ynough, & out of the Lordes house there shal flowe a spryng to water the broke of Sitim:

19 but Egipt shalbe layed waste, and Edom shalbe desolate: because they haue dealte so cruelly with þe chyldren of Iuda, and shed innocente bloude in theyr lande.

20 Agayne, Iuda shalbe inhabyted for euermore, and Ierusalem from generacion to generacyon:

21 for I wil not leaue theyr bloud vnauenged. And the Lorde shal dwel in Syon.

# Amos

## CHAPTER 1

1 These are the sermons that were shewed vnto Amos (whiche was one of the shepeherdes at Thecua) vpon Israel, in the tyme of Osiah kynge of Iuda, and in the tyme of Ieroboam the sonne of Ioah kynge of Israel, two yeare before the earthquake.

2 And he sayde: The Lorde shall roare oute of Syon, and shewe hys voyce from Ierusalem: so that the pastures of the shepherdes shalbe in a myserable case, and the tope of Charmell dryed vp.

3 Thus sayth the Lord: for thre & foure wyckednesses of Damascus, I wil not spare her, because they haue throshed Galaad with yron flales:

4 But I wyll sende a fyre into the house of Hazael, the same shal consume the palaces of Benadab.

5 Thus wyll I breake the barres of Damascus, and rote out the inhabyter from the felde of Auen, & hym that holdeth the scepter, out of the pleasaunt house: so that the people shalbe dryuen oute of fayre Syrya, sayeth the Lord.

6 Thus saith the Lord: For thre and foure wyckednesses of Gaza, I wyll not spare her: because they make the presoners yet more captyue, & haue driue them into the lande of Edom.

7 Therfore wyl I send a fyre into the walles of Gaza, whiche shall deuoure her houses.

8 I wyl rote out them the dwel at Asood & hym the holdeth the scepter of Ascalon, and stretche oute myne hande ouer Accaron, that the remnaunte of the Phylystines shal peryshe sayth the Lorde.

9 Thus sayeth the Lorde: For thre and foure wyckednesses of the cytye of Tyre, I wil not spare her, because they haue increased the captyuite of the Edomytes, and haue not remembred the brotherly couenaunt.

10 Therfore wil I sende a fyre into the walles of Tyre, that shal consume her palaces.

11 Thus sayth the Lorde: For thre and foure wickednesses of Edom I wyl not spare him, because he persecuted hys brother wyth the swearde, destroyed his mothers wombe, bare hatred very longe, and so kepte indignacyon alwaye by hym.

12 Therfore wyll I sende a fyre into Theman, which shal deuoure the palaces of Bosra.

13 Thus sayeth the Lorde: For thre and foure wyckednesses of the children of Ammon I wil not spare them, because they rypte vp the wemen greate with childe in Galaad, to make the borders of theyr landes the wyder.

14 Therefore I wyl kyndle a fyre in the walles of Rabbath that shal consume her palaces: with a great crie, in the daye of batel, in tempest & in the daye of storme,

15 so that their kinge shall go into captyuyte he and hys pryncers together, sayeth the Lorde.

## CHAPTER 2

1 Thus sayeth the Lorde: For thre & foure wyckednesses of Moab, I wil not spare him: because he brente the bones of the kyng of Edom to ashes.

2 Therfor wil I sende a fyre into Moab, which shal consume the palaces of Carioth, so that Moab shal perysh with a noyse, & the sounde of a shawme.

3 I wyl rote oute the iudge from amonge them, & slaye all hys pryncers with him, sayeth the lord.

4 Thus sayth the Lorde: for thre and foure wickednesses of Iuda, I wil not spare hym: because he hath cast a syde the lawe of the Lord, & not kepte his commaundementes: for why, they wolde nedes be disceyued with the lyes, that theyr forefathers folowed.

5 Therfore wyl I sende a fyre into Iuda, whiche shall consume the palaces of Ierusalem.

6 Thus sayth the Lorde: For thre and foure wickednesses of Israel, I wyl not spare hym:

because he hath solde the ryghteous for money, and the poore for shues.

7They treade vpon poore mens heades, in the duste of the earthe, & croke the wayes of the meke. The sonne and the father go to the harlot, to dyshonoure thy holye name,

8they lye besyde euery aulter vpon clothes taken to pledge, and in the house of theyr Goddes they drincke the wyne of the oppressed.

9Yet destroyed I the Amorite before them, that was as hye as the Cedre trees, and as stronge as the okes: notwithstandynge I destroied his frute from aboue, and his rote from vnder.

10Agayne: I broughte you oute of the lande of Egypte, and led you .xl. yeares thorowe the wyldernesse, that ye myghte haue the Amorytes lande in possession.

11I raysed vp prophetes amonge your children, and absteyners among youre younge men. Is it not so. O ye chyldren of Israel, sayeth the Lorde?

12But ye gaue the abstayners wyne to drincke, yea ye commaunded the Prophetes, sayinge: Prophecye not.

13Beholde, I will crashe you in sonder, lyke as a wayne crassheth, that is full of sheaues, 14so that the swifte shall not escape, nether the strong be able to do anye thynge: no, the gyaunt shal not saue hys owne lyfe.

15The archer shal not abyde, and the swyfte of fote shall not escape. The horsman shal not saue hys lyfe

16& he that is as manlye of stomacke as a gyaunte, shall in that day be fayne to runne hys waye naked, sayeth the Lorde.

## CHAPTER 3

1Heare, what the Lorde speaketh vnto you (O ye chyldren of Israel) namely, vnto all the tribes whome I broughte oute of Egypte, and sayd:

2you only haue I accepted from all the generacyons of the earthe: therfore wyl I vyset you in all youre wickednesses.

3Maye twayne walke together, excepte they be agreed amonge them selues?

4Doth a lyon roare in the woodde, excepte he haue a praye? Or cryeth a lyons whelpe oute of hys denne, excepte he haue gotten somthing?

5Doth a byrde fall in a snare vpon the earthe, where no fouler is? Taketh a man hys snare vp from the grounde, afore he catche somwhat?

6Crye they oute alarum wyth the trompet in the cytye, and the people not afrayed? Commeth there anye plage in a cytye withoute it be the Lordes doynge?

7Nowe doth the Lorde God no maner of thynge, but he telleth hys secrete before vnto hys seruauntes the Prophetes.

8When a lyon roareth, who wyll not be afrayed? Seynge then that the Lord God him selfe speaketh, who wyll not prophecye?

9Preache in the palaces at Asdod, and in the palaces of the lande of Egypte, and saye: gather you together vpon the mountaynes of Samaria, so shall ye se greate murther and vyolente oppressyon amonge them, for why, they regarde not the thyng that is ryght

10saith the Lorde: they gather together euyll gotten goodes, and laye vp robbery in theyr houses.

11Therfore thus sayth the Lorde God. This lande shalbe troubled and beseged rounde aboute, thy strength shalbe plucte from the, & thy palaces robbed.

12Thus sayeth the Lorde lyke as an hyrdeman taketh two legges or a pece of an eare oute of the lions mouth: Euen so the chyldren of Israel (that dwell in Samaria, hauynge theyr couches in the corner, and theyr beddes at Damascus) shalbe plucte awaye.

13Heare, and beare recorde in the house of Iacob (sayeth the Lorde GOD of hostes)

14that when I begynne to vyset the wickednes of Israel, I wyll viset the aulters at Bethell also, so that the hornes of the aulter shalbe broken of, and fall to the grounde.

15As for the wynter house and sommer house I wyll smyte them doune, and the houses of Iuery, yea, & many other houses shal perysh, and be destroyed, sayeth the Lorde.

## CHAPTER 4

1O heare thys worde ye fat kyne, that be vpon the hil of Samaria: ye that do poore men wronge, and oppresse the nedy: ye that saye to your Lordes: bring hyther, let vs drincke.

2Therfore the Lorde hath sworne by his holinesse. The dayes shal come vpon you, that ye shalbe lyft vp vpon speares, & your posteryte caryed away in fyshers panyers.

3Ye shall get you out at the gappes one after another, and in Armon shall ye be caste awaye, sayeth the Lorde.

4Ye came to Bethell for to worke vngracyousnes, and haue increased youre synnes at Galgal: ye broughte youre sacryfyces in the mornynge, and youre tythes vnto the thyrde daye.

5Ye made a thanke offerynge of leuen, ye promysed, fre wyl offerynges, and proclamed them. Suche luste had ye, O ye chyldren of Israel, sayeth the Lorde God.

6Therfore haue I geuen you ydle teeth in all youre cytyes, and carnesse of bread in all your places, yet wil ye not turne vnto me, sayeth the Lorde.

7When here were but thre monethes vnto the haruest I wythhelde the rayne from you: yea I rayned vpon one cytye, and not vpon another, one pece of grounde was moystured wyth rayne, and the grounde that I rayned not vpon was drye.

8Wherfore two, yea thre cytes came vnto one to dryncke water: but they were not satisfyed, yet wyll ye not, turne vnto me, sayeth the Lorde.

9I haue smiten you with drouth & blasting: and loke howe manye orchardes, vineyardes, fyggetrees & olyue trees ye had: the caterpyller hath eaten them vp. But yet wil ye not turne vnto me, sayeth the Lorde.

10Pestylence haue I sente amonge you, as I dyd in Egipt: youre yong men haue I slayne with the swerd, and caused youre horses be taken captyue: I made the stynkynge sauoure of youre tentes to come vp into youre nostrels: Yet wyll ye not turne vnto me, sayeth the Lorde.

11Some of you haue I ouerthrowen, as I ouerthrew Sodome and Gomorre, so that ye were as brand plucte oute of the fyre. Yet wyll ye not turne vnto me, sayeth the Lorde.

12Therfore thus wyl I handle the agayn, O Israel, yea, euen thus wyl I handle the. Make the ready then to mete thy God, O Israel.

13For lo, he maketh the mountaynes, he ordeyneth the wynde, he sheweth man what he is aboute to do: he maketh the mornynge & the darcknesse: he treadeth vpon the hye places of the earthe: the Lorde God of hostes is hys name.

# CHAPTER 5

1Heare thys worde, O ye house of Israel, & why I must make thys moue for you:

2The vyrgyn Israel shall fal, and neuer ryse vp agayne: she shalbe cast donne vpon her owne grounde, and no man shall helpe her vp.

3For thus sayth the Lorde God: Where as there dwelt a .M. in one citie there shalbe lefte scarce an hundreth therein: & where there dwelt an .C. there shal scarce ten be left for the house of Israel.

4Neuerthelesse, thus sayth the Lorde vnto the house of Israel: Seke after me, and ye shall lyue,

5but seke not after Bethel. Come not at Galgal, & go not to Bersaba, for Galgal shalbe caryed awaye captyue, & Bethel shal come to naught.

6Seke the Lorde, that ye maye lyue, leste the house of Ioseph be brente with fyre, and consumed, & lest there be none to quenche Bethel.

7Ye turne the lawe to worm wode, and caste doune ryghtuousnes vnto the grounde.

8The Lorde maketh the seuen starres and the Dryons, he turneth the nighte into daye, and of the daye he maketh darcknesse. He calleth the waters of the sea, and poureth them oute vpon the playne grounde: the Lorde is hys name:

9He rayseth destruccyon vpon the myghty people, and bringeth doune the stronge hold:

10but they owe hym euill wil, that reproueth them openly, and who so telleth them the playn truth they abhorre hi

11For so muche then as ye oppresse the poore, & robbe him of his best sustenaunce: therfore, where as ye haue buylded houses of square stone, ye shall not dwel in them. Maruelous pleasaunt vyneyardes shal ye plante, but the wyne of them shall ye not drynck: and why?

12as for the multitude of your wickednesses and your stout synnes, I know them ryghte well. Euemyes are ye of the ryghtuous, ye take rewardes, ye oppresse the poore in iudgement.

13Therfore the wyse muste nowe be fayne to holde hys tunge, so wicked a time is it.

14Seke after the thynge that is good, & not euill, so shall ye lyue: yea the Lorde God of hostes shall be wyth you, accordyng to your owne desyre.

15Hate the euil, and loue the good: set vp right agayne in the porte: & (no doute) the Lorde God of hostes shal be mercyful vnto the remnaunt of Ioseph,

16If no (sayeth the Lorde God, the God of hostes) there shal be mournynge in all stretes, yea they shal say in euerye strete: alas, alas. They shal cal the husband man to lamentacyon, and suche as can mourne to mournynge.

17In all vyneiardes there shall be heuynesse, for I wil come among you, sayeth the Lorde.

18Wo be vnto them that desyre the daye of the Lorde, Wherfore wold ye haue it? As for the daye of the Lorde, it shal be darcke and not cleare:

19Yea lyke as when a man runneth from a lyon, and a beer meteth with him: or when he commeth into the house, and leaneth hys hande vpon the wall, a serpent diteth hym.

20Shall not the daye of the Lord be darcke, and not cleare? shall it not be cloudye, and no shyne in it?

21I hate and abhorre youre holye dayes, & where as ye cense me when ye come together I wyll not accepte it:

22And though ye offre me brentofferynges, and meateofferynges, yet haue I no pleasure therein. As for youre fat thanckeofferinges, I wil not loke vpon them.

23Awaye with that noyse of thy songes, I wyl not heare thy playes of musycke:

24but se that equite flowe as the water, and ryghtuousnesse as a mightie streame.

25O ye house of Israell, gaue ye me offeringes and sacryfyces

# AMOS

those .xl. yeares long in the wyldernes?

26 yet haue ye set vp tabernacles to your Moloch, and Images of youre Idols, yea, and the starre of youre God Rempha, figures which ye made to worshyppe them.

27 Therfore will I cause you be caryed awaye beyonde Damascus, sayeth the Lorde, whose name is the God of hostes.

## CHAPTER 6

1 O wo be to the proude welthy in Syon to suche as thincke them so sure vpon the mounte of Samaria? which holde them selues for the beste of the worlde, and rule the house of Israel, euen as they lyst.

2 Go vnto Calne, and se: & from thence get you to Hemath the greate cytye, and so go doune to Gath of the Philistines: be they better at ease then these kyngedomes, or the border of theyr lande wyder then yours?

3 Ye are taken out for the euyll daye, euen ye that syt in the stole of wilfulnesse:

4 Ye that lye vpon beddes of Iuerye, and vse your wantonnesse vpon your rouches: ye that eate the beste lambes of the flocke, and the fattest calues of the droaue:

5 ye that singe to the lute, & in playenge of instrumentes compare youre selues vnto Dauid:

6 ye that drincke wyne oute of goblettes, and annoynte youre selues with the best oyle, but no man is sorye for Iosephs hurte.

7 Therfor now shal ye be the fyrst of them, that shal be led awaye captyue, and the lusty chere of the wylfull shal come to an ende.

8 The Lorde God hath sworne euen by himselfe (sayeth the Lorde God of hostes) I hate the pryde of Iacob, and I abhorre his palaces and I wyll geue ouer the cytie, with all that is therein:

9 so that thoughe there remayne ten men in one house, they shal dye.

10 So their next kynsfolkes and the dead buryers shall take them, and carye awaye theyr bones, and saye vnto hym, that is in the ynnermer house: is there yet any mo by the? And he shal answere: they are al gone, holde thy tunge (shal he say) for they wolde not remembre the name of the Lorde.

11 Beholde, the Lorde is mynded to smyte the greate houses, so that they shall decaye: & the lytle houses, that they shall cleue a sunder.

12 Who can runne with horses, or plow with oxen vpon the herde rockes of stone? For why? ye haue turned true iudgement into bytternesse, & the frute of ryghtuousnesse into worm wood:

13 Yea, euen ye, that reioyse in vayne thinges, ye that say: haue not we obtayned hornes in oure owne strength?

14 Wel, take hede, O ye house of Israel, sayeth the Lorde God of hostes: I wyll brynge a people vpon you, which shall trouble you, from the waye that goeth towarde Hemath, vnto the broke in the medowe.

## CHAPTER 7

1 The Lorde God shewed me such a vysyon: beholde, there stode one that made gresshoppers, euen when the corne was shuting forth, after the kinge had clypte hys shepe.

2 Nowe when they vndertoke to eat vp all the greue thynges in the lande, I sayd: O Lorde God, be mercyfull, I beseche the: who shuld els help vp Iacob, that is brought so lowe?

3 So the Lorde was gracyons therin, and the Lorde sayde: well, it shal not be.

4 Agayne the Lorde shewed me thys vysyon: beholde, the Lorde God called the fyre to punish withal, and it deuoured the greate depe: yea it consumed a parte already.

5 Then sayd I Lord God, holde thyne hande: for who shulde els helpe vp Iacob, that is brought so lowe?

6 So the Lorde was mercyfull therein, and the Lord God sayde: well, it shall not be.

7 Moreouer, he shewed me thys vysyon: beholde, the Lorde stode vpon a plastered wall, and a masons trowel in hys lande.

8 And the Lorde sayd vnto me: Amos, what seyst thou? I aunswered: a masons trowel. Then sayde the Lorde: Beholde, I wyl laye the trowel among my people of Israel, and wyll no more ouerse them:

9 but the hye hylchapels of Isaac must be layed waste, and the churches of Israell made desolate: and as for the house of Ieroboam, I wyl stand vp agaynst with the swerd.

10 Vpon this sent Amasiah the prest to Bethell vnto Ieroboam the kynge of Israel, sayinge: Amos maketh the house of Israel to rebell agaynst the, the lande can not awaye with his wordes.

11 For Amos sayeth, Ieroboam shall dye with the swearde, and Israel shall be led awaye captyue oute of theyr owne land.

12 And Amasiah sayde vnto Amos: Get the hence (thou that caust se so well) & fle into the lande of Iuda: get the there thy lyuynge, and prophecye there:

13 and prophecye no more at Bethell, for it is the kynges chapell, and the kynges courte.

14 Amos aunswered, and sayde to Amasiah: As for me I am neyther Prophet, nor prophetes sonne: but a keper of catell. Now as I was breakinge downe molberies, and goyng after the catell,

15 the Lorde toke me, and sayde vnto me: Go thy waye, and

prophecye vnto my people of Israel.

16 And therfore, heare thou now the word of the Lorde: Thou sayest: prophecye not agaynst Israell, & speake nothing agaynst the house of Isaac.

17 Wherfore thus sayeth the Lord: Thy wyfe shalbe defyled in the cytye, thy sonnes and daughters shall be slayne with the swearde, & thy lande shalbe measured out with the lyne. Thou thy selfe shalt dye in an vnclene lande, & Israel shalbe dryuen out of hys owne countre.

## CHAPTER 8

1 The Lorde God shewed me this vysyon: and beholde, there was a maunde wyth somer fruyte.

2 And he sayde: Amos, what seist thou? I answered: a maunde wyth sommer fruyte. Then sayde the Lorde vnto me: the ende commeth vpon my people of Israell, I wyll no more ouerse them.

3 In that daye shall the songes of the temple be turned in to sorowe, sayeth the Lorde God. Many deed bodyes shall lye in euery place, and be caste forth secretelye.

4 Heare this, O ye that oppresse the poore, and destroye the nedy in the lande, saying:

5 When wil the new moneth be gone, that we maye sell vytale, & the Sabboth, that we maye haue scarcenesse of corne: to make the busshell lesse, and the Sycle greater?

6 We shal set vp false waightes that we maye gett the poore vnder vs wyth their money, and the nedy also for shues: yee let vs sell the chaffe for corne.

7 The Lorde hath sworne agaynst the pride of Iacob: these workes of theirs wyl I neuer forget.

8 Shall not the lande tremble, and all they that dwell therin, mourne for thys? Shall not their destruccyon come vpon them lyke a water streame, and flowe ouer them, as the floude of Egypte?

9 At the same tyme (sayeth the Lorde God) I shall cause the Sunne to go downe at none, and the land to be darcke in the cleare daye.

10 Youre hye feastes wyll I turne to sorowe, and youre songes to mournynge: I wyll bringe sack cloth vpon al backes, and baldnes vpon euery head: yee soch a mournynge wyll I sende them, as is made vpon an only begotten sonne, and they shall haue a miserable ende.

11 Beholde, the tyme commeth (sayeth the Lord God) that I shal sende an hunger in to the earth: not the hunger of bread, ner the thyrst of water: but an hunger to heare the worde of the Lorde:

12 so that they shall go from the one sea to the other yee from the north vnto the east, runnyng aboute to seke the worde of the Lorde, and shall not fynde it.

13 In that tyme, shall the fayre virgins and the yonge men perysh for thyrst,

14 yee euen they that sweare in the offence of Samaria, and saye: as trulye as thy God lyueth at Dan, and as trulye as thy God lyueth at Bersaba. These shall fall, and neuer ryse vp agayne.

## CHAPTER 9

1 I sawe the Lord standynge vpon the aulter, and he sayde; smyte the dore cheke, that the postes maye shake withall. For theyr couetousnesse shal fall vpon al their heades, and their posterite shalbe slayne wyth the swerde. They shall not fle awaye, there shall not one of them escape, ner be delyuered.

2 Though they were buryed in the hell, my hande shall fetch them from thence: though they clymme vp to heauen, yet shall I cast them downe:

3 though they hyde them selues vpon the toppe of Carmell, yet shall I seke them out, and brynge them from thence: Though they crepe downe from my syght into the depe of the sea, I shall commaunde the serpente, euen there to byte them.

4 If they goo awaye before their enemyes in to captyuite, then shall I commaunde the swerde, there to slayue them. Thus wyll I sett myne eyes vpon them, for their harme, & not for their wealth.

5 For when the Lorde God of hoostes toucheth a lande, it consumeth awaye, and all they that dwell therin, muste nedes mourne: And why? theyr destruccyon shall aryse as euery streame and runne ouer them, as the floude in Egipte.

6 He that hath hys dwellynge in heauen, & groundeth hys tabernacle in the earth: He that calleth the waters of the sea, and poureth them out vpon the playne grounde: hys name is the Lorde.

7 O ye chyldren of Israell, are ye not vnto me, euen as the Moryans, sayeth the Lorde? haue not I brought Israell out of the land of Egypt, the Philystues from Capthor, and the Sirians from Cyr?

8 Beholde, the eyes of the Lorde are vpon the realme that synneth, to rote it clene out of the earth: Neuertheles, I wyll not vtterly destroye the house of Iacob, sayeth the Lorde.

9 For lo thys I promyse: though I syfte the house of Israell amonge all nacyons (like as they vse to lyfte in a syue) yet shall not the smallest grauell stone fall vpon the earth:

10 But all the wicked doers of my people, that saye: Tush, the plage is not so nye, to come so hastely vpon vs: those shall perish with the swerde.

11 At that tyme wyll I buylde agayne the tabernacle of Dauid,

that is fallen downe and hedge vp hys gappes: and loke what is broken, I shall repayre it: Yee I shall buylde it agayne, as it was a fore tyme,

12that they maye possesse the remnaunt of Edom, yee & all soch people as call vpon my name wyth them sayeth the Lorde, whyche doeth these thynges.

them sayeth the Lorde thy God.

13Beholde, the tyme commeth (sayeth the Lorde) that plowman shall ouer take the mower, & the treader of grappes, hym that soweth sede. The mountaynes shall droppe swete wyne, and the hylles shalbe fruyteful,

14and I will turne the captyuyte of my people of Israell: they shall repayre the waste cytyes, and haue them in possession: they shal plante vynyardes, and drinke the wine therof: they shal make gardens, & enioye the fruytes of them.

15And I wyll plante them vpon their owne grounde, so that I wyll neuer rote them out agayne from their lande which I haue geuen

# Obadiah

THYS is the vysyon that was shewed vnto Abdy: Thus hath the Lorde God spoken vpon Edom: We haue hearde of þe Lord that there is an embassage sent amonge the Heathen: Vp, let vs aryse, and fyght agaynst them.

2 Beholde, I wyll make the small amonge the Heathen, so þt thou shalt be vtterly despysed.

3 The pryde of thyne herte hath lyft þe vp, thou that dwellest in the strong holdes of stone, & haste made the an hye seate: Thou sayest in thyne hert: who shall cast me downe to the grounde?

4 But though thou wentest vp as hye as the Aegle, and maydest thy nest aboue amonge the starres: yet wylde I plucke the downe from thence.

5 Yf the theues and robbers came to the by nyght, thou takinge thy reste: shulde they not steale, tyll they had ynough? Yf the grape gatherers came vpon the, wolde they not leaue the some grapes?

6 But how shall they rype Esau, and seke out hys treasures?

7 Yee the men that were sworne vnto the, shall dryue the out of the borders of thyne owne lande. They that be now at one wyth the, shall dysceyue the, & ouercome the: Euen they that eate thy bread, shall betraye the, or euer thou perceyue it.

8 Shall not I at the same tyme destroye the wyse men of Edom, & those that haue vnderstandynge, from the mount of Esau?

9 Thy gyauntes (O Theman) shalbe afrayed, for thorow the slaughter they shalbe all ouerthrowne vpon the mount of Esau.

10 Shame shall come vpon the, for the malyce that thou shewedest to thy brother Iacob: yee for euermore shalt thou perysh,

11 and that because of the tyme: when thou dydest set thy selfe agaynst hym, euen when the enemyes caryed awaye his hooste, and when the aleauntes came in at hys portes, and cast lottes vpon Ierusalem, and thou thy selfe wast as one of them.

12 Thou shalt nomore se the daye of thy brother, thou shalt nomore beholde the tyme of hys captiuite: thou shalt nomore reioyse ouer the chyldren of Iuda, in the daye of their destruccyon, thou shalt tryumphe nomore in the tyme of their trouble.

13 Thou shalt no more come in at the gates of my people, in þe tyme of their decaye: thou shalt no se their mysery in the daye of their fall. Thou shalt sende out no man agaynst their hooste, in the daye of their aduersyte:

14 nether shalt thou stande waytynge any more at the corners of stretes, to murthur soch as are fled or to take them presoners, that remayne in the daye of their trouble.

15 For the daye of þe Lord is harde by vpon all the Heathen. Lyke as thou hast done, so shalt thou be dealte wythall, yee thou shalt be rewarded euen vpon thyne head.

16 For lyke wyse as ye haue droncken vpon myne holy hyll, so shall all Heathen dryncke contynually: yee dryncke shall they, and swalowe vp, so that ye shalbe, as though ye had neuer bene.

17 But vpon the mount Syon, there shall a remnaunt escape: these shalbe holye, and the house of Iacob shall possesse euen those, that had them selues afore in possessyon.

18 Moreouer, the house of Iacob shalbe a fyre, þe house of Ioseph a flame, & the house of Esau shalbe the strawe, whych they shall kyndle and consume, so that nothynge shalbe left of þe house of Esau, for the Lorde hym self hath sayde it.

19 They of the South shall haue the mount of Esau in possession: and loke what lyeth vpon the grounde, that shall the Philistines haue: the playne feldes shall Ephraim & Samaria

# OBADIAH

possesse: and the mountaynes of Galaad shal BenIamin haue.

20 And thys hoost shalbe the chyldren of Israels presoners: Now what so lyeth from Canaan vnto Zareptah, and in Sepharad, that shalbe vnder the subieccion of Ierusalem: and the cytyes of the south shall enheret it.

21 Thus they that escape vpon the hyll of Syon, shall go vp to punysh the mount of Esau and the kyngdome shallbe the Lordes.

# Jonah

## CHAPTER 1

THE worde of the Lorde came vnto Ionas þe sonne of Amithai, saying:

2 Aryse, and get the to Niniue that greate cyte: & preache vnto them, how that their wyckednes is come vp before me.

3 And Ionas made hym ready to fle vnto Tharsis from the presence of the Lord, and gat hym downe to Ioppa: where he founde a shyppe ready for to go vnto Tharsis. So he payde his fare, & wente aborde, that he myght go wyth them vnto Tharsis, from the presence of the Lorde.

4 But the Lorde hurled a greate wynde into the sea, and there was a myghtye tempest in the sea: so that the shippe was in ieoperdy of goinge in peces.

5 Then the maryners were afrayde, & cryed euery man vnto hys God: & the goodes þt were in the shyppe, they cast in to the sea, to lyghten it of them. But Ionas gat hym vnder þe hatches, where he layed hym downe and slombred.

6 So the master of the shyppe came to hym and sayde vnto hym: why slomberest thou? Vp, call vpon thy God: yf God (happely) wil thyncke vpon vs, that we peryshe not.

7 And they sayde one to another: come, lett vs cast lottes: that we maye knowe, for whose cause we are thus troubled. And so they cast lottes, and the lot fell vpon Ionas.

8 Then sayde they vnto him: tel vs, for whose cause are we thus troubled? what is thyne occupacyon? whence commest thou? what countre man art thou, and of what nacyon?

9 He answered them: I am an Ebreue, and I feare the Lorde God of heauen, whych made both the sea & drye lande.

10 Then where þe men exceadingly afrayed, & sayde vnto hym: why didest thou so? (for they knewe, that he was fled from the presence of the Lord, because he had tolde them)

11 & sayde moreouer vnto hym: What shal we do vnto the, that the sea maye ceasse from troubling vs? (for þe sea wrought & was troublous)

12 he answered them: Take me, and cast me in to the sea, so shall it let you be in rest: for I wote, it is for my sake, that this great tempest is come vpon you.

13 Neuerthelesse, the men assayed with rouwynge, to bringe the shyppe to lande: but it wolde not be, because the sea wrought so, and was so troublous agaynst them.

14 Wherfore they cryed vnto þe Lord, & sayde: O Lord lett vs not perish for this mans death, nether laye thou innocent bloude vnto oure charge: for thou, O Lorde, hast done, euen as thy pleasure was.

15 So they toke Ionas, & cast hym in to the sea, & the sea left ragyng.

16 And the men feared the Lorde exceadingly, doyng sacrifices and makinge vowes vnto the Lorde.

17 Bvt the Lorde prepared a greate fyshe, to swalow vp Ionas. So was Ionas in the bely of the fysh, thre dayes & thre nightes.

## CHAPTER 2

AND Ionas prayed vnto þe Lord his God, out of the fysshes bely,

2 & sayde: In my trouble I called vnto the Lord, & he herde me: out of the bely of hell I cryed, and thou herdest my voyce.

3 Thou haddest cast me downe depe in the myddest of the sea, and the floude compassed me aboute: yee all thy waues and roules of water went ouer me,

4 I thought that I had bene cast awaye out of thy syght: but I wyll yet agayne loke towarde thy holy temple.

5 The waters compased me, euen to the very soule, the depe laye aboute me, and the wedes were wrapte aboute myne head.

6 I went downe to the botome af the hylles, and was barred in wyth earth for euer. But thou, O Lorde my God, haste brought vp my lyfe agayne out of corrupcyon.

7 When my soule faynted within me, I thought vpon the Lord: & my prayer came in vnto the, euen in to thy holy temple.

8 They that holde of vayue vanyties, will forsake hys mercy.

9 But I wyll do the sacryfyce wyth the voyce of thankesgeuynge, and wil paye that I haue vowed: for why? saluacion commeth of the Lorde.

10 And the Lorde spake vnto the fysh, and it cast out Ionas agayne vpon the drye lande.

## CHAPTER 3

THEN came the worde of þe Lorde vnto Ionas agayne, sayenge:

2 vp, and get the to Niniue that great cytye, & preache vnto them the preachinge whyche I bade the.

3 So Ionas arose, and wente to Niniue at the Lordes commaundement. Niniue was a greate cyte vnto God, namely, of thre dayes iourney.

4 And Ionas wente to, and entred in to the cytie: euen a dayes iourney, & cryed, sayenge: There are yet .xl. dayes and then shall Niniue be ouerthrowen.

5 And the people of Niniue beleued God, and proclamed fastynge, and arayed them selues in sack cloth, as wel the greate as the small of them.

6 And the tydinges came vnto the kynge of Niniue, whyche arose out of hys seate, and dyd hys apparell of, and put on sack cloth, & sate hym downe in asshes.

7 And it was cryed and commaunded in Niniue, by the auctorite of the king and hys lordes, sayenge: se that nether man or beast, oxe or shepe taste ought at all: and that they nether fede ner drinke water:

8 but put on sack cloth both man and beast, and crye myghtely vnto God: yee se that euery man turne from hys euell waye, and from the wyckednesse, that he hath in hande.

9 Who can tell? God maye turne, & repente & cease from his fearce wrath, that we perish not.

10 And when God sawe their workes, how they turned from their wicked wayes, he repented on the euell, whych he sayde he wolde do vnto them, and dyd it not.

## CHAPTER 4

THERFORE Ionas was sore dyscontent & angrye.

2 And he prayed vnto the Lord, & sayde: O Lord was not thys my sayinge (I praye the) when I was yet in my countre? therfore I hasted rather to fle vnto Tharsis, for I know well ynough þt thou art a mercyfull God, full of compassion, long sufferyng, & of a great kyndnesse, & repentest when thou shuldest take punishment.

3 And now O Lord, take my lyfe fro me (I beseche the) for I had rather dye then lyue.

4 Then sayde the Lord: art thou so angrie?

5 And Ionas gat hym out of the cytye, & sat downe on the east side therof: & there made hym a boothe, & sat vnder it in the shadow, tyll he myght se, what shulde chaunce vnto the cytie.

6 And the Lord God prepared a wylde vyne which sprang vp ouer Ionas, that he myght haue shadowe aboue hys head, to delyuer hym out of hys payne. And Ionas was exceadynge glad of the wylde vyne.

7 But vpon the nexte morowe agaynst thespring of þe daye. The Lord ordened a worme which smote the wylde vyne, so that it wethered awaye.

8 And when the Sunne was vp God prepared a feruent east wynde: and the Sunne bett ouer the head of Ionas, that he faynted agayne, and wisshed vnto hys soule, that he myght dye, and sayde: It is better for me to dye, then to lyue.

9 And God sayde vnto Ionas: Art thou so angrie for þe wylde vyne? And he sayde: yee very angrie am I euen vnto the death.

10 And the Lorde sayde: thou hast compassion vpon a wylde vyne, wheron thou bestowdest laboure, ner maydest it growe: whyche sprange vp in one nyght & peryshed in another:

11 And shulde not I then haue compassion vpon Niniue that greate cytye, wherin there are aboue an .C. & .xx. thousand persones, that knowe not their right hand from the lefte, besyde moch catell?

# Micah

## CHAPTER 1

THYS is the worde of þe Lord that came vnto Micheas the Morastite, in the dayes of Iothan, Ahas & Iehezekiah kinges of Iuda: which was shewed hym vpon Samaria & Ierusalem.

2 Heare all ye people, marcke thys well O earth, and all that therin is: Yee the Lorde God hym selfe be wytnesse amonge you, euen the Lord from hys holy temple.

3 For why? beholde, the Lord shal go oute of his place, & come downe & treade vpon the hye thynges of the earth.

4 The mountaynes shall consume vnder hym, and the valleyes shall cleue asunder, lyke as wax consumeth at the fyre, & as the waters runne downwarde.

5 And all this shall be for the wyckednesse of Iacob, and the synnes of the house of Israell. But what is the wyckednesse of Iacob? Is not Samaria? Whiche are the hye places of Iuda? Is not Ierusalem?

6 Therfore I shall make Samaria an heape of stones in þe felde, to laye aboute the vineyarde: her stones shall I cast in to the valley, & discouer her foundacions.

7 All her Images shalbe broken downe & all her wynnynges shalbe brent in the fyre: yee all her Idols wyll I destroye: for why, they are gathered out of þe hyre of an whore, and in to an whores hyre shall they be turned agayne.

8 Wherfore I wyll mourne and make lamentacion, bare & naked wyll I go: I must mourne lyke the dragons, and take sorow as þe Estriches:

9 for their wounde is past remedy: And why? it is come in to Iuda, & hath touched þe porte of my people at Ierusalem alredy.

10 Wepe not, lest they at Geth perceyue it. Thou at Betaphra, welter thy self in the dust & asshes.

11 Thou that dwellest at Sephir get the hence with shame. The proude shall boost nomore for very sorowe: and why? her neyghboure shall take from her what she hath.

12 The rebellyous cytye hopeth, that it shal not be so euell: but for all that, þe plage shall come from the Lorde, euen in to the porte of Ierusalem.

13 The greate noyse of the charettes shal feare them, that dwell at Lachis, whyche is an occasyon of the synne of the daughter of Sion, for in the came vp the wyckednesses of Israell.

14 Yee she sent her coursers in to the lande of Geth. The houses of lyes wyll dysceaue the kinges of Israell.

15 And as for the (O thou that dwellest at Morassa) I shall brynge a possessioner vpon the, and the plage of Israel shall reach vnto Odolla.

16 Make the balde, & shaue the, because of thy tender chyldren: Make the cleane balde as an Aegle, for they shalbe caryed awaye captyue from the.

## CHAPTER 2

Owo vnto them, that Imagyn to do harme, & deuyse vngracyousnesse vpon their beddes, to perfourme it in the cleare daye: for there power is agaynst God.

2 When they couet to haue lande, they take it by vyolence, they robbe men of their houses. Thus they oppresse a man for his house, & euery man for hys heretage.

3 Therfore thus sayeth the Lorde: Beholde agaynst thys housholde haue I deuysed a plage, wherout ye shal not plucke your neckes: Ye shal nomore go so proudely, for it wyll be a perlous tyme.

4 In that daye shall thys terme be vsed, and a mournynge shalbe made ouer you on thys maner: We be vtterly desolate, the porcyon of my people is translated. When wyll he parte vnto vs the lande, that he hath taken from vs?

# MICAH

5 Neuertheles there shalbe no man to deuyde the thy porcyon in the congregacyon of the Lorde.

6 Tush, holde youre tunge (saye they.) It shall not fall vpon thys people, we shall not come so to confusyon,

7 sayeth the house of Iacob. Is the sprete of the Lorde so cleane awaye? or is he so mynded? Trueth it is, my wordes are frendly vnto them that lyue right:

8 but my people doth the contrary, therfore must I take parte agaynst them: for they take awaye both cote and cloke from the symyle. Ie haue turned youre selues to fyght,

9 the wemen of my people haue ye shot out from their good houses, and taken away my excellent gyftes from their chyldren.

10 Vp, get you hence, for here shall ye haue no rest. Because of their Idolatrye they are corrupte, & shall myserably perishe.

11 If I were a fleshlye felowe, & a preacher of lyes, & tolde them that they myght syt bebbynge & bollyng, and be droncken: O that were a Prophete for this people.

12 But I wyll gather the in dede, O Iacob, & dryue the remnaunt of Israell all together I shall cary them one wyth another, as a flocke in the folde, and as the catell in their stalles, that they maye be dysquyeted of other men.

13 Who so breaketh the gappe, he shall go before. They shal breake vp þe porte, and go in and out at it. Their kynge shall go before them, and the Lorde shallbe vpon the head of them.

## CHAPTER 3

HEARE, O ye heades of the house of Iacob, & peleders of þe house of Israel: Shulde not ye know what were lawfull and ryght?

2 But ye hate the good, and loue the euell: ye plucke of mennes skynnes, and the flesh from their bones:

3 ye eate the flesh of my people, and slay of their skynne: ye breake their bones, ye choppe them in peces as it were in to a cauldron, and as flesh into a pot.

4 Now the tyme shall come, that when they call vnto the Lorde, he shall not heare them, but hyde hys face from them, because that thorowe their owne Imaginacyons they haue dealte so wyckedly.

5 And as concernynge the prophetes that disceyue my people, thus the Lorde sayeth agaynst them: When they haue enye thynge to byte vpon, then they preach that all shalbe well: but yf a man put not some thynge is to their mouthes, they preach of warre agaynst hym.

6 Therfore youre vysyon shallbe turned to night, & youre prophecyenge to darckness. The Sunne shall go downe ouer those prophetes, and the daye shalbe darcke vnto them.

7 Then shall the vysyon seers be ashamed, and the suthsayers confounded: yee they shallbe fayne, all the packe of them, to stoppe their mouthes, for they haue not Gods worde.

8 As for me, I am full of strength, and of the sprete of the Lorde, full of iudment and boldnesse: to shewe the house of Iacob their wyckednesse, and the house of Israell their synne.

9 O heare this ye rulers of the house of Iacob, and ye iudges of the house of Israell: ye that abhorre the thynge that is laufull, and wrayst asyde the thynge that is streyght.

10 Ye that buylde vp Syon wyth bloude, and Ierusalem wyth doynge wronge.

11 O ye iudges, ye geue sentence for gyftes: O ye preastes, ye teach for lucre: O ye Prophetes, ye prophecy for monye. Yet wyll they be taken as those that holde vpon God, and saye: Is not the Lorde amonge vs? Tushe, there can no mysfortune happen vs.

12 Therfore shall Syon (for youre sakes) be plowed lyke a felde: Ierusalem shalbe come an heape of stones, and the hyll of the temple shalbe turned to an hye wodde.

## CHAPTER 4

BVT in the latter dayes it wyll come to passe, that the hyll of þe Lordes house shallbe sett vp hyer then enye mountaynes or hylles: Yee the people shall prease vnto it,

2 and the multitude of the Gentyles shall haste them thyther, sayeng: Come lett vs go vp to the hyll of the Lorde, and to the house of the God of Iacob: that he maye teach vs hys wayes, & that we maye walke in hys parthes. For the lawe shall come out of Sion, and the worde of God from Ierusalem,

3 and shall geue sentence amonge the multytude of the Heathen and refourme the people of farre countrees: so that of their sweardes they shall make plowshares, and sythes of their speares. One people shall not lyft vp a sweard agaynst another, yee they shal nomore learne to fyght:

4 but euerye man shall syt vnder hys vineyarde and vnder his fygetre, & no man to fraye hym awaye: for the mouth of þe Lord of hostes hath spoken it.

5 Therfore, where as all the people haue walcked euery man in the name of hys owne God, we wyll walcke in the name of oure God for euer and euer.

6 At the same tyme, sayeth the Lorde, wyll I gather vp the lame and the outcastes, and soche as I haue chastened:

7 & wyll geue yssue vnto

the lame, and make of the out castes a greate people: and the Lorde hym selfe shalbe their kynge vpon the mount Sion, from this tyme forth for euermore.

8 And vnto the (O thou tower of Eder, thou strong holde of the doughther Sion) vnto the shall it come: euen the lordshype and kyngdome of the daughter Ierusalem.

9 Why then art thou now so heuy? is there no Kynge in the? are they councelers awaye that thou art so payned, as a woman in her trauayle?

10 And now (O thou daughter Sion) be sory, let it greue the as a wyfe laborynge wyth chyld: for now must thou gett the out of the cytie, & dwell vpon the playne felde: Yee vnto Babylon shalt thou go, there shalt thou be delyuered, and there the Lorde shall lowse the from the hande of thyne enemyes.

11 Now also are there manye people gathered together agaynst the, sayinge: what, Sion is cursed, we shal se oure lust vpon her.

12 But they knowe not the thoughtes of the Lorde, they vnderstande not hys councell, that shal gather them together as the sheeues in the barne.

13 Therfore get the vp, O thou doughter Sion, & throsshe out the corne: For I wyll make thy horne yron, and thy clawes brasse, that thou mayest grynde many people their goodes shalt thou appropriate vnto the Lorde, and their substaunce vnto the ruler of the whole worlde.

## CHAPTER 5

AFTER that shalt thou be robbed thy selfe, O thou robbers daughter: they shall laye sege agaynst vs, & smyte the iudge of Israell wyth a rodde vpon the cheke.

2 And thou Bethleem Ephrata, art lytle among the thousandes of Iuda, Out of þe shall come vnto me, whyche shall be the gouernoure in Israell: whose out goinge hath bene from the begynnyge, and from euerlastynge.

3 In the meane whyle he plageth them for a season, vntyll the tyme that she (whyche shall beare) haue borne: then shall the remnaunt of hys brethren be conuerted vnto the chyldren of Israell.

4 He shall stande fast, and geue fode in the strength of the Lorde, and in the vyctorye of the name of the Lorde hys God: and when they be conuerted, he shal be magnifyed vnto the farthest partes of the worlde.

5 Then shall there be peace, so that the Assirian maye come in to oure lande, and treade in oure houses. We shall brynge vp seuen shepherdes and .viij. prynces vpon them:

6 these shall subdue the lande of Assur wyth the swerde, and the lande of Nymrod wyth their naked weapens. Thus shall he delyuer vs from the Assirian, when he commeth within oure lande, & setteth hys fote wythin oure borders.

7 And the remnaunt of Iacob shalbe amonge the multytude of people, as the dewe of the Lorde, and as the droppes vpon the grasse, that tarieth for no man, & wayteth of no body.

8 Yee the resydue of Iacob shalbe amonge the Gentyles and the multitude of people, as the lyon amonge the beastes of the wod, and as the Lyons whelpe amonge a flocke of shepe: whyche (when he goeth thorowe) treadeth downe, teareth in peces, and there is no man that can helpe.

9 Thyne hande shalbe lyft vp vpon thyne enemyes, and all thyne aduersaries shall perish.

10 The tyme shall come also, sayeth the Lord, that I wyll take thyne horses from the, and destroye thy charettes.

11 I wyll breake downe the cytyes of thy lande, and ouerthrowe all thy stronge holdes.

12 All witchcraftes wyll I rote oute of thyne hande, there shall no mo soyth sayinges be within the.

13 Thyne Idols and thyne Images will I destroye out of the so that thou shalt nomore bowe thy selfe vnto the worckes of thyne owne handes.

14 Thy groues wyll I plucke vp by the rotes, and breake downe the cyties.

15 Thus wyll I be auenged also, vpon all the Heathen that wyll not heare.

## CHAPTER 6

HERKEN now what the Lorde sayeth: Vp reproue the mountaynes, and let the hylles heare thy voyce.

2 O heare the punishment of the Lord, ye mountaynes, & ye myghtie foundacions of the earth: for the Lorde wyll reproue hys people, and reason with Israel:

3 O my people, what haue I done vnto the? or wherin haue I hurte the? geue me answere.

4 Because I brought the from the lande of Egypte, and delyuered the out of the house of bondage? Because I made Moses, Aaron and Miriam to lede the?

5 Remembre (O my people) what Balach þe kyng of Moab had Imagyned agaynst the, and what answeree that Balaam the sonne of Beor gaue hym, from Sethim vnto Galgal, that ye maye know the louyng kyndnesses of the Lorde.

6 What acceptable thynge shall I offre vnto the Lord? shall I bowe my knee to the hye God? Shall I come before hym wyth brentoffrynges, and wyth calues

of a yeare olde?

7 Hath the Lorde a pleasure in many thousand rammes, or innumerable streames of oyle? Or shal I geue my fyrstborne for myne offences, and the fruyte of my body for the synne of my soule?

8 I wyll shewe the, O man, what is good, & what the Lorde requyreth of the: Namely, to do right, to haue pleasure in louynge kyndnesse, to be lowlye, and to walcke wyth thy God:

9 that thou mayest be called a cytye of the Lorde, & that thy name maye be ryghtuousnesse. Heare (O ye trybes) who wolde els geue you soch warnynge?

10 Shulde I not be displeased, for þe vnrighteous good in the houses of the wycked, and because the measure hys mynyshed?

11 Or shulde I iustifie the false balaunces and the bagge of disceytfull weyghtes,

12 amonge those that be full of ryches vnryghtuously gotten: where the cyte syns deale with falshede, speake lies, & haue dysceytfull tunges in their mouthes?

13 Therfore I wyll take in hande to punysh the, and to make the desolate, because of thy sinnes:

14 Thou shalt eate, & not haue ynough: yee thou shalt bringe thy selfe downe. Thou shalt fle, but not escape: and those that thou woldest saue, wyll I delyuer to the swerde.

15 Thou shalt sowe, but not reape: thou shalt presse out oliues, but oyle shalt thou not haue to anoynte thy selfe wythall: thou shalt tread out swete must, but shalt dryncke no wyne.

16 Ye kepe the ordynaunces of Amri, & all the customes of þe house of Ahab: ye folowe their pleasures, therfore wyll I make the waste, & cause thy inhabyters to be abhorred, O my people: and thus shalt thou beare thyne owne shame.

# CHAPTER 7

Wo is me: I am become as one, that goeth a gleanynge in the haruest. There are no mo grapes to eate, yet wolde I fayne (with all my herte) haue of the best fruyte.

2 There is not a godlye man vpon earth, there is not one ryghtuous amonge men. They laboure al to shed bloud, and euery man hunteth his brother to death:

3 yet they saye: they do well, when they do euil. As the prince wyll, so sayeth the iudge: that he maye do him a pleasure agayne. The greate man speaketh what his herte desyreth: & the hearers alowe hym.

4 The best of them is but as a thistle, & the most rightuous of them is but as a breer in the hedge. But when the day of thy preachers commeth, that thou shalt be vysyted: then shall they be wasted awaye.

5 Let no man beleue hys frende, nor put his confidence in a prynce. Kepe the porte of thy mouthe, from her that lyeth in thy bosome:

6 for the sonne shall put hys father to dyshonoure, the doughter shall ryse agaynst her mother, the doughter in lawe agaynst her mother in lawe: & a mans foes shalbe euen they of hys owne houshold.

7 Neuerthelesse I wyll loke vp vnto the Lorde, I wyll pacyentlye abyde God my sauyoure: my God shall heare me.

8 O thou enemye of myne, reioyce not at my fal, for I shal get vp agayne: and thoughe I syt in my darckenesse, yet the Lorde is my lyght.

9 I wyl beare the punyshment of the Lorde (for why? I haue offended hym) tyll he sit in iudgement vpon my cause, and se that I haue ryghte. He wyll brynge me forth to the lyght, & I shall se hys ryghtuousnesse.

10 She that is myne enemy shall loke vpon it, & be confounded, which now sayth. Where is thy Lorde God? Myne eyes shall beholde her, when she shalbe troden doune, as the clay in the stretes.

11 The tyme will come, that thy gappes shall be made vp, & the lawe shall go abroade:

12 & at þe tyme shal they come vnto the, from Assur vnto the stronge cytyes, & from the stronge cytyes vnto the ryuer: from the one sea to the other, from the one mountaine to þe other.

13 Not withstandynge the land must be wasted, because of them that dwell therein, and for the frutes of theyr owne Imaginacyons.

14 Therfore fede thy people wyth thy rodde, the flocke of thyne herytage which dwell desolate in the woodde, that they maye be fedde vpon the mounte of Charmell, Basan & Galaad as afore tyme.

15 Maruelous thinges wyll I shewe them, lyke as when they came oute of Egypte.

16 This shall the heathen se, and be ashamed for all theyr power, so that they shal laye theyr hande vpon theyr mouthe, and stoppe theyr eares.

17 They shal licke the dust lyke a serpente, & as the wormes of the earthe that tremble in theyr holes. They shalbe afraid of the Lorde oure God, and they shall feare the.

18 Where is there such a God as thou? that pardonest wickednes, and forgeuest the offences of the remnaunte of thyne herytage? He kepeth not hys wrath for euer. And why? his

delyte is to haue compassyon:

19 he shal turne agayne, and be mercyfull to vs: he shall put doune oure wyckednesses, and caste all oure synnes into the botome of the sea.

20 Thou shalt kepe thy truste wyth Iacob, and thy mercye for Abraham, lyke as thou haste sworne vnto oure fathers longe agoo.

# Nahum

## CHAPTER 1

THYS is the heuye burthen of Niniue, which Nahum of Elchos dyd wryte as he sawe it.

2 The Lorde is a gelous God, & a taker of vengeaunce: yee a taker of vengeaunce is þe Lorde, and wrathfull. The Lord taketh vengeaunce of hys enemyes, and reserueth dyspleasure for his aduersaries.

3 The Lorde suffreth longe, he is of greate power, & so innocent that he leaueth no man fautlesse before hym. The Lorde goeth forth in tempest and stormy wether, the cloudes are the dust of his fete.

4 When he reproueth the sea, he drieth it vp, and turneth all the floudes to drye lande. Basan is desolate, Charmel & the pleasure of Lybanus wasteth awaye.

5 The mountaynes tremble for him, the hylles consume. At the syght of hym, þe earth quaketh: yee the whole world, and all that dwell therin.

6 Who maye endure before his wrath? Or who is able to abyde hys gryme displeasure? His anger taketh on lyke fyre, and the harde rockes burst in sunder before hym.

7 Full gracious is the Lorde, and a stronge holde in the tyme of trouble, he knoweth them that put their truste in hym:

8 when the floude renneth ouer, and destroyeth the place, and when the darcknesse foloweth styll vpon his enemyes.

9 What do ye Imagin then agaynst the Lord on this maner? (Tush, when he hath ones made an ende, there shall come nomore trouble.)

10 For lyke as the thornes that sticke together, and as the drye strawe, so shall the dronckardes be consumed together, euen when they be full.

11 There come oute of the soche as Imagin meschefe, & geue vngracious councell agaynst the Lorde.

12 Therfore thus sayeth the Lorde: Let them be as well prepared, yee and as many as they can, yet shall they be hewen downe, & passe awaye. And as for the, I wyll vexe þe, but not vtterly destroye the.

13 And now wyll I breake hys rodde from thy backe, & burst thy bondes in sonder.

14 But the Lorde hath geuen a commaundement concernynge the, þt there shall come nomore sede of thy name. The carued & casten Images wyll I rote out of the house of thy God. Thy graue shall I prepare for the, and thou shalt be confounded.

15 Beholde, vpon the mountaynes come the fete of hym, that bryngeth good tydynges, and preacheth peace. O Iuda, kepe thy holy dayes, perfourme thy promyses: for Beliall shall come nomore in the, he is vtterly roted out.

## CHAPTER 2

THE scaterer shall come vp agaynst the, & laye sege to the castell. Loke thou well to the stretes, make thy loynes stronge, arme thy self with all thy myght:

2 for the Lorde shal restore agayne the glorye of Iacob, lyke as the glory of Israell. The destroyers haue broken them downe, & marred the wyne braunches.

3 The shylde of hys gyauntes glystereth, hys men of warre are clothed in purple. Hys charettes are as fyre, when he maketh hym forward, his archers are well decke & trimmed.

4 The charettes rolle vpon the stretes, & welter in the hye wayes. They are to loke vpon lyke cressettes of fyre, & go swyftly, as the lyghtenynge.

5 When he doth but warne his giauntes, they fal in their araye, & hastely they clymme vp the walles: yee the engins of the warre are prepared all ready.

6 The water portes shalbe opened, and the kynges palace shal fall.

7 The quene her selfe shalbe led awaye captyue, and her gentil wemen shall mourne as

the doues and grone wyth in their hertes.

8 Niniue is lyke a pole full of water, but then shall they be fayne to fle. Stand, stande (shal they crye) and there shall not one turne backe.

9 Awaye with the syluer, awaye wyth the golde: for here is no ende of treasure. There shalbe a multytude of all maner costlye ornamentes.

10 Thus muste she be spoyled, emptied and clene striped out: that their hertes maye be melted awaye, their knees tremble, all their loynes be weake, and their faces blacke as a pot.

11 Where is now the dwellyng of the lyons, & the pasture of þe lyons whelpes? where the lyon & the lyonesse went wt the whelpes, & no man frayed them awaye?

12 But the lyon spoyled ynough for hys yonge ones, & deuoured for his lionesse: he filled his dennes with his pray, & his dwellynge place with that he had rauyshed.

13 Beholde, I wyll vpon the, sayeth þe lord of hostes, & wyll set fyre vpon thy charettes, that they shall smoke with all, & the swerde shal deuoure the yong lyons. I wyll make an ende of thy spoylyng from out of the earth, and the voyce of thy messaungers shal no more be hearde.

## CHAPTER 3

Wo to the bloudthurstye cytye, which is full of lyes & robbery & wyl not leaue of from rauyshyng.

2 There a man may heare scourgynge, russhyng, þe noyse of the weeles, the cryenge of the horses, & the rollynge of the charettes.

3 There the horsmen get vp with naked swerdes, & glystering speares. There lyeth a multytude slayn, & a great heape of deade bodyes. There is no ende of dead coarses, yea, men fall vpon theyr bodyes:

4 And that for the greate and manyfolde whordome, of the fayre and beutyfull harlot, which is a maistresse of witchcrafte, yea, and selleth the people thorowe her whordom, and the nacyons thorowe her witchcraft.

5 Beholde, I wyll vpon the (sayeth þe Lord of hostes) and will pull thy clothes ouer thy heade: that I maye shew thy nakednes among the Heathen, and thy shame amonge the kingdomes.

6 I wyll caste dyrte vpon the, to make þe be abhorred, and a gasyng stocke:

7 Yea al they that loke vpon the, shall starte backe, and say: Niniue is destroyed. Who wyll haue pyte vpon the: where shall I seke one to conforte the?

8 Art thou better then the greate cytie of Alexandria? that lay in the waters, and had the waters rounde about it: whiche was strongly fensed and walled with the sea?

9 Ethiopia and Egypt were her strength and that excedynge greate aboue measure. Aphrica and Lybia were her helpers,

10 yet was she dryuen away, and brought into captiuite: her yonge chyldren were smiten doune at the heade of euerye strete, the lottes were cast for the most auncient men in her, and al her mightye men were bounde in chaynes.

11 Euen so shalt thou also be droncken, and hyde thy self, and seke some helpe agaynst thyne enemy.

12 Al thy strong cities shalbe lyke figgetrees with ripe figges: which when a man shaketh, they shal fall into the mouthe of the eater.

13 Behold, thy people within the are but wemen: the portes of thy laude shalbe opened vnto thyne enemyes, and the fyre shall deuoure thy barres.

14 Drawe water nowe agaynst thou be beseged, make vp thy strong holdes, go into the claye, tempre the morter, make stronge bricke,

15 yet the fyre shall consume the, þe swerde shall destroye the, yea, as the locuste doeth, so shal it eate the vp. It shal fal heuely vpon the as the locustes, yea, right heuely shal it fal vpon þe, euen as þe greshoppers.

16 Thy marchauntes haue ben nombred with þe starres of heauen: but nowe shal they sprede abroad as the locustes, and fle theyr waye.

17 Thy Lordes are as þe greshoppers, & thy captaynes as the multytude of greshoppers: which when they be colde, remayne in the hedges: but when the Sunne is vp, they fle awaye, and no man can tel where they are become:

18 Thy shepherdes are a slepe (O kynge of Assur) thy worthyes are layed doune: thy people is scatred abroad vpon the mountaynes, and no man gathereth them together agayne.

19 Thy wounde can not be hyd, thy plage is so sore. All they that heare this of the, shal clappe theyr handes ouer the. For what is he to whom thou hast not alway ben doyng hurte.

# Habakkuk

## CHAPTER 1

THIS is the heauye burthen, whiche the Prophet Abacuc did se.

2 O lord how long shal I crye, and thou wilt not heare? How long shal I complayn vnto the, sufferynge wrong, & thou wilte not helpe?

3 Why lettest thou me se weerynesse and laboure? Tyranny & vyolence are before me, power ouergoeth righte:

4 for the lawe is toarne in peces, and there can no ryghte iudgemente go forthe. And why? the vngodly is more set by then þe rightuous: this is the cause, that wronge iudgemente procedeth.

5 Beholde, amonge the Heathen, & loke well: wondre at it, and be abashed: for I wyll do a thynge in youre tyme, whiche thoughe it be tolde you, ye shall not beleue.

6 For lo, I wyll rase vp the Caldees, that bitter and swifte people: whiche shall go as wyde as the land is, to take possessyon of dwellyng places, þt be not theyr owne.

7 A grymme and boysteours people is it, these shall sit in iudgemente, and punish.

8 Their horses are swifter then the cattes of the mountayne, & byte sorer then the wolues in the euenynge. Theyr horsmen come by greate heapes from farre, they fle hastely to deuour as the Aegle.

9 They come all to spoyle: oute of them commeth an easte wynde, whiche bloweth and gathereth theyr captyues, lyke as the sande.

10 They shall mocke the kynges, and laughe the princes to scorne. They shal not set by any stronge holde, for they shall laye ordynaunce agaynst it, and take it.

11 Then shall they take a freshe courage vnto them, to go forth, and to do more euil, & so ascrybe that power vnto theyr God.

12 But thou O Lorde my God, my holy one thou arte from the begynnynge, therfor shall we not dye. O Lorde, thou hast ordened them for a punyshment, and set them to reproue the myghtye.

13 Thyne eyes are clene, thou mayest not se euyll, thou canst not beholde the thynge that is wycked. Wherfor then doest thou loke vpon the vngodly, and holdest thy tung, when the wycked deuoureth the man that is better then hym selfe?

14 Thou makest men as the fysh in the sea, and lyke as the crepynge beastes þt haue no gyde.

15 They take vp all with theyr angle, they catche it in theyr net, and gather it in theyr yarne: whereof they reioyce, and are glad,

16 Therfore offre they vnto theyr net, and do sacryfyce vnto theyr yarne: because that thorowe it theyr porcyon is become so fat, & theyr meate so plenteous.

17 Wherfore they cast oute theyr net agayne, and neuer cease to slaye the people.

## CHAPTER 2

I stode vpon my watch, & set me vpon my bulworke, to loke & se, what he wolde saye vnto me, & what answere I shuld geue him that reproueth me.

2 But the Lord aunswered me, and sayde: Wryte the vysyon planely vpon thy tables, that who so cometh by, maye rede it,

3 for the vysyon is yet farre of for a tyme, but at the last it shal come to passe & not fayle. And thoughe he tarye, yet wayte thou for hym, for in very dede he wyll come, & not be slacke

4 Beholde, who so wyll not beleue, hys soule shall not prosper: but the iuste shall lyue by hys fayth.

5 Lyke as the wyne disceyueth the dronkarde, euen so the proud shall fayle and not endure. He openeth hys desyre wyde vp as the hell, & is as vnsacyale as death. All Heathen

gathered he to hym, and heapeth vnto hym all people.

6 But shall not all these take vp a prouerbe agaynst hym, & mocke hym with a byworde & saye: Wo vnto hym that heapeth vp other mens goodes? Howe longe wyll he lade hym selfe with thicke claye?

7 O howe sodenly wyll they stand vp that shall byte, and awake, that shal teare the in peces? yea, thou shalt be their praye.

8 Seynge thou hast spoyled many Heathen, therfore shall the remuaunte of the people spoyle the: because of mens bloude, and for the wronge done in the lande, in the cytye and vnto all them that dwell therein.

9 Wo vnto hym, that couetouslye gathereth euyll gotten goodes into hys house: that he maye set hys neste an hye, to escape from the power of mysfortune.

10 Thou hast deuysed the shame of thyne owne house, for thou haste slayne to muche people, and hast wylfully offended,

11 so that the very stones of þe wall shall crye oute of it, and the tymbre that lyeth betwixte the ioyntes of the buyldynge shal aunswere.

12 Wo vnto hym, that buyldeth þe towne wyth bloude, & maintaineth the citie wyth vnryghtuousnes.

13 Shall not the Lorde of hostes brynge thys to passe, that the laboures of the people shal be brent wyth a greate fyre, & that the thynge wherevpon the people haue weeryed them selues, shall be lost?

14 For the earth shall be full of knowledge of the Lordes honoure, lyke as the waters that couer the sea.

15 Wo vnto hym that geueth his neighboure dryncke, to get hym wrothefull dyspleasure for his dronckennesse: that he maye se his preuytees.

16 Therfore wyth shame shalte thou be fylled, in steade of honoure. Drincke thou also tyll thou slombre wyth al: for the cuppe of the Lordes ryght hande shall compasse the about and shamefull spewyng in steade of thy worshippe.

17 For the wronge that thou hast done in Lybanus, shall ouerwhelme the, and þe wylde beastes shal make the afrayd: because of mens bloude, and for the wronge done in the lande, in the cytye, and vnto all such as dwell therein.

18 What helpe then wyll the Image do, whom the worckman hath fashyoned? Or the vayne cast Image, wherein because the craftesman putteth hys trust, therfore maketh he domme Idols?

19 Wo vnto hym, that sayeth to a pece of woode: aryse, & to a domme stone: stande vp. For what instruccyon maye suche one geue? Beholde it is layed ouer wyth gold and siluer and there is no breth in it.

20 But the Lord in his holy temple is he, whome all the world shuld feare.

# CHAPTER 3

O Lord, when I hearde speake of the, I was afrayed. The worck that thou hast taken in hande, shalt thou perfourme in his tyme (O Lord): and when thy time commeth, thou shalte declare it. In thy verye wrath thou thinckest vpon mercye.

3 God commeth from Theman, and the holye one from the mounte of Pharan Selah. Hys glory couereth the heauens, and the earthe is full of hys prayse.

4 Hys shyne is as þe sunne, & beames of lyght go out of his handes, there is his power hyd.

5 Destruccyon goeth before hym, and burnynge cressettes go from his fete.

6 He standeth and measureth the earth. He loketh, and the people consume awaye, the mountaines of the worlde fall doune to poulder, & the hilles are faine to bowe them selues for hys goynges are euerlastynge and sure.

7 I sawe, that the pauylions of the Morians & the tentes of the lande of Madian were vexed for werynesse.

8 Waste thou not angrye, O Lorde, in the waters? was not thy wrathe in the floodes, and thy displeasure in the sea? yes when thou sattest vpon thyne horse, & when thy charettes had the vyctory.

9 Thou sheuedst thy bowe openly, lyke as thou haddest promised with an othe vnto the trybes. Selah. Thou diddest deuyde the waters of þe earth.

10 When the mountaynes sawe the, they were afrayed, the water streame wente awaye: the depe made a noyse at the lyftyng vp of thyne hande.

11 The sunne and mone remayned. styll in theyr habitacyon. Thyne arowes went out glysterynge, and thy speares as the shyne of the lyghtenyng.

12 Thou trodest doune the land in thyne anger, and dyddest throsshe the Heathen in thy displeasure.

13 Thou camest forth to helpe thy people, to helpe thyne annoynted. Thou smotest doune the heade the house of þe vngodlye, and dyscoueredest hys foundacyons, euen vnto the necke of hym. Selah.

14 Thou cursest hys scepters, the captayne of men of warre: whiche come as a stormy wind to scatre me abroade, and are glad when they maye eate vp the poore secretely.

15 Thou makest awaye for thyne horses in the sea, euen in the mudde of greate waters.

16 When I heare thys, my

bodye is vexed, my lyppes tremble at the voyce therof, my bones corruppe, I am afrayed where I stande. O that I myght rest in the day of trouble, that I myght go vp vnto oure people, whiche are alredye prepared.

17 For the fygge trees shall not be grene, & þe vynes shall beare no frute. The laboure of þe olyue shalbe but lost, & the lande shall bringe no corne: the shepe shalbe taken oute of þe fold & there shalbe no catel in the stalles.

18 But as for me, I wyll be glad in the Lorde, and wyll reioyce in God my sauyoure.

19 The Lord God is my strengthe, he shall make my fete as the fete of hertes: and he whiche geueth the vyctorye, shal bryng me to my hye places, synging vpon my psalmes.

# Zephaniah

## CHAPTER 1

This is the worde of þe lorde whiche came vnto Sophonye the sonne of Chusi, the sonne of Gedoliah, þe sonne of Amariah the sonne of Hezekiah in the time of Iosiah the sonne of Amon kynge of Iuda.

2 I wyl gather vp all thynges in the lande (sayeth the Lorde)

3 I wyl gather vp man and beast: I wil gather vp the foules in the ayre and the fyshe in the sea (to the greate decaye of the wycked) and wyll vtterlye destroye the men out of the lande, sayeth the Lorde.

4 I wyll stretche oute myne hande vpon Iuda, and vpon all suche as dwell at Ierusalem. Thus wyll I rote oute the remnaunte of Baal from thys place, & the names of the Remurins and priestes:

5 yea and suche as vpon theyr house toppes worshyppe and bowe them selues vnto the host of heauen: whiche sweare by the Lorde, & by theyr Malchom also:

6 whiche starte a backe from the Lord, & neyther seke after þe Lorde, nor regarde him.

7 Be styll at the presence of the Lorde God, for the daye of the Lorde is at hande: yea the Lorde hath prepareth a slayne offerynge, and called hys gestes therto.

8 And thus shall it happen in the daye of the Lordes a slayneofferyng: I wyll vpset the prynces, the kynges chyldren, and all suche as were straunge clothynge.

9 In the same daye also wyll I vyset all those, that treade ouer the tholde so proudely, which fyll theyr Lordes house with trobbery and falshede.

10 At the same time (saith the Lorde) there shalbe hearde a greate crye from the fyshporte and an howlyng from the other porte, and a greate murthur from the hylles.

11 Howle ye that dwell in the myll, for all the marchaunt people are gone, and al they that were laden with syluer, are roted oute.

12 At the same tyme will I seke thorowe Ierusalem with lanternes, and vpset them that contynue in theyr dregges, and saye in theyr hertes. Tushe, the Lorde wil do neyther good nor euyll.

13 Theyr goodes shalbe spoyled, and theyr houses layed waste: they shall buylde houses, and not dwel in them: they shal plant vyneyardes, but not drinck the wyne, therof.

14 For the greate daye of the Lorde is at hande, it is harde by, and commeth on a pace. Horryble is the tydynges of the Lordes daye, then shall the gyaunte crye oute:

15 for that daye is a daye of wrath, a daye of trouble and heuinesse, a daye of vtter destruccyon & mysery, a darcke & glomyng daye, a cloudy and stormy daye,

16 a daye of the noyse of trompettes & shawmes, agaynst the stronge cities & hye towres.

17 I wyl brynge the people into suche vexacyon, that they shal go aboute lyke blyndemen, because they haue synned agaynste the Lorde. Theyr bloude shalbe shed as the duste, & theyr bodyes as the myre.

18 Nether theyr syluer nor theyr golde shalbe able to delyuered them in þe wrothfull daye of the Lorde, but the whole lande shalbe consumed thorow the fyre of his gelousy: for he shall soone make cleane ryddaunce of all them that dwell in the lande.

## CHAPTER 2

Come together & gather you, O froward people,

2 or þe thing go forthe that is concluded, & or the tyme be passed awaye as the duste: or the fearefull wrath of the Lorde come vpon you,

3 yea or the daye of the

Lordes sore dyspleasure come vpon you. Seke the Lorde all ye meke herted vpon earth, ye that worcke after hys iudgemente, seke ryghtuousnesse: seke lowlynesse, that ye maye be defended in the wrothfull daye of þe Lorde.

4 For Gaza shal be destroyed, and Ascalon shall be layed waste. They shal caste oute Asdod at the noone daye, and Accaron shalbe pluckte vp by the rotes.

5 Wo vnto you that dwell vpon the sea cost ye murtherous people: the worde of the Lord shal come vpon you. O Canaan thou lande of the Phylistines, I wyl destroy the, so that there shall no man dwel in the any more:

6 and as for the sea coast, it shall be hyrdemens cotages & shepe foldes:

7 yea it shalbe a porcyon for suche as remayne of the house of Iuda, to fede there vpon. In the houses of Ascalon shall they reste towarde nyght: for the Lorde theyr God shal vpset them, & turne awaye theyr captyuyte.

8 I haue heard the despyte of Moab, & the blasphemyes of the chyldren of Ammon, howe they haue shamefullye intreated my people, and magnifyed them selues wythin the borders of theyr lande.

9 Therfore as truely as I lyue (sayeth the Lorde of hostes the God of Israel) Moab shalbe as Sodome, & Ammon as Gomorra: euen drye thorne hedges, salt pyttes and a perpetual wyldernes. The resydue of my folcke shall spoyle them the remnaunte of my people shall haue them in possession.

10 This shal happen vnto them for their pryde, because they haue dealte so shamefullye wyth the Lorde of hostes people, and magnified themselues aboue them.

11 The lorde shall be gryme vpon them, & destroy al the goddes in the lande. And al the Iles of the heathen shal worshippe him, euery man in hys place.

12 Ye Morians also shal perish with my swerd:

13 yea, he shall stretche oute his hande ouer the north, and destroye Assur. As for Niniue, he shall make it desolate, drye and waste.

14 The flockes & all the beastes of the people shall lye in þe middeste of it, pellicanes & storckes shall abyde in the vpperpostes of it, soules shall synge in the wyndowes, & rauens shall syt vpon the balckes, for the borders of Cedre shal be ryuen doune.

15 Thys is the proude and carelesse cytye, that sayde in her herte: I am, and there is els none. O how is she made so wast that the beastes lye therein? Who so goeth by mocketh her, and poynteth at her wyth hys fynger.

# CHAPTER 3

Wo to the abhomynable, fylthy & cruell cytie:

2 whiche will not heart, nor be refourmed. Get trust is not in the Lord, neither wyll she holde her to her goo.

3 Her rulers within her are as roaryng lyons: her iudges are as wolues in the euenynge, which leaue nothynge behynde them tyll the morowe.

4 Her prophetes are lyght persones & vnfaythfull men: her priestes vnhalowe the Sanctuarye, and do wrong vnder the pretence of the lawe.

5 But the iuste Lorde that doth no vnryghte, was amonge them, euery morning shewynge them hys lawe clearlye, and ceased not. But the vngodlye wyll not learne to be ashamed.

6 Therfore wyll I rote out thys people, and destroye theyr towres: yea, and make theyr stretes so voyd, that no man shal go therin. Theyr cytyes shalbe broken doune, so that no bodye shall be lefte, nor dwell there anye more.

7 I sayde vnto them: O feare me, and be contente to be refourmed. That theyr dwellynge shulde not be destroyed, and that there shulde happen vnto them none of these thynges, wherewyth I shall vyset them. But neuertheles they stande vp earlye, to folowe the fylthynes of theyr owne ymagynacions.

8 Therfore ye shall wayte vpon me (sayeth the Lord) vntil the tyme that I stand vp: for I am determed, to gather the people & to bring the kingedoms together, that I may poure oute myne anger, yea, al my wrothfull displeasure vpon them. For all the worlde shalbe consumed wyth the fyre of my gelousy.

9 And then wyll I clense the lyppes of the people, þt they may euerychone call vpon the name of the Lord, and serue hym with one shulder.

10 Such as I haue subdued, and my chyldren also whome I haue scatred abroade, shall brynge me presentes beyond the waters of Ethiopia.

11 In that tyme shalte thou no more be confounded, because of all thy ymagynacyons, where thorow thou haddest offended me: for I wyll take awaye the proude boasters of thyne honoure from the, so that thou shalte no more tryumphe because of my holy hyll.

12 In the also will I leaue a small poore simple people, which shal trust in the name of the Lorde.

13 The remnaunt of Israel shal do no wyckednes, nor speake lyes, neyther shall there anye disceytful tunge be founde in theyr mouthes. For they

# ZEPHANIAH

shalbe fed, and take theyr reste, and no man shall make them afrayed.

14 Geue thankes O doughter Syon, be ioyfull O Israell, reioyce and be glad from thy whole herte, O doughter Ierusalem,

15 for the Lorde hath taken awaye thy punyshemente, and turned backe thyne enemyes. The kynge of Israell, euen the Lorde hymselfe is with the: so that thou nedest no more to feare any mysfortune.

16 In that tyme it shall be sayed to Ierusalem: feare not, and to Syon: let not thyne handes be slacke,

17 for the Lorde thy GOD is with the, it is he that hath power to saue: he hath a specyall pleasure in the, & a maruelous loue towarde the: yea, he reioyseth ouer the wyth gladnesse.

18 Suche as haue bene in heuynesse, wyll I gather together, and take out of thy congregacion: as for the shame & reprofe that hath bene layed vpon the, it shalbe farre from the.

19 And lo, in that tyme wyll I destroye all those that vexe the: I wyl helpe the lame, and gather vp the caste awaye: yea I wil get them prayse and honoure in all landes, where they haue bene put to shame,

20 At the same time wyll I brynge you in, and at the same tyme wyll I gather you. I wyll get you a name and a good reporte amonge al people of the earthe, when I turne back youre captyuyte before youre eyes, sayeth the Lorde.

# Haggai

## CHAPTER 1

In the seconde yeare of Kynge Darius, in the .vi. moneth, the first day of the moneth, came the worde of the Lorde (by the Prophete Aggeus) vnto Zorobabel þe sonne of Salathiel the prynce of Iuda, and to Iesua the sonne of Iosedech the hye prieste, sayinge:

2 Thus speaketh the Lord of hostes, and sayeth: This people doth saye: The tyme is not yet come to buylde vp the Lordes house.

3 Then spake the Lord by the Prophete Aggeus, and sayde:

4 Ye your selues can fynde tyme to dwell in syled houses, and shall thys house lye waste?

5 Consydre nowe youre owne wayes in youre hertes (sayth the Lorde of hostes)

6 ye sowe muche, but ye bryng lytle in: ye eate, but ye haue not ynoughe: ye drincke, but ye are not fylled, ye decke youre selues, but ye are not warme: and he that earneth any wage, putteth it in a broken purse.

7 Thus sayeth the Lorde of hostes: Consydre your owne wayes in your hertes,

8 get you vp to the mountayne, fetche wood, and buyld vp the house, that it maye be acceptable vnto me, and that I maye shewe myne honoure, sayeth the Lorde.

9 Ye loked for much, and lo, it is come to lytle: & thoughe ye bryng it home, yet do I blowe it awaye. And why so, sayeth the Lorde of hostes? Euen because that my house lyeth so waste, and ye runne euery man vnto hys owne house.

10 Wherfore the heauen is forbidden to geue you anye dewe, and the earthe is forbidden to geue you encrease.

11 I haue called for a drouthe, both vpon the lande & vpon the mountaynes, vpon corne, vpon wyne, & vpon oyle, vpon euery thynge that the grounde bryngeth forth, vpon men and vpon catell, yea and vpon all handy laboure.

12 Now when Zorobabel the sonne of Salathiel, and Iesua the sonne of Iosedech the hye priest with the remnaunte of the people, heard the voyce of the Lorde theyr God, and þe wordes of the Prophete Aggeus (lyke as þe lorde theyr God hath sent him) the people dyd fear the Lorde.

13 Then Aggeus the Lordes angell sayde in the Lordes message vnto the people: I am wyth you, sayeth the Lorde.

14 So þe Lorde waked vp the spryte of Zorobabel the prince of Iuda, and the sprete of Iesua the sonne of Iosedech the hye priest, and the sprete of the remnaunte of all the people: that they came, and laboured, in the house of the Lorde of Hostes theyr God.

15 Vpon the .xxiiij. daye of the sixte moneth, in the seconde yeare of Kyng Darius,

## CHAPTER 2

The .xxi. daye of the seuenthe moneth, came the worde of the Lorde vp the prophete Aggeus, saying:

2 speake to Zorobabel the sonne of Salathiel prince of Iuda, and to Iesua the sonne of Iosedech the hye priest, & to the resydue of the people, and saye:

3 Who is lefte amonge you, that sawe this house in her fyrste beutye? But what thinck ye now by it? Is it not in your eyes, euen as though it were nothynge?

4 Neuerthelesse be of good chere O Zarobabel (sayeth the Lorde) be of good comforte, O Iesua thou sonne of Iosedech hye pryest: take good hertes vnto you also, all ye people of the lande, sayeth the Lorde of hostes

5 and do accordynge to the worde (for I am wt you, sayeth the Lorde of hostes) lyke as I agreed wyth you, when ye came oute of þe land of Egypte: and my spryte shalbe among you, feare ye not.

6 For thus sayth the Lorde of hostes: yet ones more wyll I shake heauen and earthe, the sea and the drye lande:

7 yea, I will moue al heathen, & the comforte of all Heathen shall come, and so wyll I fyl thys house wyth honoure, sayeth the Lorde of hostes.

8 The syluer is myne, and the gold is myne, sayth the lord of hostes.

9 Thus the glorye of the last house shalbe greater then the fyrste, sayeth þe Lorde of hostes: and in this place will I geue peace, sayeth the Lorde of hostes.

10 The .xxiiij. daye of the .ix. moneth in the seconde yeare of kynge Darius, came the word of the Lorde vnto the Prophete Aggeus, sayinge:

11 Thus sayeth the Lorde GOD of hostes: Aske the priestes concerninge the lawe, & saye:

12 yf one beare holye flesh in his cote lappe, and with his lappe do touche the bread, potage, wyne, oyle, or anye other meate: shall he be holye also? The priestes answered & sayde: No.

13 Then sayde aggeus: Nowe yf one being defyled with a dead carcase, touche anye of these: shall it also be vncleane.

14 The Pryestes gaue answers, & sayd: yea, it shalbe vncleane. Then Aggeus answered, and sayde: euen so is thys people & this nacyon before me, sayth the Lord: & so are al the worckes of theyr handes, yea, and all that they offre, is vncleane.

15 And now (I praye you) consydre from thys daye forthe, and howe it hath gone wyth you afore: or euer there was layed one stone vpon another in the temple of the Lorde,

16 that when ye came to a corne heape of .xx. bushels, there were scarce ten: and that when ye came to the wyne presse for to powre oute .C. pottes of wyne, there were scarce .xx.

17 For I smote you wyth heate, blastynge and hayle stones in all the labours of your handes: yet was there none of you, that wolde turne vnto me, sayth the Lorde.

18 Consydre then from thys daye forth and afore, namely, from the .xxiiij. daye of the .ix. moneth, vnto the daye that the foundacion of the Lordes temple was layed: marck it wel

19 is not the sede yet in the barne? haue not the vines, the fyggetrees, the pomgranates, & oliue trees bene yet vnfrutefull? but from this day forth, I shall make them to prospere.

20 Moreouer the .xxiiij. daye of the moneth came the worde of the Lorde vnto Aggeus agayne, sayinge:

21 Speake to Zorobabel the prynce of Iuda, and saye: I wyll shake bothe heauen and earthe,

22 and ouerthrowe the seat of the kyngedomes, yea; & destroye the myghtye kyngedome of the heathen. I wyll ouerthrow the charettes, and those that syt vpon them, so that both horse and man shall fall doune, euerye man thorowe hys neyghbours swearde.

23 And as for the, O Zorobabel (sayeth the Lord of hostes) thou sonne of Salathiel my seruaunt: I wil take the (sayeth the Lord) at the same tyme, and make the as a seale, for I haue chosen the, saith the Lord of hostes.

# Zechariah

## CHAPTER 1

IN the eyght moneth of the seconde yeare of kyng Darius, came the word of the Lorde vnto Zacharye the sonne of Barachias, the sonne of Addo, the prophet saying:

2 the Lorde hath ben sore dyspleased at youre forefathers.

3 And saye thou vnto them: thus sayeth the Lorde of hostes. Turne you vnto me (sayeth the Lorde of hostes) & I wyll turne me vnto you, sayth the Lorde of hostes.

4 Be not ye lyke youre forefathers, vnto whom the Prophetes cryed afore tyme, sayinge: Thus sayeth the Lord God of hostes. Turne you from youre euyll wayes, & from your wicked ymaginacyons. But thei wolde not heare, nor regarde me, sayeth the Lorde.

5 What is nowe become of your forefathers & the prophetes? are they yet styll aliue?

6 But dyd not my wordes and statutes (which I commaunded by my seruauntes the prophetes) touche your forefathers? Vpon this, they gaue aunswere and sayde: lyke as the Lord of hostes deuysed to do vnto vs, accordynge to oure owne wayes & ymagynacyons, euen so hath he dealte wyth vs.

7 Vpon the .xxiiij. daye of the .xi. moneth which is the moneth Sebat, in the second year of Darius, came the worde of the Lorde vnto Zacharye the sonne of Barachias, the sonne of Addo the Prophete, sayinge:

8 I sawe by nyght, and lo, there sate one vpon a read horse & stode styll amonge the Myrte trees, that were beneth vpon the grounde: and behynde hym were there reade, spekled, and whyt horses.

9 Then sayde I: O my Lorde, what are these? And the aungell that talcked with me, sayde vnto me: I wyll shewe the, what these be.

10 And the man that stode amonge the Myrt trees, aunswered and sayde: These are they, whom the Lorde hath sente to go thorowe the worlde.

11 And they aunswered the aungell of þe Lorde, that stode amonge the myrt trees, and sayde: We haue gone thorowe the world: and beholde, all the worlde dwell at ease, and are carelesse.

12 Then the Lordes aungell gaue aunswere, and sayde: O Lorde of hostes, howe longe wylte thou be vnmercyfull to Ierusalem and to the cytyes of Iuda, wyth whom thou hast bene dyspleased nowe these .lxx. yeares.

13 So the Lorde gaue a louynge and a confortable aunswere vnto the aungell that talcked wyth me.

14 And the aungel that commoned with me, sayde vnto me: Crye thou, and speake: Thus sayeth the Lorde of hostes: I am exceadynge gelous ouer Ierusalem and Syon,

15 and sore dyspleased at the carelesse Heathen: for where as I was but a lytle angrye, they dyd theyr best that I myghte destroye them.

16 Therfore thus sayeth the Lord: I wyl turne me agayne in mercy toward Ierusalem, so that my house shalbe buylded in it, saith the Lord of Hostes: yea and the plommet shalbe layd abroad in Ierusalem, sayeth the Lorde of hostes.

17 Crye also, and speake: thus sayeth the lorde of hostes: My cytyes shalbe in good prosperyte agayne, the Lorde shall yet comfort Sion, and chose Ierusalem.

18 Then lyfte I vp myne eyes, and sawe, and beholde, foure hornes.

19 And I sayde vnto the angel, that talketh with me: what be these? he aunswered me: These are the hornes, whiche haue scatred Iuda, Israel and Ierusalem abroade.

20 And the Lorde shewed me .iiij. carpenters.

21 Then sayde I: what wyll these do? He aunswered, and

said: Those are the hornes, which haue so strowed Iuda abroade, that no man durste lyft vp his head: But these are come to fraye them away and to caste oute the hornes of the Gentyles, whiche lyfte vp theyr horne ouer the lande of Iuda, to scatre it abroade.

## CHAPTER 2

I lyfte vp myne eyes agayne, & loked, and beholde, a man wyth a measure lyne in his hand.

2 Then sayde I: whether goest thou? And he sayde vnto me: To measure Ierusalem, that I maye se howe longe & howe broade it is.

3 And beholde, the aungell þt talked with me, wente hys way forthe. Then wente there oute another aungell to mete him

4 and sayde vnto hym: Runne, speake to thys younge man, and saye: Ierusalem shall be inhabyted wythoute anye wall, for the verye multytude of people and catell, that shal be therein

5 Yea I my selfe (sayeth the Lorde) wil be vnto her a wall of fyre rounde aboute, and wilbe honoured in her.

6 O get you forthe, O fle from the lande of the northe, sayeth the Lorde, ye whom I haue scatred into the foure wyndes vnder heauen, sayeth the Lorde.

7 Saue thy selfe, O Syon: thou that dwellest with the doughter of Babylon,

8 for thus sayeth the Lorde of hostes: Wyth a gloryous power hath he sent me out to the Heathen, which spoyled you: for who so toucheth you, shal touche the aple of his owne eye.

9 Beholde, I wyl lyfte vp myne hande ouer them, so that they shall be spoyled of those, whiche afore serued them: and ye shall knowe that the Lorde of hostes hath sente me.

10 Be glad, and reioyce, O doughter of Sion: for lo, I am come to dwell in the myddeste of the, sayeth the Lord.

11 At the same tyme there shall manye Heathen cleue to the Lorde, and shall be my people. Thus wyll I dwell in the myddest of the, & thou shalte knowe, that the Lorde of hostes hathe sente me vnto the.

12 The Lorde shall haue Iuda in possessyon for hys parte in the holye grounde, and shall chose Ierusalem yet agayne.

13 Let all fleshe be styll before the Lorde, for he is rysen oute of hys holy place.

## CHAPTER 3

AND he shewed me Iesua þe hye priest, standynge before the angell of the Lorde, and Satan stode at hys ryghte hande to resiste hym.

2 And the Lorde sayde vnto Satan: The Lorde reproue the (thou Satan) yea the Lorde that hath chosen Ierusalem, reproue the. Is not thys a brande taken out of the fyre?

3 Nowe Iesua was clothed in vnclean rayment, and stode before the aungel:

4 whiche aunswered and sayde vnto those, that stode before hym: take awaye the foule clothes from him. And vnto hym he sayd: Beholde, I haue taken away thy synne from the, and wil decke the with chaunge of rayment.

5 He sayde moreouer: set a fayre myter vpon his head. So they set a fayre myter vpon hys heade, and put on clothes vpon hym, and the aungel of the Lorde stode there.

6 Then the aungell of þe lord testyfyed vnto Iesua, and spake,

7 thus sayth þe Lorde of hostes: If thou wylte walke in my wayes, & kepe my watche: thou shalt rule my house, & kepe my courtes, and I wil geue the place amonge these that stande here.

8 Heare O Iesua thou hye priest, thou and thy frendes that dwell before the, for they are wonderous people. Beholde, I wyll brynge forthe the braunche of my seruaunt:

9 for lo, the stone that I haue layed before Iesua: vpon one stone shalbe .vij. eyes. Beholde, I wyll hewe hym out (sayeth the Lorde of Hostes) & take away the synne of that lande in one daye.

10 Then shal euery man cal for hys neyghboure vnder the vyne & vnder the fygge tree, sayeth the Lorde of hostes.

## CHAPTER 4

AND the angel that talked wyth me, came agayne, & waked me vp, as a man that is raysed out of hys slepe,

2 & sayde vnto me: What seyst thou? And I sayde: I haue loked, & beholde: a candelsticke of all golde, wyth a boll vpon vpon it and his seuen lampes therein, & vpon euery lamp .vij. stalkes.

3 And two olyue trees therby, one vpon þe right syde of the bol, and the other vpon the left side.

4 So I answered, & spake to the angell that talked with me, sayinge: O my Lorde what are these?

5 The angel that talked with me aunswered & sayde vnto me: knowest thou not what these be? And I sayde: No, my Lorde.

6 He aunswered, and sayde vnto me: Thys is the word of the Lorde vnto Zorobabel, saying: Nether thorowe an hoste of men, nor thorow strength, but thorowe my sprete, sayeth the Lorde of hoostes.

7 What art thou, thou greate mountayne, before Zorobabel: thou must be mayde euen. And he shall brynge vp the fyrst

stone, so that men shall crye vnto hym: good lucke, good lucke.

8 Moreouer the worde of the Lorde came vnto me, sayinge:

9 The handes of Zorobabel haue layed the foundacyon of thys house, his handes shal also fynysh it, that ye may know how that the Lorde of hostes hath sent me vnto you.

10 For he hath ben dispysed a lytle season, shall reioyce, when he seyth the tynne weyght in Zorobabels hande. The .vij. eyes are the Lordes, whiche go thorowe the whole worlde.

11 Then aunswered I, and said vnto him: What are these .ij. olyue trees vpon the right & left syde of the candelstycke?

12 I spake moreouer, & sayde vnto hym: what be these two olyue braunches (whiche thorow the two golden pypes) emptye them selues into the gold?

13 He aunswered me, and sayde: knoweste thou not, what these be? And I sayde: no, my Lord.

14 Then sayde he: These are the two olyue braunches, that stande before the ruler of the whole earthe.

## CHAPTER 5

So I turned me, lyftyng vp myne eyes, and loked, and beholde, a flying boke.

2 And he sayd vnto me: what seyst thou? I answered: I se a flyinge boke of .xx. cubytes longe, and ten cubytes broade.

3 Then sayd he vnto me: This is the cursse that goeth forth ouer the whole earth: for all theues shal be iudged after this boke, & all swearers shalbe iudged accordynge to the same,

4 I wyl bring it forth (sayeth the Lorde of hostes) so that it shall come to the house of the these, and to the house of hym, that falselye sweareth by my name, and shall remayne in hys house, and consume it, with the timbre & stones thereof.

5 Then the aungell that talked wyth me, wente forth, & sayde vnto me: lyfte vp thyne eyes, & se, what this is that goeth forth.

6 And I sayde: what is it? He answered: this is a measure goinge oute. He sayde moreouer: Euen thus ate they (that dwel vpon the whole earth) to loke vpon.

7 And beholde, there was lyfte vp a talent of leade: and lo, a woman sat in the myddeste of the measure.

8 And he sayde: This is vngodlynesse. So he caste her into the middest of the measure, and threwe the lompe of leade vp into an whole.

9 Then lyft I vp myne eyes, and loked: & beholde, there came oute two wemen, & þe wynd was in theyr wynges (for they had wynges lyke the wynges of a storke) & they lyfte vp þe measure betwixt the earth & the heauen.

10 Then spake I to the aungell that talcked with me: whyther wyll these beare the measure?

11 And he sayde vnto me: into the lande of Synear, to buylde them an house: which when it is prepared, the measure shalbe set there in his place.

## CHAPTER 6

Moreouer, I turned me, lyftynge vp myne eyes, and loked: and beholde there came .iiij. charettes oute from betwixte two hylles, whiche hylles were of brasse.

2 In the fyrste charet were reade horse: in the second charet were blacke horse, in the thyrde charette were whyte horse,

3 in the fourthe charet were horses of dyuerse colours and stronge.

4 Then spake I, and sayde vnto the angel that talcked with me: O Lorde, what are these?

5 The Aungell aunswered, and sayde vnto me: These are the .iiij. wyndes of the heauen, whiche be come forthe to stand before the ruler of al the earth.

6 That with the blacke horse wente into þe land of the northe, & the whyte folowed them, and the spekled horses wente forthe towarde the southe.

7 These horses were very stronge, and wente oute, and soughte to go, and take theyr iourney ouer the whole earthe. And he sayde: get you hence, & go thorowe the worlde. So they wente thorowe oute the worlde.

8 Then cryed he vpon me, and spake vnto me, saying: beholde, these that go towarde the north, shall styll my wrath in the northe countreye.

9 And the worde of the Lord came vnto me, saying:

10 Take of the presoners that are come from Babylon, namely, Heldai, Tobiah and Idaia: and come thou the same daye, and go into the house of Iosiah the sonne of Sophony.

11 Then take golde and syluer, and make crounes thereof, and set them vpon the heade of Iesua the sonne of Ioseueh, the hye pryeste,

12 and speake vnto hym: Thus sayth the Lorde of hostes: Behold the man whose name is the braunche: and he that shall sprynge vp after hym, shall buylde vp the temple of the Lorde,

13 yea euen he shall buylde vp þe temple of þe Lord. He shall beare the prayse, he shal syt vpon the Lordes trone, and haue the domynacyon. A Priest shall be also vpon hys trone, & a peaceable councell shalbe betwixte them both.

14 And the crounes shalbe in the temple of the Lorde, for a remembraunce vnto Helem, Tobiah, Idaia, and Hen the sonne of Sophony. And suche as be farre of, shal come and buylde

the temple of the Lorde,

15 that ye maye knowe, howe that the Lorde of hostes hath sent me vnto you. And this shal come to passe. Yf ye will herken diligently vnto the voyce of the Lorde youre God.

## CHAPTER 7

It happened also in the fourthe yeare of kinge Darius, that the word of the lord came vnto Zachary in the fourth daye of the .ix. monethe, whiche is called Caslew:

2 what tyme as Sarasar & Rogomelech & the men þt were with them, sent vnto Bethel for to pray before the lord:

3 & þt they should say vnto the priestes, which were in the house of the Lord of hostes, & to þe prophetes: should I wepe in the fyfte moneth, and absteyne, as I haue done now cerrtain yeares?

4 Then came the word of the Lorde of hostes vnto me, saying:

5 Speake vnto all the people of the land, & to the priestes, and saye: when ye fasted and mourneth in þe .v. & .vij. moneth (now this .lxx. yeares) dyd ye fast vnto me?

6 When ye ate also and droncke; dyd ye not eate & drincke for youre owne selues?

7 Are not these the wordes which the Lord spake by his prophetes afore tyme, when Ierusalem was yet inhabited & welthy, she and the cities round aboute her: when there dwelt men, both toward the south and in the playne countreyes?

8 And the worde of the Lorde came vnto Zachary, saying:

9 Thus sayeth the Lord of Hostes: Execute true iudgement: shew mercy & louinge kindnesse, euery man to his brother.

10 Do the widdow, the fatherlesse, the straunger, and poore no wronge: and let no man ymagen euil against his brother in his hert.

11 Neuertheles they would not take hede, but turned their backes, & stopped their eares, that they should not heare:

12 yea, they made their hertes as an Adamant stone, least they should hear the law & wordes, whiche the Lorde of hostes sent in his holy spirite by the Prophetes afore tyme. Wherfore the Lorde of hostes was verye wroth at them.

13 And thus it is come to passe, that like as he spake, & they woulde not hear: euen so they cryed, and I woulde not heare, (sayeth the Lord of hostes)

14 but scatered them among al Gentiles, whom they knew not: Thus the lande was made so desolate, that there trauayled no man in it, neyther to, nor for for that pleasaunt lande was vtterly layed waste.

## CHAPTER 8

So the worde of the lord came onto me saying:

2 Thus sayeth the Lord of hostes: I was in a great gelousy ouer Syon, yea I haue bene very gelous ouer her in a great displeasure:

3 thus sayeth the Lord of hostes: I wil turne me agayne vnto Syon & wil dwell in the middest of Ierusalem: so that Ierusalem shalbe called a faythfull, and true cytie, the hyll of the Lorde of hostes, yea an holy hill.

4 Thus sayeth the Lorde of hostes: There shal yet olde men & wemen dwell againe in the stretes of Ierusalem: yea, & such as go wt staues in their handes for very age.

5 The stretes of the citie also shalbe ful of yonge boyes & damoselles, playinge vpon the stretes.

6 Thus sayeth the Lord of Hostes: yf the residue of this people thincke it to be vnpossible in these dayes, should it therfore be vnpossible in my sight, sayeth the Lord of hostes:

7 Thus sayeth the Lord of hostes: Behold, I wil delyuer my people from the land of the east & west,

8 and will bringe them againe, that they maye dwell at Ierusalem. Then shalbe my people and I wilbe their God, in trueth & righteousnesse.

9 Thus sayeth the lord of hostes: let your handes be stronge, yea that nowe heare these wordes by the mouth of the prophetes which be in the dayes, that the foundacion is layed vpon the Lorde of hostes house, that the temple may be buylded.

10 For why? before these dayes neyther men nor cattell coulde wynne anye thinge, neyther might anye man come in and oute in rest, for trouble: but I let euery man go agaynst his neyghboure.

11 Neuerthelesse I wil now entreate the resydue of this people no more as for a time, sayeth the Lord of Hostes,

12 but they shalbe a sede of peace. The vineyarde shal geue her frute, the grounde shal geue her increase, and the heauens shall geue their dew: & I shall cause the remnaunt of this people, to haue all these in possession.

13 And it shall come to passe, that like as ye were a curse amonge the Heathen (O ye house of Iuda & ye house of Israel) Euen so wil I deliuer you, þt ye shalbe a blessing: feare not, but let your handes be stronge.

14 For thus sayeth the Lord of Hostes: lyke as I deuised to punishe you, what tyme as youre fathers prouoked me vnto wrath, sayeth the Lord of hostes, and spared not.

15 Euen so I determed now in these dayes, for to do well vnto the house of Iuda, and Ierusalem, therfore feare ye not.

16 Now the thinges that ye shall do, are these: Speake euery man the truth vnto his neyghboure, execute iudgement trulye, & peaceably within your portes,

17 none of you ymagin euill in his hert againste hys neyghboure, & loue no false othes: for al these are the thynges that I hate, sayeth the Lord.

18 And þe word of the lord of hostes, came vnto me saying:

19 Thus sayeth the lord of Hostes: The fast of the fourth moueth, the fast of the fyfth, the fast of the seuenthe, & the faste of þe tenth, shalbe ioye and gladnesse, and prosperous hye feastes vnto the house of Iuda: Only loue the treuth and peace.

20 Thus sayeth the Lorde of hostes: There shal yet come people, and the inhabiters of many cities:

21 and they that dwell in one citie, shal go to another sayeng: Vp, let vs go, and pray before the Lord, let vs seke the Lorde of Hostes, I will go with you:

22 yea much people and mightie heathen shall come and seke the Lorde of Hostes at Ierusalem, & to pray before the Lorde.

23 Thus sayeth the Lorde of Hostes: In that tyme shal ten men (out of al maner of languages of the Gentiles) take one Iew by the hemme of his garment, and saye: we wyl go with you, for we haue hearde, that God is amonge you.

## CHAPTER 9

THE worde of the Lorde shalbe receyued at Abrach, & Damascus shalbe his offering: for the eyes of all men and of the trybes of Israel shall loke vp vnto þe lord.

2 The borders of Hemath shalbe hard therby, Tyrus also and Sidon, for they are verye wise.

3 Tyrus shal make herself strong, heape vs syluer as the sande, & golde as the clay of the stretes.

4 Beholde, the lord shal take her in, & haue her in possession: he shall smyte doune her power into the sea, & she shalbe consumed with fire.

5 This shall Ascalon se, & be afraied. Gaza shalbe very sory, so shal Accaron also, because her hope is come to confusyon. For the Kinge of Gaza shal peryshe, and at Ascalon shal no man dwel.

6 Straungers shal dwel at Asdod, & as for the pryde of the Philistines, I shal rote oute

7 Their bloud wil I take away from their mouth and their abhominacyons from among their teeth Thus they shalbe left for our God, yea they shalbe as a prince in Iuda, & Accaron like as Iebusy:

8 & so wil I compase my house round about wt my men of warre goynge to & fro: that no oppressoure come vpon them any more. For that haue I sene now with myne eyes.

9 Reioyce thou greatly, O doughter Syon, be glad, O doughter Ierusalem. For lo, thy king commeth vnto the, euen the ryghteous & Sauioure: Lowly and simple is he, he rydeth vpon an asse, & vpon the foale of an asse.

10 I wil rote out the charrettes from Ephraim, & the horse from Ierusalem, the battel bowes shalbe destroyed. He shall geue the doctryne of peace vnto the heathen, & his dominion shal be from the one syde to the other, and from the flundes to the endes of the worlde.

11 Thou also thorow thy bloude of thy couenaunt, shalte let thy presoners out of the pyt, wherin is no water.

12 Turne you nowe to the strong holde, ye that be in preson, & long sore to be delyuered: And this daye I brynge the word, that I wil rewarde the double agayn.

13 For Iuda haue I bent out as a bowe for me, and Ephraim haue I fylled Thy sonnes (O Sion) will I rase vp againste the Grekes, & make the as a giauntes sweardre:

14 the Lorde God shalbe sene aboue them, and his dartes shal go forth as the lyghteninge. The Lorde God shall blowe the trompet, and shall come forth as a storme oute of the south.

15 The Lorde of hostes shall defende them, they shall consume and deuoure, & subdue them with slyng stones. They shal dryncke & rage as it were thorow wyne. They shalbe fylled like the basens, & as the hornes of the aulter.

16 The Lorde their God shall delyuer them in the day, as the flock of his people: for the stones of his Sanctuary shalbe set vp in his land,

17 O how prosperous & goodlye a thinge shall that be? The corne shall make the yong men chearefull, and the newe wyne the maydens.

## CHAPTER 10

PRAYE the Lord then by tymes to geue thou the latter rayne, so shall the Lorde make cloudes, & geue you raine ynough, for all the intreace of the felde:

2 For vayne is the answere of Idols. The sothsayers se lyes, & tel but vayn dreames: the comforthe that they geue, is nothinge worth. Therfore go they astraye lyke a flocke of shepe, & are troubled, because they haue no sheperde.

3 My wrothfull displeasure is moued at the sheperdes, & I will vpset the goates. For the

Lord of hostes wil graciously viset his flocke, the house of Iuda, and hold them as a goodlye fayre horse in the battell.

4 Out of Iuda shall come the helmet, the nale, the battelbowe, and all the princes together.

5 They shalbe as the giauntes, whiche in the batell tread doune the myre vpon the stretes. They shal fight, for the Lorde shalbe wyth them, so that the horsemen shalbe confounded.

6 I will comforth the house of Iuda, and preserue the house of Ioseph. I wil turne them also, for I pitie them: & they shalbe lyke as they were, when I had not cast them of. For I the Lord am their God, and wil hear them.

7 Ephraim shalbe as a gyaunt, and their hert shalbe chereful as thorow wine: yea, their children shall se it, & be glad, & their herte shall reioyce in the Lord.

8 I wil blow for them & gather them together, for I wil redeme them. They shal increase as they increased afore.

9 I will sow them among the people, that they may thincke vpon me in farre countreyes, they shall lyue wt their children, & turne again.

10 I wil bring them again also from the land of Egipt, & gather them out of Assiria. I wil carie them into the land of Galaad & to Libanus, & they shall wante nothing.

11 He shall go vpon the sea of trouble, & smyte the sea waues: so þt al the depe floudes shalbe dried vp. The proud boastinge of Assur shalbe cast doun, & the scepter of Egipte shalbe taken away.

12 I will comforte them in the Lord, that they maye walcke in his name, sayeth the Lorde.

## CHAPTER 11

OPEN thy dores, O Lybanus, that the fyre maye consume thy Cedre trees.

2 Howle ye fyrre trees, for the Cedre is fallen, yea, all the proude are wasted awaye. Howle (O ye oke trees of Baasan) for the mightye strong wood is cut doune

3 Men may heare the sheperdes mourne, for their glory is destroyed. Men may heare the lyons whelpes roare, for the pride of Iordan is wasted away.

4 Thus sayeth the Lorde my God: Fede the shepe of the slaughter,

5 which shalbe slaine of those that possesse them: yet they take it for no sinne, but they that sell them, say: The Lorde be thancked, I am rich: yea, their owne sheperdes spare them not.

6 Therfore will I nomore spare those that dwell in the land (sayeth the Lord) but lo, I wil delyuer the people, euerye man into his neighboures hand, and into the hande of his king, that they may smyte the lande, & out of their handes wil not I delyuer them.

7 I my self fedde the slaughter shepe (a pore flocke verely) & toke vnto me two staues: the one I called louinge mekenesse, the other I called wo, & so I kepte the shepe.

8 Thre sheperdes destroyeth I in one moneth, for I might not away wt them, neither had they any delyte in me.

9 Then sayd I: I wil fede you no more, the thing that dieth, let it dye: & þt wil perishe, let it perishe, & let the remnaunt eate, euery one the fleshe of his neyghboure.

10 I toke also my louing meke staf, & brake it, that I might disanul the couenaunt, which I made with al people.

11 And so it was broken in that daye. Then the poore simple shepe that had a respecte vnto me, knewe therby, that it was the word of the lord.

12 And I sayde vnto them: yf ye thincke it good, bring hither my pryce: yf no, then leaue. So they wayed doune .xxx. syluer pens, the value that I was prysed at.

13 And the Lorde sayd vnto me: cast it vnto the potter (a goodly pryce for me to be valued at of them) & I toke the .xxx. siluer pens, & cast them to the potter in the house of the Lorde.

14 Then brake I my other staf also (namely wo) þt I mighte lowse the brotherhead betwixte Iuda and Israel.

15 And the Lord said vnto me: Take to the also the staf of a foolish sheperd:

16 for lo, I wil rayse vp a sheperde in the lande, which shall not seke after the thinges that be lost, nor care for such as go astray: he shall not heale the wounded, he shall not norishe the thing that is whole: but he shall eate the fleshe of suche as be fat, and teare their clawes in peces.

17 O Idols sheperd, that leaueth the flocke. The swerde shall come vpon his arme & vpon his right eye. His arme shalbe cleane dryed vp, and hys ryght eye shalbe sore blinded.

## CHAPTER 12

THE heauy burthen which the lord hath deuised for Israel. Thus saieth the lord, which spred the heauens abroade, layde the foundacyon of the earth, and geueth man the breath of lyfe:

2 Beholde I will make Ierusalem a cuppe of surfet, vnto al the people that are round aboute her: Yea, Iuda him self also shalbe in the sege agaynste Ierusalem.

3 At the same tyme wil I make Ierusalem, an heauye stone for al people, so that al such as lift it vp shalbe toarne & rente, & all the people of the earth shalbe gathered together against it.

# ZECHARIAH

4 In that day, sayeth the Lorde, I will make all horses abashed, & those that ryde vpon them to be out of their wittes. I wyll open myne eyes vpon the house of Iuda, & smite all the horses of the people with blindnesse.

5 And the princes of Iuda shal say in their hertes. The inhabiters of Ierusalem shal geue me consolacion in the Lord of hostes their God.

6 In that tyme will I make the princes of Iuda lyke an hote burninge ouen with wood, & lyke a cresset of fyre among the strawe, so that they shal consume al the people rounde about them, both vpon the right hand and the left. Ierusalem also shalbe inhabited agayne: namely, in the same place, where Ierusalem standeth.

7 The Lorde shal preserue the tentes of Iuda like as afore time: so þt the glorye of the house of Dauid, & the glory of the citesins of Ierusalem, shalbe but litle regarded, in comparison of þe glory of Iuda.

8 In that day shal the Lord defende the citesins of Ierusalem: so that the weakest then amonge them shalbe as Dauid: & þe house of Dauid shalbe lyke as Gods house, and as the Angel of the Lorde before them.

9 At the same tyme wil I go about to destroy al suche people as come againste Ierusalem.

10 Moreouer, vpon the house of Dauid & vpon the cytesins of Ierusalem wil I poure oute the spirite of grace & prayer, so þt they shal loke vpon me, whom they haue pearsed: & they shal bewepe him, as men mourne for their onely begotten sonne: yea & be sory for him, as men are sorye for their fyrst childe.

11 Then shal there be a great mourning at Ierusalem, like as the lamentacion at Adremnon in þe feld of Maggadon.

12 And the land shal bewayle euery kinred by them selues. The kinred of þe house of Dauid them selues alone, & their wiues by them selues.

13 The kinred of þe house of Nathan themselues alone, & their wyues by them selues. The kinred of the house of Leui them selues alone, & their wiues by them selues. The kinred of the house of Semei themselues alone & their wiues by them selues.

14 In lyke maner, all the other generacions, euerychone by them selues alone, and their wiues by them selues.

## CHAPTER 13

IN that tyme shall the house of Dauid and the citesins at Ierusalem haue an open well, to wash of synne and vnclennesse.

2 And then (saieth the lord of hostes) I will destroye the names of Idols out of the land: so that they shal nomore be put in remembraunce. As for the false prophetes also & the vnclene spirit, I shal take them out of the land:

3 so that yf any of them prophecy any more, hys owne father and mother that begat him, shal saye vnto him: Thou shalt dye, for thou speakest lyes vnder the name of the Lord: yea his owne father and mother that begat him, shal wound him, when he prophecieth.

4 And then shal those prophetes be confounded, euery one of his vision when he prophecieth: neither shall they weer sackclothes any more, to disceyue men wt all.

5 But he shalbe fayne to saye: I am no prophete: I am an husband man, for so am I taught by Adam from my youth vp:

6 & yf it be sayd vnto him: how came these woundes then in thine handes? He shal answere: Thus am I wounded in the house of myne owne frendes.

7 Arise, O thou swerd, vpon my shepeherd, & vpon the prince of my people sayeth the lorde of hostes. Smite the sheperd, & the shepe shal be scatred abroade, & so wil I turne mine hand to the litle ones.

8 And it shal come to passe (saieth the Lord) that in all the land two partes shalbe roted oute, but the thirde parte shall remayne therin

9 And the same thyrd part wil I bring thorow the fyre, & wil clense them, as the siluer is clensed: yea, & try them like as gold is tryed. Then shall they call vpon my name and I wyll heare them: I wyl saye: it is my people. And they shal say: Lorde my God.

## CHAPTER 14

BEHOLDE, the day of the Lorde commeth, that thou shalt be spoyled, & robbed:

2 for I will gather together al the heathen, to fighte agaynste Ierusalem, so that the city shalbe woune, the houses spoyled, & the wemen defiled. The half of the city shal go away into captiuite, & the residue of the people shal not be caried out of the cyty.

3 After that shal the lord go forthe to fyght agaynste those heathen, as men vse to fight in the daye of batell.

4 Then shall his fete stand vpon the mount olyuete, that lyeth vpon the east syde of Ierusalem. And the mount olyuete shal cleue in two, eastward & westward, so that there shalbe a great valley: & the half mount shal remoue toward the north, & the other toward the south.

5 And ye shal fle vnto þe valley of my hylles, for the valley of the hylles shal reach vnto Asal. Yea, fle shal ye, like as ye fled for the earthquake in

the dayes of Osiah king of Iuda. And the lord my God shall come, and al sayntes with him.

6 In that day shal it not be light; but could & frost.

7 This shalbe that specially day, whiche is knowne vnto þe Lord: neyther day nor light, but about the euening time it shalbe light.

8 In that tyme shal the waters of lyfe runne out from Ierusalem: the half parte of them toward the east sea, & the other half toward the vttermost sea, & shal continue both somer & winter.

9 And the lord him selfe shalbe king ouer al þe earth. At that time shal there be one Lord onlye, & his name shalbe but one.

10 Men shall go about the whole earth, as vpon a feld: from Gibea to Remnon, & from the south to Ierusalem. The shal be set vp, & inhabited in her place: from BenIamins porte, vnto the place of the first port, & vnto the corner porte, & from the tower of Hananeel, vnto the kinges wine presses.

11 There shal men dwel, & there shalbe nomore cursing but Ierusalem shalbe safely inhabited.

12 This shalbe the plage, wherwith the Lorde wyll smite al people, that haue fought agaynst Ierusalem: Namely, their flesh shal consume awaye, though they stand vpon their fete: their eyes shalbe corrupt in their holes, and their tung shall consume in their mouth.

13 In that day shal the Lorde make a great sedicion amonge them, so that one man shal take another by the hande, & lay his handes vpon the handes of his neighbour.

14 Iuda shal fight also against Ierusalem, & the goodes of al þe heathen shalbe gathered together round aboute: gold & siluer, & a very great multitude of clothes:

15 & so shal this plage go ouer horses, mules, camels, asses, & al þe beastes that shalbe in the host, like as yonder plage was.

16 Euery one þt remayneth then of al the people, which came against Ierusalem, shal go vp yearly, to worshippe the king (euen the Lord of hostes) & to kepe the feast of tabernacles:

17 & loke what generacion vpon earth goeth not vp to Ierusalem for to worshippe the kinge (euen the Lorde of hostes) vpon the same shal come no rayne.

18 Yf the kinred of Egypt go not vp, and come not, it shall not rayne vpon them neyther. This shalbe the plage wherwith the Lorde wil smite al heathen, þt come not vp to kepe the feast of tabernacles:

19 yea, this shalbe the sinne plage of Egipt, & the sinne plage of al people that go not vp to kepe the feast of tabernacles.

20 At that time shall the riding geer of the horses be holy vnto the Lord, & the kettels in the Lordes house shalbe lyke the basens before the aulter:

21 yea al the kettels in Ierusalem & Iuda, shalbe holy vnto the Lord of hostes: & all they that slay offeringes, shall come take of them, & dight them therin. And at that tyme there shalbe no mo Cananites in the house of the Lorde.

# Malachi

## CHAPTER 1

THE heauy burthen, whiche the Lorde sheweth agaynst Israel by Malachi.

2 I haue loued you, sayeth the Lord: and yet ye say: wherin haste thou loued vs? Was not Esau Iacobs brother, sayeth the Lord? yet haue I loued Iacob,

3 & hated Esau: yea I haue made his hilles waste, & his heretage a wildernesse for dragons:

4 & though Edom sayd: wel, we are destroyed, we wyll go buylde vp agayne the places that be wasted: yet (sayeth the Lord of hostes) what they buylded, that brake I domie, so that is was called a cursed lande, and a people, whom the Lorde hath euer bene angrye withall.

5 Youre eyes haue sene it, & ye youre selues must confesse, that the Lord hath brought the land of Israel to great honour.

6 Should not a sonne honoure his father, & a seruaunte hys mayster? Yf I be now a father, where is mine honoure? Yf I be the Lorde, where am I feared? sayeth the Lord of hostes. Now to you priestes, that despise my name. And yf ye saye: wherin haue we despised thy name:

7 In this, that ye offre vnclean bread vpon myne aulter. And yf ye wyl say: wherin haue we offered auye vnclene thinge vnto the? In this place ye say: the aulter of the lord is not to be regarded.

8 Yf ye offre the blind, is not that euill? And yf ye offre the lame, and syck, is not that euyll? Yea, offre it vnto thy prince, shal he be content with the, or accepte thy personne, sayeth the Lorde of hostes.

9 And now make your prayer before God, that he may haue mercy vpon vs: for suche thinges haue ye done. Shal he regarde your personnes, thyncke ye, sayeth the Lorde of hostes?

10 Yea, what is he amonge you, that wyll do so muche as to shut the dores, or to kindle the fire vpon myne aulter for naught? I haue no pleasure in you, sayeth the Lord of hostes: and as for the meatofferynge, I will not accepte it at your hande.

11 For from the rysynge vp of the sunne vnto the goynge doune of the same, my name is greate amonge the Gentyles: yea, in euery place shall there sacryfice be done, & a cleane meatoffering offered vp vnto my name: for my name is great among þe heathen, sayeth the Lorde of hostes.

12 But ye haue vnhalowed it, in that ye say: the aulter of the Lorde is not to be regarded, & the thinge that is set ther vpon, not worthy to be eaten.

13 Now say ye: It is but laboure and trauail, and thus haue ye thought scorne at it (sayeth the Lorde of hostes) offeryng robbery, yea, þe lame and the sicke. Ye haue brought me in a meatoffering, shoulde I accepte it of youre hande, sayeth the Lorde?

14 Cursed be the dissembler, which hath in his flocke one that is male and when he maketh a vowe, offereth a spoted one vnto the lord. For I am a great king (sayeth the Lorde of hostes) and my name is fearfull amonge the Heathen.

## CHAPTER 2

AND now (O ye priestes) thys commaundement toucheth you:

2 yf ye wyll not heare it, nor regarde it, to geue the glorye vnto my name, sayeth the lorde of hostes, I wyll sende a curse vpon you, and wyl cursle your blessinges: yea, curse them wil I yf ye do not take hede.

3 Behold, I shall corrupte your sede, and cast dong in your faces: turn the donge of your solempne feastes, & it shal cleue faste vpon you:

4 & ye shal know, that I haue sent this commaundement vnto you: that my couenaunt which I made with Leui, myght stande, sayeth the Lorde of

Hostes.

5 I made a couenaunt of life & peace wt hym: this I gaue him, that he might stande in awe of me: & so he did feare me, & had my name in reuerence.

6 The law of truth was in his mouth and there was no wickednesse founde in hys lippe. He walcked with me in peace & equite, and dyd turne manye one awaye from their synnes.

7 For the priestes lippes should be sure knowledge, that men may seke the lawe at his mouth: for he is a messaunger of the lorde of hostes.

8 But as for you, ye are gone cleane out of the waye, & haue caused the multitude to be offended at the lawe: ye haue broken the couenaunt of Leui, sayeth the Lord of hostes.

9 Therfore wil I also make you to be despised, and to be of no reputacion among al the people, because ye haue not kepte my wayes, but bene parcial in the lawe.

10 Haue we not all one father? Hath not one God made vs? why doth euery one of vs then despyse his owne brother, and so breake the couenaunt of oure fathers?

11 Now hath Iuda offended, yea, the abhomynacyon is done in Israel & in Ierusalem, for Iuda hath defiled the Sanctuarye of the Lorde, whyche he loned, & haue kept the doughter of a straunge God.

12 But the Lorde shall destroye the man þt doth thys (yea, both the mayster and the scolar) out of the tabernacle of Iacob, with hym that offereth vp meateofferinge vnto the lord of hostes.

13 Nowe haue ye brought it to thys poynte againe, that the aulter of the Lorde is couered with teares wepyng and mourning: so that I will no more regarde the meatofferinge, neyther will I receyue or accepte anye thinge at your handes

14 And yet ye say: wherfore? Euen because that where as the Lorde made a couenaunt betwixt the & the wyfe of thy youth, thou hast despysed her: Yet is she thyne owne companion and maried wife.

15 So dyd not the one, and yet had he an excellente spirite. What dyd then the one? He sought the sede promised of God. Therfore loke well to your spirit, and let no man despise the wyfe of his youth.

16 Yf thou hatest her, put her awaye, sayeth the Lord God of Israel, & geue her a clothinge for the scorne, sayeth the Lord of hostes. Loke wel then to your spirit, & despise her not.

17 Ye greue the lord with your wordes, & yet ye say: wherwt al haue we greued him? In this, þt ye say: Al that do euil are good in the sight of god, and such please him. Or els where is the God that punisheth?

# CHAPTER 3

BEHOLDE, I wil sende my messaunger, which shall prepare the way before me: & the Lord whome, ye woulde haue, shall sone come to hys temple, yea, euen the messenger of the couenaunt, whome ye longe for. Beholde he commeth, sayeth the Lord of hostes

2 But who may abyde the day of hys commyng? Who shalbe able to endure, when he appeareth? For he is lyke a goldsmythes fire and lyke a washers sope.

3 He shall syt hym doune to trye and to clense the syluer, he shall pourge the children of Leui, & puryfye them lyke as golde and syluer: that they may bring meatofferinges vnto the Lorde in righteousnes.

4 Then shal the offering of Iuda & Ierusalem be acceptable vnto the Lord, lyke as from the beginninge, and in the yeares, afore tyme.

5 I wil come and punish you, and I my selfe will be a swyf wytnes against the witches, agaynst the aduouterers, agaynste false swearers: yea, and agaynst those, that wrongeouslye kepe backe the hyrelinges dewtye: which vexe the widdowes and the fatherlesse and oppresse the straunger, and feare not me, sayeth the Lord of Hostes.

6 For I am the lord that chaunge not, and ye (O children of Iacob) wyll not leaue of:

7 ye are gone away from myne ordinaunces, and sens the time of your forefathers haue ye not kepte them. Turne you now vnto me, and I will turne me vnto you, sayeth the Lorde of hostes: ye saye: wherin shall we turne?

8 Shoulde a man vse falshede and disceyte with God as ye vse falshede and disceyte wyth me? Yet ye saye: wherin vse we disceyt wyth the? In Tithes & heaueofferinges.

9 Therfore are ye cursed with penury, because ye dissemble with me, all the sorte of you.

10 Bringe euerye Tithe into my barne, that there maye be meat in myne house: and proue me withall (sayeth the Lorde of hostes) yf I will not open the windowes of heauen vnto you, and poure you out a blessynge with plenteousnesse.

11 Yea, I shal reproue the consumer for youre sakes, so that he shall not eate vp the frute of youre grounde, neyther shall the vineyarde be baren in the felde, sayeth the Lord of hostes.

12 In so muche that all people shall saye, that ye be blessed, for ye shalbe a pleasaunt lande, sayeth the Lorde of hostes.

13 Ye speake harde wordes agaynst me, sayeth the Lorde. And yet ye saye: What haue we spoken agaynst the?

14 Ye haue sayed. Is it but lost labour, to serue God? What profyt haue we for keping his commaundementes, and for walkinge humbly before the Lorde of Hostes?

15 Therfore maye we saye, that the proude are happye, and that they whiche deale with the vngodlynesse, are sette vp: for they tempte God, and yet escape.

16 But they that feare God, saye thus one to another: the Lord consydereth and heareth it. Yea, it is before him a memoriall boke, wryten for such as feare the Lorde, & remembre his name.

17 And in the day that I will make (sayeth the Lord of hostes) they shalbe mine own possession: and I wil fauoure them, lyke as a man fauoureth his owne sonne, that doth him seruyce.

18 Turne you therfore, and consydre what difference is betwyxt the ryghteous & vngodly: betwyxt him that serueth God, and him that serueth him not.

## CHAPTER 4

For marck, the day commeth, that shall burne as an ouen: and al the proude, yea and al such as do wickednesse, shalbe straw: and the daye that is for to come, shall burne them vp (sayeth the Lorde of hostes) so that it shall leaue them neyther rote nor braunche.

2 But vnto you that feare my name, shall the Sonne of ryghteousnesse aryse, and healthe shalbe vnder his winges: ye shal go forth, & multipply as the fat calues.

3 Ye shall treade doune the vngodlye: for they shalbe lyke the asshes vnder the soles of your fete, in the day that I shall make, sayeth the Lord of hostes.

4 Remembre the lawe of Moses my seruaunt whyche I commytted vnto hym in Oreb for al Israel, with the stratutes and ordynaunces.

5 Beholde, I wyl sende you Elias the Prophet: before the comming of the daye of the greate and fearfull Lorde.

6 He shall turne the hertes of the fathers to their chyldren, and the hertes of the children to their fathers, that I come not, & smite the earth with cursynge.

# Matthew

## CHAPTER 1

THYS is þe boke of þe generation of Iesus Christ þe sonne of dauyd, þe sonne also of Abraham.

2 Abraham begat Isaac: Isaac begat Iacob: Iacob begat Iudas and hys bretherne:

3 Iudas begat Phares & Zaram of Thamar: Phares begat Esrom: Esrom begat Aram:

4 Aram begat Amidadab: Aminadab begat Naasson: Naasson begat Salmon:

5 Salmon begat Boos of Rachab: Boos begat Obed of Ruth: Obed begat Iesse:

6 Iesse begat Dauid the kynge: Dauid the kinge begat Solomon, of her that was the wyfe of Vrye:

7 Salomon begat Roboam: Roboam begat Abia: Abia begat Asa:

8 Asa begat Iosaphat. Iosaphat begat Ioram: Ioram begat Hosias:

9 Hosias begat Ioatham: Ioatham begat Achas: Achas begat Ezechias:

10 Ezechias begat Manasses: Manasses begat Amon: Amon begat Iosias:

11 Iosias begat Iechonias & hys brethren about the tyme they were caried awaye to Babylon.

12 And after they were brought to Babylou Iechonias begat Salathiel: Salathiel begat zorobabel:

13 zorobabel begat Abiud: Abiud begat Eliachim: Eliachim begat Azor:

14 Azor begat Sadoc: Sadoc begat Achin: Achin begat Eliud:

15 Eliud begat Eliazar: Eliazar begat Matthan: Matthan begat Iacob:

16 Iacob begat Ioseph the husbande of Marie of which was borne that Iesus, that is called Christ.

17 All the generacions frome Abraham to Danid are .xiiij. generations. And from Dauid vnto the captiuitie of Babylon: are .xiiij. generations. And from the captiuitie of Babylon vnto Christe, are also fourtene generations.

18 The byrth of Iesus Christe was ou thys wise. When hys mother Mary was betrouthed to Ioseph, before they came to dwell together, she was founde with chylde by the holye Ghost.

19 Then Ioseph her husbande beinge a perfecte man and loth to make an ensample of her, was mynded to put her awaye secretly.

20 While he thus thought, behold the Aungel of the Lord appered vnto him in a dreame, sainge: Ioseph thou sonne of Dauid. fear not to take vnto the Mary thy wife. For that which is conceyued in her is of the holye Ghost.

21 She shall bryngforth a sonne, & thou shalt cal his name Iesus. For he shal saue his people from their sins.

22 All thys was done to fulfyll that whyche was spoken of the Lorde by the Prophet, saiynge:

23 Bholde a mayde shall be wyth chylde, and shal bringe forth a sonne, and they shall call hys name Emanuell, whyche is by interpretation, God wyth vs.

24 And Ioseph assone as he awoke out of slepe, did as the Aungel of the Lorde had bidden him, and toke hys wyfe vnto him,

25 and knewe her not tyl she had broughte forthe her fyrste sonne, and called hys name Iesus.

## CHAPTER 2

WHEN Iesus was born at Bethleem in Iurye, in the time of Herode the kinge: Beholde there came wise men from the east to Ierusalem

2 sayinge. Where is he þt is borne kinge of Iewes? We haue sene his star in the east, and are come to worshyppe hym.

3 When Herode the kinge had herde this, he was troubled, and al Ierusalem with him,

4 and he gathered al the chiefe priestes and scribes of the people, & axed of them where

Christe shoulde be borne.

5 And they sayd vnto hym: at Bethleem in Iury. For thus it is wrytten by the prophete.

6 And thou Bethleem in the land of Iury, art not the least concerning the Princes of Iuda. For out of the shal come the captaine, that shall gouerne my people Israel.

7 Then Herode preuily called the wyse men, and diligently enquired of them, the tyme of the starre that apeared,

8 and sent them to Bethleem sayinge: Go and searche diligentlye for the childe. And when ye haue founde hym, bringe me worde, that I may come and worshyppe him also.

9 When they hearde the kynge, they departed: and lo the starre which they sawe in the east went before them, tyll it came and stode ouer the place wher þe childe was.

10 When they sawe the starre, they were maruelously glad:

11 and went into the house, and found the chylde with Mary his mother, and kneled doune & worshypped him, and opened their treasures and offred to him giftes golde, frankinsence and myrre.

12 And after they were warned of God in a dreame, that they should not go agayne to Herode, they retourned into their owne countre another waye.

13 When they were departed: Beholde the aungell of the Lorde appeared to Ioseph in a dreame sayinge. Aryse, and take the chylde & his mother, and flee into Egipte, and abyde there tyll I bringe the worde. For Herode wil seke the chylde to destroye him.

14 Then he arose and toke the chylde and his mother by night and departed into Egypte,

15 and was there vnto the death of Herode to fulfyll that whiche was spoken of þe Lord by the prophete, which saieth out of Egipt haue I called my sonne.

16 Then Herode perceauing that he was mocked of the wyse men, was excedinge wroth, & sent forth and slue al the children that were in Bethleem, and in all the costes therof, as many as were two yere olde and vnder according to the time which he had diligently searched out of the wise men.

17 Then was fulfylled that which was spoken by the prophete Ieremy sayinge:

18 On þe hilles was a voice hearde, morning, weping & great lamentacion: Rachel weping for her children, & would not be comforted because thei were not

19 When Herode was dead: beholde, an aungel of the Lorde appeared in a dreame to Iosephe in Egipt

20 sayinge: arise and take the childe and his mother, & go into the lande of Israel. For they are dead which sought þe childes life.

21 Then he arose vp, and toke the childe and his mother, & came into the lande of Israell.

22 But when he hearde that Archelaus did raygne in Iurye, in the roume of his father Herode, he was afraide to go thither. Notwithstanding after he was warned of God in a dreame, he turned a syde into the partyes of Galile,

23 & went & dwelt in a citie called Nazareth, to fulfyl þt which was spoken by the prophetes: he shalbe called a Nazarite.

## CHAPTER 3

IN those dayes Iohn þe Baptist came and preached in þe wyldernes of Iury

2 saying: Repent the kingdome of heauen is at hande.

3 This is he of whom it is spoken by the prophete Esaye which sayeth: The voice of a cryer in wildernes prepare the Lordes way and make his pathes, strayt.

4 This Ihon had his garmente of Camels hear & a girdel of a skinne about his loynes. His meate was locustes, & wilde honye.

5 Then went out to him Ierusalem & all Iurye, & all the region rounde about Iordan,

6 & were baptised of him in Iorden, confessing their sinnes.

7 When he sawe many of the Phariseis & of the Saduces come to his baptisme, he sayd vnto them: O generacion of vipers, who hath taught you to fle from the vengaunce to come?

8 Bringe forth therfore the frutes belonging to repentaunce.

9 And se that ye once thinke not to saye in your selues, we haue Abraham to our father. For I say vnto you, that God is able of these stones rayse vp children vnto Abraham.

10 Euen now is the axe put vnto þe rote of the trees: so þt euerye tre which bringeth not forth good fruit, is hewen doun & cast into þe fire.

11 I baptise you in water in token of repentaunce, but he that cometh after me is mightyer then I, whose shues I am not worthy to beare. He shal baptise you with the holy ghost and with fyre:

12 which hath also his fan in hys hande, and will purge his floure gather the wheat into his garner, & wyl burne the chaffe with vnquenciable fyre.

13 Then came Iesus from Galylee to Iordane, vnto Ihon to be baptysed of him.

14 But Ihon forbad him sayinge: I oughte to be baptysed of the: and commest thou to me?

15 Iesus answered and sayd to hym: Let it be so nowe. For thus it becometh vs to fulfyll al righteousnes. Then he suffred him.

16 And Iesus as sone as he

was baptysed came straight out of the water. And lo heauen was open ouer him: and Ihon sawe the spirite of God descende like a doue, and light vpon him.

17 And lo ther came a voice from heauen sayinge. This is my beloued sonne in whom is my delyte.

## CHAPTER 4

THEN was Iesus led away of the spirite into wildernes, to be tempted of the deuyll.

2 And when he had fasted .xl. dayes & .xl. nightes, he was afterwarde an hungred.

3 Then came to him the temptour, & said: if thou be the sonne of God, commaunde that these stones be made bread.

4 He aunswered and said: it is written, man shall not lyue by breade onlye, but by euerye worde that procedeth out of the mouth of God.

5 Then the deuyll toke him vp into the holye cytye, and set him on a pinacle of the temple,

6 & sayd vnto him: if thou be þe sonne of God cast thy selfe doune. For it is written, he shall geue his aungels charge ouer þe, & with their handes they shal holde the vp, that thou dashe not thy fote against a stone:

7 And Iesus said to him, it is written also: Thou shalt not tempt thy lord God.

8 The deuil toke him vp again & ledde him into an exceding hye mountayne, and shewed him al þe kingdoms of the world, & al the glory of them,

9 & said to him: al these wyl I geue the, if thou wilt fall doune & worshyppe me.

10 Then sayd Iesus vnto him. Auoide sathan. For it is wrytten, þu shalt worshippe the Lord thy God and him only shalt thou serue.

11 Then the diuel left him, & beholde, the aungels came and ministred vnto him.

12 When Iesus had heard that Iohn was taken, he departed into Galile

13 and left Nazareth, and went and dwelt in Capernaum, which is a citye vpon the sea, in the coastes of Zabulon & Nephthalim,

14 to fulfil þt which was spoken by Esay the prophete, sayinge.

15 The lande of Zabulon and Nephthalym, the waye of the sea beyonde Iordan, Galile of the gentils,

16 the people which sate in darkenes, sawe great light, & to them which sate in the regyon and shadowe of death, light is begonne to shine.

17 From þe tyme Iesus began to preache, & to say repent for þe kingdom of heauen is at hand.

18 As Iesus walked by the sea of Galile, he sawe two brethren: Symon which was called Peter, and Andrew his brother, casting a net into the sea, for they were fysshers,

19 & he sayed vnto them, folowe me, and I wyll make you fysshers of men.

20 And they straight waye left their nettes, and folowed hym.

21 And he went forth from thence, and sawe other two brethren, Iames the sonne of Zebede, and Ihon his brother, in the shippe wyth Zebede their father, mending their nets, and called them.

22 And they without tarringe left þe shyp and their father and folowed hym.

23 And Iesus went about al Galile, teaching in their sinagoges, & preaching the gospel of the kingdome, & healed al maner of sickenes, & all maner of diseases among the people.

24 And his fame sprede abrode through out all Siria. And they brought vnto him all sycke people that were taken with diuers diseases & gripinges, and them that were possessed with deuils and those which were lunatike, & those that had þe palsie: & he healed them,

25 & their folowed hym a great numbre of people, from Galyle. And from the ten cities, & from Ierusalem & from Iurie & from the regions that lye beiond Iordan.

## CHAPTER 5

WHEN he sawe the people, he went vp into a mountaine, and when he was set his disciples came to him,

2 and he opened his mouth, and taught them sayinge,

3 blessed are the pore in sprete: for theirs is the kingdom of heauen.

4 Blessed are they þt morne, for they shalbe comforted.

5 Blessed are þe meke: for they shall inheret þe earth.

6 Blessed are they which honger & thurste for rightuousnes: for they shalbe filled.

7 Blessed are þe mercifull: for they shal obtaine mercy.

8 Blessed are þe pure in hert: for thei shal se God.

9 Blessed are þe peace makers: for thei shalbe called the children of God.

10 Blessed are they which suffer persecucion for rightuousnesse sake: for theirs is the kingdom of heauen:

11 Blessed are ye when men reuile you and persecute you, and shal falsely say al maner of yuel sayinges against you for my sake.

12 Reioyce & be glad, for great is your reward in heauen. For so persecuted they the prophetes which were before your dayes.

13 Ye are the salt of the earth: but & if the salt haue lost her saltnes, what can be salted

therwith? It is thensforth good for nothinge, but to be cast out, and to be troden vnder fote of men.

14 Ye are the light of þe worlde. A cytye that is set on an hill, can not be hid,

15 neither do men light a candell & put it vnder a bushell, but on a candelsticke, and it lighteth al that are in the house.

16 Let your light so shyne before men that they maye se your good workes, and gloryfye your father which is in heauen.

17 Thinke not that I am come to destroy þe lawe, or þe prophetes: no I am not come to destroy them, but to fulfil them.

18 For truly I say vnto you, til heauen & earth perish, one iote or one title of þe lawe shal not escape, til al be fulfilled

19 Whosoeuer therfore breaketh one of these lest commaundementes, & teacheth men so, he shall be called þe least in þe kingdome of heauen. But whosoeuer obserueth & teacheth, þe same shal be called great in þe kingdom of heauen.

20 For I say vnto you except your rightuousnes excede, þe rightuousnes of þe scribes & phariseis, ye can not entre into þe kingdom of heauen.

21 Ye haue heard howe it was said vnto them of þe olde time: Thou shalt not kil. For whosoeuer killeth, shal be in daunger of iudgement,

22 but I sai vnto yow, whosoeuer is angre wt his brother without a cause shal be in daunger of iudgement. Whosoeuer saieth to his brother Racha, shalbe in daunger of a counsel. But whosoeuer saieth thou fole, shalbe in daunger of hel fire

23 Therefore when thou offrest thy gift at þe altare, & their remembrest that thy brother hath ought against þe:

24 leue there thy offringe before the altare, & go thy way first & be reconciled to thy brother, & then come and offre thy gift.

25 Agre with thine aduersary quickly, whiles þu art in þe way wt him, lest þe aduersary deliuer þe to þe iudge, & the iudge deliuer þe to the minister, & then þu be cast into prison.

26 I say vnto þe verely: thou shalt not come out thence tyl thou haue payed the vttermost farthing.

27 Ye haue heard how it was sayed to them of olde time: Thou shalt not commit adultery.

28 But I saye vnto you, that whosoeuer loketh on a wife, lustinge after her, hath committed adulterye with her alredy in his herte.

29 Wherfore if thy ryght eye offende þe plucke him out, & cast him from þe. Better it is for þe that one of thy members perishe, then that thy whol body should be cast into hel.

30 Also if thy right hand offende þe, cut him of & cast him from the. Better it is that one of thy members perish, then that all thy body should be cast into hel.

31 It is sayed, whosoeuer putteth a way his wife, let him geue her a testimonial of þe deuorcement.

32 But I sai vnto you: whosoeuer putteth away his wife (except it be for fornicacion) causeth her to breke matrimony. And whosoeuer marieth her þt is deuorced, breaketh wedlocke.

33 Agayne ye haue hearde how it was sayed to them of olde time, thou shalt not forsweare thy self, but shalt performe thine othe to God.

34 But I saye vnto you, swere not at al, neither by heauen, for it is Goddes seate:

35 nor yet by the earth, for it is his fotstole: neither by Ierusalem for it is the citye of þe great kinge

36 neither shalt thou sweare by thy head, because thou canst not make one whyte hear, or blacke.

37 But your communicacion shalbe, yea, yea: nay, nay. For whatsoeuer is more than that cometh to euell.

38 Ye haue hearde how it is sayed, an eye for an eye: a tothe for a tothe.

39 But I saye to you that ye resyst not wrong. But who soeuer geue the a blowe on the right cheke, tourne to hym the other.

40 And if anye man wyll sue the at the lawe, and take awaye thy coote, let hym haue thy clooke also.

41 And whosoeuer wyll compell the to goo a myle, goo with hym twaine.

42 Geue to hym that axeth, & from him that woulde borow tourne not away.

43 Ye haue hearde how it is said: thou shalt loue thy neighbour, and hate thyne enemy.

44 But I say vnto you loue your enemies. Blesse theim that cursse you. Do good to them that hate you. Pray for them which doo you wronge and persecute you,

45 that ye may be the chyldren of youre father that is in heauen: for he maketh his sonne to aryse on the yuyll, and on the good and sendeth his raine on the iust and vniust.

46 For if ye loue them, whiche loue you: what rewarde shall ye haue? Doo not the publicanes euen so?

47 And if ye be frendly to your brethren only what synguler thinge doo ye? Do not the publycanes likewyses?

48 Ye shall therfore be perfect, euen as your father which is in heauen, is perfect.

# CHAPTER 6

Take hede to your almes, þt ye geue it not in þe sight of

men, to þe intent þt ye would be sene of them. Or els ye get no rewarde of youre father whyche is in heauen.

2 Whensoeuer therfore thou geuest thime almes, thou shalt not make a trompet to be blowen before the, as the hypocrytes do in the synagoges and in the stretes, for to be praised of men. Verely I saye vnto you, they haue their rewarde.

3 But when thou doest thine almes, let not thy lyft hande knowe what thy ryght hande doth,

4 that thyne almes may be secrete: and thy father whiche seeth in secrete, shall rewarde the openly.

5 And when thou prayest, thou shalt not be as the hipocrites are. For they loue to stande and praye in the sinagoges, and in the corners of the stretes, and because they wolde be seane of men. Verely I say vnto you, they haue their rewarde.

6 But when thou prayest, entre into thy chamber, & shut thy dore to the, & praie to thi father which is in secrete: & thy father which seeth in secrete, shall rewarde the openlye.

7 But when ye praye, bable not much as the Heathen do: for they thinke that they shalbe herde, for their muche bablynge sake.

8 Be ye not lyke them therfore. For your father knoweth wherof ye haue neade, before ye axe of him

9 after this manner therfore pray ye. Our father which art in heauen, halowed be thy name.

10 Let thy kingdome come. Thy wyll be fulfylled, as well in earth, as it is in heauen.

11 Geue vs this daye our daylye breade.

12 And forgeue vs our trespases, euen as we forgeue oure trespasers.

13 And lead vs not into temptaciou. But delyuer vs from euyll. For thyne is the kingdome and the power, and the glorye for euer Amen.

14 For and if ye shall forgeue other men their trespases, your heauenlye father shall also forgeue you.

15 But and ye wyll not forgeue men theyr trespases, no more shall your father forgeue your trespases.

16 Moreouer when ye fast, be not sad as the hipocrites are. For they disfygure their faces, that they myght be sene of men how they fast. Verely I say vnto you, they haue their rewarde.

17 But thou, when thou fastest, annoint thine head, & wash thy face

18 that it appeare not vnto men howe þt thou fastest but vnto thy father which is in secrete: & thy father which seth in secret shal reward þe openly.

19 Se that ye gater you not treasure vpon the earth, where ruste & mothes corrupte, & wher theues breake throughe & steale.

20 But gather ye treasure together in heauen, where neither rust nor mothes corrupt, & where theues neyther breake vp nor yet steale.

21 For wher soeuer your treasur is, ther wyl your hertes be also.

22 The lyght of thy body is thine eye. Wherfore if thine eye be single, al thy bodye shalbe full of light.

23 But and if thyne eye be wycked then al thy bodye shalbe ful of darkenes. Wherfore if the light that is in the, be darkenes: how great is that darckenes?

24 No man can serue two maysters. For eyther he shall hate þe one & loue þe other: yea or eles he shall leane to the one & dispise þe other. Ye cannot serue God & Mammon.

25 Therfore I saie vnto you, be not tareful for you life what ye shall eate or what ye shall dryncke, nor yet for your bodye, what ye shall put on, is not the lyfe more worthe then meate, and the body more of value then rayment?

26 Behold the foules of the ayer: for þe sowe not, neyther reape, nor yet cary into the barnes: and yet your heauenlye father fedethe them. Are ye not muche better then they?

27 Whych of you (though he toke thoughte therfore) coulde put one cubit vnto hys statuture?

28 And why care ye then for rayment? Considre the lylies of þe filde, howe they growe. They laboureth not nether spynne.

29 And yet for all that I saye vnto you that euen Solomon in all hys royaltie was not arayed lyke vnto one of these.

30 Wherfore if God so clothe þe grasse, which is to day in the felde, and to morowe shall be cast in to þe fournace: shall he not much more do the same vnto you, o ye of lytle fayth?

31 Therfore take no thought saiynge: what shall we eate, or what shall we dryncke, or wherewith shal we be clothed?

32 After all these thynges seke the gentils. For your heauenlye father knoweth þt ye haue neade of all these thynges.

33 But rather seke ye first þe kyngdome of heauen and the rightuousnes therof, & all these thynge shalbe ministred vnto you.

34 Care not then for the morow, but let the morow care for itself: for the day present hath euer ynough of his owne trouble.

# CHAPTER 7

IVDGE not, þt ye be not iudged.
2 For as ye iudge so, shall ye be iudged. And with what measur ye meate, with þe same shal it be measured to you agayne.

3 Why seiste thou a moote

in thy brothers eye, & perceyuest not the beame that is in thyne owne eye?

4 Or why saist thou to thy brother: suffer me to plucke out the moote out of thyne eye, & beholde a beame is in thyne owne eye?

5 Hypocrite, first caste out the beame out of thyne owne eye, and then shalte thou se clearelye to plucke out the moote out of thy brothers eye.

6 Geue not that whiche is holye, to dogges nether cast ye your pearles before swyne, lest they treade them vnder theyr feete, and the other tourne agayne and al to rent you.

7 Axe and it shalbe geuen you. Seke and ye shall fynde. Knocke & it shalbe opened vnto you.

8 For whosoeuer axeth receyueth, and he that seketh fyndethe, and to hym that knocketh, it shalbe opened.

9 Ys there any man amonge you whiche if his sonne axed hym bread, would offer him a stone?

10 Or if he axed fyshe, woulde he profer him a serpente?

11 Yf ye then whyche are euyll, can geue to youre chyldren good gyftes: howe muche more shall your father whiche is in heauen, geue good thinges to them that axe hym?

12 Therfore whatsoeuer ye woulde that men shoulde do to you, euen so do ye to them. Thys is the lawe and the Prophetes.

13 Enter in at the strayte gate: for wide is the gate and broade is the way that leadeth to destruction: and many there be whiche go in therat.

14 But strayt is the gate, and narrowe is the waye which leadeth vnto lyfe: & feawe there be that fynde it.

15 Beware of false Prophetes, whiche come to you in shepes clothing, but inwardly they are rauenynge wolues.

16 Ye shall knowe them by their fruites. Do men gaddre grapes of thornes? or figges of bryers?

17 Euen so euery good tre bryngeth forth good fruite. But a corrupt tree, bringeth forth euyll fruyte.

18 A good tree can not bringe forthe bad fruyte: nor yet a bad tree can bringe forth good fruite.

19 Euery tree that bryngeth not forthe good fruite shalbe hewen downe, and cast into the fyre.

20 Wherfore by theyr fruytes ye shal knowe them.

21 Not al they that saye vnto me, Maister Maister, shal enter into the kingdome of heauen: but he that doeth my fathers will which is in heauen.

22 Many will saye to me in that daye: Maister, maister, haue we not in thy name prophesied? And in thy name haue cast out deuylles? And in thy name haue done many miracles?

23 And then will I knowledge vnto them, that I neuer knewe them. Departe from me, ye workers of iniquitie.

24 Whosoeuer heareth of me these sayinges and doethe the same, I wyll lyken hym vnto a wyse man which buylt hys housse on a rocke

25 and aboundaunce of rayne descended, and the flouddes came, and the windes blew and bet vpon that same housse, and it fell not because it was grounded on the rocke.

26 And whosoeuer heareth of me these sayinges and doeth them not, shalbe lykened vnto a folyshe man whyche buylt hys housse vpon the sande

27 and abundance of rayne descended, and the floudes came, and the wyndes blewe and bet vpon that housse, and it fell, and great was the fall of it.

28 And it came to passe, that when Iesus had ended these sayinges, þe people were astonyed at his doctrine.

29 For he taught them as one hauing power, and not as the Scribes.

# CHAPTER 8

WHEN he was come downe from þe mountayne, much people folowed him.

2 And lo, there came a lepre & worshipped him saying Master, if þu wylt, þu canst make me cleane.

3 And Iesus put forthe his hand & touched him, saiyng: I will, be thou cleane, & immediatly his leprosye was clensed.

4 And Iesus sayde vnto hym. Se thou tell no man, but go and shewe thy selfe to the pryeste, and offer the gyft that Moyses commaunded in witnes to them.

5 When Iesus was entred into Capernaum there came vnto him a certayne Centurion, & besought him

6 sayinge: Master my seruaunte lyeth sycke at home of the palsy, & is greuouslye pained.

7 And Iesus saide vnto him: I wyll come and heale him.

8 The Centurion aunswered and sayd: Sir I am not worthy that thou shouldest come vnder my rofe, but speake the worde only and my saruaunt shalbe healed.

9 For I also my selfe am a man vndre power, & haue soudiers vnder me, & I say to one, go, & he goeth, and to an other come, & he cometh: and to my seruante, do this, he doeth it:

10 When Iesus hearde that, he maruailed & sayed to them that folowed him. Verely I say vnto you, I haue not founde so great faith: no, not in Israel.

11 I say therfore vnto you that many shall come from the east and west, and shal rest with

Abraham, Isaac and Iacob in the kingdome of heauen:

12 and the children of the kingdome shall be cast out in the vtter darkenes: there shalbe wepinge and gnashynge of teth.

13 Iesus sayd vnto the Centurion, go thy way, and as thou hast beleued so be it vnto the. And his seruaunt was healed the selfe houre.

14 And then Iesus went to Peters house, and sawe his wyues mother lyinge sycke of a feuer,

15 and touched her hand, & the feuer left her: and she arose, and ministred vnto them.

16 When the euen was come, they brought vnto him many that were possessed with deuyls. And he cast out the spretes with a word, and healed all that were sycke,

17 to fulfyll that which was spoken by Esaias the prophete sayinge. He toke on him oure infyrmyteis, & beare oure sycknesses.

18 When Iesus sawe muche people aboute him, he commaunded to go ouer the water.

19 And there came a scribe and sayde vnto hym: master, I wil folowe the whither soeuer thou goest.

20 And Iesus sayd vnto him: the foxes haue holes, and the birddes of the ayer haue nestes, but the sonne of man hath not wheron to rest his heade.

21 Another that was one of his disciples said vnto him: master, suffer me fyrst to go and burye my father.

22 But Iesus sayd vnto hym folowe me, and let the dead burye their deade.

23 And he entred into a shyppe, and his disciples folowed him.

24 And beholde there arose a great tempest in the sea, in so much that the shippe was couered with waues, and he was a slepe.

25 And his discyples came vnto him, and awoke him sayinge: master saue vs, we peryshe.

26 And he sayed vnto them: why are ye fearfull, O ye of lytle fayth? Then he arose, and rebuked the wyndes and the sea, and there folowed a great calme.

27 And the men maruayled and sayed: what man is this, that both wyndes and sea obey hym?

28 And when he was come to the other syde, into the countre of the Gergesytes, there mete him two possessed of deuils, which came out of the graues, & were out of measure fearce, so that no man myght go by that way.

29 And behold they cried out saying: O Iesu þe sonne of God, what haue we to do with þe? Art thou come hither to torment vs before the tyme be come?

30 And ther was a good waye of from them a great hearde of swyne fedinge.

31 Then the deuyls besoughte him sayinge: if thou cast vs out, suffer vs to go our way into the heard of swyne.

32 And he said vnto theim, go your waies. Then went they out of & departed into þe hearde of swine. And behold þe whole heard of swyne was caryed with violence headling into the sea, and peryshed in the water.

33 Then the hearde men fled & went their wayes into the cityè, and tolde euerye thynge, and what had fortuned vnto the possessed of the deuyls.

34 And beholde all the cytye came out and met Iesus, and when they sawe him they besought hym for to departe out of their coastes.

# CHAPTER 9

THEN he entred into a shyppe & passed ouer and came into his owne citie.

2 And, lo thei brought to him a man sycke of the palsye, lyinge in his bedde. And when Iesus sawe þe faith of them he said to þe sick of þe palsie sonne be of good chere, thy sinnes be forgeuen the.

3 And beholde certayne of þe scribes sayd in them selues, thys man blasphemeth.

4 And when Iesus sawe theyr thoughtes, he sayed: wherfor thinke ye euill in your hertes?

5 Whether is easyer to saye, thy synnes be forgeuen the, or to saye: aryse and walke?

6 That ye maye knowe that the sonne of man hath power to forgeue synnes in earth: then sayed he vnto the sicke of the palsie: aryse, take vp thy bed, and go home to thyne house.

7 And he arose and departed to hys owne house.

8 And when the people sawe it, they marueyled & glorifyed God whiche hath geuen suche power to men.

9 And as Iesus passed forth from thence, he saw a man syt receyuyng of custome named Mathew, and sayd to hym: folow me.

10 And he arose and folowed hym. And it came to passe, as he sate at meat in the house: beholde many Publicans, and synners came and sate doune also with Iesus and hys disciples.

11 When the Phariseis sawe that, they sayed to hys disciples: why eateth your master with Publicans and synners?

12 When Iesus heard that he sayed vnto them: The whole neade not the Phisicion, but they that are sicke.

13 Go, and learne, what that meaneth: I haue pleasure in mercye, & not in offerynge. For I am not come to cal the ryghtuouse but the synners to repentaunce.

14 Then came the disciples of Iohn to hym saying: why do we and the Pharises fast ofte: but thy

disciples fast not?

15 And Iesus sayd vnto them. Can the weddyng children morne as long as the bridegrome is with them? The tyme will come when the bridegrome shalbe taken from them, and then shal they faste:

16 No man peceth an olde garment with a pece of newe clothe. For then taketh he awaye the pece agayne from the garment, and the rente is made greater.

17 Nether do men put newe wyne into olde vessels, for then the vessels breake and the wyne runneth out, and the vessels peryshe. But they poure newe wyne into newe vessels, and so are both saued together.

18 Whyles he thus spake vnto them, behold there came a certaine rueler, and worshipped him sayinge my doughter is euen now dyseased, but come and lay thy hand on her, and she shall lyue.

19 And Iesus arose and folowed him with his disciples.

20 And beholde, a woman which was diseased with an issue of bloude .xij. yeres, came behinde him and touched the hem of his vesture.

21 For she said in her selfe: if I maye touche but euen his vesture only, I shalbe safe.

22 Then Iesus tourned him about, & behelde her saynge: Doughter be of good comforth, thy faith hath made the safe. And she was made whole euen that same houre.

23 And when Iesus came into the rulers house, and sawe the ministrels and the people raginge,

24 he sayd vnto them: Get you hence, for the mayde is not dead, but slepeth. And they laughed him to scorne.

25 Assone as the people were put forth, he went in and toke her by the hande, and the mayde arose.

26 And this was noysed through out all that lande.

27 And as Iesus departed thence, two blinde men folowed hym cryinge and sayinge: O thou sonne of Dauid haue mercy on vs.

28 And when he was come into the house, the blynde came to him. And Iesus saide vnto them: Beleue ye that I am able to do this? And they sayde vnto him: ye Lorde.

29 Then touched he their eyes, sayinge: according to your fayth, be it vnto you.

30 And their eyes were opened. And Iesus charged them sayinge: Se that no man knowe of it.

31 But they assone as they were departed, spred abrode his name through out all the lande.

32 As they were come out behold, a domme man possessed of a deuil, was brought to him.

33 And as sone as the deuyl was cast out, the domme spake: And the people meruayled: sayinge: it was neuer so sene in Israell.

34 But the pharyseis sayed: he casteth out deuils, by the power of the chiefe deuyl.

35 And Iesus went aboute all cytyes and tounes, teachinge in their synagoges and preachinge the gladde tidinges of the kingdome, and healinge all maner sicknes and disease amonge the people.

36 But when he sawe the people, he had compassyon on them, because they were pyned awaye, and scattred abroad, euen as shepe hauinge no shepeherde.

37 Then sayde he to his disciples: the herueste is greate, but the labourers are fewe.

38 Wherfore pray the Lord of the haruest to send forth labourers into his haruest.

# CHAPTER 10

AND he called his .xij. Disciples vnto him & gaue theym power ouer vncleane spyrytes, to caste them out, and to heale all maner of sycknesses, and al maner of diseases.

2 The names of the .xij. Apostles are these. The fyrst Simon called also Peter: and Andrewe his brother. Iames the sonne of Zebede, and Iohn his brother:

3 Philip and Bartlemew. Thomas and Mathewe the publican. Iames the sonne of Alphe, and Lebbius otherwyse called Taddeus.

4 Symon of Cane, and Iudus Iscarioth which also betrayed hym.

5 These .xij. sent Iesus forth after he had geuen to them commaundement sainge Go not into the wayes that lead to the gentyls, & into the cityes of the Samaritanes enter ye not.

6 But go rather to the lost shepe of the house of Israel.

7 Go and preache sayinge: that the kingdome of heauen is at hande.

8 Heale the sicke, clense the lepers, raise the dead, cast out the deuils. Frely ye haue receyued, frely geue againe.

9 Possesse not golde, nor syluer, nor brasse in your girdles,

10 nor yet scrip towardes your yourney: neither two cotes neyther shues, nor yet a staste. For the worck man is worthye to haue his meate.

11 Into whatsoeuer citye or toune ye shall come enquire who is worthye in it, & there abyde tyl ye go thence

12 And when ye come into an house salute the same.

13 And if the house be worthy, your peace shall come vpon it. But if it be not worthy, your peace shall retourne to you againe.

14 And whosoeuer shall not receiue you, nor wyll heare your preachinge: when ye departe out of that house or that cytye, shake of the duste of your fete.

15 Truly I say vnto you: it

shalbe easyer for the lande of Sodoma & Gomorra in the daye of iudgement then for þt citie.

16 Beholde I sende you forth as shepe among wolues. Be ye therfore wyse as serpentes, and innocent as doues.

17 Beware of men, for they shall delyuer you vp to the counsels, and shall stourge you in their synagoges.

18 And ye shalbe brought to the head rulers and kinges for my sake, in witnes to them & to þe gentyls.

19 But when they deliuer you vp take no thought howe or what ye shall speake, for it shalbe geuen you, euen in that same houre, what ye shal saye.

20 For it is not ye that speake, but the sprete of your father which speaketh in you.

21 The brother shall betraye the brother to death, and the father the sonne. And the children shall aryse againste their fathers & mothers, and shall put them to death:

22 and ye shal be hated of all men for my name. But he that endureth to the ende shalbe saued.

23 When they persecute you in one citye, flye into another. I tell you for a truthe, ye shall not fynishe all the cityes of Israel, tyl þe sonne of man become.

24 The discyples is not aboue his master: nor yet the seruaunt aboue his Lorde.

25 It is ynough for the discyple to be as his master is, and that the seruaunt be as hys Lorde is. If they haue called the good man of the house him selfe belzebub: how muche more shal they call them of his housholde so?

26 Fear them not therfore. Therfore is nothinge so close, þt shal not be opened, & nothing so hid, þt shal not be knowen.

27 What I tell you in darkenes, that speake ye in light. And what ye heare in the eare, that preache ye on the house toppes.

28 And feare ye not them which kil the body, and be not able to kill the soule. But rather feare him, which is able to destroy both soule & body into hell.

29 Are not two sparowes solde for a farthyng? And none of them doth lyght on the grounde, without your father.

30 And now are all þt heires of your heades numbred.

31 Feare ye not therfore: ye are of more value then many sparowes.

32 Whosoeuer therfore shall acknowlege me before men, hym will I acknowledge also before my father which is in heauen.

33 But whosoeuer shall deny me before men, hym will I also deny before my father which is in heauen.

34 Thinke not that I am come to sende peace into the earth. I came not to sende peace but a swerd.

35 For I am come to set a man at variaunce agaynst hys father, and the doughter against her mother, and the doughterlaw against her motherlaw:

36 And a mans fooes shall be they of hys owne housholde.

37 He that loueth hys father, or mother more then me, is not mete for me. And he that loueth hys sonne or doughter more then me, is not mete for me.

38 And he þt taketh not hys crosse & foloweth me, is not mete for me.

39 He that findeth hys lyfe, shal loose it: and he that looseth hys lyfe for my sake, shall fynde it.

40 He that receyueth you, receyueth me: & he that receyueth me, receiueth him that sent me,

41 He that receyueth a Prophet in the name of a prophet, shall receyue a prophetes reward. And he þt receyueth a righteouse man in þe name of a righteous man, shal receyue the rewarde of a righteous man.

42 And whosoeuer shall geue vnto one of these lytle ones to drinke, a cuppe of colde water only, in the name of a discypell: I tell you of a truthe, he shall not lose his rewarde.

# CHAPTER 11

AND it came to passe when Iesus had made an ende of commaundinge his .xij. disciples, he departed thence to teache and to preache in their cityes.

2 When Iohn beinge in prison hearde the workes of Christe, he sent two of his discyples

3 and sayd vnto him. Art thou he that shal come: or shall we loke for another.

4 Iesus anuswered and saide vnto them. Go and shewe Ihon what ye haue hearde & sene.

5 The blinde se, the halt go, the lepers are clensed: the deaf heare, the dead ryse againe, and the glade tydinges is preached to the poore.

6 And happye is he that is not offended by me.

7 And as thei departed Iesus began to speake vnto the people of Iohn. What thing went ye out into the wildernes to se? wente ye out to se a rede shaken with the winde?

8 other what wente ye out for to se? A man clothed in soft rayment? Beholde they that weare softe clothed, are in kinges houses.

9 But what went ye out for to se? A prophete. Yea, I say vnto you, and more then a prophete.

10 For this is he of whom it is written. Beholde, I sende my messenger before thy face, which shall prepare thy way before the.

11 Verely I say vnto you, amonge the children of women arose ther not a greater then Iohn the Baptist. Notwithstandinge he that is lesse in the kingdome of heauen, is greater then he.

12 From the tyme of Iohn Baptiste hitherto, the kingdome of heauen suffreth violence, and they that go to it with violence plucke it vnto them.

13 For all the prophetes and the lawe prophecyed vnto the tyme of Iohn.

14 And if ye wyll receyue it, this is that Helias which shoulde come.

15 He that hath eares to heare let hym heare.

16 But wherunto shal I lyke this generacion? It is lyke vnto children which syt in the market and call vnto their felowes,

17 and saye we haue pyped vnto you, & ye haue not daunced? We haue morned vnto you, and ye haue not sorowed.

18 For Iohn came neyther eatynge nor drinkinge, and they say, he hath the deuyl.

19 The sonne of man came eatinge and drynking, and they saye, beholde a glutton and drinker of wine, and a frende vnto publicans and synners. Neuerthelater wysdome is iustifyed of her children.

20 Then began he to vpbrayd the cytyes, in which most of his miracles were done, because they mended not.

21 Wo be to the Chorasin. Wo be to the Bethzaida: for if the miracles which were shewed in you, had be done in Tyre and Sidon, they had repented longe agone in sackcloth and ashes.

22 Neuerthelesse I saye to you: it shall be easier for Tyre and Sydon at the daye of iudgement, then for you.

23 And thou Capernaum, which art lyft vp vnto heauen, shall be brought doune to hell. For if the miracles which haue bene done in the, had be shewed in Zodome: they had remayned to this daye.

24 Neuerthelesse I saye vnto you: it shall be easyer for the lande of Zodom in the daye of iudgement, then for the.

25 At that time Iesus aunswered and said: I prayse the, O father Lorde of heauen and earth, because thou hast hid these thinges from þe wyse and prudent, and hast opened theim vnto babes:

26 euen so father, for so it pleased the.

27 All thinges are geuen vnto me of my father. And no man knoweth the sonne but the father: neyther knoweth anye man the father, saue the sonne, and he to whom the sonne wyl open hym.

28 Come vnto me all ye that labour and are laden and I wyll ease you.

29 Take my yocke on you and learne of me, for I am meke and lowly in herte: and ye shall fynde reste vnto your soules.

30 For my yocke is easy: and my burden is lyght.

# CHAPTER 12

IN that tyme went Iesus on the Saboth dayes thorowe the corne and his discyples were an hungred, and began to plucke the eares of corne and to eate.

2 When the Phariseis sawe that they sayde vnto him: Beholde, thy discyples do that which is not laufwl to do vpon the saboth daye.

3 He sayde vnto them: Haue ye not read what Dauid dyd, when he was an hungred, and they also whiche were with hym?

4 How he entred into the house of God, & eate the halowed louwes, which were not lawful, for him to eate, neyther for them which were with him but onlye for the priestes.

5 Or haue ye not read in the law, how that the pryestes in the temple breake the saboth day, and yet are blamlesse:

6 But I say vnto you: that here is one greater then the temple.

7 Wherfore if ye had wist what this sayinge meaneth: I require mercye and not sacrifyce: ye would neuer haue condemned innocentes:

8 For the sonne of man is Lorde euen of the saboth day.

9 And he departed thence, and went into their synagoge:

10 and beholde there was a man which had his hande dryed vp. And they axed hym sayinge: is it lawful to heale vpon the saboth dayes? because they myght accuse him.

11 And he sayd vnto them. Which of you wolde it be, if he had a shepe fallen into a pitte on the saboth daye, that woulde not take hym and lyft hym out?

12 And how muche is a man better then a shepe? Wherfore it is lawful to do a good dede on the saboth dayes.

13 Then sayde he to the man: stretch forth thy hande. And he stetched it forth. And it was made whole again lyke vnto the other.

14 Then the pharyseis went out, and held a counsel against him, how they might destroy hym.

15 When Iesus knewe that, he departed thence, and much people folowed hym, and he healed them all,

16 and charged them, that they shoulde not make him knowen:

17 to fulfyll that which was spoken by Esaye the prophete, which sayeth:

18 Beholde my chylde, whom I haue chosen my beloued, in whom my soule delyteth. I wyll put my sprryte on him, and he shall shew iudgement to þe gentils.

19 He shall not striue, he shal

not cry neither shal any man hear his voice in þe stretes,

20 a brosed rede shalnot he breake, & flaxe þe beginneth to burne he shal not quenche, tyll he sende forth iudgemen vnto to victory,

21 and in his name shall the gentyls truste.

22 Then was brought to him, one possessed with a deuyll which was both blinde & dombe: and he healed him, insomuch that he which was blinde and dombe, both spake and sawe.

23 And al the people were amased, and sayde: Is not this that sonne of Dauid?

24 But when the Pharyseis hearde that they sayde: This felowe driueth þe deuils no nother wyse out but by þe helpe of Belzebub the chiefe of þe deuils.

25 But Iesus knewe their thoughtes, and sayed to them. Euery Kingdome deuided within it selfe, shall be brought to naught. Neyther shall anye cytye or housholde deuided against it selfe continue.

26 So if sathan cast out sathan, then is he deuided againste him selfe Howe shall then his kingdome endure?

27 Also if I by the helpe of belzabub cast out deuils: by whose helpe do your children caste them out? Therfore they shalbe your iudges.

28 But if I cast out the deuyls by the sprete of God: then is the kingdome of God come on you?

29 Eyther how can a man enter into a strong mans house, and violently take away his goodes: except he first binde the stronge man, and then spoyle his house?

30 He that is not with me, is against me. And he that gathereth not with me, scattereth abrode.

31 Wherfore I saye vnto you, all maner of synne and blasphemy of forgeuen vnto men: but the blasphemy of the sprete, shall not be forgeuen vnto men.

32 And whosoeuer speaketh a worde against the sonne of man, it shall be forgeuen him. But whosoeuer speaketh againste the holye ghost, it shall not be forgeuen him: no, neyther in this worlde, neyther in the worlde to come.

33 Either make the tree good, and his frute good also: or els make the tree euyll, and hys frute euyll also. For the tree is knowen by his frute.

34 O generation of vipers, how can ye say well, when ye your selues are euil? For of the aboundaunce of the herte, the mouth speaketh.

35 A good man out of the good treasure of hys herte, bringeth forth good thinges. And an euill man out of his euill treasure, bringeth forth euil thinges.

36 But I say vnto you, that of euery idell worde that men shall haue spoken: they shall geue a countes at the daye of iudgement.

37 For thy wordes þu shalt be iustified: & by thy wordes thou shalt be condemned.

38 Then aunswered certaine of the scrybes and of the Phariseis sayinge. Master, we woulde fayne se a sygne of the.

39 He aunswered and said to them: The euyll and aduouterous generation seketh a sygne, but there shal no sygne be geuen to them, saue the signe of þe prophete Ionas.

40 For as Ionas was thre dayes and thre nyghtes in the whales bellye: so shall the sonne of man be thre dayes and thre nyghtes in the herte of the earth.

41 The men of Niniuye shall ryse at the daye of iudgement with this nacion, and condemne them: for thei amended at the preaching of Ionas: And beholde, a greater then Ionas is here.

42 The quene of the south shall ryse at the daye of iudgement with this generacion, and shall condemne theim: for she came from the vttermost parties of the worlde to hear the wysdome of Salomon. And beholde a greater then Salomon is here.

43 When the vncleane spirite is gone out of a man he walketh through out dry places, se kinge rest and fyndeth none.

44 Then he sayth: I wyll retourne againe into my house, from whence I came out. And when he is come, he fyndeth the house empty and swepte and garnished.

45 Then he goeth his way and taketh vnto him seuen other spirites worsse then hym selfe, and so enter they in and dwell there. And the ende of that man is worsse then the beginning. Euen so shall it be with this euill nacion.

46 Whyle he yet talked to the people: beholde his mother and his brethren stode without, desyrynge to speake with hym.

47 Then one sayd vnto: beholde thy mother and brethren stande without, desyrynge to speake with the.

48 He aunswered and sayd to hym that tolde him: Who is my mother? Who are my brethren?

49 And he stretched forth his hande ouer his disciples, and sayd: beholde my mother & my brethren.

50 For whosoeuer doth my fathers wyll which is in heauen, the same is my brother, syster and mother.

# CHAPTER 13

THE same daye wente Iesus out of the house, and sate by the sea syde,

2 and much people resorted vnto hym, so greatly that he went and sate in a shyppe, and all the

people stode on the shore.

3 And he spake many thinges to them in symilitudes, saying, beholde, the sower went forth to sowe.

4 And as he sowed, some fel by the wayes syde, and the foules came and deuoured it vp.

5 Some fell vpon stonye grounde where it hadde not muche earth: and anon it sprong vp, because it had no depth of earth:

6 & when the sunne was vp, it caughte heate, and for lacke of rotynge wyddred awaye.

7 Some fel among thornes, & the thornes sprong vp and chooked it.

8 Parte fell in good grounde, and brought forth good frute: some an hundred fold, some sixtie folde, some thyrty folde.

9 Whosoeuer hath eares to heare let hym heare.

10 And the disciples came and sayde to hym: Why speakest thou to them in parables?

11 He aunswered and sayde vnto theym: it is geuen vnto you to know the secretes of the kyngdom of heauen, but to them it is not geuen

12 For whosoeuer hath to hym shalbe geuen, and he shall haue aboundaunce. But whosoeuer hath not: from hym shalbe taken awaye euen that he hath.

13 Therfore speake I to them in similitudes: for though they se, they se not: and hearyng they heare not: neyther vnderstand.

14 And in them is fulfilled the Prophesye of Esayas, whych prophesie sayth: with the eares ye shal heare, and shal not vnderstande, and with the eyes ye shal se, and shall not perceyue.

15 For this people hertes are waxed grosse, and their eares were dull of hearynge, and their eyes haue they closed, lest they should se with their eyes, and heare with their eares, and shoulde vnderstand with their hertes, & should tourne that I myght heale them.

16 But blessed are your eyes, for they se: and your eares, for thei heare.

17 Verely I say vnto you, that many Prophetes and perfecte men haue desired to se the thinges whyche ye se, & haue not sene theim: and to heare the thynges which ye heare, and haue not heard them.

18 Heare ye therfore the similitude of the sower.

19 Whosoeuer heareth the word of the kyngedome and vnderstandeth it not, there cometh þe euill man, and catcheth awaye þt which was sowen in hys hert, and this is he whiche was sowen by the way side.

20 But he that was sowen in the stony grounde, is he which heareth the worde of God, and anone with ioye receyueth it,

21 yet hath he no rootes in hym selfe, and therefore dureth but a season. For assone as tribulation or persecucion ariseth because of the word, by and by he falleth.

22 He that was sowen among thornes, is he that heareth the worde of God: but the care of thys world, and the disceythfulnes of ryches choke the word, & so is he made vnfruteful.

23 But he whiche is sowen in þe good ground, is he that heareth the worde and vnderstandeth it, whiche also beareth frute and bryngeth forth, some an .C. folde, some sixtye folde, and some .xxx. folde.

24 Another similitude put he forth vnto them saying: The kyngedom of heauen is lyke vnto a man whiche sowed good seede in hys felde.

25 But whyle men slept there came hys foo and sowed tares amonge the wheate, and went hys waye.

26 When the blade was spronge vp, and had brought forth frute, then apeared the tares also.

27 The seruauntes came to the housholder, and sayde vnto hym: Sir sowedest not thou good seede in thy close? From whence then hath it tared?

28 He sayed to them: The enuious man hath done this. Then the seruauntes sayde vnto hym. Wilt thou then that we go and gadder them?

29 But he sayde, nay, lest whyle ye go about to wede oute the tares, ye plucke vp also wyth them the wheat by the rotes.

30 Let both growe together tyl haruest come, & in tyme of haruest, I wyl saye to the reapers, gather ye fyrst the tares, & bynde theym in shewes too be brent: but gather the wheate into my barne.

31 Another parable he put forth vnto them saying: The kyngdom of heauen is lyke vnto a grayne of mustard seede, whiche a man taketh and soweth in hys felde,

32 whych is þe leest of all seedes. But when it is growen it is the greatest among herbes, & it groweth vp into a tree: so that the byrdes of the ayre come and buylde in the braunches of it.

33 Another similitude sayde he to them. The kyngdom of heauen is lyke vnto leuen, which a woman taketh and hydeth in .iij. peckes of mele, tyll all be leuended.

34 All these thynges spake Iesus vnto the people by similitudes, and withoute similitudes spake he nothyng to them,

35 to fulfil that which was spoken by the Prophet saying: I wil open my mouth in similitudes, & will speake forth thynges whych haue ben kept secrete from þe begynnyng of the world.

36 Then sente Iesus the

people awaye, & came home. And hys disciples came vnto him sayinge: declare vnto vs the similitude of the tares of the felde.

37 Then aunswered he & sayed to them. He that soweth the good seede, is the sonne of man.

38 And the fielde is the worlde. And the chyldren of the kyngdom, they are þe good seede. And the tares are the chyldren of the wycked.

39 And the enemy that soweth them is the deuell. The Haruest is the ende of the worlde. And the reapers be the Aungels.

40 For euen as the tares are gaddred and brent in the fyre: so shall it be in the ende of thys worlde.

41 The sonne of man shall sende forth hys Aungels, and they shall gather out of hys kyngedom all thynges that offende, and them whych do iniquity,

42 and shall caste theim into a fournayce of fyre. There shalbe waylyng & gnasshyng of teth.

43 Then shall the iuste men shyne as bryght as the sunne in the kyngdom of theyr father. Whosoeuer hath eares to heare let hym heare.

44 Agayne the kyngdome of heauen is lyke vnto treasure, hidde in the fielde, the whiche a man fyndeth and hyddeth: and for ioye therof goeth and selleth all that he hathe, and byeth that felde.

45 Agayne the kyngedome of heauen is lyke vnto a marchaunt that seketh good pearles,

46 whyche when he had founde one precious pearle, went and solde all that he hadde, and bought it.

47 Agayne the kyngedome of heauen is lyke vuto a nette cast into the sea, that gathered of all kyndes of fyshes:

48 whiche when it is full, men drow to lande, and sitte and gadre the good int vessels, and cast the bad awaye.

49 So shall it be at the ende of the worlde. The aungels shall come out, and seuer the bad from þe good,

50 and shall caste them into a furnayce of the fyre: there shalbe waylyng and gnashyng of teth.

51 Iesus sayd vnto them: vnderstande ye al these thynges? They sayde, ye Lord.

52 Then sayd he vnto them. Therfore euery Scribe which is taught vnto the kyngdome of heauen is lyke an housholder, whiche bringeth forth, out of his treasur, thinges both new & old.

53 And it came to passe when Iesus had finished these similitudes, that he departed thence

54 and came into hys owne countrey, and taught them in theyr sinagoges, in so much that they were astonyed and sayde: whence cometh all thys wysdome and power vnto hym?

55 Is not thys the carpenters sonne? Is not his mother called Mary? and hys brethren be called Iames and Ioses and Simon and Iudas?

56 And are not hys sisters all here with vs? Whence hath he all these thinges.

57 And they were offended by hym. Then Iesus saide to them a Prophet is not without honor saue in his own countrey, & among his own kynne.

58 And he did not make miracles there, for their vnbeleues sake.

## CHAPTER 14

At that tyme Herode the Tetrarcha heard of the fame of Iesu,

2 & sayd vnto his seruantes. This is Ihon Baptiste. He is rysen agayne from death, and therefore are suche miracles wrought by hym.

3 For Herode had taken Ihon and bounde hym, & put hym in pryson for Herodias sake hys brother Philips wyfe.

4 For Ihon sayd vnto him. It is not lawfull for the to haue her.

5 And when he would haue put hym to deth, he feared þe people, because they counted hym as a Prophet.

6 But when Herodes byrth daie was come, the daughter of Heeodias daunsed before them and pleased Herode.

7 Wherefore he promysed with an othe, that he woulde geue her whatsoeuer she woulde axe.

8 And she beynge informed of her mother before sayd: geue me here Ihon Baptistes head in a platter.

9 And þe king sorowed. Neuertheles for hys othe sake, & for theyr sakes that satte at also at the table, he commaunded it to be geuen her:

10 and sent & beheaded Ihon in the pryson,

11 and hys headde was brought in a platter and geuen to the damsel, and she brought it to her mother.

12 And hys disciples came and toke vp the body, and buried it: and went and tolde Iesus.

13 When Iesus heard that, he departed thence by shypp into a deserte place out of the waye. And when the people had hearde therof, they folowed him a fote out of theyr cities.

14 And Iesus went forth and sawe muche people, & hys herte did melte vpon them, & he healed of theim those that were sicke.

15 When euen was come, hys disciples came to hym saying: Thys is a desert place, and the daye is spent: let the people departe, that thei may go in to the townes & bye them vitayles.

16 But Iesus sayde vnto them. They haue no nead to go away, Geue ye them to eate.

17 Then sayde they vnto hym: we haue here but .v. loues & .ij. fishes.

18 And he sayed brig them hither to me.

19 And he commaunded þe people to sit doune on the grasse: and toke the .v. loues and the .ij. fishes, and loked vp to heauen, and blessed, and brake and gaue the loues to his disciples, & the disciples gaue them to the people.

20 And they did all eate, & were suffised. And they gathered vp þe gobbets þt remayned .xij. basketsful.

21 And they þt eate, were in numbre about .v.M. men beside women and chyldren.

22 And strayght way Iesus made hys disciples into a ship, & to go ouer before him while he sent the people away.

23 And assone as he had sent the people away, he went vp into a mountayn alone to pray, & when night was come, he was there him self alone.

24 And the ship was now in the middest of the sea, & was toste wt waues, for it was a contrary wynde.

25 In the .iiij. watch of the night. Iesus came vnto them walking on þe sea.

26 And when his disciples sawe him walkinge on the sea, they were troubled, saying: it is some spirite, & cried out for feare.

27 And straight way Iesus spake vnto them saing be of good cheare, it is I, be not afrayed.

28 Peter aunswered him & saied: master: if thou be he, bid me come vnto þe on þe water.

29 And he saide come. And when Peter was come doun out of the ship, he walked on þe water, to go to Iesus.

30 But when he saw a mighty wynd, he was afrayed. And as he began to synke, he cried saying: master, saue me.

31 And immediatly Iesus stretched forth his hande & caught him, & sayed to him. O thou litle fayth wherfore diddest þu doubt?

32 And assone as they were come into the ship, the wind ceased.

33 Then they þt were in the ship came & worshipped him sayng: of a truth thou art the sonne of God.

34 And when thei were come ouer, they went into þe land of Genesareth.

35 And when þe men of þe place had knowlege of him, they sent out into all þe country rounde about, & brought vnto him al þt were sicke,

36 & besoughte him, þt thei migh touche þe hemme of his vesture only, & as many as touched it were made safe.

# CHAPTER 15

THEN came to Iesus Scribes and Phariseis from Hierusalem, sayinge:

2 why do thy disciples transgresse the tradicions of the elders? for thei washe not their handes when they eate bread.

3 He aunswered sayd vnto them: why do ye also transgresse the commaundement of God thorow your tradicions?

4 For God commaunded saying: honoure thy father and mother, and he that curseth father or mother shall suffre death.

5 But ye saye, euery man shal say to hys father or mother: þt which thou desirest of me to helpe the with: is geuen to God,

6 and so shall he not honour hys father or mother. And thus haue ye made, that the commaundement of God is without effecte, thorow your tradicions.

7 Hypocrites, well prophecied of you Esaias sayinge:

8 Thys people draweth nye vnto me with their mouthes, & honoureth me with their lippes, howe be it their hertes are farre from me:

9 but in vayne they worshippe me teaching doctrines, which are nothyng but mens preceptes.

10 And he called the people vnto hym, & sayd to them, heare and vnderstande.

11 That whych goeth into the mouth, defileth not the man: but that whych commeth out of the mouthe, defileth the man.

12 Then came hys disciples, and sayde vnto hym: Perceyuest thou not, how that the Phariseis are offended in hearing thys saying?

13 He aunswered and sayd: al plantes whiche my heauenly father hath not planted, shalbe plucked vp by the rootes.

14 Let them alone, thei be the blynde leaders of the blynd. If þe blynd leede the blynde, both shall fall into þe dytche.

15 Then aunswered Peter and sayd to hym: declare vnto vs thys parable.

16 Then sayde Iesus are ye yet without vnderstandyng?

17 Perceyue ye not that whatsoeuer goeth in at the mouth, descendeth doune into the bealy, and is cast out into the draught?

18 But those thynges, whiche procede out of the mouthe, come from the hert and they defyle the man.

19 For out of the hert come euil thoughtes, murther, breakyng of wedlocke, whoredom, thefte, false, witnes bearing, blasphemye.

20 These are the thynges which defyle a man. But to eate wt vnwashen handes, defileth not a man.

21 And Iesus went thence, and departed into the costes of Tyre and Sidon

22 And beholde a woman

whych was a Cananite came out of the same costes, and cryed vnto hym sayinge: haue mercy on me Lord the sonne of Dauid, my doughter is piteously vexed with a deuel.

23 And he gaue her neuer a woorde to aunswer. Then came to hym hys disciples, & besoughte hym saying: sende her away, for she foloweth vs criyng.

24 He aunswered, and saide: I am not sent, but vnto the lost shepe of the house of Israel.

25 Then she came and worshipped him saiyng master helpe me.

26 He aunswered & sayde: It is not good, to take thy chyldrens bread, & to cast it to dogges.

27 She aunswered & said: truth Lord, neuerthelesse the whelpes eate of the crommes, whiche fall from their masters table.

28 Then Iesus aunswered and sayd vnto her: O woman, great is thy fayth, be it to the euen as thou desirest. And her doughter was made whole, euen at that same houre.

29 Then Iesus went awaye from thence, and came vnto the sea of Galile, and went vp into a mountaine, and sate doune there.

30 And much people came vnto him, hauynge with them, halt, blynd, domme, maymed, and other many: and cast them doune at Iesus fete. And he healed them,

31 in so muche that the people wondred to se the domme speake, the maymed whole, þe halt to go, and the blynde to se, And they glorified the God of Israel.

32 Then Iesus called hys disciples to hym & sayd I haue compassion on the people, because they haue continued with me now .iij. dayes & haue nought to eate, and I wil not let them departe fasting, lest they perish in the waie.

33 And his disciples sayd vnto hym, whence shoulde we get so muche breadde in the wildernes, as should suffice so great a multitude?

34 And Iesus sayde vnto them: How many loues haue ye? And they sayde: seuen, and a fewe litle fishes.

35 And he commaunded the people to sit doune on the grounde:

36 and toke the seuen loues and the fishes, and gaue thankes, and brake them and gaue to hys disciples, & the disciples gaue them to the people.

37 And they dyd all eate and were suffised. And they toke vp of the broken meate that was lefte .vij. baskettes full.

38 And yet thei that eate were .iiij.M. men, beside women and chyldren.

39 And he sent away þe people & toke ship & came into þe parties of Magdala.

# CHAPTER 16

THEN came the Phariseis and Saduceis, and dyd tempte hym, desiring hym to shew them some signe from heauen.

2 He aunswered and saide vnto them. At euen ye saye, we shall haue fayre wedder, and that because the skye is reed:

3 and in the mornynge ye saye: to daye shalbe foule wedder, & that because the skie is cloudy and redde. O ye hypocrites ye can discerne the fashion of the skie and can ye not discerne the signes of the times

4 The froward nacion and aduouterous seketh a signe: and there shal no nother signe be geuen vnto them, but the signe of the prophet Ionas So lefte he them, and departed.

5 And when his disciples were come to the otherside of the water, they had forgotten too take bread with them.

6 Then Iesus sayd vnto them: Take hede and beware of the leuen of the Phariseis and of the Saduces.

7 And thei thoughte in theim selues sayinge: because we haue brought no breade wyth vs.

8 When Iesus vnderstode that, he sayd vnto them? O ye of litle fayth, why are your myndes cumbred because ye haue brought no bread?

9 Do ye not yet perceyue, neither remember those fyue loues when there were .v.M. men, & how many baskettes toke ye vp:

10 Neyther the seuen loues when there were .iiij. thousand, and how many baskettes toke ye vp?

11 Why perceyue ye not then, that I spake not vnto you of bread, when I sayde: beware of the leuen of the Pharises and of the Saduces.

12 Then vnderstode they, howe that he had not them beware of the leuen of breade: but of the doctrine of the Phariseis and of the Saduces.

13 When Iesus came into the costes of þe citie whych is called Cesarea Philippi, he axed his disciples sayinge: whome do men saye that I the sonne of man am?

14 They sayde: some saye that thou arte Ihon Baptist, some Helyas, som Ieremias, or one of the Prophetes.

15 He sayde vnto them: but whome saye ye that I am?

16 Simon Peter aunswered and sayde: Thou arte Christ the sonne of the liuynge God.

17 And Iesus aunswered and sayde to hym: happy arte thou Symon the sonne of Ionas, for fleshe & bloude hath not opened vnto the that, but my father which is in heauen.

18 And I saye also vnto the that thou arte Peeter: and vpon thys rocke I wil buylde my congregacion. And the gates of hell shall not preuayle against it.

19 And I wil geue vnto þe, the keyes of the kyngdome of

heauen, and whatsoeuer thou bindest vpon earth shalbe bounde in heauen, and whatsoeuer thon lowsest on earth shalbe lowsed in heauen.

20 Then he charged hys disciples, that they should tell no man, that he was Iesus Christ.

21 From that time forth Iesus beganne to shew vnto hys disciples, how that he must go vnto Ierusalem, and suffer many thinges of the elders, and of the hygh priestes, and of the scribes, and must be kylled: and ryse agayne the thyrde daye.

22 But Peter toke hym asyde, and beganne to rebuke hym saying: master fauer thy selfe: thys shall not come vnto the.

23 Then tourned he about and sayd vnto Peeter: come after me Sathan, thou offendest me, because thou sauorest not godly thynges, but worldly thynges.

24 Iesus then sayde to hys disciples. If anye man will folow me, let hym forsake hym selfe, and take vp hys crosse and folowe me.

25 For whosoeuer will saue hys lyfe, shall loose it. And whosoeuer shall loose hys lyfe for my sake shall finde it.

26 What shall it proffet a man though he shoulde wynne al the whole world if he loose hys awne soule? Or els what shall a man geue to redeme his soule agayne withall?

27 For the sonne of man shall come in þe glorye of hys father, wyth hys aungels: & then shall he rewarde euery man accordyng to his dedes.

28 Verely I saye vnto you, some there be among them that here stande, whiche shall not taste of death, till they shall haue sene the sonne of man come in hys kyngdom.

## CHAPTER 17

AND after .vi. dayes Iesus toke Peter and Iames and Ihon his brother, and broughte them vp into an hygh mountayne oute of the waye,

2 and was transfigured before them, and his face did shyne as the sunne and hys clothes were as whyte as the light:

3 & behold there appeared vnto theim Moyses & Helyas, talkyng with hym.

4 Then aunswered Peter and sayd to Iesus: master here is good beyng for vs. If thou wilt, let vs make here thre tabernacles, one for the, & one for Moses, and one for Helyas.

5 Whyle he yet speake, beholde a bryght cloude shadowed theim. And beholde there came a voyce out of the cloude, sayinge: this is my deare sonne, in whome I delite heare hym.

6 And when the disciples hearde that, they fell on theyr faces and were soore afrayed.

7 And Iesus came and touched them, and saide: arise and be not afrayed.

8 And when they loked vp, they sawe no man saue Iesus onely.

9 And as they came doune from the mountayne, Iesus charged them sayinge: se that ye shewe the vision to noman, vntyll the sonne of man be rysen agayne from death.

10 And hys disciples axed of hym saying: Why then say the Scribes, that Helyas must first come?

11 Iesus aunswered and sayde vnto them Helias shall first come and restore all thynges.

12 And I say vnto you that Helyas is come already, and they knewe hym not: but haue done vnto hym whatsoeuer they lusted. In lykewise shal also the sonne of man suffer of them.

13 Then the disciples perceiued that he spake vnto them of Ihon Baptist.

14 And when they were come to the people, there came to hym a certayne man, and kneled doune to hym, and sayde:

15 Master haue mercy on my sonne for he is francticke, and is sore vexed. For ofte tymes he falleth into the fire: and ofte into the water.

16 And I broughte hym to thy disciples, and thei could not heale him.

17 Iesus aunswered and sayde: O generation faythles and croked: howe longe shall I be wt you? how longe shal I suffre you? bryng him hydder to me.

18 And Iesus rebuked the deuel, & he came out of hym. And the chylde was healed euen that same houre.

19 Then came the disciples to Iesus secretly and sayd: Why coulde not we cast hym out?

20 Iesus sayd vnto them: Because of your vnbelefe. For I saye verely vnto you: if ye hadde faith as a grayn of a mustard seede, ye should say vnto thys mountayne, remoue hence too yonder place, and it shoulde remoue, neyther shoulde any thyng be impossible for you too do.

21 Howe be it this kynde goeth not out, but by prayer and fastynge.

22 As they passed the tyme in Galile, Iesus sayde vnto them: the sonne of man shalbe betrayed into the handes of men,

23 and they shall kyll hym, and the thyrde daye he shall ryse agayne. And they sorowed greatly.

24 And when they were come to Capernaum they that were wont to gadre poll money, came to Peter and sayde: Doeth your master paye tribute?

25 He sayd: yea. And when he was come into the house. Iesus spake fyrst to him, sayinge: What thinkest thou Simon? of whom do the kynges of the earth take tribute or pol

money? of their chyldren, or of straungers?

26 Peter sayde vnto hym: of straungers. Then sayde Iesus vnto hym agayne: Then are the chyldren fre.

27 Neuerthelesse, lest we should offende them: go to the sea and caste in thyne angel, and take the fish that first cometh vp: & when thou hast opened hys mouth, thou shalt fynde a pece of twenty pence: that take and paye for me and the.

# CHAPTER 18

THE same tyme the disciples came vnto Iesus sayinge: who is the greatest in the kyngdom of heauen

2 Iesus called a chylde vnto hym, and set hym in the middes of them:

3 and sayde. Verely I saye vnto you: excepte ye tourne, and become as chyldren, ye cannot enter into the kyngedome of heauen.

4 Who soeuer therfore humble hym selfe as thys chylde, the same is the greatest in the kyngedom of heauen.

5 And whosoeuer receyueth suche a chylde in my name, receyueth me.

6 But whosoeuer offende one of these litelone, whych beleue in me: it were better for hym, that a milstone were hanged about his necke, and that he were drowned in the depth of the sea.

7 Wo be vnto the worlde because of offences. Howe be it, it cannot be auoyded but that offences shall be geuen. Neuerthelesse woo be to the man, by whome the offence cometh.

8 Wherfore if thy hande or thy fote offende the, cut hym of and cast hym from the. It is better for the to enter into lyfe halte or maymed, rather then thou shouldest hauinge two handes or two fete, be cast into euerlastynge fyre.

9 And if also thyne eye offende the, plucke hym out and cast hym from the. It is better for the to entre into lyfe with one eye, then hauyng two eyes to be cast into hell fyre.

10 Se that ye not dispise not one of these litelones. For I saye vnto you, that in heauen their aungels alwaies behold the face of my father which is in heauen.

11 Yea, and the sonne of man is come to saue that whych is lost.

12 Howe thynke ye? If a man haue an hundred shepe, & one of them be gone astray, doth he not leaue nynty and nyne in the mountaynes, and go & seke that one whych is gone astraye.

13 If it happen that he fynde him, verely I say vnto you: he reioyseth more of that shepe, then of þe nyntye and nyne, which went not astray.

14 Euen so it is not the wil of your father in heauen, that one of these litelons shoulde perish.

15 Moreouer, if thy brother trespase agaynst the, Go and tell hym hys fault betwene hym and the alone. If he heare the, thou hast wonne thy brother.

16 But if he heare the not, then take yet with the one or two, that in the mouthe of two or thre witnesses, all thynges may be stablished.

17 If he heare not them, tell it vnto the congregacion. If he heare not the congregacion, take hym as a Heathen man, & as a publican.

18 Verely I saye vnto you, whatsoeuer ye bynde on earth, shalbe bounde in heauen. And whatsoeuer ye lowse on erth, shalbe lowsed in heauen.

19 Agayne I say vnto you, that if two of you shall agre in earth vpon any maner thyng whatsoeuer they shall desire: it shalbe geuen them of my father whyche is in heauen.

20 For where two or thre are gathered together in my name, there am I in the middes of them.

21 Then came Peter to hym, & sayde: master howe ofte shall I forgeue my brother, if he synne agaynst me, seuen tymes?

22 Iesus sayde vnto hym: I say not vnto the seuen times: but seuenty times seuen tymes.

23 Therefore is the kyngedom of heauen lykened vnto a certayne kyng, whithe woulde take a countes of hys seruauntes.

24 And when he had begon to recken: one was broughte vnto hym: which ought hym ten thousand talentes,

25 whome because he had noughte to paye, hys master commaunded him to be solde, and his wyfe, and hys chyldren, and all that he had, & payment to be made.

26 The seruaunt fel doune and besought hym sayinge: Syr geue me respyte, and I will paye it euery whyt.

27 Then had the Lord pitye on that seruaunt, & lowsed him and forgaue hym the dette.

28 And the sayd seruaunt went out & found one of hys felowes, which ought him an hundred pence, & layed handes on him, & toke hym by the throote sayinge: paye me that thou owest.

29 And hys felowe fell doune & besoughte hym, saying: haue pacience with me, and I wil pay the all.

30 But he woulde not, but wente and cast hym into pryson till he shoulde pay the det.

31 When hys other felowes sawe what was done, they were very sory, and came and told vnto theyr Lord all that had happened.

32 Then his Lorde called hym, and sayde vnto hym. O euill seruaunt I forgaue the al that det, because thou praiest me:

33 was it not mete also that thou shouldest haue had compassion on thy felow, euen as I had pitie on the?

34 And his lord was wroth and deliuered him to the iaylers, til he should paye all that was due to hym.

35 So likewyse shal my heauenly father do vnto you except ye forgeue with your hertes, eache one to hys brother theyr trespasses.

## CHAPTER 19

AND it came to passe when Iesus had finished those sayinges, he gat him from Galile, and came into the coostes of Iury beyonde Iordan,

2 and much people folowed hym, and he healed them there.

3 Then came vnto him the Pharises, tempting him, & saying to hym: Is it lawful for a man to put away his wyfe for all maner of causes?

4 He aunswered and sayde vnto them: Haue ye not reade, howe that he whiche made man at the beginnyng, made them man and woman

5 and sayd: for this thynge, shall a man leaue father and mother & cleaue vnto his wyfe, & thei twayne but one flesh.

6 Wherefore now are they not twaine, but one fleshe. Let not man therefore put a sunder, that whiche God hath couppled together.

7 Then sayd they to him: why did Moyses commaund to geue a testimoniall of diuorcement, & to put her awaye?

8 He sayde vnto them: Moyses because of the hardnes of youre hertes suffred you to put away your wyfes: But from the beginning it was not so.

9 I say therfore vnto you, whosoeuer putteth awaye hys wyfe, (except it he for fornicacion) & marieth another, breaketh wedloke. And whosoeuer maryeth her, which is diuorced, doth commit aduoutry.

10 Then sayde his disciples to him: if the matter be so betwene man and wyfe, then is it not good to marye.

11 He sayde vnto them: all men can not awaye with that sayinge, saue they to whome it is geuen.

12 There are chaste whiche were so borne out of theyr mothers bealy. And there are chaste whiche be made of men. And there be chast which haue made them selues chaste for the kyngdom of heauens sake. He that can take it let hym take it.

13 Then were brought to him iong chyldren, that he should put his handes on them & praye. And the disciples rebuked them.

14 But Iesus sayd suffer the chyldren and forbid them not to come to me: for of suche is the kyngdome of heauen.

15 And when he had put his handes on them he departed thence.

16 And beholde one came and saide to him: good master, what good thinge shall I do, that I maye haue eternall lyfe?

17 He sayde to him: why callest þu me good? there is none good but one, & that is God. But if thou wilt enter into lyfe, kepe the commaundementes,

18 The other sayd to him: Which And Iesus sayde: Breake no wedloke, kyll not, steale not: beare not false witues,

19 honoure father and mother, and loue thy neyghboure as thy selfe.

20 And the iong man sayd vnto him: I haue obserued all these thynges from my youth, what lacke I yet?

21 And Iesus sayde vnto him, if thou wilt be perfecte go and sell that thou haste, and geue it to the poore, and thou shalt haue treasure in heauen, and come and folowe me.

22 When the ionge man hearde that saying: he went away mournynge. For he had great possessions.

23 Then Iesus sayd vnto his disciples: Verely I saye vnto you: it is harde for a riche man to enter into the kyngdom of heauen.

24 And moreouer I saye vnto you, it is easier for a Camel to go thorow the eye of a nedle, then for a ryche man to entre into the kyngdom of God

25 When his disciples hearde that, thei were exceadingly amased saying: who then can be saued?

26 Iesus beheld them and sayde vnto them: with men this is impossible, but with God al thynges are possible.

27 Then aunswered Peeter and sayde vnto hym: Beholde we haue forsaken all and folowed the, what shall we haue?

28 Iesus sayde vnto them: Verely I saye vnto you: when the sonne of man shall sit in the seate of hys maiestie, yea, which folow me in the second geueracion, shall sitte also vpon .xij. seates, and iudge the .xij. tribes of Israel.

29 And whosoeuer forsaketh houses, or brethren, or systers, other father or mother, or wyfe or chyldren, or landes, for my names sake, the same shal receyue an .C. folde, & shal enherite euerlasting life.

30 Many that are firste shall be last, and the last shalbe the first.

## CHAPTER 20

FOR the kyngedom of heauen is lyke vnto an housholder, which went out early in the mornynge to hyre labourers into hys vyneyarde.

2 And he agreed with the labourers for a peny a daye, and sent them into hys vyneyarde.

3 And he went out about the

.iij. houre, and saw other standing ydel in the market place,

4 and sayd vnto them, go ye also into my vineyard: and whatsoeuer is right, I wil geue you. And they went theyr waye.

5 Agayn he went out about the sixt and nynth houre and did likewise.

6 And he went out about the eleuenth houre, and founde other standynge ydel, and sayde vnto theim: Why stande ye here all the day ydell?

7 They sayde vnto hym: because no man hath hyred vs. He sayde to them go ye also into my vyneyarde, & whatsoeuer is right, that shall ye receyue.

8 When euen was come, the Lorde of the vineyarde sayde vnto hys Stewarde: call the labourers, and geue them their hyer, beginning at the laste, tyll thou come to þe first.

9 And they whiche were hyred about the eleuenth houre, came and receyued euery man a peny.

10 Then came the first, supposing that they should receyue more, and they lykewise receyued euery man a peny.

11 And when they had receyued it, they murmured agaynst the good man of the house

12 saying: These laste haue wrought but one houre, and thou haste made theym equall vnto vs whiche haue borne the burthen, and heat of the daye.

13 He aunswered to one of them, saying: frende I do the no wrong: diddest thou not agre with me for a peny?

14 Take that which is thy duety, and go thy waye, I will geue vnto thys laste as muche as to the.

15 Is it not lawful for me to do as me lusteth with myne owne? Is thyne eye euel because I am good?

16 So þe laste shalbe firste, and the first shalbe laste. For many are called, and few be chosen.

17 And Iesus ascended to Ierusalem and toke the .xij. disciples a parte in the way, and sayde to them:

18 Beholde we go vp to Ierusalem, and the sonne of man shalbe betrayed vnto þe chief priestes and vnto the scribes: and they shal condemne hym to death,

19 and shall deliuer hym to the gentels, to be mocked, to be scourged, & to be crucified, and the thirde daye he shall rise agayne.

20 Then came to him the mother of Zebedes chyldren with her sonnes, worshippyng hym and desiring a certayn thinge of hym.

21 And he saide vnto her: what wilt thou haue? She said vnto hym: Graunt that these my two sonnes maye sitte, the one on thy right hande, and the other on the lift hande in thy kyngdome

22 Iesus aunswered and sayde: Ye wotte not what ye are. Are ye able to drinke of the cup that I shall drynke of: and to be baptised with the baptisme that I shalbe baptised wt?

23 They aunswered to hym: that we are. And he sayde vnto them: Ye shall drynke of my cup, & shal be baptised with the baptisme that I shalbe baptised with. But to sit on my right hande and on my lifte hande, is not myne to geue: but to them for whome it is prepared of my father.

24 And when the ten hearde this, they disdayned at the two brethren.

25 But Iesus called them vnto hym and sayd: Ye know that the Lordes of the gentils haue domination ouer them. And they that are great, exercyse power ouer them.

26 It shall not be so amonge you. But whosoeuer wil be great amonge you, let hym be your minister,

27 and whosoeuer wil be chief, let hym be your seruaunt,

28 euen as the sonne of man came not to be minnistred vnto, but to minister, and to geue his life for the redempcion of many.

29 And as they departed from Hiericho, much people folowed hym.

30 And beholde two blynd men sitting by the way syde, when thei heard Iesus passe by, cryed saying: Thou Lord the sonne of Dauid haue mercy on vs.

31 And the people rebuked theym: because they shoulde holde their peace. But they cried the more sayinge: Haue mercy on vs thou Lord which art the sonne of Dauid.

32 Then Iesus stode styll, & called them, and sayde: What will ye that I shoulde do to you?

33 Thei sayde to him: Lorde, that our eyes maye be opened.

34 Iesus had compassion on them, and touched their eyes. And immediatly their eyes receiued sight. And thei folowed him.

# CHAPTER 21

WHEN they drewe nygh vnto Ierusalem, and were come too Bethphage, to mount Oliuete: then sent Iesus two of his disciples,

2 sayinge to them. Go into the towne that lyeth ouer agaynste you, and anone ye shal fynde an Asse bound, & her colte with her: lose them, and bringe them vnto me.

3 And if any man saye ought vnto you, saye ye that the Lord hath nede of them: and streyght waye he will let them go.

4 All this was done, to fulfill that whiche was spoken by the Prophet saying:

5 Tel ye the doughter of

Sion: beholde thyne kyng cometh vnto the meke, and sitting vpon an Asse and a colte, the fote of an Asse vsed to the yooke.

6 The disciples went and did as Iesus commaunded them,

7 & brought the Asse and the colte, and put on theym theyr clothes, and set him thereon.

8 And many of the people spred their garmentes in the way. Other cut doune braunches from the trees, and strawed them in the waye.

9 Moreouer the people that went before, and they also that came after, cryed sayinge: Hosanna to the sonne of Dauid. Blessed be he that cometh in the name of the Lorde Hosanna in the hyest.

10 And when he was come into Ierusalem all the cytye was moued sayinge: who is thys?

11 And þe people sayd: this is Iesus þe prophet of Nazareth a citie of Galile.

12 And Iesus wente into the temple of God, and caste out all them that soulde and bought in the temple, & ouerthrewe the tables of the money chaungers, & the seates of them that solde doues,

13 and sayde to them: It is writen, my house shalbe called the house of prayer. But ye haue made it a denne of theues.

14 And the blind and the halt came to hym in the temple and he healed them.

15 When the chiefe priestes sawe the marueylles that he dyd, and the chyldren criynge in þe temple and saying: Hosanna to the sonne of Dauid, they disdayned,

16 and sayde vnto hym: hearest thou what these saye? Iesus sayde to them, yea. Haue ye neuer reade, of the mouth of babes and suckelynges thou hast ordeyned prayse?

17 And he lefte them, and wente out of þe cytye vnto Bethanye, and had hys abydynge there.

18 In the mornynge as he retourned into the cytie agayn, he hungred,

19 and spyed a fygge tree in the waye, and came to it, and found nothynge thereon, but leaues onely, and sayed to it, neuer frute growe on the hence forwardes. And anone the figge tre wyddered away

20 And when hys disciples sawe that, they marueyled sayinge: How sone is the fygge tree wyddered awaye?

21 Iesus answered, and sayd vnto them: Verelye I say vnto you: if ye shal haue fayth, and shall not dout ye shall not onely do that which I haue done to the fygge tree but also yf ye shall saye vnto thys mountayne, take thy selfe awaye and cast thy selfe into the sea it shall be done.

22 And whatsoeuer ye shall axe in prayer (yf ye beleue) ye shall receyue it.

23 And when he was come into the temple, the chiefe Priestes and the elders of þt people came vnto hym as he was teachynge, and sayde. By what auctoritie doest thou these thynges and who gaue the thys power?

24 Iesus answered, and sayed vnto them: I also wil axe of you a certayne questyon, whiche yf ye assoyle me, I in lyke wyse wyll tell you by what authoritie I do these thynges.

25 The baptisme of Iohn whence was it: from heauen or of men? Then they reasoned amonge themselues, sayinge: yf we shall saye from heauen, he wyll laye vnto vs: why dyd ye not then beleue hym?

26 But and yf we shall saye of men, then feare we the people. For all men helde Iohn as a Prophete.

27 And they answered Iesus and sayed: we cannot tell. And he lykewyse sayd vnto them: neyther tell I you by what authoritie I do these thynges.

28 What saye ye to thys? A certayne man had two sonnes, and came to the elder and sayde: sonne go and worke to daye in my vyneyarde.

29 He answered and sayde, I wyll not: but after warde repented and wente.

30 Then came he to the seconde, and sayed lykewyse. And he answered and sayed: I wyll syr: yet wente not.

31 Whether of them twayne dyd the wyll of the father? And they sayde vnto hym: the fyrst. Iesus sayde vnto them: verelye I saye vnto you, that the Publycans and the harlotes shall come into the kyngedome of God before you.

32 For Iohn came vnto you in the waye of ryghtuousnes, and ye beleued hym not. But the Publicans and the harlotes beleued hym. And yet ye (thoughe ye sawe it) were not yet moued wyth repentaunce, that ye myght afterwarde haue beleued hym.

33 Herken another similitude. There was a certayne housholder, which planted a vyneyard, and hedged it rounde aboute and made a wynepresse in it, and buylt a tower, and let it out to husbandmen, and went into a straunge countrey.

34 And when the tyme of the frute drewe neare, he sente hys seruauntes to the husbandmen to receyue the fruytes of it.

35 And the husbandmen caughte hys seruauntes and bet one, kylled another, and stoned another.

36 Agayne he sent other seruauntes, mo then the fyrste, and they serued them lykewyse.

37 But last of all, he sent vnto them hys owne sonne, sayinge: they wyll feare my sonne.

38 But when the husbandmen sawe the sonne, they sayde amonge them selues. Thys is the

heyre: come let vs kyll hym, and let vs take hys enheritaunce to oure selues.

39 And they caughte hym and thruste him out of the vyneyard, and slewe hym.

40 When the Lorde of the vyneyard cometh, what wyll he do with those husbandmen?

41 They sayed vnto hym: he wyll cruellye destroye those euyll persons, and wyll let out hys vyneyarde vnto other husbandmen, which shall delyuer hym the frute at tymes conuenient.

42 Iesus sayde vnto them: dyd ye neuer reade in the scriptures. The stone which the buylders refused, the same is set in the principall parte of the corner: thys was the Lordes doynge, and it is meruelous in oure eyes.

43 Therfore saye I vnto you the kyngdome of God shalbe taken from you, and shalbe gyuen to þe gentyles, whiche shall brynge forth the frutes of it.

44 And whosoeuer shall fall ou thys stone, he shalbe broken, but on whosoeuer it shall fall vpon, it wyll grynde hym to powder.

45 And when the chiefe priestes and pharyses hearde these similitudes, they perceyued that he spake of them.

46 And they wente aboute to laye handes on hym, but they feared the people, because they toke hym as a Prophete.

## CHAPTER 22

AND Iesus answered, and spake vnto them agayne in symylytudes sayinge.

2 The kyngdome of heauen is like vnto a certayne kynge, whiche maryed hys sonne,

3 and sent forth hys seruauntes to call them that were byd to the wedding, & they woulde not come.

4 Agayne he sent forth other seruauntes saynge. Tell them which are bydden: beholde I haue prepared my dyner, myne oxen and my fatlynges are kylled, and all thinges are redy, come vnto the mariage.

5 But they made lyght of it, and went theyr wayes: one to hys ferme place, an other about hys marchaundyse,

6 the remnaunt toke hys seruauntes and intreated them vngodly and slewe them.

7 When the kynge hearde that, he was wrothe and sente forthe hys warryers and destroyed those murtherers and brent vp theyr citie.

8 Then sayde he to hys seruauntes: the wedding was prepared. But they which were bidden: were not worthye.

9 Go ye therfore out into the hye waies, & as many as ye finde byd them to the mariage.

10 The seruauntes went out into the hye wayes, and gaddered together as many as they could fynde. Both good & bad, and the weddynge was furnyshed with gestes.

11 Then the kynge came in, to viset the gestes, and spyed there a man which had not on a weddynge garment,

12 and sayd vnto hym, frend howe fortuned it that thou camest in hyther, and hast not on a weddinge garmente? And he was euen speachlesse.

13 Then sayed the kynge to hys mynisters: take and bynde hym hande and fote, and caste hym into vtter darcknes, there shal be weping and gnashing of teeth.

14 For manye are called and fewe be chosen.

15 Then went the pharises and toke counsell how they myght tangle hym in hys wordes.

16 And they sent vnto hym theyr discyples with Herodes seruauntes sayinge: Mayster, we knowe that thou art true, & teachest the waye of God truely: neither carest for any man, for thou considerest not mennes estate.

17 Tel vs therfor how thinkest thou. Is it lawful to giue tribute vnto Cesar or not?

18 Iesus perceyued theyr wickednes, & sayd: Why tempt ye me ye hypocrites?

19 Let me se the tribute money. And they toke him a peny.

20 And he sayd vnto them: whose is thys ymage & superscripcion?

21 They sayed vnto him: Cesars. Then sayed he vnto them: Gyue therfore to Cesar, þt which is Cesars: And gyue vnto God, that which is Goddes.

22 When they hearde that they maruayled, and left hym, and went theyr waye.

23 The same day the Saduces came to hym (which say that there is no resurreccion) axed him

24 saying: Mayster, Moyses bad, yf a man dye hauyng no chyldren, that the brother marye hys wyfe, and reyse vp seed vnto hys brother.

25 There were with vs seuen brethren, and the fyrst maryed and dyseased without yssue and left hys wyfe vnto his brother.

26 Like wyse the second and the thyrde vnto the seuenth.

27 Last of all the woman dyed also.

28 Nowe in the resurreccyon whose wyfe shall she be of these seuen? For all had her.

29 Iesus answered & sayd vnto them: ye are deceyued and vnderstande not the scriptures, nor yet the power of God.

30 For in the resurrection they nether marye nor are maryed: but are as the angels in heauen.

31 As touchyng the resurreccion of the dead: haue ye not reade what is sayd vnto you of God which sayth:

32 I am Abrahams God, and Isaacks God. & the God of

Iacob? God is not the God of the dead, but of the liuynge.

33 And when the people hearde that, they were astonyed at hys doctrine.

34 When the Pharises had hearde, how that he had put the Saduces to silence, they drewe together,

35 and one of them whiche was a doctoure of lawe, axed a question temptyng hym and sayinge:

36 Mayster which is the chief commaundement in the lawe?

37 Iesus sayd to him: Loue the Lord thy God with all thyne herte, and with all thy soule, and with al thy mynd.

38 This is the fyrst and the chiefe commaundement.

39 And there is another lyke vnto thys. Loue thy neyghboure as thy selfe.

40 In these two commaundementes hange all the lawe & the Prophetes.

41 Whyle the pharyses were gaddered together. Iesus axed them

42 saying: what thynke ye of Christ? Whose sonne is he? They sayed vnto him: the sonne of Dauid.

43 He sayed vnto them: how then doeth Dauid in sprite, call him Lorde, sayenge:

44 The Lorde sayed to my Lord sit on my righthande: tyl I make thyne enemyes thy fotestole.

45 If Dauid call hym Lorde, how is he than hys sonne?

46 And none coulde aunswere hym agayne one worde, neyther durste any from that daye forth axe him any more question.

## CHAPTER 23

THEN spake Iesus to the people, & to hys disciples

2 sayinge: The Scribes and the Phariseis sit in Moyses seate.

3 All therfore whatsoeuer they bid you obserue, that obserue and do, but after their workes do not,

4 for they say and do not. Yea, and they bynd heauy burthens and greuous to be borne and lay them on mens shoulders: but they them selfs will not heaue at them with one of theyr fyngers.

5 All their workes thei do for to be sene of men. They set abroade theyr philateries, & make large borders on theyr garmentes,

6 and loue to sit vppermoste at feastes, and to haue the chiefe seates in the Synagoges,

7 and gretynges in the markettes, and too be called of men Rabbi.

8 But ye shall not suffer youre selues to be called Rabbi. For one is your master, that is to witte Christ, and all ye are brethreu.

9 And call no man your father vpon the earth, for there is but one your father, & he is in heauen.

10 Be not called masters: for there is but one your master: and he is Christ.

11 He that is greatest amonge you: shalbe your seruaunt.

12 But whosoeuer exalteth hym selfe: shalbe brought lowe, and he that humbleth hym selfe, shalbe exalted.

13 Wo be vnto you Scribes and Phariseis, hypocrites, for ye shut vp the kyngdome of heauen before men: ye youre selues go not in, neyther suffer ye them that come to enter in.

14 Wo be vnto you Scribes and Phariseis, hypocrites, ye deuoure wyddowes houses, & that vnder a coloure of praieng long prayers wherfore ye shall receyue great damnacion.

15 Wo be vnto you Scribes and Phariseis hypocrites: which compasse sea and lande, to brynge one into youre belefe: and when he is brought ye make hym two folde more þe chyld of hell: then ye your selues are.

16 Wo be vnto you blynde guydes, whyche say whosoeuer sweare by the temple, it is nothing, but whosoeuer sweared by the golde of the temple: he offendeth.

17 Ye fooles and blind, whither is greater, the golde, or the temple þt sanctifieth the gold?

18 And whosoeuer sweareth by the aultare, it is nothynge: but whosoeuer sweareth by the offeryng that lyeth on þe aulter, offendeth.

19 Ye fooles and blynde, whither is greater the offerynge, or the aulter whiche sanctifieth the offeryng?

20 Whosoeuer therfore sweareth by the aultare, sweareth by it and by all that thereon is.

21 And whosoeuer sweareth by the temple, sweareth by it and by hym þt dwelleth therin.

22 And he that sweareth by heauen sweareth by the seate of God, and by him that sitteth thereon.

23 Wo be to you Scribes and Phariseis, hypocrites, which tythe mynte, anyse and commen, and leaue the wayghtyer matters of the lawe vndone: iudgement, mercy, and faythe. These ought ye to haue done, and not to haue lefte the other vndone.

24 Ye blynde guydes whiche strayne out a gnat, and swallowe a cammell.

25 Wo be to you Scribes and Pharises hypocrites, which make cleane the vtter side of þe cuppe, & of the platter: but within they are ful of bribery and excesse.

26 Thou blynd Pharisei, clense first the ynneside of the cup & platter, þt the outside of them may be clene also.

27 Wo be to you Scribes and Phariseis hypocrytes, for ye are lyke vnto paynted tombes, whiche appeare beautifull outwarde, but are within full of

dead bones and of all filthines.

28 So are ye, for outwarde ye apeare righteouse vnto men, when within, ye are full of hypocresie and iniquitie.

29 Wo be vnto you Scribes and Phariseis hypocrites, ye buylde the tombes of the Prophetes and garnysh the sepulchres of þe righteouse,

30 and saye: if we had bene in the dayes of our fathers, we woulde not haue bene parteners with them in the bloude of the Prophetes.

31 So then ye be witnesses to your selues, þt ye are the chyldren of them whyche kylled the Prophetes.

32 Fulfil ye likewyse the measure of your fathers.

33 Ye serpentes and generacion of vppers howe shoulde ye scape the damnacion of hell?

34 Wherfore, behold I send vnto you Prophetes, wise men, & Scribes. Of them ye shal kyl and crucifye: and of them ye shall scourge in your synagoges, and persecute from citye to citye

35 that vpon you may come all the ryghtuous bloude that was shede vpon the earth, from the bloude of ryghtuous Abel, vnto the bloude of Zacharias the sonne of Barachias, whom ye slewe betwene the tempel and the aulter.

36 Verely I say vnto you, al these things shall lyght vpon this generation.

37 Ierusalem, Ierusalem which killest prophetes, and stone them which are sent to the: howe often would I haue gathered thy children together: as the henne gathered her chikens vnder her winges, but ye would not.

38 Beholde your habitation shalbe left vnto you desolate.

39 For I saye to you, ye shall not se me hence forth tyll that ye saye blessed is he that commeth in the name of the Lorde.

# CHAPTER 24

AND Iesus went out and departed from the temple: and his disciples came to hym for to shew him the building of the temple.

2 Iesus sayde vnto them: Se ye not all these thinges? Verely I say vnto you there shal not be here left one stone vpon another that shall not be cast doune.

3 And as he sate vpon the mounte Oliuet: his disciples came vnto him secretlye saying. Tell vs when these thinges shalbe: and what sygne shalbe of thy comminge and of the ende of the worlde?

4 And Iesus aunswered and sayd vnto them: take hede that no man deceyue you.

5 For many shal come in my name sayng: I am Christe: and shall deceyue many.

6 Ye shall heare of warres? and of the fame of warres: but se that ye be not troubled. For all these thinges muste come to passe, but the ende is not yet.

7 For nacion shall ryse against nacion and realme against realme: and ther shalbe pestylence, honger and earth quakes in certayne places?

8 All these are the begynnynge of sorowes.

9 Then shall they put you to trouble, and shall kyll you: and ye shalbe hated of all nacions for my names sake.

10 And then shall manye be offended, and shal betray one another, and shall hate one the other.

11 And manye false prophetes shall aryse, and shall deceyue manye.

12 And because iniquite shall haue the vpper hande the loue of manye shall abate.

13 But he that endureth to the ende, the same shall be safe.

14 And this glad tydinges of the kingdome shalbe preached in all the worlde, for a wytnes vnto all nacions: & then shal þe ende come.

15 When ye therfore shall se the abhomination that betokeneth desolation, spoken of by Daniel the prophete, stande in the holye place (let hym that readeth it, vnderstande it)

16 then let theim which be in Iurye, flye into the mountaines.

17 And let him which is on þe house toppe not come doune to fetche anye thinge out of his house.

18 Neither let him which in is þe fielde returne backe to fetche his clothes.

19 Wo in those daies to theim þt are with childe, and to them that geue sucke.

20 But praye that youre flyghte be not in the Winter, neyther on the saboth daye.

21 For then shalbe great trybulacion such as was not from the beginninge of the worlde to this tyme, nor shalbe:

22 yea, and except those dayes should be shortened, there shoulde no fleshe be saued: but for the chosens sake, those daies shalbe shortened.

23 Then if anye man shall saye vnto you: lo here is Christe, or there is christ: beleue it not.

24 For there shall aryse false Christes, and false prophetes, and shall do great myracles and wonders. In so much that if it were possyble the very electe should be deceiued.

25 Take hede, I haue tolde you before.

26 Wherfor if they shal saye vnto you: beholde he is in the deserte, in the secrete places beleue not.

27 For as the lyghteninge cometh out of the east, and shyneth into the west, so shal the comminge of the sonne of man be.

28 For whersoeuer a dead carkes is, euen thither wyl egles resort.

29 Immediatly after the

trybulations of those dayes, shall the sonne be darkened: and the mone shall not gyue hyr lyght, and the starre shal fall from heauen, & the powers of heauen shal moue.

30 And then shal apeare the sygne of the sonne of man in heauen. And then shall all the kynredes of the earth morne, and they shall se the sonne of man come in the cloudes of heauen with power and great glorye.

31 And he shall sende his aungels with the greate voyce of a trompe, and they shall gader together his chosen from the foure windes, and from the one ende of the worlde to the other.

32 Learne a symylytude of the fygge tre: when his braunches are yet tendre, and his leaues spronge, ye knowe that sommer is nye,

33 so lykewyse ye, when ye se all these thynges, be ye sure that it is neare euen at the dores.

34 Verely I say vnto you, that this generation shal not passe tyll all these be fulfylled.

35 Heauen & earth shal perishe, but my wordes shal abide.

36 But of that daye and houre knoweth no man, no not the aungels of heauen, but my father onelye.

37 As the tyme of Noe was, so lykewyse shal the commynge of the sonne of man be.

38 For as in the dayes before the floude, they did eate & drinke, mary and were maried, euen vnto the daye that Noe entred into the shippe,

39 & knew of nothinge, tyll the floude came and toke them all awaye. So shal also the comminge of the sonne of man be.

40 Then two shall be in the fielde, the one shalbe receyued, and the other shalbe refused,

41 two shalbe grindinge at the myll, the one shalbe receyued, and the other shalbe refused.

42 Wake therfor, because ye knowe not what houre your maister wyl come.

43 Of this be sure, that if the good man of the house knewe what houre the these woulde come, he would suerlye watche, and not suffer his house to be broken vp.

44 Therfore be ye also redye, for in the houre ye thinke he woulde not, wyll the sonne of man come.

45 Yf there be anye faythful seruaunt and wyse, whome his maister hath made rueler ouer his housholde to geue them meate in season conuenient:

46 happy is that seruaunt whom his maister (when he cometh) shall fynde so doyinge.

47 Verelye I saye vnto you, he shall make hym ruler ouer all hys goodes.

48 But and if that euyll seruaunt shall saye in his herte, my maister wyll defer hys commynge,

49 and begynne to smyte his felowes, yea, and to eate and to drinke with the dronken:

50 that seruauntes maister wyll come in a daye when he loketh not for him, and in an houre that he is not ware of,

51 and wyll deuide hym, and geue him his rewarde with hipocrites. There shalbe weping and gnashing of tethe.

# CHAPTER 25

THEN the kingdome of heauen shalbe lykened vnto ten virgins, which toke their lampes and went to mete the bridegrom,

2 Fyue of them were folyshe, & fyue were wise.

3 The folyshe toke theyr lampes, but toke none oyle with them.

4 But the wise toke oyle with them in their vessels with their lampes also.

5 Whyle the brydegrome taried, al slombred and slepte.

6 And euen at midnight there was a crye made: beholde, the brydegrome cometh, goo out againste hym.

7 Then all those virgins arose, and prepared their lampes.

8 And the folishe sayed to the wise: gyue vs of your oyle for oure lampes go out.

9 But the wyse aunswered sayinge not so, least there be not ynough for vs and you: but go rather to them that sell & by for your selues.

10 And whyle they went to bye the brydegrome came: and they that were redie, went in wyth hym to the weddinge, and the gate was shut vp.

11 Afterwardes cam also the other virgins sayinge: maister maister, open to vs.

12 But he aunswered and sayd: verely I say vnto you: I knowe not you

13 watche therfore: for ye knowe neither the daye nor yet the houre when the sonne of man shall come.

14 Lykewyse as a certayne man, redye to take iorney to a straunge countre, called hys seruauntes and delyuered to them his goodes.

15 And vnto one he gaue fyue talentes, to another .ij. and to another one: to euery man after his abylite, and straight waye departed.

16 Then he that had receyued the .v. talentes, went and bestowed them and wan other fyue talentes.

17 Likewise he that receiued two, gained other two.

18 But he that receiued the one, wente and digged a pit in the earth and hid his maisters money.

19 After a longe season the Lorde of those seruauntes came and rekened with them.

20 Then came he that had receyued .v. talentes, and brought other .v. talentes, sayinge: maister thou delyuerest

vnto me fyue talentes beholde I haue gained with them fyue talentes mo.

21 Then his maister sayde vnto him: Well good seruaunt and faithfull. Thou hast bene faythfull in litle, I wyll make the rueler ouer muche enter in into thy maisters ioye.

22 Also he that receiued .ij. talentes, came and sayed mayster thou deliuerest vnto me twoo talentes, beholde I haue won two other talentes with them.

23 And his maister sayde vnto hym, well good seruaunt and faithfull. Thou hast bene faithfull in litle, I wyll make the ruler ouer much: go in into thy maisters ioye.

24 Then he which had receiued the one talent, came & sayde, maister, I consydered that thou waste an harde man, which repest were thou sowest not, & gadderest where thou strawest not,

25 and was therfore afraide, and went and hid thy talente in the earth: beholde, thou hast thyne owne.

26 His maister aunswered and said vnto hym: thou euyll seruaunte and slouthful, thou knewest that I repe wher I sowed not, and gadder wher I strawed not:

27 thou oughtest therfore to haue had my money to the chaungers, then at my commynge shoulde I haue receyued myne owne with vauntage.

28 Take therfore the talent from him, and giue it vnto him which hath ten talentes.

29 For vnto euerye man that hathe shalbe geuen, and he shall haue aboundaunce, and from hym that hath not, shall be taken awaye, euen that he hath.

30 And caste that vnprofytable seruaunt into vtter darcknes: there shalbe wepinge & gnashinge of tethe.

31 When the sonne of man cometh in hys glorye, and all the holye aungels with him, then shall he sytte vpon the seate of his glory,

32 and before him shall be gathered all nations, and he shall separate them one from another, as a shephearde deuideth the shepe from the gootes.

33 And he shall set the shepe on his right haude, and the gootes on his lyfte.

34 Then shal the kinge saye to them on his right hand. Come ye blessed chyldren of my father, enheryte ye the kingdome prepared for you from the begynninge of the worlde.

35 For I was an hungred & ye gaue me meate. I thirsted and ye gaue me drinke. I was herbourles and ye lodged me. I was naked and ye clothed me.

36 I was sycke and ye visyted me. I was in pryson and ye came vnto me.

37 Then shal the rightuous aunswere him sayinge, maister, when sawe we the an houngred, & fede the, or a thyrst, & gaue the drinke

38 when sawe we the herborles, and lodged the? or naked and clothed the?

39 or when sawe we the syke or in pryson and came vnto the?

40 And the kinge shall aunswere and saye vnto theym: verelye I saye vnto you: in as much as ye haue done it to one of the least of these my brethren, ye haue done it vnto me.

41 Then shall the kinge saye vnto them that shalbe on the lyfte hande. Departe from me ye cursed, into euerlastinge fyre, which is prepared for the deuyll and hys angels.

42 For I was an hungred and ye gaue me no meate, I thyrsted and ye gaue me no drynke,

43 I was herbourles, and ye lodged me not, I was naked and ye clothed me not, I was sicke and in pryson, and ye vysited me not.

44 Then shal they answere him, sayinge: mayster when sawe we the an hungred, or a thyrst or herbourles, or naked, or sicke, or in pryson, and dyd not minister vnto the.

45 Then shall he answere them, and saye: Verelye I saye vnto you, in as much as ye dyd it not to one of these little ones: ye dyd it not vnto me.

46 And these shall go into euerlasting payne. And the righteouse into lyfe eternall.

## CHAPTER 26

AND it came to passe, when Iesus had finyshed all these sayinges, he sayed vnto hys disciples.

2 Ye know that after two dayes shalbe easter, and the sonne of man shalbe delyuered to be crucifyed.

3 Then assembled together the chiefe priestes and the scrybes and the elders of the people to the palaice of the hye priest, called Cayphas,

4 and helde a counsell, howe they myghte take Iesus by sutteltie, and kyl hym.

5 But they sayed, not on the holy daye, lest any vproure aryse amonge the people.

6 When Iesus was in Bethany, in the house of Simon the leper,

7 there came to him a woman, which had an alabaster boxe of precious oyntment, and poured it on hys heade, as he sate at the bourde.

8 When hys discyples sawe that, they had indignacyon, sayinge: what neded thys waste?

9 Thys oyntment myght haue bene wel solde, and geuen to the poore.

10 When Iesus vnderstode that, he sayed vnto them: why trouble ye the woman? she hath wrought a good worke vpon me.

11 For ye shall haue poore

folke alwaies with you, but me shall ye not haue alwayes.

12 And in that she casted thys oyntmente on my bodye, she dyd it to burye me with al.

13 Verelye I saye vnto you, wheresoeuer thys gospell shalbe preached throughout al the world, there shal also thys that she hath done, be told for a memorial of her.

14 Then one of the twelue called Iudas Iscaryoth went vnto the chiefe priestes,

15 and sayd: What wyll ye geue me, and I wyll delyuer him vnto you? And they appoynted vnto him thyrtye peces of syluer.

16 And from that tyme he sought oportunite to betraye hym.

17 The fyrst day of swete bread the disciples came to Iesus sayinge vnto hym: where wylt thou that we prepare for þe to eate the paschall lambe?

18 And he sayde: go into the cytye vnto suche a man, & saye to hym: the mayster sayth my tyme is at hande, I wyll kepe myne easter at thy house wyth my disciples.

19 And the disciples dyd as Iesus had appoynted them, and made redy the easter lambe.

20 When the euen was come, he sate doune with the .xij.

21 And as they dyd eate, he sayed: Verelye I saye vnto you, that one of you shal betraye me.

22 And they were excedynge sorowfull, and beganne euery one of them to saye vnto hym: is it I mayster?

23 He answered & sayed: he that deppeth hys hand wyth me in the dish the same shall betraye me.

24 The sonne of man goeth as it is written of hym: but wo be to that man, by whome the sonne of man shalbe betrayed. It had ben good for that man, yf he had neuer bene borne.

25 Then Iudas whiche betrayed him, answered and sayde: is it I mayster? He sayed vnto hym: thou hast sayed.

26 As they dyd eate, Iesus toke bread and gyue thankes, brake it and gaue it to the disciples and sayed: Take, eate, thys is my body.

27 And he toke the cup, & thanked, and gaue it them, saying: drynke of it euery one:

28 For thys is my bloude of the newe testament, that shalbe shedde for many, for the remissyon of synnes.

29 I saye vnto you: I wyll not drinke henceforth of this frute of the vyne tree, vntyll that daye, when I shall drinke it newe wyth you in my fathers kyngdome.

30 And when they had sayde grace, they went oute into mounte oliuete.

31 Then sayd Iesus vnto them: all ye shall be offended by me thys nyght. For it is written. I wyll smyte the shepehearde, and the shepe of the flocke shall be scattered abroade.

32 But after I am rysen agayne, I wyll goo before you into Galile.

33 Peter answered and sayd vnto hym, thoughe all men should be offended by the yet would I neuer be offended.

34 Iesus sayde vnto hym: Verelye I saye vnto the þt thys same nyghte before the cocke crowe thou shalte denye me thryse.

35 Peter sayed vnto him: Yf I should dye with the, yet would I not denye the, lykewyse also sayed all the discyples.

36 Then went Iesus with them into a place whiche is called Gethsemane, and sayde vnto the disciples: sit ye here whyle I go and praye yonder.

37 And he toke with hym Peter and the two sonnes of Zebede, and began to waxe sorowful, and to be in an agonye.

38 Then said Iesus vnto them: my soule is heauy euen to the death. Tary ye here & watche with me.

39 And he went a lytell aparte, and fell flat on hys face and prayed sayinge: O my father, yf it be possible, let thys cup passe from me: neuerthelesse not as I wyll, but as thou wilte.

40 And he came vnto the discyples, and founde them a slepe, & sayd to Peter: what, could ye not watche with me one houre:

41 watche and praye, that ye fall not into temptacion. The spirite is ready, & the fleshe is weake.

42 He wente awaye once more, & prayed, sayinge: O my father, yf thys cup can not passe awaye from me, but that I drinke of it, thy wyl be fulfylled.

43 And he came and founde them a slepe agayne. For theyr eyes were heauye.

44 And he lefte them, and went agayne and prayed þe thyrde tyme, sayinge the same wordes.

45 Then came he to hys discyples and sayde vnto them: Slepe hence forth and take youre reste. For lo the houre is at hande, and the sonne of man shalbe delyuered into the handes of synners.

46 Ryse, let vs be goynge: beholde, he is at hand that shall betraye me.

47 Whyle he yet spake: lo Iudas one of the twelue came, and with hym a great multitude with sweardes and staues, sent from the chiefe priestes and elders of the people.

48 And he that betrayed hym, had geuen them a token, saying: whosoeuer I kysse, that same is he, laye handes on hym.

49 And forthe wt al he came to Iesus, and sayed: hayle mayster and kyssed hym.

50 And Iesus sayde vnto hym: frende, wherfore arte thou come? Then came they, and layed handes on Iesus, & toke

him.

51 And behold, one of them which were with Iesus, stretched out hys hande, and drue hys swerde, and stroke a seruaunt of the hye priest and smote of hys eare.

52 Then sayed Iesus vnto hym: put vp thy swearde into hys place. For all that laye hand on the swearde, shal perysh with the swerd.

53 Eyther thynkest thou that I can not nowe praye to my father, and he shal geue me more then .xij. legyons of Angelles?

54 But how then shoulde the scriptures be fulfylled: for so must it be.

55 The same tyme sayde Iesus to the multitude: ye be come out as it were vnto a thief with sweardes and staues, for to take me. I sat daylye teachynge in the temple amonge you, and ye toke me not.

56 Al this was done that the scriptures of the Prophetes myght be fulfylled.

57 Then all the disciples forsoke hym and fled. And they toke Iesus, and ledde hym to Cayphas the hye Priest, where the Scribes & the Elders were assembled.

58 And Peter folowed him a farre of vnto the hye priestes palayce: and went in and sat with the seruauntes, to se the ende.

59 The chiefe priestes and the elders, and all the counsell, sought false wytnes agaynst Iesus, for to put hym to death,

60 but founde none in so muche that when manye false wytnesses came yet founde they none. At the laste came two false wytnesses,

61 and sayed: Thys fellowe sayed: I can destroye the temple of God and buylde it agayne in thre dayes.

62 And the chief priest arose, and sayd to hym: answerest thou nothynge? How is it that these beare wytnes agaynst the?

63 But Iesus held hys peace: And the chief Priest answered and sayed to hym: I charge the in the name of the liuynge God, that thou tell vs whyther thou be Christ the sonne of God.

64 Iesus sayd to him thou hast sayed. Neuertheles I say vnto you, hereafter shall ye se the sonne of men sittynge on the ryght hand of power, and come in the cloudes of the skye.

65 Then the hye Priest rent hys clothes sayinge: He hath blasphemed: what nede we of anye more wytnesses? Beholde nowe ye haue heard hys blasphemy

66 what thynke ye? They answered and said: he is worthy to dye.

67 Then spat they in hys face and boffeted hym wyth fistes. And other smot hym with the palme of theyr handes

68 on the face, sayinge tell vs thou Christ who is he that smote the?

69 Peter sate without in the palayce. And a damsell came to him saying: Thou also wast with Iesus of Galile:

70 but he denyed before them al sayinge: I wote not what thou sayst.

71 When he was gone oute into the poorche, another wenche sawe hym, and sayde vnto them that were there. Thys felowe was also with Iesus of Nazareth,

72 and agayne he denyed with an oth that he knew not the man.

73 And after a whyle came vnto hym they that stode by & sayde vnto Peter: surely thou art euen one of them, for thy speache bewrayeth the.

74 Then beganne he to corse and to sweare that he knew not the man. And immediatly the cocke crewe.

75 And Peter remembred the wordes of Iesu whiche sayed vnto hym: before the cocke crowe, thou shalt deny me thryse. And went out at the dores and wept bitterlye.

# CHAPTER 27

WHEN the morning was come, al the chief priestes & the elders of the people held a counsell agaynste Iesus, to put hym to death,

2 & broughte hym bounde and delyuered hym vnto Poncius Pilate the debitie.

3 Then when Iudas whiche betrayed him, saw that he was condemned, he repented him selfe, and brought agayne the .xxx. plates of syluer to the chiefe priestes and elders

4 saying: I haue synned betrayinge the innocent bloud. And they sayde: what is that to vs? Se thou to that.

5 And he caste doune the syluer plates in the temple, and departed, and wente, and honge hym selfe.

6 And the chief priestes toke þe syluer plates, & sayed: it is not lawfull for to putte them into the treasury, because it is þe pryce of bloude.

7 And they toke counsell, and bought wyth them a potters fylde to bury straungers in.

8 Wherfore that fylde is called the fylde of bloude vntyll thys day.

9 Then was fulfylled that which was spoken by Ieremy the Prophete saying: and they toke thyrty syluer plates the pryce of hym that was valewed, whom they bought of the chyldren of Israell.

10 and they gaue them for the potters fylde: as the Lorde appoynted me.

11 Iesus stode before the debitie: and the debytie axed hym saying: Art thou the Kynge of þe Iewes? Iesus sayed vnto hym: Thou sayest,

12 and when he was accused of the chief priestes & elders he

answered nothynge.

13 Then sayed Pylate vnto him: hearest thou not how many thynges they laye agaynst the?

14 And he answered hym to neuer a word: in so muche that the debitie marueyled greatly.

15 At that feast, the debitye was wont to delyuer to the people a prysoner, whom they would desyre.

16 He had then a notable prysonner called Barrabas.

17 And when they were gathered together. Pylate sayde to them whether wyl ye that I let lose vnto you Barrabas or Iesu, whiche is called Christe?

18 For he knewe well that for enuye they had delyuered hym.

19 When he was set doune to geue iudgement hys wyfe sent to hym saying: haue þu nothing to do with that iust man. For I haue suffered manye thynges thys daye in a dreame about hym.

20 But the chief priestes and the elders had perswaded the people, that they shulde axe Barrabas and destroye Iesus.

21 Then the debitye answered and sayd vnto them: whether of the twayne wyll ye that I let lose vnto you? And they sayed: Barrabas

22 Pylate sayed vnto them: what shall I do then with Iesus whiche is called Christ? They all sayed vnto hym: let hym be crucifyed.

23 Then sayed the debitie: what euyll hath he done? And they cried the more sayinge: let hym be crucifyed.

24 When Pilate sawe that he preuayled nothyng but þe more busynes was made, he toke water and washed his handes before the people sayinge I am innocent of the bloude of this iust persone, or on your perille be it.

25 Then aunswered al the people & sayed, his bloude be on vs and on oure children.

26 Then let he Barrabas louse vnto them, and schourged Iesus, and deliuered hym to be crucyfyed.

27 Then the souldiers of the debytye toke Iesus to the common hall, and gathered to hym all the companye.

28 And they strypped him, and put on him a purpyll roobe,

29 and platted a croune of thornes & put vpon his head, and a reed in his ryght hande, & bowed their knees before him and mocked hym, sayinge: hayle kinge of the Iewes,

30 and spitted vpon hym & toke the reed and smote him on the head.

31 And when they had mocked hym: they toke the robe of hym agayn, and put his owne rayment on hym, and lead him aweay to crucyfye hym.

32 And as they came out, they found a man of Cyren named Symon: him they compelled to beare his crosse.

33 And when they came vnto þe place, called Golgotha (that is to saye: a place of dead mens sculles)

34 they gaue hym veneger to drynke mengled with gall. And when he had tasted therof: he woulde not drinke.

35 When they had crucifyed hym: they parted his garmentes, and did cast lottes, to fulfyll that was spoken by the prophete. They deuided my garmentes amonge them, and vpon my vesture dyd cast lottes.

36 And they sate and watched him there.

37 And they set vp ouer his head the cause of his death written. This is Iesus the kinge of þe Iewes.

38 And ther were two theues crucifyed with him one on þe right hande, and another on the lyfte.

39 They that passed by, reuyled hym wagginge their heades

40 & sayinge: Thou that destroyest the temple of God and buyldest it in thre dayes: saue thy selfe. If thou be the sonne of God: come doune from the crosse.

41 Lykewise also the hye priestes mockynge hym with the scrybes and elders sayde.

42 He saued other, him selfe he can not saue. If he be the kinge of Israel let him now come doune from þe crosse, and we wyll beleue him.

43 He trusted in God, let hym deliuer hym now, if he wyl haue him: for he sayde I am þe sonne of God.

44 That same also the theues which were crucified with him cast in his teth.

45 From the syxte houre was there darcknes ouer all the lande vnto the ninthe houre.

46 And aboute the ninthe houre Iesus cryed with a loude voice sayinge: Eli Eli lama sabathani. That is to saye, my God, my God, why hast thou forsaken me?

47 Some of them that stode ther, when they hearde that, saied. This man called for Helias.

48 And straight waye one of them ranne & toke a sponge and fylled it full of veneger, and put it on a rede, and gaue him to drinke.

49 Other sayed, let be: let vs se whither Helias wyll come and delyuer hym.

50 Iesus cryed agayne with a loude voyce and yeldeth vp the ghost.

51 And beholde the vayle of the tempell dyd rent in twayne from the toppe to the bottome and the earth dyd quake, and the rockes did rent,

52 and graues did open, and the bodies of manye saynctes which slept arose

53 & came out of the graues after his resurreccion: and came into the holy citie and appered vnto manye.

54 When the Centurion and they that were with hym watchinge Iesus, sawe the earth quake and those thinges whiche happened they feared greatly sayinge: Of a surtye this was the sonne of God.

55 And many women were there, beholding him a farre of, which folowed Iesus from Galile, ministring vnto him.

56 Among which was Marye Magdalena and Marye the mother of Iames & Ioses, and the mother of Zebedes children.

57 When the euen was come, there came a riche man of Aramathia named Ioseph, which same also was Iesus disciple.

58 He wente to Pilate and begged the bodye of Iesus, Then Pilate commaunded the body to be deliuered.

59 And Ioseph toke the body, & wrapped it in a cleane linnen cloth,

60 & put it in his newe tombe: which he had hewen out, euen in the rocke and rolled a great stone to the dore of the sepulchre and departed.

61 And ther was Marye Magdalene and the other Mary syttynge ouer agaynste the sepulchre.

62 The nexte daye that foloweth good fryday the hye pryestes and phariseis gothe them selues to Pilate

63 and sayd: Syr, we remembre that this deceyuer sayed whyle he was yet alyue. After thre daies I will aryse agayne.

64 Commaunde therfore that the sepulchre be made sure vntyll the thirde daye lest peraduenture his disciples come, and steale him away, and saye vnto the people, he is rysen from death, & the last errourre be worste then the fyrste.

65 Pylate sayde vnto them: Take watche men: Go, and make it as sure as ye can.

66 And they went and made the sepulchre sure with watche men, and sealed the stone.

# CHAPTER 28

THE Saboth daye at euen which dauneth the morowe after þe saboth. Mary Magdalene, & the other Marye came to se þe sepulchre.

2 And beholde there was a great earthquake. For the aungell of the Lorde descended from heauen: & came & rowled backe the stone from the dore, and sat vpon it.

3 His countenaunce was lyke lyghtnyng, & his raymente whyte as snowe.

4 And for feare of him the kepers were astonnied and became as dead men.

5 The aungel aunswered & sayd to the women: feare ye not. I knowe þt ye seke Iesus, whiche was crucifyed:

6 he is not here: he is rysen as he sayd. Come & se þe place where þe Lord was put,

7 & go quickly & tel hys discyples þt he is rysen from death. And behold, he wil go before you into Galile, there ye shall se hym. Lo, I haue tolde you.

8 And thei departed quickly from the sepulchre with feare & greate ioye: & dyd runne to bring hys disciples word.

9 And as they went to tell hys disciples: beholde, Iesus met them saying al hayle. And they came & helde him by þe fete and worshypped him.

10 Then sayde Iesus vnto them: be not afrayd. Go and tel my brethren þt they go into Galile, & there shal they se me.

11 When they were gone: beholde, some of þe kepers came into the citye, & shewed vnto the hye Priestes all the thynges that were happened.

12 And they gathered them together with þe elders, and toke counsel, & gaue large money vnto the souldiers,

13 sayinge: Saye þt his discyples came by night, & stole hym away whyle ye slept:

14 and yf thys come to the rulers eares, we wyll pease him, & saue you harmles.

15 And they toke þe money & did as thei were taughte. And this saiynge is noysed amonge þe Iewes vnto thys daye.

16 Then þe .xi. disciples wente away into Galile, into a mountayne wher Iesus had appointed them.

17 And when they sawe hym they worshipped hym. But some of them doubted.

18 And Iesus came and spake vnto them saiynge: all power is geuen vnto me in heauen and in earth.

19 Go therfore & teache all nacyons, baptisyng them in the name of the father, and the sonne, & the holye ghoste.

20 Teachyng them to obserue all thynges whatsoeuer I commaunded you, And lo I am with you alwaye, euen vntyll the ende of the worlde.

# Mark

## CHAPTER 1

THE begynning of the gospell of Iesu Christ, þe sonne of God,

2 as it is written in the prophetes. Beholde, I send my messenger before thy face which shal prepare thy waye before þe

3 The voyce of a cryer in þe wildernes prepare the waye of the Lord: make hys pathes strayghte.

4 Iohn dyd baptyse in the wyldernes, and preache the baptisme of repentaunce: for the remissyon of synnes.

5 And all the lande of Iury and they of Ierusalem wente out vnto him, & were all baptysed of hym in the riuer Iordan: confessyng theyr synnes.

6 Iohn was clothed with camylles heare, & with a gerdyll of a skyn about hys loynes. And he dyd eate locustes, and wilde honey,

7 & preached saiynge: a stronger then I commeth after me, whose shoe latchet I am not worthy to stoupe doune, and vnlose.

8 I haue baptysed you with water: but he shal baptyse you with the holye ghost.

9 And it came to passe in those dayes, that Iesus came from Nazareth, a citye of Galile: and was baptysed of Iohn in Iordan.

10 And assone as he was come out of the water Iohn saw heauen open, and the holy ghost descendynge vpon him lyke a doue.

11 And there came a voyce from heauen: Thou arte my dere sonne in whom I delyte.

12 And immediatly the spirite draue hym into wyldernes,

13 & he was there in the wyldernes .xl. dayes, and was tempted of Sathan, & was with wylde beastes. And the Aungels minystred vnto hym.

14 After Iohn was taken, Iesus came into Galyle, preachynge the gospell of the kyngedom of God,

15 and sayinge: the tyme is come, & the kyngdome of God is at hande, repente & beleue the Gospell.

16 And as he walked by þe sea of Galile, he saw Simon & Andrew hys brother, castyng nettes into the sea, for they were fishers.

17 And Iesus sayde vnto them: folowe me, and I wyll make you fishers of men:

18 And strayghtwaye they forsoke theyr nettes, and folowed hym.

19 And when he had gone a lyttell further thence, he sawe Iames the sonne of Zebede, & Iohn hys brother, euen as they were in the shyppe mendynge theyr nettes.

20 And anone he called them. And they left theyr father Zebede in the shyppe with hys hyred seruauntes, & went theyr waye after hym.

21 And they entred into Capernaum: & straight waye on the Saboth dayes, he entred into þe synagoge & taught.

22 And they merueyled at hys learning. For he taught them as one that had power with hym, and not as the scrybes.

23 And there was in theyr Synagoge a man vexed with an vncleane spirite, that cryed

24 saiyng: let be: what haue we to do with the thou Iesus of Nazareth? Art thou come to destroy vs, I knowe the what thou arte, euen þe holye of God.

25 And Iesus rebuked him, saying: hold thy peace, and come out of hym.

26 And the vncleane spirite tare hym, & cryed with a loude voyce, and came out of hym.

27 And they were al amased, in so muche that they demaunded one of another, amonge them selues saying: what thyng is thys? what newe doctryne is this? For he commaundeth the foule spirites with power, and they obeye hym.

28 And immediatly hys fame spred abroade throughoute al the regyon borderynge on Galile.

29 And forth with, assone as

they were come out of the synagoge, they entred into þe house of Simon and Andrew, with Iames and Iohn

30 & Symons mother in law lay sicke of a fewer. And anone they told him of her.

31 And he came and toke her by the hande, and lyfte her vp, & the fewer forsoke her by and by: and she ministred vnto them.

32 And at euen when the sunne was doune, they brought to hym all that were dyseased, & them that were possessed with deuyls.

33 And al the cytye gathered together at the dore,

34 & he healed many that were sicke of dyuers dyseases. And he cast out manye deuyls, and suffered not þe deuyls to speake, because they knew hym.

35 And in the mornyng very early, Iesus arose and went oute into a solytarye place, & there prayed.

36 And Simon and they that were wyth hym folowed after him.

37 And when they had founde hym, they sayed vnto hym: al men seke for the.

38 And he sayed vnto them: let vs go into the next townes, that I maye preach there also: for truely I came out for that purpose.

39 And he preached in theyr synagoges, throughoute all Galile, and caste the deuyls out.

40 And there came a leper to hym, besechinge hym, and kneled doune vnto hym, and sayde to hym: yf thou wylt, thou cannest make me cleane.

41 And Iesus had compassyon on hym, and put forth hys hande, touched hym, & sayd to hym: I wyl, be thou cleane.

42 And assone as he had spoken, immediatly the leprosy departed from hym, & he was clensed.

43 And he charged hym, and sent him awaye forthwith

44 and sayde vnto hym: Se thou say nothyng to any man: but get the hence, and shewe thy selfe to the priest, and offer for thy clensing, those thinges whiche Moyses commaunded, for a testimonial vnto them.

45 But he (assone as he departed) beganne to tell many thynges, & to publyshe the dede: in so muche that Iesus coulde no more openlye enter into the citie, but was without in desert places. And they came to him from euerye quarter.

# CHAPTER 2

AFTER a feawe dayes, he entred into Capernaum agayne, & it was noysed þt he was in a house

2 And anone many gathered together, in so muche that now there was no rome to receyue them: no, not so much as about the dore. And he preached the worde vnto them.

3 And there came vnto hym that brought one sicke of the palsie, borne of foure men.

4 And because they coulde not come nye to hym for preace, they vncouered the rofe of the house, where he was. And when they had broken it open, they let doune the bed where in þe sicke of the palsye laye.

5 When Iesus saw their fayth, he sayed to the sicke of the palsie, sonne thy synnes are forgeuen the.

6 And there were certayne of the scrybes, sittynge there and reasonynge in theyr hertes:

7 how doth thys felowe so blaspheme? Who can forgeue synnes, but God onelye?

8 And immediatly when Iesus perceyued in hys spirite, þt they so reasoned in them selues, he said vnto them why thinke ye suche thynges in your hertes?

9 Whether is it easyer to saye to the sicke of the palsie, thy synnes are forgeuen the: or to saye: aryse, take vp thy bed, and walke?

10 That ye maye knowe that the sonne of man hath power in earth to forgeue synnes, he spake vnto the sicke of the palsye:

11 I saye vnto the, aryse and take vp thy bedde, and get the hence into thyne owne house.

12 And by and by he arose, toke vp the bedde, & wente forthe before them all: in so muche that they were all amased, and glorifyed God sayinge: we neuer saw it on thys fasshyon.

13 And he wente agayne vnto the sea, and all the people resorted vnto hym, and he taughte them.

14 And as Iesus passed by, he sawe Leuye the sonne of Alphey syt at the recepte of custome, and sayde vnto hym: folowe me. And he arose, and folowed hym.

15 And it came to passe as Iesus sate at meate in his house, many publicans and synners sate at meat also with Iesus and hys discyples. For there were many that folowed hym.

16 And when the Scrybes and pharyses sawe hym eate wyth Publicans and synners, they sayde vnto hys discyples: howe is it that he eateth and drinketh with Publicans and synners?

17 When Iesus heard that, he sayde vnto them: The whole haue no nede of the phisicyon, but the sicke. I came not to call the righteous, but the synners to repentaunce.

18 And the discyples of Iohn and the Pharyses dyd faste; and therfore came and sayde vnto hym. Why do the disciples of Iohn and of the Pharyses fast, and thy discyples fast not.

19 And Iesus sayde vnto them: can the chyldren of a weddyng faste, whyles the brydegrome is with them. As longe as they haue the brydegrome wyth them they

cannot fast.

20 But the dayes wil come when the bridegrome shalbe taken from them, & then shal they fast in those dayes.

21 Also no man soweth a pece of newe clothe vnto an olde garment, for then taketh he away the newe pece from the olde, and so is the rente worsse.

22 In lyke wyse no man poureth newe wyne into olde vessels, for yf he do, the newe wyne breaketh the vessels, and the wyne runneth oute, & the vessels are marred. But newe wyne must be poured into newe vessels.

23 And it chaunsed that he went thorowe the corne fieldes on the Saboth daye: and hys discyples as they wente on theyr way, began to plucke the eares of corne.

24 And the Pharyses sayde vnto hym: beholde, why do they on the Saboth dayes that which is not lawful?

25 And he sayde to them: haue ye neuer rede what Dauid dyd, when he had nede, & was an hungred both he and they that were with hym?

26 Howe he went into the house of God in the dayes of Abiathar the hye prieste, and dyd eate the halowed loues, which is not lawfull to eate, but for the priestes onely: and gaue also to them, whiche were with hym?

27 And he sayde to them: the Saboth daye was made for man, & not man for the Saboth daye.

28 Wherfore the sonne of man is Lorde euen of the Saboth daye.

## CHAPTER 3

AND he entred agayne into the synagoge, & there was a man there whiche had a wyddred hande.

2 And they watched him to se, whether he woulde heale him on the Saboth daye, that they myght accuse hym.

3 And he sayde vnto the man whiche had the widdred hande: aryse and stand in þe myddes.

4 And he sayde to them: whether is it lawful to do a good dede on the Saboth dayes, or an euyll? to saue lyfe or kyll? But they held theyr peace.

5 And he loked rounde aboute on them angerly, mournynge on the blindnes of theyr hertes, & said to þe man: stretch forth thyne hand. And he stretched it out. And hys hande was restored euen as whole as the other.

6 And the Pharyses departed, and strayght waye gathered a counsel with them that belonged to Herode agaynste hym that they might destroye hym.

7 And Iesus auoyded with hys disciples to the sea. And a great multitude folowed him from Galile, and from Iurie,

8 and from Hierusalem, and from Idumea, and from beyonde Iordane, & they that dwelled aboute Tyre and Sydon, a great multitude: whiche when they had hearde what thynges he dyd came vnto hym.

9 And he commaunded hys disciples, that a shypp shoulde wayte on hym, because of the people, leste they shoulde throunge him.

10 For he had healed many, in so much that they preased vpon hym, for to touche hym as manye as had plages.

11 And when the vncleane spirites sawe hym: they fell doune before hym, and cryed, sayinge: thou art the sonne of God

12 And he straytly charged them that they should not vtter hym.

13 And he wente vp into a mountayne, and called vnto hym whome he woulde, and they came vnto hym.

14 And he ordeyned the .xij. that they shoulde be with hym, & that he myghte sende them to preache,

15 and that they myghte haue power to heale sicknesses, and to caste oute deuyls.

16 And he gaue Simon, to name Peter.

17 And he called Iames the sonne of Zebede and Iohn, Iames brother, and gaue them Boanarges to name: whiche is to saye, the sonnes of thounder,

18 and Andrew, and Philip, & Bartelmew, and Mathew, & Thomas, & Iames the sonne of Alphey & Taddeus, & Symon of Cane,

19 and Iudas Iscaryoth, which same also betrayed hym. And they came into an house,

20 & þe people assembled together agayne, so greately þt they had not leasure so much as to eate bread.

21 And when they that longed vnto hym hearde of it, they went out to holde him. For they thought he had bene besyde hym selfe.

22 And the scribes which came from Ierusalem, sayde: he hathe Beelzebub, and by the power of the chiefe deuyll casteth out deuyls.

23 And he called them vnto hym, and sayd vnto them in similitudes. How can Sathan dryue out Satan?

24 For if a realme be deuyded agaynst it selfe, that realme can not endure.

25 Or yf a house be deuyded against it selfe, that house cannot continue:

26 So yf Satan make insurreccyon agaynst hym selfe and be deuyded, he can not contynue, but is at an ende.

27 No man can enter into a strong mans house and take awaye hys goodes, except he fyrste bynd that stronge man, and then spoyle hys house.

28 Verely I saye vnto you: al

synnes shalbe forgeuen vnto mens children and blaspheme wherwith they blaspheme:

29 But he that blasphemeth the holye ghost, shall neuer haue forgeuenes, but is in daunger of eternal damnacion,

30 because they said: he had an vncleane spirite.

31 Then came his mother and his brethren, & stode wtout, and sent vnto hym & called hym.

32 And the people sate about him, & said vnto him: beholde thy mother and thy brethren seke for þe without.

33 And he answered them saying: who is my mother and my brethren?

34 And he loked rounde about on hys disciples, which sate in compasse about him, & sayd: behold my mother & my brethren.

35 For whosoeuer doth þe wil of god he is my brother, my syster, and mother.

## CHAPTER 4

AND he began agayn to teache by the sea side. And he gathered together vnto him muche people, so greatly that he entred into a shyp, & sate in the sea, and all the people was by the sea side on the shoore.

2 And he taughte them manye thynges in similitudes: and sayde vnto them in hys doctrine.

3 Herken. Beholde, there went out a sower to sow.

4 And it fortuned as he sowed, that some fell by the waye syde, & the fowles of the ayre came & deuoured it vp.

5 Some fell on stony grounde, where it had not muche earth, & by & by sprang vp, because it had not depth of earthe,

6 but assone as the sonne was vp it caught heath, and because it had not roting widdred awaye.

7 And some fell among the thornes, and the thornes grew vp & choked it so that it gaue no frute.

8 And some fell vpon good ground, & dyd yeld frute, some thyrty folde, some sixtie folde, and some an hundred folde.

9 And he sayd vnto them: He that hath eares to heare, let hym heare.

10 And when he was alone, they that were aboute hym with the .xij. axed hym of the similitude,

11 & he sayd vnto them: To you it is geuen to knowe the mysterye of the kyngedome of God. But vnto them that are without: shal al thynges be done in similitudes:

12 þt when they se, they shall se, and not dyscerne, and when they heare, they shal heare, and not vnderstand leste at any tyme they shoulde tourne: & theyr synnes shoulde be forgeuen them,

13 and he said vnto them: Perceyue ye not thys similitude? howe then shoulde ye vnderstand all other similitudes?

14 The sower soweth the word,

15 and they that are by the wayes side, where the worde is sowen, are they to whome assone as they haue hearde it, Satan cometh immediatly, & taketh awaye the worde that was sowen in theyr hartes.

16 And lykewyse they that are sowen on the stonye grounde, are they which when they haue hearde the worde, atonce receyue it with gladnes,

17 yet haue no rotes in them selues: and so endure but a tyme: and anone as trouble and persecucyon aryseth for the wordes sake, they fall immediatlye.

18 And they that are sowen amonge the thornes; are suche as heare the worde,

19 and the care of thys worlde & the dysceythfulnes of ryches & þe lustes of other thynges, enter in, and choke the worde: and it is made vnfrutefull.

20 And those that were sowed in good grounde are they that heare the worde, & receyue it, & bryng forth frute, some thyrty fold, some sixtye folde, some an hundred folde.

21 And he sayd vnto them: is the candle lighted, to be put vnder a bushell, or vnder the table, and not rather to be put on a candelstick?

22 For there is nothyng so preuy, that shall not be opened: neyther so secrete, but that it shall come abroade.

23 Yf any man haue eares to heare let hym heare.

24 And he sayde vnto them: take hede what ye heare. With what measure ye mete, with the same shall it be measured vnto you agayne. And vnto you that heare, shall more be geuen.

25 For vnto him that hath, shall it be geuen: and from hym that hath not shall be taken away: euen that he hath.

26 And he sayde: so is the kyngdome of God euen as yf a man shoulde sowe sede in the grounde,

27 and shoulde slepe and ryse vp night and daye, and the sede shoulde spryng & grow vp, he not ware.

28 For the earth bryngeth forth frute of her selfe: fyrst the blade, then þe eares, after that full corne in the eares.

29 And assone as the frute is broughte forth, anone he thrusteth in the sykell, because the heruest is come.

30 And he sayde: where vnto shal we lyken þe kyngdome of God? or with what comparison shall we compare it?

31 It is lyke a grayne of mustarde sede, which when it is sowen in the earth, is the least of all seedes that be in the earth:

32 but after that it is sowen, it

groweth vp and is greatest of al herbes and beareth great braunches, so that the foules of the ayre maye dwell vnder the shadowe of it.

33 And with many suche similitudes he preached the worde vnto them, after as they myghte heare it.

34 And withoute similitude spake he nothyng vnto them. But when they were apart he expounded all thynges to hys disciples.

35 And the same daye when euen was come he sayde vnto them: Let vs passe ouer vnto the other syde.

36 And they lefte the people and toke hym euen as he was in the shyppe. And there were also with hym other shyppes.

37 And there arose a greate storme of wynde and dashed the waues into the shyppe, so that it was full.

38 And he was in the sterne a slepe on a pelowe. And they awoke hym, and sayde to hym: Mayster carest thou not that we peryshe?

39 And he rose vp, and rebuked the wynd and sayed vnto the sea: peace and be styll. And the wynde alayed, and there folowed a great calme.

40 And he sayde vnto them: Why are ye so fearfull? howe is it that ye haue no faythe?

41 And they feared excedynglye, and sayed one to another: What felowe is thys. For both wynde and sea obeye hym.

# CHAPTER 5

AND they came ouer to the other syde of the sea into the countre of Gaderenites.

2 And when he was come oute of the shyppe, there met hym oute of the graues a man possessed of an vncleane spirite,

3 whiche had hys abydyng among the graues. And no man coulde bynde him: no not with chaynes,

4 because that when he was often bounde with fetters and chayns, he plucked þe chayns a sunder, & brake the fetters in peces. Neyther coulde any man tame him.

5 And alwayes both nyght and daye he cryed in the mountaynes & in the graues, and bet hym self with stones.

6 When he had spyed Iesus a far of, he ranne & worshypped hym

7 and cryed with a loude voyce, and sayde: what haue I to with the Iesus the sonne of the most hyest God? I requyre the in þe name of God that thou torment me not.

8 For he had sayde vnto hym: come out of the man thou foule spirite.

9 And he axed him: what is thy name. And he answered sayinge: my name is Legyon, for we are manye.

10 And he prayed hym instantly, that he woulde not sende them awaye out of the countre.

11 And there was there nye vnto the mountaynes a great herde of swyne fedyng,

12 and al the deuyls besought hym, saying: sende vs into the herde of swyne, that we may enter into them.

13 And anone Iesus gaue them leaue. And the vncleane spirites went out and entred into the swyne. And the herde startled, and ranne hedlynge into the sea. They were aboute two .M. swyne & they were drouned in the sea.

14 And þe swyne herdes fleed, and tolde it in the cytye, and in the countre. And they came out for to se what had happened:

15 and came to Iesus, and sawe hym that was vexed with the fende, and had the legion syte, both clothed and in hys ryght mynde, & were afrayed,

16 And they that sawe it, tolde them how it had happened to him that was possessed with þe deuyl: and also of the swyne.

17 And they beganne to praye hym, that he woulde departe from their coostes.

18 And when he was come into the shyppe, he that hadde the deuel, prayed hym that he might be with him.

19 How beit, Iesus woulde not suffer him, but sayde vnto him: go home into thine owne house and to thy frendes, and shewe them what greate thinges the Lord hath done vnto the, and how he had compassion on the.

20 And he departed, & began to publishe in the ten cyties what great thinges Iesus had done vnto him, and all men did meruayll.

21 And when Iesus was come ouer agayne by ship vnto the otherside, much people gathered vnto him, and he was nye vnto the sea.

22 And beholde, there came one of the rulers of the Sinagoges, whose name was Iarius: and when he sawe him, he fell doune at his fete,

23 & besought hym greatly sayinge: my doughter lyeth at point of death, I woulde thou wouldest come and laye thy hande on her, that she might be safe and lyue.

24 And he went with hym, and muche people folowed him, & thronged him.

25 And there was a certayn woman, whiche was diseased of an yssue of bloude .xij. yeres,

26 and had suffred many thynges of many phisicions, and had spent all that she had, and felte none amendement at all, but wexed worse & worse.

27 When she had herde of Iesus: she came into the preace behinde hym, and touched hys garment.

28 For she thought: if I maye

but touch his clothes, I shalbe whole.

29 And streightway her fountayne of bloude was dryed vp, and she felft in her bodye, that she was healed of the plague.

30 And Iesus immediatly felte in hym selfe, the vertu that went out of hym, and tourned him rounde about in the preace, & sayde: who touched my clothes?

31 And his disciples sayde vnto him: seist thou the people thruste the, and yet axest, who did touche me?

32 And he loked rounde about, for to se her that had done that thing.

33 The woman feared and trembled (for she knew what was done within her) and she came and fell doune before him, and tolde the trueth of euery thinge.

34 And he sayde to her: Doughter, thy faythe hath made the whole: go in peace, and by whole of thy plage.

35 Whyle he yet spake, there came frome the ruler of the Synagoges house, certayn which sayde: thy doughter is dead: why diseasest þu the maister any further?

36 Assone as Iesus herd that worde spoken, he sayd vnto the ruler of þe Synagoge: be not afrayed, onely beleue.

37 And he suffred no man to folow him mo then Peter and Iames and Ihon the brother of Iames.

38 And he came vnto the house of the ruler of the Synagoge, and sawe the wondringe, & them that wepte and wayled greatly,

39 & went in and sayde vnto them: why make ye this a do and wepe? The mayden is not dead, but slepeth.

40 And thy laught him to scorne. Then he put them all out, and toke the father & the mother of the mayden, & them that were with hym, and entred in where the mayden laye,

41 & toke the mayden by the hande, and sayd vnto her: Talitha cumi: which is by interpretacion: mayden I saye vnto the aryse.

42 And streyght þe mayden arose, and went on her fete. For she was of the age of twelue yeres. And thei were astonyed at it out of measur.

43 And he charged them straytely that no man shoulde know of it, and commaunded to geue her meate.

# CHAPTER 6

AND he departed thence, & came into hys owne countre, and hys disciples folowed him.

2 And when the Sabboth daye was come, he began to teache in the Sinagoge And many that heard him were astonied, and sayde: From whence hath he these thinges? & what wysedome is this that is geuen vnto him? and suche vertues that are wroughte by his handes?

3 Is not this that carpenter Maries sonne, the brother of Iames and Ioses, & of Iuda and Simon? and are not his systers here with vs? And thei were offended by him.

4 And Iesus sayde vnto them: a Prophet is not dispised but in his owne countre, and amonge his owne kinne, and amonge them that are of the same housholde.

5 And he could there shewe no miracles, but layd his handes vpon a few sicke folke and healed them.

6 And he merueyled at their vnbelefe. And he went about by the tounes that lay on euery side, teachyng.

7 And he called the .xij. and began to sende them, two and two, and gaue them power ouer vncleane spirites.

8 And commaunded them, that they should take nothinge vnto their iorney saue a rod onely: Neyther scrippe, neither bread, neither money in their pourses:

9 but shoulde be shood wyth sandals. And that they should not put on two cootes.

10 And he sayde vnto them: wheresoeuer ye enter into an house, there abide till ye departe thence.

11 And whosoeuer shal not receyue you nor heare you, when ye departe thence, shake of the dust: that is vnder your fete, for a witnesse vnto them. I say verely vnto you, it shalbe easier for Zodome and Gomoree at the daye of iudgement, then for that citie.

12 And they went out and preached, that thei should repent:

13 and they cast out many deuils. And they anointed many that were sicke with oyle and healed them.

14 And kynge Herode hearde of hym (for his name was spred abroade) & sayde: Ihon Baptist is rysen agayne from death, and therefore myracles are wrought by him.

15 Other sayde: it is Helyas: and some sayde: it is a Prophet: or as one of the Prophetes.

16 But when Herode hearde of hym, he sayde: it is Ihon whome I beheaded, he is rysen from death agayne.

17 For Herode him selfe had sent forth, & had taken Ihon, and bounde him and cast him into pryson for Herodias sake, whiche was hys brother Philippes wyfe: For he had maried her.

18 Ihon sayd vnto Herode: It is not lawful for the to haue thy brothers wyfe.

19 Herodias layed wayte for him, and woulde haue killed him, but she could not.

20 For Herode feared Iohan,

knowinge that he was a iust man and an holy: and gaue him reuerence: and when he hearde hym, he did many thynges, and heard him gladly.

21 But when a conuement daye was come: Herode on his byrth day made a supper to the lordes, captaynes, and chief estates of Galile.

22 And the doughter of the sayd Herodias came in and daunsed, and pleased Herode, and them that sate at bourde also. Then the kyng sayde vnto the mayden: axe of me what thou wilt, & I wil geue it the.

23 And he sware to her, whatsoeuer thou shalt axe of me, I wil geue it the, euen vnto the halfe of my kyngdome.

24 And she went forth & sayde to her mother: what shal I axe? And she said: Ihon Baptistes head.

25 And she came in straight way with haste vnto the kynge, and axed saying: I wil that thou geue me by and by in a charger the head of Ihon Baptist.

26 And the kynge was excedinge sory: howbeit, for his othes sake, and for their sakes, whiche sate at supper also, he woulde not put her beside her purpose.

27 And immediatly the kynge sent the hang man, and commaunded his headde to be brought in. And he went and beheaded hym in the pryson,

28 and brought his head in a charger, and gaue it to the mayden, and the maiden gaue it to her mother.

29 And when his disciples heard of it, they came and toke vp his body, and put it in a tombe.

30 And the apostles gathered them selues together to Iesus, & tolde him all thinges, bothe what they had done, & what they had taught.

31 And he sayde vnto them: Come ye a parte into the wildernes and rest a while. For there were many commers and goers, that they had no leasure so muche as to eate.

32 And he went by ship out of the wai into a desert place.

33 But the people spied them when they departed: & many knew him and ranne afote thither out of all cyties, and came thither before them, & came together vnto hym.

34 And Iesus went out and sawe muche people, and had compassion on them, because they were lyke shepe, whyche had no shepeherd. And he beganne to teache them many thinges.

35 And when the daye was now farre spent, his disciples came vnto him saying: this is a deserte place,

36 and nowe the daye is farre passed, let them departe, that they maye go into the countrey roundabout, and into the tounes and bye them bread, for they haue nothing to eate.

37 He aunswered and sayd vnto them: geue ye them to eate. And they sayd vnto him: shal we go and bye .ij.C. peny worth of bread and geue them to eate?

38 He sayde vnto them: howe many loues haue ye? Go and loke. And when they had serched they sayde: fyue and .ij. fishes

39 And he commaunded them to make them all sit doune by companyes vpon the grene grasse.

40 And they sat doune, here a rowe and there a rowe, by hundredes, and fifties.

41 And he toke the .v. loues and the .ij. fishes, and loked vp to heauen, and blessed and brake the loues & gaue them to his disciples to put before theym: and the .ij. fishes he deuided amonge them all.

42 And they all did eate and were satisfied.

43 And they toke vp .xij. baskettes ful of the gobbettes and of the fishes.

44 And they that eate were aboute fyue thousand men.

45 And strayghtwaye he caused his disciples to go into the ship, and to goo ouer the water before vnto Bethsaida, whyle he sent away þe people.

46 And assone as he had sent them away, he departed into a mountayne to pray.

47 And when euen was come, the ship was in the middes of the sea, and he alone on the lande,

48 and he sawe them troubled in rowing, for the winde was contrary vnto them. And about the fourth quarter of the night he came vnto them walking vpon the sea, and woulde haue passed by them.

49 When they sawe hym walking vpon the sea, they supposed it hadde bene a spirite and cried out:

50 for they all sawe hym, and were afrayed. And anone he talked with them, and sayde vnto them. Be of good chere, it is I, be not afrayed.

51 And he went vp vnto them into the ship, and the wynd ceased, and they were sore amased in them selues beyonde measure, and meruayled.

52 For they remembred not of the loues, because their hertes were blynded.

53 And they came ouer and went into þe lande of Genezareth, and drue vp into the hauen.

54 And assone as they were come out of the ship, strayght they knewe hym,

55 and ran forth thorowout all the region round about, and began to cary aboute in beddes all that were sicke, to the place where they herde tell he was.

56 And whether so euer he entred into townes, cities, or vilages, they layed theyr sicke in the stretes and prayed hym, that they might touche, and it were

but the hemme of his vesture. And as many as touched hym were safe.

## CHAPTER 7

AND the Phariseis came together vnto hym, and diuers of þe Scribes, which came from Hierusalem.

2 And when they sawe certayne of hys disciples eate breade with commen handes (that is to say wt vnwashen handes) they complayned.

3 For the Phariseis and all the Iewes, except thei wash their handes ofte, eate not obseruinge the tradicions of the elders.

4 And when they come from the market, except they wash they eate not. And many other thinges therbe whyche they haue taken vpon them to obserue, as the wasshyng of the cuppes and cruses, and of brasen vessels, and of tables.

5 Then axed hym the Phariseis and Scribes, why walke not thy disciples accordynge to the tradicions of the elders, but eate breade with vnwashen handes?

6 He aunswered and sayde vnto them: well prophecied Esayas of you hypocrites, as it is wryten: This people honoureth me with theyr lippes, but their hert is farre from me:

7 In vayne they worship me, teachynge doctrines whyche are nothyng but the commaundementes of men.

8 For ye laye þe commaundement of God apart, and obserue the tradicions of men, as the washyng of cruses and of cuppes, and many other suche lyke thinges ye do.

9 And he sayde vnto them: wel, ye caste aside the commaundement of God too maintayne your owne tradicions.

10 For Moyses sayd: Honour thy father and thy mother: and whosoeuer curseth father or mother, let him dye for it.

11 But ye saye a man shall saye to father or mother Corban: whiche is, that thou desirest me to helpe the with, is geuen God.

12 And so ye suffer him no more to do ought for his father or his mother,

13 makynge the worde of God of none effect, thorowe youre owne tradicions, which you haue ordeyned. And many suche thinges ye do.

14 And he called all the people vnto hym, and sayde to them. Herken to me, euery one of you and vnderstande.

15 There is nothinge without a man that can defile him when it entereth into him: but those thinges which procede out of hym are those, which defile the man.

16 If any man haue eares to heare, let hym heare.

17 And when he came into an house from the people his disciples axed him of the similitude

18 And he sayde to them: Are ye so without vnderstanding. Do ye not yet perceyue that, whatsoeuer thinge from without entreth into a man it can not defile him,

19 because it entreth not into his herte, but into his bealy: and goeth out into the draught that pourgeth out all meates.

20 And he sayde that defileth a man, whiche cometh out of a man.

21 For from within, euen out of the herte of men, procede euel thoughtes: aduoutry, fornication, murther,

22 theft, coueteousnes, wickednes, deceyte: vncleanenesse and a wicked eye, blasphemy, pryde, folishenes:

23 all these euell thinges come from within and defile a man.

24 And from thense he rose and went into the borders of Tyre and Sidon, and entered into an house, and would that no man should haue knowen: but he could not be hyd.

25 For a certayn woman, whose doughter had a foule spirite hearde of him, and came & fell at hys fete.

26 The woman was a Greke out of Syrophenicia, and she besought him that he woulde caste out the deuel out of her doughter.

27 And Iesus sayde vnto her: let the chyldren firste be fedde. For it is not mete, to take the chyldrens bread and to cast it vnto whelpes.

28 She aunswered & sayde vnto him: euen so master, neuerthelesse the whelpes also eate vnder the table of þe chyldrens cromes.

29 And he sayde vnto her: for this saying go thy waye, the deuell is gone out of thy doughter.

30 And when she was come home to her house, she founde the deuell departed, & her doughter lying on the bed.

31 And departed agayne from the coostes yf Tire and Sidon, and came to the sea of Galile, thorow the middest of the coostes of the .x. cyties.

32 And they brought vnto him one þt was deafe, and stambred in his speache, and praied him to lay his hand vpon him.

33 And he toke him a side from the people, and put his finger in his eares, and did spitte and touched hys tonge,

34 and loked vp to heauen, and sighted & sayde vnto him: Ephata, that is to say be opened.

35 And straight way his eares were opened and the stringe of hys tougue was losed, and he spake playne.

36 And he commaunded them that they shoulde tell no man. But the more he forbad them, so muche the more a greate deale they published it:

37 and were beyonde measure astonyed, sayinge: He hath done all thinges well, and hath made both the deafe to heare & the domme to speake.

## CHAPTER 8

IN those dayes when there was a very great company, and had nothinge to eate. Iesus called his disciples to hym and sayde vnto them:

2 I haue compassion on this people, because they haue nowe bene with me thre dayes, and haue nothing to eate.

3 And if I shoulde send them away fastynge to theyr owne houses, they should faynte by the waye. For diuers of them came from farre.

4 And his disciples aunswered him: wher might a man haue bread here in the wildernes to satisfie these?

5 And he asked them: how many loues haue ye? They sayde seuen.

6 And he commaunded the people to sit doune on the grounde. And he toke the seuen loues, gaue thankes, brake, & gaue to his disciples to set before them. And they did set them before the people.

7 And they had a few small fishes. And he blessed them and commaunded them also to be set before them:

8 And they ate and were suffised. And they toke vp of the broken meate that was left seuen baskettes full.

9 And they that eate were in numbre about foure thousande. And he sent them awaye.

10 And anone he entered into a shyp with his disciples, and came into the partes of Dalmanutha.

11 And the Phariseis came forth and began to despute with hym, sekynge of him a signe from heauen, & tempting him.

12 And he syghed in his spirite and sayed: why doeth this generacion seke a signe. Verely I saye vnto you, there shal no signe be geuen vnto this generation.

13 And he left them and went into the shyp agayne, and departed ouer the water.

14 And they had forgotten to take bread with them, neyther had they in the shyp with them more then one lofe.

15 And he charged them sayng: Take hede of the leuen of the Phariseis, & of the leuen of Herode.

16 And they reasoned among them selues saying: we haue no bread.

17 And when Iesus knew that, he sayd vnto them: why take ye thought because ye haue no bread perceyue ye not yet, neyther vnderstande? Haue ye your hertes yet blynded?

18 Haue ye eyes and se not? and haue ye eares and heare not? Do ye not remember?

19 When I brake .v. loues among .v.M. How many baskettes ful of broken meate toke ye vp? They sayde vnto him twelue.

20 When I brake seuen among .iiij. thousande. How many baskettes of the leuynges of broken meate toke ye vp? They sayde, seuen.

21 And he sayde vnto them: How is it that ye vnderstande not?

22 And he came to Bethsaida, & they brought a blynde man vnto him, and desired him to touche him.

23 And he caughte the blynde by the hande, and leade hym out of the toune, & spat in his eyes, and put his handes vpon him, & axed hym whyther he saw oughte.

24 And he loked vp and sayde: I se the men: for I se them walke, as they were trees.

25 After that he put his handes agayne vpon his eyes, and made hym se. And he was restored to hys sight: and saw euery man clerely.

26 And he sent him home to his house saying: neyther go into the town, nor tell it to any in the towne.

27 And Iesus went out and his disciples into the townes that longe to the cytye called Cesarea Philippi. And by the way he axed hys disciples saying: whom do men say that I am?

28 And they aunswered: some say that thou arte Ihon Baptist: some say Helias: and some, one of the Prophetes.

29 And he sayde vnto them: But whome saye ye that I am? Peter aunswered and sayd vnto hym: Thou art very Christ

30 And he charged them: that they should tel no man of him.

31 And he began to teache them: howe that the sonne of man must suffer many thinges, and should be reproued of the elders and of the priestes and scribes, and be killed, and after thre dayes ryse agayne.

32 And he spake þt saying openly. And Peter toke him a syde, & beganne to chyde him.

33 Then he tourned about, and loked on his disciples and rebuked Peter saying: Go after me Sathan. For thou sauerest not the thynges of God, but the thynges of men.

34 And he called the people vnto hym, wyth his disciples also, and sayde vnto them: Whosoeuer will folowe me, let hym forsake hym self, and take vp his crosse and folow me.

35 For whosoeuer wil saue his lyfe. shall lowse it. But whosoeuer shal lowse his life for my sake and the gospels: the same shall saue it.

36 What shall it profite a man, if he shoulde wynne all the worlde, and lowse his owne soule?

37 or els what shall a man geue, to redeme his soule

agayne?

38 Whosoeuer therfore shalbe ashamed of me and of my wordes, among this aduouterous and synfull generacion, of hym shall the sonne of man be ashamed when he cometh in the glory of hys father with the holy aungels.

# CHAPTER 9

AND he sayd vnto them: Verely I saye vnto you: There be some of them that stande here, whiche shall not taste of death tyll they haue sene the kyngedom of God come wyth power.

2 And after .vi. dayes Iesus toke Peter, Iames and Iohan, and leade them vp into an hye mountayne oute of the waye alone & he was transfigured before them.

3 And hys rayment did shyne, and was made very whyte, euen as snowe: so whyte as no fuller can make vpon the earth.

4 And there apeared vnto them Helyas with Moyses, & they talke with Iesu.

5 And Peter aunswered and sayde to Iesu: Master here is a good beyng for vs, let vs make thre tabernacles, one for the, one for Moyses, and an other for Helyas.

6 And yet he wyste not what he sayde, for they were afrayde.

7 And there was a cloude þt shadowed them. And a voyce came out of the cloud saying: This is my deare sonne, heare hym.

8 And sodenly, they loked rounde aboute them, and sawe no man more then Iesus only with them.

9 And as they came doune from the hyll, he charged theym that they shoulde tell no man what they had sene, tyl the sonne of man were rysen from death agayne.

10 And they kepte þe saying with them, and demaunded one of another, what that rising from death agayn should meane?

11 And they axed him sayinge: Why then saye the Scribes that Helyas must firste come

12 He aunswered and sayde vnto them: Helias verely shal first come and restore all thinges. And also the sonne of man as it is written, shall suffer many thynges, and shalbe set at nought.

13 Moreouer I saye vnto you that Helyas is come, and they haue done vnto hym whatsoeuer pleased theym, as it is written of hym.

14 And he came to hys disciples, & saw muche people about them, and the Scribes disputing with them.

15 And strayght waye all the people when they behelde hym, were amased, & ranne to hym, and saluted hym.

16 And he sayde vnto the Scribes: what dispute ye with them?

17 And one of the company aunswered & said: Master, I haue broughte my sonne vnto the which hath a domme spirite.

18 And whensoeuer he taketh hym, he teareth hym, and he fometh and gnasheth with hys tethe, & pyneth away. And I spake to thy disciples that they should caste him out, and they coulde not.

19 He aunswered him and sayd: O generation without fayth, how long shall I be with you? How long shall I suffer you? Brynge hym vnto me.

20 And they broughte hym vnto him. And assone as þe spirite saw him, he tare him. And he fell doune on the grounde, walowing and fomynge.

21 And he axed his father: howe long is it ago, sence this hath happened him? And he sayde, of a chylde:

22 & ofte times casteth him into the fyre, and also into the water too destroye him. But if thou canste do anything, haue mercy on vs, and helpe vs.

23 And Iesus sayd vnto him: yea, if thou couldest beleue, al thinges are possible to him that beleueth.

24 And strayght way the father of the chylde cryed with teares saying: Lorde I beleue, helpe myne vnbelefe.

25 When Iesus sawe that the people came runnyng together vnto him, he rebuked the foule spirit, saying vnto him: Thou domme & deaf spirite, I charge the come out of him, & enter no more into him.

26 And the spirit cryed & rent him sore, and came out. And he was as one þt had bene dead, in so much that many sayd, he is dead.

27 But Iesus caught his hande and lyft him vp: and he rose.

28 And when he was come into the house, his disciples axed him secretly why could not we cast him out?

29 And he sayed vnto them: this kynde can by no nother meanes come forth but by prayer and fastinge.

30 And they departed thence, and toke theyr iorney through Galile, and he would not that any man should haue knowen it.

31 For he taught his disciples, and sayde vnto them: the sonne of man shalbe deliuered into the handes of men, and they shall kyll hym, and after that he is kylled he shall ryse agayne the thyrde daye.

32 But they wiste not what that saying meante, and were afrayed to axe hym.

33 And he came to Capernaum. And when he was come into an house, he axed theym: what was it that ye disputed betwene you by the waye?

34 And they helde theyr

peace: for by the waye they reasoned among them selues, who should be the chiefest.

35 And he sate doune and called the twelue vnto hym, and sayde vnto them: if any man desire to be first, the same shal be last of all, & seruaunt vnto all.

36 And he toke a chylde, & set him in the middes of them: & toke hym in his armes and sayde vnto them:

37 Whosoeuer receyueth any such a chyld in my name receyueth me. And whosoeuer receyueth me, receyueth not me, but him that sent me.

38 Ihon aunswered him saying: Maister, we sawe one castinge out deuels in thy name whiche foloweth not vs and we forbade hym, because he foloweth vs not.

39 But Iesus sayd forbid him not. For there is no man that shall do a miracle in my name, þt can lightly speake euill of me.

40 Whosoeuer is not agaynste you, is on your part.

41 And whosoeuer shall geue you a cuppe of water to drinke for my names sake, because ye belonge to Christe, verelye I saye vnto you, he shall not lowse his rewarde.

42 And whosoeuer shall offende one of these litelons, that beleue in me, it were better for him that a milstone were hanged aboute hys necke, & that he were caste into the sea.

43 Wherfore if thy hande offende the, cut hym of. It is better for the, to enter into lyfe maymed, then hauing two handes, go into hel, into fyre that neuer shal be quenched,

44 where their worme dyeth not, and the fyre neuer goeth out.

45 Likekewise if thy fote offende the, cut him of. For it is better for the to go halt into life, then hauinge two fete to be caste into hell, into fyre þt neuer shalbe quenched:

46 where their worme dyeth not, and the fyre neuer goeth out.

47 Euen so if thyne eye offende the, plucke him out. It is better for the to go into the kyngedome of God with one eye, then hauing two eies to be cast into hel fyre:

48 where their worm dieth not, and the fyre neuer goeth out.

49 Euery man therfore shalbe salted wyth fyre. And euery sacrifice shalbe seasoned with salt,

50 Salt is good. But if the salt be vnsauery what shall ye sate therwith? Se that ye haue salt in your selues, & haue peace amonge your selues, one with another.

# CHAPTER 10

AND he rose from thence, & wente into the coostes of Iury, through the region that is beyond Iordan. And þe people resorted vnto him a fresh, and as he was wont he taught them agayn.

2 And the phariseis came & axed him a question: whether it were lawfull for a man to put away his wife: to proue him.

3 And he aunswered and sayd vnto them: What did Moyses bid you do?

4 And they sayde: Moyses suffred to write a testimoniall of deuorcement, and to put her awaye.

5 And Iesus aunswered and sayde vnto them: For the hardnes of your hertes he wrote this precept vnto you.

6 But at the first creacion God made them man and woman.

7 And for this thinges seke shall man leaue his father and mother, & byde by hys wyfe,

8 and they twayne shall be one fleshe. So then are they nowe not twayne but one fleshe.

9 Therfore what God hath coupled, let not man separate:

10 And in the house hys discyples axed hym agayne of the matter.

11 And he sayed vnto them: Whosoeuer putteth awaye hys wyfe and maryeth an other breaketh wedlocke to her ward

12 And yf a woman forsake her husbande & be maryed to an other she commytteth aduoutrye.

13 And they brought chyldren to hym, þt he should touche them. And hys disciples rebuked those that brought them.

14 When Iesus sawe þt he was displeased, and sayed to them. Suffer the chyldren to come vnto me, and forbyd them not. For of suche is the kyngdom of God.

15 Verely I saye vnto you: whosoeuer shall not receyue the kyngedome of God, as a chylde, he shall not enter therein.

16 And he toke them vp in hys armes, and put hys handes vpon them and blessed them.

17 And when he was come into the way, there came one runnyng and kneled to him, & axed hym: good mayster, what shall I do, that I maye enheret eternall lyfe?

18 Iesus sayed vnto hym: why callest thou me good? There is none good but one, which is God.

19 Thou knowest the commaundementes: breake not matrimonye: kyll not: steale not: beare not false witnes: defraude no man: honour thy father & mother.

20 He aunswered to hym: mayster all these I haue oberued from my youth.

21 Iesus behelde hym, and had a fauoure to him: and sayed vnto hym: one thynge is lackynge vnto the. Go and sell all that thou haste, and geue to the poore, and thou shalte haue treasure in heauen, and come and folowe me, and take vp thy crosse.

22 But he was discomforted with that saying, and went

awaye mournynge, for he had greate possessyons.

23 And Iesus loked rounde about, and sayed vnto hys discyples: what an harde thynge is it for them that haue rychesse, to enter into the kyngedome of God.

24 And hys disciples were astonyed at his wordes. But Iesus answered agayne, and sayed vnto them: chyldren howe harde is it for them, that truste in rychesse, to enter into the kyngdome of God.

25 It is easyer for a camell to go thorowe the eye of a nedle, then for a ryche man to enter into the kyngdom of God.

26 And they were astonyed out of measure, sayinge betwene them selues: who then can be saued

27 Iesus loked vpon them & sayde: with men it is vnpossyble, but not with God, for with God all thynges are possyble.

28 And Peter beganne to saye vnto hym: Lo, we haue forsaken all, and haue folowed the.

29 Iesus aunswered and sayed: Verely I say vnto you: there is no man that forsaketh house, or brethren, or sisters, or father, or mother, or wyfe, other chyldren, or landes for my sake & the Gospels,

30 which shall not receyue an hundred folde now in this lyfe: houses, & brethren and systers, and mothers, and chyldren, and landes wyth persecucyons, and in the worlde to come eternal lyfe.

31 Many that are first, shal be last, and the laste shall be fyrste.

32 And they were in the waye goynge vnto Hierusalem. And Iesus wente before them: and they were amased, and as they folowed, they were afrayed. And Iesus toke the twelue agayne, and began to tell them what thynges shoulde happen vnto hym.

33 Beholde, we go vp to Hierusalem and the sonne of man shalbe delyuered into the handes of the hye priestes, and vnto the Scribes: and they shall condempne hym to death, and shall delyuer hym to the gentyls:

34 and they shal mocke him, & schourge him and spyte vpon hym, and kyl hym. And the thyrd daye he shall ryse agayne.

35 And then Iames & Iohn the sons of zebede came vnto hym, sayinge: Mayster, we would that thou shouldest do for vs whatsoeuer we desyre.

36 He sayed vnto them: what woulde ye I shoulde do vnto you?

37 They sayed to hym: graunte vnto vs that we may sitte one on thy ryght hande, and the other on thy lifte hande, in thy glory.

38 But Iesus sayed vnto them: Ye wote not what ye axe. Can ye drinke of the cuppe that I shall drinke of, and be baptysed in the baptime that I shalbe baptised in?

39 And they sayde vnto hym: that we can. Iesus sayde vnto them: ye shal drinke of the cup that I shall drinke of, and be baptysed with þe baptysme that I shalbe baptysed in:

40 but to sit on my ryght hande, and on my lift hande is not myne to geue, but to them for whom it is prepared.

41 And when the .x. hearde that they began to dysdayne at Iames and Iohn.

42 But Iesus called them vnto hym, and sayde to them: Ye knowe that they whiche seme to beare rule amonge the gentyls, raygne as lordes ouer them. And they that be great among them, exercyse authoritie ouer them.

43 So shall it not be among you, but whosoeuer of you wil be great among you shalbe your minister.

44 And whosoeuer wilbe chiefe, shalbe seruaunt vnto al.

45 For euen the sonne of man came not to be mynystred vnto, but to minister & to geue hys lyfe for the redempcyon of many.

46 And they came to Hierico: and as he went out of Hierico with hys discyples, and a great numbre of people, Barthymeus the sonne of Chimeus whiche was blynde, sate by the hye wayes syde begginge.

47 And when he hearde, that it was Iesus of Nazareth, he beganne to crye and to saye: Iesus the sonne of Dauid, haue mercye on me.

48 And many rebuked him that he shoulde holde hys peace. But he cryed the more a great deale: Thou sonne of Dauid haue mercye on me.

49 And Iesus stode styl, and commaunded hym to be called. And they called the blinde, sayinge vnto hym: Be of good comforte: ryse, he calleth the.

50 And he threwe awaye hys clooke, and rose, and came to Iesus.

51 And Iesus aunswered and sayde vnto hym: What wylte thou that I do vnto the. The blynde sayed vnto hym: Mayster that I myght se.

52 Iesus sayde vnto hym: Go thy waye, thy faith hath saued the. And by and by he receyued hys sight, and folowed Iesus in the waye.

# CHAPTER 11

AND when they came nye to Hierusalem vnto Bethphage and Bethanye, besydes mount Olyuete, he sent two of hys discyples,

2 and sayde vnto them: Go your wayes into the toune that is ouer agaist you. And assone as ye be entred into it, ye shal fynde a coolte tied, whereon neuer man sate: loose hym, and brynge hym hyther.

3 And yf any man say vnto you: why do ye so? Saye that the

# MARK

Lorde hath nede of hym: and strayghte waye he wyll sende hym hyther.

4 And they wente theyr waye, & founde a coolte tyed by the dore without in a place where two wayes met, and they losed hym.

5 And dyuers of them that stode there, sayd vnto them: What do ye lowsyng the coolte?

6 And they sayed vnto them euen as Iesus had commaunded them. And they let them go.

7 And they broughte the coolt to Iesus, and caste theyr garmentes on hym: & he sate vpon hym.

8 And manye spredde theyr garmentes in the way. Other cut doune braunches of the trees, and strawed them in the waye

9 And they that before, & they that folowed, cryed, saying Hosanna: blessed be he that commeth in the name of the Lord.

10 Blessed be the kyngdome that commeth in þe name of hym that is Lord of our father Dauid. Hosanna in the hyest.

11 And the Lorde entred into Hierusalem, & into the temple. And when he had loked round aboute vpon all thynges, and nowe the euen tyde was come, he wente oute vnto Bethany with the twelue.

12 And on the morowe when they were come oute from Bethany, he hungred,

13 and spied a fygge tree a farre of hauing leaues: and wente to se whether he myghte fynde any thynge theron. But when he came therto, he founde nothyng but leaues: for the tyme of fygges was not yet.

14 And Iesus aunswered & sayd to it: neuer man eate frute of the here after whyle the world standeth. And hys discyples hearde it.

15 And they came to Hierusalem. And Iesus went into the temple, and beganne to cast out sellers, and byers in the temple, & ouerthrewe the tables of the money chaungers, & the stoles of them that solde doues,

16 and woulde not suffer that anye man caryed a vessell through the temple.

17 And he taught saying vnto them: is it not wryten: my house shall be called the house of prayer vnto al nacions? But ye haue made it a den of theues.

18 And the Scrybes & hye Priestes hearde it: and soughte howe to destroy him. For they feared hym, because al the people marueyled at his doctrine.

19 And when euen was come, he wente oute of the cityne.

20 And in the mornynge as they passed by, they sawe the fygge tree dryed vp by þe rotes.

21 And Peter remembred, & sayd vnto him: maister, behold the figge tree which thou cursedest, is wythered away.

22 And Iesus aunswered, and sayed vnto them: Haue confydence in God.

23 Verelye I saye vnto you, that whosoeuer shall saye to thys mountayne: take awaye thy selfe, and caste thy selfe into the sea, and shall not wauer in hys herte, but shall beleue that those thynges whiche he sayeth, shall come to passe, whatsoeuer he sayeth, shalbe done to hym.

24 Therfore I saye vnto you, whatsoeuer ye desyre when ye praye, beleue that ye shall haue it, and it shall be done vnto you.

25 And when ye stande, and pray, forgeue, yf ye haue any thyng agaynst any man, that youre father also which is in heauen, may forgeue you your trespasses.

26 <>

27 And they came agayne to Hierusalem. And as he walked in the temple, there came to him the hye priestes and the Scribes & the elders,

28 and sayed vnto hym: by what authoritie doest thou these thynges? And who gaue the thys authoritie to do these thynges?

29 Iesus aunswered and sayed vnto them: I wyll also axe of you a certayne thynge: and aunswere ye me, and I wyll tell you by what authorite I do these thynges.

30 The baptisme of Iohn was it from heauen, or of menne? Aunswere me.

31 And they thoughte in them selues, sayinge: yf we shall saye, from heauen: he wyl saye then: why dyd ye not beleue hym?

32 But yf we shall saye, of men, then feare we the people. For al men counted Iohn that he was a very Prophet.

33 And they aunswered and sayd vnto Iesus: we can not tell. And Iesus aunswered and sayed vnto them, neyther wyll I tell you, by what authoritie I do those thynges.

# CHAPTER 12

AND he began to speake vnto them in simylitudes. A certayne man planted a vyneyarde, and compaste it wyth an hedge, and ordeyned a wyne presse, & buylde a tower in it. And let it oute to hyre vnto housband men, & went into a straunge countreye.

2 And when the tyme was come, he sente to the tenauntes a seruaunte, that he myghte receyue of the tenauntes of the frute of the vyneyarde.

3 And they caughte hym, and sent him awaye emptye.

4 And moreouer he sente vnto them another seruaunte, and at hym they cast stones, & brake hys head, & sent hym agayne all to reuyled.

5 And agayne he sente an other and hym they kylled: and manye other, beatynge some, and kyllyng some.

6 Yet had he one sonne whom he loued tenderlye, hym

also he sente at the laste vnto them, saiynge: they wyll feare my sonne.

7 But the tenauntes sayed amonge them selues: thys is the heyre: come let vs kyll hym, and the enheritaunce shall be ours.

8 And they toke hym, & kylled hym, & cast hym out of the vyneyarde.

9 What shall then the Lorde of the vyneyarde do? He wyll come and destroye the tenauntes, and let oute the vynearde to other.

10 Haue ye not read thys scrypture? The stone which the buylders dyd refuse, is made the chiefe stone in the corner:

11 thys was done of the Lorde, and is merueylouse in our eyes.

12 And they wente aboute to take hym. But they feared the people. For they perceyued that he spake that similitude agaynste them. And they lefte hym.

13 And they sente vnto hym certayne of the Pharyseis with Herodes seruauntes to take hym in hys wordes.

14 And assone as they were come, they saied vnto him: maister, we know that thou arte true, and carest for no man: for considerest not the degre of men, but teacheste the waye of God truly. Is it lawfull to paye trybute to Cesar or not.

15 Oughte we to geue, or ought we not to geue? He vnderstode theyr simulacyon, and sayde vnto them: Why tempte you me? Brynge me a peny that I maye se it.

16 And they broughte. And he sayde vnto them: Whose is thys Image and superscripcion? And they sayde vnto hym: Cesars

17 And Iesus aunswered and sayde vnto them: Then geue to Cesar that which belongeth to Cesar: and to God that whiche pertayneth to God. And they meruayled at hym.

18 Then came the Saduces vnto hym, which saye: there is no resurreccyon, and they axed hym, sayinge:

19 Mayster, Moyses wrote vnto vs, yf anye mannes brother dye: and leaue his wyfe behynde hym, and leaue no chyldren, that then hys brother shoulde take hys wyfe, and rayse vp seed vnto hys brother.

20 There were seuen brethren: and the fyrst toke a wyfe and when he dyed, he lefte no seede behynde hym.

21 And the seconde toke her and dyed: neyther lefte any seede. And the thyrde lykewyse.

22 And seuen had her, and lefte no seede behynd them. Laste of all the wyfe dyed also.

23 In the resurreccyon then, when they shal ryse agayne whose wyfe shall she be of them? For seuen had her to wyfe.

24 Iesus aunswered and sayed vnto them: Are ye not therfore deceyued, and vnderstande not the scryptures, neyther the power of GOD?

25 For when they shall ryse agayne from death, they neyther marye, nor are maryed, but are as the Aungels which are in heauen.

26 As touchynge the dead, that they shall ryse agayne: haue ye not reade in þe boke of Moyses, how in þe bushe god spake to him sayinge: I am the God of Abraham, & God of Isaac, and the God of Iacob?

27 He is not the God of the dead, but the God of the lyuyng. Ye are therfore greatly deceyued,

28 And there came one of the Scribes that had hearde them, disputynge together, & perceyued, that he had aunswered them well, and axed hym: Whiche is the fyrste of all the commaundementes?

29 Iesus aunswered hym: þe fyrst of al the commaundementes is. Heare Israel: The Lorde God is one Lorde.

30 And thou shalt loue the Lorde thy God with all thyne herte, and wyth all thy soule, & with al thy mynde, and with all thy strength. Thys is the fyrste commaundement.

31 And the seconde is lyke vnto this: Thou shalte loue thy neyghboure as thy self. There is none other commaundement greater then these.

32 And the Scribe sayd vnto him: wel master thou haste sayde the trueth, that there is one God, & that there is none but he.

33 And to loue hym with all the herte, and with al the mynd, and with all the soule, & with all the strength. and to loue a mans neyghbour as hym selfe, is a greater thyng then all burntoffrynges & sacrifices.

34 And when Iesus sawe that he aunswered discretly, he sayde vnto him: Thou art not farre from the kyngdom of God. And no man after that, durst axe him any question.

35 And Iesus aunswered & sayde, teachynge in the temple: how say the scribes that Christe is the sonne of Dauid?

36 for Dauid him self inspired with the holy ghost, sayde: The Lorde sayde to my Lorde, sit on my righthand til I make thyne enemyes thy foote stole.

37 Then Dauid him selfe calleth him Lord: & by what meanes is he then his sonne? And much people hearde him gladly.

38 And he sayd vnto them in his doctrine: beware of the Scribes, which loue to go in longe clothinge and loue salutations in the market places,

39 & the chief seates in synagoges, and to sit in the vppermoste roumes at feastes

40 & deuoure wydowes houses, and that vnder a coloure of long praiyng. These shall receyue greater dampnacion.

41 And Iesus sat ouer agaynst the treasurye, and behelde howe the people put money into the treasurye. And many that were ryche, cast in muche.

42 And there came a certayne poore wydowe, and she threwe in two mites, which make a farthynge.

43 And he called vnto hym hys discyples, and sayde vnto them. Verely I saye vnto you, that thys poore wydowe hath caste more in, then all they whiche haue caste into the treasury.

44 For they all dyd caste in of theyr superfluyte, but she of her pouertye dyd cast in all that she had, euen all her liuinge.

## CHAPTER 13

AND as he went out of the temple one of hys disciples sayde vnto hym: Maister, se what stones, & what buyldynges are here.

2 And Iesus aunswered, and sayd vnto hym: Seest thou these greate buyldinges? There shall not be left one stone vpon another, that shall not be throwen doune.

3 And as he sate on mounte Olyuete, ouer agaynst the temple, Peter, & Iames, & Iohn, & Andrewe axed hym secretelye:

4 tell vs, when shall these thynges be? And what is the sygne when all these thynges shalbe fulfylled?

5 and Iesus aunswered them, and began to saye: take hede leste any man deceyue you.

6 For manye shall come in my name, sayinge: I am Christ, and shall deceyue manye.

7 When ye shal heare of warre, and tydynges of warre, be ye not troubled. For suche thynges muste nedes be. But the ende is not yet.

8 For there shall nacyon aryse agaynst nacyon, and kingdom agaynst kyngdome. And there shalbe earthquakes in all quarters, & famyshment and troubles. These are the begynnynge of sorowes.

9 But take ye hede to your selues. For they shall brynge you vp to the counsels, and into þe synagoges, & ye shall be beaten: ye & shalbe broughte forthe rulers & kynges for my sake for a testimoniall vnto them.

10 And the Gospel muste fyrste be publyshed amonge all nacyons.

11 But when they leade you, and present you, take no thoughte afore hande, what ye, shal saye, neither ymagin: but whatsoeuer is geuen you at the same tyme, that speake. For it shall not be ye that shall speake, but the holy ghost.

12 Ye, and the brother shal deliuer the brother to death, and the father the sonne, and the children shall ryse agaynst theyr fathers and mothers, and shal put them to death.

13 And ye shal be hated of all men for my names sake. But whosoeuer shall endure vnto þe ende, the same shalbe safe.

14 Moreouer, when ye se þe abhomynacyon that betokeneth desolacion, whereof is spoken by Daniel the Prophet, stande where it oughte not, let hym that readeth vnderstand, then let them that be in Iurye, fle to the mountaynes.

15 And let hym that is on the house top, not descended doune into the house, neither enter therein, to fetche any thynge oute of hys house.

16 And let hym that is in the fielde: not tourne backe agayne vnto the thynges, which he lefte behynde hym for to take hys clothes with hym.

17 Woo is then to them that are with chyld, and to them that geue soucke in those dayes.

18 But praye, that your flight be not in þe winter.

19 For there shalbe in those dayes such trybulacyon, as was not from the beginning of creatures whiche God created, vnto thys time, neyther shalbe.

20 And except that the Lord shoulde shorten those dayes, no man shoulde be saued. But for the electes sake which he hath chosen, he hath shortened those dayes.

21 And then, yf any man say to you: lo, here is Christ, lo, he is there: beleue not,

22 for false Christes shal ryse, and false prophetes, and shall shewe myracles and wondres, to deceyue yf it were possible, euen the elect.

23 But take ye hede: beholde I haue shewed you all thynges before.

24 Moreouer in those dayes, after that trybulacyon, the sonne shall waxe darke, and the moone shal not geue her light,

25 and the starres of heauen shall fal: and the powers which are in heauen shall moue.

26 And then shall they se the sonne of man comyng in the cloudes with great power and glorye.

27 And then shal he send hys angels, & shall gather together his electe from the foure wyndes, and from the one ende of the worlde to the other.

28 Learne a symylytude of the fygge tree. When hys braunches are yet tender, & hathe brought forth leaues: ye know that þe somer is neare,

29 so in like maner when ye se these thinges come to passe: vnderstande, that it is nye euen at the dores.

30 Verelye I saye vnto you, that thys generacyon shall not passe, tyll all these thynges be done.

31 Heauen and earth shal passe, but my wordes shall not passe.

32 But of the daye & houre knoweth no man: no not the

Aungels whiche are in heauen neyther the sonne him selfe saue the father onelye.

33 Take hede, watche and pray, forth ye know not when the tyme is.

34 As a man whiche is gone into a straunge countreye, and hath left hys house, and geuen authorite to his seruauntes, and euerye man hys worke, and commaunded the porter to watche.

35 Watche therfore, for ye knowe not when the mayster of the house wyll come: whether at euen, or at mydnyght: whether at the cocke crowynge or in the dawnynge,

36 leste yf he come sodenlye, he shoulde fynde you slepynge.

37 And that I saye vnto you: I saye vnto all men, watche.

## CHAPTER 14

AFTER two dayes folowed easter and the dayes of swete breade. And the hye priestes and þe scrybes soughte meanes howe they myght take hym by crafte, and put hym to death.

2 But they sayde: Not in the feast daye least any busynes aryse among the people.

3 When he was in Bethania, in the house of Simon the leper, euen as he sate at meate ther came a woman hauynge an alabaster boxe of oyntment called narde, that was pure & costly, and she brake the boxe and powred it on hys head.

4 And there were some that were not content in them selues, and sayd: what neded this waste of oyntment?

5 For it myght haue bene solde for more then thre hundred pence, & bene geuen vnto the poore. And they grudged agaynste her.

6 And Iesus sayde: let her be in reste, why troubled ye her? she hath done a good worke on me.

7 For ye shall haue poore men with you alwayes, & whensoeuer ye wyll, ye maye do them good, but me ye shal not haue alwayes.

8 She hath done that she coulde: she came afore hande to anoynte my body to hys buryenge warde.

9 Verelye I saye vnto you: where soeuer this gospel shall be preached throughout the whole worlde, this also that she hath done shalbe rehearsed in remembraunce of her.

10 And Iudas Ischarioth one of the twelue went awaye vnto the hye priestes, to betraye hym vnto them.

11 When they hearde that, they were glad, and promysed that they woulde geue hym money. And he sought howe he myghte conuenientlye betraye hym.

12 And the fyrst daye of swete bread: when men after the pascall lambe, hys discyples sayed vnto him: where wilt thou that we go & prepare that thou mayest eat the easter lambe?

13 And he sente forthe two of his disciples, and sayed vnto them: Go ye into the cityе: and there shal a man mete you bearynge a pycher of water, folowe him.

14 And whyther soeuer he goeth in, say ye to the good man of þe house: the maister axeth: where is the gest chambre, where I shall eat þe easter lambe wt my disciples.

15 And he wyll shew you a great parloure, paued & prepared: there make readye for vs.

16 And his discyples went forth, and came to the citie, and founde as he had sayd vnto them: & made ready þe easter lambe.

17 And at euen he came with the twelue

18 and as they sate at borde, and eate. Iesus sayd: Verelye I saye vnto you: that one of you shal betraye me, whiche eateth with me.

19 And they beganne to mourne, and to say to him one by one: is it I? and another sayde: is it I?

20 He aunswered, and sayde vnto them: It is one of the .xij. & the same deppeth with me in the platter.

21 The sonne of man goeth as it is written of hym, but woo be to that man, by whom the sonne of man is betrayed: good were it for hym, yf that man had neuer bene borne.

22 And as they eate. Iesus toke bread, blessed and brake & gaue to them & sayd: Take, eat, this is my body.

23 And he toke þe cup, gaue thankes, & gaue it to them, & they all dranke of it.

24 And he sayed vnto them: This is my bloud of þe new Testament which is shed for many.

25 Verely I saye vnto you: I wyll drinke no more of thys frute of the vyne, vntil that day, that I drinke it newe in the kingdome of God.

26 And when they had grace, they went out to mount Oliuete.

27 And Iesus sayde vnto them. All ye shalbe offended through me this night. For it is written: I wyll smyte the shepeherde, and þe shepe shalbe scattered.

28 But after that I am rysen agayne: I wyll go into Galile before you.

29 Peter sayd vnto him. And though all men should be offended, yet woulde not I.

30 And Iesus said vnto hym: Verelye I saye vnto the, this daye euen in thys nyghte before the cocke crowe twyse, thou shalte denye me thryse.

31 And he spake boldelyer: no, yf I shoulde dye wt the I wyll not deuye the. Lykewyse also

sayde they all.

32 And they came into a place named Gethsemanye, and he sayde to hys discyples: Syt ye here, whyle I go a parte and praye.

33 And he toke with him Peter, Iames, and Iohn, & he began to waxe abashed, and to be in an agonye,

34 and said vnto them: My soule is very heauye euen vnto the death: tarye here & watche.

35 And he wente forthe a litle and fell doune on the grounde, and prayed: that yf it were possyble, the houre myght passe from hym.

36 And he sayde: Abba father, all thynges are possyble vnto the, take awaye this cup from me. Neuerthelesse, not that I wyll but that thou wylte, be done.

37 And he came, and founde them slepynge, and sayd to Peter: Symon slepest thou? Couldest not thou watche wt me one houre?

38 watche ye, and praye leaste ye enter into temptacyon, the spirite is ready, and the fleshe is weake.

39 And agayne he went away and prayed and spake the same wordes.

40 And he returned and found them a slepe agayn, for theyr eyes were heauy: neither wyste they what to aunswere hym.

41 And he came the thyrde tyme and sayd vnto them: slepe hence forth and take youre ease, it is ynough. The houre is come, beholde the sonne of man shalbe delyuered into the handes of synners.

42 Ryse vp let vs go. Lo, he that betrayeth me, is at hande.

43 And immediatelye whyle he yet spake, came Iudas one of the twelue, and wyth him a great numbre of people wt sweardes & staues from the hyghe Priestes & Scribes & elders.

44 And he that betrayed him, had geuen them a generall token saiyng: whosoeuer I do kysse, he it is: take hym & leade him awaye warely.

45 And assone as he was come, he went straighte waye to hym, and sayed vnto him: mayster, and kyssed him.

46 And they layde theyr handes on hym, and toke him.

47 And one of them that stode by, drue out a swerde & smote a seruaunt of the hye priest, and cut of hys eare.

48 And Iesus aunswered and sayd vnto them: ye be come oute as vnto a thefe with swerdes & with staues, for to take me.

49 I was daylye wt you in the temple teachynge, and ye toke me not: but that the scriptures shoulde be fulfylled.

50 And they all forsoke him, & ranne away.

51 And there folowed him a certayne yong man clothed in linnen vpon the bare, and the yong men caught him,

52 and he lefte hys linnen, and fleed from them naked.

53 And they leed Iesus awaye to the hyest priest of all, & to him came all the hye priestes, and the elders, and the scribes.

54 And Peter folowed him a great waye of euen into the pallaice of the hye priest, and sat with the seruauntes, and warmed hym self at the fyre.

55 And the hye priestes, and al the counsell soughte for witnes againste Iesu to put him to death, & founde none.

56 Yet manye bare false witnes againste him, but theyr witnes agreed not together.

57 And there arose certayne and brought false wytnes agaynst hym, saiinge:

58 We hearde him saye: I will destroy this temple made with handes, & within .iij. dayes I will buylde another made without handes.

59 But theyr wytnes agreed not together.

60 And the hyest priest stode vp amongest them: and axed Iesus, sayinge: answerest thou nothynge? Howe is it that these beare witnes agaynst the?

61 And he helde hys peace, and aunswered nothynge. Agayne the hyest priest axed him, and sayed vnto hym: Arte thou christe the sonne of the blessed?

62 And Iesus sayed: I am. And ye shall se the sonne of man sit on the ryght hande of power, and come in the cloudes of heauen.

63 Then the hyest prieste rent hys clothes, & sayd: What nede we any further of witnesse?

64 ye haue hearde the blasphemy, what thynke ye? And then they all gaue sentence, that he was worth of death,

65 and some began to spit at hym, and to couer hys face, and to beate hym wyth fystes, and to saye vnto him: areade vnto vs? And the seruauntes boffeted hym on the face.

66 And as Peter was beneth in the pallayce, there came one of the wenches of the hyest priest,

67 & when she sawe Peter warmyng him selfe she loked on hym, and sayd: Waste not thou also with Iesus of Nazareth?

68 And he denyed it, saying: I know hym not, neyther wot I what thou sayest. And he wente out into the porche, and the cocke crew.

69 And a damsell saw hym, and agayne beganne to saye to them that stode by: thys is one of them.

70 And he denyed it agayne. And anone after, they that stode by, sayed agayne to Peter: Surely thou art one of them, for thou arte of Galile, and thy speache agreeth therto.

71 And he began to cursse and to sweare, saiynge: I know not this man of whome ye speake.

72 And agayne the cocke

crewe, and Peter remembred the worde that Iesus sayed vnto hym: before the cocke crowe twyse, thou shalte denye me thyrse, & began to wepe.

# CHAPTER 15

AND anone in the daunynge the hye priestes helde a counsel with the elders, and the scribes, and the whole congregacion & bounde Iesus and ledde hym awaye, & delyuered hym to Pilate.

2 And Pylate axed hym: arte thou the kynge of the Iewes? And he aunswered and sayde vnto hym: thou sayest it.

3 And the hyghe Priestes accused him of manye thynges.

4 Wherfore Pylate axeth hym agayne, saying: Answerest thou nothyng? beholde how manye thinges they laye vnto thy charge:

5 Iesus yet aunswered neuer a worde, so that Pylate meruayled.

6 At that feaste Pylate was wonte to delyuer at theyr pleasure a prysoner, whosoeuer they woulde desyre.

7 And there was one named Barrabas, whiche laye bounde with them that made insurreccyon, and the insurreccyon committed murther.

8 And the people called vnto hym, & began to desyre, accordyng as he had euer done vnto them:

9 Pylate aunswered them, & sayd: Wil ye þt I lowse vnto you the kyng of the Iewes?

10 For he knew that the hye priestes had deliuered him of enuye.

11 But þe hye prestes had moued the people: that he shoulde rather delyuer Barrabas vnto them.

12 And Pylate aunswered agayne, & sayd vnto them: what wyl ye then that I do with hym, whom ye call the kynge of the Iewes?

13 And they cryed agayne: crucifye hym.

14 Pylate said vnto them: what euyl hath he done? And they cryed the more feruentlye: Crucifye hym.

15 And so Pylate wyllyng to content þe people, loused them Barrabas, and delyuered Iesus, when he had scourged hym, for to be crucifyed.

16 And the soudyers ledde hym away into the common hall, and called together the whole multytude,

17 and they clothed him wyth purple, and they platted a croune of thornes and crouned hym with al,

18 and began to salute hym: Hayle kynge of the Iewes.

19 And they smote hym on the head with a rede, and spatte vpon hym, and kneled doune & worshipped hym.

20 And when they had mocked hym, they toke the purple of hym, and put hys owne clothes on him, and led him out to crucifye him.

21 And they compelled one þt passed by, called Simon of Ciren (which came out of the feld, and was father of Alexander and Rufus) to beare hys crosse.

22 And they broughte hym to a place named Golgotha (which is by interpretacyon, the place of dead mens sculles)

23 and they gaue hym to drynke wyne myngled wyth myrre, but he receyued it not.

24 And when they had crucifyed hym, they parted hys garmentes castynge lotes for them, what euerye man shoulde haue.

25 And it was about the thyrde houre, and they crucyfyed him.

26 And the tytle of hys cause was written: The kynge of þe Iewes.

27 And they crucified wt hym two theues, the one on the ryght hande, and the other on his lyft.

28 And the scrypture was fulfylled which sayth: he was counted amonge the wycked.

29 And they that wente by rayled on hym: waggynge their heades and sayinge: A wretche, that destroyest the temple, and buyldest it in thre dayes:

30 saue thy selfe, and come doune from the crosse:

31 Lykewise also mocked him þe hye pryestes amonge them selues with the scribes and sayde: he saued other men, hym selfe he can not saue.

32 Let Christe the kinge of Israel now descende from the crosse, that we may se and beleue. And they that were crucyfyed with hym, checked him also.

33 And when the syxte houre was come, darcknes arose ouer all the earth vntyll the ninthe houre.

34 And Iesus cryed with a loude voice saying: Eloi Eloi lamasabaththany, whiche is if it be interpreted, my God my God, why hast thou forsaken me?

35 And some of them that stode by, when they hearde that: saide: behold he calleth for Helias.

36 And one ran and fylled a sponge full of vyneger and put it on a rede, and gaue him to drinke, saying let him alone, let vs se whither Helyas wyll come and take him doune.

37 But Iesus cryeth with a loude voice, and gaue vp the ghost.

38 And the vayle of the temple dyd rent in two peces from the toppe to the bottome.

39 And when the Centurion which stode before him, sawe that he so cried and gaue vp the ghost he sayde: truly this man was the sonne of God.

40 Ther were also women a good waye of beholdyng hym: among whom was Mary

Magdalen, and Marye the mother of Iames the lytle, and of Ioses, & Mary Salome:

41 whiche also when he was in Galile, folowed hym, and mynistred vnto hym: and manye other women, whiche came vp with hym vnto Ierusalem:

42 And now when night was come (because it was the euen that goeth before the Saboth)

43 Ioseph of Arimathia a noble Councelloure which also loked for the kyngdome of God, came and went in boldly vnto Pylate, & begged the bodye of Iesu.

44 And Pylate merueyled that he was already deade, and called vnto hym the Centurion, and axed of hym, whether he had bene anye whyle deade.

45 And when he knewe the truth of the Centuryon, he gaue the body to Ioseph.

46 And he bought a lynnen clothe, and toke him doune, and wrapped him in the lynnen clothe, and layde hym in a tombe that was hewen out of the rocke, and rolled a stone vnto þe dore of the sepulchre.

47 And Mary Magdalen & Marye Ioses behelde where he was layed.

# CHAPTER 16

AND when þe Saboth was past. Mary Magdalen, and Mary Iacobi, and Salome, boughte odours, þt they myghte come & anoynt hym.

2 And very early in the morninge the next daye after the Saboth daye they came to the sepulchre, when þe sunne was rysen.

3 And they sayed one to another: who shal rolle vs awaye the stone from the dore of the sepulchre?

4 And when they loked, they sawe howe the stone was rolled awaye: for it was a verye great one.

5 And they wente into the sepulchre, and sawe a yonge man syttyng on the ryght syde, clothed in a long white garment, & they were abashed.

6 And he sayed vnto them, be not afrayed: ye seke Iesus of Nazareth whiche was crucifyed. He is rysen, he is not here. Beholde the place where they put hym.

7 But go your waye, and tell hys discyples and namelye Peter: He wil go before you into Galile, there shal ye se him as he sayde vnto you.

8 And they wente oute quickly, and fled from the sepulchre. For they trembled and were amased. Neyther sayed they anye thynge to anye man, for they were afrayed.

9 When Iesus was rysen the morowe after the Saboth daye, he appeared fyrst to Marye Magdalen, out of whome he cast seuen deuils.

10 And she went and tolde them that were wyth hym as they mourned & wepte.

11 And when they heard that he was alyue, and he had appeared to her, they beleued it not.

12 After that he appered to two of them in a straunge fygure, as they walked and went into the countre.

13 And they wente and tolde it to the remnaunt. And they beleued them neyther.

14 After that he appeared vnto the eleuen, as they sate at meat, and caste in theyr tethe theyr vnbelese and hardnes of hert: because they beleued not them which had sene hym after hys resurreccyon.

15 And he sayed to them: Go ye into all the worlde, and preache the glad tydynges to all creatures,

16 he that beleueth & is baptised, shall be saued. But he that beleueth not, shalbe damned.

17 And these sygnes shall folowe them that beleue. In my name they shall caste oute deuils, & shall speake with newe tonges,

18 & shall kyll serpentes, and yf they drinke any deadly thynge, it shall not hurte them. They shal lay theyr handes on the sycke, and they shal recouer.

19 So then when the Lorde had spoken vnto them: he was receyued into heauen, and is set doune on the ryght hande of God.

20 And they wente forth and preached euerye where. And the Lorde wrought with them, and confyrmed the word wt miracles that folowed.

# Luke

## CHAPTER 1

FOR asmuche as manye haue taken in hande to compyle a treatyse of those thynges which are surelye knowen amonge vs,

2 euen as they declared them vnto vs, which from the begynnynge sawe theim their selues, and were ministers at the doyinge,

3 I determined also, assone as I had searched out dylygentlye all things from the beginning, that then I would write vnto the, good Theophilus:

4 that thou mightest knowe the certaintye of those thynges wherof thou art enfourmed.

5 Ther was in the dayes of Herode kynge of Iurye, a certaine prieste named Zacharias, of the course of Abaia. And his wyfe was of the doughters of Aaron and her name was Elizabeth.

6 Both were perfect before God, and walked in al the lawes and ordinaunces of the Lorde, that no man coulde fynde faute with them.

7 And they had no childe: because that Elyzabeth was barren, and both were well striken in age.

8 And it came to passe, as he executed the priestes office before God, as his course came

9 (accordinge to the custome of the pryestes offyce) his lot was to bourne incense.

10 And wente into the tempell of the Lorde and the whole multytude of the people were without in prayer while incense was a burninge.

11 And ther appeared vnto hym an Aungell of the Lorde standynge on the ryght syde of the altare of incense.

12 And when Zacharias sawe him, he was abashed, and feare came on him.

13 And the aungel sayde vnto him: feare not Zacharye, for thy prayer is heard: And thy wyfe Elysabeth shall beare the a sonne, & thou shalt call his name Iohn,

14 and thou shalt haue ioye and gladnes, and manye shall reioyce at his birth.

15 For he shalbe greate in the syght of the Lorde, and shall neyther drinke wyne nor stronge drinke. And he shalbe fylled with the holy ghost, euen in his mothers wombe:

16 and manye of the children of Israel shal he turne to their Lorde God.

17 And he shall go before hym in the spryte of power of Helyas, to turne the hertes of the fathers to the chyldren and the vnbeleuers to the wisdome of the iust men, to make the people redy for the Lord.

18 And Zacharias sayde vnto the aungel: wherby shal I knowe this? seynge that I am olde and my wyfe well stricken in yeares.

19 And the aungell aunswered and sayed vnto hym. I am Gabryel that stande in the presence of God, and am sente to speake to the: & shewe the these glad tidinges.

20 And behold thou shalt be dombe, and not able to speake vnto the tyme that these thinges be performed, because thou beleuest not my wordes whiche shalbe fulfylled in their ceason.

21 And the people wayted for Zacharias, and maruayled that he taryed in the temple.

22 And when he came out he coulde not speake to them. Wherby they perceyued that he had sene some vysyon in the temple. And he beckened vnto them, and remayned speacheles.

23 And it fortuned assone as the time of his offyce was out, he departed home into his owne house.

24 And after those dayes his wyfe Elyzabeth conceyued and hid hir selfe .v. monethes, sayinge.

25 This wyfe hath God dealt with me in the dayes when he loked on me, to take from me the rebuke that I suffred amonge men.

26 And in the .vi. moneth the aungell Gabriel was sent from God, vnto a citye of Galile, named Nazareth,

27 to a vyrgin spoused to a man whose name was Ioseph, of the house of Dauid, and the virgins name was Mary.

28 And the aungel wente in vnto her, & sayde Hayle full of grace, the Lorde is with the: blessed art thou amonge women.

29 When she sawe hym, she was abashed at his sayinge: and caste in her mynde what maner of salutacion that shoulde be.

30 And the aungell sayed vnto her: feare not Mary: for thou haste founde grace wyth God.

31 Lo: thou shalt conceyue in thy wombe & shalt beare a sonne, and shalt call his name Iesus.

32 He shalbe greate, and shalbe called the sonne of the hiest. And the Lorde God shal geue to hym the seat of his father Dauid,

33 and he shall raigne ouer the house of Iacob for euer, & of his kingdome shall be no ende.

34 Then sayde Mary to the aungell. How shall this be, seyinge I knowe not a man?

35 And the aungell aunswered and sayd vnto her: The holye ghoste shall come vnto the, and the power of the hyest shall ouer shadowe the. Therfore also that holye thynge whiche shall be borne shalbe called the sonne of God.

36 And beholde thy cosyn Elyzabeth hath also conceyued a sonne in her age: & thys is her syxt moneth though she be called barren:

37 for with God can nothing be vnpossyble.

38 And Marye sayde: beholde the hande mayden of þe Lord, be it vnto me euen as þu haste said. And the aungel departed from her.

39 And Mary arose in those dayes, & went into the mountaines with hast, into a cytye of Iurye,

40 and entred into the house of Zachary, and saluted Elisabeth.

41 And it fortuned as Elysabeth hearde the salutacion of Marye, the babe spronge in her belly. And Elizabeth was fylled with the holye ghost,

42 and cryed wyth a loude voice, and sayde: Blessed art thou among women, and blessed is the frute of thy wombe.

43 And whence happeneth this to me that the mother of my Lorde shoulde come to me?

44 For lo, assone as the voice of thy salutacion sounded in myne eares, the babe sprange in my bellye for ioye.

45 And blessed art thou that beleuedest: for those thinges shall be performed, whiche were tolde the from the Lorde.

46 And Marye sayde: My soule magnifyed the Lorde.

47 And my sprete reioyceth in God my sauiour.

48 For he hath loked on the poore degre of his hande maiden. Beholde now from henceforth shall all generacions cal me blessed.

49 For he that is mightye hath done to me great thinges, and holy is his name.

50 And his mercy is on them that feare hym thorowe out all generacions.

51 He sheweth strength with his arme, he scattereth them that are proude in the ymagynacion of their hertes.

52 He putteth doune the mightye from their seates, and exalteth them of low degre.

53 He fylleth the hongry with good thinges, & sendeth away the ryche empty.

54 He remembreth mercye, and helpeth his sernaunte Israell.

55 Euen as he promysed to our fathers Abraham and to his sede for euer.

56 And Marye abode with her aboute a .iij. moneths, and retourned againe to her owne house.

57 Elyzabeths time was come þt she should be delyuered, and she brought forth a sonne.

58 And her neighbours and her cosyne harde tell howe the Lorde had shewed great mercye vpon her, And they reioyceth with her.

59 And it fortuned the .viij. daye, they came to circuncyse the childe, and called his name Zacharias, after the name of his father.

60 How be it his mother aunswered, and sayde: not so, but he shalbe called Ihon.

61 And they saide vnto her: There is none of thy kinne that is named with this name.

62 And they made sygnes to his father: howe he woulde haue him called.

63 And he axeth for writtyng tables, and wrote sayinge: his name is Ihon. And they maruayled al.

64 And his mouthe was opened immediatlye, and his tonge also, and he spake laudinge God.

65 And feare came on all them that dwelt nye vnto them. And all these sayinges were noysed abrode throughout al the hyll country of Iury,

66 and all that hearde them laide them vp in their hartes sayinge: What maner chylde shall this be? And the hande of the Lorde was with him.

67 And his father Zacharias was fylled with the holye ghost, and prophecied sayinge:

68 Blessed be the Lorde God of Israel, for he hath visyted and redemed his people.

69 And hath reysed vp an horne of saluacion vnto vs in the house of his seruaunt Dauid.

70 Euen as he promised by the mouthe of his holye prophetes which were sence the worlde began.

71 That we shoulde be saued from oure enemyes, & from the power of all that hath vs.

72 To fulfyll the mercy promysed to oure fathers, and to remember his holye couenaunt.

73 And to performe the othe which he sware to oure father Abraham,

74 for to geue vs. That we delyuered out of the power of oure enemyes, might serue him without feare

75 all the dayes of our lyfe, in such holynes and ryghtuousnes as are accept before hym.

76 And thou chylde shalt be called þe prophete of the hiest: for thou shalt go before the face of the Lorde to prepare his wayes.

77 And to geue knowledge of saluacion vnto his people for the remissyon of synnes.

78 Through the tender mercye of our God, wherby the daye sprynge from on hye hath vysyted vs.

79 To geue lyght to them that sate in darcknes & in shadowe of death, and to guyde oure fete into the waye of peace.

80 And the chylde grewe and wexed stronge in spirite and was in wyldernes tyll the daye came when he shoulde shewe him selfe vnto the Israelytes.

# CHAPTER 2

AND it chaunced in those dayes: that there wente out a commaundemente from Auguste the Emperour, that al the worlde should be taxed.

2 And this taxynge was the fyrste, and executed when Syrenius was lieftenaunt in Siria.

3 And euerye man wente into his owne cytye to be taxed.

4 And Ioseph also ascended from Galyle: out of a cytye called Nazareth, into Iury: vnto the cytye of Dauid which is called Bethleem, because he was of the house and lynage of Dauid,

5 to be taxed with Marye his spoused wyfe whiche was with childe.

6 And it fortuned whyle they were there, her tyme was come that she shoulde be deliuered.

7 And she brought forth her first begotten sonne, and wrapped him in swadlynge clothes, and layed him in a maunger, because ther was no roume for them within the ynne.

8 And there were in the same region shepherdes abydinge in the fyelde, and watchinge theyr flocke by night.

9 And lo: the aungel of the Lord stode harde by them, and the brightnes of the Lord shone round about them, and they were sore afrayed.

10 But the aungel sayde vnto them: Be not afrayed. For beholde, I bringe you tydinges of greate ioye that shall come to al the people:

11 for vnto you is borne this day in the cityë of Dauid, a sauioure whiche is Christe the Lorde.

12 And take this for a sygne: ye shall fynde the chylde swadled and layed in a maunger.

13 And strayght waye there was with the aungel a multitude of heauenly souldiours, laudinge God and sayinge:

14 Glory to God on hye, and peace on the earth: and vnto men reioysynge.

15 And it fortuned, assone as the aungels were gone away from them into heauen, the shepherdes sayed one to another: let vs go euen vnto Bethleem & se this thing that is happened which the Lorde hath shewed vnto vs.

16 And they came with haste: and founde Mary and Ioseph and the babe layed in a maunger.

17 And when they had sene it, they published abroade the sayinge which was tolde them of that chylde.

18 And all that heard it, wondered at those thinges whiche were tolde them of the shepherdes.

19 But Mary kept all those sayinges, and pondered them in her herte.

20 And the shepherdes retourned, praisynge and lauding God for all that they had hearde and sene, euen as it was tolde vnto them.

21 And when the eyght daye was come, that the chylde shoulde be circuncysed, his name was called Iesus, which was named of the aungell before he was conceyued in the wombe.

22 And when the tyme of their puryfycacion (after the lawe of Moyses) was come, they brought him to Ierusalem, to presente hym to the Lorde

23 (as it is wryttem in the lawe of the Lorde: euerye male that fyrst openeth the mattrix, shall be called holye to the Lord)

24 and to offer (as it is sayde in the lawe of the Lorde) a payre of turtel doues or two yonge pygyons.

25 And beholde ther was a man in Hierusalem whose name was Symeon. And the same man was iuste and feared God, and longed for the consolacion of Israel and the holye ghost was in him.

26 And an aunswere was geuen him of the holye ghost, that he shoulde not se death, before he had sene the Lordes Christe.

27 And he came by inspiration into the tempell. And when the father and mother broughte in the childe Iesus, to do for him after the custome of the lawe,

28 then toke he him vp in hys armes and sayed.

29 Lorde. Nowe lettest thou thy seruaunt departe in peace, accordinge to thy promes.

30 For mine eyes haue sene the sauiour sent from the.

31 Which thou hast prepare before the face of all people.

32 A lyght to lighten the

gentils and the glorye of thy people Israel.

33 And his father and mother meruayled at those thinges which were spoken of him.

34 And Symon blessed them, & sayd vnto Mary his mother: beholde, this chylde shalbe the fal and resurrection of manye in Israel, & sygne which shalbe spoken againste.

35 And moreouer the swearde shall pearce thy soule, that the thoughtes of manye hertes maye be opened.

36 And ther was a prophetesse, one Anna the doughter of Phanuell of the trybe of Aser which was of a great age, and had liued with her housbande .vij. yeares from her virginitie.

37 And she had bene a weddowe aboute .iiij. score and .iiij. yeares, which went neuer out of the temple, but serued God with fastinge and prayer night & daye.

38 And the same came forth that same houre and praysed the Lorde and spake of him to all that loked for redempcion in Ierusalem.

39 And assone as they had perfourmed al thynges accordynge to the lawe of the Lorde they retourned into Galyle to their owne cytye Nazareth.

40 And the chylde grewe & waxed stronge in spyryte, and was fylled wyth wisdome, & the grace of God was with him.

41 And his father and mother went to Hierusalem euerye yeare at the feaste of easter.

42 And when he was .xij. yeare olde, they went vp to Ierusalem after the custome of the feaste.

43 And when they had fulfilled the dayes, as they returned home, the chylde Iesus bode styll in Ierusalem vnknowinge to his father and mother.

44 For they supposed he had bene in the company, and therfore came a dayes iorneye and sought him amonge their kinsfolke and acquaintaunce.

45 And when thei founde him not, they went backe againe to Ierusalem, & sought hym.

46 And it fortuned after thre dayes that they founde him in the tempell, syttynge in the middes of the doctours, both hearynge them and posynge them.

47 And all that hearde him, meruaylled at his wit and aunswers.

48 And when they sawe him, they were astonyed. And his mother sayde vnto him: sonne, why hast thou thus dealt with vs? Beholde thy father and I haue sought the, sorowing.

49 And he sayed vnto them: howe is it that ye sought me? Wyst ye not that I must go about my fathers busynes?

50 And they vnderstode not the sayinge that he spake to them.

51 And he went with them, and came to Nazareth, and was obedient to them: But his mother kepte al these sayinges in her herte.

52 And Iesus increased in wisdome and age, and in fauoure with God and man.

## CHAPTER 3

And in þe .xv. yeare of the raygne of Tiberius the Emperoure, Pontius Pilate beiynge lieftenaunte of Iury, and Herode beyinge Tethrarch of Galyle, and hys brother Philippe Tethrarchin Iturea & in the region of Traconytes, and Lysanyas the Tetrarche of Abilene,

2 when Anna and Cayphas were the hye pryestes: the word of God came vuto Iohn the sonne of Zacharias in the wildernes.

3 And he came into all the costes about Iordan, preaching the baptisme of repentaunce for the remissyon of synnes,

4 as it is written in the boke of þe sayinges of Esaias the prophete which sayeth. The voyce of a cryer in wildernes, prepare the waye of the Lorde, make hys pathes strayght.

5 Euerye valley shall be fylled, and euerye mountayne and hyll shall be brought lowe. And croked thinges shalbe made straight: and the rough wayes shalbe made smoth:

6 and all fleshe shall se the sauioure sent of God.

7 Then sayde he to the people that were come to be baptysed of him. O generacion of vipers, who hath taught you to flye from the wrath to come?

8 Bringe forth due frutes of repentaunce, and begin not to saye in your selues, we haue Abraham to our father: For I say vnto you God is able of these stones to rayse vp chyldren vnto Abraham.

9 Now also is the axe lyed vnto þe rote of the trees, so that euery tree which bringeth not forth good frute shall be hewen doune, and cast into the fyre.

10 And the people axed him sayinge: What shall we do then?

11 He aunswered and sayd vnto theim: He that hath two cotes, let him parte with him that hath none, & he that hath meate let him do lykewyse.

12 Then came there publicans to be baptysed, and sayde vnto hym: Maister, what shall we do?

13 And he sayde vnto them: require nomore then that which is appointed vnto you.

14 The souldioures lykewyse demaunded of him saiynge: and what shall we do? And he sayde to them: Do violence to no man: neither trouble any man wrongfullye: but be content with your wages.

15 As the people were in a doubte, and all men disputed in their hertes of Iohn, whither he were very Christ,

16 Iohn aunswered and sayde to them all: I baptyse you with water, but a stronger then I cometh after me, whose shoe latchet I am not worthy to vnlouse: he wyll baptyse you with the holye ghost, and with fyre.

17 Which hath his fanne in his hande, and wyll purge his floore, and wyll gather the corne into his barne, but þe chaffe wil he burne with fyre þt neuer shalbe quenched.

18 And many other thinges in his exhortacion preached he vnto the people.

19 Then Herode the Tetrarche (when he was rebuked of him for Herodias his brothers wyfe and for al the euyls, which Herode had done)

20 added this aboue al, and laied Ihon in prison.

21 And it fortuned as all the people receyued baptisme (And when Iesus was baptised and did praye) that heauen was opened,

22 and the holye ghost came doune in a bodelye shape lyke a done vpon him, and a voyce came from heauen saiynge: thou art my deare sonne, in the do I delyte.

23 And Iesus him selfe was entring the thirthy yeare of his age as men supposed hym to be the sonne of Ioseph. which was the sonne of Hely,

24 which was the sonne of Mathat, which was the sonne of Leui, which was the sonne of Melchi. which was the sonne of Ianna, which was the sonne of Ioseph,

25 which was the sonne of Mattathias, which was the sonne of Amos, which was the sonne of Nasum, which was the sonne of Esli, which was the sonne of Nagge,

26 which was the sonne of Maath, which was the sonne of Matathias, which was the sonne of Semei, which was the sonne of Iosech, which was the sonne of Iuda,

27 which was the sonne of Ioanna, which was the sonne of Rhesia, which was the sonne of Zorobabel, which was the sonne of Salathiel, which was the sonne of Neri,

28 which was the sonne of Melchi, which was the sonne of Addi, which was the sonne of Cosan, which was the sonne of Helmadam, which was the sonne of Hir,

29 which was the sonne of Ieso, which was the sonne of Heliasar, which was the sonne of Ioram, which was the sonne of Mattha, which was the sonne of Leuy,

30 which was the sonne of Simeon, which was the sonne of Iuda, which was the sonne of Ioseph, which was the sonne of Ionam, which was the sonne of Heliachim,

31 which was the sonne of Melca, which was the sonne of Menam, which was the sonne of Mathathan, which was the sonne of Nathan, which was the sonne of Dauid,

32 which was the sonne of Iesse, which was the sonne of Obed, which was the sonne of Boos, which was the sonne of Salmon, which was the sonne of Naason,

33 which was the sonne of Aminadab, which was the sonne of Aram, which was the sonne of Esrom, which was the sonne of Phares, which was the sonne of Iuda,

34 which was the sonne of Iacob, which was the sonne of Isaac, which was the sonne of Abraham, which was the sonne of Tharra, which was the sonne of Nachor,

35 which was the sonne of Saruch, which was the sonne of Ragan, which was the sonne of Phalec, which was the sonne of Heber, which was the sonne of Sala,

36 which was the sonne of Cainan, which was the sonne of Arphaxat, which was the sonne of Sem, which was the sonne of Noe, which was the sonne of Lameth,

37 which was the sonne of Mathusalem, which was the sonne of Enoch, which was the sonne of Iareth, which was the sonne of Malalehel, which was the sonne of Cainan,

38 which was the sonne of Enos, which was the sonne of Seth, which was the sonne of Adam, which was the sonne of God,

# CHAPTER 4

IESUS then full of the holye ghost returned from Iordan & was caried of the spyrite into wildernes,

2 and was .xl. dayes tempted of the deuil. And in those dayes eate he nothinge. And when they were ended he afterwarde hungred.

3 And the deuyll sayde vnto him: If thou be the sonne of God, commaunde this stone that it be bread.

4 And Iesus aunswered hym saiynge: It is written, man shall not lyue by bread onlye, but of euerye worde of God.

5 And þe deuyl toke him vp into an hye mountayne, and shewed him all the kyngdomes of the worlde euen in the twincklinge of an eye.

6 And the deuyl sayde vnto hym: al this power wyll I geue the euerye whit and the glorye of them for that is delyuered to me & to whomsoeuer I wyl, I geue it:

7 If thou therfore wilt worship me, they shalbe al thine.

8 Iesus aunswered him and sayde. Hence from me Sathan. For it is written: Thou shall honoure the Lord thy God and him onlye serue.

9 And he caryed hym to Ierusalem, and set him on a

pynacle of the tempel, and sayde vnto him. If thou be the sonne of God caste thy selfe doune from hence:

10 For it is wrytten. He shall geue his aungels charge ouer the to kepe the

11 and wyth their handes they shal sley the vp that thou dashe not thy fote agaynst a stone.

12 Iesus aunswered and sayde to hym, it is sayde: Thou shalt not tempt the Lorde thy God.

13 Assone as the deuyll had ended all his temptacion, he departed from him for a season.

14 And Iesus retourned by the power of the spyryte into Galile, and there went a fame of hym throughout all the regyon rounde about.

15 And he taught in their synagoges, and was commended of all men.

16 And he came to Nazareth wher he was nourished: and as his custome was, went into the synagoge on the. Sabboth dayes, & stode vp to reade.

17 And there was delyuered vnto hym the boke of the prophete Esayas. And when he had opened the boke, he founde the place wher it was written:

18 The spyryte of the Lorde vpon me, because he hath anoynted me: to preache the gospell to the poore he hath sent me, and to heale the broken herted, to preache deliueraunce to the captiue, and syght to the blynde, and frely to set at lyberte them that are brused,

19 and to preache the acceptable yeare of the Lorde.

20 And he closed the boke, and gaue it againe to the mynister, and sate doune. And the eyes of all that were in the synagoge were fastened on him.

21 And he began to saye vnto them. This daye is this scripture fulfylled in youre eares.

22 And all bare him witnes, and wondred at the gracious wordes which proceded out of his mouthe, and saide: Is not this Iosephs sonne?

23 And he sayde vnto them: Ye maye very wel saye vnto me these prouerbe: Phisicon, heale thy selfe. Whatsoeuer we haue hearde done in Capernaum, do the same here lykewyse in thine owne countrye.

24 And he sayed: verely I saye vnto you. No prophete is accepted in his owne countrye.

25 But I tell you of a truthe, manye wydowes were in Israel in þe dayes of Helias, when heauen was shut thre yeares & syxe moneths when great fanishment was through out all the lande,

26 and vnto none of them was Helias sent, saue vnto Sarepta besydes Sydon vnto a woman that was a wydowe.

27 And manye lepers were in Israel in the tyme of Helyseus the prophet, and yet none of them was healed, sauinge Naman of Siria.

28 And as many as were in þe synagoge when they hearde that, were fylled with wrath:

29 and rose vp, and thrust him out of the citye, & ledde him euen vnto the edge of the hyll, where on their cytye was bult, to cast hym doune hedlynge.

30 But he wente his way euen through þe myddes of them.

31 And came into Capernaum a cytye of Galyle, and there taught them on the saboth dayes.

32 And they were astonyed at his doctryne, for his preachinge was wyth power.

33 And in the synagoge ther was a man which had a spyryte of an vncleane deuyll, and cried with a loude voyce

34 saiyng: let me alone, what hast thou to do with vs, thou Iesus of Nazareth? Art thou come to destroye? I knowe the what thou arte, euen the holye of God.

35 And Iesus rebuked him saiynge: holde thy peace & come out of hym. And the deuyll throwe hym in the myddes of them and came out of hym and hurte hym not.

36 And feare come on them all and they spake amonge them selues saiynge what maner of thinge is this? For with authoryte and power he commaundeth the foule spirites, and they come out.

37 And the fame of him spread abroade through out all places of the country rounde aboute.

38 And he arose vp & came out of the synagoge, and entred into Simons house. And Simons mother in lawe was taken with a great feuer and they made intercessyon to hym for her.

39 And he stode ouer her, and rebuked the feuer, and it left her. And immediatly she arose and mynystred vnto them.

40 When the sunne was doune, all they that had sicke, taken with diuerse dyseases, brought them vnto hym, and he layde hys handes on euery one of them, and healed them.

41 And deuyls also came oute of many of them crynge and saiyng: thou arte Christ þe sonne of God. And he rebuked them, and suffered them not to speake: for they knewe that he was Christe.

42 Assone as it was daye, he departed & went awaye into a desert place, & the people sought hym and came to hym, and kept hym that he shoulde not departe from them.

43 And he sayed vnto them: I muste to other cityes also preache the kyngdome of God: For therfore am I sent.

44 And he preached in the synagoges of Galyle.

# CHAPTER 5

IT came to passe as the people preased vpon him to heare the worde of God, that he stode by

# LUKE

the lake of Genezareth:

2 and sawe two shyppes stande by the lake syde, but the fisher men were gone out of them, and were washynge their nettes.

3 And he entred into one of the shyppes, which pertayned to Symon, and prayed him, that he woulde thruste out a lytle from the lande. And he sat doune and taught the people out of the shyppe.

4 When he had left speakynge, he sayed vnto Simon: launce out into the depe, and let slip your nettes to make a draught.

5 And Simon aunswered and sayed vnto hym: Mayster, we haue laboured all nyght, and haue taken nothynge. Neuerthelater at thy worde I wyll lose forth the net.

6 And when they had so done, they enclosed a greate multytude of fyshes. And their net brake:

7 but they made sygnes to their fellowes which were in the other shyp that they shoulde come and helpe them. And they came and fylled both the shyppes that they sonke againe.

8 When Simon Peter sawe that, he fell doune at Iesus knees saiynge: Lorde go

9 from me for I am a synfull man. For he was vtterlye astonyed and all that were with hym at the draughte of fyshe, which they toke:

10 and so was Iames and Iohn the sonnes of Zebede, which were parteners with Symon. And Iesus sayed vnto Simon: feare not, from hence forth thou shalt catche men.

11 And they brought the shyppes to lande, and forsoke all and folowed hym.

12 And it fortuned as he was in a certayne citye: beholde, there was a man full of leprosye: and when he had spyed Iesus, he fell on his face, and besought him saiynge: Lorde, if thou wylt thou canst make me cleane.

13 And he stretthed forth the hande and touched him saiynge: I wyl, be thou cleane. And immediatlye the leprosye departed from him.

14 And he warned hym that he shoulde tell no man but that he should go and shewe him selfe to the pryeste and offer for his clensyng, accordinge as Moyses commaundement was, for a witnes vnto them.

15 But so much the more went there a fame abroad of him, & much people came together to heare and to be healed of him, of their infirmyties.

16 And he kepte him selfe aparte in the wyldernesse, and gaue him selfe to prayer.

17 And it happened on a certayne daye, that he taught, and there sate the phariseis and the doctours of lawe, which were come out of all the tounes of Galyle, Iurye, and Hierusalem. And the power of the Lorde was to heale them.

18 And beholde men brought a man liynge in his bedde which was taken with a palsey: & sought meanes to brynge him in, and to laye him before him.

19 And when they could not finde by what way they might bring him in, because of the prease, they went vp on the toppe of þe house, and let him doune thorowe the tyling, bedde & all in the middest before Iesus.

20 When he sawe their faith, he sayed to him: man, thy sinnes are forgeuen the.

21 And the scribes and pharyseis began to thinke saiynge: What felowe is this which speaketh blasphemy? who can forgeue synnes but God onlye?

22 When Iesus perceiued their thoughtes, he aunswered and sayd vnto them: What thinke ye in your hertes?

23 Whether is it easyer to say, thy synnes are forgeuen the, or to saye: ryse & walke?

24 But that ye may knowe that the sonne of man hath power to forgeue sinnes on earth, he said to the sycke of the paulsye, I say to the, aryse, take vp thy bed & go home to thy house.

25 And immediatlye he rose vp before them, and toke vp his bed wheron he laye, and departed to his owne house praysyng God.

26 And they were all amased, and they lauded God & were filled with fear saiyng: We haue sene straung thinges to daye.

27 And after that he wente forth and sawe a Publican named Leui, sittinge at the receite of custome and saide vnto him: folowe me.

28 And he left al, rose vp and folowed him.

29 And the same Leui made him a great feaste at home in his owne house. And ther was a great companye of publicans and of other that sate at meat with him.

30 And the scribes and pharyseis murmured againste his disciples saiynge: Why eate ye, and drinke ye with publicans and sinners?

31 Iesus aunswered and sayde vnto them: They that are whole nede not of the phisician: but thei that are sicke.

32 I am not come to cal the rightuous, but synners to repentaunce.

33 Then they sayed vnto him: Why do the disciples of Ihon faste often and praye, and the disciples of the phariseis also: and thyne eate and drinke?

34 And he sayed vnto them: Can ye make the children of the weddinge faste, as longe as the bridgrome is present with them?

35 The dayes will come, when the bridgrome shall be taken awaye from them: Then shall they faste in those dayes.

36 Then spake he vnto them

in a symylytude. No man putteth a pece of a newe garmente, into an olde vesture: for if he do, then breaketh he the newe and the pece that was taken out of the newe agreeth not with the olde.

37 Also no man poureth newe wine into olde vessels. For if he do, the newe wyne breaketh the vessels, and runneth out it selfe, and the vessels perishe:

38 But newe wyne muste be poured into newe vessels, and both are preserued.

39 Also no man that drinketh olde wyne, strayght waye can awaye with newe, for he sayeth the olde is pleasaunter.

## CHAPTER 6

It happened on an after saboth, that he wente through the corne fyelde, and that his disciples plucked the eares of corne and eate, and rubbed them in their handes.

2 And certayne of the pharyseis sayde vnto them: Why do ye that whiche is not lawfull to do on the saboth dayes?

3 And Iesus aunswered them and sayde: Haue ye not read what Dauid did when he him selfe was an hongred, and they which were with hym:

4 how he wente into the house of God and toke and eate the loues of halowed breade, & gaue also to them which were with him, which was not lawfull to eate, but for the priestes onlye.

5 And he sayed vnto them: The sonne of man is Lorde of the saboth daye.

6 And it fortuned in another saboth also, that he entred into the synagoge and taught. And there was a man whose righthande was dried vp.

7 And the scrybes and pharyseis watched him, to see whether he would heale on the saboth daye, that they myght fynde an accusacion against him.

8 But he knewe their thoughtes, and sayde to the man which had the withered hande: Rise vp and stande forth in the middes. And he arose and stepped forth.

9 Then sayde Iesus vnto them: I wyll axe you a question: Whither is it lawfull on the saboth dayes to do good or to do euyl? to saue lyfe, or for to destroye it?

10 And he behelde them al in compasse, and sayde vnto the manye: Stretche forth thy hande. And he dyd so: & his hande was restored, and made as whole as the other.

11 And thei were fylled full of madnes, and communed one with another, what they might do to Iesus.

12 And it furtuned in those dayes that he went out into a mountaine for to praye, and contynued all night in prayer to God.

13 And assone as it was daye, he called his disciples, and of them he chose .xij. whiche also he called Apostles:

14 Symon whom he named Peter, & Andrewe his brother, Iames and Ihon, Philippe and Bartelmewe,

15 Mathewe and Thomas, Iames the sonne of Alpheus, and Simon called Zelotes,

16 and Iudas Iames sonne, and Iudas Iscarioth which same was the traytour.

17 And he came doune with them & stode in the playne fyelde with the companye of hys discyples, and a great multytude of people out of all partyes of Iurye and Ierusalem & from the sea coste of Tyre and Sydon, which came to heare hym, and to be healed of their disceases,

18 and they also that were vexed with foule spyrytes, and they were healed.

19 And all the people preased to touche hym, for there wente vertue out of hym, and healed them all.

20 And he lyfte vp his eye vpon the disciples, and sayde: Blessed be ye pore: for yours is the kyngdome of God.

21 Blessed are ye that honger nowe: for ye shalbe satisfyed. Blessed are ye that wepe nowe for ye shall laughe.

22 Blessed are ye when men hate you, and thruste you out of their companye, and rayle, & abhorre youre name as an euill thinge, for the sonne of mans sake.

23 Reioyse then, and be glad: for behold your reward is great in heauen. After this maner their father entreated the prophetes.

24 But wo be to you that are riche: for ye haue therin your consolacion.

25 Wo be to you that are full: for ye shal honger. Wo be to you that nowe laugh: for ye shall wayle and wepe.

26 Wo be to you when all men prayse you: for so dyd their fathers to the false prophetes.

27 But I say vnto you which heare: loue your enemyes. Do good to them which hate you.

28 Blesse them that courrsse you. And praye for them which wrongfully trouble you.

29 And vnto hym that smiteth the on the one cheke, offer also the other. And him that taketh awaye thy gonne, forbyd not to take thy cote also.

30 Giue euerye man that axeth of the. And of hym that taketh awaye thy goodes, axe them not again.

31 And as ye woulde that men should do to you: so do ye to them likewyse.

32 Yf ye loue them which loue you, what thanke are ye worthy of? For the verye synners loue their louers.

33 And if ye do for them which do for you, what thanke are ye worthye of? For the verye synners do euen the same.

34 If ye lende to them of whom ye hope to receiue, what

thanke shall ye haue: for the very synners lende to synners to receiue much againe.

35 Wherfore, loue ye your enemyes, do good and lende, lokinge for nothynge againe, and your rewarde shall be greate, and ye shalbe the children of the hyest for he is kinde vnto the vnkinde and to the euyll.

36 Be ye therfore mercifull, as your father is mercyfull.

37 Iudge not and ye shall not be iudged. Condemne not, and ye shall not be condemned. Forgeue you, ye shalbe forgeuen.

38 Geue, and it shalbe geuen vnto you: good measure, pressed doune, shaken together and runninge ouer, shal men geue vnto your bosomes. For with what measure ye mete with the same shall men mete to you agayne.

39 And he putteth forth a symylytude vnto them: Can the blinde leade the blinde? Do they not both then fall into the dyche?

40 The discyple is not aboue his maister. Euery man shalbe perfecte if he be as his mayster is.

41 Why seist thou a moote in thy brothers eye, and consyderest not the beame that is in thyne owne eye?

42 Either howe canst thou saye to thy brother? Brother, let me pul out the moote that is thine eye: When thou perceyuest not the beame that is in thine owne eye? Ypocryte, cast out the beame that is in thine owne eye fyrst, and then shalt thou se perfectlye to pul out the mote out of thy brothers eye.

43 It is not a good tre that bryngeth forth euyll frute: neither is that au euil tre that bringeth forth good frute.

44 For euery tre is knowen by his fruite. Neyther of thornes gather men fygges, nor of bushes gather they grapes.

45 A good man out of the good treasure of his hert bringeth forth that which is good. And an euil man out of the euyll treasure of his herte bringeth forth that which is euyl. For of the aboundaunce of the herte, his mouth speaketh.

46 Why call ye me Maister Maister, and do not as I byd you?

47 whosoeuer commeth to me, and heareth my saiynges, and doth the same, I wyll shewe you to whom he is lyke.

48 He is lyke a man which builde an house and digged depe and layde the foundacion on a rocke. When the waters arose, the floud bet vpon that house, and coulde not moue it for it was grounded vpon a rocke.

49 But he that heareth and doeth not, is lyke a man that without foundacion bylt an house vpon the earth, against which the floude dyd beate and it fell by and by, and the fall of that house was greate.

# CHAPTER 7

WHEN he had ended al his saynges in the audience of þe people, he entred into Capernaum.

2 And a certayne Centuryons seruaunt was sycke and redye to dye, whom he made much of.

3 And when he heard of Iesu, he sent vnto hym the elders of the Iewes, beseechinge hym that he woulde come & heale his seruaunte.

4 And they came to Iesus and besought hym instauntlye saiynge: He is worthye that thou shouldest do this for hym.

5 For he loueth oure nacion, and hath bylt vs a synagoge.

6 And Iesus went with them. And when he was not farre from the house the Centurion sent frendes to him saiynge vnto him: Lorde trouble not thy selfe, for I am not worthy that thou shouldest enter vnder my roffe.

7 Wherfore I thought not my selfe worthy to come vnto the: but saye the worde and my seruaunte shalbe whole.

8 For I lykewise am a man vnder power, and haue vnder me souldiers, and I saye vnto one, go: and he goeth. And to an other, come: and he cometh. And to my seruaunte, do this: and he doeth it.

9 When Iesus harde this, he maruailed at him, & tourned him about & saide to þe people that folowed hym: I say vnto you, I haue not founde so greate fayth, no, not in Israel.

10 And they that were sent, turned backe home againe, and founde the seruaunte that was sycke, whole.

11 And it fortnned after that, that he wente into a cytye called Naim, and manye of hys disciples went with him and much people.

12 When he came nye to the gate of the cytye, beholde there was a dead man caryed out which was the onlye sonne of his mother and she was a wydowe, and much people of the cytye was with her.

13 And when the Lorde sawe her, he had compassyon on her and saide vnto her, wepe not.

14 And he went and touched the coffin, and they that bare hym, stode styll. And he sayde: Yonge man, I say vnto the, aryse.

15 And the dead sate vp, and began to speake. And he delyuered him to his mother.

16 And there came a feare on them all. And they glorifyed God saiynge: a greate Prophete is rysen among vs, and God hath visyted his people.

17 And this rumore of hym wente forth throughout all Iurye, and thoroweout all the regions which lye rounde about.

18 And the discyples of Ihon shewed hym of all these thinges.

19 And Ihon called vnto him

two of his discyples, and sente them to Iesus saiynge: Arte thou he that shall come? or shall we loke for another?

20 When the men were come vnto him they sayde: Ihon Baptiste sent vs vnto the saiynge. Art thou he that shall come, or shall we wayte for an other?

21 And at that same tyme he cured manye of their infyrmytyes and plages and of euyll spirites, and vnto manye that were blinde he gaue syght.

22 And Iesus aunswered and saide vnto them: Go your wayes and shewe Ihon what thinges ye haue seane and hearde: howe that the blynd se, the halt go, the lepers are clensed, the deafe heare, the dead aryse, to the poore is glad tydinges preached,

23 and happye is he that is not offended by me.

24 When the messengers of Ihon were departed, he began to speake vnto the people of Ihon. What went ye out into the wildernes for to se? Went ye to se a rede shaken with the winde?

25 But what went ye out for to se? a man clothed in softe raiment? Beholde they which are gorgeouslye apparilled, and lyue delicately are in kinges courtes.

26 But what went ye forth to se? a Prophete, yea I saye vnto you, and more then a prophete.

27 This is he of whom it is written: Behold I sende my messenger before thy face, to prepare thy waye before the

28 For I saye vnto you: a greater Prophete then Ihon, amonge womens children is ther none. Neuerthelesse one that is lesse in the kingdome of God, is greater then he.

29 And all the people that hearde and the publicans iustifyed God, and were baptysed with the baptime of Ihon.

30 But the Phariseis and scribes despised the counsel of God againste them selues, and were not baptysed of him.

31 And the Lorde sayed: Wherunto shall I lyken the men of this generacion, and what thinge are they?

32 They are lyke vnto chyldrin syttyng in the marcked place, & cryenge one to an other, and saiynge: We haue pyped vnto you and ye haue not daunsed: we mourned to you, & ye haue not wept.

33 For Ihon Baptyste came, neyther eatinge breade nor drinckinge wyne, and ye saye: he hath the deuyll.

34 The sonne of man is come and eateth and drincked, and ye saye: beholde a man which is a glotten, and a drincker of wine, a frende of publicans and synners.

35 Yet is wysdome iustyfyed of all her chyldren.

36 And one of the pharyseis desyred hym that he wolde eate with him. And he wente into the pharyseis house and sate doune to meate.

37 And beholde a woman in that citye which was a synner, assone as she knewe that Iesus sate at mete in the phariseis house, she brought an alabaster boxe of ointment,

38 and she stode at his fete behinde him wepinge, and began to washe his fete with teares, and dyd wype them wyth the heares of her head, and kyshed his fete, and annoynted them with oyntment.

39 When the pharysey which bade him, sawe that he speake within him selfe saiyng. If this man were a Prophete, he wolde surely haue knowen who and what maner woman this is which toucheth him, for she is a synner.

40 And Iesus aunswered and sayde vnto him: Simon I haue some what to saye vnto the. And he sayed: Maister saye on.

41 There was a certayne lender, which had two detters, the one ought fyue hundred pence: and the other fyfty.

42 When they had nothinge to paye, he forgaue them both. Which of them tell me, wyll loue him most.

43 Simon aunswered and saide: I suppose, that he to whom he forgaue moste. And he sayde vnto hym: Thou haste truly iudged.

44 And he turned to the woman, and sayde vnto Symon: Seist thou this woman? I entred into thy house, and thou gauest me no water to my fete, but she hath washed my fete with teares and wyped them wyth the heyres of her head.

45 Thou gauest me no kisse: but she, sence the tyme I came in, hath not ceased to kisse my fete.

46 Myne head with oyle thou dyddest not anoynte, but she hath annointed my fete with oyntmente.

47 Wherfore I saye vnto the manye synnes are forgeuen her, for she loued much. To whom lesse is forgeuen, the same doth lesse loue.

48 And he sayde vnto her, thy synnes are forgeuen the.

49 And they that sate at meate with him, began to saye with in them selues: Who is this which forgeueth synnes also?

50 And he sayde to the woman. Thy fayth hath saued the. Go in peace.

# CHAPTER 8

AND it fortuned after that, that he him selfe went thorowe out cyties and tounes preachinge and shewinge the kingdome of God, and the .xij. with hym.

2 And also certaine women, which were healed of euyll spretes and infyrmytyes: Marye called Magdalene, out of whom went seuen deuyls,

3 and Ioanna the wyfe of Chusa Herodes stewarde, and Susanna, and manye other:

which ministred to them of their substaunce.

4 When much people were gathered together, and were come to hym out of all cytyes, he spake by a symilitude.

5 A sower went out to sowe his sede: and as he sowed, some fel by the waye syde: and it was troden vnder fete, and the foules of the ayre deuoured it vp.

6 And some fell on the stone, and assone as it was spronge vp, it withered awaye because it lacked moistnes.

7 And some fell amonge thornes, and the thornes spronge vp with it, and choked it.

8 And some fell on good grounde and spronge vp and bare fruite an hundred folde. And as he sayed these thinges he cryed: He that hath eares to heare, let hym heare.

9 And his discyples axed him saiynge: what maner of symylytude is this?

10 And he sayed vnto you is it geuen to knowe the secretes of the kingdome of God: but to other in symylytudes, that when they se, they shoulde not vnderstande.

11 The symylytude is this. The sede is the worde of God.

12 Those that are besyde the waye, are they that heare, and afterwarde commeth the deuyll and taketh awaye the worde out of their hertes leste they should beleue & be saued.

13 Thei on þe stones, are thei which when they heare, receiue the worde with ioye. But these haue no rotes, whiche for a whyle beleue, & in tyme of temptacion go awaye.

14 And that whiche fell amonge thornes, are thei which heare, and go forth, and are choked with cares and with ryches, and voluptuouse liuinge, and bringe forth no fruite.

15 That in the good grounde, are they whyche with a good and pure herte, heare the worde and kepe it, and brynge forth fruyte wyth pacience.

16 No man lighteth a candell, and couereth it vnder a vessell, neither putteth it vnder a table, but setteth it on a candelstike, that thei that enter in, maye se the lyghte.

17 Nothinge in secrete, that shall not come abrode: Neyther any thynge hyd that shall not be knowen, and come to light.

18 Take hede therfore how ye heare. For who soeuer hath, to hym shall be geuen: And whosoeuer hath not, from hym shal be taken, euen that same which he supposeth that he hath.

19 Then came to hym his mother and his brethren and coulde not come at hym for preace.

20 And they tolde him sayinge: Thy mother and thy brethren stande without, and woulde se the.

21 He aunswered and sayde vnto them: my mother and my brethren are these which heare the worde of God and do it.

22 And it chaunsed on a certaine daye that he went into a shippe, and his disciples also, and he sayed vnto them: Let vs go ouer to the other syde of the lake. And they lanched forth.

23 And as they sayled he fell on slepe, and there arose a storme of winde in the lake, and they were fylled with water, and were in ieopardy.

24 And they went to him and awoke him saiyng: Maister Maister we are loste. Then he rose & rebuked the winde & the tempeste of the water, & they ceased, & it wexed calme.

25 And he sayed vnto them: Wher is your faythe? They feared and woundered saiynge one to another, what felowe is this: for he commaundeth both þe windes & water, & they obey him?

26 And they sayled vnto the region of the Gaderenites, which is ouer against Galile.

27 And as he went out to lande, there mete him a certaine man out of the citie, which had a deuil long time, & ware no clothes, neither abode in anye house: but amonge graues.

28 When he sawe Iesus he cried and fel doune before him, and with a loud voice saied: What haue I to do with the Iesus the sonne of the God moste hiest? I besech the tormente me not.

29 Then he commaunded the foule sprete to come out of the man. For oft times he caughte him, and he was bounde with chaines, and kept with fetters, and he brake the bondes, and was caried of and the fende, into wildernes.

30 And Iesus axed him saiynge: what is thy name? And he saied Legion, because many deuils were entred into him.

31 And they besought him, that he woulde not commaunde them to go out into the depe.

32 And there was therby an hearde of manie swine, feadinge on an hyl: and they besought him, that he woulde suffer them to enter into them. And he suffred.

33 Then wente the deuyls out of the man, and entred into the swine: and the hearde toke their course, and ranne headlinge into the lake, and were choked.

34 When the heardmen sawe what had chaunsed, they fled and tolde it in the cytye, and in the villages.

35 And they came out to se what was done: and came to Iesus, and founde the man out of whom the deuyls were departed syttynge at the fete of Iesus, clothed and in his ryghte mynde, and they were afrayed.

36 They also which sawe it tolde them by what meanes he that was possessed of the deuyll, was healed.

37 And all the whole

multitude of the Gaderenites, besought hym that he woulde departe from them: for they were taken with greate feare. And he gate him into the shyppe, and retourned backe againe.

38 Then the man out of whom the deuils were departed, besought him that he myght be with him. But Iesus sent hym awaye saiynge.

39 Go home againe into thine owne house, and shewe what greate thinges God hath done to the. And he wente his waye, and preached thorow out all the cytye what great thinges Iesus hath done vnto him.

40 And it fortuned when Iesus was come againe that the people receiued him. For they all wayted for hym.

41 And beholde there came a man named Iairus (and he was a ruler of the synagoge) and he fell doune at Iesus fete, and besought hym that he woulde come into his house,

42 for he had but a doughter only vpon a twelwe yere of age, and she lay a diynge. As he wente the people thronged hym.

43 And a woman hauinge an yssue of bloude twelue yeares (whiche hath spent all her substaunce amonge phisycions, neyther coulde be holpen of anye)

44 came behinde him, and touched the heme of his garment and immediatlye her yssue of bloude staunched.

45 And Iesus sayde: Who is it that touched me? When euerye man denyed, Peter and they that were with him, saide: Mayster, the people thruste the and vexe the, and sayest thou who touched me?

46 And Iesus saide: Some bodye touched me. For I perceyue that vertue is gone out of me.

47 When the woman sawe that she was not hyd, she came trimblynge, and fell at his fete, and tolde hym before all the people for what cause she had touched him, and howe she was healed immediatlye.

48 And he sayde vnto her: Doughter be of good comfort. Thy faith hath made the whole, go in peace.

49 Whyle he yet spake, there came on from the rulers of the synagoges house, which said to hym thy doughter is dead, dysease not the maister.

50 When Iesus hearde that. He aunswered the father saiynge: Feare not beleue onelye, and she shalbe made whole.

51 And when he came to the house he suffered no man to go in with him, saue Peter, Iames, and Iohn, and the father and mother of the mayden.

52 Euerye bodye wepe and sorowed for her. And he sayd: Wepe not: for she is not dead but slepeth.

53 And they laughte hym to scorne. For they knewe that she was dead.

54 And he thruste them all out, and caught her by the hand, and cried saiynge: Mayde aryse.

55 And her spiryte came againe, and she arose straight waye. And he commaundeth to geue her meate.

56 And the father and the mother of her were astonied. But he warned theim that they shoulde tell no man, what was done.

# CHAPTER 9

THEN called he the .xij. together, and gaue them power, and authoryte ouer all Deuyls, and that they myght heale diseases.

2 And he sent them to preache the kyngdome of God, and to cure the sycke.

3 And he sayed to them: Take nothinge to sucker you by the waye neither staffe, nor scrype, neyther bread neyther money, neither haue .ij. cotes.

4 And whatsoeuer house ye enter into, there abyde and thence departe:

5 And whosoeuer wyll not receyue you, when ye go out of that cytye shake of the verye dust from your fete, for a testimonye against them.

6 And they went out, and went through the tounes, preachyng the gospell: and healynge euerye wher.

7 And Herode the Tetrarch hearde of al that was done by hym, and doubted, because that it was sayde of some, that Iohn was rysen agayne from death,

8 and of some that Helyas had appeared: and of other that one of the olde prophetes was rysen agayne.

9 And Herode sayde: Ihon haue I beheaded: who then is this of whom I hearde such thinges? And he desyred to se hym.

10 And the Apollels retourned, and told him what great thinges thei had done. And he toke them and wente a syde into a solitary place nye to a cytye called Bethsayda.

11 And the people knew of it, & folowed him. And he receiued them and spake vnto them of the kingdome of God, and healed them that had nede to be healed.

12 And when the daye began to weare away then came the twelue and sayde vnto hym, sende the people awaye, that they maye go into the tounes and villages rounde aboute and lodge, and get meate, for we are here in a solytarye place or wyldernes.

13 But he sayed vnto them: Geue ye them to eate. And they sayde: We haue nomore but fyue loues and two fyshes, excepte we should goo & by meate, for al this people.

14 And they were about a fyue thousande men. And he sayd to his discyples: Cause them to syt doune by fyftyes in a

company.

15 And they dyd so, and made them all syt doune.

16 And he toke the fiue loues and the two fishes, and loked vp to heauen: and blessed them, and brake, and gaue to the discyples, to set before the people.

17 And they eate, and were all satisfyed. And there was taken vp of that remained of them, twelue baskettes full of broken meate.

18 And it fortuned as he was alone praiynge: his disciples were with him, and he axed them saiyng: Who saye the people that I am?

19 They aunswered and sayd: Iohn Baptiste. Some saye, Helyas. And some saye, one of the olde prophetes is risen agayne.

20 He sayde vnto them: who saye ye that I am? Peter aunswered and sayde: thou arte the Christe of God.

21 And he warned and commaunded them that they shoulde tell no man that thynge

22 saiynge: that the sonne of man muste suffer manye thinges, and be reproued of the elders, and of the hye pryestes and scrybes and be slayne, & the thirde daye ryse agayne.

23 And he sayed to them all, if anye man wyll come after me, let him denye hym selfe, & take vp his crosse dayly, and folowe me.

24 Whosoeuer wyll saue his lyfe, shall lose it. And whosoeuer shall lose his lyfe for my sake, the same shall saue it.

25 For what auauntageth it a man to winne the whole worlde if he lose him selfe, or runne in damage of him selfe.

26 For whosoeuer is ashamed of me, and of my saiynges: of hym shall the sonne of man be ashamed, when he cometh in his owne glory, & the glory of his father, and of the holye aungels.

27 And I tell you of a surtye.

Ther be some of them that stande here, which shall not taste of death, tyll they se the kingdome of God.

28 And it folowed about an .viij. dayes after those saiynge: that he toke Peter, Iames, and Iohn, and went vp into a mountaine to pray.

29 And as he prayed, the fashion of his countenaunce was chaunged, and his garment was white and shone.

30 And beholde, two men talked with him, and they were Moyses & Helias,

31 which appeared gloriouslye, and spake of his departinge, which he shoulde ende at Ierusalem,

32 Peter & they that were with him were heauy with slepe. And when they awoke, they sawe his glory, and two men standinge wyth hym.

33 And it chaunsed as they departed from him, Peter sayd vnto him: Maister, it is good beynge here for vs. Let vs make thre tabernacles, one for the, and one for Moyses, & one for Helyas, & wist not what the sayde.

34 Whyle he thus spake, ther came a cloude & shadowed them, and they feared when they were come vnder the cloude.

35 And ther came a voice out of the cloude saiynge. This is my deare sonne, heare hym.

36 And assone as the voyce was paste Iesus was founde alone. And they kept it close and tolde no man in those dayes anye of those thinges which they had sene.

37 And it chaunched on the nexte dayes as they came doune from the hill, much peopel mete hym.

38 And beholde a man of the company cried out saiyng: Maister, I beseche þe beholde my sonne, for he is all that I haue:

39 and se, a sprete taketh him, and sodenlye he cryeth, and he teareth him that he fometh agayne, and wyth much payne departeth from hym, when he hath rent hym,

40 and I besought thy dyscyples to cast him out, and they coulde not.

41 Iesus aunswered and sayde: O generacyon without fayth, and croked, howe longe shall I be wyth you? & shall suffer you? Bringe thy sonne hyther.

42 As he yet was a commyng, the fende rent hym, and tare hym. And Iesus rebuked the vncleane spirite and healed the chyld, and delyuered hym to hys father.

43 And they were all amased at the myghtye power of God. Whyle they wondred euerye one at al thinges, whiche he dyd, he sayde vnto hys discyples:

44 Let these sayinges sinke doune into your eares. The tyme wil come, when the sonne of man shalbe delyuered into the handes of men.

45 But they wiste not what the worde meante, & it was hyd from them, that they vnderstode it not. And they feared to axe him of that sayinge.

46 Then there arose disputacyon amonge them: who should be the greatest.

47 When Iesus perceyued the thoughtes of theyr hertes, he toke a chylde, and set hym harde by hym,

48 & sayde vnto them. Whosoeuer receyueth thys chylde in my name receyueth me. And whosoeuer receyueth me, receyueth hym that sent me. For he that is least among you all the same shalbe great.

49 And Iohn aunswered and sayeth: Mayster we sawe one castyng out deuils in thy name, and we forbad hym, because he foloweth not with vs.

50 And Iesus sayed vnto hym: forbyd ye hym not. For he that is not agaynste vs: is with

vs.

51 And it folowed when the tyme was come, that he shoulde be receyued vp, then he set his face to go to Ierusalem,

52 and sent messengers before hym. And they went and entred into a citye of the Samaritans: to make readye for hym.

53 But they woulde not receyue hym, because hys face was as thoughe he woulde go to Ierusalem.

54 When his disciples Iames and Iohn sawe that, they sayde: Lorde, wilte thou that we commaunde that fyre come doune from heauen and consume them, euen as Helyas dyd?

55 Iesus turned aboute, and rebuked them sayinge: ye wote not what maner spirite ye are of.

56 The sonne of man is not come to destroye mennes lyues, but to saue them. And they wente to another toune.

57 And it chaunsed as he went in the waye a certayne man sayde vnto hym: I wyl folowe the, whyther soeuer thou go.

58 Iesus sayd vnto him: foxes haue holes, and byrddes of the ayre haue nestes, but the sonne of man hathe not wheron to laye hys heade.

59 And he sayed vnto another: folow me. And the same sayde: Lorde suffer me fyrste to go & burye my father,

60 Iesus sayde vnto him. Let the dead burye her dead: but go thou & preach the kyngedome of God.

61 And another sayed: I wyll folowe þe Lord but let me fyrste go byd them fare wel, which are at home at my house.

62 Iesus sayed vnto hym. No man that putteth hys hande to the plough, and loketh backe, is apte to the kyngdome of God.

## CHAPTER 10

AFTER these thynges, the Lord appoynted other seuentye also: and sent them, two & two before him into euery citie and place, whyther he hym selfe woulde come.

2 And he sayed vnto them, the haruest is great, but the laborers are fewe. Praye therfore the Lorde of the harueste, to sende forth laborers into hys haruest.

3 Go youre wayes: beholde, I sende you forth as lambes among wolues.

4 Beare no wallet neyther scryppe, nor shues, and salute no man by the way.

5 Into whatsoeuer house ye enter, fyrste saye: Peace be to thys house.

6 And yf the sonne of peace be there your peace shal reste vpon hym: yf not, it shal returne to you agayne.

7 And in the same house tary styll, eatynge and drinckynge suche as they haue. For the labourer is worthy of thys rewarde. Go not from house to house,

8 & into whatsoeuer citie ye enter, yf they receyue you, eate suche thynges as are set before you,

9 and heale the sycke that are there, and say vnto them: the kyngedome of God is come nye vnto you.

10 But into whatsoeuer citie ye shall enter, yf they receyue you not, go youre wayes out into the streates of the same and saye:

11 euen the very duste, whiche cleaueth on vs of your citie, we wype of agaynste you. Notwithstandynge marke this that the kyngdome of God was come nye vpon you.

12 Yea, and I saye to you, that it shalbe easier in that daye for Zodome then for that citie.

13 Wo be to the Chorazim, wo be to the Bethsaida. For yf the myracles had bene done in Tyre and Sidon, whiche haue bene done in you, they had a great whyle a gone repented, sittynge in hayre and ashes.

14 Neuerthelesse, it shalbe easyer for Tyre and Sidon at the iudgement, then for you.

15 And thou Capernaum, which arte exalted to heauen, shalt be thruste doune to hell.

16 He that heareth you, heareth me, and he that dispyseth you, despyseth me: & he that despyseth me, despiseth hym that sente me.

17 And the seuenty returned againe with ioye saiynge. Lorde euen the very deuyls are subdued to vs throughe thy name.

18 And he sayde vnto them: I sawe Sathan, as it had bene lyghtenynge, fall doune from heauen.

19 Beholde, I geue vnto you power to treade on serpentes & scorpions, & ouer all maner power of the enemye, and nothynge shall hurte you.

20 Neuerthelesse, in thys reioyse not that the spirites are vnder youre power: but reioyse because your names are written in heauen.

21 That same time reioysed Iesus in the spirite, and sayde: I confesse vnto the father, Lorde of heauen and earth, that thou haste hyd these thynges from the wyse and prudente, and hast opened them to the babes. Euen so father for so pleased it the.

22 All thynges are geuen me of my father. And no man knoweth who the sonne is, but the father: neyther who þe father is, saue the sonne, and he to whom the sonne wyll shewe hym.

23 And he turned to hys discyples, and sayed secretely: Happy are the eyes, which se that ye se.

24 For I tell you that many prophetes and kinges haue desyred to se those thinges which ye se, and haue not sene them, and to heare those thynges whiche ye heare and haue not hearde them.

25 And beholde a certaine lawyer stode vp, & tempted hym, saiynge: Mayster what shall I do to enherite eternall lyfe?

26 He sayed vnto him: What is writen in the law? how redest thou?

27 And he aunswered and sayde: Loue thy Lorde God with all thy hert, and with al thy soule, and with all thy mynde, and thy neyghboure as thy selfe.

28 And he sayed to hym: Thou haste aunswered ryght. Thys do and thou shalte lyue.

29 He wyllinge to iustifye hym self, sayde vnto Iesus. Who is then my neyghboure?

30 Iesus aunswered, and sayde: A certayne man descended from Ierusalem into Hierico, and fell into the handes of theues, which robbed hym of hys rayment, and wounded him, and departed leuynge him halfe dead.

31 And by chance there came a certayne priest that same waye, and when he sawe hym, he passed by.

32 And lykewyse a Leuite, when he was come nye to the place, went and loked on hym, and passed by.

33 Then a certayne Samaritayne, as he iournyed, came nye vnto hym, and when he sawe hym, he had compassion on hym,

34 and went to, and bounde vp hys woundes, & poureth in oyle and wyne, and put hym on hys owne beaste, and broughte him to a common ynne, and made prouysion for him.

35 And on þe morowe when he departed, he toke oute two pence, and gaue them to the hoste, and sayde vnto hym: Take cure of him, and whatsoeuer thou spendest more, when I come agayne, I wyll recompence the.

36 Whiche nowe of these thre thinkest thou, was neyghboure vnto him that fell into the theues handes?

37 And he sayd: he that shewed mercy on hym. Then sayd Iesus vnto hym: Go, & do thou lykewyse.

38 It fortuned as they went, that he entred into a certayne toune. And a certayne woman named Martha, receyued hym into her house.

39 And this woman had a syster called Marye whiche sate at Iesus fete, and hearde his preachynge.

40 And Martha was combred aboute muche seruynge, and stode and sayed: Mayster doest thou not care, that my syster hath lefte me to mynister alone? Byd her therfore, that she helpe me.

41 And Iesu aunswered & said vnto her: Martha, Martha, thou carest, and arte troubled aboute manye thinges,

42 verelye one is nedefull. Marye hath chosen her that good part whiche shall not be taken away from her.

# CHAPTER 11

AND it fortuned as he was praiynge in a certayne place: when he ceased, one of hys discyples said vnto hym: Mayster, teache vs to praye, as Iohn taught his disciples.

2 And he sayde vnto them: When ye pray saye: O oure father whiche arte in heauen, halowed be thy name. Thy kyngedome come. They will be fulfylled euen in earthe as it is in heauen.

3 Geue vs oure daylye breade euermore.

4 And forgeue vs oure synnes: For euen we forgeue euery man that trespasseth vs: And ledde vs not into temptacyon. But deliuer vs from euyll.

5 And he sayde vnto them: Yf any of you shoulde haue a frende, and shoulde go to hym at midnight, and saye vnto hym: frende lende me thre loues,

6 for a frende of myne is come out of the waye to me, and I haue nothinge to set before him:

7 and he within shoulde aunswere & saye: trouble me not, the dore is now shut, and my seruauntes are with me in the chamber, I cannot ryse, and geue them to the.

8 I saye vnto you, thoughe he woulde not arise and geue him, because he is hys frende: yet because of hys importunitie he wold ryse, and geue him as many as he neded.

9 And I saye vnto you: axe and it shalbe geuen you. Seke, and ye shal finde. Knocke, and it shalbe opened vnto you.

10 For euery one that axeth, receyueth: and he that seketh, findeth: & to hym that knocketh shall it be opened

11 Yf þe sonne shall axe bread of any of you that is a father, will he geue him a stone? Or yf he axe fishe, will he for a fishe geue hym a serpente?

12 Or yf he axe an egge, wyl he offer hym a scorpion?

13 Yf ye then which are euill, can geue good gyftes vnto youre chyldren, howe much more shall the father of heauen geue an holy spirite to them that desyre it of hym?

14 And he was castynge oute a deuyll, which was domme. And it folowed when the deuyl was gone out, the domme spake, & the people wondred.

15 But some of them sayed: he casteth out deuyls by the power of Belzebub þe chief of the deuyls.

16 And other tempted hym, seking of him a signe from heauen.

17 But he knew their thoughtes, and sayd vnto them: Euery kingdome deuyded within it selfe, shalbe desolate: and one house shall fall vpon another:

18 So yf Satan be deuyded with in him selfe: how shal hys kyngdome endure? Because ye saye that I caste oute deuils by the power of Belzebub

19 If I by the power of Belzebub caste oute deuyls: by whom do youre chyldren caste them oute? Therefore shall they be youre iudges.

20 But yf I with the finger of God caste oute deuyls, no doubte the kyngedome of God is come.

21 When a strong man armed, watched hys house, that he possesseth is in peace.

22 But when a stronger then he cometh vpon hym & ouercommeth hym: he taketh from hym his harnes, wherin he trusted and deuydeth hys goodes.

23 He that is not with me, is agaynste me. And he that gadereth not with me, scatereth.

24 When the vncleane spirite is gone oute of a man, he walketh through waterles places, sekynge reste. And when he fyndeth none, he sayeth, I wyll returne agayne vnto my house whence I came out.

25 And when he cometh, he findeth it swepte and garnyshed.

26 Then goeth he and taketh to him seuen other spirites worse then hym selfe: and they enter in, and dwell there. And the ende of that man, is worsse then the begynnynge.

27 And it fortuned as he spake those thinges, a certayne woman of the companye lyft vp her voyce, and sayde vnto hym: Happy is the wombe that bare the, and the pappes whiche gaue the sucke.

28 But he sayde: Yea, happye are they that heare the worde of God, and kepe it.

29 When the people were gathered thycke together: he began to saye: Thys is an euyll nacyon: they seke a signe, and there shal no signe be geuen them, but the signe of Ionas the prophet.

30 For as Ionas was a signe to the Niniuites, so shall the sonne of man be to thys nacion.

31 The quene of the south shall ryse at iudgement with the men of thys generation: & condempne them: for she came from the ende of the world to heare the wysdome of Salomon. And beholde a greater then Salomon is here.

32 The men of Niniue shall ryse at the iudgement wt thys generacyon, and condempne them: for they repented at the preaching of Ionas. And beholde a greater then Ionas is here.

33 No man lyghteth a candell, & putteth in a pryuy place, neyther vnder a bushell: but on a candelsticke, that they that come in, maye se the lyght.

34 The lyght of thy body is the eye Therfor when thyne eye is single: then is al thy body full of lyghte. But yf thyne eye be euyll: then shall thy bodye also be ful of darknes.

35 Take hede therfore that the lyght whiche is in the, be not darcknes.

36 For yf all thy body shalbe lyght, hauyng no parte darke, then shal all be full of lyght, euen as when a candell doth lyght the with hys brightnes.

37 And as he spake, a certayne Pharisey besought hym to done with hym, and he wente in, & sat doune.

38 When the Pharisei sawe that he marueyled that he had not fyrste weshed before dyner.

39 And the Lorde sayde to hym: Now do ye pharyses make cleane the outsyde of the cup, and of the platter: but your inward parties are full of rauenyng and wickednes.

40 Ye foles, dyd not he that made that which is without: make that whiche is within also?

41 Neuerthelesse geue almose of that ye haue, and beholde all is cleane to you.

42 But wo be to you Pharyses: for the tyth þe mint and rew, and al maner herbes, and passe ouer iudgement and the loue of God. These ought ye to haue lefte the other vndone.

43 Wo be to you Pharises, for ye loue the vppermost seates in the synagoges, and gretynges in the markettes.

44 Wo be to you scribes and pharyses, hypocrites, for ye are as graues which appere not, and the men that walke ouer them, are not ware of them.

45 Then aunswered one of the lawyers, and sayed vnto hym: Mayster, thus saiyng, thou puttest vs to rebuke also.

46 Then he sayde: Wo be to you also ye lawyars, for ye lade men wt burthens greuous to be borne, and ye youre selues touche not the packes with one of your fyngers.

47 Wo be to you: ye buylde the sepulchres of of the Prophetes, and youre fathers kylled them,

48 truelye ye beare witnes, that ye alowe the deedes of youre fathers: for they kylled them, and ye buylde theyr sepulchres.

49 Therfore sayde the wysdome of God: I wyll send them Prophetes and Apostles, and of them they shall slea and persecute,

50 that the bloude of all Prophetes which was shede from the beginnynge of the worlde, maye be requyred of thys generacion

51 from the bloude of Abell vnto the bloude of Zacharye, whiche perysshed betwene the aulter and the temple. Verelye I saye vnto you, it shalbe requyred of thys nacyon.

52 Wo be to you lawyers: for ye haue taken away the keye of knoweledge, ye entred not in your selues, and them that came in, ye forbade.

53 When he thus spake vnto

them, the lawyers, and the Pharyses began to wexe busye aboute hym, and to stop hys mouthe with manye questyons,

54 layinge wayte for hym, and sekynge to catche some thynge of hys mouthe, whereby they myghte accuse hym.

## CHAPTER 12

As there gathered together an innumerable multitude of people (in so muche that they trode one another) he began to saye vnto hys discyples: Fyrste of all beware of the leuen of the Phariseis, which is hypocrisye.

2 For there is nothynge couered þe shall not be vncouered: neyther hydde, that shall not be knowen.

3 For whatsoeuer ye haue spoken in darknes: that same shall be hearde in lyghte. And that whiche ye haue spoken in the eare, euen in secrete places, shall be preached euen on the toppe of the housses.

4 I saye vnto you my frendes: Be not afrayde of them that kyll the bodye, and after that haue no more that they can do.

5 But I wil shew you whom ye shall feare. Feare hym whiche after he hath kylled, hath power to caste into hell. Yea I saye vnto you, hym feare.

6 Are not fyue sparrowes bought for .ij. farthynges? And yet not one of them is forgotten of God.

7 Also euen the very heares of your heades are numbred. Feare not therfore: Ye are more of value then many sparowes.

8 I saye vnto you whosoeuer confesseth me before men, euen hym shall the sonne of man confesse also before the Angels of God.

9 And he that denyeth me before men, shalbe denied before the Angels of God.

10 And whosoeuer speaketh a worde agaynste the sonne of man it shall be forgeuen hym. But vnto hym, that blasphemeth the holy ghost, it shall not be forgeuen.

11 When they brynge you vnto the synagoges and vnto the rulers and offycers take no thoughte, how or what thynge ye shall aunswere or what ye shall speake.

12 For the holye ghost shal teache you in the same houre, what ye ought to saye.

13 One of the companye sayde vnto hym: Mayster byd my brother deuyde the enherytaunce with me.

14 And he sayde vnto hym: Man who made me a iudge or deuyder ouer you?

15 Wherfore, he sayde vnto them: take hede, and beware of coueteousnes. For no mannes lyfe standeth in the abundaunce of the thynges whiche he possesseth.

16 And he put forth a simylitude vnto them, sayinge. The grounde of a certayne ryche man brought forth frutes plenteouslye,

17 and he thoughte in hym selfe sayinge: what shall I do? because I haue no roume where to bestowe my frutes?

18 And he sayed: Thys will I do. I wyl destroy my barnes, and buylde greater, and therein wyll I gather all my frutes, and my goodes,

19 and I wyll saye to my soule: Soule thou hast muche goodes layde vp in store for many yeares: take thyne ease, eate, drinke, and be mery.

20 But God sayed vnto hym: Thou fole, thys nyghte wyll they fetche awaye thy soule agayne from the. Then whose shall these thinges be which thou haste prouyded?

21 So is it with hym that gathereth ryches, and is not ryche in God.

22 And he spake vnto hys disciples: Therfor I saye vnto you: Take no thoughte for youre lyfe, what ye shal eate, neyther for your body what ye shal put on.

23 The lyfe is more then meate, and the bodye is more then raymente.

24 Consyder the rauens, for they neyther sowe, nor repe, which neyther haue store house nor barne, and yet God fedeth them. Howe muche are ye better then the fowles.

25 Which of you with takynge thoughte can adde to hys stature one cubyte?

26 Yf ye then be not able to do that thyng whiche is least: why take ye thoughte for the remnaunt?

27 Consyder the lylyes howe they growe. They laboure not, they spin not, and yet I saye vnto you: þt Salomon in all hys royaltte, was not clothed lyke to one of these.

28 If the grasse whiche is to daye in the fielde and to morowe shalbe caste into the fornace, God so cloth: howe muche more wyl he clothe you, o ye endued with lytell faythe.

29 And are not what ye shall eate, or what ye shall drinke, neyther climme ye vp an hye:

30 for all suche thynges the heathen people of the worlde seke for. Your father knoweth that ye haue nede of suche thinges.

31 Wherfore seke ye after the kyngdome of God, and all these thynges shall be ministred vnto you.

32 Feare not litel flocke, for it is your fathers pleasure, to geue you a kingdom.

33 Sell that ye haue, and geue almes. And make you bagges whiche were not old, and treasure that faileth not in heauen, where no these cometh, neyther mothe corrupteth.

34 For where youre treasure is there wyll youre hertes be also.

35 Let youre loynes be gerdde aboute, & your lyghtes brennynge,

36 and ye youre selues lyke vnto men, that wayte for theyr maister, when he wyll returne from a weddyng: that assone as he commeth and knocketh, they may open vnto hym.

37 Happye are those seruauntes, whom the Lorde when he commeth, shall fynde wakynge: Verely I saye vnto you, he wyll girde hym selfe aboute, and make them sytte doune to meate, & walke by, & mynyster vnto them.

38 And yf he come in the seconde watche, yea yf he come in the thyrd watche, and shal fynd them so: happye are those seruauntes.

39 Thys vnderstande, that yf the good man of the house knewe what houre þt these would come, he woulde surely watche, and not suffer hys house to be broken vp.

40 Be ye prepared therfore: for the sonne of man will come at an houre, when ye thynke not.

41 Then Peter sayd vnto hym: Mayster tellest thou thys similitude vnto vs, or to al men?

42 And the Lorde sayd: Yf there be any faithful seruaunte and wyse, whom hys Lorde shall make ruler ouer hys housholde, to geue them theyr dutye of meate at due season:

43 happy is that seruaunt: whom hys mayster when he commeth, shall fynde so doinge.

44 Of a truth I say vnto you: that he wyl make hym ruler ouer all that he hath:

45 But and yf þe euyll seruaunte shall saye in hys herte. My mayster wyll deferre hys commynge, & shall begynne to smyte the seruauntes, & maydens and to eate and drynke and to be droncken:

46 the lorde of that seruaunte wyll come in a daye when he thynketh not: and at an houre when he is not ware, and wyll deuyde hym, & wyll geue hym hys rewarde with the vnbeleuers.

47 The seruaunt that knewe hys maysters wyl, and prepared not hym selfe, neyther dyd accordynge to his will, shalbe beaten with many strypes.

48 But he that knewe not, & yet dyd commytte thynges worthye of strypes, shalbe beaten with fewe stripes. For vnto whome muche is geuen, of him shalbe muche requyred. And to whom men muche committe, the more of hym will they axe.

49 I am come to sende fyre on earth, & what is my desyre but that it were all ready kyndled?

50 Notwithstandyng I muste be baptysed with a baptisme, and howe am I payned tyll it be ended?

51 Suppose ye that I am come to sende peace on earth? I tell you naye, but rather debate.

52 For from henceforth there shalbe fyue in one house deuyded, thre againste two, and two agaynst thre.

53 The father shalbe deuyded agaynste the sonne, and the sonne agaynst the father. The mother agaynst her doughter, and the doughter agaynst the mother. The motherelawe agaynst her doughter lawe, and the doughterelawe agaynste her motherlawe.

54 Then sayde he to the people: when ye se a cloude ryse out of the west, strayght waye ye saye. We shall haue a sower, and so it is.

55 And when ye se the southe wynde blowe, ye saye: we shall haue heate, and it commeth to passe.

56 Hypocrites, ye can skyll of the fashyon of the earth, and of the skye, but what is the cause þt ye can not skyll of thys tyme?

57 Ye and why iudge ye not of yourselues, what is ryghte?

58 Whyle thou goest with thyne aduersarye to the ruler, as thou arte in the waye, geue dylygence that thou mayest be delyuered from hym, leaste he brynge the to the iudge, and the iudge deliuer the to the iayler, & the iayler cast the into pryson.

59 I tell the, thou departest not thence, tyll thou haue made good the vttermoste myte.

# CHAPTER 13

THERE were presente at the same season, that shewed hym of the Galileans, whose bloud Pilate mengled with theyr owne sacrifice.

2 And Iesus aunswered, and sayde vnto them: Suppose ye that these Galileans were greater synnes then all the other Galileans, because they suffred suche punishment?

3 I tell you naye: but excepte ye repente, ye shall all lykewyse perysche.

4 Or those .xviij. vpon whome the towre in Siloe fell, & slewe them, thinke ye that they were sinners aboue all men that dwell in Hierusalem?

5 I tell you naye: But excepte ye repente, ye shal al lykewyse perysche.

6 He put forth this similitude: A certayne man had a fygge tree planted in hys vyneyarde, & he came and sought frute theron, and founde none.

7 Then sayde he to the dresser of hys vyneyard: Beholde thys thre yeare haue I come and sought frute in thys fygge tre, and fynde none, cut it doune: why comvreth it the grounde.

8 And he aunswered, & sayde vnto hym: Lorde let it alone thys yeare also, tyll I digge rounde aboute it, and dounge it,

9 to se whether it wyl beare frute, and yf it beare not then, after that cut it doune.

10 And he taughte in one of

theyr synagoges on the Saboth dayes.

11 And beholde there was a woman which had a spirite of infirmytye .xviij. yeares, and was bowed together, and coulde not lyfte vp her selfe at all.

12 When Iesus sawe her, he called her to hym, and sayed to her: woman thou arte delyuered from thy dysease.

13 And he layde hys handes on her, and immediatly she was made strayght, and gloryfyed God.

14 And the ruler of the synagoge aunswered with indignacion (because that Iesus had healed on the Saboth daye) & sayed vnto the people. There are .vi. dayes, in whiche men oughte to worke, in them come and be healed, & not on þe Saboth daye.

15 Then aunswered hym the Lorde, and said: Hypocryte, doth not eache one of you on the saboth daye, lowse hys oxe or hys asse from þe stall, and leade hym to the water

16 And ought not thys doughter of Abraham, whome Satan hath bounde lo .xviij. yeares, be lowsed from thys bonde on the Saboth daye?

17 And when he thus sayde, al hys aduersaryes were ashamed, and all the people reioysed on all the excellent dedes, that were done by hym.

18 Then sayde he: what is the kyngedome of God lyke? or whereto shall I compare it?

19 It is lyke a grayne of mustarde seede, whiche a man toke and sowed in hys garden: & it grew and wexed a greate tree, and the foules of the ayre made nestes in the braunches of it.

20 And agayne he sayed, where vnto shall I lyken the kyngedome of God?

21 it is lyke leuen, which a woman toke, and hyd in thre bushels of floure, tyll all was thorowe leuended.

22 And he went thorowe all maner of cities & tounes teachynge and iorneynge towardes Hierusalem.

23 Then sayde one vnto hym: Lorde, are ther fewe that shalbe saued? And he sayde vnto them:

24 stryue with your selues to enter in at þe strayte gate: For manye I saye vnto you wyl seke to enter in, & shal not be able.

25 When the good man of the house is rysen vp, and hathe shut to the dore, ye shall begynne to stande without, and to knocke at the dore, saiynge: Lorde Lorde open to vs: and he shall aunswere and saye vnto you: I knowe you not whence ye are.

26 Then shal ye begyn to say: We haue eaten, in thy presence and dronke, and thou haste taught in oure stretes.

27 And he shall saye: I tell you I knowe you not whence ye are: departe frome me all ye workers of iniquitie.

28 There shalbe wepynge and gnashing of teth, when ye shall se Abraham and Isaac and Iacob, and all the Prophetes in the kingdome of God, and your selues thruste oute at dores.

29 And they shall come from the easte & from the west, and from the northe, and from the southe, and shall sit doune in the kyngdom of God.

30 And beholde there are laste whiche shalbe fyrste. And there are fyrste which shal be laste.

31 The same daye there came certayne of the Pharises and sayde to him: Get the out of the waye, and departe hence: For Herode wyl kil the.

32 And he sayed vnto them, Go ye and tell that foxe, beholde I caste oute deuyls, & heale the people to day and to morowe, and þe third daye I make an ende.

33 Neuertheles, I must walke to daye and to morowe and the daye folowynge. For it can not be, that a prophet perysh any other wher, saue at Hierusalem

34 O Hierusalem, Hierusalem, whiche killest Prophetes, and stonest them that are sent to the: howe often woulde I haue gathered thy chyldren together, as the hen gathered her neste vnder her wynges, but ye would not.

35 Beholde your habitacion shall be lefte vnto you desolate. For I tell you, ye shal not se me vntyll the tyme come that ye shall say, blessed is he that commeth in the name of the Lorde.

# CHAPTER 14

AND it chaunsed that he went into the house of one of the chiefe Phariseis to eate breade, on a Saboth daye: and they watched hym.

2 And beholde there was a man before hym whiche had the dropsye.

3 And Iesus aunswered and spake vnto the lawyars and Pharyseis sayinge: is it lawfull to heale on the Sabboth daye?

4 And they helde theyr peace: And he toke hym, and healed him, and let hym go:

5 and aunswered them saying, which of you shall haue an asse, or an oxe fallen into a pytte, and wyll not straighte waye pul him out on the Saboth daye?

6 And they coulde not aunswere hym agayne to that.

7 He put forth a similitude to the gestes, when he marked howe they preased to the hyest roumes, and sayed vnto them:

8 When thou arte bydden to a weddynge of anye man, sit not downe in the hyest roume, least a more honorable man then thou be bydden of hym,

9 & he that bade both hym and the, come and saye to the: geue thys man roume, and thou then begynne with shame to take

the lowest roume.

10 But rather when thou arte bydden, go and sit in the lowest roume, that when he that bade the, commeth, he maye saye vnto the frende sit vp hyer. Then shalte thou haue worshyppe in the preseuce of them that sitte at meat with the.

11 For whosoeuer exalteth him selfe, shalbe broughte lowe. And he that humbleth him selfe, shalbe exalted.

12 Then sayde he also to hym that had desyered hym to dyner. When thou makest a dyner or a supper: call not thy frendes, nor thy brethren, neyther thy kynsmen nor yet ryche neyghboures: least they byd the agayne, and a recompence be made the.

13 But when thou makest a feaste, call the poore the maymed, the lame, and the blynde,

14 & thou shalte be happy, for they can not recompence the. But thou shalte be recompensed at the resurreccyon of the iust men.

15 When one of them that sate at meate also hearde that, he sayed vnto hym: happye is he that eateth breade in the kyngdom of God.

16 Then sayde he to hym. A certayne man ordeyned a greate supper, and bade manye,

17 & sente hys seruaunte at supper tyme to saye to them that were bydden, come, for all thynges are nowe readye.

18 And they all at once began to make excuse. The fyrste sayed vnto him: I haue boughte a ferme, and muste nedes go, & se it, I pray the haue me excused.

19 And another sayed: I haue bought fyue yocke of oxen, and I go to proue them, I praye the haue me excused.

20 The thyrde sayed: I haue maryed a wyfe and therfore I can not come.

21 And the seruaunt went and brought his mayster worde therof. Then was the good man of the house displeased, and sayed to hys seruaunt: Go oute quickly into the streates and quarters of the citie, and brynge in hyther the poore, and the maymed and the halte and the blynde.

22 And þe seruaunt sayde: Lorde it is done as thou commaundest, and yet there is roume.

23 And the Lorde sayd to the seruaunt: Go oute into the hygh waies, and hedges and compel them to come in, that my house may be filled.

24 For I saye vnto you that none of those men which were bydden, shall tast of my supper.

25 There went a great companye with him, and he turned and sayde vnto them:

26 If a man come to me, and hate not hys father and mother, and wyfe, and chyldren and brethren & systers, moreouer and hys owne lyfe, he can not be my disciple.

27 And whosoeuer beare not his crosse, and come after me can not be my disciple.

28 Which of you disposed to buylde a tower, sitteth not doune before, & counteth the costes whether he haue sufficient to performe it,

29 leste after he hath layde the foundacion, and is not able to performe it, all that beholde it beginne to mocke hym,

30 saiyng: this man beganne to buylde, and was not able to make an end.

31 Or what kynge goeth to make batayle agaynste another kynge, & sytteth not doune fyrste, and casteth in hys mynd, whyther he be able with ten thousande to mete hym that cometh against him with twentye thousande.

32 Or els whyle þe other is yet a great waye of, he wyll send embassetours, and desire peace.

33 So likewise none of you that forsaketh not all that he hath, can be my discyple.

34 Salt is good, but yf salt haue loste her saltnes, what shall be seasoned therwith?

35 It is neyther good for the lande nor yet for þe doung hyll, but men caste it out at the dores. He that hath eares to heare, let hym heare.

# CHAPTER 15

THEN resorted vnto hym all the Publycans and synners for to heare hym.

2 And the Pharises & Scribes murmured saiyng. He receyued to hys company synners, and eateth with them.

3 Then put he forth thys similytude to them. saying:

4 What man of you hauynge an hundred shepe, yf he loose one of them, doth not leaue nynty and nyne in the wildernes, and go after that which is lost vntyl he fynde hym?

5 And when he hath found hym, he putteth hym on hys shoulders wyth ioye.

6 And assone as he cometh home, he calleth together his louers and neyghboures, saiyng vnto them: reioyse with me, for I haue found my shepe whiche was lost.

7 I saye vnto you, that lykewyse ioye shalbe in heauen ouer one synner, that repenteth, more then ouer nyntye and nyne iust persons whiche nede no repentaunce.

8 Eyther what woman hauyng .x. grotes yf she loose one, doth not lyght a candell, and swepe the house, and seke diligentlye, tyll she fynde it?

9 And when she hath founde it, she calleth her louers and her neyghboures, saiyng: Reioyse with me, for I haue founde the grote which I had lost.

10 Lykewyse I saye vnto you ioye is made in the presence of

the Angels of God ouer one synner that repenteth.

11 And he sayde: A certayne man had two sonnes,

12 and the yonger of them sayde to hys father: geue me my parte of the goodes that to me belongeth. And he deuyded vnto them hys substaunce.

13 And not longe after, the yonger sonne gathered all that he had together, & toke hys iorneye into a farre countrye, & there he wasted hys goodes with ryetous liuing.

14 And when he had spent all that he had, there arose a great dearth throughout all that same lande, & he began to lacke.

15 And he wente and claue to a citesyn of the same countrye, whiche sent hym to hys fielde, to kepe hys swyne.

16 And he woulde fayne haue fylled hys bellye with the codes that swyne eate. And no man gaue hym.

17 Then he came to hym selfe, and sayed: Howe many hyred seruauntes at my fathers haue breade ynough, and I dye for honger,

18 I wyll aryse, and go to my father, and will say vnto hym: father I haue synned agaynst heauen and before the,

19 and am no more worthye to be called thy sonne, make me as one of thy hyred seruauntes.

20 And he arose and wente to his father. And when he was yet a great way of, hys father sawe hym, and had compassyon and ran and fell on hys necke, & kyssed hym.

21 And the sonne sayed vnto him: father, I haue synned agaynst heauen in thy syghte, & am no more worthy to be called thy sonne.

22 But hys father sayed to hys seruauntes: brynge forthe that beste garmentes, & put it on hym, and put a rynge on hys hande, & showes on hys fete.

23 And brynge hyther the fatted caulfe and kyll hym, and let vs eate and be merye:

24 for thys my sonne was dead, and is alyue agayne, he was lost and is nowe founde. And they beganne to be mery.

25 The elder brother was in the fielde, & when he came, & drewe nye to the house, he hearde minstrelcy and daunsynge,

26 and called one of hys seruauntes, and axed what those thinges meant.

27 And he sayed vnto him: thy brother is come, & thy father hath killed þe fatted caulfe, because he hath receyued hym safe and sound.

28 And he was angrye, and woulde not go in. Then came hys father out, and intreated him

29 He aunswered and sayde to his father: Loo this many yeares haue I done þe seruice, neyther brake at any tyme thy commaundement, & yet gauest thou me neuer so muche as a kyd to make mery with my louers:

30 but assone as this thy sonne was come, which hath deuoured thy goodes with harlotes, thou hast for his pleasure kylled the fatted caulfe.

31 And he sayde vnto hym: sonne thou wast euer with me, and all that I haue, is thyne.

32 It was mete that we shoulde make merye, and be glad: for this thy brother was dead, and is aliue again and was loste, and is founde.

# CHAPTER 16

AND he sayed also vnto his disciples. There was a certayne ryche man which had a steward that was accused vnto him: that he wasted hys goodes.

2 And he called hym, and sayde vnto hym: Howe is it, that I heare thys of the? Geue a comptes of thy stewardshyppe. For thou mayest be no longer stewarde.

3 The stewarde sayde within hym selfe, what shall I do? for my mayster wyll take away from me the stewardshyppe. I can not dygge, and to begge, I am ashamed.

4 I wote what to do, that when I am put oute of stewardshyppe, they maye receyue me into theyr houses.

5 Then called he all hys maysters detters, & sayed vnto the first, how much owest thou vnto my mayster?

6 And he sayed: an hundred tonnes of oyle. And he sayed to hym: take thy bil and sit doune quicklye, and wryte fyftye.

7 Then sayed he to another: what owest thou? And he sayed: an hundred quarters of wheate. He said to hym: Take thy byll, and write foure scoore.

8 And the Lord commended the vniust steward because he had done wyslye. For the chyldren of thys worlde are in theyr kynde, wyser then the chyldren of lyght,

9 And I saye also vnto you: make you frendes, of the wycked mammon, that when ye shall depart, they maye receyue you into euerlastynge habitacyons.

10 He that is faythfull in that whiche is least, the same is faythfull in muche. And he that is vnfaythfull in the least, is vnfaythfull also in muche.

11 So then yf ye haue not ben faythfull in the wycked Mammon: who wyll beleue you in that which is true?

12 And yf ye haue not bene faythfull in another mannes busynes, who shall geue you your owne?

13 No seruaunte can serue two maysters, for other he shal hate the one and loue the other, or els he shall leane to the one, and despyse the other. Ye can not serue God and Mammon.

14 All these thynges hearde the phariseis also which were couetous, and they mocked hym.

15 And he sayde vnto them: Ye are they whiche iustifye your selues before men: but God knoweth your hertes. For that which is highly estemed amonge men, is abhominable in þe syght of God.

16 The lawe and the Prophetes raygned vntyll the tyme of Iohn: and sence that tyme the kyngdom of God is preached, and euery man stryueth to go in.

17 Soner shall heauen & earthe peryshe, then one title of the lawe shal perish.

18 Whosoeuer forsaketh his wyfe and maryeth another, breaketh matrimony. And euery man which maryeth her that is deforsed from her husbande comitteth aduoutrye also.

19 There was a certayne ryche man, whiche was clothed in purple and fyne bysse, & fared delyciously euery daye,

20 And there was a certayne begger named Lazarus, whiche laye at hys gate full of sores,

21 desierynge to be refresshed with the cromes which fell from þe riche mans bourde. Neuerthelesse the dogges came and lycked hys sores.

22 And it fortuned that the begger dyed, and was caryed by the Angels into Abrahams bosome. The ryche man also dyed and was buryed.

23 And beynge in hell in tormentes, he lyfte vp hys eyes, and sawe Abraham a farre of, & Lazarus in his bosome,

24 and he cryed & sayed: father Abraham haue mercy on me, and send Lazarus that he maye dyppe the typpe of his fynger in water, and cole my tonge, for I am tormented in this flamme.

25 But Abraham sayd vnto hym. Sonne, remembre that thou in thy lyfe tyme, receyuedest thy pleasure, and contrarywyse Lazarus payne. Nowe therfore is he conforted, and thou arte punyshed.

26 Beyonde all thys, betwene you and vs there is a great space set, so that they whiche would go from hence to you can not, neyther maye come from thence to vs.

27 Then he sayed: I praye the therfore father, sende hym to my fathers house.

28 For I haue fyue brethren, for to warne them lest they also come into thys place of tormente.

29 Abraham said vnto hym: they haue Moyses and the Prophetes: let them heare them.

30 And he sayd: nay father Abraham, but yf one came vnto them from the dead, they woulde repent.

31 He sayed vnto hym: yf they heare not Moyses, and the Prophetes, neyther wyll they beleue, though one rose from death agayne.

# CHAPTER 17

THEN sayde he to the disciples, it cannot be auoyded but that offences will come. Neuerthelesse wo be to hym: through whome they come.

2 It were better for him that a mylstone were hanged about his necke. and that he were cast into the sea, then that he shoulde offende one of these litelons.

3 Take hede to youre selues. Yf thy brother trespasse agaynst the, rebuke hym,

4 and yf he repent, forgeue hym. And thoughe he synne agaynst the seuen tymes in a day, & seuen tymes in a day tourne agayne to the saiyng: it repenteth me, forgeue hym.

5 And the Apostles sayed vnto þe Lorde: encrease oure fayth.

6 And the Lorde sayde: yf ye had fayth lyke a grayne of mustarde seede, and shoulde say vnto thys sycamine tree, plucke thy selfe vp by þe rootes, and plante thy selfe in the sea: he should obeye you.

7 Who is it of you, yf he had a seruaunt plowyng or fedynge catell, that woulde say vnto hym when he were come from the fielde. Go quickly, and sit doune to meate,

8 and woulde not rather say to him: dresse, wherwith I may suppe, and gyrde vp thy selfe, and serue me, til I haue eaten and droncken, & afterwarde eate thou, and drinke thou:

9 Doth he thanke that seruaunte, because he dyd that whiche was commaunded to hym? I trowe not.

10 So lykewyse ye, when ye haue done al those thinges: which are commaunded you, saye: we are vnprofytable seruauntes. We haue done that whiche was oure duetye to do.

11 And it chaunsed as he wente to Ierusalem that he passed through Samaria and Galile.

12 And as he entred into a certayne toune: there met hym .x. that were lepers. Whiche stode a farre

13 & put forth theyr voyces and sayde: Iesu maister, haue mercy on vs.

14 When he saw them he saide vnto them: Go and shew your selues to the priestes. And it chaunsed as they went, they were clensed.

15 And one of them when he sawe that he was clensed, turned backe agayn and with a loude voyce praysed God

16 and fel doune on his face at hys fete, & gaue him thankes. And the same was a Samaritane.

17 And Iesus aunswered and sayed: are there not ten clensed? But where are those nyne?

18 There are not founde that returned agayne to geue GOD prayse, saue only thys straunger.

19 And he said vnto him: aryse, and go thy waye, thy

faythe hath made the whole.

20 When he was demaunded of the Pharises when the kyngdom of God shoulde come: he aunswered them, and sayd: The kingdome of God cometh not with waytyng for.

21 Neyther shal men saye: Lo here, lo there. For beholde the kyngdom of God is within you.

22 And he sayed to hys disciples: The dayes wyll come, when ye shall desyre to se one daye of the sonne of man, & ye shall not se it.

23 And they shall saye to you. Se here. Se there. Go not after them, nor folowe them,

24 for as the lyghtenynge that appeareth out of the one part of the heauen, and shyneth vnto the other parte of heauen: So shall the sonne of man be in his daye.

25 But fyrste muste he suffer manye thynges, and be refused of thys nacyon.

26 As it happened in the tyme of Noe: So shal it be in the tyme of the sonne of man.

27 They ate, they dranke, they maryed wyues, and were maryed euen vnto the same daye that Noe wente into the arke, and the floude came & destroyed them all.

28 Lykewyse also, as it chaunsed in the dayes of Lot. They ate, they dranke they bought, they solde, they planted, they buylte.

29 And euen the same daye that Lot went out of Zodome, it rayned fyre and brymstone from heauen, and destroyed them.

30 After these ensamples, shal it be in the daye when the sonne of man shall appeare.

31 At that daye he that is on the house toppe, and hys stuffe in the house: let him not come doune to take it out. And lykewyse let not him þt is in the fielde turne backe agayne to that he lefte behynde.

32 Remembre Lottes wyfe

33 Whosoeuer wyll go about to saue his lyfe, shal lose it. And whosoeuer shal lose hys lyfe, shall saue it.

34 I tel you: In that nyght there shalbe two in one bed, the one shalbe receyued, & the other shal be forsaken.

35 Two shalbe also a grinding together, the one shalbe receyued, and þe other shalbe forsaken.

36 <>

37 And they aunswered, & sayde to hym: where Lorde? And he sayed vnto them: wheresoeuer the body shalbe, thyther wyl the egles resorte.

# CHAPTER 18

AND he put forth a similitude vnto them signifyeng that men ought alwaies to pray, & not to be werye,

2 saiynge. There was a Iudge in a certayne cytye, whiche feared not God, neyther regarded man.

3 And there was a certaine wedowe in the same citie whiche came vnto hym saiynge: auenge of myne aduersarye.

4 And he woulde not for a whyle. But afterwarde he sayde to hym selfe, though I feare not God, nor care for man,

5 yet because thys wedowe troubleth me. I wil auenge her least at þe least she come and hagge on me.

6 And the Lord sayed: heare what the vnrightuous iudge sayeth.

7 And shall not God aduenge his electe, which crye daye and nyghte vnto hym, ye though he defarre them?

8 I tell you, he wil auenge them, and that quickly. Neuerthelesse when the sonne of man commeth, suppose ye, that he shall fynde fayth on earth?

9 And he put forth thys similytude vnto certayne, which thrusted in them selues that they were perfecte, and despyseth other.

10 Two men went vp into the temple to praye, the one a pharise and the other a publican.

11 The Pharyse stode and prayed thus with hym selfe: God I thanke the, that I am not as other men are, extorsioners, vniust, aduouterers, or as this publican,

12 I faste twyse in the weke, I geue tythe of all þt I possesse.

13 And the Publicane stode a farre of, and woulde not lyft vp his eyes to heauen, but smote his brest, saiynge: God be mercifull to me a synner.

14 I tell you: this man departed home to hys house iustifyed more then the other. For euerye man that exalteth hym selfe, shalbe brought lowe. And he that humbleth hym selfe, shalbe exalted.

15 They broughte vnto hym also babes: that he shoulde touche them. When hys disciples saw that they rebuked them.

16 But Iesus called them vnto hym, and sayed: Suffer children to come vnto me, and forbyd them not. For of suche is the kyngdome of God.

17 Verely I say vnto you: whosoeuer receyueth not the kyngdome of God, as a chylde, he shall not enter therin.

18 And a certayne ruler axed him, saiyng: Good Maister, what ought I to do, to obtayne eternall lyfe?

19 Iesus sayde vnto hym: Why callest thou me good? No man is good, saue God onlye.

20 Thou knowest the commaundementes: Thou shalte not committe aduoutrye. Thou shalte not kyll. Thou shalt not steale. Thou shalte not beare false wytnesse: Honoure thy father and mother.

21 And he sayed: al these haue I kepte from my youth.

22 When Iesus hearde that, he sayed vnto hym. Yet lackeste thou one thynge. Sell all that

thou haste, and distrybute it vnto þe poore, and thou shalt haue treasure in heauen, and come, & folowe me.

23 When he hearde, that he was heauy: for he was very ryche.

24 When Iesus sawe hym morne, he sayed: with what difficultye shall they that haue ryches, enter into the kyngedome of God:

25 it is easyer for a camel to go thorowe a nedels eye then for a ryche man to enter into the kyngdom of God.

26 Then sayed they that hearde that: And who shall then be saued?

27 And he sayed: Thynges which are vnpossyble with men are possyble with God.

28 Then sayed Peter: Loo we haue lefte al, & folowed the.

29 And he sayed vnto them: Verelye I saye vnto you, there is no man that leaueth house, other father or mother, other brethren or wyfe or children, for the kyngdom of Goddes sake,

30 which same shall not receyue much more in thys worlde: and in the world to come, lyfe euerlastynge.

31 He toke vnto hym twelue, and sayed vnto them. Beholde we go vp to Hierusalem, & all shal be fulfylled that are wryten by þe Prophetes of the sonne of man.

32 He shalbe deliuered vnto the gentils, and shalbe mocked, and shalbe dispytefully entreated, and shalbe spitted on,

33 and when they haue scourged him, they wyll put hym to death, and the thyrde daye he shall ryse agayn.

34 But they vnderstode none of these thynges. And this saiyng was hyd from them. And they perceyued not the thynges whiche were spoken.

35 And it came to passe, as he was come nye vnto Hierico, a certayne blynde man sat by þe waye syde begginge.

36 And when he harde the people passe by, he axed what it meante:

37 And they sayed to him, that Iesus of Nazareth passed by.

38 And he cryed, saiynge: Iesus the sonne of Dauid, haue thou mercye on me.

39 And they whiche wente before, rebuked hym, that he shoulde holde his peace. But he cryed so much þe more, þu sonne of Dauid haue mercy on me.

40 And Iesus stode still, and commaunded hym to be brought vnto hym. And when he was come neare, Iesus axed hym,

41 saiyng: What wilt thou that I do vnto the? And he sayde: Lorde that I maye receyue my syght.

42 Iesus sayde vnto hym: receyue thy syght: thy fayth hath saued the.

43 And immediatly he sawe, & folowed hym, praysyng God. And all the people when they sawe it, gaue laude to God.

## CHAPTER 19

AND he entred in and went thorowe Hierico.

2 And behold, ther was a man named Zacheus, which was a ruler amonge the Publicans, and was riche also.

3 And he made meanes to se Iesus, what he shulde be, and coulde not for the prease, because he was of a lowe stature.

4 Wherfore he ran before and ascended vp into a wylde figge tree, to se him: for he should come þt same way.

5 And when Iesu came to the place, he loked vp and sawe hym, and sayed vnto hym: Zache, attonce come doune, for to daye I must abyde at thy house.

6 And he came doune hastelye & receyued hym ioyfullye.

7 And when they sawe that, they al groundged saiyng: He is gone into tarye with a man that is a synner.

8 And Zache stode forthe and sayed vnto þe Lord, beholde Lord, the haulfe of my goodes I geue to the pore, and yf I haue done anye man wronge, I wyl restore hym foure folde:

9 And Iesus sayed to him: this daye is healthe come vnto thys house, for as muche as it also is become the chyld of Abraham.

10 For þe sonne of man is come to seke, and to saue that which was loste.

11 As they hearde these thynges, he added therto a similitude, because he was nye to Hierusalem, and because also they thoughte that the kyngdome of God should shortly appere.

12 He sayde therfore: a certayne noble man wente into a farre countre, to receyue him a kyngdome, and then to come agayne.

13 And he called hys ten seruauntes, & deliuered them ten pounde saiynge vnto them? by and sell tyll I come.

14 But hys citisens hated hym, and sente messengers after hym, saiynge: we will not haue thys man to reygne ouer vs.

15 And it came to passe, when he was come agayne, and had receyued hys kyngdome, he commaunded these seruauntes, to be called to him (to whom he gaue hys money) to wyt what euery man had done.

16 Then came the fyrste saiynge: Lorde, thy pounde hath encreased ten pounde.

17 And he sayde vnto hym. Well good seruaunte, because thou waste faythful in a very lytell thynge, take thou authorityе ouer ten cities.

18 And the other came, saying: Lorde thy pounde hath encreased fyue pound.

19 And to the same he sayde,

and be thou also ruler ouer .v. cities.

20 And the .iij. came & sayde: Lorde, behold here thy pounde, whiche I haue kept in a napkyn,

21 for I feared the, because thou art a strayt man, thou takest vp that thou laydest not doune, and reapest that thou dyddest not sowe.

22 And he sayde to him: Of thyne owne mouthe iudge I the thou euil seruaunt. Knowest thou þt I am a strayte man takyng vp that I layde not doune, and reapyng that I did not sowe?

23 Wherfore then gauest not thou my money into the banke, that at my commynge I mighte haue requyred myne owne with vauntage.

24 And he sayed to them that stode by: take from hym that pounde, and geue it hym that hath ten pounde.

25 And they sayde vnto him: Lorde, he hath ten pounde.

26 I saye vnto you, that vnto all them that haue, it shalbe geuen: and from hym that hath not, euen that he hath shalbe taken from hym.

27 Moreouer those myne enemyes which woulde not that I should raigne ouer them, brynge hyther, and slea them before me.

28 And when he had thus spoken, he proceded forthe ascendyng vp to Ierusalem.

29 And it fortuned, when he was come nye Bethphage and Bethanye, besydes mounte oliuete, he sente two of hys disciples,

30 saiynge: Go ye into the toune whiche is ouer againste you, In the whiche assone as ye are come, ye shall fynde a colt tyed, whereon yet neuer man sate. Lewse him, and bring him hither.

31 And yf anye man axe you, why that ye lewse him: thus say vnto him: þe Lorde hath nede of hym.

32 They that were sente, wente theyr waye, & founde as he had sayed vnto them.

33 And as they were alewsynge the colte, the owners sayed vnto them: why lewse ye the colte?

34 And they sayed: for the Lorde hath nede of hym.

35 And they broughte hym to Iesus. And they caste theyr raymente on the colte, and set Iesus theron.

36 And as he wente, they sprede theyr clothes in the waye.

37 And when he was nowe come, where he shoulde go doune from the mount Oliuete, the whole multitude of the discyples beganne to reioyce, and to laude God with a loude voyce for all the myracles that they had sene,

38 saying: Blessed be the kyng that cometh in the name of the Lorde: peace in heauen, and glorye in þe hyest.

39 And some of the Phariseis of the companye sayde vnto him: Mayster rebuke thy disciples.

40 He aunswered and sayed vnto them: I tell you, yf these shoulde holde theyr peace, þe stones woulde crye.

41 And when he was come neare, he behelde the citie, and wept on it,

42 saiyng: Yf thou haddest knowen those thynges which belong vnto thy peace, euen at thys thy tyme. But now are they hydde from thyne eyes.

43 For þe dayes shall come vpon the, that thyne enemyes shal cast a banke aboute the, & compasse the round and kepe the on euerye syde,

44 and make the euen with the grounde, with children whiche are in the. And they shall not leaue in the one stone vpon another, because thou knowest not the tyme of thy visitacyon.

45 And he went into the temple, and beganne to cast oute them that solde therin, and them that boughte,

46 saiyng vnto them, it is wryten: my house is the house of prayer, but ye haue made it a den of theues.

47 And he taught daily in the temple. The hye Priestes and the Scribes and the chiefe of the people wente about to destroye hym,

48 but coulde not fynde what to do. For all the people stacke by hym, and gaue hym audience.

# CHAPTER 20

AND it fortuned in one of those dayes as he taught þe people in the temple, & preached þe gospel: þe hye priestes & the scribes came with the elders,

2 and spake vnto hym saiyng: Tell vs by what authoritie thou doest these thynges? Eyther who is he that gaue the this authoritie?

3 He aunswered & said vnto them: I also will axe you a question: and aunswere me.

4 The baptysine of Iohn, was it from heauen or of men?

5 And they thought wtin them selues, saiyng: yf we shal say, from heauen, he wil say: why then beleued ye him not?

6 But and yf we shall saye of men, all the people wyll stone vs. For they be perswaded þt Iohn is a Prophet.

7 And they aunswered that they coulde not tell whence it was.

8 And Iesus sayde to them: neyther tell I you by what authorite I do these thinges.

9 Then beganne he to put forthe to the people, thys similitude. A certayne man planted a vineyarde, and let it forthe to fermers, and went hym selfe into a straunge countre for a greate season.

10 And when the tyme was come, he sente a seruaunt to hys tenauntes that they shoulde geue

hym of the fruytes of the vyneyarde. And the tenauntes dyd beate hym, & sent him awaye empty.

11 And agayne he sent yet another seruaunt. And they dyd beate him, & foule entreated hym also, & sent hym awaye emptye.

12 Moreouer, he sent the third to, & hym they wounded, and cast out.

13 Then sayde the Lorde of the vineyarde: what shall I do? I wil sende my deare sonne, hym peraduenture they wyll reuerence, when they se hym.

14 But when the fermers sawe hym, they thoughte in them selues sayinge: thys is the hyre, come let vs kyl him, that the inheritaunce maye be oures.

15 And they cast hym out of the vineyarde, & kylled him. Now what shall the Lorde of the vyneyarde do vnto them?

16 He wyll come and destroye those fermers, and wyl let out his vineyarde to other: When they heard that, they sayde: God forbyd.

17 And he behelde them, and sayde: what meaneth this then that is wryten. The stone that the buylders refused, the same is made þe head corner stone?

18 Whosoeuer stomble at that stone shalbe broken: but on whomesoeuer it fal vpon it wyll grynde hym to powder.

19 And the hye priestes and the scrybes the same houre wente aboute to laye handes on him, but they feared the people. For they perceiued that he had spoken thys similitude against them.

20 And they watched hym, and sent forthe spyes whiche shoulde fayne them selues perfect, to take him in his wordes, and to delyuer hym vnto the power and authoritie of the debitie.

21 And they axed him, saiynge: Mayster, we knowe that thou sayest and teachest right, neyther consyderest thou any mans degree, but teachest the waye of God truely.

22 Is it laufull for vs to geue Cesar tribute or no?

23 He perceyued theyr craftynes, and sayde vnto them. Why tempt ye me?

24 shewe me a peny. Whose ymage and superscription hath it? They aunswered and sayde: Cesars.

25 And he sayed vnto them: Geue then vnto Cesar, that which belongeth vnto Cesar: and to God þt which partayneth to God.

26 And they coulde not reproue his saiynge before the people. But they maruayled at hys aunswere, and helde theyr peace.

27 Then came to him certaine of the Saduces which denye that there is anye resurreccyon. And they axed him,

28 saiynge: Maister, Moyses wrote vnto vs, yf anye mans brother dye hauyng a wyfe, and the same dye without yssue þt then his brother shoulde take his wyfe, and rayse vp seede vnto hys brother.

29 There were .vij. brethren, and the fyrst toke a wyfe, & dyed without chyldren.

30 And the seconde toke the wyfe, and he dyed childlesse:

31 And the third toke her, and in likewyse the residue of þe seuen. and left no chyldren behynde them, and died.

32 Laste of all the woman dyed also.

33 Nowe at þe resurreccyon whose wife of them shal she be? For seuen had her to wyfe.

34 Iesus aunswered, & sayde vnto them. The chyldren of this world mary wyues, & are maryed.

35 But they which shalbe made worthy to enioye that worlde and the resurreccyon from death, neyther marye wyues, neyther are maryed,

36 nor yet can dye anye more. For they are equal vnto the angels, & are the sonnes of god in as muche as they are the chyldren of the resurreccion.

37 And that the dead shal ryse agayne euen. Moises signifyed besides the bushe, when he sayed: The Lord God of Abraham, and the God of Isaac, and the God of Iacob.

38 For he is not the God of the dead, but of them which lyue. For al lyue in him.

39 Then certayne of the Pharises aunswered and sayd: Mayster thou haste wel sayde.

40 And after that durst they not axe him any question at all.

41 Then sayde he vnto them: how saye they, that Christe is Dauides sonne?

42 And Dauid hym selfe sayth in the boke of the Psalmes. The Lorde sayde vnto my Lorde, sitte on my ryghte hande,

43 tyll I make thyne enemyes thy fote stole.

44 Seynge Dauid called hym Lorde: howe is he then hys sonne?

45 Then in the audience of all the people, he sayed vnto hys disciples,

46 beware of the Scribes, whiche desyre to go in longe clothyng, & loue gretinges in the markettes, and the hyest seates in the synagoges, & chiefe roumes at feastes,

47 whiche deuoure wydowes houses, & that vnder a coloure of long praying: the same shall receyue greater damnacion.

# CHAPTER 21

As he behelde, he sawe the ryche men how they cast in theyr offerynges into the treasurye,

2 And he sawe a certayne poore wydowe, whiche caste in thyther two mytes.

3 And he sayde: of a truethe

I saye vnto you: this poore widow hath put in more then they all.

4 For they all haue of theyr superfluite added vnto the offering of god: but, she, of her penurye hath caste in all the substaunce that she had.

5 As some spake of the tempell, howe it was garnished wyth goodly stones and yewels, he sayde:

6 The dayes will come, when of these thinges which ye se shal not be left stone vpon stone, that shall not be throwen doune.

7 And they axed him saiynge: Maister when shall these thinges be, and what sygne wyll ther be, when such thinges shall come to passe.

8 And he sayd: take hede that ye be not deceiued. For manye wyll come in my name saiynge: I am he and the tyme draweth neare. Folowe not them therfore.

9 But when ye heare of warre and dissencion, be not afrayed. For these thinges muste fyrste come: but þe ende foloweth not by & by.

10 Then sayd he vnto them: Nacion shall ryse against nacion, and kingdom against kingdom,

11 and great earthquakes shall be in all quarters and honger, and pestilence and fearfull thinges. And great sygnes shall ther be from heauen.

12 But before all these, they shall laye their handes on you and persecute you, delyueringe you vp to the Synagoges & into pryson, and bringe you before kinges and rulers for my names sake.

13 And this shall chaunce you for a testimoniall.

14 Let it stycke therfore faste in your hertes, not once to studye before what ye shall aunswere:

15 For I wyll geue you a mouthe and wisdome, where against all youre aduersaries shall not be able to speake nor resyste.

16 Yea and ye shalbe betrayed of your fathers and mothers, and of your brethren, and kinsmen and louers, and some of you shal they put to death.

17 And hated shall ye be of all men for my names sake.

18 Yet there shal not one heare of your heades perishe.

19 With your pacience possesse your soules.

20 And when ye se Ierusalem beseged with an hoste, then vnderstande that the solacion of the same is nye.

21 Then let them which are in Iwrye fly þe to mountaines. And let them which are in the middes of it depart out. And let not them that are in other countries, enter therin.

22 For these be the dayes of vengeaunce, to fulfil all that are written.

23 But wo be to them that be with chylde, and to them that geue sucke in those dayes: for ther shalbe great trouble in the lande, and wrath ouer all this people.

24 And they shall fall on the edge of the swearde, and shalbe lead captyue into all nacyons. And Ierusalem shalbe troden vnder fote of the gentyls vntyll the tyme of þe gentyls be fulfylled.

25 And ther shalbe signes in the sunne, and in the mone, and in the starres: & in the earth, the people shalbe in such perplexitye, that they shall not tel which waye to turne them selues. The sea and the waters shall roore,

26 and mens hertes shall fayle them for feare, & for lokinge after those thinges whiche shall come on the earth. For the powers of heauen shal moue.

27 And then shall they se the sonne of man come in a cloude with power and great glory.

28 When these thynges beginne to come to passe then loke vp, and lift vp your heades, for youre redempcion draweth nye.

29 And he sheweth them a symilytude: behold the fygge tre, and all other trees,

30 when they shut forth their buddes, ye se and knowe of your owne selues that sommer is then nye at hande.

31 So likewyse ye (when ye se these thinges come to passe) vnderstande that the kingdome of God is nye.

32 Verelye I saye vnto you this generacion shall not passe tyll all be fulfylled.

33 Heauen and earth shall passe: but my wordes shall not passe.

34 Take hede to your selues, lest youre hertes be ouercome with surfetinge and dronkenes and cares of this worlde: and that that day come not on you vnwares.

35 For as a snare shall it come on all them that syt on the earth.

36 Watche therfore contynuallye and praye, that ye may obtayne grace to flye all this that shal come, and that ye may stande before the sonne of man.

37 In the daye tyme, he taught in the tempell and at night, he went out and had abiding in the mounte Oliuete.

38 And all the people came in the morninge to hym in the tempell, for to heare hym.

# CHAPTER 22

THE feast of swete bread drue nye whiche is called easter,

2 and the hye pryestes and scribes sought how to kyl hym, but they feared the people.

3 Then entred Sathan into Iudas whose syr name was Iscaryot (whych was of the number of the twelue)

4 and he went his waye and

communed with the hygh Priestes and offycers how he myght betraye him to them.

5 And they were glad, and promysed to geue him money.

6 And he consented, and sought oportunitye to betray him vnto them when the people were awaye.

7 Then came the daye of swete bread when necessyte the easterlambe muste be offered.

8 And he sent Peter and Ihon saiynge: go & prepare vs the easterlambe, that we may eate.

9 They said to hym: Where wilt thou that we prepare?

10 And he sayed vnto them: Behold when ye be entred into the citye, ther shall a man mete you bearinge a picher of water, him folowe into the same house that he entreth in,

11 & saye vnto the good man of the house: The mayster sayeth vnto the: wher is the geste chamber, where I shall eate myne easterlambe with my disciples?

12 And he shall shewe you a great parloure paued. There make redy.

13 And they went and founde as he had sayde vnto them, and made redy the easterlambe.

14 And when the houre was come, he sate doune and the twelue Apostles with him.

15 And sayde vnto them: I haue inwardlye desyred to eate this easterlambe with you, before that I suffer.

16 For I saye vnto you: henceforth I wyll not eate of it anye more, vntill it be fulfylled in the kingdome of God.

17 And he toke the cuppe and gaue thankes, and sayde: Take this and deuide it amonge you.

18 For I say vnto you: I wyll not drinke of the frute of the vyne vntyll the kyngdome of God be come.

19 And he toke bread, gaue thankes brake it, & gaue it to them, saiynge: This is my body which is geuen for you. This is the remembraunce of me.

20 Lykewyse also, when they had supped he toke the cup saiynge: This cup is the newe testamente in my bloude, whiche shall for you be shed.

21 Yet beholde, the hande of him that betrayeth me, is with me on on the table.

22 And the sonne of man goeth as it is appointed. But wo be to that man by whome he is betrayed.

23 And they beganne to enquire amonge them selues which of them it shoulde be, that shoulde do that.

24 And ther was a stryfe amonge them, which of them shoulde be taken for the greatest.

25 And he sayde vnto them: the kinges of the gentyls raigne ouer them, and they that beare rule ouer them, are called gracious Lordes.

26 But ye shall not be so. But he that is greatest amonge you, shalbe as the yongest: and he that is chiefe shal be as the minister.

27 For whether is greater, he that sytteth at meate: or he that serueth? Is not he that sytteth at meate? And I am amonge you, as he that ministreth.

28 Ye are they whiche haue bydden with me in my temptacions.

29 And I appointe vnto you a kyngdome, as my father hath appointed to me,

30 that ye maye eate and drinke at my table in my kingdome, and syt on seates, and iudge the twelue tribes of Israel.

31 And the Lorde sayde: Simon Simon beholde, Sathan hath desyred you, to syfte you, as it were wheate,

32 but I haue prayed for the, that thy faith fayle not. And when thou arte conuerted, strengthe thy brethren.

33 And he said vnto him: Lorde I am redye to go with the into prison, and to death.

34 And he saide: I tell the Peter, the cocke shal crowe this daye, tyl thou haue thrise denied that thou knowest me.

35 And he sayde vnto them: when I sente you without wallet and scrip and shoes? lacked ye any thinge? And they saide no.

36 And he sayde vnto them: but nowe he that hath a wallet let him take it vp and lykewyse his scrip. And he that hath no swerde, let him sell his cote and bye one.

37 For I saye vnto you: that yet that which is written, must be perfourmed in me: euen with the wicked was he numbred. For tose thinges which are written of me, haue an ende.

38 And they sayde: Lorde beholde here are two sweardes. And he sayde vnto them: it is ynough.

39 And he came out, and went as he was wont to mounte Oliuete. And the disciples folowed hym.

40 And when he came to the place, he sayde to them: praye, least ye fall into the temptacion.

41 And he gate him selfe from them, about a stones cast, & kneled doune, & prayed

42 saiynge: Father if thou wylt, wythdrawe this cup from me. Neuertheles, not my wyll, but thyne be fulfylled.

43 And ther appered an aungell vnto him from heauen, confortinge him.

44 And he was in agonye, and praied some what longer. And his sweate was lyke droppes of bloude trycklinge doune to the grounde.

45 And he rose vp from prayer, and came to his disciples, and founde them slepinge for sorowe,

46 and sayde vnto them: Why slepe ye? Ryse and praye, leste ye fall into temptacion.

47 Whyle he yet spake: beholde there came a company,

and he that was called Iudas, one of the twelue, wente before them, and preased nyghe vnto Iesus to kysse him

48 and Iesus said vnto hym: Iudas, betrayest thou the sonne of man with a kysse?

49 When they whiche were aboute him sawe what woulde folowe, they sayed vnto him: Lorde, shall we smite with sweardes?

50 And one of them smote a seruaunte of the hiest prieste of all, & smote of his righte eare.

51 And Iesus aunswered and saide: Suffer ye thus farre forth. And he touched his eare and healed him.

52 Then Iesus sayed vnto the hye pryestes and rulers of þe temple, and the elders which were come to him. Be ye come out as vnto a thefe with sweardes and staues?

53 When I was dayly with you in temple, ye stretched not forth handes agaynste me. But this is euen youre verye houre, and the power of darcknes.

54 Then toke they him, and ledde him and brought him to the hye priestes house. And Peter folowed a farre of.

55 When they had kindled a fyre in the myddes of the palaice, and were set doune together: Peter also sate doune amonge them:

56 And one of the wenches, behelde hym as he sate by the fyre and set good eye syght on him and sayde: this same was also with him.

57 Then he denyed hym saiynge: woman I knowe him not.

58 And after a lytle while another sawe him and said: thou arte also of them. And Peter sayed: man I am not.

59 And about the space of an houre after, another affyrmed saiynge: verelye euen this felowe was with him, for he is of Galile,

60 and Peter sayed: man I wote not what thou sayest. And immediatlye whyle he yet spake, that cocke crewe.

61 And the Lorde tourned backe and loked vpon Peter. And Peter remembred the wordes of the Lorde, howe he sayed vnto him, before the cocke crowe, thou shalt denye me thryse.

62 And Peter wente out, and wepte betterlye.

63 And the men that stode about Iesus mocked hym and smote him,

64 and blindfolded him, and smote his face. And axed him, saiynge arede who it is that smote the?

65 And manye other thinges despitfully sayed they against him.

66 And assone as it was daye the elders of the people and the hyghe priestes an scribes came together, and ledde him into their counsell saiynge:

67 are thou verye Christe? tell vs. And he sayde vnto them: If I shall tell you, ye wyl not beleue.

68 And if also I axe you, ye wyll not aunswere me or let me go.

69 Hereafter shall the sonne of man syt on the ryghthande of the power of God.

70 Then saide they all: Arte thou then the sonne of God? He sayde to them: ye say that I am.

71 Then sayde they: what nede we anye further wytnes? We our selues haue hearde of his owne mouthe.

## CHAPTER 23

AND the whole multytude of them arose, & ledde him vnto Pilate.

2 And they began to accuse hym saiynge: We haue founde thys felowe peruertinge the people & forbiddinge to paye tribute to Cesar, saiynge: that he is Christ a kinge.

3 And Pylate apposed him saiynge: art thou the kynge of the Iewes? He aunswered him and sayde: thou sayest it.

4 Then said Pilate to þe hye pryestes, & to the people: I fynde no faute in this man.

5 And they were the more fearce saiynge. He moueth the people, teachinge thorowout all Iewrye, and began at Galyle, euen to this place.

6 When Pilate hearde mencion of Galyle, he axed whether the man were of Galyle.

7 And as sone as he was knewen that he was of Herodes iurisdiccion he sent him to Herode, which was also at Ierusalem in those dayes:

8 And when Herode sawe Iesus, he was excedinglye gladde. For he was desyrous to se hym of a long season, because he had heard many thinges of him, and trusted to haue sene some miracles done by hym.

9 Then questioned he with hym of manye thinges. But he aunswered him not one worde.

10 The hye priestes and scribes, stode forth and accused him straightlye.

11 And Herode with his men of warre despysed him and mocked him, and arayed him in white, and sent him again to Pilate.

12 And the same daye Pylate and Herode were made frendes together. For before they were at variaunce.

13 And Pilate called together the hye priestes and the rulers, and the people,

14 and sayed vnto them. Ye haue brought this man vnto me, as one that peruerted the people. And beholde I haue examined him before you, & haue founde no faute in this man of those thinges wherof ye accuse him:

15 no nor yet Herode. For I sent you to him, and lo nothinge worthy of death is done of him.

16 I wil therfore chasten him and let him louse.

17 For of necessyte he muste haue let one louse vnto them at that feaste.

18 And all the people cryed at once saiynge: awaye with him and delyuer to vs Barrabas

19 which for insurreccion made in the cytye, and morther, was cast into prison,

20 Pilate spake agayne to them willinge to let Iesus louse.

21 And they cryed saiynge: Crucifye him, crucyfye him.

22 He saide vnto them the thirde tyme. What euill hath he done? I fynde no cause of death in him. I will therfore chasten him, & let him louse.

23 And they cryed with loude voice, & required that he might be crucyfyed. And the voice of them and of the hie priestes preuailed.

24 And Pilate gaue sentence that it should be as they required,

25 and let louse vnto them him that for insurreccion and morther, was cast into prison whom they desyreth, and deliuered Iesus to do with him what they woulde.

26 And as they led him awaye: they caught one Simon of Syren, coming out of the fielde and on him laide they the crosse, to beare it after Iesu.

27 And there folowed him a great companye of the people and of women, whiche women bewailed and lamented him.

28 But Iesus turned backe vnto them, and sayed: Doughters of Ierusalem, wepe not for me: but wepe for your selues and for your chyldren.

29 For beholde the dayes wyll come, when men shall saye: Happye are the baren and the wombes that neuer bare, and the pappes that neuer gaue sucke.

30 Then shall they beginne to say to the mountaynes fal on vs: to the hilles, couer vs.

31 For if they do this to a grene tre, what shalbe done to the drye?

32 And there were two euyll doers led with him to be slayne.

33 And when they were to the place which is called Caluarye, ther thei crucyfyed him and the euill doers, one on the right hande, and the other on the lifte.

34 Then said Iesus: father forgeue them, for they wote not what they do. And they parted his rayment, and cast lottes.

35 And the people stode and behelde. And the rulers mocked him with them saiyng: he holpe other men let him helpe him selfe, if he be Christ the chosen of God.

36 The souldiers also mocked him and came and gaue him vineger

37 and sayed: if thou be that kinge of the Iewes, saue thy selfe.

38 And his superscription was wrytten ouer him, in greke in latine and in Hebrew: This is the kinge of the Iewes:

39 And one of the euyll doers which hanged, rayled on him saiynge. If thou be Christ saue thy selfe and vs.

40 The other aunswered and rebuked him saiyng. Neither fearest thou God, because thou art in the same damnacion?

41 We are ryghtuously punished, for we receyued accordinge to our dedes. But this man hath done nothinge amisse.

42 And he sayd vnto Iesus: Lord remembre me when thou commeste into thy kyngdome.

43 And Iesus sayd vnto him: Verely I saye vnto the: to daye shalt thou be with me in Paradise.

44 And it was about the syxte houre. And there came a darcknes ouer all the lande, vntyl the ninthe houre,

45 and the sonne was darckened. And the vaile of the temple dyd rent euen through the myddes.

46 And Iesus cryed with a great voyce, and said: Father, into thy handes I commende my spirite. And when he thus had sayd: he gaue vp the ghoste.

47 When the Centurion sawe what had happened, he gloryfyed God saiynge: Of a suretye this man was perfecte.

48 And all the people that came together to the syght beholdinge the thinges which were done: smote their brestes, and returned home.

49 And all his acquantaunce, and the women that folowed him from Galyle, stode a farre of beholdinge these thinges.

50 And beholde there was a man named Ioseph, a counselloure, and was a good man and a iuste,

51 and did not consente to the counsell and dede of them which was of Aramathia, a cityе of the Iewes: which same also waited for the kingdome of God:

52 he wente vnto Pilate, and begged the bodye of Iesus,

53 and toke it doune, and wrapped it in a lynnen clothe, and layed it in a hewen tombe, wher in was neuer man before layed.

54 And that same day was the Saboth euen, and the Saboth drwe on.

55 The women that folowed after, which came with him from Galyle, behelde the sepulchre, and how his bodye was layed.

56 And they returned and prepared odours and ointmentes: but rested the Saboth daye, accordinge to the commaundemente.

# CHAPTER 24

On the morowe after the Saboth, early in the morninge, they came vnto the toumbe and brought the odoures which they had prepared and other women with them.

2 And they founde the stone rouled awaye from the sepulchre,

# LUKE

3 and wente in, but founde not the bodye of the Lorde Iesu.

4 And it happened, as they were amased thereat. Behold two men stode by them in shinninge vestures.

5 And as they were afrayed, and bowed doune their faces on the earth: they sayed to them: Why seke ye the lyuinge amonge the dead?

6 he is not here, but is rysen. Remember howe he spake vnto you, when he was yet with you in Galile,

7 saiynge: that the sonne of man must be delyuered into the handes of synfull men, and be crucifyed, and the thirde daye ryse againe.

8 And they remembred his wordes,

9 and returned from the sepulchre, and tolde all these thinges vnto the eleuen, and to al the remnaunte.

10 It was Mary Magdalene, and Ioanna, and Mary Iacobi, and other that were with them which tolde these thinges vnto the Apostles,

11 & their wordes semed vnto them fained thinges, neyther beleued they them.

12 Then arose Peter and ranne vnto the sepulchre, and stouped in & sawe the linnen clothes layde by them selfe, & departed wondringe in him selfe at that which had happened.

13 And beholde, two of them went that same daye to a toune which was from Ierusalem about threscore forlonges called Emaus,

14 and they talketh together of all these thinges that had happened.

15 And it chaunsed as they communed together and reasoned, that Iesus him selfe drue neare, and went with them.

16 But their eyes were holden that they coulde not knowe him.

17 And he sayed vnto them: What maner of communicacions are these that ye haue one to another as ye walke, and are sadde.

18 And the one of them named Cleophas, aunswered and sayed vnto him art thou only a straunger in Ierusalem, and hast not knowen the thinges which haue chaunsed therin in these dayes?

19 To whom he sayde: what thinges? And they sayde vnto him: of Iesus of Nazareth which was a Prophete, mighty in dede and worde before God, and all the people.

20 And howe the hye priestes and oure rulers delyuered him to be condempned to death: and haue crucifyed him.

21 But we trusted that it shoulde haue bene he, that shoulde haue delyuered Israell. And as touchinge all these thinges, to daye is euen the thirde daye, that they were done.

22 Yea and certayne women also of our companye made vs astonied, whiche come earlye vnto the sepulchre,

23 and founde not his bodye: and came saiynge, that they had sene a visyon of aungels, whiche saide that he was aliue.

24 And certaine of them which were with vs went their waye to the sepulchre, and founde it euen so as the women had sayde: but hym they sawe not.

25 And he sayed vnto them: O fooles and slowe of hert to beleue all that the Prophetes haue spoken.

26 Ought not Christ to haue suffred these thinges and to enter into his glorye?

27 And he began at Moyses, and at all the Prophetes, & interpreted vnto them in all scryptures, which were written of hym.

28 And they drue me vnto the toune which they wente to. And he made as though he woulde haue gone further?

29 But they constrayned him saiynge, abyde with vs, for it draweth towardes nyght, and the daye is farre passed. And he wente into tarye wyth them.

30 And it came to passe as he sate at meate with them, he toke breade, blessed it, brake and gaue to them.

31 And their eyes were opened and they knewe him: and he vanyshed out of their sight.

32 And they sayde betwene them selues: did not our hertes burne within vs whyle he talked with vs by the waye, and as he opened to vs the scryptures?

33 And they rose vp the same houre, and returned agayne to Ierusalem and founde the eleuen gathered together, and them that were with them,

34 which sayde: The Lorde is rysen in dede, and hath appeared to Simon.

35 And they tolde what thinges were done in the waye, and howe they knewe him in breakinge of breade.

36 As they thus spake. Iesus him selfe stode in the middes of them, and saide: Peace be with you.

37 And thei were abashed and afraied, supposynge that they had sene a spirite.

38 And he sayde vnto them: Why are ye troubled, and why do thoughtes aryse in your hertes?

39 Beholde my handes and & my fete, that it is euen my selfe. Handle me & se: for spyrytes haue not flesh and bones as ye se me haue.

40 And when he had thus spoken, he shewed them his handes and his fete.

41 And while they yet beleued not for ioye, and wondred, he said vnto them: haue ye here anye meate?

42 And they gaue him a pece of broiled fyshe, and of an hony combe.

43 And he toke it, and eate it before them.

44 And he sayde vnto them: These are the wordes which I spake vnto you, whyle I was yet with you: that al muste be fulfilled which was written of me in lawe of Moyses and in the prophetes and in the Psalmes.

45 Then opened he their wittes, that they myght vnderstande the scriptures,

46 and sayde vnto them: Thus is it written, and thus it behoued Christ to suffer: and to ryse agayne from death the thirde day,

47 and that repentaunce and remissyon of synnes shoulde be preached in his name amonge all nacions. And must begynne at Ierusalem.

48 And ye are witnesses of these thinges.

49 And beholde, I wyl sende the promes of my father vpon you. But tary ye in the citye of Ierusalem, vntyll ye be endewed with power from an hye.

50 And he led them out into Bethany, and lift vp his handes, & blessed them.

51 And it came to passe, as he blessed them, he departed from them, and was caryed vp into heauen.

52 And they worshipped him, and returned to Ierusalem, with great ioye,

53 and were contynuallye in the temple, praysynge and laudinge God. AMEN.

# John

## CHAPTER 1

In the begynnynge was the worde, and the word was with God, & the worde was God.

2 The same was in the begynnynge wyth God.

3 All thynges were made by it and without it was made nothynge that was made.

4 In it was lyfe, and the lyfe was the lyght of men,

5 & the lyght shyneth in the darknes, but the darknes comprehended it not.

6 Ther was a man sent from God, whose name was Iohn.

7 These same came as a wytnes to beare wytnes of the lyght, that all men through him myght beleue.

8 He was not that lyght but to beare witnes of the lyght.

9 That was a true lyght, which lyghted all men that come into the worlde.

10 He was in the worlde, & the worlde was made by him, & yet the worlde knewe him not.

11 He came amonge his (owne) & his owne receiued him not.

12 But as manye as receyued him to them he gaue power to be the sonnes of God in that they beleued on his name

13 & which were borne not of the bloude nor of the wyl of the flesh, nor yet of the wyll of man: but of God.

14 And the worde was made flesh & dwelt amonge vs, and we sawe the glorye of it, as the glory of the onlye begotten sonne of the father, which worde was ful of grace & verite.

15 Iohn bare witnes of him & cried saiyng: This was he of whom I spake, he that cometh after me was before me, because he was yer then I.

16 And of his fulnes haue all we receyued, euen (grace) for grace.

17 For the lawe was geuen by Moyses, but grace and truthe came by Iesus Christ.

18 No man hath sene God at anye tyme. The onlye begotten sonne which is in the bosome of the father, he hath declared hym.

19 And this is the recorde of Iohn: When the Iewes sent pryestes and Leuites from Ierusalem, to axe him what arte thou?

20 And he confessed and denied not, and sayd plainlye: I am not Chryste.

21 And they axed hym: what then? Art thou Helias? And he sayed: I am not. Art thou a Prophete? And he aunswered no.

22 Then sayed they vnto him: what art thou? that we may geue an aunswere to them that sent vs? What sayest thou of thy selfe?

23 He sayde: I am the voice of a cryar in the wyldernes, make strayght the waye of the Lorde, as sayde the Prophete Esaias.

24 And they which were sent, were of the pharyseis.

25 And they axed him: and sayd vnto him: why baptysest thou then if thou be not Christ, nor Helias, neyther a Prophete?

26 Iohn aunswered them saiynge: I baptyse with water, but one is come amonge you whom ye knowe not,

27 he it is that cometh after me, which was before me, whose shoe latchet I am not worthy to vnlose.

28 These things were done in Bethabara beyonde Iordaine wher Iohn did baptyse.

29 The nexte daye Iohn sawe Iesus commynge vnto him, and sayde: beholde the lambe of God, which taketh away the synne of the worlde.

30 This is he of whom I sayde. After me cometh a man which was before me, for he was yer then I,

31 and I knowe him not: but that he shoulde be declared to Israel, therfore am I come baptysynge with water.

32 And Iohn bare recorde saiynge: I saw the sprete descende from heauen, lyke vnto a doue, and abide vpon him,

33 and I knewe him not. But

he that sent me: to baptyse in water, the same sayde vnto me: vpon whom thou shalt se the sprete descende and tarye styll on him, the same is he, whych baptyseth wyth the holye ghost.

34 And I sawe and beare recorde that this is the sonne of God.

35 The next daye after Iohn stode againe, and two of his disciples.

36 And he behelde Iesus as he walked by, & sayde: beholde the lambe of God.

37 And the .ij. disciples hearde him speake & foloweth Iesus.

38 And Iesus turned aboute and sawe them folowe, and sayde vnto them: what seke ye? They sayde vnto him: Rabbi (which is to saye by interpretacion, Maister) wher dwellest thou?

39 He sayed vnto them: come and se. They came and sawe wher he dwelte: and abode with him the daye. For it was aboute the tenth houre.

40 One of the two which hearde Iohn speake and folowed Iesus, was Andrew Simon Peters brother.

41 The same founde his brother Simon fyrst, and sayde vnto him: we haue founde Messias, which is by interpretation, anointed:

42 and brought him to Iesus. And Iesus behelde him and saide: thou art Simon the sonne of Ionas, thou shalt be called Cephas: which is by interpretacion, a stone.

43 The daye folowinge Iesus woulde go into Galyle, and founde Philip, and saide vnto him: folow me.

44 Philip was of Bethsaida the citye of Andrewe and Peter.

45 And Phylyp founde Nathanaell, and sayde vnto hym. We haue founde hym of whom Moyses in the lawe, and the prophetes did write: Iesus the sonne of Ioseph of Nazareth.

46 And Nathanael said to him: Can there any good thing come out of Nazareth? Philip saide to him: come and se.

47 Iesus sawe Nathanael comminge to him and sayde of him: Beholde a right Israelyte, in whom is no gyle.

48 Nathanael, saide vnto hym: wher knewest thou me? Iesus aunswered, and sayde vnto him: Before that Philyp called the when thou wast vnder the fygge tree, I sawe the.

49 Nathanael aunswered & sayde vnto him: Rabbi, thou art the sonne of God, thou art the kynge of Israel.

50 Iesus aunswered and sayde vnto him: Because I sayde vnto the: I sawe the vnder the fygge tree, thou beleuest. Thou shalt se greater thinges then these.

51 And he sayed vnto him: Verely verely, I saye vnto you: here after shall ye se heauen open, and the aungels of God ascendinge and descendinge ouer the sonne of man.

# CHAPTER 2

AND þe thyrd day, was ther a Maryage in Cana a citie of Galile: & the mother of Iesus was ther.

2 And Iesus was called also & his disciples vnto the mariage.

3 And when the wyne fayled, the mother of Iesus sayde vnto him: they haue no wine.

4 Iesus said vnto her: woman, what haue I to do with the? Myne houre is not yet come.

5 His mother sayd vnto the mynisters: whatsoeuer he saith vnto you, do it.

6 And ther were standing there, sixe water pots of stone after the maner of the puryfiyng of the Iewes containinge two or thre fyrkins a pece.

7 And Iesus sayd vnto them: fill the waterpottes with water. And they filled them vp to þe bryme.

8 And he sayd vnto them: drawe out now, & beare vnto þe gouerner of þe feaste. And they beare it.

9 When the ruler of þe feaste had tasted the water þt was turned vnto wyne, & knew not whence it was (but the mynysters whyche drue the water, knewe) He called the brydegrome,

10 and sayed vnto him: Al men at þe beginning, set forth good wine and when men be dronke, then that which is worsse. But thou hast kept back þe good wine vntil now.

11 This beginning of miracles did Iesus in Cana of Galile, and shewed his glory, & hys disciples beleued on him.

12 After that he descended into Capernaum, and his mother and his brethren, and his disciples: but continued not manye dayes there.

13 And the Iewes easter was euen at hande, & Iesus went vp to Ierusalem,

14 and founde syttinge in the temple those þt solde oxen & shepe and doues and chaungers of money.

15 And he made a scourge of smal cordes: and draue them all out of the temple with the shepe and oxen, and poured out the chaungers money, and ouerthrue the tables,

16 and sayd vnto them that solde doues: Haue these things hence & make not my fathers house an house of marchaundise.

17 And his dyscyples remembred how that it was written: the zele of thyne house hath euen eaten me.

18 Then aunswered the Iewes & saied to him: what token shewest thou vnto vs, seyng that thou dost these thinges?

19 Iesus aunswered and said vnto them: destroy thys temple & in thre dayes. I wyll reare it vp

again.

20 Then said the Iewes .xlvi. yeres was thys temple a buildynge, and wylt thou reare it vp in .iij. daies?

21 But he spake of the temple of hys bodie.

22 Assone therfore as he was risen from death agayne, his disciples remembred that he thus said. And they beleued the scrypture, and the wordes whyche Iesus had sayd.

23 When he was at Ierusalem at easter in the feaste many beleued on his name, when they sawe his miracles which he dyd,

24 but Iesus put not himself in their handes, because he knewe all men,

25 and neded not that any man shuld testyfy of man. For he knew what was in man.

## CHAPTER 3

THER was a man of þe Pharises named Nicodemus a ruler amonge the Iewes.

2 The same came to Iesus by nyghte & sayed vnto him: Rabbi, we knowe that thou art a teacher whiche art come from God. For no man coulde do such miracles as thou doest, except God were wt him.

3 Iesus aunswered & said to him: verely verely, I said vnto the: except a man be borne a new, he can not se the kingdome of God.

4 Nicodemus said vnto him: how can a man be borne when he is olde? can he enter into his mothers wombe and be borne againe?

5 Iesus aunswered: verely, verely, I saye vnto the: except that a man be boren of water and of the spyryte, he can not enter into the kyngdome of God.

6 That whyche is borne of the fleshe is fleshe: and that whiche is borne of the spyryte, is spyrite.

7 Marueyle not that I said to þe, ye must be borne a newe.

8 The wynde bloweth wher it listeth: and thou hearest the sounde therof: but canst not tell whence it cometh and whyther it goeth: So is euery man that is borne of the spyryte.

9 And Nicodemus aunswered and said vnto him: how can these thinges be?

10 Iesus aunswered & said vnto him: art thou a maister in Israel, and knowest not these thinges?

11 Verely, verely, I say vnto þe we speake that we know and testify that we haue sene, & ye receiue not our witnes.

12 Yf when I tel you earthly thinges ye beleue not: howe shoulde ye beleue if I shal tell you of heauenly thinges?

13 And no man ascendeth vp to heauen, but he that came doune from heauen, that is to say, the sonne of man which is in heauen.

14 And as Moyses lyfte vp the serpent in the wyldernes, euen so muste the sonne of man be lyft vp,

15 that none that beleueth in him perish, but haue eternall life.

16 For God so loueth the worlde, þt he hath geuen his only sonne, that none that beleue in him, should perishe: but should haue euerlastinge lyfe.

17 For God sent not his sonne into þe world, to condempne the worlde: but that the world through him, might be saued.

18 He that beleueth on him, shal not be condempned. But he that beleueth not is condempned allready, because he beleueth not in the name of the onlye sonne of God.

19 And this is the condempnacion, that light is come into the worlde, and the men loued darknes more then lyght, because their dedes were euyll.

20 For euerye man that euyll doth, hateth the light: nether commeth to the lyghte: lest his dedes shoulde be reproued.

21 But he that doeth truth commeth to the light that hys dedes myght be knowen, how that they are wrought in God.

22 After these thinges came Iesus & his dysciples into the Iewes lande, and ther he haunted wyth them & baptised.

23 And Iohn also baptysed in Enon besides Salim, because ther was much water there, & they came and were baptised.

24 For Iohn was not yet cast into pryson.

25 And ther arose a question betwene Iohns disciples and the Iewes aboute purifyinge.

26 And they came vnto Iohn, and sayed vnto hym: Rabbie, he that was with þe beyond Iordan, to whom thou bareste witnes, Beholde the same baptyseth, and al men come to him.

27 Iohn aunswered, and sayed: a man can receiue nothing at al except it be geuen him from heauen.

28 Ye youre selues are witnesses how that I saide: I am not Christ, but am sent before him.

29 He that hath the bryde is þe brydegrome. But the frend of the brydegrom, whiche standeth by and heareth him reioyseth greatlye of the brydegromes voyce. Thys my ioye is fulfilled.

30 He muste increace: and I muste decreace.

31 He that commeth from an hye is aboue al. He that is of the earth, is of the earth, & speaketh of the earth. He that commeth from heauen, is aboue all,

32 and what he hath sene and hearde: that he testifyeth: but no man receiueth his testimony.

33 Howbeit he that hath receiueth his testimony hath set to his seale that God is true.

34 For he whom God hath sent, speaketh the wordes of God: For God geueth not þe spirite by measure.

35 The father loueth þe sonne and hath geuen all thinges into his hand.

36 He that beleueth on the sonne, hath euerlasting life, and he that beleueth not þe sonne shall not se life: but þe wrath of God abydeth on him.

# CHAPTER 4

As sone as the Lord had knowledge, how the Phariseis had hearde, that Iesus made & Baptysed more disciples then Iohn

2 (though that Iesus him self baptysed not: but his disciples)

3 he lefte Iewry, & departed agayne into Galile.

4 And it was so þt he must nedes go thorowe Samaria.

5 Then cam he to a citie of Samaria called Sichar, beside the possessyon that Iacob gaue to hys sonne Iosephe.

6 And there was Iacobs wel, Iesus then weried in hys iorny, sate thus on the wel. And it was about the .vi. houre:

7 and ther came a woman of Samaria to draw water. And Iesus sayed vnto hyr: geue me drinke.

8 For hys disciples were gone awaye vnto the town to bye meate.

9 Then sayde the woman of Samarya vnto hym: howe is it, þt thou beynge a Iewe, axest drynke of me which am a Samaritan? for the Iewes medle not with the Samaritans.

10 Iesus aunswered & sayd vnto hyr: if thou kneweste the gyfte of God, and who it is that sayeth to the geue me drynke, thou wouldeste haue axed of hym, and he woulde haue geuen the water of lyfe.

11 The woman sayd to hym: Syr thou hast nothinge to drawe wyth, and the well is depe: from whence then hast thou that water of lyfe?

12 Art thou greater, then our father Iacob, whyche gaue vs this well, and he him selfe dranke therof, and hys chyldren, and his catell?

13 Iesus aunswered & sayde vnto hyr: whosoeuer drynketh of thys water: shall thyrste agayne.

14 But whosoeuer shall drinke of þe water that I shall geue hym, shall neuer be more a thyrste: but the water that I shall geue him, shall be in him a well of water, springinge vp into euerlasting lyfe.

15 The woman sayde vnto him: Syr geue me of that water, that I thyrst not neyther come hyther to draw.

16 Iesus sayd vnto hyr. Go and call thy husbande, and come hyther.

17 The woman aunswered and sayde to him: I haue no husbande.

18 Iesus sayde to hyr, Thou hast well sayed, I haue no husbande. For thou haste had fyue husbandes and he whome thou nowe haste is not thy husbande. That saydest thou trulye.

19 The woman sayd vnto him: Syr I perceiue that thou art a prophete.

20 Oure fathers worshipped in this mountayne: and ye saye þt in Hyerusalem is the place where men ought to worship.

21 Iesus sayd vnto hyr: woman beleue me, the houre cometh, when ye shal neyther in this mountayne, nor yet at Hierusalem worshyppe the father.

22 Ye worshype, ye wote not what: we knowe what we worshype. For saluation cometh of the Iewes.

23 But the houre cometh and nowe is, when the true worshyppers shal worshyp the father in spyrite and in trueth. For verelye suche the father requireth to worshyp him.

24 God is a spyryte, and they that worshyp hym, must worshyp hym in spiryte and trueth.

25 The woman sayd vnto him: I wot well Messias shal come, whiche is called Christe. When he is come, he wyll tell vs all thinges.

26 Iesus sayd vnto hyr: I that speake vnto the am he.

27 And euen at that poynte, came hys disciples, & merueyled that he talketh with the woman. Yet no man said vnto him: what meanest thou, or why talkest thou with hyr?

28 The woman then left hyr waterpotte, and went hyr way into the citie, and sayed to the men.

29 Come se a man whiche told me all thynges that euer I dyd. Is not he Christ?

30 Then they went out of the cytye, and came vnto hym.

31 And in the meane while his disciples praied hym saying: Maister, eate.

32 He said vnto them: I haue meate to eate, that ye knowe not of.

33 Then saied the discyples betwene them selues: hath anye manne brought hym meate?

34 Iesus saied to them: my meate is to do the wil of him that sent me. And to fynishe his workes.

35 Saye not ye: there are yet foure monethes, and then cometh heruest? Behold I saye vnto you, lyfte vp youre eyes, and loke on the regyons: for they are whyte al ready vnto harueste.

36 And he that reapeth receyueth rewarde, and gathereth fruite vnto lyfe eternall: that both he that soweth, and he that reapeth might reioyce together.

37 And herein is the sayinge true, that one soweth, and another reapeth.

38 I sente you to reape that wheron ye bestowed no laboure. Othere men laboured, and ye are entred into theyr laboures.

# JOHN

39 Manye of the Samarytanes of that citie beleued on hym for the sayinge of the woman, whyche testified, he tolde me all thynges that euer I did.

40 Then when the Samaritans were come vnto him they besought hym þt he woulde tary with them. And he abode ther .ij. daies.

41 And manye more beleued because of his owne wordes,

42 & sayd vnto þe woman. Now we beleue not because of thy saying. For we haue heard hym oureselues, & knowe þt thys is euen in dede Christe the Sauioure of þe worlde.

43 After .ij. daies he departed thence, and wente awaye into Galile.

44 And Iesus hym selfe testifyed, that a Prophet hath no honoure in hys own countrye.

45 Then assone as he was come into Galyle, the Galyleans receyued hym whych had sene al the thynges that he dyd at Hierusalem at þe feaste. For they went also vnto þe feaste daye.

46 And Iesus came againe into Cana of Galile: wher he turned water into wine. And there was a certayne ruler, whose sonne was sicke at Capernaum.

47 Assone as the same heard þt Iesus was come out of Iury into Galile, he wente vnto hym, and besoughte hym, that he woulde descende and heale hys sonne: For he was euen ready to dye.

48 Then sayed Iesus vnto hym: except ye se sygnes and wonders ye can not beleue.

49 The ruler sayd vnto him: Syr come awaie or euer my chylde dye.

50 Iesus sayd vnto hym: Go thy waie, thy sonne liueth. And the man beleued the wordes that Iesus had spoken vnto hym, and went hys way.

51 And anone as he went on his waye, hys seruauntes mette hym and tolde hym sayinge, thy chylde lyueth.

52 Then enquered he of them the houre when he began to amende, and they saied vnto hym: yester daye the seuenth houre þe feuer lefte hym.

53 And the father knewe that it was the same houre in whyche Iesus sayed vnto hym: Thy sonne lyueth. And he beleued and al his housholde.

54 This is againe the, seconde miracle, that Iesus dyd after he was come out of Iury into Galile.

## CHAPTER 5

AFTER that there was a feast of the Iewes and Iesus went vp to Ierusalem.

2 And ther is at Ierusalem by the slaughterhouse, a pole called in the Ebrue toung Bethesda, hauing .v. porches,

3 in which lay a greate multitude of sycke folke, of blinde halt and withered, waitinge for the mouyng of the water.

4 For an angell went doune at a certaine ceason into the pole and troubled the water. Whosoeuer then fyrste after þe steringe of the water, stepped in, was made whole of whatsoeuer disease he had.

5 And a certayne man was there whyche had ben diseased .xxxviij. yeares.

6 When Iesus sawe hym lye and knewe that he nowe longe tyme had bene diseased, he said vnto hym: Wylt thou be made whole?

7 The sicke man aunswered hym. Syr I haue no man when þe water is troubled to put me into þe pole. But in þe meane time while I am about to come, another steppeth doune before me.

8 And Iesus sayde vnto him: ryse take vp thy bed, and walke.

9 And immediatly the man was made whole, and toke vp his bedde, and went. And the same day was the saboth daye.

10 The Iewes therfore sayd to him þt was made whole it is the saboth day, it is not lawful for the to carye thy bed.

11 He answered them: he that made me whole, said vnto me: take vp thy bed, and get the hence.

12 Then axed they hym what man is þt whiche saied vnto þe, take vp thy bed & walke.

13 And he þt was healed, wiste not who it was. For Iesus had gotten him selfe awaie, because þt there was prease of people in the place.

14 And after that, Iesus found him in þe temple & said vnto him: behold thou arte made whole, synne no more, lest a worsse thinge happen vnto the.

15 The man departed & told þe Iewes that it was Iesus, which had made him whole.

16 And therfore the Iewes dyd persecute Iesus, and soughte þe meanes to slea him, because he had done these thinges on the saboth daye.

17 And Iesus answered them: my father worketh hither to & I worke.

18 Therfore the Iewes sought the more to kill him not only because he had broken the saboth, but sayd also that God was hys father, and made hym selfe equal with God.

19 Then aunswered Iesus and sayed vnto them: verely verely, I say vnto you: the sonne can do nothinge of hym selfe, but that he seeth the father do. For whatsoeuer he doth, that doeth the sonne also.

20 For the father loueth þe sonne, & sheweth hym all thinges, whatsoeuer he him selfe doeth. And he wyll shewe hym greater workes then these, because ye should maruaile.

21 For lykewyse as the father rayseth vp the dead, and quickeneth them: euen so the

sonne quickeneth whom he wyll.

22 Neyther iudgeth the father anye man: but hath committed all iudgement vnto the sonne,

23 because that all men should honoure the sonne, euen as they honoured the father. He that honoureth not the sonne: þe same honoureth not þe father, which hath sent him.

24 Verely, verely I say vnto you he that heareth my wordes, and beleueth on him that sent me, hath euerlasting lyfe, & shal not come into damnacion: but is escaped from death vnto lyfe.

25 Verely verely, I saye vnto you: The tyme shall come, and nowe is, when the dead shall heare the voyce of the sonne of God. And they that heare shall lyue.

26 For as the father hath lyfe in him selfe, so lykewyse hath he geuen to the sonne to haue lyfe in him selfe,

27 and hath geuen him power also to iudge, in that he is the sonne of man.

28 Maruaile not at this, the houre shall come in the which all that are in the graues, shal heare his voice,

29 and shall come forth: they that haue done good, vnto the resurreccion of lyfe, and they that hath done euil, vnto the resurreccion of damnacion.

30 I can of myne owne selfe do nothinge at all. As I heare. I iudge: and my iudgement is iust, because I seke not mine owne wyll but the wyll of my father which hath sent me.

31 If I beare witnes of my selfe, my witnes is not true.

32 Ther is another that beareth witnes of me, and I am sure that the wytnes which he beareth of me, is true.

33 Ye sent vnto Iohn, and he bare witnes vnto the truth.

34 But I receiue not the recorde of man Neuerthelesse, these thinges I say that ye might be safe.

35 He was a burninge and a shyninge lyght and ye woulde for a season haue reioysed in his lyght:

36 But I haue greater witnes then the witnes of Iohn. For the workes which the father hath geuen me to fynyshe the same workes which I do, beare witnes of me that the father sent me.

37 And the father himselfe which hath sent me, beareth witnes of me. Ye haue not hearde his voice at anye tyme nor ye haue sene his shape:

38 therto his wordes haue ye not abydinge in you. For whom he hath sent, him ye beleue not.

39 Searche the sciptures, for in them ye thinke ye haue eternall lyfe: and they are they which testifye of me.

40 And yet wyll ye not come to me that ye might haue lyfe.

41 I receyue not prayse of men.

42 But I knowe you, that ye haue not the loue of God in you.

43 I am come in my fathers name, and ye receyue me not. If another shall come in his owne name, him wyll ye receyue.

44 Howe can ye beleue which receyue honoure one of another, and seke not the honoure that commeth of God onlye?

45 Do not thinke that I wyll accuse you to my father. There is one that accuseth you euen Moyses in whom ye truste.

46 For had ye beleued Moises ye would haue beleued me for, he wrote of me.

47 But seynge ye beleue not hys writting: how should ye beleue my wordes?

# CHAPTER 6

AFTER these thynges Iesus went his way ouer the sea of Galyle, nye to a cytye called Tyberias.

2 And a great multitude folowed hym, because they had sene his miracles which he did

on them that were diseased.

3 And Iesus went vp into a mountayne, and there he sate with his disciples.

4 And easter a feast of the Iewes was nye.

5 Then Iesus lift vp his eyes, and sawe a company come vnto him, and sayd vnto Phylip: whence shalt we bye bread þt these might eate?

6 This he sayde to proue hym, for he him selfe knewe what he would do.

7 Philip aunswered him, two hondred peny worth of bread are not sufficient for them, that euerye man haue a litel.

8 Then sayde vnto hym one of his disciples, Andrew Simon Peters brother.

9 Ther is a lad here, which hath fyue barly loues and two fyshes: but what is that among so many?

10 And Iesus sayde: make the people sytte downe. There was much grasse in the place. And the men sate doune, in numbre, about fyue thousande.

11 And Iesus toke the bread and gaue thankes, and gaue to the disciples, and his disciples to them that were set doune. And likewise of the fyshes as much as they would.

12 When they had eaten ynough, he said vnto his disciples: gather vp the broken meate that remayneth: that nothinge be lost:

13 And they gathered it together and fylled twelue baskettes with the broken meate, of the fyue barly loues and two fyshes which broken meate remained vnto them that had eaten.

14 Then the men when they had sene the miracle that Iesus did, saide: this is of a truthe the prophete that shoulde come into the worlde.

15 When Iesus perceiued that they woulde come, & take him vp to make him king, he

departed againe into a mountaine him selfe alone.

16 And when euen was come his disciples went vnto the sea

17 and entred into a shyppe and went ouer the sea vnto Capernaum. And anone it was darke, and Iesus was not come to them.

18 And þe sea arose wt a great winde þt blewe.

19 And when they had rowen about a .xxv. or a .xxx. furlonges, they sawe Iesus walke on the sea, and drawe nye vnto the shippe and they were afrayed.

20 And he sayde to them. It is I: be not afrayed.

21 Then would they haue receyued him into the shyppe, and the shyppe was by and by at the lande whither they wente.

22 The daye folowinge, the people which stode on the other syde of the sea, sawe that ther was none other shyp ther saue that one wherinto his disciples were entred and that Iesus went not in with his discyples into the shyp but that his disciples were gone awaye alone.

23 How be it ther came other shyppes from Tiberias nye vnto the place wher they eate bread when the Lorde hath blessed.

24 Then when the people sawe that Iesus was not there neyther his disciples, they also toke shyppinge and came to Capernaum sekinge for Iesus.

25 And when they had found him on the other syde of the sea, they sayde vnto hym: Rabbi when camest thou hither?

26 Iesus aunswered them and sayde verelye, verelye I say vnto you ye seke me, not because ye sawe the miracles, but because ye eate of the loues, and were fylled.

27 Laboure not for the meate which perysheth, but for the meate that endureth vnto euerlasting lyfe, which meate the sonne of man shall geue vnto you. For hym hath God the father sealed.

28 Then sayde they vnto him: what shall we do þt we might worke the workes of God?

29 Iesus aunswered and saide vnto them: This is the worke of God, that ye beleue on him: whom he hath sent.

30 They said vnto him: what sygne shewest thou them that we may se and beleue the? What doest thou worke?

31 Our father did eate manna in the desert as it is written. He gaue them bread from heauen to eate.

32 Iesus sayde vnto them: verelye, verelye I say vnto you: Moyses gaue you not breade from heauen: but my father geueth you the true breade from heauen.

33 For the bread of God is he which commeth doune from heauen, and geueth lyfe vnto the worlde.

34 Then sayde they vnto hym: Lord, euermore geue vs this breade.

35 And Iesus sayde vnto them: I am that breade of lyfe. He that commeth to me, shall not honger: and he that beleueth on me shall not thurste.

36 But I saye vnto you: that ye haue sene me, and yet beleue not.

37 All that the father geueth me shall come to me, and him that cometh to me, I cast not awaye.

38 For I came doune from heauen: not to do myne owne wyll, but his wyll which hath sent me.

39 And this is the fathers wyll which hath sent me, that of all whiche hath geuen me, I shoulde loose nothinge: but shoulde rayse it vp agayne at the laste daye.

40 And this is the wyll of him that sent me: that euerye man which seeth the sonne and beleueth on him haue euerlasting lyfe. And I wyll rayse him vp at the laste daye.

41 The Iewes then murmured at him, because he sayd: I am that bread which is come doune from heauen.

42 And they sayde: Is not this Iesus the sonne of Ioseph, whose father and mother we knowe? Howe is it then that he saieth: I came doune from heauen?

43 Iesus aunswered and saide vnto them. Murmure not amonge your selues.

44 No man can come to me: except the father which hath sent me drawe him. And I wyll rayse him vp at the laste day.

45 It is written in the prophetes: that they shalbe al taught of God. Euery man therfore thath hath heard and hath learned of the father commeth vnto me.

46 Not that anye man hath sene the father, saue which is of God, the same hath sene the father.

47 Verely, verelye, I say vnto you, he that beleueth on me, hath euerlasting lyfe

48 I am that bread of lyfe.

49 Youre fathers did eate Manna in the wyldernes and are dead.

50 This is that bread which commeth from heauen that he which eateth of it, shoulde also not dye.

51 I am that lyuinge bread: which came doune from heauen. If any man eate of this bread, he shall lyue for euer. And the bread that I wyll geue is my flesh, which I will geue for the life of the worlde.

52 And the Iewes stroue amonge them selues saiynge: How can this felowe geue vs his flesh to eate?

53 Then Iesus saide to them. Verely, verely, I say vnto you: excepte ye eate the fleshe of the sonne of man and drinke his bloude, ye shall not haue lyue in you.

54 Whosoeuer eateth my flesh, and drinketh my bloude, hath eternal lyfe: and I wyll rayse him vp at the laste day.

55 For my flesh is meate in dede, and my bloude is drinke in dede.

56 He þt eateth my flesh, and drinketh my bloude, dwelt in me and I in him.

57 As the liuinge father hath sent me, euen so lyue I by my father, and he that eateth me shall lyue by me.

58 This is the bread which came from heauen: not as your fathers haue eaten Manna and are dead. He that eateth of this breade, shall lyue euer.

59 These things sayed he in the synagoge as he taught in Capernaum.

60 Many therfore of his disciples, when they had hearde this, sayd this is anhearde saiynge: who can abide the hearinge of it?

61 Iesus knewe in him selfe, that his disciples murmured at it, and sayde vnto them: Doth this offende you?

62 What and if ye shall se the sonne of man ascende vp wher he was before?

63 It is the spirite that quickeneth, the flesh proffetteth nothing. The wordes that I speake vnto you, are spirite and lyfe.

64 But there are some of you that beleue not. For Iesus knewe from the beginninge, which they were that beleued not, and wo should betraye him.

65 And he sayde: therfore said I vnto you that no man cometh vnto me, except it were geuen vnto him of my father.

66 From that tyme manye of his discyples wente backe, and walked no more with him.

67 Then sayde Iesus to the twelue: will ye also go awaye?

68 Then Symon Peter aunswered: Maister to whom shall we go? Thou hast the wordes of eternall lyfe,

69 and we beleue and knowe thou arte Christe the sonne of the lyuinge God.

70 Iesus aunswered them: Haue not I chosen you twelue, and yet one of you is the deuyll?

71 He spake it of Iudas Iscarioth þe sonne of Simon: For he it was that shoulde betraye him, and was one of the twelue.

## CHAPTER 7

AFTER that Iesus went about into Galile, and would not go about in Iewry, for the Iewes sought to kyll him.

2 The Iewes tabernacle feaste was at hande.

3 His brethren therfore sayde vnto hym: get the hence, & go into Iewry that thy disciples maye se thy workes that thou doest.

4 For ther is no man that doeth any thing secretly, and he him selfe seketh to be knowen openly. If thou do such thinges shew thy selfe to the worlde.

5 For as yet his brethren beleued not in him.

6 Then Iesus sayde vnto them: My tyme is not yet come, your tyme is alway redye.

7 The worlde can not hate you. But me it hateth: because I testifye of it, that the workes of it are euyll.

8 Go ye vp vnto this feaste, I wyl not go yet vnto this feaste for my tyme is not yet full come.

9 These wordes he sayde vnto them, and abode styll in Galyle.

10 But assone as his brethren were gone vp, he wente also vp vnto the feast: not openly, but as it were priuelye.

11 Then sought him the Iewes at the feaste, and sayde: where is he?

12 And much murmuringe was ther of him amonge the people. Some sayde: He is good. Other sayd nay, but he deceiued the people.

13 How beit no man spake openlye of him, for feare of the Iewes.

14 In the middes of the feaste, Iesus wente vp into the temple and taught

15 And the Iewes maruayled saiynge: How knoweth he the scriptures, seiyng that he neuer learned?

16 Iesus aunswered them, and sayde: My doctryne is not myne: but his that sent me:

17 If any man wil do his wyll he shall knowe of the doctryne, whither it be of God, or whither I speake of my selfe.

18 He that speaketh of him selfe, seketh his owne prayse. But he that seketh his prayse that sent him, the same is true and no vnrightuousnes is in him.

19 Dyd not Moises geue you a lawe, and yet none of you kepeth the lawe? Why go ye about to kill me?

20 The people aunswered and sayde: thou hast the deuyl: who goeth about to kyll the?

21 Iesus aunswereth and saide to them: I haue done one worke, and ye all maruayle.

22 Moyses therfore gaue vnto you circuncisyon: not because it is of Moises, but of the fathers. And yet ye on the Saboth daye, circumcyse a man.

23 If a man on the Saboth daye receyue circumcisyon without breakinge of the lawe of Moyses: disdayne ye at me because I haue made a man euery whit whole on the Saboth daye?

24 Iudge not after the vtter aperaunce: but iudge rightuouse iudgemente.

25 Then sayde some of them of Hierusalem: is not this he whom they go aboute to kyll?

26 Beholde he speaketh boldly, & they say nothinge to him: Do the rulers knowe in dede that this is very Christe?

27 Howe be it we knowe this

man whence he is: but when Christ cometh, no man shall knowe whence he is.

28 Then cried Iesus in the temple as he taught saiyng: ye knowe me, and whence I am ye knowe. And yet I am not come of my selfe, but he that sent me is true, whom ye knowe not.

29 I knowe hym: for I am of hym, and he hath sent me.

30 Then they sought to take hym: but no man layde handes on hym, because his tyme was not yet come.

31 Many of the people beleued on him and sayd: when Christe cometh wyl he do mo miracles then this man hath done?

32 The pharyseis hearde that the people murmured such thinges about him. Wherfore the phariseis and hye priestes sente ministers forth to take him.

33 Then sayde Iesus vnto them: Yet am I a lytle while with you, and then go I vnto hym that sent me.

34 Ye shall seke, and shal not fynde me: and where I am, thither can ye not come.

35 Then sayd the Iewes amonge them selues: whither wyll he go, that we shall not fynde him? Wyll he go amonge the gentyls which are scattered all abrode and teache the gentyls:

36 What maner of saiynge is this that he saide: ye shall seke me, and shall not fynde me: and wher I am thither can ye not come?

37 In the last day, that great daye of the feaste Iesus stode and cried saiynge: If a man thirste, let him come vnto me and drinke.

38 He that beleueth on me, as sayeth the scripture, out of hys bellye shall flowe riuers of water of lyfe.

39 This spake he of the spirite which they that beleueth on him, shoulde receyue. For the holye ghost was not yet because that Iesus was not yet gloryfyed.

40 Manye of the people, when they hearde that saiynge sayed: of a truthe this is a Prophete,

41 other sayeth: this is Christe, some saide: shal Christ come out of Galile?

42 Saieth not the scriptuture þt Christ shal come of þe sede of Dauid, & out of the toune of Bethleem wher Dauid was?

43 So was there dissencydu among þe people aboute hym?

44 And some of them woulde haue taken him: but no man layed handes on hym.

45 Then came the ministers to the hye priestes and Phariseis. And they sayd vnto them: why haue ye not brought hym?

46 The seruauntes aunswered: neuer man spake as thys man doth.

47 Then aunswered them the Phariseis: are ye also deceyued?

48 Doth anye of the rulers or the Phariseis beleue on hym?

49 But the commune people whiche know not the lawe, are cursed.

50 Nicodemus sayed vnto them. He that came to Iesus by night, and was one of them.

51 Doeth our lawe iudge anye man, before it heare him and knowe what he hath done?

52 They aunswered and sayed vnto hym: art thou also of Galile? Searche and loke, for oute of Galile aryseth no Prophete.

53 And euery man wente vnto hys owne house.

# CHAPTER 8

AND Iesus wente vnto mounte Oliuete,

2 and earlye in the mornynge came agayne into the temple, and all the people came vnto him, and sate doune & taught them.

3 And the Scribes and Phariseis brought vnto hym a woman taken in aduoutrye, and set her in the middest,

4 and sayed vnto hym: Mayster, thys woman was taken in aduoutrye, euen as the dede was a doynge.

5 Moyses in the lawe commaunded vs þt suche shoulde be stoned. What sayest thou therfore?

6 And this they sayed to tempte hym, that they myghte haue, whereof to accuse hym. Iesus stouped doune, and with hys fynger wrote on the ground.

7 And whyle they continued axynge hym, he lyfte hym selfe vp, and sayd vnto them: let hym that is amonge you without synne caste the fyrst stone at her.

8 And agayne he stouped doune, and wrote on the grounde.

9 And assone as they hearde that, they went out one by one, the eldest fyrst. And Iesu was left alone, and the woman standynge in the myddes.

10 When Iesus had lyft vp hym self agayn and sawe no man but the woman, he sayd to her. Woman where are those thyne accusers? Hath no man condemned the?

11 She sayed no man Lorde. And Iesus sayde: Neyther do I condempne the. Go, and synne no more.

12 Then spake Iesus agayne vnto them, saiynge. I am the lyghte of the worlde. He that foloweth me, shall not walke in darkenes: but shall haue the lyghte of lyfe.

13 The Phariseis sayde vnto hym: thou bearest recorde of thy selfe thy recorde is not true.

14 Iesus aunswered and sayed vnto them: though I beare recorde of my selfe, yet my recorde is true: for I know whence I came, and whether I go. But ye can not tel, whence I came, and whither I go.

15 Ye iudge after the flesh. I

iudge no man.

16 Thoughe I iudge, yet is my iudgement true. For I am not alone: but I and the father that sent me.

17 It is also written in your lawe, that the testimony of two men is true.

18 I am one that beare witnes of my selfe, and the father that sent me beareth witnes of me.

19 Then sayde they vnto hym: where is thy father? Iesus aunswered: ye neyther knowe me nor yet my father. Yf ye had knowen me, ye shoulde haue knowen my father also.

20 These wordes spake Iesus in the treasury, as he taught in the temple, and no man layde handes on hym, for hys tyme was not yet come.

21 Then sayde Iesus agayne vnto them. I go my waye, and ye shall seke me, & shall dye in youre synnes. Whether I go, thither can ye not come.

22 Then sayde the Iewes: will he kyll hym selfe, because he sayth: whether I go thyther can ye not come?

23 And he sayde to them: ye are from beneth. I am from aboue. Ye are of thys worlde. I am not of thys worlde.

24 I sayd therfore vnto you, þt ye shall dye in your synnes. For except ye beleue that I am he, ye shall dye in youre synnes.

25 Then sayed they vnto hym, who arte thou? And Iesus sayde vnto them: Euen the very same thynge that I saye vnto you,

26 I haue manye thynges to saye, and to iudge of you: but he that sent me is true. And I speake in þe worlde, those thinges which I haue hearde of hym.

27 Howe be it, they vnderstode not that he spake of hys father.

28 Then sayde Iesus vnto them: when ye haue lyfte vp an hye the sonne of man, then shall ye knowe, that I am he, and þt I do nothynge of my self: but as my father hath taught me, euen so I speake:

29 and he that sente me, is with me. The father hath not left me alone, for I do alwayes those thynges, that please him.

30 As he spake these wordes, many beleued on hym. Then sayde Iesus to those Iewes whiche beleued on hym.

31 Yf ye continue in my wordes: then are ye my very discyples,

32 and shal know the truth, and the truthe shall make you free.

33 They aunswered hym. We be Abrahams seede, and were neuer bonde to any man: why sayest thou then: ye shalbe made, fre?

34 Iesus aunswered them: verelye, verelye I say vnto you, that whosoeuer committeth synne

35 is the seruaunte of synne. And the seruaunte abydeth not in the house for euer.

36 But þe sonne abydeth euer. Yf the sonne therfore shal make you fre, then are ye free in dede.

37 I knowe that ye are Abrahams sede, but ye seke meanes to kyl me, because my sayinges haue no place in you.

38 I speake that I haue sene with my father: and ye do that which ye haue sene with youre father.

39 They aunswered, & sayde vnto hym. Abraham is oure father. Iesus sayde vnto them: yf ye were Abrahams chyldren, ye woulde do þe dedes of Abraham.

40 But nowe ye go about to kyll me, a man that haue tolde you the truthe whiche I haue hearde of God, thys dyd not Abraham,

41 ye do the dedes of your father. Then sayde they to him: we were not borne of fornicion. We haue one father, whiche is God.

42 Iesus sayde vnto them: yf God were youre father, then woulde ye loue me. For I proceaded forth, and come from God. Neyther came I of my selfe, but he sente me.

43 Why do ye not knowe my speache? Euen because ye cannot abyde the hearynge of my wordes.

44 Ye are of youre father the deuyl, and þe lustes of your father ye wyll do. He was a murtherer from the begynnyng, and abode not in the truth, because there is no truthe in hym. When he speaketh a lye, then speaketh he of hys owne. For he is a lyar, and the father therof.

45 And because I tell you the truthe, therfore ye beleue me not.

46 Which of you can rebuke me of synne? Yf I saye the truth, why do not ye beleue me?

47 He that is of God, heareth Goddes wordes. Ye therfor heare them not, because ye, are not of God.

48 Then answered the Iewes, and sayd vnto hym: Saye we not well that thou arte a Samaritane, and hast the deuyll?

49 Iesus aunswered: I haue not the deuyll: but I honoure my father, & ye haue dishonoured me.

50 I seke not myne owne prayse: but there is one that seketh, and iudgeth.

51 Verely verely I saye vnto you, yf a man kepe my saiynges, he shall neuer she death.

52 Then sayed the Iewes to hym. Nowe knowe we that thou haste the deuyll. Abraham is dead, and also the Prophetes, and yet thou sayest, yf a man kepe my saiynges he shall neuer tast of death.

53 Art thou greater then oure father Abraham which is dead? And the Prophetes are dead: Whome makest thou thy selfe?

54 Iesus answered. Yf I honoure my selfe, myne honoure

is nothynge worthe. It is my father, that honoureth me, which you saye is youre God,

55 and ye haue not knowen hym: but I knowe hym, And yf I shoulde saye: I knowe hym not, I shoulde be a lyer lyke vnto you. But I knowe hym, and kepe hys saiynge.

56 Your father Abraham was glad to se my daye and he sawe it, and reioyced.

57 Then sayed the Iewes vnto hym: thou arte not yet .l. yeares olde, and hast thou sene Abraham?

58 Iesus said vnto them: Verelye verely I saye vnto you: yer Abraham was I am.

59 Then toke they vp stones to caste at hym. But Iesus hyd him self and wente oute of the temple.

## CHAPTER 9

AND as Iesus passed by, he saw a man which was blynde from hys byrthe.

2 And his disciples axed hym: Mayster, who dyd synne: thys man or his father and mother: that he was borne blynd?

3 Iesus aunswered: Neyther hath thys man synned nor yet hys father and mother: but that the workes of God shoulde be shewed on him.

4 I must work the workes of hym that sente me, whyle it is daye. The nyghte cometh, when no man can worke.

5 As longe as I am in the worlde, I am the lyght of the worlde.

6 Assone as he had thus spoken; he spatte on the grounde, and made claye of the spetle, and rubbed the claye on the eyes of the blynd,

7 and sayed vnto hym: Go, washe the in the pole of Syloe, whiche by interpretacyon, signifyeth sente. He went hys waye, and washed & came agayne, sayng:

8 The neyghboures and they þt had sene him before, how that he was a beggar, sayed: is not thys he that satte & begged.

9 Some sayed: this is he. Other saied: he is like hym. But he hym selfe sayd: I am euen he.

10 They sayed vnto hym: Howe are thyne eyes opened then?

11 He aunswered and sayde. The man that is called Iesus, made claye, & anoynted myne eyes, and sayed vnto me: Go to the pole Siloe, and washe. And I wente and washed & receyued my syghte.

12 They sayde vnto him: where is he? He sayde: I can not tell.

13 Then brought they to the Pharises, hym that a litle before was blynde:

14 for it was the Saboth day, when Iesus made the claye and opened hys eyes.

15 Then agayne the Pharises also axed him, how he had receyued his sight. He sayed vnto them: He put claye vpon my eyes, and I washed and do se.

16 Then sayd some of the Phariseis: thys man is not of God, because he kepeth not the Saboth daye. Other sayed: howe can a man that is a synner, do such miracles? And there was stryfe among them.

17 Then spake they vnto the blynde agayne. What saiest thou of hym, because he hath opened thyne eyes? And he sayed: He is a Prophete.

18 But the Iewes dyd not beleue on the felowe, howe that he was blynde and receyued hys sighte, vntyll they had called the father & mother of hym that had receyued his sighte.

19 And they axed them, saiynge: Is thys youre sonne, whom ye say was borne blynde? How doth he now se then?

20 His father and mother aunswered them, and sayed: We wote well þt thys is oure sonne, & that he was borne blind,

21 but by what meanes he now seeth, that can we not tell, or who hath opened hys eyes, can we not tell. He is olde ynoughe, axe him, let hym answere for hym self.

22 Such wordes spake his father and mother, because they feared þe Iewes. For the Iewes had conspyred al ready, that yf any man dyd confesse that he was Christe, he shoulde be excommunicate oute of the synagoge,

23 therfore sayd hys father & mother: he is olde ynough, axe hym.

24 Then agayne called they the man that was þe blynde, & sayd vnto him: Geue God þe prayse we knowe that this man is a synner.

25 He aunswered and sayde: Whither he be a synner or no. I can not tell, one thyng I am sure of: that I was blynde, and now I se.

26 Then sayd they to hym agayne: What dyd he to the? Howe opened he thyne eyes?

27 He aunswered them: I tolde you per whyle, and ye dyd not heare. Wherfore woulde ye heare it agayne? wyl ye also be hys discyples?

28 Then rated they him, & sayde: thou arte hys disciple: we be Moyses discyples.

29 We are sure that God spake wyth Moyses, thys felowe we knowe not from whence he is.

30 The man aunswered, and sayd vnto them: Thys is a merueylous thynge, that ye wote not whence he is, seyng he hath opened myne eyes.

31 For we be sure that God heareth not synners. But yf any man be a worshypper of God, and do hys wyl, hym heareth he.

32 Sence the worlde began: was it not hearde that any man opened the eies of one that was

borne blynde.

33 If thys man were not of God, he coulde haue done nothynge.

34 They answered, and sayde vnto hym: thou arte all together borne in synne, and doest thou teach vs? And they cast hym oute.

35 Iesus hearde, that they had excommunicat hym, he sayde vnto hym: doest thou beleue on the sonne of God?

36 He aunswered, and sayde: Who is it Lord that I myght beleue on him?

37 And Iesus sayde vnto hym: Thou haste sene hym, and he it is that talked with the.

38 And he sayde: Lorde I beleue & worshypped hym.

39 Iesus sayed: I am come vnto iudgement into this worlde, that they which se not myght se, and they which se, myght be made blynd.

40 And some of the Pharises whiche were with him, hearde these wordes, and sayde vnto hym: are we then blynde?

41 Iesus sayde vnto them: yf ye were blynde, ye shoulde haue no synne. But nowe ye saye: we se, therfor your synne remayneth.

# CHAPTER 10

Verelye verelye I saye vnto you: he that entreth not in by the dore, into the shepe folde: but climmeth vp some other waye, the same is a thefe and a robber.

2 He that goeth in by the dore, is the shepeherde of the shepe,

3 to him the porter openeth, and the shepe heare hys voyce, and he calleth hys owne shepe by name, and leadeth them oute.

4 And when he hath sente forth hys owne shepe, he goeth before them, and the shepe folowe hym, for they knowe hys voyce.

5 A straunger they wyll not folowe, but wyll flye from hym, for they know not the voyce of straungers.

6 Thys similitude spake Iesus vnto them: But they vnderstode not what thynges they were whiche he spake vnto them.

7 Then Iesus sayed vnto them agayne Verelye I saye vnto you: I am the dore of þe shepe.

8 Al, euen as manye as came before me, are theues and robbers: but the shepe dyd not heare them.

9 I am the dore: by me yf any man enter in, he shalbe safe, and shall go in & oute, and fynde pasture.

10 The thefe cometh not, but for to steale, kyll, and destroye. I am come, that they might haue lyfe, and haue it more aboundauntlye.

11 I am the good shepeherde. The good shepe herde geueth hys lyfe for the shepe.

12 An hyred, seruaunte, which is not the shepeherde, neyther the shepe are hys own, seeth the wolfe commynge, and leaueth the shepe, and fleeth, and the wolfe catcheth them, & scatiereth þe shepe.

13 The hyred seruaunte fleeth, because he is an hyred seruaunte, and careth not for the shepe.

14 I am that good shepeherde, and knowe myne and am knowen of myne.

15 As my father knoweth me, euen so knowe I my father. And I geue my lyfe for the shepe:

16 and other shepe I haue whiche are not of thys folde. Them also muste I brynge that they maye heare my voyce, and that there maye be one flocke, and one shepeherde.

17 Therfore doth my father loue me, because I put my lyfe from me, that I myght take it agayne.

18 Noman taketh it from me,
but I put it awaye of my selfe. I haue power to put it from me, and haue power to take it agayne. Thys commaundemente haue I receyued of my father.

19 And there was a dissencyon agayne among the Iewes for these saiynges,

20 & many of them sayd: he hath the deuil, and is madde: why heare ye hym?

21 Other sayd: these are not the wordes of hym that hath the deuyll. Can the deuyll open the eyes of the blynde?

22 And it was at Hierusalem the feaste of the dedicacion of the temple, and it was wynter,

23 & Iesus walked in Solomons porche.

24 Then came the Iewes rounde about hym, & sayed vnto hym: Howe longe dost thou make vs doubte? Yf thou be Christe, tell vs playnely.

25 Iesus aunswered them: I tolde you, and ye beleue not. The workes þt I do in my fathers name, then beare witnes of me.

26 But ye beleue not because ye are not of my shepe. As I said vnto you:

27 my shepe heare my voice, & I know them, and they folowe me,

28 and I geue vnto them eternall lyfe, and they shall neuer perish neyther shall any man plucke them out of my hande.

29 My father whiche gaue them me, is greater then all, and no man is able to take them out of my fathers hande.

30 And I and my father are one.

31 Then the Iewes agayne toke vp stones to stone hym with all.

32 Iesus aunswered them: manye good workes haue I shewed you from my father: for whiche of them wyll ye stone me?

33 The Iewes aunswered him, saiynge: For thy good workes

sake we stone þe not, but for thy blasphemye, and because that thou beynge a man, makest thy selfe God.

34 Iesus aunswered them: is it not wrytten in youre lawe. I saye: ye are Goddes?

35 Yf he called them Goddes vnto whom the worde of God was spoken (& the scripture can not be broken)

36 saye ye then to hym, whom the father hath sanctifyed, & sent into the worlde, thou blasphemest, because I sayed. I am the sonne of God?

37 yf I do not the workes of my father, beleue me not.

38 But yf I do: then thoughe ye beleue not me, yet beleue the workes, that ye maye knowe and beleue, þt the father is in me, and I in hym.

39 Agayne they went about to take hym: but he escaped out of theyr handes,

40 and went awaye agayne beyonde Iordan, into the place where Iohn before had baptysed, and there abode.

41 And manye resorted vnto hym, & sayed: Iohn dyd no myracle, but all thynges that Iohn spake of thys man, are true.

42 And manye beleued on hym there.

## CHAPTER 11

A certayne man was sicke, named Lazarus of Bethania, the toune of Marye and her syster Martha.

2 It was that Marye whiche annoynted Iesus with oyntment and wyped hys fete with her heyre, whose brother Lazarus was sicke,

3 and hys systers sente vnto hym, saiynge: Lorde, beholde, he whome thou louest, is sicke.

4 When Iesus hearde, that he sayed: this infirmitie is not vnto death, but for the laude of God that the sonne of God myght be praysed by the reason of it.

5 Iesus loued Martha and her sister and Lazarus.

6 Then after he had hearde þt he was sicke, yet abode he two dayes styll in the same place, where he was.

7 Then after that sayde he to hys disciples: Let vs go into Iewry agayne.

8 His discyples sayde vnto hym: Mayster, the Iewes latelye sought meanes to stone the, and wylt thou go thyther agayne?

9 Iesus aunswered: are there not .xij. houres in the daye of a man walke in the daye, he stombleth not, because he seeth the lyght of thys world.

10 But yf a man walke in the nyght, he stombleth, because there is no lyght in him.

11 This sayed he, and after that, he sayed vnto them: oure frende Lazarus slepeth but I go to wake him out of slepe.

12 Then sayed hys discyples: Lorde yf he slepe, he shall do well ynough.

13 Howe be it Iesus spake of hys death: but they thought that he had spoken of the naturall slepe.

14 Then sayd Iesus vnto them plainly: Lazarus is dead,

15 and I am glad for youre sakes, that I was not there, because ye may beleue. Neuerthelesse let vs go vnto him.

16 Then sayde Thomas whiche is called Dydymus, vnto the discyples: Let vs also go, that we maye dye with hym.

17 Then wente Iesus, and founde that he had lyen in hys graue foure dayes already.

18 Bethanye was nye vnto Hierusalem aboute .xv. furlonges of,

19 and manye of the Iewes were come to Martha and Marye to comforte them ouer theyr brother.

20 Martha assone as she hearde that Iesus was commynge, went, and met hym: but Mary sat styll in the house.

21 Then sayde Martha vnto Iesus: Lorde, yf thou haddest bene here, my brother had not ben dead:

22 but neuerthelesse, I know that whatsoeuer thou axest of God, God wyl geue it þe.

23 Iesus sayde vnto her: thy brother shall ryse agayne.

24 Martha sayed vnto him: I knowe þt he shall ryse agayne in the resurreccyon at the laste daye.

25 Iesus sayed vnto her: I am the resurreccion and the lyfe. He that beleueth on me, ye though he were dead, yet shall he lyue.

26 And whosoeuer lyueth, and beleueth on me, shall neuer dye. Beleuest thou thys?

27 She sayd vnto hym: ye Lorde I beleue that thou arte Christe the sonne of God, which should come into the worlde.

28 And assone as she had so sayd, she went her waye, and called Marye her syster secretelye, saiynge: The mayster is come, and calleth for the.

29 And she assone as she hearde that, arose quickly, and came vnto hym.

30 Iesus was not yet come into the toune, but was in the place where Martha met hym.

31 The Iewes then which were with her in the house and comforted her, when they sawe Mary, that she arose vp hastely, and went out, and folowed her, saiynge: She goeth vnto the graue, to wepe there.

32 Then when Mary was come, where Iesus was, and sawe hym, she fell doune at hys fete, saiynge vnto hym: Lorde yf thou haddest bene here, my brother had not ben dead.

33 When Iesus sawe her wepe, and þe Iewes also wepe which came with her, he groned in the spirite, and was troubled in hym self,

34 & sayd: Where haue ye layed hym? They sayde vnto

hym: Lorde, come and se.

35 And Iesus wepte.

36 Then sayde the Iewes: Beholde, howe he loued him.

37 And some of them sayde: coulde not he which opened the eyes of the blynde, haue made also that thys man shoulde not haue dyed?

38 Iesus agayne groned in hym selfe, and came to the graue: it was a caue and a stone layde on it.

39 And Iesus sayde: take ye away the stone. Martha the syster of hym that was dead, said vnto him: Lorde by thys tyme he stinketh: for he hath bene dead four dayes.

40 Iesus sayed vnto her: Sayd I not vnto the, that yf thou dyddest beleue, thou shouldest se þe glory of God.

41 Then they toke awaye the stone from þt place where the dead was layde. And Iesus lyft vp hys eyes, and sayde: Father I thanke the because that thou haste hearde me.

42 I wote that thou hearest me alwayes: but because of the people that stande by, I sayed it, that they may beleue that thou hast sent me.

43 And when he thus had spoken: he cryed wt a loude voyce: Lazarus come forth.

44 And he þt was dead, came forth, bounde hand and fote with graue boundes, and his face was bounde with a napkin. Iesus sayed vnto them, lowse him, and let hym go.

45 Then many of the Iewes which came to Marye, and had sene the thynges whiche Iesus dyd, beleued on hym.

46 But some of them went theyr wayes to the Pharises, and tolde them what Iesus had done.

47 Then gathered the hye Priestes and Pharyses a counsel and sayd: What do we? This man doth many myracles:

48 yf we let hym scape thus, all men wyll beleue on hym, & the Romaynes shall come and take away our countrey and the people.

49 And one of them named Cayphas which was the hye prieste that same yeare sayde vnto them: ye perceyue nothynge at all, nor yet consyder that

50 it is expedyent for vs, that one man dye for the people, & not that all the people peryshe.

51 Thys spake he not of hym selfe, but beynge hye Prieste that same yeare he prophesyed that Iesus shoulde dye for the people,

52 and not for the people only, but that he shoulde gather together in one the children of God which were scattered abrode.

53 From that daye forth they helde a counsell together, for to put hym to death.

54 Iesus therfore walked no more openlye amonge the Iewes, but went hys waye thence vnto a countrye nyghe to the wyldernes, into a cytye called Ephraim, & ther haunted wt his disciples.

55 And the Iewes Easter was nye at hande, and manye wente oute of the countrye vp to Hierusalem before the Easter, to purifie them selues.

56 Then soughte they for Iesus, and spake amonge them selues, as they stode in þt temple: What thynke ye, seynge he commeth not to the feast

57 The hye priestes and Pharyseis had geuen a commaundement, that yf any man knewe, where he were, he shoulde shew it, that they myght take hym.

# CHAPTER 12

THEN Iesus .vi. dayes before Easter, came to Bethanye where Lazarus was which was dead, and whom Iesus raysed from death.

2 There they made hym a supper, & Martha serued: but Lazarus was one of them that sate at the table with hym.

3 Then toke Mary a pounde of oyntment called Nardus, perfecte and precyous, and annoynted Iesus fete, and wepte hys fete with her heare, and the house was fylled wyth the sauoure of the oyntmente.

4 Then sayed one of hys disciples named Iudas Iscarioth Simons sonne. whiche afterwarde betrayed him:

5 why was not thys oyntment solde for thre .C. pens and geuen to the poore?

6 Thys sayed he, not that he cared for the poore, but because he was a thiefe, and kepte the bagge, and bare that whiche was geuen.

7 Then sayed Iesus Let her alone, agaynste the daye of my buriynge the kept it.

8 The poore alwayes shall ye haue with you, but me shall ye not alwayes haue.

9 Muche people of the Iewes had knoweledge that he was there, & they came not for Iesus sake onely, but that they myghte se Lazarus also whom he raysed from death:

10 The hye priestes therfore helde a counsel, that they myght put Lazarus to death also,

11 because that for hys sake many of the Iewes went away, and beleued on Iesus.

12 On the morowe muche people that were come to the feast, when they hearde that Iesus shoulde come to Hierusalem,

13 toke braunches of palme trees, and went and met hym, and cryed: Hosanna, blessed is he that in the name of the Lorde cometh kynge of Israell.

14 And Iesus gotte a yong asse, and sate theron, accordynge to that which was wrytten,

15 feare not doughter of Syon, beholde thy kynge

cometh, sittynge on an asses colte.

16 These thinges vnderstode not hys discyples at the fyrst: but when Iesus was glorifyed, then remembred they that suche thynges were written of him, and that suche thynges they had done vnto hym.

17 The people that was with hym, when he called Lazarus out of hys graue, and raysed hym from death, bare recorde.

18 Therfore met hym the people, because they hearde that he had done suche a myracle.

19 The Phariseis therfore sayed amonge them selues: perceyue ye howe we preuayle nothing? beholde þe worlde goeth awaye after hym.

20 There were certayne Grekes among them, that came to praye at the feaste:

21 the same came to Phylyppe which was of Bethsayda a citie in Galile, and desiered hym, saiynge: Syr we woulde fayne se Iesus.

22 Phylip came and told Andrewe. And agayne Andrewe and Philip tolde Iesus.

23 And Iesus aunswered them sayinge: The houre is come that the sonne of man must be glorifyed.

24 Verelye verelye I saye to you, excepte the wheate corne fall into the grounde and dye, it bydeth alone. If it dye, it bringeth forth much frute.

25 He that loueth hys lyfe, shall destroy it: and he that hateth hys lyfe in this world, shal kepe it vnto lyfe eternall.

26 If any man minister vnto me, let hym folowe me, and where I am, there shal also my minister be. And yf any man minister vnto me, hym wyll my father honoure.

27 Nowe is my soule troubled, and what shal I saye? Father delyuer me from thys houre: but therfore came I vnto thys houre.

28 Father, glorifye thy name. Then came there a voyce from heauen: I haue glorifyed it, and wil glorifye it agayne.

29 Then sayde the people that stode by, and hearde: it thoundreth, Other sayd an angell spake to him.

30 Iesus aunswered and sayed: thys voyce came, not because of me, but for your sakes.

31 Now is the iudgement of thys world: now shall the prince of thys worlde be caste oute.

32 And I, yf I were lyft vp from the earth, will drawe all men vnto me.

33 This sayde Iesus, signifyenge what death he shoulde dye.

34 The people aunswered hym: We haue hearde oute of the lawe, that Christe bydeth euer: and howe sayest thou then that the sonne of man muste be lyfte vp? who is that sonne of man?

35 Then Iesus sayed vnto them: yet a lyttell whyle is the lyght with you. Walke, whyle ye haue lyght, lest the darcknes come on you. He that walketh in the darcke, woteth not whether he goeth.

36 Whyle ye haue lyghte, beleue on the lyght, that ye maye be the chyldren of light. These thynges spake Iesus, and departed, and hyd hym selfe from them.

37 And though he had done so many myracles before them, yet beleued not they on hym,

38 that the saiynge of Esayas the Prophete myght be fulfylled, that he spake. Lorde, who shall beleue our saiyng? And to whome is the arme of the Lorde opened?

39 Therfore coulde they not beleue, because that Esayas sayth agayne:

40 he hath blynded theyr eyes and hardened theyr hertes, þt they shoulde not se with theyr eyes, and vnderstand with theyr hertes, and shoulde be conuerted, and I shoulde heale them.

41 Such thynges said Esayas when he sawe hys glorye, and spake of hym.

42 Neuerthelesse among the chief rulers many beleued on hym. But because of þt Pharyses they woulde not be a knowen of it, least they shoulde be excommunicate,

43 for they loued the prayse, that is geuen of men, more then the prayse that commeth of God.

44 And Iesus cryed and sayde: he that beleueth on me, beleueth not on me, but on hym that sente me.

45 And he that seeth me, seeth hym that sent me.

46 I am come a lyght into the worlde, that whosoeuer beleueth on me, shoulde not byde in darknes.

47 And yf anye man heare my wordes, & beleue not, I iudge him not. For I came not to iudge the worlde, but to saue the worlde.

48 He that refuseth me, and receiueth not my wordes, hath one þt iudgeth hym. The wordes that I haue spoken, they shall iudge hym in the laste day.

49 For I haue not spoken of my selfe: but the father which sent me, he gaue me a commaundement what I shoulde say, & what I should speake.

50 And I knowe that thys commaundement is lyfe euerlasting. Whatsoeuer I speake therfore, euen as the father bade me, so I speake.

# CHAPTER 13

BEFORE the feast of Easter when Iesus knew that hys houre was come, that he shulde depart oute of thys worlde vnto the father. When he loued his which were in the worlde, vnto the ende he loued them.

2 And when supper was

ended, after that the deuyl had put in the herte of Iudas Iscarioth Simons sonne, to betraye hym.

3 Iesus knowyng that the father had geuen all thynges into hys handes, and that he was come from God, and went to God,

4 he rose from supper, and layde asyde hys vpper garmentes, & toke a towell, and gyrde hym selfe.

5 After that poured he water into a bason, & began to wash hys discyples fete, and to wype them wyth a towell, wherewith he was gyrde.

6 Then came he to Symon Peter. And Peter sayde vnto hym: Lorde shalt thou washe my fete?

7 Iesus aunswered, and sayed vnto him: what I do, thou wotest not nowe, but thou shalt knowe hereafter.

8 Peter sayed vnto him: thou shalt not washe my fete whyle þe worlde standeth. Iesus aunswered hym: yf I washe the not, thou shalte haue no parte with me.

9 Simon Peter sayed vnto him: Lord not my fete onelye: but also my handes and my heade.

10 Iesus sayed vnto hym: he that is washed, neadeth not saue to washe hys fete, and is cleane euery whyt. And ye are cleane: but not al.

11 For he knewe hys betrayer. Therfore sayed he: ye are not all cleane.

12 After he had washed theyr fete, and receyued hys clothes, and was set doune agayne, he sayed vnto them. Wote ye what I haue done to you?

13 Ye call me mayster and Lorde, & ye saye well, for so am I.

14 Yf I then your lord and mayster haue washed your fete, ye also ought to wash one anothers fete.

15 For I haue geuen you an ensample, that ye shoulde do as I haue done to you.

16 Verelye verelye I say vnto you: the seruaunte is not greater then hys mayster, neyther the messenger greater then he that sent hym.

17 Yf ye vnderstande these thynges, happye are ye yf ye do then.

18 I speake not of you all. I knowe whome I haue chosen. But that þe scripture myght be fulfylled, he that eateth bread with me hath lyft vp hys hele agaynst me.

19 Nowe tell I you before it come, that when it come to passe, ye myght beleue that I am he.

20 Verelye verelye I saye vnto you. He that receyueth whomesoeuer I sende, receyueth me. And he that receyueth me, receyueth him that sent me.

21 When Iesus had thus sayed, he was troubled in the spirite, and testifyed, saiynge: verelye verelye I saye vnto you, that one of you shall betraye me.

22 And then the disciples loked one on another, doubtinge of whom he spake.

23 There was one of hys disciples which leaned on Iesus bosome whome Iesus loued.

24 To him beckened Simon Peter that he shuld axe who it was, of whom he spake.

25 He then as he leaned on Iesus breste sayed vnto hym: Lorde who is it?

26 Iesus aunswered, he it is to whom I geue a sop, when I haue depte it. And he wet a soppe, and gaue it to Iudas Iscaryoth Simons sonne.

27 And after the sop Satan entred into hym. Then sayde Iesus vnto hym: that thou doest, do quickly.

28 That wist no man at the table, for what intent he spake vnto hym.

29 Some of them thought, because Iudas had þe bagge, that Iesus had sayed vnto hym, bye those thinges that we haue nede of agaynst the feast: or that he shoulde geue some thyng to the poore.

30 Assone then as he had receyued the sop, he went immediatlye out. And it was nyght.

31 When he was gone oute, Iesus sayde: nowe is the sonne of man glorifyed. And God is glorified by hym.

32 Yf God be glorifyed by hym, God shall also glorifye hym in hym selfe, and shall strayghte waye glorifye hym.

33 Deare chyldren, yet a lytell whyle am I with you, ye shall seke me, and as I sayde vnto the Iewes: whyther I go, thyther can ye not come. Also to you saye I now:

34 A newe commaundement geue I vnto you, that ye loue together, as I haue loued you, that euen so ye loue one another.

35 By thys shall all men knowe that ye are my discyples, yf ye shall haue loue one to another.

36 Simon Peter sayed vnto hym. Lorde whyther goest thou? Iesus aunswered hym: Whether I go thou canste not folowe me now, but thou shalt folow me afterwarde.

37 Peter sayde vnto him: lorde, why can not I folowe the now? I wyll geue my lyfe for thy sake.

38 Iesus aunswered hym: wilte thou geue thy lyfe for my sake? Verelye verelye I saye vnto the, the cocke shall not crowe, tyll thou haue denyed me thryse.

# CHAPTER 14

AND he sayd vnto hys disciples: Let not youre hertes be troubled. Beleue in God & beleue in me.

2 In my fathers house are manye mansyons. Yf it were not

so, I wolde haue told you. I go to prepare a place for you.

3 And yf I go to prepare a place for you, I wyl come agayne, and receyue you euen vnto my self, that wher I am, there may ye be also.

4 And whyther I go, ye knowe, and the waye ye knowe.

5 Thomas sayde vnto him: Lorde we know not whether thou goest Also how is it possyble for vs to knowe the waye?

6 Iesus sayd vnto hym: I am the waye, the truthe and þe lyfe. And no man commeth to the father, but by me.

7 Yf ye had knowen me, ye had knowen my father also. And nowe ye knowe hym, & haue sene hym.

8 Philip sayde vnto hym: Lorde shewe vs the father, and it suffyseth vs.

9 Iesus sayd vnto hym. Haue I bene so longe tyme with you, and yet haste thou not knowen me? Philip, he that hath sene me, hath sene the father. And how sayest thou then: shew vs the father?

10 Beleuest thou not þt I am in the father & þe father in me? The wordes that I speake vnto you, I speake not of my selfe: but the father þt dwelleth in me, is he that doeth the workes.

11 Beleue ye not þt I am in the father, and the father in me? At the least beleue me for the very workes sake.

12 Verely, verely I saye vnto you, he that beleueth on me, the workes that I do, the same shal he do, and greater workes then these shal he do, because I go vnto my father.

13 And whatsoeuer ye axe in my name that will I do þt þe father myght be glorifyed by the sonne.

14 Yf ye shall axe any thyng in my name, I wyl do it.

15 Yf ye loue me, kepe my commaundementes

16 & I will praye the father, and he shal geue you another conforter, that he may byde with you euer

17 which is the spirite of truth whom the worlde can not receyue, because the world seeth hym not, neyther knoweth hym. But ye knowe hym. For he dwelleth with you, & shal be in you.

18 I wyll not leaue you comfortlesse, but wyll come vnto you.

19 Yet a lytel whyle and the worlde seeth me no more: but ye shal se me. For I lyue, and ye shall lyue.

20 That daye shall ye knowe that I am in my father, and you in me, and I in you

21 He that hathe my commaundementes and kepeth them, the same is he that loueth me. And he that loueth me, shal be loued of my father: And I will loue hym, and will shewe myne owne selfe to him.

22 Iudas sayd vnto hym (not Iudas Iscarioth) Lord what is the cause that thou wilte shewe thy selfe vnto vs, & not vnto the worlde?

23 Iesus aunswered and sayd vnto hym, yf a man loue me, and will kepe my saiynges, my father also will loue hym & we will come vnto hym, and will dwell to hym.

24 He that loueth me not, kepeth not my saiynges. And the wordes whiche ye heare, are not myne, but the fathers which sent me.

25 Thys haue I spoken vnto you, beynge yet present with you.

26 But that comforter whiche is the holy ghost (whome my father wil send in my name) he shal teache you all thinges, & brynge all thynges to youre remembraunce whatsoeuer I haue tolde you.

27 Peace I leaue with you, my peace I geue vnto you. Not as the worlde geueth, geue I vnto you. Let not your hertes be greued, neyther feare ye.

28 Ye haue hearde how I sayde vnto you. I go and come agayne vnto you. Yf ye loued me, ye would verely reioyce, because I sayde: I go vnto the father. For the father is greater then I.

29 And nowe haue I shewed you before it come, þt when it is come to passe, ye myght beleue.

30 Here after will I not talke manye wordes vnto you. For the ruler of thys world cometh and hath noughte in me.

31 But that the worlde maye knowe that I loue the father: therfore as the father gaue me commaundement euen so do I. Ryse, let vs go hence.

# CHAPTER 15

I am the true vyne, and my father is on husband man.

2 Euery braunche that beareth not frute in me, he wyll take awaye. And euerye braunche that beareth frute, wil he pourge, that it maye bryng more frute.

3 Now are ye cleane thorowe the wordes which I haue spoken vnto you.

4 Byde in me, and let me byde in you. As the braunche can not beare frute of it selfe, except it byde in the vyne no more can ye except ye abyde in me.

5 I am the vyne, and ye are the braunches. He that abydeth in me, and I in him, the same bryngeth forth muche frute. For without me can ye do nothynge.

6 Yf a man byde not in me, he is cast forth as a braunche, and is wythered: and men gather it, and cast it into the fyre, and it burneth.

7 Yf ye hyd in me and my wordes also hyd in you: axe what ye wyll, and it shalbe done to you.

8 Here is my father glorifyed that ye beare muche

fruyte, and be made my disciples.

9 As the father hath loued me, euen so haue I loued you. Continue in my loue.

10 Yf ye shal kepe my commaundementes, ye shall byde in my loue, euen as I haue kepte my fathers commaundementes, and abyde in hys loue.

11 These thynges haue I spoken vnto you, that my ioye myght remayne in you, and þt youre ioye myght be full.

12 This is my commaundement, that ye loue together as I haue loued you.

13 Greater loue then thys hath no man, then þt a man bestowe hys lyfe for hys frendes.

14 Ye are my frendes, yf ye do whatsoeuer I commaunde you.

15 Henceforth call I you not seruauntes: for the seruaunt knoweth not what hys lorde doth. But you haue I called frendes, for all thynges þt I haue heard of my father, I haue opened vnto you.

16 Ye haue not chosen me, but I haue chosen you and ordeyned you, þt ye go & bringe forth frute, and that your frute remayne, and that whatsoeuer ye shall axe of the father in my name, he shoulde geue it to you.

17 Thys commaunde I you, that ye loue together.

18 Yf the worlde hate you, ye knowe that it hated me before it hated you.

19 Yf ye were of the worlde, the worlde woulde loue his owne. Howe be it because ye are not of the worlde, but I haue chosen you out of the worlde, therfore hateth you the worlde.

20 Remember þe saiyng that I sayde vnto you: the seruaunt is not greater then þe lorde, yf they haue persecuted me, so wyll they persecute you: yf they haue kept my saiynges, so wyll they kepe yours.

21 But all these thinges wyll they do vnto you, for my names sake, because they haue not knowen him that sent me.

22 Yf I had not come, and spoken vnto them, they should not haue had synne: but now haue they nothynge to cloke theyr synne with all.

23 He that hateth me, hateth my father.

24 If I had not done workes among them which none other man dyd, they had not had synne. But now haue they sene, & yet haue hated both me & my father:

25 euen þt the saiyng might be fulfilled that is writen in their lawe: they hated me without a cause.

26 But when the comforter is come, whome I will sende vnto you from the father, which is the spirite of truth, which proceadeth of þe father, he shall testify of me.

27 And ye shall beare witnes, also because ye haue bene with me from the begynnynge.

## CHAPTER 16

THESE thynges haue I sayed vnto you, because ye shoulde not be offended.

2 They shall excommunicate you: ye the tyme shall come, that whosoeuer kylleth you, wil thinke that he doeth god seruice.

3 And suche thinges shall they do vnto you, because they haue not knowen the father, neyther yet me.

4 But these thynges haue I tolde you, that when that houre is come ye myghte remember them that I tolde you so. These thynges sayde I not vnto you at the begynnynge, because I was present with you.

5 But nowe I go my waye to hym that sent me, and none of you axeth me, whyther goest thou?

6 But because I haue sayde suche thinges vnto you, youre hertes are full of sorowe.

7 Neuerthelesse I tell you the trueth, it is expediente for you that I go awaye. For yf I go not awaye, that comforter wil not come vnto you. But yf I departe, I wil sende hym vnto you.

8 And when he is come, he wil rebuke þe world of synne, and of ryghteousnesse, and of iudgement

9 Of synne, because they beleue not on me:

10 of ryghteousnesse, because I go to my father, and then ye shall not se me,

11 and of iudgement, because the chiefe ruler of this worlde is iudged already.

12 I haue yet many thinges to say vnto you, but ye cannot beare them awaye now.

13 Howe be it when he is come (I meane the spirite of truth) he wyll lead you into all truth. He shall not speake of hym self, but whatsoeuer he shal heare, that shall he speake, and he wyll shewe you thynges to come.

14 He shall glorifye me, for he shall receyue of myne, and shall shewe vnto you.

15 Al thynges that the father hath, are myne. Therfore sayd I vnto you, that he shal take of myne, and shewe vnto you.

16 After a whyle ye shall not se me: & agayne after a whyle ye shall se me: for I go to the father.

17 Then sayed some of hys disciples amonge them selues: what is this that he sayeth vnto vs: after a whyle ye shall not se me, & agayne after a whyle ye shall se me, and that I go to the father.

18 They sayd therfore: what is it that he sayeth, after a whyle? we can not tell what he sayth.

19 Iesus perceyued that they woulde axe him and sayde vnto them. This is it that ye enquyre

# JOHN

of amonge your selues that I sayde after a whyle ye shall not se me, and agayne after a whyle ye shall se me.

20 Verely verely I say vnto you: ye shall wepe and lament, & the world shall reioyce. Ye shall sorowe, but your sorow shalbe turned into ioye.

21 A woman when she trauayleth, hathe sorowe, because her houre is come: but assone as she is deliuered of þe child she remembreth no more the anguish, for ioye that a man is borne into the worlde.

22 And ye now are in sorow: but I wyll se you agayne, and youre hertes shall reioyce, and youre ioye shall no man take from you.

23 And in that day shal ye axe me no question. Verely verely I say vnto you: whatsoeuer ye shall axe the father in my name, he wyll geue it you.

24 Hytherto haue ye axed nothyng in my name. Axe and ye shall receyue it, that your ioye maye be full.

25 These thynges haue I spoken vnto you in prouerbes. The tyme will come when I shall no more speake to you in prouerbes: but I shall shewe you plainly from my father.

26 At that daye shall ye axe in my name. And I say not vnto you that I wyll speake vnto my father for you.

27 For the father hym selfe loueth you, because ye haue loued me, and haue beleued, that I came out from God.

28 I wente oute from the father, and came into the world, and I leaue the world agayne, and go to þe father.

29 Hys disciples sayde vnto him: lo now speakest thou plainly, and thou vsest no prouerbe.

30 Nowe knowe we that thou vnderstandest all thynges, and nedest not that any man should axe the any question. Therfore beleue we that thou camest from God.

31 Iesus aunswered them: Now ye do beleue.

32 Beholde, the houre draweth nye, and is all readye come that ye shalbe scatered euerye man hys wayes, and shall leaue me alone. And yet am I not alone. For the father is with me.

33 These wordes haue I spoken vnto you, þt in me you myght haue peace. For in þe worlde shall you haue tribulacyon: but be of good cheare. I haue ouercome the worlde.

# CHAPTER 17

THESE wordes spake Iesus, & lyfte vp hys eyes to heauen, and said: father the houre is come: glorify thy sonne, that thy sonne maye glorifye the:

2 as thou haste geuen hym power ouer all flesh, that he should geue eternall lyfe to as manye as thou hast geuen hym.

3 This is lyfe eternall that they myghte knowe, the that onely very God, and whome thou haste sente Iesus Christ.

4 I haue glorifyed the on the earthe. I haue finyshed the worke whiche thou gauest me to do.

5 And nowe glorifye me thou father with thyne owne selfe with the glorye which I had with the, yer the worlde was

6 I haue declared thy name vnto the men which thou gauest me out of the worlde. Thyne they were and thou gauest them me, and they haue kepte thy saiynges.

7 Now they knowe that all thynges whatsoeuer thou hast geuen me, are of the.

8 For I haue geuen vnto them the wordes whiche thou gauest me, and they haue receyued them and knowe surely that I came out from the, and do beleue that thou dyddest sende me.

9 I praye for them, and praye not for þe worlde but for them whome thou haste geuen me, for they are thyne.

10 And all myne are thyne, and thyne are myne, and I am glorifyed in them.

11 And now am I no more in þe world, but they are in the worlde, and I come to the. Holy father kepe in thyne owne name, them whom thou hast geuen me, that they maye be one, as we are.

12 Whyle I was with them in þe worlde, I kept them in thy name. Those that thou gauest me, haue I kept, and none of them is lost, but that loste chylde, that the scripture myght be fulfylled.

13 Nowe come I to the, and these wordes speake I in the worlde, that they myghte haue my ioye full in them.

14 I haue geuen them thy wordes, and the worlde hath hated them, because they are not of the worlde, euen as I am not of the worlde.

15 I desyre not that thou shouldest take them out of the world: but that thou kepe them from euyl.

16 They are not of the worlde, as I am not of the world.

17 Sanctifye them with the truthe, thy saiyng is truthe,

18 As þu diddest sede me into the world, euen so haue I sent them into the worlde,

19 & for theyr sakes sanctifye I my selfe, that they also myght be sanctifyed through the truth:

20 I praye not for them alone: but for them also which shall beleue on me through theyr preachyng

21 that they all maye be one, as thou father art in me, and I in the that they maye be also one in vs, that the worlde maye beleue þt thou haste sent me.

22 And that glorye that thou gauest me, haue I geuen them, that they may be one, as we are

one,

23 I in them, and thou in me, that they maye be made perfect in one, & that the worlde maye knowe that thou haste sent me, & hast loued them as thou haste loued me.

24 Father, I will that they which thou haste geuen me, be with me where I am, that they maye se my glory which thou hast geuen me. For thou louedest me before the makynge of the worlde.

25 O righteous father, þe very world hath not knowen the: but I haue knowen the, and these haue knowen that thou haste sente me.

26 And I haue declared vnto them thy name, & will declare it that the loue where with þu haste loued me, be in them, and that I be in them.

## CHAPTER 18

WHEN Iesus had spoken these wordes, he wente forth with his disciples ouer the broke Cedron, where was a garden into the whiche he entred with his discyples.

2 Iudas also which betrayed hym, knewe the place: for Iesus oftetymes resorted thither with hys disciples.

3 Iudas then after he had receyued a bande of men, and ministers of the hye priestes and Phariseis, came thyther wt lanternes and fyrebrandes, and weapons.

4 Then Iesus knowing all thynges that should come on hym, wente forth, and sayed vnto them: whom seke ye?

5 They aunswered hym: Iesus of Nazareth. Iesus sayed vnto them: I am he. Iudas also which betrayed hym, stode wt them.

6 But assone as he had sayd vnto them: I am he, they went backwardes, and fell to the grounde.

7 And he asked them agayne: whome seke ye? They aunswered: Iesus of Nazareth.

8 Iesus aunswered: I sayde vnto you: I am he. Yf ye seke me, let these go theyr waye.

9 That the saiynge myght be fulfylled which he spake: of them which thou gauest me, haue I not loste one.

10 Simon Peter hadde a swerde, & drue it, and smote the hye Pryestes seruaunte, and cut of hys ryght eare. The seruauntes name was Malchus.

11 Then sayed Iesus vnto Peter: put vp thy swerde into the sheath: shall I not drinke of the cup whiche my father hathe geuen me?

12 Then the company and þe captaine and the ministers of the Iewes, toke Iesus & bounde hym,

13 and led hym awaye to Anna fyrste: For he was fatherinlawe vnto Cayphas, whiche was the hye prieste that same yeare.

14 Cayphas was he that gaue counsell to the Iewes, that it was expedient, that one man shoulde dye for the people.

15 And Simon Peter folowed Iesus, & another disciple: that disciple was knowne of the hye prieste, and went in with Iesus into the palayce of the hye prieste.

16 But Peter stode at the dore without. Then went oute that other disciple whiche was knowne vnto the hye prieste, and spake to the damsell that kepte the dore, & brought in Peter.

17 Then sayed the damsel that kepte the dore, vnto Peter: Arte not thou one of thys mans disciples? He sayed: I am not.

18 The seruauntes and the ministers stode there and had made a fyre of coles, for it was colde, and they warmed them selues. Peter also stode amonge them, and warmed hym selfe.

19 The hye Prieste axed Iesus of hys disciples and of hys doctryne.

20 Iesus aunswered him: I spake openly in the world. I euer taught in the synagoge, and in the temple whyther all the Iewes resorted, and in secrete haue I sayde nothynge.

21 Why axest thou me? Axe them whiche hearde me, what I sayde vnto them. Beholde, they can tell what I sayde.

22 When he had thus spoken, one of the ministers which stode by, smote Iesus on the face, saiyng: aunswerest thou the hye prieste so?

23 Iesus aunswered hym: Yf I haue euyll spoken, beare wytnes of the euyll, yf I haue well spoken, why smytest thou me?

24 And Annas sent him bounde vnto Cayphas the hye priest.

25 Symon Peter stode and warmed him self and they sayed vnto hym: arte not thou also one of hys discyples? He denyed it, and sayde: I am not.

26 One of the hye priestes seruauntes (hys cosin whose eare Peter smote of) sayde vnto him: dyd not I se the in the garden with him?

27 Peter denyed agayne, and immediatlye the cocke crewe.

28 Then led they Iesus from Cayphas into the hall of iudgement. It was in the morning and they themselues went not into the iudgement hall leaste they shoulde be defyled, but that they might eate the paschall lambe.

29 Pylate then wente oute vnto them, and sayde: what accusacion bringe ye agaynste this man?

30 They aunswered, and sayed vnto him. If he were not an euyli doer, we woulde not haue delyuered him vnto the.

31 Then sayed Pilate vnto them: take ye him, and iudge hym after your owne lawe. Then the Iewes sayed vnto hym: It is not laufull for vs to put any man

to death

32 That the wordes of Iesus might be fulfylled, whiche he spake, signifiynge what death he shoulde dye.

33 Then Pilate entred into the iudgemente hall agayne, and called Iesus, and sayd vnto hym: arte thou the kynge of the Iewes?

34 Iesus aunswered: saiyest thou that of thy self, or dyd other tell it the of me?

35 Pylate aunswered Am I a Iewe? Thyne owne nacyon and hye priestes haue delyuered the vnto me, What hast thou done?

36 Iesus aunswered my kingdome is not of thys worlde. If my kingdome were of thys worlde, then woulde my mynisters surely fyght, that I shoulde not be delyuered to the Iewes, but now is my kyngdom not from hence.

37 Pilate sayed to him: Arte thou a kynge then? Iesus aunswered: Thou sayest that I am a kynge. For thys cause was I borne, and for thys cause came I into the worlde, that I shoulde beare wytnes vnto the trueth. And al that are of the trueth heare my voyce.

38 Pylate sayde vnto hym: what thynge is trueth? And when he had sayd that, he wente oute agayne to the Iewes, and sayd vnto them: I fynd in him no cause at al.

39 Ye haue a custome that I shoulde deliuer you one lose at Easter. Wyll ye that I lose vnto you the kyng of the Iewes.

40 Then cryed they all agayne, sayinge: Not hym, but Barrabas, that Barrabas was a robber.

# CHAPTER 19

THEN Pylate toke Iesus & scourged him.

2 And the souldyers wound a croune of thornes, and put it on hys heade. And they dyd on hym a purple garment

3 & sayde: hayle kyng of the Iewes: and they smote him on the face.

4 Pylate went forth agayne, & sayd vnto them: behold I bryng hym forth to you, that ye maye knowe, that I fynde no faute in hym.

5 Then came Iesus forthe wearynge a croune of thornes and a purple robe. And Pylate sayde vnto them: Beholde the man.

6 When the hye Priestes and ministers saw him, they cryed, saiyng: Crucifye him, crucifye him. Pylate sayde vnto them: Take ye hym, and crucifye hym; for I finde no cause in him.

7 The Iewes aunswered hym: we haue a lawe, and by our lawe he oughte to dye: because he made hym selfe the sonne of God.

8 When Pilate hearde that saiyng: he was the more afrayd,

9 and went agayne into þe iudgement hall, and sayde vnto Iesus: whence are thou? But Iesus gaue hym none aunswere.

10 Then sayde Pylate vnto him: Speakest thou not vnto me? knowest thou not that I haue power to crucify the, and haue power to louse the?

11 Iesus aunswered: Than couldest haue no power at all agaynst me, except it were geuen the from aboue. Therfore he that delyuered me vnto the, is more in synne.

12 And from thence forth sought Pylate meanes to louse him: but the Iewes cryed, saiynge: yf thou let hym go, thou arte not Cesars frende. For whosoeuer maketh hym selfe a kynge, is agaynst Cesar.

13 When Pylate heard þt saiyng: he brought Iesus forth, and sate doune to geue sentence in a place called the pauement: but in the Hebrue tong Gabbatha.

14 It was the Saboth euen which falleth in the easter feast, and about the sixt houre. And he sayed vnto the Iewes. Beholde your kynge.

15 They cryed, awaye wyth hym, awaye with hym, crucifye hym. Pylate sayd to them: Shall I crucifye your kynge? The hye Priestes aunswered: we haue no king but Cesar.

16 Then delyuered he him vnto them to be crucifyed. And they toke Iesus, & led hym awaye,

17 & he bare his crosse, & went forth into a place called the place of dead mens sculles, which is named in Hebrewe Golgatha,

18 Where they crucifyed hym, and two other with hym, on eyther syde one, and Iesus in the myddest.

19 And Pylate wrote hys tytle and put it on the crosse. The wrytyng was Iesus of Nazareth, kynge of the Iewes.

20 Thys tytle red manye of the Iewes. For the place where Iesus was crucifyed, was nye to the cytye. And it was wrytten in Hebrue, Greke and Latyn.

21 Then sayde the hye priestes of þe Iewes to Pylate. Wryte not kynge of the Iewes: but that he sayde. I am kyng of þe Iewes.

22 Pilate aunswered: what I haue wrytten that haue I wrytten.

23 Then the souldyers, when they had crucyfyed. Iesus toke hys garmentes, and made foure partes, to euery souldyour a parte, and also hys cote. The cote was withoute seame, wroughte vpon thorow out.

24 And they sayde one to another. Let vs not deuyde it, but caste lottes, who shall haue it: That the scripture myght be fulfylled which sayeth. They parted my raymentes among them, and on my cote dyd they caste lottes. And the souldiours dyd such thynges in dede.

25 There stode by the crosse of Iesus his mother, and hys

mothers sister. Marye the wyfe of Cleophas, and Mary Magdalen.

26 When Iesus sawe his mother, and the discyple standyng whome he loued, he sayed vnto his mother: woman beholde thy sonne.

27 Then sayed he to the discyple: beholde thy mother. And from that houre the discyple toke her for hys owne.

28 After that when Iesus perceyued that all thynges were perfourmed, that the scrypture myght be fulfylled, he sayed: I thyrst.

29 There stode a vessell full of vyneger by. And they fylled a sponge with vyneger, and wounde it aboute with ysope, and put it to hys mouthe.

30 Assone as Iesus had receyued of the vyneger he sayed: It is fynyshed: and bowed hys head, and gaue vp the ghoste.

31 The Iewes then because it was the saboth euen, that the bodyes shoulde not remayne vpon the crosse on the saboth day (for that Saboth daye was an hye daye) besought Pylate that theyr legges myghte be broken, and that they myghte be taken doune.

32 Then came the souldyers, and brake the legges of the fyrst & of the other, which was crucified with Iesus.

33 But when they came to Iesus, and sawe that he was dead already, they brake not hys legges:

34 but one of the souldyers with a speare thruste hym into the syde and forth with came there out bloude and water.

35 And he that sawe it, bare recorde, and hys recorde is true. And he knoweth that he sayth true, that ye myghte beleue also.

36 These thynges were done, that the scripture shoulde be fulfylled: Ye shall not breake a bone of hym.

37 And agayne another scripture sayeth: They shall loke on hym whome they pearled.

38 After that Ioseph of Arimathia (whiche was a disciple of Iesus, but secretely for feare of the Iewes) besought Pylate that he myght take doune the bodye of Iesus. And Pylate gaue him licence.

39 And there came also Nicodemus whiche at the begynnyng came to Iesus by nyght, and broughte of myrre & aloes myngled together aboute an hundred pounde wayght.

40 Then toke they the body of Iesu, & wound it in lynnen clothes with the odoures, as the maner of the Iewes is to burye.

41 And in the place where Iesus was crucifyed, was a garden, and in the garden a new sepulchre, wherein was neuer man layde.

42 There layde they Iesus because of the Iewes saboth euen, for the sepulchre was nye at hande.

## CHAPTER 20

THE morowe after the Saboth daye came Mary Magdalene early when it was yet darcke, vnto the sepulchre, and saw the stone taken awaye from þt toumbe.

2 Then she ranne, and came to Simon Peter, and to the other discyple whom Iesus loued, and sayde vnto them. They haue taken away the Lorde out of the toumbe, and we cannot tell where they haue layde hym.

3 Peter went forth & that other disciple & came vnto the sepulchre.

4 They ranne both together, & that other disciple dyd out runne Peter, & came fyrste to the sepulchre.

5 And he stouped doune, and saw the lynnen clothes liyng, yet went he not in.

6 Then came Symon Peter folowyng him and wente into the sepulchre, and sawe þe lynnen clothes lye,

7 and the napkyn that was aboute hys head, not liynge with the lynnen clothe, but wrapped together in a place by it selfe.

8 Then wente in also that other discyple which came fyrste to the sepulchre, and he saw & beleued.

9 For as yet they knew not the scriptures that he should ryse agayne from death.

10 And the discyples went awaye agayne vnto theyr owne home.

11 Mary stode without at the sepulchre wepynge. And as she wepte. she bowed her self, and loked into the sepulchre,

12 and sawe two angels in whyte sittynge, the one at the heade, & the other at the fete, where they had layde the bodye of Iesus.

13 And they sayd vnto her: Woman, why wyppest thou? She sayed vnto them: For they haue taken awaye my Lorde, and I wote not where they haue layed hym.

14 When she had thus sayde, she tourned her self backe, and sawe Iesus standynge, and knewe not, that it was Iesus.

15 Iesus sayde to her: woman why wepest thou? Whome sekest thou? She supposynge that he had bene the gardener, sayed vnto him: Syr yf thou haue borne him hence, tell me where thou hast layed hym, that I maye fet him.

16 Iesus sayde vnto her: Mary. She turned her selfe, and sayd vnto him: Rabbony, whiche is to saye: Mayster.

17 Iesus sayd vnto her touch me not, for I am not yet ascended to my father. But go to my brethren, & saye vnto them: I ascende vnto my father and youre father: to my God and your God.

18 Mary Magdalene came

and tolde the dyscyples that she had sene the Lord, and that he had spoken suche thinges vnto her.

19 The same day at night, which was the morowe after the saboth day, when þe dores wer shut, wher the disciples were assembled together for fear of the Iewes, came Iesus and stode in the myddes, and saide to them: peace be wyth you.

20 And when he had so sayed, he shewed vnto them his handes, and hys syde. Then were the dyscyples glade when they sawe the Lorde.

21 Then sayde Iesus to them agayne: peace be with you. As my father sente me euen so sende I you.

22 And when he had sayd that he brethed on them and sayde. Receyue the holy ghost.

23 Whosoeuers synnes ye remyt they are remitted vnto them. And whosoeuers synnes ye retayne, they are retayned.

24 But Thomas one of the twelue, called Didymus, was not wyth them when Iesus came,

25 The other disciples saide vnto him: we haue sene the Lorde. And he said vnto them: excepte I se in hys handes the prent of the nailes, and put my fynger into the holes of the nayles, and thruste my handes into hys syde, I wyl not beleue.

26 And after .viij. dayes agayne, hys dyscyples were wythin, and Thomas wyth them. Then came Iesus when the dores were shut, and stode in the middes and sayd: peace be wyth you.

27 After that sayde he to Thomas: brynge thy fynger hyther, and se my handes, and brynge thy hande and thrust it into my syde: and be not faithlesse, but beleuinge.

28 Thomas aunswered and said vnto hym: My Lord and my God:

29 Iesus sayd vnto hym: Thomas because thou hast sene me, therfore thou beleuest. Happye are they that haue not sene, and yet haue beleued.

30 And manie other sygnes dyd Iesus in the presence of hys dyscyples, whyche are not written in this boke.

31 These are written that ye myght beleue, that Iesus is Christe the sonne of God, and that in beleuinge ye might haue lyfe thorow hys name.

# CHAPTER 21

After that Iesus shewed hym selfe agayne at the sea of Tyberias. And on thys wise shewed he hym selfe.

2 Ther were together Symon Peter and Thomas, whyche is called Didimus, and Nathaniell of Cana a cytie of Galile, and the sonnes of Zebedei, and two other of the disciples.

3 Simon Peter sayd vnto them: I go a fyshinge. They sayd vnto hym: we also wyll go wyth the. They went theyr way and entred into a shyppe strayght waie, and that nighte caught they nothyng.

4 But when the mornyng was nowe come, Iesus stode on the shore: neuerthelesse the dyscyples knewe not that it was Iesus.

5 Iesus sayd vnto them: syre, haue ye anye meate? They aunswered him: no.

6 And he sayd vnto them: caste out the net on the ryght syde of the shyppe, and ye shall fynde. They caste out, and anone they were not able to draw it for the multytude of fyshes.

7 Then sayde the disciple whom Iesus loued vnto Peter: It is the Lord. When Simon Peter hearde that it was the Lorde, he gyrde hys mantel to him (for he was naked) and sprange into þe sea:

8 The other disciples came by shippe for they were not farre from land, but as it were two hundred cubites, and they drewe the net wyth fyshes:

9 Assone as they were come to land, they sawe hote coles and fyshe, layde thereon and breade.

10 Iesus said vnto them: bringe of the fishe which ye haue now caught.

11 Simon Peter stepped forth, and drewe the net to lande full of great fyshes an hundred and .liij. And for all there were so many, yet was not the net broken.

12 Iesus sayde vnto them: come and dyne. And none of the discyples durst axe him, what art thou? for they knewe that it was the Lord.

13 Iesus then came and toke bread, and gaue them, and fyshe lykewyse.

14 And thys is nowe the thyrde tyme that Iesus appeared to hys discyples after that he was rysen agayne from deathe.

15 When they had dyned. Iesus sayd to Simon Peter: Simon Ioanna, louest thou me more then these? He sayd vnto him: ye Lorde thou knowest that I loue the. He saide vnto him: fede me lambes.

16 He saied to him again the seconde tyme? Simon Ioanna, louest thou me? He saied vnto him: yea Lorde thou knowest that I loue the. He saied vnto him: fede me shepe:

17 He saied vnto him the thyrde tyme: Simon Ioanna, louest thou me? And Peter sorowed, because he saied to him the thirde time, louest thou me, and said vnto him: Lord, thou knowest all thinge: thou knowest that I loue the. Iesus sayd vnto him: fede me shepe.

18 Verelie verelye, I saie vnto the, when thou waste yonge, thou girdest thy selfe, and walkedst whither thou wouldest: but when thou arte olde, thou shalt stretche forth thy handes, and another shall gyrd the, and lead the whither thou wouldest

not:

19 That spake he, signyfyeng by what death he should glorifie God. And when he had saied thus, he sayed to hym: folowe me.

20 Peter tourned aboute, and sawe that disciple whom Iesus loued folowinge which also leaned on his breste at supper and saied: Lord which is he that shal betraye the?

21 When Peter saw him, he sayde to Iesus: Lord what shall he here do?

22 Iesus sayde vnto him: Yf I wyll haue him to tarye tyll I come, what is that to the? folow thou me.

23 Then went this saiynge abrode amonge the brethren, that that disciple shoulde not dye. Yet Iesus sayde not to hym, he shall not dye, but if I wyl that he tary tyll I come, what is that to the?

24 The same dyscyple is he which testifyeth of these thinges, and wrote these thinges. And we know þt his testimonie is true.

25 Ther are also many other thinges whych Iesus dyd, the whiche if they shoulde be written euery one I suppose the worlde could not contayne the bokes that shuld be written.

# Acts

## CHAPTER 1

IN the former treatyse (deare frende Theophilus) I haue written of all that Iesus beganne to do and teache,

2 vntyll the day in whyche he was taken vp after that he, through the holy ghost, had geuen commaundementes vnto þe Apostles whiche he had chosen:

3 to whom also he shewed him selfe aliue after his passion by many tokens, apperynge vnto them fourty dayes, & speakinge of the kyngdome of God,

4 & gathered them together, and commaunded them, that they shoulde not departe from Hierusalem: but to wayt for the promys of the father, wherof ye haue hearde of me.

5 For Iohn baptysed with water: but ye shal be baptised with the holy ghost, and that wyth in thys feawe dayes.

6 When they were come together they axed of him saiynge: Lorde wylt thou at thys tyme restore againe the kyngdome to Israel?

7 And he sayed vnto them: It is not for you to know the tymes or the seasons which the father hath put in hys owne power

8 but ye shall receiue power of the holy ghost, whiche shall come on you. And ye shall be witnesses vnto me in Hierusalem, and in al Iewrye, and in Samary and euen vnto the worldes ende.

9 And when he had spoken these thynges whyle they beheld, he was taken vp, and a cloud receiued him vp out of their sighte,

10 And while they loked stedfastlye vp to heauen as he went, beholde two men stode by them in whyt apparell,

11 whyche also sayde: ye men of Galile, why stande ye gasynge vp into heauen? This same Iesus which is taken from you into heauen, shal so come, euen as ye haue sene hym go into heauen.

12 Then returned they vnto Hierusalem from mounte Oliuete, whiche is nie to Hierusalem counteynynge a saboth dayes iorney.

13 And when they were come in, they went vp into a parler where abode bothe Peter, and Iames, Iohn and Andrew, Philip & Thomas, Bartlemew and Matthewe, Iames the sonne of Alpheus and Simon zelotes, and Iudas Iames sonne.

14 These all continued wyth one accorde in prayer and supplicacion with the women and Mary the mother of Iesu, and with hys brethren.

15 And in those dayes Peter stode vp in the myddes of the dyscyples and sayde (the numbre of names that were together, were about an hundred and twenty)

16 Ye men and brethren this scripture muste haue nedes ben fulfilled, which the holy ghost through þe mouth of Dauid spake before of Iudas, whiche was gyde to them that toke Iesus.

17 For he was noumbred wyth vs and had obtayned felowshype in this ministracion.

18 And the same hath now possessed a plot of grounde with the rewarde of iniquitie, and when he was hanged, brast a sondre in the myddes. and all his bowels gushed out.

19 And it is knowen vnto all the inhabiters of Ierusalem, in so much that, that felde is called in theyr mother tonge Acheldama, that is to say, the bloude fielde.

20 It is written in the boke of Psalmes: His habitacion be voide, and no man be dwelling ther in: and his Byshoprycke let another take.

21 Wherfore of these men whiche haue companyed with vs all the tyme that the Lorde Iesus went in and oute among vs,

22 beginning at þe baptisme of Iohn, vnto that same daye that he was taken vp from vs, muste one be ordeyned to beare wytnes with vs of hys resurreccion.

23 And they apoynted two, Ioseph called Barsabas (whose syr name was Iustus) and

Mathias.

24 And they praysed saiynge: thou Lorde whyche knowest the hertes af all men, shewe whether of these two thou hast chosen,

25 that the one may take the roume of this mynystracion and Apostleshippe, from þt which Iudas by transgression fel, that he myght go to his owne place.

26 And they gaue forth theyr lottes, and the lot fell on Mathias, and he was counted with the eleuen Apostles.

# CHAPTER 2

WHEN the fyfty daye was come, they were all with one accorde together in one place.

2 And sodainly there came a sounde from heauen, as it had bene the comynge of a myghty wynd, and it filled al the housse where they sate.

3 And there appeared vnto them clouen tounges, lyke as they had bene fyre, and it sate vpon eche of them,

4 and they were all filled with the holye ghoste, and began to speake wyth other tounges, euen as the spyryte gaue them vtteraunce.

5 And there were dwelling at Hierusalem Iewes, deuout men, whyche were of all nations vnder heauen.

6 When thys was noysed aboute, the multitude came together & were astonied, because that euery man hearde them speake hys owne toung.

7 They wondred all & merueyled sayinge among them selues: Behold are not al these which speake of Galile?

8 And how heare we euery man his own tounge wherin we were borne?

9 Parthians, Medes, and Elamites, and the inhabiters of Mesopotamia, of Iewry, and of Cappadocia, and of Ponthus and Asia,

10 Phrysia, Pamphilia, and of Egypte, and of the parties of Libia, which is besyde Syren, and straungers of Rome, Iewes, and conuertes,

11 Grekes, and Arabians: we haue heard them speake: wyth our owne tounges the great workes of God.

12 They were all amased, and woundered saiynge one to another: what meaneth thys?

13 Other mocked them sayinge: they are full of newe wyne.

14 But Peter stepped forth wyth the eleuen, and lyfte vp his voyce, and sayed vnto them: Ye men of Iewrye, and all ye that inhabite Hierusalem: be thys knowen vnto you, and wyth youre eares heare my wordes.

15 These art not drounke, as ye suppose, for it is yet but the thyrde houre of the day.

16 But thys is that which was spoken by the Prophet Iohel:

17 It shal be in the laste daies saith God, of my spirite: I wil pour out vpon all flesh. And your sonnes and daughters shal prophesie, & your youngmen shal se visions, and your oldmen shall dreame dreames.

18 And on my seruauntes and on my handmaydens, I wyll pour out of my spirite in those dayes, and they shall prophesye.

19 And I wyll shewe wounders in heauen aboue, and tokens in the earth beneth, bloude & fyre, and the vapoure of smoke.

20 The sonne shalbe turned into darckenes, and the mone into bloude, before that greate and notable day of the Lorde come.

21 And it shall be, that whosoeuer shall call on the name of the Lord shall be saued.

22 Ye men of Israel heare these wordes: Iesus of Nazareth, a man approued of God amonge you wyth miracles, woundres, and signes whiche God dyd by hym in the middes of you, as ye your selues knowe:

23 hym haue ye taken by the handes of vnryghtuous persons after he was delyuered by the determinate counsell and for knowledge of God, and haue crucifyed and slayne:

24 whom God hath raysed vp and lowsed the sorowes of deathe, because it was vnpossible þt he shoulde be holden of it.

25 For Dauid speaketh of hym afore hand. I sawe the Lorde alwayes before me: For he is on my ryghte hande, that I shoulde not be moued.

26 Therefore dyd my herte reioice, and my tounge was glad. Moreouer also my fleshe shall reste in hope,

27 because thou wylt not leaue my soule in hel, neyther wylte suffer thine holy, to se corruption.

28 Thou hast shewed me the wayes of lyfe, and shalte make me full of ioye, wt thy countenaunce.

29 Men and brethren, let me frely speake vnto you of þe patriarche Dauid: For he is both dead and buryed, and hys sepulchre remaineth wyth vs vnto this daye.

30 Therfore seiyng he was a Prophet, and knew that God had sworne wyth an othe to hym, that the fruyte of hys loynes shoulde sit on hys seat (in that Christ shoulde ryse agayne in the flesh)

31 he sawe before: and spake of the resurreccion of Christ, that hys soule shoulde not be lefte in hell: neyther hys fleshe should se corruption.

32 Thys Iesus hath God raised vp wher of we all are witnesses.

33 Sence nowe that he by the ryght hand of God is exalted, and hath receiued of þe father the promyse of the holy ghost, he hath shed forth, that whyche ye now se and heare.

34 For Dauid is not ascended into heauen: but he sayd: The Lord said to my Lord, syt on my ryght hande

35 vntyll I make thy fooes thy fote stole.

36 So therefore let all the house of Israell knowe for a surety, that God hath made the same Iesus whom ye haue crucifyed, bothe Lord and Christe.

37 When they hearde this, they were prycked in their hertes, and sayd vnto Peter and vnto the other Apostles. Ye men and brethren, what shall we do?

38 Peter sayde vnto them: repent and be baptysed euerye one of you in the name of Iesus Christe for the remission of sinnes, and ye shall receiue the gifte of the holye ghost.

39 For the promyse was made vnto you and to your chyldren, & to all that are a farre, euen as manye as the Lorde oure God shall call.

40 And wyth manye other wordes bare he wytnes and exhorted them saiynge: Saue your selues from thys vntowarde generacion.

41 Then they þt gladlye receiued his preachinge, were baptysed, and the same daye there were added vnto them about thre thousande soules.

42 And they continued in the Apostles doctrine and fellowshyppe, and in breakyng of bread, and in praier.

43 And feare came ouer euery soule. And many woundres & signes were shewed by the Apostles.

44 And all that beleued kept them selues together, and had all thinges commen,

45 and solde their possessions and goodes, and departed them to all men as euery man had nede.

46 And they contynued dayly wyth one accorde in the temple and brake bread in euerye house, and dyd eate their meate together, with gladnes and singlenes of hert

47 praisynge God, and had fauour wyth all þe people: And the Lorde added to the congregacion dayly suche as should be saued.

# CHAPTER 3

PETER and Iohn wente vp together into the temple at þe nynth houre of prayer.

2 And ther was a certayne man halte from hys mothers wombe, whome they broughte and layed at the gate of the temple called beutifull, to axe almes of them that entred into the temple.

3 Whyche same when he sawe Peter and Iohn, that they woulde into the temple, desiered to receiue an almes.

4 And Peter fastened hys eyes on hym wyth Iohn and sayed: loke on vs.

5 And he gaue heede vnto them, trustynge to receyue somethinge of them.

6 Then sayed Peter: Syluer and gold haue I none, suche as I haue geue I the. In the name of Iesu Christ of Nazareth, ryse vp & walke.

7 And he toke hym by the right hande, and lyft him vp. And immedyatlye hys fete and ancle bones receyued strength.

8 And he sprange, stode and also walked, and entred wyth them into the temple, walkynge and leaping and laudinge God.

9 And all the people sawe hym walke and laude God.

10 And they knewe hym that it was he whyche sate and begged at the beutyfull gate of the temple. And they wondred & were sore astonied at that, which had happened vnto hym.

11 And as the halte whych was healed held Peter and Iohn, all the people ran amased vnto them in Solomons porche.

12 When Peter saw that, he aunswered vnto the people: ye men of Israel why maruaile ye at this or why loke ye so stedfastly on vs as though by our owne power or holines, we had made this man go.

13 The God of Abraham Isaac and Iacob, the God of our fathers hath glorified hys sonne Iesu, whom ye delyuered and denyed in the presence of Pylate, when he had iudged hym to be lowsed.

14 But ye denyed the holye and iuste: and desyred a mortherer to be geuen you

15 and kylled the Lorde of lyfe, whom god hath raysed from death, of the whiche we are wytnesses.

16 And hys name through the fayth of his name, hath made this man sound: whom ye se and knowe. And the fayth whych is by hym, hath geuen to hym thys health in the presence of you all.

17 And nowe brethren I wote well þt through ignoraunce ye dyd it, as did also your heades.

18 But those thinges whyche God before had shewed, by the mouth of all hys prophetes, howe that Christe shoulde suffer, he hath thus wyse fulfilled.

19 Repent ye therfore and turne, that youre synnes maye be done away. When the tyme of refreshing commeth, which we shall haue of the presence of þe Lorde,

20 and when God shal sende hym, which before was preached vnto you, that is to wytte, Iesus Christe,

21 whiche he must receiue heauen, vntyl the tyme that al thinges (which God hath spoken by the mouthe of all hys holye Prophetes sence the worlde beganne) be restored agayne.

22 For Moyses sayd vnto the fathers: A Prophete shall the Lorde youre God raise vp vnto you, euen of youre brethren lyke vnto me: hym shall ye heare in

all thynges, whatsoeuer he shall saye vnto you.

23 For the tyme wyll come, that euerye soule, whyche shal not heare that same prophete, shal be destroyed from amonge the people.

24 Also all the Prophetes from Samuel and thence forth, as manye as haue spoken, haue in lykewyse tolde of these dayes.

25 Ye are the chyldren of the prophetes and of the couenaunt, which God hath made vnto our fathers saiynge to Abraham: Euen in thy sede shall all þe kynredes of the earthe be blessed.

26 Fyrste vnto you hath God raysed vp his sonne Iesus, and hym he hath sent to blesse you, that euery one of you shuld turne from your wickednes.

## CHAPTER 4

As they spake vnto the people: the Priestes and the Rular of the Temple, and the Saduces came vpon them,

2 taking it greuouslye that they taughte the people and preached in Iesus the resurreccion frome deathe.

3 And layed handes on them, and putte them in holde vntyll the nexte daie, for it was nowe euen tyde.

4 Howe be it, manye of them which hearde the wordes, beleued: and the numbre of þe men was about fyue thousande.

5 And it chaunced on the morowe that theyr rulars, and elders, and scribes,

6 as Annas the chiefe Prieste, and Cayphas, and Iohn, and Alexander, and as many as were of the hye priestes gathered together at Ierusalem,

7 and set them before them, & axed: by what power or in what name haue ye done this syrs?

8 Then Peter full of the holy ghost sayed vnto them: ye rulars of the people, and elders of Israel,

9 if we thys day are examined of the good dede done to the sicke man by what meanes he is made whole:

10 be it knowen vnto you all and to all the people of Israel, that in the name of Iesus Christe of Nazareth, whom ye crucifyed, and whom God raysed agayne from deathe, euen by hym doth thys man stande here presente before you whole.

11 This is the stone cast asyde of you builders, which is set in the chiefe place of the corner.

12 Neither is ther saluacion in any other. Nor yet also is there any other name geuen to men wherin we muste be saued.

13 When they sawe the boldnes of Peter & Iohn and vnderstode that, they were vnlerned men and lay people, they meruailed, and they knew then that they were with Iesu:

14 and beholdinge also the man whiche was healed standynge wyth them, they coulde not saye agaynst it.

15 But they commaunded them to go a syde out of the counsell, and counceled amonge them selues

16 saiynge: what shall we do to these men? For a manifeste signe is done by them, and is openlye knowen to all them that dwell in Hierusalem, and we can not denie it.

17 But þt it be noised no further among the people, let vs threaten and charge them that they speake henceforth to no man in this name.

18 And they called them and commaunded them that in no wyse they should speake or teache in the name of Iesu.

19 But Peter and Iohn aunswered to them and sayd: whether it be ryght in þe syght of God to obey you more then God, iudge ye.

20 For we can not. But speake that whiche we haue sene and heard.

21 So threatened they them and let them go, and founde nothinge howe to punyshe them, because of the people. For all men lauded God for the myracle which was done,

22 for the man was aboue fourty yeare olde, on whom thys myracle of healynge was shewed.

23 Assone as they were let go, they came to their fellowes, and shewed all that the hye priestes and elders had sayed to them.

24 And when they hearde that, they lifte vp their voices to God with one accorde, and saied: Lorde, thou art God, whiche haste made heauen and earth, the sea and al that in them is,

25 whiche by the mouth of thy seruaunt Dauid hast said: Why dyd the heathen rage, and the people imagyn vaine thinges.

26 The kinges of þe earth stode vp and þe rulers came together, againste Lorde and agaynste his Chryste.

27 For of a trueth againste thy holy childe Iesus, whom thou hast anointed, both Herode and also Poncius Pilate, with the Gentyls & the people of Israel, gathered them selues together,

28 for to do whatsoeuer thy hande and thy councell determined before to be done.

29 And nowe Lorde, beholde their threateninges, and graunte vnto thy seruauntes with all confidence to speake thy worde.

30 So þt thou stretche forth thy hande, that healing and signes and wounders be done by the name of thy holye chylde Iesus.

31 And assone as they had prayed, the place moued where they were assembled together, and they were all filled with the holy ghoste, and they spake the worde of God boldlye.

32 And the multitude of them that beleued were of one herte, and of one soule. Also none of them said that anye of the thinges whyche he possessed, was his owne: but had all thinges commune.

33 And with greate power gaue the Apostles wytnes of the resurreccion of the Lorde Iesus. And greate grace was geuen wt them all.

34 Neyther was there anye amonge them that lacked. For as manie as were possessours of landes and houses, sold them and broughte the price of the thinges, that were solde,

35 and layed it doune at the Apostles fete. And distribution was made vnto euery man accordinge as he had nede.

36 And Ioses who was also called of þe Apostles Barnabas (that is to say the sonne of consolation) beynge a Leuite, and of the country of Cipers,

37 had lande, and solde it, and laied the pryce doune at the Apostles fete.

# CHAPTER 5

A certain man named Ananyas with Saphira his wyfe solde a possession,

2 and kept awaye parte of the price (hys wyfe also beyng of counsel,) and brought a certain parte, and layd it doune at þe Apostles fete.

3 Then said Peter. Ananias, how is it, that Sathan hath fylled thyne hert, þt thou shouldest lye vnto the holy ghost, and kepe awaye part of the pryce of the lyuelod:

4 Pertained it not vnto the onelie, and after it was solde, was not the price in thine owne power? Howe is that, thou hast conceiued this thinge in thyne herte? Thou hast not lied vnto men, but vnto God.

5 When Ananias hearde these wordes, he fell doune and gaue vp the ghost. And great feare came on all them that hearde these thinges.

6 And the younge men rose vp, and put him a parte and caryed hym out, and buried him.

7 And it fortuned as it were aboute þe space of thre houres after that hys wyfe came in, ignoraunt of that whiche was done.

8 And Peter sayed vnto her: Tell me, gaue ye þe lande for so much? And she said: ye for so much.

9 Then saied Peter vnto her: why haue ye agreed together to tempte þe spiryte of þe Lorde? Beholde, þe fete of them whiche haue buried thy husbande, are at the dore, and shal cary the out.

10 Then she fell doune straighte waye at his fete, and yelded vp the ghoste. And the yonge men came in and founde her dead, and caryed her out & buried her by her housbande.

11 And great feare came on al the congregation, and on as manie as hearde it.

12 By the handes of the Apostles were manie signes and wounders shewed amonge the people. And they were all together wyth one accorde in Solomons porch.

13 And of other durst no man ioyne him selfe to them: neuerthelater the people magnifyed them.

14 The numbre of them that beleued in the Lorde, both of men and women, grewe more and more:

15 in so much that they broughte the sycke into the stretes, & layed them on beddes and palettes, that at the leaste waye, the shaddowe of Peter when he came by, myght shadowe some of them.

16 There came also a multitude out of the cyties round about vnto Hierusalem, bringinge sicke folke, and them whiche were vexed wyth vncleane spirites. And they were healed euery one.

17 Then the chiefe Prieste arose vp & al they that were with hym (which is the seete of the Saduces) and were full of indignacion,

18 and laied handes on the Apostles, and put them in the commune prison.

19 But the Aungell of þe Lorde by nyght opened the prison dores, and broughte them forth, & sayed:

20 go, steppe forthe, and speake in the temple to the people all the wordes of this lyfe.

21 When they heard þt, they entred into the temple early in the mornynge and taught. The chiefe Prieste came & they that were with him, and called a counsell together, and all the elders of the children of Israell, & sent to the prison to fetche them.

22 When the mynisters came and founde them not in the prison, they returned and tolde

23 saiynge: the pryson founde we shut as sure as was possible, and the kepers standynge wyth out before the dores. But when we had opened, we founde no man with in.

24 When the chiefe Priest of al and the ruler of the temple and the hye Priestes heard these thinges, they doubted of them whervnto thys woulde growe.

25 Then came one and shewed them: beholde the men that ye put in prison, stande in the temple, and teache the people.

26 Then went the ruler of the temple with ministers, and brought them without violence. For they feared þe people: least they should haue bene stoned.

27 And when they had brought them, they set them before the counsell. And the chiefe prieste axed them

28 saiynge: dyd not we straytely commaunde you, that

ye shoulde not teach in this name. And behold ye haue fylled Hierusalem with your doctrine, and ye intended to brynge this mannes bloude vpon vs.

29 Peter and the other Apostles aunswered & saied. We ought more to obey God, then men.

30 The God of our father raysed vp Iesus whom ye slewe and hanged on tree.

31 Hym hath God lyfte vp with his ryght hand to be a ruler and a sauiour, for to geue repentaunce to Israell and forgeuenes of synnes?

32 And we are hys recordes concerninge these thinges, & also the holy ghost, whom God hath geuen to them that obey him.

33 When they heard that they claue a sunder, & sought meanes to slea them.

34 Then stode ther vp one in the counsel, a pharisey named Gamaliel, a doctoure af law, had in aucthorite amonge all the people, and commaunded to put the Apostles a syde a litel space,

35 and saide vnto them: Men of Israel take hede to youre selues what ye entende to do as touching these men.

36 Before these dayes rose vp one Theudas bostynge him selfe: to whom resorted a numbre of men, aboute a foure hundred which was slaine, and they all which beleued him: were scatred abroade, & brought to nought.

37 After this man, arose ther vp one Iudas of Galile in the tyme when tribute began, and drewe awaie muche people after him. He also perished, and all euen as manye as harkened to hym: are scattered abroade.

38 And nowe I saye vnto you: refrayne youre selues from these men, let them alone. For if the counsel of this worke be of men, it wil come to nought.

39 But and if it be of God ye can not destroye it, leaste haply ye be found to striue against god.

40 And to him they agreed, and called the Apostles, and beate them, and commaunded that they shoulde not speake in the name of Iesu, and let them go.

41 And they departed from the counsel, reioysinge that they were counted worthy, to suffer rebuke for his name.

42 And dayly in the temple and in euerye house they ceased not, teachinge and preachinge Iesus Christe.

## CHAPTER 6

IN those dayes as the numbre of the disciples grewe, ther arose a a grudge amonge the Grekes agaynste the Hebrues, because their widdowes were despysed in the dayly ministracion.

2 Then þe twelue called the multitude of the dysciples together and saide: it is not mete that we shoulde leaue the worde of God and serue at the tables.

3 Wherfore brethren, loke ye out amonge you seuen men of honeste reporte, and full of the holye ghoste and wysdome, whyche we maye apoint to this nedfull busines.

4 But we wyl geue our selues continually to prayer, and to the ministracion of the word.

5 And the saiynge pleased the whole multitude. And they chose Stephan a man full of faieth and of the holye ghost, and Philip, and Prochorus, and Nichanor, and Timon, and Permenas, and Nicholas a conuerte of Antioche.

6 Whiche they set before the Apostles, and they praied and laide their handes on them.

7 And the worde of God encreased, and the numbre of the disciples multiplyed in Hierusalem greatly, and a great companye of the priestes were obedient to the faith.

8 And Stephane ful of fayth and power, dyd greate wounders and miracles amonge the people.

9 Then arose certaine of the Synagoge, whyche are called Lybertines and Syrenites, and of Alexandria, and of Cilicia, and Asia, and disputed with Stephan.

10 And they could not resist the wysdome, and the spyryte wt whyche he spake.

11 Then sent they in men, whiche said: we haue heard him speake blasphemous wordes against Moyses and against God.

12 And they moued the people and the elders and the scribes: and came vpon him and caught hym,

13 and brought him to the counsell and brought forth false witnesses whiche sayde. This man ceaseth not to speake blaspemous wordes against thys holy place, and the lawe,

14 for we hearde him saie: this Iesus of Nazareth shall destroye this place, and shal chaung the ordinaunces, which Moises gaue vs.

15 And al that sate in the counsel loked stedfastlye on hym, and saw hys face as it had bene the face of an aungel.

## CHAPTER 7

THEN sayde the chiefe priest: is it euen so?

2 And he sayde: ye men, brethren, and fathers, harken to. The God of glorye appeared vnto our father Abraham whyle he was yet in Mesopotamia, before he dwelt in Charran,

3 & saied to him: come oute of thy countrey & from thy kynred, and come into the lande, whiche I shall shewe the.

4 Then came he out of the lande of Chaldey, and dwelt in Charran. And after that assone as his father was dead he brought him into thys lande, in whiche ye now dwell,

5 and he gaue him none inheritaunce in it, no not the

bredeth of a fote: but promised that he would geue it to hym to possesse, and to his seed after him, when as yet he had no chylde.

6 God verely spake on this wyse that his sede should be a dweller in a straung land, & that they should kepe them in bondage & entreate them euyll .iiij.C. yeares.

7 But the nacion to whome they shalbe in bondage, will I iudge, sayed God. And after that shall they come forth and serue me in this place.

8 And he gaue hym the couenaunt of circumcision. And he begat Isaac, and circumcised him the .viij. daye and Isaac begatte Iacob, and Iacob þe twelue Patriarches.

9 And the patriarches hauinge indignacion sold Ioseph into Egypt. And God was wyth him,

10 and deliuered him out of all his aduersities and gaue him fauoure and wysdome in the sight of Pharao kynge of Egypt, whiche made him gouerner ouer Egypte, and ouer al his houshold.

11 Then came there a derth ouer all the land of Egypt and Canaan, and great affliction, that our fathers founde no sustenaunce.

12 But when Iacob hearde that there was crone in Egypt: he sent our fathers first.

13 And at the seconde tyme, Ioseph was knowen of hys brethren, and Iosephes kinred was made knowen vnto Pharao.

14 Then sente Ioseph and caused hys father to be brought and all his kyn, thre score and .xv. soules.

15 And Iacob descended into Egypte, and dyed both he and our fathers,

16 and were translated into Sichem, and were put in the sepulcher, that Abraham bought for money of the sonnes of Emor, at Sichem.

17 When the tyme of the promys drue nye, (which God had sworne to Abraham) þe people grew and multiplied in Egypte,

18 tyll another kyng arose, whiche knew not of Ioseph.

19 The same dealt subtely wyth oure kynred, & euyll intreated oure fathers, and made them to caste out theyr yonge chyldren, þt they should not remayne aliue.

20 The same time was Moises borne, and was a proper chylde in þe sight of God, whiche was nourished vp in hys fathers house thre monethes.

21 When he was cast out Pharaos doughter toke him vp, & nourished hym vp for her owne sonne.

22 And Moises was learned in al maner wysdome of the Egyptians, and was mighty in dedes and in wordes.

23 And when he was full forty yeare old, it came into his herte to vysyte his brethren the chyldren of Israell.

24 And when he sawe one of them suffer wronge, he defended hym and auenged his quarel that had the harme done to hym, and smote the Egyptian.

25 For he supposed his brethren woulde haue vnderstande how that God by his handes should saue them. But they vnderstode not.

26 And the nexte daye he shewed hym selfe vnto them as they stroue, and woulde haue set them at one againe saiyng: Syrs, ye are brethren, why hurte ye one another?

27 But he that dyd his neighboure wronge, thrust him awaie sayinge: who made the a ruler and a iudge amonge vs?

28 What, wilt thou kyll me, as thou dydest the Egyptian yester daye?

29 Then fled Moyses at that saiyng, and was a straunger in the lande of Madyan, where he begatte two sonnes.

30 And when .xl. yeares were expired, ther appeared to him in the wyldernes of mount Sina, an aungel of the Lord in a flamme of fyre in a bushe.

31 When Moyses saw it he woundred at the sight. And as he drue near to behold, the voice of the Lord came vnto hym.

32 I am the God of thy fathers, the God of Abraham the God of Isaac, and the God of Iacob? Moises trembled and durst not behold.

33 Then sayde the Lorde to him: Put of thy shewes from thy fete, for the place where thou standeste, is holye grounde.

34 I haue perfectly sene the affliction of the people, which is in Egipt and I haue heard their groninge, & am come doune to deliuer them. And nowe come, and I wyl sende the into Egypte.

35 This Moyses whom they forsoke saiyng: who made the a ruler and a iudge, the same God sente both a ruler and a deliuerer, by the handes of the angell, whiche appeared to him in the bushe.

36 And the same brought them out shewing woundres and signes in Egypte, & in the red sea, and in the wildernes .xl. yeares.

37 This is that Moises which said vnto the children of Israell: A Prophet shall the Lorde your God rayse vp vnto you of youre brethren, lyke vnto me, him shal ye heare.

38 This is he that was in the congregation, in the wyldernes wyth the aungell, whyche spake to hym in the mounte Syna, and wyth oure fathers. This man receiued the worde of lyfe to geue vnto vs,

39 to whom our fathers woulde not obey, but cast it from them, and in their hertes turned backe againe into Egipt,

40 saiynge vnto Aaron: Make

vs Gods to go before vs. For this Moises that broughte vs out of the lande of Egipte, we wote not what is become of him.

41 And they made a calfe in those dayes, and offred sacrifices, vnto the ymage, and reioysed in the workes of their owne handes.

42 Then God turned him selfe, and gaue them vp that they shoulde worship the starres of þe skye, as it is written in the boke of the Prophetes. O ye of the house of Israell, gaue ye to me sacrifyces and meate offeringes by the space of .xl. yeare in the wildernes?

43 And ye toke vnto you the tabernacle of Moloch, & the star of your God Remphan, figures which ye made to worshippe them. And I wil translate you beyonde Babylon.

44 Our fathers had the tabernacle of witnes in the wildernes, as he had apoynted them speaking vnto Moyses, that he shoulde make it accordynge to the fashyon that he had sene,

45 Whiche tabernacle our fathers receiued, and brought it in with Iosue into the possession of the Gentils, whiche God draue out before þe face of our fathers vnto the tyme of Dauid.

46 Which found fauour before God, and desired that he myght fynde a tabernacle for the God of Iacob.

47 But Solomon buylt hym an house.

48 Howe be it he that is hyest of all, dwelleth not in temples made with handes, as sayth the prophet:

49 Heauen is my seate, and earth is my fotestole, what house wil ye builde for me sayed þe Lorde? or what place is that I should reste in?

50 hath not my hande made all these thinges.

51 Ye styfe necked, and of vncyrcumcysed hertes and eares, ye haue al wayes resisted þe holye ghoste as your fathers dyd, so do ye.

52 Whyche of the prophetes haue not your fathers persecuted? And they haue slayne them, which shewed before of the comminge of þe iuste whom ye haue nowe betrayed and mordred.

53 And ye also haue receiued a lawe by the ordinaunce of aungels, and haue not kepte it.

54 When they heard these thinges, their hertes claue a sunder, and they gnashed on him with theyr tethe.

55 But he beynge full of the holye ghoste: loked vp stedfastly wyth his eyes into heauen, and sawe the glorye of God, & Iesus standynge on the ryghte hand of God,

56 & sayde: beholde, I se the heauens open, and the sonne of man standynge on the ryght hande of God.

57 Then they gaue a shut wyth a loude voice, and stopped their eares, and ranne vpon hym al at once,

58 and cast him out of the cytie, & stoned him. And the witnesses layde doune theyr clothes at a yonge mannes fote named Saul.

59 And they stoned Stephan calling on & saiyng: Lord Iesu receiue my spyryte.

60 And he kneled doune and cryed with a loude voice: Lord laye not thys sinne to their charge. And when he had thus spoken: he fel a slepe.

# CHAPTER 8

SAUL had pleasure in hys death. And at þe tyme ther was a great persecution agaynste þe congregation, whiche was at Ierusalem, & they were all scattered abroade thorowout þe regions of Iury & Samaria, excepte þe Apostles.

2 Then deuout men dressed Stephan, & made great lamentation ouer hym.

3 But Saul made hauoke of þe congregacion entring into euery house, and drewe oute bothe man and woman, and thruste them into prysone.

4 They that were scatered abroade, wente euery where preaching the word.

5 Then came Philyp into a cytye of Samarya, and preached Christe vnto them.

6 And the people gaue hede vnto those thinges, whiche Philippe spake, wyth one accord, in that they heard and sawe the miracles which he dyd.

7 For vncleane spyrites criynge with loude voyce, came out of manye that were possessed of them. And manye taken wyth palsyes, and manye that halted, were healed.

8 And ther was greate ioye in þe cytye.

9 And ther was a certaine man called Simon, which before tyme in þe same citye, vsed wytchcraft and bewitched the people of Samarye, sayinge that he was a man that coulde do greate thinges.

10 Whom they regarded, from the lest to the greatest, saiyng: this felow is the great power of God.

11 And hym they set much by: because that of long tyme he had mocked them with sorcery.

12 But assone as they beleued Philippes preachinge of the kyngedome of God and of the name of Iesu Christe, they were baptysed both men and women.

13 Then Symon hym selfe beleued also, and was baptysed, and continued wyth Philip, and woundred beholdinge the miracles & signes whiche were shewed.

14 When the Apostles whiche were at Ierusalem hearde saye, that Samaria had receiued the word of God, they sente vnto them Peter and Iohn.

15 Whyche when they were

come prayed for them that they myght receiue the holy ghost.

16 For as yet he was come on none of them, but they were baptysed onlye in the name of Christ Iesu.

17 Then laied they theyr handes on them & they receiued þe holy ghost.

18 When Simon saw that thorow laiyng on of the Apostles handes on them, þe holy ghoste was geuen, he offred them money

19 saiyng: Geue me also this power, that on whomsoeuer I put the handes, he may receiue the holy ghost.

20 Then sayd Peter vnto him: thy money perishe with the, because thou wenest that the gift of God maye be obteyned wt money.

21 Thou hast neither parte nor fellowshippe in thys busynes. For the hert is not ryght in the sight of God.

22 Repent therfore of this thy wyckednes, and praye God, that the thought of thyne herte maye be forgeuen the.

23 For I perceiue, þt thou art full of bitter gal, & wrapped in iniquitie.

24 Then aunswered Simon, and said: praye ye to the Lord for me, that none of these thinges, which ye haue spoken fal on me.

25 And they when they had testified and preached þe worde of the Lorde returned towarde Ierusalem, & preached the Gospel in manie cities of the Samaritans.

26 Then the aungel of the Lorde spake vnto Philippe, saiynge: aryse and go Southward vnto the way, that goeth doune from Ierusalem vnto Gaza, which is in the desert.

27 And he arose and wente on. And beholde a man of Ethiopia, whiche was a chamberlayne, and of greate auctorite with Candace quene of the Ethiopians, and had the rule of all her treasure, came to Hierusalem for to praye.

28 And as he returned home againe sittinge in hys charet, he reade Esay the prophete.

29 Then the spyrite sayed to Phylippe: God neare, and ioyne thy selfe to yonder charete.

30 And Philippe ranne to him, and hearde hym reade the Prophete Esaias and saied: Vnderstandeste thou what thou readeste?

31 And he saied: how can I excepte I had a gyde? And he desiered Philyp, that he woulde come vp and syt wyth hym.

32 The tenoure of the scripture whiche he reade, was thys. He was led as a shepe to be slaine, and lyke a Lambe dombe before his sherar, so opened he not his mouth:

33 Because of hys humblenes, he was not estemed: who shall declare hys generacyon? for his lyke is taken from the earth.

34 The chamberlayne aunswered Phylippe, and sayed: I pray the of whom speaketh the Prophete this? of him selfe, or of some other man?

35 And Philippe opened his mouth, and began at the same scripture, and preached vnto him Iesus.

36 And as they wente on their waye, they came vnto a certaine water, and the chamberlaine sayed: Se here is water, what shall let me to be baptysed?

37 Philyp saide vnto him: If thou beleue with all thyne herte, thou maieste. He aunswered and saied, I beleue that Iesus Christe is the sonne of God.

38 And he commaunded the charete to stande styll. And they went doune both into the water: both Philippe and also the chamberlayne, and he baptysed him.

39 And assone as they were come out of the water, the spyryte of the Lorde caught awaye Phylip, that the chamberlayne sawe him no more. And he went on his waie reioysinge:

40 but Philippe was found at Azotus. And he walked thorow out the countrie preachynge in theyr cytyes, tyll he came to Cesarea.

# CHAPTER 9

AND Saul yet breathynge out threatening & slaughter against the Disciples of the Lorde, went vnto þe hye priest,

2 and desired of him letters to Damasco to the synagoges that if he founde anye of thys way, whether they were men or women, he mighte bring them bound vnto Hierusalem.

3 But as he went on his iorneye, and was come nye to Damasco, sodenly there shyned round aboute him a lyght from heauen,

4 & he fell to þe earth, and hearde a voice saiyng to him: Saul, Saul why persecutest thou me?

5 And he saide: what art thou Lorde? And the Lorde saide: I am Iesus whom thou persecutest it shalbe hearde for the to kycke agaynste the prycke.

6 And he both tremblinge and astonied sayde: Lorde what wylt thou haue me to do? And þe Lorde sayde vnto hym: aryse, and go into the cytye, and it shal be tolde what thou shalt do.

7 Then the men whiche iornyed wyth hym stode amased, for they heard a voice, but sawe no man.

8 And Saul arose from the earth, and opened his eyes, but saw no man. Then led they hym by the hande, and broughte him into Damasco.

9 And he was thre dayes wt out sight & neyther eate nor dranke.

10 And ther was a certaine

disciple at Damasco, named Ananias, & to hym sayd þe Lorde in a vision: Ananias. And he sayd: beholde I am here Lorde.

11 And the Lorde sayd vnto him: aryse, and go into the streat, whiche is called strayght, and seke in the house of Iudas, after one called Saul of Tharsus. For beholde he prayeth,

12 & hath sene in a vision a man named Ananias comminge in to hym, and putting hys handes on him that he myght receiue hys sight.

13 Then Ananias aunswered: Lord, I haue heard by many of this man, how much euyll he hath done to thy sainctes at Ierusalem,

14 and here he hath auctorite of the hye Pryestes to bynd all that call on thy name.

15 The Lorde said vnto him: go thy wayes for he is a chosen vessel vnto me, to beare me name before the gentyls and kynges, and the chyldren of Israel.

16 For I wil shew hym howe greate thinges he muste suffer for my names sake.

17 Ananias went hys waye and entred into the house, and put his handes on him, & said: brother Saul the Lord that appeared vnto þe in the waye as thou camest, hath sent me, that thou myghtest receiue thy sight, and be fylled with the holy ghoste.

18 And immediatly ther fel from hys eyes as it had bene scales, and he receiued sight and arose and was baptised,

19 and receiued meate, and was conforted. Then was Saul certaine dayes wyth the dyscyples whyche were at Damasco.

20 And straight way he preached Christ in the Synagoges, howe that he was the sonne of God.

21 All that heard him, were amased and sayde: is not this he that spoiled them, whiche called on this name in Hierusalem, and came hyther for the intente that he shoulde brynge them bounde vnto the hye priestes?

22 But Saul encreased in strengthe, and confounded þe Iewes whiche dwelte at Damasco affirminge that this was verye Christe.

23 And after a good whyle, the Iewes toke counsell together to kyl him.

24 But their laying awaite was knowen of Saule. And they watched at the gates day and night, to kyl hym,

25 then the disciples toke hym by nyght and put hym thorow the wall, and let him doune in a basket.

26 And when Saule was come to Hierusalem he assaied to couple him selfe wyth the dyscyples and they were all afraied of him and beleued not that he was a dyscyple.

27 But Barnabas toke hym and broughte hym to the Apostles and declared to them, howe he had sene the Lorde in the waye, and had spoken wyth hym: and howe he had done boldlye at Damasco in the name of Iesu.

28 And he had his conuersation wyth them at Hierusalem,

29 and quit hymselfe boldlie in the name of the Lorde Iesus. And he spake and disputed with the Grekes: and they wente aboute to slea him.

30 But when the brethren knew of that, they brought him to Cesaria, and sent him forth to Tharsus.

31 Then had the congregations reste thorowe out all Iewry and Galile and Samarie, and were edified, and walked in the feare of the Lorde, and multiplied by the confort of the holy ghoste.

32 And it chaunced that as Peter walked thorow out al quarters, he came to the sainctes, whiche dwelt at Lydda,

33 and there he founde a certaine man named Eueas, which had kepte his bed .viij. yere sycke of þe palsey.

34 Then saied Peter vnto hym: Eneas, Iesus Christe make the whole. Aryse, and make thy bed. And he arose immediatlie.

35 And all that dwelte at Lidda and Assaron, sawe hym, and turned to the Lorde.

36 Ther was at Ioppa a certaine woman, (which was a disciple named Tabitha, which by interpretation is called Doreas) the same was ful of good workes and almes dedes, whiche she did.

37 And it chaunsed in those daies that she was sicke and dyed. When they had washed her, and layed her in a chamber:

38 Because Lidda was nye to Ioppa, and the discyples had hearde, that Peter was there, they sent vnto hym, desieringe hym that he would not be greued to come vnto them.

39 Peter arose and came wyth them & when he was come, they brought him into the chamber. And all the wydowes stode round about him wepynge and shewynge the cotes & garmentes, whyche Dorcas made whyle she was wyth them.

40 And Peter put them al forth and kneled doune, and praied and turned him to the bodye, and saied: Tabitha, aryse. And she opened her eyes, and when she sawe Peter she sat vp.

41 And he gaue her the hande, and lyfte her vp, and called the Sayntes and wydowes, and sheweth her alyue.

42 And it was knowen thorowe out all Ioppa, and many beleued on the Lorde.

43 And it fortuned that he taried manye dayes in Ioppa wyth one Simon a tanner.

# CHAPTER 10

THERE was a certain man in Cesaria, called Cornelius, a captaine of the souldiers of Italy,

2 a deuout man, & one þt feared God wt al his houshold whiche gaue much almes to the people, and prayed God alway.

3 The same man saw in a vision euydently aboute the ninth houre of the daye, an aungel of God commyng in to hym, and saiyng vnto him: Cornelius.

4 When he loked on hym he was afraid and said, what is it Lord? He sayed vnto hym: Thy prayers and all thy almeses are come vp into remembraunce before God.

5 And now send men to Ioppa and call for one, Symon named also Peter.

6 He lodgeth wt one Symon a tanner, whose house is by the sea syde. He shall tell the, what thou oughtest to do.

7 When the aungell whiche spake vnto Cornelius, was departed, he called two of his housholde seruauntes, and a deuout souldier of them that waited on him

8 and told them all the mater, and sent them to Ioppa.

9 On the morow as they wente on theyr iourneye, and drewe nye vnto the cytie, Peter wente vp into the toppe of the house to praye about the .vi. houre.

10 Then wexed he an houngred, and woulde haue eaten. But whyle they made ready, he fell into a traunce,

11 and sawe heauen opened, and a certaine vessel come doune vnto hym as it had bene a greate sheete knyte at the .iiij. corners, and was let doune to the earth,

12 wherin were all maner of .iiij. foted beastes of the earth, and vermen and wormes, and foules of the ayer.

13 And ther came a voyce to hym: ryse Peter kyll and eate.

14 But Peter sayed: God forbydde Lorde, for I haue neuer eaten anye thynge that is comen or vncleane.

15 And the voyce spake vnto hym agayne the seconde tyme: what God hath clensed, that make thou not commen.

16 This was done thrise, and the vessell was receyued vp againe into heauen.

17 While Peter mused in himself: what this vision, whiche he had sene, meant: beholde, the men whiche were sente from Cornelius had made inquiraunce for Simons house, & stode before the dore.

18 And called oute one and axed, whither Simon, whiche was also called Peter were lodged there.

19 While Peter thoughte on thys vision, the spyryte sayed vnto hym: Beholde men seke the,

20 aryse therfore, get the doune, and go with them, and doubt not, for I haue sent them,

21 Peter went doune to the men, whiche were sent vnto hym from Cornelius, and saide. Beholde, I am he whom ye seke, what is the cause, wherfore ye are come?

22 And they sayde vnto him: Cornelius the captaine, a iuste man, and one that feareth God, and of good reporte amonge al the people of the Iewes, was warned by an holye aungel to sende for the into hys house, and to heare wordes of the.

23 Then called he them in, and lodged them. And on the morowe Peter wente awaye wyth them, and certaine brethren from Ioppa accompanyed him.

24 And the thyrd daye entred they into Cesaria. And Cornelius wayted for them, and had called together his kinsmen, and speciall frendes.

25 And as it chaunsed Peter to come in, Cornelius met him, and fel doune at his fete, and worshipped him.

26 But Peter toke him vp saiynge: stand vp: for euen I me selfe am a man.

27 And as he talked wyth him he came in, and founde manye that were come together.

28 And he sayde vnto them: Ye knowe howe that it is an vnlawfull thynge for a man that is a Iewe, to companye or come vnto an aliaunte: but God hath shewed me that I should not cal any man commen, or vncleane:

29 therfore came I vnto you wyth out saiynge naye, assone as I was sente for I axe therfore, for what intente haue ye sent for me?

30 And Cornelius sayde: Thys daye nowe .iiij. dayes I fasted and at the nynthe houre I prayde in my house: and beholde, a man stode before me in brighte clothinge,

31 and sayd: Cornelius, thy prayer is hearde, and thine almes deades are had in remembraunce in the sight of God.

32 Send therfore to Ioppa, and call for Simon whiche is also called Peter. He is lodged in the house of one Simon a tanner by the sea syde, the which assone as he is come, shall speake vnto the.

33 Then sent I for the immediatly, and thou hast wel done for to come. Nowe are we all here present before God, to heare al thinges that are commaunded vnto the of God.

34 Then Peter opened hys mouth and saide: Of a trueth I perceyue, that God is not partyall,

35 but in all people he that feareth hym and worketh rightuousnes, is accepted wyth hym.

36 Ye knowe the preachinge that God sent vnto the chyldren of Israel, preachynge peace by Iesus Christe, whiche is Lorde

ouer all thinges.

37 Whiche preaching was published thorow out all Iewry, and beganne in Galile, after the baptisme, whiche Iohn preached,

38 howe God had annoynted Iesus of Nazareth wyth the holy ghost, and wyth power. Whiche Iesus went about doynge good, and healinge all that were oppressed of the deuils for God was wyth him.

39 And we are witnesses of al thinges whiche he did in the lande of the Iewes and at Ierusalem: whom they slewe and honge on tree.

40 Hym God reysed vp the thyrd daye, and shewed hym openlye,

41 not to all the people, but vnto vs witnesses chosen before of God, whiche eate and dronke wyth him, after he arose from death.

42 And he commaunded vs to preache vnto the people & testifye that it is he that is ordeined of God a iudge of quicke and deade.

43 To hym geue all the Prophetes witnes, that thorowe hys name, all that beleue in hym, shall receyue remission of sinnes.

44 Whyle Peter yet spake these wordes the holye Ghoste fel on all them whyche hearde the preaching.

45 And they of the circumcision, whyche beleued, were astonied, as manye as came wyth Peter, because that on the Gentils, also was shede out the gyfte of þe holy ghoste.

46 For they heard them speake wyth tounges & magnified God. Then aunswered Peter.

47 Can anye man forbydde water that these shoulde not be baptysed, whiche haue receyued the holye ghoste as well as we?

48 And he commaunded them to be baptysed in the name of the Lorde. Then prayed they hym to tarye a fewe dayes.

# CHAPTER 11

AND the Apostles and the brethren þt were thorowout Iewry, harde say that the heathen had also receyued the word of God.

2 And when Peter was come vp to Hierusalem, they of the circuncysyon reasoned with him

3 saiyng: Thou wentest into men vncircumcysed, and eatest with them.

4 Then Peter began and expounded the thing in order to them saiyng:

5 I was in the cytie of Ioppa praiynge, and in a traunce I sawe a vision, a certaine vessell descende, as it had bene a large linnen cloth, let doune from heauen by the fower corners, and it came to me.

6 Into the which when I had fastned myne eyes, I consydered and sawe fower foted beastes of the earth, and vermen, wormes, and foules of the aier.

7 And I hearde a voice saiyng vnto me, aryse Peter sley & eate.

8 And I saide: God forbid Lord, for nothing commen or vncleane, hath at anye tyme entred into my mouth.

9 But the voice aunswered me agayne from heauen, count not thou those thinges commen, whiche God hath clensed.

10 And this was done thre times: And all were taken vp againe into heauen.

11 And beholde immediatly there were thre men come vnto the house where I was, sent from Cesarea vnto me,

12 that I should go with them, wythout doubting. More ouer these sixe brethren accompanied me: and we entered into the mans house.

13 And he shewed vs how he had sene an Angel in hys house, whiche stode and sayed to him. Sende men to Ioppa, and call for Simon named also Peter,

14 he shal tell the wordes, wherby both thou and all thyne housse shal be saued.

15 And as I began to preach, the holy ghost fell on them, as he dyd on vs at the beginninge.

16 Then came to his remembraunce þe wordes of the Lorde, howe he sayed: Iohn Baptised with water, but ye shal be baptysed wyth the holy ghost.

17 For as much then as God gaue them lyke giftes, as he dyd vnto vs, when we beleued on the Lord Iesus Christe: what was I that I shoulde haue withstand God?

18 When they heard thys, they helde their peace & gloryfyed God, sayinge: then hath God also to the gentyls graunted repentaunce vnto lyfe.

19 They whiche were scattered abroade thorowe the affliction that arose aboute Stephan, walked thorowe oute tyll they came to Phenices and Cypers, and Antioche, preachinge the worde to no man, but vnto the Iewes onely.

20 Some of them were men of Cypers & Syrene, whyche when they were come into Antioche spake to the Grekes, and preached the Lorde Iesus.

21 And the hande of the Lorde was with them, and a greate numbre beleued and turned to the Lorde.

22 Tydinges of these thynges came to the eares of the congregation, which was at Hierusalem. And they sent forth Barnabas that he should go vnto Antioche.

23 Which when he was come, and had sene the grace of God, was gladd, and exhorted them all that wyth purpose of hert they woulde continually cleaue vnto the Lorde.

24 For he was a good man, and ful of the holy ghoste and of

faith: and much people was added vnto the Lord.

25 Then departed Barnabas to Tharsus for to seke Saul.

26 And when he had founde hym, he brought him vnto Antioche. And it chaunced that a whole yere they had theyr conuersation with þe congregation there, and taught much people: in so much that the disciples of Antioche were þe fyrst that were called christians.

27 In those dayes came Prophetes from Hierusalem vnto Antioche.

28 And there stode vp one of them, named Agabus, and signified by the spyrite that there shoulde be greate derth thorowe out all the world, whiche came to passe in the Emperour Claudius daies.

29 Then the disciples euery man according to his abilite, purposed to send succoure vnto the brethren, which dwelt in Iewry.

30 Whiche thynge they also dyd, and sente it to the elders, by the handes of Barnabas and Saule.

## CHAPTER 12

IN that tyme Herode the Kinge stretched forth hys handes to vexe certayne of the congregacyon.

2 And he killeth Iames the brother of Iohn wt the swearde

3 and because he sawe that it pleased the Iewes he proceaded forther, and toke Peter also. Then were the dayes of swete bread.

4 And when he had caught hym, he put hym in pryson, & deliuered hym to .iiij. quaternions of soudyers to be kept, entendynge after Easter to bryng hym forth to the people.

5 Then was Peter kept in pryson. But prayer was made without ceasing of the congregacyon vnto God for hym:

6 And when Herode woulde haue brought him out to the people, the same nyght slept Peter betwene two souldiours bound with two chaynes, and the kepers before the dore kepte the pryson.

7 And beholde the aungell of the lorde was there presente, and a light shyned in þe lodge. And he smote Peter on the syde, and stered hym vp, saiyng: aryse vp quickly. And hys chaynes fell of from hys handes.

8 And the aungell sayed vnto him: gyrde thy selfe, and bind on thy sandales. And so he dyd. And he sayed vnto hym: cast thy mantle aboute the, & folow me.

9 And he came out, and folowed hym, and wist not that it was truthe, whiche was done by the aungell, but thought he had sene a vysion.

10 When they were past the fyrste and the second watche, they came vnto the Iron gate, that leadeth vnto the citie which opened to them by his owne accorde. And they went oute and passed thorowe one strete, and by and by the aungell departed from hym.

11 And when Peter was come to hym selfe, he sayde. Nowe I knowe of a suretye, that the Lorde hath sent hys aungell, and hath delyuered me out of the hande of Herode, and from all the waytyng for of the people of þe Iewes.

12 And as he consydered the thynge, he came to the house of Mary the mother of one Iohn which was called Marke also, where manye were gathered together in prayer.

13 As Peter knocketh at the entry dore, a damsell came forth to herken, named Rhoda,

14 when she knew Peters voyce, she opened not the entrey for gladnes, but ran in and tolde, how Peter stode before the entrey.

15 And they sayde vnto her: thou arte mad. And she bare them doune that it was euen so. Then sayde they: it is hys Aungel.

16 But Peter contynued knockynge. And when they had opened the dore, and sawe hym, they were astonyed.

17 And he beckened vnto them with the hande to holde theyr peace, and tolde them by what meanes the Lord hath brought hym out of the pryson. And he sayde: go shew these thynges vnto Iames, and to the brethren. And he departed, and went into another place.

18 Assone as it was daye, there was no litell a do amouge the soudyers, what was become of Peter.

19 When Herode had called for hym, and founde hym not, he examined the kepers, and commaunded them to be caryed awaye. And he descended from Iewry to Cesarea, & there abode.

20 Herode was displeased with them of Tyre & Sydon, And they came all at once, and made intercessyon vnto Blastus þe kinges chamberlayne, & desyred peace, because theyr countrey was nouryshed by the kynges lande.

21 And vpon a daye appoynted Herode arayed hym in royall apparell, and set hym in hys seate, and made an oracyon vnto them.

22 And þe people gaue a shout, saiyng: it is the voyce of a God, and not of a man.

23 And immediatly þe aungell of the Lorde smote hym, because he gaue not God the glorye, and he was eaten of wormes, and gaue vp the ghost.

24 And the worde of God grew and multyplyed.

25 And Barnabas and Paul returned to Hierusalem, when they had fulfylled theyr offyce, and toke with them Iohn whiche also called Marcus.

## CHAPTER 13

THERE were at Antioche in the congregacyon certayne Prophetes and teachers: as Barnabas and Symon called Niger, and Lucius of Cyrene, & Manahen. Herode the Tetrarkes noursfelowe. and Saule.

2 As they ministred to the Lorde and fasted, the holy ghost sayde: separate me Barnabas and Saule, for the worke where vnto I haue called them.

3 Then fasted they and prayed, and put theyr handes on them, & let them go.

4 And they after they were sent of the holye ghost, came vnto Seleutia, & from thence they sayled to Cyprus.

5 And when they were come to Salamyne, they shewed þe word of God in the synagoges of the Iewes. And they had Iohn to theyr minister.

6 When they had gone thorowout the yle vnto the citie of Paphos, they founde a certayne sorcerer, a false Prophet which was a Iewe named Bariesu,

7 whiche was with the ruler of the countrey one Sergius Paulus a prudent man. The same ruler called vnto hym Barnabas and Saule, and desyred to heare the word of God.

8 But Elymas the sorcerer (for so was hys name by interpretacyon) withstode them, & sought to turne awaye the ruler from þe faith.

9 Then Saul which also is called Paul being full of the holy ghost set hys eyes on hym,

10 & sayde. O full of all subteltie and disseytfulnes the chylde of the deuyll, and the enemye of all ryghteousnes, thou ceasest not to peruerte the strayghte wayes of the Lorde.

11 And nowe beholde the hande of the Lorde is vpon the, and thou shalbe blynde, and not se the sunne for a season. And immediatlye there fell on hym a myste and a darcknes, and he wente about sekynge them that shoulde leade hym by the hande.

12 Then the rular when he saw what had happened, beleued, and wondered at the doctryne of the Lorde.

13 When they that were with Paule, were departed by shippe from Paphus, they came to Perga a cytie of Pamphilia: and there Iohn departed from them, and returned to Ierusalem.

14 But they wandred thorow the countreys from Perga to Antioche a citie of the countrye of Pisidia, and went into the synagoge on the Saboth daye, and sat doune.

15 And after þe law and the prophetes we read, the rulers of the synagoge sent vnto them, saiyng: Ye men and brethren, yf ye haue anye sermon to exhort the people, saye on.

16 Then Paule stode vp, and beckened wyth the hande, and sayde: Men of Israell, and ye that feare God, geue audience.

17 The God of thys people chose our fathers, and exalted the people when they dwelt as straungers in the lande of Egypt, and with a myghtye arme brought them out of it,

18 and aboute the tyme of .xl. yeares suffred he theyr maners in þe wyldernes.

19 And he destroyed .vij. nacyons in the lande of Canan, and deuyded theyr lande to them by Lot.

20 And afterwarde he gaue vnto them iudges about the space of .iiij.C. and .l. yeares vnto the tyme of Samuel the prophet.

21 And after that, they desyred a kyng, and God gaue vnto them Saul the sonne of Cis, a man of the trybe of Beniamin by the space of .xl. yeares.

22 And after he had put him doune, he set vp Dauid to be theyr kynge of whom he reported sayinge: I haue founde Dauid þe sonne of Iesse, a man after myne owne hert, he shall fulfyll all my wyll.

23 Of thys mans seed hath God (accordynge to hys promes) brought forth to the people of Israell a sauyour, one Iesus,

24 when Iohn had fyrste preached before hys commyng the baptisme of repentaunce to Israel.

25 And when Iohn had fulfylled hys course he sayde: whome ye thinke that I am, the same am I not. But behold ther cometh one after me, whose shewes of hys fete I am not worthy to lowse.

26 Ye men and brethren, chyldren of the generacyon of Abraham, and whosoeuer amonge you, feareth God, to you is this worde of saluacyon sente.

27 The inhabiters of Ierusalem & theyr rulers, because they knowe him not, nor yet the voices of þe prophetes which are reade euerye Saboth daye, they haue fulfylled them in condempnyng hym.

28 And when they found no cause of death in hym, yet desyred they Pylate to kyll hym.

29 And when they had fulfilled all that were written on hym, they toke hym doune from the tree, and put hym in a sepulchre.

30 But God raysed hym agayne from death,

31 and he was sene manye dayes of them whiche came with hym from Galile to Ierusalem, Which are hys wytnesses vnto the people.

32 And we declare vnto you, how that the promes made vnto the fathers,

33 God hath fulfylled vnto vs theyr children, in that he raysed vp Iesus agayne, euen as it is wryten in the fyrste psalme: Thou arte my sonne, thys same daye begat I the.

34 As concernyng that he raysed hym vp from death, nowe

no more to returne to corrupcion, he sayed on thys wyse. The holy promyses made to Dauid, I wyll geue them faythfully to you.

35 Wherfore he sayth also in another place: Thou shalte not suffer thyne holy one to se corrupcyon.

36 Howbeit Dauid after he had in hys tyme fulfylled the wyll of God, he slepte, and was layde with hys fathers, and sawe corrupcyon.

37 But he whome God raysed agayne, sawe no corrupcyon.

38 Be it knowen vnto you therfore ye men & brethren, that thorowe thys man is preached vnto you the forgeuenes of synnes,

39 and that by hym are all that beleue iustifyed from all thynges from the which ye coulde not be iustifyed by the lawe of Moses.

40 Beware therfore leste that fall on you, whiche is spoken of in þe Prophetes:

41 Beholde ye despysers, and wonder, and peryshe ye: for I do a worke in your dayes, whiche ye shall not beleue, yf a man woulde declare it you.

42 When they were come out of the Sinagoge of the Iewes, the gentyls besought þt they woulde preache the folowyng wordes to them on the Saboth.

43 When the congregacyon was broken vp, many of the Iewes & vertuouse conuertes, folowed Paule and Barnabas, which spake to them, and exhorted them to continue in the grace of God.

44 And the next Saboth day came almost the whole citie together, to heare the worde of God.

45 When the Iewes saw the people, they were ful of indignacyon & spake agaynste those thynges, whiche were spoken of Paule, speakynge agaynst it, and railynge on it.

46 Then Paule and Barnabas wexed bolde, and sayed: it was mete that the worde of God shoulde fyrste haue ben preached to you. But seynge, ye put it from you, and thynke youre selues vnworthy of euerlastyng lyfe: lo, we turne to the gentyls:

47 For so hath the Lorde commaunded vs: I haue made the a lyghte to the gentyls, that thou be the saluacion to the ende of the worlde.

48 The gentyls hearde and were glad & glorifyed the worde of the Lorde, and beleued euen as many as were ordeyned vnto eternal lyfe.

49 And the worde of the Lorde was publyshed thorowout all the regyon.

50 But the, Iewes moued the worshypfull and honorable women, & the chiefe men of the citie, and raysed persecucion agaynste Paule and Barnabas, & expelled them out of theyr costes.

51 And they shoke of þe dust of theyr fete agaynst them, and came vnto Iconium.

52 And the discyples were fylled wt ioye and with the holy ghoste.

# CHAPTER 14

AND it fortuned in Iconium, that they went both together into þe synagoge of the Iewes, and so spake that a greate multitude bothe of the Iewes, and also of the grekes beleued.

2 But the vnbeleuynge Iewes stered vp, and vnquieted the myndes of the gentyls agaynst the brethren.

3 Long tyme abode they there, and quyt them selues boldely with the helpe of the Lorde, which gaue testimonye vnto the worde of hys grace, & caused signes and wondres to be done by theyr handes.

4 The people of the citie were deuyded: and parte helde with the Iewes, and parte wt the Apostles.

5 When there was a sault made both of the gentyls, and also of the Iewes with theyr rulars, to put them to shame and to stone them,

6 they were ware of it, and fled vnto Lystra & Darba, cities of Lycaonia, and vnto the regyon that lyeth rounde aboute,

7 and there preached the Gospel.

8 And there sate a certayne man at Listra weake in hys fete, beyng creple from hys mothers wombe, and neuer walked.

9 The same hearde Paule preache. Whiche behelde hym, and perceyued that he had faythe to be whole,

10 and sayed with a loude voyce stande vpryght on the fete. And he sterte vp, & walked.

11 And when the people sawe, what Paule had done, they lyfte vp theyr voyces, saiynge in the speache of Lycaonia: Goddes are come doune to vs in the lykenes of men.

12 And they called Barnabas Iupiter and Paul Mercurius, because he was the preacher.

13 Then Iupiters prieste whiche dwelte before theyr citie, brought oxen and garlandes to the churche porche, and woulde haue done sacrifice with þe people.

14 But when the Apostles Barnabas & Paul hearde that, they rent theyr clothes, and ran in amonge the people, criynge,

15 and saiynge: Syrs why do ye thys? We are mortall men lyke vnto you, and preache vnto you, that ye shoulde turne from these vanities vnto the liuynge God, which made heauen and earthe and the sea, and all that in them is:

16 the whiche in tymes paste suffered all nacyons to walke in theyr owne wayes.

17 Neuerthelesse he lefte not hym selfe without wytnes, in that he shewed hys benefytes, in

geuynge vs rayne from heauen, and fruteful ceasons, fyllyng our hertes with fode and gladnes.

18 And with these saiynges scace refrayned they the people þt they had not done sacrifyce vnto them.

19 Thyther came certayne Iewes from Antioche and Iconium, and obtayned the peoples consent, and stoned Paul, and drewe him out of the citie, supposyng he had bene dead.

20 Howbeit as the disciples stode rounde about him, he arose vp, and came into the citie. And þe next daye, he departed with Barnabas to Derba.

21 After they had preached to that citie, and had taughte manye, they returned agayne to Lystra, and to Iconium and Antioche,

22 and strengthed the disciples soules exhortynge them to continue in the faith, affyrmyng that we must thorowe muche tribulacion enter into the kingdome of God.

23 And when they had ordeyned them elders by election in euery congregacion, and after they had prayed and fasted, they commended them to God on whom they beleued.

24 And they wente thorowout Pisidia and came into Pamphilia,

25 and when they had preached the worde of God in Perga, they descended into Attalia,

26 and thence departed by shyppe to Antioche, from whence they were delyuered vnto the grace of god, to the worke which they had fulfylled.

27 When they were come & had gathered the congregation together, they rehearsed all that God had done by them, and how he had opened the dore of fayth to the gentyls.

28 And there they abode longe tyme with the discyples.

# CHAPTER 15

THEN came certayne from Iewrye, and taughte the brethren: excepte ye be circumcised after the maner of Moyses, ye can not be saued.

2 And when there was rysen dissention and disputyng not a lytle vnto Paul and Barnabas against them. They determyned that Paule and Barnabas, and certayne other of them, should ascende to Hierusalem vnto the Apostles and elders about this question.

3 And after they were brought on theyr waye by the congregacyon, they passed ouer Phenices and Samaria declarynge the conuersyon of the Gentyls, and they brought great ioye vnto all the brethren.

4 And when they were come to Ierusalem, they were receyued of the congregacyon, and of þe Apostles and elders. And they declared what thynges God had done by them.

5 Then arose there vp certayne that were of the secte of the Pharises which dyd beleue, saying, þt it was nedefull, to circumcyse them and to enioyne them to kepe the lawe of Moyses.

6 And the Apostles and elders came together to reason of thys matter.

7 And when there was muche disputynge, Peter rose vp, and sayde vnto them: Ye men and brethren ye knowe howe that a good whyle a go, God chose amonge vs that the gentils by my mouth shoulde heare the worde of the Gospell, and beleue.

8 And God which knoweth þe herte bare them wytnes, and gaue vnto them the holy ghost, euen as he dyd vnto vs:

9 and he put no difference betwene them and vs, but with fayth purified theyr hertes.

10 Now therfore why tempte ye God, that ye woulde put a yoke on the disciples neckes, which neyther our fathers nor we were able to beare.

11 But we beleue that through the grace of the Lorde Iesu Christ, we shalbe saued, as they do.

12 Then all the multitude was peased, and gaue audience to Barnabas and Paul which told what sygnes and wondres God had shewed among the gentyls by them.

13 And when they helde theyr peace, Iames aunswered, saiynge: Men and brethren herken vnto me.

14 Simon told, how God at the beginnynge dyd visite the gentyls, and receyued of them people vnto hys name.

15 And to this agreeth the wordes of the Prophetes, as it is wryten.

16 After thys I wyll returne, and wyll buyld agayne the tabernacle of Dauid which is fallen doune, and that whiche is fallen in dekeye of it, wyll I buylde agayne, & I wyll set it vp,

17 that the resydue of men myghte seke after the Lorde, and also the gentyls vpon whome my name is named (sayth the Lorde) which doth all these thynges:

18 knowen vnto God are all hys workes from the beginning of the worlde.

19 Wherfore my sentence is that we trouble not them whiche from among the gentyls are turned to God,

20 but that we write vnto them, that they abstayne them selues from fylthynes of ymages, from fornicacyon, from stranglyde and from bloude.

21 For Moses of olde tyme hath in euerye cytie that preache hym, and he is reade in the synagoges euerye saboth daye.

22 Then pleased it the Apostles and elders with the whole congregacion, to sende chosen men of theyr owne

companye to Antioche wt Paule and Barnabas. They sent Iudas called also Barsabas and Sylas, whiche were chiefe men among the brethren,

23 and gaue them letters in theyr handes after thys maner. The Apostles, elders, and brethren sende gretynges vnto the brethren whiche are of the gentyls in Antioche, Syria, and Celicia.

24 For as muche as we haue hearde that certayne whiche departe from vs, haue troubled you with wordes, and combred your myndes, saiynge: Ye must be circumcysed, and kepe the lawe, to whom we gaue no suche commaundement.

25 It semed therfore to vs a good thynge, when we were come together with one accord to sende chosen men vnto you, with our beloued Barnabas and Paule,

26 men that haue ieoperded theyr lyues for the name of our Lorde Iesu Christ.

27 We haue sent therfore Iudas & Sylas, whiche shall also tell you, the same thinges by mouth.

28 For it semed good to the holye ghost & to vs, to put no greuous thyng to you more then these necessarye thynges,

29 that is to saye that ye abstayne from thynges offered to ymages, from bloude, from strangled and fornicacion. From which yf ye kepe your selues ye shall do well. So fare ye well.

30 When they were departed, they came to Antioche, and gathered the multitude together, and delyuered the Epistle.

31 When they had reade it, they reioysed of that consolacion.

32 And Iudas and Sylas beynge prophetes, exhorted the brethren with muche preachyng, and strengthed them.

33 And after they had taryed there a space they were let go in peace of the brethren vnto the Apostles.

34 Notwithstandynge it pleased Sylas to abyde there styll.

35 Paule and Barnabas contynued in Antioche teachynge and preachynge the worde of the Lorde with other manye.

36 But after a certayne space, Paule sayd vnto Barnabas: Let vs go agayn and visite our brethren in euery citie where we haue shewed the worde of the Lorde, and se howe they do.

37 And Barnabas gaue counsell to take with them: Iohn called also Marke.

38 But Paule thoughte it not mete to take hym vnto theyr companye whiche departed from them at Pamphilia, and went not with them to the worke.

39 And the dissencyon was so sharpe betwene them, that they departed a sunder one from þe other, so that Barnabas toke Marke and sayled vnto Cypers.

40 And Paule chose Sylas and departed, delyuered of the brethren vnto the grace of God.

41 And he went throughe al Ciria and Cilicia, stablyshynge the congregacions, commaundyng to kepe the preceptes of þe Apostles and elders.

# CHAPTER 16

THEN came he to Derba and to Lystra. And beholde a certayne disciple was there named Timotheus, a womans sonne whiche was a Ieweas and beleued: but hys father was a Greke.

2 Of whom reported well, the brethren of Lystra and Iconium.

3 The same Paule woulde that he shoulde go forthe with hym, and toke and circumcysed him, because of the Iewes whiche were in those quarters: for they knewe all, that hys father was a Greke.

4 As they went through the cities, they delyuered them the decrees for to kepe, ordeyned of the Apostles and elders, whiche were at Ierusalem.

5 And so were the congregacions stablysheth in the fayth, and encreased in noumbre daylye.

6 When they had gone through oute Phrygia, and the regyon of Galacia, and were forbidden of the holy ghost to preache the worde in Asia

7 they came to Misia, and sought to go into Bethinia. But the spirite suffered them not.

8 Then they went ouer Misia, and came doune to Troada.

9 And a visyon appeared to Paule in the nyght. There stode a man of Macedonia, and prayed hym, saiynge: come into Macedonia, and helpe vs.

10 After he had sene the vysyon, certified that the Lorde had called vs for to preache the Gospell vnto them.

11 Then loused we forth from Troada, and with a strayght course came to Samothracia, and the nexte daye to Neapolym,

12 and from thence to Phylyppos, which is the chiefe citie in the partes of Macedonia, and a fre citie. We were in that citie abydynge certayne dayes.

13 And on the Saboth dayes we wente out of the citie besydes a ryuer, where men were wonte to praye. And we sate doune, and spake vnto the women which resorted thyther.

14 And a certayne woman named Lydia a seller of purple of the citie of Thiatyra, which worshypped God, gaue vs audience. Whose hart the Lorde opened, that she attended vnto the thynges whiche Paul spake.

15 When she was baptysed and her housholde, she besoughte vs saiyng: Yf ye

thynke that I beleue on þe Lord come into my house, and abyde there. And she constrayned vs.

16 And it fortuned as we went to prayer, a certayne damsell possessed with a spirite that prophesyeth, met vs, which brought her mayster and maysters muche vauntage with prophesiynge.

17 The same folowed Paul and vs, & cryed, saiynge: These men are the seruauntes of the moste hye God, which shew vnto vs þt waye of saluacyon.

18 And thys dyd she manye dayes. But Paule not content turned aboute, and sayed to the spirite: I commaunde the in the name of Iesu Christe, that thou come oute of her. And he came out the same houre.

19 And when her maister and maysters saw, that the hope of theyr gaynes was gone, they caughte Paule and Sylas, and drue them into the market place vnto the rulars,

20 & brought them to the offycers saiynges: These men trouble oure citie, whiche are Iewes,

21 and preache ordinaunces whiche are not laufull for vs to receyue, neyther to obserue, seynge we are Romayns.

22 And the people came on them, and the offycers rent theyr clothes, and commaunded them to be beaten with roddes.

23 And when thei had beaten them sore, they caste them into pryson, commaundynge the iayler to kepe them surelye.

24 Which iaylar when he had receyued such commaundemente thruste them into the ynner pryson, and made theyr fete fast in the stockes.

25 At mydnyght Paule and Sylas prayed, & lauded God. And the prysoners hearde them.

26 And sodenly there was a great earthquake, so that the foundacion of the pryson was shaken, and by and by all the dores opened, and euery mannes bondes were loused.

27 When þe keper of the pryson waked oute of hys slepe, and sawe the pryson dores open, he drue oute hys swearde, and woulde haue kylled hym selfe, supposynge the prysoners had bene fled.

28 But Paule cryed with a lowde voyce, saiyng: do thy selfe no harme, for we are all here.

29 Then he called for a lyght, and sprang in, and came tremblyng, and fell doune before Paule and Sylas,

30 and brought them out and sayde: Syr what muste I do to be saued?

31 And they sayd: beleue on þe Lord Iesus & þu shalt be saued & thy housholde.

32 And they preached vnto him the worde of the Lorde, & to all þt were in hys house.

33 And he toke them the same houre of the nyght, and washed theyr woundes, and was baptysed with all that belonged vnto him strayght waye.

34 When he had broughte them into hys house: he set meate before them, and ioyed that he with all hys housholde beleued on God.

35 And when it was daye, the offycers sente the ministers sayinge: Let those men go.

36 The keper of the pryson tolde this saiyng to Paul: the officers haue sent word to loose you. Now therfore get you hence, and go in peace.

37 Then sayde Paule vnto them. They haue beaten vs openly vncondempned, for all that we are Romaynes, and haue caste vs into pryson: & now woulde they sende vs awaye priuely? Naye not so, but let them come them selues, and set vs out.

38 When the ministers tolde these wordes vnto the offycers, they feared when they hearde that they were Romaynes,

39 and came and besought them, and brought them oute, & desyered them to departe out of the cytie.

40 And they went oute of the pryson, and entred into the housse, of Lydya, and when they had sene the brethren, they comforted them, and departed.

# CHAPTER 17

As they made theyr iorney thorowe Amphipolis, and Appolonia, they came to Thessalonica, where was a synagoge of þe Iewes.

2 And Paule as his maner was, went in vnto them, and thre Saboth dayes declared oute of the scripture vnto them,

3 openynge and aledgynge that Christe muste nedes haue suffered and rysen agayne from death, and that thys Iesus was Christe, whom (sayed he) I preache to you.

4 And some of them beleued and came, and compayned with Paul and Sylas: also of the honorable Grekes a greate multytude, and of the chief women not a fewe.

5 But the Iewes which beleued not, hauing indignacyon, toke vnto them euyl men which were vagabondes, and gathered a companie, and set all the citie on a rore, and made asaulte vnto the house of Iason, and sought to bryng them out to the people.

6 But when they found them not, they drue Iason and certayne brethren vnto the heades of the citie, criynge: these that trouble the worlde are come hyther also,

7 which Iason hath receyued pryuely. And these all do contrary to the decrees of Cesar, affyrmyng another kynge, one Iesus.

8 And they troubled the people and the officers of the citie, when they hearde these

thynges.

9 And when they were suffyciently aunswered of Iason, and of the other, they let them go.

10 And the brethren immediatly sente awaye Paule and Sylas by nyghte vnto Berrea. Whiche when they were come thyther, they entred into the synagoge of the Iewes.

11 These were the noblest of byrthe among them of Thessalonia whiche receyued the worde with al diligence of mynde, and searched the scriptures daylye whether those thynges were euen so.

12 And many of them beleued: also of worshipfull women which were Grekes, and of men not a feawe.

13 When the Iewes of Thessalonia had knowledge that the worde of GOD was preached of Paul at Berrea, they came and moued the people there.

14 And then by and by the brethren sente awaye Paule to go as it were to the sea: but Sylas and Timotheus abode there styll.

15 And they that gyded Paule brought hym vnto Athens, and receyued a commaundement vnto Sylas & Timotheus for to come to hym at once and came theyr waye.

16 Whyle Paule wayted for them at Athens, hys spirite was moued in hym, to se the cytye geuen to worshyppynge of ymages:

17 Then he disputed in the synagoge with the Iewes, and with the deuoute persones and in þe market daylye with them that came vnto hym.

18 Certayne Philosophers of the Epicures and of the Stoickes, disputed with him. And some there were, whiche sayed. What wyll this babler saye? Other said he semeth to be a tydynges brynger of newe deuyls, because he preached vnto them Iesus and the resurreccyon.

19 And they toke hym, and broughte hym into Marsestrete, saiynge: maye we not knowe what thys newe doctrine whereof thou speakest is?

20 For thou bryngest straung tydynges to oure eares. We woulde knowe therfor what these thynges meane.

21 For all the Athenians and straungers which were there, gaue them selues nothynge els, but eyther to tell or to heare newe tydynges.

22 Paule rode in the myddes of Marsestrete, and sayd: Ye men of Athens I perceyue that in all thynges ye are to supersticyous.

23 For as I passed by, and behelde the master, howe ye worshyppe youre Goddes, I founde an Altare wherein was wrytten: vnto the vnknowen God. Whom ye then ignorauntelye worshyppe hym, shew I vnto you.

24 God that made the worlde, and all that are in it, seynge that he is Lorde of heauen and earth, he dwelleth not in temples made with handes, neyther is worshypped wt mennes handes,

25 as though he neded of any thing seynge he hym selfe geueth lyfe and brethe to al men euerye where,

26 and hath made of one bloude all nacyons of men, for to dwell on al the face of the earth, and hath assygned before howe longe tyme, and also the endes of theyr inhabitacyon,

27 that they shoulde seke God, yf they myght fele and fynde hym though he be not far from euerye one of vs.

28 For in him we lyue, moue, and haue our beyng, as certayne of your own Poetes sayd. For we are also hys generacion.

29 For as muche then as we are the generacyon of God, we ought not to thinke that the God hede is lyke vnto golde, syluer, or stone grauen by crafte and ymagynacyon of man.

30 And the tyme of thys ignoraunce God regarded not. But now he byddeth all men euerye where repent,

31 because he hath appoynted a daye, in the whiche he will iudge the world accordynge to ryghteousnes, by that man whom he hath apoynted, and hath offered fayth to all men, after that he had raysed hym from death.

32 When they hearde of the resurreccion from death, some mocked, and other sayd: we wyll heare the agayne of thys matter,

33 So Paul departed from amonge them.

34 Howbeit certayne men claue vnto Paule, and beleued, amonge the which was Dionisius a senatoure, and a woman named Damaris and other wyth them.

# CHAPTER 18

AFTER that Paule departed from Athens, and came to Corinthum

2 and founde a certayne Iewe named Aquila, borne in Ponthus, latelye come from Italye wyth hys wyfe Priscilla (because that the Emperour Claudius had commaunded all Iewes to depart from Rome) and he drewe vnto them.

3 And because he was of þe same craft, he abode with them and wroughte: theyr crafte was to make tentes.

4 And he preached in the Synagoge euerye Saboth daye and exhorted the Iewes and the gentyls.

5 When Silas and Timotheus were come from Macedonia, Paule was constrayned by the spirit to testify to the Iewes that Iesus was very Christ.

6 And when they sayde contrary and blasphemed, he shoke his raymente and sayed

vnto them, youre bloude vpon youre owne heades, & frome henceforth I go blameles vnto the gentils.

7 And he departed thence, & entered into a certayne mannes house named iustus a worshypper of God, whose house ioyned harde to the synagoge.

8 How be it one Crispus the chiefe rular of the Synagoge beleued on the Lorde wyth al his houshold, & manye of the Corinthians gaue audience & beleued, and were baptised.

9 Then spake the Lorde to Paule in the nyght by a vision: be not afrayde, but speake, and hold not thy peace:

10 for I am with the, and no man shal inuad the that shal hurt the. For I haue much people in this citie.

11 And he continued there a yeare and six monethes, and taught them the word of God.

12 When Gallio was ruler of the countre of Achaia the Iewes made insurrection with one accorde agaynst Paule, & brought him to the iudgement seate

13 saiynge: this felowe councelleth men to worship God contrary to the lawe.

14 And as Paul was aboute to open hys mouthe. Gallio sayde vnto the Iewes: yf it were a matter of wronge, or an euyl dede (o ye Iewes) reason would that I should hear you:

15 but if it be a question of words or of names, or of your law, loke ye to it your selues. For I wil be no iudge in suche matters

16 and he draue them from the seate.

17 Then toke all þe grekes Sostenes the chiefe ruler of the Synagoge, & smote hym before the iudges. seate. And Gallio cared for none of those thinges.

18 Paule after this, taried there, yet a whyle, and then toke his leaue of the brethren, & sayled thence into Ciria, Priscilla and Aquila accompaniynge him. And he shore hys heade in Ceuchrea, for he hadde a vowe.

19 And he came to Ephesus and lefte them there: but he him self entred into þe sinagoge, and reasoned with the Iewes.

20 When they desyred him to tary longer tyme with them, he consented not

21 but bad them fare well saiynge. I must nedes at this feaste þt cometh, be in Ierusalem: but I will returne agayne vnto you, yf God will. And he departed from Ephesus

22 and came vnto Cesarea: & ascended and saluted the congregacion, and departed vnto Antioch,

23 and when he had taryed there a while he departed. And went ouer al the countrey of Galacia and Phrigia by order, strenthinge al the disciples.

24 And a certayne Iewe named Apollos, borne at Alexandria, came to Ephesus, an eloquente man and mighty in the scriptures.

25 The same was informed in the waye of the Lorde, and spake feruently in the spirit, and taught diligently the thinges of the Lorde, and knewe but the baptysme of Iohn only.

26 And the same began to speake boldely in the Synagoge. And when Aquila & Priscilla had hearde him, they toke him vnto them & expounded vnto him þe way of God more perfectly.

27 And when he was disposed to goe into Acaia, the brethren wrote exhortynge the disciples to receyue hym. After he was come thethere, he holpe them muche whych hadde beleued thorowe grace.

28 And myghtely he ouercame the Iewes, and that openly, shewinge by the scriptures that Iesus was Christe.

# CHAPTER 19

IT fortuned, whyle Appollo was at Corinthum, that Paule passed thorowe þe vtter costes and came to Ephesus, & founde certayne disciples

2 and sayed vnto them: haue ye receyued the holy ghoste sence ye beleued? And they sayd vnto hym: no we haue not heard whether there be anye holy Ghost or no.

3 And he sayed vnto them: wherewyth were ye then baptised? And they said wyth Iohns baptisme.

4 Then sayed Paule: Iohn verelye baptised with the baptisme of repentaunce, sayinge vnto the people that they should beleue on hym whyche shoulde come after hym: that is on Christe Iesus.

5 When they hearde that they were Baptised in the name of the Lorde Iesus,

6 and Paule layed hys handes vpon them, and the holy Ghoste came on them, and they spake wyth tonges and prophecied,

7 & all the men were about .xij.

8 And he went into the synagoge, & speake boldelye for the space of thre monethes, disputynge and geuynge them exhortacions of the kyngedome of God.

9 When diuers waxde hard herted & beleued not, but spake euyll of the waye, and that before the multitude: he departed from them, and seperated the disciples. And disputed dayly in the schole of one called Tyrannus.

10 And thys continued by the space of two yeares: so that all they whyche dwelt in Asia, hearde the worde of the Lorde Iesu, both Iewes & Grekes.

11 And God wrought no small miracles by the handes of Paule,

12 so þt from his bodye, were brought vnto the sycke, napkyns or partletes, and the diseases departed from them, and the euill spirites went out of them.

13 Then certayne of the vagabounde Iewes exorcistes toke vpon them to call ouer them whyche had euyl spirites, the name of the Lorde Iesus saiynge: We adiure you by Iesu whom Paul preacheth.

14 And there were seuen sonnes of one Sceua a Iew and chiefe of the priestes which did so.

15 And þe euyl spirite answered and said: Iesus I know and Paull I know: but who are ye?

16 And þt man in whom the euyll spyryte was ranne on them and ouercame them, and preuayled agaynste them, so that they fledde out of that house naked and wounded.

17 And this was knowen to al the Iewes and Grekes also, which dwelt at Ephesus, and feare came on them al, and they magnified the name of the Lord Iesus.

18 And many that beleued, came and confessed, and shewed their workes.

19 Manye of them, whiche vsed curious craftes, broughte their bokes and burned them before al men, and they counted the price of them, & founde it fyfty thousand syluerlinges.

20 So myghtyly grew the word of God, and preuayled.

21 After these thynges were ended, Paul purposed in the spyryte, to passe ouer Macedonia and Achaia, and to go to Ierusalem, saiynge: After I haue ben there, I must also se Rome.

22 So sent he into Macedonia two of them that ministred vnto him Timotheus & Erastus: but he hym selfe remayned in Asia for a season.

23 The same tyme there arose no lytell ado about that way.

24 For a certain man named Demetrius, a siluersmith, whiche made siluer shrynes for Diana, was not a litel beneficial vnto the craftes men.

25 Whiche he called together with the workemen of like occupacion, & sayde: Syrs: ye knowe that by thys crafte we haue vauntage.

26 Moreouer ye se & heare that not alone at Ephesus, but almoste thorough out al Asia, this Paule hath persuaded and turned away muche people: saying that they be not Goddes, whiche are made wyth handes.

27 So that not onelye thys our craft cometh into pacel to be set at nought: but also that the temple of the great Goddas Diana shoulde be despised, and her magnificence should be destroied, which al Asia, and the world worshyppeth.

28 When they hearde these sayinges, they were full of wrath, and cryed oute sayinge: Great is Diana of the Ephesyans.

29 And all the cytye was on a rore, and they rushed into the commune hal wyth one assent, & caughte Gayus and Aristarcus, men of Macedonia, Paules companyons.

30 When Paul woulde haue entered in vnto the people, the dyscyples suffered hym not.

31 Certayne also of the chiefe of Asia, whiche were hys frendes, sent vnto him, desiringe hym that he woulde not prease into the commen hall.

32 Some cryed one thynge, and some another, and the congregacyon was all oute of quyete, and the more parte knewe not wherfore they were come together.

33 Some of the company drewe forth Alexander, the Iewes thrusting hym forwardes. Alexander beckened with the hand, & would haue geuen the people an aunswere.

34 When they knewe that he was a Iewe, there arose a shoute almost for the space of two houres, of all men crynge, greate is Diana of the Ephesyans.

35 When the towne clarke had ceased the people he saied: ye men of Ephesus, what man is it that knoweth not how that the cytye of the Ephesyans is a worshypper of the great God as Diana, and of the ymage, which came from heauen.

36 Seyng then that no man sayth her agaynst, ye oughte to be contente, & to do nothyng rashlye,

37 for ye haue brought hether these men, which are neither robbers of churches, nor yet despysers of your Godas.

38 Wherfore yf Demetrius and the craftes men, whiche are wyth him haue any saiynge to any man, the law is open, and there are rulars let them accuse one another.

39 Yf ye go aboute any other thynge, it may be determined in a lawful congregacion.

40 For we are in ieoperdy to be accused of this dayes busines. For as much as there is no cause wherby we may geue a rekening of this concourse of people.

41 And when he had thus spoken he let the congregacyon departe.

# CHAPTER 20

AFTER the rage was ceased: Paule called the disciples vnto him, & toke his leaue of them, & departed for to go into Macedonia.

2 And when he had gone ouer those partyes, and geuen them large exhortacyons he came into Grece,

3 and there abode thre monethes. And when the Iewes layde wayte for him as he was about to sail into Syria, he purposed to returne thorough

Macedonia.

4 There accompanyed hym into Asia, Sopater of Berrea, and of Thessalonia Aristarcus and Secundus, & Gaius of Derba, and Timotheus, and out of Asia, Tichycus and Trophimos.

5 These wente before, & taryed vs at Troas.

6 And we sayled awaye from Philippus after the easter holy daies, and came vnto them do Troas in .v. dayes where we abode seuen dayes.

7 And on the morowe after the saboth day þe disciples came together for to breake bread and Paule preached vnto them (readye to departe on the morowe) and contynued the preachynge vnto midnyght.

8 And there were manye lyghtes in the chamber where they were gathered together,

9 and there sate in a wyndowe a certayne yonge man named Eutichos, fallen into a depe slepe. And as Paule declared, he was the more ouercome with slepe, and fell doune from the thyrde lofte, and was taken vp dead.

10 Paule wente doune and fell on hym, and embrased hym, and sayed: make nothynge a do, for hys lyfe is in hym.

11 When he was come vp again, he brake bread and tasted, and commened a longe whyle euen tyll the mornynge, and so departed.

12 And they brought the yonge man alyue, and were not a lytle comforted.

13 And we went afore to shyppe, and loused vnto Asson there to receyue Paule. For so had he appoynted and woulde hym self go afore.

14 When he was come to vs to Assone, we toke hym in and came to Mitelenes.

15 And we sailed thence, and came the next daye ouer agaynste Chios. And the next daye we aryued at Samos, and taryed at Trogilio. The nexte daye we came to Mileton,

16 for Paule had determyned to leaue Ephesus as they sayled, because he woulde not spende the tyme in Asia. For he hasted to be (yf he coulde possible) at Ierusalem at the daye of Pentecoste.

17 Wherfore from Myleton he sent to Ephesus, and called the elders of the congregacyon.

18 And when they were come to hym, he sayde vnto them. Ye knowe from the fyrste daye that I came into Asia, after what maner I haue ben with you at al ceasons

19 seruynge the Lorde with all humblenes of mynde, and with many teares, and temptacyons whiche happened to me by the laiynges awayte of the Iewes,

20 and howe I kept backe nothyng that was profytable, but that I haue shewed you, and taughte you openlye, and at home in your houses,

21 wytnessyng both to the Iewes, and also to the Grekes, the repentaunce towarde God and fayth towarde oure Lorde Iesus.

22 And now beholde I go bounde in the spyryte vnto Ierusalem, and knowe not what shal come on me there,

23 but that the holy ghost wytnesseth in euerye citie, saiynge: that bondes and trouble abyde me.

24 But none of these thinges moue me: neyther is my lyfe dere vnto my selfe: that I myght fulfyl my course with ioye, and the ministracyon whiche I haue receyued of þe Lord Iesus, to testifye the gospell of the grace of God.

25 And now beholde, I am sure that henceforth ye al (through whom I haue gone preachyng þe kingdom of God) shal se my face no more.

26 Wherfore I take you to recorde this same daye that I am pure from þe bloud of all men.

27 For I haue kept nothynge backe, but haue shewed you all the counsell of God.

28 Take hede therfore vnto youre selues, and to all the flocke wherof the holy ghoste hath made you ouersears, to rule the congregacyon of God, which he hath purchased wt hys bloude.

29 For I am sure of this, that after my departing shall greuous wolues enter in amonge you, which wyll not spare the flocke.

30 Moreouer of your own selues shal men aryse speakyng peruerse thinges to draw disciples after them.

31 Therfore awake & remember, that by the space of .iij. yeares I ceased not to warne euerye one of you both night and daye with teares.

32 And nowe brethren I commende you to God, and to the worde of hys grace, which is able to buylde further, and to geue you an inheritaunce amonge all them which are sanctifyed

33 I haue desyred no mans syluer, golde or vesture.

34 Ye knowe well that these handes haue ministred vnto my necessities, & to them that were with me,

35 I haue shewed you all thinges, how that so laborynge ye ought to receyue þe weake & to remember the wordes of the lorde Iesu, how that he sayde: it is more blessed to geue then to receyue.

36 When he had thus spoken, he kneled doune & prayed with them all.

37 And they wept al aboundauntly, and fell on Paules necke, & kyssed him

38 sorowynge moste of all for the wordes which he spake, that they should se hys face no more. And they accompanied hym vnto the shyppe.

# CHAPTER 21

AND it chaunsed that assone as we had launched forthe, & were departed from them, we came with a strayght course vnto Choon, & the daye folowing vnto þe Rhodes, and from thence vnto Patara.

2 And we found a shyppe ready to sayle vnto Phenices & went a bourde and set forthe.

3 Then appeared vnto vs Cyprus, and we left it on the lefte hand, & sayled vnto Syria, & came vnto Tire. For ther the shyp vnladed her burthen.

4 And when we had founde brethren, we taryed there .vij. dayes. And they tolde Paule throughe the spirite þt he shoulde not go vp to Hierusalem.

5 And when the dayes were ended, we departed and went our wayes, & they al brought vs on our way, with theyr wyues and children, tyll we were come out of the cityre. And we kneled doune in the shore and prayde.

6 And when we had taken our leaue one of another, we toke shyp, and they returned home agayne.

7 When we had full ended the course from Tyre we arryued at Ptolomaida, and saluted the brethren, and abode with them one daye.

8 The nexte daye, we that were of Paules companye, departed and came vnto Cesarea. And we entred into the house of Philip the Euangeliste, whiche was one of the .vij. deacones, & abode wyth hym.

9 The same man had foure doughters virgens which dyd prophesy.

10 And as we taryed there a good manye of dayes, there came a certayne Prophete from Iewry, named Agabus.

11 When he was come to vs, he toke Paules gyrdell, and bound hys handes and fete, and sayed: thus sayeth the holye Ghoste: so shall the Iewes at Hierusalem bynde the man that oweth thys gyrdell, and shall delyuer hym into the handes of the gentyls.

12 When we hearde thys, both we and other of the same place, besoughte hym, þt he would not go vp to Ierusalem.

13 Then Paul aunswered and sayd: what do ye wepynge and breakyng myne hert? I am ready not to be bound onelye: but also to dye at Hierusalem for the name of the Lorde Iesus.

14 When we coulde not turne hys mynde, we ceased saiynge: the wyll of the Lorde be fulfylled.

15 After those dayes we made oure selues readye, and went vp to Hierusalem.

16 There wente vp with vs also certayne of the discyples of Cesarea, and brought with them one Mnason of Cyprus, an olde disciple with whom we should lodge.

17 And when we were come to Hierusalem, the brethren receyued vs gladlye.

18 And on the morowe Paule wente in wyth vs vnto Iames. And all the elders came together.

19 And when he had saluted them, he tolde by ordre al thynges that God had wroughte amonge the Gentyles by hys ministracyon.

20 And when they hearde it, they glorifyed the Lorde, and sayed vnto hym: thou seest brother, howe manye thousande Iewes there are that beleue, & they are all zelous ouer the lawe.

21 And they are informed of the, that thou teacheste all the Iewes whiche are amonge the gentyls, to forsake Moyses, and sayest, that they oughte not to circumcyse theyr chyldren, neyther to lyue after the customes.

22 What is it therfore? The multytude muste nedes come together. For they shal heare that thou arte come.

23 Do therfore thys that we saye to the. We haue foure men which haue a vowe on them.

24 Them take and purifye thy self wt them, and do coste on them that they maye shaue theyr heades, and all shall knowe that those thinges, whiche they haue heard, concerning the, are nothinge: but that thou thy selfe also walkest and kepest the lawe.

25 For as touching the Gentylles whiche beleue, we haue writen and concluded, that they obserue no such thinges: but that they kepe them selues from thynges offered to Idols, from bloude, from strangled, and from fornicacyon.

26 Then the next daye Paule toke the men, and puryfyed hym selfe with them, and entred into the temple, declarynge that he obserued the dayes of the purifycation, vntyll that an offerynge shoulde be offered for euerye one of them.

27 And as the seuen dayes shoulde haue ben ended, the Iewes which were of Asia when they sawe hym in the temple, they moued all the people, and layed handes on hym,

28 criyng: Ye men of Israell, healpe. Thys is the man that teacheth all men euerye where agaynste the people and the lawe, and this place. More ouer also he hath brought Grekes into the temple, & hath polluted thys holy place.

29 For they sawe one Trophimus an Ephesyan with him in the cytie. Hym they supposed Paule had brought into the temple.

30 And all the citie was moued, and the people swarmed together. And they toke Paule, and drue hym out of þe temple, and forthwith the dores were shut to.

31 As they wente aboute to kyll hym, tydinges came vnto the hye captayne of the

souldyers, that all Ierusalem was moued.

32 Whiche immediatlye toke souldyers and vndercaptaynes, and ran doune vnto them. When they sawe the vpper captayne and the souldyers, they left smittynge of Paule.

33 Then the captayne came neare, and toke hym: and commaunded hym to be bounde with two chaynes, and demaunded what he was, and what he had done.

34 And one cryed thys, another that, among the people, And when he coulde not know the certaintye for the rage, he commaunded hym to be caryed into the castle.

35 And when he came vnto a grece, it fortuned that he was borne of the souldyers, for the violence of the people.

36 For the multitude of the people folowed after cryenge awaye with hym.

37 And as Paule shoulde haue bene caryed into the castle, he sayde vnto the hye captaine: maye I speake vnto the? Which sayde: canste thou speake Greke?

38 arte not thou that Egyptian whiche before these dayes made an vproure, and led oute into the wyldernes .iiij.M. men that were mortherers?

39 But Paule sayd: I am a man which am a Iewe of Tharsus a citie in Cicyll, a cytisyn of no vyle cytie, I beseche the, suffer me to speake vnto the people.

40 When he had geuen hym licence. Paul stode on the stoppes, and beckened with the hande vnto the people, and there was made a great silence. And he spake vnto them in the Hebrew tonge, saiynge.

# CHAPTER 22

Ye men, brethren, and fathers: heare myne aunswere whiche I make vnto you.

2 When they heard that he spake in the Hebrue tonge to them: they kept þe more silence. And he sayd:

3 I am verely a man which am a Iewe borne in Tharsus, a citie in Cicil: neuerthelesse yet brought vp in thys citie at þe fete of Gamaliel, and informed diligentlye in the lawe of the fathers, and was feruent mynded to godwarde, as ye all are this same day,

4 and I persecuted thys waye vnto the deathe, byndynge and delyuerynge into pryson both men and women,

5 as the chief priest doth beare me wytnes and all the elders, of whome also I receyued letters vnto the brethren, and went to Damasco to bring them which were there bounde vnto Ierusalem for to be punyshed.

6 And it fortuned as I made my iorney and was come nye vnto Damasco aboute none, that sodenlye there shone from heauen a greate lyght rounde aboute me,

7 and I fell to the earthe, and heard a voyce, saiynge vnto me: Saul, Saule, why persecutest thou me?

8 And I aunswered: what arte thou Lorde? And he sayde vnto me: I am Iesus of Nazareth whom thou persecutest.

9 And they that were with me sawe verelye a lyghte and were afrayde: but they hearde not the voyce of hym that spake with me.

10 And I sayde, what shall I do Lord? And the Lorde sayed vnto me. Aryse and go into Damasco, and there it shalbe tolde the of all thynges which are appoynted for the to do.

11 And when I sawe nothynge for þe brightnes of that lyght, I was ledde by the hand of them þt were with me, and came into Damasco.

12 And one Ananias a perfecte man, and as pertaynynge to the lawe hauynge good reporte of all the Iewes whiche there dwelte,

13 came vnto me, and stode, and sayde vnto me: brother Saule, loke vp. And that same houre I receyued my sighte, and sawe hym.

14 And he sayde: the God of oure fathers hath ordeyned the before, that thou shouldeste knowe hys wyll, and shouldeste se that which is ryghtfull: and shouldest heare the voyce of hys mouth:

15 for thou shalte be hys wytnes vnto all men of those thynges whiche thou haste sene and hearde.

16 And now, why taryest thou? aryse and be baptysed, and washe awaye thy synnes in callynge on the name of the Lorde.

17 And it fortuned when I was come agayn to Ierusalem, and prayde in the temple that I was in a traunce,

18 and sawe hym, saiyng vnto me: Make hast, and get the quickly out of Ierusalem: for they wyll not receyue the wytnes that thou bearest of me.

19 And I sayde: Lorde, they knowe that I prysoned and beate in euery synagoge then that beleued on the,

20 and when the bloude of thy witnes Stephan was shede: I also stode by, and consented vnto his death, and kepte the rayment of them that slew hym.

21 And he sayd vnto me: depart, for I wyl sende the a farre hence vnto the gentyls.

22 They gaue audience vnto thys worde, and then lyft vp theyr voyces, and sayde: awaye with suche a felowe from the earthe, it is pytye that he shoulde lyue.

23 And as they cryed, and caste of theyr clothes, and thrue duste into the ayer,

24 þe captayne bad him to be brought into the castel and

commaunded hym to be scourged, and to be examyned, that he myght knowe wherfore they cryed on hym.

25 And as they bounde hym with thonges, Paule sayde to the Centuryon that stode by. Is it lawfull for you to scourge a man that is a Romayne and vncondempned?

26 When the Centuryon hearde that, he wente, and tolde the vpper captayne saiynge: What intendest thou to do? This man is a Romayn.

27 Then the vpper Captayne came, and said to hym: tell me, arte thou a Romayne? He sayde: Yea.

28 And the captayn aunswered: with a great some obtayned I thys fredome: And Paul sayd: I was free borne.

29 Then strayght waye departed from hym, they which should haue examyned hym. And the hye Captayne also was afrayde, after he knewe that he was a Romayne: because he had bounde hym.

30 On the morowe because he woulde haue knowen the certaintye wherfore he was accused of the Iewes, he loused hym from his bondes, and commaunded the hye Priestes and all the counsell to come together, and brought Paule and set hym before them.

# CHAPTER 23

PAUL behelde the counsell & said: men and brethren. I haue liued in al good conscience before God vntyll thys day.

2 The hye priest Ananias commaunded them that stode by, to smyte hym on the mouth.

3 Then sayde Paul to hym: God smite the thou paynted wall. Sittest thou and iudgest me after the lawe, and commaundest me to be smyten contrarye to the lawe?

4 And they that stode by, sayde: reuylest thou Gods hye priest?

5 Then sayde Paule: I wyste not brethren that he was the hye priest. For it is writen: thou shalt not cursse the ruler of thy people.

6 When Paule perceyued that the one part were Saduces, and the other Pharyses: he cryed oute in the counsell: Men and brethren, I am a Pharisey, the sonne of a Pharysey. Of the hope and resurreccyon from death. I am iudged.

7 And when he had so sayde, there arose a debate betwene the Pharyseis and the Saduces, and the multytude was deuyded:

8 For the Saduces saye, that there is no resurreccyon, neyther aungell, nor spirite. But the Pharyseis graunte both.

9 And there arose a great crye, and the Scrybes whiche were of the Phariseys parte arose and stroue, saiyng: we fynde none euyll in thys man. Thoughe a spirite or an angell haue appeared to hym, let vs not stryue agaynst God.

10 And when there arose great debate, the captayne fearynge lest Paule shoulde haue bene plucked a sundre of them, commaunded the souldyers to go doune, and to take hym from among them, and to bryng hym into the castle.

11 The nyght folowynge, God stode by hym and sayed: be of good cheare Paule: for as thou haste testifyed of me in Ierusalem, so must thou beare wytnes at Rome.

12 When daye was come, certayne of the Iewes gathered them selues together, & made a vowe, saiynge, that they woulde neyther eate nor drynke, tyll they had kylled Paul.

13 They were about .xl. which had made thus conspiracyon.

14 And they came to the chiefe priestes and elders, and sayde: we haue bounde our selues with a vowe, that we wyll eate nothynge vntyll we haue slayne Paule.

15 Nowe therfore geue ye knoweledge to the vpper captayne & to the counsell, that he brynge hym forthe vnto vs to morowe as thoughe we woulde knowe some thynge more perfectlye of hym: But we, or euer he come neare, are readye in the meane season to kyll hym.

16 When Paules systers sonne heard of theyr laiyng awayt: he went & entred into the castle, and tolde Paul.

17 And Paul called one of the vnder captaynes to hym, and sayde: brynge thys yongemen to the hye captayne, for he hathe a certayne thinge to shewe hym.

18 And he toke hym, & led hym to the hygh captayne, & sayde: Paul the prysoner called me vnto hym, and prayed me to brynge thys yonge man vnto the whiche hath a certayne matter to shewe the.

19 The hye captayne toke him by the hande, and wente aparte with hym oute of the way, and axed hym, what haste thou to saye vnto me?

20 And he sayde: the Iewes are determyned to desyre the that thou wouldest brynge forthe Paule to morowe into the counsell, as though they woulde enquyre some what of him more perfectely.

21 But folowe not theyr myndes: for there lye in wayte for hym of them, moo then .xl. men, which haue bounde them selues with a vowe, that they wyll neyther eate nor drinke tyll they haue kylled hym. And now are they readye, and loke for thy promes.

22 The vpper captayne let the yonge man departe, & charged hym: se thou tel it out to no man that thou hast shewed these thynges to me.

23 And he called vnto hym two vnder captaynes, saiynge: make readye two hundred souldyers to go to Cesarea, and horsmen thre score and ten, and speare men two hondred at the thyrde houre of the nyght.

24 And delyuer them beastes that they may put Paule on, and bryng hym safe vnto Felix the hye debitie,

25 and wrote a letter in thys maner.

26 Claudius Lisias to the moste myghtye rular Felix sendeth gretynges.

27 Thys man was taken of the Iewes, and shoulde haue ben kylled of them. Then came I with souldiers and reserued hym, and perceyued that he was a Romayne.

28 And when I woulde haue knowen þe cause, wherfor they accused him, I brought hym forth into theyr counsell:

29 there perceyued I that he was accused of questyons of theyr lawe: but was not gyltye of any thynge worthy of death or of boundes.

30 Afterward when it was shewed me, how that the Iewes layde wayte for the man, I sent him strayght waye to the, and gaue commaundement to hys accusars, yf they had oughte agaynste hym to tell it vnto the. Fare well.

31 Then the souldyours as it was commaunded them, toke Paule and broughte hym by nyght to Antipatras.

32 On the morowe they lefte the horsmen to go with hym and returned vnto the castle.

33 Whiche when they came to Cesarea, they delyuered the Epistle to the debitie, and presented Paul before hym.

34 When the debitie had redde þe letter, he axed of what countreye he was: and when he vnderstode þt he was of Cicill,

35 I wyll heare the (sayde he) when thyne accusars are come also: and commaunded hym to be kepte in Herodes Pallayce.

## CHAPTER 24

AFTER fyue dayes Ananias the hye prieste descended wt the elders and with a certayne oratour named Tertullus, and enformed the rular of Paul.

2 When Paule was called forth. Tartullus began to accuse hym, saiynge: Seynge that we lyue in a great quietnes by the meanes of the: & that manye good thynges are done vnto thys nacyon throughe thy prouidence:

3 that alowe we euer and in all places, most myghty Felix, wt all thankes.

4 Notwithstandyng that I be not tedyous vnto the. I praye the that thou wouldest heare vs of thy curtesy a fewe wordes.

5 We haue founde thys man a pestylent felowe, and a mouer of debate vnto all the Iewes thoroughout the world, and a mayntayner of the secte of the Nazarites,

6 and hath also enforsed to pollute the temple. Whome we toke, and woulde haue iudged accordynge to our law,

7 but the hye captayne Lysyas came vpon vs, and with great violence toke hym awaye out of our hande,

8 commaundyng hys accusars to come vnto the. Of whome thou mayest (yf thou wilt enquyre) knowe the certaintye of al these thynges, wherof we accuse hym.

9 The Iewes lykewyse affirmed, saiyng: that it was euen so.

10 Then Paule (after that the ruler him selfe had beckened vnto hym that he should speake) aunswered I shall with a more quyet mynde aunswere for my selfe, for as muche as I vnderstande that thou haste bene of manye yeares a iudge vnto thys people,

11 because þt thou mayest know that there are yet but .xij. dayes sence I wente vp to Ierusalem for to praye,

12 & that they neyther founde me in the temple disputynge with anye man, eyther raysynge vp the people neither in the synagoges, nor in the citie.

13 Neyther can they proue the thynges wherof they accuse me.

14 But thys I confesse vnto the, that after that waye (which they call heresye) so worshyppe I the God of my fathers, beleuynge al thynges which are written in the lawe and the Prophetes,

15 and haue hope towardes God that the same resurreccyon of the dead (which they them selues loke for also) shall be both of iuste and vniuste.

16 And therfore studye I to haue a cleare conscience towarde God, and towarde man also.

17 But after many yeares I came & brought almes to my people and offerynges,

18 in the whiche they founde me puryfyed in the temple, neyther with multytude, nor yet with vnquyetnes. Howe be it there were certayne Iewes oute of Asia,

19 which ought to be here present before the, & accuse me, yf they had ought agaynste me:

20 or els let these same here saye, yf they haue founde anye euyll doynge in me, whyle I stand here in the councell:

21 excepte it be for thys one voyce that I cryed standynge amonge them, of the resurreccyon from death, am I iudged of you thys daye.

22 When Felix heard these thinges he deferred them, for he knewe verye well of that way, and sayed when Lisias the captayne is come, I wil knowe the vtmost of youre matters.

23 And he commaunded an

vnder captaine to kepe Paul, and that he shoulde haue reste, and that he shoulde forbidde none of hys acquaintaunce to minister vnto hym, or to come vnto him.

24 And after a certaine daies came Felix and his wyfe Drusilla, which was a Iewas, and called forth Paul, and heard him of the fayth which is towarde Christ.

25 And as he preached of rightuousnes, temperaunce and iudgement to come. Felix trembled and aunswered: thou haste done inough at this tyme, departe. When I haue a conueniente tyme, I wil send for the.

26 He hoped also, that money should haue bene geuen hym of Paul, that he myght louse him: wherfore he called him the oftener, and communed wyth hym.

27 But after .ij. yeare Festus Porcius came into Felix roume. And Felix wyllynge to shewe the Iewes a pleasure, left Paule in prison bounde.

## CHAPTER 25

WHEN Festus was come into þe prouince, after .iij. dayes, he ascended from Cesarea to Hierusalem.

2 Then enfourmed hym the hye priestes and the chiefe of the Iewes, of Paule. And they besoughte hym,

3 and desiered fauoure agaynste him, that he would sende for him to Hierusalem: and layed awayte for him in the waye to kyl him.

4 Festus aunswered, that Paul shoulde be kepte at Cesaria, but that he him selfe would shortly departe thyther.

5 Let them therfore (saied he) whyche amonge you are able to do it, come doune with vs and accuse him, if there be any faulte in the man.

6 When he had taried there more then .x. dayes he departed vnto Cesarea, and the next daye sate doune in the iudgemente seate, and commaunded Paule to be broughte.

7 When he was come, the Iewes, whiche were come from Hierusalem, came about hym and layd many and greuous complayntes agaynste Paul, whiche they could not proue

8 as longe as he aunswered for him selfe, that he had neither againste the lawe of the Iewes, neither againste the temple, nor yet against Cesar, offended any thynge at al.

9 Festus willing to do the Iewes a pleasure, aunswered Paule & sayd. Wylt thou go to Hierusalem, and there be iudged of these thinges before me?

10 Then saied Paule: I stand at Cesars iudgement seate, where I oughte to be iudged. To the Iewes haue I no harme done, as thou verye wel knowest.

11 Yf I haue hurte them, or committed anye thinge worthye of deathe, I refuse not to dye. Yf none of these thinges are, wherof they accuse me, no man ought to deliuer me to them. I appeale vnto Cesar.

12 Then spake Festus wyth deliberation, and aunswered. Thou haste appealed vnto Cesar, vnto Cesar shalt thou go.

13 After certaine daies, kynge Agrippa and Bernice came vnto Cesaria to salute Festus.

14 And when they had bene ther a good ceason, Festus rehersed Paules cause vnto the Kinge saiynge: there is a certaine man left in prison of Felix,

15 about whom when I came to Hierusalem, the hye priestes, and elders of þe Iewes enfourmed me, and desiered to haue iudgemente againste him.

16 To whome I aunswered: It is not the maner of the Romaynes to deliuer any man that he shoulde perishe, before that he whiche is accused, haue the accusers before hym, & haue licence to aunswere for him selfe concerninge the crime layde against him:

17 when they were come hither, without delaye on þe morowe, I sate to geue iudgemente, and commaunded the man to be brought forth.

18 Againste whom when the accusers stode vp, they brought none accusation of such thinges as I supposed,

19 but had certayne questyons againste him of their owne supersticion, and of one Iesus, whiche was dead, whom Paul affirmed to be alyue,

20 And because I doubted of such maner questions, I axed him whether he would go to Ierusalem, and there be iudged of these matters.

21 Then when Paul had appealed to be kept vnto the knowledge of Cesar: I commaunded him to be kept, tyll I might send him to Cesar.

22 Agrippa saied to Festus: I woulde also heare the man my selfe. To morowe (saide he) thou shalt heare him.

23 And on the morow when Agrippa was come, and Bernice with greate pompe, & were entred into the counsel house wyth the captaines, and chiefmen of the cytye: at Festus commaundement Paule was brought forth.

24 And Festus said. Kinge Agrippa, and al men which are here present with vs: ye se this man about whom all the multitude of the Iewes haue bene with me both at Hierusalem & also here, crying that he ought not to lyue anye lenger.

25 Yet founde I nothinge worthy of death that he had committed. Neuertheles seynge that he hath appealed to Cesar: I haue determined to sende him.

26 Of whom I haue no certaine thynge to writte vnto my Lorde. Wherfore I haue broughte

him vnto you, and specially vnto the, Kynge Agrippa, that after examination had, I myght haue some what to writte.

27 For me thinketh it vnreasonable, for to sende a prysoner, & not to shewe the causes, whiche are layed againste hym.

# CHAPTER 26

AGRIPPA sayd vnto Paule: thou art permitted to speake for thy selfe, Then Paule stretched forthe the hand, and aunswered for him selfe,

2 I thinke my selfe happye kynge Agrippa, because I shall aunswere this day before þe, of all thinges wherof I am accused of þe Iewes,

3 namely because thou art exparte in all customes and questions, which are amonge the Iewes. Wherfore I beseche the to heare me paciently.

4 My liuinge of a childe, whiche was at the fyrst amonge myne owne nacion at Ierusalem, knowe all the Iewes,

5 whyche knew me from the beginninge if they woulde testyfye it. For after the most strayteste secte of oure laye, lyued I a phariseye,

6 and now I stand, & am iudged for the hope of the promis made of God vnto our fathers

7 vnto whyche promys our .xij. trybes instantlye, seruynge God daie and nighte hope to come. For whiche hopes sake, king Agrippa, I am accused of þe Iewes.

8 Why should it be thought a thinge vncredible vnto you, that God shoulde raise agayne the dead?

9 I also verely thought in my selfe, that I ought to do manie contrarye thinges, clene agaynste the name of Nazareth,

10 which thinge I also dyd in Ierusalem. Where manye of þe sainctes I shut vp in prison, and had receiued authorite of the hye priestes. And when they were put to death, I gaue the sentence.

11 And I punyshed them ofte, in euerye synagoge, and compelled them to blaspheme, and was yet more madde vpon them, and persecuted them euen vnto straunge cities.

12 Aboute which thinges as I wente to Damasco with authoryte and licence of the hye priestes,

13 euen at mydday (O king) I saw in the way alyght from heauen, aboue the bryghtnes of the sunne, shyne rounde aboute me, and them whyche iorneyed wyth me.

14 When we were all fallen to the earth: I heard a voice speakinge vnto me, and saiynge in the Hebrue tonge: Saul Saul, why persecutest þu me? It is hard for the to kicke against the pricke.

15 And I said. Who art thou Lorde? And he sayd: I am Iesus whom thou persecutest,

16 but ryse and stand vp on thy fete. For I haue appeared vnto the for this purpose, to make the a minister, and a wytnes both of those thinges, whiche thou hast sene, and of those thinges in the which I wil appeare

17 vnto the deliuering the from the people, and from the gentils, vnto whiche nowe I sende the,

18 to open theyr eyes, that they myght turne from darckenes to lyght, and from the power of Satan vnto God: that they maye receiue forgeuenes of synnes, and inheritaunce amonge them whyche are sanctyfyed by fayth in me.

19 Wherfore kynge Agrippa I was not disobedient vnto the heauenly vision:

20 but shewed fyrst vnto them of Damasco, and at Hierusalem and through out all the coastes of Iewry, and to the gentyls, that they should repent, & tourne to God, and do the ryght workes of repentaunce.

21 For this cause the Iewes caught me in the temple, and went aboute to kyll me.

22 Neuerthelesse I obtained helpe of God, and continue vnto this daye wytnessinge both to smal and to great, saiyng none other thinges, then those which the prophetes and Moyses dyd saye shoulde come

23 that Christe shoulde suffer, and that he shoulde be the fyrste, that shoulde ryse from death, and shoulde shewe lyghte vnto the people, and to the gentyls.

24 As he thus aunswered for him selfe, Festus saied with a loude voyce. Paul, thou art besides thy selfe. Muche learninge hath made the mad.

25 And Paul saied: I am not mad, most deare Festus, but speake the wordes of trueth & sobernes.

26 The kinge knoweth of these thinges, before whom I speake frelye, neither thinke I that anye of these thinges are hydden from hym. For this thinge was not done in a corner.

27 Kinge Agrippa beleuest thou the prophetes? I wote well thou beleuest.

28 Agrippa saied to Paule: Some what thou bringest me in mynd for to become a Christian,

29 And Paul sayde: I would to God that not onlye thou: but also all that heare me to daye, were not some what onelye but altogether suche as I am, excepte these bondes.

30 And when he had thus spoken: the kynge rose vp, and the debitie, and Bernice and they that sate with them.

31 And when they were gone aparte: they talketh betwene them selues saiyng. Thys man doth nothinge worthy of death,

nor of bondes.

32 Then sayde Agrippa vnto Festus: Thys man might haue bene loused if he had not appealed vnto Cesar.

## CHAPTER 27

WHEN it was concluded that we shoulde sayle into Italye, they deliuered Paule, and certaine other prisoners vnto one named Iulius, an vnder captayne of Cesars souldiers.

2 And we entred into a ship of Adramicium, and lowsed from land, appointed to saile by the coastes of Asia, one Aristarcus out of Macedonia, of the countrey of Thessalia, beinge with vs.

3 And the next day we came to Sidon. And Iulius courteously entreated Paule, and gaue hym libertie to go vnto his frendes, and to refreshe him selfe.

4 And from thence lanched we, and sayled hard by Cypers, because the windes were contrarie.

5 Then sayled we ouer the sea of Cylycia, and Pamphilia, and came to Mira a citie in Lycia.

6 And there the vnder captaine founde a shyp of Alexander redy to sayle into Italy & put vs therin.

7 And when we had sailed slowly manye dayes, and scace were come ouer againste Gnidou (because the wynde withstode vs) we sayled harde by the coastes of Candy, ouer againste Salmo,

8 and with much worcke sayled beyonde it, and came vnto a place called good porte. Nye wherunto was a cytie called Lasea.

9 When muche tyme was spente and sailinge was nowe ieoperdous, because also that we had ouerlonge fasted, Paule put them in remembraunce,

10 and sayed vnto them Sirs: I perceiue that thys viage wilbe wyth hurte and much domage, not of the lodynge. And ship onely: but also of oure liues.

11 Neuerthelater the vndercaptaine beleued the gouerner & the maister, better then those thinges, which were spoken of Paule.

12 And because the hauen was not commodious to winter in, many toke counsell to departe thence, if by anye meanes they mighte attaine to Phenices, and there to winter, which is an hauen of Candy, and serueth to the southwest and northwest wind.

13 When the south wind blewe, they supposynge to obtayne theyr purpose, loused vnto Asson and sailed paste al Candy.

14 But anone after there arose againste their purpose, a flowe of winde out of þe northeaste.

15 And when the shyp was caughte, and coulde not resiste the winde, we lette her go & draue with the wether.

16 And we came vnto an yle named Clauda, and had muche worke to come by a bote,

17 whiche they toke vp an vsed helpe, vndergerdinge the shippe, fearinge lest they shoulde haue fallen into Syrtes and we let doune a vessell and so were caried.

18 The nexte daye, when we were tossed with an excedinge tempest, they lightened the shippe,

19 & the third daye we cast out with oure owne handes, the tacklinge of the shippe.

20 When at the laste nether sunne nor starre in manye dayes appeared, and no smal tempest laye vpon vs, all hope that we shoulde be saued, was then taken awaye.

21 Then after longe abstinence, Paul stode forth in the middest of them and saied: Syrs ye shoulde haue herkened to me, and not haue loused from Candy, neyther to haue brought vnto vs this harme and losse.

22 And nowe I exhorte you to be of good chere, for there shall be no losse of anye mans lyfe amonge you, saue of the shyppe onelye.

23 For there stode by me this nyght the aungell of God. Whose I am, and whom I serue,

24 sayinge. Feare not Paule, for thou muste be broughte before Cesar. And lo, God hath geuen vnto the all that sayle wyth the.

25 Wherfore Syrs be of good cheare: for I beleue God, that so it shal be euen as it was tolde me.

26 How be it we must be cast into a certaine Ilande.

27 But when the fourtenth nyghte was come, as we were caryed in Adria about midnyght, the shipmen demed that there appeared some countreye vnto them:

28 and sounded, and founde it .xx. feadoms. And when they had gone a litle further, they sounded againe, and founde .xv. feadoms.

29 Then fearing lest they should haue fallen on some Rocke, they cast .iiij. ancres out the sterne, and wyshed for the day.

30 As the shipmen were about to flee out of the shyp, & had let doune the bote into the sea, vnder a coloure, as though they woulde haue cast ancres out of the forshyppe:

31 Paule sayed vnto the vnder captaine, and the souldiers: excepte these abyde in the shyp, ye can not be safe.

32 Then the souldiers cut of the rope of the bote, and let it fall away.

33 And in the meane tyme betwixt that and daye, Paule besoughte them al to take meate, sayinge: thys is the fourtenth daye, that ye haue taried, and continued fastinge, receiuinge

nothinge at all.

34 Wherfore I praye you take meate: for thys no doubte is for your health: for there shall not an heire fal from the heade of anye of you.

35 And when he had thus spoken, he toke bread, and gaue thankes to God in presence of them all, and brake it, and began to eate.

36 Then were they all of good cheare, and they also toke meate.

37 We were all together in the shippe, two hundreth three score and sixtene soules.

38 And when they had eaten inough, they lyghtened the shippe, & cast out the wheate into the sea.

39 When it was daye, they knewe not the land, but they spied a certaine hauen wyth a banke, into the which they were minded (if it were possible) to thrust in the shippe.

40 And when they had taken vp the ancres, they committed them selues vnto the sea, and loused þe rudder bondes, and hoysed vp the manye sayle to the winde and drue to lande.

41 But they chaunsed on a place, whiche had the sea on both the sydes, and thruste in the ship. And the fore part stucke fast and moued not, but þe hinder brake wyth the violence of the wawes.

42 The souldiers counsel was to kyll þe prysoners, lest anye of them, when he had swome out, shoulde flee awaye.

43 But the vnder captaine willing to saue Paule, kepte them from their purpose, and commaunded that they þt could swyme, should cast them selues first into the sea, and scape to land.

44 And the other he commaunded to go, some on bourdes, & some on broken peces of the shyp. And so it came to passe, that they came al safe to lande.

# CHAPTER 28

AND when they were scaped, then they knewe that the Ile was called Milete.

2 And þe people of the countrey shewed vs no lytel kyndnes: for they kindled a fyre, and receiued vs euery one, because of the presente rayne, and because of the colde.

3 And when Paule had gathered a boundel of styckes, and put them into the fyre, there came a viper out of the heate, and lept on his hand.

4 When the men of the countrey sawe the worme hange on his hande, they sayd amonge them selues: this man must nedes be a murtherer. Whom (though he haue escaped the sea) yet vengeaunce suffreth not to lyue.

5 But he shouke of the vermen into the fyre and felt no harme.

6 Howe be it they wayted when he should haue swolne or fallen doune dead sodenly. But after they had loked a greate whyle, and sawe no harme come come to him, they chaunged their mindes, and said that he was a God.

7 In the same quarters the chiefe man of the yle whose name was Publius had a lordeshyp: the same receiued vs, and lodged vs thre dayes courteouslye.

8 And it fortuned that þe father of Publius laie sicke of a fieuer and of a blouddy flixe. To whom Paule entred in and prayed, and layed his handes on him, and healed him.

9 When this was done, other also which had dyseases in the yle came and were healed.

10 And they dyd vs great honoure. And when we departed they loded vs with thinges necessary.

11 After thre monethes we departed in a shyppe of Alexandria, whiche had wintred in the yle whose badge was Castor and Pollux:

12 And when we came to Cyracusa, we taried ther .iij. dayes.

13 And from thence we set a compasse and came to Regium. And after one daye the south wynd blew, and we came the next daye to Putiolus:

14 where we founde brethren, and were desired to tarye wyth them seuen daies, and so came to Rome.

15 And from thence, when the brethren hearde of vs, they came against vs to Apiphorum, and to þe thre tauernes. When Paule sawe them, he thanked God, and waxed bold.

16 And when he came to Rome, the vndercaptaine deliuered the prisoners to the chiefe captaine of the host: but Paule was suffred to dwelle by him selfe with one souldier that kepte him.

17 And it fortuned after thre dayes that Paul called þe chiefe of the Iewes together. And when they were come, he saide vnto them: Men and brethren though I haue committed nothinge againste the people or lawes of oure fathers: yet was I deliuered prisoner from Ierusalem into the handes of þe Romaynes.

18 Whiche when they had examyned me, woulde haue let me go, because they found no cause of death in me.

19 But when the Iewes cryed contrary, I was constrayned to appeale to Cesar: not because I had ought to accuse my people of.

20 For thys cause haue I called for you, euen to se you, and to speake wyth you: because that for the hope of Israell, I am bounde wyth thys chayne.

21 And they saide vnto him: We neyther receiued letters out of Iewrye partaininge vnto the, neyther came any of the brethren

that shewed or spake anye harme of the.

22 But we wyll heare of the what thou thynkest. For we haue hearde of this secte that euery where it is spoken agaynste.

23 And when they had appoynted him a daye, there came manye vnto him into hys lodgynge, to whom he expounded and testifyed the kingedome of God, and preached vnto them of Iesu: both out of the Prophetes, euen from morninge to nyghte.

24 And some beleued the thinges, whyche were spoken, and some beleued not.

25 When they agreed not amonge them selues, they departed, after that Paule had spoken one word: Welspake the holy ghoste by Esay the prophet vnto youre fathers, saiyng: go vnto thys people,

26 and saye: wyth youre eares shall ye heare, & shall not vnderstande: and wyth youre eies shal ye se and shall not perceiue.

27 For the hert of this people is waxed grosse and their eares were thicke of hearinge, and theyr eyes haue they closed: lest they should se with their eyes, and heare with their eares, and vnderstande with their hertes, and should be conuerted, and I should heale them.

28 Be it knowen therfore vnto you, that this saluation of God is sente to the gentyls, and they shall heare it.

29 And when he had sayed that, the Iewes departed, and had greate despicions among them selues.

30 And Paule dwelt two yeares full in his lodgynge, and receyued all that came to hym,

31 preaching those thynges, whyche concerned the Lorde Iesus wyth all confydence vnforboden.

# Romans

## CHAPTER 1

PAULE the seruaunte of Iesus Christ called to be an Apostle, put aparte to preache the Gospel of God,

2 whiche he promised afore by hys Prophetes in the holye scriptures

3 that make mention of hys sonne, the whyche was begotten of the sede of Dauid (as perteininge to the fleshe)

4 and declared to be the sonne of God, wyth power of the holye ghoste that sanctifyeth, sence the tyme that Iesus Christ our Lorde rose againe from death,

5 by whom we haue receyued grace and Apostleshyp, to brynge all maner heathen people vnto the obedience of the fayth that is in his name:

6 of the whyche heathen are ye a parte also, whyche are Iesus Christes by vocation.

7 To all you at Rome beloued of God, and sainctes by callynge Grace be wyth you and peace from God our father, and from our Lorde Iesus Christ.

8 Fyrste verelye I thanke my God thorowe Iesus Christe for you all, because your fayth is publyshed throughout all the worlde.

9 For God is my wytnes, whom I serue wyth my spyryte in the Gospel of hys sonne, that wythout ceasinge I make mencion of you alwayes in my prayers,

10 besechinge that at one tyme or other, a prosperous iorneye (by the wyll of God) myghte fortune me, to come vnto you.

11 For I longe to se you that I myght bestowe amonge you some spyrytuall gyfte, to strength you wyth all,

12 that is that I might haue consolacion together wyth you through the common fayth, whiche both ye and I haue.

13 I woulde that ye shoulde knowe bretherne, howe that I haue often tymes purposed to come vnto you (but haue bene let hitherto) to haue some fruite amonge you, as I haue amonge other of the Gentyls.

14 For I am detter both to the Grekes and to them, whyche are no Grekes, vnto the learned and also vnto þe vnlearned.

15 Lykewyse as much as in me is. I am redy to preache þe Gospel to you of Rome also.

16 For I am not ashamed of the Gospel of Christ, because it is the power of God vnto saluacion to all that beleue, namely to þe Iewe and also to the gentyle.

17 For by it the rightuousnes, which commeth of God is opened from fayth to fayth.

18 As it is written: the iust shal liue by faith. For the wrath of God appeareth from heauen agaynste all vngodlynesse and vnryghtuousnes of men, whiche wythholde the trueth in vnryghtuousnes,

19 saiyng: what maye be knowen of God, that same is manifest amonge them. For God dyd shewe it vnto them.

20 So that his inuisible thinges, that is to saye, hys eternall power and Godhead, are vnderstand & sene by the workes from the creation of the worlde. So that they are wythout excuse,

21 in as muche as when they knewe God, they glorifyed him not as God, neither were thankful, but waxed full of vanities in theyr Imaginations, and their folishe hertes were blinded.

22 When they counted them selues wyse, they became foles,

23 and tourned the glorye of the immortall God, vnto the þe similitude of þe Image of mortall man, and of byrdes, and foure foted beastes, and of serpentes.

24 Wherfore God lykewyse gaue them vp vnto their hertes lustes vnto vncleanes, to defyle theyr owne bodies betwene them selues:

25 whyche turned hys truth vnto a lye, and worshipped and serued the creatures more then the maker, whyche is blessed for

euer. Amen.

26 For this cause God gaue them vp vnto shamefull lustes. For euen theyr women dyd chandge the natural vse vnto the vnnaturall.

27 And lykewyse also the men lefte the naturall vse of the woman, and brent in theyr lustes one on another. And man with man wroughte fylthynes, and receiued in them selues the reward of theyr errour, as it was accordinge.

28 And as it semed not good vnto them to be a knowen of God, euen so God deliuered them vp vnto a leud minde, þt they should do those thinges, whiche were not comly,

29 beyng ful of al vnryghtuous doing, of fornicacion, wickednes, couetousnes, maliciousnes, full of enuye, murther, debate, disceite, euyl condicioned, whisperers,

30 backbiters, haters of God, doers of wronge, proude, bosters, bryngers vp of euyll thinges, disobedient to father and mother,

31 wythout vnderstandynge, couenaunt breakers, vnlouinge, truce breakers and mercyles.

32 Whyche men though they knewe the ryghtuousnes of God, howe that they which such thinges commit, are worthy of death, yet not onely do the same, but also haue pleasure in them that do them.

## CHAPTER 2

THERFORE arte þu inexcusable (O man) whosoeuer thou be that iudgest. For in that same wherin thou iudgest another, thou condemnest thy selfe. For thou that iudgeste doest euen þe same selfe thynges.

2 But we are sure that the iudgement of God is accordynge to trueth agaynst them, which committe suche thinges.

3 Thinkest thou this (O thou man that iudgeste them, whiche do suche thinges) and yet dost euen the very same, that thou shalt escape the iudgement of God?

4 Eyther despysest thou the riches of hys goodnes, pacience and longe sufferaunce? and remembreste not howe that the kindnes of God leadeth the to repentaunce?

5 But thou after thyne harde herte that can not repente, heapeste the together the treasure of wrath againste the daye of vengaunce, when shall be opened the righteous iudgement of God,

6 whyche wyll rewarde euerye man according to hys dedes:

7 that is to say, prayse, honoure and immortalytye, to them whyche continue in good doynge and seke eternall lyfe.

8 But vnto them that are rebellious and disobey the trueth, and folowe iniquitie, shall come indignacion and wrath,

9 tribulacion and anguishe, vpon the souls of euerye man that doeth euyll: of the Iewe fyrst, and also of the gentyll.

10 To euery man that doth good, shall come prayse, honoure, and peace, to the Iewe fyrst, and also to the gentil.

11 For ther is no parcialitie with God. But whosoeuer hath synned without lawe,

12 shall perishe wythout lawe. And as many as haue synned vnder the lawe, shalbe iudged by the law.

13 For before God they are not ryghtuous whiche heare the lawe: but the doers of the lawe shalbe iustifyed.

14 For yf the Gentyls whiche haue no lawe do of nature the thinges contayned in the lawe: then they hauynge no lawe, are a law vnto them selues,

15 which shew the dedes of the lawe wrytten in theyr hertes: whyle theyr conscience beareth witnes vnto them, and also theyr thoughtes, accusyng one another, or excusynge

16 at the daye when God shall iudge the secretes of men by Iesus Christ accordynge to my Gospell.

17 Beholde, thou art called a Iewe, and trustest in the lawe, and reioysest in God,

18 & knowest hys wyll, and haste experience of good, and bad, in that thou arte infourmed by the lawe,

19 and beleuest that thou thy selfe arte a guyde vnto the blynde, a lyght to them which are in darknes,

20 an infourmer of them whiche lacke discrecyon, a teacher of vnlearned, which haste the ensample of that whiche ought to be knowen, and of the trueth, in the lawe.

21 But thou whiche teachest not another, teacheste not thy selfe. Thou preachest, a man shoulde not steale, and yet thou stealest.

22 Thou sayst, a man shoulde not commyt aduoutrye: and thou breakest wedlocke. Thou abhorreste ymages, and robeste God of hys honoure.

23 Thou reioysest in the lawe and thorow breakynge the law, dishonourest God.

24 For the name of god is euyll spoken of amonge the gentyls thorow you, as it is wrytten.

25 Circumcysyon verelye auayleth, yf thou kepe the lawe. But yf thou breake the lawe, thy circumcysyon is made vncircumcisyon.

26 Therfore yf the vncircumcised kepe the right thynges conteyned in the lawe: shall not hys vncircumcysyon be counted for circumcision?

27 And shall not vncircumcysyon whiche is by nature (yf it kepe the lawe) iudge

the, whiche beynge vnder the letter and circumcysyon, doest transgresse the lawe?

28 For he is not a Iewe, whiche is a Iewe outwarde. Neyther is that thynge circumcysyon, whiche is outewarde in the fleshe:

29 but he is a Iewe, which is hyd within, and the circumcisyon of the herte is the true circumcisyon, whiche is in þe spirite & not in the letter, whose prayse is not of men, but of God.

## CHAPTER 3

WHAT preferment then hathe the Iewe? other what auauntageth circumcysyon?

2 Surelye verye muche. Fyrste vnto them was commytted the word of God.

3 What then though some of them dyd not beleue? shall theyr vnbelefe make the promes of God withoute effecte?

4 God forbyd. Let God be true and all men lyars, as it is wrytten: That thou myghtest be iustifyed in thy saiynge, and shouldest ouercome when thou art iudged.

5 If our vnryghtuousnes make the ryghtuousnes of God more excellent: what shall we saye? Is God vnrightuous which taketh vengeaunce? I speake after the maner of men,

6 God forbyd. For how then shall God iudge the worlde?

7 Yf the veritie of God appeare more excellent thorow my lye, vnto hys praise why am I hence forth iudged as a synner?

8 & saye not rather (as men euyl speake of vs, and as some affyrme that we saye) let vs do euyll that good maye come thereof. Whose damnacyon is iuste.

9 What saye we then? Are we better then daye? No, in no wyse. For we haue alreadye proued, howe that both Iewes and Gentyls are all vnder synne:

10 as it is wrytten: There is none righteous, no not one:

11 there is none that vnderstandeth, there is none that seketh after God,

12 they are all gone out of the waye, they are all made vnprofytable, there is none that doeth good, no not one.

13 Theyr throte is an open sepulchre, with theyr tonges they haue disceyued, the poyson of aspes is vnder their lippes.

14 Whose mouthes are full of curssyng and bytternes.

15 Theyr fete are swyfte to sheed bloude.

16 Destruccyon and wretchednes are in theyr wayes.

17 And the way of peace they haue not knowen.

18 There is no feare of God before theyr eyes.

19 Yea and we knowe that whatsoeuer þe law sayeth, he saith it to them which are vnder the lawe. That all mouthes maye be stopped, and all the world be subdued to God,

20 because that by the dedes of the lawe, shall no fleshe be iustifyed in the syght of God. For by the lawe commeth the knoweledge of synne.

21 Nowe verelye is the ryghteousnes that commeth of God, declared withoute the fulfyllynge of lawe, hauynge wytnes yet of þe lawe and of the Prophetes.

22 The ryghteousnes no doubte whiche is good before God commeth by the fayth of Christe, vnto all and vpon all that beleue. There is no difference:

23 for al haue sinned, and lacke the prayse that is of valoure before God,

24 but are iustifyed frelye by hys grace thorowe the redempcion that is in Christe Iesus,

25 whome God hath made a seate of mercye thorowe fayth in hys bloude, to shewe þe rightuousnes whiche before hym is of valoure, in that he forgeueth the synnes that are passed, whiche God dyd suffer

26 to shewe at thys time the ryghteousnes that is alowed of hym that he myghte be counted iuste, and iustifyar of hym which beleueth on Iesus.

27 Where is then thy reioysynge? It is excluded. By what lawe? by the lawe of workes? Naye, but by the lawe of faythe.

28 For we suppose that a man is iustified by fayth withoute the dedes of the lawe.

29 Is he þe God of Iewes onely? Is he not also the God of the gentyls? Yes, euen of the gentyls also.

30 For it is God onelye which iustifyeth circumcysyon whiche is of fayth, and vncircumcysyon thorowe fayth.

31 Do we then destroye the lawe thorowe fayth? God forbyd. But we rather mayntayne the lawe.

## CHAPTER 4

WHAT shall we saye then, that Abraham oure father as pertaynyng to the fleshe, dyd fynde?

2 Yf Abraham were iustifyed by dedes, then hath he wherein to reioyce but not with god.

3 For what sayth the scripture? Abraham beleued God, and it was counted vnto hym for ryghteousnes.

4 To hym that worketh, is the rewarde not reckened of fauoure: but of dutye.

5 To hym that worketh not, but beleueth on hym that iustifyeth the vngodly, is hys fayth counted for ryghteousnes.

6 Euen as Dauid descrybeth the blessedfulnes of the man vnto whome God ascrybeth ryghteousnes withoute dedes.

7 Blessed are they, whose

vnryghteousnes are forgeuen, and whose synnes are couered.

8 Blessed is that man to whome the Lord imputeth not synne.

9 Came thys blessednes then vpon the circumcysed or vpon the vncircumcysed? We say verelye how that fayth was rekened to Abraham for ryghtuousnes.

10 Howe was it rekened: in þe tyme of circumcysyon? or in the tyme before he was circumcysed? Not in tyme of circumcisyon: but when he was yet vncircumcysed.

11 And he receyued the sygne of circumcysyon, as a seale of the ryghtuousnes whiche is by fayth, whiche fayth he had yet beynge vncyrcumcysed: that he shoulde be the father of all them that beleue, thoughe they be not circumcysed, that ryghtuousnes myght be imputed to them also:

12 and that he myghte be the father of the circumcysed, not because they are circumcysed only: but because they walke also in the steppes of that faythe that was in oure father Abraham before the tyme of circumcysyon.

13 For the promes that he shoulde be þe heyre of the worlde, was not geuen to Abraham or to hys sede thorowe the lawe: but thorow the ryghtuousnesse which commeth of fayth.

14 For yf they whiche are of the lawe, be heyres, then is fayth but vayne, and the promes of none effecte.

15 Because the lawe causeth wrath. For where no lawe is, there is no transgressyon.

16 Therfore by fayth is the inheritaunce geuen, that it myght come of fauoure: and the promes myghte be sure to all the seed. Not to them onelye, which are of the lawe: but also to them whiche are of the fayth of Abraham, which is the father of vs all.

17 As it is written: I haue made the a father to manye nacyons, euen before God whome thou haste beleued, whiche quickeneth the deade, and called those thinges whiche be not, as thoughe they were.

18 Whiche Abraham contrary to hope, beleued in hope that he shoulde be the father of manye nacyons, accordynge to that whiche was spoken.

19 So shall thy seed be. And he fainted not in the fayth, nor yet consydered hys owne bodye which was now dead, euen when he was almost an hondred year olde: neyther yet that Sara was past chylde bearynge.

20 He stackered not at the promes of God thorowe vnbelefe: but was made stronge in the fayth and gaue honoure to God,

21 full certifyed, that what he had promysed, that he was able to make good.

22 And therfore was it reckened to hym for ryghteousnes.

23 It is not wryten for hym only, that it was reckened for hym for ryghteousnes: but also rekened to hym for ryghtuousnes:

24 but also for vs, to whom ye shalbe counted for rightuousnes, so we beleue on hym that raysed vp Iesus oure Lorde from death.

25 Whiche was deliuered for oure synnes and rose agayne for to iustifye vs.

# CHAPTER 5

BECAUSE therfore that we are iustifyed by fayeth we are at peace wyth God thorowe oure Lorde Iesus Christe

2 by whom we haue a waye in thorowe fayeth vnto thys grace where in we stande & reioye in hope of the prayse that shalbe geuen of God.

3 Nether do we so only: but also we reioice in tribulacion. For we know that tribulation bryngeth pacience,

4 pacience bringeth experience, experience bringeth hope.

5 And hope maketh not ashamed, for þe loue of God is sheed abroade in our hertes by the holye ghost, which he is geuen vnto vs.

6 For when we were yet weake accordyng to the tyme: Christ died for vs whiche were vngodly.

7 Yet scrace will anye man dye for a ryghtuouse man. Parauenture for a good man durst a man dye.

8 But God setteth out his loue þt he hath to vs, seing þt whil we wer yet sinners, Christ died for vs.

9 Much more then now (seing we are iustified in hys bloud) shall we be saued from wrath thorowe hym.

10 For yf when we were enemyes, we were reconciled to God by the death of hys sonne muche more, seynge we are reconciled, we shall be preserued by his lyfe.

11 Not only so, but we also ioy in god by the means of oure Lorde Iesus Christ, by whom we haue receiued the attonment.

12 Wherfore as by one man synne entred into the worlde, and death by the means of synne:

13 And so death went ouer all men, in so much that al men synned. For euen vnto the tyme of the lawe was synne in the worlde, but sinne was not regarded, as long as there was no lawe:

14 neuerthelesse death reygned from Adam to Moyses, euen ouer them also that synned not, with lyke transgression as did Adam: whyche is the similytude of hym that is to come.

15 But the gyfte is not lyke as the synne. For yf thorowe the

synne of one, manye be dead: muche more plentuous vpon manye was the grace of God and gyfte by grace: Which grace was geuen by one man Iesus Christe.

16 And the gyfte is not ouer one that sinned. For damnacion came of one synne vnto condemnation but the gyfte came to iustify from many synnes.

17 For if by þe synne of one death reygned by the meanes of one: muche more shall they whiche receyue aboundaunce of grace & of the gyfte of ryghtuousnes reigne in life by the meanes of one (that is to saye) Iesus Christe.

18 Lykewyse then as by the synne of one, condemnacion came on al men: euen so by the iustifiyng of one commeth the ryghtuousnes that bryngeth lyfe vpon al men.

19 For as by one mans disobedience many became synners: so by the obedience of one, shall manye be made ryghtuouse.

20 But the law in the meane tyme entred in, that sinne should encreace. Neuerthelater where aboundaunce of synne was, there was more plentuousnes of grace,

21 that as synne had reygned vnto death, euen so myght grace raygne thorow rightuousnes vnto eternall lyfe, by the helpe of Iesus Christe.

## CHAPTER 6

WHAT shall we saye then? Shal we continue in synne, that there maye be aboundaunce of grace?

2 God forbide. How shal we that are deade as touchynge synne, lyue any lenger therin?

3 Remembre ye not þt al we which are baptised in the name of Iesus Christe, are baptised to dye wyth hym?

4 We are buried wyth hym by baptisme, for to dye that lykewyse as Christe was raysed vp from death by the glorye of the father: euen so we also shoulde walke in a newe lyfe.

5 For yf we be grafted in deathe lyke vnto hym: euen so muste we be in the resurrection.

6 Thys we muste remember, that oure olde man is crucified wyth hym also, that þe bodye of synne myght vtterlye be destroyed, that hence forthe we should not be seruauntes of synne.

7 For he that is dead is iustifyed from synne.

8 Wherefore yf we be deade wyth Christe, we beleue that we shall lyue with hym:

9 remembrynge that Christe ones raysed from death, dieth no more, death hath nomore power ouer hym.

10 For as touchynge that he dyed, he died concernynge synne, ones. And as touchinge that he liueth, he liueth vnto God.

11 Lyke wyse ymagyne ye also, that ye are dead concernynge synne: but are a lyue vnto God thorowe Iesus Christe oure Lorde.

12 Lette not synne reygne therefore in youre mortall bodyes, þt ye shoulde thereunto obey in the lustes of yt.

13 Neyther geue ye youre members as instrumentes of vnrightuousnes vnto sinne: but geue yourselues vnto god, as they that are aliue from death. And geue your membres as instrumentes of ryghtuousnes vnto God,

14 Let not synne haue power ouer you. For ye are not vnder the lawe, but vnder grace.

15 What then? Shall we synne, because we are not vnder þe lawe: but vnder grace? God forbyd.

16 Remember ye not howe that to whomsoeuer ye commit your selues as seruauntes to obey, hys seruauntes ye are to whom ye obey: whether it be of synne vnto death, or of obedience vnto rightuousnes?

17 God be thanked þt though ye were ones the seruauntes of synne ye haue yet obeyed with herte vnto the forme of doctrine wherunto ye were delyuered.

18 Ye are then made fre from sinne, & are become the seruauntes of rightuousnes.

19 I will speake grossely because of the infirmitie of youre fleshe. As ye haue geuen your members seruauntes to vnclennes and to iniquitie: from iniquitie vnto iniquitie: euen so now geue your membres seruauntes vnto rightuousnes, that ye may be sanctifyed.

20 For when ye were þe seruauntes of synne, ye were not vnder rightuousnes.

21 What fruit had ye then in those thynges, where of ye are nowe ashamed. For the ende of those thynges is deathe.

22 But nowe are ye deliuered from synne, and made the seruauntes of God, and haue youre fruyte that ye shoulde be sanctified, & the ende euerlastynge lyfe.

23 For the rewarde of sinne is death: but eternal lyfe is the gyfte of God, thorow Iesus Christ oure Lorde.

## CHAPTER 7

REMEMBRE ye not brethren (I speake to them that knowe the lawe) howe that the lawe hath power ouer a man as longe as yt endureth?

2 For the woman whiche is in subiection to a man, is bounde by the lawe to the man as longe as he liueth. If the man be dead, she is lowsed from the lawe of the man.

3 So then if whyle þe man liueth the completh her selfe wyth an other man, she shall be counted a wedlocke breaker. But yf þe man be dead, she is fre

from the law, so þt she is no wedlocke breaker, though she couple her selfe wyth an other man.

4 Euen so ye my brethren, are dead concerning the lawe by the bodye of Christ, that ye shoulde be coupled to another (I meane to hym that is risen agayne from death) that we shoulde brynge forth fruite vnto God.

5 For when we were in the fleshe the lustes of synne whych were sterred vp by the law reygned in oure membres, to brynge forthe fruyte vnto deathe.

6 But nowe are we deliuered from the lawe, & dead from that where vnto we were in bondage, that we should serue in a newe conuersacion of the spirite, and not in the olde conuersacion of the letter.

7 What shall we saye then? Is the lawe synne? God forbid: but I knewe not what synne meante but by the law. For I had not knowne what luste had meant, except the lawe had sayed, thou shalte, not lust.

8 But synne toke an occasion by the meanes of the commaundement, and wrought in me al maner of concupiscence. For without the lawe, synne was dead.

9 I ones liued without lawe. But when the commaundemente came, synne reuyued, & I was deade.

10 And the verye same commaundemente which was ordeyned vnto lyfe, was founde to be vnto me an occasion of death,

11 for synne toke occasion by the meanes of the commaundement and so disceyued me, and by the selfe commaundemente slewe me.

12 Wherfore the lawe is holye and the commaundemente holy, iuste and good.

13 Was that then whiche is good, made death vnto me? God forbid. Naye, synne was death vnto me, that yt might appere,

howe that synne by þe meanes of that which is good, had wrought death in me: that sinne which is vnder þe commaundemente, myghte be out of measure synfull.

14 For we knowe þt the lawe is spirituall but I am carnal, sold vnder synne,

15 because I wote not what I do. For what. I would do, that I do not: but what I hate, that do I.

16 Yf I do nowe that which I would not. I graunt to the lawe þt it is good.

17 So then now, yt is not I that do yt, but sinne that dwelleth in me.

18 For I knowe that in me (that is to saye in my fleshe) dwelleth no good thynge. To wyll is present wyth me: but I fynde no meanes to performe that whiche is good.

19 For I doo not the good thynge whyche I woulde: but that euyll do I which I woulde not.

20 Finallye, if I do that I woulde not, then is yt not I that do it, but synne that dwelleth in me, doeth it.

21 I fynde then by the lawe that when I woulde do good, euyll is present with me.

22 I delite the lawe of God, concernynge the inner man.

23 But I se another lawe in my membres rebellynge agaynst the lawe of my mynde and subduynge me vnto þe lawe of synne whyche is in my membres.

24 O wretched man that I am: who shall deliuer me frome this bodye of deathe?

25 I thanke God thorowe Iesus Christe oure Lorde. So then I my selfe in my mynde serue the law of God, & in my flesh the lawe of synne.

# CHAPTER 8

THERE is then no damnation to them which are in Christ Iesu, which walke not after the flesh: but after þe spirite.

2 For the law of the spirite that bringeth lyfe through lyfe through Iesus Christe, hath delyuered me from the lawe of synne & death.

3 For what the lawe coulde not do in as much as it was weake because of the fleshe: that performed God, and sente hys sonne in the similitude of synfull fleshe,

4 and by synne dampned synne in the fleshe: that the ryghtuousnes requyred of the law myghte be fulfylled in vs, which walke not after the flesh but after the spirite.

5 For they that are carnally, are carnally mynded. But they that are spirituall, are ghostly minded.

6 To be carnally mynded is death. But to be spiritually minded is lyfe and peace.

7 Because that the fleshlye minde is enemy agaynste God: for it is not obediente to the lawe of eyther can be.

8 So then they that are geuen to the fleshe, can not please God.

9 But ye are not geuen to the fleshe, but to the spirite yf so be þt the spirite of God dwell in you. Yf there be any man þt hath not the spirite of Christ, the same is none of hys.

10 Yf Christe be in you, the bodye is deade because of synne: but the spirite is lyfe for ryghtuousnes sake.

11 Wherfore yf the spirit of him that raysed vp Iesus frome deathe dwell in you, euen he þt raysed vp Christe from death shall quicken your mortall bodyes, because that his spirite dwelleth in you.

12 Therfore brethren we are nowe detters not to the fleshe,

13 to lyue after the fleshe. For yf ye liue after the, fleshe, ye muste dye. But if ye mortifye the dedes of the bodye, by the helpe of þe spirite, ye shall liue.

14 For as many as are led by the spirite of God:

15 they are the sonnes of God. For ye haue not receiued the spirite of bondage to feare anye more: but ye haue receiued the spirite of adoption, where by we crye Abba father.

16 The same spirite certifieth oure spirite that we are the sonnes of God.

17 Yf we be sonnes, we are also heyres, the heyres I meane of God, and heyres annexed with Christe yf so be that we suffer together, that we maye be glorified together.

18 For I suppose that the afflictions of thys lyfe are not worthy of the glory which shall be shewed vpon vs.

19 Also the feruente desyre of the creatures abydeth lokynge when the sonnes of God shal appere,

20 because þe creatures are subdued to vanitie agaynst their wyl but for his will which subdueth them in hope.

21 For the verye creatures shall be deliuered from the bondage of corruption into the glorious libertye of the sonnes of God.

22 For we knowe þt euerye creature groneth with vs also & traueyleth in payne euen vnto this tyme.

23 Not they onely, but euen we also which haue the fyrst fruytes of the spirite, mourne in oure selues and wayte for the (adoption) & luke for þe deliueraunce of oure bodyes.

24 For we are saued by hope, But hope that is sene is no hope. For howe can a man hope for that which he seyth?

25 But and yf we hope for that we se not, then do we with pacience abyde for yt.

26 Lykewyse the spirite also helpeth our infirmityes. For we knowe not what to desyre as we ought: but þe spirite maketh intercession mightelye for vs wyth gronynges whiche can not be expressed with tonge.

27 And he that searcheth the hertes knoweth what is the meanynge of the spirite: for he maketh intercession for the sayntes accordinge to the pleasure of God.

28 For we knowe that all thynges worke for the beste vnto them that loue God, whyche also are called of purpose.

29 For those which he knewe before he also ordeyned before, that they shoulde be like fashioned vnto the shape of hys sonne that he myght be the fyrste begotten sonne amonge manye brethren.

30 More ouer whiche he appointed before, them he also called. And which he called, them also he iustified, whiche he iustified, them he also glorifyed.

31 What shall we then say vnto these thynges? yf God be on oure syde: who can be agaynste vs?

32 whyche spared not his owne sonne but gaue hym for vs all: how shall he not wyth hym geue vs all thynges also?

33 Who shall laye anye thynge to the charg of Goddes chosen? It is God that iustifieth

34 who then shall condempne? It is Christe whyche is dead, ye rather which is rysen agayne, which is also on the right hande of God, and maketh intercession for vs.

35 Who shall seperate vs from the loue of God shall tribulation? or anguyshe? or persecution? othere honger? other nakednesse? other peryll? other swearde?

36 As it is wrytten: For thy sake are we killed al day longe, and are counted as shepe appointed to be slayne.

37 Neuerthelesse in all these thynges we ouercome stronglye thorowe hys helpe that loued vs.

38 Yea and I am sure that neyther death, neither life, neyther angels, nor rule, neythere power, neythere thinges presente, neyther thynges to come,

39 neyther heyght, neyther loweth, neyther any other creature? shall be able to depart vs from the lowe of God, shewed in Christ Iesu our Lord.

# CHAPTER 9

I say the trueth in Christe and lye not, in that where of my conscience beareth me wytnes in the holy goste,

2 that I haue great heauines and continuall sorowe in my hert.

3 For I haue wyshed my selfe to be cursed from Christ, for my brethren and my kynsmen (as pertaynynge to the fleshe)

4 whiche are the Israelites. To whom pertayneth the adoption, and the glory, and the couenauntes, & þe lawe that was geuen, & the seruice of God, & þe promises:

5 whose also are the fathers & they of whom (as concerninge the flesh) Christe came, whiche is God ouer al thynges blessed for euer. Amen.

6 I speake not these thinges as though the wordes of God had taken none effect. For they are not al Israelites whiche came of Israell,

7 neither are they al chyldren strayght way, because they are the seede of Abraham. But in Isaac shall thy seede be called:

8 that is to saye, they whiche are the chyldren of the fleshe, are not the chyldren of God. But the chyldren of promise are counted the seede.

9 For this is a worde of promyse, aboute this tyme wyll I come, and Sara shall haue a sonne.

10 Neither was it so with her onely: but also when Rebecca

was wyth childe by one, I meane by oure father Isaac,

11 yer the children were borne, when they had neither done good nor bad: that the purpose of God whiche is by election, might stand, it was sayed vnto her, not by the reason of workes, but by grace of the caller:

12 the elder shall serue the yonger.

13 As it is wrytten: Iacob loued, but Esau he hated.

14 What shall we saye then? is there any vnrightuousnes with God? God forbid.

15 For he sayth to Moyses: I will shewe mercy to whom I shewe mercy: and wyll haue compassion

16 on whom I will haue compassion. So lyeth it not then in a mans wil or cunnynge, but in the mercy of God.

17 For the scripture sayeth vnto Pharao. Euen for this same purpose haue I sterred the vp, to shewe my power on the and that my name myghte be declared thorowout al the worlde.

18 So hath he mercie on whom he wyll, and whom he wyll, he maketh harde herted.

19 Thou wylt saye then vnto me: why then blameth he vs yet? For who can resist hys wyll?

20 But O man, what arte thou whiche disputeste wyth God? Shall the worke saye to the workeman, why haste thou made me on thys fashion?

21 Hath not the potter power ouer the clay euen of the same lumpe to make one vessell vnto honoure, and another vnto dishonoure?

22 Euen so God wyllynge to shewe his wrath, and to make his power knowen, suffered wyth longe pacience the vessels of wrath, ordeined to damnacion,

23 that he myght declare þe riches of his glory on the vesseles of mercye, whiche he had prepared vnto glorye:

24 that is to saye, vs whom he called, not of the Iewes only, but also of the gentils.

25 As he sayeth in Osee I wyll call them my people which were not my people: and her beloued which was not beloued.

26 And it shall come to passe in the place where it was sayed vnto them, ye are not my people: that there shalbe called the children of the liuinge God.

27 But Esayas cryeth concernynge Israell, thoughe the number of the chyldren of Israel be as the sande of the sea, yet shall a remnaunt be saued.

28 He fynysheth the worde verely, and maketh it shorte in ryghtuousnes. For a short worde wyll God make on earth.

29 And as Esayas sayed before. Excepte the Lorde of Sabaoth had left vs seede, we had bene made as Zodoma, and had ben lykened to Gomorra.

30 What shall we saye then? We saye that the Gentyles which folowed not ryghteousnes haue ouertaken ryghtuousnes: I meane the ryghtuousnes whiche cometh of faythe.

31 But Israell whiche folowed the lawe of rightuousnes, coulde not attayne vnto the lawe of ryghtuousnes.

32 And wherfore? Because they sought it not by fayth: but as it were by the workes of the lawe. For they haue stombled at the stomblynge stone.

33 As it is wrytten. Beholde I put in Syon a stomblyng stone, and a rocke which shall make men faule. And none that beleue on hym, shalbe a shamed.

## CHAPTER 10

Bretherne, my hertes desyre, and prayer to God for Israell is þt they myghte be saued.

2 For I beare them recorde that they haue a feruent mynde to Godwarde, but not accordynge to knoweledge.

3 For they are ignoraunte of the ryghteousnes whiche is alowed before God, and go aboute to stablish theyr owne ryghtuousnes, and therfore are not obediente vnto the ryghtuousnes whiche is of valoure before God.

4 For Christe is þe ende of the lawe, to iustifye all that beleue.

5 Moyses descrybeth the ryghtuousnes whiche cometh of the lawe, howe that the man which doeth the thynges of the lawe, shal liue therein.

6 But the ryghtuousnes which cometh of fayth, speaketh on thys wyse. Saye not in thyne herte who shall ascende into heauen? (þt is nothyng els, but to fetch Christ doune)

7 Other who shall descende into the depe? (that is nothynge els, but to fetche vp Christe from death).

8 But what sayeth the scripture? The worde is nye the, euen in thy mouth & in thyne herte. Thys worde is the word of faith which we preache.

9 For yf thou shalt knoweledge with thy mouthe that Iesus is the Lorde, and shalte beleue with thyne herte that God raysed hym vp from death, thou shalte be safe.

10 For the beliefe of the herte iustifyeth: and to knoweledge with the mouth, maketh a man safe.

11 For the scripture sayth whosoeuer beleueth on hym, shall not be ashamed.

12 There is no difference betwene þe Iewe, & the gentyll. For one is Lorde of all whiche is ryche vnto all that call on hym.

13 For whosoeuer shall call on the name of the Lorde, shalbe safe.

14 But how shall they call on hym, on whom they beleued not? howe shall they beleue no hym of whom they haue not

hearde? howe shall they heare withoute a preacher?

15 And howe shall they preache except they be sent? As it is wrytten: howe beautyfull are the fete of them whiche brynge glad tydynges of peace, and bryng glad tydynges of good thynges.

16 But they haue not all obeyed to the Gospell. For Esayas sayeth: Lorde, who shal beleue oure saiynges?

17 So then fayth cometh by the worde of God.

18 But I axe. Haue they not hearde? No doubte, theyr sounde went out into all landes, and theyr wordes into the endes of the worlde.

19 But I demaund, whether Israel dyd knowe or not? Fyrste Moyses sayth: I will prouoke you for to enuye, by them that are no people, and by a folyshe nacyon I will anger you.

20 Esayas after that is bolde and sayth: I am founde of the, that soughte me not, & haue appeared to them that axed not after me.

21 And agaynste Israell he sayth: All daye long haue I stretched forth my handes vnto a people þt beleueth not, but speaketh agaynste me.

## CHAPTER 11

I saye then: hath God cast away hys people? God forbyd. For euen I verelye am an Israelite, of the sede of Abraham, and of the trybe of Beniamin,

2 GOD hath not caste away hys people whiche he knewe before. Eyther wote ye not what the scripture sayth by the mouth of Helyas, how he maketh intercessyon to God agaynst Israel, saiynge:

3 Lorde they haue killed thy prophetes and dygged downe thyne alters: and I am lefte onelye, and they seke my lyfe?

4 But what sayth the aunswere of God to hym agayne? I haue reserued vnto me seuen thousande men whiche haue not bowed the knee to Baal.

5 Euen so at thys tyme is there a remnaunte left thorow the election of grace.

6 Yf it be of grace, then is it not of workes. For then were grace no more grace. Yf it be of workes, then is it no more grace. For then were deseruynge no lenger deseruynge.

7 What then? Israell hath not obtayned þt, that he soughte. No but the electyon hath obtayned it. The remnaunte are blynded,

8 accordynge as it is wrytten. God hath geuen them þe spirite of vnquyetnes: eyes that they should not se, and eares that they shoulde not heare euen vnto thys daye.

9 And Dauyd sayth: Let theyr table be made a snare to take them wyth all, and an occasyon to fall, and a reward vnto them.

10 Let theyr eyes be blynded that they se not: and euer bowe doune theyr backes.

11 I saye then: Haue they therfore stombled, that they shoulde but falle onelye? God forbyd: but thorowe theyr fall is saluacyon happened vnto the gentyles for to prouoke them withall.

12 Wherfore yf the fall of them, be the ryches of the worlde: and the minyshynge of them the ryches of the gentyles: Howe much more shoulde it be so, yf they all beleued?

13 I speake to you gentyls, in as much as I am þe Apostle of the gentyls: I wil magnify myne offyce,

14 that I myght prouoke them which are my fleshe, and myght saue some of them.

15 For yf the castynge awaye of them, be the reconcilinge of the worlde: what shall the receyuing of them be but lyfe agayne from death?

16 For yf one piece be holye, the whole heape is holy & yf the rose be holy, þe braunches are holy also.

17 Thoughe some of the braunches be broken of, and thou beynge a wylde olyue tree, arte grafte in among them, and made partaker of the rote and fatnes of the olyue tree,

18 bost not thy selfe agaynst the braunches. For yf thou boste thy selfe, remember that thou bearest not the rote, but the rote the.

19 Thou wylte saye then: the braunches are broken of, that I might be grafte in.

20 Thou sayeste well: because of vnbelefe they are broken of, & thou standest stedfaste in faythe.

21 Be not hye mynded, but feare seyng that God spared not the naturall braunches, leste happlye he also spare not the.

22 Beholde the kyndnes and rigorousnes of God on them which fell, rygorousnes: but towardes the kyndnes, yf thou contynue in hys kyndnes. Or els thou shalte be hewen of,

23 and yf they byde not styll in vnbelefe, shalbe graffed in agayne. For God is of power to graffe them in agayn.

24 For yf thou wast cut out of a naturall wylde olyue tree, and waste graffed contrary to nature into a true olyue tre, howe muche more shall the naturall braunches be graffed into theyr owne olyue tree agayne.

25 I woulde not that thys secrete shoulde be hyd from you my brethren (leste ye should be wyse in youre owne conceptes) that partelye blyndenes is happened in Israell, vntyll the fulnes of the gentyls be come in:

26 and so al Israel shalbe saued. As it is wrytten: There shal come oute of Syon he that doeth delyuer, and shall turne away the vngodlynes of Iacob.

27 And this is my couenaunte

vnto them, when I shall take awaye theyr synnes.

28 As concernynge the Gospell, they are ennemyes for youre sakes: but as touchynge the eleccyon, they are beloued for the fathers sakes.

29 For verelye the giftes and callyng of god are suche, that it cannot repente hym of them,

30 for loke as ye in time passed, haue not beleued God, yet haue nowe obtayned mercy thorow theyr vnbelefe:

31 euen so nowe haue they not beleued the mercye whiche is happened vnto you, that they also maye obtayne mercy.

32 God hath wrapped all nacyons in vnbelefe, that he myght haue mercye on all.

33 O the deapnes of the abundaunte wysedome and knoweledge of God: howe vnsearcheable are his iudgementes, and hys wayes paste fyndynge out?

34 For who hath knoweth the mynde of the Lord? Or who was his counseller?

35 Other who hath geuen vnto hym fyrst that he myghte be recompensed agayne?

36 For of hym, and thorowe hym, and for hym, are all thynges. To hym be glorye for euer. Amen

# CHAPTER 12

I beseche you therfore brethren, by the mercyfulnes of God, þt ye make your bodyes a quicke sacrifyce holye and acceptable vnto God, which is youre reasonable seruynge of God:

2 And fashyon not youre selues lyke vnto thys worlde. But be ye chaunged in youre shape, by the renuynge of youre wyttes, that ye may fele what thynge that good, that acceptable, and perfect wyll of God is.

3 For I say (thorowe the grace that vnto me geuen is) to euery man among you, that no man esteme of hym selfe more then it becommeth hym to esteme: but that he discretelye iudge of hym selfe, accordynge as GOD hath dealt to euery man the measure of fayth.

4 As we haue many members in one bodye, & all members haue not one offyce:

5 so we beyng many, are one body in Christ & euery man (amonge our selues) one anothers members.

6 Seynge that we haue dyuers gyftes, accordynge to the grace that is geuen vnto vs: yf any man haue the gyft of prophesy, let him haue it that it be agreyng vnto the fayth.

7 Let hym that hath an offyce, wayte on hys office. Let hym that teacheth, take hede to hys doctryne.

8 Let hym that exhorteth, geue attendaunce to hys exhortacyon. Yf any man geue, let hym do it with singlenes. Let him that ruleth do it with diligence. Yf anye man shew mercy let hym do it with cherfulnes.

9 Let loue be without dissimulacyon. Hate that whiche is euyll, and cleaue vnto þt which is good.

10 Be kynde one to another with brotherlye loue. In geuynge honoure, go one before another.

11 Let not the busynes whiche ye haue in hande, be tedyous to you. Be feruente in the spirite. Applye youre selues to the time.

12 Reioyce in hope. Be pacyent in trybulacyon. Contynue in prayer.

13 Distribute vnto the necessitie of the Saynctes, and be diligente to harboure.

14 Blesse them whiche persecute you: blesse, but cursse not.

15 Be merye with them that are merye. Wepe with them that wepe.

16 Be of lyke affeccyon one towardes an other. Be not hyghe mynded, but make youre selues equall to them of the lower sorte. Be not wyse in youre owne opinions.

17 Recompence to no man euyll for euyll. Prouyde afore hande thynges honest in the syght of all men.

18 If it be possyble, how be it of your part, haue peace with all men.

19 Derely beloued auenge not youre selues, but geue roume vnto the wrathe of God. For it is wrytten: vengeaunce is myne, and I wyll rewarde sayeth þe Lorde.

20 Therfore yf thyne enemye hunger, feede hym: yf he thurste, geue hym drinke, for in so doyng thou shalt heape coles of fyre on hys head.

21 Be not ouercome of euyl: But ouercome euil with goodnesse.

# CHAPTER 13

Let euery soule submit him selfe vnto the authoritie of the hygher powers. For there is no power but of God.

2 The powers that be are ordeyned of God. Whosoeuer therfore resisteth power, resisteth the ordinaunce of GOD. And they that resiste, shall receyue to them selfe damnacyon.

3 For rulars are not to be feared for good workes, but for euyll. Wylte thou be wyth oute feare of the power? Do well then: and so shalte thou be praysed of the same.

4 For he is the minister of GOD, for thy welth. But and yf thou do euyll, then feare: for he beareth not a swearde for noughte, but is the minister of God, to take vengeaunce on them that do euyll.

5 Wherfore ye muste nedes obeye, not for feare of

vengeaunce onelye, but also because of conscience.

6 And euen for thys cause paye ye trybute. For they are Goddes ministers, seruynge for the same purpose.

7 Geue to euerye man therfore hys dutye: Tribute to whom trybute belongeth: Custome to whom custome is due: feare to whome feare belongeth: Honoure to whom honoure pertayneth.

8 Owe nothynge to anye man: but to loue one another. For he that loueth another, fulfylleth the lawe.

9 For these commandementes Thou shalte not commyt aduoutrye: Thou shalte not kyll: Thou shalt not steale: Thou shalte not beare false wytnesse: Thou shalte not desyre: and so forth (yf there be anye other commaundente) they are all comprehended in thys saiynge: Loue thyne neyghboure as thy selfe.

10 Loue hurteth not hys neyghbour. Therfore is loue the fulfyllynge of the lawe.

11 Thys also we knowe, I meane the season, howe that it is tyme, that we should now awake oute of slepe. For nowe is oure saluacyon nearer, then when we beleued.

12 The night is passed, and the day is come ny. Let vs therfore caste awaye the dedes of darcknes, & let vs put on the Armoure of lyghte.

13 Let vs walke honestlye as it were in the daye lyght: not in eatynge and drynkynge: neyther in chamburynge and wantonnes, neyther in stryfe & enuiynge:

14 but put ye on the Lorde Iesus Christ. And make not prouysyon for the fleshe, to fulfyll the lustes of it.

# CHAPTER 14

HYM that is weake in þe fayth, receyue vnto you, not in disputynge and troublyng hys conscience.

2 One beleued that he maye eate all thynge. Another whiche is weake, eateth herbes.

3 Let not hym that eateth, dispyse hym that eateth not. And let not hym whiche eateth not, iudge him that eateth. For God hath receyued hym,

4 What arte thou, that iudgeste another mans seruaunte? Whether he stande or fall that pertayneth vnto hys mayster: yea he shall stande. For God is able to make him stande.

5 Thys man putteth difference betwene day and daye. Another man counted all dayes a lyke. Se that no man wauer in hys owne meanynge.

6 He that obserueth one daye more then another, doth it for the Lordes pleasure. And he that obserueth not one day more then another, doeth it to please the Lorde also. He that eateth, doeth it to please the Lorde, for he geueth God thankes.

7 And he that eateth not, eateth not to please the Lorde with all, & geueth God thankes.

8 For none of vs lyueth his owne seruaunt: neyther doeth anye of vs dye hys owne seruaunte. Yf we lyue, we lyue to be at the Lordes wyll. And yf we dye, we dye at the Lordes wyll. Whether we lyue therfore or dye, we are the Lordes.

9 For Christe therfore dyed, and rose agayne, and reuyued that he myght be Lord both of dead & quicke.

10 But why doest thou then iudge thy brother? Other why doeste thou despyse thy brother? We shall all be brought before the iudgement seate of Christe.

11 For it is wrytten: as truelye as I lyue sayth the Lorde: all knees shall bowe to me, and all tonges shall geue a knowledge to God.

12 So shall euery one of vs, geue accomptes of hym selfe to GOD.

13 Let vs not therfore iudge one another anye more. But iudge thys rather, that no man put a stumblynge blocke or an occasyon to falle in hys brothers waye.

14 For I knowe and am ful certifyed in the Lorde Iesus, that there is nothynge comen of it selfe, but vnto hym that iudgeth it to be commen: to hym is it comen.

15 Yf thy brother be greued with thy meat, now walkest thou not charytablye. Destroye not him with thy meate, for whome Christ dyed.

16 Cause not youre treasure to be euyll spoken of.

17 For the kyngedome of God is not meate and drynke, but ryghtuousnes, peace, & ioye in the holye ghoste.

18 For whosoeuer in these thynges serueth Christe, pleaseth well God, & is commendeth of men.

19 Let vs folowe those thynges which make for peace, and thynges wherewith one maye edifye another.

20 Destroye not the worke of God for a lytell meates sake. All thynges are pure: but it is euyll for that man, whiche eateth with hurte of hys conscience.

21 It is good neyther to eate flesh, neyther to drynke wyne neyther anye thynge whereby thy brother stombleth, eyther falleth, or is made weake.

22 Haste thou faythe? haue it wyth thy selfe before GOD. Happye is he that condempneth not hym selfe in that thynge whiche he aloweth.

23 For he that maketh conscience, is dampned yf he eate, because he doeth it not of faythe. For whatsoeuer is not of faythe, that same is synne.

# CHAPTER 15

WE whiche are strong, ought to beare the fraylnes of

them whiche are weake, and not to stande in our owne conceptes.

2 Let euery man please his neyghboure vnto his wealth and edifiynge.

3 For Christe pleased not hym selfe, but as it is writen: The rebukes of them whiche rebuke the, fell on me.

4 Whatsoeuer thynges are wrytten afore tyme, are wrytten for oure learnyng, that we thorowe pacyence and comforte of the scrypture myght haue hope.

5 The God of pacience and consolatyon, geue vnto euery one of you, that ye be lyke mynded one towardes another after the ensample of Christe Iesu,

6 that ye all agreynge together, maye with one mouthe prayse God the father of oure Lorde Iesus,

7 Wherfore receyue ye on another, as Christe receyued vs, to the prayse of God.

8 And I saye that Iesu Christ was a mynyster of the circumcysyon for the trueth of God is to confyrme the promyses made vnto the fathers.

9 And let the Gentyles prayse God for hys mercye, as it is written: For thys cause I wyll prayse the amonge the Gentyles, & sing in thy name.

10 And agayne he sayth: reioyse ye Gentyles with his people.

11 And agayn. Prayse the Lorde all ye gentyles, and laude hym all nacyons.

12 And in another place Esayas saith: there shalbe the rote of Iesse, and he that shall ryse to reygne ouer the Gentyles: in hym shal the Gentyles truste.

13 The God of hope fil you with all ioye, and peace in beleuynge, that ye maye be ryche in hope thorowe the power of the holye ghoste.

14 I my selfe am full certifyed of you my brethren. that ye your selues are full of goodnes and fylled with all knoweledge, and are able to exhorte one another.

15 Neuerthelesse brethren I haue some what boldelye wrytten vnto you, as one that putteth you in remembraunce thorowe the grace that is geuen me of God,

16 that I should be the minister of Iesu Christe amonge the Gentyles, and should minister þe glad tydynges of God, that þe gentils myghte be an acceptable offerynge, sanctifyed by the holye ghoste.

17 I haue therfore where of I maye reioyce in Christe Iesu, in those thynges which partayne to God.

18 For I dare not speake of anye of those thynges whiche Christe hath not wrought by me, to make the gentyls obedient, with worde and dede,

19 in myghty sygnes and wonders, by the power of the spirite of God: so that from Hierusalem and the coastes rounde about vnto Illiricum, I haue fylled al countreys with the glad tydynges of Christe.

20 So haue I enforced my selfe to preache the Gospell, not where Christe was named, leste I shoulde haue buylt on another mannes foundacyon:

21 but as it is wrytten: To whom he was not spoken of, they shall see, and they þt heard not, shall vnderstande.

22 For thys cause I haue ben ofte let to come vnto you:

23 but nowe seyng I haue no more to do in these countreys, & also haue ben desyrous manye yeares to come vnto you,

24 when I shall take my iorneye into Spayne, I wyll come to you. I truste to set you in my iourneye, and to be broughte on my way thytherwarde by you after that I haue somwhat enioyed you.

25 Now go I vnto Hierusalem, and ministre vnto the saynctes.

26 For it hath pleased them of Macedonia and Achaia to make a certayne distribution vpon the pore saynctes, whiche are at Hierusalem.

27 It hath pleased them verely, and theyr detters are they. For yf the gentyles be made partakers of theyr spirituall thynges, theyr dutye is to ministre vnto them in carnall thynges.

28 When I haue perfourmed thys, and haue broughte them thys frute sealed. I wyll come backe agayne by you into Spayne.

29 And I am sure when I come, that I shall come with aboundaunce of the blessinge of the Gospell of Christe.

30 I beseche you brethren for oure Lorde Iesus Christes sake, and for the loue of the spyryte, that ye healpe me in my busynes, with your prayers to God for me,

31 that I maye be delyuered from them whiche beleue not in Iewry, and that thys my seruyce, whiche I haue to Hierusalem, maye be accepted of the saynctes,

32 that I maye come vnto you wyth ioye, by the wyll of God, and maye with you be refreshed.

33 The God of peace be with you. Amen.

# CHAPTER 16

I commende vnto you Phebe our syster (whiche is a minister of the congregacion of Cenchrea)

2 that ye receyue her in the Lorde as it becommeth saynctes, & þt ye assiste her in whatsoeuer busynes she neadeth of youre ayde. For she hath suckered many, & myne owne selfe also.

3 Grete Prisca & Aquyla my helpers in Christe Iesu,

4 whiche haue for my lyfe layde doune theyr owne neckes. Vnto which not I onlye geue

thankes, but also þe congregacyon of the gentyls.

5 Lykewyse grete all the companye that is in her house. Salute my welbeloued Epenetos, whiche is the fyrst frute amonge them of Achaia.

6 Grete Marye whiche bestowed much laboure on vs.

7 Salute Andronicus and Iunia my cosyns, whiche were prysoners with me also, which are well taken among the Apostles, and were in christ before me.

8 Grete Amplias my beloued in the Lorde.

9 Salute Vrban oure helper in Christ, & Stachys my beloued.

10 Salute Appelles approued in Christ. Salute them whiche are of Aristobolus housholde.

11 Salute Herodion my kynsman. Grete them of the houshold of Narcissus whiche are in the Lorde.

12 Salute Tryphena and Triphosa, whiche women dyd laboure in the Lorde. Salute the beloued Persis, which laboured in the Lorde.

13 Salute Rufus chosen in the Lorde, and hys mother and myne.

14 Grete Asincritus, Phlegon, Herman, Patrobas, Hermen, and the brethren whiche are with them.

15 Salute Philologus & Iulia, Nereus and hys syster, and Olympha, and all the saynctes whiche are with them.

16 Salute one another with an holye kysse. The congregacyons of Christe salute you.

17 I beseche you brethren, marke them which cause diuisyon, and geue occasyons of euyl, contrary to the doctryue which ye haue learned: and auoyd them.

18 For they that are such, serue not the Lorde Iesus Christ: but theyr owne bellyes, and with swete preachynges & flatterynge wordes deceyue the hertes of the innocentes.

19 For youre obedience extendeth to all men I am glad no doubte of you. But yet I woulde haue you wyse vnto that whiche is good, and to be innocent as concernyng euill.

20 The God of peace treade Sathan vnder your fete shortelye. The grace of oure Lorde Iesu Christe be with you.

21 Timotheus my worcke felowe and Lucyos and Iason and Sosipater my kynsmen, salute you.

22 I Tertius salute you, whiche wrote thys Epistle in the Lorde.

23 Gayus myne hoste and the hoste of all the congregacion, saluteth you. Erastus the chamberlayne of the citie saluteth you. And Quartus a brother, saluteth you.

24 The grace of oure Lorde Iesus Christ be with you all. Amen.

25 To hym that is of power to stablysh you, accordynge to my Gospell and preachinge of Iesus Christe, in vtterynge of the mysterye whiche was kepte secrete sence the worlde began,

26 but nowe is opened by the scriptures of prophesye, at the commaundemente of þe euerlastynge God, to stere vp obedience to the fayth publyshed among all nacions:

27 To the same God, which alone is wyse, be all prayse thorowe Iesus Christe for euer. AMEN.

# 1 Corinthians

## CHAPTER 1

Paule by vocacyon an Apostle of Iesus Christe thorow the wyll of God, & brother Sostenes.

2 Vnto the congregacyon of GOD whiche is at Corinthum. To them that are sanctifyed in Christ Iesu, saynctes by callyng with al that call on the name of oure Lorde Iesus Christe in euerye place, bothe of theyrs and of oures.

3 Grace be with you and peace from God oure father, and from the Lorde Iesus Christ.

4 I thanke my God alwayes on youre behalfe, for the grace of God whiche is geuen you by Iesus Christ,

5 that in all thynges ye are made ryche by hym, in all learnynge and in al knoweledge

6 euen as the testimony of Iesus Christ was confyrmed in you,

7 so that ye are behynd in no gyfte, and wayte for the appearynge of oure Lorde Iesus Christe,

8 which shal strength you vnto the ende, that ye may be blamelesse in the daye of oure Lorde Iesus Christ.

9 For God is faythfull, by whome ye are called vnto to the felowshyppe of hys sonne Iesus Christ oure Lorde.

10 I beseche you brethren in the name of oure Lorde Iesus Christe, that ye all speake one thynge, and that there be no dissencyon amonge you: but be ye knyt together in one mynde, and in one meanynge.

11 It is shewed vnto me (my brethren) of you, by them that are of the housse of Cloe, that there is stryfe amonge you. And thys is it that I meane,

12 how þt communly among you, one saith: I hold of Paul, another I holde of Apollo, the thyrd I holde of Cephas, the fourth I holde of Christ.

13 Is Christe diuided? was Paule crucifyed for you? eyther were ye baptysed in the name of Paule?

14 I thanke God, that I christened none of you, but Crispus & Gaius,

15 lest any should say that I had baptysed in myne own name.

16 I baptysed also the housholde of Stephana. Furthermore knowe I not whether I baptysed anye man or no.

17 For Christe sente me not to baptyse, but to preache the gospel, not with wysdom of wordes leaste the crosse of Christe shoulde haue bene made of none effecte.

18 For the preachyng of the crosse is to them that peryshe folyshnes, but vnto vs whiche are saued, it is the power of God.

19 For it is written: I will destroye the wysdome of the wyse, and wyll caste awaye the vnderstandinge of the prudent.

20 Where is the wyse? Where is the scribe? Where is the searcher of this worlde?

21 Hath not God made the wysdome of thys worlde folyshnes? For when the world thorough wysdome knewe not God, in þe wisdom of God, it pleased God thorough folishnes of preachynge to saue them that beleue.

22 For the Iewes require a signe, and the Grekes seke after wisdom.

23 But we preache Christe crucifyed vnto the Iewes an occasion of fallinge, and vnto the Grekes folishnes,

24 but vnto them, whiche are called both of Iewes and Grekes we preache Christe the power of God, and the wisdome of God.

25 For the folyshnes of God is wyser then men, and the weaknes of God is stronger then men.

26 Brethren loke on youre callinge howe þt not manye wyse men after the fleshe, not manie myghty, not manye of hye degre are called:

27 but God had chosen the folyshe thynges of the worlde, to confounde the wise. And God hath chosen the weake things of

the worlde, to confounde thynges, whyche are myghty.

28 And vile thinges of the world, and thinges whiche are despysed, hath God chosen, yea and thinges of no reputation for to bringe to nought thinges of reputation,

29 that no flesh shoulde reioise in his presence.

30 And vnto him partaine ye in Christe Iesus, whiche of God is made to vs wysdome, and also rightuousnes, and sanctifiynge and redemption.

31 That accordynge as it is written: he whiche reioyseth should reioyse in the Lorde.

## CHAPTER 2

AND I brethren when I came to you, came not in gloriousnes of wordes, or of wysdome, shewynge vnto you the testimonye of God.

2 Neither shewed I my selfe that I knew any thinge amonge you saue Iesus Christe, euen the same that was crucified.

3 And I was amonge you in weaknes, & in feare and in muche tremblinge.

4 And my wordes and my preachinge were not wyth entisynge wordes of mannes wysdome but in shewinge of the spirite, and of power,

5 þt youre fayth shoulde not stande in the wysdome of men, but in the power of God.

6 That we speake of, is wisdome amonge that are perfecte: not þe wisdome of this world (whiche go to nought)

7 but we speake þt wysdome of God, whiche is in secrete and lyeth hyd, whiche God ordeined before the world vnto oure glory,

8 whiche wisdome none of the rulars of this worlde knewe. For had they knowen it, they would not haue crucified the Lorde of Glorye.

9 But as it was written: The eye hath not sene, and þe eare hath not hearde, neither haue entred into the herte of man the thinges, which God hath prepared for them that loue him.

10 But God hath opened them to vs by hys spirite. For the spirite searcheth al thinges, ye the bottome of Goddes secretes.

11 For what man knoweth the thynges of a man, saue the spyryte of a man, whiche is wythin him. Euen so the thinges of God knoweth no man, but the spirite of God.

12 And we haue not receiued the spirite of the world: but the spyryte whiche cometh of God, for to knowe þe thinges, that are geuen to vs of God,

13 which thinges also we speake, not in the conninge wordes of mannes wysdome, but wyth the conning wordes of the holye ghost, makinge spyrytual comparisons of spirituall thinges.

14 For the naturall man perceiueth not the thinges of þe spyrite of God. For they are but folishnes vnto him. Neither can he perceiue them, because he is spiritually examined.

15 But he that is spyrytuall, discusseth all thinges: yet he hym selfe is iudged of no man.

16 For who knoweth the minde of the Lorde? other who shall informe him? But we vnderstand the minde of Christ.

## CHAPTER 3

AND I coulde not speake vnto you brethren as vnto spiritual, but as vnto carnal, euen as it were to babes in Christ:

2 I gaue you milke to drinke, & not meat. For ye then were not stronge, no neyther yet are. For ye are yet carnall.

3 As longe verelye as there is amonge you enuiynge, stryfe and dissencion: are ye not carnall, and walke after the maner of men?

4 As long as one sayeth, I holde of Paul, and another I am of Apollo, are ye not carnall?

5 What is Paule? What thinge is Apollo? Dulye ministres are they, by whom ye beleued, euen as the Lorde gaue euerye man grace.

6 I haue planted, Apollo watred: but God gaue the increase.

7 So then neyther is he that planteth anye thinge neyther he that watreth: but God that gaue the increase.

8 He that planteth and he that whathereth, are neither better then the other. Euerye man yet shall receyue hys rewarde accordynge to hys laboure.

9 We are Goddes labourer, ye are Goddes husbandrye ye are Goddes buyldinge.

10 According to the grace of God geuen vnto me, as a wyse buylder haue I layde the foundation. And another buylte theron. But let euery man take hede how he buildeth vpon.

11 For other foundation can no man laie, then that whiche is layde, whiche is Iesus Christ.

12 Yf any man buylde on this foundacion, golde, syluer, precyous stones timber, haye or stobble:

13 euerye mans worke shall appeare. For the daye shal declare it, & it shalbe shewed in fyre. And the fyre shall trye euery mannes worke, what it is.

14 Yf any mannes worke that he hath buylt vpon, byde: he shall receiue a rewarde.

15 If any mannes worke burne, he shall suffer losse: but he shalbe safe him selfe: neuerthelesse yet as it were thorow fyre.

16 Are ye not ware that ye are the temple of God, and how that the spyryte of God dwelleth in you?

17 Yf anye man defyle the temple of God him shall God destroy. For the temple of God is holy, whyche temple ye are.

18 Let no man deceyue hym selfe. Yf anye man seme, wyse amonge you, let hym be a fole in thys worlde that he maye be wyse.

19 For the wysdome of this worlde is folyshnes wyth God. For it is wrytten: he compaseth the wyse in theyr craftynes.

20 And agayne, God knoweth the thoughtes of the wyse that they be vayne.

21 Therfore let no man reioice in men. For all thinges are youres

22 whether it be Paule, other Apollo, other Cephas: whether it be þe world, other lyfe, other deathe, whether they be present thynges or things to come: all are youres,

23 and ye are Christes & Christ is Gods.

## CHAPTER 4

LET men thus wyse esteme vs, euen as the ministers of Christ, and disposers of the secretes of of God.

2 Furthermore it is requyred of the dysposers, that they be found faithfull.

3 Wyth me it is but a very smal thinge, that I shoulde be iudged of you, eyther of (mans daye). No I iudge not myne owne selfe.

4 I knowe nought by my selfe: yet am I not therby iustified. It is the Lorde that iudgeth me.

5 Therfore iudge nothing before the tyme vntill the Lorde come, who wyll lyghten thinges, that are hyd in darckenes, and open the counsels of the hertes. And then shall euery man haue praise of God.

6 These thinges brethren I haue described in myne owne person and Apollos for youre sakes, that ye myght learne by vs, that no man counte of him selfe beionde that, which is aboue written: that one swell not against another for anye mans cause.

7 For who preferreth the? What haste thou, that thou hast not receyued? Yf thou haue receyued it ewhy reioyseste thou as thoughe thou haddeste not receiued it?

8 Now ye are ful: now ye are made rych: ye reigne as kinges without vs: and I would to God ye dyd reygne that we might reygne wyth you.

9 Me thinketh that God hath sente forth vs, which are Apostles for the lowest, of al as it were men appointed to death. For we are a gasyng stoke vnto the world, and to the aungels, and to men.

10 We are foles for Christes sake and ye are wise thorow Christe. We are weake, and ye are stronge. Ye are honorable, and we are despised.

11 Euen vnto this daye we honger and thyrst, and are naked, and are boffetted wyth fystes, and haue no certayne dwellinge place,

12 and labour workinge wyth oure handes. We are reuiled, & yet we blesse. We are persecuted and suffer it.

13 We are euyl spoken of and we pray. We are made as it were the filthines of the worlde, þe ofscowring of all thynges, euen vnto this time.

14 I wryte not these things to shame you but as my beloued sonnes I warne you.

15 For thoughe ye haue ten thousand instructours in Christ: yet haue ye not many fathers. In Christe Iesu, I haue begotten you thorowe þe Gospell.

16 Wherfore I desyre you to folowe me.

17 For this cause haue I sent vnto you Tymotheus, which is my deare sonne, and faithfull in the Lorde, whiche shall put you in remembraunce of my waies, whiche I haue in Christ euen as I teache euery wher in all congregations.

18 Some swell as though, I would come no more at you.

19 But I wil come to you shortly yf God wil: and will knowe not the wordes of them, which swel, but the power,

20 for the kyngdom of God is not in wordes, but in power.

21 What wyll ye? Shall I come vnto you with a rodde, or els in loue and in the spyryte of mekenes?

## CHAPTER 5

THERE goeth a commen, saiynge: that there is fornicacion amonge you, and such fornication as is not ones named amonge þe Gentiles: that one should haue his fathers wyfe.

2 And ye swell and haue not rather sorowed, that he whiche hath done this dede, myght be put from amonge you.

3 For I verelye as absent in bodye, euen so present in spirite, haue determined alredye (as though I were present) that he that hath done this dede,

4 in þe name of oure Lord Iesus Christ, when ye are gathered together, in my spyryte, wyth the power of the Lorde Iesus Christe,

5 be delyuered vnto Sathan, for the destruccion of the fleshe, that the spirite maye be saued in the daye of the Lorde Iesus.

6 Your reioysing is not good: knowe ye not that a lytle leuen sowreth the whole lompe of dowe.

7 Pourge therfore the olde leuen, that ye may be new dowe, as ye are swete bread. For Christ oure easterlambe is offered vp for vs.

8 Therfore let vs kepe holy daye, not wyth olde leuen, neither with the leuen of malycyousnes and wyckednes, but with the swete bread of purenes and trueth.

9 I wrote vnto you in an Epystle that ye shoulde not companye wyth fornicatours.

10 And I meant not at al of the fornicatours of this worlde, eyther of the couetous, or of extorsioners, eyther of the ydolaters: for then muste ye nedes haue gone oute of the world.

11 But nowe I writte vnto you, that ye companye not together, if anie that is called a brother be a fornicatour, or couetous, or a worshiper of ymages, eyther a raylar, either a drounkard, or an extorcionar: with him that is such, se that ye eate not.

12 For what haue I to do, to iudge them which are without? Do ye not iudge them, that are within?

13 Them that are wythout, God shal iudge. Put awaye from amonge you, that euyl person.

## CHAPTER 6

Howe dare one of you hauynge busines wyth another, go to law vnder the wycked, and not rather vnder the sainctes?

2 Do ye not knowe that the sainctes shall iudge the worlde? Yf the world shal be iudged by you: are ye not good ynoughe to iudge smal tryfles:

3 know ye not how that we shal iudge the aungels? Howe much more maye we iudge thinges that pertayne to the lyfe?

4 Yf ye haue iudgementes of worldlye matters, take them whiche are despised in the congregacion, and make them iudges.

5 Thys I saye to youre shame. Is there vtterlye no wyse man amonge you. What, not one at al, that can iudge betwene brother and brother,

6 but one brother goeth to lawe with another, and that vnder the vnbeleuers?

7 Nowe therfore, there is vtterlye a faute amonge you, because ye go to law one wyth another. Why rather suffer ye not wronge? Why rather suffre ye not youre selues to be robbed?

8 naye, ye youre selues do wronge, and robbe: and that the brethren.

9 Do ye not remember, howe that the vnrightuous shall not inheret the kyngdome of God? Be not deceyued. For neither fornicatours, neither worshipers of ymages, neither whormongers, neyther weaklinges, neither abusers of them selues wyth the mankynde,

10 neither theues, neythe couetous, neither dronkardes, neither cursed speakers, neither pyllars, shall inherete þe kyngedome of God.

11 And suche were ye verelye, but ye are washed, ye are sanctifyed, ye are iustifyed by the name of the Lorde Iesus, and by the spyryte of our God.

12 All thinges are lawfull vnto me: but all thinges are not profitable. I may do all thynges, but I wil be brought vnder no mans power,

13 Meates are ordeyned for þe belly, and the belly for meates, but God shall destroye both it and them. Let not the bodye be applied vnto fornication, but vnto the Lorde, and the Lorde vnto the body.

14 God hath raysed vp the Lorde, and shal rayse vs vp by his power.

15 Either remembre ye not, that youre bodyes are the membres of Christe, shal I now take the membres of Christ, and make them the membres of an harlotte? God forbid.

16 Do ye not vnderstande, that he whiche coupleth him selfe with an harlot, is become one body? For two (sayth he) shalbe one flesh.

17 But he that is ioyned vnto the Lorde, is one spyryte.

18 Fle fornycatyon. Al synnes that a man doth, are without the body. But he that is a fornicatour, sinneth agaynst his owne bodye.

19 Either knowe ye not howe that youre bodies are the temple of the holye ghoste, whyche is in you, whome ye haue of God, and how that ye are not your owne?

20 For ye are dearlye boughte. Therfore glorifye ye God in youre bodyes, and in youre spyrytes, for they are Goddes.

## CHAPTER 7

As concerninge, wherof ye wrote vnto me, it is good for a man, not to touche a woman.

2 Neuerthelesse to avoide fornication, let euery man haue his wyfe: and let euerye woman haue her husbande.

3 Let the man geue vnto the wyfe due beneuolence. Lykewyse also the wyfe vnto the man.

4 The wyfe hath not power ouer her owne bodie, but the husbande. And lykewyse the man hath not power ouer his owne bodye, but the wyfe.

5 Withdrawe not your selues one from another, excepte it be wyth consente for a tyme, for to geue your selues to fastinge, and prayer. And afterward come agayne to the same thinge, leste Sathan tempte you for your incontinencye.

6 Thys I saye of fauoure, and not of commaundement.

7 For I woulde that all men were as I my selfe am: but euerie man hath hys proper gyfte of God, one after this maner, another after that.

8 I saye vnto the vnmaryed men and wyddowes: it is good for them, if they abyed euen as I do.

9 But and if they cannot abstayne, let them mary. For it is

better to mary, then burne.

10 Vnto the maryed commaunded not I but the Lorde: that the wyfe separate not her selfe from the man.

11 Yf she separate her selfe, let her remayne vnmaryed, or be reconcilied to her husband againe. And let not the husband put away his wife from him.

12 To the remnaunte speake I and not the Lord. Yf anye brother haue a wyfe that beleued not, if she be contente to dwel with hym, let him not put her awaye.

13 And the woman, which hath to her husband an infidele, if he consente to dwell with her, let her not put him awaie.

14 For the vnbeleuinge husbande, is sainctified by the wyfe: and the vnbeleuinge wife, is sainctified by the husbande. Or els were youre chyldren vnclene: but nowe are they pure.

15 But and if the vnbeleuinge departe, let him departe. A brother or a syster is not in subieccion to suche. God hath called vs in peace.

16 For howe knowest thou O woman, whether thou shalt saue that man or no? Other howe knoweste thou O man, whether thou shalt saue that woman or no?

17 but euen as God hath distributed to euery man. As the Lorde hath called euery person so let him walke: and so ordeine I in all congregations.

18 If any man be called beynge circumcised, let him adde nothing thereto. If any be called vncircumcised: let him not be circumcised.

19 Circumcison is nothinge, vncircumcision is nothinge, but the kepinge of the commaundementes of God is altogether.

20 Let euery man abyde in the same state, wherin he is called.

21 Art thou called a seruauntes, care not for it. Neuertheles if thou maiest be fre, vse it rather.

22 For he that is called in the Lord beynge a seruaunte, is the Lordes freman. Lykewyse he that is called beynge fre, is Christes seruaunte.

23 Ye are dearlye bought, be not mennes seruauntes.

24 Brethren let euery man wherin he is called, therin abide with God.

25 As concerninge virgins, I haue no commaundemente of the Lorde: yet geue I counsel, as one that hath obteyned mercy of the Lord to be faithfull.

26 I suppose that it is good for the presente necessitie. For it is good for a man so to be.

27 Arte thou bounde vnto a wife? seke not to be loused. Arte thou loused from a wife? seke not a wife.

28 But and if thou take a wyfe, thou sinnest not. Lykewise if a virgine mary: she sinneth not. Neuerthelesse such shal haue trouble in theyr fleshe: but I fauoure you.

29 This saye I brethren the tyme is short. It remaineth that they which haue wiues, be as though they had none,

30 and they that wepe be as though they wept not, and they that reioyse be as though they reioysed not: & they that bye, be as though they possessed not:

31 and they that vse this worlde, be as though they vsed it not. For the fashion of this world goeth away.

32 I would haue you without care. The single man careth for the things of the Lorde howe he maye please the Lorde.

33 But he that hath maried, careth for þe thinges of þe worlde howe he may please his wyfe.

34 There is difference betwene a virgine and a wyfe. The single woman careth for the things of þe Lorde, that she maye be pure both in bodye and also in spyryte. But she that is maried, careth for the things of the worlde, howe she maye please her husbande.

35 This speake I for youre profite, not to tangel you in a snare, but for þt whiche is honeste and comely vnto you, and that ye maye quietly cleaue vnto the Lorde without separacion.

36 If anye man thinke that it is vncomelye for his virgine if we passe þe tyme of mariage, and yf so nede require, let hym do what he listeth, he sinneth not: let them be coupled in mariage.

37 Neuerthelesse, he that purposeth surely in his herte, hauing none nede, but hath power ouer his owne wyll, and hath so decreed in his herte that he wyl kepe his virgin, doeth well. So then he that ioyneth his virgine in mariage doeth well.

38 But he that ioyneth not his virgine in mariage doeth better.

39 The wife is bounde to the lawe as longe as her husband liueth. If her husbande slepe, she is at libertye to mary with whome she wyll, onely in the Lorde.

40 But she is happyer if she so abyde, in my iudgemente. And I thinke verely that I haue the spirite of God.

# CHAPTER 8

To speake of thinges dedicate vnto Idols, we are sure that we all haue knowledge, knowledge maketh a man swel, but loue edyfyeth.

2 If anye man thinke þt he knoweth anie thinge, he knoweth nothinge yet as he ought to knowe.

3 But yf anye man loue God, the same is knowen of hym.

4 To speake of meate dedicate vnto Idols, we are sure that there is none Idol in þe world and that there is none

other God but one.

5 And though there be that are called Goddes, whether in heauen other in earthe (as there be Goddes manye and Lordes manye)

6 yet vnto vs is there but one God, whiche is the father, of whom are al thinges, and we in him: and one Lorde Iesus Christ, by whom are all thinges, and we by hym.

7 But euery man hath not knowledge. For some suppose that there is an Idole, vntyll this houre, and eate as of a thinge offered vnto the Idole, and so their consciences beynge yet weake are defyled.

8 Meate maketh vs not acceptable to God. Neither yf we eate are we the better. Neither, yf we eate not, are we the worsse.

9 But take hede that your libertye cause not the weake to faule.

10 For yf some man se the, whiche hast knowledge, syt at meate in the Idoles temple, shall not the conscience of him which is weake, be boldened to eate those thinges, whiche are offered vnto the Idole?

11 And so thorowe thy knowledge shal the weake brother perishe for whom Christ dyed.

12 When ye synne so againste the brethren, and wound theyr weake consciences, ye synne agaynste Christe.

13 Wherfore yf meate hurte my brother, I wyll eate no fleshe, whyle the worlde standeth, because I wyll not hurte my brother.

## CHAPTER 9

AM I not an Apostle? am I not free? haue I not sene Iesus Christ our Lorde?

2 Are not ye my worke in the Lorde? Yf I be not an Apostle vnto other, yet am I vnto you. For the seale of myne Apostleshyppe are ye in the Lord.

3 Mine aunswere to them that axe me, is this.

4 Haue we not power to eate, and to drinke?

5 Either haue we not power to leade aboute a syster to wyfe as well as other Apostles, and as the brethren of the Lord, and Cephas?

6 Either onely I and Barnabas haue not power this to do?

7 who goeth a warfare anye time at hys owne cost? Who planteth a vineiarde, and eateth not of the fruite? Who fedeth a flocke and eateth not of the mylke?

8 Saye I these thinges after the maner of men? Or sayeth not the lawe the same also?

9 For it is written in þe lawe of Moyses. Thou shalt not mosell the mouth of þe oxe that treadeth out the corne. Doeth God take thought for oxen?

10 Either saith he it not altogether for our sakes? For our sakes no doubte this is written: þt he whiche eareth, shoulde eare in hope: & þt he whych thresheth in hope, should be partaker of hys hope.

11 Yf we sowe vnto you spyrytuall thinges: is it a great thinge yf we reape youre carnall thinges.

12 Yf other be partakers of this power ouer you: wherfore are not we rather? Neuerthelesse we haue not vsed thys power but suffer all thinges leste we shoulde hinder the Gospell of Christe

13 Do ye not vnderstande howe that they whiche minister in the temple, haue their fyndynge of the temple? And they whych wayte at the aulter, are partakers of the aulter?

14 Euen so also dyd the Lord ordaine, that they which preach the Gospel, shoulde lyue of the Gospel.

15 But I haue vsed none of these thinges. Neither wrote I these thinges, þt it should be so done vnto me. For it were better for me to dye, then that anye shoulde take this reioysinge from me.

16 In that I preache the Gospel, I haue nothinge to reioyce of. For necessytye is put vnto me. Wo is it vnto me yf I preach not the Gospel.

17 Yf I do it wyth a good wil, I haue a rewarde. But yf I do it against my wyl, an offyce is committed vnto me.

18 What is my reward then? Verelye, that when I preache the Gospell, I make the Gospell of Christ fre, that I misuse not myne authoryte in the Gospell.

19 For though I be fre from all men, yet haue I made my selfe seruaunte vnto all men, that I myght winne the mo.

20 Vnto þe Iewes, I became as a Iewe, to winne the Iewes. To them that were vnder the lawe, was I made as though I had ben vnder þe lawe, to winne them that were vnder the lawe.

21 To them that were without lawe, became I as though I had ben without the lawe (when I was not without lawe as perteyninge to God, but vnder a lawe as concerninge Christe) to wynne them that were without lawe.

22 To the weake became I as weake, to wynne the weake. In all thinge I fashioned my selfe to all men, to saue at the lest waye some.

23 And thys I do for the Gospel sake, that I might haue my parte thereof.

24 Perceyue ye not howe that they whyche runne in a course, runne all, yet but one receiueth the reward. So runne that ye maye obtayne.

25 Euery man that proueth maysters abstaineth from all thinges. And they do it to obtaine a corruptible croune: but we to

obtaine an vncorruptible croune.

26 I therfore so runne, not as an uncertaine thinge. So fight I not as one that beateth the ayer:

27 but I tame my bodye and bringe it into subieccion, leste after that I haue preached to other, I my selfe should be a cast away.

## CHAPTER 10

BRETHREN I would not þt ye should be ignoraunte of this, howe that oure fathers were all vnder a cloude, and al passed thorowe the sea,

2 and were all baptysed vnder Moyses, in the cloude, and in the sea:

3 and dyd al eate of one spyrytual meate,

4 and dyd al drincke of one maner of spyrytual drincke. And they drancke of that spyrytuall rocke that folowed them, which rocke was Christe.

5 But in manie of them had God no delite. For they were ouerthrowen in the wyldernes.

6 These are ensamples to vs that we should not luste after euyll thinges, as they lusted.

7 Neyther be ye worshippers of Images as were some of them accordynge at it is written: The people sate doune to eate and drynke, and rose vp agayne to playe.

8 Neyther let vs committe fornicacion as some of them committed fornycacyon, and were destroied in one day .xxiij. thousand.

9 Neither let vs tempte Christe as some of them tempted, and were destroyed of serpentes.

10 Neyther murmure ye as some of them murmured, and were destroyed of the destroyer.

11 Al these thinges happened vnto them for ensamples, and were written to put vs in remembraunce, whom the endes of the world are come vpon.

12 Wherfore let him that thynketh he standeth, take hede leste he fall.

13 There hath none other temptacion taken you, but suche as foloweth the nature of man. But God is faythful whiche shall not suffre you to be tempted aboue your strength: but shall in the middest of the temptacion make a waye to escape out.

14 Wherfore my deare beloued, fle from worshipping of Idols.

15 I speake as vnto them, whiche haue dyscrecion, iudge ye what I saye.

16 Is not þe cuppe of blessinge whiche we blesse, partaking of that bloude of Christe?

17 is not the breade which we breake, partakinge of the bodye of Christ? because that we (thoughe we be manye) yet are one bodye in as muche as we all are partakers of one breade.

18 Beholde Israell whiche walketh carnally. Are not they which eate of the sacrifyce, partakers of the aultre?

19 What saye I then? that the Image is any thinge? or that it whiche is offered to Images is anye thinge?

20 Naye, but I saye, that these thinges, whiche the Gentyles offer, they offer to deuyls, and not to God. And I woulde not þt ye should haue felloushippe wt the deuyls.

21 Ye can not drinke of the cuppe of the Lorde: and of the cuppe of the deuils. Ye can not be partakers of the Lordes table, and of the table of the deuils.

22 Either shall we prouoke the Lorde? Or are we stronger then he? All thinges are laufull vnto me, but all thinges are not expedient.

23 All thinges are lauful to me, but all thinges edifye not.

24 Let no man seke his owne profyte: but let euerye man seke anothers wealth.

25 Whatsoeuer is solde in the market, that eate and axe no questions for consciens sake.

26 For the earth is the Lordes, and all that therin is.

27 Yf anye of them whiche beleue not, byd you to a feste, & yf ye be disposed to go, whatsoeuer is set before you, eate, axing no question for conscience sake.

28 But and yf anye man saye vnto you: this is dedicate vnto Idols, eate not of it for his sake that sheweth it, and for hurtyng of conscience (The earth is the Lordes, & al that therin is)

29 Conscience I saye, not thine but the conscience of that other. For why should my libertie be iudged of another mannes conscience?

30 For yf I take my parte wyth thankes: why am I euil spoken of for þe thinge, wherfore I geue thankes.

31 Whether therfore ye eate or drynke, or whatsoeuer ye do, do al to the praise of God.

32 See that ye geue occasion of euil, neither to þe Iewes, nor yet to the Gentiles, neither to the congregation of God:

33 euen as I please al men in al thinges, not sekinge myne owne profite, but the profit of manye, that they myghte be saued.

## CHAPTER 11

FOLOWE me, as I do Christe.

2 I commende you brethren that ye remembre me in al thinges, & kepe the ordinaunces euen as I deliuered them to you.

3 I woulde you knewe that Christ is the heade of euery man. And the man is the womans heade. And God is Christes heade.

4 Euery man praiynge or prophesiynge hauing any thinge on his heade, shameth his head.

5 Euery woman that prayeth or prophesyeth bare headed,

dishonesteth her heade. For it is euen all one, and the very same thinge, euen as though she were shauen.

6 If the woman be not couered, let her also be shoren. If it be shame for a woman to be shorne or shauen let her couer her head.

7 A man oughte not to couer his heade, for as muche as he is the ymage and glorye of God. The woman is the glorye of the man.

8 For the man is not of the woman, but the woman of the man.

9 Neither was the man created for the womans sake: but the woman for the mannes sake.

10 For thys cause ought þe woman to haue power on her heade, for þe aungels sakes.

11 Neuerthelesse, neyther is the man wythout the woman neyther the woman wythout the man in the Lorde.

12 For as þe woman is of the man, euen so is the man by the woman: but al is of God.

13 Iudge in your selfes whether it be comelye, that a woman praye vnto God beare headed.

14 Or els doeth not nature teache you that it is a shame for a man,

15 yf he haue longe heyr, & prayse to a woman, yf she haue longe heyre? For her heyre is geuen her to couer her wythall.

16 If there be anye man amonge you, that lusteth to striue let hym knowe that we haue no suche custome, neither the congregations of God.

17 This I warne you of, and commende not that ye come together: not after a better maner but after a worsse.

18 Fyrste of all when ye come together in the congregacion, I heare that there is dyssencyon amonge you, and I partely, beleue it.

19 For there muste be sectes amonge you, that they whyche are perfecte amonge you, myghte be knowen.

20 When ye come together a man can not eate the Lordes supper. For euery man beginneth afore to eate hys owne supper.

21 And one is houngerye, and another is drounken. Haue ye not houses to eate and to drinke in?

22 Or els despise ye the congregacion of God and shame them that haue not? What shall I saye vnto you? shall I prayse you: In thys prayse I you not.

23 That whiche I delyuered you, I receiued of the Lorde. For the Lorde Iesus þe same nyght, in whyche he was betrayed, toke breade,

24 and thanked and brake, and sayde. Take ye, eate ye thys is my bodye whiche is broken for you. Thys do ye in the remembraunce of me.

25 After the same maner he toke the cuppe, when supper was done, saying. Thys cuppe is the newe testamente in my bloude. Thys do as ofte as ye drynke it, in the remembraunce of me.

26 For as often as ye shal eate thys breade, and drincke this cuppe, ye shall shewe the Lordes death tyll he come.

27 Wherfore whosoeuer shall eate of this bread, or drinke of the cuppe vnworthely, shall be gyltie of the bodye and bloude of the Lorde.

28 Let a man therfore examen hym selfe, and so let hym eate of the breade and drynke of the cuppe.

29 For he that eateth or drinketh vnworthelye, eateth and drynketh his owne dampnation, because he maketh no difference of the Lordes bodye.

30 For this cause manye are weake and sycke amonge you, and manye slepe.

31 Yf we had truely iudged our selues, we should not haue ben iudged.

32 But when we are iudged of the Lorde, we are chastened, because we shoulde not be dampued wyth the worlde.

33 Wherfore my brethren, when ye come together to eate, tary one for another.

34 If any man hunger, let hym eate at home, that ye come not together vnto condempnation. Other thynges wil I set in order when I come.

# CHAPTER 12

In spiritual thinges brethren I would not haue you ignoraunt.

2 Ye knowe that ye were Gentyles, and wente your wayes vnto domme Idols, euen as you were led.

3 Wherfore I declare vnto you, that no man speakinge in the spirite of God, defieth Iesus. Also no man saye that Iesus is the Lorde: but by the holye ghoste.

4 There are diuersities of gyftes verelye, yet but one spirite.

5 And there are differences of administracions, & yet but one Lorde.

6 And there are diuerse maners of operations, and yet but one God, which worketh all thinges that are wrought, in all creatures.

7 The giftes of the spirite are geuen to euerie man to profite the congregation.

8 To one is geuen thorowe the spirite the vtteraunce of wysdome. To another is geuen the vtteraunce of knowledge by the same spirite.

9 To another is geuen fayth by the same spirite. To another the giftes of healinge, by the same spirite.

10 To another power to do miracles. To another prophecie. To another iudgement of spirites. To an other diuerse tounges. To another the interpretation of tounges.

11 And these all worketh

euen the selfe same spyryte, deuydynge to euerye man seuerall gyftes, euen as he wyll.

12 For as the bodye is one, and hath manye membres, and all the membres of one bodye though they be many, yet are they but one bodye: euen so is Christ.

13 For in one spyryte are we al baptysed to make one body, whether we be Iewes or Gentiles, whether we be bounde or fre: and haue al drounke of one spirite.

14 For the body is not one member, but manye.

15 Yf the fote saye: I am not the hand, therfore I am not of the bodye: is he therfore not of the bodye?

16 And yf the eare saye, I am not the eye: therfore I am not of the bodye: is he therfore not of the bodie?

17 If al þe bodye were an eye, where were then the eare? If all were hearinge? wher were the smellynge?

18 But nowe hath God disposed the membres euerye one of them in the bodye, at hys owne pleasure,

19 If they were al one member: where were the bodye?

20 Nowe are there manye membres, yet but one bodye.

21 And the eye can not saye vnto the hand: I haue no nede of the: nor the heade also to the fete. I haue no nede of you.

22 Yea rather a greate deale those members of the bodye, whyche seme to be moste feble, are moste necessarye.

23 And vpon those membres of the bodie, which we thinke leste honest, put we moste honestye on. And oure vngodlye parties haue most beauty on.

24 For our honeste members nede it not. But God hath so disposed the bodye, and hath geuen moste honoure to that parte whyche lacked,

25 lest there should be anye stryfe in the bodye: but that the membres shoulde indifferentlye care one for another.

26 And yf one member be had in honoure, all the membres be glad also.

27 Ye are the bodye of Christe, and membres one of another.

28 And God hath also ordeined in the congregation, fyrst the Apostles, secondarely prophetes, thyrdely teachers then them that do miracles: after that þe giftes of healinge, helpers, gouernes, diuersitie of tounges.

29 Are all Apostles? Are all Prophetes? Are all teachers? Are all doers of miracles:

30 Haue al the gyftes of healinge? Do all speake with tounges? Do al interprete?

31 Couet after the beste gyftes. And yet shewe I vnto you a more excellente waye.

## CHAPTER 13

THOUGHT I speake with tounges of men and angels, and yet had no loue, I were euen as soundinge brasse, or as a tynklinge Cimbal.

2 And though I could prophecye, and vnderstande all secretes, and all knowledge: yea, yf I had all fayth so that I coulde moue mountaines out of theyr places, and yet had no loue, I were nothing.

3 And thought I bestowed all my goodes to fede the pore, and though I gaue my bodye euen that I burned, and yet had no loue, it profeteth me nothinge.

4 Loue suffreth longe, and is curteous. Loue enuieth not. Loue doth not frowardelye, swelleth not, dealeth not dishonestlye,

5 seketh not her owne, is not prouoketh to anger, thinketh not euil,

6 reioiceth not in iniquitie: but reioiseth in the trueth,

7 suffreth all thinge, beleueth all things, hopeth al thinges, endureth in all thinges.

8 Though that propheciynge fayle, other tounges shall cease, or knowledge vanishe awaye, yet loue falleth neuer awaye.

9 For oure knowledge is vnperfect, & oure prophesiynge is vnperfecte.

10 But when that which is perfect, is come: then þt which is vnperfect, shal be done awaye:

11 When I was a child, I spake as a chylde, I vnderstode as a child, I Imagined as a chylde. But assone as I was a man, I put away childishnes.

12 Nowe we se in a glasse euen in a darke speakinge, but then shall we se face to face. Nowe I knowe vnperfectlye, but then shall I knowe euen as I am knowen.

13 Nowe abideth fayth, hope, and loue, euen these thre: but the chiefe of these is loue.

## CHAPTER 14

LABOURE for loue, and couete spyrytuall gyftes: and moste chiefely for to prophecye.

2 For he that speaketh wyth tounges speaketh not vnto men, but vnto God, for no man heareth hym, howe be it in the spyryte he speaketh mysteryes.

3 But he that prophecyeth, speaketh vnto men, to edifiynge, to exhortation and to comforte.

4 He that speaketh wyth tounges profyteth hym selfe: he that prophecieth edifyeth the congregation.

5 I woulde that ye all spake with tounges: but rather that ye prophecyed. For greater is he that prophecieth, then he that speaketh with tounges, excepte he expounde it also, that the congregacion maye haue edifiyng.

6 Nowe brethren yf I come vnto you speakinge with tounges, what shall I profite you,

excepte I speake vnto you, other by reuelation or knowledge, or propheciynge, or doctryne.

7 Moreouer when thynges wythout lyfe, geue sounde: whether it be a pipe or an harpe excepte they make a distinction in the soundes, howe shal it be knowen what is piped or harped?

8 And also yf the trompe geue an vncertaine voice, who shall prepare him selfe to fyght?

9 Euen so likewyse when ye speake with tounges, excepte ye speake wordes that haue signifycacion, howe shall it be vnderstande what is spoken? For ye shall but speake in the ayer.

10 Manye kindes of voices are in the worlde and none of them are wythout significacion.

11 If I knowe not what the voice meaneth, I shalbe vnto hym that speaketh, an alient: and he that speaketh shall be alient vnto me

12 Euen so ye (for as much as ye couete spiritual gyftes) seke that ye maye haue plentye vnto the edifiyng of the congregation.

13 Wherfore let him that speaketh with tounges praye, that he maye interprete also.

14 If I praye wyth tounges, my spyryte prayeth: but my mynde is wythout fruite.

15 What is it then? I wyl praye with the spirite, and wyll praye with mynde also. I wil singe with the spyrite, and wil singe with the minde also.

16 For els when thou blessest with the spirite howe shal he that occupieth the roume of the vnlearned saye amen at thy geuynge of thankes, saynge: he vnderstandeth not what thou sayeste?

17 Thou verelye geueste thankes wel, but the other is not edifyed.

18 I thanke my God, I speake with tounges more then ye all.

19 Yet had I leuer in the congregation, to speake fyue wordes with my mynd to the information of other, rather then .x. thousand wordes with the tounge.

20 Brethren be not chyldren in wyt howebeit as conceringe maliciousnes be children: but in wyt be perfect.

21 In the lawe it is written, wyth other tounges, and with other lippes wyl I speake vnto thys people, and yet for al that wil they not heare me, sayeth the Lorde.

22 Wherfore, tounges are for a signe, not to them that beleue, but to them that beleue not. Contrarywyse propheciyng serueth not, for them that beleue not: but for them whiche beleue.

23 Yf therfore when all the congregation is come together, and all speake wyth tounges, there come in they that are vnlearned, or they whyche beleue not: wyll they not saye that ye are out of your wyttes?

24 But and yf all prophecye, and there come in one that beleueth not, or one vnlearned, he is rebuked of al men, and is iudged of euerye man:

25 and so are the secretes of hys herte opened, and so falleth he doune on hys face, and worshyppeth God, & sayeth that God is wyth you in dede.

26 Howe is it then brethren? When ye come together, euerye man hath his songe, hath his doctryne, hath his tounge, hath hys reuelation, hath hys interpretation. Let al thynges be done vnto edifiynge.

27 If anye man speake wyth tounges, let it be two at ones, or at the moste thre at ones, and that by course: and let another interprete it.

28 But yf there be no interpreter, let him kepe silence in the congregation, and let him speake to him selfe and to God.

29 Let the Prophetes speake two at ones, or thre at ones, and let other iudge.

30 And yf anye reuelation be made to another that sitteth by, let the fyrste holde hys peace.

31 For ye maye all prophecye, one by one that all maye learne, and all maye haue comforte.

32 For the spirites of the Prophetes are in the power of þe Prophetes.

33 For God is not causer of strife, but of peace, as he is in all other congregations of the sainctes.

34 Let your wyues kepe silence in the congregations. For it is not permitted vnto them to speake: but let them be vnder obedience, as sayeth the lawe.

35 If they wil learne anye thynge, let them axe theyr husbandes at home. For it is shame for women to speake in the congregation.

36 Spronge the worde of God from you? Eyther came it vnto you onelye.

37 Yf anye man thinke hym selfe a Prophet, either spyrytuall. let him vnderstand, what thinges I write vnto you. For they are the commaundementes of the Lorde.

38 But and yf anye man be ignoraunte, let him be ignoraunt.

39 Wherfore brethren couete to prophecye, and forbyd not to speake wyth tounges.

40 And let al thynges be done honestlye and iu ordre.

# CHAPTER 15

BRETHREN as pertaininge to the Gospel, whiche I preached vnto you, whiche ye haue also accepted, and in the whiche ye continue,

2 by whiche also ye are saued: I do you to wit, after what maner I preached vnto you yf ye kepe it, except ye haue beleued in vaine.

3 For fyrste of al I deliuered vnto you that which I receiued how that Christe dyd for oure synnes, agreinge to the scriptures:

4 and that he was buried, and that he rose agayne the thyrde daye accordinge to the scriptures

5 and that he was sene of Cephas, then of the twelue.

6 After that he was sene of more then fyue hundred brethren at ones of whiche manie remaine vnto this daie, and many are fallen a slepe.

7 After that appeared he to Iames, then to al the Apostles.

8 And last of al, he was sene of me, as of one that was borne out of due time.

9 For I am the leste of al the Apostles, whiche am not worthy to be called an Apostle, because I persecuted the congregation of God.

10 But by þe grace of God I am that I am. And his grace which is in me, was not in vaine, but I laboured more aboundantly then they al, not I but the grace of God which is with me.

11 Whether it were I or they, so we preache, and so haue ye beleued.

12 If Christe be preached howe that he rose from death: howe saye some? that are amonge you, that there is no resurreccion from death?

13 If ther be no rysinge agayne from death, then is Christe not rysen.

14 If Christ be not rysen, then is our preachinge vayne, and your faith is also in vaine.

15 Ye and we are founde false witnesses of God. For we haue testifyed of God, howe that he raysed vp Christe, whom he raysed not vp yf it be so that the deade ryse not vp againe.

16 For yf the dead rise not againe then is Christ not rysen againe.

17 Yf it be so þt Christe rose not, then is youre faith in vayne, and yet are ye in youre synnes.

18 And ther to they which are fallen a slepe in Christ, are peryshed.

19 If in thys lyfe onelye we beleue on Christ, then are we of all men the miserablest.

20 But now in Christ rysen from the dead, and is become the fyrste fruytes of them that slepte.

21 For by a man came death, and by a man came the resurceccion of the dead.

22 For as by Adam all dye: euen so by Christe, shall all be made aliue,

23 and euery man in his owne order. The fyrste is Christe, then they that are Christes at his comminge.

24 Then commeth the ende when he hath delyuered vp the kyngedome to God the father, when he hath put doune all rule, authoritie, and power.

25 For he muste reigne tyll he haue put all hys enemies vnder his fete.

26 The laste enemy that shalbe destroied is death.

27 For he hath put all thinges vnder hys fete. But when he sayeth, all thinges are put vnder hym it is manifest that he is excepted, whyche dyd put all thinges vnder him.

28 When all thinges are subdued vnto hym: then shall the sonne also him selfe be subiecte to him that put al thinges, vnder him that God maye be all in all thinges.

29 Eyther els what do they, which are baptysed ouer the dead, yf the dead ryse not at all? Why are they then baptysed ouer the dead?

30 yea and why stande we in ieoperdy euerye houre?

31 By our reioysinge, whyche I haue in Christe Iesu our Lorde, I dye dayly.

32 That I haue fought wyth beastes at Ephesus, after the maner of men what auauntageth it me, yf þe dead rise not againe? Let vs eate and drincke, to morowe we shall dye.

33 Be not deceiued: malicious speakinges corrupte good maners.

34 Awake truelye out of slepe and synne not. For some haue not the knowledge of God. I speake this vnto you: rebuke.

35 But some man wyl saye: howe aryse the dead? wyth what bodyes come they in?

36 Thou fole, that whiche thou sowest is not quickened except it dye.

37 And what sowest thou? Thou sowest not that bodye that shall be, but are corne (I meane either of what, or of some other)

38 and God geueth it a body at his pleasure, to euery seede a seuerall body.

39 Al fleshe is not one maner of fleshe: but there is one maner fleshe of men, another maner fleshe of beastes, another maner fleshe of fyshes, and another of byrdes.

40 There are celestiall bodyes, and there are bodyes terrestriall. But the glorye of the celestiall is one, and the glorye of the terrestriall another.

41 There is one maner glory of þe sunne and another glorye of the mone, and another glory of the starres. For one starre dyffereth from another in glorye.

42 So is the resurreccion of the dead. It is sowen in corruption, and ryseth in incorruption.

43 It is sowen in dishonoure, and ryseth in honoure. It is sowen in weakenes, and ryseth in power. It is sowen a naturall bodye, and ryseth a spyrytuall bodye.

44 There is a naturall bodye, and there is a spiritual bodye,

45 as it is written: the fyrste man Adam was made a lyuinge soule, and the last Adam was made a quickeninge spirite.

46 Howbeit that is not fyrste whiche is spyrytual: but that which is naturall, and then that which is spyrytual.

47 The fyrste man is of the earth, earthlye: the seconde man

is the Lorde from heauen.

48 As is the earthlye, such are they that are earthlye. And as is the heauenlye, suche are they that are heauenlye.

49 And as we haue borne þe ymage of the earthly so shal we beare the Image of the heauenlye.

50 This saye I brethren, that fleshe and bloude can not inheryte the kyngedome of God. Neyther corruption inheryte: vncorruption.

51 Beholde I shewe you a mysterye. We shal not al slepe: but we shal al be chaunged,

52 and that in a momente & in the twinkling of an eye, at the sound of the last trompe. For the trompe shall blowe, and the dead shal rise incorruptible and we shal be chaunged.

53 For this corruptible must put on incorruptibilitie; and this mortal muste put on immortalytye.

54 When this corruptible, hath put on incorruptibilitie, and this mortal hath put on immortalite, then shalbe brought to passe the saiyng that is written.

55 Death is consumed into victory. Death wher is thy stynge? Hel wher is thy victory?

56 The stinge of death is sinne: & the strength of sinne is the lawe.

57 But thankes be vnto God, which hath geuen vs victory, thorowe our Lorde Iesus Christ.

58 Therfore my deare brethren, be ye stedfast and vnmouable alwayes ryche in the workes of þe Lorde, for as much as ye knowe, howe that your labour is not in vaine in the Lorde.

## CHAPTER 16

OF the gatheringe for the sainctes, as I haue ordeined in the congregations of Galatia, euen, so do ye.

2 Vpon some sonday let euerye one of you put a syde at home, and laye vp whatsoeuer he thinketh meate that there be no gatheringes when I come.

3 When I am come, whomsoeuer ye shall alowe by youre letters, them will I sende to bringe your liberalitie vnto Ierusalem.

4 And yf it be mete that I go, they shal go with me.

5 I wyl come vnto you after I haue gone ouer Macedonia. For I wyl go throughout Macedonia.

6 With you peraduenture I wil abide a while, or els winter, that ye maye bringe me on my waye whethersoeuer I go.

7 I wil not se you nowe in my passage: but I truste to abyde a while wyth you, yf God shal suffer me.

8 I wyll tary at Ephesus vntyl whitsontyde.

9 For a greate dore, and a frutefull is opened to me, and there are manye aduersaryes.

10 If Timotheus come, se that he be with you. For he worketh the worke of the Lorde as I do.

11 Let no man despyse hym: but conuaye hym forthe in peace, that he maye come vnto me. For I loke for hym wyth the brethren.

12 To speake of brother Apollo: I greatlye desyred hym to come vnto you wyth the brethren but hys mynd was not at all to come at this tyme. Howbeit he wil come when he shal haue conueniente tyme.

13 Watche ye, stande faste in the fayth, quyte you lyke men and be stronge,

14 & let youre busynes be done in loue.

15 Brethren (ye know the house of Stephana, howe that they are the fyrste fruites of Achaia, and that they haue appoynted them selues to minister vnto the sainctes)

16 I beseche you that ye be obedient vnto suche, and to all that helpe and laboure.

17 I am glad of the comminge of Stephana, Fortunatus and Achaichus: for that which was lackinge on youre parte, they haue supplied.

18 They haue comforted my spyrite and youres. Loke therfore that ye knowe them that are suche.

19 The congregations of Asia salute you. Aquila and Priscylla salute you muche in the Lorde, and so doth the congregation that is in theyr house.

20 Al the brethren grete you. Grete ye one another wyth an holy kysse.

21 The salutation of me Paule with myne owne hande.

22 Yf anye man loue not the Lorde Iesus Christ the same be anathema maranatha.

23 The grace of the Lorde Iesus Christe be wyth you all,

24 My loue be wyth you all in Christe Iesus. Amen.

# 2 Corinthians

## CHAPTER 1

Paule an Apostle of Iesu Christ by the wyll of God, and brother Timotheus. Vnto the congregation of God, whithe is at Corinthum, with all the sainctes, which are in all Achaia.

2 Grace be wyth you, and peace from God oure father, and from the Lorde Iesus Christ.

3 Blessed be God the father of oure Lorde Iesus Christ, the father of mercy, and þe God of all comforte,

4 whiche comforteth vs in all oure tribulacion, in so muche that we are able to comforte them, which are troubled in whatsoeuer tribulation it be, with the same comforte wherwith we our selues are comforted of God.

5 For as the affliccions of Christ are plenteous in vs: euen so is our consolacion plenteous by Christe.

6 Whether we be troubled for youre consolacion & saluacion, whiche saluacion, sheweth her power in that ye suffer the same afflictions which we also suffer: or whether we be comforted for your consolacion, and saluation,

7 yet oure hope is stedfast for you, in as muche as we knowe howe that as ye haue youre parte in affliccions, so shall ye be partakers of consolacion.

8 Brethren I woulde not haue you ignoraunt of oure trouble, whiche happened vnto vs in Asia. For we were greued out of measure passinge strength, so greatlye that we despeared euen of lyfe.

9 Also we receiued and aunswere of death in our selues, and that because we woulde not put oure truste in oure selues: but in God, whiche rayseth þe dead to lyfe again,

10 & which delyuered vs from so greate a death, and doth delyuer. On whom we truste that yet here after he will delyuer,

11 by the helpe of your prayer for vs: that by the meanes of manye occasions, thankes maye be geuen of manye on our behalfe, for þe grace geuen vnto vs.

12 Oure reioysinge is this, the testimony of oure conscience, that in synglenes and Godly purenes, and not in fleshely wysdome, but by the grace of God, we haue had oure conuersation in the worlde, and moste of all to youwardes.

13 We write no nother thinges vnto you, then that ye read and also knowe, yea & I truste ye shall fynde vs vnto the ende euen as ye haue founde vs partelye,

14 for we are your reioysinge, euen as ye are oures in the day of the Lorde Iesus.

15 And in this confidence was I minded the other tyme to haue come vnto you, that ye myghte haue had yet one pleasure more,

16 and to haue passed by you into Macedonia, and to haue come againe out of Macedonia vnto you, & to haue bene led forth to Iewryward of you.

17 When I thus wyse was mynded: dyd I vse lyghtnes? Or thynke I carnallye those thinges, which I thinke? that with me should be yea yea, and nay nay?

18 God is faithfull. For oure preaching vnto you, was not yea & nay.

19 For Gods sonne Iesus Christe, whiche was preached amonge you by vs (that is to saye, by me and Siluanus and Timotheus) was not yea and naye, but in him it was yea:

20 For all the promyses of God, in him are yea, and are in him Amen, vnto the lande of God thorow vs.

21 For it is God, whiche stablisheth you and vs in Christ, and hath annointed vs,

22 which hath also sealed vs, and hath geuen the earnest of the spyryte into oure hertes.

23 I call God for a recorde vnto my soule that for to fauer you withall I came not anye more to Corinthum.

24 Not that we be lordes ouer youre fayth but helpers of youce ioye. For by fayth ye stand.

## CHAPTER 2

But I determyned thys in my selfe, þt I wold not come agayne to you in heauynes.

2 For yf I make you sorye, who is it that shoulde make me glad, but the same which is made sorye by me?

3 And I wrote thys same Epistle vnto you, leste yf I came, I shoulde take heauines of them, of whome I ought to reioyce. Certaynely thys confidence haue I in you al, that my ioye is the ioye of you al.

4 For in great affliction and anguyshe of herte I wrote vnto you with many teares: not to make you sory, but that ye myght perceyue the loue which I haue most specially vnto you.

5 Yf anye man haue caused sorowe the same hath not made me sory, but partelye: leaste I shoulde greue you all.

6 It is suffycyente vnto the same man, that he was rebuked of many.

7 So that nowe contrarywyse ye ought to forgeue hym, and comforte hym: leaste that same persone shoulde be swalowed vp, with ouer muche heauynes.

8 Wherfore I exhorte you, þt loue maye haue strengthe ouer hym.

9 For this cause verely dyd I wryte, that I might know the profe of you, whether ye shoulde be obedyent in all thynges.

10 To whom ye forgeue any thynge, I forgeue also. And verelye yf I forgeue anye thynge, to whome I forgaue it, for your sakes forgaue I it in the roume of Christe,

11 leaste Sathan shoulde preuente vs. For thys thoughtes are not vnknowen vnto vs.

12 When I was come to Troada for Christes gospels sake (and a greate dore was opened vnto me of the Lorde)

13 I had no rest in my spyryte, because I founde not Titus my brother: but toke my leaue of them, and wente awaye vnto Macedonia.

14 Thankes be vnto God whiche alwayes geueth vs the victorye in Christ, and openeth the sauour of hys knowledge by vs in euerye place.

15 For we are vnto God the swete sauoure of Christe, bothe amonge them that are saued, and also among them whiche peryshe.

16 To the one part are we the sauoure of death vnto death. And vnto the other parte are we the lauoure of lyfe vnto lyfe. And who is mete vnto these thynges?

17 For we are not as many are which choppe & chaunge with the worde of god: but euen out of purenes, and by the power of God, and in the syghte of God, so speake we in Christe.

## CHAPTER 3

We begynne to prayse oure selues agayne. Nede we as some other, of Epistles, of recommendacion vnto you? or letters of recommendacyon from you?

2 Ye are oure Epistle wrytten in oure hertes, which is vnderstande and read of, all men,

3 in that ye are knowen, howe that ye are the Epistle of Christe, ministred by vs and writen, not wyth ynke, but wyth the spirite of the lyuyng God, not in tables of stone, but in fleshly tables of the herte.

4 Suche truste haue we throughe Christe to Godwarde

5 not that we are suffyciente of our selues to thynke any thynge as it were of our selues, but our ablenes cometh of God,

6 which hath made vs able to minister the new testament, not of the letter, but of the spirite. For the letter killeth, but the spirite geueth lyfe.

7 Yf the mynystracyon of death throughe þe letters fygured in stones was gloryous, so that the chyldren of Israell coulde not behold the face of Moyses for the glory of hys countenaunce (whiche glory neuerthelesse is done awaye)

8 why shall not the ministracion of the spiryte be muche more gloryous?

9 For yf the ministrynge of condempnacyon be glorious, muche more doeth the ministracyon of ryghtuousnes excede in glorye.

10 For no doubte that which was there glorifyed is not once gloryfyed in respecte of thys excedynge glorye.

11 Then yf that whih is destroyed was gloryous muche more shall that whiche remayneth, be gloryous.

12 Seynge then that we haue suche trust, we vse great boldnes,

13 and do not as Moyses, whiche put a vayle ouer hys face that þe children of Israell shoulde not se, for what purpose that serued whiche is put awaye.

14 But theyr myndes were blynded. For vntil thys daye remayneth the same couerynge vntaken awaye in the olde testament when they reade it, whiche in Christe is put awaye.

15 But euen vnto thys daye when Moyses is reade, the vayle hangeth before theyr hertes.

16 Neuerthelesse when they turne to the Lorde, the vayle shalbe taken awaye.

17 The Lorde no doubte is a spiryte. And where the spiryte of the Lorde is, there is libertye.

18 But we all beholde the glorye of the Lorde with hys face open, and chaunged vnto the same similitude, from glorye to glory, euen of the spirite of the Lorde.

## CHAPTER 4

Therfore seynge that we haue suche an offyce, euen

as mercye is come on vs, we faynte not:

2 but haue caste from vs the clokes of vnhonestye, and walke not in craftynes, neyther corrupte we þe word of God: but walke in open trueth, & reporte our selues to euerye mans conscience in the syght of God.

3 Yf oure Gospell be yet hyd, it is hyd among them that are loste,

4 in whome the God of thys worlde hath blynded the myndes of them which beleue not, leste the lyght of the gloryous gospell of Christe which is the ymage of God shoulde shyne vnto them.

5 For we preache not oure selues, but Christ Iesus to be the Lorde, and oure selues youre seuauntes for Iesus sake.

6 For it is God that commaunded the lighte to shyne out of darknes, whiche hath shyned in oure hertes, for to geue the lyghte of the knoweledge of the glorye of God, in the face of Iesus Christe.

7 But we haue thys treasure in earthen vessels that the excellent power of it myght appeare to be of God, and not of vs.

8 We are troubled on euerye syde, yet are we not withoute shyfte. We are in pouerte, but not vtterlye withoute some what.

9 We are persecuted, but are not forsaken. We are caste doune, neuerthelesse we peryshe not.

10 And we alwayes beare in oure bodyes the dyinge of the Lorde Iesus, that the lyfe of Iesus myght appeare in oure bodyes.

11 For we whiche lyue are alwayes delyuered vnto deathe for Iesus sake, that the lyfe also of Iesu myghte appeare in oure mortall fleshe.

12 So then death worketh in vs, and lyfe in you.

13 Seynge then we haue the same spirite of fayth, accordynge as it is written: I beleued, & therfor haue I spoken. We also beleue, & therfore speake.

14 For we knowe þt he which raysed vp þe Lord Iesus, shal rayse vp vs also by the meanes of Iesus, & shall set vs wt you.

15 For all thynges do I for youre sakes, that the plentuous grace by thankes geuen of manye, maye redounde to the prayse of God.

16 Wherfor we are not weryed, but though oure outwarde man perysh: yet the inwarde man is renewed daye by daye.

17 For oure excedynge trybulation whiche is momentanye and lyghte, prepareth an excedynge and eternall wayghte of glory vnto vs,

18 whyle we loke not on the thinges whiche are sene, but on the thinges which are not sene. For thynges whiche are sene, are temporall, but thynges whiche are not sene, are eternall.

# CHAPTER 5

We knowe surelye yf oure earthy mansyon wherin we nowe dwell were destroyed, that we haue a buyldynge ordeyned of God an habitacyon not made with handes, but eternall in heauen.

2 And therfore syghe we, desyrynge to be clothed wyth oure mansyon which is from heauen

3 so yet yf that we be founde clothed, and not naked.

4 For as longe as we are in thys tabernacle, we syghe and are greued, for we woulde not be vnclothed, but woulde be clothed vpon, þt mortalitye myghte be swalowed vp of lyfe.

5 He that ordeyned vs for thys thynge, is God whiche very same hath geuen vnto vs þe earnest of the spiryte.

6 Therfore we are alwaye of good chere, & knowe well that as longe as we are at home in the bodye, we are absente from God.

7 For we walke in fayth, and se not.

8 Neuerthelesse we are of good comforte, and had leuer be absente from the bodye, and to be presente with the Lorde.

9 Wherfore whether we be at home or from home, we endeuoure oure selues to please hym.

10 For we muste all appeare before the iudgement seate of Christ, that euery man maye receyue the workes of hys bodye accordyng to that he hath done, whether it be good or badde?

11 Seynge then that we know, how the Lorde is to be feared, we fare fayre with men. For we are knowen well ynoughe vnto God. I truste also that we are knowen in your consciences.

12 We prayse not oure selues agayne vnto you, but geue you an occasyon to reioyce of vs that ye maye haue somewhat agaynst them whiche reioyce in the face, and not in the hert,

13 For yf we be to feruente, to God we are to feruente. Yf we kepe measure, for youre cause kepe we measure.

14 For the loue of Christ constrayneth vs, because we thus iudge, yf one be dead, for all that then are all dead,

15 and that he dyed for all, that they which lyue, shoulde not hence forth lyue vnto them selues, but vnto hym, whiche dyed for them, and rose agayne.

16 Wherfore hence forthe knowe we no man after the fleshe. In so muche though we haue knowen Christe after the fleshe, nowe hence forth knowe we hym so no more.

17 Therfore yf anye man be in Christe, he is a newe creature. Olde thynges are passed awaye, beholde all thynges are become newe.

18 Neuerthelesse all thynges

are of God, whiche hath reconcyled vs vnto hym selfe by Iesus Christe, and hath geuen vnto vs the offyce to preache the attonement.

19 For God was in Christe, and made agrement betwene the worlde and hym selfe, and imputed not theyr synnes vnto them, & hathe committed to vs the preachynge of the atonnement.

20 Nowe then are we messengers in the roume of Christ: euen as thoughe God dyd beseche you thorowe vs: So praye we you in Christes stede, that ye be atone with God,

21 for he hath made hym to be synne for vs, whiche knewe no synne, þt we by hys meanes should be that ryghtuousnes whiche before God is allowed.

## CHAPTER 6

We as healpers therfore exhorte you, that ye receyue not the grace of God in vayne.

2 For he sayeth: I haue hearde the in a tyme accepted: and in the day of saluacyon. haue I succoured the. Beholde nowe is that well accepted tyme: behold now is that daye of saluacyon.

3 Let vs geue no man occasyon of euyll, that in our offyce be founde no faulte,

4 but in al thynges let vs behaue our selues as the ministers of God. In muche pacience, in afflictions, in necessitie, in anguishe,

5 in strypes, in prysonnement in stryfe, in laboure, in watchynge, in fasting

6 in purenes, in knoweledge, in longe suffering in kyndnes, in the holye ghoste, in loue vnfayned,

7 in the wordes of trueth, in the power of God, in the armour of ryghtuousnes on the ryght hande, and on the lyfte,

8 in honoure and dishonour, in euyll reporte, & good reporte: as disceyuers & yet true:

9 as vnknowen, & yet knowen: as dying, & beholde we yet liue: as chastened and not kylled:

10 as sorowyng, & yet alway mery: as poore, and yet make many ryche: as hauynge nothynge, and yet possessynge all thynges.

11 O ye Corinthyans, oure mouth is open vnto you. Oure hertes made large:

12 ye are in no strayte in vs, but are in a strayte in youre owne bowelles:

13 I promyse you lyke rewarde with me, as to my chyldren.

14 Sette your selues therfore at large, and beare not a straungers yoke with the vnbeleuers. For what feloweshyppe hath ryghtuousnes with vnryghtuousnes? What companye hath lyght with darkenes?

15 What concorde hath Christe with Belyall? Eyther what parte hath he that beleueth with an infydele?

16 Howe agreeth the temple of God with Images. And ye are the temple of that lyuynge God, as sayed God. I wyll dwell amonge them, and walke among them, and wyll be theyr God, and they shall be my people.

17 Wherfore come out from among them, and separate youre selues (sayeth the Lorde) and touche none vncleane thynge: so wyll I receyue you,

18 and wyll be a father vnto you, and ye shall be vnto me sonnes and doughters, sayth the Lorde almyghtye.

## CHAPTER 7

Seynge that we haue such promyses dearely beloued, let vs cleanse oure selues from al fylthynesse of the fleshe & spyrite, and grow vp to full holynesse in the feare of God.

2 Vnderstande vs. We haue hurte no man: we haue corrupt no man: we haue defrauded no man.

3 I speake not thys to condempne you: for I haue shewed you before, þt ye are in oure hertes to dye, and lyue wyth you.

4 I am very bolde ouer you, and reioyce gentelye in you. I am fylled with comforte, and am excedynge ioyouse in all oure trybulatyons.

5 For when we were come into Macedonia, our flesh had no rest, but we were troubled on euerye syde. Outwarde was fyghtynge, inwarde was feare.

6 Neuerthelesse GOD that comforteth the abiect, comforteth vs at the comming of Tytus.

7 And not with hys commynge onelye: but also wyth the consolacyon wherewith he was comforted of you. For he tolde vs youre desyre, youre mournyng, youre feruent mynde to me warde, so that I now reioyce the more.

8 Wherfore thoughe I made you sory with a letter, I repent not, though I dyd repent. For I perceyue that, that same Epistle made you sory, thoughe it were but for a season.

9 But I nowe reioyce, not that ye were sory, but that ye so sorowed, that ye repented. For ye sorowed Godlye, so that in nothyng ye were hurt by vs.

10 For Godly sorowe causeth repentaunce vnto saluacyon, not to be repented of: when worldlye sorowe causeth death.

11 Beholde, what diligence thys Godlye sorowe that ye toke, hath wroughte in you: yea it caused you to cleare your selues. It caused indignacyon, it caused feare, it caused desyre, it caused a feruent mynde, it caused punyshement. For in all thynges ye haue shewed your selues that

ye are cleare in that matter.

12 Wherfore thoughe I wrote vnto you: I dyd it not for hys cause that dyd hurte, neyther for hys cause that was hurt: but that our good mynd whiche we haue towarde you in the syght of God, myght appeare vnto you.

13 Therfore we are comforted, because ye are comforted: yea and excedynglye the more ioyed we, for the ioye that Titus had, because his spyryte was refreshed of you all.

14 I am therfore, not nowe ashamed, though I bosted my selfe to hym of you. For as all thynges which I preached vnto you are true, euen so is oure bostyng, that I bosted my selfe to Titus with all, founde true.

15 And nowe is his inwarde affection more aboundante towarde you, when he remembreth the obedience of euerye one of you, howe with feare and tremblynge ye receyued hym,

16 I reioyce that. I maye be bolde ouer you in all thynges.

## CHAPTER 8

I do you to wyt brethren, of the grace of God, which is geuen in the congregacyons of Macedonia,

2 howe that the aboundaunce of theyr reioysynge is, that they are tryed with muche trybulacyon. And therto thoughe they were excedynge poore, yet haue they geuen excedynge richelye, and that in synglenesse.

3 For to theyr powers (I beare recorde) ye and beyonde theyr power, they were wyllynge of theyr owne accorde,

4 & prayed vs with great instaunce that we would receyue theyr benefyte, and suffer them to be partakers with other in mynystrynge to the saynctes.

5 And thys they dyd, not as we loked for: but gaue theyr owne selues fyrste to the Lorde, and after vnto vs by the wyl of God:

6 so that we coulde not but desyre Titus to accomplyshe the same beneuolence amonge you also, euen as he had begonne.

7 Nowe therfore, as ye are ryche in al partties in fayth, in worde, in knoweledge, in all feruentnes, and in loue, which ye haue to vs: euen so se that ye be plenteous in thys beneuolence.

8 Thys saye I not as commaundyng: but because other are so feruente, therfore proue I youre loue, whether it be perfecte or no.

9 Ye knowe the lyberalytie of oure Lorde Iesus Christe, whiche though he were ryche, yet for youre sakes became pore that ye thorowe hys pouertye myght be made ryche.

10 And I geue counsell hereto. For thys is expediente for you, whiche beganne, not to do onelye, but also to wyll, a yeare a go.

11 Nowe therfore performe the dede: that as there was in you a redynes to wyll, euen so ye may performe the dede of that whiche ye haue.

12 For yf there be fyrste a wyllynge mynde, it is accepted accordyng to that a man hath, and not accordynge to that he hath not.

13 It is not my mynde that other be set at ease, and ye broughte into combraunce:

14 but þt there be equalnes nowe at thys tyme, þt youre aboundaunce succoure theyr lacke: that theyr aboundaunce maye supplye youre lacke:

15 that there may be equalitie, agreyng to that which is wryten. He that gathered muche, had neuer the more aboundaunce, and he that gathered lyttell had neuerthelesse.

16 Thankes be vnto God, which put in the hert of Titus the same good mynde towarde you.

17 For he accepted þe requeste, yea rather he was so well willyng þt of hys owne accorde he came vnto you.

18 We haue sente with him that brother whose lande is the Gospell thorowe out all the congregacyons,

19 and not so onely, but is also chosen of the congregacyons to be a felowe with vs in oure iorneye concernynge thys beneuolence that is ministred by vs vnto the prayse of the Lorde, and to stere vp youre prompte mynde.

20 For this we eschue, that anye man shoulde rebuke vs in thys plentuous distribucyon, þt is ministred by vs,

21 and therfore make prouision for honest thynges, not in the syghte of God onelye, but also in the syght of men.

22 We haue sent with them a brother of ours whome we haue oftentimes proued diligente in many thinges, but now much more diligent.

23 The greate confydence whiche I haue in you hath caused me thus to do, partely for Tytus sake, whiche is my felowe and helper as concernynge you, partely because of other which are oure brethren, and the messengers of the congregacyons, and the glorye of Christe.

24 Wherfore shewe vnto them the profe of your loue, and of the reioysynge that we haue of you, that the congregacyons maye se it.

## CHAPTER 9

Of the ministrynge to the sayncles, it is but superfluous for me to wryte vnto you:

2 for I knowe your redynes of mynde whereof I boste my selfe vnto them of Macedonia, and saye that Achaia was

prepared a yeare a go, and youre feruentnes hath prouoked manye.

3 Neuerthelesse yet haue I sent these brethren, lest oure reioysynge ouer you shoulde be in vayne in thys behalfe, and that ye (as I haue sayed) prepare your selues,

4 lest parauenture yf they of Macedonia come with me, and fynde you vnprepared, the bost þt I made in thys matter, shoulde be a shame to vs. I saye not vnto you.

5 Wherfore I thought it necessarye to exhorte the brethren, to come before hande vnto you, for to prepare your good blessyng promysed afore, that it myght be redye, so that it be a blessynge, and not a defraudynge.

6 Thys yet remember, howe that he whiche soweth lyttell, shal reape lyttell, & he that soweth plentuously, shall reape plentuously.

7 And let euery man do accordyng as he hath purposed in hys hert, not groundgingly, or of necessitie. For God loueth a chearefull geuer.

8 God is able to make you ryche in al grace that ye in al thynges hauyng suffycyent vnto the vttermoste, maye be ryche vnto all maner good workes,

9 as it is wrytten. He that sparsed abroade, and hath geuen to the pore, hys ryghtuousnes, remayneth for euer.

10 He that fyndeth the sower seed, shall minister breade for fode, and shall multyplye your seede and increace the frutes of youre ryghtuousnes that on all partyes,

11 ye maye be made riche in all synglenes, whiche causeth thorowe vs, thankes geuynge vnto God.

12 For the offyce of thys ministracyon, not onelye supplyeth the neede of the saynctes: but also is aboundaunte herein, that for thys laudable mynystrynge, thankes myghte be geuen to God of many,

13 whiche prayse God for the obedience of youre professyng the Gospell of Christe, and for youre synglenes in distrybutynge to them and to all men,

14 and in theyr prayers to God for you, long after you, for the aboundaunce grace of God geuen vnto you.

15 Thankes be vnto God for hys vnspakeable gyfte.

## CHAPTER 10

I Paule my selfe beseche you by the mekenesse and softenes of Christe, whiche when I am present amonge you, am of no reputacion, but am bolde toward you beynge absent,

2 I beseche you, that I nede not to be bolde, when I am present (with that same confydence, wherewith I am supposed to be bolde) agaynste some whiche repute vs as though we walked carnally.

3 Neuerthelesse thoughe we walke compassed wt the fleshe, yet we ware not fleshly.

4 For the weapens of oure warre are not carnal thynges, but thynges myghtye in God to caste doune stronge holdes,

5 wherewith we ouerthrowe Imaginations and euerye hye thynge that exalteth it selfe agaynste the knoweledge of God, and brynge into captiuite all vnderstandynge to the obedience of Christe,

6 and are redye to take vengeaunce on all disobedience, when youre obedience is fulfylled.

7 Loke ye on thynges after the vtter apparence? Yf any man truste in hym selfe that he is Christes, let the same also consydre of him self that as he is Christes, euen so are we Christes

8 and thoughe I shoulde boste my selfe some what more of oure authoritie which the Lord hath geuen vs to edifye, and not to destroye you, it shoulde not be to my shame.

9 This say I, leste I shoulde seme, as thoughe I went about to make you afrayde with letters.

10 For þe Epystles (sayeth he) are sore and stronge, but hys bodely presence is weake, and hys speach rude.

11 Let hym that is suche, thynke on thys wyse, þt as we are in wordes by letters when we are absent, such are we in dedes when we are present.

12 For we can not fynde in oure hertes to make oure selues of the numbre of them, or to compare oure selues to them, whiche laud them selues, neuerthelesse while they measure them selues wyth them selues, and compare them selues with them selues, they vnderstande nought.

13 But we wyll not reioyce aboue measure: but accordynge to the quantitye of the measure, whiche God hath distrybuted vnto vs, a measure that reacheth euen vnto you.

14 For we stretche not oure selues beyonde measure, as thoughe we had not reacheth vnto you. For euen vnto you haue we come with the Gospell of Christe,

15 and we boste not oure selues out of measure in other mens labours. Yea, and we hope, when your fayth is increased amonge you, to be magnifyed accordynge to oure measure more largelye,

16 and to preache the Gospell in those regyons, whiche are beyonde you: and not to reioyce of that whiche is by another mans measure prepared already.

17 Let hym that reioyceth, reioyce in þe Lord.

18 For he that prayseth hym self, is not allowed: but he whom the Lorde prayseth.

# CHAPTER 11

WOLDE to God ye coulde suffre me a lytell in my folyshenes: yea, and I praye you, forbeare me.

2 For I am gelous ouer you with godly gelousye. For I coupled you to one man, to make you a chaste virgyn to Christe.

3 But I feare leste as þe serpente begyled Eue thorowe hys suttelty, euen so youre wyttes shoulde be corrupte from the synglenes that is in Christe.

4 For yf he that commeth, preache another Iesus then hym whom we preached: or yf ye receyue another spiryte then that whiche ye haue receyued: other another Gospell then that ye haue receyued, ye mygth ryghte well haue bene content.

5 I impose that I was not behynde þe chief Apostles.

6 Though I be rude in speakynge, yet I am not so in knoweledge. Howe be it amonge you: we are knowen to the vttermoste what we are in all thynges.

7 Dyd I therein synne, because I submytted my selfe, that ye myght be exalted, and because I preached to you the Gospell of God fre?

8 I robbed other congergacyons, and toke wages of them, to do you seruyce with al.

9 And when I was present with you, and had nede, I was greuous to no man, for that whiche was lackynge vnto me, the brethren whiche came from Macedonia, supplyed: and in all thynge I kept my selfe that I shoulde not be greuous to you, & so wyl I kepe my selfe.

10 Yf the trueth of Christe be in me, thys reioysynge shall not be taken from me in the regyons of Achaia.

11 Wherfore? Because I loue you not? God knoweth.

12 Neuerthelesse what I do, that wyll I do, to cut awaye occasyon from them which desyre occasyon, that they myght be founde lyke vnto vs in that wherein they reioyce.

13 For these false Apostles are disceytfull workers, and fashyon them selues lyke vnto the Apostles of Christe.

14 And no maruail for Satan hym selfe is chaunged into the fashyon of an angell of lyghte.

15 Therfore it is no greate thynge, thoughe hys mynysters fashyon them selues as thoughe they were the mynisters of rightuousnes, whose end shalbe accordynge to theyr dedes.

16 I saye agayne, lest anye man thynke that I am folyshe, or els euen nowe take me as a fole, that I maye boaste my selfe a lyttell.

17 That I speake, I speake it not after the wayes of the Lorde, but as it were folishly, while we are nowe come to bostynge.

18 Seyng that manye reioyce after the fleshe, I will reioyse also.

19 For ye suffer foles gladly, because that ye youre selues are wyse.

20 For ye suffre euen yf a man brynge you into bondage: yf a man deuoure, yf a man take yf a man exalte hym selfe, yf a man smite you on the face.

21 I speake as concernynge rebuke, as thoughe we had bene weake. Howe be it, wherein soeuer any man dare be bolde (I speake folyshly) I dare be bolde also.

22 They are Hebrues, so am I: They are Israelytes, euen so am I. They are the seede of Abraham, euen so am I.

23 They are the ministers of CHRISTE (I speake as a fole) I am more: In labours more aboundaunte: In strypes aboue measure: In pryson more plentuouslye: In death ofte.

24 Of the Iewes .v. tymes receyued I euerye tyme .xl. strypes saue one.

25 Thryse was I beaten with roddes. I was once stoned. I suffered thryse shipwracke. Nyght and daye haue I bene in the depe of the sea.

26 In iorneyeyng often: in parils of waters: in parylles of robbers: in ieoperdyes amonge the heathen. I haue bene in peryls in cytyes, in peryls in wyldernes, in peryls in the sea, in peryls among false brethren,

27 in laboure and trauayle, in watchyng often, in hunger, in thyrste, in fastynges often, in colde, and in nakednes.

28 And besyde the thynges whiche outwardelye happen vnto me, I am combered dayelye, and do care for all congregations.

29 Who is weake, and I am not weake? Who is hurte in the faythe, and my herte burneth not?

30 Yf I muste nedes reioyce, I wyll reioyce of myne infirmities.

31 The God and father of oure Lorde Iesus Christ, whiche is blessed for euermore, knoweth that I lye not

32 In the citie of Damascon the gouerner of the people vnder king Aretas, layd watche in the citie of the Damascens, and woulde haue caught me,

33 and at a wyndowe was I let doune in a basket thorow the wall, and so scaped hys handes.

# CHAPTER 12

IT is not expedyent for me (no doubte) to reioyce. Neuerthelesse I wyll come to visions and reuelations of the Lorde.

2 I knowe a man in Christe aboue .xiiij. yeares agone (whether he were in the bodye I cannot tell, or whether he were oute of the bodye I cannot tell, God knoweth) whiche was taken vp into the third heauen.

3 And I knowe the same man (whether in the bodye, or oute of the bodye, I cannot tell,

God knoweth)

4 howe that he was taken vp into paradyse, and hearde wordes not to be spoken, whiche no man can vtter.

5 Of thys man wyll I reioyce, of my selfe wyll I not reioyce, excepte it be of myne infyrmytyes.

6 And yet thoughe I woulde reioyce, I shoulde not be a fole: for I shoulde saye the trueth: Neuerthelesse I spare, lest anye man shoulde thynke of me aboue that he seeth me to be, or heareth of me.

7 And lest I shoulde be exalted out of measure thorowe the aboundaunce of reuelacions there was geuen vnto me vnquyetnes of þe fleshe, the messenger of Satan to buffete me: because I shoulde no be exalted oute of measure.

8 For thys thynge besought I the Lorde thryse, that it myght departe from me.

9 And he sayde vnto me: my grace is suffycyent for the. For my strengthe is made perfecte thorowe weakenes. Very gladly therfor wil I reioyce of my weakenes, that the strength of Christe maye dwell in me

10 Therfore haue I delectacyon in infyrmities, in rebukes, in nede, in persecutions, in anguyshe, for Christes sake. For when I am weake, then am I stronge.

11 I am made a fole in bostynge my selfe. Ye haue compelled me: I ought to haue bene commended of you. For in nothynge was I inferyor vnto the chiefe Apostles. Thoughe I be nothynge

12 yet the tokens of an Apostle were wroughte amonge you with al pacience: with signes, and wonders and myghty dedes.

13 For what is it wherein ye were inferyours vnto other congregacyons except it be therein that I was not greuous vnto you. Forgeue me thys wrong done vnto you.

14 Behold the now thyrde time I am redy to come vnto you, and yet wyll I not be greuouse vnto you. For I seke not yours, but you. Also the chyldren ought not to lay vp for the fathers & mothers but the fathers a mothers for the chyldren.

15 I wyll very gladly bestowe, and wyll be bestowed for youre soules: thoughe the more I loue you, the lesse I am loued agayne.

16 But be it that I greued you not: neuerthelesse I was crafty and toke you with gyle.

17 Dyd I pyl you by any of them which I sent vnto you?

18 I desyred Titus, and with hym I sent a brother. Did Tytus defraude you of any thing? walked we not in one spyryte? walked we not in lyke steppes?

19 Agayne, thynke ye that we excuse oure selues. We speake in Christe in the syght of God. But we do all thynges dearelye beloued for youre edifiynge.

20 For I feare least it come to passe, that when I come, I shall not fynde you suche as I woulde, and I shalbe founde amonge you debate, enuiynge, wrath, stryfe, backbytynges, whisperynges, swellynges & discorde.

21 I feare leste when I come agayne, God brynge me lowe amonge you, and I be constrayned to bewayle many of them which haue synned already, and haue not repented of the vncleanes, fornicacyon, and wantonnes, whiche they haue commytted.

## CHAPTER 13

Nowe come I the thyrde time vnto you. In the mouthe of two or three wytnesses shall euery thing stande.

2 I tolde you before, & tell you before, and as I sayd when I was presente with you the seconde tyme, so wayte I now beynge absent to them which in tyme paste haue synned, and to all other, that yf I come agayne, I wyll not spare,

3 seyng þt ye seke experience of Christe, whiche speaketh in me, which amonge you is not weake, but is myghty in you.

4 And verely thoughe it came of weakenes that he was crucyfyed, yet liueth he thorowe the power of GOD. And we no doubte are weake in hym: but we shall lyue with hym by the myght of God among you.

5 Proue youre selues whether you be in þe fayth or not. Examen your owne selues: know ye not your owne selues, howe that Iesha Christe is in you, except ye be casteawayes?

6 I truste that ye shall knowe that we be not cast awayes.

7 I desyre before God that ye do none euyll, not that we shoulde seme commendale, but that ye shoulde do that which is honest: and let vs be counted as leude persons.

8 We can do nothynge agaynste the truth. But for the trueth,

9 we are glad when we are weake, & ye strong. Thys also we wyshe for, euen that ye were perfecte.

10 Therfore wryte I these thinges beynge absente, leste when I am presente I shoulde vse sharpenesse accordynge to the power whiche the Lorde hath geuen me, to edifye, and not to destroye.

11 Finally brethren fare ye well, be perfeccte, be of good comforte, be of one mynde, lyue in peace, and the God of loue, and peace, shal be with you.

12 Grete one another in an holy kysse.

13 All the saynctes salute you.

14 The grace of oure Lorde Iesus Christ, and the loue of God, and the feloweshyppe of the holye ghoste be with you all. Amen.

# Galatians

## CHAPTER 1

Paul an Apostle, not of men, neyther by man, but by Iesus christ and by God the father, which raysed hym from death:

2 and all the brethren whiche are with me. Vnto the congregacyons of Galacia.

3 Grace be with you and peace from God the father, and from our Lorde Iesus Christ,

4 whiche gaue hym selfe for oure synnes, to delyuer vs from thys present euyll worlde, thorow the wyll of God our father,

5 to whom be prayse for euer and euer. Amen.

6 I maruayle that ye are so sone turned from hym that called you in the grace of Christ, vnto an other Gospell:

7 whiche is nothynge els, but that there be some which trouble you, and entende to peruert the Gospell of Christe.

8 Neuerthelesse thoughe we oure selues, or an Angell from heauen, preache any other Gospell vnto you then that whiche we haue preached vnto you, holde hym as accurssed.

9 As I haue sayed before, so saye I nowe agayne, yf anye man preache any other thynge vnto you, then that you haue receyued, holde hym accursed.

10 Preache I mans doctryne or Goddes? Eyther go I aboute to please men? Yf I studyed to please men, I were not the seruauat of Christe.

11 I certifye you brethren, that the Gospell which was preached of me, was, not after the maner of men,

12 neyther receyued I it of man, neyther was I taughte it, but receyued it by the reuelacyon of Iesus Christ.

13 For ye haue hearde of my conuersacyon in tyme paste, in the Iewes wayes, howe that beyonde measure I persecuted the congregacyon of God, & spoyled it,

14 and preuayled in the Iewes lawe, aboue many of my companyons, which were of myne own nacyon, & was a much more feruent mayntayner of the tradicions of þe elders.

15 But when it pleased God (whiche separated me from my mothers wombe, and called me by hys grace,

16 for to declare hys sonne by me) that I shoulde preache hym amonge the heathen immediatly I communed not of the matter with fleshe and bloude,

17 neyther returned to Hierusalem to them whiche were Apostles before me, but went my wayes into Arabia, and came agayne to Damasco.

18 Then after .iij. yere I returned to Ierusalem to se Peter and abode with hym .xv. dayes,

19 no nother of the Apostles sawe I, saue Iames the Lordes brother.

20 The thynges which I wryte beholde God knoweth I lye not.

21 After that I went into the costes of Syria, and Cilicia,

22 and was knowen as touchynge my person vnto the congregacyons of Iewry, whiche were in Christe,

23 But they hearde onlye that he which persecuted vs in tyme past nowe preacheth the fayth which before he destroyed.

24 And they gloryfyed God on my be halfe.

## CHAPTER 2

Then .xiiij. yeares after that, I went vp agayne to Hierusalem with Barnabas, and toke with me Titus also.

2 Yea and I wente vp by reuelacion, and communed with them of the Gospell which I preache amonge the gentyls: but a part with them which were counted chiefe, lest it shoulde haue bene thought, that I should runne or had runne in vayne.

3 Also Tytus which was wt me, though he were a Greke, yet was not compelled to be circumcysed,

4 and that because of incommers beynge false brethren which came in amonge other to spye out our lybertye

which we haue in Christe Iesus, that they myghte brynge vs into bondage.

5 To whom we gaue no roume, no not for the space of an houre, as concernynge to be brought into subieccion, & that because that the truth of þe Gospel might contynue with you.

6 Of them whiche seme to be great (what they were in time passed, it maketh no matter to me: God loketh on no mans person) neuerthelesse they whiche seme great, added nothing to me.

7 But contrary wyse, when they sawe þt the Gospel ouer þt vncircumcysyon was committed vnto me, as the gospell ouer þe circumcisyon was vnto Peter:

8 for he þt was mighty in Peter in the Apostleshyppe ouer the circumcisyon the same was myghty in me amonge the Gentyls,

9 and therfore when they perceyued the grace that was geuen vnto me, then Iames, Cephas, and Iohn, whiche semed to be pyllars, gaue to me & Barnabas the ryght handes, & agreed with vs, that we should preach amonge the Heathen, and they amonge the Iewes,

10 warnyng onely, that we should remembre the pore. Whiche thyng also I was dylygently to do.

11 And when Peter was come to Antioche, I withstode hym in the face, for he was worthy to be blamed.

12 For yer that certayne came from Iames, he eate with the Gentyls. But when they were come, he withdrue and separated hym selfe, fearyng them which were of the circumcysyon.

13 And the other Iewes dissembled lykewyse, in so muche þt Barnabas was brought into theyr simulacyon also.

14 But when I sawe, that they went not the ryghte waye after the truth of the Gospell, I sayde vnto Peter before all men, yf thou beynge a Iew, lyuest after the maner of the Gentyls, and not as do the Iewes: why causeste þu the Gentyls to lyue as do the Iewes?

15 We whiche are Iewes by nature, and not sinners of the Gentyls,

16 knowe that a man is not iustifyed by the dedes of the lawe, but by the fayth of Iesus Christe. And therfore we haue beleued on Iesus Christe that we myghte be iustifyed by the fayth of Christe, and not by the dedes of the lawe, because that by the dedes of the lawe no fleshe can be iustifyed.

17 Yf then whyle we seke to be made ryghtuousnes by Christe, we our selues are founde synners, is not then Christe the mynister of synne? God forbyd,

18 For yf I buylde agayne that whiche I destroyed, then make I myself a treaspaser.

19 But I thorowe the lawe, am dead to the law: that I myght lyue vnto God

20 I am crucyfyed with Christ. I lyue verelye: yet now not I, but Christe lyueth in me. For the lyfe which I now lyue in the, flesh I lyue by the faythe of the sonne of God whiche loued me, and gaue hym selfe for me.

21 I despyse not the grace of God. For yf ryghteousnes come of the lawe, then Christ dyed in vayne.

# CHAPTER 3

O folyshe Galathyans: who hath wytched you, that ye should not beleue the truthe? To whom Iesus Christ was descrybed before the eyes, and among you crucyfyed.

2 Thys onelye woulde I learne of you, receyued ye the spyryte by the dedes of the law, or els by preachynge of the faith?

3 Are ye so vnwyse that after ye haue begonne in the spyryte, ye woulde nowe ende in the fleshe?

4 So many thinges then ye haue suffered in vaine, yf that be vayne.

5 Which mynistred to you the spyryte, and worketh myracles among you, doth he it thorowe the dedes of that lawe or by preachynge of the fayth?

6 Euer as Abraham beleued God, and it was ascrybed to hym for ryghtuousnes.

7 Vnderstande therfore, that they whiche are of fayth, the same are the chyldren of Abraham.

8 For þe scripture sawe afore hand, that God woulde iustifye the heathen thorow fayth, & therfore shewed before hand glad tydynges vnto Abraham. In the shall all nacyons be blessed.

9 So then they whiche be of faythe are blessed with faythful Abraham.

10 For as many as are vnder the dedes of the lawe, are vnder malediccyon. For it is wrytten: cursed is euery man that contynueth not in all thynges, whiche are wrytten in the boke of the law, to fulfyll them.

11 That no man is iustifyed by the lawe in the syght of God, is euydente. For þe iuste shall lyue by fayth.

12 The lawe is not of fayth: but the man that fulfylleth the thinges contayned in the lawe, shall lyue in them.

13 But Christ hath delyuered vs from the curse of þe lawe, and was made accursed for vs. For it is wrytten: cursed is euery one that hangeth on tre,

14 that the blessyng of Abraham myghte come on the Gentyles thorowe Iesus Christ and that we myght receyue the promes of the spyryte thorow fayth.

15 Brethren I wyll speake after the maner of men. Thoughe it be but a mans testamente, yet no man despyseth it, or addeth any thyng there to when it is once alowed.

16 To Abraham and hys seede were the promyses made. He sayth not in the sedes as in manye: but in thy sede as in one, whiche is Christe.

17 Thys I saye, that the lawe which beganne afterward beyonde: .iiij.C. and .xxx. yeares doth not disanull the testament, that was confyrmed afore of God vnto Christe warde, to make the promes of none effecte.

18 For yf the inherytaunce come of the lawe, it commeth not of promes. But God gaue it vnto Abraham by promes

19 Wherfore then serueth the lawe? The law was added because of transgressyon (tyll the sede came to whiche the promes was made) & it was ordeyned by angels in the hande of a mediator,

20 he is not a mediator of one. But God is one.

21 Is the lawe then agaynst the promes of God? God forbyd. Howbeit yf there had bene a lawe geuen whiche could haue geuen lyfe: then no doubt ryghteousnes should haue come by the lawe.

22 But the scrypture concluded all thynges vnder synne that the promes by the fayth of Iesus Christe shoulde be geuen vnto them that beleue.

23 Before that fayth came, we were kept and shut vp vnder the lawe, to the fayth which shuld afterward be declared.

24 Wherfore the lawe was our scholemaster to the tyme of Christ, that we might be made ryghtuouse by fayth.

25 But after that fayth is come, nowe are we no lenger vnder a scholemayster.

26 For ye are al the sonnes of God, by the fayth whiche is in Christe Iesus.

27 For al ye þt are baptysed, haue put on Christ.

28 Nowe is there no Iewe neyther gentyle, ther is neyther bonde nor free: there is neyther man nor woman, but ye are all one thyng in christ Iesu.

29 Yf ye be Christes, then are ye Abrahams seede and heyres by promes.

# CHAPTER 4

AND I say that the heyre as longe as he is a chylde, differeth not from a seruaunt thoughe he be Lorde of all,

2 but is vnder tutours and gouernours, vntyll the tyme appoynted of the father.

3 Euen so we as longe as we were chyldren, were in bondage vnder the ordinaunces of the world.

4 But when the tyme was full come, God sente hys sonne made of a woman, and made bonde vnto the lawe,

5 to redeme them which were vnder the lawe: that we thorowe eleccyon myght receyue the enheritaunce that belongeth vnto the naturall sonnes.

6 Because ye are sonnes, God hath sent the spyryte of hys sonne into our hertes, whiche cryeth Abba father.

7 Wherfore now thou art not a seruaunt but a sonne. Yf thou be the sonne, thou arte also the heyre of God thorowe Christe.

8 Notwithstandynge when ye knewe not God ye dyd seruyce vnto them, which by nature were no Goddes.

9 But nowe seynge, ye knowe God (yea rather are knowen of God) how is it that ye turne agayne to the weake & beggerly ceremonies, wherevnto agayne ye desyre a freshe to be in bondage?

10 Ye obserue dayes, and monethes, and tymes, and yeares.

11 I am in feare of you lest I haue bestowed on you laboure in vayne.

12 Brethren I beseche you, be ye as I am, for I am as ye are. Ye haue not hurte me at all.

13 Ye knowe howe thorowe infyrmytye of the fleshe, I preached the Gospell vnto you at the fyrste.

14 And my temptacion whiche I suffered by reason of my flesh, ye dispysed not, neyther abhorred, but receyued me as an Angell of God: yea as Christe Iesu.

15 How happye were ye then? for I beare you recorde that yf it had bene possyble, ye woulde haue plucked oute youre owne eyes, and haue geuen them to me.

16 Am I therfore become your enemye, because I tell you the truth?

17 They are gelous ouer you amysse. Yea, they intende to exclude you, that ye should be feruent to them ward.

18 It is good always to be feruent, so it be in a good thinge, and not onelye when I am presente with you.

19 My lytle chyldren (of whome I trauayle in byrth agayne vntyll Christe be fashyoned in you)

20 I woulde I were with you now, and coulde chaunge my voyce, for I stande in a doubte of you.

21 Tell me ye that desyre to be vnder the law haue ye not heard of the law?

22 For it is writen, that Abraham had two sonnes, the one by a bonde mayd the other by a fre woman.

23 Yea and he whiche was of the bond woman, was borne after the fleshe: but he whiche was of þe fre woman, was borne by promes.

24 Whiche thynges betoken misterye. For these women are

two testamentes the one from the mounte Syna, whiche gendreth to bondage whiche is Agar.

25 For mounte Syna is called Agar in Arabia, and bordreth vpon the citie, which is nowe Hierusalem, and is in bondage with her chyldren.

26 But Hierusalem, whiche is aboue, is fre, whiche is the mother of vs all.

27 For it is written: Reioyce thou baren, that bearest no chyldren: breake forth and crye, thou that trauaylest not. For the desolate hath many more children then she whiche hath an husband.

28 Brethren we are after the maner of Isaac children of promes.

29 But as then he that was borne carnally, persecuted him that was borne spirytuallye. Euen so is it nowe.

30 Neuerthelesse what sayth the scripture: put awaye the bond woman and her sonne. For the sonne of þe bond woman shall not be heyre with the sonne of þe fre woman.

31 So then brethren we are not chyldren of the bonde woman, but of the fre woman.

## CHAPTER 5

STANDE fast therfore in the lybertye wherewith Christ hath made vs free and wrappe not your selues againe in the yoke of bondage.

2 Beholde I Paule saye vnto you, that yf ye be circumcysed Christe shall profyte you nothynge at all.

3 I testifye agayne to euery man whiche is circumcysed that he is bounde to kepe the whole lawe.

4 Ye are gone quyte from Christe as manye as are iustifyed by the law, and are fallen from grace.

5 We loke for, and hope in the spiryte, to be iustifyed thorow fayth.

6 For in Iesu Christ nether is circumcysion any thing worth, neyther yet vncircumcysyon, but fayth which by loue is myghtye in operacyon.

7 Ye dyd runne wel: who was a let to you, that ye shoulde not obeye the trueth?

8 Euen that counsell that is not of hym that called you.

9 A lytell leuen doeth leuen the whole lumpe of dowe.

10 I haue trust towarde you in the Lorde, that ye wyll be none otherwyse mynded. He that troubleth you, shall beare hys iudgemente, whatsoeuer he be.

11 Brethren, yf I yet preache circumcysyon: why do I yet suffer persecutyon? For then had the offence whiche the crosse geueth, ceased.

12 I woulde to God they were separated from you, whiche trouble you.

13 Brethren ye were called into lybertye onelye let not youre lybertye be an occasyon vnto the fleshe, but in loue serue one another.

14 For all the lawe is fulfylled in one worde: whiche is thys: thou shalte loue thyne neyghboure as thy selfe.

15 Yf ye byte and deuour one another: take hede leaste ye be consumed one of another.

16 I saye: walke in the spyryte, and fulfyl not the lustes of the fleshe.

17 For the flesh lusteth contrarye to the spirite, and the spirite contrarye to the fleshe. These are contrarye one to the other, so that ye cannot do that which ye would.

18 But and yf ye be led of the spyryte, then are ye not vnder the lawe.

19 The dedes of the flesh are manyfeste, which are these aduoutrye, fornicacyon, vncleannes, wantonnes,

20 Idolatrye wytchecrafte, hatred, varyaunce, zele, wrathe stryfe, sedityon, sectes,

21 enuiynge, murther, dronkennes, glottonye, and suche lyke: of the whiche I tell you before, as I haue tolde you in tymes past, that they whiche commytte suche thynges shall not enheryte the kingdome of God.

22 But the frute of þe spiryte, is loue, ioye peace, longe sufferynge, gentylnes, goodnes, faithfulnes,

23 mekenes, temperauncye. Against suche there is no lawe.

24 They that are Christes haue crucyfyed the fleshe with the appetytes and lustes.

25 If we lyue in the spyryte: let vs walke in the spyryte.

26 Let vs not be vayne gloryouse, prouokynge one another, and enuyinge one another.

## CHAPTER 6

BRETHREN, yf any man be fallen by chaunce into any faute: ye which are spyrytuall helpe to amende hym, in the spyryte of mekenes, consyderynge thy selfe leste thou also be tempted.

2 Beare ye one anothers burthen, and so fulfyl the lawe of christ.

3 Yf anye man seme to hym selfe, that he is somwhat, when in dede he is nothynge the same deceyueth hym selfe in hys ymaginacyon.

4 Let euerye man proue hys owne worke, and then shall he haue reioysynge in hys owne selfe, & not in another.

5 For euery man shal beare his owne burthen.

6 Let hym that is taughte in the worde, mynyster vnto him that teacheth hym, in al good thynges.

7 Be not deceyued, God is not mocked. For what soeuer a man soweth, that shal he reape.

8 He that soweth in hys

fleshe: shall of the fleshe reape corrupcion. But he that soweth in the spyryte, shall of the spyryte reape lyfe euerlastynge.

9 Let vs not be werye, of wel doynge. For when the tyme is come, we shall reape withoute werynes.

10 Whyle we haue therfore tyme, let vs do good vnto all men, and specially vnto them which are of the houshold of faythe.

11 Beholde how large a letter I haue writen vnto you with myne owne hande.

12 As manye as desyre with vtwarde apperaunce to please carnallye, they coustrayne you to be circumcysed, onelye because they woulde not suffer persecucyon with the crosse of Christe.

13 For they them selues which are circumcysed kepe not the lawe: but desyre to haue you circumcysed that they myght reioyce in your fleshe.

14 God forbyd that I shoulde reioyce but in the crosse of oure Lorde Iesu Christe, wherby the worlde is crucifyed as touchyng me, and I as concernynge the worlde.

15 For in Christe Iesu neyther circumcisyon auayleth any thing at all, nor vncircumcysyon but a newe creature.

16 And as many as walke accordynge to thys rule peace be on them, and mercye, and vpon Israel þt pertayneth to God.

17 From hence forthe let no man put me to busynes. For I bare in my bodye the markes of the Lord Iesu.

18 Brethren the grace of oure Lorde Iesu Christe be with youre spyryte. Amen.

# Ephesians

## CHAPTER 1

Paule an Apostle of Iesu Christe by the wyll of God. To þe Saynctes whiche are at Ephesus, & to them whiche beleue on Iesus Christe.

2 Grace be wyth you, and peace from God oure father, and from the Lorde Iesus Christe.

3 Blessed be God the father of oure Lorde Iesus Christe, which hath blessed vs wyth all maner of spyrytuall blessynges in heauenlye thynges by Christe,

4 accordynge as he had chosen vs in hym, before the foundacyon of the worlde was layde that we shoulde be Saynctes and wythoute blame before hym thorow loue.

5 And ordeyned vs before thorowe Iesus Christe to be heyres vnto hym selfe, according to the pleasure of hys wyll,

6 to the prayse of þe glory of hys grace, wherewith he hath made vs accepted in the beloued.

7 By whome we haue redemption thorowe hys bloude, euen the forgeuenes of synnes accordyng to the ryches of hys grace

8 he shedde on vs aboundauntlye in all wysdome & perseueraunce.

9 And hath opened vnto vs the misterye of hys wyll accordyng to hys pleasure and purposed the same in hym selfe

10 to haue it declared, when the tyme were full come, þt all thynges, bothe the thynges whiche are in heauen, & also thynges whiche are in earth shoulde be gathered together euen in Christ:

11 that is to saye in hym in whome we are made heyres, and were thereto predestinate accordynge to the purpose of hym which worketh all thynges after the purpose of hys owne wyll,

12 that we whiche before beleued in Christ shoulde be vnto the prayse of hys glorye.

13 In whome also ye (after that ye hearde the worde of trueth. I meane the Gospel of your saluacyon, wherein ye beleued) were sealed with the holye spiryte of promes,

14 whiche is þe ernest of oure inheritaunce, to redeme the purchased possessyon, and that vnto the lande of hys glorye.

15 Wherfore euen I (after that I hearde of the faythe whiche ye haue in the Lorde Iesu, and loue vnto all the saynctes)

16 cease not to geue thankes for you: makyng mencyon of you in my prayers,

17 that the God of oure Lord Iesus Christ, and the father of glorye myghte geue vnto you the spyryte of wysdome, and open to you the knoweledge of hym selfe,

18 and lyghten the eyes of youre myndes that ye myght knowe what that hope is, where vnto he hath called you, and what the ryches of hys gloryous inheritaunce is vpon the saynctes,

19 and what is the excedynge greatnes of hys power to vs warde, whiche beleue accordynge to the workynge of that hys myghtye power,

20 whiche he wrought in Christe, when he raysed hym from the dead, and set hym on hys ryght hande in heauenly thynges,

21 aboue all rule, power, and myghte, and domynyon, and aboue all names that are named, not in thys worlde onely, but also in the worlde to come,

22 and hath put all thynges, vnder hys fete, and hath made hym aboue all thynges the heade of the congregacyon,

23 which is hys bodye, and the fulnes of hym that fylleth all in all thynges.

## CHAPTER 2

And you hath he quickened also that were deade in treaspas & synne,

2 in the whiche in time passed, yet walked accordynge

to the course of thys worlde, & after the gouerner that ruleth in the ayer, the spyrite that nowe worketh in the chyldren of vnbelefe,

3 amonge whiche we also had our conuersation in tyme paste, in the lustes of oure fleshe, and fulfylled the wyll of the fleshe and of the mynde, and were naturallye the chyldren of wrath, euen as well as other.

4 But God whiche is ryche in mercye thorow his great loue wherewith he loued vs,

5 euen when we were dead by synne, hath quickened vs together in Christ (for by grace are ye saued)

6 and hath rayseth vs vp together, & made vs sitte together in heauenly thynges thorowe Christ Iesu,

7 for to shewe in tymes to come the excedinge riches of hys grace in kyndnes to vswarde in Christe Iesus.

8 For by grace are ye made safe thorowe fayth, and that not of youre selues. For it is the gyfte of God,

9 and commeth not of workes, leste anye man should bost him selfe.

10 For we are his worckmanshyp created in Christe Iesus to good workes, vnto the, whyche God ordeined vs before, þt we should walke in them.

11 Wherfore remember that ye, beynge in tyme passed Gentyles in fleshe, and were called vncircumcision to them whiche are called circumcision in the fleshe, whiche circumcision is made by handes:

12 Remember I saye, that ye were at that tyme without Christe, and were reputed aliantes from the commen welth of Israel, and were straungers from the testamentes of promes, and had no hope and were wythout God in thys worlde.

13 But nowe in Christ Iesu, ye whych a whyle ago were farre of are made nygh by the bloud of Christe.

14 For he is our peace, whiche had made of both one, and hath broken doune the wall þt was a stop betwene vs,

15 and hath also put awaye thorowe hys fleshe the cause of hatred (that is to saye, the lawe of commaundementes contayned in the lawe written) for to make of twayne one newe man in hym selfe, so makinge peace:

16 and to reconcile both vnto God in one body thorowe his crosse, and slew hatered therby:

17 and came and preached peace to you, whiche were a farre of, and to them that were nygh.

18 For thorowe hym we both haue an open waye in, in one spyrite vnto the father.

19 Nowe therfore ye are no more straungers and foreners, but citizyns with the sainctes, and of the houshold of God:

20 and are buylt vpon the foundation of the Apostles & Prophetes, Iesus Christe beynge the head corner stone,

21 in whom euerye buyldinge coupled together, groweth vnto an holye temple in the Lorde,

22 in whom ye also are buylde together, and made an habitacion for god in the spyryte.

## CHAPTER 3

For this cause I Paule am in the bondes of Iesu Christ for your sakes, whiche are heathen.

2 Yf ye haue hearde of the ministration of the grace of God, whiche is geuen me to youward.

3 For by reuelation shewed he this misterie to me as I wrote aboue in fewe wordes,

4 wherby when ye reade, ye maye knowe myne vnderstandinge in the misterye of Christe.

5 Which mysterye in tymes passed was not opened to the sonnes of men, as it is now declared vnto his holye Apostles and Prophetes by the spyrite

6 that the Gentyles shoulde be inheritours also, and of the same bodye, and partakers of hys promes that is in Christe, by the meanes of the Gospell,

7 wherof I am made a mynyster, by the gyfte of the grace of God geuen vnto me thorowe the workynge of hys power.

8 Vnto me the leaste of all sainctes is this grace geuen, that I shoulde preache amonge the Gentyls the vnsearcheable ryches of Christe,

9 and to make all men se what the fellowshyp of the mysterye is, whiche from the beginninge of the worlde hath bene hyde in God, whiche made all thinges thorowe Iesus Christ,

10 to the entente, that nowe vnto the rulers & powers in heauen myght be knowen (by the congregation) the manifolde wysedome of God,

11 accordinge to the eternal purpose, whiche he purposed in Christe Iesu our Lorde,

12 by whom we are bold to drawe nighe in that truste, whyche we haue by fayth on on him.

13 Wherfore I desyre that ye faynte not because of my tribulations for your sakes, whiche is your prayse.

14 For this cause I bowe my knees vnto the father of oure Lorde Iesus Christ,

15 whiche is father ouer all that is called father, in heauen and in earth,

16 that he woulde graunt you accordinge to the ryches of his glorie, that ye maye be strengthed wyth mighte by his spirite in the inner man,

17 that Christ may dwell in your hertes by fayth, that ye beinge roted and grounded in loue,

18 might be able to comprehende wyth all sainctes, what is þe bread and length, deapt and height:

19 and to knowe, what is the loue of Christe, whyche loue passeth knowledge, that ye myghte be fulfylled wyth all maner of fulnes, whiche cometh of God.

20 Vnto hym that is able to do excedinge aboundantly aboue all þt we are or thinke, according to the power that worketh in vs,

21 be prayse in the congregation by Iesus Christe, thorowout al generacions, from time to time. Amen.

## CHAPTER 4

I therfore whiche am in boundes for the Lordes sake, exhorte you, that ye walke worthy of the vocation wherwyth ye are called,

2 in all humblenes of mynde, and mekenes, and longe sufferynge, forbearinge one another thorowe loue,

3 and þt ye be diligente to kepe the vnitie of the spirite in the bounde of peace,

4 beynge one bodye, & one spirite, euen as ye are called in one hope of your callinge.

5 Let there be but one Lorde, one fayth, one baptysme,

6 one God and father of all, whiche is aboue al thorowe all and in you all.

7 Vnto euery one of vs is geuen grace according to the measure of þe gyfte of Christ.

8 Wherfore he sayth: He is gone vp on hye, and had led captiuitie captiue, and hath geuen gyftes vnto men.

9 That he ascended, what meaneth it, but that he also descended fyrste into the loweste parties of the earth?

10 He that descended, is euen the same also that ascended vp euen aboue all heauens, to fulfyll al thinges.

11 And the very same made some Apostles, some Prophetes, some Euangelistes, some sheperdes, some teachers,

12 that the saynctes myghte haue all thinges necessarye to worke and ministre wythal, to the edifiynge of the bodye of Christ,

13 tyl we euerie one (in the vnitie of fayth, and knowledge of the sonne of God) growe vp into a perfecte man, after the measure of age of the fulnes of Christ.

14 That we henceforth be no more chyldren, wauerynge and caryed wyth euerye wynde of doctryne, by the wylynes of men and craftynes, wherby they laye awayte for vs to deceyue vs.

15 But let vs folowe the truethe in loue, and in al thinges growe in him which is þe head, that is to saye, Christe,

16 in whom all the body is coupled and knyt together in euerye ioynt, wherwyth one ministreth to another (accordynge to the operation, as euerye parte hath hys measure) and encreaseth the bodye, vnto the edifiynge of it selfe in loue.

17 Thys I saye therfore and testifye in the Lorde, that ye henceforth walke not as other Gentyles walke, in vanitie of theyr mynde,

18 blynded in theyr vnderstandynge, beynge straungers from the lyfe whiche is in God thorowe the ignoraunce that is in them, because of the blyndnes of theyr hertes:

19 whiche beyng paste repentaunce, haue geuen them selues vnto wantonnes, to worke al maner of vncleanes, euen wyth gredines.

20 But ye haue not so learned Christ,

21 yf so be ye haue heard of hym, and are taughte of hym, euen as the trueth is in Iesu.

22 So then as concernyng the conuersacyon in tyme past, laye from you that olde man, whyche is corrupte thorowe the deceyueable lustes

23 and be ye renued in the spyrite of your mindes,

24 and put on that newe man, whyche after the Image of God is shapen in ryghteousnes & true holynes.

25 Wherfore put awaye lyinge, and speake euerye man trueth vnto hys neyghboure, for as muche as we are membres one of another.

26 Be angrye, but synne not, let not the sunne go doune vpon your wrath,

27 neyther geue place vnto the backebyter.

28 Let hym that stole, steale no more, but let hym rather laboure wyth his handes some good thynge, that he maye haue to geue vnto hym that nedeth.

29 Let no fylthy communication procede out of your mouthes: but that whiche is good to edefye wyth all, when nede is: that it maye haue fauoure with the hearers.

30 And greue not the holye spirite of God, by whom ye are sealed vnto the daye of redemption.

31 Let all bitternes, fearsnes and wrath, roring and cursed speakinge, be put awaye from you, wyth all maliciousnes.

32 Be ye courteouse one to another and mercyfull, forgeuynge one another, euen as God for Christes sake forgaue you.

## CHAPTER 5

Be ye folowers of God as deare children,

2 and walke in loue euen as Christe loued vs, and gaue hym selfe for vs, an offeringe, and a sacrifice of a swete sauoure to God.

3 So that fornicacion and vncleanes, or couetousnes be not

ones named amonge you, as it becommeth sainctes:

4 neyther fylthynes, neyther folyshe talkinge, neither gestinge whiche are not comely: but rather geuinge of thankes.

5 For this ye knowe, that no whormonger, other vncleane persone, or couetous person, whyche is the worshypper of Images, hath anye inheritaunce in the kyngdome of Christe and of God.

6 Let no man deceiue you with vayne wordes. For thorowe suche thinges commeth the wrath of God vpon the children of vnbelefe.

7 Be not therfore companions wyth them.

8 Ye were ones darckenes, but are nowe lyghte in the Lorde. Walke as chyldren of lyghte.

9 For the fruite of the spirite is in all goodnes, ryghtuousnes and trueth.

10 Accepte that whiche is pleasinge to the Lorde:

11 and haue no fellowshyp wyth the vnfruitfull workes of darckenes: but rather rebuke them.

12 For it is shame euen to name those thinges, whiche are done of them in secrete:

13 but all thinges, when they are rebuked of the lyghte are manifeste. For what soeuer is manifeste, that same is lyght.

14 Wherfore he sayth: awake thou that slepest, and stand vp from death, and Christ shall geue the lyght.

15 Take hede therfore that ye walke circumspectlye: not as foles, but as wyse

16 redeminge the time, for the dayes are iuel.

17 Wherfore be ye not vnwise, but vnderstande what þe wyll of the Lorde is,

18 and be not drounke wt wyne. wherin is excesse, but be fulfylled wyth þe spirite,

19 speakinge vnto your selues in Psalmes, and Hymnes, and spiritual sounges, singing and makinge melodye to the Lorde in your hertes,

20 geuinge thankes alwayes for al thinges vnto God the father, in the name of oure Lorde Iesu Christe,

21 submittinge your selues one to another in the feare of God.

22 Women submitte youre selues vnto your owne husbandes, as vnto the Lorde.

23 For the husbande is the wyues head, euen as Christe is the heade of the congregation, and þe same is the sauiour of the body.

24 Therfore as the congregation is in subieccion to Christe, lykewyse let the wyues be in subieccion to theyr husbandes in all thynges.

25 Husbandes loue youre wyues, euen as Christe loued the congregation, and gaue him selfe for it,

26 to sanctifye it, and cleansed it in the fountayne of water thorowe the worde

27 to make it vnto hym selfe a glorious congregation wythout spotte or wrinckle, or anye suche thinge: but that it shoulde be holy and wythout blame.

28 So ought men to loue theyr wyues, as their owne bodies. He that loueth hys wyfe, loueth him selfe.

29 For no man euer yet hated hys owne fleshe, but norisheth and cherisseth it euen as the Lorde doeth the congregation.

30 For we are members of his bodie, of his fleshe, and of hys bones.

31 For this cause shall a man leaue father and mother, and shall continue wyth hys wyfe, and two shalbe made one fleshe.

32 Thys is a greate secrete, but I speake betwene Christe and the congregation.

33 Neuerthelesse do ye so that euerye one of you loue his wyfe truely euen as hym selfe: And let the wyfe se that she feare her husbande.

# CHAPTER 6

CHYLDREN obeye youre fathers and mothers in the Lorde: for so is it ryght.

2 Honoure thy father and mother, that is the fyrst commaundemente that hath anye promes,

3 that thou mayeste be in good estate, and liue longe on the earth.

4 And ye fathers, moue not youre children to wrath, but bringe them vp with the norter and information of the Lorde.

5 Seruauntes be obedient vnto youre carnall maisters, wyth feare and tremblinge, in singlenes of youre hertes, as vnto Christe,

6 not wyth seruice in þe eye sight, as men pleasers, but as the seruauntes of Christe, doynge the wyll of God frome the herte

7 wyth good wyll seruynge the Lorde, & not men.

8 And remembre that, whatsoeuer good thinge any man doeth, that shall he receiue agayne of the Lorde, whether he be bounde or fre.

9 And ye maisters, do euen the same thinges vnto them puttinge awaye threateninges: and remembre that euen your maister also is in heauen, neither is ther anye respect of person wyth hym.

10 Finally my brethren, be stronge in þe Lord and in the power of his myghte.

11 Put on the armoure of God, that ye maye stande stedfaste agaynste the crafty assautes of the deuyll.

12 For we wrestle not againste fleshe and bloude: but against rule, agaynst power, and againste worldlye rulers of the darckenes of thys worlde, againste spyrytuall wickednes, for heauenly thynges.

13 For thys cause take vnto you the armoure of God, that ye maye be able to resiste in the euyl daye, and stande perfect in al thinges.

14 Stande therfore, and your loynes gyrde about wyth veritie, hauinge on þe breste plate of rightuousnes,

15 and shoed with shoes prepared by the Gospel of peace.

16 Aboue all take to you the shelde of fayth, wherwith ye maye quench all þe fyrie dartes of the wycked.

17 And take the helmet of saluacion and the swerd of the spyrite, which is the word of God.

18 And praye all wayes wyth all maner prayer and supplicacion: and that in the spirite, and watch therunto with all instaunce and supplication for all sainctes,

19 and for me, that vtteraunce maye be geuen vnto me, that I maye open my mouth bloudly, to vtter the secretes of the Gospel,

20 wherof I am a messenger in boundes that therin I may speake frely, as it becommeth me to speake.

21 But that ye maye also knowe what condicion I am in and what I do. Tichicus my deare brother and faythfull mynyster in the Lorde, shal shewe you of all thinges,

22 whom I sent vnto you for the same purpose, that ye myght knowe what case I stand in, and that he myght comforte your hertes.

23 Peace be with the brethren, and loue with fayth from God the father, and from the Lorde Iesus Christe.

24 Grace be with al them whiche loue oure Lorde Iesus Christe in purenes. Amen.

# Philippians

## CHAPTER 1

Paule and Tymotheus þe seruauntes of Iesu Christe. To all þe sainctes in Christe Iesu, which are at Philippos, wyth the Bishops and Deacons.

2 Grace be wyth you and peace from God oure father, and from the Lorde Iesus Christe.

3 I thanke my God wyth all remembraunce of you,

4 all wayes in al my prayers for you, and praye wyth gladnes,

5 because of the fellowshyppe, whyche ye haue in the Gospell from the fyrste daye vnto nowe:

6 and am surelye certifyed of this, that he whyche began a good worke in you, shall go forth wyth it vntyll the daye of Iesus Christe,

7 as it becommeth me so to iudge of you al, because I haue you in my herte, and haue you also euerye one companions of grace wyth me, euen in my boundes as I defende and stablishe the Gospel.

8 For God beareth me recorde howe greatlye I longe after you all from the very herte rote in Iesus Christe.

9 And this I praye, that youre loue maye increase more and more in knowledge, and in al fealinge,

10 that ye myght accepte thinges moste excellent, that ye might be pure and such as should hurte no mannes conscience, vntyll the daye of Christe,

11 fylled with the fruites of rightuousnes, which fruites come by Iesus Christ vnto the glory and laude of God.

12 I woulde ye vnderstode brethren that my busines is happened vnto the greater furtheringe of the Gospel.

13 So that my boundes in Christe are manifeste thorowe out al the iudgement hal and in al other places:

14 In so much that many of the brethren in the Lorde are boldened thorowe my boundes, & dare more largely speake the worde without feare.

15 Some there are whiche preache Christ of enuie and stryfe, and some of good wyll.

16 The one parte preacheth Christe of strife and not purelye supposinge to adde more aduersitye to my boundes.

17 The other parte of loue, because they se that I am set to defende the Gospell.

18 What then? So, that Christe be preached al maner wayes, whether it be by occasion, or of true meaninge, I therin ioye: ye & will ioye.

19 For I knowe that this shall chaunce to my saluacion, thorowe your prayer and mynystringe of the spyryte of Iesu Christe,

20 as I hertely loke for and hope that in nothinge I shalbe ashamed, but that wyth all confydence as always in tymes paste, euen so nowe Christe shall be magnyfyed in my bodye, whether it be thorowe lyfe, or else death.

21 For Christe is to me lyfe, and death is to me auauntage.

22 Yf it chaunce me to lyue in the fleshe, that is to me frutefull for to worke, and what to chose

23 I wote not. I am constrayned of two thinges: I desire to be lowsed and to be wyth Christe, whiche thinge is best of all.

24 Neuerthelesse to abyde in the fleshe is more nedeful for you.

25 And thys am I sure of that I shall abyde, and wyth you all continue for the furtheraunce and ioye of your faith,

26 that ye may more abundantly reioyce in Iesus Christe thorowe me, by my comminge to you again.

27 Onlye let your conuersation be as it becommeth the Gospell of Christ, that whether I come and se you, or els be absent, I maye yet heare of you, that ye continue in one spyrite, and in one soule, labouringe as we do, to

mayntayne the fayth of the Gospell,

28 and in nothing fearing your aduersaries: whiche is to them a token of perdicion, and to you of saluation, and that of God.

29 For vnto you it is geuen, that not onely ye should beleue on Christ, but also suffre for his sake,

30 and haue euen the same fyght, whiche ye sawe me haue and now heare of me.

## CHAPTER 2

If there be amonge you anye consolation in Christ, yf there be anye comfortable loue, yf there be anye feloweshyp of spirite, yf there be any compassion or mercye,

2 fulfyll my ioye that ye drawe one waye hauinge one loue, being of one accorde, and of one minde,

3 that nothing be done thorowe stryfe or vaine glorye, but that in mekenes of mynde euerye man esteme other better then him selfe,

4 & that no man considere his owne, but what is meate for other.

5 Let the same mynde be in you that was in Christ Iesu:

6 Whiche beinge in the shap of God, and thought it not robbery to be equal wt God.

7 Neuerthelesse he made hym selfe of no reputation, & toke on him the shap of a seruaunt, and became lyke vnto men,

8 and was founde in hys aparell as a man. He humbled hym selfe, and became obediente vnto þe death euen the death of the crosse.

9 Wherfore God hath exalted hym, and geuen hym a name aboue al names,

10 that in the name of Iesus should euerye knee bowe, both of thinges in heauen and thinges in earth, and thinges vnder the earth,

11 and that al tounges should confesse that Iesus Christ is the Lorde vnto the prayse of God the father.

12 Wherfore my dearlye beloued, as ye haue alwayes obeyed, not when I was presente onelye, but nowe much more in myne absence euen so worke out your owne saluacion wt feare and trembling.

13 For it is God, whyche worketh in you, both the wyll and also the dede, euen of good wyl.

14 Do al thinge wythout murmuringe and disputynge,

15 that ye maye be fauteles & pure, the sonnes of God wythout rebuke, in the middes of a croked and a peruerse nacyon, amonge whiche se that ye shine as lightes in the worlde,

16 holding fast the worde of life, vnto my reioysing in the daye of Christe, that I haue not runne in vayne, neyther haue laboured in vaine.

17 Yea, and though I be offered vp vpon the offeringe and sacrifyce of youre fayth: I reioyce, and reioyce wyth you al.

18 For the same cause also, reioyce ye, and reioyce ye wyth me.

19 I truste in the Lord Iesus for to sende Timotheus shortely vnto you, that I also maye be of good comforte, when I knowe what case ye stand in.

20 For I haue noman that is so lyke mynded to me, whiche with so pure affeccion careth for youre matters.

21 For al other seke theyr owne, and not that whiche is Iesus Christes.

22 Ye knowe the profe of hym, howe that as a sonne with the father, so with me bestowed he his laboure vpon the Gospel

23 Hym I hope to send assone as I knowe, howe it wyl go with me.

24 I truste in the Lord I also my selfe shal come shortly.

25 I supposed it necessarye to sende brother Epaphroditus vnto you, my companion in laboure and felow souldier, youre Apostle & my minister at my nedes.

26 For he lounged after you, and was full of heauines, because þt ye had hearde saye, that he shoulde be sycke.

27 And no dout he was sicke, and that nye vnto death. But God had mercye on hym not on hym onely, but on me also, lest I should haue had sorowe vpon sorowe.

28 I sent him therfore the diligentliar, that when ye shoulde se hym, ye might reioyce againe, and I myght be the lesse sorowfull.

29 Receiue him therfore in the Lorde wyth al gladnes, and make muche of suche:

30 because that for the worke of Christ he went so farre, that he was nye vnto death, and regarded not hys lyfe, to fulfyll that seruice, whiche was lackinge on your part towarde me.

## CHAPTER 3

Moreouer my brethren, reioyce in the Lorde. It greueth me not to write one thinge often to you. For to you it is a sure thynge.

2 Beware of dogges, beware of euyll workes. Beware of dyssencyon.

3 For we are cyrcumcysion, whyche worship God in the spirite, and reioyce in Christe Iesu, and haue no confidence in the fleshe,

4 though I haue wherof I might reioice in the fleshe. If any other man thinke that he hath wherof he mighte truste in the fleshe, much more I,

5 circumcised the eighte daye, of the kynred of Israel, of

the tribe of Beniamin, an Hebrue borne of the Hebrues: as concerninge the lawe, a pharisey,

6 and as concerning feruentnes, I persecuted the congregation, & as touching the ryghtuousnes, whiche is in the lawe, I was vnrebukeable.

7 But the thinges that were vauntage vnto me. I counted losse for Christes sake.

8 Yea I thinke al thinges but losse for that excellent knowledge sake of Christ Iesu my Lord. For whom I haue counted al thinges losse, and do iudge them but dounge, that I myght wynne Christe,

9 and might be founde in hym, not hauinge mine owne rightuousnes, which is of the lawe, but that whyche spryngeth of the fayth, is in CHRISTE. I meane the rightuousnes, whiche commeth of God thorowe faith

10 in knowinge him and the vertue of his resurreccion, & the fellowshippe of hys passyons, that I myghte be conformable vnto his death,

11 yf by anye meanes I myght atteyne vnto the resurreccyon from death.

12 Not as though I had alreadie atteined to it, either were already perfecte: but I folowe yf that I maye comprehende that, wherin I am comprehended of Christ Iesu.

13 Brethren I count not my selfe that I haue gotten it: but one thinge I say. I forget that, whiche is behinde, & stretche my selfe vnto that whiche is before,

14 and prease vnto the marke appointed, to obteine the reward of the high callinge of God in Christe Iesu.

15 Let vs therfore as many, as be perfect be thus wyse minded, & yf ye be other wise minded, I pray God open euen this vnto you.

16 Neuertheles in þe, whervnto we are come, let vs procede by one rule, that we may be of one accord.

17 Brethren be folowers of me, and loke on them which walke euen so, as ye haue vs for an ensample.

18 For many walke (of whom I haue tolde you often, and nowe tel you weping) that they are the enemies of the crosse of Christ,

19 whose ende is dampnation, whose God is theyr belye, and whose glorye is to theyr shame, whiche are worldlye minded.

20 But oure conuersation is in heauen, from whence we loke for a sauiour, euen the Lorde Iesus Christ,

21 whiche shal chaunge oure vyle bodies, that they maie be fashioned like vnto his glorious bodie, accordinge to þe working, wherby he is able to subdue all thinges vnto him selfe.

# CHAPTER 4

THERFORE my brethren dearlye beloued & lounged for my ioye & crowne, so continue in the Lord, ye beloued.

2 I praye Euodias, & beseche Sintiches that they be of one accorde in the Lorde.

3 Yea, and I beseche the faythfull yockefelowe, helpe the women, whiche laboured wyth me in þe Gospell, and with Clemente also, and with other my labour felowes, whose names are in the boke of my lyfe.

4 Reioyce in the Lorde alway, and agayne I say reioyce.

5 Lette your softnes be knowen to all men. The Lorde is euen at hande.

6 Be not carefull: but in all thinges shewe your petition vnto God in prayer and supplication, wyth geuinge of thankes.

7 And the peace of God, whiche passeth al vnderstandynge, kepe your hertes and myndes in Chryste Iesu.

8 Furthermore brethren, whatsoeuer thynges are true, whatsoeuer things are honest, whatsoeuer thinges are iuste, whatsoeuer thinges are pure, whatsoeuer thinges pertaine to loue, whatsoeuer thinges are of honeste report: yf there be anie vertuous thinge yf there be anye laudable thinge,

9 those same haue ye in your minde, whiche ye haue both learned and receiued, hearde, and also sene in me: those thinges do, and the God of peace shall be wyth you.

10 I reioyce in the Lorde greatly, that nowe at the last ye are reuiued agayne to care for me, in that wherin ye were also carefull, but ye lacked opportunitie.

11 I speake not because of necessitie. For I haue learned in whatsoeuer estate I am therwyth to be content.

12 I can both cast doune my selfe. I can also excede. Euery where, and in all thinges I am instructed, both to be ful, and to be houngrie, to haue plentie, and to suffre nede.

13 I can do al thinges thorowe the helpe of Christe whiche strengtheth me.

14 Notwithstandinge ye haue well done, that ye beare parte with me in my tribulation.

15 Ye of Philippos knowe that in the beginninge of the Gospel, when I departed from Macedonia, no congregacion beare parte wyth me, as concerning, geuinge, and receiuinge, but ye onely.

16 For when I was in Thessalonica, ye sente ones, and afterwarde agayne vnto my nedes:

17 not that I desire gyftes, but I desire aboundaunte frute on youre part.

18 I receiued al, and haue plentie. I was euen fylled after that I had receyued of Epaphroditus, that which came

from you, & odour that smelleth swete, a sacrifyce accepted and pleasaunt to God.

19 My God fulfill youre nedes thorowe hys gloriouse ryches in Iesus Christ.

20 Vnto God and oure father be prayse for euermore. Amen.

21 Salute all the sainctes in Christ Iesus. The brethren which are with me grete you.

22 All the sainctes salute you, and most of all they, which are of the Emperours houshholde.

23 The grace of our Lord Iesus Christe be wyth you all. Amen.

# Colossians

## CHAPTER 1

Paule an Apostle of Iesu Christe by the wyll of God, and brother Tymotheus.

2 To the sainctes, whiche are at Colossa, and brethren that beleue in Christe. Grace be wyth you and peace from God oure father, and from the Lorde IESVS Christe.

3 We geue thankes to God the father of oure Lorde Iesus Christe, alwaies prayinge for you,

4 sence we hearde of your fayth, which ye haue in Christ Iesu, and of the loue, which ye beare to all saynctes,

5 for the hopes sakes, whiche is layde vp in store for you in heauen of whiche hope ye haue heard before by the true worde of the Gospel

6 which is come vnto you, euen as it is into all the world, and is frutefull, as it is amonge you, from the fyrste daye in the, whiche ye hearde of it, and had experience in the grace of God in the trueth,

7 as ye learned of Epaphra oure deare felowe seruaunte, whiche is for you a faythfull minister of Christe,

8 whiche also declared vnto vs your loue, whiche ye haue in the spirite.

9 For this cause we also, sence the daye we heard of it, haue not ceased prayeng for you, and desiring that ye myght be fulfilled with the knowledge of his will, in all wysdome, and spiritual vnderstandinge,

10 that ye mighte walke worthy of the Lorde in all thinges, that please him beyng frutefull in all good workes, and encreasing in the knowledge of God

11 strengthed wyth all myghte thorowe his glorious power, vnto al pacience & longe suffering with ioyfulnes,

12 geuing thankes vnto the father, which hath made vs mete to be partakers of the inheritaunce of sainctes in lyght.

13 Which hath deliuered vs from the power of darcknes and hath translated vs into the kyngdome of his deare sonne,

14 in whom we haue redempcion thorowe his bloude, that is to saye: the forgeuenes of synnes,

15 whyche is the ymage of the inuisible God, fyrste begotten of creatures.

16 For by hym were all thynges created, things that are in heauen, and things that are in earth: thinges visible and thinges inuisible, whether they be maiestye or Lordeshyp, eyther rule or power. Al thynges are created by hym and in hym,

17 and he is before all thinges, and in hym all thinges haue theyr beynge.

18 And he is the head of the body, that is to wyt of the congregation: he is the beginning and fyrst begotten of the dead, that in all things he might haue the preeminence.

19 For it pleased the father that in him shoulde all fulnes dwel,

20 and by hym to reconcile all thinge vnto him selfe, and to set at peace by him thorowe þe bloude of his crosse, both thinges in heauen, and things in earth.

21 And you (which were in tymes past straungers and enemyes, because your myndes were set in euyl workes) hath he now reconciled

22 in the body of his fleshe thorowe death, to make you holye vnblamable and without faut in his owne syght,

23 yf ye continue grounded and stablyshed in the fayth, and be not moued away from the hope of the Gospell, where of ye haue hearde, how that it is preached amonge al creatures which are vnder heauen, wherof I Paule am made a minister.

24 Nowe ioye I in my sufferinges which I suffer for you, and fulfyll that whiche is behinde of the passions of Christe in my fleshe for his bodies sake, which is the congregacion,

25 wherof I am made a minister accordinge to the ordinaunce of God, whiche ordinaunce was geuen me vnto you warde, to fulfyll þe worde of God,

26 that mistery hyd sence the world beganne, and sence the begynnynge of generacyons: but now is opened to hys sainctes

27 to whom God woulde make knowen the glorious riches of this misterye amonge the Gentyls, whiche ryches is Christ, in you the hope of glorye,

28 whome we preache, warning all men and teaching all men in all wisdom, to make all men perfect in Christ Iesu.

29 Wherin I also labour and stryue euen as farforth as his workinge worketh in me mightely.

## CHAPTER 2

I woulde ye knewe what fightinge I haue for your sakes, & for them of Laodicia, and for as many as haue not sene my person in the fleshe,

2 that their hertes mighte be comforted and knit together in loue, and in all riches of full vnderstandinge for to knowe the mystery of God the father and of Christe,

3 in whom are hyd al the treasures of wysdom and knowledge.

4 This I saye leaste anye man shoulde begyle you with entisyng wordes.

5 For though I be absent in fleshe: yet am I present with you in the spirite ioyenge and beholdinge the order that ye kepe, and your stedfast faith in Christ.

6 As ye haue therfore receiued Christe Iesus þe Lorde, euen so walke,

7 roted and builte in him and stedfaste in the fayth as ye haue learned, and therin be plentuous in geuing thankes.

8 Beware least anye man come and spoyle you thorowe philosophie and disceitful vanitie, thorowe the tradicions of men, and ordinaunces after the world, and not after Christ.

9 For in him dwelleth al the fulnes of þe Godhead bodely,

10 and ye are complete in hym, whiche is the head of al rule and power,

11 in whom also ye are circumcysed with circumcision made withoute handes, by puttinge of the synful body of the fleshe thorow the circumcision, that is in Christ,

12 in that ye are buried, wt him thorow baptisme in whom ye are also risen again thorow fayth, þt is wroughte by the operacion of God, which raysed hym from death.

13 And ye which were dead in sinne thorow the vncircumcision of youre fleshe, hath he quyckened with him, and hath forgeuen vs al oure treaspases.

14 And hath put out the hande wryttinge that was againste vs, contayned in the lawe wrytten, and that hath he taken out of the waye, and hath fastened it to his crosse,

15 and hath spoiled rule and power and hath made a shewe of them openlye, and hath tryumphed ouer them in hys owne persone.

16 Let no man therfore trouble youre consciences aboute meate and drincke, or for a peace of an holye daye, as the holy daye of the new mone, or of the Saboth dayes,

17 whyche are nothinge, but shaddowes of thinges to come, but the bodye is in Christe.

18 Let no man make you shoute at a wronge marke which after his owne ymaginacion walketh in the humblenes and holynes of aungels, thynges which he neuer sawe: causelesse puft vp with his fleshely minde,

19 and holdeth not the head, wherof all the bodye by ioyntes and couples receyueth nouryshment, & is knyt together, & encreaseth wyth the increasynge that cometh of God.

20 Wherfore yf ye be deade wyth Christe from the ordinaunces of the world, why as though ye yet liued in the worlde, are ye ledde wyth tradicions of them that saye?

21 Touche not, tast not, handel not,

22 whiche all perishe wyth the vsynge of them, and are after the commaundementes and doctrines of men,

23 which thinges haue the symilitude of wysdome in chosen holines and humblenes, and in that they spare not the bodye, and do the fleshe no worship vnto his nede.

## CHAPTER 3

IF ye be then rysen agayn with Christ seke those thinges which are aboue where Christe sitteth on the right hand of God.

2 Set youre affeccion on thinges that are aboue, and not on thinges, which are on the earth.

3 For ye are dead and youre lyfe is hid with Christ in God.

4 When Christ which is our life, shal shew him selfe then shal ye also appere wyth him in glorye.

5 Mortifie therfore, youre members whiche are on the earth, fornicacion, vnclenes, vnnatural, lust euil concupiscence, and couetousnesse, which is worshippinge of Idolles,

6 for which thynges sakes the wrathe of God commeth on the chyldren of vnbeliefe.

7 In whyche things ye walked ones, when ye liued in them.

8 But now put ye also awaye from you all things, wrath,

fearnes, maliciousnes, cursed speaking fylthy speaking out of your mouthes.

9 Lye not one to another, that the olde man wyth hys workes be put of,

10 and þe newe put on, whiche is renued in knowledge after the ymage of hym, that made hym

11 where is neyther Gentile nor Iew, circumcysion nor vncircumcision, Barbarous or Sythian, bond or fre: but Christ is all in al thinges.

12 Nowe therfore as electe of God, holy and beloued, put on tender mercye, kyndnes, humblenes of mindes, meaknes, longe sufferynge,

13 forbearing one another, and forgeuing one another, yf anye man haue a quarel to another, euen as Christe forgaue you, euen so do ye.

14 Aboue all these thynges put on loue, which is the bond of perfectnes.

15 And the peace of God rule in your hertes, to the which peace ye are called in one bodye. And se that ye be thankfull.

16 Let the word of Christ dwell in you plenteouslye in all wysdome. Teache and exhorte youre owne selues, in psalmes, and hymnes, and spirituall songes, whiche haue fauoure with them, singinge in your hertes to the Lorde.

17 And all thinges (whatsoeuer ye do in word or dede) do it in the name of the Lorde Iesu geuinge thankes to God the father by hym.

18 Wyues submitte youre selues vnto youre owne husbandes, as it is comly in the Lorde.

19 Husbandes loue your wyues, and be not bitter vnto them.

20 Chyldren obey your fathers & mothers in all thinges, for that is wel pleasynge vnto the Lorde.

21 Fathers, rate not your children, leaste they be of a desperate mynde.

22 Seruauntes, be obediente vnto your bodelye maisters in al thinges, not wyth eye seruice as men pleasers, but in synglenes of herte fearinge God.

23 And what soeuer ye do, do it hertelye as though ye dyd it to the Lord, and not vnto men

24 for as muche as ye know that of the Lorde ye shall receiue the reward of inheritaunce, for ye serue the Lorde Christ.

25 But he that doeth anye wronge, shall receiue for the wronge that he hath done, for there is no respect of persons wyth God.

# CHAPTER 4

YE maisters do vnto your seruauntes, that which is iuste and equall, sayng: ye know that ye also haue a maister in heauen.

2 Contynue in prayer & watch in the same wyth thankes geuynge,

3 prayeng also for vs þt God open vnto vs the dore of vtteraunce, that we maye speake the misterye of Christe (wherfore I am also in bondes)

4 that I maye vtter it, as it becometh me to speake.

5 Walke wiselye to them that are wythout and redeme the tyme.

6 Let youre speache be always well sauoured and poudred with salte, that ye maye knowe, howe to answere euery man.

7 The deare brother Tichicus shal tell you of al my busines, whiche is a faithfull minyster, and felow seruaunt in the Lorde,

8 whom I haue sent vnto you for the same purpose, that he mighte knowe howe ye do, & myght comforte your hertes,

9 wyth one Onesimus, a faythfull and a beloued brother, whiche is one of you. They shall shewe you of al thinges, whiche are adoing here.

10 Aristarchus my pryson felowe saluteth you and Marcus, Barnabas sisters sonne: touching whom ye receiued commaundementes. Yf he come vnto you, receiue him,

11 and Iesus which is called Iustus, which are of the circumcision. These onely are my worke felowes vnto the kyngdome of God, whiche were vnto my consolacion.

12 Epaphras the seruaunte of Christe, which is one of you, saluteth you, and alwaies laboureth feruentlye for you in prayers, that ye maye stande perfecte and full in all that is the wyll of God.

13 I beare hym recorde, that he hath a feruent minde toward you and toward them of Laodicia and them of Hierapolis.

14 Deare Lucas the Phisician greteth you, and Demas.

15 Salute the brethren whiche are of Laodicia, and salute Nimphas, and the congregacion, which is in hys house.

16 And when the Epistle is read of you, make that it be read in the congregacion of the Laodicians also and that ye lykewyse read the Epistle of Laodycya.

17 And saye to Archippus: take hede to the offyce that thou hast receyued in the Lord, that thou fulfill it.

18 The salutation by the hande of me Paule. Remembre my bondes. Grace be with you Amen.

# 1 Thessalonians

## CHAPTER 1

**P**AULE, Siluanus, and Tymotheus. Vnto the congregation of the Thessalonyans in God the father, and in the lord Iesus Christ. Grace be with you, & peace from God our father, & from the Lord Iesus Christ.

2 We geue God thankes alwayes for you all, makinge mention of you in oure prayers

3 wythoute ceasinge, and cal to remembraunce your worke the fayth, and laboure in loue & perseueraunce in the hope of our Lord Iesus Christ, in the syght of God oure father,

4 because we know brethren beloued of God, how that ye are electe.

5 For oure Gospell came not to you in worde onelye, but also in power, and in the holye Ghoste, and in muche certaintie, as ye know after what maner we behaued our selues among you, for your sakes.

6 And ye became folowers of vs and of the Lord, and receyued the worde with much affliccion, with ioye of the holye ghoste:

7 so that ye were an ensample to al that beleue in Macedonia and Achaia.

8 For from you sounded out the worde of the Lord, not in Macedonia & in Achaia onelye: but your fayth also which ye haue vnto God, sprede her selfe abrode in all quarters, so greatlye that it neadeth not vs to speake any thynge at all.

9 For they them selues shewe of you, what maner of entering in we had vnto you, and howe ye turned vnto God from Images, for to serue the liuing and true God,

10 and for to loke for hys sonne from heauen, whom he raised from death. I meane Iesus which deliuered vs from wrath to come.

## CHAPTER 2

**F**OR ye youre selues knowe brethren of oure entraunce in vnto you, how þt it was not in vaine:

2 but euen after that we had suffred before, and were shamefullye entreated at Philippos (as ye wel know) then were we bolde in our God to speake vnto you the Gospel of God wyth muche stryuynge.

3 Oure exhortacyon was not to bringe you to erroure, nor yet to vnclennes, neyther was it wyth gile,

4 but as we were allowed of God, that the Gospel shoulde be committed vnto vs, euen so we spake, not as though we entended to please men, but God whyche tryeth oure hertes.

5 Neither was our conuersacyon at anye tyme wyth flatterynge wordes, as ye well knowe neyther in cloked couetousnes, god is record:

6 neyther sought we prayse of men neyther of you, nor yet of anye other, when we mighte haue bene chargeable, as the Apostles of Christe,

7 but we were tender amonge you, euen as a noursse cheryshed his children,

8 so was our affeccion toward you, oure good wil was to haue dealte to you, not the Gospel of God onely, but also our owne soules because ye were deare to vs.

9 Ye remember brethren our labour and trauayle. For we laboured day and night, because we would not be greuous vnto any of you, and preached vnto you the Gospel of God.

10 Ye are wytnesses, and so is God, howe holily and iustlye and vnblameably we behaued our selues among you that beleue

11 as ye know howe that we exhorted and comforted, and besoughte euerye one of you, as a father hys chyldren,

12 that ye woulde walke worthye of God, whiche hath called you vnto his kingdome & glory.

13 For thys cause thanke we God wythout ceasyng, because

that when ye receiued of vs the word, wher with God was preached, ye receiued it not as the worde of man: but euen as it was in dede, the worde of God: whiche worketh in you that beleue.

14 For ye brethren became folowers of the congregacions of God, which in Iewrye are in Christ Iesu, for ye haue suffred lyke thinges of your kinsmen, as we our selues haue suffred of the Iewes.

15 Which as they kylled the Lorde Iesus and theyr owne prophetes, euen so haue they persecuted vs, and God they please not, and are contrarye to all men,

16 and forbid vs to preache vnto the Gentyls, that they might be saued to fulfyll theyr synnes alwaye. For the wrathe of God is come on them, euen to the vtmost.

17 For as muche brethren as we are kepte from you for a season as concernynge the bodely presence, but not in the herte we enforsed the more to se you personallye wyth greate desyre.

18 And therfore we woulde haue come vnto you I Paule ones and agayne: but Sathan withstode vs.

19 For what is oure hope or ioye, or crowne of reioysynge: are not ye it in the presence of our Lord Iesus Christ at hys coming?

20 yes ye are our glory and ioye.

## CHAPTER 3

Wherfore sence we could no longer forbeare, it pleased vs to remayne at Athens alone,

2 & sente Timotheus our brother and minister of God, and our laboure felowe in the Gospel of Christe, to stablishe you and to comforte you ouer youre fayth,

3 that no man should be moued in these afflicons. For ye your selues knowe þt we are euen appointed there vnto.

4 For verelye when I was wyth you, I tolde you before that we shoulde suffer tribulacion, euen as it came to passe, and as ye know.

5 For this cause when I coulde no longer forbeare, I sente, þt I might haue knowledge of your fayth, least haplye the tempter had tempted you, and that oure labour had bene bestowed in vayne.

6 But nowe lately when Timotheus came from you vnto vs, and declared to vs youre fayth & your loue, & howe that ye haue good remembraunce of vs alwayes, desyring to se vs as we desyre to se you.

7 Therfore brethren we had consolacion in you and in all our aduersyte and necessitie, thorow your fayth.

8 For nowe are we alyue, yf ye stande stedfast in þe Lorde.

9 For what thankes can we recompence to God again for you, ouer al the ioy that we ioy for your sakes before oure God

10 whyl we nighte and daye praye excedinglye that we mighte se you presently, and might fulfill that which is lackynge in youre fayth.

11 God him selfe our father, and our Lord Iesus Christ guide oure iorney to you:

12 and the Lorde increase you and make you flow ouer in loue one towarde another and toward all men euen as we do toward you,

13 to make your hertes stable & vnblameable in holynesse before God oure father, at the comminge of our Lorde Iesus wyth al hys sainctes.

## CHAPTER 4

Fvrther more we beseche you brethren and exhorte you in the Lord Iesus, that ye increase more and more, euen as ye haue receiued of vs, howe ye oughte to walke and to please God.

2 Ye remember what commaundementes we gaue you in oure Lorde Iesu Christ.

3 For this is the will of God, euen that ye shoulde be holy, and that ye shoulde abstayne from fornicacion,

4 that euerye one of you should know, howe to kepe his vessell in holynes and honoure,

5 and not in the luste of concupiscence, as do the heathen, which know not God,

6 that no man go to far and defraude his brother in bargaining: because the Lorde is a reuenger of al suche thinges as we tolde you before tyme and testified.

7 For God hath not called vs to vncleanes, but vnto holines.

8 He therfore that despiseth, despiseth not man, but God, whiche hath sente his holye spirite amonge you.

9 But as touchinge brotherly loue, ye nede not þt I write vnto you. For ye are taught of God to loue one another.

10 Yea and that thing verelye ye do vnto all the brethren, which are thorowout all Macedonia. We beseche you brethren, that ye encrease more and more,

11 and that ye studye to be quyete, and to medle with youre owne busines, and to worke wyth youre owne handes, as we commaunded you:

12 that ye may behaue your selues honestly towardes them that are wythout, and that nothinge be lackinge vnto you.

13 I woulde not brethren haue you ignoraunt concerninge them whiche are fallen a sleepe, that ye sorowe not as other do which haue no hope.

14 For yf we beleue that Iesus Christe dyed and rose agayne

euen so them also, whyche slepe by Iesus, wyl God brynge agayn with hym.

15 And thys saye we vnto you in the worde of the Lorde, that we whyche lyue and are remaynynge in the commynge of the Lorde, shal not come yerre they which slepe.

16 For the Lord hym selfe shall descende from heauen with a shoute, and the voice of the Archangell and trompe of God. And the deade in Christ shall arise fyrste:

17 then shal we which lyue and remayne, be caught vp with them also in the cloudes, to meate the Lorde in the ayer. And so shall we euer be with the Lord.

18 Wherfore comforte youre selues one another with these wordes.

## CHAPTER 5

OF the tymes and seasons brethrne ye haue no nede, that I wryte vnto you:

2 for ye youre selues knowe perfectly that the daie of the Lorde shall come euen as a thefe in the nyght.

3 When they shal say peace and no daunger, then commeth on them soden destruccion, as the trauaylynge of a woman wyth chyld, and they shal not escape.

4 But ye brethren are not in darckenes, that that daye shoulde come on you as it were a thefe.

5 Ye are all the chyldren of lyght and the chyldren of the daye. We are not of the nyghte neither of darckenes.

6 Therfore let vs not slepe as do other: but let vs watche & be sober.

7 For they that slepe, slepe in the nyght: and they that be droncken, are droncken in the nyght.

8 But let vs whiche are of the daye, be sober, armed wyth þe breste plate of fayth and loue, and wyth hope of saluacyon as an helmet.

9 For God hath not annoynted vs vnto wrath: but to obtayne saluacyon by the meanes of oure Lord Iesu Christ

10 whyche dyed for vs: that whether we wake or slepe, we shoulde liue together wyth hym.

11 Wherfore comforte your selues together, and edifye one another, euen as ye do.

12 We beseche you brethren, that ye knowe them, whiche laboure amonge you, and haue the ouersight of you in the Lord

13 and geue you exhortacyon, that ye haue them the more in loue for theyr workes sake, and be at peace wyth them.

14 We desyre you brethren, warne them that are vnruly, comforte the feble minded, forbeare the weake, haue contynuall pacience towarde all men.

15 Se that none recompence euyll for euyll vnto any man: but euer folowe that which is good, both among your selues, and to all men.

16 Reioyse euer.

17 Praye contynuallye.

18 In all thinges geue thankes. For thys is the wyll of God in Christe Iesu towarde you.

19 Quenche not the spyryte.

20 Despyse not prophesyenge.

21 Examen all thinges, and kepe that which is good.

22 Absteyne from all suspicious thinges.

23 The very God of peace sanctifye you thorowout. And I praye God that your whole spyryte, soule and bodye, be kept faultles vnto the comming of oure Lorde Iesus Christe.

24 Faythfull is he whiche called you: which wyl also do it.

25 Brethren, praye for vs.

26 Grete all the brethren wyth an holy kysse.

27 I charge you in the Lorde, that thys Epistle be read vnto all the holy brethren.

28 The grace of the Lord Iesus Christ be wyth you. Amen.

# 2 Thessalonians

## CHAPTER 1

Paule, Syluanus & Timotheus. Vnto the congregacyon of the Thessalonians, whiche are in God oure father, and in the Lorde Iesus Christe.

2 Grace be with you and peace from God oure father, and from the Lorde Iesus Christe.

3 We are bounde to thanke God alwayes for you brethren, as it mete, because that your fayth groweth excedingly, and euerye one of you swimmeth in loue towarde another betwene youre selues,

4 so that we oure selues reioyse of you in the congregacions of GOD ouer youre pacience and fayth in al youre persecucyons and trybulacyons that ye suffer,

5 whiche is a token of the ryghtuouse iudgement of God that ye are counted worthye of the kyngdome of God, for whiche ye also suffer.

6 It is verely a ryghteous thing with God to recompence trybulacyon to them that trouble you:

7 and to you whiche are troubled, reste wyth vs, when the Lorde Iesus shall shewe hym selfe from heauen wyth hys myghtye Aungels,

8 in flammynge fyre, rendrynge vengeaunce vnto them that knowe not God, and to them that obeye not vnto the Gospel of our Lorde Iesus Christ,

9 which shall be punyshed wyth euerlastyng dampnacyon from the presence of the Lorde, and from the glory of hys power,

10 when he shall come to be gloryfyed in hys saynctes, and to be made marueylous in all them that beleue: because oure testimonye that we had vnto you, was beleued euen the same daye that we preached it.

11 Wherfore we praye alwayes for you that oure God make you worthye of the callynge and fulfyll al delectacyon of goodnes and the worke of fayth, wyth power

12 that the name of oure Lorde Iesus Christe maye be gloryfyed in you, and ye in hym, thorowe the grace of oure God, and of the Lorde Iesus Christe:

## CHAPTER 2

We beseche you brethren by the commynge of oure Lorde Iesu Christe, and in that we shal assemble vnto hym,

2 that ye be not sodenly moued fome your mynd, and be not troubled, neyther by spirite neyther by wordes, nor yet by letter whiche shoulde seme to come from vs, as thoughe the daye of Christe were at hande.

3 Let no man deceyue you by any meanes, for the Lord commeth not, except there come a departyng first, and that, that sinful man be opened, the sonne of perdicyon

4 whiche is an aduersarye, and is exalted aboue all that is called God, or that is worshypped: so that he shall sytte as God in the temple of God, and shewe hym selfe as God.

5 Remember ye not, that when I was yet with you, I tolde you these thynges?

6 And nowe ye knowe what withholdeth: euen that he myght be vttered at his tyme.

7 For the mysterye of that iniquitie doeth he al ready work whiche onelye loketh vntyll it be taken out of the waye.

8 And then shall that wicked be vttered, whome the Lorde shall consume with the spirite of hys mouth, and shall destroye wt the aperaunce of hys commynge.

9 euen hym whose commynge is by the workynge of Sathan, with all liynge power, signes and wonders:

10 and in all deceyuablenes of vnryghtuousnes, amonge them that peryshe: because they receyued not the loue of the truethe, that they myght haue bene sayed.

11 And therfor God shall sende them stronge delusyon,

971

that they shoulde beleue lyes:

12 that all they myghte be damned which beleued not the trueth but had pleasure in vnryghtuousnes.

13 But we are bounde to geue thankes alwaye to God for you brethren beloued of the Lorde, because that God hath from the beginnynge chosen you to saluacyon, thorow sanctifiynge of the spyryte, and thorowe beleuing the trueth

14 whereunto he called you by oure Gospell, to obtayne the glorye that commeth of oure Lorde Iesu Christe.

15 Therfore brethren stande fast and kepe the ordinaunces which ye haue learned: whether it were by oure preachynge or by epistle.

16 Our Lorde Iesu Christe hym selfe, and God oure father whiche hath loued vs and hath geuen vs euerlastynge consolatyon and good hope thorow grace,

17 comforte youre hertes, and stablyshe you in all doctryne and good doynge.

## CHAPTER 3

Fvrthermore brethren praye for vs, that the worde of God maye haue free passage and be glorifyed, as it is with you:

2 and that we maye be delyuered from vnreasonable and euyll men. For all men haue not fayth:

3 but the Lorde is faythfull, whiche shall stablyshe you, and kepe you from euyll.

4 We haue confydence thorowe the Lorde to you warde, that ye both do, and wyll do þt whiche we commaunde you.

5 And the Lorde guide your hertes to the loue of God and pacience of Christe.

6 We requyre you brethren in the name of oure Lorde Iesu Christ, that ye wythdrawe your selues from euerye brother that walketh inordinatelye and not after the institucyon whiche ye receyued of vs.

7 Ye youre selues knowe howe ye oughte to folowe vs. For we behaued not oure selues inordinately among you.

8 Neyther toke we bread of anye man for nought: but wroughte wyth laboure and trauayle nyght and daye, because we would not be greuous to anye of you:

9 not but that we had authorytye: but to make oure selues as ensample vnto you, to folowe vs.

10 For when we were with you thys we warned you of, that yf there were any whiche woulde not worke, that the same shoulde not eate.

11 We haue hearde say no doubte that there are some whiche walke amonge you inordinately and worke not at all, but are besye bodyes.

12 Them that are suche we commaunde and exhorte by oure Lorde Iesu Christe, that they worke wyth quietnes, and eate theyr owne breade.

13 Brethren be not werye in well doyng.

14 Yf any man obeye not oure sayinges send vs worde of hym by a letter: and haue no companye wyth hym that he maye be ashamed.

15 And counte hym not as an enemy, but warne hym as a brother.

16 The verye Lorde of peace geue you peace alwayes, by all meanes. The Lorde be wyth you all.

17 The salutacyon of me Paule wyth myne owne hande. Thys is the token in al Epistles. So I wryte.

18 The grace of oure Lorde Iesus Christe be with you all. AMEN.

# 1 Timothy

## CHAPTER 1

Paule an Apostle of Iesus Christe, by the commaundemente of God our sauyour, and Lord Iesus christ whiche is oure hope.

2 Vnto Timothe hys naturall sonne in the fayth. Grace, mercye, and peace from God oure father and Lorde Iesus Christe oure Lorde.

3 And I besought the to abyde styl in Ephesus, when I departed into Macedonia, euen so do, that thou commaunde some, that they teache no nother wyse:

4 neyther geue hede to fables and genealogyes whiche are endelesse, & brede doubtes more then Godlye edifiynge whiche is by fayth:

5 for the ende of the commaundement is loue that commeth of a pure hert, & of a good conscience, and of fayth vnfayned:

6 from the which things some haue erred & haue turned vnto vayne iangelyng,

7 because they woulde be doctours in the scrypture, and yet vnderstand not what they speake, nether wherof they affyrme.

8 We knowe that the lawe is good, yf a man vse it lawfullye,

9 vnderstandynge thys, howe that the lawe is not geuen vnto a ryghtuous man but vnto the vnryghtuous and disobedient, to the vngodly and to synners, to vnholy and vncleane, to murtherers of fathers, and murtherers of mothers to manstears

10 & whor mongers: to them that defyle them selues wyth mankynde: to menstealers, to lyars & to periured, and so forth yf there be any other thynge that is contrarye to holsome doctrine

11 accordynge to the Gospell of the glorye of the blessed God, whiche Gospell is committed vnto me.

12 And I thanke Christe Iesus oure Lorde which hath made me stronge: for he counted me true, and put me in offyce,

13 when before I was a blasphemer and persecuter, and a tyraunte. But I obtayned mercye, because I dyd it ignoraunlty thorowe vnbelefe.

14 Neuerthelater the grace of oure Lorde was more aboundaunt wyth fayth and loue whiche is in Christ Iesu.

15 Thys is a true saiynge and by all meanes worthy to be receyued, that Christ Iesus came into the worlde to saue synners, of whom I am chiefe.

16 Not wythstandyng for this cause was mercye geuen vnto me that Iesus christ shoulde fyrste shewe on me all longe pacience vnto the ensample of them whiche shal in tyme to come beleue on hym vnto eternall lyfe.

17 So then vnto God, kyng euerlastyng, immortall, inuysyble, and wyse onely, be honoure & prayse for euer and euer. Amen.

18 Thys commaundement committe I vnto the sonne Timotheus, accordyng to the Prophesyes whiche in tyme paste were Prophesyed of the that thou in them shouldest fyght a good fyghte

19 hauynge fayth and a good conscience whiche some haue put away from them and as concernyuge faythe, haue made shypwracke.

20 Of whose numbre is Himeneus and Alexander whome I haue delyuered vnto Sathan that he myghte be taught not to blaspheme.

## CHAPTER 2

I exhorte therfore, that aboue al thynges, prayers, supplicacyons intercessyons, and geuynge of thankes be had for all men:

2 for kynges, and for all that are in authorytye, that we maye lyue a quyete and a peasable lyfe, in all godlynes and

honestye.

3 For that is good and accepted in the syghte of God oure sauyoure,

4 whiche wyll haue all men saued, and to come vnto the knoweledge of the trueth.

5 For there is one God, and one Meadiatoure betwene God and man, which is the man Christ Iesus

6 which gaue hym self a raunsome for al men, that it shoulde be testifyed at hys tyme,

7 where vnto I am ordeyned a preacher and an Apostle: I tell the trueth in Christe and lye not, beynge the teacher of the gentyles in fayth and verytye.

8 I wyll therfore that the men praye euerye where lyfting vp pure handes wythout wrath or doubtyng.

9 Lykewyse also the women that they araye them selues in comlye apparell wyth shamefastnes and discrete behauyoure not wyth broyded heare other golde, or pearles, or costlye araye:

10 but wyth suche as becommeth women that professe the worshyppyng of God thorowe good workes.

11 Let the woman learne in silence with all subieccyon.

12 I suffer not a woman to teache, neyther to haue authoritie ouer a man: but for to be in silence.

13 For Adam was fyrste formed, and then Eue.

14 Also Adam was not deceyued, but the woman was deceyued, and was in a transgressyon.

15 Notwythstandyng thorow bearyng of chyldren they shalbe saued, so they continue in faythe, loue & holynes with discrecion.

## CHAPTER 3

THYS is a true saiyng. If a man couete the offyce of a byshop, he desyreth a good worke.

2 Yea and a bishop muste be fautlesse the husband of one wyfe, sober discrete, hone style apparelled, harberous, apt to teache,

3 not dronken, no fyghter, not geuen to fylthy lucre: but gentle, abhorrynge fyghtyng, abhorrynge couetousnes,

4 and one that ruleth hys owne house honestlye, hauing children vnder obedience, wyth all honestye.

5 For yf a man can not rule hys owne house, howe shall he care for the congregacion of God.

6 He maye not be a yong scholer, lest he swell and fall into the iudgement of the euyll speaker.

7 He muste also be well reported of amonge them whiche are wythout forth, lest he fall into rebuke and snare of the euyll speaker.

8 Lykewyse muste the Deacons be honest, not double tonged, not geuen vnto much drinkynge, neyther vnto fylthy lucre:

9 but hauing the mystery of the fayth in a pure conscience.

10 And let them fyrste be proued, and then lette them mynyster, yf they be founde fautlesse.

11 Euen so muste theyr wyues be honeste, not euyll speakers, but sober and faythfull in all thynges.

12 Let the deacons be the husbandes of one wyfe, and suche as rule theyr chyldren well, and theyr owne housholdes.

13 For they that mynyster wel, get them selues good degree and greate lybertye in the faythe whiche is in Christ Iesu.

14 These thynges wryte I vnto the, trusting to come shortely vnto the:

15 but and yf I tarye longe, that then thou mayeste yet haue knowledge howe thou oughtest to behaue thy selfe in the housse of God, whiche is the congregacyon of the lyuynge God, the pyllar & ground of trueth.

16 And wythout naye greate is that mysterye of godlynes: God was shewed in þe fleshe, was iustified in the spirite, was sene of aungels, was preached vnto the gentils, was beleued on in earth and receyued vp in glory.

## CHAPTER 4

THE spyryte speaketh euydentlye that in the later tymes some shal departe from the fayth, & shall geue heed vnto spyrytes of erroure, and deuelysh doctryne of them

2 which speake false thorowe hypocrisye, and haue theyr consciences marked with an hote Iron,

3 forbyddyng to marye, and commaundynge to abstayne from meates which God hath created to be receyued wyth geuyng thankes, of them which beleue and know the trueth.

4 For all the creatures of God are good & nothynge to be refused, yf it be receyued with thankes geuynge.

5 For it is sanctifyed by the worde of God and prayer.

6 Yf thou shalt put the brethren in remembraunce of these thynges: thou shalt be a good mynyster of Iesu Christe, whiche hast bene noryshed vp in the wordes of the fayth and good doctryne, which doctryne thou haste contynuallye folowed.

7 But cast awaye vnghostly and olde wyues fables. Exercyse thy selfe vnto Godlynes.

8 For bodely exercyse profyteth lytell: But godlynes is good vnto all thynges, as a thynge whiche hath promyses of the lyfe that is now, and of the

# 1 TIMOTHY

lyfe to come.

9 Thys is a sure saiyng and of all partyes worthy to be receyued.

10 For therfore we laboure and suffer rebuke, because we beleue in the lyuyng God, whiche is the sauyoure of all men: but specyally of those that beleue.

11 Suche thynges commaunde and teache.

12 Let no man despyse thy youthe: but be vnto them that beleue, an ensample, in worde in conuersacyon, in loue, in spyryte, in fayth & in purenes.

13 Tyll I come, geue attendaunce to reading to exhortacyon and to doctryne.

14 Despyse not the gyfte that is in the, whiche was geuen the thorow Prophesye, and wyth layinge on of the handes of an elder.

15 These thynges exercyse, and geue thy selfe vnto them, that it maye be sene howe thou profytest in all thynges.

16 Take hede vnto thy selfe and vnto learnyng, and contynue therein. For yf thou shalte so do, thou shalte saue thy selfe and them that heare the.

## CHAPTER 5

REBUKE not an elder: but exhorte hym as a father, and the yonger men as brethren

2 the elder women as mothers, the yonger as systers, with all purenes.

3 Honour wyddowes, whiche are true wyddowes.

4 Yf any wyddowe haue chyldren or neues, let them learne fyrst to rule theyr owne houses godlye and to recompence theyr elders. For that is good and acceptable before God.

5 She that is a verye wydowe and fryndelesse, putteth her trust in God & contynueth in supplicacyon & prayer nyghte and daye.

6 But she that lyueth in pleasure, is dead euen yet alyue.

7 And these thynges commaunde, that they may be wythout faute.

8 Yf there be anye that prouideth not for hys owne, & namely for them of hys housholde the same denyeth the fayth, & is worsse then an infydele.

9 Let no wydowe be chosen vnder thre score yere olde, and suche a one as was the wyfe of one man,

10 and well reported of in good workes: yf she haue nouryshed chyldren, yf she haue bene lyberall to straungers, yf she haue washed the sayncts fete, yf she haue mynystred vnto them whiche were in aduersitie, yf she were contynually geuen vnto all maner good workes.

11 The yonger wydowes refuse. For when they haue begonne to waxe wanton to the dyshonoure of Christe, then wyll they marye,

12 hauynge damnacion because they haue broken theyr fyrst fayth.

13 And also they learne to go from house to house ydle, ye not ydle onelye, but also tryflynge and busybodyes speakynge thynges whiche are not comely.

14 I wyll therfore that the yonger women marye and beare children, and guyde þe house and geue none occasyon to the aduersarye to speake euyll.

15 For many of them are alreadye turned backe and are gone after Sathan.

16 And yf any man or woman that beleueth haue wydowes, let them mynyster vnto them, & lette not the congregacion be charged: that it maye haue suffycyent for them that are wyddowes in dede.

17 The elders that rule well, are worthye of double honoure, most specyally they whiche laboure in the worde and in teachynge.

18 For þe scrypture sayeth: Thou shalt not mousell the mouthe of the oxe that treadeth out the corne. And the labourer is worthye of hys rewarde.

19 Agaynste an elder receyue none accusacyon: but vnder two or thre wytnesses.

20 Them that synne, rebuke openly, that other maye feare.

21 I testyfye before God & the Lorde Iesus Christ, and the electe aungels, that thou obserue these thynges wythout hasty iudgement and do nothynge parcyally.

22 Laye handes sodenly on no man, neyther be partakers of other mennes synnes: kepe thy self pure.

23 Drink no lenger water, but vse a lytle wyne for thy stomakes sake, and thyne often dyseases.

24 Some mennes sinnes are open before hand and go before vnto iudgemente: some mennes synnes folowe after.

25 Lykewyse also good workes are manyfest before hande, and they that are otherwyse can not be hyd.

## CHAPTER 6

LET as manye seruauntes as are vnder the yoke, count theyr maysters worthy of all honoure that the name of God and hys doctryne be not euyll spoken of.

2 Se that they whiche haue beleuynge maysters, despyse them not because they are brethren: but so muche the rather do seruyce, for asmuch as they are beleuynge and beloued and partakers of the benefyte.

3 These thynges teache and exhorte. Yf any man teache otherwyse, and is not contente wt the holsome wordes of our Lord Iesus christ, and wyth the doctryne of Godlynes,

4 he is puft vp, and knoweth nothyng: but wasteth hys braynes about questyons and stryfe of wordes, whereof sprynge enuye, stryfe, raylynges, euyll surmysynges

5 and vayne disputacyons of men wyth corrupte myndes, and destytute of the trueth, whiche thynke that lucre is Godlines, from suche separate thy self.

6 Godlynes is greate ryches, yf a man be content with that he hath.

7 For we broughte nothynge into thys worlde & it is a playne case that we can carye nothyng out.

8 When we haue fode and raymente, let vs therwyth be content.

9 They that wyll be rych, fall into temptacyon and snares, and into many folysh and noysome lustes which drowne men in perdicyon and destruccyon.

10 For couetousnes is the rote of all euyll, whiche whyle some lusted after, they erred from the faythe and tangled them selues wyth manye sorowes.

11 But thou which arte the man of GOD, flye suche thynges. Folowe ryghtuousnes. Godlynes, loue, pacyence and mekenes.

12 Fyghte þe good fyght of fayth. Laye hande on eternall lyfe, wherevnto thou arte called and hast professed a good professyon before manye wytnesses.

13 I geue the charge in the syght of GOD, whiche quickeneth all thynges, & before Iesu Christe whiche vnder Poncyus Pylate wytnessed a good wytnessynge,

14 that thou kepe the commaundement, and be wythout spot and vnrebukeable, vntyll the appearynge of our Lorde Iesus,

15 whiche appearynge (when the tyme is come) he shal shew that is blessed and myghtye onelye, kynge of kynges, & Lord of Lordes,

16 whiche onelye hath immortalitie, and dwelleth in lyght that no man can attayne, whome neuer man sawe, neyther can se, to whom be honoure and rule euerlastynge. Amen.

17 Charge them that are ryche in this worlde shal they be not exceadyng wyse, and þt they truste not in the vncertayne ryches, but in the lyuyng God, which geueth vs aboundauntly al thynges to enioy them,

18 and that they do good and be ryche in good workes, and readye to geue and to distrybute,

19 layinge vp in store for them selues a good foundacyon agaynste the tyme to come that they maye obtayne eternal lyfe.

20 O Timothe saue that whiche is geuen the to kepe, and auoyde vnghostlye vanytyes of voyces and opposicyons of science falslye so called,

21 whiche science whyle some professed, they haue erred as concernyng the fayth. Grace be with the. AMEN.

# 2 Timothy

## CHAPTER 1

Paule an Apostle of Iesu Christ by the wyll of God to preache þe promes of life which lyfe is in Christe Iesu.

2 To Tymothe his beloued sonne. Grace, mercy and peace from God the father, and from Christe Iesu oure Lorde.

3 I thanke God, whom I serue from myne elders with pure conscience, that wythout ceasyng I make mencyon of the in my prayers nyghte and daye,

4 desyrynge to se the, myndefull of thy teares: so that I be fylled with ioy,

5 when I call to remembraunce the vnfayned fayth, that is in the, whiche dwelte fyrste in thy graundmother Loys, and in thy mother Eunica: and am assured that it dwelleth in the also.

6 Wherfore I warne the that thou stere vp the gyfte of God whiche is in the, by the puttynge on of my handes.

7 For God hath not geuen to vs the spiryte of feare, but of power and of loue, and of sobrenes of mynde.

8 Be not ashamed to testifye oure Lorde, neyther be ashamed of me, whiche am bounde for hys sake: but suffre aduersitye also wyth the Gospell thorowe the power of God,

9 whiche saued vs and called vs with an holye callynge, not accordynge to hys owne purpose & grace whiche grace was geuen vs thorowe Christe before the worlde was,

10 but is nowe declared openlye by the appearynge of oure sauyoure Iesu Christ whiche hath put awaye deathe, & hath broughte lyfe and immortalitye to light thorow the Gospell,

11 whereunto I am appointed, a preacher and an Apostle and a teacher of the Gentyls:

12 for the whiche cause I also suffer these thinges. Neuerthelesse I am not ashamed. For I know whom I haue beleued, and am sure that he is able to kepe that whiche I haue commytted to hys kepyng, agaynst that daye.

13 Se thou haue the ensample of the holsome wordes, whiche thou heardest of me in faythe and loue whiche is in Iesus Christe.

14 That good thynge, whiche was commytted to thy kepynge, kepe in the holy ghoste which dwelleth in vs.

15 Thys thou knowest howe that all they whiche are in Asia, be turned from me. Of whiche sorte are Phygelos and Hermogenes.

16 The Lorde geue mercye vnto the house of Onesiphoras, for he ofte refreshed me, and was not ashamed of my chayne:

17 but when he was at Rome, he sought me oute very dylygently, and founde me.

18 The Lorde graunte vnto hym that he maye fynde mercye with þe Lorde at that daye. And in howe manye things he mynystred vnto me at Ephesus thou knowest very well.

## CHAPTER 2

Thou therfor my sonne, be strong in the grace that is in Christ Iesus.

2 And what thynges thou hast hearde of me, manye bearyng wytnes, the same delyuer to faythfull men, whiche are apte to teache other.

3 Thou therfore suffer affliccyon as a good souldyer of Iesu Christe.

4 No man that warreth entangleth hym selfe with worldye busynes, and that because he woulde please hym that hath chosen hym to be a souldyer.

5 And though a man stryue for a masterye, yet is he not crouned, except he stryue lawfullye.

6 The husbandman that laboureth must fyrste receyue of the frutes.

7 Consyder what I saye. The Lorde geueth vnderstandynge in

all thinges.

8 Remember that Iesus Christe beynge of the sede of Dauid, rose agayne from death accordynge to my Gospell,

9 wherein I suffer trouble as an euyll doar, euen vnto bondes. But the worde of God was not bounde.

10 Here fore I suffre all thynges, for the electes sakes, that they myghte also obtayne the saluacyon, which is in Christe Iesus, with eternal glory.

11 It is a true saiyng, yf we be deade wt hym we also shall lyue with hym.

12 Yf we be pacyente, we shal also raygne with hym. Yf we denye hym, he also shall denye vs

13 Yf we beleue not yet abydeth he faythfull. He can not deny hym selfe.

14 Of these thynges put them in remembraunce, and testifye before the Lorde, þt they stryue not aboute wordes: which is to no profyte, but to peruerte the hearers.

15 Studye to shewe thy selfe laudable vnto God a workeman that nedeth not to be ashamed dyuydynge the worde of truste iustelye.

16 Vnghostly and vayne voices passe ouer. For they shall encreace vnto greater vngodlynes,

17 and theyr wordes shall frete euen as doeth a cancre: of whose number is Himeneos & Phyletos:

18 which as concernyng the truethe haue erred, saiynge that the resurreccyon is past alredy, and do destroye the fayth of diuers persons.

19 But the sure grounde of God remayneth, and hath thys seale: the Lord knoweth them þt are his, & let euerye man that calleth on the name of Christe departe from iniquitie.

20 Notwtstandyng in a greate house are not onelye vessels of golde and of syluer: but also of woode and of earthe, some for honoure, and some vnto dyshonoure.

21 But yf a man purge hym self from suche felowes, he shalbe a vessell sanctyfyed vnto honoure, mete for the Lorde, & prepared vnto all good workes.

22 Lustes of youth auoyde, and folow ryghtuousnes, fayth, loue, & peace, with them that call on the Lorde with pure herte.

23 Folyshe & vnlearned questions put from the, remembring that they do, but gendre stryfe.

24 But the seruaunt of the Lorde must not stryue, but must be peasable to all men, and apte to teache, and one that can suffre

25 the euyll in meakenes, and can informe them that resiste: yf that God at any tyme wyll geue them repentaunce for to know the trueth,

26 that they may come to them selues agayne out of the snare of the deuyll, whiche are nowe taken of hym at hys wyll.

# CHAPTER 3

THYS vnderstand, that in the last dayes shall come perylous tymes.

2 For the men shall be louers of theyr owne selues coueteous, bosters, proude, cursed speakers, dysobedyent to father and mother, vnthankefull, vnholye,

3 vnkynde, truce breakers, stubborne false accusars, ryatours, fierce despysers of them whiche are good,

4 traytours, headye, hye mynded, gredy vpon voluptuousnes more then the louers of God,

5 hauynge a simylytude of Godly lyuynge, but haue denyed þe power thereof: and suche abhorre.

6 Of thys sorte are they which enter into houses, & bring into bondage women laden wyth synne which women are lede of dyuers lustes,

7 euer learnynge, and neuer able to come vnto the knowledge of the trueth.

8 As Iannes and Iambres withstode Moyses, euen so do these resiste the trueth, men they are of corrupte myndes, and lewde, as concernyng the fayth,

9 but they shall preuayle no longer. For theyr madnes shalbe vttered vnto all men as theyrs was.

10 But thou haste sene the experience of my doctryne, fashyon of lyuyng, purpose, fayth, long suffering, loue, pacience,

11 persecucyons, and affliccyons which happened vnto me at Antioche, at Iconium and at Lystra: whiche persecucyons I suffered pacyently. And from them all, the Lorde delyuered me.

12 Yea and all that wyll lyue Godlye in Christe Iesu, must suffer persecucyons.

13 But þe euyll man and disceyuers shal waxe worsse & worsse whyle they deceyue, and are deceyued them selues.

14 But continue thou in the thynges whiche thou hast learned, which also were committed vnto the seyng thou knowest of whome thou hast learned them,

15 and for as muche also as thou haste knowen holy scrypture of a chyld, whiche is able to make the wyse vnto saluacion thorowe the fayth which is in Christ Iesu.

16 For al scripture geuen by inspyracion of God, is profytable to teache, to improue, to amende and to instruct in ryghtuousnes,

17 that the man of God maye be perfecte and prepared vnto all good workes.

# CHAPTER 4

I testifye therfore before God, & before the Lord Iesu

Christe, which shall iudge quycke and deade in hys appearyng in his kyngedome,

2 preache the word, be feruent, be it in season or out of season. Improue, rebuke, exhorte, wyth all long suffering and doctryne.

3 For the tyme wyll come, when they wyll not suffer wholsome doctryne: but after theyr owne lustes shall they (whose eares ytch) get them an heape of teachers,

4 & shal turne theyr eares from the trueth, and shalbe geuen vnto fables.

5 But watche thou in all thynges, and suffre aduersitye and do þe work of an Euangelist, fulfyll thyne offyce vnto þe vtmost.

6 For I am now ready to be offered, and the tyme of my departynge is at hande.

7 I haue fought a good fyght, and haue fulfylled my course, and haue kepte the fayth.

8 From henceforth is layde vp for me a croune of ryghtuousnes which the Lorde that is a ryghtuous iudge shall geue me at that daye: not to me only, but vnto all them that loue hys comynge.

9 Make spede to come vnto me at once.

10 For Demas hath left me & hath loued this present worlde, and is departed into Thessalonica. Crescens is gone to Galacia, & Titus vnto Dalmacea.

11 Onelye Lucas is wyth me. Take Marke and brynge hym wyth the for he is necessarye vnto me, for to minister.

12 And Tichicus haue I sent to Ephesus.

13 The cloke that I lefte at Troada wyth Carpus, when thou comest, bryng wyth the, and the bokes but specially the partchement.

14 Alexander the coppersmyth dyd me muche euyll, the Lorde rewarde him, according to hys dedes,

15 of whom be thou ware also. For he wythstode our preachyng sore.

16 At my fyrste aunsweryng, no man assisted me, but all forsoke me. I praye God that it maye not be layed to theyr charges:

17 Notwithstandynge the Lord assisted me, & strenghthed me, that by me the preachynge shoulde be fulfylled to the vttermoste, and that al the Gentyles shoulde heare. And I was delyuered out of the mouth of the Lyon.

18 And the Lord shall delyuer me from all euyll doynge, and shall kepe me to his heauenly kyngdome. To whom be prayse for euer and euer, Amen.

19 Salute Prisca and Aquila, and the housholde of Onesiphorus.

20 Erastus abode at Corinthum. Trophimos I lefte at Myletum sycke.

21 Make spede to come before wynter. Eubolus greteth the, and Pudens, and Linus, & Claudia, and all the brethren.

22 The Lorde Iesus Christ be with thy spyryte. Grace be with you. Amen.

# Titus

## CHAPTER 1

Paule the seruaunt of God and an Apostle of Iesu Christ, to preache þe faythe, of Goddes elect, & the knowledge of that truethe, whiche is after Godlynes,

2 vpon the hope, of eternall lyfe, whiche lyfe God þt can not lye, hath promysed before the worlde beganne:

3 but hath opened hys worde, at the tyme appoynted thorowe preachynge which preachynge is commytted vnto me by the commaundement of God oure sauyoure.

4 To Titus hys naturall sonne in the common fayth. Grace, mercy, and peace from God the father and from the Lorde Iesu Christe oure sauyoure.

5 For thys cause left I the in Crete, that thou shouldest performe that whiche was lackynge, and shouldest ordeyne elders in euery cytye as I appoynted the.

6 Yf any be fautelesse, the husbande of one wyfe hauyng faythfull chyldren, whiche are not sclaundred of ryote, neyther are dysobedyent.

7 For a byshoppe must be fautelesse, as it becommeth the mynister of God: not stubborne, not angrye, no dronkarde, no fyghter, not geuen to fylthy lucre:

8 but herberous one that loueth goodnes, sober mynded, ryghtuous, holy temperate,

9 and suche as cleaueth vnto the true worde of doctryne, that he maye be able to exhorte wyth wholesome learnynge, and to improue them, that saye agaynste it.

10 For there are many dysobedyent: & talkers of vanitye and disceyuers of myndes, namely they of the circumcision,

11 whose mouthes must be stopped: whiche peruerte whole houses teachynge thynges whiche they oughte not because of fylthy lucre.

12 One beyng of them selues, which was a poete of theyr owne, said: The Cretians are alwayes lyars, euil beastes and slowe belyes.

13 Thys wytnesse is true, wherfore rebuke them sharply that they may be sounde in the fayth,

14 and not takyng hede to Iewes fables and commaundementes of men that turne from the truethe.

15 Vnto the pure are all thynges pure, but vnto them that are defyled and vnbeleuynge, is nothynge pure: but euen the very myndes and consciences of them are defyled.

16 They confesse that they knowe God: but wyth the dedes they denye hym, and are abhomynable and dysobedient, and vnto all good workes discommendable.

## CHAPTER 2

But speake thou þt whiche becommeth wholsome learnyng.

2 That the elder men be sober, honest, discret, sounde in the fayth, in loue, and in pacience.

3 And the elder women lykewyse, that they be in such rayment as becommeth holynes, not false accusars, not geuen to muche drynkynge, but teachers of honest thinges

4 to make the yong women sobre mynded, to loue theyr husbandes, to loue their chyldren,

5 to be dyscret, chast, huswyfly, good & obedyent vnto theyr owne husbandes, þt the word of God be not euyl spoken of.

6 Young men lykewyse exhort that they be sobre mynded.

7 Aboue all thynges shewe thy selfe an ensample of good workes wyth vncorrupt doctryne wyth honesty,

8 and wyth the wholesom worde, which cannot be rebuked, that he which

wythstandeth, maye be ashamed, hauyng nothynge in you that he maye dysprayse.

9 The seruauntes exhort to be obedient vnto theyr owne maysters, and to please in al thynges, not aunswerynge agayne,

10 neyther be pyckers, but þt they shewe all good faythfulnes, that they maye do worshyp to þe doctryne of oure sauyoure God in all thynges.

11 For the grace of God, þt bringeth saluacion vnto al men, hath apered

12 & teacheth vs þt we shoulde denye vngodlynes & worldly lustes, and that we shoulde lyue sobre mynded ryghtuouslye and Godly in this present worlde,

13 lokynge for that blessed hope and gloryous apperyng of the myghtye God, and of oure sauyoure Iesu Christe,

14 whiche gaue hym selfe for vs, to redeme vs from al vnryghtuousnes and to pourge vs a peculyar people vnto him selfe, feruently geuen vnto good workes.

15 These thynges speake, and exhorte, and rebuke, wyth all commaundyng. Se that no man despyse the.

# CHAPTER 3

WARNE them that they submytte them selues to rule and power to obeye the offycers that they be ready vnto al good workes

2 that they speake euyll of noman that they be no fyghters, but softe, shewynge all meakenes vnto all men.

3 For we our selues also in tymes paste, vnwyse, dysobedient, deceyued, in daunger to lustes, and to dyuers maners of voluptuousnes, lyuyng in malycyousnes and enuye, ful of hate, hatyng one another.

4 But after that the kyndnes and loue of our sauyoure God to man warde appered,

5 not of the dedes of rightuousnes, which we wrought but of hys mercy he saued vs, by the fountayne of the newe byrth, & with the renuyng of þe holye ghost,

6 which he shed on vs aboundauntly, thorowe Iesus Christe oure sauyoure,

7 that we ones iustifyed by hys grace, shoulde be heyres of eternall lyfe, thorow hope.

8 Thys is a true saiynge. Of these thynges I would thou shouldest certyfye, that they whiche beleue God, might be dylygent to go forwarde in good workes. These thynges are good and profytable vnto men.

9 Folysh questions and genealogyes, and braulynge and stryfe aboute the law auoyde: for they are vnprofytable and superfluous.

10 A man that is geuen to heresye, after the fyrst & the seconde admonicyon auoyde,

11 remembring that he that is suche, is peruerted, and synneth euen damned by hys owne iudgement.

12 When I shall sende Artemas vnto the or Tichicus, be diligente to come to me vnto Nichopolis. For I haue determyned there to wynter.

13 Brynge zenas the lawyar and Apollos on theyr iorneye dilygentlye, that nothing be lackyng vnto them.

14 And let oures also learne to excell in good workes as farforthe, as nede requyreth, that they be not vnfruteful.

15 All that are with me salute the. Grete them that loue vs in the faythe Grace be wt you all. AMEN.

# Philemon

PAUL the prysoner of Iesu Christe and brother Timotheus. Vnto Philemon the beloued, & oure healper,

2 and to the beloued Appia, and to Archyppus our felowe souldyer, & to the congregacyon of thy house.

3 Grace be wyth you and peace from God our father, and from the Lorde Iesus Christ.

4 I thanke my God, makynge mention alwayes of the in my prayers,

5 when I heare of thy loue and fayth, which thou hast towarde the Lorde Iesu, and towarde all saynctes:

6 so that the fellowshyppe that thou haste in the fayth, is frutefull thorowe knowledge of all good thynges, whiche are in you by Iesus Christe.

7 And we haue greate ioye, and consolation ouer thy loue: For by the (brother) the sainctes hertes are conforted.

8 Wherfore though I be bolde in Christe to enioyne the, that whiche becommeth the:

9 yet for loues sake I rather beseche the, thoughe I be as I am euen Paule aged, and now in bondes for Iesu Christes sake.

10 I beseche the for my sonne Onesimus, whom I begat in my bondes,

11 whiche in tyme passed was to the vnprofytable both to the, and also to me,

12 whome I haue sente home agayne. Thou therfore receyue hym, that is to say, myne owne bowels

13 whome I woulde fayne haue receyued with me, that in thy stede he myght haue ministred vnto me in the bondes of the Gospell.

14 Neuer thelesse, wythout thy mynde, woulde I do nothynge, that the good whiche spryngeth of þe shoulde not be as it were of necessytie, but wyllynglye.

15 Happelye he therfore departed for a season that thou shouldest receyue hym for euer,

16 not nowe as a seruaunte, but aboue a seruaunte I meane a brother beloued, specyally to me: but howe muche more vnto the, bothe in the fleshe and also in the Lorde?

17 Yf thou count me a felowe, receyue hym as my selfe.

18 Yf he haue hurte the, or oweth the oughte that laye to my charge.

19 I Paule haue wryten it wt myne owne hande, I wyll recompence it. So that I do not saye, to the, howe that thou owest vnto me euen thyne owne selfe.

20 Euen so brother, let me enioye the in the Lorde. Comforte my bowelles in the Lord.

21 Trusting in thyne obedyence, I wrote vnto the, knowing, that thou wylt do more then I saye for.

22 Moreouer prepare me lodgynge: for I truste thorowe the healpe of your prayers, I shall be geuen vnto you.

23 There salute the Epaphras my felowe prysoner in christ Iesu.

24 Marcus, Aristarchus Demas, Lucas, my helpers.

25 The grace of our Lorde Iesu Christe be with youre spyrytes Amen.

# Hebrews

## CHAPTER 1

GOD in tyme paste diuerselye and manye wayes, spake vnto the fathers by Prophetes,

2 but in these laste dayes he hath spoken vnto vs by hys sonne, whom he hath made heyre of all thynges, by whom also he made the worlde.

3 Whyche sonne beyng the bryghtnes of hys glorye, and verye Image of his substaunce, bearinge vp al thinges wyth the worde of hys power, hath in his owne persone pourged our synnes, and is sitting on the right hand of the maiestie on hygh,

4 and is more excellente then the Angelles, in as muche as he hath by enheritaunce obteyned an excellenter name then haue they.

5 For vnto whyche of the Angelles sayed he anye tyme: Thou arte my sonne, thys day begat I the? And agayne: I wyll be hys father, and he shall be my sonne.

6 And agayne: when he bringeth in the fyrst begotten sonne into the worlde, he sayeth: And al the Angels of God shal worshyppe him.

7 And of the Angels he sayth: He maketh his Angels spyrytes, and hys mynysters flammes of fyre.

8 But vnto the sonne he sayeth: God thy seate shall be for euer and euer. The cepter of thy kyngdome is a ryghte ceptre.

9 Thou hast loued ryghtuousnes, and hated inyquytye. Wherfore God, whiche is thy GOD, hath anoynted the wyth the oyle of gladnes aboue thy felowes.

10 And thou Lorde in the beginninge hast layed the foundacion of the earth. And the heauens are the workes of thy handes.

11 They shal peryshe, but thou shalt endure. They all shal wexe olde as doth a garment,

12 and as a vesture shalt thou chaunge them, and they shalbe chaunged. But thou arte alwayes, and thy yeares shal not fayle.

13 Vnto which of the Angels sayed he at anye tyme? Sitte on my ryghte hande, tyll I make thyne enemies thy fote stole.

14 Are they not al ministringe spirites, sent to minister for their sakes, whiche shal be heyres of saluation?

## CHAPTER 2

WHERFOR we ought to geue þe more heede to the thynges which we haue heard, lest we perishe.

2 For yf the word which was spoken by Angels was stedfast, so that euery transgression and disobedience receyued a iuste recompence to rewarde,

3 howe shal we escape, yf we despise so great saluacyon, whyche at the fyrst began to be preached of the Lorde hym selfe, and afterward was confirmed to vswarde, by them that hearde it,

4 God bearynge wytnesse therto, both wyth signes and wonders also, and with diuers miracles, and giftes of the holy ghoste, according to his own will.

5 He hath not vnto the Angelles put in subieccion the world to come, wherof we speake.

6 But one in a certaine place wytnessed, saying. What is man, that thou arte mindfull of him?

7 After thou haddeste for a season made him lower then the Angelles: thou crownedst him with honoure and glorye, and hast set him aboue the workes of thy handes.

8 Thou hast put all things in subieccion vnder hys fete. In that he put al things vnder hym, he lefte nothing that is not put vnder him.

9 Neuertheles we yet se not all things subdued, but him that was made lesse then the Angelles, we se that it was Iesus, whiche is crowned with glory and honoure for the suffering of death, that he by the grace of God, should taste of death for al

men.

10 For it became him, for whom are al thynges and by whom are al thinges, after that he had brought many sonnes vnto glory, that he should make the Lorde of their saluacyon perfect thorowe sufferinge.

11 For he that sanctifieth, and they which are sanctified, are all of one: For whiche causes sake, he is not ashamed to cal them brethren

12 sayinge: I wyll declare thy name vnto my brethren and in the middes of the congregacion wil I praise the.

13 And again: I wil put my truste in him. And agayne: beholde here am I and the chyldren, which God hath geuen me.

14 For as muche then as the children were partetakers of fleshe and bloude, he also him selfe lyke wyse toke part wyth them, for to put doune thorowe death, that is to saye the deuyll,

15 and that he mighte delyuer them, which thorowe feare of death weare all theyr lyfe tyme in daunger of boundage.

16 For he in no place taketh on him the angels, but the seade of Abraham taketh he on hym.

17 Wherfore in al thinges it became him to be made like vnto his brethren, that he myghte be mercyfull and a faythful hye prieste in thinges concerninge God, for to pourge the people synnes.

18 For in that he hym selfe suffered and was tempted, he is able to sucker them that are tempted.

## CHAPTER 3

THERFORE holye brethren, partakers of the celestiall callinges, consider the ambassatoure and hye prieste of oure professyon, Christe Iesus

2 which was faithfull to him that made him euen as was Moises in al his house.

3 And yet was this man counted worthy of more glorye then Moyses: In as muche as he which hath prepared þe house hath most honoure in the house.

4 Euery house is prepared of some man. But he that ordeyned al thinges is God.

5 And Moyses verelye was faythfull in al hys house as a minyster, to beare wytnes of those thynges, whyche shoulde be spoken afterwarde.

6 But Chryste as a sonne hath rule ouer the house, whose house are we, so that we holde faste the confidence and the reioysynge of that hope, vnto the ende.

7 Wherfore as the holy ghoste sayeth, to daye yf ye shal heare his voice,

8 harden not youre hertes, after the rebellion in the day of temptacion in the wyldernes,

9 where youre fathers tempted me, proued me, and sawe my workes .xl. yeares longe.

10 Wherfore I was greued wyth that generacion and sayde. They erre euer in their hertes, they verely haue not knowen my wayes,

11 so that I sware in my wrath, that they should not enter into my reste.

12 Take hede brethren, that there be in none of you an euyll herte in vnbeleue, that he shoulde departe from the lyuinge God:

13 but exhorte one another dayly, whyle it is called to daye, leste anye of you wexe harde herted thorowe the deceythfulnesse of synne.

14 We are partakers of Christe, yf we kepe sure vnto the ende the fyrste substaunce,

15 so longe as it is sayde, to daye yf ye heare hys voyce, harden not youre hartes, as when ye rebelled.

16 For some, when they hearde, rebelled, how be it not al that came out of Egypte vnder Moyses.

17 But wyth whome was he depleased .xl. yeares? Was he not displeased wyth them that synned, whose carkases were ouerthrowen in the deserte?

18 To whom sware he, that they should not enter into hys reste, but vnto them that beleued not?

19 And we se þt they could not enter in because of vnbeleue.

## CHAPTER 4

LET vs feare therfore leste anye of vs forsakinge the promes of entringe into his reste, shoulde seme to come behinde.

2 For vnto vs was it declared, as well as vnto them. But it profiteth not them that they hearde the worde, because they which hearde it, coupled it not wyth fayth.

3 But we whiche haue beleued, do enter into his reste, as contrarywyse he sayde to þe other: I haue sworne in my wrath, they shal not enter into my rest. And that spake he verely longe after that the workes were made, and the foundacion of the worlde layde.

4 For he spake in a certaine place of the seuenth day, on this wyse: And God dyd reste the seuenth daye from all his workes.

5 And in this place againe: They shall not come into my reste.

6 Seynge therfore it foloweth that some must inter therinto, and they to whom it was fyrst preached, intred not therin for vnbeleues sake:

7 Againe he appointeth in Dauid a certaine present day after so longe a tyme, saiynge as it is rehearsed, this daye yf ye heare his voice, be not harde herted.

8 For yf Iosue had geuen

them reste, then woulde he not afterwarde haue spoken of another day.

9 There remayneth therfore yet a rest to the people of God.

10 For he that is entred into his reste doth cease from his owne workes, as God dyd from his.

11 Let vs study therfore to enter into þe reste, leste anye man falle after the same ensample, into vnbelefe.

12 For the word of God is quicke and myghty in operacion, and sharper then anye two edged swerde, and entreth through, euen vnto the diuiding a sonder of the soule and the spirite, and of the ioyntes and the marie, and iudgeth the thoughtes and the ententes of the herte:

13 neyther is there anye creature inuisible in the syght of him. For all things are naked and bare vnto the eyes of him, of whom we speake.

14 Seyng then that we haue a great hye prieste, which is entred into heauen (I meane Iesus the sonne of God) let vs holde our profession.

15 For we haue not an hye prieste, whiche can not haue compassion on our infirmities, but was in all pointes tempted, lyke as we are, but yet without sinne.

16 Let vs therfore go boldely vnto the seate of grace, that we may receiue mercye, and fynde grace to healpe in time of nede.

# CHAPTER 5

FOR euerye hye prieste that is taken from amonge men, is ordeined for men, in thinges perteininge to God, to offer gyftes & sacrifices for synne:

2 whiche can haue compassion on the ignoraunt, and on them that are out of the waye, because that he him selfe also is compassed with infirmitie:

3 For the which infirmities sake, he is bounde to offer for synnes, as well for his own part, as for the peoples.

4 And no man taketh honoure vnto him selfe, but he that is called of God, as was Aaron.

5 Euen so lykewyse, Christe glorified not himselfe, to be made the hye prieste, but he þt sayde vnto him, thou art my sonne, this daye begat I the, glorified him.

6 As he also in another place speaketh: Thou arte a prieste for euer after þe order of Melchisedech.

7 Which in the daies of his flesh did offer vp praiers and supplications, wyth strong criynge and teares, vnto him that was able to saue hym from death, and was also hearde because of his Godlines.

8 And though he were Goddes sonne, yet learned he obedience, by those thinges which he suffred,

9 and was made perfect, and the cause of eternall saluacyon vnto all them that obey him,

10 and is called of God an hyghe prieste, after the order of Melchisedech.

11 Wherof we haue manye thinges to saye whiche are harde to be vttered, because ye are dull of hearinge.

12 For when as concerneinge the tyme, ye oughte to be teachers, yet haue ye nede agayne, that we teache you the fyrst pryneiples of the word of God, and are become such as haue nede of milk and not of stronge meate:

13 For euerye man that is fed wyth mylke, is inexperte in the word of rightuousnes. For he is but a babe.

14 But stronge meate belongeth to them that are perfecte, which thorow custome haue theyr wittes exercised to iudge both good and euil also.

# CHAPTER 6

WHERFORE let vs loue the doctrine pertaininge to the beginninge of a Christen man, & let vs go vnto perfeccion, & nowe no more lay þe foundacion of repentaunce from deade workes, and of faythe towarde God,

2 of baptyme, of doctryne, and of layinge on of handes, and of resurreccion from death, and of eternal iudgemente.

3 And so wil we do, yf God permytte.

4 For it is not possible that they whiche were ones lyghted, and haue tasted of the heauenly gyft, and were become partakers of the holy ghoste,

5 and haue tasted of the good worde of God, and of the worlde to come:

6 yf they fall, shoulde be renued agayne vnto repentaunce: for as muche as they haue (as concernynge them selues) crucifyed the sonne of God a freshe makynge a mocke of hym.

7 For that earthe whiche drincketh in the rayne whiche commeth ofte vpon it, and bryngeth forth herbes mete for them that dresse it, receyueth blessynge of God.

8 But that ground which beareth thornes and bryars, is reproued, and is nye vnto curssynge: whose ende is to be burned.

9 Neuerthelesse deare frindes, we truste to se better of you, and thynges whiche accompanye saluacyon, though we thus speake.

10 For God is not vnryghtuous þt he should forget your worke and laboure that procedeth of loue, which loue you shewed in hys name, whiche haue mynystred vnto the saynctes, & yet mynyster.

11 Yea, and we desyre that euerye one of you shew the same

dylygence, to the stablyshynge of hope euen vnto the ende:

12 that ye faynt not, but folowe them, whiche thorowe fayth & pacience inheret the promyses.

13 For when God made promes to Abraham, because he had no greater thynge to sweare by, he sweare by hym selfe,

14 saiynge: Surelye I wyl blesse the, and multyplye the in deede.

15 And so after that he had taryed a longe tyme, he enioyed the promes.

16 Men verelye sweare by hym that is greater then them selues, & an othe to confyrme the thynge, is amonge them an ende of all stryfe.

17 So God wyllynge verye aboundauntlye to shewe vnto the heyres of promes, the stablenes of hys counsayle, he added an othe,

18 that by two immutable thynges (in which it was vnpossyble that GOD shaulde lye) we myghte haue perfecte consolacyon, whiche haue fled, for to holde faste the hope that is set before vs,

19 whiche hope we haue an ancre of the soule both sure and stedfast. Whiche hope also entreth in, into those thynges that are wythin the vayle,

20 whether the fore runner is for vs entred in I meane Iesus that is made an hye prieste for euer, after the order of Melchysedech.

## CHAPTER 7

THYS Melchysedech, kynge of Salem (whiche beynge prieste of the moost hye God met Abraham, as he returned agayne from the slaughter of the kynges, & blessed him:

2 to whom also Abraham gaue tythes of all thynges) fyrste is by interpretacyon kynge of ryghtuousnes: after that he is kynge of Salem that is to saye, kynge of peace,

3 wythoute father, wythout mother, wythout kynne, & hath neyther begynnyng of hys tyme, neyther yet ende of hys lyfe: but is lykened vnto þe sonne of God, and contynueth a prieste for euer.

4 Consyder what a man this was, vnto whom the patriarke Abraham gaue tythes of þe spoyles.

5 And verely those chyldren of Leuy, which receyue the offyce of the priestes, haue a commaundemente to take accordynge to þe lawe, tythes of the people, that is to say of theyr brethren, yea thoughe they sponge oute of the loynes of Abraham.

6 But he whose kynred is not counted amonge them, receyued tythes of Abraham, and blessed hym that had the promises.

7 And no man denyeth but that whiche is lesse, receyueth blessyng of that which is greater.

8 And here men that dye, receyue tythes. But there he receyueth tythes of whome it is wytnessed, that he lyueth.

9 And to say þe trueth. Leuy hym selfe also whiche receyueth tythes, payed tythes in Abraham.

10 For he was yet in the loynes of hys father Abraham when Melchysedech mete hym.

11 Yf nowe therfore perfeccyon came by the priesthode of the Leuytes (for vnder that presthode the people receyueth the lawe) what nedeth furthermore that another prieste shoulde aryse after the ordre of Melchisedech, and not after the ordre of Aaron?

12 Nowe no doubte, yf the priesthode be translated, then of necessitye must the lawe be translated also.

13 For of whome these thynges are spoken pertayneth vnto another trybe, of whiche neuer man serued at the aulter.

14 For it is euident, that oure Lorde sprong of the trybe of Iuda, of whiche trybe spake Moyses nothyng concernynge priesthode.

15 And it is yet a more euydent thynge, yf after the similitude, of Melchisedech, there arise an other prieste:

16 which is not made after the lawe of the carnall commaundement: but after the power of the endelesse lyfe.

17 (For he testifyeth thou arte a prieste for euer, after the ordre of Melchysedech).

18 Then the commaundement that wente before, is dysanulled, because of her weakenes and vnprofytablenes.

19 For the lawe made nothynge perfecte: but was an introduccion of a better hope, by which hope we drawe nye vnto God.

20 And for thys cause it is a better hope, that it was not promysed without an oth

21 (those pryestes were made wythout an othe, but thys prieste wyth an othe, by hym that layed vnto hym. The Lorde sware, and wyl not repente: Thou arte a prieste for euer after the order of Melchisedech)

22 And for þe cause was Iesus a stablisher of a better testament.

23 And amonge them many were made priestes, because they were not suffered to endure by the reason of death.

24 But thys man, because he endureth euer hath an euerlastyng priestehode.

25 Wherfor he is able also euer to saue them that come vnto God by hym, seyng he euer lyueth, to make intercessyon for vs.

26 Suche an hye Prieste it became vs to haue which is holy, harmlesse, vndefyled, separate from synners, and made hyer then heauen.

27 Whiche nedeth not dayelye (as yonder hye priestes) to offer vp sacrifyce, fyrste for hys own synnes, and then for the peoples synnes. For that dyd he at once for all, when he offered vp hym selfe.

28 For the lawe maketh men priestes, which haue infyrmytye: but þe worde of the othe that came sence the lawe, maketh the sonne pryeste, whiche is perfecte for euermore.

## CHAPTER 8

OF the thynges which we haue spoken this is the pythe: that we haue suche an hye prieste that is sytten on the ryght hande of the seate of maiestye in heauen,

2 and is a mynyster of holye thynges, and of the verye tabernacle whiche God pyghte, & not man.

3 For euerye hye prieste is ordeyned to offer gyftes and sacryfyces: wherfore it is of necessitye that thys man haue some what also to offer,

4 for he were not a prieste, yf he were on þe earth, where are priestes that according to the lawe offer gyftes,

5 whiche priestes serue vnto the ensample and shadowe of heauenly thynges: euen as the aunswer of God was geuen vnto Moses when he was aboute to fynyshe the tabernacle. Take hede (sayde he) that thou make all thynges accordynge to the patrone shewed to the in the mounte.

6 Nowe hath he obtayned a more excellente offyce, in as muche as he is the medyator of a better testamente, whiche was made for better promyses.

7 For yf that fyrste testamente had bene faultlesse then shoulde no place haue bene soughte for the seconde.

8 For in rebukyng them he sayth: beholde the dayes wyll come (sayeth the Lorde) and I wyll fynyshe vpon the house of Israel, and vpon the house of Iuda,

9 a newe testamente: not lyke the testament that I made wyth theyr fathers at that tyme when I toke them by the handes, to leade them oute of the lande of Egypte, for they continued not in my testamente, and I regarded them not sayth the Lorde.

10 For thys is the testament that I will make wyth the house of Israel: After those dayes sayth the Lorde: I wyl put my lawes in their myndes, and in theyr hertes I wyl wryte them and I wyll be theyr God, and they shall be my people.

11 And they shall not teache euerye man hys neyghboure, and euerye man hys brother, saiynge: knowe the Lorde: For they shall knowe me, from the leste to the most of them:

12 For I wyll be mercyfull ouer theyr vnryghtuousnes, and on theyr synnes & on theyr iniquities.

13 In that he sayth a newe testament he hath abrogate the olde. Now that which is dysanulled and waxed olde, is readye to vanyshe awaye.

## CHAPTER 9

THAT fyrste tabernacle verelye had ordinaunces, and seruinges of God, and worldly holynes.

2 For there was a fore tabernacle made, wherein was the candelstycke and the table, & the shewe bread which is called holye.

3 But wythin the second vayle was there a tabernacle, whiche is called holyeste of all

4 whiche had the golden senser, and the arcke of the testament ouerlayde roundabout wyth gold, wherein was the golden pot with manna, and Aarons rodde that sprong, and the tables of the testament.

5 Ouer the arcke were the cherubes of glorye shadowynge the seate of grace. Of whiche thynges we wyll not nowe speake perticularlye.

6 When these thynges were thus ordeyned the priestes wente always into the tabernacle and executed the seruyce of God.

7 But into the seconde wente the hye priest alone, once euerye yeare, and not wythout bloude, whiche he offered for hym selfe, and for the ignoraunce of the people.

8 Wherewith the holy ghost this signifyinge, that the waye of holy thynges, was not yet oppened, whyle as yet the fyrst tabernacle was standynge.

9 Whyche was a simylytude for the tyme then present, and in whyche were offered gyftes and sacrifices þt coulde not make the mynyster perfecte, as pertaynynge to the conscience,

10 wyth onelye meates and drynkes and dyuers washynges and iustifiynges of the fleshe, whyche were ordeyned vntyll the tyme of reformacyon.

11 But Christe beynge an hye prieste of good thynges to come, came by a greater & a more perfecte tabernacle, not made wyth handes: that is to saye, not of thys maner buyldynge,

12 neyther by the bloude of gotes and calues, but by hys owne bloude he entred once for al into the holye place, and founde eternal redempcyon.

13 For yf the bloude of oxen and of gotes and the ashes of an heyfer, when it was sprinkled, puryfyed the vncleane, as touchyng the puryfiynge of the fleshe:

14 Howe muche more shall the bloude of Christe (which thorow the eternall spyryte offred hym selfe without spot to God) pourge youre conscyences from dead workes, for to serue the lyuyng God?

15 And for thys cause is: he the medyatour of the new testament, that thorowe death whiche chaunsed for the redempcyon of those transgressyons that were in the fyrst testament, they whiche were called myght receyue the promes of eternall inherytaunce.

16 For wheresoeuer is a testamente, there muste also be the death of hym that maketh þe testament.

17 For the testament taketh authoritie when men are dead. For it is of no value as longe as he that made it, is alyue.

18 For whiche cause also, neyther that fyrst testament was ordeyned without bloude.

19 For when al the commaundementes were reade of Moyses to all the people, he toke the bloude of calues and of gotes, whiche water and purple woul and ysope, and sprynkled both the boke and all the people

20 saiynge: thys is the bloud of the Testamente, with GOD hath appoynted vnto you.

21 More ouer he sprinkled the tabernacle wyth bloude also, and all the mynystrynge vessels.

22 And also all moost all thynges, are by the lawe pourged wyth bloude, and wythout sheddynge of bloude is no remyssyon.

23 It is then nede that the simylytudes of heauenly thinges be puryfyed wyth such thinges but the heauenly thynges them selues are puryfyed with better sacryfyces then are those.

24 For Christe is not entred into the holye places that are made wyth handes, whiche are but simylytudes of true thynges: but is entred into verye heauen, for to appere nowe in the syghte of God for vs:

25 not to offer hym selfe, often as the hye prieste entreth into the holye place euerye yeare wt straunge bloude

26 for then must he haue often suffered sence the worlde beganne. But nowe in the ende of the worlde hath he appered ones to put synne to flyghte by the offerynge vp of hym self.

27 And as it is appoynted vnto men that they shall ones dye, and then commeth the iudgemente,

28 euen so Christ was ones offered to take away the synnes of many, and vnto them that loke for hym, shall he appere agayne wythoute synne vnto saluacyon.

# CHAPTER 10

FOR the lawe whyche hath but the shadowe of good thinges to come, and not the thynges in theyr owne fashyon can neuer wyth the sacrifyces whych they offer yere by yere continuallly, make the commers thereunto perfect.

2 For woulde not then those sacryfyces haue ceased to haue bene offered, because that the offerers once pourged shoulde haue had no more consciences of synnes?

3 Neuertheles in those sacryfyces is ther mencyon made of synnes euery yeare.

4 For it is vnpossyble that the bloude of oxen and of gotes shoulde take awaye synnes.

5 Wherfore, when he commeth into þe world he sayth: Sacrifyce and offerynge thou wouldest not haue: but a body hast thou ordeyned me.

6 In sacryfyces and synne offerynges thou hast not luste.

7 Then I saide: Lo I come, in the cheyfest in the boke it is wrytten of me, that I should do thy wil, O God.

8 Aboue when he had sayd sacryfyce and offerynge, and burnte sacrifices and synne offerynges thou wouldest not haue, neither hast alowed (whyche yet are offered by the lawe)

9 and then sayd, Lo I come to do thy wyll, O God: he taketh awaye the fyrste to stablysshe þe latter.

10 By the whiche wyll we are sanctyfyed, by the offerynge of the bodye of Ieu Christ once for all.

11 And euery priest is redy daylie mynistring and ofte tymes offereth one maner of offerynge whyche can neuer take awaye synnes.

12 But thys man after he had offered one sacryfyce for synnes, satte hym downe for euer on the right hande of God,

13 and from henceforth taryeth tyl hys foes be made hys fote stole.

14 For wyth one offeryng hath he made perfecte for euer, them that are sanctyfyed.

15 And the holy ghost also beareth vs record of thys, euen when he told before:

16 Thys is the testamente that I wyl make to them: after those dayes sayth the Lorde. I wyll put my lawes in theyr hertes and in theyr mynde I wyll wryte them

17 and theyr synnes and iniquities wyll I remember no more.

18 And where remyssyon of these thynges is, there is no more offerynge for synne.

19 Seynge brethren that, by the meanes of the bloude of Iesu, we may be bold to enter into that holy place,

20 by the newe and lyuynge waye, whych he hath prepared for vs, thorow the vayle, that is to say hys flesh.

21 And seynge also that we haue an hye pryest which is ruler ouer the house of God

22 let vs draw nye wyth a true herte in a full fayth, sprynkeled in our hertes from an euyl conscyence, and washed in our bodyes wyth pure water,

23 and let vs kepe the professyon of our hope, wythout wauerynge (for he is faithful that promysed)

24 and let vs consyder one another to prouoke vnto loue, and to good workes:

25 and let vs not forsake the feloshyppe that we haue among our selues, as the maner of some is: but let vs exhort one another and that so muche the more, because ye se that the day draweth nye.

26 For yf we synne wyllyngly after that we haue receyued þe knowledge of the trueth, ther remayneth no more sacryfyce for synnes,

27 but a fearful lokynge for iudgement, and vyolente fyre, whyche shal deuoure the aduersaryes.

28 He that despyseth Moyses lawe, dyeth wythout mercye vnder two or thre wytnesses

29 Of howe muche sorer punyshement suppose ye shal he be counted worthy, whych treadeth vnder fote the sonne of God: and counted the bloud of the testament as an vnholy thynge wherwyth he was sanctyfyed, and doth dishonour to the spyryte of grace.

30 For we knowe hym that hath sayde: vengeaunce belongeth vnto me. I wyll recompence sayth the lorde. And agayne: the lord shall iudge hys people.

31 It is a fearfull thynge to falle into the handes of the lyuynge God.

32 Cal to remembraunce the dayes that are passed in the whyche after ye had receyued lyght ye endured a great fyght in aduersities

33 partely whyle all men wondred and gased at you for the shame and trybulacyon that was done vnto you, and partly, whyle ye became companyons of them whyche so passed theyr tyme.

34 For ye suffered also wyth my bondes, and toke in worth the spoyllyng of your gootes, & þt wyth gladnes, knowynge in youre selues howe that ye had in heauen a better & an endurynge substaunce.

35 Caste not awaye therfore youre confidence whiche hath great reward to recompence.

36 For ye haue nede of pacyence, that after ye haue done the wyll of God, ye myght receyue the promes.

37 For yet a very lyttel whyle, and he that shall come wyll come, and wyll not tarye.

38 But the iuste shall lyue by fayth. And yf he wythdrawe hym selfe my soule shal haue no pleasure in him.

39 We are not whych wythdrawe our selues vnto dampnacyon, but partayne to faith, to the winnynge of the soule.

# CHAPTER 11

FAYTH is a sure confydence of thynges which are hoped for, & a certayntye of thynges which are not sene.

2 By it the elders were wel reported of.

3 Thorow faythe we vnderstande that the worlde was ordeyned by the worde of God: and that thinges whiche are sene, were made of thynges whiche are not sene.

4 By fayth Abel offred vnto God a more plentuous sacrifyce then Cayn: by whiche he obtayned wytnes that he was ryghtuous, God testifiynge of his gyftes: by which also he beynge dead, yet speaketh.

5 By fayth was Enoch translated that he shoulde not se death, neyther was he founde: for God had taken hym away. Before he was taken awaye, he was reported, of, that he had pleased God:

6 but wythout fayth it is vnpossybleto please hym. For he that cometh to God muste beleue that God is, and that he is a rewarder of them that seke hym.

7 By faythe Noe honoured God, after that he was warned of thynges whiche were not sene, and prepared the arcke to the sauynge of hys housholde, thorow the whiche arcke, he condemned þe worlde, and became heyre of þe righttuousnes that commeth by faythe.

8 By fayth Abraham, when he was called obeyed, to go out into a place, which he shoulde afterward receyue to inherytaunce, and he wente oute not knowynge whyther he should go.

9 By fayth he remoued into the lande that was promysed hym, as into a straunge countreye, and dwelte in tabernacles: and so dyd Isaac and Iacob, heyres wyth hym of the same promes.

10 For he loked for a cytie hauing a foundacyon, whose buylder and maker is God.

11 Thorow fayth Sara also receyued strength to be with chyld, and was delyuered of a child when she was past age, because she iudged hym faythfull which had promysed.

12 And therfore spronge thereof one (& of one whiche was as good as deade) so manye in multitude, as the starres of the skye, and as the sande of the sea shore whiche is innumerable.

13 And they all dyed in fayth, and receyued not the promyses: but sawe them a farre of, & beleued them; and saluted them: and confessed that they were straungers and pylgrems on the earthe.

14 They that saye suche thynges, declare that they seke a countreye.

15 Also yf they had bene myndefull of that countreye from whence they came oute, they had leasure to haue returned agayne.

16 But nowe they desyre a better, that is to saye an heauenlye. Wherfor God is not ashamed of them euen to be

called theyr God: for he hath prepared for them a cytye.

17 In fayth Abraham offered vp Isaac, when he was tempted, and he offered hym beynge hys onelye begotten sonne, whiche had receyued the promyses,

18 of whom it was sayde, in Isaac shal thy sede be called,

19 for he considered that God was able to rayse it vp agayne from death. Wherfore receyued he hym, for an ensample.

20 In faith Isaac blessed Iacob and Esau concernynge thynges to come.

21 By fayth Iacob when he was a diynge, blessed both the sonnes of Ioseph, and bowed hym self towarde the top of hys cepter.

22 By fayth Ioseph when he dyed, remembred the departynge of the chyldren of Israel, and gaue commaundemente of hys bones.

23 By faith Moses when he was borne, was hyd thre monethes of hys father and mother, because they sawe he was a proper chyld, neyther feared they the kynges commaundement.

24 By fayth Moyses when he was great, refused to be called the sonne of Pharaos doughter,

25 and those rather to suffer aduersitie wyth the people of God, then to enioy the pleasures of synne for a season,

26 and estemed the rebuke of Christe greater ryches then the treasure of Egypte. For he had respect vnto the reward.

27 By fayth he forsoke Egypte, and feared not the fearcenes of the kynge. For he endured euen as he had sene hym whiche is inuysyble.

28 Thorowe fayth he ordeyned the Easter Lambe and the effusyon of bloud, lest he that destroyed the fyrst borne shoulde touche them.

29 By fayth they passed thorowe the redde sea, as by drye lande, whiche when the Egypcyans had assayed to do, they were drouned.

30 By fayth the walles of Hierico fel doune after they were compassed about seuen dayes.

31 By faythe the harlot Raab peryshed not wyth the vnbeleuers, when she had receyued the spyes to lodgynge peaceably.

32 And what shall I more saye? the tyme woulde be to short for me to tell of Gedeon, of Baroch, and of Sampson, and of Iephtae: also of Dauid and Samuel, and of the Prophetes:

33 which thorowe fayth subdued kingdomes wrought ryghtuousnes, obtayned the promyses, stopped the mouthes of Lyons,

34 quenched the vyolence of fyre, escaped the edge of the swearde, of weake were made stronge, waxed valyaunte in fyght, turned to flyghte the armyes of the alientes.

35 And the women receyued theyr dead raysed to lyfe agayne. Other were racked, and woulde not be delyuered, that they myghte receyue a better resurreccyon.

36 Other tasted of mockynges and scourgynges, moreouer of bondes and prysonmente,

37 were stoned, were hewen a sounder, were tempted, were slayne wyth swerdes, walked vp and doune in shepes skynnes, in gotes skynnes, in nede, trybulacyon, and vexacyon,

38 whiche the world was not worthy of, they wandred in wyldernes, in mountaines, in dennes and caues of the earth

39 And these all thorowe fayth obtayned good report, and receyued not the promys,

40 God prouydynge a better thynge for vs, that they wythoute vs shoulde not be made perfecte.

# CHAPTER 12

WHERFORE let vs also (seyng that we are compassed wyth so great a multytude of witnesses) laye away all that presseth doune, and the synne that hangeth on and let vs runne, wyth pacience vnto the batayle that is set before vs

2 lokynge vnto Iesus the author and fynysher of our fayth, whiche for the ioye that was set before hym, abode þe crosse, and despised the same, and is set doune on the ryght hande of the throne of God.

3 Consydre therfore how that he endureth such speakyng agaynst him of synners least ye should be weryed and faynte in youre myndes.

4 For ye haue not yet resysted vnto bloude sheding stryuynge agaynst synne.

5 And ye haue forgotten consolacyon, which speaketh vnto you as vnto chyldren: my sonne despyse not the chastenynge of the Lorde, neyther faynte when thou arte rebuked of hym:

6 For whom þe Lord loueth, hym he chasteneth: yea, and he scourgeth euerye sonne that he receyueth.

7 Yf ye endure chastenynge, God offereth hym selfe vnto you as vnto sonnes. What sonne is that whom the father chasteneth not?

8 Yf ye be not vnder correccyon (whereof all are partakers) then are ye bastardes and not sonnes.

9 Moreouer seynge we had fathers of oure fleshe whiche corrected vs, and we gaue them reuerence: shoulde we not muche rather be in subieccyon vnto the father of spyrytuall gyftes, that we myght lyue?

10 And they verely for a few dayes, nurtured vs after their owne pleasure, but he learneth vs vnto that whiche is profytable that we myght receyue of hys holynes.

11 No maner chastisynge for the presente tyme semeth to be

ioyeous, but greuous: neuerthelesse afterwarde, it bryngeth þe quyet frute of ryghtuousnes vnto them whiche are therein exercysed.

12 Stretche forth therfore agayne the handes whiche were let doune and the weake lines

13 & se that ye haue strayght steppes vnto your fete, least any halting, turne you oute of þe way: yea let it rather be healed.

14 Embrace peace wt all men and holynes, wythout the whiche no man shall se the Lorde.

15 And loked to, that no man be destitute of the grace of God, and þt no rote of bytternes sprynge vp and trouble, and therebye manye be defyled,

16 & that there be no fornicator or vncleane person, as Esau whiche for one breakfast solde his byrthright.

17 Ye know how that afterwarde when he wolde haue inheryted the blessyng, he was put by & he found no meanes for to come therby again no thoughe he desyred it with teares.

18 For ye are not come vnto the mounte that can be touched, and vnto burnynge fyre, nor yet to mist and darkenes, and tempest of wether,

19 neyther vnto the sounde of a trompe and the voyce of wordes: whiche voyce they that hearde it wyshed awaye, that the communicacyon shoulde not be spoken to them.

20 For they were not able to abyde that whiche was spoken. Yf a beaste had touched the mountayne, it must haue bene stoned, or thrust thorowe wt a darte:

21 euen so terryble was the syght which appeared, Moyses sayde: I feare and quake.

22 But ye are come vnto the mounte Syon, and to the cytye of the lyuyng God, the celestiall Ierusalem: and to an innumerable syghte of Angels,

23 and vnto the congregacyon of þe first borne sonnes, which are wrytten in heauen, and to God the iudge of all, and to the spyrytes of iuste and perfecte men,

24 and to Iesus the medyatoure of the newe testament, and to the sprycklynge of bloude that speaketh better then the bloude of Abell.

25 Se that ye despyse not hym, that speaketh. For yf they escaped not whiche refused hym, that spake on earth: muche more shall we not escape, yf we turne awaye from hym that speaketh from heauen:

26 whose voyce then shouke the earth, and now declareth saiyng: yet ones more wyll I shake not the earth only, but also heauen.

27 No doubte that same that he sayeth yet ones more, signifyeth the remouyng away of those thynges, whiche are shaken as of thynges whiche haue ended theyr course: that the thynges whiche are not shaken maye remayne.

28 Wherfore yf we receyue a kingdom which is not moued, we haue grace, wherby we may serue God, and please hym wyth reuerence & Godly feare.

29 For our God is a consumynge fyre.

# CHAPTER 13

LET brotherlye loue continue.
2 Be not forgetfull to lodge straungers. For therebye haue diuers receyued Angels into theyr houses vnwares.

3 Remembre them that are in bondes, euen as thoughe ye were bounde wyth them. Be myndefull of them whiche are in aduersitye, as ye which are yet in youre bodyes.

4 Let wedlocke be had in pryce in all poyntes, and let the chambre be vndefyled: for whorekepers and aduouterers God wyll iudge.

5 Let your conuersacyon be wythoute couetuousnes, and be content wyth that ye haue alreadye. For he verelye sayed: I wyll not fayle the, neyther forsake the:

6 that we maye boldelye say: the Lorde is my helper and I wyll not feare what man doethe vnto me.

7 Remembre them whiche haue the ouersyght of you, whiche haue declared vnto you the worde of God. The ende of whose conuersacyon se that ye loke vpon, and folowe theyr faythe.

8 Iesus Christe yesterdaye and to daye, and the same contynueth for euer.

9 Be not caryed aboute wyth dyuerse and straunge learnynge. For it is a good thynge that the herte be stablyshed wyth grace, and not with meates, whiche haue not profyted them that haue had theyr pastyme in them.

10 We haue an altar whereof they maye not eate whiche serue in þe tabernacle.

11 For the bodyes of those beastes whose bloude is broughte into the holye place by the hygh priest to pourge synne, are burnt wythout the tentes.

12 Therfore Iesus to sanctyfye the people wyth hys owne bloude, suffered wythout the gate.

13 Let vs go forth therfore out of the tentes, and suffre rebuke with him.

14 For here haue we no continuynge cytye: but we seke one to come.

15 For by hym offre we the sacryfyce of laud always to God: that is to saye, the frute of those lyppes, whiche confesse hys name.

16 To do good, and to distrybute, forget not, for wt suche sacryfyces God is pleased.

17 Obeye them that haue the ouersyghte of you, and submyt

your selues to them, for they watche for youre soules, euen as they þt muste geue accomptes: that they maye do it wyth ioye, and not wyth griefe. For that is an vnprofytable thynge for you.

18 Praye for vs. We haue confydence because we haue a good conscience in all thynges, and desyre to lyue honestlye.

19 I desyre you therfore some what the more aboundauntly, that ye so do, that I may be restore to you quickely.

20 The God of peace that brought agayne from death oure Lorde Iesus, the great shepe herde of the shepe, thorowe the bloude of the euerlastynge testament,

21 make you perfecte in all good workes, to do hys wyl, workynge in you that whiche is pleasaunte in hys syghte thorowe Iesus Christe. To whom be prayse for euer whyle the worlde endureth. Amen.

22 I beseche you brethren, suffre the wordes of exhortacyon: For we haue wrytten vnto you in fewe wordes:

23 knowe the brother Tymothe, whome we haue sent from vs, with whom (yf he come shortly) I wyll se you.

24 Salute them that haue the ouersyghte of you, and all the sainctes. They of Italye salute you.

25 Grace be wyth you all. AMEN.

# James

## CHAPTER 1

IAMES the seruaunte of God and of the Lorde Iesus Christ sendeth gretyng to the twelue trybes whiche are scattered here and there.

2 My brethren, count it excedyng ioye when ye fal into dyuers temptacyons,

3 for as muche as ye knowe howe that the triynge of youre fayth bryngeth pacience:

4 and let pacyence haue her perfect worke, that ye maye be perfecte and sounde, lackynge nothynge.

5 Yf anye of you lacke wysedome, let hym axe of God whiche geueth to all men indyfferentlye, and casteth no man in the teath: and it shal be geuen hym.

6 But let hym axe it in faith and wauer not. For he that doubteth is lyke þe waues of the sea, toste of the wyndes & caried wyth vyolence.

7 Neyther let that man thynke that he shal receyue any thynge of the Lorde.

8 A waueryng mynded man is vnstable in all hys wayes.

9 Let the brother of low degre reioyce in that he is exalted,

10 and the ryche in that he is made lowe. For euen as the flower of the grasse, shal he vanysh away.

11 The sonne riseth with heat, and the grasse widereth, and hys flower falleth awaye, & the beautye of the fashyon of it perysheth: euen so shal the ryche man peryshe wyth hys aboundaunce.

12 Happy is the man that endureth in temptacyon, for when he is tryed, he shal receyue þe croune of lyfe, which the Lorde hath promised to them that loue hym.

13 Let no man saye when he is tempted, that he is tempted of God. For god tempteth not vnto euyl, neyther tempteth he any man:

14 But euerye man is tempted, drawne awaye, & entysed of hys owne concupiscence.

15 Then when luste hath conceyued, she bringeth forth sinne, & sinne when it is fynyshed bryngeth forthe death.

16 Erre not my deare brethren.

17 Euery good gyfte, and euerye perfecte gyfte, is from aboue and commeth doune from the father of lyght wyth whome is no varyablenes, neyther is he chaunged vnto darkenes.

18 Of hys owne wyll begat he vs wyth the worde of lyfe, that we shoulde be the fyrste frutes of hys creatures.

19 Wherfore deare brethren, let euerye man be swyfte to heare, slowe to speake, and slow to wrath.

20 For the wrath of man worketh not that whiche is ryghtuous before God.

21 Wherfore laye a parte all fylthynes, all superfluytye of malycyousnes, and receyue wyth mekenes the worde that is grafted in you, whiche is able to saue your soules.

22 And se that ye be doars of the worde & not hearers onely, deceyuyng your owne selues wyth sophystrye.

23 For yf any heare the word, and do it not, he is lyke vnto a man that beholdeth his bodly face in a glasse.

24 For assone as he hath loked on hym selfe, he goeth hys waye, and forgetteth immediatly what hys fashyon was.

25 But who so loketh in þe perfecte lawe of lybertye, and contynueth therin (yf he be not a forgetfull hearer, but a doar of þe worke) the same shall be happye in hys dede.

26 Yf anye man amonge you seme deuoute, & refrayne not his tonge, but deceyue his owne hert: thys mannes deuocyon is in vayne.

27 Pure deuocyon and vndefyled before God the father is thys: to visite the fatherlesse

and wyddowes in theyr aduersitye, and to kepe hym selfe vnspotted of the worlde.

## CHAPTER 2

Brethren haue not the faythe of oure Lorde Iesus Christe the Lorde of glorye in respect of persons.

2 If there come into your company a man wyth a golden ring and in goodly apparell, and there come in also a pore man in vyle raymente,

3 and ye haue a respecte to hym that weareth the gaye clothynge, and saye vnto hym. Sitte thou here in a good place: and saye vnto the pore, stande thou there, or sitte here vnder my fotestole:

4 are ye not parcyall in your selues, and haue iudged after euyll thoughtes?

5 Harken my deare beloued brethren. Hath not God chosen the pore of thys world, which are ryche in faythe, and heyres of the kyngedome whiche he promysed to them that loue hym?

6 But ye haue despysed the pore. Are not the ryche they whiche oppresse you: and they which drawe you before iudges?

7 Do not they speake euyll of the good name after whiche ye be named?

8 Yf ye fulfyll the royall lawe accordynge to the scripture whiche sayeth. Thou shalte loue thyne neyghboure as thy self, ye do wel.

9 But yf ye regarde one personne more then another, ye commytte sinne, and are rebuked of the lawe as transgressours.

10 Whosoeuer shall kepe the whole lawe, and yet fayle in one point he is gyltye in all.

11 For he that sayde: Thou shalte not committe adultery, sayed also, thou shalte not kyll. Thoughe thou do none adulterye: yet yf thou kyll, thou arte a transgresser of the lawe.

12 So speake ye, and so do, as they þt shalbe iudged by the lawe of lybertye.

13 For there shalbe iudgemente mercyles to hym, þt sheweth no mercy, & mercy reioyseth against iudgemente.

14 What auayleth it my brethren, thoughe a man saye he hath faythe, when he hath no deedes? Can fayth saue hym?

15 If a brother or a sister be naked or destitute of dayly fode,

16 and one of you saye vnto them: Departe in peace, God sende you warmnes and fode: not wyth standynge ye geue them not those thynges which are nedefull to the bodye: what helpeth it them?

17 Euen so faythe, yf it haue no dedes is dead in it selfe.

18 Yea and a man myghte saye: Thou haste faythe, and I haue dedes: Shewe me thy faith by thy dedes, and I wyll shew the my faythe by my dedes.

19 Beleuest thou that there is one God? Thou doest well. The deuyls also beleue and tremble.

20 Wylt thou vnderstande (O thou vayne man) that fayth without dedes is dead?

21 Was not Abraham oure father iustifyed thorowe workes when he offered Isaac hys sonne vpon the aultare?

22 Thou seyste howe that faythe wroughte wyth hys dedes, & through the dedes was faythe made perfecte:

23 and the scrypture was fulfylled whiche sayeth: Abraham beleued God, and it was reputed vnto hym for ryghtuousnes: and he was called the frende of God.

24 Ye se then how þt of dedes a man is iustifyed, and not of fayth onely.

25 Lykewyse also was not Raab the harlot iustifyed thorowe workes, when she receyued the messengers, and sente them out another way?

26 For as the bodye, without the spyryte is dead euen so fayth wythout dedes is dead.

## CHAPTER 3

My brethren be not euery man a mayster, remembrynge howe that we shal receyue the more damnacyon:

2 for in many thinges we synne all. Yf a man synne not in worde, the same is a perfect man and able to tame al the bodye.

3 Beholde we put bittes into the horsses mouthes that they shoulde obeye vs, and we turne aboute all the body.

4 Behold also the shyppes, which though they be so greate and are dryuen of fyers wyndes, yet are they turned aboute wyth a verye smale helme, whether soeuer the vyolence of the gouerner wyll

5 euen so the tonge is a lyttell member, and boasteth greate thinges. Beholde howe greate a thynge a lyttell fyre kyndleth,

6 and the tonge is fyre, and a worlde of wickednes. So is the tong set among our members, that it defyleth the whole body and setteth a fyre all that we haue of nature, & is it selfe set a fyre euen of hell.

7 All the natures of beastes, and of byrdes, and of serpentes, and thynges of the sea, are meked and tamed of the nature of man.

8 But the tonge can no man tame. It is an vnrulye euyll ful of deadly poyson.

9 Therewyth blesse we God the father, and therewyth cursse wemen which are made after the similitude of God.

10 Out of one mouth proceadeth blessynge and curssynge. My brethren these thynges ought not so to be.

11 Doth a fountayne sende forth at one place swete water & bitter also?

12 Can the fygge tree, my Brethren, beare olyue beryes: other a vyne beare fygges?

13 So can no fountayne geue both salte water & freshe also. If any man be wyse and endued wyth learnynge amonge you, let hym shewe the workes of hys good conuersacyon in mekenes that is coupled with wysdome.

14 But, yf ye haue bitter enuyinge and strife in youre hertes, reioyce not: neyther be lyars agaynste the trueth.

15 Thys wysedome descendeth not from aboue: but is earthye, & naturall, and deuelyshe:

16 For where enuiynge and stryfe is there is vnstablenes and all maner of euyll workes.

17 But the wysedome that is from aboue, is fyrste pure, then peasable, gentle, and easye to be entreated, full of mercye & good frutes, wythoute iudgynge, and wythout simulacyon:

18 yea, & the frute of ryghtuousnes is sowen in peace, of them that maintayne peace.

## CHAPTER 4

FROM whence commeth warre & fyghtynge amonge you: come they not hear hence? euen of your voluptuousnes, that rayne in youre membres.

2 Ye luste & haue not. Ye enuye and haue dignacyon, and cannot obtayne. Ye fyght and war and haue not, because ye axe not.

3 Ye axe and receyue not, because ye axe a mysse: euen to consume it vpon youre voluptuousnes

4 Ye aduouterers, & women that breake matrimonye: knowe ye not, how that the frendeshyppe of the worlde is enmitie to God warde? Who so euer wyl be a frende of the worlde, is made the enemy of God.

5 Eyther do ye thynke that the scrypture sayeth in vayne. The spyryte that dwelleth in you lusteth euen contrarye to enuye:

6 but geueth more grace.

7 Submytte your selues to God, and resiste the deuyl, and he wyll flye from you.

8 Drawe nye to God, and he wyll drawe nye to you. Clense youre handes ye synners, and purge youre hertes ye wauerynge mynded.

9 Suffer afflictyons: sorowe ye and wepe. Let youre laughter be turned to mornynge and youre ioye to heauynes.

10 Cast doune your selues before the Lorde, and he shal lyfte you vp.

11 Back byte not one another, brethren. He that backbyteth hys brother, and he that iudgeth hys brother, backbyteth the lawe, and iudgeth the lawe. But and yf thou iudge the law, thou art not an obseruer of the law, but a iudge.

12 There is one law geuer, which is able to saue & to destroy. What arte thou that iudgest another man?

13 Go to nowe ye that saye: to daye, and to morowe let vs go into suche a cytye and contynue there a yeare and bye and sel, and wynne:

14 and yet can not tell what shall happen to morowe. For what thynge is youre lyfe? It is euen a vapoure that appeareth for a lyttel tyme, and then vanysheth awaye:

15 For that ye oughte to saye: yf the Lorde wyll and yf we lyue, let vs do thys or that.

16 But nowe ye reioyce in youre bostynges. All suche reioysing is euyl.

17 Therfor to hym that knoweth how to do good, and doeth it not to him it is sinne.

## CHAPTER 5

GO to nowe ye ryche men. Weepe, and howle on your wretchednes þt shal come vpon you.

2 Youre ryches is corrupte youre garmentes are motheaten.

3 Your gold and your siluer are cankered, & the ruste of them shal be a witnes vnto you, and shall eate your fleshe, as it were fyre. Ye haue heaped treasure together in your laste dayes:

4 Beholde the hyre of the labourers which haue reped doun your fieldes (which hyer is of you kept backe by fraude) crieth: & the cryes of them whiche haue reped, are entred into the eares of the Lorde Sabaoth

5 Ye haue lyued in pleasure on the earth, & in wantonnes. Ye haue norished your hertes, as in a day of slaughter

6 Ye haue condempned, & haue kylled the iuste, & he hath not resisted you.

7 Be ye pacyente therfore brethren, vnto the commynge of the Lord. Behold the husbande man wayghteth for the precious frute of the earth & hath long pacience therevpon, vntyll he receyue (the early and the latter rayne.)

8 Be ye also pacyent therfor, and setle your hertes, for the commynge of the Lorde draweth nye.

9 Grudge not one agaynst another brethren lest ye be damned. Beholde the iudge standeth before the dore.

10 Take (my brethren) the Prophetes for an ensample of sufferyng aduersitye, & of longe pacience, whiche spake in the name of the Lorde.

11 Beholde we count them happye whiche endure. Ye haue hearde of the pacience of Iob, & haue knowen what ende the Lorde made. For the Lorde is verye pytyfull and mercyfull.

12 But about al thinges my brethren, sweare not, neyther by heauen, neyther by earth, neyther by anye other othe. Let

your yea be yea and youre naye, naye: leaste ye falle into hypocrysye.

13 Yf any of you be euyll vexed, let hym praye. Yf anye of you be merye, let hym singe Psalmes.

14 Yf anye be deseased amonge you, let hym call for the elders of the congregacyon, and let them praye ouer him, and annoynte hym wyt oyle in the name of þe Lord

15 and the prayer of fayth shall saue þe sicke, & the Lorde shall rayse hym vp: and yf he haue commytted synnes, they shalbe forgeuen him.

16 Knoweledge youre fautes one to another; and praye one for another, that ye maye be healed. The prayer of a ryghtuous man auayleth muche yf it be feruente.

17 Helias was a man mortall, euen as we are, and he prayed in hys prayer, that it might not rayne: and it rayned not on the earth by the space of thre yeares & sixe monethes.

18 And he prayed againe, and the heauen gaue rayne, and the earthe broughte forth her frute.

19 Brethren yf anye of you erre from þe trueth and an other conuerte hym,

20 let the same know that he which conuerted the synner from goyng astraye out of hys waye, shall saue a soule from death, and shall hyde the multytude of synnes.

# 1 Peter

## CHAPTER 1

PETER an Apostle of Iesu Christe to them that dwell here & there as straungers thorowout all Pontus, Galacia, Capadocia Asia, and Bithinia, electe

2 by the for kneweledge of God the father, thorowe the sanctifiynge of the spyryte, vnto obedience & sprinklyng of the bloude of Iesus Christe. Grace be wyth you & peace be multiplied.

3 Blessed be God the father of oure Lorde Iesus Christe, whiche thorowe his aboundaunt mercye begat vs agayne vnto lyuely hope by the resurreccyon of Iesus Christe from death,

4 to enioye an enherytaunce immortall & vndefyled, and that putryfyeth not, reserued in heauen for you,

5 whiche are kept by the power of God thorowe fayth, vnto saluacyon, whiche saluacyon is prepared all ready to be shewed in the laste tyme,

6 in the whiche tyme ye shall reioyce, thoughe nowe for a season (yf nede requyre) ye are in heauynes, thorow manyfolde temptacyon,

7 that youre faythe ones tryed beynge muche more precyous, then golde that perysheth (though it be tryed with fyre) myghte be founde vnto laude, glory, and honoure, at the apearynge of Iesus Christe

8 whome ye haue not sene, and yet loue hym, in whome euen nowe, thoughe ye se hym not, yet do you beleue: and reioyce with ioye vnspeakeable and gloryous:

9 receyuynge the ende of youre faythe, the saluacyon of youre soules.

10 Of whiche saluacyon haue the Prophetes enquyred and searched, whiche prophesyed of the grace that shoulde come vnto you,

11 searchynge when or at what tyme of the spyryte of Christe whiche was in them, shoulde signifye, whiche spyryte testyfyed before, the passyons that shoulde come vnto Christe, and the glorye that shoulde folowe after:

12 vnto which Prophetes it was declared, that not vnto them selues, but vnto vs, they shoulde mynyster the thynges whiche are nowe shewed vnto you of them whiche by the holye ghoste sent doune from heauen, haue preached vnto you the thynges whiche the aungels desyre to beholde.

13 Wherfore gyrde vp the loynes of youre myndes, be sober, and trust perfectelye on the grace that is broughte vnto you, by the declarynge of Iesus Christe,

14 as obedyent chyldren not fashyonynge youre selues vnto your old lustes of ignorauncye:

15 but as he whiche called you is holye, euen so be ye holy in all maner of conuersacyon,

16 because it is wrytten. Be ye holy, for I am holy.

17 And yf so be that ye call on the father, whiche wythout respecte of person, iudgeth accordynge to euery mannes workes se that ye passe the tyme of youre pylgrymage in feare.

18 For as muche as ye know howe that ye were not redemed wyth corruptyble syluer and golde, from youre vayne conuersacyon whiche ye receyued by the tradicyons of þe fathers:

19 but wyth the precyous bloud of christ as of a lambe vndefyled, and wythout spotte,

20 whiche was ordeyned before the worlde was made, but was declared in the laste tymes for youre sakes,

21 whiche by hys meanes haue beleued on God that raysed hym from death, & gloryfyed hym, that youre faythe and hope myght be in God.

22 And for as muche as ye haue puryfyed, youre soules thorowe the spyryte, in obeying the truethe for to loue brotherlye wythout faynynge, se that ye loue one another with a pure herte feruentlye:

23 for ye are borne a newe, not of mortal seede, but of immortall, by the word of God whiche lyueth, and lasteth for euer.

24 For all fleshe is as grasse, and all the glorye of man is as the floure grasse. The grasse wyddereth, and the floure falleth awaye,

25 but the worde of the Lorde endureth euer. And thys is the worde whiche by the gospell was preached amonge you.

## CHAPTER 2

WHERFORE laye a syde all malycyousnes, and all gyle, and dyssymulacyon, and enuye, and all backbytynge:

2 and as newe bourne babes, desyre that reasonable mylke whiche is wythout corrupcyon that ye maye growe therein.

3 If so be that ye haue tasted howe pleasaunt the Lorde is,

4 to whome ye come as vnto a lyuinge stone dysalowed of men, but chosen of God and precyous:

5 and ye as lyuynge stones, are made a spirytuall housse, and an holye priesthode, for to offer vp spyrytuall sacryfyce, acceptable to God by Iesus Christe.

6 Wherfore it is contained in the scrypture: beholde, I put in Syon an head corner stone, electe and precyous: and he that beleueth on hym, shall not be ashamed.

7 Vnto you therfor whiche beleue, he is precyous, but vnto them whiche beleue not, the stone whiche the buylders refused the same is made the head stone in the corner,

8 and a stone to stomble at, and a rocke to offende them whiche stomble at the word, and beleue not that whereon they were set.

9 But ye are a chosen generacyon, a royall priesthode, an holye nacyon and a peculyar people that ye shoulde shewe the vertues of hym that called you oute of darkenes into his marueylous lyght,

10 whiche in tyme past were not vnder mercye, but nowe haue obtayned mercye.

11 Dearely beloued, I beseche you as straungers and pylgremes, obstayne from fleshely lustes, which fyght agaynste the soule,

12 and se that ye haue honest conuersacyon amonge the Gentyls, that they whiche backbyte you as euyll doars, maye se youre good workes and prayse God in the daye of visitacyon.

13 Submyt youre selues vnto all maner ordinaunce of man for the Lordes sake, whether it be vnto the kynge as vnto the chiefe heade:

14 other vnto rulars, as vnto them that are sent of hym, for the punyshemente of euyll doars: but for the laude of them that do wel.

15 For so is the wyll of God, that ye put to sylence the ignorauncye of the folyshe men:

16 as fre, and not as hauynge the lybertye for a cloke of maliciousnes, but euen as the seruauntes of God.

17 Honoure all men. Loue brotherlye felowship. Feare God, and honour the kynge.

18 Seruauntes obeye your maysters wyth al feare, not onelye yf they be good, and courteous: but also thoughe they be frowarde.

19 For it is thanke worthy yf a man for conscience towarde God endure griefe, suffering wrongfullye.

20 For what prayse is it, yf when ye be buffeted for your faultes, ye take it pacientlye? But and yf when ye do well, ye suffre wrong and take it pacyently, then is there thanke wt God.

21 for here vnto verelye were ye called: for Christe also suffered for vs, leauynge vs an ensample that we shoulde folowe his steppes,

22 whiche dyd no synne, neyther was there gyle founde in hys mouth:

23 which when he was reuyled, reuyled not agayne: when he suffered, he threatened not: but commytted þe cause to him that iudgeth ryghtuously,

24 which hys owne selfe bare oure synnes in hys body on the tree, that we shoulde be delyuered from synne, and shoulde lyue in ryghtuousnes. By whose strypes ye were healed.

25 For ye were as shepe goynge astraye: but are nowe returned to the shepeherde and byshop of your soules.

## CHAPTER 3

LYKEWYSE let the wyues be in subiectyon to theyr husbandes, that euen they which beleue not the worde, maye wythoute the worde be wonne by the conuersation of the wiues:

2 whyle they beholde your pure conuersacion coupled wyth feare.

3 Whose apparell shall not be outewarde wyth broyeded heare, and hangynge on of golde, other in puttynge on of gorgyous apparell:

4 but let the hyd man of the harte be vncorrupte with a meke and a quyete spyryte, whiche spyryte is before God a thynge muche set by.

5 For after thys maner in the olde tyme dyd the holye women whiche trusted in God, tyer them selues, and were obedyente to theyr husbandes

6 euen as Sara obeyed Abraham, and called hym Lorde: whose doughters ye are as longe as ye do well, and be not afrayde of euerye shadowe.

7 Lykewyse ye men dwell wyth them accordynge to knoweledge, geuynge honoure vnto the wyfe, as vnto the weaker vessell, and as vnto them that are heyres also of the grace of lyfe, that youre prayers be not let.

8 In conclusyon be ye all of one mynd, one suffer wyth another, loue as brethren, be petifull, be curteous,

9 not rendringe euyll for euyll, neyther rebuke for rebuke, but contrarywyse, blesse, remembryng that ye are thervnto called, euen that ye shoulde be heyres of blessinge.

10 If anye man longe after lyfe, and loueth to se good dayes, let him refrayne his tonge from euil, & his lippes that they speake not gyle.

11 Let hym eschue euyll and do good, let him seke peace, and ensue it.

12 For the eyes of the Lorde are ouer the rightuous, and his eares are open vnto theyr prayers. But the face of the Lorde beholdeth them that do euil.

13 Morouer who is it that wyll harme you, yf ye folowe that whiche is good?

14 Notwithstanding happy are ye, yf ye suffre for ryghtuousnes sake. Yea and feare not though they seme terrible vnto you, neither be troubled,

15 but sanctifie the Lorde God in your hertes. Be ready alwaies to geue an answere to euery man that axeth you a reason of the hope, that is in you, and that with mekenes & feare,

16 hauinge a good conscience, that when they backbyte you as euyl doers, they maye be ashamed, for as muche as they haue falsely accused your good conuersation in Christ.

17 It is better (yf the wyll of God be so) þt ye suffre for wel doyng, then for euil doinge.

18 For as much as Christ hath ones suffered for sinners, the iuste for the vniuste, for to bringe vs to God, and was kylled, as perteininge to the fleshe: but was quickened in the spirite.

19 In which spirite, he also wente and preached vnto the spirites that were in prison,

20 which were in tyme passed disobedient, when the longe sufferinge of God abode excedinge paciently in þe dayes of Noe, whyle the arcke was a preparing wherin fewe (that is to saie .viij. soules) were saued by water,

21 which signifyeth baptisme that nowe saueth vs, not þe puttinge awaye of the fylth of the fleshe, but in that a good conscience consenteth to God, by the resurreccion of Iesus Christe,

22 whyche is on the right hande of God, and is gone into heauen, aungelles, power, and mighte, subdued vnto him.

# CHAPTER 4

FOR as much as Christ hath suffred for vs in the fleshe, arme your selues lykewise wyth the same mynde: for he which suffereth in the fleshe ceaseth from synne,

2 that he hence forwarde shoulde lyue as muche tyme as remayneth in the fleshe, not after the iustes of men, but after the wyl of God.

3 For it is sufficient for vs, þt we haue spent the time that is past of the lyfe, after the wil of the Gentiles, walking in wantonnes, lustes, dronckennes, in eatinge, drinkinge & in abominable Idolatrie.

4 And it semeth to them a straunge thynge, that ye runne not also with them vnto the same excesse of riote, and therfore speake they euyl of you,

5 whiche shall geue a comptes to hym that is redy to iudge quicke & dead.

6 For vnto this purpose verely was the Gospel preached vnto the dead that they shoulde be iudged lyke other men in the fleshe, but shoulde lyue before God in the spirite.

7 The ende of al thinges is at hande. Be ye therfore discrete and sober, that ye maye be apt to prayers.

8 But aboue all thinges haue feruente loue among you. For loue couereth the multitude of synnes.

9 Be ye herberous one to another, & that without grudginge.

10 As euerye man hath receyued þe gifte, minister the same one to another as good mynisters of the manifolde grace of God.

11 Yf anye man speake let hym talke as though he spake the wordes of God. If any man mynistre, let hym do it as of the habilitie, whyche God ministreth vnto hym. That God in all things may be glorifyed thorowe IESUS Christ, to whom be prayse and domynyon for euer, and whyle the worlde standeth. Amen.

12 Dearely beloued, be not troubled in hys heate, whiche nowe is come amonge you to trye you as though some straunge thing had happened vnto you:

13 but reioice in as much as ye are partakers of Christes passions, that when his glory appereth, ye maye be mery and glad.

14 If ye be railed vpon for the name of Christ, happie are ye. For the spyryte of glorye, and the spyryte of Gad resteth vpon you. On theyr parte he is euyll spoken of, but on your parte he is glorified.

15 Se that none of you suffer as a murtherer or as a thefe, or an

euil doar, or as a busibody in other mens matters.

16 Yf any man suffer as a Christen man, let him not be ashamed, but let him glorifie God on this behalfe.

17 For the time is come that iudgemente must beginne at the house of God. Yf it fyrst begynne at vs, what shal the ende be of them, whiche beleue not the Gospel of God?

18 And yf the rightuous scasly be saued, where shal the vngodly and the sinner appere?

19 Wherfore let them that suffer according to the wil of God, commit their soules to him with wel doing, as vnto a faythfull creator.

# CHAPTER 5

THE elders whiche are amonge you, I exhorte, whiche am also an elder, and a wytnes of the affliccions of Christe, and also a partaker of the glory that shallbe opened,

2 se that ye fede Christes flocke, which is amonge you, takinge the ouersight of them, not as though ye were compelled therto, but wyllingly, not for the desire of fylthy lucre, but of a good minde,

3 not as though ye were Lordes ouer the parishes, but that ye be an ensample to þe flocke.

4 And when þe chiefe shephearde shal appere, ye shal receiue an incorruptible crowne of glorie.

5 Lykewyse ye yonger submit youre selues vnto the elder. Submit youre selues euerye man, one to another, knyt youre selues together in lowlines of mynde. For God resisteth the proude & geueth grace to humble.

6 Submit youre selues therfore vnder the myghty hande of God, that he maye exalte you, when the tyme is come.

7 Caste all your care to him: for he careth for you.

8 Be sober and watch, for your aduersary þe deuyll as a roringe Lyon walketh aboute, sekinge whom he may deuour,

9 whom resist stedfast in the fayth remembring, that ye do but fulfill the same affliccions, which are appointed to youre brethren that are in the worlde.

10 The God of al grace, which called you vnto his eternal glory by Christe Iesus, shall hys owne selfe after ye haue suffred a little affliccion make you perfecte, shall settle, strength and stablishe you.

11 To hym be glorie and dominion for euer, and whyle the worlde endureth. Amen.

12 By Syluanus a faythfull brother vnto you (as I suppose) haue I wrytten brefly, exhortynge and testifyenge howe that this is the true grace of God wherin ye stande.

13 The companions of youre election, that are of Babylon, salute you, and Marcus my sonne.

14 Grete ye one another wyth the kysse of loue. Peace be wyth you all, which are in Christe Iesus. AMEN.

# 2 Peter

## CHAPTER 1

SIMON Peter a seruaunte, and an Apostle of Iesus Christe, to them whyche haue obtained lyke precyous faith wyth vs in the rightuousnes that commeth of oure God and sauiour Iesu Christ.

2 Grace wyth you, and peace be multiplied in the knowledge of God and of Iesus Christ oure Lorde.

3 Accordyng as hys godlye power hath geuen vnto vs al thinges that pertayne vnto lyfe and godlines, thorowe the knowledge of him that hath called vs by vertue & glory,

4 by the meanes, wherof are geuen vnto vs excellent and most great promises, that by the helpe of them ye should be partakers of the godly nature, in that ye flee the corruption of worldelye luste.

5 And herunto geue al diligence, in youre fayth, mynyster vertue, and in vertue knowledge,

6 and in knowledge temperancie, and in temperauncie, pacience, in pacience, Godlynes,

7 in Godlines brotherly kyndnes, in brotherlye kindnes, loue.

8 For yf these things be amonge you and are plenteous, they wyll make you, that ye neyther shalbe ydle nor vnfruteful in the knowledge of oure Lord Iesu Christe.

9 But he that lacketh these thinges, is blind and gropeth for the waye with his hand, and hath forgotten that he was pourged from his olde synnes.

10 Wherfore brethren, geue the more diligence for to make your callinge and eleccion sure. For if ye do suche thinges, ye shal neuer erre.

11 Yea and by this meanes an entringe in, shalbe minystred vnto you aboundantlye into the euerlastinge kingdome of oure Lorde and sauiour Iesus Christ.

12 Wherfore I wyll not be negligente to put you always in remembraunce of such thynges, though that ye knowe them your selues, and be also stablyshed in the presente trueth.

13 Notwithstanding I thinke it mete, (as long as I am in this tabernacle) to stere you vp by puttynge you in remembraunce

14 for as muche as I am sure how that the tyme is at hande, that I must put of my tabernacle, euen as our Lord Iesus Christ hath shewed me.

15 I wil enforce therfore that on euerye syde ye myght haue wherwith to stere vp the remembraunce of these thynges after my departinge.

16 For we folowed not deceiuable fables, when we opened vnto you the power and comminge of our Lord Iesus Christ, but wyth our eyes we saw his maieste, euen then verelye,

17 when he receiued of God the father honoure and glory, and when there came such a voice to hym from the excellente glorie: This is my deare beloued sonne in whome I haue delyte.

18 This voice we hearde when it came from heauen beynge wyth hym in the holy mounte.

19 We haue also a ryght sure worde of prophesye, whervnto yf ye take hede, as vnto a light, that shineth in a darcke place, ye do wel vntyll the daye dawne, and the daye starre aryse in youre hertes.

20 So that ye fyrste knowe this, that no prophesye in the scripture hath any priuate interpretacion.

21 For the scrypture came neuer by the wyl of man, but holye men of God spake as they were moued by the holy ghoste.

## CHAPTER 2

THERE were false prophetes among the people, euen as there shalbe false teachers amonge you, which priuilie shal bringe in damnable sectes, euen denyenge the Lorde that hath bought them and bringe vpon them selues swyft dampnacion,

2 and many shal folowe theyr damnable wayes, by whiche the way of trueth shalbe euyl spoken of,

3 and thorowe couetousnes shal they wyth fayned wordes make marchaundyse of you, whose iudgement is not farre of, and theyr dampnacion slepeth not.

4 For yf God spared not the aungels that sinned but cast them downe into hell, and deliuered them into chayns of darckenes, to be kept vnto iudgement,

5 neyther spared the olde worlde, but saued Noe the ryght preacher of rightuousnes, and brought in the floud vpon the worlde of the vngodly,

6 and turned the cyties of Sodom and Gomor into ashes, ouerthrowe them, dampned them, and made on them an ensample vnto all that after shoulde lyue vngodly.

7 And iust Lot vexed with the vnclenly conuersacyon of the wicked, deliuered he.

8 For he beinge rightuouse and dwellinge amonge them, in seinge and hearinge, vexed his rightuouse soule from daye to daye wyth theyr vnlawfull dedes.

9 The Lorde knoweth howe to deliuer the Godlye out of temptacion, and howe to reserue the vniuste vnto the daye of iudgement for to be punyshed,

10 namely them that walke after the fleshe in the luste of vncleanes, and despyse the rulars. Presumpteous are they, & stubborne and feare not to speake euyl of them that are in authoritie.

11 When the angels which are greater both in power and might, receiue not of the Lorde railing iudgement agaynste them.

12 But these as brute beastes naturallye made to be taken and destroyed, speake euyll of that they knowe not, and shal perishe thorow their owne destruccion,

13 and receiue the reward of vnrightuousnes. They count it pleasure to lyue deliciously for a season. Spottes they are and filthines, liuinge at pleasure, and in disceiueable waies feastinge with you,

14 hauinge eyes full of aduoutrye, and that can not cease to synne, begilinge vnstable soules. Hertes they haue exercised with couetousues. They are cursed children,

15 and haue forsaken the ryght waye, and are gone astray folowing the waye of Balam the sonne of Bosor, whiche loued the rewarde of vnrightuousnes,

16 but was rebuked of hys iniquitye. The tame and dome beaste, speakinge with mannes voice, forbade the folishnes of the Prophete.

17 These are welles wythout water, & cloudes caried about of a tempest, to whom the miste of darkenes is reserued for euer.

18 For when they haue spoken the swellinge wordes of vanitie, they begyle with wantonnes thorowe the lustes of the fleshe, them that were cleane escaped, but nowe are wrapped in errours.

19 They promis them libertie, and are them selues the bonde seruauntes of corrupcyon. For of whomsoeuer a man is ouer come, vnto the same is he in bondage.

20 For yf they, after they haue escaped from the fylthines of the worlde thorowe the knowledge yf þe Lord and of the sauiour Iesus Christe, are yet tangled agayne therin and ouercome, then is the latter ende worsse wyth them then the beginninge.

21 For it had bene better for them not haue knowen the way of rightuousnes then after they haue knowen it to turne from the commaundementes geuen vnto them.

22 It is happened to them according to the true prouerbe: The dogge is turned to his vomet againe, and the sowe that was washed, to her wallowing in the mire.

# CHAPTER 3

THIS is the seconde epistle that I nowe wryte to you (beloued) wherwith I stere vp & warne youre pure myndes, to cal to remembraunce

2 the wordes, which were tolde before of the holy prophetes, and also the commaundementes of vs the apostles of the Lorde and sauiour.

3 This fyrst vnderstande, that there shall come in the laste dayes mockers, which wyll walke after their own lustes

4 and say. Where is the promes of hys comminge? For sence the fathers dyed, al thinges continue in the same estate, wherin they were at the beginninge.

5 This they knowe not (and that willinglie) howe that the heauens a greate whyle ago were, & the earth that was in the water, appered vp out of the water by the worde of God,

6 by the which thinges, the worlde that then was, perished ouer flowen with the water.

7 But the heauens verely and earth, which are now are kept by the same worde in store, and reserued vnto fyre, agaynste the daye of iudgemente, and perdycyon of vngodlye men.

8 Dearly beloued, be not ignoraunt of thys one thinge, howe that one daye is wyth the Lorde, as a thousande yeare, and a thousande yeare as one daye.

9 The Lord is not slacke to fulfyl hys promyse, as some men count slaknes, but is patient to vsward and would haue no man loste, but would receyue al men to repentaunce.

10 Neuertheles the daye of the Lord wyl come as a thiefe in

the nyght in þe which daye, the heauens shal peryshe wyth terryble noyse, and the elementes shal melte wyth heate, and the earth wyth the workes that are therin shal burne.

11 If al these thinges shal perishe, what maner persons ought ye to be in holye conuersacyon and Godlynes:

12 lokynge for and hasting vnto the comminge of the daye of God, in which the heauens shall perishe with fyre, & the elementes shalbe consumed wyth heat.

13 Neuertheles we loke for a new heauen and a newe earth, accordinge to his promys, wherin dwelleth rygtuousnes.

14 Wherfore dearly beloued, seynge that ye loke for such thinges, be diligent that ye may be found of hym in peace, wythout spotte and vndefyled

15 And suppose that the longe suffering of the Lord is saluacion, euen as oure dearlye beloued brother Paule accordinge to the wysdome geuen to hym wrote vnto you,

16 yea, almoste in euery epistle speakinge of such thinges, amonge whiche are manye thinges harde to be vnderstande, which they that are vnlearned, and vnstable, peruert, as they do other scriptures vnto their owne destruccion.

17 Ye therfore beloued, seynge ye knowe it before hand, beware lest ye be also plucked away with the errour of the wycked, and fall from your own stedfastnes,

18 but grow in grace, and in the knowledge of oure Lorde and Sauiour Iesus Christe. To whom be glorye both nowe and foreuer. Amen.

# 1 John

## CHAPTER 1

THAT whyche was from the begynninge, whyche we haue hearde, whyche we haue sene with oure eyes, which we haue loked vpon and our handes haue handeled, of the word of the lyfe.

2 For the life appeared, and we haue sene, and beare wytnes, and shewe vnto you that eternall lyfe, whyche was wyth the father, and appeared to vs.

3 That whyche we haue sene and hearde declare we vnto you, that ye maye haue felowshyp wyth vs, and that our felowshype may be wyth the father and hys sonne Iesus Christ.

4 And this wryte we vnto you that youre ioye may be ful.

5 And this is the tydinges that we haue heard of him, and declare vnto you, that God is lyghte and in him is no darckenes at al,

6 yf we saye that we haue felowshippe with him, and yet walke in darckenes, we lye, and do not the trueth,

7 but and yf we walke (in light) euen as he is in lighte, then haue we felowshyppe wyth hym, and the bloude of Iesus Christe his sonne clenseth vs from all sinne.

8 If we saye that we haue no sinne, we deceiue oure selues, and trueth is not in vs.

9 If we knowledge oure sinnes, he is faythfull and iust, to forgeue vs our sinnes, and to clense vs from al vnrightuousnes.

10 If we say we haue not sinned, we make him a liar, and his word is not in vs.

## CHAPTER 2

MY lytle chyldren, these thinges wryte I vnto you, that ye sinne not, yf anye man synne, yet we haue an aduocate with the father, Iesus Christe, whiche is rightuouse,

2 and he it is that obtayned grace for our sinnes, not for oure sinnes onelye, but also for the synnes of al the worlde.

3 And herby we are sure that we knowe him, yf we kepe his commaundementes.

4 He that sayth I knowe him, and kepeth not his commaundementes, is a liar, and the veritie is not in him.

5 Whosoeuer kepeth his worde, in him is the loue of God, perfecte in dede. And there by knowe we that we are in him.

6 He that sayeth he abydeth in him ought to walke euen as he walked.

7 Brethren I wryte no newe commaundemente vnto you, but that olde commaundemente, which ye hearde from the beginning.

8 The olde commandement is the word, which ye heard from the beginninge. Againe a new commaundement I write vnto you, a thinge that is true in him, and also in you, for the darkenes is past, and the true light now shineth.

9 He that sayeth how that he is in the light, and yet hateth his brother, is in dackenes euen vntill this tyme.

10 He that loueth his brother, abideth in the lyghte, and there is none occasion of euill in him.

11 He that hateth his brother, is in darckenes and walketh in darckenes, and can not tell whether he goeth, because that darckenes hath blinded his eyes.

12 Babes I wryte vnto you, how that youre sinnes are forgeuen you for his names sake.

13 I wryte vnto you fathers, how that ye know him, that was from the beginninge. I wryte vnto you yong men, how that ye haue ouercome the wicked. I write to you lytel children, howe that ye knowe the father,

14 I wryte vnto you fathers, how that ye knowe him, that was from the beginninge. I wryte vnto you young men, how that ye are stronge and the word of God abyeth in you, & ye haue ouercome that wycked.

15 Se that ye loue not the world, neyther the thynges that are in the worlde. Yf anye man loue the worlde the loue of the father is not in him.

16 For all that is in the world (as the luste of the fleshe, the lust of the eyes, and the pryde of goodes) is not of the father, but of þe world.

17 And the world vanysheth away, and the lust therof, but he that fulfilleth the will of God, abideth euer.

18 Litel chyldren, it is the last time, and as ye haue hearde how that Antichriste shall come, euen nowe are there many Antichristes come alredye. Wherby we knowe that it is the last tyme.

19 They went out from vs, but they were not of vs. For yf they had bene of vs: they woulde no doubte, haue continued wyth vs. But that fortuned, that it myghte appeare, that they were not of vs.

20 And ye haue an oyntment of the holye ghost and ye knowe all thinges.

21 I wrote not vnto you, as though ye knewe not the trueth, but as though ye knewe it, and knowe also that no lye commeth of trueth.

22 Who is a liar but he that denyeth that Iesus is Christ? The same is the Antechrist that denyeth the father and the sonne.

23 Whosoeuer denyeth the sonne, the same hath not þe father.

24 Let therfore abyde in you that same, whiche ye hearde from the beginninge, shall remaine in you, ye also shal continue in the sonne, and in the father.

25 And this is the promes, that he hath promysed vs euen eternal lyfe.

26 This haue I written vnto you concerning them, that disceyue you.

27 And the anointinge, whiche ye haue receiued of him, dwelleth in you. And ye nede not that anye man teache you, but as the anointing teacheth you al thinges, and is true, and is no lye, & it is taught you, euen so byde therin.

28 And now babes abide in him, that when he shal appeare, we maye be bolde, and not be made ashamed of him at his comming:

29 If ye knowe that he is righteous, knowe also that he whiche foloweth rightuousnes, is borne of hym.

# CHAPTER 3

BEHOLDE what loue þe father hath shewed on vs, that we shoulde be called þe sonnes of God. For this cause the worlde knoweth you not, because it knoweth not him.

2 Dearly beloued, now are we the sonnes of God, and yet it doeth not appeare, what we shalbe. But we knowe that when it shal appere, we shalbe like him. For we shall se him as he is.

3 And euery man that hath thys hope in him, pourgeth him selfe, euen as he is pure.

4 Whosoeuer committeth synne, committeth vnrightuousnes also, for synne is vnrightuousnes.

5 And ye knowe that he appered to take awaye oure synnes, & in him is no sinne.

6 As many as byde in him synne not, whosoeuer synneth, hath not sene him, neyther hath knowen him.

7 Babes let no man deceiue you. He that doth rightuousnes is rightuous, euen as he is righteous.

8 He that committeth sinne, is of the deuil, for the deuil sinneth sence the beginninge. For this purpose appered the sonne of God to lowse the workes of the deuil.

9 Whosoeuer is borne of God, sinneth not, for hys seed remaineth in him, and he can not sinne, because he is borne of God.

10 In this are the chyldren of God knowen, and the chyldren of the deuil. Whosoeuer doth not righteousnes, is not of God, neyther he that loueth not his brother.

11 For this is the tidinges, that ye hearde from the beginninge, that ye should loue one anothere

12 not as Cayn, which was of the wicked & slewe his brother. And wherfore slewe he him? Because his own workes were euyll, and his brothers good.

13 Maruaile not my brethren though the worlde hate you.

14 We know that we are translated from death vnto lyfe, because we loue the brethren. He that loueth not his brother, abydeth in death.

15 Whosoeuer hateth his brother, is a man slear. And ye know þt no man slear hath eternal life abidinge in him.

16 Hereby perceyue we loue, that he gaue hys lyfe for vs, & therfore oughte we also to geue our lyues for the brethren.

17 Whosoeuer hath this worldes good, and seeth his brother haue nede, and shutteth vp his compassion from him, howe dwelleth the loue of God in hym?

18 My babes, let vs not loue in worde neyther in tonge, but wyth the dede and in veryty:

19 For therby we know that we are of the verytye, and can before him quyete oure hertes.

20 But if our hertes condempne vs, God is greater then our hertes, and knoweth all thinges.

21 Beloued, yf our hertes condempne vs not, then haue we trust to Godward,

22 and whatsoeuer we are, we shall receiue of him, because we kepe his commaundementes, and do these thinges, which are pleasyng in hys sight.

23 And this is his commaundement, that we beleue on þe name of his sonne Iesus Christ and loue one another, as he gaue commaundemente.

24 And he that kepeth hys commaundementes, dwelleth in hym and he in him, & therby we know that there abydeth in vs of the spyryte, which he gaue vs.

## CHAPTER 4

YE beloued, beleue not euery spirite, but proue the spirites whether they be of God, or not, for manye false prophetes are gone out into the world.

2 Hereby shall ye knowe the spyryte of God. Euerye spyrite that confesseth that Iesus Christe is come in the fleshe, is of God.

3 And euerye spyryte þt confesseth not that Iesu Christe is come in the fleshe, is not of God. And this is that spyrite of Antechrist, of whom ye haue hearde, how that he shoulde come, and euen nowe alreadye is he in the worlde.

4 Lytel chyldren, ye are of God, and haue ouercome them, for greater is he that is in you, then he that is in the world.

5 They are of the world, & therfore speake they of þe world, and the world heareth them.

6 We are of God. He that knoweth God heareth vs, he that is not of God, heareth vs not. Here by knowe we þe spyryte of verity, & the spirite of erroure.

7 Beloued, let vs loue one another, for loue commeth of god. And euery one þt loueth is borne of God, & knoweth God.

8 He that loueth not, knoweth not God: for God is loue.

9 In this appered the loue of God to vsward, because that God sent his onely begotten sonne into the world, that we myght lyue thorow him:

10 Herin is loue, not that we loued God, but that he loued vs, & sente his sonne to make agrement for our synnes.

11 Beloued yf God so loued vs we oughte also to loue one another.

12 No man hath sene God at anyetime. Yf we loue one another, god dwelleth in vs, and his loue is perfect in vs.

13 Hereby knowe we þt we dwel in him, and he in vs, because he hath geuen vs of his spyrite.

14 And we haue sene and do testifye, that the father sent the sonne, whyche is the sauyour of the world.

15 Whosoeuer confesseth, that Iesus is the sonne of God, in him dwelleth God and he in God.

16 And we haue knowen & beleued the loue that God hath to vs. God is loue, and he that dwelleth in loue, dwelleth in God, and god in hym.

17 Herin is the loue perfect in vs, that we shoulde haue trust in the daye of iudgement: For as he is, euen so are we in thys worlde.

18 There is no feare in loue, but perfecte loue casteth out all feare, for feare hath paynfulnes. He that feareth is not perfect in loue.

19 We loue him, for he loued vs fyrste.

20 Yf a man saye, I loue God, and yet hate his brother, he is a lyar. For howe can he that loueth not his brother whom he hath sene, loue god, whom he hath not sene?

21 And this commaundemente haue we of him that he which loueth God, should loue his brother also.

## CHAPTER 5

WHOSOEUER beleueth that Iesus is Christ, is borne of God. And euerye one that loueth hym whiche begat, loueth hym also whyche was begotten of hym.

2 In thys we know, that we loue the children of God, when we loue God and kepe his commaundementes.

3 This is the loue of God, that we kepe his commaundementes, and his commaundementes are not greuous.

4 For all that is borne of God, ouercommeth the world. And this is the victorye, that ouercommeth the worlde, euen oure fayeth.

5 Who is it that ouercommeth the worlde, but he which beleueth, that Iesus is the sonne of God?

6 This Iesus Christ is he that came by water and bloude, not by water onelye, but by water and bloud. And it is the spirite that beareth witnes, because the spirite is trueth.

7 (For there are thre which beare recorde in heauen, the father, the worde, and the holye Ghoste. And these thre are one.)

8 For there are thre, whiche beare recorde in earth the spyrite and water, and bloude, and these thre are one.

9 If we receyue the wytnes of men, the wytnes of God is greater. For thys is the wytnes of God, whiche he testified of his sonne.

10 He that beleueth on the sonne of God, hath the wytnes in him selfe. He that beleued not God, hath made hym a lyar, because he beleued not the recorde, that God gaue of hys sonne.

11 And thys is that recorde, howe that God hath geuen vnto vs eternal lyfe, and this lyfe is in his sonne.

12 He that hath the sonne, hath lyfe: and he that hath not sonne of God, hath not lyfe.

13 These things haue I wryten vnto you, that beleue on the name of the sonne of God, that ye maye know, how that ye haue eternal lyfe, and that ye may beleue on the name of the

sonne of God.

14 And this is the truste that we haue in him, that yf we axe any thinge, accordinge to hys will he heareth vs.

15 And yf we knowe that he heareth vs whatsoeuer we axe, we knowe, that we shall haue the peticyons that we desyre of hym.

16 If any man se his brother synne a synne that is not vnto death, let him axe, and he shal geue him lyfe, for them that synne not vnto death. There is a synne vnto death, for which saye I not that a man shoulde praye.

17 All vnryghtuousnes is synne, and there is sinne not vnto death.

18 We knowe that whosoeuer is borne of God, synneth not, but he that is begotten of God kepeth him selfe, and that wycked toucheth him not.

19 We knowe that we are of God, and that the world is altogether set on wyckednes.

20 We know, that the sonne of God is come, & hath geuen vs a minde to know him which is true, & we are in him, that is true thorowe his sonne Iesus Christ. This same is verye God, and eternal lyfe.

21 Babes kepe your selues from Images. Amen.

# 2 John

THE elder to the electe Lady, and her children, whiche I loue in the trueth: and not I onelye, but also all that knowe the trueth,

2 for the truethes sake, whyche dwelleth in vs, and shalbe in vs for euer.

3 Wyth you be grace, mercye, and peace from God the father, and from the Lord Iesus Christ the sonne of the father, in trueth and loue.

4 I reioysed greatly, that I founde of thy children walking in trueth, as we haue receiued a commaundemente of the father.

5 And nowe beseche I the Ladye, not as though I wrote a newe commaundemente vnto the, but that same which we had from the beginning, that we should loue one another.

6 And this is the loue, that we shoulde walke after his commaundementes. Thys commaundemente is (that as ye haue hearde from the beginninge) ye shoulde walke in it.

7 For many deceyuers are entred into the worlde, whiche confesse not that Iesus Christe is come in the fleshe. Thys is a deceyuer and an Antichriste.

8 Loke on youre selues, that we lose not that we haue wrought but that we maye haue a full rewarde.

9 Whosoeuer transgresseth and bydeth not in the doctryne of Christe, hath not God. He that endureth in the doctrine of Christe, hath both the father and the sonne.

10 Yf there come any vnto you, and bringe not this learninge, him receiue not to house, neither byd hym God spede.

11 For he that biddeth him God spede, is partaker of his euyll dedes.

12 I had manye things to wryte vnto you, neuerthelesse I woulde not wryte wyth paper & ynke: but I trust to come vnto you, & speake wyth you mouth to mouth, that oure ioye maye be full.

13 The sonnes of thy electe sister grete the. Amen.

# 3 John

THE elder vnto the beloued Gaius, whom I loue in the trueth.

2 Beloued, I wyshe in all thynges, that thou prosperedst, and faredest well euen as thy soule prospereth.

3 I reioysed greatly, when the brethren came and testifyed of the trueth that is in the, how thou walkest in the trueth.

4 I haue no greater ioye, then for to heare howe that my sonnes walke in veritye.

5 Beloued, thou doest faythfullye whatsoeuer thou doest to the brethren, and to straungers,

6 whiche beare wytnes of thy loue before all the congregacion. Whiche brethren when thou bringest forwards on their iourney (as it besemeth God) thou shalt do wel,

7 because that for his names sake they wente forth, and toke nothinge of the Gentiles.

8 We therfore ought to receyue suche, that we also myght be healpers to the trueth.

9 I wrote vnto the congregacion, but Diotrephes, which loueth to haue the preeminence amonge them, receiueth vs not.

10 Wherfore yf I come, I wyl declare his dedes, whiche he doth, resting on vs wyth malicious wordes, neyther is there wyth contente. Not onlye he hym selfe receyueth not the brethren, but also he forbyddeth them that woulde, and thrusteth them out of the congregacyon.

11 Beloued, folowe not that whiche is euyll, but that which is good. He that doth well, is of God, but he that doth euyl, seeth not God.

12 Demetrius hath good report of al men, and of the trueth, yea: & we our selues also beare recorde, and ye knowe that oure recorde is true.

13 I haue many thynges to wryte, but I wyll not wyth ynke and penne wryte vnto the.

14 For I trust I shal shortly se the, and we shall speake mouth to mouth. Peace be wyth the. The louers salute the. Grete the louers by name.

# Jude

Iudas the seruaunte of Iesus Christ, the brother of Iames. To them whyche are called & sanctyfied in God the father, and preserued in Iesu Christe.

2 Mercye vnto you, and peace, and loue be multiplyed.

3 Beloued, when I gaue all dylygence to wryte vnto you of the commen saluacyon: it was nedefull for me to wryte vnto you, to exhorte you, that ye should contynuallye labour in the faythe whiche was ones geuen vnto þe saynctes.

4 For there are certayne craftely crept in, of which it was wrytten afore tyme vnto suche iudgement. They are vngodlye & turne the grace of oure God vnto wantonnes, and denye God the onelye Lorde, and oure Lord Iesus Christe.

5 My mynd is therfore to put you in remembraunce, for as muche as ye ones knowe this, how that the Lord (after that he had deliuered the people out of Egypt) destroyed them which afterwarde beleued not.

6 The aungels also whiche kepte not theyr fyrste estate: but lefte theyr habytacyon, he hath reserued in euerlastyng chaynes vnder darkenes vnto the iudgement of the greate daye:

7 euen as Sodome and Gomor, and the cytyes about them (which in lyke maner defyled them selues with fornicacyon, and folowed straunge fleshe) are sette forth for an ensample, and suffer the vengeaunce of eternal fyre.

8 Likewyse these dremers defyle the flesh, despyse rulars and spake euil of them that are in authorytye.

9 Yet Michael the Archangel when he stroue agaynst the deuyl, and dysputed aboute þe bodye of Moyses, durste not geue raylyug sentence, but sayed: the Lorde rebuke the.

10 But these speake euyl of those thynges they know not, and what thynges they knowe naturally as beastes which are wythout reason, in those thynges they corrupte them selues.

11 Wo be vnto them, for they haue folowed the waye of Cayn, and are vtterlye geuen to the errour of Balam for lukers sake, and peryshe in the treason of Core.

12 These are spottes which of youre kyndnes feast together, wythoute feare, fedyng themselues. Cloudes they are wythout water, caryed aboute of wyndes, and trees wythout frute at gatherynge tyme, twyse dead & plucked vp by rotes.

13 They are the ragynge waues of the sea, fomyng out theyr owne shame. They are wandryng starres to whome is reserued the myste of darcknes for euer.

14 Enoch the seuenth from Adam, prophesyed fore of suche, saying: Beholde, the Lorde shall come wt thousandes of saynctes,

15 to geue iudgemente agaynst al men, & to rebuke al that are vngodly among them, of all theyr vngodly dedes, whiche they haue vngodlye commytted and of all theyr cruell speakynges; whiche vngodly synners haue spoken agaynste him.

16 These are murmurers, complayners, walkyng after theyr owne iustes, whose mouthes speake proud thinges. They haue men in great reuerence because of vauntage.

17 But ye beloued, remembre the wordes whiche were spoken before of the Apostles of oure Lord Iesu Christe,

18 howe that they tolde you that there shoulde be begylers in the laste tyme whiche shoulde walke after theyr owne vngodlye lustes.

19 These are makers of sectes fleshlye, hauynge no spyryte.

20 But ye dearely beloued, edifye your selues in your moste holy faythe, praying in the holye ghost,

21 and kepe your selues in the

loue of God, lokynge for the mercye of oure Lorde Iesus Christe, vnto eternall lyfe.

22 And haue compassyon of some, separatynge them:

23 and other saue wyth feare, pullynge them oute of the fyre, and hate the fylthy vesture of þe flesh.

24 Vnto hym that is able to kepe you, that ye fal not, and to preserue you fautles before the presence of hys glorye wyth ioye,

25 that is to saye, to God oure sauyoure whiche onelye is wise be glorye maiestye, dominion and power, now and for euer. Amen.

# Revelation

## CHAPTER 1

THE Reuelacyon of Iesus Christe which God gaue vnto hym, for to shew vnto his seruauntes thinges whiche muste shortely come to passe. And he sent and shewed by hys angel vnto hys seruaunt Iohn

2 whiche bare recorde of the word of God, and of the testimonye of Iesus Christe, and of all thynges that he sawe.

3 Happye is he that readeth, and they that heare the wordes of the prophecye, and kepe those thynges which are wrytten therein. For the tyme is at hande.

4 Iohn to the .vij. congregacyons in Asia. Grace be wyth you and peace, from hym which is, and whiche was, and whiche is to come, & from the .vij. spyrites which are present before hys throne,

5 and from Iesus Christ, whiche is a faythfull wytnes, and fyrst begotten of the dead, and Lorde ouer the kynges of the earth. Vnto him, that loued vs and washed vs from synnes in his owne bloude,

6 & made vs kinges and priestes vnto God his father: be glorye and dominyon for euer more. Amen.

7 Behold he commeth wyth cloudes, and al eyes shal se him: and they also whiche persed hym. And all kynredes of þe earth shal waile. Euen so. Amen:

8 I am Alpha and Omega, the begynnynge and the endynge, sayeth the Lorde almyghty, whiche is, which was, and whiche is to come.

9 I Iohn your brother and companyon in trybulacyon, and in the kyngdome and pacyence whiche is in Iesu Christe, was in the yle of Pathmos for the worde of God, and for þe wytnessynge of Iesu Christe

10 I was in the spirite on a sondaye, and hearde behynde me a great voyce, as it had bene of a trompe,

11 saiynge. I am Alpha and Omega, the fyrst and the laste. That thou seest wryte in a boke, and sende it vnto the congregacyons which are in Asia, vnto Ephesus, and vnto Smyrna, & vnto Pergamos, and vnto Sardis, & vnto Phyladelphia, and vnto Laodicia.

12 And I turned backe to se the voyce þt spake to me. And when I was turned, I sawe .vij. golden candelstickes,

13 and in the myddes of þe candelstickes, one lyke vnto the sonne of man clothed wyth a lynnen garment doune to the grounde, and gyrde aboute the pappes with a golden gyrdle.

14 Hys heade and hys heares were whyte, as whyte woul and as snowe: & hys eyes were as a flamme of fyre:

15 & hys fete lyke vnto brasse, as thoughe they brent in a fornace: & his voice as the sound of many waters.

16 And he had in hys ryghthande .vij. starres. And out of his mouth went a sharp two edged sweard. And hys face shone euen as þe sonne in hys strength.

17 And when I sawe hym, I fell at hys fete, euen as dead. And he layde hys ryght hande vpon me, saiynge vnto me: feare not, I am þe fyrste, and the laste,

18 and am alyue, and was dead. And beholde I am alyue for euer more and haue the kayes of hell, & of death.

19 Write therfore the thynges, whiche thou hast sene, & the thynges whiche are, & the thynges which shalbe fulfylled here after:

20 and the misery of the .vij. starres which thou sawest in my right hande, and the .vij. golden candelstickes. The .vij. starres are the messengers of the .vij. congregacions: And the .vij. candelstyckes which thou sawest are the .vij. congregacyons.

## CHAPTER 2

VNTO the messenger of the congregacion of Ephesus writte, these thinges, sayeth he þt holdeth the .vij. starres in his right hand, and walketh in the middes of the seuen golden candelstickes:

2 I knowe thy workes, and thy laboure, & thy pacience, and howe thou cannest not forbeare them, whyche are euyl, and examinedst them which saye they are Apostles and are not, & hast found them lyars

3 and dydest washe thy selfe. And hast pacience, and for my names sake hast labored and hast not faynted:

4 Neuertheles I haue somwhat agaynste the, for thou hast left thy fyrst loue.

5 Remember therfore from whence thou arte fallen, and repente, and do the fyrste workes. Or els I wil come vnto the shortlye, and wil remoue thy candelsticke out of his place, excepte thou repent.

6 But this thou hast because thou hatest the dedes of the Nicolaytans, which dedes I also hate.

7 Let him that hath eares heare, what the spirite sayeth vnto the congregacions. To him that ouercommeth, wyl I geue to eate of the tree of lyfe, whyche is in the middes of the Paradyse of God.

8 And vnto the angell of the congregacion of Smyrna wryte: These thynges sayeth he that is fyrst, and the last, which was dead & is alyue.

9 I knowe thy workes and tribulacion and pouertye, but thou art rych: And I know the blasphemy of them, whiche call them selues Iewes and are not, but are the congregacion of Sathan.

10 Feare none of those thynges, which thou shalt suffre. Behold, the deuil shal caste of you into pryson, to tempte you, and ye shal haue tribulacion .x. dayes. Be faythful vnto the death, & I wyl geue the a croune of life.

11 Let him that hath eares, heare what the spyryte sayth to the congregacyons. He that ouercommeth, shall not be hurte of the second death.

12 And to the messenger of the congregacion in Pergamos wryte: Thys sayth he, whych hath the sharpe sweard, wyth two edges.

13 I know thy workes, and where thou dwellest euen where Sathans seate is, and thou kepest my name, and hast not denyed my fayth. And in my dayes, Antypas was a faithful wytnes of myne whych was slaine among you, where Sathan dwelleth.

14 But I haue a fewe thinges against the, that thou hast there, them that maintaine the doctryne of Balam, whiche taught in Balake, to put occasyon of synne before the chyldren of Israel, that they shoulde eate of meate dedicate vnto ydoles & committe fornicacion.

15 Euen so hast thou them that mayntaine the doctryne of the Nicolaytans whiche thinge I hate.

16 But be conuerted, or els I wyll come vnto the shortlye, and wil fyght agaynst them wyth the swearde of my mouth.

17 Let him that hath eares, heare what the spyryte sayeth vnto the congregacyons. To hym that ouercommeth will I geue to eate Manna, that is hyd and wyll geue hym a whyte stone, and in the stone a new name wrytten, whiche no man knoweth sauynge he that receiueth it.

18 And vnto the messenger of the congregacion of Thiatyra wryte. This sayth the sonne of God, which hath hys eyes lyke vnto flame of fyre, whose feete are lyke brasse:

19 I knowe thy workes and thy loue, seruyce, and fayth, and thy pacience, and thy dedes, whyche are mo at the laste then at the fyrst.

20 Notwithstandinge I haue a fewe thinges against the, that thou sufferest that woman Iesabel, which called her selfe a prophetisse, to teache and to deceyue my seruauntes to make them commit fornicacion, and to eate meates offered vp to Idols.

21 And I gaue her space to repent of her fornicacion and she repented not.

22 Beholde I wyl caste her into a bed, and them that commit fornicacyon wyth her into greate aduersytie, except they turne from their dedes.

23 And I will kyl her chyldren wyth death. And all the congregacions shal know, that I am he, whiche searched the reynes and hertes. And I will geue vnto euery one of you according vnto youre workes.

24 Vnto you I say, and vnto eyther of them of Thiatyra, as manye as haue not knowen this learning, and whiche haue not knowen the depnes of Sathan (as they say) I wyl put vpon you none other burthen,

25 but that whiche ye haue allreadye. Hold faste, tyll I come,

26 and whosoeuer ouercommeth and kepeth my workes vnto the ende, to hym wyl I geue power ouer nacions,

27 and he shal rule them with a rodde of yron: and as the vessels of a potter, shall he breake them to sheuers. Euen as I receyued of my father,

28 so wyll I geue him, the morninge starre.

29 Let hym that hath eares, heare what the spyryte sayeth to the congregations.

# CHAPTER 3

AND write vnto the messenger of the congregation of Sardis, this sayth he that the spyryte of God & the .vij. starres. I know thy workes, thou hast a name, thou lyuest and thou arte deade.

2 Be awake & strengthe the

thinges whiche remayne, that are ready to dye. For I haue not founde thy workes perfecte before God.

3 Remember therfore howe thou hast receiued and hearde, and hold faste & repent. Yf thou shalt not watche, I wyl come on the as a thiefe, and thou shalt not knowe, what hour I wil come vpon the.

4 Thou hast a fewe names in Sardys, whyche haue not defyled their garmentes: and they shal walke wyth me in whyte, for they are worthy.

5 He that ouercommeth, shalbe clothed in whyte araye, and I wyll not put out hys name out of the boke of lyfe, and I wyll confesse his name before my father, and before his angels.

6 Let hym that hath eares, heare what the spyryte sayeth vnto the congregacions.

7 And wryte vnto the tydinges bringer of the congregacyon of Philadelphia, this sayeth he that is holy and true, which hath the keye of Dauid, which openeth and no man shutteth, and shutteth & no man openeth.

8 I know thy workes. Beholde I haue set before the an open doore, and no man can shut it, for thou hast a lytel strength, and hast kept my saiynges: and hast not denyed my name,

9 Behold I make them of the congregacion of Sathan, which cal them selues Iewes and are not, but do lye: Beholde: I wyl make them that they shal come and worshyppe before thy fete, and shal knowe that I loue the.

10 Because thou hast kepte the wordes of my pacience, therfore I wyll kepe from the houre of temptacyon, which wyll come vpon al the worlde, to tempte them that dwell vpon the earth.

11 Beholde: I come shortlye. Holde that, which thou hast, that no man take away thy croune.

12 Hym that ouercommeth, wyl I make a pyller in the temple of my God, and he shal go no more out. And I wyl wryte vpon him, the name of my God, and the name of the cytye of my God, newe Ierusalem, which commeth doune out of heauen from my God, & I wyl wryte vpon him my newe name.

13 Let him that hath eares, heare what the spirite sayeth vnto the congregacions.

14 And vnto the messenger of the congregacion, which is in Laodicia wryte: Thys sayth (Amen) the faythful and true wytnes, the beginninge of the creatures of God.

15 I knowe thy workes, that thou art neyther colde nor hote. I would thou were colde or hote.

16 So then because thou arte betwene both, and neyther colde nor hote. I wyll, spewe the out of my mouth:

17 because thou art ryche and increased wyth goodes, and hast nede of nothinge, and knowest not howe thou art wretched and miserable, poore, blind and naked.

18 I counsel the to bye of me golde tryed in the fyre, that thou mayest be ryche, and whyte raymente, that thou mayest be clothed, that thy fylthye nakednes do not appere, & annointe thine eyes wyth eye salue, that thou maiest se.

19 As manye as I loue, I rebuke and chastes. Be feruent therfore and repente.

20 Behold I stande at the dore and knocke. Yf anye man heare my voice and open the dore. I wil come in vnto him, and will suppe with him, and he wyth me.

21 To hym that ouercommeth, wyl I graunt to sit with me in my seate euen as I ouercame and haue sitten wyth my father, in his seate.

22 Let him that hath eares, heare what the spyrite sayth vnto the congregacions.

# CHAPTER 4

AFTER thys I loked, and beholde a dore was open in heauen, and the fyrst voyce which I hearde, was as it were of a trompete, talkynge wyth me which sayd: come vp hether, and I wyll shewe the thynges, whyche must be fulfylled herafter.

2 And immediatly I was in the spyryte: and behold a seate was put in heauen, and one sate on the seate.

3 And he that sate was to loke vpon, lyke vnto a Iaspar stone and a Sardin stone: And there was a rayne bowe aboute the seate, in syght lyke to an emeralde.

4 And about þe seate were .xxiiij. seates. And vpon the seates .xxiiij. elders syttynge clothed in whyte rayment, & had on their heades crounes of golde.

5 And out of the seate proceded lyghteninges, and thonderinges, and voyces, and there were seuen lampes of fyre, burninge before þe seate, whiche are the seuen spirites of God.

6 And before the seate there was a sea of glasse lyke vnto a Crystal, and in the middes of the seate, and roundabout the seat were .iiij. beastes full of eyes before and behinde,

7 and the fyrste beast was lyke a Lyon, the second beast lyke a calfe, and the thyrde beast had a face as a man, and the fourth beaste was lyke a fliyng egle.

8 And the .iiij. beastes had eche one of them .vi. wynges about him, and they were full of eies wythin. And they had no reste, daye neither nyghte sayinge. Holye, holye, holy, Lord God almyghtye, whyche was and is, and is to come.

9 And when those beastes gaue glorye and honour, and thankes to him that sate on the seate, whiche lyueth for euer and

euer,

10 þe .xxiiij. elders fel doune before him that sate on the throne, and worshypped him that lyueth for euer, and cast their crounes before the throne, saiynge:

11 thou art worthy Lorde to receiue glory and honour and power, for thou hast created al thinges, and for thy wylles sake they are and were created.

## CHAPTER 5

AND I saw in the ryghte hand of him that sate in þe throne, a boke wrytten, wythin and on the backsyde, sealed with .vij. seales.

2 And I sawe a stronge angel, which cryed wyth a loude voyce: Who is worthy to open the boke, and to lose the seales therof?

3 And no man in heauen nor in earth, neyther vnder the earth, was able to open the boke, neyther to loke theron.

4 And I wepte muche, because no man was founde worthy to open and to reade the boke, neyther to loke theron.

5 And one of the elders sayd vnto me: wepe not: beholde a Lyon beinge of the tribe of Iuda, the rote of Dauid, hath obtayned to open the boke, and to lowse the .vij. seales therof.

6 And I beholde, and lo, in the middes of the seate, and of the .iiij. beastes, and in the myddes of the elders, stode a lambe as though he had bene kylled, whyche had .vij. hornes and .vij. eyes, which are the spirites of God, sente into all the worlde.

7 And he came and toke the boke out of the ryght hand of him that sate vpon the seate.

8 And when he had taken the boke, the .iiij. beastes, and .xxiiij. elders fel doune before the lambe, hauinge harpes and golden vialles full of odoures, whyche are the prayers of saynctes,

9 and they songe a new songe saiyng: thou art worthy to take the boke, and to open the seales therof: for thou wast kylled, & hast redemed vs by thy bloud out of al kynredes, and tonges, and people, and nacions

10 and hast made vs to our God, kynges, and priestes, & we shal reigne on the earth.

11 And I behelde, and I heard the voyce of many angels about the throne, and about the beastes, and the elders, and I heard thousande thousandes,

12 sayinge wyth a loud voyce: Worthy is the lamb that was kylled to receiue power, and riches, and wysdome, and strength, and honoure, & glorye and blessing.

13 And al creatures whiche are in heauen, and on the earth, and vnder the earth, and in the sea, and al that are in them hearde I saiynge: blessing, honour, glory, and power be vnto him that sytteth vpon þe seate, and to the Lambe for euermore.

14 And þe foure beastes sayd Amen. And the .xxiiij. elders fel vpon theyr faces, and worshypped hym that liueth for euermore.

## CHAPTER 6

AND I saw when the Lambe opened one of the seales, and I hearde one of the .iiij. beastes saye, as it were the noyse of thonder, come and se.

2 And I sawe, and beholde there was a whyte horsse, and he that sate on him had a bow, & a croune was geuen vnto him, and he went forth conquerynge and for to ouercome.

3 And when he opened the seconde seale, I hearde the seconde beaste saye, come and se.

4 And there wente out another horsse that was red, and power was geuen to him that sate theron, to take peace from the earth, and that they should kyl one another. And there was geuen vnto hym a greate swerde.

5 And when he opened the thyrde seale, I hearde the thyrde beast say: come and se. And I behelde, and lo a blacke horsse: and he that sate on him, had a payre of balances in hys hand.

6 And I heard a voyce in the myddes of the .iiij. beastes say: a measure of wheat for a penye, and .iij. measures of barly for a peny, and oyle and wyne se thou hurte not.

7 And when he opened the fourth seale, I heard the voyce of þe fourth beaste saye: come and se.

8 And I loked, and behold a pale horsse, and hys name that sate on him was death, and hell folowed after him, and power was geuen vnto him ouer the fourth parte of the earth, to kyll with swerd and wyth honger, and wyth death, that cometh of vermen of the earth.

9 And when he opened the fyft seale, I saw vnder the aulter, the soules of them that were kylled for the word of God, & for the testymonye, whych they had,

10 and they cryed wyth a loude voyce sayinge: Howe longe tariest thou Lord holy and true, to iudge and to auenge oure bloud on them that dwell on the earth?

11 And longe whyte garmentes were geuen vnto euery of them. And it was sayde vnto them that they should reste for a litle season vntyll the number of their felowes and brethren, & of them that should be kylled as they were, were fulfylled.

12 And I behelde when he opened the syxte seale, and lo there was a greate earth quake, and the sunne was as blacke as

sacke cloth, made of heare. And the mone wexed euen as bloude,

13 and the starres of heauen fell vnto þe earth, euen as a fygge tree casteth from her her fygges, when she is shaken of a myghty wynde.

14 And heauen vanished awaye, as a scrole, when it is rolled together. And al mountaines and Iles, were moued out of their places.

15 And the kynges of the earth, & the greate men and the ryche men, and the chiefe captaines, and the myghty men, and euerye bonde man, and euery free man, hyd them selues in dennes, and in rockes:

16 fal on vs, and hyde vs from the presence of hym that sitteth on the seate, and from the wrath of the lambe,

17 for the great day of his wrath is come: And who can endure it?

## CHAPTER 7

And after that I sawe .iiij. angeles stand on the .iiij. corners of the earth, holding the .iiij. wyndes of the earth, that the windes should not blow on the earth, neyther on the sea, neyther on any tree.

2 And I sawe another angell ascende from the rysinge of the sunne, whiche had the seale of the lyuing God, and he cried wyth a loud voyce to the .iiij. angelles (to whom power was geuen to hurte the earth and the sea)

3 sayinge: Hurte not the earth, neyther the sea, neither the trees, tyl we haue sealed the seruauntes of oure God in their forheades.

4 And I heard the numbre of them whyche were sealed, and there were sealed an .C. and .xliiij.M. of all tribes of the chyldren of Israell.

5 Of the trybe of Iuda were sealed .xij.M. Of the trybe of Ruben were sealed .xij.M. of the trybe of Gad were sealed .xij.M.

6 Of the trybe of Asser were sealed .xij. thousand. Of the trybe of Neptalim were sealed twelue thousande. Of the Trybe of Manasses were sealed twelue thousand.

7 Of the tribe of Simeon were sealed twelue thousand. Of the tribe of Leuy were sealed .xij. thousande. Of the tribe of Isacar were sealed .xij.M.

8 Of the tribe of Zabulon were sealed twelue thousand. Of þe tribe of Ioseph were sealed twelue thousand. Of the tribe of Beniamin were sealed twelue thousande.

9 After this I behelde, and lo a greate multitude (which no man coulde numbre) of al nacions and people, and tonges, stode before the seate, and before the lambe, clothed wyth longe whyte garmentes, and palmes in their handes,

10 and cried with a loude voyce, saying: saluacion be ascribed to him that sitteth vpon the seate of our God, and vnto the lamb.

11 And all the Angelles stode in the compasse of the seate, and of the elders, and of the .iiij. beastes, and fell before the seate on theyr faces, & worshipped God

12 saying, Amen: Blessing and glory, wisdome, and thankes, and honoure, and power & mighte, be vnto our God for euermore: Amen.

13 And one of the elders aunswered, saying vnto me: what are these, which are arayed in longe whyte garmentes, and whence came they?

14 And I sayd vnto hym: Lorde thou wotest. And he said vnto me: these are they which came out of great tribulacion, and made their garmentes large and made them white, in the bloude of the lambe,

15 therfore are they in the presence of the seate of God and serue hym daye and nyghte in his temple, and he that sitteth in the seate wyl dwell amonge them.

16 They shal honger no more neyther thyrste, neyther shal the sunne lyghte on them, neyther anye heate:

17 For the lambe, which is in the middes of the seate shall feede them, and shall leade them vnto fountaynes of lyuinge water, and God shall wype awaye al teares from theyr eyes.

## CHAPTER 8

And when he had opened the seuenth seale, there was silence in heauen about the space of halfe an houre.

2 And I saw angelles standing before God, and to them were geuen .vij. trompettes.

3 And another angel came and stode before the aultare hauynge a golden senser, and muche of odoures was geuen vnto hym, that he shoulde offer of the prayers of al sainctes vpon the golden aultare, which was before the seate.

4 And the smoke of the odoures, whiche came of the prayers of al sainctes ascended vp before God out of the angelles hand.

5 And the angell toke the senser, and fylled it wyth fyre of the aultare, and caste it into the earth, and voyces were made, and thonderinges and lighteninges, and earth quakes.

6 And the .vij. angelles, whiche had the .vij. trompettes prepared them selues to blowe.

7 The fyrste angel blewe, and these was made hayle and fyre, whiche were myngled wyth bloude, and they were cast into the earth, and the thyrde parte of the trees was burnte, and al grene grasse was brente.

8 And the seconde angel

blewe: and as it were a greate mountaine burning wyth fyre was caste into the sea, and the thyrde parte of the sea turned to bloud,

9 and the thirde parte of the creatures, whiche had lyfe, dyed, and the thyrd parte of shyppes were destroyed.

10 And the thyrd angel blewe, and there fell a great starre from heauen burninge, as it were a lampe, and it fell into the thyrde parte of the riuers, and into fountaines of waters,

11 & the name of the starre is called wormwod. And the thyrde parte was turned to wormwode. And manye men dyed of the waters, because they were made bitter.

12 And þe fourth angel blew, and the thyrde parte of the sunne was smytten and the thyrd part of the mone, and the thirde parte of the starres, so that the thirde part of them was darckened. And the daye was smitten, that the thirde parte of it shoulde not shyne, and lykewise the nyghte.

13 And I behelde and hearde an angell fliynge thorowe the middes of heauen, sayinge wyth a loude voyce: Wo, wo, to the inhabiters of the earth, because of the voyces to come of the trompe of the .iij. angels, whyche were yet to blowe.

## CHAPTER 9

And the fyfte Angel blewe, and I sawe a starre fall from heauen vnto the earth, And to hym was geuen the keye of the bottomlesse pyt.

2 And he opened the bottomlesse pyt, and there arose the smoke of a great fornace. And the sunne, and the ayer were darkened by the reason of the smoke of the pytt.

3 And there came out of the smoke locustes vpon the earth, and vnto them was geuen power as the Scorpions of the earth haue power.

4 And it was commaunded them, that they should not hurt the grasse of the earth, neyther any grene thinge, neither any tree, but onely those men which haue not the seale in their foreheades,

5 and to them was commaunded that they should not kyll them, but that they should be vexed fyue monethes, and theyr payne was as the payne that commeth of a scorpion, when he hath stonge a man.

6 And in those dayes shal men seke death, and shal not finde it, and shall desyre to dye, and death shal flye from them.

7 And the similitude of the locustes was lyke vnto horsses prepared vnto battayl, and on theyr heades were as it were crounes, lyke vnto gold and their faces were as it had bene the faces of men.

8 And they had heere as the heere of women. And theyr teeth were as the teeth of Lyons.

9 And they had habbergions, as it were habbergyons of Iron. And the sounde of theyr wynges, was as the sounde of charettes, when many horsses runne together to battayle.

10 And they had tayles lyke vnto Scorpyons, and there were stynges in theyr tayles. And their power was to hurte men fyue monethes.

11 And they had a kynge ouer them, whych is the angel of the bottomlesse pyt, whose name in the Hebrue tonge, is Abodon, but in the Greke tonge, Appollion.

12 One wo is paste, and behold two woes come after thys.

13 And the syxte angel blewe, and I hearde a voyce from the .iiij. corners of the golden aultare, which is before God,

14 sayinge to the syxte angel, which had the trompe, louse the .iiij. angelles, whyche are bounde in the great riuer Euphrates.

15 And the .iiij. angels were loused, whyche were prepared for an houre, for a daye, for a moneth, and for an yere, for to slea the thyrd parte of men.

16 And the number of horsmen of warre, were twenty tymes ten thousand. And I heard the numbre of them.

17 And thus I sawe the horsses in a vision, and them that sate on them hauynge fyry habbergions of a Iacinct colour, and brimstone, and the heades of the horsses were as the heades of Lyons. And out of their mouthes wente forth fyre and smoke, and brymstone.

18 And of these .iij. was the thirde parte of men kylled, that is to say, of fyre, smoke, and brymstone, whych proceded out of the mouthes of them.

19 For theyr power was in their mouthes and in theyr tayles, for theyr tayles were lyke vnto serpentes, and had heades, and wyth them they dyd hurt.

20 And the remnaunt of the men which were not kylled by these plages, repented not of the dedes of their handes, that they should not worship deuyls, and Images of gold, and syluer, and brasse, and stone, and of wood, whych neyther can se, neyther heare, neyther go.

21 Also they repented not of theyr murther, and of theyr sorcery, neyther of their fornicacion, neither of their thefte.

## CHAPTER 10

And I sawe an other myghtye angel come doune from heauen, clothed wyth a cloude, and the rayne bowe vpon hys heade. And hys face as it were the sunne, and hys fete as it were pyllars of fyre

2 and he had in hys hand a lyttel boke open, & he put hys ryghte fote vpon the sea, and hys lyfte fote on þe earth

3 And cryed wyth a loude voyce, as when a Lyon roreth.

And when he had cried, seuen thonders spake their voyces.

4 And when the .vij. thonders had spoken their voyces, I was aboute to wryte. And I harde a voice from heauen saying vnto me, seale vp those thynges, which the .vij. thonders spake, and wryte them not.

5 And the angell whyche I sawe stand vpon the sea, and vpon the earth, lyfte vp hys hand to heauen,

6 and swore by hym that lyueth for euer more, whiche created heauen, and the thynges that therin are, and the sea, and the thynges whyche therin are: that there shoulde be no longer tyme,

7 but in the dayes of the voyce of the seuenth aungel, when he shal begyn to blow, euen the mistery of God shalbe fynished as he preached by his seruauntes the prophetes.

8 And the voyce, whych I hard from heauen, spake vnto me agayne, and sayde, go and take the lytle boke, which is open in the hande of the angell, whyche standeth vpon the sea, and vpon the earth.

9 And I went vnto the angell, and sayd to hym, geue me the lytel boke, and he sayde vnto me take it, and eate it vp, and it shall make thy belly bytter, but it shal be in thy mouth as swete as hony,

10 and I toke the lytle boke out of hys hand, and eate it vp, and it was in my mouth as swete as honye, and assone as I had eaten it, my bealy was bitter.

11 And he sayd vnto me: thou muste prophesye againe amonge the people, and nacyons, and tonges, and to many kynges.

# CHAPTER 11

AND then was geuen me a rede lyke vnto a rodde, and it was sayde vnto me: Ryse and meate the temple of God, and the aultare, and them that worshyppe therin,

2 and the quyre whiche is wythin the temple caste out and meate it not: for it is geuen vnto the Gentyles and the holy cytye shal they treade vnder fote .xlij. monethes.

3 And I will geue power vnto my .ij. witnesses, & they shal prophesy .M.ij.C. & .lx. daies, cloteth in sacke cloth.

4 These are two olyue trees, and two candelstickes, standyng before the God of the earth.

5 And yf any man wyl hurte them, fire shal proceade out of theyr mouthes, and consume theyr enemyes. And yf anye man wyll hurte them this wyse muste he be killed.

6 These haue power to shut heauen, that it rayne not in the daies of they: Prophesiyng, and haue power ouer waters to turne them to bloud, and to smyte the earth wyth al maner plages, as often as they will.

7 And when they haue fynished theyr testymonye, the beast that came out of the bottomlesse pyt, shal make warre agaynst them, and shal ouercome them, and kyl them.

8 And theyr bodies shal lye in the stretes of the great city, whiche spyrytually is called Sodome and Egypte, where oure Lorde was crucyfyed.

9 And they of the people and kynredes, and tonges, and they of the nacyons, shal se theyr bodyes thre dayes and an halfe, and shall not suffer theyr bodies to be put in graues.

10 And they that dwell vpon the earth, shall reioyse ouer them and be glad, and shal sende gyftes one to another for these two prophetes vexed them that dwelt on the earth.

11 And after .iij. dayes and an halfe the spyryte of lyfe from God, entred into them. And they stode vp vpon theyr fete, and great feare came vpon them, whiche sawe them.

12 And they harde a greate voyce from heauen, saying vnto them. Come vp hether. And they ascende vp into heauen in a cloud and their enemies sawe them.

13 And the same houre was there a greate earth quake, and the tenth parte of the cytye fell, and in the earth quake were slayne names of men seuen thousande, and the remnaunte were feared, and gaue glorye to GOD of heauen.

14 The seconde wo is past, and beholde the thyrde wo wyll come anone.

15 And the seuenth angell blewe, and there were made greate voyces in heauen, sayinge: the kyngdomes of thys worlde are oure Lordes and hys Christes, & he shall raygne for euer more.

16 And the .xxiiij. elders, whyche sit before God on their seates, fell vpon theyr faces, and worshipped God,

17 sayinge: we geue the thankes Lord GOD almyghty, whyche arte and wast, and arte to come, for thou hast receyued thy greate myght and hast reigned.

18 And the nacyons were angrye, and thy wrath is come, and the tyme of the dead that they shoulde be iudged and that thou shouldeste geue rewarde vnto thy seruauntes the Prophetes and saynctes, and to them that feare thy name small and greate, and shouldeste destroye them, whyche destroye the earth.

19 And the temple of God was opened in heauen, and there was sene in hys temple the arcke of hys testamente, and there folowed lyghtenynges, and voyces, and thonderynge and eartquake and muche hayle.

# CHAPTER 12

AND there appered a greate wonder in heauen: A

woman clothed with the sunne, and the mone vnder her fete, and vpon her heade a croune of .xij. starres.

2 And she was wyth chylde and cryed trauailling in byrth, and payned redy to be deliuered.

3 And there appered another wonder in heauen, for behold a great Dragon, hauinge .vij. heades, and ten hornes & crounes vpon his heades,

4 and hys tayle drewe the thyrde parte of the starres, and cast them to the earth. And the dragon stode before the woman, whyche was redye to be delyuered, for to deuoure her chyld assone as it were borne.

5 And she brought furth a man chyld, which should rule al nacyons wyth a rod of Iron. And her sonne was taken vp vnto God, and to hys seate.

6 And the woman fled into wyldernes, where she had a place prepared of God, that they should feede her there a thousand .ij. hundred and .lx. dayes.

7 And there was great battayle in heauen, Michael and his angels fought with the dragon, and the dragon fought and his angells,

8 and preuayled not, neyther was theyr place found any more in heauen.

9 And the great dragon, that olde serpente called the deuyll and Sathanas was caste out. Whiche deceyueth al the worlde. And he was cast into the earth, and his angelles were cast out also.

10 And I hearde a loude voyce sayinge: in heauen is nowe made saluacyon, and strength and the kyngdome of our God, and þe power of hys Christe. For he is caste doune, whyche accused them before God daye and nyghte.

11 And they ouercame hym by the bloude of the lambe, and by the worde of theyr testimony, and they loued not theyr liues vnto the death.

12 Therfore reioyse heauens, and ye that dwell in them, Wo to the inhabiters of the earth, & of the sea, for the deuyll is come doune vnto you, which hath great wrath, because he knoweth that he hath but a shorte tyme.

13 And when the dragon sawe, that he was caste vnto the earth, he persecuted the woman, which broughte forth the man chyld.

14 And to þe woman were geuen two winges of a greate egle, þt she might flye into the wildernes, into her place, where she is noryshed for a tyme, tymes, & halfe a time from the presence of the serpente.

15 And the dragon cast out of his mouth water after the woman as it had bene a riuer, because she should haue be caught of þe floud.

16 And the earth holpe the woman, & the earth opened her mouth, and swalowed vp þe ryuer which the dragon cast out of his mouth.

17 And the dragon was wroth wyth the woman, and went and made warre wyth the remnaunt of her seede, whiche kepe the commaundementes of God, and haue the testimonye of Iesus Christe. And I stode on the sea sande.

# CHAPTER 13

AND I sawe a beaste ryse out of the sea, hauyng .vij. heades, and .x. hornes, and vpon his hornes ten crounes, and vpon his heade the name of blasphemye.

2 And the beaste whych I sawe, was lyke a cat of the mountayne, and hys fete were as the fete of a beare, and his mouth as the mouth of a Lyon. And the dragon gaue him hys power and hys seale, and great authorytye,

3 & I sawe one of his heades as it were wounded to death and his deadlye wounde was healed. And al the worlde wondred at the beaste,

4 & they worshipped the dragon, which gaue power vnto the beaste, and they worshipped the beast saiynge: who is lyke vnto the beast? who is able to warre with him?

5 And there was mouth geuen vnto hym, that spake greate thinges and blasphemies, and power was geuen vnto hym, to do .xlij. monethes.

6 And he opened hys mouth vnto blasphemy agaynste God, to blaspheme hys name, and his tabernacle and them that dwell in heauen.

7 And it was geuen vnto hym to make warre wyth the Saynctes, and to ouercome them. And power was geuen hym ouer al kynredes, tonges and nacions,

8 and al that dwel vpon þe earth worshipte him, whose names are not written in the boke of lyfe of þe lambe, which was killed from the beginning of the worlde.

9 Yf any man haue an eare, let hym heare.

10 He that leadeth into captiuitie shal go into captiuitie, he that kylleth wt a sweard, must be kylled wyth a sweard. Here is the pacience and the fayth of the sainctes.

11 And I behelde another beast commyng vp out of the earth, and he had two hornes lyke a lambe, and he spake as dyd the dragon.

12 And he, dyd al that the fyrste beast could do in his presence, and he caused the earth, and them which dwel therin, to worship the fyrst beast, whose deadly wounde was healed.

13 And he dyd greate wonders, so that he made fyre come doune from heauen in the syght of men.

14 And deceiued them that

dwelt on the earth by the meanes of those sygnes, which he had power to do in the syght of the beaste, saying to them that dwelt on þe earth, that they should make an ymage vnto the beaste, whyche had the wounde of a swearde, and dyd lyue.

15 And he had power to geue a spyryte vnto the ymage of the beaste, and that þe ymage of the beast should speake, and shoulde cause that as manye as would not worshyppe the ymage of the beaste, shoulde be kylled.

16 And he made al both smale and greate, ryche and poore, free and bonde, to receyue a marke in theyr ryght handes, or in theyr forheades.

17 And that no man myghte by or sell, saue he that had the marke, or the name of the beaste, other the numbre of his name.

18 Here is wysdom. Let him that hath wyt counte the numbre of the beaste. For it is the numbre of a man, and hys numbre is syxe hundred thre score and syxe.

## CHAPTER 14

And I loked, and lo a lamb stode on the mounte Syon, and wyth him an hundred & .xliiij. thousand hauyng hys fathers name wrytten in theyr forheades.

2 And I hearde a voice from heauen, as the sounde of manye waters, and as the voice of a greate thunder. And I hearde the voyce of harpers harping with their harpes.

3 And they songe as it were a newe songe, before the seate, & before þe foure beastes, & the elders, & no man coulde learne þe songe, but the hundred and .xliiij.M. which were redemed from the earth.

4 These are they, whiche were not defyled wt women for they are virgins. These folowe þe lamb whether so euer goeth. These were redemed from men being þe fyrst frutes vnto God & to the lamb,

5 & in their mouthes was founde no gyle. For they are without spot before þe trone of God.

6 And I sawe an angel flye in the middes of heauen hauinge an euerlastinge Gospell to preache vnto them that sytte and dwell on the earth, & to al nacions, kinredes, & tonges, and people,

7 sayinge with a loude voice: Feare God, & geue honoure to him, for the houre of his iudgemente is come, and worshyp hym, that made heauen and earth & the sea, & fountaynes of water.

8 And there folowed another angel, sayinge: Babylon is fallen, is fallen, that great city, for she made al nacions drinke of the wine of her fornicacion.

9 And the thyrd angel folowed them saying wt a loude voice: Yf any man worship the beast & his ymage, and receiue his marke in his forhead, or in his hand,

10 the same shall drynke of the wine of the wrath of God, which is poured in the cup of this wrath. And he shalbe punished in fyre & brimstone before the holy angels, and before the lambe.

11 And the smoke of their tormente ascendeth vp euermore. And they haue no rest daye nor night, which worship the beaste & his ymage, and whosoeuer receiueth the prynt of hys name.

12 Here is the pacience of saynctes. Here are they that kepe the commaundementes & the fayth of Iesu.

13 And I heard a voice from heauen, sayinge vnto me: wryte. Blessed are the dead, whyche here after dye in the Lorde euen so sayth the spyryte, that they may reste from their laboures, but their workes shal folowe them.

14 And I loked and beholde a whyte cloude, & vpon the cloude one setting like vnto the sonne of man, hauinge on his head a golden croune, & in his hand a sharpe sykle.

15 And another angel came out of the temple, criynge wyth a loude voyce to him þt sate on þe cloud. Thruste in thy sykle and reape for the time is come, to reape, for the corne of the earth is rype.

16 And he that sate on the cloude, thruste in hys sykle on the earth, and the earth was reaped.

17 And another angel came out of the temple which is in heauen hauing also a sharpe sikle.

18 And another angel came out from the aulter, whiche had power of fyre, and cryed wyth a loude crye to him that had the sharpe sykle, & sayed: thruste in thy sharpe sykle, and gather the clusters of þe earth for her grapes are rip.

19 And the angel thruste in his sykle on þe earth, and cut doune the grapes of the vineyarde of the earth, and caste them into the great wynfat of the wrath of God,

20 and the wynfat was troden wythout the cyty, and bloud came out of the fat, euen vnto the horsse brydelles by the space of a thousand and .vi. hundred furlonges.

## CHAPTER 15

And I saw another signe in heauen greate and maruellous .vij. angels, hauynge the seuen laste plages, for in them is fullfylled the wrath of GOD.

2 And I sawe as it were a glassy sea, mingled wt fyre, & them that had gotten victory of the beast and of his ymage, and

of his marke, & of the numbre of his name, stande on the glassye sea, hauinge the harpes of God,

3 and they songe the songe of Moises the seruaunt of God, & they songe of the lamb, sayinge: Great & maruelous are thy workes Lorde God almighty, iuste & true are thy wayes kynge of sainctes.

4 Who shal not feare. O Lorde, & glorify thy name? For thou only arte holy and al Gentyls shal come and worshippe before the for thy iudgementes are made manifeste.

5 And after that, I loked & behold the temple of the tabernacle of testimony was open in heauen,

6 & the .vij. angels came out of the temple, which had the .vij. plages, clothed in pure and bryght linnen, & hauing their breastes gyrded wt golden gyrdels.

7 And one of the .iiij. beastes gaue to the .vij. angels .vij. golden vialles, ful of the wrath of God, whiche liueth for euermore.

8 And the temple was ful of the smoke of the glory of God and of his power, & no man was able to enter into the temple, tyll the seuen plages of the seuen angels were fulfylled.

## CHAPTER 16

AND I hearde a great voice out of the temple saying to the .vij. angels: go youre wayes, poure out your vialles of wrath vpon the earth.

2 And the fyrste wente and poured out his vial vpon the earth, and there fel a noisome and a sore botche vpon the men, which had the marke of the beaste, & vpon them whiche worshipped his ymage.

3 And the seconde angel shed oute his vial vpon the sea, & it turned as it were into the bloud of a dead man, & euery liuing thing dyed in þe sea.

4 And the thyrde angel shed out his vial vpon the riuers & fountaines of waters & they turned to bloud.

5 And I heard an angel say: Lord which art & wast, thou art rightuous & holy, because thou hast geuen such iudgementes,

6 for they shed out the bloud of sainctes, & prophetes, & therfore hast thou geuen them bloud to drinke, for they are worthy.

7 And I heard another out of the aulter saye, euen so Lord God almyghty, true, and ryghtuous are thy iudgementes.

8 And the fourth angel poured out his vial on the sunne, & power was geuen vnto hym to vexe men with heate of fire.

9 And the men raged in great heate, & spake euyl of þe name of God which hath power ouer those plages, & they repented not, to geue him glory.

10 And the fyfte angel poured out his vial vpon the seate of the beast, & his kingdome waxed darcke, & they gnew their tounges for sorowe,

11 & blasphemed the God of heauen for sorowe and payne of their sores, and repented not of theyr dedes.

12 And the .vi. aungel poured out hys vyall vpon the great riuer Euphrates, & the water dried vp that the wayes of the kynges of the este should be prepared.

13 And I sawe thre vncleane sprytes, lyke frogges come out of the mouth of the dragon and out of the mouth of the beast, & out of the mouth of the false prophete.

14 For they are the spirites of deuils working miracles to go out vnto the kinges of þe earth, & to the whole worlde to gather them to þe batayle of þe greate daye of God almighty.

15 Beholde I come as a thefe. Happye is he that watcheth & kepeth his garmentes, least he be founde naked, and men se hys filthynes.

16 And he gathered them together into a place, called in the Hebrue tonge Armagedon.

17 And the .vij. angel poured out his vial into the aire. And there came a voice out of heauen from the seate, sayinge: it is done.

18 And there folowed voices thonderinges & lighteninges, & there was a greate earth quake suche as was not sence men were vpon the earth so mighty an earthquake & so great.

19 And the greate city was deuided into three parties, & the cyties of al nacions fel. And great Babilon came in remembraunce before God, to geue vnto her the cup of þe wine of the fyercenes of his wrath.

20 Euery Ile fleed away, & the mountaines were not founde.

21 And there fell a greate hayle, as it had bene talentes, out of heauen vpon the men, & the men blasphemed God, because of þe plage of þe haile, for it was great, & þe plage of it sore?

## CHAPTER 17

AND there came one of the seuen angelles, which had þe seuen vialls, and talked with me, saiynge vnto me, come I wil shew the, the iudgement of the great whore that sytteth vpon manye waters,

2 wt whom haue committed fornicacion the kinges of the earth so that the inhabiters of þe earth, are drounken wyth the wyne of her fornicacion.

3 And he caryed me awaye into the wildernes in the spirite. And I saw a woman sit vpon a rose colored beaste ful of names of blasphemye, which had .x. hornes.

4 And the woman was arayed in purple & rose coloure, and decked wyth golde, precious

stones and pearles, and had a cuppe of golde in her hand full of al abominacions and fylthines of her fornicacion.

5 And in her forhead was a name wrytten, a mystery, great Babylon the mother of whoredome and abominacions of the earth.

6 And I saw the wyfe drounken with the bloude of Sainctes, and with the bloud of the wytnesses of Iesu. And when I saw her, I wondred wyth great maruayle.

7 And the angel said vnto me, wherfore maruailest thou? I wil shewe the þe mistery of the woman, & of the beast þt beareth her, whyche had seuen heades & .x. hornes.

8 The beaste that thou seest, was, & is not, & shal ascende out of the bottomlesse pyt, & shal go into perdition, and they that dwel on the earth, shal wondre (whose names are not wrytten in the boke of lyfe from the beginninge of the worlde) when they beholde the beaste that was, and is not.

9 And here is a minde that hath wysdome. The seuen heades are seuen mountaines, on which the woman sytteth,

10 they are also .vij. kynges. Fyue are fallen, and one is, and another is not yet come. When he commeth he muste continue a space.

11 And the beast that was, and is not, is euen the eyghte, and is one of the seuen, and shall go into destruccion.

12 And the .x. hornes, which thou seest, are .x. kinges, which haue receiued no kingdom, but shal receiue power as kynges at one hour with þe beast.

13 These haue one minde, & shal geue their power & strength vnto þe beast.

14 These shal fyght wt the lamb, & the lamb shal ouercome them. For he is Lorde of Lordes, & kinge of kinges, & they that are on his syde, are called the chosen and faithful.

15 And he sayde vnto me, the waters whyche thou saweste, where the whore sitteth are people, and folke, and nacions & tounges.

16 And þe ten hornes, which thou sawest vpon the beast, are they that shal hate the whore, & shal make her desolate and naked, and shal eate her flesh and burne her wyth fyre.

17 For God hath put in their hertes to fulfil his wil, & to do wt one consent, for to geue her kingdom to the beast, vntil the wordes of God be fulfilled.

18 And the woman, which thou sawest is that great city, which reigneth ouer the kinges of the earth.

## CHAPTER 18

AND after that I saw another angel come from heauen, hauinge greate power, & the earth was lightened wt his brighnes.

2 And he cryed mightely with a strong voyce, saing: Great Babylon is fallen, is fallen: and is become the habitacion of deuilles, and the holde of al foule spyrytes, and a cage of al vncleane and hateful byrdes,

3 for al nacyons haue dronken of the wyne of the wrath of her fornicacion. And the kinges of the earth haue committed fornicacion wyth her, & her marchauntes are wexed riche of the aboundance of her pleasures.

4 And I hearde another voice from heauen say: Come awaye from her my people, þt ye be not partakers in her sinnes, & that ye receiue not of her plages.

5 For his sonnes are gone vp to heauen, & God hath remembred her wickednes.

6 Reward her euen as she rewarded you, & geue her double accordinge to her workes. And youre in double to her in þe same cuppe, which she fylled vnto you.

7 And as muche as she glorified her selfe and lyued wantonly, so muche poure ye in for her of punishment, & sorowe, for she said in her herte: I sytte being a quene and am no wydowe, and shall se no sorowe.

8 Therfore shal her plages come at one daye, death, and sorowe, and honger, and she shalbe brente wyth fyre, for stronge is the Lorde God, whiche iudgeth her.

9 And þe kynges of the earth shal bewepe her & wayle ouer her, which haue committed fornicacion with her, & haue lyued wantonly with her, when they shal se þe smoke of her burning,

10 & shal stand a farre of, for feare of her punishmente, saying: Alas, Alas, that great citie Babilon, that myghty cytie. For at one houre is her iudgemente come.

11 And the marchauntes of the earth, shal wepe and wayle in them selues, for no man wil bye their ware anye more,

12 the ware of gold, & syluer, & precious stones, neither of pearle, sylke, and raynes, & purple, & skarled, and al thin wode, & all maner vessels of iuory, & al maner vessels of most precious wode, and of brasse, and of Iron,

13 & sinamome, and odoures, and oyntmentes, & frankinsence, and wine, and oyle, and fine floure, and wheat, beastes, and shepe, and horsses, & charrettes, and bodyes, and soules of men.

14 And the apples that thy soule lusted after are departed from the. And al thinges which were deyntye, & had in price are departed from the, & thou shalt finde them no more.

15 The marchauntes of these

thinges, which were wexed riche shal stand a farre of from her, for feare of the punishment of her, weping & waylynge,

16 & saying: alas, alas that great city, that was clothed in raines, & purple, and scarlet, & decked wt gold, & precious stones, & pearles,

17 for at one hour so great riches is come to nought. And euery shyp gouerner, & al they that occupied shippes, & shipmen which worke in the sea, stode a farre of

18 & cried, when they saw the smoke of her burninge, sayinge: what citie is lyke vnto this great citie?

19 And they cast duste on their heades, & cried weping, & wailing, & said: Alas, alas the greate citye wherin were made riche al that had shippes in the sea, by the reason of her costlines, for at one houre is she made desolate.

20 Reioice ouer her thou heauen, and ye holy Apostles, & prophetes: for God hath geuen your iudgemente on her.

21 And a mighty angel toke vp a stone lyke a greate mylstone, & cast it into the sea, saying: wyth such violence shal that greate citie Babilon be caste, and shalbe found no more.

22 And the voice of harpers, & musicions, and of pipers, & trompeters, shalbe hearde no more in the, and no craftes man, of whatsoeuer crafte he be, shalbe founde any more in the, & the sound of a myl, shalbe hard no more in the,

23 and the voice of the brydegrome and of the bryde, shalbe hard no more in the, for thy marchauntes were the greate men of the earth. And wt thyne inchauntment were deceiued al nacions,

24 & in her was found the bloud of the prophetes, and of the sainctes and of al that were slayne vpon the earth.

## CHAPTER 19

AND after þt, I heard the voice of much people in heauen saying Alleluia. Saluacion and glory and honoure, & power be ascribed to the Lorde oure God,

2 for true and ryghteous are his iudgementes, for he hath iudged that great whore, whiche dyd corrupte the earth with her fornicacion, & hath auenged the bloude of his seruauntes of her hand.

3 And again they said: Alleluia. And smoke rose vp for euermore.

4 And þe .xxiij. elders, & þe .iiij. beastes fel doune, & worshipped God that sate on þe seat sayinge: Amen Alleluia.

5 And a voice came out of the seate, saying: prayse our Lord God all ye that are his seruauntes, and ye that feare him both smalle and great.

6 And I heard the voice of much people, euen as the voice of many waters & as the voice of strong thondringes, saying: Alleluia, for God omnipotent reigneth.

7 Let vs be glad & reioyse & geue honour to him, for the mariage of the lambe is come, and hys wyfe made her selfe readye.

8 And to her was graunted that she shoulde be arayed wyth pure and goodlye Raynes. For the Raynes is the ryghtuousnesse of Saynctes.

9 And he sayed vnto me, happye are they whyche are called vnto the Lambes supper. And he said vnto me, these are true sayinges of God.

10 And I fell at his feete, to worshippe him. And he sayed vnto me, se thou do it not. For I am thy felowe seruaunt, & one of thy brethren, & of them þt haue the testimony of Iesus. Worshippe God. For þe testimony of Iesus is the spirit of prophesye.

11 And I sawe heauen open, & beholde a whyt horsse: and he that sate vpon hym was faythful and true, & in rightuousnes dyd he iudge & make battayl.

12 His eyes were as a flame of fyre, and on hys head were manye crounes, and he had a name wrytten, that no man knewe but he hym self.

13 And he was clothed with a vesture dipt in bloud, & his name is called the worde of God.

14 And the warryers whiche were in heauen, folowed hym vpon whyte horsses, clothed with whyte & pure raynes:

15 & out of hys mouthe went out a sharpe swearde, þt with it he should smyte the heathen. And he shal rule them wyth a rod of Iron, & he trode the wine fat of þe fiercenes & wrath of almightye God.

16 And hath on hys vesture & on hys thighe a name wrytten: king of kinges, & Lord of Lordes,

17 And I sawe an angel stand in þe sunne & he cryed wyth a loud voyce, saiyng to al the foules that flye by the myndes of heauen come & gather youre selues together vnto þe supper of the great God,

18 þt ye may eate þe flesh of kinges, & of hye captaynes, & the fleshe of myghty men, and the flesh of horsses, & of them that sit on them, & the flesh of all free men & bonde men, & of small & great.

19 And I sawe the beast and the kynges of the earth, & theyr warriers gathered together to make battayl against him that sat on the horse & agaynst hys souldyers.

20 And the beast was taken, & with hym that false prophete þt wrought miracles before him with which he deceyued them that receiued þe beastes marke, & them þt worshipped his Image These both were cast into a ponde of fyre burnyng with

brimstone:

21 and the remnaunte were slayne with þe swerd of him that sate vpon the horse, which swerd proceded out of his mouth & all the foules were fulfilled with their flesh.

# CHAPTER 20

And I saw an angel come doune from heauen, hauing the keye of the bottomlesse pytte, & a greate cheyne in his hand.

2 And he toke the dragon that olde serpent which is the deuyl and Satanas, & he bound him a thousand yeares:

3 and cast him into the botomles pyt, and he bounde hym, and set a seale on him, that he shuld deceyue the people nomore, tyl the thousand yeares were fulfilled. And after that he must be loused for a lytle season.

4 And I saw seates and they sate vpon them and iudgement was geuen vnto them: & I saw the soules of them that were beheaded for the wytnes of Iesu, & for þe worde of God, which had not worshypped þe beast, nether his Image, nether had taken hys marke vpon theyr forheades, or on theyr handes: and they lyued, and reygned with Christ a thousande yere:

5 but the other of the dead men lyued not agayne, vntil þe .M. yeres were fynyshed. This is þe fyrste resurreccion.

6 Blessed & holy is he that hath part in the fyrst resurreccyon. For on suche shall þe seconde death haue no power, for they shalbe the priestes of God and of christe, and shall raygne wyth hym a thousande yeare.

7 And when the thousand yeres are expired, Sathan shal be loused out of hys pryson,

8 & shal go out to deceiue þe people which are in þe four quarters of the earthe Gog & Magog, to gether them together to battayle, whose nomber is as the sande of the sea,

9 & they went vpon þe playne of the earth, & compassed the tentes of þe saynctes about & the beloued cytye. And fyre came doune from God, out of heauen, & deuoured them:

10 & the deuyll that deceyued them, was caste into a lake of fyre and brymstone, where the beast and the false Prophet were & shalbe tormented daye and nyghte for euermore.

11 And I sawe a great whyte seate and hym that sate on it, from whose face fled away bothe the earthe & heauen, & theyr place was no more founde.

12 And I sawe the deade, both great and small stande before God: & the bokes were opened, & an other boke was opened, which is the boke of lyfe, and the dead were iudged of those thynges: which were wrytten in the bokes accordyng to theyr deedes:

13 & the sea gaue vp her deade, which were in her, & death & hel delyuered vp the deade which were in them: & they were iudged euery man according to hys deedes.

14 And death & hell were cast into þe lake of fyre. Thys is that seconde death.

15 And who so euer was not founde wrytten in the boke of lyfe, was caste into the lake of fyre.

# CHAPTER 21

And I sawe heauen & a new earthe. For the fyrst heauen, & the first earth were vanyshed away & there was no more sea.

2 And I Iohn saw that holye cyty new Ierusalem come doune from God out of heauen prepared as a bryd garnyshed for her husband

3 And I heard a great voyce out of heauen saying: beholde, the tabernacle of God is wt men, and he wyll dwell with them. And they shal be his people, & God hym selfe shalbe with them & be theyr God.

4 And god shal wipe away al teares from their eyes. And there shalbe no more death, neyther sorow neither criyng, neither shal there be any more paine, for the olde thinges are gone.

5 And he that sate vpon the seate, said: Behold I make al things new. And he sayd vnto me: wryte for these wordes are faythfull and true.

6 And he said vnto me: it is done, I am Alpha & Omega, þe beginning & the ende. I will geue to hym that is a thyrst of the wel of the water of lyfe free.

7 He that ouercometh, shal inherete all thynges, & I wilbe his God, & he shall be my sonne.

8 But the fearful and vnbeleuing, & the abhominable, & murtherers, & whoremongers, & sorcerers, & ydolaters, & al lyars shall haue their parte in the lake which burneth wt fyre & brymstone, which is the seconde death.

9 And there came vnto nie one of the .vij. aungels which had the .vij. vials ful of the .vij. last plages: & talked with me saiyng: come hyther I wil shewe the the bryde, the lambes wyfe.

10 And he caryed me away in þe spirite to a great & hygh mountayne, & he shewed me the great citie, holy Ierusalem, descendyng out of heauen from God,

11 hauyng the bryghtnes of god And her shinyng was lyke vnto a stone most precyous, euen a Iasper cleare as Chrystal,

12 & had walles great and hye, and had twelue gates, & at the gates .xij. angelles: & names wrytten, which are the twelue trybes of Israel:

13 on the easte parte thre gates, & on the northe syde thre

gates, & towardes the south .iij. gates, and from the west thre gates,

14 & the wal of the citie had .xij. foundacyons, & in them the names of the lambes twelue Apostles.

15 And he þt talked with me, had a golden rede to measure the cytie with al & the gates therof & the wal thereof.

16 And the citie was buylt .iiij. square, & the length was as large as þe bredth of it, & he measured the citie with the rede .xij.M. furlonges: & the length and the bredth, & the heyth of it were equall.

17 And he measured the wal therof an .cxliiij. cubites, the measure that the angel had, was after the measure þe man vseth.

18 And the buyldyng of the wall of it was of Iaspar. And the citie was pure golde lyke vnto cleare glasse,

19 and the foundacyons of the wall of the cytye were garnyshed with all maner of precious stones. The first foundacyon was Iaspar, the seconde saphyre, the thyrde a calcedony, the fourth an emerald:

20 the fyft sardonix: the .vi. sardeos: the .vij. chrysolite the .viij. beral: the .ix. a topas, the tenth a chrisoprasos: the .xi. a Iacint: and the .xij. an amatist.

21 The .xij. gates were .xij. pearles, euery gate was of one pearle, & the strete of the cytie was pure golde, as thorowe shynyng glasse.

22 And there was no temple therein. For the Lord God almyghty & the lambe are the temple of it

23 & the cytye hath no nede of the sunne neyther of the mone to lyghten it. For the bryghtnes of God dyd lyght it, & the lambe was the lyght of it.

24 And the people which are saued, shall walke in the light of it: & the kinges of the earth shal brynge theyr glory vnto it.

25 And the gates of it are not shut by daye. For there shalbe no myght there.

26 <>

27 And there shal enter into it none vncleane thyng, neyther whatsoeuer worketh abominacyon: or maketh lyes: but they onely which are wrytten in the lambes boke of lyfe.

# CHAPTER 22

And he shewed me a pure ryuer of water of life cleare as cristal: procedyng out of the seat of god and of the lambe.

2 In the middes of the strete of it, and of eyther syde of the ryuer was the wode of lyfe: which bare .xij. maner of frutes: & gaue frute euerye moneth: and the leaues of the wodde serued to heale the people wythall.

3 And there shall be no more cursse, but the seate of God, and the lambe shalbe in it: and hys seruauntes shall serue hym.

4 And shall se his face, & hys name shall be in theyr foreheades.

5 And there shalbe no nyght there, and they nede no candel neyther lyghte of the sunne: for the Lorde geueth them lyghte, & they shall rayne for euermore.

6 And he said vnto me, these sayinges are faythfull, & true. And the Lord God of sainctes and prophetes sente hys angel to shew vnto hys seruauntes, the thynges whiche muste shortly be fulfylled.

7 Beholde I come shortly. Happy is he that kepeth the saiyng of the prophesy of this boke.

8 I am Iohn which saw these thynges and harde them. And when I had hearde and sene, I fell doune to worshyppe before the fete of the aungell whiche shewed me these thynges.

9 And he sayed vnto me: se thou do it not, for I am thy felowe seruaunte, & the felowe seruaunte of thy brethren the Prophetes, & of them which kepe the sayinges of thys boke. But worshyppe God.

10 And he sayd vnto me: seale not the sayinges of the prophesye of thys boke. For the tyme is at hande

11 He that doeth euill, let hym do euyll styll, & he whiche is filthy, let him be filthy still: & he þt is ryghteous, let hym be more righteous: & he þt is holy, let him be more holy

12 And beholde I come shortlye, & my rewarde wyth me, to geue euerye man accordynge as hys dedes shall be.

13 I am Alpha & Omega, þe beginnynge and the ende: the fyrst & the laste.

14 Blessed are they that do his commaundementes that theyr power maye be in the tree of lyfe, & maye enter in thorowe the gates into the cite.

15 For without shal be dogges & inchaunters, & whoremongers, and murtherers & Idolaters and whosoeuer loueth or maketh leasynges.

16 I Iesus sent myne angell, to testifye vnto you these thinges in the congregacyons. I am the rote and the generacion of Dauid and the bryghte mornyng starre.

17 And the spiryte and the bride said: come. And let him that heareth, saye also come. And let hym that is a thyrste, come. And let whosoeuer wyll, take of the water of lyfe, fre.

18 I testifye vnto euerye man that heareth þe wordes of the prophesye of thys boke. Yf any man shall ad vnto these thynges, God shall adde vnto him the plages that are written in thys boke.

19 And yf any man shal mynyshe of the wordes of the boke of this prophesy, God shall take awaye hys part out of the boke of lyfe, & out of the holye citie and from those thinges

which are wrytten in this boke.

20 He which testifyeth these thynges sayeth: be it, I come quickly, Amen. Euen so: come Lord Iesu.

21 The grace of our Lord Iesu Christe be wyth you all. Amen.

Printed in Dunstable, United Kingdom